Early Greek Myth

Early Greek Myth

A Guide to Literary and Artistic Sources

Timothy Gantz

The Johns Hopkins University Press *Baltimore and London*

© 1993 The Johns Hopkins University Press
All rights reserved
Printed in the United States of America on acid-free paper

The Johns Hopkins University Press
2715 North Charles Street
Baltimore, Maryland 21218-4319
The Johns Hopkins Press Ltd., London

Library of Congress Cataloging-in-Publication Data

Gantz, Timothy.
    Early Greek myth : a guide to literary and artistic sources / Timothy Gantz.
       p.   cm.
    Includes bibliographical references and index.
    ISBN 0-8018-4410-X (hc)
    1. Mythology, Greek.   I. Title.
BL782.G34   1993
292.1'3—dc20   92-26010

A catalog record for this book is available from the British Library.

In memoriam
Kyle Meredith Phillips, Jr.

Contents

xiii

Contents

Preface

Handbooks of Greek myth are certainly nothing new. Indeed, the very word *handbook* has an eminent Greek pedigree in the term *encheiridion*, and Greek, too, is the concept of assembling stories from different literary sources into a more or less homogeneous narrative that traces events from the first gods and mortals to the time of the Trojan War. The poems of the so-called Epic Cycle, that is, those recounting events before and after the action of the *Iliad*, were perhaps a step in this direction. But the first work we know of to actually compile traditions from the whole range of Greek myths was the poem that came to be called the *Ehoiai*, or *Catalogue of Women*. Produced probably in the first part of the sixth century B.C. by a man we know only as the Catalogue Poet, this undertaking arranged myths on a genealogical basis—organizing, systematizing, grouping, all the while employing as reference points the various unions between mortal women and gods, whose offspring and the stories surrounding them could then be enumerated. To what extent this labor of systemization, of bringing together into a whole previously unrelated figures, was achieved by the Catalogue Poet himself, and to what extent he found such groupings already in his sources, we do not know. With the emergence of prose in the later sixth century such handbooks took on more the look of early history, with as always a certain amount of local bias at work. Two names in particular which we know of are Akousilaos of Argos, writing perhaps at the end of the century, and Pherekydes of Athens (not to be confused with the Presocratic philosopher from Syros), who produced his account in the early part of the fifth century. These, in turn, were followed by numerous other prose writers, including Hellanikos and the Atthidographers, or local historians of Athens, who employed similarly systematic arrangements of mythic traditions for a variety of purposes.

All these works, however, are lost to us, save for bits and pieces in citations and (for the *Ehoiai*) occasional papyrus fragments. Our first preserved handbook is that of Palaiphatos in (probably) the fourth century B.C., although this is a modest effort relating few myths, and its author's sole purpose is to rationalize their more fantastic elements, such as Daidalos' flight from Krete and Atalanta's conversion into a lioness. Other works of similar scope include the tales enumerated by Konon in the first century B.C. But the first truly comprehensive collection of myths we have is that ascribed to one Apollodoros and written, we think, in the second century A.D. This Apollodoros (the ascription seems in error, but the name is as good as any other) presents us with a continuous narrative account beginning with the family of Deukalion and ending with the returns of the Achaians who fought at Troy. In a verse preface to the work, the author boasts that his readers will have no further need to consult Homer, or elegy, or tragedy, or even painting, because everything is contained within the covers of this one book. Seen from that perspective he is, of course, right; the readers he envisions for his compilation are those eager to find everything neatly assembled in one package, thus obviating the consultation of numerous literary works with their inevitable gaps and conflicts. Admittedly, variants of name or detail are not entirely lacking, and at times the specific sources from which Apollodoros has drawn (or claims to have drawn) his information are cited—Homer on five occasions, "Hesiod" and Pherekydes perhaps a dozen each, Akousilaos ten, Euripides four, sometimes the tragic poets as a group. Yet these occasional ascriptions do not alter the fact that Apollodoros' handbook, valuable though it may be, is an avowed synthesis, one designed to knit together disparate elements from many different sources (or earlier compilations of those sources) into a relatively seamless whole. As such, it inevitably promotes the concept of Greek myths as a cultural commodity, the product of a united Greek mind rather than contributions from many different tellers of tales in many different contexts over a great span of time.

Modern handbooks of Greek mythology offer, in many cases, the same kind of synthesis as Apollodoros and for the same valid reasons. Indeed, given that modern audiences have far less access to the original sources, such handbooks are often essential, and certainly there is no one interested in the subject who has not read and profited by them; in English, one thinks most readily of works by H. J. Rose and Karl Kerényi, which annotate (far more copiously than Apollodoros) the places from which they have drawn their information.[1] Still, these annotations are relegated to small print in the back of each volume (where few of us bother to look for them, save on particular points), and they do not obscure the impression that ancient Greeks by and large knew and retold the same myths over and over again in much the same form throughout their history as a culture.

What I have tried to do in the present volume is to stress rather the opposite point of view, to "uncompile" these myths back into what we know of their constituent forms (even when that is very little) and to try to envision when those forms might have arisen. To that end, individual myths are not so much retold as broken down to see what we can establish regarding the origin of each narrative detail; in general, I have tried to determine where each such detail first appears in our literary or artistic sources. In most cases, of course, given the state of preservation for our sources, the answer to that question provides nothing more than a *terminus post quem*, which in turn leads to more questions and unprovable hypotheses. Nevertheless, these are important starting points for a better understanding of how myths develop: only when we know how early a detail does survive, and in what context, are we really in a position to speculate on where it might have come from and why. Some details are clearly attested for pre-fifth-century epic and lyric; others surface first in authors such as Apollodoros who often draw on early works (or epitomes of them), while still others emerge in Euripides, Kallimachos, Ovid, and the like, writers whom we suspect do not hesitate to rework, on occasion, the traditions they have inherited for the need of the moment. Whether a tale like Leda's dalliance with a swan, first found in Euripides—as opposed to the earlier attested union of Zeus and Nemesis as geese—could be his invention is in no way assured (and is probably not the case), but we do begin to see more clearly the possibilities.

Mention of specific authors leads us to the use of the word *early* in the book's title. I had originally projected a far more modest volume isolating only that information about the various myths guaranteed in one way or another for the Archaic period (defined as from Homer down through roughly Aischylos and Bakchylides). In practice, however, such a method involved far too many gaps, places where details that must have existed in some form or other in the earliest versions survived only in post-Archaic accounts. Then, too, it seemed pointless to ignore Apollodoros, whose fondness for early sources appears all the more palpable now that we can appreciate his probable debt to the organizational structure of the *Ehoiai*.[2] And finally, a significant portion of our evidence for these early versions derives from less than certain authorities, in many cases scholiasts who assure us that the contents of their summaries are found in a given work but may mean only that the said work mentioned something on the subject (see below). Accordingly, the book's scope has been expanded, and while the focus is still on what stories were told (and in what forms) in earlier times, the range now includes details as they appear for the first time throughout Greek and Roman literature. By "earlier times," I continue to mean basically the Archaic period; I am interested above all in the versions of myths which would have been known to people like Aischylos and Pherekydes. This is, admittedly, an arbitrary cutoff point, and the sixth century (with Stesichoros depriving Helen of her flight to Troy) was perhaps no more conservative in its treatment of myths than Euripides in the later fifth. Given, however, that later authors are also represented when they have something new to offer, the consequences of such a dividing line are not very great. In practice, I have tried to report everything of narrative interest attested in literary sources down through Aischylos, even when they duplicate other early sources; for later authors and artifacts the criteria are narrowed to include only material that seems to have some possibility of going back to an early source. This may seem subjective, but as the size of the book indicates I have tried not to exclude anything that might reasonably be of any interest on these terms, and sources such as Apollodoros and the Roman mythographer Hyginus are almost always cited. What the reader will not find is any systematic treatment of a myth's development in later times for its own sake, for example, how motifs fully attested earlier are reworked or manipulated by Kallimachos or Ovid.

Regarding this so-called early period, the emphasis is primarily chronological, that is, on assembling the evidence for the period as a whole and naming the source(s) for each detail. Inevitably, discussion of what might or might not have been found in individual authors is involved, but I have not gone out of my way to reconstruct individual lost works, or to interpret the use of myths in preserved ones, save where it seemed necessary to the book's overall intent. On the whole, I adhere to the concept of a general corpus of traditional tales known to professional storytellers of the time of Homer and earlier, and while each of these storytellers made his own selection (and, no doubt, some innovations), the appeal of this corpus surely derived from a certain canonical element maintained despite the diversity of individual treatment. From that viewpoint, the attestation of a particular detail as seventh- or sixth-century, in general, matters far more than our ability to assign it to Lesches' *Little Iliad* rather than Arktinos' *Iliou Persis*. For much the same reason, I have allowed the term "Homer" to stand in the text when referring to the *Iliad* and the *Odyssey*, even though I believe, with many, that these are not the work of the same poet; for present purposes, authorship is not crucial and the actual poem meant is always specified in the parenthetical references.

Likewise given little consideration in the discussion, though for different reasons, is the matter of place. Unquestionably, local traditions in different parts of the Greek world played an enormously important role in the development of narratives, especially those designed to justify occupation of territory or to explain the first settlement of the various regions. If the present work is less diachoric than it is diachronic, that is only because I am not confident that we can, on the whole, recover these distinctions, at least not without speculation far greater than would be appropriate to a handbook. And however local in origin, many such traditions may have become considerably more widespread by the end of the Archaic period; the allusions of Pindar to quite a variety of myths, even when composing for non-Theban audiences, suggests that these tales were now "international" in their form, and could be exported without conflict or confusion.

In presenting what we know of the early literary sources for the myths passed down to us, I have also tried where possible, as befits a handbook, to avoid subjective evaluations of source quality. One has only to follow the trail of Aristarchean criticism a short way through the scholia of Homer to discover that many of our most valuable references to myths in that author can be (and have been) athetised with relatively few strokes. I assume, in any case, that most of the supposed interpolations utilize material found elsewhere in the literature of the Archaic period; again, since specific citations are always given, I leave the reader to draw his or her own conclusions about the ancestry of the information involved. Only in the case of the eleventh book of the *Odyssey*, which contains much extraneous material whose dating is of interest, have I thought it worthwhile to indicate potential outside influence with the standard book title *Nekuia*. In the case of missing works, however, the matter is sometimes far more serious. Some references to the lost epic and lyric poets consist of direct quotes, or attestations by known writers that such-and-such a work contained such-and-such a detail. In other cases, however, including almost all those involving lost mythographers, our sources are late epitomators or scholiasts who often relate a given tale at length, adding at the end, "the story is found in [e.g.] Pherekydes." Such a subscription may mean that their source made that claim, having actually drawn from the work in question, or that (in some few cases) they themselves did so, but it may also mean that they have copied their information from a handbook and then (to look more scholarly) added the name of an author who (we hope) related or at least mentioned the story somewhere. Again, I have taken these citations at face value, usually with indications where handbook-type summaries are involved, but anyone relying on this kind of information needs to evaluate the texts firsthand, something I hope this book will encourage.

As for the artistic material utilized, no attempt has been made to offer anything like a complete assessment of the artifacts illustrating myths in Archaic times; unlike the literary sources, the numbers of these are legion, and they are well documented in the invaluable *Lexicon Iconographicum Mythologiae Classicae,* now close to completion. What I have tried to do rather is to select out those artifacts that attest for the first time to the presence of a myth, or (as with the literary sources) add some new detail to our knowledge of the narrative and its possible variations. Extremely early representations (i.e., of the Late Geometric period) are treated with some caution, as they are rarely specific enough in detail to guarantee that a myth is intended (the Moliones are an exception), and in any case do not usually advance our knowledge of the story. For later periods, there is often controversy over the interpretation of clearly mythic scenes; I have tried to indicate both the uncertainties and the possibilities. Variations of purely iconographic interest (i.e., pose, dress, composition) have been omitted, as has consideration of the relative popularity of myths in different areas and time periods. This last body of evidence has (here again) undoubtedly important things to say about influence from lost literary works and even the existence of unsuspected ones, but it is again too speculative and too vast to fit into the present confines. The same is true of regional variants or versions of myths as represented in art; attempts have been made to separate a Peloponnesian tradition of tales (seen especially in shield-bands at Olympia) from that found in Athens, but on the whole it cannot be said that we have a very clear idea of what sources either group of artists drew from, and for many other important items we have no firm notion of ultimate origin at all. The numerous pictorial representations that have been included as relevant to establishing narrative details are identified by museum number wherever possible; these can be used to refer to the Catalogue of Artistic Representations (Appendix C) at the back of the book, where further bibliography is available. For items of a highly disputed nature, I have tried to indicate in the brief endnotes places where fuller discussions (of whatever persuasion) and references can be found. I have also included in the notes some of the valuable recent monographs and books cataloguing certain scenes from myth in art; again, these will point the way to other literature in what is a much vaster field than one might imagine. I have not as a rule referred to the articles in the new *Lexicon Iconographicum* noted above; these, like the material in Pauly-Wissowa's *Real-Encyclopädie* or any work organized as an encyclopedia, should be both self-explanatory and, for the artistic tradition on any aspect of myth, the first point of consultation for the reader who has access to them. Appendix C includes *LIMC* item/illustration numbers for all pieces cited here which are now included in that work (through the first five volumes).

I append here just a few remarks on procedure. In citing literary sources I have usually found it more economical to paraphrase than to quote directly, but these paraphrases are intended to be rigidly accurate, implying (or supplying) nothing that is not in the original, and noting any obscurities or uncertainties in the text. The parenthetical references to the original texts are likewise intended to indicate for precisely what details each source is or is not responsible. To avoid excessively long parentheses, the names of sources have been abbreviated more drastically than usual (see Abbreviations), but as most of them appear quite frequently, it is hoped they will become familiar with a minimum of effort on the part of the reader. As for the method by which the material is set forth, I had originally thought it might be possible to arrange all the sources—both literary and artistic—in strict chronological sequence, regardless of the information they contained. In many cases, however, that proved impractical; evidence with an earlier pedigree often required immediate support from something later if it was to make sense, and the artistic tradition was often better taken as a body. Accordingly I have improvised, depending on the nature of the information in each case: at times, all the literary evidence is taken first, followed by that from art, while in others the two are interspersed, and in some instances it has even seemed advisable to begin from the latest literature and work backwards, on the grounds that the early material was too fragmented to mean anything without a frame of reference. No doubt such reliance on one own's train of thought to bring coherence to scattered references, however objectively meant, has brought with it an undesired degree of subjectivity. But I hope this has not interfered too seriously with the goal of the book as a whole, which is to refer Greek myths, where we can, back to the specific writers, taletellers, and artists who gave them to us, and to reconsider what part of our world of Greek myth each of those sources knew.

The shield-band illustrations throughout the book are from E. Kunze, *Archaische Schildbänder (Olympische Forschungen II)* (Berlin, 1950), and P. Bol, *Argivische Schilder (Olympische Forschungen XVII)* (Berlin, 1989).

It remains only to thank several people for their welcome assistance. Jocelyn Penny Small of the U.S. Center of the *Lexicon Iconographicum Mythologiae Classicae* and Frances Van Keuren of the University of Georgia were both kind enough to read several chapters and make salutary comments from which the book has certainly profited. Johnna Hodges, Christopher Gregg, Erika Thorgerson, and Lawrence Dean, all graduate students in my department at the university, rechecked many of the references for typing errors and other aberrations. The university's Research Foundation generously provided a grant to enable firsthand study of artifacts in London, Paris, Berlin, and Munich, and as well a small subvention toward the book's publication. My brother Jeffrey I thank for invaluable help in extricating materials from Widener Library at Harvard on a number of occasions, and my wife Elena for contributing the results of her research-in-progress on the Erinyes in Archaic thought and art, as if her support and encouragement over the many years of this book's writing were not contribution enough. I want also to express my appreciation to the Press for permitting (indeed, inviting) the inclusion of notes citing secondary literature (something no longer customary in handbooks), and in general for their sympathetic reception of such a lengthy work. It goes without saying that a number of the Press's anonymous readers made valuable suggestions, and I must thank as well Therese Boyd, whose copy-editing has restored numerous idiosyncracies to the realm of recognizable convention, and benefited the manuscript in countless other ways as well. The teacher of many years past who provided the impetus to this undertaking (whatever its merits) is mentioned in the dedication.

Early Greek Myth

1 The Early Gods

Theogonies and the Like   Before proceeding to the actual narratives that will make up this chapter, we might do well to review briefly those ancient literary works known or assumed to contain information on the earliest stages in the world and the Greek gods who peopled it. We have first of all the authority the Greeks themselves most revered, Hesiod, whose *Theogony* (not necessarily Hesiod's title) offers a brief account of the origins of the cosmos as preface to the extolling of Zeus' rule.[1] Since the purpose of the poem is largely to contrast Zeus' organization of the world with the absence of such order in previous times, the lack of any great detail in this account is not surprising. Whether Greek storytelling had actually developed further details by the seventh century B.C. is a more difficult question. Homer speaks only rarely of the period before Zeus; references to Kronos and the other Titans in Tartaros (where Zeus put them), to Okeanos as the *genesis* of all the gods (whatever that means), to Tethys as caring for Hera, and to a first union of Zeus and Hera unknown to their parents, are about the extent of the information that the *Iliad* and the *Odyssey* offer. Such brief glimpses guarantee at least that Homer knew of an era before the reign of Zeus, and of Zeus' seizure of power from his father, but we cannot be sure that the poet possessed anything like complete stories on these topics or, if he did, that they were the same as Hesiod's. Indeed, Homer's apparent view of Okeanos' role in the beginnings of things might suggest that they were not the same, or that he invented pertinent details as he needed them, without worrying about a consistent whole.

Of other works to be considered in this context, the most important was probably the lost epic *Titanomachia* with its account of the battle between the Olympians and the Titans, and presumably what led up to that battle.[2] As always, discussion of such a source inevitably involves us in the problems connected with the antiquity of the Epic Cycle: we simply do not know if the events recounted in those poems were concocted in a post-Homeric/Hesiodic period to flesh out earlier references, or drawn from a genuine pre-Homeric tradition, or combined from both. Photios does tell us that the Epic Cycle began with the union of Gaia and Ouranos and the birth of the Hundred-Handers and Kyklopes (as in Hesiod: Cyclus Epicus *test* 13 *PEG*), but it is not absolutely certain that he is referring to the *Titanomachia*.[3] On the other hand, definitely

1

from that work is the information that Ouranos is a son of Aither (*Tit* frr 1, 2 *PEG*), that Helios sailed in a cauldron (fr 8 *PEG*), and that Aigaion, son of Gaia and Pontos, fought on the side of the Titans (fr 3 *PEG*). These points suggest that the *Titanomachia*, like Hesiod's poem, contained some description of the beginning of things as preface to the account of the battle. On the other hand, the first and last items are in direct contrast to Hesiod (if, as in Homer, Aigaion and Briareos are the same figure), so that the author of the *Titanomachia* may have made use of a version not simply fuller than what Hesiod has left us but in some respects different. In all, we really know very little of the extent to which the work may have resembled, influenced, or copied Hesiod's account.

Still other sources dealing with first causes bring us a variety of details, not always consistent with what we have seen above. In the sixth century, there surface (in fragments) the versions of early mythographers and philosophers such as Akousilaos of Argos and Pherekydes of Syros, and an entire *Theogony* was also credited to the Kretan Epimenides, with Aer and Nyx as the two first principles. Akousilaos would be extremely valuable if only we had more of him (as in Hesiod, everything began from Chaos); Pherekydes of Syros seems for his part more interested in the possibilities of new philosophic beliefs than in preserving traditions, and what survives from his work is here relegated (together with the "Orphic" cosmogonies) to Appendix A.

As for Epimenides, the *Theogony* recorded under his name is probably a product of the fifth century; with its novel ideas (Aphrodite as daughter of Kronos) it is no less interesting for that, but very little survives.[4] Definitely of the fifth century is Pherekydes of Athens, who like Hesiod produced an account (or section thereof) referred to as a "Theogony"; Typhoeus and Tityos were included, and we hear of a few other minor gods, but we cannot assess the scope of the work. Perhaps a bit later is the *Eumolpia* ascribed to "Mousaios," where all things began from a union of Tartaros and Nyx (2B14), although the poem seems to have focused primarily on Zeus.[5]

Of post-Archaic sources the most obviously relevant is the first section of Apollodoros' *Bibliotheke*, where we find an account mirroring for the most part that of Hesiod. There are, however, several differences, notably that the Titans release the Kyklopes and Hundred-Handers before Kronos reimprisons them, Gaia and Ouranos predict to Kronos his overthrow by an offspring, Zeus on Krete is cared for by Adrasteia and Ida (daughters of Melisseus) and guarded by the Kouretes, and Zeus defeats Kronos with the aid of Metis and an emetic (Ap*B* 1.1–2). On the other hand, Briareos here fulfills the same role as in Hesiod (i.e., supporter of Zeus). Thus (again, *if* Briareos and Aigaion are the same figure), we might well conclude that while Apollodoros did not use Hesiod exclusively for his account, neither can he have drawn exclusively from the *Titanomachia*, since there Aigaion aids the Titans. He might, of course, have fused the two works together, but similarities with Orphic versions have prompted the suggestion that an Orphic *Theogony* (as part of the Epic Cycle) was his source;[6] we will return to the question in Appendix A.

As for artistic representations of these early events and divinities, there are few clear examples; Greek artists understandably preferred as subjects heroes and those gods actually worshipped. Nyx does appear in her chariot on occasion, alone or in conjunction with Helios and Selene (e.g., Berlin:Ch F2524), and Gaia, as we shall see in subsequent chapters, is often shown defending her children Tityos and the Gigantes, or rising up out of the earth to proffer the child Erichthonios to Athena. But the fact remains that our knowledge of the origins of the gods is largely dependent on Hesiod, without our being really certain how widely held his views were in his own time or in the Archaic era that followed.

Primal
Elements

In the beginning, according to the *Theogony*, there was (or came into being, since the Greek will allow both) Chaos, a neuter noun meaning "yawning" or "gap" (*Th* 116). Between what objects, precisely, Chaos might have been a gap, Hesiod does not say, and perhaps did not know; since this entity comes first, there is logically nothing to frame it. Later references in the poem suggest a place beneath the earth but not beyond Tartaros, one capable of feeling the heat of Zeus' thunderbolts (*Th* 813–14, 700; cf. 740, where a *chasma* is located at the roots of Tartaros and Earth). If this is right, then Chaos is a kind of foundation. It has also been proposed, although it does not easily suit these passages, that Chaos was originally the gap between heaven and earth, here reused by Hesiod in a different fashion.[7] In any case Chaos is followed by the appearance of Gaia, the Earth, broad-bosomed and a secure seat for the gods yet to come (*Th* 117–18). Next is Tartaros (here in the neuter plural form *Tartara*), mistily dark in the recesses of the earth, and then Eros, the limb-loosener who conquers the hearts of mortals and gods (*Th* 119–22). Tartaros is elsewhere in the poem the lowest part of the cosmos (even lower than Chaos: *Th* 814) and the place of imprisonment for certain figures. On one occasion, however, he is sufficiently personified to father a child (Typhoeus) on Gaia (*Th* 821–22).

As for Eros, the third of these primal forces, the remainder of Hesiod's poem mentions him on one occasion only, as attendant at Aphrodite's birth (*Th* 201); thus his chief function here seems to be as symbol of the process of sexual union and procreation that will populate the world. As a god he does not appear in Homer at all (note, however, the impact of love at *Od* 18.208–13). Plato quotes a dactylic couplet, possibly from a *Homeric Hymn*, in which he is called Pteros because of his wings (*Phaidros* 252b). In Simonides we first find his familiar role as the offspring of Aphrodite and Ares (575 *PMG*), but this was not as commonly agreed upon as we might suppose: Sappho makes him the child of Ouranos and Gaia according to one source, of Ouranos and Aphrodite according to another (198 LP), while Alkaios calls him the offspring of Zephyros and Iris (a quote: 327 LP), Akousilaos that of Erebos and Nyx or Aither and Nyx (2F6), and the undatable "Olen" the child of Eileithuia (Paus 9.27.2). Such variation is obviously due to the appeal of allegory in the case of this particular figure, and perhaps a certain inability to pin down his identity. His most common parentage in later times—that of Aphrodite and Ares—is probably no more than a by-product of their own popularity as a couple. In Anakreon, Eros comports himself as the playful tempter to love, the role that later becomes his stock-in-trade (358 *PMG*). Yet the bow and arrows with which we are so familiar do not appear in literature until the late fifth century, when Euripides speaks of them as the god's weapon of love in the *Medeia* (530–31), and in the *Iphigeneia at Aulis* as producing good and bad effects (543–51); previously, Sappho has used the notion of being shaken when she discusses his power (47, 130 LP).

The artistic evidence suggested at one time a similar development, with Erotes in the earlier fifth century wielding a whip (so Athens 15375) or goad (Berlin:Lost F2032: Zeus and Ganymedes). But a Red-Figure lekythos, assigned to the Brygos Painter or his time and now in Fort Worth, does display an appropriate winged figure with bow (Kimbell Coll AP 84.16); probably, too, on the Parthenon's east metope 11, Eros carried this weapon.[8] Pindar (*Nem* 8.5; fr 122.4 SM), Bakchylides (9.73), and Aischylos (A:*Hik* 1043) all present the god as a plurality (i.e., Erotes), as often in art, but say little about his activities; Pindar does state, and Bakchylides and Aischylos imply, that his mother was Aphrodite. We will see him from time to time in this book as a small winged figure (or figures) in Attic vase-painting, attending his mother or hovering overhead on suitable occasions, such as the abduction of Helen by Paris. The preserved cast (the actual panel is now lost) of Slab 6 of the east frieze of the Parthenon shows him as a boy of about twelve, naked and winged, standing at his mother's side. Although Eros and Psyche are popular allegorical figures in later Greek thought (and art[9]), the actual narrative about the god's love for a mortal of that name and their subsequent problems is a story found first in Apuleius in the second century A.D. With regard to all three of these figures—Gaia, Tartaros, and Eros—we should note that Hesiod does not say they arose *from* (as opposed to *after*) Chaos, although this is often assumed. Plato's Phaidros believes just the opposite (i.e., that Eros in Hesiod has no parents: *Sym* 178b), and the succeeding lines of the *Theogony*, where other parentages are explicitly detailed, may indeed suggest that in Hesiod's mind these first entities simply appear, much as Chaos did.

Next, and definitely born from Chaos, arise Erebos (Darkness) and black Nyx (Night) (*Th* 123–25). Erebos has virtually no character of his own; in both the *Iliad* and *Odyssey*, the word is used to indicate the Underworld (*Il* 8.368, 16.326–27; *Od* 10.528, 11.37), while later in the *Theogony* it becomes the place below the earth into which Menoitios is thrown down and from which the Hundred-Handers are brought up (*Th* 514–15, 669). This Erebos does, however, mate with Nyx (the first sexual union) to produce Aither (Brightness) and Hemere (Day), figures who constitute in the remainder of the poem strictly physical aspects of the cosmos (compare the description of their alternate forays out into the world at *Th* 748–57).

Nyx's other children, produced without the aid of Erebos or any other partner, are detailed subsequently in the poem: Moros (Doom, Destiny), Ker (Destruction, Death), Thanatos (Death), Hypnos (Sleep), the Oneiroi (Dreams), Momos (Blame), Oizus (Pain, Distress), the Hesperides who care for the golden apples and fruit trees beyond the streams of Okeanos, the Moirai (Fates), here named as Klotho, Lachesis, and Atropos, the Keres who punish the transgressions of gods and men (unless these lines refer to the Moirai: see below), Nemesis (Indignation and Retribution), Apate (Deceit), Philotes (Love, here probably sexual), Geras (Old Age), and Eris (Strife) (*Th* 211–25).

Some of these figures are strictly allegorized personifications, but others do have occasional functions to serve in the myths. The scholia minora to *Iliad* 1.5–6 tell us, for example, that Momos advised Zeus to marry Thetis to a mortal and himself beget a daughter (Helen) in order to precipitate the Trojan War; the scholiast adds that the story is found in the *Kypria*, though the lines he then quotes from that poem would seem to preclude Momos' role (*Kyp* fr 1 *PEG*). Thanatos and Hypnos are sent by Apollo (at the command of Zeus) to carry the body of Sarpedon back to Lykia in book 16 of the *Iliad* (681–83); the scene is illustrated on several vases, including the late sixth-century Euphronios Krater in New York where both divinities have wings and armor (NY 1972.11.10). Homer specifically calls them twins, although he does not name the mother. Hypnos also appears in *Iliad* 14, when Hera approaches him with a proposal to lull Zeus to sleep (*Il* 14.231–91). In reply, he reminds her that once before he performed this service, when Herakles was leaving Troy, and that Zeus, upon awakening, would have thrown him into the sea had he not fled to Nyx, whom Zeus feared to anger. Nonetheless, the bargain is concluded upon Hera's promise of Pasithea, one of the Charites, to wife, and Hypnos awaits his task in the highest fir on Ida, disguised as a bird. Subsequently, he even exceeds his commission by reporting events to Poseidon, so that the latter might stir up the Achaians (*Il* 14.354–60).

Elsewhere, Hypnos and Thanatos are mentioned together again in the *Theogony*'s description of the ends of the earth, where Nyx and these two of her children have their homes (*Th* 756–66). Here Hypnos is described as roaming the earth with calm and benevolence for men, but Thanatos as having an iron pitiless heart, which makes him hated even by the gods. In fact, Thanatos is a curious divinity; Hades' role as lord of the dead, and Hermes' as conductor of souls, leaves this personification of death with very little to do in most myths. Nor is he always impossible to defeat: Pherekydes relates how, sent by Zeus to claim Sisyphos, the god is instead held in strong bonds by his intended victim, so that no one can die; finally, Ares contrives in some way to release him (Pher 3F119). Thanatos also had a role in Phrynichos' lost *Alkestis*, apparently appearing on stage (as in Euripides' play) and cutting off a lock of his victim's hair to consecrate her (fr 3 Sn). Whether he, like Euripides' Thanatos, wrestled with Herakles and lost we do not know, although it seems likely. Last, he is mentioned in Aischylos' *Niobe* as a god who loves not gifts, and from whom persuasion stands apart (fr 161 R); probably this is for the most part poetic personification of an abstract concept. In literature Hypnos has little to do after the *Iliad,* but we will encounter him frequently in artistic versions of Herakles' slaying of Alkyoneus, where as a small Eros-like figure he hovers overhead or actually sits on the sleeping giant.

Of Nyx's other children, the Oneiroi as a race of dreams form part of the landscape to the far west (beyond Okeanos) on the suitors' journey to the Underworld at *Odyssey* 24.12, while a single destructive Oneiros is Zeus' instrument to deceive Agamemnon at *Iliad* 2.5–6. The Hesperides are apparently included in the same family by virtue of their association with evening and the West, although one might have expected their name to indicate descent from a god of evening, Hesperos (so Paus 5.17.2). Elsewhere in the *Theogony* they are called "shrill-voiced" (*Th* 275: several post-Archaic sources make them singers) and located near Atlas and the Gorgons at the limit of Okeanos, toward the edge of night (*Th* 517–18). Hesiod will later describe as well the snake offspring of Phorkys and Keto who guards similar apples in the hollows of dark earth at its limits (a difficult geographical concept: *Th* 333–35).

The initial reference to the Hesperides in the *Theogony* is the only mention in Archaic *literature* of their role as tenders of the golden apples (the next preserved allusion is Euripides' *Hipp* 742; cf. *HF* 394–99), but for them and the snake there is some further evidence from art. A cedar-wood group by the mid-sixth-century Lakonian sculptor Theokles, apparently for Byzantion's treasury at Olympia, portrayed Herakles, snake, tree, and five Hesperides; two Hesperides with apples also appeared on the throne of Pheidias' Zeus statue (Paus 6.19.8, 5.17.2, 5.11.6). For his part, Pherekydes tells us that Gaia brought apple trees bearing golden fruit to Hera as a gift on the occasion of her wedding, and that Hera promised to plant them in the garden of the gods near Atlas, with a snake (Apollonios is the first to call him Ladon: AR 4.1396–98) to guard the apples from the depredations of Atlas' daughters (3F16); another source adds in this connection that Pherekydes made the Hesperides daughters of Zeus and Themis (Σ *Hipp* 742 = 3F16d; Jacoby argues confusion with the Eridanos Nymphai here). Akousilaos instead makes the Harpuiai the guardians (2F10), and the Epimenides *Theogony* identified these last with the Hesperides, if Philodemos is to be trusted (3B9). From the latter writer we learn that the author of the epic *Titanomachia* also discussed the matter, but Philodemos' text breaks off just as the guardians are about to be named (*Tit* fr 9 *PEG*).

Of Archaic poets, Mimnermos too places the Hesperides in the West (12.8 W), and a fragment of Stesichoros describes their golden homes on a lovely island, presumably in connection with Herakles' acquisition of the apples as one of his Labors (or as part of the *Geryoneis*?: 8 *SLG*). For Apollonios they are three in number (Hespere, Erytheis, Aigle) and located in Libya, where the Argonautai encounter them mourning the recent death of the snake, guardian of the apples, at the hands of Herakles (AR 4.1396–1449). The later account of Apollodoros locates garden and Hesperides, instead, near the Hyperboreans (thus presumably in the far north), and names them Aigle, Erytheia, Hesperia, and Arethousa (Ap*B* 2.5.11, after emendation).[10] The Hellenistic historian Agroitas (Σ AR 4.1396a = 762F3a) and Diodoros Siculus both discuss the possibility that what the Hesperides guarded were after all sheep, not apples (since the Greek word *mêla* can mean both); Diodoros also adds an unlikely tale about one Hesperis, daughter of Atlas' brother Hesperos, who lay with Atlas and became the mother of seven Hesperides (DS 4.26–27). South Italian art often shows the Hesperides in their garden alone, with one of them usually giving the snake something to drink (so Ruvo 1097). But we will also see them (and the snake) together with Herakles on numerous fifth- and fourth-century vases, for in some earlier accounts, as well as in Apollonios, Herakles secures the apples from them directly, rather than using Atlas as an intermediary.

Next are the Moirai. Homer mentions them just once by their collective name, at *Iliad* 24.49, when they are described as giving enduring hearts to men, but *Iliad* 24.209–10 also gives us a singular Moira who spins with her thread a particular fate for Hektor at his birth, and Aisa substitutes for Moira in a similar phrase at *Iliad* 18.20.127–28. For its part, *Odyssey* 7.197–98 speaks of both Aisa and the stern Klothes (Spinners) jointly in this same role; these latter are surely the Moirai under a descriptive epithet (the form *Klothes* is elsewhere unattested). Finally, even Zeus (*Od* 4.207–8), or the gods as a whole (*Od* 1.17–18), can do the spinning at times. *Moira* as a singular noun is, of course, quite common in both epics, but except for the above instances never clearly personified.

In Hesiod we first find the goddesses' number and individual names: Klotho (the Spinner), Lachesis (the Apportioner), and Atropos (the Unavoidable), who give good and evil to men at their birth (*Th* 217–19, 904–6). In the earlier of these two passages, where they and the Keres are children of Nyx, these individual names follow awkwardly in 218 after the mention of the Keres, as does the subsequent task of pursuing wrongdoers in 219: very likely both these lines (West brackets them) are in fact intruders, with the wrongdoers originally hunted down by the Keres. The later passage at 904 revises their genealogy in accordance with the new order and makes them the offspring of Themis and Zeus, who is the source of their power. In the Hesiodic *Aspis*, the three resurface (on the shield itself), with Atropos the shortest and oldest (258–63), but these lines too are probably interpolated; certainly the following reference to a role in battle, if genuine, indicates again the preceding Keres.[11] Elsewhere the Moirai are not much in evidence. Klotho appears in Pindar's *Olympian* 1 as the goddess supervising the rebirth of Pelops (*Ol* 1.26: a rare story of bringing the dead to life, in seeming violation of *moira*, and perhaps invented by Pindar), and Lachesis is present in the same author's *Paian* 12 at the birth of Artemis and Apollo to Leto, as well as at the allotment of honors to the Olympians in *Olympian* 7 (*Pa* 12.16–17; *Ol* 7.64–67). In *Olympian* 6 all three attend (with Eileithuia) the birth of Iamos (*Ol* 6.41–42: cf. *Nem* 7.1), and likewise in *Olympian* 10 they are present at Herakles' founding of the Olympian games (*Ol* 10.51–52). More unusually, in a fragment of Pindar they bring Themis as wife to Zeus, thus suggesting that they cannot here be his children by her (fr 30.3 SM). Another fragment, which may be simply poetic recasting, calls Tyche the most powerful Moira (fr 41 SM). In this connection we may also note an unassigned lyric fragment (Simonides?) with a prayer to Aisa, Klotho, and Lachesis, the daughters of Nyx (1018 *PMG*).

Turning to Aischylos, we find Apollo accused of deceiving and persuading the Moirai (in the matter of Admetos) with the help of wine—a most surprising notion of which no other trace exists (*Eum* 723–28: one wonders what Phrynichos' *Alkestis* might have said on the matter). The *Prometheus Desmotes* mentions them in a more respectful vein, as helmsmen (with the Erinyes) of necessity (*PD* 515–16); to Io's query whether they are stronger than Zeus there is, alas, no direct answer. One other story in which we might have expected to encounter them is that of Althaia and the brand given to her at Meleagros' birth. Bakchylides tells this tale in his Ode 5 (140–44), but names simply *moira* as weaving such a fate for Meleagros; how Althaia learned of the brand's significance, or who created such a situation, we are not told. Phrynichos dramatized the myth in his *Pleuroniai*, and there the Moirai may have played a greater role, though presumably not on stage, since the action surely revolved around Meleagros' death years later. As matters stand we must turn to Ovid, Apollodoros, and Hyginus for accounts of their involvement in this tale (*Met* 8.451–57; Ap*B* 1.8.1; *Fab* 171). Of the three, Hyginus has the most interesting feature, that when they appeared to Althaia Klotho promised that the child would be magnanimous (or noble?), Lachesis that he would be strong, and Atropos that he would live as long as the brand on the hearth lasted, conceivably a gift rather than a curse. Whatever the details, it is an odd story—not fully in accord with other early accounts of Meleagros' fate, and the only preserved suggestion that the Moirai ever communicate directly with mortals regarding their lot. In art they are virtually unknown, but they do appear as three women (inscribed "Moirai") among the guests at Thetis' wedding on both the François Krater (Florence 4209) and the Erskine Dinos (London 1971.11–1.1).

Closely linked to the Moirai, it seems, are the Keres. Homer knows this word, which means "death" or "destruction," in the plural, but in both poems it appears simply as a synonym for death or divinities bringing death (e.g., *Il* 2.302, 18.535–38; *Od* 17.547). Of these, the *Iliad* 18 passage (from the description of Achilleus' shield) is especially noteworthy for its picture of a Ker in bloodstained garment on the battlefield, dragging away a victim by the foot. In Hesiod, on the other hand, if *Theogony* 218–19 is indeed an interpolation (see above), the Keres pursue wrongdoing of men and gods, never ceasing from their anger until they have brought evil to the transgressor; such a role sounds far more like the task usually assigned to the Erinyes. Subsequently, Keres appear in Mimnermos as twin bearers of evils to men, the one of old age, the other of death (2.5–7 W), while on the shield in the Hesiodic *Aspis* they fight with each other to drink the blood of the newly dead or dying, gnashing their white teeth and snatching up bodies with their claws (*Aspis* 248–57), and on the Chest of Kypselos a single Ker stands behind Polyneikes, displaying teeth like those of a wild beast and long hooked nails (Paus 5.19.6). These last examples again remind us of Aischylos' Erinyes, who may have taken over some of the functions and character of the Keres. Hesiod's own Erinyes are the offspring of Ouranos' blood, as we shall see shortly.

Last of Nyx's children among those requiring comment are Nemesis and Eris. Nemesis (Indignation or Retribution), although she had a cult at Rhamnous in Attika, would scarcely qualify as a mythological figure, were it not for a fragment cited from the *Kypria* (fr 9 *PEG*). There we are told that Zeus pursued Nemesis with amorous intent, that she fled over land and sea, changing into every form of animal (including fish) to avoid him, and that, finally captured, she bore to the god a daughter, Helen.[12] Philodemos adds that in the same poem Zeus too in the form of a goose pursued her (implying that she had herself become one), and that their mating resulted in an egg from which Helen was born (fr 10 *PEG*).[13] We will see (in chapter 11) that later sources confirm this union of birds (whether geese or swans), with the egg thus produced brought to or found by Leda so that she might raise Helen just as she does when (as in the *Iliad*) the child is hers; the story was in some way parodied in Kratinos' lost comedy *Nemesis*.

By contrast, Eris (Strife) is largely just a personification of her name (see, e.g., *Il* 4.440–43), but Zeus does send her to rouse the Achaians (by shouting) in a memorable passage in *Iliad* 11 where she comes holding the *teras* of battle (*Il* 11.3–14). She also plays one crucial role in Greek mythology as instigator of the Judgment of Paris. Homer knows of this event but just barely alludes to it in the *Iliad* (24.27–30), with no direct mention of Eris. Our epitome of the *Kypria*, however, clearly makes her the guilty party (though as part of the plan of Zeus and Themis), and adds that she stirred up the quarrel among the three goddesses at the wedding feast for Peleus and Thetis (pp. 38–39 *PEG*). That she was not invited to the feast, or used an apple marked "for the fairest," are details that may or may not have been in the *Kypria*; we find them first in Loukianos (*DMar* 7.1), Hyginus (*Fab* 92) and (apple only) Apollodoros (Ap*E* 3.2), although the apple probably goes back to the fifth century in art (see chapter 16). Sophokles wrote a play entitled *Eris*, but nothing survives to indicate even the plot.

In art we find Eris first on the Chest of Kypselos, where she stands between Aias and Hektor, having a most base *(aischistê)* appearance (Paus 5.19.2), and then named in the tondo of a mid-sixth-century Black-Figure cup, where she is portrayed as quite normal in appearance apart from her wings and winged sandals (Berlin:Ch F1775).[14] The later fifth century (*c.* 430 B.C.) adds to this a Red-Figure calyx krater confirming the narrative of the *Kypria*: while the lower section presents the Judgment of Paris in its usual form, the upper shows Eris with her hand on the shoulder of Themis (both named) as the two lean toward each other in animated discussion (Leningrad St 1807). Hesiod's account goes on to list Eris' own children, born with no father mentioned and virtually all allegorizings: Ponos (Labor), Lethe (Forgetfulness), Limos (Famine), Algea (Pains), Hysminai (Combats), Machai (Battles), Phonoi (Slaughterings), Androktasiai (Slayings of Men), Neikea (Quarrels), Pseudea (Falsehoods), Logoi (Words), Amphillogiai (Unclear Words), Dysnomia (Bad Government), Horkos (Oath), and Ate (Folly) (*Th* 226–32). Of this list, only the last has any identity, and she, when she appears in the *Iliad* to deceive Zeus (in the matter of Herakles' birthright: *Il* 19.91–133), is a daughter of Zeus himself (no mother is mentioned). With regard to that story it may be noted that Hera is the one who actually carries out the deception by rearranging the order of births; Ate merely clouds Zeus' mind so that he does not notice the trick.

Gaia and Ouranos

From Nyx and her children we return in Hesiod to Gaia, who brings into being (1) Ouranos (Sky) to enclose her and be a home for the gods (does this mean she foresees the coming of the Olympians?), (2) the Ourea (Mountains), and (3) Pontos (Sea), all expressly without sexual congress (*Th* 126–32). The Ourea are clearly just a feature of the landscape, but Gaia mates with both Ouranos and Pontos to produce further offspring. To Ouranos she bears first twelve relatively normal children, six male and six female, whom Hesiod will later call "Titans": Okeanos, Koios, Kreios, Hyperion, Iapetos, Kronos, Theia, Rheia, Themis, Mnemosyne, Phoibe, and Tethys (*Th* 132–38). Of these, Kronos is named expressly as the youngest and "crooked-planning" (probably the sense Hesiod gave to the word, even if originally it referred rather to Kronos' sickle[15]), the most terrible of the group, who hated his father.

Next born are the Kyklopes, three in number, and like to the other gods in all things save for the single round eye in their foreheads (*Th* 139–46). Their names—Brontes, Steropes, and Arges—are connected with lightning and thunder, and indeed they will be the ones to forge the thunderbolt for Zeus.

Last come three more brothers, the Hundred-Handers, the most monstrous of all with their fifty heads and hundred hands, Kottos, Briareos (or Obriareos), and Gyges (*Th* 147–53). What follows in Hesiod is not entirely clear—Ouranos hates his children, perhaps just the last six but more likely all eighteen, and as soon as they are born imprisons them deep within the earth, that is, both underground and in the womb of their mother. The reason for his hatred may be their terrible appearance, though Hesiod does not quite say this (*Th* 155 comes close to implying it as the reason). In any event, he delights in the deed, and Gaia in her anger and distress fashions a sickle of adamant, after which she asks her children to take revenge on their father. Only Kronos has the courage to volunteer, and is placed by his mother in ambush (inside her body, we will understand, if he too is a prisoner) to await Ouranos. When the latter comes to lie with Gaia, bringing with him night, and stretches out beside her, his son reaches out with the sickle and castrates him. The severed testicles are then thrown behind Kronos into the sea, while Gaia receives the drops of blood that fall from them, and thus produces in time the Erinyes, the Gigantes, and the Melian Nymphai. The testicles themselves float past the island of Kythera to Cyprus, where Aphrodite is born and, accompanied from the very beginning by Eros and Himeros (Desire), assumes her role as goddess of erotic encounters (*Th* 154–206). In passing, Hesiod makes explicit the derivation of her cult titles ("Kytherea" and "Kyprogeneia") from Kythera and Cyprus, as well as the supposed formation of her name from the foam *(aphros)* surrounding the testicles. This section of the *Theogony* then concludes with Ouranos' prediction that retribution will come to the Titans for their deed (*Th* 207–10).

Homer, as we have seen, relates none of this; indeed, in *Iliad* 14, Okeanos and Tethys seem elevated to the status accorded Ouranos and Gaia in Hesiod (*Il* 14.200–210, 245–46), while Aphrodite is throughout the poem clearly the daughter of Zeus (by the Okeanid Dione, *Il* 5.370–71). The first of these points is especially difficult to assess: Hera tells Zeus as part of her *Trugrede* that she is on her way to the ends of the earth to visit "Okeanos the *genesis* of gods and mother Tethys, they who raised me well in their home, receiving me from Rheia when Zeus cast Kronos down beneath the earth and the barren sea." Mother Tethys here need be no more than a stepmother to Hera herself, and the phrase "*genesis* of gods" might be simply a formulaic epithet indicating the numberless rivers and springs descended from Okeanos; so, for example, at *Iliad* 21.195–97 he is that from which all rivers and springs and the whole sea derive. But in Hera's subsequent interview with Hypnos, the latter describes the great river as the "*genesis* for all," leaving us to wonder whether Homer could have supposed Okeanos and Tethys the parents of the Titans (Kronos' father is never specified), for how else can they fit this description? The second part of Hera's statement also seems problematic, for in the *Theogony* she is swallowed by her father and presumably emerges from his belly full grown, ready to aid her brother; even if she is not in that poem swallowed, as might be argued following Hyginus (*Fab* 139),[16] she should be full grown by the time of the overthrow, and have no need of a nurse. Just possibly Homer, in contrast to Hesiod, did think of her as still an infant on re-emerging, and thus needing to be cared for, though if he believed this true of all five siblings he probably did not believe in a general battle between Olympians and Titans (see below). Elsewhere, for what it is worth, the *Iliad* on several occasions calls the Olympians "Ouraniones," presumably meaning "descendants of Ouranos" (*Il* 1.570: cf. *Il* 5.898, where the same term clearly applies to the Titans). "Ouraniones" is also used twice at the end of the *Theogony*, both times of the Olympians (*Th* 919, 929). In Akousilaos, Ouranos certainly seems to hold his Hesiodic position, since he is said to have thrown the Hundred-Handers down into Tartaros, lest they be greater than he (2F8).

From a later time we have Plato's *Timaios*, where the genealogy offered looks very much like an attempt to bridge a presumed Homer/Hesiod divergence in *Iliad* 14: Ouranos and Gaia here beget Okeanos and Tethys who in their turn beget Kronos, Rheia, and the others, plus Phorkys (*Tim* 40d-e). Just possibly, of course, it is instead an early tradition, and the basis for Homer's description of Okeanos.[17] Also puzzling are the scattered references to Ouranos as Akmonides, or son of Akmon. A comment that this genealogy appeared in Hesiod (fr 389 MW) is probably a mistake based on manuscript corruption; it first appears for certain in the Hellenistic Simias' *Pteruges* (c. 290 B.C.: Eros succeeds Akmonides as ruler of the world) and in Eustathios, who ascribes it to Alkman (with "Akmon" derived from the Greek for "unwearying": 61 *PMG*). Perhaps the word was not in the beginning intended as a proper name. As a matter of strict accuracy, we should also in passing observe that neither *Iliad* nor *Odyssey* ever uses the term "Titan" to denote anything except those Titans under the earth with Kronos; as a result we cannot say with certainty, however likely it may seem, that Homer thought of figures such as Hyperion, Themis, Mnemosyne, Leto, and Atlas as related to Kronos, or indeed that he thought of their parentage at all.

The second difference between Homer and Hesiod here, that of the otherwise unpretentious Dione (Homer says nothing about her parents either) as Aphrodite's mother, is at least in keeping with the *Iliad's* general tendency to avoid the magical and fantastic, at any rate in comparison with lost epics.[18] Yet we have no basis on which to insist that Homer invented rather than selected a version. The beginning of the *Theogony* lists a Dione (together with Hebe) among those divinities whom the poem will celebrate (*Th* 17), as if Hesiod involuntarily recognized the Homeric version (or a line was interpolated here); later on in the poem a Dione will appear as one of the Okeanides (*Th* 353). Apollodoros follows Homer, but with Dione given the rank of a thirteenth Titan offspring of Ouranos and Gaia (Ap*B* 1.1.3). This is probably an attempt to elevate her status after the fact, since later in the same work a Dione is one of the Nereides (Ap*B* 1.2.7), but we cannot be certain that Apollodoros did not find it in early sources.[19] The usual interpretation of Dione's name as a feminine form of Zeus, if correct, may also indicate a greater early importance than Hesiod allows. The epic *Titanomachia*, with its presumed beginning from Gaia and Ouranos (the latter sprung from Aither), might have contributed much in this regard. Different altogether is the view of the Epimenides *Theogony:* a two-line fragment quoted by a scholiast makes Aphrodite, the Moirai, and the Erinyes all offspring of the same father, whom the scholiast identifies as Kronos (3B19). One other point of interest comes to us from Proklos' comments on the *Timaios:* he cites seven lines of a hexameter poem, probably of Orphic origin, in which Okeanos ponders whether to join Kronos and his other brothers in the attack on their father, as their mother desires, or to remain safely at home (fr 135 Kern). As the fragment breaks off we leave Okeanos in his halls, brooding and angry with his mother and especially his brothers; Proklos tells us that he did not in fact join them.

As for other details in Hesiod's account, the Kyklopes of this early period could scarcely be more different from those encountered by Odysseus in Book 9 of the *Odyssey*. The latter are expressly described as uncultured shepherds, sons of Poseidon (actually Homer *says* only that Polyphemos is a son of Poseidon) who have little use for the gods and share with their Hesiodic namesakes just the feature of the single eye (if in fact they are all so equipped, and not just Polyphemos: the general description at *Od* 9.106–15 says nothing on the subject). In the later sections of the *Theogony*, the Ouranian Kyklopes recede into the background as the Hundred-Handers become more prominent. We will certainly expect them to be immortal, and yet the *Ehoiai* presents them as slain by Apollo, presumably in anger over the killing of his son Asklepios by Zeus' thunderbolt (Hes frr 52, 54 MW). Pherekydes confirms this story and motive but makes Apollo's victims the *sons* of the Kyklopes (3F35a: we hear nothing elsewhere about their having offspring). And a fragment of Pindar suggests that Zeus himself killed them, lest they forge weapons for anyone else (fr 266 SM). The Catalogue Poet's version of their fate reappears in the prologue to Euripides' *Alkestis* as motive for Apollo's exile; the later history of the Hundred-Handers will be considered in connection with the battle of the Olympians and Titans.

Of the birth of the Erinyes, later authors say little, save for the Epimenides *Theogony* (see above) and Aischylos, who makes them daughters of Nyx in his *Eumenides* (416). Such a descent is logical enough, yet Hesiod's version, in which they are sprung from an act of violence by son against father, seems highly consistent with their general character in Homer. In the *Iliad*, Amyntor calls upon them to curse Phoinix after the son has taken his father's concubine (*Il* 9.453–56); Althaia's prayers are heard by them when her son Meleagros kills her brother(s) (*Il* 9.571–72); Iris reminds Poseidon that these goddesses always support the elder brother (*Il* 15.204); and Athena suggests to Ares that his defeat is caused by them because he abandoned his mother's side in the Trojan War (*Il* 21.412–14). Likewise in the *Odyssey*, Telemachos speaks of the potential curses of Penelope if he should expel her from his house, and Odysseus describes the Erinyes of Epikaste working against her son Oidipous (*Od* 2.134–36; 11.279–80). In all the above instances an intrafamilial offense, usually child against parent, is involved. At other moments, however, a broader range of functions seems indicated. In *Iliad* 19, the Erinyes are described as punishing under the earth those who have sworn false oaths, and at the end of the same book they, rather than the Moirai, check the voice of the horse Xanthos (*Il* 19.259–60 [cf. 3.278–79]; 19.418), while at *Odyssey* 17.475 we hear of the Erinyes of beggars. Several other references remain uncertain, including the complaint of the Erinyes against Melampous (*Od* 15.233–34), and the handing over to them of the daughters of Pandareos (to be attendants?: *Od* 20.77–78), though in this last case one of the daughters (not necessarily one of those handed over) seems to have by mistake killed her own son (*Od* 19.518–23 and scholia ad loc.).

In most of these passages the actual chastisement imposed by the Erinyes remains lamentably unclear. True, Phoinix is afflicted with childlessness as the curse of his father requested, but Meleagros suffers nothing like the death Althaia prayed for (unless we are to understand that this happens subsequently), nor does Ares' humiliation at the hands of Athena seem very substantial. Again, in the *Odyssey*, Melampous' quest suffers some obstacles but is ultimately quite successful, and it is difficult to say how the Erinyes might punish Oidipous if he neither blinds himself nor loses his kingdom. Only in the cases of the hypothetical oath-breaker and the daughters of Pandareos do they seem to act directly, and even then we do not learn exactly what they do.

Post-Homeric sources add to this picture some new ideas on their activities. *Theogony* 472–73 suggests that Kronos' overthrow will be in part aided by the Erinys of Ouranos, although Zeus seems to do all the work; line 473 apparently makes the Erinys concerned about Kronos' treatment of his children, but this is a difficult verse grammatically and may well be an explanatory interpolation. In the *Works & Days* Erinyes assist at the birth of Horkos (Oath) from Eris, thus confirming their interest in falsely sworn statements (*W&D* 803–4), and Herakleitos remarks that if the sun should stray from its course the Erinyes, helpers of Dike, would track it down (22B94: this reassertion of natural law on their part seems of a piece with the halting of Xanthos' speech in *Iliad* 19). Moreover, an unassigned lyric fragment appears to make them responsible for the changing of Hekabe into a dog (965 *PMG*).

But the Erinyes' best-known roles in Greek myth are their pursuit of the matricides Orestes and Alkmaion, and their involvement with the family of Oidipous. Of the harassment of Orestes Homer knows nothing, but since his Orestes serves as a model for the punishment of faithless wives, such a silence is hardly surprising. Stesichoros at least told the story, if a papyrus commentary on his value as a source may be trusted; apparently he had Apollo give Orestes a bow with which the latter might ward off the goddesses (217 *PMG*). Subsequently, of course, the tale appears in Aischylos' *Eumenides*, where the Erinyes are given full stage exposure as disgusting, loathsome creatures, dripping with blood and crawling around on all fours to scent their prey. Yet even here their exact function remains obscure: we are told that they want to drink Orestes' blood (like the Keres of the *Aspis*) and drag him down to the Underworld, but with no indication of the order or consequences of these torments (*Eum* 264–68). In the same way, their stated purpose of avenging kindred bloodshed seems especially tailored to the needs of the play, and even then that purpose will not explain why they did not punish Agamemnon for the slaying of his daughter, or Atreus for that of his nephews. At one point, too, they appear to claim responsibility for the protection of strangers, much as was suggested for beggars in the *Odyssey* (*Eum* 545–49). Ultimately, they reveal fertility connections in their prayers for and against the welfare of Athens, a detail that may or may not arise strictly from the poet's dramatic purposes. Earlier in the same trilogy, Kassandra has suggested that they have brought about disaster to the house of Atreus in response to Thyestes' adultery with his brother's wife (*Ag* 1188–93), and the chorus has involved an Erinys in the destruction of Troy, possibly in the guise of or at least by using Helen (*Ag* 744–49). The story of Alkmaion's killing of Eriphyle is largely a blank in early sources; Homer mentions her crime in the *Nekuia*, but says nothing of her fate (*Od* 11.326–27). And though Stesichoros obviously dealt with the tale in his lost *Eriphyle*, the few preserved fragments do not cover this part; the same is true for the shadowy epic *Alkmaionis* mentioned by Apollodoros (Ap*B* 1.8.5). Whether the epic *Epigonoi* or Aischylos' play of the same name could have extended so far is unknown. In chapter 14, we will consider whether an Erinys might be included (as snake or woman) on an Attic Black-Figure version of Eriphyle's death (Berlin:PM VI 4841), and in chapter 17, whether an Erinys might be shown as a snake wrapped around Orestes on a metope from Foce del Sele (no #). Later accounts of the Alkmaion myth indicate that he secured relief from the Erinyes through long travel and purification, much as Orestes does in the *Eumenides* (Ap*B* 3.7.5). If this was also the early version, it might suggest that their function was ordeal by pursuit, rather than a specific punishment. But possibly, too, Alkmaion's harassment is simply modeled on that of Orestes, or vice versa.

From matricides we turn to the house of Oidipous. We have seen that in Homer the Erinyes of Epikaste cause trouble of some sort for her son; presumably his offense was marrying his mother, though Homer might know of other deeds that we do not. In Pindar's *Olympian* 2, on the other hand, the Erinys destroys the sons of Oidipous with mutual slaughter, having seen their father slay his father as Delphi had predicted (*Ol* 2.38–42). This notion, that the Erinyes might punish anyone but the transgressor himself for his crime, appears here for the first time in the preserved literature. Subsequently, we find the goddesses exercising an important role in *Seven against Thebes*, the last play of Aischylos' trilogy on the legend. But the loss of the first two plays, *Laios* and *Oidipous*, leaves us very uncertain as to the goddesses' significance. Clearly Eteokles believes, and Aischylos probably meant the audience to agree, that an Erinys brings about his fatal meeting with his brother Polyneikes. But we do not know whether such intervention was caused by an offense of Laios, or Oidipous, or Eteokles himself, as we shall see later in discussing the assault on Thebes. Here again, however, it may be noted that the Erinyes operate through manipulation of mortals, as often in Homer, rather than by direct intervention. The name "Eumenides," which forms the title of Aischylos' play on the fate of Orestes (but does not actually appear in the preserved drama), represents perhaps Aischylos' own fusion of the Erinyes with these divinities of Kolonos and elsewhere, as well as with the Semnai Theai of the Areopagos.[20] The individual names—Alekto, Tisiphone, and Megaira—first occur in the *Aeneid* (although it is not clear whether Vergil thought of them all as Erinyes: *Aen* 6.570–72; 7.324–26 [Alekto as daughter of Plouton]; 12.845–48 [Megaira and the twin Dirae]). Subsequently, Apollodoros confirms these names as those of the three Erinyes born from the blood of Ouranos (Ap*B* 1.1.4).

The other major offspring of Ouranos' blood, the Gigantes, do not share the same obvious rationale for birth in this unusual fashion, and indeed there is little mention of them in Archaic sources. Homer notes a people of this name

ruled by one Eurymedon, and adds that he and his *atê*-possessed subjects perished, but we are not told how (*Od* 7.58–60; possibly this is the same Eurymedon guilty of the rape of Hera [see chapter 2]). Bakchylides confirms what
the name "Gigantes" implies, that they were children of the earth; he speaks
of the hybris that destroyed them, but he too does not offer details (15.63–64).
The equally sparse tradition of the Gigantes' battle with the Olympians will be
discussed later, in the context of Herakles' exploits. As for the Melian Nymphai, the final product of Ouranos' castration, we shall return to them in our
consideration of minor divinities in chapter 3. We should, however, note that
Alkaios (441 LP) and Akousilaos (2F4) both add another set of offspring, the
Phaiacians, as resulting from the castration.

Turning to Aphrodite's birth, we find that sources after Homer and Hesiod
have little to add. The opening of *Homeric Hymn* 6, the only other Archaic
evidence, rather supports Hesiod's view of the matter, since it makes the goddess arise from the sea foam near Cyprus (though with no direct mention of
Ouranos). One notable change here is that, after the birth, the Horai, rather
than Hesiod's Eros and Himeros, come to adorn her and accompany her to
Olympos; in Hesiod's account the Horai, as daughters of Zeus, have not yet
been born. Oddly enough, nothing we have from Pindar, Bakchylides, or Aischylos commits itself on the subject of Aphrodite's father. In later literature,
she is almost universally the daughter of Zeus, though the Epimenides *Theogony* as noted before does make her spring from Kronos (3B19). Artistic representations of her rising up from the sea (in presumably a birth scene) do not
begin before the mid-fifth century.

Gaia and Pontos

Next in Hesiod's account are the children sprung from Gaia and her other
offspring/consort, Pontos. These are five in number (though the first is not
actually called a child of Gaia): Nereus, Thaumas, Phorkys, Keto, and Eurybia
(*Th* 233–39). For Nereus, Hesiod offers a brief description—honest and unly-
ing, knower of laws and just counsels, gentle and unerring—but his primary
function, like that of his siblings, is to produce further offspring. His one real
appearance in myth occurs when Herakles seizes and holds him in a successful
attempt to extract information necessary to his Labors (the way to the Cattle
of Geryoneus, or to the Hesperides). According to Pherekydes, the sea god
turns himself into fire and water in an effort to escape, but to no avail (3F16).
Prior to the fifth century, Attic Black-Figure shows this tale, with Triton sometimes unaccountably the wrestler while Nereus watches (see chapter 13).

Nereus marries Doris, a convenient daughter of Okeanos and Tethys, and
their children—all female—are the fifty Nereides, for whom Hesiod gives a
complete set of names (*Th* 240–64). Of these daughters, only four—Amphitrite, Thetis, Galateia, and Psamathe—will have any further role to play in
Greek myth as individuals, though as a group the fifty appear with Thetis in
the *Iliad* to lament the death of Patroklos, rising up together from the depths
of the sea and their cave where they live with their father (*Il* 18.35–51).

Homer, on this occasion, names thirty-four Nereides (thirteen on his list do not appear on Hesiod's), although he specifies that all the others came as well. The same mourning of Patroklos was dramatized by Aischylos in his *Nereides*, where the daughters were presumably the chorus, as they may have been also in the *Hoplôn Krisis*, if in that play Thetis actually came in response to the request that she judge the contest for her dead son's arms (fr 174 R). In any case, the *Odyssey* certainly presents the Nereides as attending also the funeral of Achilleus (*Od* 24.47–59), and this is repeated in Proklos' summary of the *Aithiopis* (in both sources they are accompanied by the Mousai). Aischylos and Pindar (*Is* 6.6) further agree that they were fifty in number.

Pontos' second son, Thaumas, also marries an Okeanid, Elektra, by whom he fathers Iris and the two Harpuiai, Aello and Okypetes (*Th* 265–69). For Iris we must look to the *Iliad*, for she is never mentioned in the *Odyssey*, and only rarely in subsequent literature (despite her popularity in vase-painting). Oddly enough, Homer never discusses her parentage (although *Il* 11.201 comes close to calling Zeus her father); the epithets applied to her focus rather on her speed and her function as the messenger of the gods. In this latter capacity she plays a variety of roles. On three occasions she is sent by Zeus to bear his commands to other gods (Hera and Athena, Poseidon, Thetis: *Il* 8.398–425; 15.55, 144–200; 24.77–99), while on two others he sends her to mortals (Hektor, Priam, both times in her own form: *Il* 11.185–210; 24.143–88). For her part, Hera sends the goddess to Achilleus (again in her own form) to advise him, in secret from Zeus (*Il* 18.165–202). On two further occasions Iris appears to mortals (Priam, Helen) disguised as a human; here we are not specifically told that she has been sent by anyone, and what she offers is basically information combined with practical advice (*Il* 2.786–807, where she comes "from the side of Zeus"; 3.125–40). Finally, there are two points at which she clearly acts of her own accord, first in helping Aphrodite to leave the battlefield (by chariot) after her wounding by Diomedes (*Il* 5.353–69 [note that she also unhitches the chariot and feeds the horses]), and second in conveying Achilleus' prayer to Zephyros and Boreas by flying to the former's home (*Il* 23.198–212). In this last instance she stresses that, upon completion of her errand, she will return to the land of the Aithiopes to share in the sacrifices they are preparing for the gods. To be fair, we should add that the *Odyssey* certainly knows of her, even if she is not mentioned, since the beggar Arnaios is nicknamed "Iros" after her (*Od* 18.6–7).[21]

In Hesiod, she makes only one real appearance, as the divinity who journeys to the Styx and brings back water when one of the gods wishes to take an oath (*Th* 780–86). Proklos' summary of the *Kypria* shows her revealing to Menelaos the departure of Helen with Paris, and in two of the Homeric Hymns she also functions as a messenger: in that to Apollo she is sent by the other goddesses to fetch Eileithuia to Leto's lying-in (*HAp* 102–14), while in the Hymn to Demeter Zeus sends her (unsuccessfully) to summon Demeter to Olympos after the famine has arisen (*HDem* 314–24). In this last instance we should note that, after Iris has failed, Zeus sends Hermes to Hades; thus, both gods serve as messengers in the same work. The only other early mention of Iris is the one already noted in a fragment of Alkaios, where she becomes by Zephyros the mother of Eros (327 LP). In Attic Black-Figure vase-painting, she has a standard function as the escorter of the gods to the wedding of Peleus and Thetis (so on the François Krater, the Erskine Dinos, and probably Athens Akr 587; Hermes stays well to the rear). She also appears on a number of occasions as cupbearer for the gods (e.g., Berlin:Ch F2278; Munich 2304). Attic Red-Figure vase-painting shows her in a variety of roles: with the infant Hermes (Munich 2426), with Memnon, as Hypnos and Thanatos carry him away (London E12), with Kentauroi whom she must perhaps ward off (Florence 4218), and with Silenoi, who similarly pursue her (London E65; Boston 08.30a; Berlin:PM F2591). On the London cup with Memnon she is wingless and holds the kerykeion; conceivably, then, she may here usurp Hermes' role as *psychopompos*, although (since Eos appears on the other side of the corpse) she *might* be bringing the bereaved mother the news of Memnon's blissful afterlife. Her encounter with the Silenoi seems in all three cases to have been triggered by her visit to an altar, from which she has picked up an ox-tongue or some such part of the sacrificial offering.[22] The London cup (by the Brygos Painter) shows the Silenoi reaching for both her and the offering; Dionysos stands by in astonishment, but presumably he will come to her rescue (unless the offerings belong to him).[23] A satyr play should be at work here, though the only known candidate, Achaios' satyric *Iris*, is too late in time. Iris holds the kerykeion already on the François Krater (Florence 4209), and probably also the Erskine Dinos (London 1971.11–1.1), reasonably enough since she, rather than Hermes, leads the procession; on the other hand, the Antimenes Painter shows her following Hermes as the two of them together (both with the kerykeion) bring the goddesses to Paris (Berlin:PM F1895). Red-Figure often gives her this same distinctive staff (so, e.g., Berlin:PM F2264 [Oltos] and London E12 and E65 above); on Munich 2426, she seems to carry Hermes *and* the staff, perhaps to identify the child. Apart from London E12, she is almost always represented with wings (the *Iliad*, in fact, twice calls her *chrysopteros*, "golden-winged": *Il* 8.398; 11.185).

The Harpuiai would appear to share parentage with Iris on the basis of their tremendous speed; the Epimenides *Theogony*, however, calls them daughters of Okeanos and Gaia (3B7), while Pherekydes of Syros assigns as their father Boreas (and as sister Thyella: 7B5). In a separate fragment the Epimenides *Theogony*, as we have seen, also equates them with the Hesperides (3B9), and in this same connection both that work and Akousilaos put them in charge of the apples (2F10); Pherekydes has them guard Tartaros. In the *Iliad*, we find mention of a single Harpuia, Podarge, who mates in the form of a mare with Zephyros and produces Xanthos and Balios, the horses of Achilleus (*Il* 16.150–51). The *Odyssey* offers the more familiar plural "Harpuiai" for wind-spirits whom Telemachos and Eumaios describe, perhaps figuratively, as carrying off Odysseus, and to whom Penelope refers as the abductors of the daughters of Pandareos (*Od* 1.241; 14.371; 20.77–78); their role in this last event seems to be as agents of the Erinyes, to whom they hand over the daughters. In the same context, Penelope calls them *thuellai* (storm-winds), and that may have been another name for them. We see the two of them illustrated in flight on a spouted bowl by the Nessos Painter, with the word "Arepuia" inscribed; the artist has depicted them as normal-looking women marked out only by their large wings (Berlin:Lost F1682). Their tormenting of Phineus and their flight from the sons of Boreas is not a story for which we have early sources (although it was recounted in the *Ehoiai*); we will return to it when discussing the voyage of the Argo in chapter 12.

Pontos and Gaia's third son, Phorkys, marries his own sister Keto, and the resulting offspring are the most monstrous of all Pontos' progeny—the two Graiai, three Gorgons, Echidna, and the snake Ophis (*Th* 270–336). As for Phorkys himself, the *Odyssey* calls him "old man of the sea" like his brother Nereus (*Od* 13.96, 345), and makes him the grandfather of Polyphemos through a daughter, Thoosa (*Od* 1.72). Elsewhere in Archaic literature (assuming he is not the Porkos of Alkman 1.19 PMG²⁴), he appears only as progenitor of the Graiai, a role he serves in Akousilaos, Pherekydes, Pindar, and Aischylos, as well as in Hesiod (Akousilaos makes him the son of Eidothea [daughter of Proteus], rather than of Pontos and Gaia: 2F11).

The Graiai are described in the *Theogony* simply as gray from birth (*Th* 270–73). Aischylos gives them one eye among them and one tooth at *Prometheus Desmotes* 792–97; it is not clear whether the tooth is also shared, or whether they have one each. The same play makes them three in number, long-lived, and "swan-shaped"; whether this should be taken literally, or simply refers to their white hair, is a difficult point. Whatever Aischylos intended, they live near their sisters, the Gorgons, somewhere far to the east (and apparently on dry land, where Io could reach them). Aischylos' lost Perseus trilogy included a play entitled *Phorkides* in which Perseus encountered the Graiai on his way to find the Gorgons (fr 262 R). Various references make clear that here the Graiai guarded their sisters, and that Perseus stole the eye (and threw it away) so as to thwart their task; unfortunately, we cannot be certain that they appeared in the play (though it seems very likely), and if so, whether they were chorus or actors. Neither does there survive from the play any indication of where the sisters are located (save that the eye is thrown into the Tritonian lake). The same is true of Pherekydes' account, where the sisters are named as Pemphredo, Enyo, and Deino (3F11). Here they clearly have one eye *and* one tooth among them, and Perseus steals both in order to obtain information needed for his task. The information acquired, he returns both items and continues on his journey. Pindar's brief mention, with its use of the word "darkened" for Perseus' treatment of the Graiai (*Py* 12.13), rather suggests agreement with Aischylos' version. We shall see later (chapter 10) that there are Attic illustrations of these sisters (and the theft) from the latter part of the fifth century; although the tableau there presented confirms the basic situation, it offers no help on the above questions.

Unlike the Graiai, the Gorgons are from the beginning (in Hesiod) three in number (*Th* 274–83). Hesiod names them as Sthenno, Euryale, and Medousa, and places them toward the edge of night, beyond Okeanos, near the Hesperides, in other words to the far west (he does not say whether the Graiai lived near them). Of the three, Sthenno and Euryale are immortal and ageless, but Medousa is mortal (Hesiod offers no explanation of this odd situation). She alone mates with Poseidon (assuming that Kyanochaites is here, as elsewhere, an epithet of the sea god), and after her beheading by Perseus, Chrysaor and the horse Pegasos spring forth from her neck. Pegasos we shall meet again in the story of Bellerophontes (referred to briefly in passing at *Th* 325); Hesiod here says simply that he flew up to Olympos to carry the lightning and thunderbolt for Zeus. Chrysaor marries another convenient Okeanid, Kallirhoe, who bears the three-headed Geryoneus later to be slain by Herakles (*Th* 287–94; 979–83).

In contrast to the *Theogony*, Homer, although he describes several Gorgon heads on bucklers (e.g., *Il* 11.36–37) and conjures up yet another to frighten Odysseus in the *Nekuia* (*Od* 11.633–35), never directly alludes to the tale of Medousa, save perhaps in *Iliad* 5, where the description of Zeus' aigis worn by Athena includes the Gorgon head customarily donated by Perseus (*Il* 5.738–42). In the *Kypria* (context not clear, although the point of reference seems to be Phorkys and Keto), the Gorgons are pictured as living on a rocky island named Sarpedon in the stream of Okeanos (fr 32 *PEG*). Pherekydes also puts them somewhere in Okeanos; the summary of his account says little about their physical appearance, but does note that Medousa's face turned men to stone, and adds that the head was ultimately given to Athena for the aigis (3F11). The *Aspis* offers a typically garish portrait: Gorgons with twin snakes— glaring and gnashing their teeth—wrapped around their waists (for artistic confirmation of this point, see below), and *possibly* a vague reference to snakes for hair (*Aspis* 229–37). Snaky locks are in any case well attested by Pindar (*Py* 10.46–48; 12.9–12), and here again Medousa's head lithifies, while Euryale's lament becomes the model for the song of the flute. In *Pythian* 10, also see Perseus journeying to the land of the Hyperboreans in the far north on his quest for the head; the Gorgons may or may not have been located there. For Aischylos, we must again be content with the description in *Prometheus Desmotes*, since there are no relevant fragments from the *Phorkides*. As noted above, his Gorgons live near their sister Graiai to the far east; they have wings and snaky hair, and no mortal can look upon them and live (*PD* 798–800). This last detail suggests that Aischylos believed all three sisters could turn men to stone, but he may be exaggerating for effect, or perhaps he refers to their generally ferocious character. The tale that Medousa was once beautiful, and fell prey to Athena's anger by mating with Poseidon in the goddess' temple, first appears in Ovid (*Met* 4.790–803); something of the same sort also surfaces in

Apollodoros, who says that Medousa wished to rival Athena in beauty (Ap*B* 2.4.3). Such an idea may have been developed at some late point in time to dignify Poseidon's union with the Gorgon; certainly it will not explain the equally hideous condition of her two sisters. Euripides' surprising statement in the *Ion* that Athena herself slew a Gorgon (not actually called Medousa) at Phlegra, where the gods fought the Gigantes, might be relevant to a tale of rivalry, though the text's implication is that Gaia spawned the monster especially for that battle (*Ion* 989–96).

Artistic representations of Gorgons are much too abundant to list in detail here, but we may note a few special features. On a Boiotian relief amphora of *c.* 650 B.C., a figure in traveling garb cuts off the head of a female represented as a Kentauros (Louvre CA 795).[25] The attitude of the beheader, with face averted from his victim, seems not only to guarantee that this is an early Medousa, but to offer our earliest evidence for the Gorgon's perilous qualities. On the contemporary Protoattic Eleusis Amphora, the sisters appear as monstrous (albeit shapely) insect-faced creatures with no wings but distinct snakes around their heads (Eleusis, no #). By the time of the name vases of the Nessos and Gorgon Painters of Athens (end of the seventh century: Athens 1002, Louvre E874), canonical features, such as the tripartite nose and lolling tongue (perhaps developed in Corinthian painting), are basically in force; for the wings and snakes there is also a slightly earlier ivory relief from Samos depicting the decapitation (Samos E 1). The same time period also offers our first look at Medousa and her family, that is, Medousa shown intact and, at her side, her children, Pegasos and Chrysaor, who will in fact emerge from her neck only after her head has been cut off. We find this composition on a shield-band from Olympia (B 1687: wings, but apparently no snakes) and again on the famous Medousa pediment from the Temple of Artemis on Kerkyra (no #), where the wings and snakes are both in evidence. In this latter example, the two snakes knotted around her waist repeat the image found in the *Aspis* and seen again in Attic Black-Figure of the early sixth century. Two other architectural reliefs of this period, a metope from Temple C at Selinous and the antepagmentum from Gela, present Pegasos alone with Medousa, perhaps due to considerations of space. On two cups by the C Painter we actually see the head of Pegasos rising up from Medousa's severed neck as she collapses to the ground (London B380; Berlin:Ch F1753); the London cup shows as well a naked young man between the pursuing Gorgons (presumably Chrysaor, though he appears again behind Medousa). Black-Figure of the late sixth and early fifth century will complete the birth by presenting Pegasos leaping completely clear of the neck (e.g., NY 06.1070). Chrysaor's presence on the Olympia shield-band, the Kerkyra pediment, and the London cup constitutes the sum of our evidence for his appearance; in general, he seems normal enough, but the sculptor of the pediment has twisted his face and mouth in a grotesque fashion.[26] His name, which is sometimes used as an epithet of Apollo, means "golden sword"; there are no preserved stories about him, and nothing to explain such an appellation.

Neither is there any obvious reason why his son should be triple-bodied, except that this branch of the early divine family is prone to monsters. Stesichoros, who had ample occasion to describe the characteristics of Geryoneus for his *Geryoneis*, gives him six arms and six wings as well (186 *PMG*; 10–15 *SLG*). As we might imagine, the wings usually do not survive in artistic versions; either Geryoneus is given three bodies from the waist up, or else is represented as three completely separate human figures against whom Herakles must battle (see chapter 13).

After the Graiai and Gorgons, Phorkys and Keto produce Echidna, half fair maiden (presumably the upper half) and half terrible snake, a monster who lives alone in a cave under the earth, far from men and gods (though Hesiod may intend this habitation rather for Keto: the syntax of the prepositional phrase at *Th* 300 is unclear). If the following lines are genuine, the cave is in the land of the Arymoi, but that location is itself much disputed.[27] The one variant of her parentage comes from the Epimenides *Theogony*, where she is the offspring of Styx and one Peiras (3B6). Whatever we make of this and wherever she lives, Echidna mates in Hesiod with Typhoeus, the challenger of Zeus, and the results are all animals: Orthos, the watchdog of Geryoneus, Kerberos, the fifty-headed watchdog of Hades, the snaky Hydra of Lerna, and possibly the fire-breathing Chimaira with its three heads, one of a lion, one of a goat, and one of a snake, arranged respectively at the front, middle, and back (*Th* 304–25). Alternatively (since the pronoun referent at 319 is uncertain), the mother of the Chimaira would be the Hydra (by an unnamed father) or even, less probably, Keto.[28] To this list, Akousilaos (2F13) and Pherekydes (3F7) agree in adding the eagle who devoured Prometheus' liver; Hesiod gives it no parentage.

About Orthos we find nothing more than that he was killed by Herakles during the raid on Geryoneus' cattle. Artistic representations sometimes include him (always dead, usually with arrows protruding from his body) in scenes of the combat; on several occasions (including the earliest), he has two heads. Kerberos' duties as watchdog (and devourer of any who try to leave Hades) are described later in the *Theogony* (769–74). He is mentioned in connection with Herakles' task in both the *Iliad* and the *Odyssey* (*Il* 8.367–68; *Od* 11.620–26), but without any further details of his appearance, and the same is true in Bakchylides, where his parentage from Echidna is repeated (5.60–62). Pindar's lost dithyramb on Herakles in the Underworld seems, however, to have given the creature one hundred heads, if the scholia minora to the *Iliad* can be trusted (fr 249a SM). The earliest artistic portrayal, a Middle Corinthian kotyle from Argos, shows only one head, but has snakes growing out all over his body (lost; cf. the Caeretan hydria Louvre E701). A Lakonian cup from the middle of the sixth century increases the number of heads to three and adds a snake for tail as well (Erskine Coll), and this (with sometimes only two heads) becomes the standard representation in both art and literature. On the Corinthian kotyle mentioned above, Kerberos appears to run from Herakles, but on all subsequent examples it is Herakles (and even his divine helpers) who display caution. Presumably the frequent variant of two heads arose from logistical problems in draftsmanship.

As for the Hydra, Hesiod says simply that Hera raised her to be a danger to Herakles, and that he slew her with the aid of Iolaos, but a scholion adds that Alkaios gave her nine heads, and Simonides fifty (Al 443 LP; Sim 569 PMG). Pausanias adds that, in his opinion, she had originally just one, and that the epic poet Peisandros added additional heads in order to make her more fearsome (fr 2 PEG); whether he is right to suppose Peisandros the first in this respect we cannot, of course, say. The representations in vase-painting usually show a multitude of snaky heads and bodies (joined together toward the tail), often as many as ten. For the actual detail that two heads grew from each severed neck, or that one head was immortal, we must await Ovid (Met 9.69–74: two heads only) and Apollodoros (ApB 2.5.2); nevertheless the sickle (usually for Iolaos) is a standard element in early representations of the battle (together with a sword or club for Herakles). As for the searing of the necks to prevent regrowth, the first evidence is a late sixth-century Black-Figure amphora on which Iolaos holds a torch (VG 106465); Euripides in the *Herakles Mainomenos* adds that Herakles "burnt out" the Hydra, which may well confirm this idea (HF 420). Sophokles' *Trachiniai* together with the *Herakles* appear to be our earliest firm sources for the idea that the blood of the Hydra was poisonous and could be applied to Herakles' arrows (Tr 831–40), but in chapter 13 we will look more closely at a recently discovered fragment of Stesichoros' *Geryoneis*.

The Chimaira, as we have seen, is the offspring of either Echidna or the Hydra. Hesiod's description (heads of lion, goat, snake, fire-breathing capacity) is paralleled word for word in the *Iliad*'s account of Bellerophontes' exploits (Il 6.179–82); later in the poem a certain Amisodaros of Lykia is named as the one who raised the monster (Il 16.328–29), and in the *Homeric Hymn to Apollo*, Apollo boasts that neither Typhoeus nor Chimaira will avail the dead Python (HAp 367–68). Typhoeus (earlier in the poem the Python's fosterling) is reasonable here, but the Chimaira remains unexplained. Her capacity for breathing fire recurs in an extremely fragmentary remnant of the *Ehoiai* (Hes fr 43a.87 MW). The artistic tradition, beginning with Protocorinthian vessels of the early seventh century, interprets the creature as a lion with the goat's head growing out of the back (not from the same neck as the lion's) and the snake serving in place of the tail (in one early Black-Figure example, the whole rear of the body may end in a snake: Kerameikos 154). Whether the goat's head was responsible for the name "Chimaira" or vice versa is an open question. In any case, she (or just possibly Echidna) mates with the dog Orthos (her brother, if she is descended from Echidna, and uncle, if from the Hydra), and the results here are both lion types, the Phix (elsewhere Sphinx) and the Nemean Lion (Th 326–32).

Hesiod calls the Phix a bringer of destruction to the Thebans, but says nothing about physical appearance or method of operation. Sphinxes as a type, with the canonical lion's body, woman's head, and wings, are well known in sculpture and metalwork from the Near East and Crete, and in painting from Protocorinthian vase designs; in the Greek world the Sphinx also becomes a popular crowning device on columns and grave stelai. The name "Sphinx" (or "Sphix") is assured for the type from its use on an Attic Black-Figure band cup of about 540 B.C. (Munich 2243). But in all these representations, the creature is employed without mythological context. Our earliest portrayal in which she actually does something is probably the architectural relief from Mycenae of about 630 B.C. on which two sphinxes are reconstructed as standing over a nude male body (Athens 2870). Subsequently, a Siana cup by the C Painter shows a Sphinx pursuing a number of men (one of whom she seems to have caught: Syracuse 25418), and several other Black-Figure pots of the sixth century repeat that pattern (CabMéd 278, Athens 397, Syracuse 12085).[29] The first recorded association of Sphinx with Oidipous dates to about 530 B.C., a Chalkidian amphora on which Oidipous sits before the Sphinx (Stuttgart 65/15), as he does on the famous Red-Figure cup in the Vatican (16541). Here the solving of her riddle (first attested in literature in Sophokles' *Oidipous Tyrannos*) is obviously the primary consideration, but we will see in chapter 14 that she has a complex dual role as riddle-poser and snatcher of young men. The epic *Oidipodeia* (where she kills Kreon's son Haimon) might have told us much about these matters, and likewise Aischylos' lost satyr play *Sphinx*. As to appearance, both Aischylos and Sophokles call her a dog, and while this might be figurative language, it might also reflect a variant tradition: the bodies of lions and dogs, minus the head, are not so very different (Ais fr 236 R; *OT* 391: Palaiphatos [4] actually says that she had the body of a dog, though he may be drawing from these same passages of tragedy). No early author gives any motive for her assault on the Thebans, although as a monster perhaps she did not need one; later writers will at times make her an agent of various gods who visit disaster on Thebes for one reason or another. All of these traditions, and her odd demise by suicide, will be discussed more fully in the context of Oidipous' exploits.

The Chimaira's other child, the Lion of Nemea, presents no special features, save for his invulnerable hide. Hesiod, who does not mention this characteristic, says simply that Hera raised him, as she did the Hydra (but here without reference to Herakles), and that Herakles overcame him (*Th* 328–32). Bakchylides makes the same two points and adds that this was the first of Herakles' Labors, but he too does not tell us whether Hera's tendance had her enemy's destruction as a goal (9.6–9). Elsewhere he and Pindar are the first to describe the skin as impenetrable (Bak 13.46–54; *Is* 6.47–48). The scene of combat between the Lion and Herakles, one of the most popular in Greek vase-painting, shows the hero usually wrestling with the Lion, but on occasion brandishing a sword, and even stabbing with it (see chapter 13). If this is not ignorance of the tradition of invulnerability, it may represent Herakles' initial attempt to slay the creature. The resulting lionskin adorns Herakles as his trademark in much of Archaic art, beginning about 570 b.c., and seems to be as early as the epic account of Peisandros (fr 1 *PEG*; Athen 12.512f attributes the idea rather to Stesichoros). One final reference of an odd sort comes from the Epimenides *Theogony*, where the Lion (like Epimenides himself) is said to be sprung from (or shaken off by) Selene, probably in her role as the moon rather than as a goddess (3B2).[30]

Of Ophis, fourth and last of Phorkys and Keto's brood, we have already spoken in the discussion of the Hesperides. Hesiod, as we saw, makes him guard the apples (though the location—under the earth?—is difficult), Theokles carves him in wood at Olympia (together with fruit tree, Hesperides, and Atlas: Paus 6.19.8), and Pherekydes gives him the same task at the behest of Hera (in fear of illicit apple-munching by the daughters of Atlas: 3F16, where he also has ninety heads). A Black-Figure lekythos of about 500 b.c. shows him (with two heads) wrapped around his tree and menacing Herakles (Berlin:PM VI 3261: chapter 13 offers other examples). No Archaic source describes his combat with the hero, though the vase illustrations suggest discretion on Herakles' part; Sophokles probably and Euripides definitely say that the hero killed him to get the apples (*Tr* 1099–1100; *HF* 397–99).[31]

Finally, we come to the fifth and last child of Pontos and Gaia, Eurybia, the second daughter. She marries Kreios, one of the twelve Titans, and thus joins together the lines of descent from Gaia through Pontos and Ouranos (*Th* 375–77). This union is to some extent the result of the fact that four of the other Titan males marry their sisters, while the two remaining sisters, Themis and Mnemosyne, are reserved for the subsequent attentions of Zeus. Thus, the two remaining brothers must find spouses outside the immediate family. Iapetos will adopt the same solution as did Nereus and Thaumas, his half-brothers, by wedding an Okeanid (in his case, Klymene), while Kreios here takes his half-sister. The children of Kreios and Eurybia are three: Astraios, Pallas, and Perses. Astraios weds his cousin Eos, the dawn (daughter of Hyperion and Theia), and produces three winds, Boreas, Zephyros, and Notos, plus the morning star Heosphoros and the stars in general (*Th* 378–82). Zephyros, we have already observed, is at his house with Boreas when Iris comes to summon them to Achilleus in *Iliad* 23, and appears as the sire of Achilleus' horses in *Iliad* 16; he will reappear in chapter 2 as a contender (with Apollo) for the affections of Hyakinthos. Boreas is best known for his abduction of Oreithuia, daughter of Erechtheus, a tale dramatized by Aischylos in his lost *Oreithuia*; we will return to him in chapter 7, but it might be noted here that Pausanias found him depicted on the Chest of Kypselos, with snake's tails instead of feet, as he carried off his love (5.19.1).[32] The children of the union, as both Simonides (534 *PMG*) and Akousilaos (2F30) tell us, are Zetes and Kalais, who sail with the Argo. We have already discovered that Pherekydes of Syros makes Boreas the father of the Harpuiai as well (7B5).

The second son, Pallas, marries his cousin Styx (daughter of Okeanos and

Tethys); their children are Zelos (Glory), Nike (Victory), Kratos (Power), and Bia (Force) (*Th* 383–85). These last two appear briefly in the *Prometheus Desmotes*, but basically all four are personifications.

The third son, Perses (oddly noted for his wisdom), then marries his cousin Asterie (daughter of Koios and Phoibe and sister of Leto), and their one child is Hekate (*Th* 409–13). In his long discourse on the powers of this figure, Hesiod makes her a general helper of men, bringing victory and success to their various endeavors *if* she wishes, and honored by Zeus as she was by the Titans, but with no chthonic or lunar associations mentioned.[33] In the *Homeric Hymn to Demeter* (where she is the daughter of Persaios), she hears Persephone's cries of despair from her cave and later informs Demeter, torch in hand, of that fact, but her role is markedly less than that of Helios (*HDem* 24–25, 51–63: in later authors, she is more prominently involved in assisting Demeter). At the end of the poem she does become an attendant of Persephone (*HDem* 438–40), and this may suggest previous cultic links with Persephone and/or the Underworld. The *Megalai Ehoiai* makes her the mother of Skylla by one Phorbas (Hes fr 262 MW); Akousilaos agrees, but makes the father Phorkys, which leaves little doubt that he supposes this Skylla the sea monster of the *Odyssey* (2F42). Whatever its origin, the idea of Hekate as parent of such an offspring gains some currency, for Apollonios repeats it in the *Argonautika* (4.828–29) while fusing Hekate with Krataiis, Skylla's mother in the *Odyssey* (12.124). In the *Eumolpia* of "Mousaios," Hekate is the child of Asterie by *Zeus*, who only subsequently bestows his paramour upon Perses (2B16: on Asterie and Zeus, see further below, under the children of Koios and Phoibe). For Pherekydes, she is the daughter of Aristaios, son of Paion (3F44), and Bakchylides calls her the torch-bearer, daughter of Nyx (fr 1B SM). Pindar, who has nothing whatever to say about her parents, seems to connect her with the moon in the fragmentary *Paian* 2 (75–79). An Orphic tradition calls her the daughter of Demeter (fr 41 Kern), and so too Kallimachos, where her father is again Zeus (fr 466 Pf).

This last evidence, and her role in the Hymn, might make Hekate seem almost a doublet of Persephone. By contrast, however, Pausanias claims that the *Ehoiai* equated Hekate with the Iphimede (i.e., Iphigeneia) rescued by Artemis (1.43.1). We have what we think is the passage in question, and although the rescue part is probably an addition to the original concept of Iphigeneia's death,[34] the papyrus does say that Artemis saves the girl and makes her Artemis *einodia*, Artemis "of the road" (Hes fr 23b MW). But nowhere is Hekate specifically mentioned (in a section that appears to be complete), so that we must ask on what basis Pausanias has drawn his conclusion. In Sophokles' *Antigone* we find a messenger speaking of Kreon's prayers to both Plouton and the *einodia theos* when he buries Polyneikes (*Ant* 1199–1200), while a fragment of the same poet's *Rhizotomoi* appeals to the goddess (with Helios) as "*einodia* Hekate," she who dwells on Olympos and at crossroads on the holy earth (fr

535 R; cf. *Hel* 569–70). It would appear, then, that by the fifth century, if not before, *einodia* was a title of Hekate, thus explaining Pausanias' deduction. Philodemos apparently supposed the same thing, and adds further that Stesichoros followed Hesiod in equating Iphigeneia with Hekate (215 *PMG*), thus strengthening the likelihood that Pausanias is here correct.

If a fusion of Iphigeneia and Hekate under the name of Artemis *einodia* was the intention of the *Ehoiai*, then that poem will have suggested an identity, or at least a very strong link, between Hekate and Artemis, and scholars have seen this same link in both the *Hiketides* of Aischylos (676: Artemis Hekate) and the *Phoinissai* of Euripides (109–10: Hekate child of Leto). The problem is that the word "Hekate" in these two passages could be simply an epithet, much as *Hekatos* (far-darter) is sometimes applied to Apollo (e.g., Sim 573 *PMG*).[35] Thus our evidence for Hekate as a by-form of Artemis in early times remains tantalizingly unclear. The speech from the *Rhizotomoi* may or may not also intend an association of Hekate as the moon with Helios the sun; our ignorance as to the point at which Artemis became linked with the moon (Aischylos? see below) is one more uncertainty here. But Sophokles does clearly connect Hekate with crossroads, while Euripides' Medeia regards her as a patroness, perhaps with an eye toward skill in the preparing of drugs and poisons (*Med* 395–97). In art, her most notable appearance is on a Red-Figure bell krater by the Persephone Painter on which she (name inscribed) holds two torches as Hermes brings Persephone up from within the earth (NY 28.57.23). Pausanias claims that the Athenian sculptor Alkamenes in the latter part of the fifth century B.C. was the first to represent her as triple-bodied (2.30.2), and she takes that form also in the preserved Gigantomachy on the Altar of Zeus at Pergamon. But on present evidence these and other such representations denoted a tripling of the same divinity, not a joining together of Hekate, Artemis, and Selene or the like.[36]

The Titans Our survey of the children of Gaia and Pontos has already led us to consider one of the Titans, Kreios, and his offspring, since he marries Eurybia, one of their two daughters. Of the other Titans, as noted above, four (Okeanos, Hyperion, Koios, and Kronos) marry their own sisters (Tethys, Theia, Phoibe, and Rheia) while Iapetos, like Kreios, must look elsewhere. Okeanos, whatever his Homeric role in fathering the gods, is clearly in all accounts the great stream surrounding the world, to be found at the ends of the earth (*Th* 791–92) and in Homer somehow crossed in order to arrive at the entrance to Hades (*Od* 11.13–19). Later writers tell us that the sun sails at night from west to east through his waters (Mim 12 W; Stes 185 *PMG*; probably *Tit* fr 8 *PEG*). Homer also gives Okeanos an encircling role on the shield of Achilleus (*Il* 18.607–8), and calls him in *Iliad* 21 the source of all rivers and springs and wells and the whole sea (*thalassa: Il* 21.195–97; Pontos never appears in Homer). At other early points, too, the distinction between fresh and salt water fails to assert itself: in the *Theogony*, we have seen two sons of Pontos (Nereus and Thaumas) marry Okeanides, while *Iliad* 18 presents Thetis and the Okeanid Eurynome dwelling together (*Il* 18.398–99).

Hera's deception speech in *Iliad* 14 involves the story that Okeanos and his consort Tethys are quarreling and refrain from love, a detail that may or may not be part of the deception (*Il* 14.205–7). Otherwise, the god is normally a place rather than a person, the major exception being Aischylos' *Prometheus Desmotes*. Here Okeanos visits the bound Prometheus on a winged griffin or hippocamp and offers some rather feeble advice (*PD* 284–396). At one point, Prometheus appears to imply that his fellow Titan aided him in putting Zeus on the throne (*PD* 330–32), but the lines are questionable and may simply reflect sarcasm at Okeanos' present "daring."[37] Earlier in this chapter we considered the Orphic fragment in which Okeanos hesitated and demurred when the other Titans made their attack against Ouranos (fr 135 Kern). Though it may be simply a stock formula, the *Theogony* does say that Styx and her children went over to Zeus' side on the advice of her father (*Th* 397–98). In one way or another, all storytellers (or rather, all those who made Okeanos a Titan) had of course to explain Okeanos' continuing liberty (a cosmological necessity) when his brother Titans were imprisoned in Tartaros or otherwise punished. For Tethys, there are no myths at all, save for Hera's comment in the *Iliad* that she was given by Rheia to Tethys to raise when Zeus was deposing Kronos (*Il* 14.201–4). Artistic representations appear in the illustrations of the wedding of Peleus and Thetis on the François Krater (Florence 4209) and the Erskine Dinos (London 1971.11–1.1), where Okeanos and Tethys form part of the procession as invited guests; in both cases, Okeanos is presented as human in form (albeit with bull's head or horns) from the waist up, but with a fish's body from the waist down.

The children of Okeanos and Tethys are a series of sons, the rivers (Hesiod names nineteen, including Acheloos, Peneios, and Skamandros: *Th* 337–45), and daughters, the Okeanides, who with Apollo and the rivers aid in the bringing up of young men (*Th* 346–70). Hesiod names forty-one of these, including Elektra, Doris, Klymene, Kallirhoe, Dione, Perseis, Metis, Kalypso, and Styx, but he also stresses that the total number of offspring, male and female, is six thousand (three thousand each), of which no mortal knows all the names. Akousilaos calls Acheloos the eldest of the group (2F1); Homer mentions him together with Okeanos as a mighty river (though weaker than Zeus: *Il* 21.193–95). The story of this offspring's transformation into a bull and his combat with Herakles for Deianeira was apparently recounted by Archilochos (287 W) and Pindar (fr 249a SM); our summary of the latter also says that Herakles broke off one of his horns, and that the river god ransomed it back by offering a horn acquired from Amaltheia, daughter of Okeanos (the latter not mentioned in Hesiod; for other notions about this horn, see below on Zeus' infancy). But a full account of the battle is not preserved until the prologue to Sophokles' *Trachiniai*, where Deianeira herself tells the story. Vase-painting portrays Acheloos for this occasion as a Kentauros or human-headed bull or fish, horn prominent (see chapter 13). His brother Skamandros' conflict with Achilleus forms a major part of *Iliad* 21. Of the sisters, we have seen Elektra married to Thaumas, Doris to Nereus, Klymene to Iapetos, Kallirhoe to Chrysaor, and Styx to Pallas, while Dione and Metis consort with Zeus and Kalypso with Odysseus; Perseis will wed Helios. Not mentioned in Hesiod's list, in addition to Amaltheia, is Hesione, whom Akousilaos (2F34) and Aischylos (*PD* 555–60) make the wife of Prometheus.

Of all these children of Okeanos, Styx is given special prominence through her role in Hesiod's Titanomachy: when Zeus summons the gods to Olympos and promises to maintain the honors of those who take his side, the Okeanid (as we saw, on the advice of her father) is the first to join him, and brings with her her children by Pallas (*Th* 389–401). In return for these tokens of victory, Zeus makes her the oath by which the gods swear. Such oaths are not overly common in Homer (often a nod suffices, and indeed Zeus once calls this the greatest witness: *Il* 1.525–26), but Hera swears twice by the Styx (among other things) to Hypnos and Zeus in the *Iliad* (14.271; 15.37–38), and Kalypso gives the same pledge to Odysseus in the *Odyssey* (5.185–86). From the Homeric Hymns there is also Leto to Delos (*HAp* 85–86) and Demeter to Metaneira (*HDem* 259), while Apollo suggests such an oath to Hermes (although he in fact nods: *HHerm* 518–19). The rather strange description of the oath later in the *Theogony* states that whenever someone of the immortals lies and there is a dispute on Olympos, Iris is sent to fetch water from the Styx in a golden pitcher, and the gods swear pouring it out (*Th* 780–806). Elsewhere, as we have seen, it is enough to name the river in making the oath. In this passage, Hesiod goes on to define the penalty for breaking such an oath, though one might have thought it unbreakable: the god who forswears lies for a year breathless and voiceless in an artificial sleep, and when this penalty has ended he suffers the worser torment of expulsion from the gods' company and table for nine years. There is no other record anywhere in Greek literature of this (save for Empedokles 31B115 and the Orphic Theogonies [fr 295 Kern]), and certainly nothing to indicate that the penalty was ever enforced. It should be noted that oaths are generally given by gods to other gods, not to mortals; Demeter's voluntary oath to Metaneira and that of Kalypso to Odysseus are exceptions.

The Styx as river is also described in this section of the *Theogony*: one-tenth of Okeanos' waters are allotted to her, and she runs far under the earth, coming up to pour forth from a rock (*Th* 775–79, 786–92). As an actual stream of the Underworld she is mentioned by Athena at *Iliad* 8.369, and Kirke makes the Kokytos an offshoot of her at *Odyssey* 10.514. In the *Homeric Hymn to Demeter*, she is also named by Persephone as one of her companions (together with numerous other Okeanides; the poet gives twenty-one names here, of whom six are not in the *Theogony*: *HDem* 418–23) at the time of her abduction. Moving down to the fifth century, the Epimenides *Theogony* says that she does not live with Pallas (the father of her children), and that she bore Echidna to one Peiras (3B6). Pindar mentions her oath in *Paian* 6 (155), but the context is too fragmentary to say more. As a group, the Okeanides come up from their cave beneath the earth to form the chorus of the *Prometheus Desmotes*, and may or may not share Prometheus' fate of being overwhelmed by a cataclysm as the play ends.[38] Whether they were mentioned at all in the *Lyomenos* (where the chorus was composed of Titans) is not clear.

Third in the group of Titan unions is that of Hyperion and Theia. For these two, as for most of the other Titans, there are no stories and no functions. Their three children, on the other hand, are quite prominent: Helios, Selene, and Eos (note that *Homeric Hymn* 31 calls their mother Euryphaessa, "broad-shining one," though still a sister of Hyperion). Helios is clearly in Homer and Hesiod the sun god who travels across the sky (e.g., *Il* 8.68). As such, he sees all things, and thus makes a convenient witness for oaths (as in the case of Agamemnon at *Il* 3.277 and 19.259) and an observer of transgressions. In this latter role, he informs Hephaistos of the affair of Ares and Aphrodite at *Odyssey* 8.302, and is finally prevailed upon to reveal the identity of Persephone's abductor in the *Homeric Hymn to Demeter* (62–89, where he has officially for the first time the horses and chariot never mentioned in Homer or Hesiod: cf. *Tit* fr 7 *PEG*; Mim 12 W; *HHerm* 68–69; *HomH* 31). He is not named in the *Iliad* as the son of Hyperion, but the *Odyssey, Theogony,* and the *Hymn to Demeter* each refer to him once as Hyperionides (*Od* 12.176; *Th* 1011; *HDem* 74; cf. *HDem* 26 [son of Hyperion]). Elsewhere in the *Iliad* and *Odyssey,* however, he is called Helios Hyperion, as if the latter name were itself a patronymic or other epithet (*Il* 8.480; *Od* 12.133, etc.), and so too at *Iliad* 19.398 and *Hymn to Apollo* 369 he is simply Hyperion; otherwise in that Hymn, as in the *Iliad,* his name is clearly Helios. Subsequent writers (Eumelos fr 3 *PEG*; Mim 12 W; Stes 185 *PMG*; *Ol* 7.39) maintain the distinction of father and son between the two figures.

Helios' chief role in the *Odyssey* is, of course, his ownership of sheep and cattle on Thrinakia, ageless animals whom his daughters (by Neaira), Phaethousa and Lampetie, shepherd (*Od* 12.127–36). When Odysseus' men have taken and eaten the best of them, Lampetie rushes to tell her father, and he appeals to Zeus and the other gods for vengeance, threatening to take his light down to Hades if he is not satisfied (*Od* 12.374–88: Zeus heeds the threat and takes appropriate action against the miscreants). Alteration of the sun's normal behavior is touched on again in *Iliad* 18, when Hera forces him to set unwillingly, thus presumably before his time (*Il* 18.239–40). Unfortunately, we have no early source for the story that the sun traveled backward in the sky after Thyestes had seduced the wife of his own brother Atreus. Euripides suggests that Zeus caused this event (E:*El* 699; *Or* 996); Sophokles, in his lost *Atreus,* may have made the sun go backward of its own accord in horror at the feast of Thyestes' children (*AP* 9.98). On a less serious note, *Homeric Hymn* 28 makes Helios come to a stop when he first sees Athena. If Athenaios and his sources are to be trusted, the *Titanomachia* provided the first description of the cauldron or cup in which the god travels from west to east at night (fr 8 *PEG*). Mimnermos, whose lines on the subject Athenaios preserves, calls it a hollow bed, made by Hephaistos and golden with wings, in which Helios rides through Okeanos at night to the land of the Aithiopes, where his horses stand waiting (12 W). This cup (or whatever) is the same one loaned by Helios to Herakles for his journey to the far west (either for the cattle of Geryoneus or the apples of the Hesperides) in a story noted by Peisandros, Aischylos, and Stesichoros, among others; the latter mentions that, on recovering the cup, Helios prepares for his nightly voyage to his mother and wife and children (185 *PMG*). We will return to the tale of this loan in chapter 13, but we should note here several charming late Black-Figure vases on which Herakles waits as Helios and his horses rise up from Okeanos at dawn in order to ask him for the cup (e.g., Athens 513, NY 41.162.29, Boston 93.99). Apollo's usurpation of Helios' functions as the sun (or identification with him) first appears for certain in Euripides (see below); Aischylos may have preceded him in such a notion, if an account linked to his *Bassarides* is, in fact, entirely from that play (discussion under "Apollo" in chapter 2). One other tale survives only in Pindar (and may well represent local tradition or poetic invention), namely that Helios was inadvertently excluded when the Olympians held their original apportionment, and that he took the nymph/island Rhodos as bride in compensation (*Ol* 7.54–76).

Surprisingly absent from our preserved early sources, however, is the story of Helios' son Phaethon. Hesiod mentions such a person in the *Theogony*, but as a son of Eos and Kephalos snatched away by Aphrodite, and thus presumably a different figure altogether (*Th* 986–91).[39] Since the Helios Phaethon is (at least later) the offspring of a god and mortal woman, one might have expected his story and the ill-fated chariot ride to have found a place in the *Ehoiai*, but our first evidence that it did so comes from Hyginus, where the tears of Phaethon's sisters hardening into electrum are ascribed to Hesiod (*Fab* 154 = Hes fr 311 MW).[40] Hyginus' version here follows for the most part the account well known from Ovid; the Hesiodic Corpus may have related the same tale, or a different one, or nothing beyond the hardening of the tears. In any case, the story was dramatized in full by Aischylos in his lost *Heliades*, with as chorus Phaethon's sisters, who grieved for him after his death (frr 68–73 R). Details are lacking, but with such a chorus the scene was very probably Helios' palace, and the emphasis thus on Phaethon's divine family, not his mortal one. Indeed, perhaps in this version he had no mortal family, as we will see below. But our only certain information for the play (from Pliny) is the transformation of the Heliades into poplars beside the Eridanos, the river in the Western Mediterranean into which their brother presumably fell (*HN* 37.31).

By contrast, Euripides' lost *Phaethon* was set in a mortal landscape, with Phaethon here nominally the offspring of Klymene (an Okeanid) and her husband Merops, but in reality, of course, the child of Klymene and Helios. The scene is Merops' kingdom in Aithiopia, very close in fact to the home of Helios, and as the play opens Merops has planned his supposed son's wedding to an unidentified goddess, most likely one of the Heliades (although Aphrodite has also been suggested).[41] In the opening scene, to judge from fragments, Klymene attempts to persuade a reluctant Phaethon to accept the marriage. The basis for his hesitation is not clear, but in the end Klymene tries to allay his doubts by sending him to his real father, Helios, for confirmation of his parentage, noting as she does so that Helios promised her a favor at the time of their union (fr 773 N²). That Phaethon requests and receives permission to drive his father's chariot may be deduced from the fact that Helios gives his son guidance and even accompanies him, riding beside the chariot on his horse and shouting instructions (this is reported back to Klymene in a later messenger speech: fr 779 N²). Subsequently, the still-smoking corpse of Phaethon is brought on stage, so that presumably he was struck down by Zeus, as in most later accounts, but we have no details. The remainder of the plot may have concerned Merops' discovery of his son's death and the child's real father. But how the proposed marriage and the fatal ride fit together and why the marriage was necessary to the plot at all remain unclear. (Those supporting Aphrodite as the intended bride suggest that she planned Phaethon's destruction from the very beginning, as vengeance for Helios' revelation of her adultery with Ares.) Since Phaethon's corpse is brought back on stage immediately after the disaster, we must probably conclude that his journey did not proceed as far as the Eridanos in the far west. One other point to note—the earliest sure linking of the sun with Apollo—presents itself in a speech of Klymene near the end of the play, when she laments that Helios has destroyed her child, Helios whom men rightly call "Apollo" (the "Destroyer": fr 781 N²).

To this evidence for Aischylos and Euripides we may add, since it claims to derive "from the tragedians," the *Odyssey* scholion at 17.208. Here Helios and Rhode, daughter of Asopos, are the parents of no less than four children, Phaethon, Lampetie, Aigle, and Phaethousa. But although Rhode might thus seem to be Helios' proper wife, Phaethon proceeds as in other accounts to seek the identity of his father, whereupon Rhode sends him to Helios. The latter unwillingly grants his request to drive the chariot, he loses control, scorching the earth, and Zeus strikes him with the thunderbolt, causing him to fall into the Eridanos and perish. His sisters lament him unceasingly, until Zeus in pity turns them into electrum-dripping poplars. The contradiction in this narrative between the presence of Phaethon's sisters and his seemingly fatherless status may well argue a conflation from several different plays, perhaps even those of Aischylos and Euripides, although of course we cannot be sure that the *entire* scholion is taken from tragedy. Still, with no mention of any marriage to a goddess here or in later accounts, the idea looks increasingly like a Euripidean invention.

As for those other accounts, in the fourth century Plato's *Timaios* confirms that Phaethon was unable to keep his father's chariot on the proper course, and burned the earth until he was destroyed by a thunderbolt (*Tim* 22c); Palaiphatos specifies that he obtained the chariot from his father with many tears, but here there is no thunderbolt: unable to control the horses, he passes very near the earth and is thrown out into the Eridanos, where he drowns (Pal 52). In Apollonios the thunderbolt returns, and the Eridanos is once more Phaethon's grave, surrounded by his sisters as poplars (AR 4.595–611; cf. DS 5.23.2–4). Among Roman tellers of the tale Ovid is preceded by Lucretius, where Zeus hurls the thunderbolt in anger and Helios brings the horses back on course (5.396–405). To all this the *Metamorphoses* has little new to add: as in Euripides Phaethon is brought up by Merops and Klymene in Aithiopia, and sent by his mother to Helios when her claim that he is the god's son is disputed (*Met* 1.750–2.400). Helios' rash promise of anything the boy wants leads to Phaethon's (solo) journey, a scorched Gaia's appeal to Zeus, and the reluctant hurling of the thunderbolt. Klymene wanders all the way to the Eridanos to find the tomb of her son, accompanied, curiously enough, by Heliades (Phaethousa and Lampetie, among others) who are here her daughters, presumably by Merops despite their name. The anomaly suggests a relocating of events (here again) which were originally more at home in the world of Helios and his family.

Further evidence of such a shift may perhaps be found in Hyginus. We saw above that his *Fabula* 154 cites Hesiod for at least the detail of the amber tears. The beginning of the same *fabula* offers a more surprising picture, with Phaethon the child of one Klymenos, son of Helios and Merope the Okeanid (admittedly the sort of confusion of names often found in our text of this author). But otherwise the account proceeds much as we would expect. By contrast, in the same mythographer's *Fabula* 152A, where Phaethon is simply the son of Helios and Klymene, we find quite a different version of these same events, namely that Phaethon takes the chariot of the sun without his father's permission, that his sisters harness the horses for him (again without their father's knowledge), and that Phaethon comes to ruin solely from his own terror, which causes him to fall from the chariot into the Eridanos; the sisters turn into poplars as usual.[42] By itself this might represent only an aberration, but taken together with hints we have seen above, it offers a remarkably coherent narrative for a hypothetical early version in which Helios is, like his sisters, the offspring of a legitimate marriage and raised from childhood in his father's house. Under such circumstances there would be, of course, no need for proof of parentage and thus no ill-fated promise by Helios; instead, his son expresses a natural desire to emulate his father, and when refused takes matters (disastrously) into his own hands. Some scholars have credited this version to the Hesiodic Corpus, although any real evidence is lacking. More likely, I think, are the prospects for Aischylos' *Heliades*, which stressed Phaethon's divine sisters and was probably set in the home of his divine father. The first part of the *Odyssey* scholia at 17.208, with Phaethon as full brother to three Heliades, might then well be taken from this play, like the detail of the fall into the Eridanos which we found to be non-Euripidean. Indeed, if these assumptions are correct, Euripides may well have invented not only the proposed marriage with a goddess, but also the concept of the child brought up in uncertainty as to his real father, the essence of the story as we find it in Ovid. Artistic representations of the story, oddly enough, seem not to begin much before the time of the Roman Empire, but we should note one remarkable version on an Arretine bowl dating near the birth of Christ: here the chariot has just been destroyed and, while Phaethon falls to earth, Apollo mounted on a horse of his own (as in Euripides) tries to lasso two of the escaping steeds (Boston 98.828). On the other side of the chariot, Artemis aims her bow toward Phaethon, as if she had taken an active part in his destruction, while Zeus looks on and another female figure behind him moves rapidly away with one of the chariot wheels. To judge from Valerius Flaccus this last figure is Tethys, for he notes that she collected the axle and yoke (VF 5.431), but one does not immediately see why her role should be thus emphasized (though she is the grandmother of Phaethon on his mother's side). In any case, there remains the tantalizing possibility that this vase preserves numerous details from Euripides' play.

As to other children of Helios, we have already encountered in the *Odyssey* two daughters, Lampetie and Phaethousa (merely a feminine form of Phaethon) by one Neaira. In the *Theogony*, the god weds rather the Okeanid Perseis, and produces two children, Aietes and Kirke (*Th* 956–57); both are confirmed as offspring of such a union by the *Odyssey* (10.136–39). In Eumelos, the children are Aietes and Aloeus, and the mother one Antiope (fr 3 *PEG*). The *Odyssey* scholia we saw to assign him four children—Phaethon, Lampetie, Phaethousa, and Aigle—by Rhode, daughter of Asopos (Σ *Od* 17.208). Finally, for the tale of two other mortal lovers of Helios, Klytie and Leukothea, our primary source is again Ovid. As he tells the story, Klytie is one of those whom Helios has loved in the past; still longing for the god, she is struck with jealousy when his attentions turn toward Leukothea, daughter of Orchamos and Eurynome, and she reveals the affair to the girl's father, who buries his daughter alive (*Met* 4.192–270). Helios' efforts to uncover her are in vain, and Klytie, scorned by him ever after, becomes the heliotrope. A comment by Lactantius Placidus repeats this story and assigns it to "Hesiod," but scholars have generally been dubious (Hes fr 351 MW).

Hyperion and Theia's second child, Selene, is simply mentioned by Hesiod as an offspring. Likewise in Homer she appears only in her capacity as the moon, without reference to any stories. The *Hymn to Hermes* calls her, oddly enough, a daughter of Pallas, son of Megamedes, whoever he is (*HHerm* 99–100). Her most extensive description in Archaic literature occurs in the Hymn addressed to her (32), where, like Helios, she is given a chariot to drive across the sky. This same Hymn also notes a mating with Zeus, the result of which is the goddess Pandeia. In Aischylos' *Xantriai*, on the other hand, we find the phrase "star-faced eye of the daughter of Leto" after a reference to the sun, suggesting that the process of identification between the moon and Artemis has already begun (fr 170 R).

As for the famous love affair with Endymion, this does not appear where we might expect it, at the end of the *Theogony* together with other matings of goddesses and mortals, but Sappho apparently referred to it (199 LP). Our source on this point, a scholiast to Apollonios, goes on to offer various bits of further information about Endymion. Hesiod, he says, makes him the offspring of Aethlios (son of Zeus) and Kalyke, and given by Zeus the right to choose when he would dispense death to himself (Hes fr 245 MW); Pherekydes (3F121), Akousilaos (2F36), and Peisandros *mythographus* (16F7) are cited in this same connection, and Alkaios may also have mentioned the story (317 LP). The scholiast then moves to quite a different tale in the *Megalai Ehoiai*, where an Ixion-like Endymion is taken up to Olympos by Zeus, falls in love with Hera (actually a cloud), and is cast out of Olympos as punishment, going down into Hades (Hes fr 260 MW). From "Epimenides," he relates a version in which Endymion, after consorting with the gods and desiring Hera, requests eternal sleep (as his punishment?) from an aggrieved Zeus (3B14); finally, from "others," comes the idea that Endymion was made a god because of his just character, but (committing some transgression?) sought from Zeus the eternal sleep (Σ AR 4.57–58). The explicit notion of apotheosis in this last account may provide a clearer explanation of earlier ones: if Endymion was actually a god, then punishing some mild offense or resolving an awkward situation (such as a passion for Hera) would become more difficult, and sleep one viable solution. But nowhere, save at the very beginning of this whole note (where Endymion is visited in a cave, unattested), does our scholiast mention Selene. Sappho, as we saw, is said to have told something of her love, but the first actual account of it does not surface until the passage of Apollonios annotated by the scholiast (*AR* 4.57–58: Selene speaks of her passion for Endymion and her visits to the Latmian cave). In Theokritos 3.49–50, the singer calls his sleep enviable, clearly (in the context) because of her love. Apollodoros repeats the Aethlios-Kalyke parentage of the Hesiodic Corpus, adding that because of his beauty Selene fell in love with him, and Zeus granted him a wish, which was to sleep forever, remaining deathless and ageless (as also in the Corpus: Ap*B* 1.7.5). Unfortunately, this account does not make clear whether Zeus' offer was the result of Endymion's beauty or Selene's love, and whether Endymion's choice was at all prompted by the latter (so that she might look upon his youth forever?). No source claims that the sleep was her idea, and likely enough (given its role in some quarters as a punishment, and his love for Hera), she was not always a part of his story.[43] Loukianos' dialogue between Selene and Aphrodite suggests that she has become enamored of him while seeing him asleep each night, and that when she descends to him he awakens to fulfill her desires (*DD* 19). Vases and other artifacts from the second half of the fifth century on may possibly show Selene leaving an awake Endymion.[44] A variant of sorts occurs in the late fifth-century B.C. dithyrambist Likymnios of Chios, who suggests that Hypnos fell in love with the youth and lulled him to sleep with his eyes open so that he might have the pleasure of looking at them (whether once for all time or every night is not clear: 771 *PMG*). The one other tale of Selene involves an affair with Pan. Vergil says that Pan won her favors with the gift of a sheep (*G* 3.391–93), but the scholia thereto make the god cover himself with a sheepskin (i.e., turn into a sheep?) and ascribe the story to Nikandros. In art we find at least one elegant portrayal of the goddess in her chariot on a Red-Figure cup by the Brygos Painter (Berlin:Ch F2293).[45]

Hyperion's third child, Eos the dawn, is rather more active in the romantic sphere. Homer mentions several of her amours, including Orion, of whose favored status the gods were jealous until Artemis slew him on Ortygia (*Od* 5.121–24: cf. Ap*B* 1.4.5), and Kleitos, grandson of Melampous, whom she snatched away to live among the gods because of his beauty (*Od* 15.249–51). Hesiod adds Kephalos, to whom she bore the above-mentioned Phaethon carried off by Aphrodite (*Th* 986–87; Pausanias saw her abduction of him on the Amyklai Throne [3.18.12]). Whether this is the same Kephalos as the son of Deioneus and husband of Prokris whom Eos fruitlessly carries off in Ovid (*Met* 7.700–713) and Antoninus Liberalis (41) seems dubious; indeed the source used by those two writers may have gotten the idea of adding her to the tale of Prokris and Kephalos from this very passage of Hesiod with its similarly named victim (for the story of this Hesiodic Kephalos, presumably the son of Hermes and Herse, see chapter 7, with *Hipp* 454–58 [where he is taken to Olympos], and Ap*B* 3.14.3 and 1.9.4; for Kephalos, son of Deioneus, see chapter 7 as well). For what it is worth, Pherekydes (3F34) tells Ovid's story *without* Eos. In art there are quite a number of Red-Figure paintings of a winged divinity pursuing a young man in hunter's garb, and on at least four occasions, beginning with a cup by Douris, these are named as Eos and Kephalos (Getty 84.AE.569; CabMéd 423; Madrid 11097; Berlin:Ch F2537).[46] To these we can add Pausanias' mention of an Eos-Kephalos acroterion on the Stoa Basileios in Athens (1.3.1).

Kephalos, however, is not Eos' only abductee in art. Another series of Red-Figure vases features the same winged figure reaching for a boy with a lyre, and this pair is confirmed (albeit by just one inscription) as Eos and her most famous lover, Tithonos (CabMéd 846).[47] The *Iliad* knows him as the son of Laomedon and brother of Priam (*Il* 20.237), and the same lines in both *Iliad* and *Odyssey* describe the goddess as rising each morning from his bed (*Il* 11.1–2 = *Od* 5.1–2); Hesiod adds that she bore to him Memnon and Emathion (*Th* 984–85). The fullest account, however, and the first reference to Tithonos' old age, appears in the *Homeric Hymn to Aphrodite,* where Aphrodite relates the affair as a parallel to her own seduction of Anchises (*HAph* 218–38). The Hymn tells us that Eos snatched Tithonos away, and then asked Zeus for immortality, which he granted, but not for youth. While her lover remained young, he enjoyed the goddess' bed, but when he grew old she shunned his love, although she continued to care for him until he became so old that she shut him up in a room by himself; there he babbles inaudibly, with no strength left. Sappho also alludes to his problems (58 LP), and Mimnermos notes his old age as if it were almost an intended evil or punishment from Zeus (4 W). But the first preserved source to turn him into a grasshopper or cicada seems to be Hellanikos (4F140); the idea does not reappear until we reach the commentators to later Latin works (e.g., Servius at *G* 3.328).

Of the sons, Proklos' summary of the *Aithiopis* tells us that Memnon was slain at Troy by Achilleus, and that after his death his mother obtained for him immortality from Zeus. The same sequence of events was dramatized by Aischylos in a trilogy containing the *Memnon* and the *Psychostasia*; although our evidence is very slim, Eos seems to have appeared in the latter play (together with Thetis) to plead unsuccessfully before Zeus for her son's life (see *testimonia* in Radt). Whether in this version also she was able to give him immortality when he died we do not know. An East Greek hydria in the Villa Giulia (the "Ricci Hydria," no #) shows the two goddesses before Zeus while their sons prepare to fight, and a Red-Figure cup by Douris emphasizes the full pathos of the situation, as the goddess holds the corpse of her dead son in her arms (Louvre G115). According to Pherekydes her other son, Emathion, is slain by Herakles when the latter is on his way to obtain the apples of the Hesperides (3F73). At no point in any of these sources is there a suggestion of conflict between Eos' affairs and her marriage to Astraios, by whom we saw her in Hesiod to bear the winds and the stars; indeed, in Homer and a number of later authors she is pictured as living with Tithonos, as if she had no other obligations. Whether Homer knows of Tithonos' fate is also a question; possibly the picture of Eos leaving Tithonos each morning had become a poetic *topos* that overrode awareness of his aging.

One other story not preserved before Apollodoros is that Aphrodite found Eos in bed with Ares, and as punishment condemned her to be always falling in love (Ap*B* 1.4.4). Whether or not this is very old, it certainly offers an explanation for what is rather unbridled behavior on the part of a goddess. An additional figure perhaps to be noted here is Heosphoros ("Dawn-conveyor"), who in *Iliad* 23 appears before Eos as a harbinger of the dawn (*Il* 23.226), and in the *Theogony* is one of her children, together with the other stars (*Th* 381); as the morning star he is involved in few tales, but does serve in Apollodoros as the father of the Keyx who marries Alkyone, daughter of Aiolos (Ap*B* 1.7.4; cf. Σ*Ab* 9.562, where he is Phosphoros).

The fourth marriage of Titans is that of Koios and Phoibe (*Th* 404–9). Neither figure performs any noteworthy deeds, save for Aischylos' story that Phoibe gave Delphi to Apollo as a present (*Eum* 4–8), but they do produce two daughters, Leto and Asterie. From Homer onward, Leto is consistently the mother of Apollo and Artemis. Hesiod, who takes some pains to describe the Titaness as gentle to men and gods (*Th* 406–8), mentions the birth only briefly (*Th* 918–20), but we have a detailed narrative from the first part of the *Ho-*

meric *Hymn to Apollo* (*HAp* 14–126). In this account, the delivery of the two children is separated: Apollo is born on Delos, Artemis on Ortygia, and only the birth of Apollo is actually related. We hear that Leto went to many places across the Aegean, seeking not merely a place for the delivery but rather a home for her son. At every point she is turned away out of fear (we are not told of what), until she reaches Delos. At first this island also refuses, on the grounds that Apollo would despise such a poor place, but after Leto has sworn that he will build a temple there for his worship, it agrees gladly. Throughout this exchange, there is no mention at all of Hera's possible anger. But when Leto is ready to deliver Apollo, and various goddesses—Dione, Rheia, Themis, and Amphitrite, among others—have come to attend her, Hera remains on Olympos out of jealousy, and does not tell the birth goddess Eileithuia that she will be needed. Nine days pass, and then the other goddesses send Iris to summon Eileithuia, offering in the bargain a golden necklace. As soon as the latter arrives on Delos, the birth is accomplished by Leto leaning against Mount Kynthos, and Themis gives the child nectar and ambrosia.

Subsequent accounts reflect much the same picture: Theognis relates the birth more briefly, but includes the palm tree and the harbor (5–10), while Pindar in a fragment of a lost paian has Zeus watching from the hills above as the twin children (here both born on Delos) come into the light and Eileithuia and Lachesis shout in triumph (*Paian* 12: cf. 886 *PMG*). Pindar is also, in a different poem, our first source for the story that, prior to Leto's arrival, Delos was tossed about on the waves, but that when the goddess came, four columns rose up from the roots of the earth and fixed the island firmly on their capitals (fr 33d SM). In later times, Apollodoros suggests that Artemis was born on Delos before Apollo, and then served as midwife to help deliver him (Ap*B* 1.4.1). Hyginus offers yet another version, in which the snake Python in his prophetic role at Delphi knows that Leto is fated to bring to birth his destruction, and thus pursues her when he learns of her pregnancy (*Fab* 140). As a result (and because Hera has dictated that Leto shall not give birth in any place reached by the sun), Zeus has Boreas take her to Poseidon, who installs her on Ortygia and covers it over with water to hide her. When Python abandons the search the sea god then reveals again the upper part, which becomes Delos, and the children are born. Following the birth (in some late sources), Leto takes the child Apollo to Delphi (where he kills Python) or else goes herself in order to claim the oracle; we will return to these stories in chapter 2.[48]

Subsequent to the birth of her children, Leto has (like most other mothers of Olympians) no real role to play. She does, however, seem to have been a permanent resident on Olympos, as we see from both the beginning of the *Hymn to Apollo* (where she holds an honored place beside Zeus when Apollo makes his entrance) and the battle of the gods in *Iliad* 21 (where she is the recipient of Hermes' humorous surrender at 497–504 after having come down from Olympos with the other gods at *Il* 20.38–40). Part of the humor in this latter scene may in fact have derived from her reputation as a gentle goddess, and there is a touching moment in which she picks up Artemis' bow and arrows and follows her defeated daughter back to Olympos. Earlier in the *Iliad*, she and Artemis together heal Aineias after he has been wounded by Diomedes (*Il* 5.447); the role is unusual for both mother and daughter.

The one other story involving Leto is that of Tityos' assault upon her found in the *Nekuia* (*Od* 11.576–81). Homer here says simply that the assailant was a son of Gaia, and that he tried to carry off Leto as she was on her way to Delphi. For this he was punished by being tied down to the ground in the Underworld, with vultures on either side of him to devour his liver. The *Ehoiai* seems to have made him a son of Elara (Hes fr 78 MW); Pherekydes adds that his father was Zeus, and tells the story (perhaps to square with Homer) that Zeus hid the pregnant Elara under the earth in fear of Hera, and that the child was thus born from the earth (3F55). Pherekydes also says that Apollo and Artemis together killed Tityos (3F56); Pindar mentions only Artemis (*Py* 4.90–92). This notion of his death at the hands of Leto's children (not mentioned by Homer) requires, of course, that he be mortal; thus his crime would parallel those of Ixion and Peirithoos in seeking to rise above his station.

In the artistic tradition, Leto frequently appears on vase-paintings in generic scenes with her children, or mounting a chariot. The abduction by Tityos was also a common subject, with the pursuit by Apollo and Artemis usually added to the scene, as on the Amyklai Throne (Paus 3.18.15) and the metopes from Foce del Sele (no #). These last presented the story on two (presumably) adjacent carvings: that to the left shows the children closing in with drawn bows, while to the right their quarry Tityos flees with Leto on his shoulder, looking backward and seemingly pulling an arrow out of his eye. An Attic Black-Figure neck-amphora of the period offers the same pursuit, but here Tityos strides off with Leto to the right, while between them and the pursuing Apollo stands a cloaked female who must be Tityos' mother, facing left to protect her son (VG 106341; cf. Tarquinia RC 1043). A similar amphora in Paris omits Leto but names the intervening female as Gaia; Tityos again has an arrow through his head (Louvre E864). On a shield-band type from later in the century Leto (with veil) appears to watch as Apollo, his bow cast to the ground, closes in on the abductor with a sword (Basel Lu 217, and Olympia B 4836). The fifth century brings as usual a gentler touch: Apollo and Artemis reach out their hands in protest as Tityos between them raises Leto off the ground on an amphora by Phintias (Louvre G42). Later vase-painting often restricts the field to Apollo and Tityos, the latter accompanied at times by a woman who could equally be Gaia or Leto (or neither: puzzling is Louvre G164, a calyx krater by the Aigisthos Painter on which the woman has several arrows protruding from an enigmatic blob [a clod of earth?] on her shoulder). Tityos' death also appeared as one of a series of undated sculptural groups set up by the Knidians near the Sikyonian Treasury at Delphi (Paus 10.11.1). That Leto's father was always Koios is surely the case, but we should note that when the matter is mentioned in the *Hymn to Apollo* the manuscripts say *Kronos*

(*HAp* 62); emendation to Koios is presumably required. Homer, as we saw above, does not specify her parentage.

Leto's sister, the other daughter of Koios and Phoibe, was Asterie. In Hesiod, we have seen her as the wife of her cousin Perses, by whom she is the mother of Hekate (*Th* 409–11), and in Mousaios as the mother of this same child by Zeus, who then gives her (Asterie) to Perses (2B16). Pindar for his part preserves a more violent version: pursued by Zeus (presumably for amatory purposes), she is unwilling, and then (Pindar grants that this may seem unbelievable) she is cast into the sea as a rock, and becomes the island Ortygia, which is tossed about in the sea (*Pa* 7b.43–52). At this point the fragment breaks off, but the remaining words appear to say that Zeus brought into being on this island Apollo and Artemis, and a fragment of *Paian* 5 tells us that Pindar identified Asterie and Delos (*Pa* 5.40–42). Thus Asterie would become the island on which her sister gives birth to both gods (since Pindar appears to equate the birthplaces of the two). We find the story in no other Archaic source; Kallimachos repeats it in his *Hymn to Delos* (4.36–40), as do Apollodoros (who says that Asterie changed herself into a quail [*ortyx*] before becoming an island: *ApB* 1.4.1) and Hyginus (who says that Zeus changed her into the quail: *Fab* 53). In any case, the tale is clearly not known to (or else not accepted by) the author of the *Homeric Hymn to Apollo*, where Leto and Delos for all their amicability say nothing about being sisters. The same Hymn, as we have seen, regards Ortygia as an island quite distinct from Delos, and the birthplace of Artemis. Hyginus' solution, as we have also seen, is to make Delos the upper part of Ortygia, after it has reemerged from the waves.

Fifth of the Titan sons of Ouranos and Gaia is Iapetos, who, like Kreios, must marry outside the immediate circle of his sisters. He chooses Klymene, a daughter of his brother Okeanos, and their children in Hesiod are Menoitios, Atlas, Prometheus, and Epimetheus (*Th* 507–11). Iapetos himself is the one Titan mentioned specifically by Homer as being in Tartaros with Kronos (*Il* 8.478–81). Of Menoitios Hesiod says that he was *hubristês*, and that Zeus, striking him with the thunderbolt, cast him down into Erebos because of his folly and excessive abilities. No other Archaic writer mentions this event, and we cannot be sure whether it was a part of the Titans' war against the Olympians, or some other incident altogether (as the word "folly" [*atasthalia*] might seem to suggest); the later account of Apollodoros (*ApB* 1.2.3) does make it part of the Titanomachy. Atlas' fate, too, would seem linked to a defiance of Zeus in that battle but Hesiod again does not say so, while for Prometheus we can only note that, whatever his role (or lack of it) in the conflict, he does survive to deceive Zeus at Mekone. The fourth brother, Epimetheus (who looks very much like a specially invented foil for Prometheus), also survives but only to become the receiver of Pandora. We shall return to Atlas in discussing Zeus' early rule, and to Prometheus and Epimetheus in chapter 4 when we consider Hesiod's picture of the earliest stages of human existence, for as we shall see, these last two offspring are strangely involved in the fortunes of the first men. Atlas' problematic daughters—the Pleiades and Hyades—will be discussed in chapter 6.

The sixth and last pairing of Titans is that of Kronos, youngest of the twelve, with his sister Rheia. From their union come six children, and Kronos swallows, or means to swallow, all of them (*Th* 453–62). What else he may have done since volunteering to castrate his own father we cannot say, for Hesiod has no account of what followed that deed; we do not see the son assume rule or take any other action, although later Hesiod calls him ruler of the earlier generation of gods (*Th* 491). He does eventually receive a prophecy from his parents to the effect that he is fated to be overthrown by one of his own children, and to forestall this, the first five—Hestia, Demeter, Hera, Hades, and Poseidon—are swallowed as soon as they are born (or, less probably, just the male children).[49] When the sixth is about to arrive, Rheia appeals to Gaia and Ouranos—who seem now on more amiable terms with each other— for a plan to save him. Following their counsel, she goes to Lyktos on Krete to deliver Zeus, and hands him over to Gaia to rear, while she herself gives Kronos a stone wrapped in swaddling clothes to swallow (*Th* 463–91).

Hesiod adds to this account only that Zeus grew swiftly, but the *Eumolpia* of "Mousaios" says that he was given to Themis, his aunt, who in turn gave him to Amaltheia, who had a goat nurse him (2B8, apud *Katast* 13). The account of Ps-Eratosthenes from which this last information is drawn goes on to claim that the goat in question was a child of Helios, with an appearance much feared by the Titans, who requested Gaia to hide her in a cave on Krete. Gaia did so, but also gave her into Amaltheia's safekeeping. Subsequently, in this same account, Zeus is advised that the skin of that goat will protect him in his battle with the Titans, being invulnerable and much feared by them (it has as well a Gorgoneion on its back). Our epitome of the *Katasterismoi* goes no further than this, but Hyginus (*Astr* 2.13.4) provides the clearly intended conclusion that this skin is the aigis, and both Hyginus and the Germanicus scholia make it the source of Zeus' epithet *aigiochos*. Kallimachos (*Hymn* 1.47–48) seems the first to assign the name "Amaltheia" to the goat itself; so too Σb *Iliad* 15.229, which offers much the same information as Ps-Eratosthenes, with the addition that Themis was the source of the advice to use the skin of the goat as protection. Ovid (like most other authors) returns us to the idea that Amaltheia was the owner of the goat; he adds, however, that the goat broke one of her horns against a tree, and that Amaltheia carried the horn, filled with fruits, to the child Zeus (*Fasti* 5.111–28). This seems the earliest preserved source we have to relate this origin of the horn of plenty, but already in the Archaic period Anakreon has referred to "the horn of Amaltheia" as something highly desirable (361 *PMG*; likewise Phokylides [fr 7 Diehl]), and Pherekydes says that it had the power to furnish whatever food and drink one might desire (3F42). We saw, too, earlier in this chapter that Pindar has Acheloos trade a horn obtained from Amaltheia in order to get back the one he lost to Herakles (fr 249a SM). By contrast, in Ovid's *Metamorphoses* the horn of plenty is Acheloos' own broken-off horn, which the Naiades fill with fruits (*Met* 9.85–88), and we encounter something of the same sort in Apollodoros, who says that Amaltheia's horn was the horn of a bull (this just before citing Pherekydes, who may be his source: Ap*B* 2.7.5). Lactantius Placidus repeats the information found in the *Metamorphoses* but adds to it that Herakles took the horn with him down to Hades (Σ St: *Theb* 4.106); we will reconsider this surprising detail in chapter 13.

Returning to the matter of Zeus' infancy, we find in the Epimenidean *Theogony* that the god turns himself into a snake and his nurses into bears to deceive Kronos, and is nursed together with Aigikeros, who aids him against the Titans (3B23, 24). Ps-Eratosthenes, our source for the latter point, adds that this Aigikeros was sprung from Aigipan with Aix (or "the goat") as mother, and had horns and the tail of a fish, the latter appropriately since he used a conch shell to frighten the Titans (*Katast* 27). He was, of course, made into a constellation for his services, Aigikeros to the Greeks, Capricornus to the Romans (*Astr* 2.28).

Far better known than this figure, however, and probably much more crucial to Zeus' safety, are the Kouretes, the attendants of his mother who supposedly clashed their weapons to drown out his cries. If Korinna could be dated to the Archaic period, she would constitute valuable early evidence for their existence, for she says that they hid the god from Kronos (654 *PMG*). Otherwise we have nothing at all until the poem of "Epimenides" on the birth of the Kouretes and Korybantes (a poem that may have prefaced the Epimenidean *Theogony*), and nothing of any substance until Euripides. This last poet's *Kretes* links the Kouretes with Idaian Zeus, Zagreus, and the "mountain mother" (fr 472 N²) while *Bakchai* 120–34 *may* allude to their protective role. For the concrete action of concealing Zeus' infant cries by the clashing noise of their weapons, however, our first source is again Kallimachos (*Hymn* 1.51–53). Similar stories about the Korybantes (who seem to have been drawn into this myth through their connection with Kybele) will be found in chapter 3. Both Kallimachos (Hymn 1.46) and Apollonios (3.133) speak too of a nurse Adrasteia (another name for Nemesis?[50]), and Apollodoros adds to her Ida, both as daughters of Melisseus (Ap*B* 1.1.6–7; see Appendix A for possible Orphic sources). In Hyginus, the account of the noisemaking of Kouretes or Korybantes is prefaced by a story in which Kronos has cast Poseidon into the sea and Hades down to the Underworld, rather than swallowing them; Hera (also not swallowed) then asks her mother to give her the child Zeus when he is born, and Rheia substitutes the stone for Kronos to swallow (*Fab* 139). Kronos soon discovers the trick but cannot find the child, suspended as he is in a cradle between sky, earth, and sea by Amaltheia. Rheia's entrusting of the swaddling-wrapped stone to a surprised husband is charmingly depicted on several Red-

Figure pots of the later fifth century (Louvre G366; NY 06.1021.144); otherwise these events, in whatever form, have left little trace in art.

Other tales of Kronos are limited to his mating with Phillyra, daughter of Okeanos, in the form of a horse, thus producing the biformed Cheiron, as Pherekydes tells the story (3F50: cf. *Th* 1001–2 ["Cheiron Phillyrides"] and *AR* 2.1231–41), and his role in the Epimenides *Theogony* as the father of the Moirai, the Erinyes, and Aphrodite (3B19). It is true that Hesiod in the *Works & Days* makes him ruler during the original Golden Age (*W&D* 111), but that is probably an unavoidable consequence of the author's overall scheme at this point, rather than a genuine piece of mythmaking. The question of Kronos' ultimate fate we will come to shortly, after the battle of the Olympians and the Titans.

As for Rheia, she appears subsequently in the Homeric Hymns at Leto's delivery of Apollo, and as Zeus' messenger to announce the settlement regarding Persephone to Demeter (*HAp* 93; *HDem* 441–43), while in Bakchylides she is the one to bring Pelops back to life (fr 42 SM). Her identification with Kybele must be subsequent to the time of that divinity's entry into the Greek world. As far as literature is concerned, the name "Kybele" first appears in Aristophanes' *Ornithes* (876–77), where she is, like Sabaizos, of Phrygian origin and mother of gods and men. But the cult of the "Meter" is clearly much older, as evidenced by an early *Mêtrôon* in the Athenian Agora and by Pindar's reference in a dithyramb to the Great Mother for whom drums sound on Olympos (fr 70b.8–9 SM).[51] Euripides' *Kretes* (fr 472 N², as above) mentions this Meter in connection with Idaian Zeus and Zagreus, and the *Bakchai* makes the link almost certain by naming Rheia as co-inventor of the Phrygian drums with which are celebrated the rites of the Great Mother Kybele (*Bkch* 58–59, 78–79).

But there were also other views on the Greek divinity most suited to represent the Mother: Euripides' contemporary, Melanippides, seems to have equated her with Demeter (764 *PMG*), and Euripides himself in the *Helen* calls Demeter (as she searches for her daughter) the "mountain mother of the gods," with a characterization of her worship and attributes unmistakably that of Kybele (*Hel* 1301–52). Such a link between Kybele and Demeter, rather than Kybele and Rheia, may have arisen from the Phyrigian's role as mother of all the gods (indeed, the mother of all life), in contrast to Rheia, the mother only of the Olympians. But we shall see in Appendix A that the situation is still more complicated, for the Derveni papyrus now suggests that the fusion of Rheia and Demeter as the mother of Zeus *and* of his daughter Persephone in Orphic theogonies may go back to the beginning of the fifth century.[52] One wonders whom sixth-century viewers saw when they gazed at the goddess in her lion-drawn chariot fighting against the Gigantes on the north frieze of the Siphnian Treasury at Delphi (no #). I suspect the Meter alone, with assimilations to Rheia and Demeter coming only in the course of the fifth century, but even if that is correct, the sequence of these assimilations is impossible to establish, and perhaps the question should not be asked.

The Titanomachia and Zeus' Rise to Power

Upon coming of age, Zeus sets about to overthrow his father and recover his brothers and sisters. Hesiod is quite circumspect about these events, perhaps because he has compressed a longer account but perhaps, too, because they involve violence by Zeus against a parent; later authors are not much help in filling the gap (though Aischylos, in the lost play from which our Dike fragment 281a R comes, apparently treated the matter as a legal question, and someone in the play says that Kronos began the quarrel). Here again the epic *Titanomachia* might have added much to our knowledge, but as matters stand we must await Apollodoros for anything like a complete account. What Hesiod does say is that Kronos was deceived into disgorging his children by the stratagems of Gaia, but also by the skills and strength of Zeus (*Th* 492–500). The stone comes up first, and then, presumably, the children in reverse order, as the *Homeric Hymn to Aphrodite* attests by making Hestia oldest and youngest (*HAph* 22–23; cf. *Il* 13.354–55 and 15.166, with Zeus older in the first passage and Poseidon older in the second).[53] But what happens after that we do not learn in the *Theogony*; it is not clear whether Kronos retires from the field gracefully, suffers further violence from Zeus, or escapes to participate in the war between the Olympians and Titans.[54]

In Apollodoros, events are much the same, but we are told that Metis gave Kronos an emetic to swallow (Ap*B* 1.2.1); this may or may not be the version to which Hesiod refers, though it does seem more likely than the Orphic tradition in which Kronos is drugged with honey (at the suggestion of Nyx), then bound and castrated (fr 154 Kern; cf. Lyk 761–62). I am likewise dubious about Pausanias' mention of the two engaging in the first wrestling match at Olympia (5.7.10; 8.2.2). But whatever the *Theogony* supposed Kronos to endure in the process of his overthrow, the poem clearly puts him in Tartaros with the other Titans (*Th* 851: the line is formulaic, resembling several in the *Iliad* where the same situation holds). Art offers several scenes that *might* represent the struggle between father and son, but their identification is highly questionable and would in any case add little to our understanding of the story; they include, for the record, a seated figure (gender not certain) threatened by a standing one in the pediment of the Temple of Artemis on Kerkyra, and a Lakonian cup on which a large figure is seized and pulled forward by a smaller one (Athens 13910).[55]

In Hesiod, Zeus' first act after recovering the other Olympians is to release the Kyklopes; they remember the favor, and in return give him the thunderbolt, which Gaia had previously hidden (*Th* 501–6). Subsequently (after the story of Prometheus, out of sequence as it were), we find the same tale related at greater length of the Hundred-Handers, with the addition that Gaia advised the release so that the Olympians might win victory (*Th* 617–23). Earlier, Zeus had also pronounced that none of those who had honors before should lose them if they sided with him, and that those who had none should receive them (*Th* 383–403). As seen above, Styx is the first to accept this offer; accompanying her are her children Zelos, Nike, Kratos, and Bia. At this point, the battle between the Olympians and the Titans begins, with the Olympians fighting from Mount Olympos, the Titans from Mount Othrys to the south; Hesiod's account does not quite say whether the Hundred-Handers were freed before the conflict or only in the tenth year. Either way, the gods appeal to these older powers for help, and Kottos promises their assistance.

The actual battle is described in only the most general terms, with no names (perhaps not surprising, since there can be no real casualties), but we are told that both males and females participated (*Th* 687–735). Eventually, if not at the beginning, the Hundred-Handers are fighting, but the battle is not turned until Zeus strides forth from Olympos with his thunderbolt. The heat stuns the Titans, the glare blinds them, and the Hundred-Handers, after pelting them with stones, bind them up and cast them down into Tartaros, as far below earth as heaven is above. There the Hundred-Handers guard them (though Briareos is later married to Poseidon's daughter Kymopoleia: *Th* 817–19) by the will of Zeus. This Briareos is a more complex figure than one might expect, since in both the *Iliad* and the *Titanomachia* he has an alter ego, Aigaion, to whom we will return in discussing Zeus' rule (*Il* 1.400–406; *Tit* fr 3 *PEG*). We saw above, too, that in Ps-Eratosthenes (probably drawing from the Epimenides *Theogony*) the goat-fish-child Aigikeros raised with Zeus assisted him in the battle by discovering the use of the conch shell as trumpet, with which he frightened the Titans (3B24, apud *Katast* 27). Apollodoros would seem acquainted with a more detailed version of some events than that given by Hesiod, for he tells us that Zeus slew a female guard named Kampe in order to release those under the earth (*ApB* 1.2.1). Hyginus' account offers even more novelty, for he says that Hera, angered at the vast territory of Epaphos, son of Io, called upon the Titans to rise up against Zeus and restore Kronos; Zeus, as elsewhere, throws them down to Tartaros (with the help of Athena, Apollo, and Artemis: *Fab* 150). Likely enough, Hyginus has here confused stories of Hera's summoning of the Gigantes to her aid (as in the *Homeric Hymn to Apollo*) with the overthrow of the Titans. But such confusion serves to underline how little we really know about the conflict of Olympians and Titans; apart from Hesiod, no preserved Archaic work describes it, there are no relevant fragments from the *Titanomachia*,[56] and as noted above no sure (and certainly no useful) artistic representations.

We have seen that the ensconcement of the Titans in Tartaros is mentioned several times in the *Iliad*, chiefly when Zeus is threatening to send other Olympians to the same place (*Il* 8.478–81; 14.203–4, 273–74, 278–79; 15.225). On most of these occasions, Kronos is noted specifically as the god who resides there (or was driven there by Zeus), with the other Titans gathered around him (including, in particular, Iapetos). The same picture emerges from the *Theogony* (Kronos alone named) and the *Homeric Hymn to Apollo* (where

Hera calls on the Titans for aid, much as if they were chthonic spirits: *HAp* 334–36), and likewise in *Prometheus Desmotes*, where Kronos is again named (*PD* 219–21). On the other hand, the female Titans appear to be very much at large: Leto and Tethys in the *Iliad*, Themis and Mnemosyne in the *Theogony*, Rheia and Leto in the *Homeric Hymns*, and Phoibe in Aischylos. Okeanos and Hyperion, who also seem at liberty in Homer (if the latter is in any way the sun), and Okeanos again in Aischylos are probably special cases, since they represent physical elements of the cosmos from which they can hardly be separated. Apart from all these, Atlas, son of Iapetos, suffers the unique fate of being condemned to bear up the sky on his shoulders. But though this punishment is mentioned by Homer (*Od* 1.52–54, where he stands at least partly in the sea and holds up columns), Hesiod (*Th* 517–20), Pindar (*Py* 4.289–90), and Aischylos (*PD* 347–50),[57] none of them actually says that Atlas' role in the Titanomachy was the cause, nor is it stated before Hyginus that Atlas led the Titans in battle (*Fab* 150); possibly the punishment is older than the crime. Again, the lost *Titanomachia* might have answered many if not all of these questions, and it is curious that so little of its information is quoted (at least by name) in later accounts. Two other stories concerning Atlas deserve mention here. One, that he assisted Herakles in obtaining the apples from the garden of the Hesperides, seems guaranteed as early by shield-band reliefs, sixth-century vase-paintings, and the well-known metope from the temple of Zeus at Olympia where Atlas returns from the garden with the apples while Herakles holds up the sky (see chapter 13 for all of these). The other, that Perseus changed the Titan into stone by holding up the head of Medousa, is preserved no earlier than Ovid's *Metamorphoses* (4.631–62), but told already, according to the Lykophron scholia, by the dithyrambist Polyidos (837 *PMG*). This earlier version made Atlas simply a shepherd who questioned Perseus about his identity as the latter passed by; when Perseus' answers failed to satisfy him the Gorgon head was needed to resolve the situation. In Ovid, Atlas is a more prepossessing figure, and as usual a son of Iapetos, but here too he does not support the sky; instead he is envisioned as ruling over a vast realm in the West, with many flocks and a tree with golden fruit. When Perseus seeks from him a place to rest for the night, he recalls (from Themis) a prophecy according to which a son of Zeus will deprive him of the fruit, and rebuffs his visitor; Perseus uses Medousa's head as before, and only now, after he is lithified, does the sky rest upon him. Such a tale, of course, whatever mountain(s) it may account for, leaves Herakles (the true object of the prophecy) with no one to help him get the apples in time to come, and is probably a late invention, although we will see that in some early versions of Herakles' Labor the hero procures the apples by himself.

As to the ultimate fate of the Titans, after they have arrived in Tartaros, there is some variance of tradition. For Homer and the *Theogony*, they certainly remain in Tartaros, Kronos included. But in two papyrus versions of a passage of the *Works & Days*, the description of the Fourth Age heroes who go to the Isles of the Blessed includes mention of Kronos, who is said to rule over those there, having been released by Zeus (*W&D* 173a-c). That the lines conflict with *Theogony* 851 is not absolutely damning, but they do not fit into their grammatical context very well either, they are not found in our other versions of the text, and while Zeus might release his father in Hesiod's world, it is hard to see why he would reward him. If with most editors we take the lines as a later interpolation into some manuscripts,[58] the next earliest appearance of such a tradition occurs in Pindar and Aischylos. In Pindar's *Olympian* 2, securely dated to 476 B.C., Kronos appears as lord in the marvelous afterlife pictured by the poet for his Sicilian patron Theron (*Ol* 2.76–77). Admittedly, this world has a number of aspects that do not reflect anything known from earlier eschatology, but nonetheless Kronos' role ought to have some foundation in a previous story of his release. Nor does Pindar stop with Kronos: in *Pythian* 4, dated to 462 B.C., he observes that though Atlas still remains holding up the sky (one can scarcely release him), the other Titans have been freed by Zeus (*Py* 4.289–91; cf. fr 35 SM). Since the point of this comment is to encourage Arkesilas to pardon Demophilos, one would expect the poet's reference to be to a well-accepted or at least familiar myth, rather than something completely new to the tyrant. And since Atlas is pointedly excluded from the amnesty, one might assume that Kronos is not. The one other Archaic reference to the event is from Aischylos' lost (and undated) *Prometheus Lyomenos*, where the chorus is composed of Titans clearly released from Tartaros (frr 190–93 R), perhaps in part for the purpose of persuading Prometheus to divulge his secret. Nothing is said about Kronos in what remains of this trilogy; he may or may not have been mentioned by name as one of the parolees (Philodemos [p. 39 Gomperz] perhaps attempts to address this point). Relevant in this regard is perhaps the exchange between Apollo and the Erinyes in Aischylos' *Eumenides* 640–66. Apollo stresses the importance of fathers; the Erinyes ask if Zeus showed such respect when he bound his own father. It would have been easy enough, and more appropriate to the point Apollo wishes to make, if he had answered that Zeus had since that time released his father; instead, he limits himself to remarking that bonds *might* be undone. Either Kronos was not released with the other Titans in the *Lyomenos*, or there is a difference of situation between the two plays. The fragment of the same poet's Dike-play has too many gaps to permit certainty, but it does seem that Zeus there supports Dike because she approved his treatment of his father, and nothing is said about any later clemency toward Kronos (fr 281a R). From Tertullian we learn that Aristotle made reference to a sleeping Kronos (*De anima* 46.10); Plutarch adds that this sleep (in a cave) is an imprisonment devised by Zeus, and that in the course of it he dreams what Zeus plans to do (*Mor* 941f-42a). Finally, in the Aristotelian *Athenaion Politeia*, the tyranny of Peisistratos is compared to life under Kronos as a kind of Golden Age (*AthPol* 16.7). Likely this refers to Hesiod's original Golden Age, set in the time of Kronos (cf. *Pol* 272a-b), but it could also mean the overlordship of the Isles of the Blessed. In either case, Kronos' association with some such world seems to be a common notion by the latter half of the fourth century; whether it gained impetus from Pindar or some other source is harder to say.

After the Titans have been defeated and cast down into Tartaros, there is in most accounts an allotment of powers among the Olympians. The earliest description is found in the *Iliad*, when Poseidon displays a small outburst of resentment at being ordered by Zeus to retreat from the battlefield (*Il* 15.187–95). He describes an apportionment made among just the three sons of Kronos and Rheia, in which he received the sea, Hades the underworld, and Zeus the heavens (so too Ap*B* 1.2.1). The earth, he continues, and Olympos are common to all three. This last suggestion scarcely concurs with Zeus' opinion of his position or with the balance of power as presented in the *Iliad*; Poseidon subsequently concedes the point. The notion of a shared earth conjures up as well puzzling images of Hades, who never leaves his realm to enjoy the earth or Olympos, save for the occasion on which he abducts Persephone (and, it seems, one other, when he is wounded by Herakles: see *Il* 5.395–402). The same three-way division, without details, is mentioned in the *Homeric Hymn to Demeter* (*HDem* 85–86). In the *Theogony*, with its emphasis on Zeus' power, the account is rather different. Here Zeus relies much more heavily on the thunderbolt, the weapon with which the Titans and Typhoeus are defeated, as the source of his authority. He has also from his political conciliations the support of the children of Styx, who personify strength and victory. Thus, he is presented by Hesiod as a natural leader, and toward the end of the poem we are told that on the advice of Gaia the other gods invited him to rule over them. He then apportioned out honors himself (*Th* 881–85), as opposed to the version of the *Iliad*, where lots were clearly involved. In Pindar's *Olympian 7*, a primal division is again featured; the use of the words *ampalos* and *lachos* strongly suggest that what Pindar has in mind is in fact apportionment by chance (*Ol* 7.54–63). The story told by Pindar is that Helios missed the division (of *land*) and, rather than accept the recasting offered by Zeus, asked for the island of Rhodes (just then risen from the sea) as his share. The notion that *all* the gods participated in the division is new, and the overall frame of the story sounds suspiciously like a Pindaric invention created to further the themes of his poem. Yet many of the lesser divinities do have specific areas of jurisdiction assigned to them, and perhaps there was at some earlier point a tradition in which a great many figures received their functions by a drawing. Elsewhere in Archaic literature, Zeus' power is simply accepted, and no other author presumes to tell us what its basis is.

At some point very early in Zeus' reign (Hesiod puts it just before his official installation as king), his rule is challenged by the monstrous Typhoeus/Typhaon (the *Theogony* gives both forms). In the *Theogony* itself, this creature is the offspring of Gaia after sexual union with Tartaros (*Th* 821–22); this is the only time Tartaros appears in such a role, and no reason is given why Gaia, who elsewhere in Hesiod always supports Zeus, should here issue a pretender to his throne. The arrival of such a challenger does, however, give Zeus a chance to show off his power when the other gods can do nothing, and this is surely intended by Hesiod, if not Gaia. Typhoeus is not fully described, but he has on his shoulders one hundred snake heads that breathe fire (perhaps: 845 is unclear) and imitate every conceivable kind of noise (*Th* 823–35). The combat itself is short-lived, for Zeus throws his thunderbolt, and Typhoeus crashes down to earth as a fiery mass. Zeus then hurls him into Tartaros, and nothing is left but his offspring—the minor winds and the children he had by Echidna (or Keto?) earlier in the poem (Orthos, Kerberos, Hydra, Chimaira). The version of the *Homeric Hymn to Apollo* covers only Typhoeus' birth and infancy, with the important difference that here he is a child of Hera alone, born in retaliation for Zeus' bearing of Athena (*HAp* 305–55). Hera prays to Gaia for a son stronger than Zeus, slaps the earth with her hand, and becomes impregnated. The offspring, however, is like neither gods nor men, and she gives it to the Python to rear (which might suggest a resemblance to snakes). Aside from these details, the poet says only that Typhoeus became a great bane to *mortals*—seemingly a strange description, if he was to challenge the gods. The one reference in the *Iliad* is also brief—a simile mentions how Zeus strikes the earth around Typhoeus in anger, where he lies in the Arima (or among the Arimoi: *Il* 2.782–83). This certainly implies that Zeus disposed of Typhoeus, but does not specify any cause for the conflict.

As for later Archaic sources, the *Etymologicum Magnum* tells us that Stesichoros, in contrast to Hesiod, made Hera bear Typhoeus alone because of her anger at Zeus (239 *PMG*); thus he uses the same version as the author of the *Homeric Hymn to Apollo*. The Epimenides *Theogony* agrees that Typhoeus attempted to take the rule of Zeus, and may have pictured him stealing into the palace while Zeus slept, only to be struck down when the latter awoke (3B8). Pindar has a number of references, several of them quite useful. In *Olympian* 4, he mentions that Zeus holds the hundred-headed Typhoeus prisoner under Aitna (*Ol* 4.6–7). The longer description in *Pythian* 1 places him in Tartaros, but at the same time stretched out on a hard bed under both Aitna and Cumae (presumably therefore Vesuvius); this passage also calls him "enemy of the gods" and has him raised in a Cilician cave (*Py* 1.15–28). *Pythian* 8 makes him Cilician as well, and says specifically that he was conquered by the thunderbolt (*Py* 8.16–17). Fragments of lost poems repeat the imprisonment under Aitna, stress that Zeus alone conquered him, reduce the number of his heads to fifty, and, in a context where divine transformations are being considered, apparently had all the gods change into animals as they fled him (frr 92, 93, 91 SM). Prometheus, in Aischylos' *Prometheus Desmotes*, offers an account along what thus appear to be fairly standard lines: Typhoeus is "earth-born" (hence born of Gaia?), Cilician, hundred-headed (*PD* 351–72). He challenges the gods, shrieking and flashing dreadfully from his eyes, and hopes to take the throne of Zeus, but the thunderbolt strikes him down, and he is imprisoned under Aitna. From there his anger still pours forth on occasion in streams of fire.

Pherekydes also told the story; a summary of his account relates that Typhoeus flees to the Caucasus and then, when those mountains begin burning (from a thunderbolt?), to Italy, where the island of Pithekoussai is thrown up around him (3F54). From Akousilaos, we have the statement that snakes arose from Typhoeus' blood (2F14), and agreement with Hesiod that he was the father (by Echidna) of Kerberos, as well as the Promethean eagle (2F13). This exhausts the early literary evidence, but a Chalkidian hydria now in Munich (596) shows Zeus on one side aiming his thunderbolt, and Typhoeus (named) on the other, a creature with a human head and torso, but from the waist down a body consisting of two snake's tails. Based on this one example, the scenes with Zeus and a similar creature on shield-band reliefs from Olympia (B 988, B 1636, etc.) are taken to represent the same combat (and the numerous single-snake-tailed figures in Corinthian vase-painting designated as "Typhons"[59]). Earlier than any of these but highly conjectural is the Protocorinthian aryballos in Boston with Zeus aiming his thunderbolt at a human-legged Kentauros as both clutch the same scepter or staff (Boston 95.12). That Typhoeus is represented here is certainly a possibility if the object held by his opponent is indeed a thunderbolt, but even that is not quite certain.[60]

Of later literary accounts, that of Nikandros (preserved in AntLib 28) has Typhoeus as a monstrous child of Gaia with snakes growing from various parts of his body. All the gods flee to Egypt save for Zeus and Athena, changing (as in Pindar) into various animals (Apollo to a hawk, Hermes an ibis, Ares a scaly fish, Artemis a cat, Dionysos a goat, Herakles a fawn, Hephaistos a cow, and Leto a mouse). Zeus, however, throws his thunderbolt, causing Typhoeus to plunge into the sea to put out the fire, and then places Aitna on top of him. The same transformation into animals, with still more detail, appears in Apollodoros: here Gaia, angered at the death of her children the Gigantes, produces Typhoeus (as in Hesiod) after union with Tartaros (ApB 1.6.3). The monster has (as in Nikandros) snake tails springing from his thighs, and wings, but apparently only one head, from which he breathes fire. On seeing him approach, the gods again flee to Egypt and change into animals, but Zeus attacks with thunderbolt and sickle. At close quarters, however, Typhoeus wrests the sickle away, cuts out the sinews from Zeus' hands and feet, and thus renders the god helpless. Only when Hermes and Aigipan (a by-form of Pan?) have stolen the sinews back does Zeus recover his strength and take up again the pursuit of Typhoeus with his thunderbolt. Meanwhile, at Mount Nysa, the Moirai deceive Typhoeus into eating fruit that will bring about his downfall, and he is then defeated by Zeus in Thrace and imprisoned under Aitna. Much of this is unique, though Nonnos also knows of the stealing of the sinews, after a fashion, and has Kadmos disguised as a shepherd get them back by proposing to make them into a lyre (1.362–534: what precedes this is actually the theft of Zeus' thunderbolt). One other late account of interest comes from the b scholia to the *Iliad*: angry with the gods over the death of the Gigantes, Gaia complains (or slanders Zeus?) to Hera, who in turn goes to Kronos and receives two eggs smeared with his own seed to bury underground (Σb *Il* 2.783). She does so at Arimon in Cilicia, but when Typhoeus is born she relents, revealing the fact to Zeus, and he strikes Typhoeus with the thunderbolt. These latter two narratives have elements that might seem to be too primitive to represent later interventions, and the last in particular may have Orphic features.[61]

From Zeus' conquests we move, with Hesiod, to his initial amatory affairs. As a first wife, we are told, he takes Metis (presumably the daughter of Okeanos and Tethys), who knows most of men and gods (*Th* 886–900). When she is about to bear Athena, however, he deceives her with soft words and swallows her, on the advice of Gaia and Ouranos, lest she bear not only Athena, with strength and wisdom equal to her father's, but also a son to be king over men and gods. In this way Metis counsels him as to good and evil, and in time Athena (but not the son) is born from his head. An alternate version of these lines quoted by Chrysippos and probably from the Hesiodic Corpus retains the conceiving of Athena by Metis and the swallowing, and the fear of a child greater than his father, but not the specific prediction (Hes fr 343 MW). Moreover, in this account Zeus turns to Metis in anger after Hera has produced Hephaistos all by herself (a reversal from the situation in the *Homeric Hymn to Apollo*, where Hera bears Typhoeus in anger because Zeus produced Athena). Of course, Zeus does not thereby create a child unilaterally—he still needs the help of a woman—but at least he gives it birth. Unique to the *Iliad* scholia is the version in which Metis is already pregnant with Athena by the Kyklops Brontes when Zeus swallows her (ΣbT *Il* 8.39). Ignoring this last, we probably have a conflation of several different stories: one in which Zeus produces Athena from his head spontaneously, one in which he swallows Metis to gain her wisdom, and one in which he swallows her to prevent the birth of a rival. The second and third tales were then seen as a way of rationalizing the more unlikely elements in the first, and a somewhat unwieldy compound was created. Homer, as one might expect, says nothing about any of these stories; in both the *Iliad* and *Odyssey*, Athena is simply Zeus' daughter. Later accounts are likewise silent about Metis, but the birth itself of Athena from the head of Zeus proves very popular. *Homeric Hymn* 28 describes her as leaping forth in full armor (the Chrysippos fragment says that Metis provided this), to the amazement of heaven and earth; Stesichoros apparently gave the same picture (233 *PMG*), and a scholiast (to Apollonios) names him as the first to put her in armor at birth (Σ AR 4.1310). We have also a reference to the telling of the birth in Ibykos (298 *PMG*), but not until Pindar is there explicit literary mention of Hephaistos' expediting of matters with his axe (*Ol* 7.35–38 and fr 34 SM). Long before this, however, the birth and Hephaistos' part in it were popular topics in the artistic tradition. The earliest representation now seems to be that on a relief amphora from Tenos dating to the first half of the seventh century: a winged, helmeted figure holding two uncertain objects leaps forth from the head of a similarly winged seated male.[62] Neither of the two flanking figures here (Eileithuia and Hermes?) has much possibility of being Hephaistos. Certain in this respect, on the other hand, are the shield-band reliefs from Olympia dating to perhaps 600 B.C., where all the major details are clearly shown, including the blacksmith god with axe, and Athena in armor (B 1687, etc.). The same group appears over and over in Attic Black-Figure painting, beginning with a tripod pyxis by the C Painter of about 570 B.C. (Louvre CA 616). But how old the motif of Hephaistos cleaving Zeus' head is in literary terms, or where it first appeared, remains unclear.

Second of Zeus' unions with other goddesses is that with Themis, one of the two daughters of Ouranos and Gaia who have not previously mated (*Th* 901–11). She appears three times in Homer, once as the ruler of feasts on Olympos when Hera returns from a quarrel with Zeus (*Il* 15.87–91), once when Zeus orders her to assemble all the gods (*Il* 20.4–6), and once when Telemachos appeals to her as the convener and dissolver of assemblies (*Od* 2.68–69). Her role, then, as her name implies, seems that of imposing some kind of order or control over gatherings; nothing is said in Homer of any mating with Zeus or children. A similar sort of role may be indicated in the *Homeric Hymn to Apollo,* where Themis gives the newborn god nectar and ambrosia (*HAp* 123–25); this action might symbolize recognition of his divine status (for which a Moira would also have been appropriate) but it could also be an extension of her authority over divine feasts. The title "Ichnaia" applied to her earlier in the same poem (*HAp* 94) remains of uncertain meaning: literally "Tracker," it could be simply a cult title based on a place name. In Hesiod, Themis becomes mother of both the Horai and the Moirai, although these last were earlier in the same poem the children of Nyx. Elsewhere, she is portrayed as Zeus' confidant (a role rarely given to Hera): in *Homeric Hymn* 23.2–3 she thus assists him, and at the beginning of the *Kypria* she is a co-planner of the Trojan War. A fragment of Pindar adds a bit of elegance to their union: Themis is brought by the Moirai (here not her daughters) from the springs of Okeanos to Olympos to be the first wife of Zeus, and the Horai are born (fr 30 SM). These last are not inappropriately connected with concepts of order and law, and are mentioned several other times by Pindar, but only Dike has any mythology to speak of, as discussed below. The one other story concerning Themis also occurs in Pindar: she appears in *Isthmian* 8 as the revealer of the secret of Thetis' fate (*Is* 8.30–45). Here again we have a role that might have been more appropriate to the Moirai, and one that would seem traditional, since Aischylos acknowledges it in identifying Themis with Gaia for purposes of transferring the secret to Prometheus in *Prometheus Desmotes* (*PD* 209–10). This identification could, of course, also be traditional (at least post-Hesiodic traditional) but it is made very pointedly in the *Desmotes,* and more likely Aischylos has here innovated in order to give his protagonist some leverage over Zeus. If that is correct, then the secret is originally Themis', and revealed as part of the preservation of the current order. From these brief appearances, one might suspect that Themis was once rather more important in

---

the power structure of Olympos. On the other hand, a fragment of Philodemos seems to attest that in the *Kypria* and "Hesiod" Thetis was married to Peleus simply because Zeus was angry at her refusal of his attentions (*Kyp* fr 2 *PEG* = Hes fr 210 MW); it might therefore be the case that the theme of a son greater than his father originally belonged to Metis, and that Themis is given knowledge of this doublet of that tale only at a relatively late point, perhaps in deference to her name. Although equating her with Gaia for his Prometheus plays, Aischylos returns to the traditional descent from Gaia in the *Eumenides* (2–3) and calls her *Themis Dios* in the *Hiketides* (360). Such a conjunction with the genitive form of Zeus' name might make us think that she is his daughter, but more likely Aischylos means that she acts in some way as his representative.[63]

Themis' first set of daughters, the Moirai, have already been discussed as the children of Nyx; only the *Theogony* names them as her offspring, but it is rare that any author mentions their parentage. The second set, the Horai, are noted by Homer only as keepers of the cloud-gates on Olympos, which they twice open for Hera and Athena (*Il* 5.749–51 = 8.393–95); on the second of these occasions they also take charge of chariot and horses when the goddesses return (8.433–35). This seems an odd role for a group of goddesses whose collective name means already in Homer (and Hesiod) "Seasons," to judge by the descriptions used. And the individual names that Hesiod (not Homer) assigns them—Dike (Justice), Eirene (Peace), and Eunomia (Lawful Government)—suggest that their sphere of activity should be among men, not the gods. In the *Works & Days* they crown Pandora with spring flowers (*W&D* 74–75), and in one of the shorter *Homeric Hymns* to Aphrodite, they greet the newborn goddess on her arrival at Cyprus, clothe and adorn her, and escort her to Olympos, where they themselves go to dance with the gods (*HomH* 6.5–13). Later Archaic sources follow more often than not the model of the *Theogony* in making them representatives of civic virtue: Pindar, Bakchylides, and an unassigned lyric fragment all refer to them by individual name (*Ol* 13.6–8; Bak 15.53–54; Ades 1018b *PMG*), and Pindar goes so far as to call Dike the "sure foundation of cities." This last of the three has as well her own separate role to play in the *Works & Days* and in the unplaced fragment of Aischylos noted above. In Hesiod, she sits beside Zeus and reports back to him when mortals have been unjust, a task for which there is absolutely no parallel in Homer (*W&D* 257–62). The fragment of Aischylos is extremely uncertain, but apparently Dike is sent down to earth to offer her services to mankind, rewarding the good and punishing (Aischylos stops short of saying how) the wicked (fr 281a R). Other aspects of the Horai's activity are all from Pindar: at *Pythian* 9.54–65 they foster Kyrene's son Aristaios, at *Paian* 1.6–9 they seem to bring round the year, and in another fragment (fr 75.14–15 SM) they are associated with spring. In all, then, these goddesses appear to have four different functions: doorkeepers on Olympos, adorners of beauty (and supporters of the young?), promoters of social order, and representatives of the seasons. What original conception led to these separate prerogatives, and whether some are older than others, is as so often difficult to say.

Third to mate with Zeus is Eurynome, another daughter of Okeanos, who bears the Charites, by name Aglaia, Euphrosyne, and Thalia (*Th* 906–11). Eurynome's one real appearance in myth is in tandem with Thetis as a harborer of Hephaistos after Hera has thrown him out of Olympos (*Il* 18.398–405). Hephaistos, in fact, emphasizes that she is an Okeanid, leaving us to wonder why she is in the sea with a Nereid. Possibly there is a connection with Hephaistos' wife on this occasion, who is called simply "Charis," perhaps a proper name, perhaps not; it would be logical for Hephaistos to marry a daughter of his benefactress, although he does not here refer to Eurynome as his wife's mother, in contrast to what we might expect. We will see that in the *Theogony* he is specifically married to Aglaia (*Th* 945–46). Elsewhere in epic and later literature, there are frequent references to the Charites in the plural but no real myths about them and very little indication of any concrete function. In the *Iliad*, they make a robe for Aphrodite (*Il* 5.338), and Hera promises one of the younger sisters, Pasithea, as a wife to Hypnos (*Il* 14.267, 275). This last occurrence may well indicate more than three sisters, and with other names; Hesiod's recur only in Pindar (*Ol* 14.13–16). In the *Odyssey*, they bathe and dress Aphrodite after her entrapment in Hephaistos' net (*Od* 8.364–66), and do so again (in the same words) in the *Homeric Hymn to Aphrodite*, before she goes to encounter Anchises (*HAph* 61–62). Otherwise, the references are rather general and relate mostly to their bestowal of beauty or their patronage of song, the latter especially in Pindar, where they not only contribute praise, but seem at times to grant victory (or just the tokens thereof?: *Ol* 2.49–52). On occasion they are also mentioned in connection with dancing, but this scarcely characterizes them, any more than it does the Horai or the Mousai (*Od* 18.194; *HAph* 194; *HomH* 27.15).

By Mnemosyne, the other unclaimed sister of Kronos, Zeus then begets the Mousai, as Hesiod has already told us at the beginning of the *Theogony* (*Th* 53–79). Nine nights the ruler of the gods goes up into her bed, apart from the other gods, and nine daughters are produced, whom Hesiod names: Kleio, Euterpe, Thaleia, Melpomene, Terpsichore, Erato, Polymnia, Ourania, Kalliope. The place of birth appears to be Pieria, just north of Mount Olympos, although Mnemosyne herself is described as ruling (being worshipped at?) Eleutherai, near Mount Kithairon. So far there are no problems. But Diodoros Siculus claims that while this is the most widely reputed parentage, some poets, among them Alkman, made the Mousai daughters of Ouranos and Gaia (67 *PMG*), and Pausanias says that for Mimnermos the older Mousai had this parentage, while the younger Mousai were sprung from Zeus (13 W, with *apparatus*). A fragment of Alkman that suggests that Mnemosyne was the mother after all may indicate that he shared such a solution (8.9 *PMG*); the same idea resurfaces in a fragment of the *Eumolpia*, where we find two births and two generations of Mousai, one in the time of Kronos (no parents are given), the other from Zeus and Mnemosyne (2B15). Pausanias' claim that the three Mousai of Helikon were Melete, Mneme, and Aoide may indicate various local traditions that the Hesiodic version eventually overcame (9.29.2). Homer generally speaks of just one such figure, but at *Odyssey* 24.60 all nine appear for the funeral of Achilleus. In Hesiod and numerous other authors, the Mousai's primary function seems to be singing and dancing, on earth or on Olympos, and often in the company of Apollo. On occasion they bear children (often musically talented): Kalliope is commonly the mother of Orpheus, and an unnamed Mousa the mother of the title figure in Euripides' *Rhesos* (*Rh* 915–25), while in Apollodoros we find Pieros and Kleio producing Hyakinthos, Apollo and Thalia the Korybantes, Acheloos and Melpomene the Seirenes, and Strymon and Euterpe (or Kalliope) Rhesos (ApB 1.3.3–4). The A scholia to *Iliad* 10.435 add Linos from Terpsichore or Euterpe, Palaiphatos from Thaleia, Thamyris of Thrace from Erato, and Triptolemos from Polymnia (cf. Σ *Rh* 346). On the whole, though, the Mousai appear in only one real story, that of the Thracian Thamyris (here presumably not the son of one of them). Homer says that they caused him to be maimed (*pêros*) and deprived of his musical skills, angered by his challenge to them as a superior musician (*Il* 2.594–600).[64] In later accounts, this maiming is more specifically the loss of his eyes; so, apparently, the *Ehoiai* (Hes fr 65 MW) and the epic *Minyas*, where the singer also pays a penalty in Hades for his boasts (Paus 4.33.7; cf. his appearance in Polygnotos' *Nekuia* at 10.30.8). Of Sophokles' version of the tale in his lost *Thamyras* (Attic spelling) we have virtually nothing. Aischylos may have referred to or dramatized the same misfortune, if a scholiast to the *Rhesos* is correct;[65] the *Rhesos* itself calls Thamyris a son of Philammon whom the Mousai blind for criticizing their skills (*Rh* 915–25). In Asklepiades, according to this *Rhesos* scholion, Thamyris is of a wondrous appearance, with one white eye (the right) and one black one (the left: 12F10). Ascribed to the same source is the tale that when the Mousai arrive in Thrace the singer proposes to lie with all nine of them, claiming such polygamy to be a local custom. A contest in music is then agreed to, with the stakes the right of the Mousai to do whatever they wish with Thamyris against his right to consort with as many of them as he pleases; upon winning they take his eyes. Apollodoros (calling him a son of Philammon and Argiope) likewise reports his desire to lie with all nine Mousai and the contest on said terms; again eyes *and* musicianship are taken (ApB 1.3.3; so too ΣA *Il* 2.595). He also tells us that Thamyris loved Hyakinthos, being the first to become enamored of other males. As for his curious eyes, in the b scholia at *Iliad* 2.595 they are gray (*glaukos*) and black, and so too in Pollux, where we learn that Thamyris on the stage wore a mask thus designed (4.141).[66] Art offers several examples of his fate, including a Red-Figure hydria of about 440 B.C. on which, flanked by several of the Mousai, we see him blind and casting away his lyre (Oxford G291).

With Mnemosyne, the role of the older gods in Greek mythology comes to a virtual end; henceforth, the tales told involve almost exclusively the Olympian gods and humans (Prometheus is a notable exception). The *Theogony* does add two more figures who as offspring of the Titans contribute to the rolls of the Olympian pantheon: Leto, who as we have seen bears Apollo and Artemis, and Maia, daughter of Atlas, who gives birth by Zeus to Hermes. This last event, like the birth of Apollo and Artemis, is mentioned only briefly by Hesiod and just once by Homer (*Od* 14.435), but is fully detailed in the *Homeric Hymn to Hermes,* as we shall see in the next chapter.

2   The Olympians

The Children of Kronos	ZEUS The closing section of Hesiod's *Theogony* brings Zeus, after his previous dalliances, to his own sister Hera, who will become his actual wife, thus heralding the beginning of a more stable career as ruler of the gods (*Th* 921–23). As we saw in the preceding chapter, the *Iliad* offers one very odd reference to this union of brother and sister: in Book 14, when Zeus sees Hera coming toward him with the *himas* (love charm) of Aphrodite, he says that he desires her as he did when they first went to bed together, unknown to their parents (*Il* 14.295–96). If indeed Kronos did swallow his daughters as well as his sons in the *Theogony*, the young couple could not have comported themselves thus before Zeus seized power from his father (and forced the disgorging of his sister), at which point Kronos' knowledge or ignorance of his children's sexual activities would seem rather irrelevant. Possibly, then, Homer alludes rather to an account in which Kronos swallows only his sons (as we saw in Orphic fr 58 Kern) or otherwise imprisons them (as in *Fab* 139), for then the grown Zeus will be free to emerge from hiding and mate with his sister before his father becomes aware of his existence. But even in this version Zeus will remain unknown to his father, and his union with his sister will be the least of Kronos' eventual worries. Hera's reference in this same Book 14 of the *Iliad* to her rearing by Tethys might or might not be a further indication of a version in which she is not swallowed; by contrast, the *Homeric Hymn to Hestia* alludes to the swallowing of the daughters in a manner that certainly suggests audience familiarity.

When we turn for help to the *Iliad* scholia for 14.295–96, we are offered two stories. One (Ab [credited to Euphorion] and, in part, T) suggests that Hera, while still in the house of her parents, was raped by Eurymedon (one of the Gigantes) and bore Prometheus, to whom Zeus was thus understandably hostile. Though indubitably intriguing, this idea does little to resolve our present concern. The second tale (bT) relates that, after Kronos had been sent down to Tartaros, Hera was betrothed (as a presumed virgin) to Zeus by Okeanos and Tethys but promptly gave birth to Hephaistos, having anticipated her marriage by lying with Zeus in secret on the island of Samos; to cover the deed she claimed that the birth was without benefit of intercourse (cf. ΣA *Il* 1.609). This last is closer to what we want, but by strict logic will explain the Homeric situation only if Okeanos and Tethys can be taken as the parents of Zeus and Hera, and it seems very doubtful that Homer ever believed that; more likely, the story represents a scholiast's attempt to explain an allusion whose real referent was unknown to him (and possibly no more than a Homeric invention of the moment). Whatever the truth of the matter, the idea of a secret tryst between the two gods reappears in Kallimachos, who hints that some such event is the *aition* for a Naxian prenuptial ritual (fr 75.4–5 Pf). Adding further uncertainty is the remark by Theokritos that all women know how Zeus married Hera, together with the scholiast's explanation (citing Aristotle) that Zeus transformed himself into a cuckoo so as to effect contact with her (Σ Theok 15.64; so too Paus 2.17.4, 2.36.2). Conceivably, the god contrived this metamorphosis to escape detection by Kronos, but the motive we would expect (and so Pausanias) is the deception of the intended lover, not her parents. Nor can we be sure that Theokritos himself did not intend by his allusion something quite different from what the scholiast supposes.

For any other information about the early passions of Zeus and Hera, the closest we come in Archaic literature is Pherekydes, where (as we found in chapter 1) the wedding at least is well publicized, and all the gods bring gifts to the new bride (in particular, Gaia brings a tree bearing golden apples: 3F16). Of that event too, however, nothing else survives. As regards offspring of the marriage, Zeus begets by his wife in all accounts three children—Ares, Hebe, and Eileithuia—and frequently a fourth, Hephaistos (in Hesiod and some other authors the blacksmith god is the child of Hera alone; see below under "Hephaistos"). Together with this union, Hesiod, of course, does speak of several other matings with goddesses of Zeus' own generation: that with his second sister Demeter, who bears to him Persephone (*Th* 912–14), that with Leto, as discussed in chapter 1 (*Th* 918–200), and that with Maia, daughter of Atlas, to produce Hermes (*Th* 938–39). His third sister, Hestia, remains as always a virgin.

Of the character of Zeus and the nature of early tales involving him, only a brief summary can be attempted here. We have seen that his rule derives, in Hesiod, from the express approval of all the gods. In the *Iliad*, although there is the previously noted dissent by Poseidon (with the suggestion that the three sons of Kronos are equal in rank), the latter ultimately retreats, in fear of Zeus' power if not his authority (*Il* 15.187–95). Power does seem in the *Iliad* a key feature of Zeus' reign; when he threatens the other gods, as he sometimes must to obtain their obedience, it is generally with the prospect of physical violence. Occasionally this is the thunderbolt, as in *Iliad* 8, when he tells Hera and Athena that he will shatter their chariot if they do not turn back from the battlefield (*Il* 8.397–408), but more usually the force involved is simply that of his bare hands, particularly to throw gods out of Olympos. So in *Iliad* 1, Hephaistos relates that this was done to him when he tried to help his mother (*Il* 1.590–91), and the same is said of the gods in general (quite possibly referring to the same occasion) at *Iliad* 15.22–24. Previously Zeus has threatened to hurl

Ares (*Il* 5.897–98) or any other gods who oppose him (*Il* 8.13–14) into Tartaros, and in *Iliad* 14 he is about to throw Hypnos into the sea until Nyx, whom he fears to anger (because she is a primal element?), restrains him (*Il* 14.254–61). A more vivid expression of his superior power occurs (again in *Iliad* 8) when he boasts that in a tug-of-war all the gods together could not pull him down from Olympos, but that he could easily pull them all up (*Il* 8.19–27). Even more bizarre, perhaps, is the punishment of which he reminds Hera in *Iliad* 15: hands bound by a golden chain, she was suspended by a rope with anvils attached to her feet, and none of the gods was able to help her (*Il* 15.18–22). In all this, Zeus' greater strength seems absolute; the other Olympians protest and mutter, but they do not deny what he says, or ever successfully challenge him. On the one occasion on which Hera, Athena, and Poseidon do make a serious attempt, by plotting to bind him, Thetis summons Briareos/ Aigaion to his side, and the conspirators hastily abandon their plans (*Il* 1.396–406). This story survives only in the *Iliad,* and leaves much to be explained (for example, what the conspirators might have hoped to accomplish); if it is not a spontaneous creation of Homer, it *could* refer to a time earlier in the Trojan War, when the gods in question (these are the Achaian supporters) plotted to gain the advantage for their own side. Ion of Chios seems to have told the tale as well, or at least mentioned the summoning of Aigaion to Olympos by Thetis (741 *PMG*); we cannot say whether he had other sources besides Homer. Though the *Iliad* scholia also reflect puzzlement, the A group recounts Didymos' story that Hera, Poseidon, Athena, and Apollo plotted against Zeus because of his high-handedness and outspoken nature; when Aigaion saved him, he hung up Hera in her own chains and bound Poseidon and Apollo to serve Laomedon (ΣA *Il* 1.399). The b and T groups also know this last part, and add that some scholars actually substituted Apollo's name for Athena's in the text, on the grounds that she would not threaten the father to whom she was so close. But most of their commentary is devoted to an allegorical explanation of the conspiracy, suggesting that they had few real myths to fall back on. In the *Iliad* itself, we should note, Hera's suspension in air stems from an entirely different matter, that of her driving Herakles to Kos in a storm.

Elsewhere in Archaic literature, even in the *Odyssey,* conflicts between Zeus and the other gods are few, and his authority, rather than his power, predominates. The *Odyssey* offers us gods who are almost totally united in their support of Odysseus, and a Zeus who is a model of diplomacy, not threats, in dealing with Poseidon. From later literature one thinks primarily of Apollo, who in the *Ehoiai* is about to be hurled by Zeus into Tartaros for killing the Kyklopes when someone (probably Leto) intervenes (Hes fr 54 MW, with Akousilaos [2F19] also named as source). But beyond this point, Zeus is presented more and more as a god who dominates by wisdom, and the other Olympians as implementers of his designs; for example, his role in the *Homeric Hymn to Hermes* is entirely one of good-natured arbiter in the dispute between his two sons. Indeed, even in the *Iliad* he spends much of his time reconciling other gods to what must happen, and very little attending to his own wishes. His one notable area of personal indulgence is, naturally, his affairs with mortal women, but even these are often regarded as necessary steps in the propagation of mortal heroes (e.g., *Aspis* 27–29, of Herakles). To be sure, Hera sees matters differently, and this remains a point of contention between them; the *Ehoiai* tells us that Zeus pardons all false mortal oaths made in the name of love after his own false statements to his wife (Hes fr 124 MW).

As to Zeus' control over events, divine and human, we see that in the *Iliad* the broader patterns of fate reside with the Moirai, whose dictates Zeus cannot alter without consequences too disastrous to contemplate. Thus, Sarpedon and Hektor must die, and Troy must fall, whether Zeus wills it or not. But in the smaller details of the war, and the gods' intervention therein, he clearly has a great deal of room to maneuver, and even where he cannot, he seems to know before the other gods what is fated to happen. Thus, when Thetis asks him to turn the tide of battle temporarily, he replies that it will be awkward from a domestic standpoint, but never suggests that he lacks the ability, and indeed once he has acceded to the request he has no difficulty in carrying it out (*Il* 1.518–27). Likewise, he may punish mortals as he wishes, without considering the ordinances of the Moirai. In all this there is much that manifestly serves the needs of the storyteller without involving the restrictions of a clearly defined theology. One might observe as well that the Zeus of the *Iliad*, though not in total control of events, spends a great deal of time meditating, often in seclusion from the other gods. And while he is not totally immobile, descending as he does at times to Mount Ida to observe the course of events, he never confronts mortals directly, and usually sends other gods to accomplish what he does not do himself from Olympos.

In the *Odyssey* much of this is changed; the gods represent a world in which human justice is generally rewarded, and there is little sign of conflict between their wishes and the designs of the Moirai. Moreover, Athena is here from beginning to end the representative of Zeus, and thus he is not required to do much after his initial mandate, except to approve his daughter's actions. In the *Theogony* and *Works & Days*, we see more of the systems he has created to organize human existence than any of his actual contacts with men (and those very systems suggest that such contacts will be rarer), but he is, of course, in the *Theogony* the father of the Moirai, and thus presumably the ultimate determiner of all that happens. In later authors he tends to be more worshipped and less described. Pindar, for example, has remarkably little to say about him in the mythic portions of his odes; to Aischylos (even if we discount the *Prometheus Desmotes*[1]), the supreme god was obviously a concept to be explored and reevaluated, but we cannot say with confidence, in the present state of Aischylean criticism, what conclusions he reached. One point offered by the parodos of the *Hiketides* does, though, seem representative of Greek thought in general: Zeus alone of the gods can accomplish what he wishes from Olympos, without moving from his throne (A: *Hik* 96–103). The equally famous fragment from the *Heliades* in which Zeus is called "the aither, the earth, the heavens, all things, and whatever is beyond them" (fr 70 R) might take us still further, if only we could be sure that the poet supported the sentiments of his character on this occasion.[2]

As for the myths in which Zeus actually appears, these are primarily unions with mortal women. His protestation of desire for Hera in *Iliad* 14 offers us a basic list—Dia, Danae, Europa, Semele, Alkmene—to which we may add from other sources Io, Aigina, Antiope, Kallisto, Leda, and, different in gender but sharing the same category, Ganymedes. Elsewhere he protects guests and hosts in his role as Zeus Xenios, purifies Ixion of the first homicide (and subsequently punishes him and Tantalos for hybris), sends a flood to destroy all mankind except for Deukalion and Pyrrha, plots with Themis to relieve the earth of overcrowding by starting the Trojan War (in the *Kypria*), and strikes down various mortals with his thunderbolt when they have committed extreme transgressions, as witness Salmoneus, Kapaneus, Asklepios, and Phaethon (if his story is early). The tale of Lykaon involves him rather more directly, since there we find him as a guest in Lykaon's home, where the host (as in the case of Tantalos) serves to him a child, perhaps as a test of his perspicacity (see chapter 18). His role as father of various mortals, like that of other gods, is generally restricted to the act of procreation; Herakles is one of the few mortals in whom he shows subsequent interest. For the most part the guiding divine forces in Greek mythology are other gods, most especially Hera, Hermes, Apollo, and Athena, whether or not we understand them to be operating at Zeus' bidding. His oracle at Dodona is alluded to at *Iliad* 16.233–35; in the *Odyssey* we first hear (via a fictitious journey of Odysseus) of the power of the lofty-leaved oaks there to convey the god's will (*Od* 14.327–28; cf. Hes fr 240 MW).

HERA   Of Hera, second of Kronos' children, we see a great deal in the *Iliad*, but rather less after that. Her role as the chief opponent of Zeus' purposes in the Trojan War, and her ultimate defeat in opposing him, have already been described. In the *Odyssey* she is scarcely mentioned at all, and among the *Homeric Hymns* she appears prominently only in that to Apollo, where she (somewhat irrelevantly to the story being told) gives birth to the monster Typhoeus. Otherwise her primary role in Greek myths is as jealous wife, harassing the unwilling lovers (or offspring) of Zeus, in particular Io, Semele, and Herakles; in many other cases, however, she is not heard from at all (e.g., Dia-Peirithoos, Danae-Perseus, Europa-Minos, Aigina-Aiakos [but in this last case see *Met* 7.523–24 and *Fab* 52]). Naturally, as the goddess who defends the proprieties of marriage, she has no lovers herself.

Her relationship with her son Hephaistos provides material for two stories, one that she threw him out of Olympos, the other that he imprisoned her in a magical throne; we will return to both of these in discussing Hephaistos himself. She is also desired by Ixion (who mates with a cloud in her form) and

Endymion, aids the hero Iason and, of course, participates in the Judgment of Paris, which leads to her involvement in the Trojan War. Of the strange story told by Dione that Hera was once wounded by Herakles with an arrow there is no other trace (*Il* 5.392–94); the tale that he protected her from the advances of the Silenoi is known to us primarily from Attic Red-Figure vase-painting (see chapter 13, under "Herakles and the Gods"). Likewise we have no additional support for the notion of the *Iliad* scholia discussed above, that she became the mother of Prometheus after being assaulted by Eurymedon (ΣAb *Il* 14.295), although the two of them appear together (Hera seated holding out a phiale, Prometheus before her) in the tondo of a Red-Figure cup by Douris (CabMéd 542). Her anger against Semele assumed an especially vivid form in Aischylos' play of that name, in which she disguised herself as a mortal priestess in order to bring about Semele's doom (fr 168 R);[3] in connection with the same philandering we should remember the madness she sent to Ino's family after the latter had agreed to raise Dionysos, and her attempts in some accounts to destroy Dionysos himself by sending Titans to rend him apart. The story of her wrath against the nymph Echo for distracting her until Zeus' lovers could escape is not found before Ovid (*Met* 3.359–68). On the whole, her character emerges as rather severe, not generally inclined to offer assistance to mortals and certainly with no sense of humor. But perhaps her marital situation is sufficient cause for that.

POSEIDON   Poseidon, Zeus' oldest brother before the rebirth from Kronos (if *presbutaton* at *Od* 13.142 has its literal sense), like his sister is quite active in the *Iliad* (and plays a major if limited role in the *Odyssey*), but he too becomes less of a factor in later mythical accounts. The *Theogony* marries him off to the Nereid Amphitrite, and gives him as offspring Triton (*Th* 930–33); the same union is mentioned by Pindar (*Ol* 6.104–5) and Bakchylides (17.109–11), and illustrated on numerous pinakes and vases, including the wedding processions on the François Krater (Florence 4209) and Erskine Dinos (London 1971.11–1.1). The *Theogony* also portrays him as a mate to Medousa, and father by her of Pegasos and Chrysaor by a rather unorthodox birth after she is decapitated (*Th* 278–81). This connection with (and ability to sire) horses reappears in the story of his mating in the form of a horse with an Erinys (ΣAb *Il* 23.346; ΣT *Il* 23.347), or a Harpuia (ΣT *Il* 23.347), or Demeter (Ap*B* 3.6.8; Paus 8.25.4–7), and thus fathering Adrastos' steed, Areion. Both scholia cited refer the version with the Erinys back to the Epic Cycle (= *Theb* fr 8 *PEG*), while that of the Harpuia is credited to the *neôteroi*. Apollodoros claims that Demeter likened herself to an Erinys before the mating, and Pausanias that she was called an Erinys because of her anger at the deed. Accounts of Poseidon's children in the *Odyssey* are more flattering: Polyphemos, his son by Thoosa (*Od* 1.68–73), is admittedly a bit ungainly, but the two sets of twins—Otos and Ephialtes (the Aloadai) by Iphimedeia, Neleus and Pelias by Tyro—seem normal enough, if at times violent and arrogant. The *Nekuia* is our source for both these latter matings (*Od* 11.305–20, 235–57), and offers the odd tale of Poseidon wooing Tyro in the guise of the river god Enipeus, the only occasion in early Greek mythology when a god impersonates another god. The *Odyssey* offers as well Alkinoos' father Nausithoos, who is the child of Poseidon and Periboia, daughter of Eurymedon (*Od* 7.56–62). Amphitrite, meanwhile, although she is never in the *Odyssey* called Poseidon's wife, does appear as a controller of sea monsters (*Od* 5.422–23) and general sea goddess; from the *Iliad* she is absent altogether.

In later literature we also find the god of the sea seducing the fiftieth Danaid, Amymone, who bears a son, Nauplios; Pherekydes attests this union (3F4), and we know Aischylos to have dramatized it in a satyr play *Amymone*, with Poseidon actually on stage to accomplish the seduction (after rescuing the girl from a Silenos: pp. 131–32 R). Other children include Boutes (Hes fr 223 MW), Euadne (by Pitane: *Ol* 6.28–30), and Orion (by Euryale, daughter of Minos: Hes frr 148, 149 MW; Pher 3F52). More uncertain is the siring of Theseus. Bakchylides says that Poseidon is the father (17.33–36), in a poem in which Theseus' divine paternity is set against that of Minos, and while the matter is not elsewhere discussed in Archaic literature, there are a number of Red-Figure pots on which Poseidon pursues Theseus' mother, Aithra.[4] Against this stand we have the *Aspis* (182 = *Il* 1.265, a line perhaps interpolated[5]) and Theognis (1233), where the patronymic Aigeides is an apparent vote in favor of Aigeus. It must be admitted, though, that such terminology could refer without too much trouble to Aigeus' role as stepfather or reputed father of Theseus. In the later sources, Aigeus' claim usually prevails, although there is mention of Aigeus and Poseidon both visiting Aithra on the same night; we will return to the question in more detail in chapter 7.

Other than his activity as a father, and his frequent championing of the Achaians in the *Iliad*, Poseidon is not as common a figure in Greek mythology as one might expect. He aids Apollo in building the walls of Troy (for reasons that are never explained: *Il* 21.441–57 and see above on ΣA *Il* 1.399), disputes the homecoming of Odysseus after Polyphemos is blinded, and contends with Zeus for Thetis until her peculiar destiny is made clear (*Is* 8.27–29). His jealous concern for his status is also demonstrated by his protest against the fortification wall of the Achaians in the *Iliad* (7.445–53), and his threatened walling-up of the Phaiacians for traveling too confidently on his domain in the *Odyssey* (13.149–64). Dione in the *Iliad* does *not* mention him among those gods wounded by Herakles, but Pindar's *Olympian* 9 notes a conflict between them, and Attic vase-painting seems to confirm this, as we shall see in chapter 13. But there is no trace in the early literature of his role in the misfortunes of Minos and Pasiphae, or of his attempt to win the patronage of Athens or other territories.

DEMETER Demeter, the fourth of Kronos' children, makes only two appearances in Homer, and both of those by virtue of references to earlier times.

In the *Iliad*, Zeus names her to Hera as one of those whom he has loved; no offspring is mentioned (*Il* 14.326). In the *Odyssey*, Kalypso includes her among those goddesses whose unions with mortal men are envied by the gods; the mortal in question here is Iasion, the mating takes place in a thrice-plowed fallow field (again, no offspring is mentioned), and Zeus on learning of it slays the lover with his lightning bolt (*Od* 5.125–28). The *Theogony* for its part recognizes both these unions and assigns children to them: Persephone is named as Demeter's daughter by Zeus, and Ploutos as her son by Iasion, or Iasios as he is called here (*Th* 912–14; 969–74). In this Hesiodic account, as in the *Odyssey*, Iasion is clearly mortal, although Ploutos, with a name meaning "wealth" and a description as bringer of wealth and fortune, certainly seems intended as a god, in contrast to the normal rule for matings between gods and men. The thrice-plowed field (here in Krete) also reappears as the scene of the union, but no mention is made of Zeus' anger, or any untimely demise. Iasion makes one other certain appearance, in the *Ehoiai*, but the context is too fragmentary to say more than that genealogy is involved, and that he seems referred to as dear to the gods (Hes fr 185 MW). A second fragment of the *Ehoiai* may well have related his liaison with Demeter, if "Iasion" was there (as certainly in Hellanikos) another name for Eetion, brother of Dardanos (Hes fr 177.8–12 MW; Hell 4F23, 4F135). One of the Hellanikos references also contains, however, the odd idea that this Iasion/Eetion was struck by a thunderbolt because he maltreated an *agalma* (statue? honor?) of Demeter (4F23).

By contrast, Persephone is found a number of times in the *Iliad* and *Odyssey*, always in consort with Hades and the Underworld. Homer never once calls her the daughter of Demeter, but there is, perhaps, never any compelling reason to do so; the *Odyssey* does on one occasion call her the daughter of Zeus (*Od* 11.217). In both poems, but especially the *Odyssey*, she seems to share Hades' powers and control over the dead, as when she grants to Teiresias the retention of his reasoning ability; Theognis, in fact, suggests that it was she from whom Sisyphos obtained his deceitful furlough (704). Phersephatta (or variations thereof) appears as her name in Aischylos (*Cho* 490), on vase-painting (e.g., Dresden 350), and in Attic prose inscriptions; see, too, Plato's discussion of Pherrephatta (more frightening as a name) versus Phersephone (*Kratylos* 404c). "Kore" appears on the whole more as a cult title, possibly used as a proper name in the *Homeric Hymn to Demeter* (439), definitely in a fragment of Lasos (702 *PMG*), early Red-Figure pots (e.g., Eleusis 596), and Euripides' *Herakles Mainomenos* (609). Curiously enough, when Apollodoros first mentions Persephone he calls her a daughter of Zeus and Styx (ApB 1.3.1), reverting back to the usual parentage only when he comes to the story of the abduction. Just possibly then, Kore, daughter of Demeter, and Persephone, queen of Hades, are not in origin the same person, although they are certainly so by the time of *Theogony* 912–14, when Hades' wife is clearly the daughter he steals from Demeter rather than any offspring of the Underworld.[6]

The primary tale involving Persephone and Demeter is, of course, the former's snatching away by Hades, noted briefly in the *Theogony* (Zeus bestows her; no mention of a return: 913–14) and told at great length in the *Homeric Hymn to Demeter*.[7] In this latter account as well, Hades snatches away his niece with the full permission of Zeus (and without that of Demeter) while she is gathering flowers (in particular the narcissus, grown by Gaia to abet the theft) in the company of the Okeanides in the Nysian plain. Hekate and Helios alone hear her cries; Helios apparently sees the abductor as well (why the Okeanides have witnessed nothing is not explained, nor the role of Athena and Artemis, whom Persephone, much later in the Hymn [424–25], describes to her mother as also present). For nine days, Demeter roams the earth with torches, eating nothing; on the tenth, Hekate comes to her, and the two of them together confront Helios, who now reveals both Hades' role and Zeus' complicity. Demeter in her anger shuns the company of the gods, going instead to the habitations of men and Eleusis, where she sits at the Maidens' Well near the house of the king Keleos, son of Eleusinos. To the king's daughters who encounter her she feigns a mortal identity as Doso, a woman kidnapped from Krete by pirates, and asks for work in the house. The daughters offer her the care of their infant brother Demophoon, and this is confirmed by their mother Metaneira. But Demeter's care is not of the usual kind: by day she anoints the child with ambrosia, and by night she buries him in the embers of the hearth. The purpose of this treatment is to make him immortal and unaging (much as we will see Thetis and Medeia attempt to do), but Metaneira discovers the plan, and in her ignorance of the goddess' intentions arouses her anger. As a result, the child remains mortal, though still promised honors, and Demeter commands the Eleusinians to build for her a great temple where she may teach her rites.

Following this event, Demeter continues her wandering and mourning on earth. For a year the land lies wasted; the race of men is threatened and the gods' sacrifices are thus endangered, until Zeus sends Iris to bring his sister to him. But Iris fails, and one by one all the other gods fare the same in their attempts to persuade her. Finally, Zeus addresses the heart of the problem and sends instead Hermes down to Hades to ask for the return of Persephone. Hades consents, but gives his bride a pomegranate to eat before Hermes takes her back. When Demeter receives her daughter she perceives the trick immediately, and concedes that if Persephone has tasted any food at all in the Underworld, she must return to her husband for a third of each year, the winter months. Hekate then joins Persephone as her companion and attendant, and Rheia comes from Zeus to ask Demeter to restore the fertility of the earth. With Demeter's agreement the Hymn comes to an end, as the goddess teaches her holy rites—not to be divulged—to the leaders of Eleusis, including Triptolemos. These rites in some way promise a reward to men after death, although whether in the Underworld or elsewhere is not clear, while to those whom they favor of men the goddess and her daughter send Ploutos (here no parentage is given) to bring wealth in this life.

Brief references establish that other poets in the Archaic period also told this tale, as we might imagine, and there were one or more "Orphic" versions in circulation which may well have overlapped with the account known at Eleusis. What survives, though, are chiefly minor variations in detail. Pausanias alludes, for example, to a hymn by one Pamphos, with such events as Demeter's disguised sojourn in Eleusis the same but with some small differences (of Attic origin?) in detail (1.38.3; 1.39.1; 9.31.9). Panyasis seems to have spoken of a Triptolemos, son of Eleusis, as more centrally involved in entertaining the goddess (or, less likely, the child cared for by her: fr 13 *PEG*), while Bakchylides locates the abduction in Krete (fr 47 SM); in neither case do we know if the story was fully recounted or just mentioned in passing. Of later authors Phanodemos puts the event rather in Attika, likely reflecting local traditions developed at Eleusis itself (325F27). What we have from Orphic traditions follows the Hymn fairly closely, but with the child Demophoon perhaps killed by the fire (so definitely in Ap*B* 1.5.1; cf. VM II 97) and Demeter learning from Eubouleus and Triptolemos (sons of Dysaules: see below) what has happened to her daughter (frr 49, 51 Kern). This last point, admittedly, motivates much better than the Hymn Demeter's stay in Eleusis (she has come there in search of her child) and her gift to the people (after they have helped her).

Another feature with perhaps Orphic associations is the presence of Athena and Artemis to aid Demeter in her search or even to resist Hades at the time of the abduction; the former situation is implied by Euripides (*Hel* 1310–18), the latter described in detail by Claudian (RP 2.204–31). In both cases Zeus intervenes (with a thunderbolt in Claudian) to discourage pursuit of the abductor. We saw before (although the line *might* be interpolated) that at a late point in the *Homeric Hymn* the presence of these same two goddesses at the theft is suddenly recalled. Probably then the Hymn's author knew of their role as in Claudian, but preferred a narrative in which Demeter searches for some time before Helios tells her the truth. Diodoros, who places the abduction in Sicily, near Enna, speaks of Athena, Artemis, and Kore growing up there and weaving a robe for Zeus; he does not mention any role played by the first two at the abduction itself (DS 5.3.1–4). Kallimachos' *Hymn to Demeter* concerns a different story altogether (Erysichthon), but he names in passing Hesperos as the one who persuaded the goddess to break her fast, apparently when she had come to the far west and the garden of the Hesperides (H 6.6–10).

Of other late authors, Ovid retains the names of Keleos and Metaneira, but makes the child whose mortality the goddess tries to burn away Triptolemos (*Fasti* 4.502–60); Hyginus does the same, but with Eleusinos and Kothonea as parents (*Fab* 147). In both cases, after Demeter is interrupted this child survives, and she sends him forth (in Hyginus with a chariot drawn by dragons) to sow the earth. Panyasis may perhaps be the source for this notion, although as Apollodoros cites the latter Triptolemos seems to be the host, not the child; we will return to him shortly. Ovid (*Met* 5.533–50) and Apollodoros (Ap*B* 1.5.3, 2.5.12) are the first to mention Askalaphos, a figure who saw

Persephone swallowing the pomegranate seeds in the Underworld and reported this to Hades; Demeter turned him into an owl (or put a stone on top of him, and then turned him into an owl after his rescue by Herakles). The story of Antoninus Liberalis (from Nikandros) seems a variant of this, that when Demeter came to Attika she was thirsty and gulped down water given her by one Misme; on being mocked by the latter's child, Askalabos, for her greed she threw the remaining water on him and changed him into the same owl as above (AntLib 24). Mockery leads us to another minor detail, the moment in the *Homeric Hymn* when one Iambe gladdens the distraught Demeter in the house of Keleos with some form of jeering or other verbal humor (*HDem* 198–205). Seemingly this event had an alternate form in which the hosts were Dysaules and Baubo, figures known at least as early as Asklepiades (12F4) and hence appearing on the tragic stage. Clement tells of Baubo that she received the bereaved Demeter and, when the goddess refused refreshment, pulled up her skirts and exposed herself, much to the goddess' delight (Cl: *Pro* 2.20). From Ovid (*Met* 5.564) and Hyginus (*Fab* 146) comes the idea that Persephone's time in Hades was to be six rather than four months. For what it is worth, no account of the Underworld ever suggests that Persephone is not present; she is, as noted above, a well-established figure there.

In art we find no certain scene of the abduction before the fifth century,[8] when an Attic Red-Figure neck-amphora by the Oionokles Painter offers a Hades (with cornucopia) pursuing Persephone (Naples H3091), and fragments of a skyphos from about 440–30 B.C. show the two together descending into the earth in Hades' chariot (Eros, Hermes, and perhaps Demeter look on: Eleusis 1804).[9] In this second example, the two women following are probably Athena (spear preserved) and Artemis; certainly they appear (before the chariot, Athena in challenging pose, thunderbolt descending) on an Apulian hydria of the later fourth century in Bari (Macinagrossa Coll 26) and other South Italian vases.[10] For the return we have (possibly) an Attic Black-Figure neck-amphora of the Leagros Group with Hermes, Persephone, a graying Hades (seated), and Sisyphos struggling with his rock (London B261); this might be a generic scene, although I suspect that it intends to portray the start of the journey upward. The finish of that same journey is certainly (and strikingly) depicted on a bell krater of about 440 B.C.: Persephone here emerges from the earth (only her lower legs are still hidden) while Hermes stands in full frontal view beside her; to the right Hekate draws back in amazement with torches in each hand, and beyond her Demeter waits patiently (NY 28.57.23; names included for all figures). Also interpreted to show this scene is a krater by the Alkimachos Painter with Hermes leading a young woman by the hand, flanked by a Silenos bearing a chest and a woman with torches (Bologna 236), although Hermes wedding the mother of Pan is perhaps more likely. Other pots present us with a potentially more puzzling conception of the *anodos*. Certain is a krater of the Polygnotos Group in Dresden with Persephone (named) rising from the earth as Hermes stands waiting and Silenoi (with goat horns) cavort about (Dresden 350). From this sure point we move to others on which Hermes disappears and the Silenoi assume center stage with Persephone (e.g., Berlin: Lost VI 3275), and then still others where only the upper body of the goddess has emerged and the Silenoi wield hammers that they swing in her direction, as if summoning her forth by their pounding on the earth (e.g., Ferrara 3031; Stockholm:NM 6). Most impressive of all is the one Black-Figure piece, a lekythos of about 470 B.C. on which the goddess' head and hands alone are visible, and two Silenoi seemingly bring their hammers down on that head (CabMéd 298). If these do show Persephone, they may intend her annual return from the Underworld (as the burgeoning grain?) rather than the first such instance. We should note that most of these scenes have also been interpreted as representing Pandora, based on a volute krater in Oxford which definitely shows the latter (without Silenoi, however: Oxford G275). Of the two, the Dresden krater offers, I think, some grounds for preferring Persephone, but there is clearly something here that we do not entirely understand.[11]

Turning to other tales of Demeter, we saw above that her transformation into a horse to avoid (unsuccessfully) the advances of Poseidon is preserved only in late sources. Presumably, though, the idea itself is early, and the equation Demeter/Erinys is ascribed by Pausanias (in a direct quote) to an Antimachos who is probably the epic poet of Teos, since the line comes from a poem about the attack on Thebes (8.25.4). In chapter 1 we also found the goddess on occasion as the mother of Hekate (by Zeus). One of our sources for that idea, Kallimachos, provides as well our first account of her anger against Erysichthon, the son of Triopas, son of Poseidon and Kanake (*Hymn* 6). As he tells the story, Erysichthon goes to a holy grove of the goddess with twenty of his men to cut down the trees for a banquet hall. When Demeter tries to dissuade him (in the guise of her own priestess Nikippe) he threatens her with his axe, and in consequence she sends upon him an unending hunger that causes him to consume everything in his father's house (even the cat) and then beg at crossroads. In all this there is no mention of any daughter Mestra or his ultimate fate. A daughter of this name does, however, appear in the *Ehoiai* as the mate of both Glaukos and Poseidon, and while there seems no room in the fragment for a complete account of her father's problems, there is a reference to hunger (Hes fr 43a MW). Hellanikos similarly calls Erysichthon "insatiate of food" (4F7), Palaiphatos derides the idea that his daughter Mestra could change her shape at will (saying that it was instead her beauty that caused suitors to bring her father gifts: Pal 23), and Lykophron speaks of the shapechanging daughter of the man hateful to Demeter who daily lightened her father's fierce hunger (Lyk 1391–96). Thus we can reasonably suppose that the story known from Ovid is essentially old: Erysichthon's crime and punishment are narrated as in Kallimachos, but when the miscreant sells his daughter to get more food, her one-time lover Poseidon changes her into a man and she escapes (*Met* 8.738–878). On learning of her power, Erysichthon then resells her numerous times (she assumes various different forms to return to him) but finally even such proceeds are not enough and he consumes his own body. A Red-Figure pelike of the mid-fifth century seems our only illustration: Erysichthon raises the axe to strike the tree while a female figure (Demeter? a Dryad?) rises up from the ground to protest (Bonn 2661).

Somewhere in the Hesiodic Corpus there was also the story of the snake Kychreides that came from Salamis to Eleusis and was made the attendant of Demeter (Hes fr 226 MW). We have already seen in chapter 1 that the fusion of Rheia and the Phrygian Mother of the Gods (Kybele) is accompanied by a fusion between Demeter and that same Mother, as attested by Euripides (*Hel* 1301–45) and Melanippides (764 *PMG*) in the second half of the fifth century. The mating of Zeus (as a serpent) with Persephone (his own daughter by Rheia/ Demeter, his mother) to produce a child Dionysos (subsequently dismembered and eaten by Titans) is for the most part a tale restricted to Orphic texts which we will consider more fully in Appendix A. Its earliest sure appearance might be Pindar, *if* the words "atonement for the ancient grief of Persephone" do refer to the loss of her child (mankind sprung from the ashes of the guilty Titans would be the atoners) and *if* Plato is in fact quoting Pindar here (*Meno* 81b = fr 133 SM). The child is sometimes named Zagreus, although not perhaps in Orphic contexts; this and other references to Zagreus in literature will be treated later in this chapter.

Finally, there is Triptolemos.[12] We have seen that in the *Homeric Hymn to Demeter* he is simply a leading citizen of Eleusis, but that in Orphic tradition he and his brother reveal the secret of Persephone's disappearance, thus becoming the recipients of Demeter's agricultural knowledge. Likewise, in Ovid and Hyginus he is the child nearly immortalized by Demeter, and subsequently promoted to sower of grain over the whole earth. Pausanias, our source for "Orpheus," says that in "Mousaios," Triptolemos is the son of Okeanos and Gaia, in Choirilos the son of Raros and a daughter of Amphiktyon (the same woman who bore Kerkyon to Poseidon), and to other Athenians the son of Keleos (1.14.2–3), as he is to Ovid; Hyginus makes him a son of Eleusinos (*Fab* 147), Servius a son of Ikarios or Eleusinos at one point (Σ G 1.19), of Keleos at another (Σ G 1.163). Sophokles wrote a *Triptolemos* play at the very beginning of his career, and we know that in it Demeter described the places to which the hero would travel (in a dragon chariot), but we cannot tell if this was the core of the drama or only a small part of it. Pausanias relates that at Patrai Triptolemos' dragon chariot was stolen by Antheias while its owner was sleeping; Antheias' attempt to sow the land was, however, foiled by his fall from the chariot and death (7.18.2–3). In Ovid we find a somewhat similar tale, that a king Lynkos of Scythia planned to kill Triptolemos in his sleep so that he himself might be the bestower of the grain; Demeter changed him into a lynx as he raised the sword (*Met* 5.645–61; cf. *Fab* 259). Plato's *Apology* mentions Triptolemos together with Minos, Rhadamanthys, Aiakos, and others of the just among the *hêmitheoi* in the Underworld (*Apol* 41a); the initial reference to at least some of these as judges there may or may not be meant to include

Triptolemos, but the latter does seem to appear as such on an Apulian volute krater of the mid-fourth century (Naples H3222: heavily restored in places). As for the rest of the artistic tradition, we see Triptolemos first on an amphora in Reggio Calabria from the circle of Exekias: he stands by, holding grain, as Demeter mounts a horse-drawn chariot; Herakles, Athena, Hermes, and one Ploutodotas are also in attendance (Reggio 4001). But from the last third of the sixth century in Attic Black-Figure he himself is seated in a two-wheeled chariot without horses, clutching his ears of grain while Demeter and Persephone (or groups of mortals) flank him (so Göttingen J14 and Brussels A130, both by the Swing Painter). On none of these vases is there any sign of dragons, wings, or other means of propulsion; only in Red-Figure are wings sometimes added, and a snake springing from the hub of the wheel (e.g., London E140).[13] For what it is worth, Dionysos sometimes appears in the winged chariot, and as well Hephaistos (or Dionysos with an axe: Florence 81600; Berlin: Lost F2273).

HADES   Kronos and Rheia's fifth child, Hades, plays as one might expect a rather retiring role in the corpus of tales about the Olympians. The allotment Poseidon speaks of in *Iliad* 15 applies also to this third brother, who draws as his share the "misty darkness" of the Underworld (*Il* 15.187–91: cf. *HDem* 84–87). His only certain reappearance from this kingdom is the foray recounted above, to abduct Persephone (in later sources he is said to have pursued several other maidens on other occasions: Str 8.3.14). There remains, though, a curious story, told by Dione in the *Iliad* (5.395–402) and perhaps alluded to by Pindar (*Ol* 9.29–35), to the effect that the god was wounded by Herakles with his arrows at Pylos among the dead, and was forced to go up to Olympos to be cured. Uncertain is whether Pindar's allusion refers to a direct confrontation between Hades and Herakles, and whether he means that Herakles fought Hades, Poseidon, and Apollo together or separately; the scholiast here argues for three separate conflicts, but Pindar's mention of the locale of the Poseidon combat as Pylos seems suspicious, if in fact Homer's "Pylos among the dead" indicates the same place. On the other hand, Herakles might well be imagined as coming to blows with Hades in the Underworld when he arrives there to fetch Kerberos, and the *Iliad* scholia do relate such an incident, with a wounding of Hades, as part of the quest for the dog (ΣbT *Il* 5.395). Both Pausanias (6.25.2) and Apollodoros (ApB 2.7.3) envision a single occasion, namely Herakles' attack against Neleus (so too ΣA *Il* 11.690, with Hades, Poseidon, and Hera against Athena and Zeus), but they in their turn may have been led astray by the reference to Pylos; it is difficult to see why Hades should be involved in this venture. Not impossibly Homer manufactured the event, which like much else in Dione's speech is problematic, and Pindar and other writers then attempted to flesh out his reference. Yet this solution will not explain the conflict with Poseidon (not in Homer) attested both by Pindar and sixth-century vase-painting. It may be therefore that an important narrative really has been lost. We will return to this question in chapter 13, where we will also consider several puzzling vase-paintings showing Herakles carrying a figure (with a cornucopia), who may be Hades.

Elsewhere in *Iliad* 5 we learn that Hades possesses a cap that makes the wearer invisible: Athena has borrowed it so that she might deceive Ares (*Il* 5.844–45). The origins of this cap are nowhere mentioned in our early sources; Apollodoros says that the Kyklopes gave Hades a cap (no special properties mentioned, although it is very likely this one) when they gave Zeus the thunderbolt and Poseidon the trident (ApB 1.2.1). That a god whose name is taken to mean "the unseen one" would properly own such a cap seems obvious at first, but Hades is presumably unseen by mortals because he remains under the earth, not because he roams the world unobserved (indeed, neither he nor any other Homeric god needs a cap for that). In any case, while in his realm of darkness Hades has little use for it, and we need not be surprised that Perseus in his quest for Medousa's head is allowed to wear it (*Aspis* 226–27). Surprisingly, though, our sources do not show Perseus acquiring the cap from Hades himself, or even from other major divinities; instead, both a mid-sixth-century Chalkidian amphora (London B155) and Pherekydes (3F11) send him to certain Nymphai to obtain it. The amphora does not label the item in question, but both the *Aspis* and Pherekydes (or rather, our summary of him) say specifically that what Perseus wears belongs to Hades; they do not explain why the Nymphai would have it. Apollodoros offers one other use of this same cap: Hermes wears it in the battle of the gods and Gigantes (ApB 1.6.2). In none of these myths is it ever used to deceive mortals.

Hades has also, in the passage of Pindar cited above, a *rhabdos* or staff, which he uses to bring mortals down to the Underworld, thus (apparently) usurping Hermes' functions as *psychopompos* (*Ol* 9.33–35). Most likely, Pindar does *not* mean that he has the power to apportion out death here, as that would be an unparalleled assumption of powers allotted to the Moirai (unless he is somehow defending himself in a battle context). The god's responsibilities as Lord of the Underworld are largely to rule the dead (who presumably need little ruling) once they have entered his realm, and to keep them from leaving again. Only in two somewhat curious passages of Aischylos (one in the *Hiketides*, the other in the *Eumenides*) does he actually appear to judge in any fashion the deeds that the dead committed while they were alive (A: *Hik* 228–31; *Eum* 273–75), and in virtually no case does he punish mortals in Hades (the "Tartaros" transgressors constitute an extremely small exception, as we will see in chapter 3, nor is it clear that they are under Hades' jurisdiction, save for Sisyphos). There is, however, a passage from *Iliad* 3 to be noted in this regard: when Agamemnon takes the oath on behalf of the Achaians before the single combat between Menelaos and Paris, he calls upon Zeus and Helios and "those under the earth who punish the dead who have sworn falsely in life" (*Il* 3.278–79). Normally, Zeus is the guarantor of oaths, and in this particular instance Athena punishes the oath-breaker Pandaros, so that it is not clear how seriously we should consider the idea of chthonic forces here, even if the phrase "those under the earth" does indicate Hades and Persephone. Related perhaps are two passages of the *Iliad* involving punishment of transgressors while still on earth. In the first of these, Althaia calls upon Hades and Persephone to avenge the loss of her brothers with death (*Il* 9.566–71: the Erinyes hear the prayer, although we are not told whether they carry it out); in the second, Hades and Persephone fulfill Amyntor's wish for the childlessness of his son Phoinix (though the prayer was made to the Erinyes: *Il* 9.456–57). We will hardly be surprised that in their chthonic capacity these gods have such powers, but rarely elsewhere in myth do they abandon their role as innocuous underworld rulers and actually use them.

Such tales otherwise told of Hades involve those few heroes who descend to the Underworld while still alive, that is, Herakles, Theseus and Peirithoos, and Orpheus (Odysseus scarcely counts, since he does not actually enter the realm of the dead), or those like Sisyphos, Protesilaos, and Eurydike, who are given permission to leave. In many of these tales, the ruler of the dead shows himself to be surprisingly compassionate; one wonders how he (or Persephone?) was portrayed by Aischylos when the latter presented his Sisyphos play(s). One other point in the *Iliad* at which Hades appears (or almost appears) occurs during the gods' preparation to join battle by the sides of their favorites on the Trojan plain; the clamor is such that he starts up in fear from his throne, lest Poseidon should break open the earth, and the dead be revealed to the living (*Il* 20.61–65: his concern seems to be for the feelings of the gods, rather than those of the dead).

As for names, in Homer he is Aides or Aidoneus but, on one occasion, Zeus Katachthonios, Zeus under the earth (*Il* 9.457). So too in the *Theogony* he is the chthonian god (*Th* 767), and in Aischylos the "other Zeus" (A:*Hik* 231), "the earthly, the much-visited Zeus of the dead" (A:*Hik* 156–58), "chthonian Zeus" (fr 273a R), or "Zeus who is beneath the earth" (*Ag* 1386–87: *kata chthonos Dios*). But a line of the *Works & Days* offers the phrase "chthonian Zeus" of the god who with Demeter fosters the crops, which would seem to denote rather he who sends rain, that is, Olympian Zeus (*W&D* 465).[14] Thus it appears that at times Zeus and Hades represented simply different facets of a single extended divine power. The name "Plouton" for the god *may* appear in a list of gods on an inscription of the early fifth century from Eleusis (if this is correctly supplemented: IG³ I 5).[15] Subsequently, we find it for certain in Sophokles' *Antigone* (1200; Plouton at *PD* 806 denotes a river), but well before that it surfaces on fragments of a cup by Douris on which Plouton (head only preserved) is accompanied by Persephone (also named) and probably Demeter (Getty 86.AE.18.1–9 plus 86.AE.185.1–3 and 81.AE.213).[16] From perhaps 430 B.C. comes a second example by the Kodros Painter: here the bearded Plouton (again so named) reclines on a banquet couch and holds a cornucopia in one hand and phiale in the other while Pherrephatta sits facing him (London E82). Thus, there seems no doubt that, by the fifth century at least, "Plouton" was another name for Hades, as well as the name of the anonymous bearded figure with cornucopia shown elsewhere on numerous occasions in Attic vase-painting (so Louvre G209 [Oionokles Painter]; Athens 16346; Madrid 11017; we have already identified such a figure as Hades in his pursuit of Persephone on Naples H3091).[17]

How the name "Plouton" might have originally related (if at all) to that of the child Ploutos borne by Demeter to Iasios is unclear, but a fragment from Sophokles' lost *Inachos* creates a pun between the two names (fr 273 R; cf. *OT* 30), and Plato etymologizes *Plouton* as giver of the wealth that lies within the earth (presumably metals: *Kratylos* 403a). Given the presence of the inscription at Eleusis, we may wonder exactly who (or what) Athenians saw in the (bearded) Ploutodotas who appears with Demeter and Triptolemos on the amphora by Exekias noted above (Reggio Calabria 4001). As for the cornucopia (sometimes empty, usually full), we cannot say whether it holds metals or agricultural produce, but it would seem that Hades has assumed a more positive role in Athenian thinking, perhaps by way of Eleusis. We will see in chapter 13 a tradition according to which Herakles brought this horn (or at least one like it) down to Hades when he came for Kerberos. One last name, "Klymenos," appears first in Lasos toward the end of the sixth century (702 *PMG*). Since it refers to the husband of Demeter's daughter it can scarcely denote anyone but Hades, though the reason for the application of such a term is not entirely clear; inscriptions do show it as a title of the god in Hermione, Lasos' homeland.

HESTIA   Last (and least seen, at any rate) of Kronos' children is Hestia. Homer never mentions her at all, and indeed there seem to be no real myths about her until Priapos makes an unwitting attempt upon her honor in Ovid's *Fasti* (6.319–48). But she does appear in the *Theogony* briefly as the first-born child of Kronos, and the *Homeric Hymn to Aphrodite* gives her the same role, calling her first- and last-born, presumably because of Kronos' disgorging of his children (*HAph* 21–32). This Hymn also recounts that she was wooed by Poseidon and Apollo, but rejected both of them and swore, touching Zeus' head, an oath of eternal chastity; no reasons are given for her decision. Zeus as compensation then assigns her great honor in the homes of men. Two other short Hymns are addressed to her. In one she is said to tend the temple of Apollo at Delphi (meaning perhaps only that there is a hearth there: *HomH* 24); in the other she is linked with Hermes in a common prayer, although no special relationship between the two seems intended (*HomH* 29). Pindar and Bakchylides each mention her once, but simply as an object of prayer (*Nem* 11.1–2; Bak 14B.1). Our representations of the wedding procession to the nuptials of Peleus and Thetis do however demonstrate that she is not completely housebound; on the François Krater she is shown next to Chariklo, while on both Sophilos vases she enjoys the company of her sister Demeter, with Leto and Chariklo immediately following (Florence 4209; London

1971.11–1.1; Athens Akr 587). She is also remembered on a Red-Figure kylix by Oltos, appearing with the rest of the Olympians in a typical gathering on Olympos (Tarquinia RC 6848).

The Children of Zeus

HEPHAISTOS[18] From the children of Kronos and Rheia we proceed to the offspring of Zeus, whose amatory activities will complete the basic pantheon of the Olympians. By his own wife Hera he begets three or four children, depending on whom we read. The doubt occurs, as we have already seen, in the case of Hephaistos, who is clearly Hera's child but may or may not have a father. In *Iliad* 1 the blacksmith god does call Hera mother and Zeus father, but there lurks a possibility that this last could be a general title (*Il* 1.577–79). Similarly, in *Iliad* 14, Zeus calls him son, but he could well mean Hera's son (*Il* 14.338). In *Odyssey* 8, however, Hephaistos clearly reproaches his "two parents," and these, it would seem, can only be Zeus and Hera (*Od* 8.312). For the story that Hera alone conceived him we must turn to the *Theogony*, where his birth without a father is described immediately after a reference to Athena's birth (*Th* 927–29). We are told here that Hera is angry, but Athena's birth as the source of her anger is not made explicit, although it seems very likely. In the version that Chrysippos found elsewhere in "Hesiod," an *eris*, or quarrel, is again the cause of Hera's deed (Hes fr 343 MW), but now the conception of Hephaistos comes *before* that of Athena, so that, barring an earlier reference to Athena's birth (or confusion in the narrative), the quarrel in question springs from some other cause.[19] The motif of the goddess' annoyance over her husband's venture into childbirth also appears in the *Homeric Hymn to Apollo*, but here the child conceived by Hera without a father is Typhoeus, not Hephaistos (*HAp* 331–52; cf. Stes 239 *PMG*, where the same result follows from a "grudge" against Zeus). We saw at the beginning of this chapter the tale of the *Iliad* scholia, that Hera conceived Hephaistos (by Zeus) before her marriage, then pretended there was no father so as to conceal the deed (ΣbT *Il* 14.296).

In the same *Hymn to Apollo* noted above, Hera, contrasting Athena with Hephaistos whom *she* has borne (presumably with Zeus, or else the following tale of Typhoeus would have no point), says that he was crippled in his feet, and that (a line giving her motivation, which was probably her son's appearance, is missing here) she picked him up and threw him down into the sea, where Thetis and her sisters cared for him (*HAp* 316–21). This admission of guilt from Hephaistos' own mother tallies perfectly with what the god himself says in *Iliad* 18: told that Thetis has come to see him, he recalls how she and the Okeanid Eurynome saved him when he fell into the sea by the will of Hera, who wanted to hide him because he was lame (*Il* 18.395–405). We learn too that he stayed with his hosts for some time in a cave near the stream of Okeanos, making elegant jewelry for them, and that neither gods nor men knew where he was. In *Iliad* 1 we receive quite a different account: Hephaistos here says that on one occasion he attempted to defend his mother from Zeus, and for his trouble was picked up by the latter and hurled from the threshold; he fell for an entire day, and at evening landed heavily on Lemnos, where the Sintians cared for him (*Il* 1.590–94). At no point in this story (although it may have been its original rationale, and is asserted by Apollodoros: Ap*B* 1.3.5) is it said that Hephaistos became lame because of the fall; we have seen that in *Iliad* 18 (and probably *Odyssey* 8) he is lame from birth. Neither are we told the details of the quarrel that provoked this second fall, but it seems likely (and again can be found in Apollodoros) that the event was the punishment of Hera described in *Iliad* 15, when she was hung up in the air with anvils tied to her feet after having driven Herakles' ship to Kos (*Il* 15.18–30). Zeus says here that if he caught anyone trying to aid Hera he flung them down to earth, which certainly sounds like a reference to Hephaistos. Nevertheless, even if Homer did understand these two expulsions as two distinctly separate events, we should probably suppose them in origin variant methods of explaining the same phenomenon: either Hephaistos is lame because he is thrown out of Olympos, or he is thrown out of Olympos because he is lame.

The second of these versions, that in which Hera throws out her son, forms the basis for the further tale of Hephaistos' revenge against his mother by means of the magical throne. Apparently, both Alkaios and Pindar told this story (Al 349 LP; Pind fr 283 SM), and it was a favorite with Attic Black-Figure vase-painters, but for any details at all we must await Pausanias (1.20.3), Hyginus (*Fab* 166), and the account in the fable collection falsely ascribed to Libanius (*Narrationes* 30.1 Westermann). These last three are in accord that the chair was sent to Hera in the guise of a present, and held her fast as soon as she sat down in it. Already in Alkaios, it seems, Ares set forth in hopes of bringing Hephaistos back to undo the power of his craftsmanship;[20] we know, however, that only Dionysos was able to perform that task, by plying Hephaistos with large quantities of wine. In the "Libanius" account, too, Ares attempts Hephaistos' return, but is beaten off with fire-brands by his brother; when Dionysos does bring Hephaistos back, the latter pointedly presents to his mother her benefactor, and she accommodates him by persuading the other gods to admit Dionysos to their company. Hyginus refers to the chair as floating or swinging in the air, once Hera is stuck to it. In this latter account Hephaistos after his return obtains from Zeus a wish in return for freeing his mother, and on Poseidon's spiteful advice asks for the hand of Athena (the spilled seed and birth of Erichthonios follow as in that story elsewhere).

Pausanias mentions Hera's binding as one of the scenes on the Amyklai Throne (3.18.6), and her release as depicted somewhere on the bronze temple of Athena in Sparta (3.17.3). But the earliest preserved artistic representation of the story occurs on a Middle Corinthian amphoriskos in Athens, if the rider with sharply turned-around feet escorted by Dionysos and padded dancers is in fact Hephaistos (Athens 664).[21] Certain, and more useful, is the François Krater, on which we view the actual arrival of the procession at the house of Zeus (Florence 4209). The Olympians are represented by Zeus himself and Hera, both on thrones (Hera for obvious reasons), then Athena looking back at a kneeling and sullen-faced Ares. Since Ares had tried and failed to bring back Hephaistos, his lack of enthusiasm over Dionysos' success might seem natural enough without further explanation. At the center of the composition, however, is a surprise: Aphrodite has come out to stand in front of Zeus and observe the arrival firsthand. Possibly her special interest in the event stems from the assumption that Hephaistos is here, as in *Odyssey* 8, her husband, in which case her look probably denotes disappointment at his return. But it has also been suggested that Hephaistos has demanded her hand in marriage (rather than, as in Hyginus, that of Athena) if he is to release his mother.[22] This last interpretation has, unfortunately, no evidence whatever from antiquity to support it, but it would certainly explain a very unusual marriage and perhaps better account for what seems here to be very real agitation on Aphrodite's part.

Other representations of the tale generally favor Hephaistos en route to Olympos over the actual arrival, and thus offer no useful information; exceptions include an Olympia shield-band (B 8402, *c*. 550 B.C.), an Apulian amphora (Foggia 132723, *c*. 310 B.C.), and a Lucanian volute krater (Leningrad 988), all of which show Hephaistos beside Hera in her chair (in the last instance actually undoing the bonds). In a lighter vein, we see what is very likely Hephaistos' combat with Ares (before Hera on her chair) on an Apulian Phlyax krater of the mid-fourth century, as each god brandishes a spear (London F269).[23] Some form of the story was certainly told in Epicharmos' comedy *Hephaistos* or *Komastai* (Revelers), and probably too in Achaios' satyric *Hephaistos*, but we have no details beyond the titles.

Of Hephaistos' other exploits there is not as much to say. We have seen that in *Odyssey* 8 he is married to Aphrodite, but this is the only place in early literature or art where they are explicitly so associated; in assemblages of the gods in art Aphrodite is usually placed next to Ares, as for example in the case of the wedding of Peleus and Thetis on the François Krater (and probably already on a Cycladic amphora of the mid-seventh century: Naxos, no #). In *Iliad* 18 Hephaistos is married to Charis, who seems to be a kind of alternative to the idea of three Charites (*Il* 18.382–83); in the *Theogony* he marries Aglaia, the youngest of the Charites (*Th* 945–46). Elsewhere, he is not mentioned as being married at all, but the similarity of concept in a marriage of the lame, deformed god with Charis on the one hand and Aphrodite on the other is certainly striking. In the *Iliad* we also see him as the artisan of numerous objects, including the homes of the gods themselves (*Il* 1.606–8), the aigis of Zeus (*Il* 15.309–10), golden attendants who move of their own accord (*Il* 18.417–21), and a scepter given to Zeus and passed from him to Hermes to Pelops (*Il* 2.101–4). Hephaistos' workmanship often seems, in fact, to become the possession of mortals: in addition to Achilleus' armor (both sets, usually) there is Diomedes' breastplate at *Iliad* 8.194–95, plus the two-handled amphora given by Dionysos to Thetis and thence to Achilleus (*Od* 24.73–75). Possibly this last was a wedding gift or, as Stesichoros recounts, a present in gratitude to her for his rescue from Lykourgos (234 *PMG*); if the former, we may see the amphora carried by Dionysos on the François Krater. From the *Odyssey* in this category we might think of the silver mixing bowl Menelaos gives to Telemachos (*Od* 15.115–19 = 4.615–19) and the gold and silver dogs before the palace of Alkinoos (*Od* 7.91–94), while the *Ehoiai* refers to Peleus' sword (the one hidden by Akastos: Hes fr 209 MW, so also Anakreon 497 *PMG*) and something (the beginning of the line is lost, but the item is presumably a necklace) made by Hephaistos for Zeus to give to Europa (Hes fr 141 MW). From the *Aspis* there are greaves for Herakles (*Aspis* 122–23), and from Simonides we hear of the bronze Talos made for Minos (568 *PMG*). As for other deeds, we have already seen the god in the role of peacemaker in *Iliad* 1; subsequently in *Iliad* 5 he saves one of the sons (Idaios) of his priest Dares from death at the hands of Diomedes (*Il* 5.22–24: his only intervention in the fighting among humans) and combats with his fire the river Xanthos when the latter tries to drown Achilleus (*Il* 21.330–82). In the *Odyssey* his only real action is his shrewd (though predictably pointless) ensnaring of Ares and Aphrodite (*Od* 8.266–366).

One possible reason for the god's lack of greater involvement in stories may be that, in preserved Archaic literature at least, he has virtually no children; the one exception appears in Pherekydes, where he is made the father of Kabeiros and the Kabeirides (3F48). Later, in Apollonios, we will find him named as father of the (crippled) Palaimonios, one of the Argonautai (AR 1.202–4). And Ovid, Apollodoros, and Pausanias identify one Periphetes (a victim of Theseus at Epidauros) as an offspring of Hephaistos (*Met* 7.436–37; Ap*B* 3.16.1; Paus 2.1.4); such a brigand is conspicuously absent from early rosters of Theseus' opponents on his journey to Athens, but he does seem present on several Theseus-cycle pots and perhaps too on the Hephaisteion metopes. To be sure, if Hephaistos' failed union with Athena and the spilling of his seed upon the ground counts as parenthood, then he is the father of Erichthonios; this is also a late story in its complete form, but Pausanias reports Hephaistos pursuing Athena on the Amyklai Throne (3.18.13), the epic *Danais* speaks of Erichthonios *and* Hephaistos appearing from the earth (fr 2 *PEG*: "and" often emended to "son of"), and Hellanikos certainly knows of an Erichthonios sprung from Hephaistos (4F39). We will return to the whole story in detail in chapter 7, where Erichthonios (name given as "Erechtheus") will prove a child of earth as far back as Homer, although Homer offers no father or explanation for the event. For the moment we may simply note that the tale of Hephaistos' passion for Athena which led to the birth of the child survives first in Ps-Eratosthenes (*Katast* 13), who refers it back to Euripides (*Erechtheus?*; a satyr play?). Kallimachos must also have recounted it in his *Hekale* (ΣA *Il* 2.547; bits of the actual text in fr 260.18–23 Pf), and it appears in Apollodoros (Ap*B* 3.14.6) and Hyginus (*Fab* 166); the latter, as we saw, suggests that Athena was promised to Hephaistos after he returned to Olympos and released his mother. Whatever his motivation, there seems no doubt that Athena had her own ideas on the matter.

If not then the most prolific of fathers (other sons in *Fab* 158),[24] Hephaistos does play a unique role in the bringing to birth of two important females—Athena and Pandora. His task in opening Zeus' head for the first delivery is not attested in literature before Pindar (*Ol* 7.35–37), but he is a frequent (though not inevitable) component of the scene in much earlier artistic representations, beginning with the shield-bands from Olympia and continuing on through a good many Attic Black-Figure pots. On the basis of such a well-established iconography one might assume that he was also present at the birth of the goddess on the east pediment of the Parthenon. Unfortunately, the center of the east pediment was where the apse of the later Christian church was constructed, and thus the statues from that area had disappeared well before Carrey drew the pediments in 1674.[25] As for Pandora, Hephaistos is here creator, not just midwife; in both the *Theogony* and the *Works & Days* Zeus instructs him to fashion her out of earth (in the *Works & Days* earth and water: *Th* 571–72, *W&D* 60–63). We will see later (chapter 4) in discussing Pandora's story that hammers *may* have been involved in her making in some versions, which might help to explain a blacksmith god's involvement.

Blacksmith skills also involve Hephaistos (tangentially) in one other story (his only appearance in preserved tragedy): on Zeus' command he binds and nails Prometheus to a rock in the prologue of Aischylos' *Prometheus Desmotes*. Here he emerges, as elsewhere, as a sympathetic character, who feels for the suffering he must cause another. Aischylos is our first source for the idea that the fire Prometheus gave to man was stolen from Hephaistos, not directly from Zeus. If the lost *Prometheus Pyrphoros* was indeed the first play in the presumed Prometheus trilogy, then this latter action might have been dramatized or at least recounted, but there is perhaps better reason for thinking that the play came third (see chapter 4). In any case, one suspects that Hephaistos was a popular figure in satyr plays, both as the avenging son returning to Olympos and in other guises. On the basis of the new fragment of Aischylos' *Theoroi/Isthmiastai* (fr 78a R), it has even been suggested that he was a major character in that play, forging for the Silenoi the javelins with which they hoped to compete in the Isthmian Games.[26] His epithet of "Amphigueeis" (used at times as a name) appears frequently in epic (*Iliad*, *Odyssey*, and Hesiod), but although it is frequently taken to mean "lame or hobbling in both legs" (less frequently, "skilled with both hands"), its sense for Homer and Hesiod remains quite uncertain.[27] At one point in Homer (*Il* 2.426) the word "Hephaistos" clearly functions as a synonym for fire, as often in later literature.

ARES Zeus and Hera's other son is Ares, whose name in the *Iliad* is often synonymous with war (*Il* 2.385, 440, etc.). Not surprisingly he plays a major part in this poem, in contrast to the *Odyssey* where his only appearance is in Hephaistos' bed. On a figurative level he is often said to bestow martial valor on men (so, e.g., Hektor, *Il* 17.210–12), and various heroes are compared to him as they prepare to confront opponents (*Il* 2.627, 11.295, etc.), or described as "offshoots" *(ozos)* of Ares (*Il* 2.540, etc.). He incites the Trojans in the normal divine way (much as Athena and Poseidon do the Achaians) with shouts and personal exhortations while disguised: see, for example, *Iliad* 5, where he rallies his forces in the guise of Akamas (*Il* 5.461–69), and the remarkable scene in *Iliad* 20 where he runs back and forth to the hill of Kallikolone like a dark storm while shouting (*Il* 20.51–53). But he also does something that no other god at Troy does (excepting perhaps Apollo's intervention with Patroklos): he actually fights against the Achaians as if he were a normal warrior, and is even found stripping the armor from the corpse of Periphas, as if he could have any need for such spoils (*Il* 5.842–44). This gruesome and rather unsportsmanlike behavior in fact prompts Hera to ask Zeus for his removal from the battle, and leads directly to his defeat at the hands of Diomedes and Athena. Earlier in *Iliad* 5 we see, however, what he can do even without fighting, as he strides with Hektor holding his great spear and appearing now before the Trojan, now behind him (*Il* 5.592–95). And earlier still he had wrapped the battlefield in night at Apollo's bidding to aid their side (*Il* 5.506–8). But if he has little trouble controlling the battle, he is no match for his counterpart, Athena. The ease with which she inspires Diomedes to wound him and send him bellowing up to Olympos (to be reproached by Zeus for his hateful character: *Il* 5.835–909) is matched by her rough treatment of him again in *Iliad* 21. There she seems surprised that he would even think to try his strength against her, and has no trouble knocking him down with a large stone, which puts an end to the combat (*Il* 21.391–414). We have already seen him discomfited by Hephaistos when he tried to bring his brother back to Olympos, and there is as well the strange story told by Dione of Otos and Ephialtes, namely that they imprisoned the god in bonds in a bronze jar for thirteen months, and that he would have perished, overcome by the bonds, if Hermes had not stolen him away (*Il* 5.385–91). No reason is given for this undertaking by the Aloadai; although it seems to reflect little credit on Ares, we may perhaps wonder if they did not thus intend to rob the Olympian gods of their warlike valor before making their assault on Olympos (the scholia suggest as their motive rather anger at Ares' slaying of Adonis, who had been placed in the care of the Aloadai: ΣbT *Il* 5.385). We should note also Ares' encounters with Herakles in the *Aspis*, one recounted, the other forming the climax of the tale (*Aspis* 357–67, 424–66). In each case Ares is defeated, and both times wounded in the thigh, but the first occasion is said by Herakles to have been when Ares stood against him on behalf of Pylos and thus offers yet another vague reference to some mysterious combat between Herakles and the gods in the western Peloponnesos. In any case, it is clear that Ares has his problems in combat with all but the weakest opponents.

In the field of love the war god fares somewhat better, as we have already had reason to note. His relationship with Aphrodite in the *Iliad* is at times close, as when he lends his chariot to her so that she might leave the battlefield (*Il* 5.355–63), but never made explicit, and of course they are allies on the same side of the war. Only in *Iliad* 21, when Aphrodite comes up to help him away after his defeat at the hands of Athena, might we conceivably see stronger emotions at work (*Il* 21.416–17). For what it is worth, though, in *Iliad* 5 when Aphrodite does borrow the chariot she calls Ares "dear brother" (*Il* 5.359), and one is left with the suspicion that the *Iliad* does not recognize their erotic relationship. In any event, the *Odyssey* makes up for this reticence by publicizing to the full their encounters, in a situation that is now adultery (as it would not have been in the *Iliad*, since there Hephaistos is married to Charis). Ares comes to Hephaistos' house after he has seen its master leave, and makes the proposal to put his rival's absence to good use, but after the trap is sprung neither he nor Aphrodite has anything to say (*Od* 8.266–366). When the net is finally loosed he goes to Thrace; whether he ever pays the adulterer's fine promised by Poseidon we do not learn. In the *Theogony* (where Hephaistos is married to Aglaia), Aphrodite bears to the war god three children, all somewhat personified abstractions: Harmonia, Phobos, and Deimos (*Th* 933–37). The first of these takes on a more personal aspect by marrying Kadmos and bearing the royal line of Thebes; the others, as their names imply, serve as Ares' attendants, and are found as such in both the *Iliad* (*Il* 4.439–40, 15.119–20) and the *Aspis* (463–66: they bring up a chariot to help him away to Olympos after his defeat by Herakles). In the *Iliad* Phobos is also at one point said to be his child (*Il* 13.298–99). His further parenting of Eros by Aphrodite appears first in Simonides and is probably just a logical convenience based on their long-term relationship. Other children who are definitely Ares' in the *Iliad* are the mortal Achaians, Askalaphos and Ialmenos, whose mother Astyoche went to the god in secret in an upper room of her father's house (*Il* 2.512–15: cf. Hermes' similar tryst with a mortal at 16.181–86). It is the death of Askalaphos in *Iliad* 13 (although Ares learns of it only in *Iliad* 15) that prompts the god to don his armor and start down to the battlefield for revenge (although one wonders what he would have done, since the slayer—Deiphobos—is one of the heroes on his own side: *Il* 15.110–20). Here as elsewhere Athena takes charge, pulling him back and reminding him of what Zeus will do to any god who intervenes at this point in the battle (*Il* 15.121–42). The continuing link between the two divine colleagues in war may in fact suggest that Athena was regularly thought of as representing a more rational counterweight to Ares' battle fury. It is of interest, too, that Athena twice complains that Ares has reneged on a promise to fight on the side of the Achaians; he does not deny the charge (*Il* 5.831–34; 21.412–14).

Before leaving Ares in epic we may also note two other figures with whom he is associated. In *Iliad* 4, Eris who marches with him is called his sister (*Il* 4.440–41); in the *Theogony*, she is one of the many children of Nyx. Likewise in *Iliad* 5 we twice find the goddess Enyo, for whom no genealogy is given (the Enyo of the *Theogony* is one of the Graiai), as a companion of war (*Il* 5.333,

592–93). Her name is likely related to "Enyalios," which, though it sometimes appears in the *Iliad* as an isolated term, is on three separate occasions clearly a title of Ares (*Il* 13.518–19; 17.210–11; 20.69; see also *Aspis* 371). Alkman seems at times to have made Ares and Enyalios the same figure, at other times different ones (44 *PMG*); the scholiast who tells us this also knows a version in which Enyalios is the son of Ares and Enyo, or of Kronos and Rheia.

In later Archaic literature Ares is not much in evidence, save for when there are direct references to war. We have seen that he is the father of the Kyknos whom Herakles defeats in the *Aspis* (despite Ares' help; so too Stes 207 *PMG*). Pindar, in a fragment narrating the same hero's capture of the flesh-eating mares, also makes their master Diomedes of Thrace a son of Ares (fr 169 SM), and this is the standard later version. In the *Ehoiai*, Ares is probably the father of Thestios and Euenos by Demodike, daughter of Agenor (Hes fr 22 MW; this is not actually confirmed until Apollodoros), and possibly of Meleagros (Hes fr 25 MW and Ap*B* 1.8.2). Apollodoros offers as well Parthenopaios (by Atalanta), Tereus of Thrace, and even the dragon slain by Kadmos (Ap*B* 3.11.1; 3.14.8; 3.4.1). Equally appropriate is his Amazon daughter Penthesileia, as attested by the opening lines of the *Aithiopis* (fr 1 *PEG*), although here as elsewhere the linking of warlike figures to the war god as father is too obvious a device to be very interesting. But there is one other daughter with a more intriguing function, that of involving Ares in a primordial murder trial, a story first mentioned by Euripides (E: *El* 1258–62; *IT* 945–46) and Hellanikos (4F38; cf. Dem 23.66 and Phil 328F3) and subsequently by Apollodoros (Ap*B* 3.14.2) and Pausanias (1.21.4). According to Euripides, Ares was judged by the gods on the Areopagos (and cleansed of pollution by Zeus) after slaying Halirrhothios, a son of Poseidon, in anger over an unholy union (i.e., rape) with his daughter. Hellanikos adds that the girl in question was Alkippe, Ares' child by Aglauros, daughter of Kekrops, and that Ares was opposed at the trial by Poseidon, but says nothing about the outcome. In Apollodoros, Ares appears before twelve gods, and is acquitted, as Euripides would seem to imply (*IT* 945–46).[28] A remark by someone to Herakles in Panyasis includes Ares (by the command of his father) among gods who have endured to serve mortals (fr 3 *PEG*), and it is not impossible that this was a condition of the acquittal. But, though at times ready to help his children, Ares nowhere aids any heroes, nor does he ever become involved in stories of offended divine honor (save perhaps for his release of Thanatos after the latter is bound by Sisyphos: Pher 3F119). Not surprisingly, given these limitations, his role in Greek art is usually confined to standing or sitting next to Aphrodite at gatherings of the gods (on the Chest of Kypselos they have a whole panel to themselves), assisting Kyknos against Herakles, and of course participating in the battle of the gods and Gigantes.[29]

HEBE AND EILEITHUIA   In addition to sons, Zeus and Hera are credited with two daughters, Hebe and Eileithuia, according to the *Theogony* (*Th* 922). Presumably the former, judging from her name, was always a goddess of youth, though given that the Olympians seem to possess eternal youth as a natural attribute, it is a bit difficult to appreciate her importance. One might guess that at some point in time her presence on Olympos was what kept the gods from aging, but this is never specified in the surviving literature, and no one ever attempts to strike at the gods by abducting her. She appears three times in the *Iliad*, once to pour nectar for the gods (*Il* 4.2–3), once to bathe Ares after he has been wounded by Diomedes (*Il* 5.905), and once to help Hera hitch up her chariot (*Il* 5.722, much as Iris unhitches the chariot that has brought Aphrodite back to Olympos in the same book). On none of these occasions is her parentage mentioned, so we cannot be sure whether the poet of the *Iliad* would have agreed with Hesiod on that point. In the *Odyssey* she is certainly called the daughter of Zeus and Hera (*Od* 11.602–4), but the context is her marriage to Herakles on Olympos; since his apotheosis is scarcely much earlier than the beginning of the sixth century (see chapter 13), these lines are an obvious interpolation, and we thus know no more for the *Odyssey* than we do for the *Iliad*. The same problem holds for the reference to Hebe's wedding and parents near the end of the *Theogony* (950–55), and for that in the *Ehoiai* (Hes fr 25.26–29 MW). Since there are no other sources or stories about her, we cannot say at what point her parentage was established, or whether her role as cupbearer of the gods (mentioned only the one time in the *Iliad*) was a well-established function (we have seen Hephaistos serving in that capacity in *Iliad* 1, although this was apparently a special occasion; elsewhere Iris is also cup-bearer, as frequently in vase-painting). But the interpolations in the *Odyssey*, *Theogony*, and *Ehoiai* are surely earlier than the fifth century, and indeed Pindar calls her a sister of Eileithuia (*Nem* 7.4), thus implying her ancestry. In any case, her marriage to Herakles can hardly precede his apotheosis, so that that part of her story, too, must be later than Homer. Most likely it arose from the fact that Hebe was a minor deity and conveniently available, but her parentage from Hera may also have been a factor, serving as it would to reinforce the latter's reconciliation with Herakles. In art she appears, as one might expect, primarily in scenes of Herakles' arrival on Olympos, although she does find a place on the Erskine Dinos, alone, between Dionysos and Cheiron (London 1971.11–1.1), and to the far left in Oltos' divine assembly (Tarquinia RC 6848).

The other daughter, Eileithuia, is mentioned four times in the *Iliad* and once in the *Odyssey*. All four references in the *Iliad* show her as a goddess who assists in childbirth (*Il* 11.269–72; 16.187–88; 19.103–4, 117–19), but on two occasions the form is pluralized as Eileithuiai (*Il* 11.270; 19.117–19), and on one of those the goddesses are called "daughters of Hera" (*Il* 11: no father is mentioned and this is the only allusion to her/their parentage in Homer). In the one instance where she has a specific task, we see that Hera holds her (or rather them) back, so that Alkmene might not be delivered of Herakles before the wife of Sthenelos should bear Eurystheus; Hera herself speeds up the birth of the latter child, who is in only his seventh month (*Il* 19.117–19). In the *Odyssey*, the reference is simply to the cave of Eileithuia at Amnisos, with no word at all about her functions (*Od* 19.188). However, Eileithuia does play a brief but crucial role in the *Homeric Hymn to Apollo* (*HAp* 97–116). Here again, in the matter of the birth of Apollo, Hera restrains her daughter (or keeps her in ignorance of the situation), so that Leto is racked with labor pangs for nine days and nights. At last, the other goddesses send Iris to fetch the birth goddess, armed with persuasive words and the offer of a great long necklace with golden threads; as soon as Eileithuia arrives on Delos, the birth is accomplished. We see from this account, as from that of Alkmene in the *Iliad,* that apparently Eileithuia must be physically present in order to assist in events. An original function as an actual helper in delivery might be the reason for her sometimes plural (and probably earlier) form, given that many hands would be useful in such endeavors. Otherwise her appearances in Archaic literature are limited to four citations in Pindar. In one of these she aids Euadne to bear Iamos (*Ol* 6.41–42), in another she is addressed as daughter of Hera sitting beside the Moirai (*Nem* 7.4), and in yet another she and Lachesis shout together as Apollo and Artemis are born (*Paian* 12.16–17), but none of these passages adds anything to what we have already seen of her character. We should perhaps add to this Pausanias' mention of a hymn by "Olen" in which she is called the "deft spinner," as if she were a Moira, and "older than Kronos" (8.21.3). In art she also appears with the other gods at the wedding of Peleus and Thetis on the Erskine Dinos (London 1971.11–1.1) and, more individually, in one other context, at the birth of Athena. Very likely this role occurs as early as the shield-bands from Olympia, for though B 1687 (600 B.C. or earlier) merely shows a woman standing behind the throned Zeus with her hands on his shoulders, B 847 (575–50 B.C.) has a similar woman holding Zeus' head as Athena springs forth. In Attic Black-Figure we can be even more certain, for in this same context Eileithuia is sometimes named as she stands beside Zeus (so Berlin:Ch F1704, London B147; Louvre E851). In many cases he is flanked by two women who both seem to attend him and might be intended as twin Eileithuiai, but the fondness of vase-painters for symmetrical composition may be a consideration here (on the Berlin pot cited above, this second woman is named as Demeter).

ATHENA Next of Zeus' children we come to Athena, the child who is all his (unless swallowing the mother counts). The circumstances of her birth have already been discussed in connection with Zeus' mating with Metis and Hephaistos' role in the deed. Homer, as we might expect, is silent about such a physically abnormal event, but it *may* be implied in Ares' speech at *Iliad* 5.880, when he reproaches Zeus for letting Athena do as she pleases just because he (bore? begat? the Greek verb is *egeinato*) her. This verb normally means "give birth" when used of a woman and "beget" when used of a man, but since Zeus also begat Ares the latter meaning would not have much point here, so that

Zeus in both roles may be what is intended. In any case, we can say that Homer never attempts to provide her with a more normal mother. We have seen that both Hesiod and the Hesiodic Corpus tell the tale of her unusual delivery, and post-Hesiodic sources allow the story to stand; indeed, Aischylos' *Eumenides* depends heavily on the notion that Athena is the daughter of Zeus alone (*Eum* 736–38). Both the *Iliad* and the *Odyssey* show her as a clear favorite of his, knowing well her father's temper and likely to get what she asks for. Uncharacteristic, and yet indicative of their relationship, is her outburst (to Hera, not Zeus) in *Iliad* 8, when she suggests that all her help to Herakles (which she now regrets) was done to please Zeus, and at his command (*Il* 8.360–72).

Of Athena's many activities in the *Iliad* we should note especially her tempting of Pandaros in *Iliad* 4, her support of Diomedes in *Iliad* 5 (during which she brings about Pandaros' death), and her impersonation of Deiphobos to lure Hektor to his death in *Iliad* 22; we have already seen her rough treatment of Ares in our discussion of that god. In the *Odyssey*, after initiating the question of divine aid for Odysseus, she represents all the gods (save Poseidon) in bringing about his return, and assumes a variety of disguises, male and female, in the process. Her additional name of Pallas is also frequently found in both poems, but never without Athena as a complement; the *Homeric Hymn to Demeter* is the first instance in which the name "Pallas" is used by itself (*HDem* 424). No Archaic source attempts to explain this name; the tale that Athena accidentally killed a playmate Pallas, daughter of Triton, comes to us from Apollodoros (*ApB* 3.12.3), as does the idea that she slew Pallas, one of the Gigantes (and used his skin as a shield: *ApB* 1.6.2).[30] Two other names (or at least titles used independently) in both *Iliad* and *Odyssey* are "Tritogeneia" (born from Lake Tritonis? born on the third of the month?: first *Il* 4.515)[31] and "Atrytone" (the unwearied one?: first *Il* 2.157).[32]

Of all Athena's attributes, the most curious is surely the aigis. Exactly what this object was remains unclear, even after its many appearances in Homer.[33] Zeus, of course, has "aigis-bearing" (probably in truth, "aigis-riding": *aigiochos*[34]) as one of his most common epithets, but he seems never to wear (or ride) it, and on only two occasions to use it. From *Iliad* 15 we learn that Hephaistos made it for Zeus (*Il* 15.309–10: cf. Hes fr 343 MW, where Metis makes it for Athena), and from *Iliad* 2 that it has one hundred golden tassels (*Il* 2.448–49). In *Iliad* 5 Athena clearly dons it as a piece of clothing (*Il* 5.738–42), and in *Iliad* 21 she is again wearing it, a defense that not even the thunderbolt can pierce, when Ares attacks her (*Il* 21.400–401). Its primary use, however, seems to be as something held in the hands and shaken, usually to produce fear. Athena does employ it to hearten the shipward-bound Achaians at *Iliad* 2.450–52, but Apollo (on Zeus' invitation) panics those same Achaians with it in a memorable passage (*Il* 15.229–30, 318–22), and later Zeus himself does likewise (bringing up dark clouds, and shaking the aigis to the accompaniment of lightning and thunder: *Il* 17.593–96); in Book 4, we are told that he will hold it over Troy on the day of the city's destruction (*Il* 4.166–68). On the

---

other hand, Athena on one occasion casts it over Achilleus (*Il* 18.203–4: to protect him?), and Apollo uses it to guard Hektor's corpse when Achilleus drags the latter before Patroklos' funeral pyre (*Il* 24.20). From the description in *Iliad* 5 we learn too that it was decorated with a Gorgon head; Medousa is not specifically mentioned (*Il* 5.741–42). The *Odyssey* has far less to offer; in fact, there is only one reference, when Athena holds up the aigis before the suitors in Book 22, and they recognize her sign (*Od* 22.297–98). The Hesiodic *Aspis* adds to all this Athena's shaking of the aigis to inspire Herakles just before his combat with Kyknos (343–44). In sixth- and fifth-century Greek art Athena is almost always shown wearing the aigis, which seems to be a combination breastplate and cloak (e.g., London B380, by the C Painter); often it has snake heads for tassels (cf. Pind fr 70b.17–18 SM), and sometimes the Gorgon. Unfortunately, there is no further evidence of its function after Homer. Euripides, in his *Ion*, offers the strange idea that the aigis was the skin of the Gorgon, who was slain by Athena (*Ion* 986–96); we have seen already that later authors make it the skin of the goat that nourished Zeus as a child (e.g., *Katast* 13).[35] One other common feature of Athena in Homer is her attribute *glaukôpis*, variously translated "gray-eyed," "flashing-eyed," or "owl-eyed." Its real meaning may have been unknown even to Homer.[36]

Of Athena's patronage of crafts or domestic arts we hear less than we might have expected in the two epics. But she certainly weaves clothing on occasion, for in *Iliad* 5 she takes off a peplos that she made for herself (*Il* 5.734–35), and in *Iliad* 14 Hera also has a robe that Athena made (*Il* 14.178–79). In *Iliad* 9, Achilleus speaks more generally of rejecting a daughter of Agamemnon "even if she matched Athena in handicrafts" (*Il* 9.390), while earlier she seems to have inspired Phereklos, a Trojan who knew how to build all manner of things, including ships for Paris (*Il* 5.59–61; cf. *Il* 15.410–12 of Athena and shipbuilders in general). In the *Odyssey*, she is also linked with Hephaistos as an instructor of men in the working of precious metals (*Od* 6.233–34). But only with the *Homeric Hymn to Aphrodite* is she formally assigned such interests (*HAph* 7–15): teaching men the manufacture of chariots, and women those things that they should know how to do in their homes (presumably weaving, though this is not specified).

References to Athena in later literature are rarer, and generally confined to the story of her birth. We have seen that her assistance to Herakles was already known to the poet of the *Iliad*; in Attic art her presence is commonplace in scenes of his exploits. She is likewise a standard feature of Perseus' decapitation of Medousa, beginning with the Protoattic Eleusis amphora of the mid-seventh century (given the limit on actors, one wonders whether she appeared in Aischylos' trilogy on this subject), and according to Pindar gave Bellerophontes the bridle with which he tamed Pegasos (*Ol* 13.63–72). The Panaitios Painter of the fifth century shows her aiding Theseus on his visit to Amphitrite in the depths of the sea (Louvre G104), and the Syleus Painter has her advising the same hero while Dionysos leads away Ariadne (Berlin:PM

F2179). But her aid to Iason in building the Argo and fitting it with a speaking timber from Dodona is first preserved in Apollonios (AR 1.524–27), although we shall see in chapter 12 that the timber itself is early. From Pindar's account of the Argo's voyage in *Pythian* 4 she is conspicuously absent. By contrast, in art she appears at Iason's side as he attempts to win the Fleece on both a cup by Douris in the Vatican and a krater by the Orchard Painter in New York (Vat 16545; NY 34.11.7). Her assistance to the Kalydonian hero Tydeus (Argive by adoption) is documented in the *Iliad* by her conversations with his son Diomedes (*Il* 5.800–805), while the tale that she meant to make him immortal until she found him gnawing on the brains of Melanippides before the walls of Thebes survives in Bakchylides (fr 41 SM) and apparently Pherekydes (3F97); so too clearly on a mid-fifth-century Etruscan terracotta relief plaque from Temple A at Pyrgi (VG, no #). In any case, Pindar (who often likes to deify heroes) is our earliest source for the notion that she did immortalize the son Diomedes (*Nem* 10.7).

Athena is, of course, one of the three virgin goddesses of Olympos; no attempts on her honor are even contemplated, save for that by Hephaistos already noted (after which she rather oddly assumes responsibility for the child borne not by her but by Gaia). One may wonder, too, why such a goddess would present herself as an aspirant for the title offered by Eris, however alluring her physical charms. In general, Athena's relationship with mortals seems more benevolent than that of any other deity except perhaps Hermes, and characterized by only occasional moments of anger. The tale that she blinded Teiresias because he saw her bathing appears first in Pherekydes (3F92), then Kallimachos' *Hymn to Athena*, while Arachne's challenge to her weaving and consequent metamorphosis into a spider must wait for Vergil (*G* 4.246–47) and Ovid (*Met* 6.5–145). The less well-known story of her (quite pardonable) wrath against the Arkadian Ornytos is first referred to by the Hellenistic writer Polemon (apud Cl:*Pro* 2.31) and told by Pausanias; in the latter's account, Ornytos (also called Teuthis) has come to Aulis with a contingent of troops, but proposes to return home when the adverse winds arise (Paus 8.28.4). Athena in the guise of one Melas tries to dissuade him, but is wounded in the thigh for her trouble; subsequently, both Ornytos and his homeland fall into a wasting sickness and must placate Athena with a statue, wounded thigh and all. This sounds like a legend based on local cult, but we cannot say for certain that it did not appear in the *Kypria*. We must also not forget that as early as Pindar the goddess makes a contribution to music in the form of the flute, after hearing the death dirge of Medousa's sisters (*Py* 12.6–8). That she threw the instrument away, to be recovered by Marsyas, is guaranteed for the early fifth century by Melanippides of Melos' dithyramb (758 *PMG*) and by Myron's bronze statue group on the Athenian Akropolis (*HN* 34.57; Paus 1.24.1). The reason for this forfeiture of a possible musical career, namely annoyance over the unseemly puffing-out of her cheeks while she played, is also given by Melanippides, and by many later writers, including Palaiphatos (47), Propertius

(2.30.16–18), and Ovid (*Fasti* 6.697). In art we find it on an Apulian vase of about 370 B.C. on which the goddess watches herself in a mirror while playing (Boston 00.348).

APOLLO   By Leto, as we have seen, Zeus is the father of Apollo and Artemis; their remarkable birth on Delos (or on Delos and Ortygia) is described in detail in the opening of the *Homeric Hymn to Apollo*. As soon as he is born, Apollo receives nectar and ambrosia, and immediately springs up to stride forth into the world, declaring that the lyre and bow will be his special care, and that he will prophesy to men the will of Zeus. Thus we see at an early point his three major interests, although the first item conflicts with the story in the *Homeric Hymn to Hermes* that he receives the lyre from that god as compensation for his stolen cattle (unless he is here already speaking "prophetically"). That Apollo was a god connected with herding as well is suggested perhaps by several other stories about him (i.e., his tendance of the herds of Admetos and Laomedon); his own Hymn says nothing on that count.

Whatever his other early interests, no source prior to the fifth century ever calls him the sun (the latter is always Helios or Hyperion). Parmenides and Empedokles may have done so, if a late source can be trusted, but seemingly in the context of philosophic structures that found physical equivalents for many of the gods (28A20 DK = 31A23 DK). Eventually, and for perhaps the same reasons, the idea also surfaces in Orphic texts. But the first sure literary identification of Apollo with the sun occurs no earlier than Euripides, in a fragment of his lost *Phaethon* (fr 781.10–12 N²), and we cannot tell from the text whether the innovation is his or something previously in circulation. Earlier in the century there are admittedly some suspect moments in Aischylos on this point: we have seen that the playwright probably does link the moon with Artemis (fr 170 R), and his *Hiketides* (212–14) has been thought by some to call the rays of the sun Apollo. In addition, the same poet's lost *Bassarides* may have contained a reference to the dismemberment of Orpheus by those women, who we are told were sent by Dionysos because Orpheus ignored him and worshipped only Helios, whom he called Apollo (p. 138 R). I must confess that I am skeptical of most of this evidence: the tale of Orpheus comes from Ps-Eratosthenes, who cites Aischylos for one brief point near the end of the story, suggesting that the rest of the account (including Helios/Apollo) derives from other sources (*Katast* 24).[37] As for the *Hiketides*, the link between Apollo and the sun there is achieved largely by emendation of an (admittedly corrupt) text that originally implied just the opposite.[38] And while different plays are entitled to different views, we should note that in the *Choephoroi* Helios is addressed by Orestes in a way that emphasizes his separation from Apollo (*Cho* 984–86). Still, there is the reference to Artemis as the moon, if we have read the fragment correctly. Whenever the connection between god and sun was made, it was surely fostered by Apollo's title of Phoibos, used so often by Homer and the *Hymn to Apollo* (with or without Apollo added), and meaning (or thought to mean) "shining." But on balance we should probably conclude that the myths of the Archaic period (virtually) always made Helios and Apollo two separate figures; they are never confused in early art.

Apollo's birth occupies the so-called Delian section of his Hymn; his subsequent exploits on the mainland (whether or not by the same author) make up the Pythian section.[39] Desiring to find a suitable place for his oracle, he passes from Euboia (the Lelantine Plain is rejected) through Boiotia and finally to Telphousa. Here, though the god is pleased, the place persuades him to continue on to Krisa and Parnassos, since Telphousa does not wish to share her site with anyone else. At Krisa Apollo does in fact found his oracle, after slaying the monstrous female snake *(drakaina)* who had previously raised Typhoeus, the child of Hera. He then sets out to find priests for the sanctuary, and for these he chooses a group of Cretan sailors on their way to Pylos. To bring them to Delphi he takes the form of a dolphin who leaps onto the ship's deck and shakes the vessel ominously, while sudden breezes send it in the desired direction. Once the ship has been brought to shore, the new priests are taken by a disguised Apollo to their appointed service, and with this the *Hymn to Apollo* ends. Given the laudatory nature of this type of literature, it is perhaps not surprising that no mention is made of any anger on the part of Gaia for the killing of the snake, or any purification undergone by Apollo at Tempe; this last is hinted at by the third-century b.c. poet Aristonoos (where the god is "cleansed at Tempe" by the will of Zeus, though he has "persuaded" Gaia and Themis to surrender Delphi: 1.17–24 Pow), but first made explicit only in Plutarch (*Mor* 293c, 421c). Pindar also seems to have related that Apollo got control of Delphi by force (for which Gaia wanted him cast down into Tartaros: fr 55 SM), but in Aischylos' *Eumenides* we find a quite different version, that Gaia voluntarily gave the site to her daughter Themis, Themis gave it to her sister Phoibe, and Phoibe gave it in turn to her grandson Phoibos Apollo (*Eum* 1–8). Since the peaceful transfer of power from female to male forms a very appropriate prologue to the content of this particular play, we should probably suspect Aischylean invention here, though certainly to good effect.

Later sources, in fact, do return to the notion of some kind of conflict: in Euripides' *Iphigeneia among the Tauroi* the infant Apollo is taken to Delphi by his mother (*IT* 1239–58). When (still held in his mother's arms) he sees the snake he immediately kills it, and takes over control of the oracle. There is here to be sure a protest by the displaced parties: Gaia had intended to give the site to Themis, and in anger at Apollo sends prophetic dreams to men. But Apollo complains to Zeus about this competition, and Zeus halts the dreams (*IT* 1259–83). Hyginus offers something similar to the first part of this: in his version Apollo on the third day after his birth goes to Delphi and kills Python (the snake's usual name in later sources) to avenge the serpent's pursuit of his mother (*Fab* 140). Several vases would seem to reflect some version of this youthful exploit: a White-Ground lekythos of *c.* 460 b.c. presents Leto holding Apollo on her shoulder as he aims his bow at Python (CabMéd 306), while a lost Apulian (?) amphora of the fourth century has Leto with a small child (no weapons) in each arm shrinking back before the menacing snake.[40] The Cyzicene Epigrams take a slightly different approach, for in their account, although Apollo again shoots the monster he does so to defend his mother, and appears to be full-grown (*AP* 3.6); the accompanying introduction claims that she had gone to Delphi to take possession of the oracle.

The other *Homeric Hymn* in which Apollo plays a major role is that to his brother Hermes. Here he is the possessor of cattle (for what purpose is not clear) which he must track down after they have been abducted by the newborn god of thieves. The story is an odd one, and requires among other things that he overlook his prophetic powers in seeking the cattle as any normal human would. For a while Hermes' youth seems likely to fool him, but he stands his ground and finally takes the culprit before Zeus, where the cattle are returned and a reconciliation effected through Hermes' proffering of his newly invented lyre. All of this characterizes Hermes more than Apollo, but it does show the older god in a light somewhat similar to that revealed by his affairs with women (although in the present case he is ultimately successful).

In the *Iliad* Apollo is of course the defender of the Trojans and, until Hektor's fate is sealed, a powerful ally. Like Poseidon and Athena he operates primarily by encouraging his side (and on one occasion luring Achilleus away from battle in the form of Agenor), but in *Iliad* 16, after Patroklos has ignored his warnings to withdraw from the walls of Troy, he intervenes directly to strip the Myrmidon of his armor and leave him helpless before Euphorbos and Hektor (*Il* 16.787–96). From Proklos' summary of the *Aithiopis* we learn that Paris and Apollo together slew Achilleus (as predicted at *Il* 22.358–60); Pindar's *Paian* 6 is too mangled in the surviving papyri to permit certainty, but here Apollo appears to do the deed in the guise of Paris (fr 52f SM). Such action might seem to overstep the normal bounds permitted to the gods in the Trojan War, but we should remember that in both cases *moira*, in which Apollo as Zeus' spokesman has a special interest, was about to be transgressed (Achilleus had broken through the Skaian gate and was about to take the city); so, too, the god inspires the Trojans at *Iliad* 21.515–17, lest the Achaians capture Troy "before its appointed time." In fact, the god seems much more resigned to the dictates of *moira* (or Zeus) in the *Iliad* than are, say, Athena or Hera. Perhaps for this reason he abandons Hektor without making any attempt to help him when the scales of the latter's fate sink down (though in fairness he also initiates the recovery of the body from Achilleus).

Unlike Athena, Apollo rarely if ever aids mortal endeavors outside the framework of the *Iliad*; perhaps storytellers felt such support to be incompatible with his role as prophet at Delphi. Those exploits that we do find fall into two main categories: affairs with mortal women (there is scarcely any record of liaisons with other divinities) and defense of challenges to his musical abilities. Regarding the former, the only tale told in Homer is that of Marpessa, daughter of Euenos, whom Apollo appears to have kidnapped away from her intended husband Idas; the latter gives pursuit with his bow, and Marpessa is returned to bear Kleopatra (the future wife of Meleagros), though Homer does not say how this return was effected (*Il* 9.555–64). For the detail that Zeus intervened in the dispute and gave Marpessa her choice (an unparalleled action) we must await Simonides (563 *PMG*), who adds that Marpessa very sensibly chose Idas because she knew that Apollo would abandon her when she was old (he seems not to have thought to offer her youth or divinity). On the Chest of Kypselos, Idas was represented as leading a "not unwilling" Marpessa back after her abduction by Apollo, according to the inscription (Paus 5.18.2). In surviving art, we encounter the story first on a Red-Figure psykter of perhaps 480 B.C. by the Pan Painter: the two rivals raise their bows against each other, while Marpessa (next to Idas) urges him on and Euenos (?) tries to intervene; from the other side of the pot Zeus approaches with Hermes, presumably to resolve the matter (Munich 2417).[41] Idas' original wooing of Marpessa and the consequent death of her father Euenos we will return to in chapter 5.

From Homer we return to the (Pythian) *Hymn to Apollo*, where we find tantalizing references to the courting of at least two women, but unfortunately also a lacuna at a critical point (*HAp* 208–13). Still, the daughter of Azan for whom Ischys, son of Elation (or Elatos), is his rival is apparently Koronis (see below), while mention of Leukippos (against whom the god races, on foot against horses) and his wife might conceivably lead us to Daphne. The link in this latter case is a story attributed to Phylarchos (third century B.C.) in which Leukippos, son of Oinomaos, falls in love with the huntress Daphne, daughter of Amyklas, and disguises himself as a woman in order to be near her; unfortunately a jealous Apollo puts the idea into her head to bathe, and when Leukippos refuses she and her friends discover the truth and kill him (81F32, apud Parthenios; cf. Paus 8.20.2–4). There is here, however, no formal competition between Leukippos and Apollo, and Daphne certainly does not become anyone's wife, so that the Hymn may have had another story in mind. Phylarchos went on to relate Apollo's pursuit of Daphne and her prayer to Zeus for escape, resulting in her metamorphosis into the laurel.

The Palaiphatean corpus has a slightly different account: Daphne's parents are Gaia and the river Ladon (presumably in Arkadia: Pal 49). When Apollo sees her he gives chase, and the girl calling upon her mother to take her back is received by the earth; the laurel tree grows up on that very spot and Apollo refuses to part with it. The Lykophron scholia repeat this version in somewhat clearer terms, with Gaia sending forth the plant of the same name as the swallowed-up girl as a consolation to the god (Σ Lyk 6). Ovid, in a justly famous narrative that has become the standard, employs the transformation motif as opposed to that of the substitution, and makes Daphne's father (here the river Peneios) responsible for her rescue (*Met* 1.452–567). He is also our first source for the prologue to the tale in which Apollo taunts Eros, leading the latter to unleash his arrows and provoke the unrequited passion for Daphne. Red-Figure painting of the fifth century offers several scenes with Apollo pursuing an unidentified girl who may be Daphne (e.g., London E64, *c.* 500 B.C.), but there is no certainty, and no illustration of the metamorphosis until Roman times.

Next, we may consider Apollo's (again not entirely successful) passion for Koronis. We have seen above that the *Hymn to Apollo* made reference to a clash between Apollo and Ischys, while somewhere in the Hesiodic Corpus a raven comes to inform Apollo that Koronis (daughter of Phlegyas here) has married Ischys Eilatides (Hes fr 60 MW). Unfortunately, the quote ends at just this point, without telling what (if any) child she bore to the god. If Koronis did appear in the *Ehoiai*, as a second "Hesiod" quote seems to suggest (fr 59 MW, with its *ê hoiê* formula and maiden washing her feet in the Boibias lake [cf. *Py* 3.34]), then this child will pose a problem, since the *Ehoiai* elsewhere makes Asklepios (the usual offspring of Apollo and Koronis) the son rather of Apollo and Arsinoe, daughter of Leukippos (Hes fr 50 MW: cf. Ap*B* 3.10.3). But probably the safest solution given the evidence is to assume that the *Ehoiai* either ignored her or told some other story about her.[42] Asklepios himself is as old as the *Iliad*, where he learns healing from Cheiron (or at least obtains medicines from him: *Il* 4.193–94, 218–19); alas no parents are mentioned. His status as son of Apollo (and Koronis) is attested by *Homeric Hymn* 16, but the circumstances surrounding the birth are not divulged to us until the fifth century, in Pindar's *Pythian* 3. In this ode, after Apollo learns (from the raven *and* his own divining) of Koronis' infidelity with Ischys, he sends Artemis to slay her (curiously, many of her neighbors also perish; perhaps they connived at the wedding) but snatches the unborn child from her womb as the flames cover her funeral pyre (*Py* 3.8–46). Asklepios is given to Cheiron to raise, and here too learns from the latter (not Apollo) the art of healing. Akousilaos (2F17) and Pherekydes (3F3) also told the story, but in how much detail we cannot say; Akousilaos does suggest that Koronis chose Ischys willingly, fearing the god's (eventual?) scorn, and Pherekydes adds that Apollo killed his rival himself, while Artemis (as in Pindar) slew many women. The story that Apollo in anger at the raven's message turned the bird from its original white to black comes to us from the scholia to Pindar, who ascribe it to the Hellenistic Artemon (Σ *Py* 3.52b = 569F5). A Red-Figure skyphos from the mid-fifth-century does in fact show Apollo with a white bird overhead (Mormino Coll, no #).

The son Asklepios has his own peculiar fate: having angered Zeus by attempting to heal death itself and raise someone from Hades, he is struck down by the thunderbolt. On this form of his fate the *Ehoiai* (Hes fr 51 MW), Stesichoros (194 *PMG*), Akousilaos (2F18), Pherekydes (3F35), and Pindar (*Py* 3.55–58) all agree; that the crime was an attempt to raise the dead is mentioned only by Stesichoros, Pherekydes, and Pindar. The identity of the intended beneficiary of his skills varies greatly from author to author. Stesichoros (the work is his lost *Eriphyle*) says Kapaneus and Lykourgos, two of the Seven against Thebes; Pherekydes makes the revived "those dying at Delphi" but offers no names, while Pindar notes simply that money was the motive. In later writers other names are given, including Hippolytos, the son of Theseus, in the accounts of Ps-Eratosthenes (*Katast* 6) and Hyginus (*Fab* 49); Apollo-doros also mentions this possibility and attributes it to the seventh- or sixth-century epic *Naupaktia* supposedly written by one Karkinos of Naupaktos (Ap*B* 3.10.3–4). It should be noted that some of these versions imply a successful raising of the dead before the thunderbolt struck.

What happened after Asklepios' death is likewise told as early as the *Ehoiai*: Apollo slays the providers of the thunderbolt, the Kyklopes (despite their presumed immortality), in anger over the loss of his son (Hes fr 54 MW, with supplements). This deed in turn prompts Zeus to threaten to hurl Apollo down to Tartaros (compare the threat to Ares in *Iliad* 5), but someone (Leto?) intervenes, and the punishment is commuted to serving a mortal for a year; so too Akousilaos (2F19), while Leto definitely appears in this role in Apollodoros (Ap*B* 3.10.4). *Iliad* 2.766, where Apollo is said to have reared the mares of Eumelos (son of Admetos) in Pereia, may allude to the same series of events. Pherekydes adds two points: in his version the victims are the *sons* of the Kyklopes (perhaps he felt the incongruity involved in killing senior divinities), and the mortal served is Admetos (3F35; 3F131). For the further development that Apollo rescues Admetos from death at the cost of his wife we have nothing before Euripides' play *Alkestis*, though Phrynichos earlier in the century is known to have written a play of the same title. We should also observe here that in some late versions Apollo's servitude is linked rather to his slaying of Python.

About yet another unfortunate infatuation of the god, that with Kassandra, there is much less to say. Kassandra is never made by Homer to possess prophetic powers, although she seems to have done so in the *Kypria*, where she prophesies to Paris (p. 39 *PEG*), and Pindar calls her *mantis*, "seer," at *Pythian* 11.33. The same poet's *Paian* 8 (where her predictions are probably vain) and Bakchylides' Ode 23 (see *apparatus*) present a similar view. But predictions that no one believes (if they had, matters would obviously have taken much less interesting turns) do not necessarily require Apollo; Kassandra's relationship with the god as we know it first appears in Aischylos' *Agamemnon*, where we read that she promised herself to him, received the gift of inspiration, and then reneged on the promise (*Ag* 1202–12). The notion of a woman who can refuse a god, even at cost, is a strange one, and it is hard to say how this situation relates to the rest of the play. Kassandra implies as well that because Apollo was angry her prophecies have persuaded no one, although she does not state that condition as a formal or irreversible punishment. The fact that in the *Kypria* she tells Paris what will happen if he sails to Sparta and does not convince him would carry more weight were it not that Helenos apparently also prophesies to him, with no better luck. Of course we have only a bald summary; possibly Helenos foretold the success of the immediate venture to Spartan, and only Kassandra predicted the ultimate disaster. But we should not overlook the possibility that Apollo's involvement with her is a late Archaic development. Euripides in his *Troades* has Hekabe tell us that Apollo granted to Kassandra to be forever virgin (*Tro* 253–54), but this is perhaps to underline the impieties of Aias and Agamemnon in ignoring that concession. Several other points in the play stress that Kassandra is inspired, and that Apollo is the source (*Tro* 366, 408, 500). The similar story of Apollo's failure with the Cumaean Sibyl, to whom he gave one thousand years of life (but no youth to match it, after she had refused him), surfaces no earlier than Ovid (*Met* 14.129–53); it may or may not be based on that of Kassandra.[43]

On a happier note, we may turn to Apollo's mating with Kyrene, which again is first found in the *Ehoiai*. To be perfectly strict, the preserved two lines attest only that Kyrene dwelt by the waters of the Peneios river (Hes fr 215 MW), but of course the point of the poem is to celebrate unions of gods and mortal women, and Servius tells us that Aristaios (the traditional offspring) was called Apollo *pastoralis*, that is, Apollo *nomios*, in the Hesiodic Corpus (Σ *G* 1.14), so there seems little doubt that the *Ehoiai* told the story. Full details, with perhaps some personal elaboration, come to us from Pindar's *Pythian 9*, in which this myth forms the heart of the poem (*Py* 9.5–70). Here Apollo sees the maiden in the vales of Pelion and falls in love with her as he observes her wrestling a lion. Her father is Hypseus, king of the Lapithai, who in his turn is a son of Peneios, and her own nature is very much that of the huntress. Spurred on by the approval of Cheiron, Apollo persuades the maiden of his desires, and they proceed from Thessaly to Libya, where the union is accomplished and the child Aristaios born. This child is then taken by Hermes (whose name appears in connection with that of Aristaios in a fragmentary scrap of the *Ehoiai*: Hes fr 217 MW), and brought to the Horai and Gaia, who give him nectar and ambrosia and make him, if not quite a god, at least a cult hero, with the names "Agreus" and "Nomios." Kyrene wrestling with the lion appears on a Lakonian cup of about 510 B.C. (Taranto 4991).[44] The locating of the union with Apollo in Libya might seem to postdate the establishment there by people from Thera of a colony named Kyrene in the late seventh century, but the general story could well be much older, and in its Hesiodic form have excluded Libya (and the lion) altogether.[45] A more difficult question involves the relationship of this Aristaios to the one who marries Kadmos' daughter Autonoe and becomes the father of Aktaion (*Th* 977). Pindar does not relate any further events in the history of Kyrene's son, and perhaps it is, on the whole, best to regard them as separate figures. Aristaios as bee-keeper and giver of honey does make a memorable appearance in Vergil's *Fourth Georgic;* probably this aspect of his character was part of his early status as a bringer of good things to men.

Other liaisons of a less important nature, and generally attested by only one source, include that with the Okeanid Melia, who bears Teneros (*Pa* 9.34–49; 7.1–12: a rare union with a goddess), Euadne, daughter of Poseidon, who bears Iamos (*Ol* 6.35), Thero, daughter of Phylas, who bears Chairon (Hes fr 252 MW), Psamathe, daughter of Krotopos, who bears Linos (killed by dogs: Konon 26F1.19), and Philonis, daughter of Deion, who (after lying with Apollo and Hermes in the same day) bears to Apollo Philammon, the first man to train choruses of maidens (Pher 3F120).[46] To Ion, offspring of the Erechtheid Kreousa, we shall return in chapter 7; the *Ehoiai* appears to make him the son of Kreousa by her husband Xouthos (Hes fr 10a.20–24 MW). Apollo does not in fact beget a great many children, and only one daughter (in Hyginus, *Astr* 2.25.2, where he and a Chrysothemis have a child, Parthenos, who dies young and becomes the constellation Virgo).

We cannot, however, close this catalogue of the god's affairs without mentioning two young boys, Hyakinthos and Kyparissos. Both return Apollo's love, and yet both die tragically, the first of an accidental blow from a discus thrown by Apollo, the second of grief over the death of his pet stag. Their stories are best known to us from Ovid (*Met* 10.162–219; 10.106–42) who, in the case of Kyparissos, is the only preserved source. For Hyakinthos we have fragments of the *Ehoiai* which mention a discus and a son of Diomede (Hes fr 171 MW: in Ap*B* 3.10.3, Hyakinthos is the son of Amyklas and Diomede), and thus that poem probably told the whole story of the accidental slaying. Euripides also alludes to Hyakinthos and the discus (*Hel* 1469–74), but it is first in Palaiphatos that we find Zephyros as a jealous rival causing the discus to swerve (46). That same version appears in Loukianos (*DD* 16), but not in Ovid. Completely absent from all these accounts (or what we have of them) is the idea that Hyakinthos (and his sister Polyboia) went up to Olympos, escorted by various gods, but Pausanias found this scene on the altar-shaped base of the statue standing on the Amyklai Throne, an apotheosis perhaps encouraged by the cult of Hyakinthos at that site (3.19.4). The same scene may appear on a sixth-century Lakonian cup in New York (NY 50.11.7), although there the much larger size of the female who precedes (and leads) the male probably argues rather for Athena and Herakles.[47]

Seemingly there are no illustrations of Apollo and Hyakinthos together; possibly though the latter appears alone as the boy riding a swan (the bird of Apollo) in early fifth-century Red-Figure (e.g., Athens no # [*ARV*² 17]). Likewise he has been seen as the young man carried off or otherwise pursued by a beardless winged figure (i.e., Zephyros, as on Boston 95.31).[48] The latter view in particular must remain tentative, given the predominance of winged Erotes in this time period (though admittedly Eros is not otherwise known to pursue males). One other youth, Hymenaios, is mentioned only by Antoninus Liberalis, who credits the *Megalai Ehoiai* and Nikandros, among others: Apollo's passion for him permits Hermes to steal the god's cattle, but we never learn the outcome of the romance (AntLib 23). On the whole, Apollo's amatory adventures are more impressive for their frustration than anything else; perhaps if we had the entire *Ehoiai*, the picture would be altered.

The god's anger against those who challenge him is likewise not well documented in early literature. We have seen in discussing Leto that he joins with Artemis in rescuing his mother from Tityos as early as the *Nekuia*, and the similar deed of destroying the children of Niobe to defend his mother's honor is recounted in *Iliad* 24.602–9 (Telesilla [721 *PMG*] and Hyginus [*Fab* 9] have him slay the father Amphion as well). There is also in the *Odyssey* his slaying of Otos and Ephialtes when they attempt to challenge the reign of the gods by climbing up to Olympos (*Od* 11.318–20). The tale of Marsyas is more difficult: Myron's statue of Athena with a Silenos on the Akropolis gives us a beginning point for the latter's discovery of the flute discarded by the goddess, but there are no Archaic literary references to guarantee Apollo's subsequent involvement.[49] Our first evidence for his role arrives in fact only with Attic Red-Figure of the latter part of the fifth century, when Apollo and Marsyas appear together (note NY 12.235.4, where Marsyas [named] holds a flaying knife). One assumes that Melanippides told some form of the story in his lost *Marsyas,* but the earliest actual record of the contest and subsequent flaying appears to be that of Herodotos (7.26), and for full details we must turn to Xenophon (*Anab* 1.2.8) and Diodoros Siculus (3.59). The story of Midas, to whom Apollo gave asses' ears because he preferred the music of Pan to Apollo's own, comes from Ovid (*Met* 11.146–93) and Hyginus (*Fab* 191); Midas' possession of such ears, however, shows up in late fifth-century Red-Figure scenes of himself with Silenos (e.g., London E447), and is mentioned by Aristophanes in his *Ploutos* (286–87).

On one other occasion Apollo needed the help of his father to withstand a mortal's assault, namely in the matter of Herakles' seizing of the Delphic tripod. Literary evidence is late (see below) but already on a bronze tripod leg from Olympia, *c.* 700 B.C., we find two figures on either side of and clutching a tripod, thus possibly an early representation of the story (B 1730).[50] Quite certain, subsequently, is the Foce del Sele metope (no #) on which a clearly recognizable Herakles has picked up the tripod and is carrying it away on his shoulder, while Apollo tries to hold him back; the scene was also quite popular in Attic vase-painting, where Athena and Artemis often add their respective support. Late sixth-century Black-Figure (and the east pediment of the Siphnian Treasury at Delphi) indicate that Zeus himself (or Hermes) intervened to resolve matters (evidence in chapter 13). The fullest literary account is in Apollodoros, where Herakles seizes the tripod after the Pythia refuses to tell him how he might be purified for the murder of Iphitos; Apollo protests, and Zeus separates them with a thunderbolt (*ApB* 3.16.42). Briefer references can be found in Cicero (*ND* 3.16.42) and Hyginus (*Fab* 32). One possible early allusion is that of Pindar in the difficult passage of *Olympian* 9 concerning Herakles' battles with the gods (*Ol* 9.29); the scholiast on the passage would have us see here a reference to this event, but it seems at best doubtful. Despite the evidence for Zeus' aid, Attic Red-Figure often presents just Herakles and a magisterial-looking Apollo, as if the god was believed to have settled the matter on his own.

It remains to note Apollo's connection with healing. We have seen that Pindar, though scarcely one to deprive the gods of their accomplishments, credits Asklepios' knowledge of medicine not to his father but to Cheiron, and we find in the *Iliad* that both Achilleus and Asklepios have learned their skills from that Kentauros (*Il* 11.831–32, 4.218–19). It is true that in *Iliad* 16 Apollo does cure Glaukos' wound, or rather checks the pain (*Il* 16.527–29). But this is no more than Leto and Artemis have done for Aineias earlier in the same poem (*Il* 5.447–48), nor does Glaukos specifically call upon Apollo as a healer. On the contrary, there is a god of healing, Paieon, who appears twice in the *Iliad* and is clearly distinct from Apollo (*Il* 5.401, 899); the same is probably true of a reference in the *Odyssey* (4.432). A scholiast on this latter passage cites two lines from "Hesiod" (fr 307 MW) which also pointedly distinguish the two gods, although their mention together may after all associate Apollo with the same skills attributed to Paieon. A line in the *Homeric Hymn to Apollo,* when the Cretan priests sing in praise of their new god, is likewise difficult, since the term "Paian" may here be a term of address or only the name of the song (*HAp* 517; cf. *Il* 1.473). But Sappho (44 LP) suggests and Sophokles (*OT* 145) confirms that the two figures have fused, and that Apollo is now the healer among the gods. In one sense, of course, Apollo is always a healing god, for as one who sends plagues he is also the one who can halt them. But whether his role as healer of those already sick is the result of his connection with Asklepios, or the cause of it, or neither, remains open.

Epithets that are applied to Apollo in Homer include *hekatêbolos* and *hekêbolos,* whose meaning somehow involves archery and may mean "shooting from afar" or "shooting at will," *hekatos* (perhaps a short form of the preceding), and *smintheus,* whose sense is quite unclear (from *sminthos,* "mouse?" Or Sminthe the city? See ΣA *Il* 1.39). "Lykeios," whether connected with wolves, light, Lycia, or something else, appears first in Aischylos' *Seven against Thebes* (145); as a cult title it is perhaps much older.[51] The first attested use of the name "Loxias" ("slanting?") is at Bakchylides 13.148, a poem dated to about 485 B.C.; subsequently it surfaces in Aischylos' *Seven* (618) and quite frequently in the *Oresteia* (so too *PD* 669).

One final (perhaps darker) aspect of Apollo's activity emerges from his involvement in two no-longer-preserved Aischylean productions. In the first of these, the trilogy for which the above-mentioned *Seven against Thebes* is the final play (preceded by the lost *Laios* and *Oidipous*), Apollo apparently prophesied to Laios that he could save Thebes by not having children; Laios of course did so, but this was scarcely an act likely to arouse the god's anger. Yet Eteokles in the *Seven* speaks on several occasions of Apollo's hostility and even hatred of Laios' race (*Hepta* 689–91, 743–49, 800–802); presumably there were reasons (the rape of Chrysippos?)[52] that have disappeared with the first two plays. The other occasion arises from a quote (no play is named) given to us by Plato in which Thetis accuses the god of having predicted long life and happiness for her child, then played a role in Achilleus' early death (fr 350 R, apud *Rep* 2.383b). We can only assume that, bad as the evidence looks, Aischylos somehow vindicated Apollo, perhaps in the context of Achilleus' transfer to the Isles of the Blessed.[53]

ARTEMIS   The birth of Apollo's sister Artemis has also been noted in connection with the story of their mother Leto in chapter 1. Hesiod says that they are
both children of Zeus and Leto, but offers nothing about the place of birth (*Th*
918–20). In the *Homeric Hymn to Apollo*, the two children are delivered separately, Artemis on Ortygia, Apollo on Delos; the sequence is left unclear, although Artemis is mentioned first (*HAp* 14–18: in Apollodoros she is clearly
born first, and aids in the delivery of Apollo [*ApB* 1.4.1]). Pindar's *Paian* 12 is
the earliest preserved work to actually locate the birth of both children on
Delos, or to call them twins (fr 52m.14–17 SM). In Homer, however, as in
Hesiod, they are clearly brother and sister, and offspring of Zeus and Leto.
Homer's favorite epithet for Artemis is *iocheiaira*, "she who showers down
arrows," and a passage in *Odyssey* 6 describes her hunting exploits in the hills
and vales as a standard activity (*Od* 6.102–8). The *Homeric Hymn to Aphrodite* (16–20) likewise says that the bow and the slaying of animals are dear to
her, and as well the lyre and dancing, piercing cries and shadowy groves, and
the cities of just men (cf. *HomH* 27).

But for all her love of hunting in the wilds, her arrows in the *Iliad* and
Odyssey are more often directed at humans. Her slaying of mortals appears to
fall into two distinct categories. On the one hand, she is responsible for the
sudden, unexplained death of women; thus Odysseus in the Underworld asks
his mother Antikleia if Artemis struck her down (*Od* 11.171–73), Eumaios
relates the same fate of the Phoenician woman who kidnapped him (*Od*
15.478), and Andromache likewise of her mother (*Il* 6.428). Similarly in the
Iliad Achilleus wishes that Artemis had slain Briseis before she caused so much
trouble (*Il* 19.59–60), and Penelope several times prays that the goddess might
bring death to her, to save her from her plight (*Od* 18.202–4; 20.60–63,
80–81). On the other hand, there are clearly also occasions on which Artemis
acts in anger, and the death (here of both men and women) is in some way
merited. Thus we are told in *Iliad* 6 that Laodameia, daughter of Bellerophontes, suffered this fate, although we do not learn why the goddess was
angry (*Il* 6.205). In *Odyssey* 5 Kalypso complains that the gods are jealous of
mortal men who consort with goddesses; therefore, it seems, Artemis has
killed (with painless arrows, unless this is a misapplied formula) Orion, the
lover of Eos (*Od* 5.121–24). Orion's death is a complicated matter, to be considered more fully in chapter 8: later accounts often have him slain by a scorpion sent by Artemis because he had made advances to her or one of her followers. Strictly speaking, Kalypso does not actually say that Artemis slew
Orion *because* he had lain with Eos, although that is the most obvious assumption. In any case we see that the goddess does not hesitate to bring death to
those who displease her. In *Iliad* 9 we find a more indirect method in the form
of the Kalydonian Boar, sent to ravage the countryside after Oineus has forgotten to offer up first fruits (*Il* 9.533–40); the same account appears in Bakchylides (5.94–110). More mysteriously, in the *Nekuia* we learn that Artemis
has slain Ariadne on Dia on the evidence of Dionysos (*Od* 11.321–25). No

reasons for this strange reversal of the usual marriage to that god are given, but we may notice that on several other occasions the same pattern applies. We have already seen that Artemis kills Koronis at Apollo's request in Pindar, though she has no quarrel with the girl herself. And while the familiar version of Aktaion's death is that he saw Artemis bathing, the account of our early sources (Stes 236 *PMG*, Akou 2F33) suggests that here too the goddess acts as agent for someone else, namely Zeus, who fears Aktaion as a rival for Semele's affections; the story that Artemis herself was offended survives first in Kallimachos, though given the artistic tradition such offense (in some form) is probably much older (see chapter 14). The vengeance taken against the daughters of Niobe for the affront offered her mother Leto and the rescue of Leto from the clutches of Tityos (both in concert with her brother) likewise illustrate the dangers of crossing this divinity, whose relationship with mortals is rarely supportive.[54]

One other area of Artemis' activity displays similar characteristics. She is of course one of the three virgin goddesses of Olympos, and although she does not defend chastity in general she does seem to expect it of those huntress maidens who follow her. Two particular cases emerge from our Archaic sources. In the *Ehoiai*, Kallisto, daughter of Lykaon, is listed as one such follower who is seduced by Zeus; when Artemis discovers her pregnancy she turns her into a bear, and in that form she gives birth to a son, Arkas (Hes fr 163 MW; for other versions see chapter 18). One of Aischylos' lost plays, *Kallisto*, was clearly on this topic, although the dramatic difficulties must have been considerable; one would give much to know how Artemis was presented (unless the emphasis was primarily on Zeus). A second such figure, mentioned by Homer and described by Pherekydes, is Maira, daughter of Proitos (probably not the brother of Akrisios), who follows Artemis in the wilds but is seduced by Zeus and then shot by Artemis (again, see chapter 18). A third figure of this type is mentioned only in passing by Euripides in the *Helen*, though the very casualness of the allusion (we are not even given a name) suggests that the story was well known: the daughter of Merops is turned into a golden-horned hind and banished from Artemis' company because of her beauty (*Hel* 381–83). There is no indication whether the goddess was simply jealous or feared that such a follower would attract the attention of men. Given the golden horns, this story would seem to offer a variant explanation for the existence of the hind of Keryneia, sacred to Artemis, which Herakles must catch as one of his Labors; we will consider other (more plausible) possibilities in chapter 13.

Returning to the Trojan War, we come to what is probably the most famous instance of Artemis' anger, that occasioned by Agamemnon as he prepares to depart for Troy. Homer says nothing whatever about such an event; the *Kypria* however knows of it and ascribes as cause Agamemnon's boast, after shooting a stag, that he surpasses even the goddess. Sophokles in his *Elektra* gives essentially the same account, adding that the deer was in a sacred precinct

(S:*El* 566–72); Euripides in *Iphigeneia among the Tauroi* suggests that Agamemnon had rashly promised to Artemis the fairest thing produced in the year of his daughter's birth (*IT* 17–24). In Aischylos' *Agamemnon* no reason is given at all, save perhaps that the goddess wishes to dissuade Agamemnon from the sacking of Troy. In any case, the sacrifice of Iphigeneia follows—or seems to, since as early as the *Kypria* Artemis rescues her and substitutes a stag, while Iphigeneia is taken off to the land of the Tauroi and made immortal. A fragment of the *Ehoiai* appears to tell the same story—at least insofar as Iphigeneia (here called Iphimede) is rescued and made an immortal attendant of the goddess—but the lines relating the rescue have been seen (convincingly, I think) as an interpolation (Hes fr 23 MW; see chapter 16). With or without additions, the papyrus in question offers no clear cause for anger on Artemis' part, any more than it tells us (in the same fragment) why the goddess makes Klytaimestra's sister Phylonoe immortal. On present evidence Aischylos and Pindar (*Py* 11.22–23) emerge as the first to say that Artemis really did require Iphigeneia's death, but we must allow that the *Ehoiai* may have preceded them. Of Aischylos' lost play *Iphigeneia*, in which Artemis surely played an important part (and in which the girl perhaps survives), we have nothing.

In the *Iliad* itself Artemis' role is rather limited. At no point does she engage in the fighting, even to urge on the Trojans, and one is left with the impression that she supports them merely for the sake of her brother. Her one actual contribution is to heal (with her mother) Aineias after he has been wounded by Diomedes (*Il* 5.447–48). Later, of course, she participates in the so-called battle of the gods in *Iliad* 21, first reproaching Apollo for refusing to fight Poseidon, then being soundly trounced by Hera and running away in tears to her father (*Il* 21.470–513). In the *Odyssey*, like many of the other gods, she plays no role at all; the few references to her as goddess of the hunt or bringer of sudden death have already been discussed. One other mention, in *Iliad* 5, deserves special notice because of its unusual character: Menelaos kills the Trojan Skamandrios, whom Artemis herself has trained to hunt all manner of wild beasts (*Il* 5.51–52). This may be simply epic characterization, yet it seems odd that Artemis should be thought to consort with men as opposed to women; such a relationship may perhaps prefigure the one that Euripides offers between the goddess and Hippolytos.

APHRODITE   On the birth of the next Olympian, Aphrodite, we have observed already that Hesiod and Homer offer widely varying accounts: in Hesiod she is born from the severed testicles and foam of the sea after Kronos has castrated his father Ouranos (*Th* 188–206), while in both *Iliad* and *Odyssey* she is the daughter of Zeus (*Il* 3.374, etc.; *Od* 8.308, 320), and in the *Iliad* her mother is clearly Dione (*Il* 5.370–71). Such a descent is for both poems something more than just repetition of the formulaic expression *Dios thugatêr*; in the *Iliad* Aphrodite goes so far as to call Ares *brother* on one occasion (*Il* 5.359), and in the *Odyssey* Hephaistos threatens to reclaim the bride gifts he paid to her father Zeus after her infidelity with Ares has been revealed (*Od* 8.306–20). Thus her parentage seems well established in the Homeric tradition. On the other hand, her birth from the sea and the seed of Ouranos has a crude, early look, and one can well understand why Hesiod's organization of the world's beginnings was not satisfied to leave such a primal force to a stage as late as that of Zeus' children. Hesiod gives us all three of the goddess' names— Aphrodite, Kyprogene (or Kypris), and Kythereia—and after his account of her birth has little trouble explaining them (though linguists are not quite as convinced): she is born of the foam *(aphros)* that drifts past Kythera to Cyprus (*Th* 195–99).[55] Interestingly enough, the *Iliad* calls her Kypris five times (all in *Iliad* 5, with four of them related to her wounding by Diomedes: *Il* 5.330, 422, 458, 760, 883),[56] but never Kythereia, while the *Odyssey* calls her Kythereia twice (*Od* 8.288; 18.193) but never Kypris (although in *Odyssey* 8 she does go to Cyprus where she has a cult). In the *Homeric Hymns* she is Kythereia five times (*HAph* 6, 175, 287; *HomH* 6.18; 10.1) and Kyprogene once (*HomH* 10.1 again). Her common epithet *philommeidês* may or may not mean "laughter-loving" (the *Theogony* etymologizes it in relation to the testicles [*mêdea*] of Ouranos).[57]

Aphrodite's role in the *Iliad* has been touched on above in connection with those of other gods. In *Iliad* 3 she saves Paris from an ignominious defeat at the hands of Menelaos by breaking his chin-strap and sweeping him up in a cloud back to his own bedroom (*Il* 3.373–82). The subsequent interview with Helen, in which she first disguises herself as an old Lakonian woman who has accompanied her mistress, offers us the unusual (in fact, unparalleled) spectacle of a god ordering a mortal on pain of his/her displeasure to act in a fashion contrary to that mortal's wishes: when Helen declares that she has become disenchanted with Paris, the goddess makes clear that Helen's desires are not a consideration (*Il* 3.383–417). Possibly this extraordinary behavior can be explained by the fact that Helen has already made (by all accounts of her own free will, albeit with Aphrodite's help) a decision from which she cannot now retreat, but possibly, too, Aphrodite enjoys special privileges as the goddess of desire, a force that even the gods cannot control. In any event, we note that Aphrodite definitely stands behind the promise she made many years ago, when she offered Helen to Paris. But although she can create infatuation, it is not as evident that she can create love.

She fares less well in *Iliad* 5: attempting to save her son Aineias from certain death on the battlefield, she intervenes, much as she did with Paris, but this time, for the sake of the story, she is less adroit, and Diomedes succeeds in scratching her hand (*Il* 5.311–80). Aineias is instantly dropped and forgotten (Apollo has to rescue him), and only with the help of Iris and the loan of Ares' chariot does she make her way back to Olympos to throw herself on the knees of her mother Dione for consolation (*Il* 5.418–30). The subsequent jests of Hera and Athena at her expense are well received by Zeus, despite his predilection for Troy. From this point on she is totally absent from the poem until *Iliad*

14, when Hera comes to her to ask for the loan of the *himas,* or strip of embroidered material (not, it seems, an actual garment), which she wears attached in some way to whatever apparel encloses her breasts (*Il* 14.188–223). The functions of this embroidery are not entirely clear: charms, desire, whispers, and sexual union are woven into it, to steal away the minds of even the clear-thinking. But the purpose for which Hera presumes to need it (the bringing together of Okeanos and Tethys) does not seem very appropriate, unless she proposes to give it to Tethys as a sexual charm. Quite the contrary, however, what she does is to tuck it into her own bosom, and Aphrodite approves, saying that thus her request to the older gods will not be refused. As matters turn out, the use Hera does make of the *himas* is more what we might expect: she becomes (without uttering a single word of love or persuasion) so attractive to Zeus that he cannot wait to lie with her. Of the return of the *himas* to its owner, or any reproach for its misuse, we hear nothing.[58]

Aphrodite makes two other appearances in the *Iliad,* one in the mock battle of the gods in *Iliad* 21, the other to protect Hektor's corpse in *Iliad* 23. In the battle she does not face off against any of the other gods, but after Ares has been defeated by Athena she helps him off the field of battle, whereupon, at Hera's urging, Athena runs after them and with her hand knocks both to the ground (*Il* 21.416–33). In *Iliad* 23 Aphrodite plays the odd role of keeping dogs away from Hektor's body, and works together with Apollo to prevent the body from rotting (*Il* 23.184–87). It also appears from the end of *Iliad* 22 that she gave Andromache a circlet or veil on the day of her wedding to Hektor (*Il* 22.468–72). As with many of Hephaistos' gifts to mortals, this identification of source is primarily a way of expressing an object's divine quality.

In the *Odyssey* Aphrodite is, like most of the other gods, little in evidence, save for her moment in the net with Ares. We have seen before that in this poem she is married to Hephaistos, but that in the *Iliad* such is manifestly not the case because he is instead married to Charis. We saw, too, that of an amorous relationship between Aphrodite and Ares in the *Iliad* there is no clear evidence, although they seem close, fighting as they do on the same side. In any case, Demodokos in the *Odyssey* leaves little to the imagination in his description of the affair; missing only is the goddess' reaction after the trap is sprung (*Od* 8.266–364). From the jesting of Apollo and Hermes one might gather too that although much desired by the gods, she has not been especially promiscuous with her favors. Indeed, this moment and her union with Anchises that produced Aineias are the only references to sexual activity by the goddess in Homer, and we will see that the subsequent literature does not add as much as we might expect. The one other mention of Aphrodite in the *Odyssey* (aside from the usual comparisons to her beauty) is the curious tale of her raising of the orphaned daughters of Pandareos (*Od* 20.67–78); no author attempts to tell us why she would do this, but the implication is perhaps that she felt a responsibility to bring the girls to sexual blossoming and to find consorts for them.

The other work of preserved Archaic literature in which Aphrodite is extensively involved is, of course, the *Homeric Hymn* in her honor narrating her affair with Anchises. Here she is described as a matchmaker who causes other gods to desire mortals, rather than an active participant in such unions. Indeed, Zeus causes her to fall in love with Anchises precisely so that she, too, will have suffered the humiliation of an affair with a mortal. How Zeus brings this about, usurping a power that should belong to Aphrodite alone, is not explained (and is probably not a question to be asked, since the story requires this detail). In any event she comes to Anchises, disguised as a mortal woman, bearing the most unlikely tale that she has been kidnapped by Hermes and brought to Anchises to be his wife. Yet more improbable, though her purported father Otreus is still alive, she proposes to consummate the marriage on the spot, and Anchises is only too willing. Toward evening she arouses him from his slumber and reveals the truth, admitting her identity but also conceding a certain regret that she cannot make him immortal and her husband. She then predicts the birth of Aineias, whom the Nymphai of the mountains will raise until the child reaches five years. The Hymn concludes with a warning that Zeus' thunderbolt will strike Anchises if he should be foolish enough to speak to anyone of his union with a goddess. Both the *Iliad* and the end of the *Theogony* mention this same affair and the resulting child, but without details (*Il* 2.819–21; *Th* 1008–10). Our earliest source to actually say that Anchises was struck by lightning is Sophokles, in a fragment of the lost *Laokoon* which describes Aineias with his crippled father on his shoulders (fr 373 R). The reference is very much in passing (Anchises' clothing hangs down over his "thunderbolted back"), so that, barring some exposition earlier in the play, the audience must already know the cause of the affliction. Vergil also ascribes Anchises' debility to a thunderbolt from Zeus (*Aen* 2.648–49), but only with Hyginus do we find a specific connection between that thunderbolt and Anchises' indiscretion in revealing his dalliance with Aphrodite (*Fab* 94). Given such a state of affairs one becomes a bit uncertain about the many sixth-century Attic vases that show Aineias carrying his father out of burning Troy: is the latter here crippled, or merely old? Most likely, Aphrodite's last words in the Hymn are a hint to an audience already aware of subsequent disaster, but perhaps too those parting words created only in the mind of some later author a tale in which the threat of Zeus' anger became a reality. Whatever the cause, Anchises' enfeebled condition well represents the fate that he himself in the Hymn fears will befall men who lie with goddesses (*HAph* 189–90).

Of Aphrodite's other well-known mortal love, Adonis, our Archaic sources have virtually nothing to say. An Adonis was mentioned somewhere in the Hesiodic Corpus, probably in the *Ehoiai*, as the son of Phoinix Agenorides and Alphesiboia (Hes fr 139 MW: she is not the mother of Phoinix's other children), and Apollodoros, our source for this information, clearly supposes him the familiar figure of that name (*ApB* 3.14.4). He also cites, however, the version of Panyasis in which Smyrna is the mother by her own father Theias (= fr 27 *PEG*), so that there was some variation in the matter (fuller discussion in chapter 18). The place where we would have expected to find at least a mention of this famous affair is in the last section of the *Theogony*, where other unions between goddesses and mortal men (including that of Aphrodite and Anchises) are recalled, but there the tale is conspicuously absent. Possibly the fact that no offspring resulted from the union (in contrast to all the others named) caused the poet to exclude it. In any case, Adonis does not surface again until Euripides' *Hippolytos*, and then only by inference: Artemis promises at the end of the play to kill with her arrows whomever Aphrodite next loves (*Hipp* 1420–22). The allusion is generally taken to mean Adonis, even though in our preserved late versions he is killed by a boar (whether or not sent by Artemis), not by arrows. Actual mention of Aphrodite as lover of Adonis comes only with Theokritos (3.46–48: cf. Sappho 140 LP, where Aphrodite advises his mourning), although several late fifth-century vases show the two of them together (e.g., London E699; Florence 81948), and the fourth-century comic poet Euboulos referred in his *Astutoi* to her burial of him (so Athen 2.69c-d). His death on the tusks of a boar first appears in Bion's *Lament for Adonis*. Later Ovid, among others, gives a vivid account (*Met* 10.503–739). Apollodoros adds a number of variant details, including the notion that Artemis sent the boar, and the story that Persephone contested for the youth with Aphrodite, the two ultimately sharing him much as Persephone herself is shared between Hades and Demeter (Ap*B* 3.14.4; cf. *Astr* 2.7.3, and see chapter 18); this latter tale is linked in Apollodoros to the idea, not supported in his main narrative, that Adonis is the product of incest, and may well derive from the same source, Panyasis. The death takes on a somewhat different look in the *Iliad* scholia and Servius, for those commentaries tell us that Ares caused Adonis' demise while the latter was hunting (ΣbT *Il* 5.383; Σ *Ecl* 10.18, cf. Σ *Aen* 5.72); the *Iliad* scholia imply, and Servius states explicitly, that the motive was jealousy over Adonis' affair with Aphrodite.

One other incident of a perhaps amatory nature from the end of the *Theogony* should also be recalled here: Aphrodite's abduction of Phaethon, son of Kephalos and Eos, to be an attendant in her temple (*Th* 987–91). Clearly it is his beauty that has attracted her, but the story is told simply as a coda to the mating of Kephalos and Eos, and the poet makes no mention of an actual union, as one might have expected him to do if that were the case. The tale that the ferryman Phaon took her, disguised as an old woman, across the Aegean without charge, gaining as his reward youthful beauty, survives first in Palaiphatos (48); Aelianus and Servius add that she gave him a jar of unguent with which he made himself desired by many women (*VH* 12.15 [where he dies taken in adultery]; Σ *Aen* 3.279). On a Red-Figure calyx krater of about 420 we see the goddess about to step into the skiff, with Phaon sitting in the stern (Bologna 288 bis). Other vases of this period show Phaon surrounded by women and looking perhaps a bit bored. Only Athenaios, citing a play by Kratinos in which Aphrodite hides Phaon in a lettuce-bed, states that she herself was in love with him (Athen 2.69d; the lettuce-bed appears also in *VH* 12.15).

As we have seen, the *Theogony* does credit the goddess with bearing Deimos, Phobos, and Harmonia to Ares, as well as Aineias to Anchises; Eros is, of course, missing from the list because he is (even more so than Aphrodite herself) a primal element in the poem, and thus present from the very beginning. His various parentages have already been discussed in chapter 1; Sappho (198 LP) and Simonides (575 *PMG*) are the first preserved sources to take the obvious step of making him the son of Aphrodite (Sappho by Ouranos and Simonides by Ares). Two other children surface no earlier than Diodoros Siculus, and have the look of late imports or inventions: Priapos as son of Aphrodite and Dionysos (DS 4.6.1), and Hermaphroditos as son of Aphrodite and Hermes (DS 4.6.5).[59] Diodoros rather suggests that this last is bisexual from birth; the fusion with Salmacis to produce that condition occurs first in Ovid (*Met* 4.285–388). From Sappho (200 LP) we have also record of a daughter, Peitho, an obvious allegory along the lines of Eros who, like her counterpart, is popular in vase-painting. Diodoros is likewise our source for Eryx as son of the Argonaut Boutes and Aphrodite (DS 4.83.1; cf. Boutes' rescue by the goddess at AR 4.912–19). Finally, Pindar's *Olympian* 7 calls the island/bride Rhodos who mates with Helios a child of Aphrodite, perhaps simply to emphasize her beauty (*Ol* 7.14); the scholia attribute to one Herophilos her birth from Aphrodite and Poseidon, this last surely reflecting Rhodos' ascent as an island from the bottom of the sea.

Aside from Homer and these (relatively few) amatory encounters, Aphrodite's role in myth is limited to isolated instances of aiding lovers or punishing those who reject love. In the first category one thinks immediately of Hippomenes and his winning of Atalanta, but though the *Ehoiai* apparently told the story at length (Hes frr 72–76 MW: three apples were used to secure victory), we must wait for Ovid to be assured that Aphrodite supplied those apples (*Met* 10.560–680). The tale may or may not have appeared, too, in Aischylos' lost *Atalanta*; we do not know whether this work concerned the Boiotian maiden who refused all suitors or the Arkadian Atalanta and her role in the Kalydonian Boar Hunt. Similar uncertainty over date surrounds the goddess' role in the coda of Hippomenes' story: Ovid is our first source to say that she became angry with the two lovers because they were insufficiently grateful, and turned them into lions (*Met* 10.681–707). The notion of their transformation does, however, appear as early as Palaiphatos, where it is attached to Atalanta and Meilanion (Pal 13); thus Ovid may or may not have transferred it from the tale of the Arkadian Atalanta, where it may or may not have involved Aphrodite. One other instance in which the goddess aided a mortal to win the object of his affections—that of Pygmalion and Galatea—is found only in Ovid (*Met* 10.243–97). Otherwise, save for the obvious affair of Paris and Helen, Aphrodite does not specifically cause any human to fall in love in our Archaic sources, although Sappho's poetry repeatedly credits her with this power. One can only guess what role she might have played in lost accounts of Ariadne's love for Theseus, or that of Medeia for Iason.

Aphrodite's other main category of activity, punishing those who reject love, does also sometimes involve arousing feelings of passion in mortals, but for rather different purposes; the outcome of Hippomenes' race is a happy exception to the normal pattern. Most notable in this respect are the fates of Hippolytos and Phaidra: the former angers the goddess, but it is the latter who is forced into a state of mind she does not desire in order to effect the punishment, when it would have been easy enough to afflict the miscreant directly. We must remember, of course, that Aphrodite's role in the story comes to us first in Euripides' second *Hippolytos* (the preserved one). Quite possibly she did not have the same impact at all in the first version, and may even constitute a Euripidean addition to earlier accounts in which Phaidra's own shamelessness (and Theseus' absence) was sufficient to motivate the subsequent chain of events, much as in the similar myths of Astydameia and Stheneboia. Less well known, but coming from Stesichoros, is the idea that Tyndareos on one occasion forgot to sacrifice to Aphrodite when he remembered all the other gods, and that in anger she made his daughters (Helen and Klytaimestra surely; perhaps also Timandra and Phylonoe) "twice-married and thrice-married and abandoners of their husbands" (223 *PMG*: Helen makes no mention of this possibility when she blames Aphrodite for her actions in Euripides' *Troades*). A somewhat similar notion, that Smyrna rejected Aphrodite (or else that her mother boasted of her beauty) and for this was made to fall in love with her own father, survives no earlier than Apollodoros (Ap*B* 3.14.4, again perhaps drawing from Panyasis) and Hyginus (*Fab* 58).

Finally, though the evidence is a scant seven-line fragment, notice should be taken of Aphrodite's dramatic appearance in the *Danaides*, the final play of Aischylos' Danaid trilogy (fr 44 R). In what one suspects is a scene contrived especially for the drama, the goddess speaks not surprisingly on behalf of Hypermestra's choice to spare her husband, and against that of her sisters. But that Aphrodite should speak of erotic love in such cosmic terms, and make of herself a basic principle in the fertility of the earth, goes beyond anything we have seen in our other sources, and perhaps paves the way for Lucretius' portrait of her at the beginning of his *De Rerum Natura*.

HERMES   Of Hermes, the god of thieves, trade, messages, and mischief, the birth is recorded in the *Homeric Hymn to Hermes*, as well as in *Homeric Hymn* 18 and, of course, the *Theogony* (*Th* 938–39). The latter describes the blessed event in just two lines, noting that Maia, daughter of Atlas, went into the bed of Zeus, and bore Hermes, herald of the gods (a phrase—*kêryx athanatôn*—not found in Homer of either Hermes or Iris, though Zeus in *Od* 5.29 calls Hermes "messenger" [*angelos*] as one of his many roles). The two Hymns on the other hand say—in almost the same words—that Zeus went to the cave of Maia, who lives apart from the other gods, in the dead of night, and lay with her unbeknownst to Hera (*HHerm* 1–9; *HomH* 18.1–9). No reason is offered in either poem for this odd isolation of Maia. The *Hymn to Hermes* continues with the narrative of the god's first day, calling him among other things a thief, cattle rustler, and conductor of dreams. His first deed is to spring from his cradle and encounter a tortoise outside the cave; this he takes back inside and uses to create the first lyre. Next, as night falls, he makes his way from Kyllene to Pieria, where Apollo's herds are kept; of these he takes fifty head and drives them backward for a while to confuse pursuit. At the Alpheios river he finally halts, invents fire, or at least the art of kindling it, and sacrifices two cows, arranging twelve portions for the gods. That a god—even one striving for recognition—should sacrifice to other gods is unparalleled in Greek mythology, as is the subsequent idea that Hermes must restrain himself from eating some of the meat. When he finally does return to his home toward morning, he tells his mother that he intends to have his share of honor as a god, and to live with the other Olympians. There follows Apollo's arrival, and Hermes' unsuccessful attempt to persuade him that he is a small, naïve child, knowing nothing of thefts or cattle. At last Apollo takes him to Olympos, and before Zeus the two are reconciled, with Hermes giving Apollo the lyre to soothe his anger. In conclusion, Apollo observes that Zeus has charged the new god with the overseeing of deeds of trade; the poet of the *Hymn* adds to this his sovereignty over birds of omen, lions, boars, dogs, and all flocks of sheep, and as well his task as messenger down to Hades. The word used for this last role—*angelos* again (*HHerm* 572–73)—does not however suggest the escorting of souls; rather it reminds us of the *Hymn to Demeter*, where Hermes is sent down to the Underworld by Zeus to bring back Persephone. Much of the *Hymn to Hermes'* tale of the youthful Hermes seems also to have been told by Alkaios, though nothing survives except the novel idea that the god also purloined Apollo's quiver while the latter was threatening him (309 LP). In the fifth century, Sophokles dramatized the story in his partly preserved *Ichneutai* ("Trackers"), with Silenos and a chorus of Satyroi promised gold and freedom if they can find the cattle, and Hermes again inventing the lyre; unfortunately, the resolution of the play, which might have added some new details, is lost.

The *Iliad* does not mention Maia, but *Odyssey* 14.435 describes Hermes as her son, and in both poems his father is explicitly Zeus. Each poem also presents him in a variety of subordinate roles, but rarely as a main actor. In the *Iliad* he favors the Achaian side (*Il* 15.214), and stands with his fellow gods for the *theomachia* (*Il* 20.34–35), but he is never shown influencing the human combat in any way whatever. Throughout the *Iliad* Iris acts as the gods' messenger; only in the *Odyssey* (where Iris is never mentioned) does Hermes assume his most familiar function. Nevertheless, the story in *Iliad* 2.103–4 of his conveying a scepter from Zeus to Pelops probably denotes some sort of courier activity.

Elsewhere in the *Iliad* we learn that of all the Trojans Hermes loved Phorbas (though we are not told why, and he does nothing to prevent the death of the man's son, Ilioneus: *Il* 14.489–92), that he has a son, Eudoros, by Polymele among the Myrmidones (*Il* 16.179–86: the seduction in her bedchamber is described much as Ares' of Astyoche in *Iliad* 2), and that he rescued Ares when the latter was imprisoned by the Aloadai (*Il* 5.388–91). This last exploit, when combined with proposals for the rescue of Hektor's body at the beginning of *Iliad* 24 (23–24), suggests a world in which Hermes' powers of stealth were far more important than they are in the main narrative of the *Iliad*, where Zeus and the other gods generally have the capacity to simply take what they want. Only in *Iliad* 24, where Zeus doubts if even Hermes could steal the body away from Achilleus, do we see this world reflected directly. In a late-preserved story already noted (ApB 1.6.3), it is likewise Hermes who recovers Zeus' sinews from Typhoeus. His one other appearance, aside from the gracious and kindly help he gives to Priam in reaching Achilleus' camp, is also typical: in the *theomachia* of *Iliad* 21 he refuses to fight Leto, and suggests that she may if she likes tell all the other gods that she defeated him (*Il* 21.497–501). It is difficult to imagine any of the other Olympians wearing their honor so lightly.

As to attributes, an important garbing scene in *Iliad* 24 is paralleled word for word by a similar scene in *Odyssey* 5 (*Il* 24.339–45 = *Od* 5.43–49). On both occasions Zeus has sent his son on a mission, and Hermes puts on golden sandals that bear him over land and sea with the wind (Homer does not say that they are winged; note that Athena has the same sandals at *Od* 1.96–98). He also takes a *rhabdos*, or wand, with which he can put men to sleep or wake them up. Presumably this is the forerunner of the kerykeion or herald's wand that Hermes almost invariably carries in Greek art; it may or may not be the same as the one that Apollo gives to Hermes at the end of the latter's *Homeric Hymn* (528–30). This last is golden and three-petaled, but the only power Apollo assigns it is that of warding off harm. In *Iliad* 24, Hermes does put the Achaian sentries to sleep; elsewhere, only the herdsman Argos is so treated, and both Bakchylides (19.29–39) and Ovid (*Met* 1.583–723) say rather that a soothing song was the culprit (though Ovid concedes that Hermes possesses a sleep-producing wand, and it is used later to seduce Chione [11.307–9: see below]). The god is addressed by the epithet *chrysorrhapis*, "with golden wand," three times in the *Odyssey* and several more times in the *Hymns*, but never in the *Iliad* (*Od* 5.87; 10.277, 331). The *Hymn to Hermes* calls him a conductor of dreams, which *might* refer to the bringing of sleep (*HHerm* 14). In any case, we will see another use for Hermes' wand shortly, when we come to his role as *psychopompos*. In art the familiar wand with crossing curves at the top appears (top part only intact) as early as the Protocorinthian Chigi Vase in the Villa Giulia (VG 22679) and then fully preserved on the Gorgon Painter's name vase (Louvre E874: *c.* 600 B.C.) From then on it becomes standard equipment for the god; Sophokles' lost *Philoktetes at Troy* refers to it specifically as having twin snake heads (fr 701 R).

In the *Odyssey* the god's activity is similarly restricted to a few appearances in which he again plays subordinate roles. Zeus, we learn in *Odyssey* 1, sent him to warn Aigisthos not to take Klytaimestra or kill her husband (*Od* 1.37–42), and at Athena's suggestion now prepares to send him to advise Kalypso that she cannot keep Odysseus (*Od* 1.84–87). This latter task is only carried out in *Odyssey* 5, and this is the point at which Zeus calls his son a messenger (*Od* 5.28–32); Hermes carries out the assignment, and imparts his message politely but firmly, after partaking of nectar and ambrosia (*Od* 5.75–148). In *Odyssey* 7 we encounter a more surprising notion of the god: as Odysseus enters the palace of Alkinoos, he finds the Phaiacians pouring a last libation—to Hermes—before turning their thoughts toward bed (*Od* 7.136–38). Conceivably, this refers to the god's previously mentioned power of bringing men sleep, but we might have expected to hear more of such an ability, especially in view of the various bouts with insomnia in Homer (in *Odyssey* 1 it is Athena who sends sleep to Penelope). Perhaps we should think rather that the prayer is for the protection of the household and its occupants at night, given Hermes' patronage of nocturnal prowling (cf. *HHerm* 15). *Odyssey* 8 brings back the fun-loving Hermes, who, in answer to Apollo's query whether he would wish to suffer the same fate as Ares in the net, confounds Hephaistos by declaring that the prize is certainly worth the penalty (*Od* 8.335–42). From the account of Odysseus' wanderings we find Hermes warning the hero against the enchantments of Kirke and offering him the plant that will save him (*Od* 10.277–308). Odysseus, as narrator, cannot tell us who sent the god, and Hermes himself does not address that question. Whether or not the god acts on his own, he does have full power and authority to thwart Kirke's intentions, and seems to have been something of a social acquaintance, since she says later that he had told her many times of Odysseus' coming (*Od* 10.330–32). Likewise, when Odysseus must explain how he knows that Helios brought about the death of his men, he falls back on the explanation that he heard it from Kalypso, who in turn heard it from Hermes (*Od* 12.389–90). From such examples, if they are more than simply narrative devices, we may perhaps conclude that Hermes is the standard link between Olympos, with its omniscience of human events, and those gods or goddesses who remain tied down to the earth. One other function often ascribed to him is demonstrated at the start of *Odyssey* 24, when he herds the souls of the dead suitors down to the Underworld with his wand (*Od* 24.1–10). This is Hermes' first appearance as a *psychopompos*, or conductor of souls, and very nearly his last in Archaic literature, since he does not reappear in that role until Aischylos (*Cho* 622). We have seen, though, that he is made the gods' messenger to Hades at the end of his *Homeric Hymn*, and the Euphronios Krater in New York adds him to the scene of Sarpedon's death as the central figure (NY 1972.11.10). Since Hypnos and Thanatos here carry away the body, Hermes must surely be responsible for the *psyché*, and indeed on fifth-century White-Ground lekythoi he is shown bringing the dead to Charon (e.g., Berlin:Ch F2455; Munich

2777). But whether this concept of Hermes as escorter of souls was a novelty introduced by *Odyssey* 24, or an inherent part of his early character, is not clear. *Odyssey* 11 does remind us that he and Athena together helped Herakles to descend into the Underworld to capture Kerberos (*Od* 11.625–26; cf. *Ai* 831–32), but this service obviously relates to his function as messenger and one familiar with the terrain.

Other references to Hermes in Homer add that he gives grace and fame to the handiwork of men (in particular Eumaios' skills at wood-chopping and fire-building: *Od* 15.319–24), and that he taught Autolykos the art of thievery and cleverly phrased oaths in return for the latter's sacrifices to him (*Od* 19.394–98). His standard epithets are, like those of many other gods, not entirely clear. Both *Iliad* and *Odyssey* use *argeiphontês* as a substitute for his name, often accompanied by *diaktoros*. The former term is usually rendered as "slayer of Argos," although this would constitute an unusual linguistic formation (*argei-* instead of *argo-*), and we must allow for the possibility that the myth was generated by the (no longer understood) epithet.[60] Hermes appears in this tale (in one case clearly dispatching Argos) as early as sixth-century Black-Figure (see chapter 6); the earliest literary reference is the *Ehoiai* (Hes fr 126 MW), followed by Aischylos' *Hiketides* (305), Bakchylides (19), and Pherekydes (3F66). *Diaktoros* is similarly an odd word to result from the Greek verb *diago*; the usual translation here is "guide" or "messenger," but again the word may originally have had a completely different meaning. On one occasion in the *Odyssey*, and two in the *Homeric Hymns*, he is *dôtôr heaôn*, "giver of good things" (although there is some doubt about the original sense of the word translated "good things": *Od* 8.335; *HomH* 18.12, 29). At several points in both *Iliad* and *Odyssey* he is called strong (*kratus*) Hermes, a word perhaps surprising for an Olympian god, and applied to no one else in either poem (e.g., *Il* 16.181; *Od* 5.49; and five times in the *Hymns*, always in combination with *argeiphontês*). Lastly, both poems occasionally call him *eriounios* (or *eriounês*, at the end of a line), which is usually (and again doubtfully) translated as "helpful" or "kindly"; even the *Phoronis*, which tells us that Zeus gave his son this name because he surpassed all men and gods at cunning and thieving devices, seems not to have any real understanding of it (fr 5 *PEG*). Possibly the word refers rather to Hermes' speed as a messenger. In any case, like *argeiphontês* this epithet can at times stand in place of the god's name.

We have already seen that Hermes sires Eudoros in the *Iliad* (*Il* 16.179–86), and if we go down as far as Diodoros, Hermaphroditos by Aphrodite (DS 4.6.5). Pherekydes makes him the parent as well (by Philonis, daughter of Deion) of Autolykos, a child who inherits his father's talents as a thief (3F120); the *Odyssey* passage noted above where Hermes *gives* Autolykos those skills (in return for sacrifices) neither mentions nor (it seems) understands any such blood relationship. Pherekydes' account adds that Philonis mated with Hermes and Apollo on the same day. The scholiast's summary that is our source for the mythographer gives no further details, but Ovid claims that both gods saw the girl (now Chione, daughter of Daidalon[61]) at the same moment of her budding beauty: while Apollo deferred his desire until evening (disguised as an old woman), Hermes took his pleasure on the spot, using his sleep-inducing wand (*Met* 11.301–27). The child born to Apollo in Pherekydes and Ovid is Philammon; Chione herself we have seen is in the *Metamorphoses* slain by Artemis for boasting of her greater beauty. As early as the *Ehoiai*, Autolykos (no parents here named) has the capacity to make things "unseen," or change their skin color *(chroia)*, or somehow alter their markings *(sphragides)*; these talents bring him many of other men's herds and flocks. So too in Pherekydes he can change the nurslings of herds into whatever shapes he wishes, and in Ovid and Hyginus (*Fab* 201) make white from black and black from white, or (Hyginus only) put horns on animals without them and take them away from those with them. We will return to this master thief and his magical skills in chapter 5, when he uses those skills in an attempt to steal the herds of Sisyphos.

A still more famous child of Hermes is Pan, whose birth and chief characteristics are recounted in *Homeric Hymn* 19. We learn that Hermes fell in love with the daughter of Dryops (she is not named) and for her sake tended the sheep of her father.[62] How the mating was actually brought about we do not hear, but the offspring, with its goat feet, horns, and a beard, understandably unnerves the child's nurse. Hermes, however, is pleased with his son and takes him to Olympos to show to the gods, all of whom like the newcomer, but especially Dionysos. Earlier in the poem Pan appears as a creature of the mountains, keeping company with Nymphai, slaying wild beasts, and playing his reed pipes. The Hymn does also at one point call him a *daimôn*, even though his mother is a mortal. For his name, the author cannot resist the obvious: he is called Pan because he is pleasing to all the gods. Other references to him in Archaic literature are rare, but it does emerge that his parentage was quite disputed: Hekataios (1F371: note emendation) and Pindar (fr 100 SM; fuller texts in Bowra's edition [fr 90]) apparently make him the son of Apollo and Odysseus' wife Penelope, while for Herodotos (2.145), Cicero (*ND* 3.22.56), Loukianos (*DD* 2), Apollodoros (Ap*E* 7.38), and Hyginus (*Fab* 224), he is the son of Hermes and Penelope, and the Theocritean *Syrinx* makes Odysseus himself the father; Aischylos even speaks of two Pans, one the offspring of Zeus, the other of Kronos (fr 25b R).[63] Pindar further describes him as the companion of the Great Mother, and as her dog (presumably in the best sense: frr 95, 96 SM). In art he appears most conspicuously on the Pan Painter's name vase in Boston, where he pursues a youth (Boston 10.185); his form is here as elsewhere that of a young man with a goat's head and a very short goat tail. Stories of his amours are found only later, and like Apollo's are sometimes unreciprocated. His passion for Echo survives first in the corpus of Moschos (6) and the *Syrinx*, only to take a distressing turn in the novel *Daphnis and Chloe*, where the god, rejected, causes shepherds to tear the girl apart (3.23; cf. Nonnos 2.117–19, where he pursues her until she becomes an echo). Syrinx, too, first appears in the *Syrinx*, with the full story coming from Ovid (Hermes tells the tale to put Argos to sleep: *Met* 1.689–712). Third, there is Pitys, also in the *Syrinx* but explained only by Nonnos, where we find the predictable account of her pursuit by Pan until she becomes a pine tree (42.258–61). We have already considered the god's successful seduction of Selene (with or as a sheep) in Vergil's *Georgics* (3.391–93) and the scholia thereto. Ovid elsewhere relates a contest between Pan and Apollo, but only Midas seems to question the verdict in Apollo's favor (*Met* 11.146–93). The story of Pan's "death" comes from Plutarch (*Mor* 419b-d). Aischylos and Sophokles also appear to have spoken at times of Pans as a generic group, like Silenoi or Satyroi, and this concept may well be an early one. We will consider in chapter 3 possible evidence for Hermes as father of the Silenoi/Satyroi as well.

Moving from Hermes' offspring back to his own role in myth, we find that, although he is a popular figure in both literature and art, his function continues to be, as it was in Homer, to escort or accompany as a peripheral figure. Already in the *Kypria* he has the task of guiding Hera, Athena, and Aphrodite to Paris, as he regularly does in the artistic representations. We have seen that he rescues Io from Argos, brings Persephone back from Hades, and probably intervenes in the dispute between Apollo and Herakles over the Delphic tripod (see above and note that Ap*B* 2.6.2–3 follows this story with Hermes' sale of Herakles to Omphale). In Alkaios (447 LP) and apparently also Sappho (141 LP) he is the wine-pourer of the gods, while quite a number of vase-paintings show him doing the actual holding of the scales for Zeus when the lots of Achilleus and Hektor (or Achilleus and Memnon) are being weighed (e.g., London B639; VG 57912; Boston 10.177). He is also a standard element in Perseus' beheading of Medousa, providing as he does a special sword, and accompanying the hero for moral support. Encouragement is likewise offered to Herakles in the matter of Kerberos, and the god frequently appears as well in the company of Silenoi. In Pindar's *Pythian* 4 he is the father of two Argonautai, Echion and Erytos (*Py* 4.178–79); the same author calls him *enagônios* and makes him a patron of athletic contests (*Py* 2.10; *Ol* 6.78–79; so also Ais fr 384 R). In Aischylos we have as well a number of references to Hermes *chthonios*, or Hermes in his role of communicator of the wishes of the living to the dead (*Cho* 1, 124, 727). But the most startling appearance of Hermes in early literature is surely his characterization, by Aischylos or whomever, in the *Prometheus Desmotes*; here the light-hearted, playful messenger becomes, like Kratos and Bia, a proponent of power politics, with no preference for any but the winning side, and contempt for those who believe otherwise. Elsewhere one presumes (and hopes) that he remained a carefree god of mischief. Likely he appeared as helper to the hero in one or more parts of Aischylos' Perseus trilogy.

One or two other stories of Hermes deserving of mention are preserved only in very late accounts. In Apollodoros he is the father of Oinomaos' charioteer, Myrtilos (Ap*E* 2.6), and while this in itself is not remarkable, a scholiast to Euripides' *Orestes* 812 claims that Hermes, in anger over the death of his son at the hands of Pelops, provided the golden lamb that began the quarrel between Atreus and Thyestes; the same may be implied at *Orestes* 997, where the lamb seems to come from Hermes' flocks, but there no motive is given. The allusiveness of Euripides' reference does suggest that the story was known earlier, possibly from Sophokles' *Atreus*, or perhaps from Euripides' own *Kressai*, if not an earlier epic. Hermes is also in Apollodoros the lover of Kekrops' daughter, Herse (Ap*B* 3.14.3; so too *Met* 2.708–832), and father by her of Kephalos (a difficult figure, as we shall see in chapter 7). In a rare role as bringer-up of the dead, he restores Protesilaos to Laodameia for one night before she joins her husband in death (Ap*E* 3.30; *Fab* 103). Finally, there is the tale of Tantalos, Pandareos, and the golden dog, which we will deal with in discussing the House of Tantalos in chapter 15.

DIONYSOS   Last of the major Olympians is Dionysos, the only such god to be born of a mortal woman. Both the *Iliad* and the end of the *Theogony* acknowledge him as the child of Zeus and Semele, daughter of Kadmos (*Il* 14.323–25; *Th* 940–42); their affair and her ultimate fate will be treated among the stories of the children of Kadmos. The unusual nature of Dionysos' birth is not mentioned explicitly in the early sources, but *Homeric Hymn* 1 does say that Zeus "gave birth" to him (the verb in question, *tiktein*, can mean "beget," but here the context makes it quite clear that the woman's role is what is intended). A fifth-century Red-Figure lekythos by the Alkimachos Painter (Boston 95.39) actually shows the god emerging from his father's thigh;[64] our first preserved literary account is in Herodotos (2.146.2), followed by Euripides' *Bakchai* (89–98). The location of this event in the *Hymn* (and Pindar: fr 85a SM) was the mountain of Nysa, which at some point was made an explanation for the latter part of the god's name. In *Homeric Hymn* 26, Hermes then conveys the child to the Nymphai of that place, who rear him. The role of Semele's sister Ino and her husband Athamas in his upbringing remains unclear: Pherekydes apparently brought them into the story after the Nymphai had become afraid of Hera's anger (3F90), although such an evasion was scarcely likely to be successful. Apollodoros more logically makes Ino the first choice, with the child going to the Nymphai only after her misfortune (Ap*B* 3.4.3: Ino disguises him as a girl, and when this fails Zeus turns him into a goat kid and smuggles him to the Nymphai). On Red-Figure vases, matters are more direct, with Zeus handing the child over to Nymphai (Ferrara 2737) or Hermes taking him to a house that must be that of Ino (Kyrou Coll). There is also the Throne of Amyklai, on which Pausanias claims to have seen Hermes carrying the infant Dionysos to heaven (3.18.11); more likely, he is seeking a nurse for the child, though conceivably the young god is just snatched from the womb of Semele and being taken up to Zeus. The alternate tale of his birth, that he sprang from a union of Zeus and the latter's own daughter Persephone and was torn apart by Titans, comes to us first from an Orphic theogony that Martin West dates in its codified form to the latter part of the fifth century (see Appendix A). In one attempt to reconcile this account with more traditional views, Demeter puts the pieces back together so that the child can be resuscitated (DS 3.62.6); in another, the heart of Dionysos (as always, saved from the Titans) is ground up by Zeus and served to Semele in a drink, so that the god is born again from her body (*Fab* 167).

Regarding Dionysos' divinity we find, however, doubters, and while the usual explanation of his traditional parentage (god from mortal) is that Semele was in origin really a goddess, one cannot help noting the difficulties he has in establishing his identity. The *Iliad* mentions him only two times, both casual references outside the action of the Trojan War, in which like Demeter he plays no part. The first as we have seen is the noting of his birth from Semele, the second the tale of his clash with the Thracian Lykourgos (*Il* 6.130–40). In this cautionary story, told by Diomedes to Glaukos, Lykourgos (the local king) attacks Dionysos and his party of nurses from Nysa; the latter throw down their *thusla* (*thyrsoi?*) and flee when they are struck by the ox-goad, while Dionysos himself in fear dives into the sea, where Thetis receives and comforts him. That any god, even a young one, should fear men is remarkable, and we should also observe that, though the point of the tale is for men not to anger the gods, the gods who are angered here are those up on Olympos, not Dionysos; the latter is nowhere actually called a god in the *Iliad*, though this is surely coincidence. Neither is there mention of wine here, but Dionysos is *mainomenos,* "maddened," before Lykourgos disrupts matters, and in *Iliad* 14 he is a "joy to mortals." On the issue of his divinity we might also note that at *Homeric Hymn* 26.6 he is said to be "numbered among the gods," as if there could be some doubt. The end of the *Theogony* (942) clearly calls him immortal, but this section also involves the apotheosis of Semele, and may represent a later addition. At any rate, Lykourgos' punishment in the *Iliad* is blindness from Zeus, and as one hated by the gods he does not live long after that. The lost epic *Europeia* (of Eumelos?: fr 11 *PEG*, where Hera is the cause), Stesichoros (234 *PMG*), and Pherekydes (3F90) also told the story of this assault on the god (the latter making the nurses the Hyades, seven in number), while Aischylos detailed it at length in one of his tetralogies (*Edonoi, Bassarides, Neaniskoi, Lykourgos*). The titles of these plays, however, are anything but helpful, and reconstructions depend almost entirely on Apollodoros and other late sources.[65] In Apollodoros his punishment is to kill his son Dryas with an axe, imagining that he is striking vines; subsequently his people on command of the god put him to death (apparently torn apart by horses: Ap*B* 3.5.1). Hyginus has him become drunk, attempt to rape his own mother, then kill his wife and son, and finally cut off his own foot, mistaking it for a vine, or (in another *fabula*) kill himself (*Fab* 132, 242). By contrast, in Sophokles' *Antigone* he seems merely to be imprisoned in a rocky cave, where his madness apparently abates, although some of this may be invented for the sake of the parallel with Antigone (*Ant* 955–65). What part of the above Aischylos might have used is another matter. But certainly Lykourgos must have had a prominent role in the satyr play that bears his name; while the action of this last could fall at any point in the overall story, it might indicate that the protagonist did not die (or suffer irreparable harm) in Aischylos' version of the overall tale. One other suggestion, that the second tragedy of this production focused on Orpheus and the worship of Apollo as a sun god, is quite uncertain. One of the earliest illustrations is a Red-Figure hydria of the mid-fifth century: Lykourgos raises an axe to strike his son, who has taken shelter at an altar and raises his hands to his father in a vain plea (Cracow 1225). Between the two of them a woman (surely the mother) crouches, pulling at her hair, while to the far side of the altar Dionysos raises vine tendrils over the victim, fostering, it would seem, the illusion that the child is a vine, as in Apollodoros. Subsequently the madness and slaughter become quite popular on South Italian vases, with Lykourgos killing his wife (Munich 3300: Lyssa present) or attacking her after having slain his son (London F271; Naples 3237).[66]

As there are two references to Dionysos in the *Iliad*, so there are only two in the *Odyssey*. One, concerning the fate of Ariadne on Dia, we will return to shortly; the other relates that for Achilleus' burial Thetis used an amphora given to her by Dionysos (who received it from Hephaistos: *Od* 24.73–77). Stesichoros adds, what we might have supposed anyway, that the gift was in gratitude for Thetis' protection from Lykourgos (234 *PMG*); we may see Dionysos carrying it to the wedding of Thetis on the François Krater (Florence 4209). Nonbelievers also provide the theme for *Homeric Hymn* 7, in which the god in the guise of a young man is taken on board ship by pirates who suppose he will bring a ransom. When the bonds fall away from him the helmsman perceives that he is a god, but the other sailors persist in their folly, until wine flows through the ship, and vines and ivy twist around the mast. Dionysos himself becomes a lion, and roars until all except the helmsman have flung themselves into the sea and become dolphins. The reference to wine is almost, but not quite, the first concrete reference to Dionysos in this connection; earlier Hesiod, in the *Works & Days*, speaks of drawing the "gift of Dionysos" from the vats (see also *HomH* 26.11). In art the scene of the sailors' metamorphosis is clearly illustrated on an Etruscan Black-Figure kalpis of about 520 B.C.: as the men fall into the sea (head first) the upper parts of their bodies turn into those of dolphins, while human legs are still visible (Toledo 82.134).

Other literary references to Dionysos before the fifth century are few, although Alkaios mentions him as the god of wine in a memorable drinking fragment (346 LP), and he is a standard element in much of sixth-century Attic vase-painting.[67] Most of the latter scenes portray him simply as the god of wine, often surrounded by Silenoi and/or Mainades, but in a few instances an actual myth is involved, most frequently of course the triumphal escorting back of Hephaistos to Olympos, an event that might or might not be responsible for Dionysos' full membership in the company of the gods.[68]

Another figure associated with the god on vases is Ariadne, whom Dionysos marries at the end of the *Theogony*, and whom Zeus for that reason makes immortal (*Th* 947–49). Obviously such a grant of immortality is necessary if a marriage between god and mortal is to succeed. In conflict with this status, however, and with the marriage itself, are the tales of Ariadne's death. In the *Nekuia*, Odysseus sees her in the Underworld and notes that she was being taken to Athens by Theseus, but that before he could bring her there and enjoy her, Artemis slew her on sea-girt Dia (Naxos? or the small island off Iraklion on Krete?), by reason of the evidence given by Dionysos (*Od* 11.321–25). That Ariadne should here die before reaching her rendezvous with Dionysos is difficult enough; that she dies at the instigation of the god who is elsewhere her eternal husband may well seem intolerable. Nor is this seeming aberration of the *Nekuia* without echoes in the subsequent literature. Pherekydes, who may be trying to join two separate traditions, recounts the more familiar version in which Ariadne is abandoned by Theseus after falling in love with him and fleeing Krete (3F148). The ship here puts in at Dia, where Theseus, who has fallen asleep, is told by Athena to leave Ariadne and return to Athens alone. Dionysos then arrives, takes the girl in marriage, and gives her a golden crown. To this account, preserved in the scholia to the *Nekuia* passage (Σ *Od* 11.322), the scholiast adds, "and they say that she was slain by Artemis, having thrown away her virginity [*parthenian*]," then concludes with the standard formula, "the story is from Pherekydes." As a result, it is not clear whether the reference to Artemis and Ariadne's death is part of the same version as the rest, nor whether the sense is that Artemis slew the girl *after* she married the god. If this last is so, then the deed can hardly have been done at Dionysos' bidding. A further remark in the scholia, that what Dionysos testified to in Homer was Ariadne's sexual union with Theseus in the god's precinct on Naxos (Σ *Od* 11.325), is probably no more than a commentator's guess, since it would seem to conflict with Homer's statement that Theseus derived no enjoyment from his leading away of Ariadne (and does not explain why Artemis should be involved, unless the deed offended her [through Ariadne's inchastity] as well as Dionysos: see below).

In this whole context we must consider, too, the statement of "Epimenides" that when Dionysos came to Minos, wishing to seduce *(phtheirai)* Ariadne, he gave her the crown, by which she was deceived (3B25, apud *Katast* 5 [R]). This last phrase (or its fuller original) is rendered by the Germanicus scholia and Hyginus to mean simply that Ariadne was pleased with the gift and so did not refuse the god, whose intentions (given the word *phtheirai*, literally "ruin" [by seducing]) will scarcely have been honorable. Adding that information to the *Nekuia*'s idea that Theseus did not "enjoy" Ariadne, one might perhaps suspect that divine jealousy is involved in the *Odyssey*, with Ariadne having there, too, some commitment to Dionysos before she met Theseus. If so, we might imagine that the Artemis of the *Nekuia* slew Ariadne because of her infidelity to Dionysos, much as the goddess slays Koronis in Pindar because of her infidelity to Apollo. But again the *Nekuia* scholia's notion of lost virginity (whether or not from Pherekydes) presents a problem, unless we suppose that Ariadne promised herself to the god but gave herself to Theseus instead. In any case, since Dionysos is not likely to forgive a mortal lover's dalliance with a rival, we must assume that those versions in which he marries her after Theseus leaves her preclude any notion of an earlier seduction of her on Krete. We would seem then to have three different lines of narratives: (1) Dionysos seduces Ariadne, Theseus carries her off, Dionysos prevails on Artemis to kill her; (2) Dionysos and/or Theseus seduce Ariadne, Artemis kills her for inchastity; (3) Theseus carries her off, Dionysos supplants him and marries her. The divergence between tragedy and bliss in all this is oddly captured by Euripides' *Hippolytos*, where Phaidra calls her sister both wretched and the wife of Dionysos in the same line (339). As noted above, Ariadne and the god do appear together frequently in vase-paintings, so that the *Theogony's* version might seem the better established. Several illustrations show (or anticipate) the moment of their blissful meeting on Naxos: so, for example, on the hydria by the Syleus Painter noted earlier, where Dionysos escorts Ariadne off on one side of the scene, Athena dismisses Theseus on the other (Berlin:PM F2179). Ariadne here wears a headband that could be the crown mentioned by Pherekydes and Epimenides; the story that she possessed a crown, whether this or another, which shone in the dark will be considered in connection with the exploits of Theseus on Krete in chapter 8.

Surprisingly, the *Theogony* does not mention any offspring from the union of Dionysos and Ariadne, and in fact the god of wine has no children at all in the preserved Archaic sources. Though he appears on several occasions in Black-Figure next to a woman who carries a child (or children), this woman is never named, and her status as Ariadne uncertain.[69] On a neck-amphora by Exekias, however, the god is attended by a young man named Oinopion (London B210). This last name recurs in Diodoros (5.79.1), Apollodoros (ApE 1.9), and other authors as a son of Dionysos and Ariadne (Apollodoros also names Thoas, Staphylos, and Peparethos as sons by the same mother), so that it might seem logical to make the connection and suppose parentage the intent of the sixth-century painters. On the other hand, Plutarch knows of a tradition that would make Oinopion and Staphylos the children of Theseus (despite the implication of wine in their names) and cites Ion of Chios to that effect (*Thes* 20). Possibly Theseus acquired them during his general increase in popularity among the Athenians in the first half of the fifth century. Whether this Oinopion was thought in early times to be the same as the mythical king of Chios who blinded Orion remains uncertain.[70] Other children of Dionysos are attested only late, and can be briefly listed: Phanos and Staphylos (again) as Argonautai (ApB 1.9.16), Priapos as a son of Dionysos and Aphrodite (DS 4.6.1), and surprisingly Deianeira as daughter of Althaia and the god, rather than her husband Oineus (ApB 1.8.1: so too *Fab* 129). Just prior to reporting this last tradition, Apollodoros has noted Dionysos' gift of a vine to Oineus, and there seems likely to have been some connection between the two events. For what it is worth, Bakchylides 5 appears to regard Deianeira as Oineus' daughter (5.165–73), while the *Ehoiai* (Hes fr 25 MW) and Sophokles' *Trachiniai* (6) are quite certain of that fact.

Dionysos' other major conflict with an unbeliever, following that with Lykourgos, takes place upon his return to his mother's city of Thebes. Here Pentheus, the grandson of Kadmos from his daughter Agaue, doubts the divinity of his first cousin and offers like Lykourgos an ill-conceived violence. Unfortunately, Pentheus is not mentioned in any of the preserved literature before Aischylos, who wrote a trilogy about the encounter (titles were probably *Bakchai, Pentheus, Xantriai*)[71] which is entirely lost. Euphronios gives us a Red-Figure psykter of about 515 B.C. on which the tearing-apart of Pentheus is shown (Boston 10.221), but this tells us little about the part Dionysos plays in the story; one inevitably wonders how much the god's forceful role in Euripides' version of the tale draws from Aischylos, and how much from Euripides' own view of divinity. Less disastrous but also traumatic is the god's reception by the daughters of Proitos (and perhaps the other women of Argos) if we believe with the *Ehoiai* (Hes fr 131 MW) that this was the divinity they insulted (Bakchylides, Akousilaos, and Pherekydes agree that it was Hera; see chapter 10). The *Ehoiai* follows the standard later account that they were driven mad, and adds a detail about *machlosynê* (licentiousness?). We do not know if Dionysos eventually relented; in later accounts either Melampous or the gods bring about their cure (e.g., Ap*B* 2.2.2). By contrast, a story in which Dionysos was accepted by a mortal is totally missing from the Archaic sources: Ikarios' unfortunate dismemberment after he had shared the wine of the god with his friends, who thought themselves bewitched. The tale, which is credited to Eratosthenes in the *Iliad* scholia (ΣAb *Il* 22.29), goes on to relate the hanging death of the man's daughter, Erigone, after she finds his body, and may or may not have been the subject of Sophokles' drama *Erigone* (the title might also refer to Aigisthos' daughter).

All these stories—Ariadne, Lykourgos, the Proitides, Pentheus, Ikarios—result in catastrophe for the mortals involved. But we have seen that in some accounts Ariadne does profit quite handsomely from her experience of the god, and the idea that his mother Semele becomes a goddess on Olympos after her death is known as early as the end of the *Theogony* (*Th* 942), the Amyklai Throne (with Ino: Paus 3.19.3), and Pindar (*Ol* 2.25–27; *Py* 11.1), although the further elaboration that Dionysos went down into Hades to fetch his mother is found first in Pausanias (2.31.2) and Apollodoros (Ap*B* 3.5.3). As we will see in chapter 14, she appears (named) with Dionysos on a sixth-century cup in Naples (Stg 172), and likewise on a hydria in Berlin where Dionysos mounts a chariot (Berlin:Lost F1904). I have speculated elsewhere that Aischylos wrote an entire trilogy on the events surrounding Semele's death;[72] if that is right, Dionysos' role in her apotheosis might well have been known this early.

It remains to note some of the god's other titles. Bakchos in its adjectival form, "Bakcheios," is applied to Dionysos first in *Homeric Hymn* 19 (early fifth century?[73]) and Pindar (fr 70b SM), but the noun as an actual name does not appear before Sophokles (*OT* 211) and Euripides (fr 477 N²), or possibly Aischylos, depending on the reading of a textually difficult fragment (where he is perhaps called the "ivied Apollo": fr 341 R). The term "Bakchai" for his followers may be as early as Alkman, if the words "Kadmeian Bakchai" in a commentary on his work are (1) correctly supplemented and (2) in fact a direct quote (7 *PMG*). Certainly those followers are called "Bakchai" in Aischylos' *Eumenides* (*Eum* 25), and presumably the title of the lost Aischylean *Bakchai* also referred to them, though the subject matter of that play is uncertain. Yet another name for the god, "Bromios," apparently derives from *bromos* and signifies "noisy, boisterous"; it first appears in Pratinas (708 *PMG*) and in two dithyrambs of Pindar describing Dionysiac celebrations (on Olympos, where there is special stress on percussion instruments [fr 70b SM], and in Athens [fr 75 SM]). Subsequently we find it, too, in Aischylos' *Eumenides* (25). A third name, "Iakchos," remains highly controversial. Seemingly evolving from (or a personification of) the shout *(iakchê)* uttered by initiates during their procession to Eleusis, he became perhaps a kind of patron god of the procession, complete with cult statue carried along, but his role in the mysteries themselves, if any, we do not know, nor is he mentioned in the *Homeric Hymn to Demeter*. His identification with Dionysos begins perhaps in the fifth century; already the first literary references to him, from Sophokles, attest to it (*Ant* 1149–54; fr 959 R).[74] One other name, "Theoinos," occurs only in a one-line fragment of Aischylos (fr 382 R).

Zagreus, a figure also at times identified with Dionysos, is a more complicated matter. His name survives first in the epic *Alkmaionis*, where he is paired with Gaia as a powerful god (fr 3 *PEG*). Aischylos in one of his *Sisyphos* plays seems to have made him a personage of the Underworld with Hades (quite possibly his son: fr 228 R), but in the *Aigyptioi* (or the *Hiketides*?) Hades himself (fr 5 R). In his *Kretes* Euripides offers a chorus of Kretan *mystai* ("initiates") who have become *mystai* of Idaian Zeus and herdsmen of "night-wandering Zagreus, celebrating the feasts of raw flesh," so that, holding up torches for the mountain mother, they acquire the title of "Bakchos" (fr 79 Aus, revised from 472 N²); this and the rest of the context may suggest some fusion with Dionysos. That link would seem definite by the time of Kallimachos, who somewhere refers to the birth of Dionysos Zagreus (fr 43.117 Pf and *apparatus*); the Byzantine sources for this quote add that "Zagreus" is the poets' name for Dionysos, Zeus having mated with Persephone to create a Dionysos who is *chthonios*. One might suppose such an alter ego of the wine god ideally suited to the Orphic notion of the child torn apart by Titans and reborn, since it provides a separate identity for the Dionysos born of Persephone. But in fact the Orphic sources preserved seem not to use the name "Zagreus" in this (or any other) context. Kallimachos, on the other hand, may well have done so, given that the Byzantine works in question clearly refer to that child before quoting his line on Dionysos-Zagreus' birth; we know in fact that he did relate the tale of the dismemberment (fr 643 Pf; so too Euphorion).[75] Certain in any case are Nonnos (5.563–67; 6.206–10) and the Lykophron scholia (at 355) as places where the child's name (or one of the names, together with Dionysos) is Zagreus. From such evidence it seems likely that the fusion of Zagreus with Dionysos-as-dismembered-child is a secondary development, and that originally he may well have been a son of Hades and Persephone (though Hades' identity as Zeus' *katachthonios* alter ego might lead us back to Zeus after all).

3　Olympos, the Underworld, and Minor Divinities

Olympos　We have seen that a great number of gods, in fact far and away the majority, dwell on earth, either in the sea or in connection with specific points of local topography. But the major gods inhabit Olympos, and indeed one of Homer's standard epithets uses precisely that fact to identify them. What Homer imagines Olympos to be is a more difficult question.[1] The story of the Aloadai in the *Nekuia* will illustrate some of the problems. Here we are told that Otos and Ephialtes threatened war against the gods who are on Olympos, and then, immediately following, that they intended to do so by stacking Ossa on Olympos, and Pelion on Ossa, so that they might reach *ouranos* (*Od* 11.313–16). Thus on the one hand the gods are to be found on Olympos, but on the other Olympos is a terrestrial mountain, useful only for reaching the heavens where the gods seem to be located. This part of the *Nekuia* is from its catalogue of heroines, and may well be later than its surroundings, but nonetheless it presents a conflict in conception which pervades the rest of the *Odyssey* and *Iliad* as well. In *Iliad* 16, a cloud is said to go from Olympos to *ouranos* (*Il* 16.364–65), and at numerous points in both poems epithets describing the divine residence portray it as a mountain with crags, peaks, etc.; in three instances it is even snowy (*Il* 1.420; 18.186, 616). Then, too, when Hera leaves Olympos in *Iliad* 14 to go to Lemnos (*Il* 14.225–30), and Hermes in *Odyssey* 5 to visit Kalypso (*Od* 5.50), they both pass Pieria as the first local landmark, which suggests that Olympos is indeed the real mountain of that name in Thessaly. On the other hand, there are also moments in which the gods clearly reside up in the sky (or beyond it), and indeed where Olympos and *ouranos* appear to be the same thing. When Thetis rises from the sea to visit Zeus in *Iliad* 1, for example, she goes to "great *ouranos* and Olympos," and finds Zeus sitting on a peak of many-ridged Olympos, apart from the other gods (*Il* 1.497–99). Here we can at least say that Olympos is as high as *ouranos*, if not equivalent to it, and hence scarcely a mountain. Yet it nonetheless retains vestiges of what is probably its former identity as a mountain. The same ambiguity seems inherent in Zeus' boast to the other gods at the beginning of *Iliad* 8, when he claims that he could tie a rope to a peak of Olympos and pull up all the others with the earth and sea as well (*Il* 8.18–26); thus, sometimes Olympos cannot even be attached to the earth.

120

Links between Olympos and *ouranos* also emerge from the two passages of the *Iliad* in which Hera and Athena harness up a chariot in order to reach the Trojan battlefield. In *Iliad* 5, they pass through the gates held by the Horai, "to whom are entrusted great *ouranos* and Olympos, both to open the thick clouds and to close them" (*Il* 5.749–54; cf. 8.393–96). Certainly this suggests that *ouranos* and Olympos are the same, and while we might suppose that *ouranos* is on one side of the gates and Olympos on the other (or that Olympos is that part of *ouranos* on one side), when the two goddesses do exit through the gates, they find Zeus on the other side sitting, once again, "on a peak of many-ridged Olympos." It is of course possible that here too, as in the *Nekuia* passage, there is internal confusion, but it seems more likely that Olympos is on both sides of the gates (which would then simply protect the gods' residences within Olympos) and coexists to some extent with *ouranos*. Such a conclusion is also in accord with numerous other passages in both poems where the gods are said to come down from or return to Olympos or *ouranos* indifferently, and there is a formula (twice in the *Iliad*, quite common in the *Odyssey*) in which the gods actually hold *ouranos* rather than the usual Olympos or Olympian homes (*Il* 20.299; 21.267; *Od* 1.67, etc.). Yet *ouranos* can after all be simply the heavens, unoccupied by the gods, and as Poseidon reminds us in *Iliad* 15, while Zeus is master of the meteorological sky, Olympos is the common property of all the Olympians (*Il* 15.191–92).

We have seen that Olympos is snowy, and that somewhere within it are gates made of clouds; such details are surely meant to emphasize its great height. But one scarcely imagines Zeus making his way through snowdrifts or dense fog when he leaves his palace in the morning, and thus we are not surprised to find, in *Odyssey* 6, that the home of the gods is unacquainted with wind or rain or snow or even clouds; instead it is perpetually bathed in a brilliant light (*Od* 6.42–46). For both *Iliad* and *Odyssey* Olympos seems in the last analysis a fantasy world, something not quite mountain, not quite sky, but a combination of whatever serves to set the gods apart in their own realm. Here, as *Iliad* 1 tells us, their primary activity is communal feasting, the music of Apollo's lyre, and the singing of the Mousai (*Il* 1.601–4). Hephaistos' remarks on that occasion suggest that, at least for this function of the gods, being together is important, and indeed we never see them feasting separately, or in smaller groups (cf. *HDem* 484; *HAp* 186). Whenever Zeus sits apart from the others, his absence from the group as a whole is always noted as a point of special interest (*Il* 1.498–99; 5.753–54). In the same way, we are told that the gods sit severally in their own homes in *Iliad* 11 when they are angry with Zeus; again the intention seems to mark that this is not normal behavior (*Il* 11.75–77). From the close of *Iliad* 1 we have already learned that the gods do indeed have separate homes, made for them by Hephaistos, to which they repair at night to sleep (*Il* 1.606–8). But the same passage implies what is later confirmed explicitly in *Iliad* 15 and *Odyssey* 1, namely that the gods assemble in the house of Zeus (*Il* 15.84–85; *Od* 1.26–27). *Iliad* 15 also shows Themis as perhaps presiding, at least in Zeus' absence. The location of the assembly that Zeus calls on the highest peak of Olympos in *Iliad* 8.2–3 may well be outside, perhaps for better scrutiny of the situation down below. That the gods should choose Zeus' home for their gatherings is, of course, obvious. But why Athena should choose the threshold of Zeus' palace as a place in which to divest herself of her peplos and arm for battle (*Il* 5.733–47) remains a mystery (Hera, by contrast, has her own chamber [with a secret lock] to which to retreat when she prepares to seduce her husband: *Il* 14.166–69). It has been suggested, based on a study of the various formulae used to denote movement to and from Olympos, that this was the home of Zeus before it was that of the other gods, and such a conclusion may well be right.[2]

From Hesiod and the *Homeric Hymns* can be culled most of the same formulae used in the *Iliad* and *Odyssey*, and the conception of Olympos seems essentially the same: mountain peaks and snow, and the home of the gods (*Th* 42–43, 113). Some of the contradictions apply as well: when the children of Kronos prepare to battle the Titans, they do so from Olympos, while the Titans come forth from Othrys, which is the name of an actual mountain in the southern part of Thessaly (*Th* 632–34). Thus, Hesiod seems to conceive of the gods as being on Mount Olympos, at the northern end of the Thessalian plain. But when the battle is actually joined and Zeus comes forth to hurl his thunderbolts, he does so "from *ouranos* and from Olympos" (*Th* 689–90), thus presenting us with much the same problem as when Thetis went to *ouranos* and Olympos to find Zeus in *Iliad* 1. We should also note the description of Zeus' offer of privileges to those who will join him: on this occasion he summons the gods to Olympos, as if he was originally there alone (*Th* 390–91). But perhaps we are to understand that his brothers and sisters are already with him, as natural allies, and that the invitation is to the still undecided gods of earlier generations; the other Olympians, of course, have not yet been born. In the *Homeric Hymns* we find various scattered references to the gatherings of the gods, here again in the home of Zeus. The one description that offers some novelty is that at the beginning of the Pythian section of the *Hymn to Apollo*, when the god arrives on Olympos and in Zeus' house sets all the gods to thoughts of music (*HAp* 189–206). Here affairs are a bit livelier than in Homer: the Mousai sing of the sorrows of men, while the Charites and the Horai dance with Harmonia and Hebe and Aphrodite and Artemis, and even Ares and Hermes sport in some undefined way. A fragment of a Pindaric dithyramb shows us something of the same sort, with torches and timbrels, all apparently under the inspiration of Dionysos and the Meter (fr 70b SM); how gods can be inspired by the gift of wine when they drink only nectar is no doubt a question we are not intended to ask.

From later sources, other than the Pindaric fragment just mentioned, there is really nothing at all of Olympos, perhaps not surprising when we consider that post-epic literature usually restricts itself to a mortal frame of reference and thus has no possibility of viewing the gods in their own domain. On vase-paintings we do occasionally see the gods at home, sometimes for the arrival of Herakles or Dionysos and on the François Krater for the return of Hephaistos.[3] But these scenes add no new information, and show only the gods we would expect to find. Mortals who are elevated to Olympos seem to number only a few—Herakles, Ganymedes, Semele, Ariadne, Kephalos, perhaps Hyakinthos—and of these only Herakles is really brought to Olympos to become a god; the others gain entrance through the affections of gods who want them near at hand. We might also add Tantalos, who in the *Nostoi* (if *Return of the Atreidai* is this poem) at least visits the gods (fr 4 *PEG*). Pindar uses the same story in his *Olympian 1*, and here we have as well the son Pelops, whom Poseidon brings up to Olympos, much as Zeus brought Ganymedes. But the experiment with Tantalos fails, and Pelops is sent back to earth; one might be pardoned for suspecting that much of this is Pindar's own invention. At any rate the list ends here; for other mortals destined to escape Hades (or Tartaros) the goal is always Elysion, as we will see shortly.

From Olympos we descend to what may be considered its polar opposite, the Underworld. Both *Iliad* and *Odyssey* make clear that this place for departed shades is, in fact, underground, even though in the *Odyssey* the approach to it is from the ends of the earth. The *Iliad* has no further information to offer on the subject; the poet does not take us down to the Underworld or even follow any of the many souls who go there (although in *Il* 8.369 the Styx is mentioned as a river to be crossed). From the *Odyssey* we have, of course, both Odysseus' visit to the edge of Hades and the actual entrance of the shades of the dead suitors in *Odyssey* 24. The hero receives before he departs from Aiaia sailing instructions from Kirke: the ship is to sail before the north wind across Okeanos to the far shore, where Odysseus will find the grove of Persephone, with its willows and poplars (*Od* 10.504–40). From there he will proceed into Hades, where Pyriphlegethon and Kokytos (a branch of the Styx) come together into Acheron, and there dig his trench for the blood of the sheep.

The beginning of *Odyssey* 11 generally follows this same course in actually bringing the ship to Hades: after a day's sailing it comes to Okeanos and the land of the Kimmerians, over whom there is eternal darkness (*Od* 11.13–50). Here the crew disembark, and walk along the bank of Okeanos until they reach the place specified. The sacrifice is then carried out, and the souls come up from out of Erebos to drink the blood that will restore to them something of their senses (cf. Erebos at *Od* 11.564). First, however, comes Elpenor, Odysseus' recently deceased companion, who seems not to need the blood in order to speak, nor to have any desire for it (*Od* 11.51–80). Rather, Odysseus associates his presence at the head of the shades with the fact that he is unburied, and indeed this is the sole purpose of Elpenor's lament, to request a proper burial. We might therefore suppose that he requires burial in order to join the other souls, but his words imply a much different preoccupation. He speaks of being bewailed and cremated with his weapons and full armor, and then having a conspicuous mound by the shore of the sea, so that he might be known to future generations. This concern with reputation, or at least with leaving some mark upon the world, is typical of Homeric epic, but here it surfaces just where we might have expected some interest in the effects of burial on the condition of the shade in the afterlife. Of course this section of the poem has good reason to disregard any questions that might involve the crossing of a river in the Underworld, since either Odysseus or the shades he encounters would then have to negotiate it, and this would require awkward explanations. Still, the fact remains that Elpenor does not appear to suppose that burial will alter his status except insofar as the living remember him. The same picture emerges from a consideration of the situation at the beginning of *Odyssey* 24; here Hermes leads the shades of the dead suitors into Hades without any mention of difficulty, and they enter into full social intercourse with the shades of those already dead. Yet they have clearly not been buried; that is what part of the conflict of *Odyssey* 24 is about. There is, however, one point in the *Odyssey* (from the *Nekuia* itself, in fact) where the existence of rivers is stressed: when Odysseus' mother Antikleia sees him, she wonders how he could have arrived, noting that to reach the Underworld great rivers and terrible streams— Okeanos first of all—must be crossed (*Od* 11.157–58). Actually Odysseus has traversed only Okeanos in our preserved account, but we surely have vestiges of a tradition in which rivers in the Underworld itself constituted a further barrier, at least to the living; Antikleia does not say that they are difficult for the dead, whether buried or not.

In the *Iliad* matters are rather different. As noted, Book 8 (Athena's description of her aid to Herakles) establishes the existence of a river Styx that must be crossed when the hero descends into Hades to obtain Kerberos (*Il* 8.369). And in *Iliad* 23, Patroklos' shade visits Achilleus and asks to be buried as quickly as possible, "so that I might pass through the gates of Hades. For the *psychai*, the likenesses of the dead, keep me far away, and do not permit me to mingle with them on the other side of the river. But always in the same way I roam about outside of Hades of the wide gates" (*Il* 23.71–74). Thus we see for the first and only time in Homer the idea of a river bounding Hades which cannot be crossed unless one has received burial. Neither Achilleus, Priam, nor even the gods mention such a consideration in the lengthy treatment of the disposal of Hektor's body; rather, the issue seems entirely one of honor and the feelings of the deceased's relatives. In the same way, as we saw, the question is never broached with regard to the dead suitors in the *Odyssey*.

Post-Homeric sources do not add much on these points. Hesiod, who has a good deal to say about the Styx one way and another, does not ever say that she forms a boundary in the Underworld; the first hint of this idea after the *Iliad* comes from Alkaios, who mentions Acheron as the river back across which the dead cannot pass (38A LP; cf. Sappho 95 LP). Acheron as a river (or lake) leading to or somehow typical of the Underworld also appears in Aischylos (*Hepta* 854–60; cf. Kokytos at *Hepta* 690 and *Ag* 1558) and in Sophokles'

Antigone (816), a play in which, contrary to what one might suppose, there is never any mention of advantage to *Polyneikes* from his burial (the same is true for the Argive dead in Euripides' *Hiketides*). The figure we are accustomed to think of as controlling passage across this body of water, whether Acheron or Styx, is of course Charon, but he is conspicuously absent from Homer and other early sources. His first appearance of certain date is actually no earlier than Polygnotos' painting of Hades for the Knidian Lesche at Delphi in the second quarter of the fifth century. Pausanias, however, in describing this painting for us, quotes two lines of the otherwise obscure epic *Minyas* which show Theseus and Peirithoos failing to find the old ferryman Charon or his boat when they arrive at its mooring-place (10.28.2). The poem is probably of the Archaic period, but given the scant remains we have no absolute proof that it predates the execution of Polygnotos' painting (*c.* 470–60 B.C.).[4] Fifth-century in date, like that painting, are the earliest preserved representations of a boatman of the dead, presumably Charon, on Attic White-Ground funerary lekythoi. The series actually begins with a Black-Figure fragment of a portable hearth or grave vase on which an old man sits in the stern of his boat manning the rudder while around him hover small winged figures (who should not therefore logically need his services: Frankfurt:Lieb 560).[5] The White-Ground examples, however, show him in the more familiar role of boat-punter, with Hermes leading an unwinged deceased to his craft (so Athens 1926, where there still remain very tiny winged figures as well). In preserved literature after the *Minyas* fragment our first reference is Euripides' *Alkestis*, where Charon is variously named as the ferryman of corpses, the *psychopompos* (elsewhere always Hermes' title), and one who crosses the lake of Acheron in his two-oared skiff (*Alk* 252–55, 361, 439–44; cf. 786 *PMG*). The notion of Charon's charging for his services survives first in Aristophanes' *Batrachoi*, where the fare is two obols (*Batr* 139–40); archaeological evidence for the practice of leaving a coin in the mouth of the deceased does not seem to surface earlier than the Hellenistic period in Attika, and perhaps likewise elsewhere.[6]

To return now to the *Odyssey*'s account of the Underworld, after discovering Elpenor's plight and promising to redress the situation Odysseus speaks with Teiresias (who gives him some, but not all, of what he came for) and his mother (*Od* 11.84–224). In both cases there is mention of Persephone, who gives Teiresias his retained powers of thought and prevents Odysseus from embracing his mother. The bride of Hades ushers in the succeeding scene as well when she sends up the wives and daughters of famous heroes, and scatters them after a time (*Od* 11.225–330). Next, Odysseus speaks with Agamemnon and Achilleus (*Od* 11.385–540); the latter, despite his grim words on the unpleasantness of death, is the only shade here or elsewhere to display any joy in the Underworld, this coming upon the report of his son Neoptolemos' exploits. It may or may not be coincidence that Achilleus, as we shall see, is a figure whom Homer's listeners might have expected to find elsewhere, in happier surroundings. Aias' silence then concludes this group of interviews, and we move to the most suspect part of Odysseus' visit, the witnessing (seemingly without abandoning the blood-filled trench) of six figures, three of whom at least are immobile and usually to be found in Tartaros (*Od* 11.566–635). The series begins with Minos in his role as judge, and we might suppose that his task here, as later in Plato and Dante, is to pass judgment on deeds committed by men in their lifetime. But the text seems clearly to indicate that the shades bring their *disputes* to Minos to be resolved. That beings as insubstantial as those the *Odyssey* describes could find anything about which to dispute, much less a way of paying back the offended party, strikes one as unlikely; probably we see here simply a reflection of Minos' role on earth, much as seems the case with Orion, the next figure viewed by Odysseus. This shade simply drives across the meadows of asphodel the wild beasts he slew while alive, not a reward or blissful existence, perhaps, but hardly a punishment either. The same situation holds for the shade of Herakles, who stalks about with drawn bow and arrow, as if ready to shoot.

But between Orion and Herakles come three transgressors who are clearly punished for their misdeeds on earth: Tityos, stretched along the ground with vultures tearing at his liver (because he dared attack Leto), Tantalos, who stands in his pool of water reaching vainly for fruit (the crime is not specified), and Sisyphos, who rolls his rock up a hill (again no crime is specified). Thus, the principle (if any) unifying this last group of shades remains uncertain. After Herakles has departed, Odysseus hopes to see still other heroes, in particular Theseus and Peirithoos, and the mention of these two together suggests that he expects to find both of them held fast on their bench. But fear of the massed shades and the thought that Persephone (here again emphasized rather than Hades) might send up a Gorgon head finally overwhelm him and drive him back to his ship. The crew casts off, and this time the craft appears to travel along rather than across Okeanos, and perhaps to follow the river back to Kirke; in any case, once they have left Okeanos, both the sea and Aiaia come into view quite quickly.

To Odysseus' account in *Odyssey* 11 we must add that in 24, where the shades of the dead suitors, guided by Hermes, make their way down into the Underworld. These also cross Okeanos (how we are not told) and as well the Leukas rock, the gates of Helios, and the land of dreams, but here again, no rivers in the Underworld itself. From here they pass quickly to the actual residence of the dead, once again in meadows of asphodel. But before they join the others, we are treated to a lengthy exchange between the shades of Achilleus and Agamemnon, who seem not at all hindered by the general incognizance of the dead which was the rule in *Odyssey* 10 and 11. Likewise, when the suitors do arrive, Agamemnon questions Amphimedon on the reason for his demise, and Amphimedon has no difficulty in responding. This detail is no doubt a narrative convenience: if shades cannot speak intelligently to each other, there is no point in staging an Underworld scene of this sort. Nevertheless, the poet's seeming ability to maneuver freely in concocting this (relatively unnecessary) encounter may tell us something about early conceptions of the land of the dead. Subsequent to Homer there is very little preserved on the geography or rationale of Hades. The rather confused section of Hesiod's *Theogony* after the defeat of the Titans seems to place the entrance near the homes of Nyx and her children, Hypnos and Thanatos, before which Atlas stands (*Th* 736–66). The remainder of the description is devoted to the watchdog Kerberos, who wags his tail at those coming down but eats anyone attempting to leave (*Th* 767–73). Homer, it should be noted, never mentions Kerberos by name, and he is conveniently absent when Odysseus arrives (perhaps because Odysseus does not actually enter the Underworld), but both the *Iliad* (8.367–68) and the *Odyssey* (11.263) are acquainted with Herakles' task of fetching "the dog." The Hesiodic Corpus seems to have included an account of the descent of Theseus and Peirithoos into Hades to abduct Persephone, but the only surviving fragment is a dialogue between Theseus and Meleagros (Hes fr 280 MW); we have already seen that there was similarly an account of this *katabasis* in the shadowy epic *Minyas*. According to Pausanias (10.28.7) the *Nostoi* also included some description of the Underworld, perhaps in connection with Agamemnon's death. Stesichoros seems to have written an entire poem entitled *Kerberos* of which we know nothing; one would suspect that it dealt with Herakles' exploits, like the *Kyknos* and *Geryoneis* of the same author. Possibly it contained some of the same material as Bakchylides' Ode 5, where Herakles (rather than Theseus) interviews Meleagros on route to obtaining the dog (5.56–175). As often in this genre, however, Bakchylides' story begins and ends abruptly, and there is no attempt to set the scene; we learn only that the shades are gathered by the river Kokytos.

In Theognis' brief reference to Sisyphos (707–12), there is mention of the dark gates of Hades, but nothing about rivers. From our list of Aischylos' lost plays there are two titles actually dealing with Sisyphos: *Sisyphos Drapetes* ("Runaway") and *Sisyphos Petrokylistes* ("Stone-roller"). If these really are two separate plays,[7] it would seem likely that the *Petrokylistes* actually took place in the Underworld, with perhaps even a personal appearance by Hades or Persephone. But we may be also dealing with alternate titles for a play set above ground, after Sisyphos has escaped from the Underworld. Another lost play, the *Psychagogoi* ("Shade-summoners"), appears to have dramatized Odysseus' encounter with the shades in the *Nekuia*, since it contained a prediction of his death by (presumably) Teiresias (fr 275 R). But the title in any case suggests that here, as in the *Odyssey*, the shades come up out of Hades, so that Aischylos may not have presented a great deal in the way of eschatology.

Finally, we return to Polygnotos' painting for the Knidians at Delphi. In addition to the ferryman, Polygnotos' version of Hades has two other surprising elements: ordinary men punished for their deeds on earth (cf. *Batr* 145–51, where perjurers and various other wrongdoers are in a pool of mud), and a death demon named Eurynomos (10.28.7). Among these ordinary men are one who was not just to his father (and is being strangled by that same father), and one who had stolen holy things (being tormented in some unspecified way by a woman skilled in the use of drugs). Eurynomos is described as between dark blue and black (like the color of meat flies), showing his teeth, and reclining on a vulture's hide. Pausanias adds that neither the *Odyssey,* the *Nostoi,* nor the *Minyas* mentions this creature; he notes also that, according to the local guides, Eurynomos is accustomed to eating flesh from the bones of corpses. Here again we seem to be in a world very much in contrast with that of Homer's incorporeal shades. But from this point on, the painting reverts back to familiar themes: a series of mythological figures, all shown in relaxed postures. Among them, as in the *Nekuia,* are famous women (not always the same ones), heroes from Troy, and transgressors, including Peirithoos and Theseus, Sisyphos, Tantalos, and Tityos (who is said to have been wasted away by his punishment). From folktales, one presumes, is the figure called Oknos (Sloth) who sits plaiting a rope that a donkey next to him promptly eats. Finally, Pausanias describes two women, one young, one old, who are carrying water in broken pots, with a common inscription calling them "of the noninitiated women" (10.31.9). Shortly thereafter he comes to four more such figures, a boy, a young woman, and an old man and woman, all carrying water to a pithos (10.31.11); he supposes (rightly or wrongly) that these, like the others, are people who ignored the rites of Eleusis. We will consider below in discussing Tartaros some further pictorial evidence for these so-called Amyetoi.

So much our Archaic sources offer on the nature of the Underworld and existence there; if the emergence of people like Charon and Eurynomos no earlier than the fifth century is not simply an accident of preservation, it may be that this period saw a general influx of new ideas drawn from folktale beliefs. About Tartaros we are rather better informed, although here the rules for admittance are in some doubt. The *Odyssey* never mentions the name, not even in the *Nekuia* when the punishment of classic transgressors is described (perhaps because there is no suggestion that these transgressors are in a separate place). But in the *Iliad* Zeus threatens to send any god who opposes him down to Tartaros (*Il* 8.10–16), and here we learn that the place is the deepest gulf *(berethron)* under the earth, closed in by iron gates and a bronze threshold and as far below Hades as *ouranos* is from earth. Two other references in the *Iliad* place the Titans (specifically Iapetos and Kronos) in this darkness, at the lowest limits of earth and sea, where they delight in neither sun nor winds, sitting with deep Tartaros all about them (*Il* 14.274, 278–79; 8.478–91). Presumably this is also the intent of *Iliad* 5.898, where Ares almost winds up "lower than the children of Ouranos."

In the *Theogony* we find an actual account of the placing of the Titans in this grim prison (*Th* 713–45). The Hundred-Handers rush out onto the battlefield between Olympos and Othrys after Zeus has hurled his thunderbolt, bind their opponents, and send them as far beneath the earth as earth is from *oura-*

nos, into gloomy Tartaros. The distance is made more impressive by the image of the bronze anvil falling nine days and nights to reach earth from *ouranos*, and nine more days and nights to reach Tartaros from earth, but we must still note that this is not quite as deep as in the *Iliad's* version, where the second distance is measured from Hades, not earth. Hesiod goes on to speak of a brazen wall or fence, and of night poured in three layers about the neck, as if he envisioned Tartaros as a bottle. What follows this description, however, is rather more confused, and has often been considered as a later addition not entirely worked out (*Th* 734–43).⁸ We are told that in this place where the Titans are imprisoned (guarded, as we have already seen, by the Hundred-Handers) are the sources and limits of all things, of earth and Tartaros and sea and starry *ouranos*, a harsh, gloomy, dank realm. Here too (or perhaps it is the same thing) is a great chasm, the bottom of which one might not reach in a year, so strong are the blasts of wind. The home of Nyx then appears, and we are suddenly in the far west, with no further explanation of how this chasm relates to Tartaros or the roots of all things. Possibly the poet meant to suggest something of the *Theogony's* original Chaos as the first condition of things.

We have seen that both the *Iliad* and the *Theogony* know of Tartaros only as the prison of the Titans (and a place into which Olympians might be hurled as well); no human transgressors of the sort required are mentioned in either poem. Neither does Hesiod think to place Prometheus there (Atlas is obviously not a possibility). In the *Odyssey*, as we found, the opposite holds; a few select mortals are punished after death, but not in Tartaros or any other special place. From the *Homeric Hymn to Apollo* we have again a reference to the Titans dwelling in Tartaros (*HAp* 335–36), while in the *Ehoiai* Apollo himself is nearly cast down there after he has slain the Kyklopes (Hes fr 54 MW), and in the *Hymn to Hermes* the son of Leto threatens Hermes with the same fate if the latter does not reveal the whereabouts of the stolen cattle (*HHerm* 256–59). After the customary mention of great darkness and gloom, this last threat continues rather cryptically with the idea that there Hermes would rule among few men (meaning the Titans?). The passage of the *Return of the Atreidai* (probably the *Nostoi* of the Cycle) mentioned above shows Tantalos punished by being placed under a large rock that perpetually threatens to fall (*Nostoi* fr 4 PEG). From the nature of his transgression here (asking for the pleasures of the gods), we might have expected that this fate would be carried out on Olympos or else at his home in Sipylos, but Pausanias does say that the *Nostoi* discussed the Underworld, and this would be the most likely place for what after all must be a digression. Even so, there is no guarantee that the *Nostoi* mentioned Tartaros at all, or placed Tantalos in it. Similarly, Pausanias claims that the *Minyas* dealt with the punishment of Amphion in Hades occasioned by his rejection of Leto and her children (9.5.8–9); we have no idea what such a punishment would be.

If this assessment from admittedly scanty material is correct, it would appear that Tartaros in the beginning is a place of confinement for gods alone, that is, Titans and (though in threat only) recalcitrant Olympians who do not mind their betters. Confinement or punishment of *mortals* anywhere under the earth (Hades or Tartaros) occurs only in the *Nekuia* (precisely that section of it most likely to be a post-Homeric addition[9]), the *Nostoi*, and the *Minyas*, to which we should add Sisyphos and his rock from the Foce del Sele metopes (no #) and numerous Attic Black-Figure pots. And not until the *Ehoiai* do we find a mortal (namely Salmoneus) specifically cast down into *Tartaros* for wrongdoing (Hes fr 30 MW). The source in question is a papyrus fragment not without gaps, but it seems clear that Salmoneus suffers for his presumption in imitating Zeus, who personally imprisons him; no more specific chastisement is mentioned. One wonders, since men (unlike gods) must die and leave the light of the sun in any case, whether simple confinement in such a place was thought more terrible than an existence in Hades.

From other Archaic sources there is little evidence. In the *Aspis* we see that after the Keres have disposed of warriors on the battlefield, the shade goes down to chill Tartaros, just as if that were the normal residence of the dead (254–55). The text as transmitted to us adds the words "to Hades" in apposition, as if the poet supposed the two places to be identical, but the line in question contains a metrical anomaly, and "to Hades" probably represents an attempt to fill in a gap.[10] Even so, we are beginning to see some imprecision in the use of terms, if a writer can describe Tartaros rather than Hades as the normal receiver of the shades of the dead. The same development appears in a poem of Anakreon where the poet, in describing the terrors of old age and impending death, says that he frequently weeps, fearing Tartaros, and adds "for the pit of Hades is dreadful" (395 *PMG*). Here Tartaros and Hades must denote the same place. There is no discussion of transgressions while on earth; the poet simply fears Tartaros because he fears the end of life. So too in Pindar's *Paian* 4 (42–45), a land and people are cast down by the gods into Tartaros. Elsewhere we find that both Stesichoros (254 *PMG*) and Alkaios (286 LP) mention the place, but with no usable context. On the other hand, Pherekydes of Syros offers some interesting ideas in a comment on Zeus' treatment of Hephaistos in *Iliad* 1: the Harpuiai and Thyella (Storm-wind) guard Tartaros, and it is a place to which Zeus banishes gods for transgressions (7B5). Possibly the presence of Thyella is related to Hesiod's notion of a chasm with strong blasts of wind; in any case, here again Tartaros is a prison for gods.

From the fifth century there is likewise almost nothing. In Aischylos' *Prometheus Desmotes* the Titan is threatened with transfer to a place that is not named but is certainly Tartaros, to judge from its description (*PD* 1018–21, 1028–29, 1050–52; earlier in the same play Kronos and his colleagues are, as usual, placed there (*PD* 219–21). The *Desmotes* also confirms that Tartaros is below Hades and thus not for this poet identical with it (*PD* 152–54). In the *Eumenides* we are told that the Erinyes dwell in Tartaros, but this may be just a means of characterizing them as fearsome creatures. Both this play and the *Hiketides* offer certain intimations of punishment after death, as we have seen in discussing the god Hades, yet nowhere is Tartaros mentioned in such a context, not even when the Erinyes threaten Orestes with various torments. Still another Aischylean drama already noted, the *Sisyphos Petrokylistes*, might actually have been set in Tartaros if it was different from the *Drapetes*. Here, however, we might ask whether Sisyphos is ever in Tartaros, even though the *Nekuia* does associate him with Tantalos and Tityos. His punishment after all is decreed by Hades as a means of keeping him in his realm, whereas those in Tartaros are placed there by Zeus, and it is perhaps territory not governed by the lord of the Underworld. In all, were it not for the papyrus fragment from the *Ehoiai*, one would be very tempted to say that the equation of Tartaros with a place where mortal transgressors are punished is no earlier than Plato's *Gorgias*, where the closing vision makes the idea quite explicit (523b). As it is, there must be more to the picture than we can see, but one can still suggest with some confidence that Tartaros was not originally intended for any but gods, and then simply for their imprisonment, a purpose considered its sole function for much of the Archaic period. One might also wonder if the appearance of mortals in Tartaros is in any way connected with the exit of the older gods from that place after they have been released by Zeus.

Finally, there are several puzzling representations of watercarriers in the Underworld to be considered in conjunction with those from Polygnotos' Nekuia noted above.[11] On a Black-Figure amphora of about 525 B.C., we see the familiar figure of Sisyphos with his rock, thus guaranteeing that we are in the Underworld, but we also see, to his left and given equal prominence in the composition, four smaller winged figures in short tunics bringing water in jugs to a large pithos and pouring it in (Munich 1493). From their attire the figures are presumably male; there is no indication that either jugs or pithos fail to hold the water. On a slightly later lekythos we find a similar scene of watercarriers but without Sisyphos; the figures, now clearly male and female and no longer winged, carry the jugs on their heads as they hasten to the pithos (Palermo 996). In front of this pithos is a donkey and to the left an old man looking lost in thought, possibly Oknos as Pausanias saw him with a donkey in the Nekuia of Polygnotos.

From these puzzling illustrations we turn to Plato, in whose *Gorgias* Sokrates tells Kallikles that the licentious and unperceiving are the Amyetoi, the uninitiated, and that in the Underworld they will be fated to carry water in pierced sieves to an equally pierced pithos (493b; cf. *Rep* 2.363d). Obviously Plato here creates his own, ethically oriented definition of what uninitiated means, but comparison with Polygnotos' watercarriers and the inscription over the first two of them suggests that Plato has borrowed an idea from mysteries of some sort in which those who did not participate, the Amyetoi, were condemned like Sisyphos to an endless task. As a result we should probably conclude that the figures on the two sixth-century Attic vases are suffering a similar penalty. Their crime, however, is less certain; even in Polygnotos' painting we cannot say for sure what mysteries they are accused of ignoring, or if the punishment shown was always the traditional one. One doubts though that they are figures from any specific Greek myth; the one obvious group of candidates, the Danaides, are surely excluded by the presence of males in the paintings. We will see in chapter 6 that this or any other penalty for the Danaides is probably a relatively late idea.

Last in our survey of mythical Greek afterlife, there is the Elysian plain or, in its other manifestation, the Isles of the Blessed. We first encounter this concept in the *Odyssey*, from the sea god Proteus, who tells Menelaos in *Odyssey* 4 that the latter will not die or come upon his fate in Argos, but that the immortals will send him to the Elysian plain and the ends of the earth, where dwells Rhadamanthys and where there is the easiest possible way of life for mortals: no snow or rain, but always soft cooling breezes from Okeanos (*Od* 4.561–69). The reason for this reward is then added in one line: Menelaos is married to Helen, and is thus a son-in-law of Zeus. Such information, which Proteus furnishes rather gratuitously, raises several questions. If Menelaos is not even to die, when will he arrive at this paradise, and what will become of his old age? Will Helen go with him? Why is he singled out for this honor, when Zeus has so many mortal children? (Admittedly, he has no other mortal daughter, and thus no son-in-law, but when does he ever appear fond of Helen?) And why is Rhadamanthys there but not (in the *Nekuia* at least) his brother Minos? Such queries remain unanswered, but we should note that in Alkman (7 *PMG*) Menelaos seems to be living with the Dioskouroi in Therapnai after death; Therapnai is a place where, in Pindar, we also find the Dioskouroi when they are not on Olympos or in Hades (*Py* 11.61–64; *Nem* 10.55–57; cf. Pher 3F109, where one Aithalides [at AR 1.51–55 a son of Hermes and an Argonaut] by the grace of that god spends time in "places under the earth, as well as in Hades" [one day in turn in each, according to Σ AR 1.643f]). Thus, there seems to be a general tradition of special treatment for this Atreid, perhaps linked to the unusual afterlife of his brothers-in-law. The *Iliad* knows nothing of any such place; given the emphasis on the inevitability of death in the poem, even for Achilleus, we may safely assume that it plays no part in the poet's worldview. In the *Odyssey*, magical elements (and the opportunity to become a god) are more in evidence, but nevertheless the *Nekuia* shows us a wide range of people, including Achilleus, Agamemnon, and Aias, with no suggestion that they might have found another fate. Odysseus himself, who might have been promised such a reward, is told by Teiresias only of his old age and death, and we are left to conclude, if we think about such matters, that one's shrewdest course of action is to marry into high places.

Turning from Homer to Proklos' summary of the *Aithiopis*, we see that after Memnon has been slain by Achilleus, Eos obtains for her son immortality from Zeus (p. 69 *PEG*). Nothing is said about where he will live in this summary, but at its end, after Achilleus in turn has been slain, Thetis comes, mourns for her child, and then, snatching him up from the pyre, takes him to the White Island *(Leukê Nêsos)*. Proklos has no more details, and we are left to guess that some sort of blissful future existence is intended. In lyric poetry, Ibykos not only brings Achilleus to the Elysian plain, but also unites him to Medeia in marriage (291 *PMG*); our scholiast source tells us that Simonides did likewise. The same source specifies that Ibykos was the first to offer "this" innovation; presumably he refers to the marriage rather than the translation. Either way, the use of the actual term "Elysian plain" by these two poets is less than certain: since the scholion in question is a comment on lines from Apollonios' *Argonautika* in which the Elysian plain is named, the scholiast may have picked up the phrase from his text rather than from Ibykos or Simonides. For what it is worth, the word "Elysian" does not otherwise surface between its appearances in *Odyssey* 4 and Apollonios (it does appear in *AP* 2.13, but as part of the introduction to one of the Cyzicene Epigrams, not the actual text). Ibykos seems to have made Diomedes immortal as well, perhaps even married to Hermione and living with the Dioskouroi (294 *PMG*: ascription of this last part uncertain).

On the other hand, the *Works & Days* of Hesiod has its own ideas about a blissful afterlife. The fourth race of men was created by Zeus, we are told, and these were the *hêmitheoi*, or demi-gods (*W&D* 156–73). Some perished at Thebes fighting over the flocks of Oidipous, others at Troy trying to bring back Helen. And of these heroes some (or all) the limit of death has covered over, but to others (or again all)[12] apart from men Zeus gives a life at the ends of the earth, and they have uncaring spirits on the islands of the blessed ones next to deep-eddying Okeanos. Here the earth produces food for them three times a year, and so presumably they have a life of ease. The similarity of location between this paradise and that predicted for Menelaos in the *Odyssey* is obvious, and we may suppose that they are probably two versions of the same idea, but Hesiod is not much clearer than Homer on the details. If in fact not all heroes of this age are found there (as I suspect), he certainly offers no criteria by which Zeus might select some members of the race but not others, nor whether the fortunate ones bypass death. Not surprisingly for Hesiod, the major characteristic of this world is that the earth produces food in abundance; one does not have to labor over the land. Whether from the beginning it was the residence of heroes is another uncertain question: *makarôn* ("blessed ones") is a term usually applied to the gods, so that these islands may have been conceived in origin as a habitation of the Olympians. Alternatively, since we do see these gods dining with the Aithiopes at the beginning of the *Iliad*, perhaps the Isles of the Blessed were originally intended as a place where mortals and gods might come together. One last complication in Hesiod's version is the presence in some papyrus texts of three lines, following those just discussed, which relate that Kronos rules over those on the islands, having been released (presumably from Tartaros) by Zeus. We saw in considering Kronos that these lines are completely missing from our manuscript tradition as well as from a third papyrus; since it is much easier to understand why they should have been added than dropped, they are probably a subsequent accretion.[13]

Yet another problem arises when we turn to the fragment of the *Ehoiai* in which the suitors of Helen gather (Hes fr 204 MW). At the point in question (ll. 95–103) the papyrus is quite mutilated, but Zeus is somehow preparing to destroy or eliminate a race of *hêmitheoi*, so that the "children of the gods" will not be further associated with mere mortals, who must suffer and die, but rather that these "blessed ones" might live as before apart from men. If "blessed ones" could here mean the gods themselves, the sense would be that in future they will cease to consort with mortals, thus bringing the age of heroes to an end. But, given the demonstrative, they seem rather the children of the gods, the heroes themselves (as at *W&D* 141) who return to some sort of primeval golden age, perhaps inspired by that envisioned for Hesiod's first race. Not impossibly the Catalogue Poet here intends to align himself with *Works & Days* 156–73; if so (since he cannot mean that *all* heroes of the Fourth Age are brought to some paradise when certain lesser mortals are left behind) we must consider whether in his view those directly descended from the gods were chosen and others excluded. But little else in the Archaic tradition suggests that such children stood apart from other men (even if they were often more favored) and perhaps the poet meant something else that we have not yet guessed.

From the fifth century we have Pindar's description of the other world that hopefully awaits his patron Theron of Akragas in *Olympian* 2.56–83. Here details are in greater abundance—golden flowers growing on trees and in the water, soft breezes, the rule of Rhadamanthys *and* Kronos—and the term "islands of the blessed" is specifically used. It is a world, too, without labor and without tears. Pindar clearly means to describe a future accessible to people of his own time, rather than mythological heroes, and thus his somewhat mystical criteria for access need not concern us. He does, however, name three more occupants, in addition to Rhadamanthys and Kronos: Kadmos, Peleus, and Achilleus, the last brought by his mother after she has persuaded Zeus. A fragmentary passage from one of Pindar's dirges appears to speak of the same place, although this must be guessed from the context (fr 129 SM). In this account we find eternal sunlight, meadows with red roses, incense, and golden fruit, while the residents occupy themselves with horses, or the lyre, or draughts, the first mention of the need for entertainment. But the fragment says nothing further, and we must remember again that this was a world envisioned primarily for real people. Pindar at *Nemean* 10.7 also makes Diomedes immortal (as has Ibykos before him), and Hellanikos adds one other name: Lykos, son of Poseidon and Kelaino, an otherwise totally obscure offspring whom his father settles on the islands of the blessed (4F19).

Finally, we have a brief reference in a line from what was apparently a popular song, in which it is claimed that the Athenian Harmodios, slayer of Peisistratos' son Hipparchos, is not dead, but rather on the islands of the blessed together with Achilleus and Diomedes (894 *PMG*). The date of the song cannot be determined precisely, but presumably it falls somewhere in the fifth century B.C., and at least demonstrates that the notion of such an afterlife was by this time a widely based concept. Yet there is oddly no trace of it in any of our preserved tragedies, not even in Euripides (where predictions of a happy future are such a staple feature), save for a passing reference to Achilleus as ruling somewhere in the Propontis (*And* 1259–62). But we should remember that Aischylos seems to have written a play about the death of Achilleus, to judge from the fragment of it which Plato quotes in the second book of the *Republic* (fr 350 R), and the question of an afterlife may have been taken up there. Certainly it surfaces again in Pausanias, where we find Achilleus and Helen blissfully joined together on the same White Island found in the *Aithiopis* (3.19.13). On the whole, and leaving aside the puzzling case of Menelaos, one might speculate that the epic tradition was not happy with the fate assigned to Achilleus in the *Iliad* and *Odyssey,* and that the creation of a special afterlife for him then paved the way for a select group of heroes to follow. But it may also be that such ideas are much older than the *Iliad* and *Odyssey,* and reflect a world in which great heroes commonly avoided the dark realms of Hades.

Minor Divinities

The great majority of minor gods in Greek myth are generated from divinities of the times prior to the coming of the Olympians, and have been treated above in chapter 1 according to the sequence in which they appear in the *Theogony*. There are, however, yet other figures, perhaps known to Hesiod, perhaps not, who also leave their mark in the Archaic period. First among these, we may consider the Satyroi and Silenoi. Neither entity is mentioned at all by Homer or Hesiod. Satyroi first appear in a fragment of the *Ehoiai* dealing with the offspring of Doros, son of Hellen (Hes fr 10a.17–19 [*olim* 123] and 10b MW); here someone ("Hekateros": corrupt) and a daughter of Phoroneus beget five daughters who in turn become the mothers of these creatures. No father is named, and no physical description given, only the information that the Satyroi are worthless and not suited for work. From these same five daughters, according to the fragment, spring the mountain Nymphai and the Kouretes, who are thus siblings of the Satyroi. But nowhere do we find mention of Dionysos, either in the three lines of the fragment quoted by Strabo, or the larger context of the papyrus now shown to be the home of those lines. That larger context does, though, give us the name "Iphthime" (Hes fr 10a.13 MW), and since she reappears in Nonnos as a daughter of Doros and mother of the Satyroi (or a good many of them) by the god Hermes (14.105–17), it seems very likely that the name "Hekateros" in Strabo conceals Doros (with the first syllable the preposition *ek*). The *Ehoiai* then probably made Iphthime and her sisters daughters of Doros who consort with gods (perhaps others besides Hermes) to produce the Satyroi (plus the Nymphai and Kouretes). That Hermes should be the father is perhaps the most logical way to explain the unusual form of these creatures, given that he serves the same role in the begetting of the goatish Pan.

For the Silenoi, on the other hand, the first reference is in the *Homeric Hymn to Aphrodite* (262–63): after her union with Anchises the goddess instructs him that the child Aineias will be reared by the mountain Nymphai, "with whom the Silenoi and the watcher Argeiphontes mingle in love in the recesses of fair caves." Again no physical description, and this is the entire extent of our knowledge of either group in the eighth and seventh centuries. In the sixth we begin to find artistic representations, and these constitute our first real evidence for appearance.[14] Foremost is the François Krater, on which three figures, named "Silenoi," and sporting equine ears, tails, and hind legs, accompany Dionysos as he brings Hephaistos back to Olympos: one carries a wineskin, one plays the double pipes, and the third embraces one of the Nymphai (so named) who are bringing up the rear (Florence 4209). Similar figures also appear in the same scene on a Black-Figure dinos of the mid-sixth century now in Paris (Louvre E876), but here they mingle with human-legged counterparts who also possess equine tails. On a slightly later amphora in Würzburg the same combination is found in a context of pursued women (Würzburg 252). Elsewhere in sixth-century Black-Figure the human-legged type is on the whole more common (beginning with the creature on Agora P334[15]), and often shown in great numbers without any presence of the equine type (so, e.g., on Lydos' New York Return of Hephaistos: NY 31.11.11). Yet the equine type does not entirely disappear: even toward the end of the century a belly-amphora by the Painter of Berlin 1686 shows three human-legged figures with the appropriate ears and tails moving toward one who is equine-legged (Berlin:PM F1697), while a neck-amphora from the circle of the Antimenes Painter has two such creatures with human feet to either side of a third with hooves, as all three proceed in the same direction and play the cithara (Berlin:Ch Inv 1966.1). From these examples it seems unlikely that sixth-century Athenians at least made any serious distinction between the equine- and human-legged versions of the beings under discussion. Possibly the first were originally thought of as Silenoi and the second as Satyroi, but as early as the middle of the century a kylix signed by Ergotimos presents a figure named "Silenos" with human legs and a horse's tail (Berlin:Ch VI 3151); thus, if there was any such distinction it would seem to be lost early.[16] As a final piece of the puzzle we should add an Attic Red-Figure kylix of the last quarter of the sixth century (Ambrosios Painter) in Würzburg (474 [H1646]). Here the name "Satyros" appears for the first time on a pot (and for the first time anywhere since the Hesiodic Corpus). The figure to which the name is attached has again human legs and a horse's tail; part of his form has been broken away, but the top of the tail is clear, and the fully preserved companion on the other side of the centrally placed Dionysos provides a means to check the artist's intention. This companion, however, is specifically named ("Eukrates"), and thus the possibility arises that "Satyros," too, was here (and elsewhere?) understood as a personal rather than a generic name.

Elsewhere in the sixth century we also find both these types of Satyroi/ Silenoi, but with no indication at all of how they were named. The equine format with horse's hind legs occurs on two of the metopes from Heraion I at

Foce del Sele; each metope shows two such figures striding left, with stones poised for throwing. Unfortunately, the target of their aggression was on a third metope that cannot be definitely identified in what remains; the usual interpretation derives from the later-attested tale that Herakles defended Hera from assault by such creatures, and there is a metope preserved which may well show Hera and Herakles together in an appropriate pose.[17] Equine legs are likewise found on the Chalkidian Phineus cup in Würzburg (164: *c.* 530 B.C.) where the figures in question are creeping up on unsuspecting women. In Sparta, on the other hand, sixth-century bronze statuettes offer figures who have all the requisite qualities from the neck up, but human legs and no tails whatever (e.g., Athens 7544, perhaps from a tripod).

As Attic art moves toward the end of the century the human-legged (and horse-tailed) variety appear more and more frequently as the retinue of Dionysos. What Athenians normally called them at this time is, as we saw, unclear. But we do know that eventually the Attic tragedies of the last quarter of the century were joined by satyr plays, and that these featured choruses made up to look like Satyroi/Silenoi. Illustrations of such productions (for example, lascivious attacks on Iris and Hera) certainly seem to appear in fifth-century Attic vase-painting, and what we find there are the familiar horse tails and ears, and human feet.[18] In drama, then, at any rate, these creatures were commonly known as Satyroi. Whether they were also called (there or in other contexts) Silenoi is another matter, but certainly at some point the two names fused, since in both Sophokles' *Ichneutai* and Euripides' *Kyklops* the chorus of Satyroi is accompanied by a leader named "Silenos" who is their father. By this time, too, such figures have taken on more goatish qualities, with a much shorter tail and hooves, to judge from their appearance on Attic vases after 450 B.C. Aischylos' lost *Prometheus Pyrkaeus*, presented in 472 B.C., might seem to anticipate that development, since a preserved fragment tantalizingly compares the chorus of Satyroi to goats (fr 207 R). Yet the joke involved does not guarantee that Satyroi looked like goats, but only that they had beards. In all, we must admit severe limits to our information for the Archaic period. Perhaps Satyroi and Silenoi were originally different figures, but perhaps too one of those names was originally personal and the other generic, or both were generic and designated the same creature in different regions.

The activities of the figures we do find on sixth- and early fifth-century pottery are largely what one would expect of Dionysos' companions: drinking, flute-playing, dancing and acrobatics, and erotic endeavors, mostly directed toward Mainades and innocent-looking young women (Nymphai?), but occasionally toward the donkey that Dionysos rides. On quite a number of vases the ladies involved seem to be warding off their admirers, although no great force is employed on either side, and the effect is presumably meant to be comic. The same should probably be said of a cup by Epiktetos in London on which Satyroi are portrayed armed for battle (to support Dionysos against the Gigantes?: London E3). Several Black-Figure pots also show them engaged with

Dionysos in a more constructive activity, namely the collecting of grapes and making of wine (e.g., Boston 63.952; Basel Kä 420). On what evidence we have, however, their amatory inclinations are the oldest part of their character, and it has even been suggested that their link with Dionysos is a subsequent development.

Of one other related tale, the capture of a figure named "Silenos" by Midas, there are a number of illustrations in the Archaic period.[19] Earliest is probably the Black-Figure kylix signed by Ergotimos as potter mentioned above, showing Silenos (so named) being led away as prisoner between two men, the first of whom holds a wineskin (Berlin:Ch VI 3151); as with the Würzburg cup showing a Satyros, we cannot say whether the name was meant to be personal or generic. The usual assumption is that this and later such scenes reflect the capture of Silenos as noted by Herodotos (8.138: the capture takes place in Midas' rose garden) and Xenophon (who sets the event at a fountain and calls the victim a Satyros: Anab 1.2.13). From close to the same period (c. 560 B.C.) are two Lakonian cups, each with a Silenos figure approaching the fountain house (clearly denoted) as his pursuers close in (VG 57231; Berlin:Ch WS 4). The conclusion of this whole action is first shown on a sieve (or other spherically shaped) vase in Eleusis from after the middle of the century: Hermes stands before a seated man, surely Midas, with behind the god a Silenos approaching, hands bound and tethered to another man who accompanies him (Eleusis 1231). Toward the end of the sixth century the Acheloos Painter presents this Silenos engaged in drinking from the fountain's lion-spout as two men with spears crouch behind him (NY 49.11.1); on a lekythos (London 1910.2–12.1) and a Red-Figure column krater (Cahn Coll 191) of the period we see one or more of these ambushers (with coiled ropes) on the roof of the fountain house as their quarry drinks.

The emphasis on drinking in these scenes is no doubt explained by the fourth-century writer Theopompos, who has the capture accomplished by putting wine in the fountain so as to make Silenos drunk (115F75a, b). Another reference to the same author says nothing about such a capture but does have Silenos and Midas converse with each other, in the course of which Silenos recites to Midas wondrous tales of faraway places (115F75c; cf. TD 1.48.114, where Silenos secures his release with some highly pessimistic philosophizing). In Ovid, Silenos simply becomes separated from Dionysos and finds Midas celebrating Bacchic revels; the king entertains him as an honored guest of the festival for ten days and then takes him back to the god, who in gratitude grants him a wish, the ill-fated power of turning things to gold (Met 11.89–105; so too Fab 191). Silenos as an individual character also appears in a fragment of Pindar (fr 156 SM), where he is very strong, a dancer, raised on Maleia, and the husband of Nais. Since Nais is here the personified archetypal river-Nymph, it may be that her husband is simply the archetypal Silenos. In passing we may note, too, that Herodotos calls Marsyas a Silenos (7.26); unfortunately, there are no preserved early artistic representations of his story.

Finally, there are two items that, although late, are of interest: Apollodoros says that the Kentauros Pholos was the offspring of Silenos and a Nymph (Ap*B* 2.5.4), while Pausanias comments that the oldest of the Satyroi are called Silenoi (1.23.5). This last remark recalls what we found above in Sophokles and Euripides: a Father Silenos who probably reflects a common belief of that time and later. Based on the artistic evidence, it would not appear to have been a conception of the Archaic period, though the balding Silenos/Satyros face on many Greek and Etruscan terracotta antefixes of the sixth century may indicate otherwise.

Satyroi and Silenoi lead inevitably, as the *Hymn to Aphrodite* has already demonstrated, to the Nymphai. In the *Iliad* the word *nymphê* appears some nine times. On one occasion it is used to address Helen (*Il* 3.130), on another it refers to Marpessa as a bride (*Il* 9.560), and on Achilleus' shield it denotes brides in general (*Il* 18.492). But elsewhere it clearly describes nature spirits. Three of these bear sons to mortals, and these sons fight and die at Troy (*Il* 6.21–26; 14.444–45; 20.383–85). In each case the Nymph is also a *nêis*, "river/spring spirit," which seems to be a subcategory of Nymph. Another such category is represented by the *nymphai orestiades*, mountain Nymphai and daughters of Zeus, who plant elms around the tomb of Andromache's father Eetion (*Il* 6.419). In *Iliad* 24, Sipylos, where Niobe goes to mourn, is called the site of the beds of the *theaôn nymphaôn*, "goddess Nymphai" (*Il* 24.615–16). And at the beginning of *Iliad* 20, when Zeus instructs Themis to assemble all the gods, even the Nymphai who dwell in groves, springs, and meadows are present (*Il* 20.8–9).

In the *Odyssey*, the term "Nymph" is used somewhat more loosely. Eurykleia applies it to Penelope in direct address (*Od* 4.743), as Iris did to Helen in the *Iliad*, but it is also used repeatedly (in narration, not address) of Kalypso (*Od* 1.14 and *Od* 5 *passim*), and even once of Kirke (although that occasion represents a formulaic line previously used for Kalypso: *Od* 10.543 = 5.230). Thoosa, daughter of Phorkys and mother by Poseidon of Polyphemos, is likewise called Nymph (*Od* 1.71–73), and so too the daughters of Helios (*Od* 12.132). But there are, nevertheless, some real Nymphai as well: these flush out goats for Odysseus and his men (*Od* 9.154), and sport with Artemis as part of a comparison with Nausikaa (*Od* 6.105–8); in both cases, they are daughters of Zeus. On the latter occasion Odysseus also thinks of Nymphai who dwell in mountains, springs, and meadows when he wakes from his exhausted slumber on the beach of Phaiakia (*Od* 6.122–24). And there is one particular class of Nymphai, here again Naiades, whom we encounter only on Ithaka: a cave in the harbor of Phorkys is sacred to them, and Odysseus, who used to sacrifice to them there, calls them daughters of Zeus as he prays to them for assistance (*Od* 13.103–4, 347–50, 355–60; 17.210–11, 240–46).

Turning from Homer to Hesiod, we find only two brief references to Nymphai, both in the *Theogony*: they are said as goddesses to inhabit the glades of the hillsides (*Th* 129–30), and those of them called Meliai are sprung, like the Erinyes and the Gigantes, from the blood of the castrated Ouranos (*Th* 187). As we will see in chapter 4, these Meliai are the source of the race of bronze which Zeus fashions *ek melian* in the *Works & Days* that is, out of ash trees or from the Nymphai of those trees (*W&D* 145). From the Hesiodic Corpus there are three notices. In one, spoken by a Naiad (who calls herself a Nymph), we learn that the lifespan of the Nymphai, daughters of Zeus, is ten times that of the phoenix, which in turn is nine times that of the raven, and so forth (Hes fr 304 MW); the final total is uncertain, since everything is based on the lifespan of humans, but it is clear that the Nymphai, although extremely long-lived, do not live forever (the passage does not call them goddesses). The second passage, that already noted in connection with the first appearance of the Satyroi, makes them sisters of those Satyroi and of the Kouretes (all as offspring of the daughters of [probably] Doros), and does call them goddesses, as well as mountain Nymphai (Hes fr 10a.17–19 MW). The third fragment names five particular Nymphai—Phaisyle, Koronis, Kleia, Phaio, and Eudore—whom men call the Hyades (Hes fr 291 MW); we shall come back to these in chapter 6.

The *Homeric Hymns* also offer some information. The poet of the *Hymn to Hermes* calls the god's mother Maia a Nymph on six different occasions, and on one of these a mountain Nymph (*oureiê nymphê* at *HHerm* 244: she lives, after all, in a cave on Mount Kyllene). She is never called daughter of Atlas in this poem, although that title surfaces in *Hymn* 18, where the word "Nymph" is again found (*HomH* 18.4, 7); we might remember, for whatever it is worth, that Kalypso is also a daughter of Atlas. In *Hymn* 19, Pan dances with choruses of mountain Nymphai, and his mother is so named, although she is the daughter of one Dryops and the word here probably means no more than "marriageable girl" (*HomH* 19.19–23, 34). In *Hymn* 26, the Nymphai receive Dionysos as a child from Zeus, rear him on Mount Nysa, and follow him as leader when he is grown (*HomH* 26.3–10); these last details should make us wonder whether the poet does not intend us to understand the nurses of Dionysos frightened off by Lykourgos in *Iliad* 6. These same nurses are in some accounts (e.g., Pherekydes; see chapter 6) the Hyades, who at least in later authors are the daughters of Atlas.

Last and most interesting of the references to Nymphai in the *Hymns* is the one from the *Hymn to Aphrodite* already considered in connection with the Silenoi (*HAph* 97–98). Previously in this tale Anchises has wondered if the disguised Aphrodite might actually be one of the Nymphai who inhabit glens, or perhaps Ida itself, and the springs and meadows. She of course persuades him that she is a mortal maiden carried to Ida by Hermes, and her desires are thus consummated. Toward evening, when the goddess reveals the truth, she tells Anchises that their child Aineias will be reared by

deep-girdled mountain Nymphai, those who dwell on this great and holy mountain. They are numbered neither with mortals nor immortals: long they live, and partake of the food of the gods, and dance with the immortals in lovely choruses. And the Silenoi and the watcher Hermes mingle in love with them in the depths of fair caves. But at their birth firs or lofty-crowned oaks are also born, trees fair and flourishing in the high mountains, and they are called precincts of the gods. These trees men do not ever cut down, but when their allotted death comes, first they wither and their bark dries up and the branches fall away, and then in the same way the souls of the Nymphai leave the light of the sun. [*HAph* 256–75]

Thus we see a concept similar to that expressed in fragment 304 MW of the Hesiodic Corpus, and one fairly unique in Greek myth, namely the notion of creatures who are in almost all respects similar to gods, but who will nevertheless die, as all things in nature do. The link between Nymphai and trees, familiar from many later mythographers and especially Ovid, also seems to have appeared in a fragment of Pindar, where again the life of the Nymph is equated with the life of the tree (fr 165 SM). Possibly he called such Nymphai Hamadryades, as Plato (*AP* 9.823) and Apollonios (*AR* 2.476–83) were later to do.

From the lyric poets there are only scattered and mostly unimportant references. Alkman calls the Nymphai Naiades, Lampades, and Thuiades (63 *PMG*); the scholiast who quotes the line explains Lampades as denoting the carrying of torches for Hekate, and Thuiades the inspired raving with Dionysos, but these are more likely his own interpretations, whatever their validity. Anakreon links Nymphai with Dionysos (357 *PMG*), and Alkaios offers non-formulaic support for Homer's view that they are daughters of Zeus (343 LP). Alkaios also seems (the papyrus is fragmentary) to have called Thetis a sea-Nymph (44 LP); elsewhere Nymphai are always connected with fresh springs and woods and mountains, and perhaps the poet meant no more than "bride." Semonides suggests that with Hermes they share in the protecting of shepherds (20 W), while Pindar speaks of the Naiad Kreousa (mother of Hypseus) as a daughter of Gaia (*Py* 9.16–17), thus perhaps agreeing with Hesiod's notion of generation from the earth and Ouranos' blood.

In tragedy, we find in Aischylos an important reference that extends the role of the Nymphai beyond what we have so far seen. They are named in a fragment from the playwright's lost *Semele* (or *Xantriai*)[20] in which Hera (in disguise) addresses the chorus (fr 168 R); from her speech it appears that she is posing as a priestess collecting offerings for the "life-giving Nymphai who are the children of Argive Inachos." She goes on to describe these Nymphai as attending all human endeavors, and as especially concerned with the rites of marriage and the begetting of children. As children of Inachos, whether literally or figuratively, they are connected with rivers, something we have not seen stressed previously, and thus the extension of their concern to the fostering of new life adheres to the standard pattern of Greek religion. One other role of the Nymphai, that of aiding Perseus in locating the Gorgons, appears first on a Chalkidian amphora of about 520 B.C., where three figures named "Neides" approach Perseus with *kibisis*, cap (of Hades), and winged sandals (London B155); subsequently (although it may have been omitted in Aischylos' *Perseus* trilogy), we find the same detail in Pherekydes, with Hermes accompanying Perseus as he seeks out the necessary items from the Nymphai (3F11). Unfortunately, the scholiast's summary of Pherekydes' account gives us no further information about these Nymphai, nor does it say why the items should be in their possession. Curious also is the fact that although Perseus is assisted by Hermes (and Athena) he must still visit the Graiai to locate the Nymphai. As he requires the latter's help, so too in Pherekydes Herakles must consult the Nymphai of the Eridanos (daughters of Zeus and Themis) in order to secure directions to Nereus (3F16).

In sum, the term "Nymph" presents us with a variety of different aspects, but nothing that contradicts their basic essence as creatures ultimately linked to physical manifestations of nature (although the word can be used more broadly of nubile young women). There seem to be at least two basic categories, the Nymphai of springs and the Nymphai of mountains; Nymphai inhabiting forests and meadows, and those connected with specific trees, may or may not be subcategories of the above. For Hesiod those called after ash trees are born from Gaia; in the *Iliad* mountain Nymphai, in the *Odyssey* Naiades, are called daughters of Zeus (no mother is ever named, though Pherekydes as we just saw makes Themis the mother of at least some). Daughters of Atlas may also have had some special claim to the title. For the *Hymn to Aphrodite*, the Hesiodic Corpus, and Pindar, Nymphai, though they are elsewhere often called goddesses, are subject to death; in the *Hymn* and Pindar this death is linked to the life of a tree, while in the Corpus mortality refers rather to Naiades. The *Hymn* also tells us that they consort with Silenoi (and we have already seen this confirmed by the Return of Hephaistos band on the François Krater) but they may mate with mortal men as well on occasion. A primary activity would appear to be dancing; one particular group become the nurses of Dionysos, and later devotees of his rites. Perhaps related to this is the association of Nymphai in later sources (e.g., DS 5.70.2–3) with the Kouretes and the upbringing of Zeus. In most of their appearances the Nymphai are simply part of the natural environment, but both the *Odyssey* and Aischylos hint at broader capacities to help those who pray to them.

The idea of Nymphai who accompany Dionysos (and consort with his attendants the Silenoi) brings us to the seemingly related and certainly better-known type of Bakchic companion, the Mainad. Unfortunately, the evidence for these figures is extremely limited. In *Iliad* 22, Andromache is compared to one as she dashes to the city's walls, fearing that Hektor has been killed (*Il* 22.460), but there is no further context, and the word may simply mean "raving woman." In the *Homeric Hymn to Demeter,* the goddess herself is compared to such a woman as she rushes to meet the recovered Persephone (*HDem* 386); here the mention of wooded mountains may indicate a general state of inspiration. But there is no definite link with Dionysos until Aischylos, who in an unassigned fragment calls the god the "yoker of Mainades" (fr 382 R). Sophokles offers much the same idea in the *Oidipous Tyrannos* (OT 212; cf.

Bkch 103), but again without elaboration. Given this paucity of reference, one begins to suspect that the word *Mainad* is really just a descriptive epithet, and not like Silenos or Nymphai a generic category. We have already seen, of course, that Dionysos is accompanied by inspired attendants—his nurses, who may have been Nymphai—as early as the *Iliad*, but the formalizing of this retinue could still have taken place later. The same picture emerges from scrutiny of the term *Bakchê*, which does not actually appear until Aischylos' *Eumenides* (25–26), where it describes the Theban women who dismembered Pentheus; an earlier Aischylean play entitled *Bakchai* was probably part of the lost Pentheus trilogy. That group, or the one relating Dionysos' clash with Lykourgos, might have had more to say on the subject of the women who accompany the god (although in the latter case the titles establish that such women were never the chorus). We should remember perhaps, too, that in the fragment of Euripides' *Kretes* noted above (fr 472 N²) the term *Bakchos* refers to a grade of initiation, that is, something open to all. From Sophokles' *Antigone* there is mention of Thebes as the mother city of the Bakchai (*Ant* 1122) and, more interestingly, a reference to Nymphai Bakchides, also of Thebes (*Ant* 1128–29). The context of this last, in a choral ode to Dionysos, seems to guarantee that real Nymphai are being spoken of, and thus furnishes a non-Nysaian link between them and the god. A third point in the same play describes Thuiades ("raving ones": *Ant* 1150–52) who attend Dionysos and, maddened, dance all night. From art there are of course myriad representations of what we call "Mainades," but this name seems not actually to be found on any of the pots in question, and thus constitutes an arbitrary term of convenience. Nevertheless, if we look at the Nymphai on the François Krater and then at Dionysos' companions on the krater by Lydos in New York (31.11.11), we see what may be an important divergence. Kleitias' Nymphai, clad in peploi, walk in a sober and dignified fashion (even if one of them is being embraced by a Silenos). Lydos' women, on the other hand, all wear fawnskins over their chitons, and are engaged in an ecstatic dance with the Silenoi. These are among the earliest representations of Dionysos and his followers: the fawn- or feline-skin and the ecstatic movements, together with the thyrsos, will become standard equipment in the decades that follow.[21] Whether an Attic vase-painter of the sixth century would have called such women Mainades is uncertain. Neither, and more important, can we say whether these women were permanent companions of the god, or only temporarily inspired; perhaps it is not a question an artist of the period would have thought to ask.

From Silenoi, Nymphai, and Mainades we turn to another race of woodland creatures who, though generally mortal, may be considered here: the Kentauroi. Both the *Iliad* and *Odyssey* are acquainted with the term, but they tell us less than we might have wished. In *Iliad* 1 Nestor speaks to the assembled Achaians of a time when he came from Pylos to fight with Peirithoos, Kaineus, and others against the strongest foes of that age, mountain beasts (*Il* 1.266–68). No further description is given, and the word "Kentauros" is not used, but since Nestor's comrades are unquestionably Lapithai, it seems clear that the Kentauroi are meant. What they looked like is another matter, although the word "beast" *(phêr)* should signify that they had some animal component; we may note here that Pindar will use that same term to denote both Cheiron (*Py* 4.119) and the Lapithai's combatants (fr 166 SM). In *Iliad* 2, the Catalogue of Ships mentions Polypoites as son of the Peirithoos who chased the shaggy beasts away from Pelion; again the word "Kentauros" does not appear (*Il* 2.742–44). Where we do find it used is rather for Cheiron, who in *Iliad* 11 as Achilleus' tutor is called the "most just of the Kentauroi" (thus not the only one: *Il* 11.832). From the *Odyssey* there is only one reference of any sort, in *Odyssey* 21 where Antinoos says that wine was the undoing of the Kentauros Eurytion in the halls of the Lapith Peirithoos (*Od* 21.295–303). That there is no mention of creatures who are half-horse, half-man in Homer is perhaps not surprising in view of his tendency to suppress fantastic elements, but we must also allow for the possibility that his Kentauroi looked rather different from what we are familiar with. In any case the familiar form was certainly known in Homer's time, as we see from a bronze statuette group from the end of the Geometric Period showing a horse/man in apparent combat with a normal human (NY 17.190.2072); usually (and probably rightly) this group is taken to represent Herakles and Nessos, although we have seen in chapter 1 other suggestions, chief among them Typhoeus.[22] Even earlier is the terracotta statuette found at Lefkandi on Euboia and apparently to be dated before 900 B.C.[23] Unfortunately this piece is without context, and one cannot say who or what the artist had in mind. The last quarter of the eighth century brings a sudden outpouring of such *Mischwesen* in Attic vase-painting: helmeted at times, carrying branches and present singly and in groups, but not on the whole hostile in appearance.[24] So on an ovoid krater from Lord Elgin's collection (now Ortiz Coll) a horse/ man strides forward with pine branch and dead deer,[25] matching to be sure the iconography that we later recognize for Kentauroi. But seemingly this same horse/man type could be used for other purposes as well, as indicated by two other artifacts discussed in chapter 1, a Protocorinthian aryballos (Boston 95.12) and a Cycladic relief pithos (Louvre CA 795), both from the first half of the seventh century. The aryballos shows a figure with raised thunderbolt (or firebrand?) and scepter moving toward a creature of canonical Kentauros form. If this figure is Zeus, as seems very likely, then (considering that no myth of any sort is known [or conceivable] which would link Zeus with a Kentauros) we should probably interpret the horse/man creature as Typhoeus or some other early opponent. The pithos offers even clearer evidence: here Perseus, clearly identified by his cap, bag, winged sandals, and averted face, cuts off the head of a horse/woman who can only be Medousa. Thus the combination of human and horse seems in the early Archaic period a device utilized to represent several different kinds of monsters, while we cannot even be absolutely certain that the earliest Kentauroi were conceived in this form.

Likewise flexible is the exact appearance of early half-man/half-horse creatures. The horse/man renditions we have discussed so far show the type as a complete human figure all the way down to its feet, with the barrel and hindquarters of the horse joined onto the human buttocks; this is true even for the Medousa figure on the Louvre pithos, despite the fact that she wears a dress. The two possible exceptions to this mode of presentation are the Lefkandi Kentauros (though probably the forelegs do have knees[26]) and a Cycladic sealstone in Paris showing perhaps Herakles and Nessos (CabMéd M5837); on this last (though it is hard to be sure) the human part does seem to end at the waist, and the human legs to be replaced by equine ones. In the seventh century, this latter type definitely appears on a late Protocorinthian kotyle from Perachora[27] and an ivory relief plaque from Sparta depicting (again probably) Herakles and Nessos (Athens 15350). But most of the evidence we have for the rest of the century—for example, a Protocorinthian aryballos in Berlin (Berlin:PM F336: Herakles in the cave of Pholos), a Protoattic amphora in New York (NY 11.210.1: definitely Herakles and Nessos), and a bronze relief from Olympia (BE 11a: Kaineus and Kentauroi)—shows a retention of the more "human" form. Only when we come to the Peiraieus and Nessos Painters of Attic Black-Figure toward the end of the century does the equine type reassert itself (Kerameikos 658; Athens 1002); from this point on, it becomes the standard for Attic vase-painting, as the François Krater's presentation of the Lapithai and Kentauroi demonstrates. Nevertheless, though the equine Kentauros is the rule for the more hostile representatives of the breed, the friendly Kentauros Cheiron is usually portrayed with the more human form, and even elegantly clothed. A similar logic seems to have been applied in designing the metopes for Heraion I at Foce del Sele, where Herakles fights equine Kentauroi while a clearly human-fronted Pholos looks on (elsewhere on the same building Herakles does battle with an equine Nessos), and the same combination applies on a Lakonian dinos of about 540 B.C. (Louvre E662: that one other Kentauros besides Pholos is also human is presumably a mistake, although the three Kentauroi on the same slab with Herakles on the Temple of Assos frieze are human, the others equine). In Attic art of this time Pholos is equine in some instances (London B226; Vat 388; VG 50626), human in others (Palermo 45; Boston 93.100).[28] Elsewhere in the sixth century, human Kentauroi remain common: Peirithoos' guests on an Ionian hydria (Bonn 2674), Nessos on a Caeretan hydria (Louvre C 10228), and virtually all Corinthian examples.

Of the origin of these creatures there is surprisingly no consistent early account. The end of the *Theogony* calls Cheiron the offspring of Phillyra (*Th* 1001–2), and this information is expanded by the author of the *Gigantomachia* (probably the *Titanomachia*: fr 10 *PEG*) and Pherekydes (3F50), both of whom tell us that Kronos took the form of a horse to mate with Phillyra, daughter of Okeanos, with the biformed Cheiron the result. The same parentage is given by Pindar (*Py* 3.4; 4.102–3, 115), and for him, as for the *Gigantomachia*, Cheiron is married to Chariklo (Pindar does not actually say this, but it seems the obvious conclusion from *Pythian* 4, where Phillyra, Chariklo, and Cheiron's daughters all live with him in his cave). This Chariklo is a figure otherwise unknown in Archaic literature, but she does appear on all three preserved representations of the wedding of Peleus and Thetis in the early sixth century: Sophilos' Akropolis fragments (Athens Akr 587), the same painter's Erskine Dinos (London 1971.11–1.1), and Kleitias' François Krater (Florence 4209). On all three, oddly enough, she is found in the company of the same two goddesses, Demeter and Hestia. Although Cheiron is preserved on the latter two vases, she is not immediately next to him as she might be, but presumably she is present because of the relationship between Peleus and Cheiron. In all three cases she is entirely human, and one supposes that the children (who are called *kourai* in *Pythian* 4) are the same (Hippo/Hippe, the daughter of Cheiron, is a girl who *becomes* a horse by intervention of the gods in Euripides' *Melanippe Sophe* and later sources: see chapter 18). Thus Cheiron emerges as a one-time product of an unusual mating, unable to reproduce his own form. Something of the same sort is found, although only in Apollodoros (ApB 2.5.4), for Pholos: as we saw earlier, this Kentauros is made the offspring of Silenos (or a Silenos?) and a Melian Nymph. But an explanation for the existence of a whole race of Kentauroi comes only in Pindar's *Pythian* 2, where Ixion, having mated with a cloud in the form of Hera, produces a child named "Kentauros." No description is given, but from what follows it appears that he is human in form, for he mates with mares on Mount Magnesia, and the resulting offspring resemble their father above, their mother below (*Py* 2.25–48). Obviously such a story leaves some points unexplained: no motivation at all is offered for the mating of man and horse, and the name "Kentauros" is here applied only to the human father, not the half-horse children. We might perhaps wonder if an original single Kentauros (most likely Cheiron) had his form appropriated and given to the beast-like creatures who battled the Lapithai, thus creating the need for a different and broader generation myth; Pindar's account (which is designed primarily to illustrate the full force of Ixion's mental aberration) may even be his own invention. But this remains only speculation. The Thessalian Souidas of the fourth or third century makes Cheiron like the other Kentauroi a son of Ixion (602F1; his failure to follow Pindar in making those others grandsons of Ixion may be just carelessness). Plato (*Phaidros* 229d) and Xenophon (*Kyn* 4.3.17) are the first authors to use the term *Hippokentauros* (cf. DS 4.69–70).

Two other points to be noted in regard to Kentauroi are those of gender and mortality. We have already seen in the figure of Medousa on the Louvre relief pithos a female human/horse form, but this scarcely counts as a female Kentauros. In fact, Loukianos does describe such a creature, complete with twin Kentauroi children, as depicted in a painting of the late fifth- or early fourth-century painter Zeuxis (*Zeuxis* 3–6).[29] But he then goes on to stress as his primary point the absolute novelty of Zeuxis in thinking up something new and strange; thus, we should probably conclude that the concept of female Kentauroi was unknown in the Archaic period. As for mortality, the *Iliad* says only that Peirithoos chased his enemies away from Pelion, not that he killed them (*Il* 2.742–44). But certainly artistic representations of the Kentauroi attacking Herakles on Mount Pholoe show dying victims of his arrows, as for example on the Foce del Sele metopes, and then there is of course the story of Nessos, whose death is a necessary forerunner to that of Herakles. On the other hand, Cheiron is said by Sophokles (*Tr* 714–15) and Apollodoros (ApB 2.5.4, 2.5.11) to have been immortal, and such a *moira* would square well with his separate birth (from two gods, in fact). Apollodoros' context for his remark is Herakles' wounding of Cheiron and the latter's apparent surrender of his immortality to Prometheus in order to be free of his pain. Unfortunately, textual problems concerning who is exchanged for Cheiron intrude here.[30] Hermes' mysterious allusion to a liberator at the end of Aischylos' *Prometheus Desmotes* (1026–30) is commonly taken to support the notion that Prometheus is the beneficiary. But as we shall see in chapter 4, Prometheus as a Titan should not need any such favor (certainly not in Aischylos, where he is clearly immortal). What Apollodoros actually seems to have said is that Cheiron gives his immortality to *Herakles* (who, though mortal, must become immortal in some fashion), and probably we should accept that solution for the *Desmotes* as well. In any case, Apollodoros does clearly attest to both Cheiron's immortality and his death after he has traded away that immortality. From the earlier sources there is only Pindar's acknowledgment in *Pythian* 3 that Cheiron is dead (*Py* 3.1–4), and Ovid's brief allusion to the wounding and death (but unfortunately not to the way in which it was brought about: *Met* 2.649–54; in Loukianos [*DMor* 8] he desires to die because of boredom). The death of one other Kentauros, Pholos, is mentioned by both Diodoros (4.12.8) and Apollodoros; supposedly he dropped one of Herakles' poisoned arrows on his foot and died instantly. The poet Lasos apparently wrote a work entitled *Kentauroi* that might have touched on many of the above matters, but nothing survives (704 *PMG*).

Yet another group of minor divinities have already appeared in connection with the fragment of the *Ehoiai* in which the daughters of Doros (emendation) give birth to the mountain Nymphai, the Satyroi, and the Kouretes (Hes fr 10a.17–19 MW). These last, the Kouretes, are said to be playful and dancers. The lines were originally quoted by Strabo (10.3.19), but have now been restored to their original context on a papyrus that does not seem to leave much room for further details about their nature. Strabo goes on to say that in the epic *Phoronis* they are Phrygians and flute players (fr 3 *PEG*); elsewhere they are generally placed on Krete, while their frequent companions the Korybantes come from Phrygia. Diogenes Laertius tells that "Epimenides" wrote an account of the birth of the Kouretes and the Korybantes that, together with the *Theogony* ascribed to him, totaled 5,000 lines (DL 1.111 = 3A1 DK). Whether or not this account is simply a preface to the *Theogony*, the prominence given to these two groups is notable. How they came to be linked together is another question; the Korybantes are, for Pherekydes, offspring of Apollo and Rhetia

(3F48, apud Strabo) but do not otherwise survive in the Archaic period. Later sources make them attendants of Kybele and, as noted, put their origin in Phrygia (Str 10.3.19; DS 3.55.8; ApB 1.3.4). Both groups are tantalizingly alluded to in Euripides' *Bakchai*, where the chorus tells of the cave of the Kouretes in Krete where Zeus was born and where the Korybantes invented the drum that they gave to Rheia (*Bkch* 120–34); the Greek might or might not intend to equate the two groups here. In any case, their presence together at the birth of Zeus likely results from the frequent identification of Kybele with Rheia. The lost *Hypsipyle* of Euripides adds to this that the Kouretes of Krete were mortal (12.75–76 GLP). Korinna, whatever her date, also seems aware that the Kouretes hid Zeus away from Kronos (654 i.12–18 *PMG*), in contrast to the *Theogony*, which never mentions such a detail, or even the existence of either of these groups. Kouretes as guards of the child also appeared in at least one branch of the Orphic tradition (fr 151 Kern). But the generally familiar story that the Kouretes rattled their armor so that Kronos might not hear the infant Zeus' cries survives first in Kallimachos' *Hymn to Zeus* (1.51–53: cf. ApB 1.1.6–7; DS 5.65); it is not clear whether the Korybantes' drum in the *Bakchai* might have served the same purpose.

A group of far more uncertain function and status are the Kabeiroi, about whom Aischylos wrote an entire play of which we know virtually nothing, save that the Argonautai visited them and became drunk (Athen 10.428f). Strabo, in connection with his account of the Kouretes and Korybantes, cites several different versions of their origin: according to Pherekydes they are three in number, offspring of Hephaistos and Kabeiro, daughter of Proteus, and they have three sisters (3F48); according to Akousilaos they are also three, but offspring of Kadmillos or Kamillos, who is, in turn, the child of Hephaistos and Kabeiro (2F20). Herodotos too makes them sons of Hephaistos (3.37). For Mnaseas of Patrai they are four in number, Axieros, Axiokersa, Axiokersos, and Kasmilos (Σ AR 917). Still other writers, unnamed by Strabo, identify them with the Korybantes (as children of Zeus and Kalliope) and locate them on Samothrace (Str 10.3.19). That they were linked to Samothrace is likewise the opinion of Herodotos (2.51) and Stesimbrotos (107F20, apud Strabo), but Strabo himself says that they were most honored in Imbros and Lemnos (10.3.21), the last in particular confirmed by inscriptional evidence. Aischylos' play must have involved them in some sort of myth, even if only as hosts of the Argonautai; the setting might equally have been Samothrace (where the Argo could have stopped on her way to Kolchis) or Lemnos (the latter perhaps more likely if the *Kabeiroi* was part of a trilogy with *Lemniai* and *Hypsipyle*).

Mention should here be made as well of the Idaian Daktyloi. According to the *Souda*, the Hesiodic Corpus contained a work devoted to them in which they seem to have discovered the working of iron on Krete (Hes fr 282 MW). The *Phoronis* calls them sorcerers (*goêtes*), Phrygians from Ida who dwelt in the mountains, Kelmis and Damnameneus and Akmon, servants of Adrasteia who were the first to discover iron and its forging (as their names imply: fr 2

PEG). Pherekydes speaks of two groups, those of the "left" (thirty-two in number, the sorcerers), and those of the "right" (twenty in number, the dissolvers of spells:[31] 3F47). In Sophokles there are males and females (five each, thus Daktyloi: fr 366 R). Probably this information is from the lost satyr play *Kophoi*, where Kelmis as one of the group insulted his mother Rheia when she came to Ida (fr 365 R). For Hellanikos, however, they were called Daktyloi because meeting Rheia by chance on Ida they took her fingers in greeting (4F89). Strabo adds that in all sources the Daktyloi initiate the use of iron and function as *goêtes*, dwelling with the mother of the gods near Mount Ida in the Troad (Str 10.3.22); according to Diodoros they have the former skill from her (DS 17.7.5). Clearly their association with the Mother and with Ida facilitated their establishment in Krete as well as the Troad; Pausanias says that Rheia gave the care of Zeus into their hands and that they were the same as the Kouretes (Paus 5.7.6).[32]

Very similar to the Daktyloi in many respects are the Telchines. Our only Archaic references to them are Stesichoros, who somehow links them with the Keres (265 *PMG*), and Bakchylides, who according to Tzetzes made them children of Tartaros and Nemesis (fr 52 SM; the same writer notes that others make them children of Pontos and Gaia). Pindar may perhaps also allude to them if the Rhodians to whom Athena grants skills in the working of statues are indeed these craftsmen (*Ol* 7.50–53). Kallimachos (*H* 4.30–31) adds that they made Poseidon's trident for him, while at the beginning of his *Aitia* they are creatures of envy, and a later fragment of the same work has them (now residents of Keos) destroyed by Zeus' thunderbolt because of their hybris (fr 75.64–69 Pf). By Kallimachos' own admission this story comes from the pen of the fifth-century historian Xenomedes (442F1); its details are not entirely clear, but there is a Demonax who scorns the gods and an old woman, Makelo, with her daughter Dexithea. These last two are saved when the gods overturn the island, an event tallying with Pindar's *Paian* 4, where Euxantios, son of Dexithea, remarks that Zeus and Poseidon once sent countless men of Keos down to Tartaros with thunderbolt and trident, but spared his mother and her home (*Pa* 4.40–45). We cannot be sure, however, that Pindar also thought of these Keans as Telchines; Ovid returns them to Rhodes, where Zeus submerges them because their eyes harm all things with their gaze (*Met* 7.365–67). Nothing else survives of this myth, and further information of any sort on the Telchines comes only, once again, from Diodoros and Strabo. Diodoros tells us that they were the first inhabitants of Rhodes, that Rheia gave them Poseidon to raise, and that they were sorcerers, makers of statues of the gods, and, in general, discoverers of useful things for mankind (DS 5.55.1–3). Strabo for his part knows of traditions that would equate the Telchines with the Kouretes, or else make the latter a subcategory of the former; he also knows of their reputation as sorcerers, and the notion that they were the first to work with bronze and iron, even fashioning the sickle for Kronos (Str 10.3.7, 19; 14.2.7).

For a completely different kind of divinity, the Thriai, we have essentially only the *Homeric Hymn to Hermes*. Here Apollo tells Hermes that although the new god may not possess Apollo's gift of prophecy, he can still learn from the three winged, elderly sisters who live on Parnassos and reveal the truth in a frenzy when they have tasted of honey (*HHerm* 552–63). Pherekydes adds, what we might have guessed, that they are daughters of Zeus (3F49). Certainly they sound like creatures who were once all or in part bees. Of a similar sort, perhaps, are the Seirenes. Alkman in the Louvre Partheneion recognizes them as beautiful singers and calls them goddesses (1.96–98 *PMG*); another very brief fragment seems to equate (surely figuratively) Seiren and Muse (30 *PMG*). Otherwise we have for the Archaic period only the *Odyssey*, where we are told by Kirke that the Seirenes (two in number) deliberately try to lure men to their deaths with their song (*Od* 12.39–46). They themselves, when they do appear later in Book 12, offer to Odysseus knowledge in which he will delight, although they then proceed, somewhat paradoxically, to assert that they know all that happened at Troy, something with which Odysseus is already acquainted (*Od* 12.184–91). Possibly the poet means that they offer men a clearer or more complete understanding of what said men have already experienced. The *Odyssey* says nothing of their physical appearance or family pedigree. Vase-painting, however, does offer help on the former point: a Corinthian aryballos of *c.* 560 B.C. shows clearly the two Seirenes sitting on a rock while on the other side of the vase the ship with Odysseus bound to the mast sails by (Boston 01.8100). What the artist has portrayed (and what will become the standard mode of representation) is the bird with the head of a woman long familiar from nonnarrative scenes in Corinthian vase-painting. Whether this type of figure was always thought of as a Seiren, or whether it was appropriated when artists decided to draw this scene, remains open. Toward the end of the century appear several Attic vases on which they have lyres and even double pipes (Stockholm:Med, no #; Berlin:Ch VI 3283). From (much) later sources there is a plethora of suggestions as to their parentage (Acheloos and Terpsichore in Apollonios [4.895–96], Acheloos and Melpomene in Apollodoros [ApB 1.3.4]) but very little that would explain their form or function. Simonides does seem to have compared the Attic tyrant Peisistratos to a Seiren (607 *PMG*), presumably in reference to the former's abilities of persuasion.

Last in this category of lesser (at least for narrative purposes) divinities comes Tyche. The name (or for that matter even the word) does not appear in Homer in any form, although, of course, the root verb *tunkhanô* does. Hesiod assigns "Tyche" as a name to one of the Okeanides (*Th* 360), but with no special emphasis; the *Homeric Hymn to Demeter* offers the same (420). A fragment of Alkman employs it more as we would expect, that is, for a figure in some way connected with chance, but the genealogy given suggests that she is little more than allegory: sister of Eunomia and Peitho, and daughter of an otherwise unattested Prometheia (64 *PMG*). Someone (perhaps Archilochos) also notes in a one-line fragment that *tychê* and *moira* give all things to men (16 W); he may or may not have personified such a concept in his own mind.

From Pindar, finally, we do have an appeal to Tyche, as the daughter of Zeus, to watch over the city of Himera (*Ol* 12.1–2). This suggests that she works for good, or at least can be requested to do so. But there are no myths whatever about her, and clearly she did not capture the Greek mind of the Archaic period, however sensitive that mind may have been to the changing winds of fortune.

4 Prometheus and the First Men

Although Homer frequently refers to Zeus as the father of men and gods, this appellation is not to be taken too literally. He is not, of course, the father of all the gods, or indeed of any great number of them, and the same is true of his relationship with mortals. What Homer presumably means is that Zeus exercises a paternal role in his control of various situations and his mediating between humans and gods in conflict. We must remember that in neither the *Iliad* nor the *Odyssey* do the gods ever display any sense of responsibility for humanity's existence or its problems, save for instances in which they are obligated to reciprocal action by sacrifices or the like. Mortals for Homer are simply there, as part of the dispensation of Moira, and no one questions where they have come from. But, obviously, for a poet like Hesiod the temptation to create (or at least use) tales about the origin of humans as a means of better illustrating their place in the world was great, and obviously, too, for subsequent writers such as the Catalogue Poet and Pherekydes who used genealogy as the organizational basis of their work, such questions would be difficult to avoid.

Hesiod's account of Prometheus and humankind's fall from an early life of ease appears in both the *Theogony* and the *Works & Days*. In the latter poem, however, this explanation of the human condition is immediately followed by another, quite different one, the tale of the Five Ages of Man. This second account does not actually contradict the first in any specific way, but it clearly operates on its own terms, and exists primarily for the sake of the point it wants to make. In Hesiod's telling of the story there are in fact features suggesting that the concept of these Ages had not been worked out fully or made to cohere with other stories told about the early days of men and gods.[1] As with the dual birth of the Moirai in the *Theogony*, we see that at this (relatively) early stage of our tradition the historical concreteness of events can be highly flexible, depending on what those events are thought to mean.

Since Hesiod's "Prometheus" version of humankind's early misfortunes has no account at all of their creation, we will turn first to the Five Ages' view of affairs. In the beginning, the *Works & Days* tells us, there was a golden race of *anthrôpoi*, made by the immortals who have homes on Olympos, and these lived in the time of Kronos, when he ruled the sky (*W&D* 109–26). The phrase

152

"immortals who have homes on Olympos" is perhaps here no more than an unconscious formula, since Hesiod's more detailed look at the gods' evolution in the *Theogony* makes Kronos' offspring (including Zeus) the first gods to inhabit Olympos. At any rate, the implication of these lines would certainly seem that Kronos created this first race, an idea scarcely in keeping with Hesiod's general portrait of the god in the *Theogony*. But that idea is not made explicit, and possibly the poet intended simply to suggest the antiquity of this earliest race by putting it back in Kronos' time. In any event, this race of mortals lives like gods, without toil or cares, without even old age, and they feast constantly, as the earth produces an abundance of food for them. And yet, even without old age they die, as if falling asleep, and are buried, and become *daimones* who roam the earth and ward off evil from humans (how this is done Hesiod does not say, and said *daimones* do not appear elsewhere, unless they are the watchers of *W&D* 252–55).

Next, the Olympians (denoted by the same expression as before, but now with no mention of Kronos) create a silver race, not like the golden one in appearance or wisdom, and much inferior (*W&D* 127–42). As children these mortals require a hundred years to grow up, staying by their mothers, and then live only a little while, bringing pains on themselves by their folly and arrogance and refusal to sacrifice to the gods. The reference to mothers is probably included simply to make the extended childhood of this race more vivid, but it also reminds us that Hesiod has so far said nothing about women or procreation or whether there is more than one generation in any of the races. Zeus destroys this second race because of their failure to honor the gods, and the earth covers them too, although here again there is honor after death, and they are called "the blessed ones under the earth."

Third comes the bronze race, this time specifically created by Zeus rather than the Olympians and sprung from ash-trees, or else from the Meliai, ash-tree Nymphai (the Greek will allow both, though if Hesiod here intended normal human birth, he says nothing about any fathers, and the Greek text will not allow Zeus to play that role).[2] We are told that this is a warlike race, loving battle above all else, that they do not eat bread (we are not told what they do eat), and that they destroy each other and go down to Hades (*W&D* 143–55).

Fourth, and when we might have expected an iron age, we find the race of heroes, the *hêmitheoi*, this also "made" by Zeus, although the very term *hêmitheoi* might lead us to believe that these ought to be the offspring of gods and mortals through sexual union (*W&D* 156–73). We have already considered this race in discussing views on the afterlife, for these are the recognizable heroes of Greek mythology who fight at Thebes and Troy; either some of them go to Hades and others to the islands of the blessed ones, or all of them have this latter fate.[3] This is the race before Hesiod's own; he does not say why it ceases (although as seen in chapter 3 the *Ehoiai* suggests a conscious decision by Zeus to separate them from other men: Hes fr 200.95–104 MW).

The final race is that of iron; unfortunately, the expected introduction telling us who created it is preserved only as part of the dubious group of lines at *Works & Days* 173a-e found in several papyri but not in our manuscript tradition.[4] Hesiodic or not (the lines are also fragmentary), these verses name Zeus once again, although this time as having *placed* the race on earth. At this point we have left the era of myths, and while Hesiod has a good deal more to say about the shortcomings of his own age, we shall turn here to his two versions of Prometheus' clash with Zeus. In the *Theogony* Prometheus is clearly identified as the son of Iapetos and Klymene, and is thus a second-generation Titan and first cousin to Zeus; his siblings are Atlas, Menoitios, and Epimetheus (*Th* 507–11). Of these, Menoitios is immediately struck by Zeus' thunderbolt and sent down to Erebos (*Th* 514–16); it is not clear whether Hesiod means by this Tartaros, or that Menoitios met the fate of a mortal (in contravention of his Titan status). Neither are we told what transgression he had committed. Hesiod says simply that he was *hubristês* (arrogant), and suffered for his *atasthalia* (presumption?) and excessive *ênoria* (manly strength), which might refer to a role in the Titanomachy but sounds rather more like a preemptive strike by Zeus. The same situation applies to his brother Atlas; Zeus assigns to this figure the *moira* of holding up the sky, but no reason is given. By contrast Epimetheus fares perhaps better; we will return to him shortly in connection with Pandora. Likewise left unexplained by Hesiod is how Prometheus and Epimetheus survived the Titanomachy, and what role (if any) they played in it.

Hesiod's account of Prometheus in the *Theogony* begins with an overview of the story and Prometheus' final punishment, then backtracks to detail the two transgressions (*Th* 521–616). At no point does he actually call Prometheus a god, but *Theogony* 523–24 does speak of the latter's immortal liver, and divine status seems implicit in the nature of his punishment. Yet there are obviously also mortals in existence at this time (albeit unexplained), since they serve as the recipients of Prometheus' benefactions. We are not told why Prometheus chooses to represent them in the division at Mekone, only that he presents a great cow to be shared between humans and gods, intending already to deceive Zeus. Presumably the understanding was that Prometheus would divide the animal into what he judged to be equal shares and then offer first pick of those shares to Zeus, thus making it in his own best interest to be as equitable as possible. But instead the Titan offers Zeus the appearance of profit by arranging the piles of meat unequally and then disguising them—covering the good flesh and entrails with the cow's stomach, and the white bones with a piece of fat.[5] Hesiod is in some embarrassment at this point, for his Zeus is not the sort to be fooled by such an obvious trick, and the poet says so. On the other hand, the story cannot continue if Zeus does not take up the wrong share, and this he does, receiving the bones and becoming exceedingly angry with mortals, since his choice will be the gods' portion forever. In recompense he does not give mankind fire (the Greek says "withhold," not "take back"), but Prometheus deceives him again by stealing fire in the stalk of a fennel plant (no further details are given). When we next see that fire, two lines later, it is in the possession of men, and Zeus is once more angry. Accordingly he plots a further evil for them; at his request Hephaistos molds together earth in the form of a maiden. Athena dresses her, including a veil, floral wreaths, and a wondrous crown made by Hephaistos with all kinds of monsters on it. This is all; no other gods contribute to her charms, and she is not in fact called "Pandora" or given any name at all in the *Theogony*. Instead she is brought forward into a gathering of men and gods, and both wonder at her beauty. But, Hesiod continues, she will be an inextricable snare and evil for mankind, for from her will be born the (or a, since the Greek could mean either) race of women, who will be lazy and drain men of their prosperity. Hesiod's further comments on the general character of women need not concern us here. Earlier, at the beginning of the entire story, he tells us that Epimetheus was the first to receive a woman, a *parthenos*, fabricated by Zeus. Those words might be taken to mean that other less dangerous women were known from other sources (Zeus' creation is never actually called the first woman), but her primacy seems the obvious conclusion from the statement that she is the source of women as we know them. In that case there would be only men, not women, before this act of Zeus' compensation, and no means of human regeneration. But to inquire about such matters is probably to expect more than Hesiod intended to offer. Presumably Epimetheus marries Pandora, and when Hesiod says that the race of women is through her, he means us to understand through the normal process of sexual procreation.

As for Prometheus, Hesiod has him chained to a column in harsh bonds that Zeus probably makes to pass through the middle of that column (*Th* 521–22).[6] The exact means of securing the miscreant is of interest because several vase-paintings of the sixth century appear to show Prometheus impaled on a column, a notion that may have resulted from a misunderstanding of this passage with its admittedly compressed language (Athens 16384; Berlin: Ch F1722; cf. the Lakonian cup Vat 16592, where Prometheus—if it is he—is clearly bound *to* the column).[7] In any case, such punishment is much in accord with the imprisonment of the Titans, for as Hesiod presents the matter Prometheus is like them a troublemaker, well intentioned perhaps, but nonetheless causing harm to both gods and men with his deceiving of Zeus, and needing restraint if the world is to function properly. But Zeus' chastisement here goes well beyond mere imprisonment: he sends against his adversary an eagle who feeds on Prometheus' liver, which in turn grows back equally each night (*Th* 523–25). This part of the punishment is subsequently abated in the following lines of the poem, when Herakles arrives and slays the eagle with the approval of Zeus, who allows the deed in order that his son might win still greater fame (and because, though still angry, he has ceased from the wrath that he had before: *Th* 533). It is often assumed that Hesiod's further statement that Herakles "freed Prometheus from anxiety" (*Th* 527–28) means that Prometheus was freed from his bondage as well as from the eagle. But at *Theogony* 616 (a line variously emended or even excised to remove the contradiction) the poet says clearly that great bonds still hold Prometheus fast, and this after all is what we should expect from Hesiod: so long as Prometheus, like Atlas and the Titans in Tartaros, remains under restraint, the reign of Zeus, and the order which it brings, will be better secured. In all probability the words "freed from anxiety" simply relate in different terms, through its effect, the slaying of the eagle; the imprisonment itself is not remitted, and Prometheus remains chained to his column.[8] Only with Aischylos will matters clearly take a different turn, as we will see.

In the *Works & Days* we receive a much briefer account of these events, focusing primarily on Pandora (*W&D* 42–105). Here we learn that mortals lived at one time a life of ease, producing enough in one day to last a whole year. But then Prometheus deceived Zeus (the poem does not say how) and in anger the ruler of the gods hid fire. The story continues with the same sequence of events as in the *Theogony*: Prometheus steals the fire, this time specifically from Zeus in a fennel stalk, and Zeus counters with Pandora (here named), who will be, as he tells Prometheus, an evil that men will embrace and delight in to their own ruin. This time Hephaistos is ordered to mix together earth and water, to give the result voice and strength, and to liken her in face to the goddesses. Athena is then to teach her skill of hands, including weaving, Aphrodite is to pour *charis* and the inciting of desire about her, and Hermes to give her the mind of a bitch and a thievish character. When these orders are carried out, however, they take a slightly different direction. Athena dresses the new creation, as in the *Theogony*, but with help from the Charites and Peitho, who put golden chains around her, and the Horai, who give her a crown of spring flowers. Hermes then places in her heart lies and flattering words and the thievish character requested by Zeus, and a voice as well, and he names her "Pandora," because all the gods on Olympos together are giving her to man as a gift (the common alternative that all the gods give to her a gift is really not what Hesiod's Greek says).[9]

At this point, rather than present her to an assembled multitude, Zeus sends Hermes to take her to Epimetheus, who does not remember that his brother warned him never to accept any gift from Zeus, and realizes what he has received only too late. In such an account there emerges some minor sleight-of-hand, more obvious here perhaps than in the *Theogony's* version: Zeus' gift to mankind is transacted as a gift to the immortal Titan Epimetheus, much as if he were an early mortal, and he now becomes in some unexplained way the predecessor (perhaps even the progenitor) of those mortals through his union with Pandora. But in contrast to the *Theogony* his role as procreator of future women is not here stressed; instead the *Works & Days*, despite the clear previous hints that Pandora's own character is the source of men's ills, now presents the story of the jar. Where this jar comes from is never said; we learn simply that Pandora removed the great lid from the vessel with her own hands and scattered into the world evils, and sicknesses, and painful labor. Thus,

Hesiod says, she brought about mournful cares for humanity. The Greek verb used in this last sentence *(emêsato)* usually connotes contrivance or at least intention, as if to say that Pandora understood in advance the consequences of her action. But as noted above, we know nothing about the jar, not even whether she brought it with her when she came into the house of Epimetheus. In any event she does manage (by the planning of Zeus) to put the lid back on the jar before Elpis can fly out. If this Elpis is, as generally translated, "hope," then we have another clear (and seemingly unnecessary) illogicality in the story: mortals ought not to possess both hope *and* the aforementioned evils if one stays in the jar and the others do not. Perhaps, though, we have credited Hesiod with more optimism than he intended. If rather than "hope," Elpis could mean "expectation" (i.e., a realistic awareness of just how bad things are and are likely to get: not an impossible sense for the Greek), then the logic of the narrative would be fully restored.[10] Humankind would indeed have hope, but that hope would consist of the absence, the withholding, of expectation, so that we might not understand or be weighed down by the full realization of our predicament.

When we move from Hesiod to the seventh and sixth centuries we find extremely little on any of the above material. Proklos records in the scholia to the *Works & Days* a variant in which Prometheus gets the jar from the Satyroi (Σ *W&D* 89); possibly this is early, but we must obviously suspect a satyr play (perhaps Aischylos' *Prometheus Pyrkaeus* or Sophokles' *Pandora*). Eumelos makes Epimetheus' wife the Okeanid Ephyra in his *Korinthiaka*, so that he probably ignored the Pandora story altogether (fr 1 *PEG*). Servius does attribute to Sappho (as well as to Hesiod) the statement that the gods in anger over the theft of fire sent to man two evils, women and sicknesses (Σ *Ecl* 6.42 = 207 LP), but it does not seem likely that Sappho would have treated the story in any detail. As noted, there are some artistic representations of Prometheus' imprisonment, including a gem from Krete, a seventh-century ivory relief from Sparta (Athens 15354), a bronze shield-relief from Olympia (B 4992), and a number of Attic and Lakonian Black-Figure pots (one of which is attributed to the Nessos Painter: Athens 16384). All of these show basically the same scene: either a bound Prometheus and the eagle, or these two figures with the addition of Herakles moving in from left or right, bow in hand, to shoot the eagle. As we also saw, several of these pots represent Prometheus as impaled on a column (with in three instances his hands left free);[11] in other cases he is sitting on a rock. In every one of these compositions the eagle is the main focus of events; we cannot say what the artists might have supposed to happen next, but certainly nothing will prove that they believed Prometheus released from his bonds.

Just possibly there is also an illustration of Pandora's creation in Attic Black-Figure: on an amphora in Berlin a bearded figure with scepter holds before him in his hands a small, doll-like woman, while a female figure opposite him holds out garlands with which to adorn her and Hermes moves away to the right (Berlin:Ch F1837). Furtwängler interpreted this scene as perhaps the birth of Athena,[12] but there are no weapons or other identifying criteria for that goddess, while for Pandora the presence of an adorning figure (Aphrodite or one of the Charites) and Hermes (preparing to escort Pandora down to earth) are suggestive. On fifth-century Attic ware there are several scenes of Pandora's adornment: by Athena and Hephaistos on a White-Ground cup of *c.* 460 B.C., where she is named "Anesidora" (London D4), and by Athena alone (as Zeus, Poseidon, Ares, Hermes, Iris, and perhaps Aphrodite watch) on a slightly earlier calyx krater (London E467).[13] The Red-Figure volute krater in Oxford with its curious (but certain) representation of Pandora rising up from the earth as Epimetheus looks on we will consider in more detail when we come to Sophokles' *Pandora* below.

From the fifth century in literature the most prominent evidence for Prometheus' story should be Aischylos' dramatic trilogy consisting (probably) of the *Prometheus Desmotes, Prometheus Lyomenos,* and *Prometheus Pyrphoros.* That Aischylos wrote some such group seems certain, but recent scholarship has reawakened doubts as to whether the *Desmotes* that alone survives today is indeed the one he composed, rather than a later effort.[14] For our purposes authorship is of relatively limited importance, especially as the time period (fifth century B.C.) seems the same in any case. In what follows, however, I will assume Aischylean authorship, at least insofar as the play's thought and the relationship of that thought to what we know of the two lost plays are concerned. Also ascribed to Aischylos (and lost) is a satyr play entitled *Prometheus Pyrkaeus* ("Firekindler") that burlesqued Prometheus' gift of fire to the first men (i.e., Satyroi). This satyr play we know to have been presented not with the other Prometheus plays, as one might expect, but rather with the *Persai-Phineus-Glaukos Potnieus* production of 472 B.C. (so the hypothesis to the *Persai*). The date and satyr play of the Prometheus trilogy remain unknown, and it should be noted, too, that while Aischylos' *Lyomenos* certainly followed his *Desmotes,*[15] the *Pyrphoros* has been thought by some to be a variant name for the *Pyrkaeus,* leaving us without a third title here.[16] Also uncertain is whether this third title (*Pyrphoros* or not) was the first of the three plays, detailing Prometheus' theft of fire, or the last, in which in case it *might* further develop the problem of Zeus' reconciliation with Prometheus and/or Herakles.[17] On the theory that the beginning of the *Desmotes* contains a good deal of expository material, and that Prometheus does, after all, say quite a bit about the theft of fire and his other deeds in the course of that play, most scholars argue that the *Desmotes* began the trilogy and that the *Pyrphoros* concluded it, but the issue remains open.

In any event, as the preserved *Desmotes* begins Prometheus is led out on stage by Zeus' agents, the personified Kratos (Power) and Bia (Force), who instruct Hephaistos to chain the Titan (he is frequently so named) to a rock as Zeus' punishment for his theft of fire; the setting is hazily envisioned as somewhere to the far north of Greece and west of the Black Sea, perhaps not too remote from Okeanos itself.[18] Prometheus is duly chained (with a wedge apparently driven through his chest, perhaps a development from the notion of impalement), and the others depart the stage. The title figure is thus left to await the arrival of the chorus, to whom he can tell his side of the story. These presently appear in the person of the Okeanides, and through question and answer the details of Prometheus' dealings with Zeus emerge. There are several surprising deviations from Hesiod. Missing is any mention whatever of the sacrificial division at Mekone, or Pandora, or even Epimetheus. On the other hand, we learn that Prometheus is now the son of Gaia (*PD* 209–10: she in turn is equated with Themis, and no father of Prometheus is specified), that he aided Zeus in his rise to power by telling him to release the Kyklopes and secure the thunderbolt (*PD* 219–21), that he prevented Zeus from eliminating the human race when the latter wished to do so (*PD* 232–36), and that his gifts to mortals go far beyond the simple presentation of fire. These last include architecture, advanced methods of agriculture, the domestication of animals, divination, and writing (*PD* 442–506). There is also in the category of new material the matter of a certain prophecy, to which we will return shortly.

Such innovations and omissions (as measured against Hesiod) clearly reflect a consistent program on the part of the playwright. From the opening lines the drama is shaped in such a way that it cannot but work against Zeus. Kratos and Bia (Dike might have come in their place) summarize power politics in its most unattractive form, while Hephaistos' sympathy for Prometheus (this from the offended party in the case) undermines the seriousness of the charges. Prometheus' binding is described in harsh and repulsive terms, and later he will levy against Zeus charges of ingratitude (for the assistance in the latter's rise to power) and conspiracy to obliterate humanity. Then there is the brutal treatment of the wholly innocent Io (clearly brought into arbitrary conjunction with Prometheus for just this purpose) and the play's closing scene, in which a self-serving Hermes brings the threat of the eagle's torment if Prometheus does not divulge the secret of the prophecy. Under such circumstances, it should come as no surprise that Prometheus' misdeeds at Mekone are omitted while his services both to Zeus and humanity become more elaborate. The absence of Pandora, who could have reflected further discredit on the ruler of the gods, perhaps depends on a less misogynistic outlook; possibly the trilogy holds Pandora in reserve, to be presented later as a boon to men.

The most striking difference between Hesiod's and Aischylos' versions of the story, however, occurs not in our preserved play, but in the lost *Lyomenos*, and is guaranteed by the very title of that drama: Prometheus is released not just from the eagle's depredations, but from his bonds. Given the total gap in our evidence between Hesiod and the fifth century we cannot say with any certainty that Aischylos himself devised this deviation from the *Theogony*, but the Hesiodic version was still current in the latter's time, for Pherekydes, whose work may pre- or postdate the Prometheus trilogy, relates that Herakles, in search of the garden of the Hesperides, encounters Prometheus, takes pity on him, and shoots the eagle that has been devouring his liver (3F17). In return for this service, as the text clearly states, Prometheus advises Herakles to seek out Atlas and let him obtain the apples. Admittedly this text, like much of Pherekydes, is a scholiast's summary rather than an actual quote, but even in such a summary the scholiast would surely have mentioned the much greater service of Prometheus' release had he found that in his source. If that is true, an Athenian writing at about the time of Aischylos' production supposed like Hesiod that Prometheus' confinement was forever. But there is also evidence (some of it perhaps earlier than this production) that the release was a familiar idea in Athens at this time. Certainly Aischylos' own (lost) *Sphinx* of 467 B.C. knew of it, for a crown/garland is there called "the best of bonds, according to the word of Prometheus" (fr 235 R), and the quoter of these lines, Athenaios, tells us that Zeus in the *Lyomenos* caused the newly freed Prometheus to wear a garland as a substitute for his imprisonment (15.674d; in Hyginus the object serving this purpose is a ring [*Astr* 2.15.4], while Probus mentions both items [Σ *Ecl* 6.42]). Then, too, the Athenians possessed a cult of Prometheus, one associated with that of Hephaistos and celebrated by a torch race; one wonders whether this Prometheus (or Promethos) was ever different from the Titan chastised by Zeus.[19] In art of this period (as earlier) we do not see Prometheus' release from his bonds, but we do find him standing before a seated Hera in the tondo of a cup by Douris showing the return of Hephaistos on the exterior (CabMéd 542).[20] With a date of *c.* 475 B.C., this cup, too, may reflect or antici- pate Aischylos' release of the Titan. But clearly there were times and traditions in which he was released, and times and traditions in which he was not.

One other element of note regarding this release in Aischylos concerns its cause. We might suppose that Zeus simply softened his attitude toward Pro- metheus, as elsewhere he is made to do in the case of the other Titans and even Kronos. But Aischylos supplies quite a different motivation that seems likely to be his own. In the *Desmotes* we find that knowledge of the *moira* of Thetis to bear a son greater than his father, assigned by Pindar to Themis in his *Isthmian* 8, is here given to Prometheus as something learned from his mother Gaia (Pindar's version may well explain why Aischylos conflates Gaia and Themis). Thus he will be able to bargain with Zeus for his freedom, although in the *Desmotes* the Titan shows no very clear grasp of how matters will turn out.

This much stated, the action of our preserved play is simple enough. Pro- metheus in bits and pieces describes his situation to the Okeanides. Their fa- ther, Okeanos, visits and offers to intercede with Zeus, but is easily dissuaded by Prometheus' emphasis on the possible risks. The bound Titan in further conversation with the chorus reveals the existence of the secret and some of its nature. Io appears and turns the chorus (and presumably the audience) wholly against Zeus with her pitiable condition; Prometheus relates her past and pre- dicts her future. Finally Hermes arrives: Zeus has heard Prometheus' boasts about the secret and is prepared to plunge him into Tartaros to extract from him the name of the goddess who has such a *moira*. If that fails, Prometheus will be brought back up into the light, and an eagle will come to gnaw at his liver. Thus what began as a simple punishment for a transgression is transformed into a test of wills, and Prometheus will have to decide if he wants to wait Zeus out or negotiate a settlement.

From the lost *Lyomenos* we do have a few fragments that give us the essential action, but not always the answers to the crucial questions. Prometheus has now been returned to the earth's surface, not however to his original place of punishment but to the Caucasian Mountains, if Strabo (4.1.7 = fr 199 R) and Cicero (*TD* 2.23–25 = fr 193 R) are correct; in the *Desmotes*, at least, these mountains were envisioned as north of the Black Sea, since Io was to reach them *before* the Kimmerian Bosporos (*PD* 717–35). Wherever located, the Titan does indeed suffer the torment of the eagle, as had been predicted. The chorus for the play consists of his fellow Titans who have come to this spot specifically to view his tribulations (fr 190 R). Since Prometheus told us clearly in the first play that these were in Tartaros, we are left to deduce that they have been freed since that time, and freed by Zeus. At some point in their travels, they have been down to (or come from?) the red sea (Indian Ocean?) and the land of the Aithiopes near Okeanos, where the sun rests himself and his horses (fr 192 R); this could be their route from Tartaros, but it might also have something to do with the islands of the blessed ones. As one might expect, Prometheus discusses his situation with these newcomers; the fragment preserved (actually a translation into Latin by Cicero: *TD* 2.22 = fr 193 R)[21] describes the dreaded visit of the eagle every second day. At this juncture Gaia may appear (her name is erroneously included in the cast of characters for the *Desmotes*, suggesting that she appeared somewhere else in the trilogy[22]), but if so we do not know what her purpose was; possibly she tried to persuade Prometheus to relent and divulge the secret. At some point, too, Herakles certainly enters, and receives from the Titan information on his past and future wanderings, much as Io did in the first play. In fact, given the parallelism between these fragments and the preserved play, we may wonder if there is not some intentional link between Io and Herakles, since both are apparently innocent victims of Hera's jealousy. We know also that Herakles shoots the eagle, although we cannot say whether he does this before, during, or at the end of their conversation. The title of the play guarantees that Prometheus will be released from his bonds in the course of the drama, and certain hints in the *Desmotes* would seem to assure us that Herakles will be his releaser. Yet the crucial details of the release—when and why—fail us. A line cited by Plutarch from this play has Prometheus call Herakles "dearest son of a most hateful father" *after* he has been saved (fr 201 R). If this means saved from the eagle, then a considerable amount of dramatic time might elapse between the slaying of the eagle and the breaking of the bonds, during which Zeus and Prometheus might become reconciled. If, on the other hand, it means saved from imprisonment, then Herakles may have released Prometheus without Zeus' permission. Against the latter conclusion, however, we have information from

Philodemos, who says (in a very fragmentary passage) that the Aischylean Prometheus was released because (or when) he revealed the secret about Thetis, namely that she was fated to bear a son greater than his father (p. 41 Gomperz = p. 306 R). A scholiast on *Desmotes* 167 adds (although he does not say that this is drawn from Aischylos) that Zeus is pursuing Thetis through the Caucasians when Prometheus stops him; the scholia at *Isthmian* 8.56b do state that in Aischylos Prometheus prevented Zeus from mating with her, and we saw above that Athenaios claims the reconciliation of the two sides came in this play. Most complete of all (but here too without direct reference to Aischylos) is Probus' statement that Herakles slew the vulture but feared to release Prometheus lest he offend his father; Zeus did, however, permit him to do this *after* Prometheus had revealed the necessary name (Σ *Ecl* 6.42). Such evidence seems to point in one direction; if it is all relevant, perhaps matters came to a head in the middle of the play, with the following sequence: Herakles slays the eagle, discusses his fate and that of Prometheus, Zeus is seen (offstage) pursuing Thetis, Prometheus decides to reveal her *moira* (Gaia perhaps bears the message), and Zeus in consequence permits Herakles to accomplish the release. But even if this reconstruction is correct, we do not quite grasp the grounds on which Prometheus' crucial decision is made, and it becomes very difficult to see what a concluding *Pyrphoros* might have contained.

As to that presumed third play (unless it really was the first), the *Pyrphoros*, we have virtually no evidence at all. Loose ends that might be tied up could include an aetiology for the torch races held in Prometheus' honor (assuming that release and races predated Aischylos' play). There is also, as noted above, the possibility of Pandora's creation, and there does exist an unassigned Aischylean fragment that refers to her (fr 369 R). In this connection we should perhaps remember a remark made by Prometheus in the *Desmotes* to the effect that Zeus wanted to eliminate the current human race and create a new one (*PD* 231–36). The reason for this odd intention is never given, although it inevitably reminds us of Deukalion's flood, or even the notion of the *Kypria* and the *Ehoiai* that Zeus intended the Trojan War to reduce the human population (see chapter 16). Stranger still is Prometheus' statement that he opposed Zeus and saved mankind from destruction. How he did this is not clear; his gifts to mortals have certainly improved their status, but nothing in those gifts could make them a match for Zeus, and Prometheus himself is now chained up and unable to protect them further. Possibly the question of Zeus' attitude toward humankind is more complex than the *Desmotes* allows, perhaps even being treated in a concluding play through the presentation of Pandora as Zeus' benevolent gift to men. Alternatively, it has been suggested that the unassigned Aischylean fragment in which Zeus sends his daughter Dike down to earth to bring Justice to men might have been part of such a play (fr 281a R);[23] this, too, would effectively resolve some of the tensions of the *Desmotes* (and re-scrutinize Zeus' rise to power) by allowing the ruler of the gods to demonstrate his own concern for the welfare of the human race with a gift markedly absent from Prometheus' catalogue of benefits. Whatever we conclude, it should be remembered that Io in the *Desmotes* and presumably Herakles in the *Lyomenos* are told (by Prometheus) of their ultimate blissful fate; the reasons for their sufferings are admittedly obscure, but surely the Zeus who emerges at the end of this trilogy must look far different from the harsh and callous ruler presented to us at its beginning.

One final detail of the trilogy's resolution has already been discussed in connection with the immortality of Cheiron (see chapter 3). The passage in question is *Desmotes* 1026–30, where Hermes tells Prometheus, "Do not expect any end to this suffering before someone of the gods presents himself to be a recipient of your pain, and volunteers to go down into sunless Hades and the murky depths of Tartaros." Possibly Hermes himself simply meant this as an *adunaton*, something that would never happen. Nevertheless Prometheus will be released, and it seems reasonable to suppose that Aischylos intended the remark as a reference to some real future event, even if Hermes does not. But we have seen that Cheiron cannot be the one meant here; Prometheus is clearly immortal, and what Cheiron wants in going down to Hades is to get rid of his own pain, not take on that of Prometheus. We found in chapter 3 that the real solution to this riddle may lie in the person of Herakles, who must descend into Hades to fetch Kerberos.[24] Admittedly there is a problem: Herakles may *become* a god, but he is not one at the time he performs this particular feat. Perhaps the riddle was intended to turn on this ambiguity; if not, then we must admit that we do not know who made the descent, or exactly what he/she did to facilitate Prometheus' release.

Such is virtually the sum of our material concerning Prometheus' conflict with Zeus in the Archaic period. Epicharmos did write a play entitled (depending on one's source) *Pyrrha and Prometheus* or *Pyrrha or Prometheus* or even *Deukalion* (pp. 112–13 Kaibel), but of course this would have been a parody of whatever narrative was familiar to Greeks, and the fragments suggest that it dealt not with Prometheus and Zeus, but rather with the Flood, as we would expect (see below). In Sophokles, the Titan surfaces at least twice: a digression in the lost *Kolchides* apparently offered some part of the plot of the *Desmotes* (by Medeia, explaining the source of her potions?: pp. 316–17 R) while a lost satyr play was entitled *Pandora or Sphyrokopoi* ("Hammerers"). As a possible illustration of the latter drama we may note the Attic Red-Figure volute krater in Oxford already mentioned in chapter 2 (Oxford G275: *c.* 450 b.c.). Zeus stands to the left, with Hermes moving away from him; to the right is Epimetheus (so named on the pot) holding a hammer and looking at Pandora (also named), who is in the act of rising up out of the earth and holding her arms out to him. From the look on Epimetheus' face it seems clear that he is already smitten (an Eros hovers overhead as well). The hammer in the Titan's hand strikes one as an odd detail, but certainly in keeping with the dual title of Sophokles' play. Whether hammers were there required for Pandora's creation (and how Epimetheus would be involved in that case) is unclear, as nothing is known about the play's action (although there was a reference to the kneading of mud).[25] Complicating the problem further are the other fifth-century vases we considered in chapter 2 with a woman (who in one case is specifically named "Pherophatta," i.e., Kore) arising from the earth in a similar fashion. In several of these examples the woman is flanked by Silenoi holding hammers (or tools for breaking up the earth?), and in one a Silenos appears to actually bring his hammer down on the emerging head of the goddess. Perhaps, as was suggested in discussing Persephone, the hammers are part of a ritual summoning of Pandora, or else a means of releasing her from the earth. But the Hesiodic version of her is formed from earth and water, and the artist may mean no more than that. We cannot, after all, say for certain that the hammer in Epimetheus' hand (curious though it is) has anything to do with Pandora's emergence from the earth to be bestowed upon him, or even that the Oxford vase was definitely inspired by Sophokles' play.[26]

Prometheus' career does not quite end with his release from bondage; as he was the helper of mankind in Hesiod, so in the *Ehoiai* of the Catalogue Poet he and his brother Epimetheus seem to become ancestors of the human race. Unfortunately, our chief evidence, a scholion to Apollonios, has probably garbled something in transmission, for it says that the *Ehoiai* makes Deukalion the son of Prometheus and Pandora, and Hellen the son of either Prometheus or Deukalion and Pyrrha (Hes fr 2 MW). Possibly this reflects an earlier version of the whole story in which Pandora as the punishment for Prometheus' misadventures is appropriately enough given to Prometheus himself rather than his brother. But such an account does not square with the *Theogony* (the poem of which the *Ehoiai* is supposed to be a continuation), or with the nearly unanimous arrangement of later authors, or (probably) with evidence of fragment 4 of the same poem (see below); we might add that it also does not account for the birth of Pyrrha. On the whole, then, it seems better to presume miscopying and emend the scholion.[27] In that case we would have, as usual, Prometheus producing a son, Deukalion, and Epimetheus (or Zeus)[28] and Pandora producing a daughter, Pyrrha; these two offspring would then marry and give rise to a number of children, including Hellen (cf. ApB 1.7.2). But the mother of Deukalion remains a difficult matter, even after we have excluded Pandora. Neither the *Theogony* nor the *Works & Days* gives Prometheus a wife; Aischylos in the *Desmotes* makes her Hesione daughter of Okeanos (*PD* 560), and Akousilaos does the same (2F34). But apparently the Catalogue Poet did not agree, because the same scholiast who gives us the information about Akousilaos cites the *Ehoiai* as offering a different name, either "Pryneia" or "Prynoe" (Hes fr 4 MW: both spellings are probably corruptions, but we cannot guess of what). No parentage is given for this figure, and since we cannot identify her with any known personage, we cannot say whether she was mortal or divine. But certainly Hesione as a daughter of Okeanos and Tethys ought to be immortal, and so should children born to her and Prometheus; no doubt this is the sort of inconsistency we are meant not to notice, given the obvious difficulties in making the transition from gods to men. Likewise is the case of Epimetheus and Pandora, where we cannot even say what status Pandora should occupy. In any event Deukalion and Pyrrha, though at times preceded by shadowy predecessors, do emerge as the first named man and woman in Greek myth, or at least in the Deukalionid tradition of northern Greece. As such they serve two functions: to become ancestors for those who will in turn father the familiar figures of story, and to be survivors of the Great Flood.

Unfortunately no surviving fragment of the *Ehoiai* mentions the Flood. There is to be sure a quote from the poem in Strabo which relates that Zeus created men from the earth and gave them to Deukalion (Hes fr 234 MW), but we cannot say for certain that the previous absence of manpower arose from the same cause as in later accounts—indeed, since the end of the *Theogony* and the following *Ehoiai* begin from the beginning, we should perhaps assume that it does not.[29] Akousilaos for his part specifies that Deukalion and Pyrrha cast stones behind them to create new men (2F35), but here too we are not told what went before. Not until Pindar's *Olympian* 9, in fact, do we actually hear of the Flood: Zeus then causes the waters to recede, and Deukalion and Pyrrha come down from Parnassos and make people out of stones (*Ol* 9.42–46, 49–53). Alas, Pindar does not say who caused the flood to begin with or why. Epicharmos' *Pyrrha*, or whatever it was titled (see above), also contained this idea of people created from stones; recent finds from Oxyrhynchus now suggest that Pyrrha was indeed a character in the play, that Deukalion's ark (or chest: *larnax*) for riding out the flood was described, and that Pyrrha may have been concerned about Prometheus stealing the possessions of her household (POxy 25.2427 fr 1). The person she speaks to here would appear to be her husband, and since she is more likely to accuse her father-in-law than her father we should probably assume that here too she is the (at least nominal) daughter of Epimetheus married to Deukalion (or Leukarion?), son of Prometheus. Whether a second fragment actually says that Prometheus' debts (stealing of fire?) are the cause of the Flood is more difficult (POxy 25.2427 fr 27). For further details we must await Ovid, who tells us that Zeus deliberately destroyed everyone except Deukalion and Pyrrha with the Flood because of man's wickedness (*Met* 1.163–312: here too we find, as in Akousilaos, the version alluded to by Pindar in which the pair cast stones [the bones of their mother Earth] over their shoulders), and Apollodoros, who makes the Flood Zeus' method of eliminating the race of bronze (ApB 1.7.2: in the *Works & Days* they destroyed each other). Since Greek mythology largely deals with Hesiod's fourth age, that of the heroes, putting Deukalion and Pyrrha at the very end of the previous one makes good sense, but we cannot say for certain that anyone before Apollodoros thought of it (cf. Σ *W&D* 85a). His further account features Prometheus advising Deukalion to build an ark and take shelter in it with Pyrrha; the ark floats for nine days and nights before coming to Parnassos, where, as the rain ceases, Hermes arrives and allows Deukalion and Pyrrha to create new men and women by throwing stones over their heads. As we shall see in the following chapters, Deukalion and Pyrrha themselves do not account for all the figures that populate the myths, but they do play a major part in the beginnings of the human race.[30] The one other legend in this regard, that the gods created men from earth and fire and called on Epimetheus to distribute to these and other creatures their various qualities (with Prometheus then stealing fire to compensate for the failure to properly equip mortals), survives first in Plato (*Prot* 320–21), and may well be largely that philosopher's own invention, if he did not find it in one of the Presocratics.[31]

5   The Line of Deukalion

*The
Children of
Deukalion
and Pyrrha*
The immediate offspring of Deukalion and Pyrrha, including indeed several
generations, are primarily eponymous ancestors or intermediate place-holders
rather than actors in any real narratives.[1] The fragments of the *Ehoiai* assign
to the two of them three offspring: the son Hellen whom we have already
encountered, and two daughters, Thuia and Pandora (Hes frr 9, 7, 5 MW). We
should note that for the Catalogue Poet Hellen *may* be in reality a son of Zeus
(Σ *Od* 10.2).[2] Pherekydes adds a third daughter (Protogeneia: 3F23), Hekataios
three more sons (Pronoos, Orestheus, and Marathonios, with Hellen the son
of Pronoos: 1F13), and Apollodoros one Amphiktyon (Ap*B* 1.7.2). Of the
daughters, Thuia bears to Zeus Magnes and Makedon (Hes fr 7 MW), and
Magnes in his turn begets Diktys and Polydektes (Hes fr 8 MW), whom we
will encounter again in the story of Perseus. Pandora bears to Zeus Graikos
(Hes fr 5 MW). Pherekydes does not assign the third daughter, Protogeneia,
any children, but both Apollodoros (Ap*B* 1.7.3) and Pausanias (5.1.3) make her
by Zeus the mother of Aethlios, who will marry Kalyke, daughter of Aiolos
(see below), and become the father of Endymion.

    To Hellen, son of Deukalion (or Zeus), the *Ehoiai* gives three sons of his
own, Doros, Xouthos, and Aiolos (Hes fr 9 MW). To Doros were born Aigimios
and seemingly other children, and somewhere in the very fragmentary lines of
this section must be the Nymphai, Satyroi, and Kouretes, probably as offspring
of five of his daughters by Hermes (Hes fr 10a.17–19 MW).[3] Xouthos for his
part marries Kreousa, daughter of Erechtheus, just as in Euripides' *Ion*, and
they have three children, Achaios, Diomede, and a third whose name is missing
but is very likely Ion, since the space to be filled in the papyrus gap is quite
small (Hes fr 10a.21–24 MW). In that case, however, Ion is certainly here the
child of Xouthos, not of Apollo.[4] Aiolos (not to be confused with the Aiolos
son of Hippotes visited by Odysseus as keeper of the winds) has the largest
family; his wife (the name is lost: in Ap*B* 1.7.3 she is Enarete) bears seven
sons and five daughters. Of the sons the names "Kretheus," "Athamas," "Sisyphos," "Salmoneus," and "Perieres" are preserved; Apollodoros offers "Deion"
and "Magnes" as the others, and while "Deion" would fit well in the papyrus,
"Magnes," as we have seen, conflicts with the *Ehoiai's* use of that name elsewhere. We will consider below the evidence for Minyas as the seventh son in

the *Ehoiai*. The poem then moves to the daughters and, as often, having named them last deals with all their offspring before returning to those of the sons.

The daughters named are Peisidike, Alkyone, and Perimede, with two missing (Hes fr 10a.100, 96, 34 MW); Apollodoros calls these Kalyke and Kanake, names that certainly would fit well into the *Ehoiai's* available gaps. No Archaic source mentions Melanippe, a supposed daughter of Aiolos and Hippo, daughter of Cheiron, who appears first as the heroine of two of Euripides' lost plays, the *Melanippe Sophe* and the *Melanippe Desmotis* (for her story see chapter 18). In the succeeding list of offspring for these five daughters there are again many gaps that must be filled in from Apollodoros or the like, a surely justifiable procedure given the many correspondences between the Catalogue Poet and Apollodoros in this particular family. Nevertheless, in what follows I do bracket those details added from later sources.

1. <Perimede bears to the river god Acheloos two sons, Orestes and Hippodamas (ApB 1.7.3).> Hippodamas marries (unknown woman) who bears to him Antimachos and Eureite; the latter marries Porthaon, son of the son of Pleuron (i.e., Agenor), and bears Oineus, Alkathoos, Agrios, <Melas,> and youngest of all, Pylos (Hes fr 10a.45–57 MW: *Il* 14.115–18 has a Portheus [rather than Porthaon] beget Agrios, Melas, and Oineus, while ApB 1.7.10 omits Pylos and adds Leukopeus). These latter four—Alkathoos, Agrios, Melas, and Pylos—are slain by their nephew Tydeus, son of Oineus, because they had wrested power from his father (Pher 3F122 has other accounts).

2. <Kalyke marries Aethlios (a grandson, like her father, of Pyrrha and Deukalion) and bears Endymion (so too Hes fr 245 MW), whom Zeus honors> and assigns gifts, and he is a steward of old age and death. <He is the father of Aitolos, and Aitolos in turn is the father of> Kalydon and Pleuron, and Pleuron is the father of Agenor (Hes fr 10a.58–65 MW; ApB 1.7.6–7).

3. Alkyone marries Keyx, and here the papyrus becomes extremely fragmentary (Hes fr 10a.94–96 MW). But another papyrus attests that in their folly the couple called each other Zeus and Hera, and this not surprisingly angered the real Zeus, who changed them into birds (Hes fr 10d MW). The Hesiodic Corpus also contains a poem entitled *The Wedding of Keyx*, but the few fragments offer no further information, and the Keyx there named may well be someone different. After this there is nothing until Ovid and Apollodoros. Ovid omits the transgression and has Keyx simply drowned at sea; when Alkyone sees the body floating offshore she throws herself into the sea, and is transformed like her husband into a bird (*Met* 11.410–748; so too Hyg *Fab* 65). Apollodoros gives the same version as that of the *Ehoiai* (ApB 1.7.4).

4. Peisidike marries Myrmidon and has two children, Antiphos and <Aktor> (Hes fr 10a.99–101 MW; ApB 1.7.3).

5. Last, <Kanake> lies with Poseidon and bears children twice, but here the papyrus breaks off altogether (Hes fr 10a.102–4 MW; Ap*B* 1.7.4). Apollodoros names five children in all (Hopleus, Nireus, Epopeus, Aloeus, and Triops), and while in theory all these could have come from the *Ehoiai*, one does not see in that case why the poet should specify the number of deliveries required. If, as seems likely, he knew of only two children, they were probably Aloeus and Triops, since Aloeus certainly appears in the *Ehoiai* as the nominal father of the Aloadai (Hes fr 19 MW), and the mother of these last, Iphimedeia, is in Apollodoros the daughter of Aloeus' brother Triops (Ap*B* 1.7.4). In Kallimachos we find that Triops (here Triopas) is as well the father of Erysichthon (*H* 6.31–32, 96–100).

Although as noted above Aiolos, son of Hellen, is quite different from the Aiolos encountered by Odysseus in Homer, the two are inevitably (at times even deliberately) identified, and so we will consider here briefly the namesake. The author chiefly responsible for confounding the two seems Euripides, in whose lost *Aiolos* a daughter Kanake plays a major role. What the *Odyssey* tells us is that Aiolos, son of Hippotes, lived with his wife and twelve children (six sons and six daughters) on a kind of island paradise free from care, that he married the six sons to the six daughters, and that they all lived happily together (*Od* 10.1–12). Euripides is clearly inspired by this, or something like it, but in his play matters take a rather different turn.[5] From Plutarch (*Mor* 312c-d) and other references we get the following story: Makareus, the youngest (or oldest) of the six sons, has fallen in love with and raped his sister Kanake. Fearful lest her pregnancy (and his deed) be discovered, he proposes to their father that all six sons marry their six sisters. Unfortunately, he does not receive Kanake in the resulting allotment. Their father then discovers the truth, and probably sends Kanake a sword with which she kills herself; Makareus may follow suit. As it stands, this tale has only the name of Kanake in common with the family of Aiolos, son of Hellen, but Euripides began his play with a prologue that mentioned Aiolos, son of Hellen and father of Sisyphos, Athamas, Kretheus, and Salmoneus (fr 14 N²); it would seem then that either he fused the two Aioloi together (with the twelve new children offspring of a second marriage?) or made his Aiolos somehow related to this original one. Not impossibly, given the large number of sons and daughters assigned to each of them, they were in a more distant past the same person. Kanake's tragic story also appears in epistle form in Ovid's *Heroides* (11), where the father is clearly the ruler of the winds, and the child apparently thrown to the dogs. In art we encounter it on a Lucanian hydria of about 410 B.C. now in Bari: Kanake slumps over in death on her couch, the fatal knife still in her hand, while Aiolos on one side raises his staff to point at a bound Makareus on the other (Bari 1535).

The above genealogies exhaust (more or less) the immediate family of Deukalion and Pyrrha. From the various branches two names stand out as progenitors of future figures prominent in myth: Aiolos, son of Hellen (through his sons), and Agenor, son of Pleuron, from the line of Kalyke, daughter of Aiolos. The progeny of these two persons—taken together with the offspring of Inachos, Atlas, Asopos, Kekrops, and Tantalos—will form a basic cast of characters populating most of the major narratives.

The Aloadai We saw above that Apollodoros has Aloeus, son of Kanake, marry Iphimedeia, daughter of his brother Triops (ApB 1.7.4). Of these details a scholiast (to Apollonios) guarantees for the *Ehoiai* at least the marriage of Aloeus and Iphimedeia, and as well the children that she bore to Poseidon (Hes fr 19 MW), but we have no direct fragments and cannot say for certain whether their story was told in full. In the *Nekuia*, Iphimedeia is one of the women seen by Odysseus, and there too she states that, although the bedpartner of Aloeus, she has lain also with Poseidon and borne to the god two children, Otos and Ephialtes (*Od* 11.305–20).[6] These sons, according to the *Nekuia*, are the largest and most handsome of mortals after Orion, and indeed grow at an alarming rate: by the age of 9 they are nine cubits in width and nine fathoms in height. They threaten war against the gods by planning to set Mount Ossa on Mount Olympos and then Mount Pelion on Mount Ossa, and thus reach *ouranos*, and Homer says that they would have accomplished this had they grown to manhood. But Apollo destroys them (we are not told how) before their beards have begun to grow. In the *Iliad* we find a completely different story, that of the imprisoning of Ares (*Il* 5.385–91). Here the children are again named and now called the sons of Aloeus; no mention is made of Poseidon or Iphimedeia, and the poet may or may not have meant that they were Aloeus' natural sons. In any case they bind the god of war in strong bonds and place him in a bronze jar for thirteen months. No reason is given; possibly they believed that Ares' absence from Olympos would cripple the gods militarily and facilitate their own assault (the scholia for their part suggest that they were angry with the war god because he had slain Adonis after the latter was entrusted to their care by Aphrodite [ΣbT *Il* 5.385]). The imprisonment ends only when the stepmother of the children, one Eeriboia, reveals to Hermes where Ares is, and the messenger god steals his brother away (in the scholia this Eeriboia is the daughter of Eurymachos, son of Hermes). The one other preserved Archaic source to speak of the brothers is Pindar, who says in *Pythian* 4 simply that Otos and Ephialtes died on Naxos (*Py* 4.88–89), and speaks in a fragment of a ladder leading up to *ouranos* (fr 162 SM).

Apollodoros repeats essentially what is found in Homer, but with no further details (ApB 1.7.4). He does, however, add two new stories, (1) that the brothers sought to court Hera (Ephialtes) and Artemis (Otos), and (2) that Artemis brought about their deaths on Naxos by becoming a hind and causing them to throw their spears at each other (so too Σ *Py* 4.156a, ΣbT *Il* 5.385). Hyginus has a slightly different version of this, namely that Artemis was unable to fend off their advances, but that Apollo sent a hind to distract their (maddened) attention, and while trying to kill it they slew each other as above (*Fab* 28). Something similar certainly appears on an Attic Red-Figure bell krater of about 450 B.C.: two hunters attack a deer (one with spear, the other with sword), while to the right Artemis aims her bow at the hunters (Basel:ASM Kä 404). Given the deer, and the fact that nothing distinguishes either of the two hunters as Orion, the Aloadai are probably intended; the goddess' active role here may arise from a need to make the story visually comprehensible.

The Aiolidai   SALMONEUS, TYRO, AND KRETHEUS   Of Aiolos' seven sons, four play quite important roles in myth. Salmoneus, the first of them, is the archetypal mortal usurper of the functions of Zeus, and of course pays the penalty. Our only Archaic source for his story is the papyrus fragment from the *Ehoiai* noted in chapter 3 (Hes fr 30 MW). While this has the usual gaps, it is clear that bronze pots are being attached to a chariot, and torches waved around, so that Salmoneus might pretend to be the god of thunder and lightning (a chance reference elsewhere adds that in Hesiod he actually called himself Zeus: Hes fr 15 MW). Naturally the real Zeus is quite incensed, thundering and shaking the earth; he then leaves Olympos and goes down to visit the people of Salmoneus. The king himself is struck by the thunderbolt and hurled into Tartaros as an object lesson to other mortals; the people—women, children, servants, even houses— are totally wiped out. This last penalty seems unusually harsh, but possibly these people did indeed accept Salmoneus as Zeus, in which case they would have only themselves to blame. That possibility is strengthened by the fact that one person was spared, namely Tyro, daughter of Salmoneus, and this specifically because she quarreled with her father and opposed his attempt to equal the gods. This is all the fragment gives us; had we more at the beginning of it, we might know more about what prompted Salmoneus to his insane action. Somewhat surprisingly, Attic tragedy is of little help; although the tale seems ideal material for such a medium, the only *Salmoneus* title to which we have reference is a satyr play by Sophokles. The remains do not supply any idea of the plot; presumably the Satyroi of the chorus narrowly escape the king's fate. Another Sophoklean play, the *Aias Lokros*, does have Athena call him the "hide-roarer Salmoneus" (fr 10c R), which alludes surely to a second means of mimicking thunder, and Euripides in the *Aiolos* spoke of his hurling of fire (fr 14 N²). In Vergil he demands divine honors, and the imitation is accomplished "with bronze and the pounding of horses' hooves," whatever that means (*Aen* 6.585–94). In Apollodoros, where the destruction of the entire town in Elis (Salmoneus has migrated there from Thessaly[7]) again appears, the miscreant orders Zeus' sacrifices transferred to himself (ApB 1.9.7), which confirms perhaps our guess about Zeus' reasons for destroying the town in the *Ehoiai*; alternatively (since Apollodoros also says that Salmoneus founded the town) the god may have wished by such an act to blot out his impostor's memory. In vase-painting we have a Red-Figure column krater of about 460 B.C. showing Salmoneus with his pseudo-thunderbolt and a sword, and as well a greave on his left arm and chain on his left ankle; two women (one winged) dart away to either side (Chicago 89.16).[8]

Salmoneus' daughter Tyro is not simply saved by Zeus in the *Ehoiai;* he immediately takes her to the home of her father's brother Kretheus, who welcomes her joyfully and raises her (she seems now to be younger than she was when she opposed her father). When she does reach an appropriate age Poseidon falls in love with her, and here our fragment ends, although another fragment adds bits and pieces of Poseidon's speech to Tyro telling her that she will bear two children (Hes fr 31 MW). We learn rather more from the *Nekuia,* where she is, like Iphimedeia, one of the women seen by Odysseus (*Od* 11.235–59). Here, as well as being the daughter of Salmoneus and the wife of Kretheus, she is said to have fallen in love with the river god Enipeus, whose waters she visited frequently. This in itself is strange enough (few other heroines fall in love with gods), but what follows is stranger still—Poseidon takes the form of Enipeus and lies with Tyro at the outpourings of the river, and a dark wave towers up over them, to hide them. Here, too, there is a speech (several of whose lines are identical to lines in the *Ehoiai*) in which Poseidon identifies himself and calls upon Tyro to bring up the children, but also exhorts her to keep silent about the matter. Why she should do so is not clear, but may relate to themes exploited later in tragedy (see below). Tyro then bears Pelias and Neleus; the former settles in Iolkos, the latter in Pylos.[9] The *Nekuia* finishes its story with the names of the three children whom Tyro bore to Kretheus: Aison, Pheres, and Amythaon, all, like their half-brothers, important in later stories.

No other Archaic source mentions Tyro. Sophokles did write two plays with her name as title, but we cannot tell whether they covered two separate phases of her tale, or were two different versions of the same play.[10] The few references mention a recognition scene (involving the boat in which the children were exposed), and seem to indicate that Tyro is ill-treated by a woman named Sidero (pp. 463–64 plus frr 657, 658 R). In Menander's *Epitrepontes* of the following century the twins are found by a goatherd who brings them up and eventually gives them a wallet with tokens of recognition (*gnôrismata,* presumably items found with them: *Epitr* 326–33). Somehow from these they perceive their true identity and become kings. The Cyzicene Epigrams tell us that Salmoneus himself imprisons Tyro, and that his new wife, Sidero (thus Tyro's stepmother), torments her; no reason is given in the epigram itself, but the introduction attributes the maltreatment to her seduction (*AP* 3.9: her children confront Salmoneus and release her). So too less explicitly Diodoros, where Salmoneus' first wife is Alkidike and the second is Sidero, who treats Tyro cruelly (before the latter's children are born) on general principles in her role as stepmother (DS 4.68.2). Apollodoros has Tyro (like Antiope) expose her children and suffer badly at the hands of her stepmother Sidero; presumably here, too, the cause is the disgrace she has brought upon herself (Ap*B* 1.9.8). The children are found and raised by horse breeders (after Pelias has been kicked in the face by one of their mares). Years later these children return full grown, release their mother, and kill the wicked stepmother (Pelias does the deed, in a sanctuary of Hera). The *Iliad* scholia claim that Neleus was nursed by a dog, and Pelias kicked by the horse *before* they are found by the horse breeders (ΣA *Il* 10.334); Aelianus adds that Pelias was raised by a horse (*VH* 12.42). All this is likely enough material for one or both of Sophokles' plays, with the children returning much like Hypsipyle's sons and being recognized, then saving their mother. Certainly the injunction by Poseidon in the *Nekuia* to conceal his identity as father of her children would provide an appropriate backdrop to such events, although they cohere less well with Poseidon's exhortation to bring up those children, a command found in both the *Nekuia* and the *Ehoiai*. Possibly the abandonment goes back to a tradition in which Enipeus was the real father and Tyro, uninstructed as to her offspring, quite naturally left them on their father's banks.[11] But perhaps, too, the tale of abandonment, recognition, and revenge was developed rather for the tragic stage. In any case we are left uncertain to whom Sidero was married in Sophokles' version. We have seen that in the *Ehoiai* Kretheus brings up his niece after her father's demise, and Apollodoros tells the same story (Ap*B* 1.9.8, as above). But subsequently in Apollodoros she is tormented by her stepmother *(mêtruia)*, who is presumably then (unless Apollodoros has conflated conflicting sources) the wife of her adopted father, not her real one. Likely this was the situation in Sophokles as well, with Kretheus conveniently available to marry Tyro after the death of his first wife at the hands of her children (might Poseidon appear to order this union?). The alternative notion, that Salmoneus himself married Sidero, as in the Cyzicene Epigrams and Diodoros, keeps him less plausibly alive when his own story demands otherwise; perhaps it arose from the supposition that where a wicked stepmother is at work a father must exist to marry her. In contrast to this whole plot we have, finally, the account of the *Odyssey* scholia in which Tyro is sent to another of her uncles, Deion, and then given by him to Kretheus in marriage after her seduction by Poseidon (Σ *Od* 11.290). Such a sequence is far more direct and logical than anything considered above, and for what it is worth would allow Tyro the possibility of bringing up her first two children, as Poseidon commands in the *Ehoiai* and the *Nekuia*.

SISYPHOS   Third of the sons of Aiolos is Sisyphos. The *Iliad* knows of him by that name and parentage, and as the father of Glaukos, father of Bellerophontes (all this in the great-great-grandson Glaukos' speech to Diomedes: *Il* 6.153–55). In the *Odyssey* he is somewhat less well regarded, appearing in the *Nekuia* together with other transgressors (*Od* 11.593–600). As we saw in chapter 3, this account describes the rock he must push uphill, and how it rolls back down again, but says nothing at all about what he did to arrive at such a pass. Alkaios notes that he was almost too clever to die (38 LP), and Theognis relates how he persuaded Persephone to let him come back up into the sunlight

(702–12), but only with Pherekydes do we find any real explanation of his misdeeds (3F119). After Zeus has fallen in love with Aigina, daughter of Asopos, and taken her from Phlious to the island (presumably Oinone) that will bear her name, Sisyphos reveals to the searching father the author of the abduction. For this he incurs Zeus' anger, and the latter sends Thanatos to him. But Sisyphos contrives to bind Thanatos, and for a while no one can die, until Ares (we might have expected Hermes) releases him and hands Sisyphos over to him to meet his fate. The trickster has yet another device, however: before dying, he has instructed his wife Merope (a daughter of Atlas in Hell 4F19a) not to perform the customary funeral rites, and thus Hades sends him back up to reproach her. Naturally, when he arrives in Korinth he stays there until he dies of old age. Returned to the Underworld, he is given by Hades a rock to roll lest he run away again.

We have already seen in chapter 3 that Aischylos wrote one and perhaps two plays about Sisyphos, and Pherekydes may well have drawn heavily on these, although both authors could, of course, also be using earlier sources. The two Aischylean titles are *Sisyphos Drapetes* ("Sisyphos the Runaway"), as preserved in the Medicean Catalogue, and *Sisyphos Petrokylistes* ("Sisyphos the Rock-roller"), as given by three citations. The *Drapetes* took place on earth, and seems to have been a satyr play that related Sisyphos' escape from Hades, although what action might have taken place onstage is harder to say (a celebration? Hades' coming to get Sisyphos?). The *Petrokylistes* offers no information at all on its content, nor does one see very clearly how one could find a tragedy in such material. Given Aischylos' fondness for connected tetralogies we might possibly have such a group here, with the other titles (concerning Sisyphos-Zeus-Aigina and Sisyphos-Thanatos?) missing. But more likely the two titles refer to the same satyr play, and Aischylos compressed events so that Sisyphos' return to Hades could form the finale. Of the *Sisyphos* plays of Sophokles (one reference only, perhaps mistaken) and Euripides (satyric) nothing is known. In art the stone-rolling appears as early as the metopes from Heraion I at Foce del Sele (no #). Here our escape artist is clearly depicted pushing his rock up a hill, while a small winged figure hovers behind, probably to make sure his pace does not slacken.[12] The tale may also be shown on a Lakonian cup of the same period (Kassel S 49b, now lost),[13] and was certainly well known in the second half of the sixth century in Athens, as there are some nine Black-Figure representations preserved (e.g., Munich 1494, 1549). All examples present Sisyphos with his rock in Hades, as we might expect, and thus have nothing new to offer from a narrative standpoint.

What survives of the *Ehoiai* says nothing about these events, but we do find Sisyphos in another quite different context as the seeker of a wife for his son Glaukos (Hes fr 43a MW). As we saw earlier, the woman in question is Mestra, daughter of Erysichthon, and Sisyphos is himself, it seems, deceived, for although he offers many bride gifts and some sort of bargain is concluded, Mestra darts off back to her father's house, perhaps in the form of some animal (there are massive gaps in the papyrus here). A quarrel ensues between Sisyphos and Erysichthon which no mortal can resolve; it is thus referred to one of the goddesses, who apparently decides in favor of Sisyphos and the contract. But Sisyphos, although surpassing all mortals in intelligence, does not grasp the will of Zeus, who does not intend that Glaukos shall beget children by Mestra. She is taken instead by Poseidon to Kos, where she bears to the god Eurypylos, father of Chalkon and Antagores. After this, she apparently makes her way back to Athens and her father, while Sisyphos sets his sights on a second prospective daughter-in-law, this time the offspring of Pandionides (i.e., of Nisos? *Fab* 157 speaks of Bellerophontes' mother as "Eurynome, daughter of Nisos"; in Ap*B* 1.9.3 "Eurymede" is the name of Glaukos' wife). This marriage appears to involve fewer problems, but once again Zeus denies Glaukos offspring, and the son Bellerophontes whom the wife bears in Glaukos' halls is actually the child of Poseidon. We shall see in chapter 10 that Pindar comes close to suggesting this parentage in his *Olympian* 13; neither Homer nor Apollodoros suggest anything of the sort. Eumelos for his part offers the surprising idea that Glaukos was by Panteiduia the real father of Leda; he had gone to Lakedaimonia to look for lost horses, and sired the child by the woman who later married Thestios, the putative father (fr 7 *PEG*). Almost certainly a desire to impose Corinthian ancestry upon a broader range of mythological figures is at work here.

We should note, too, that this son Glaukos is identified by Asklepiades with the Glaukos of Potniai who was killed by his own mares (12F1). As Asklepiades tells the story, Glaukos raised these mares on human flesh so that they might be more aggressive and ferocious in battle. When their accustomed food failed, however, they devoured their master at the funeral games for Pelias. Likely enough, much of this derives from Aischylos' lost play *Glaukos Potnieus*, which obviously dealt with the same story; from the play itself almost nothing survives. In the fourth century Palaiphatos, too, attests that Glaukos was devoured by his horses (Pal 25), and subsequently both Pausanias (6.20.19) and Hyginus (*Fab* 250, 273) agree with Asklepiades on the victim's parentage and the locale of the event. Servius, however, offers somewhat different causes, that Aphrodite maddened the mares because Glaukos scorned her rites, or that she did so because he had kept the horses from mating to improve their speed (Σ *G* 3.268). In the *Nostoi*, Sisyphos seems to have had another son, one Thersandros who becomes the father of a Proitos (fr 6 *PEG*). This Proitos is either identical to or becomes conflated with the Iliadic Proitos of Argos usually considered the son of Abas; about Thersandros himself nothing else is recorded. Pausanias, our source for the *Nostoi*, likewise calls him a son of Sisyphos at one other point in his work, where he adds to the family as well Ornytion and Almos (2.4.3).

One other well-remembered exploit of Sisyphos is preserved first in a fragment of Aischylos' lost *Hoplôn Krisis* ("Judgment of Arms") in which Aias tells Odysseus that Sisyphos approached the latter's mother Antikleia (fr 175

R). The fragment breaks off here, but the context of the citation makes clear that Aias is charging Odysseus with being a bastard, sprung from Antikleia and Sisyphos rather than her husband Laertes. The idea was picked up by both Sophokles and Euripides, and subsequently became a staple of the Odyssean tradition; whether it is any earlier than Aischylos (e.g., the *Aithiopis* or *Little Iliad*) we cannot say. Later sources report that Autolykos, the father of Antikleia (so already *Od* 11.85), had used his skills in thievery and metamorphosis to increase his own herds at the expense of Sisyphos', but was nevertheless caught when Sisyphos began carving a monogram of his name on the hooves of his animals (*Fab* 201; Σ Lyk 344). While visiting Autolykos to reclaim his property (Tzetzes says the two men had become friends), Sisyphos then found time to deflower Antikleia, who was thus pregnant with Odysseus when she married Laertes. Part of this tale appears as early as an Apulian volute krater from the end of the fifth century: in one scene Laertes introduces his new bride to surprised friends (one of whom points a finger indelicately at her belly), while the other shows Laertes handing to Autolykos a heart-shaped token with the name "Sisyphos" on it, presumably the latter's means of announcing (after his departure) responsibility for Antikleia's condition (Munich 3268). A Megarian bowl from the second century actually shows Sisyphos and Antikleia (both named) embracing in a bed-chamber, and before that are scenes in which Autolykos (also named) seems to be removing cattle from a protesting Sisyphos, and in which Sisyphos takes back the cattle as Autolykos and Laertes look on (Berlin:Lost 3161a).[14] Very possibly some form of this tale was the subject of Euripides' satyric *Autolykos*. From other early literature of the fifth century there is only a mention of Sisyphos as "shrewdest in contrivances like a god" in Pindar (*Ol* 13.52), and the story in a fragment of the same poet (fr 6.5 SM) that the Nymphai appeared to Sisyphos and ordered him to found the Isthmian games in honor of his dead nephew Melikertes (for whom see below on Athamas). The curious tale that he was at odds with his brother Salmoneus, and on the advice of an oracle begot twin sons upon his own niece Tyro to serve as his avengers (Tyro, however, killed them when she realized his scheme) survives only in Hyginus (*Fab* 60).

ATHAMAS The fourth of the sons of Aiolos has an extremely checkered career, with different and conflicting stories about his marriages and children which make him appear to be two or even three separate persons. On the one hand he is married to Nephele and has as offspring Phrixos and Helle, who must contend with a variously named hostile stepmother. On the other, he is the husband of Ino who bears Learchos and Melikertes and thus he is head of a family grievously afflicted by Hera's anger after Ino accepts custody of her sister's son Dionysos. And there is as well a third marriage, with still more children, to be considered in due course.

The *Odyssey* knows of Ino, daughter of Kadmos, who becomes the sea nymph Leukothea and rescues Odysseus, but says nothing of any husband or past history (*Od* 5.333–35). The *Ehoiai* for its part recounted something about a golden ram and Phrixos (Hes fr 68 MW), Ino's fate (and probably her role as Dionysos' nurse: Hes fr 70.6–7 MW), and daughters Euippe and Hyperippe from a son of Athamas (Leukon?: cf. ApB 1.9.2; Paus 9.34.9); alas the papyrus fragment in question (PSI 1383) does not take us further, which is especially unfortunate in view of the seeming conflation of traditions at some point in the development of the story. In Pherekydes' account a (wicked?) stepmother Themisto appeared, Phrixos willingly offered himself to be sacrificed when a crop failure occurred (3F98), and (as in the *Ehoiai*) a golden ram was involved (3F99). Pindar surely knew something of the same story, since he refers in passing to Phrixos' flight from his stepmother on the golden ram (*Py* 4.159–62). A scholion to this passage (one of our sources for Pherekydes, in fact: Σ *Py* 4.288a) also mentions versions in which the stepmother, not content with simple jealousy, has fallen in love with Phrixos, and consequently (having presumably been rebuffed) plots his destruction; no source is given, but Pindar's *Hymns* are immediately cited for the name of the stepmother as Demodike (fr 49 SM; cf. the fuller version of *Astr* 2.20, where Demodike, the would-be seducer, is the wife of Kretheus and hence no one's stepmother). Aischylos wrote a play, *Athamas*, which is completely lost. If it was part of a connected trilogy, then it was probably linked to the *Toxotides* (concerning the death of Semele's suitor, Aktaion) and the *Semele* (about Semele's pregnancy and death); in that case it would obviously have concerned the disasters attendant upon the upbringing of Dionysos. The scholion mentioned above also tells us that for the sophist Hippias of Elis the stepmother was neither Themisto nor Demodike but Gorgopis (6F11), and we will see below that even this does not exhaust the possibilities.

Still in the fifth century, Sophokles wrote two separate *Athamas* plays; one of these dealt with Athamas' near death (Herakles rescues him) as punishment for the sacrifice of Phrixos, while the content of the other is uncertain, although Dionysos seems to be involved. There was also a *Phrixos* play about which we know, as so often, nothing. And all these questions become still more complex when we turn to Euripides' *Ino*; if Hyginus can be trusted, Athamas here marries Themisto after Ino has run off to join a Bakchic revel (*Fab* 4). Years later Ino returns and is unwittingly employed as a nurse by Themisto, who confides to Ino her plan to kill Ino's children. Naturally Ino effects an exchange; Themisto kills her own children by mistake and then commits suicide. This might seem more than enough for one play, but Hyginus adds in this same *fabula* the madness of Athamas and consequent slaying of Learchos while hunting, and as well Ino's leap into the sea with Melikertes. Euripides also wrote two separate *Phrixos* plays, to which we shall return below, and asserts in the *Medeia* that Ino's madness caused her to kill both her children *before* jumping into the sea (*Med* 1282–89); this slight variation on the normal story may be for the sake of a better parallel with Medeia.

For any coherent fleshing out of these bits and pieces we must, as elsewhere, turn to Hyginus and Apollodoros. Hyginus, who as we have just seen devotes an entire *fabula* to Euripides' *Ino*, also has separate (unascribed) *fabulae* for Themisto, Ino, and Phrixos (*Fab* 1, 2, 3). From these we obtain the following story. Athamas marries three times and has six children: Phrixos and Helle by Nephele, Learchos and Melikertes by Ino, and Sphinkios and Orchomenos by Themisto. At some point Themisto tries to destroy Ino's children, with the consequences described above. Ino plots to destroy Nephele's children by persuading the women of the land to parch the grain before it is sown. Athamas then sends a messenger to Delphi to inquire about alleviating the consequent famine, and Ino bribes this man to report back that Phrixos must be sacrificed. Athamas refuses to do this, but Phrixos volunteers himself. At the last minute, however, the messenger repents his actions and reveals the truth. Athamas hands Ino and Melikertes over to Phrixos to be killed; Dionysos intervenes by sending a mist, and snatches his old nurse Ino away. He also drives Phrixos and Helle mad, and they are wandering lost in a forest when their mother, Nephele, arrives with a golden ram, which she tells them to mount and ride to Kolchis. Much of this smacks of tragedy, and indeed a hypothesis to the second of Euripides' *Phrixos* plays found at Oxyrhynchos in recent years confirms that playwright's use of the material. The first section is largely missing, but we know from other sources that grain bins were mentioned in this play (*Phrixos B*: fr 827 N²), and the end of the hypothesis tells of Ino's escape, Dionysos' attempt to destroy Phrixos and Helle precisely as in Hyginus, and Nephele's rescue of them through the ram (POxy 2455 fr 17 = Hypothesis 32 Aus).[15] Hyginus goes on in this same *Fabula* 2 to repeat the story of Athamas' madness and Ino's leap, but this seems unlikely to have been a part of either *Phrixos*, especially if it was included in the *Ino*.

Apollodoros covers much the same ground as Hyginus (Ap*B* 1.9.1). Athamas has Phrixos and Helle by Nephele; he marries Ino (we are not told what happens to Nephele, but her name and subsequent events suggest that she is a goddess) and begets Learchos and Melikertes. Ino's plot with the grain and the messenger to Delphi ensues, and Athamas is forced by the people of the land to sacrifice Phrixos. But in this account Nephele intervenes directly, sending the golden ram to rescue her son from the altar and take him and Helle to Kolchis (cf. Σ *Th* 993a, where events are as above and the children are thrown into the sea before being rescued by the ram). There follows the tale of Athamas' madness caused by the anger of Hera (presumably over the upbringing of Dionysos): he slays Learchos with an arrow and Ino performs her usual leap with Melikertes. Subsequently, he wanders to a new land (Thessaly?) and marries Themisto, daughter of Hypseus; the children are Leukon, Erythrios, Schoineus, and Ptoos.

One other account survives chiefly in the A scholia to *Iliad* 7.86, with the story as a whole credited to one Philostephanos of the third century B.C.: here Athamas marries Ino first, by whom he begets Learchos and Melikertes, but then puts her aside by order of Hera and marries Nephele, who bears Phrixos and Helle. Nephele, however, catches Athamas continuing to consort with Ino and leaves him; Ino, once more in command of the household, plots against Nephele's children with the stratagem of the parched seed-corn, as above. The rest follows as we would expect, save that Learchos' death and Ino's plunge into the sea with Melikertes result not from a separate madness sent by Hera, but from Athamas' justifiable anger against the woman who tried to destroy his other children. Such an arrangement knits together various different strands with remarkable logic, arguing perhaps for an origin in a drama, although one in that case making remarkably little impact on other surviving versions.

Thus, as suggested at the beginning of this section, we seem to have in origin three separate stories, one relating Ino's attempt to kill Phrixos and Helle (Nephele-Phrixos-Ino), a second Ino's leap and the death of her children (Ino-Learchos-Melikertes), and a third Themisto's foiled plot to kill Ino's children (Ino-Themisto). The *Ehoiai* and Pherekydes both seem to have related the first two, though we cannot be sure of the details (or the names), and the *Odyssey* must have known of Ino-Learchos-Melikertes in some form. Aischylos probably used this latter story for his play *Athamas*. Sophokles dramatized the aftermath of Nephele-Phrixos-Ino in his *Athamas A*; *Athamas B* could concern Ino-Learchos-Melikertes, since Dionysos is mentioned, but there are other possibilities, such as the actual events of Nephele-Phrixos-Ino (although these could have formed a part of his *Phrixos*). Euripides' *Phrixos B* used Nephele-Phrixos-Ino for its plot, while his *Ino* is based on Ino-Themisto, with possibly Ino-Learchos-Melikertes tacked on at the end. We saw that the *Ehoiai* clearly knows of a son of Athamas who is neither Phrixos, Melikertes, nor Learchos (given the daughters named: Hes fr 70.8–10 MW); if this is Leukon, as Pausanias suggests (see below), we might assume knowledge by the Catalogue Poet of Themisto in some form. But on the present evidence Ino-Themisto is unique to Euripides, and we may wonder whether he could have invented it; Apollodoros ignores it, although he is familiar with Themisto as Athamas' wife. The story pattern was in any case familiar from the *Odyssey*'s tale of Aedon, wife of Zethos, and her killing of her own child, Itylos, when she meant to kill those of her sister-in-law, Niobe (*Od* 19.518–23). Surprising on the above analysis is the Pindaric scholiast's naming of the stepmother from whom Phrixos flees as Themisto in Pherekydes. If he is right, then Themisto may at one time have played Ino's role in the Nephele-Phrixos-Ino sequence. But possibly, too, the scholiast is confused; it is not encouraging that the same scholion makes Nephele the stepmother in Sophokles' *Athamas*, which surely cannot be right.

One other point on which we should like more information is that of Phrixos' rescue: does Apollodoros' simpler account in which Nephele sends the ram directly to the altar represent an older version than the one (used probably by Euripides) in which the messenger confesses his guilt to save the children and a mist sent by Dionysos resolves the immediate crisis? If our guesses on the contents of the *Athamas* plays of Aischylos and Sophokles are correct, then Euripides might have been the first playwright to actually dramatize Phrixos' sacrifice; we must remember, however, that Sophokles' *Phrixos* is a complete blank to us. In Palaiphatos, the ram actually tells Phrixos that Athamas is about to sacrifice him (Pal 30); quite possibly this idea is more clearly explained by the A scholia at *Iliad* 7.86, where Phrixos on his father's instructions brings the finest ram of the flock for sacrifice, and that ram reveals to Phrixos that he himself is the victim. By contrast, we saw that in the scholia to *Theogony* 993a Phrixos and Helle are to be thrown into the sea rather than sacrificed at an altar, and the ram appears first in the water to save them. Phrixos and the ram appeared on one of the metopes of the Sikyonian *monopteros* at Delphi, but we cannot say if other parts of the story were also shown.[16] On a Red-Figure amphora of about 430 B.C. by the Munich Painter, Phrixos flees right, holding on to the horn of the ram, while to the left a woman pursues with a raised axe, suggesting perhaps that the stepmother intended to perform the sacrifice herself (Naples Stg 270). Unfortunately, there are no names, so that we cannot be sure what the artist would have called this particular stepmother.[17] The following century offers a Paestan calyx krater of *c.* 350 with Phrixos and Helle (here for the first time) on the ram together (Naples H3412); only slightly later is an Apulian dish on which Helle is shown falling off the ram as her brother clings to it (Münster 673).[18]

Of children from Athamas' children there is little to say. The *Ehoiai* lists, as we saw, two and likely three daughters of a son of Athamas who is probably Leukon, to judge from Pausanias (9.34.9), where Leukon's daughter Euippe agrees with the one name preserved in Hesiod fragment 70 MW. These daughters all seem to have had children—one marries Kopreus, grandson of Orchomenos, and produces Hippoklos, and another (Euippe?) marries Eteoklos, son of Andreus and likewise grandson of Orchomenos. But no names of any importance for further stories emerge. Neither Learchos nor Melikertes have descendants; the offspring of Phrixos (and Helle) we shall encounter below. The Schoineus mentioned by Apollodoros as a brother of Leukon (ApB 1.9.2) is likely to be the same Schoineus who in the *Ehoiai* fathers the Boiotian Atalanta.

PERIERES, DEION, MINYAS Aiolos' other three sons play no role in myths themselves, but they do have children or (more often) grandchildren who will interest us. Perieres seems to have married an Alkyone (not the same as the wife of Keyx) in the *Ehoiai*, and to have been the father of Halirrhothios, who in turn was the father of Semos and Alazygos (Hes fr 49 MW: the scholiast does not quite assign this information to the *Ehoiai*, but presumably that is where he is looking). As children of Perieres, Apollodoros (ApB 1.9.5) and Pausanias (4.2.4) add two more sons, Leukippos and Aphareus, although they alter the name of the mother to Gorgophone, daughter of Perseus, and fail to mention Halirrhothios in this context. In addition, Pausanias would have Perieres disappear from view (at 2.21.8 he in fact dies) and Gorgophone then marry Oibalos, son of Kynortes (from the line of Atlas), and bear Tyndareos (and Ikarios?: 3.1.3–4). But Apollodoros subsequently cites Stesichoros for the idea that it was a Perieres, son of Kynortes (as opposed to a Perieres, son of Aiolos, or an Oibalos, son of Kynortes), who married Gorgophone and begat all four children—Aphareus, Leukippos, Tyndareos, and Ikarios (227 *PMG*; still no sign of Halirrhothios). Certainly all four of these would have been mentioned, with their ancestry, in a poem such as the *Ehoiai*, but the only preserved information we have is that Tyndareos is the son of Oibalos (Hes fr 199.8 MW; no mother noted). Seemingly, then, two separate families have been brought together, that of Perieres and his children Aphareus and Leukippos (either by Alkyone or Gorgophone) on the one hand, and that of Oibalos and his children Tyndareos and Ikarios (by Gorgophone) on the other.[19] On Stesichoros' evidence this would seem to have happened early, since he not only assigns these children a common mother but also a single male parent who conflates the two previous fathers by having the name of one and the ancestry of the other. As a variant on this process we find in the scholia to the *Orestes* Oibalos, son of Perieres, as father to Tyndareos and Ikarios (plus Arene and the bastard Hippokoon: Σ *Or* 457).

As for the children of these four siblings, Pindar makes Aphareus the father of Idas and Lynkeus (*Nem* 10.65), and this represents the standard tradition, although Simonides somewhere called Idas at least a child of Poseidon raised by Aphareus (563 *PMG*). In Apollodoros we find as well one Peisos (ApB 3.10.3). We have already discussed Idas' challenging of Apollo to win back Marpessa; his taking of her from her father Euenos will be considered later in this chapter, and his and Lynkeus' deaths in chapter 11. Leukippos, brother of Aphareus, is traditionally the father of three daughters, of whom two, Phoibe and Hilaeira, are carried off by the Dioskouroi, leading at times to the battle with their cousins the Apharetidai. The third daughter, Arsinoe, is probably attested already in the *Ehoiai* as a child of Leukippos, and definitely appears in that work as the mother of Asklepios by Apollo (Hes fr 50 MW; so too ApB 3.10.3); as we have seen, the usual mother is Koronis. There is one other point of note: Pausanias tells us that, although Hilaeira and Phoibe are called Leukippides (i.e., daughters of Leukippos) in their shrine at Sparta, the author of the *Kypria* makes them daughters of Apollo (3.16.1 = fr 11 *PEG*). Possibly Leukippos was in that tradition their stepfather. The families of the other two brothers, Tyndareos and Ikarios, we will consider in chapters 6 (as part of the line of Atlas) and 11.

Deion's marriage is not preserved in the *Ehoiai* or any other early source. But Pherekydes does give him a daughter, Philonis, who bears to Apollo Philammon and to Hermes Autolykos (3F120; see chapter 2); quite possibly this was covered in Hesiod fragment 64 MW. In Apollodoros, this same Deion weds

Diomede, daughter of Xouthos, a woman whom we have already encountered with that parentage in the *Ehoiai* (Ap*B* 1.9.4; Hes fr 10a.20–24 MW), so that such a marriage may also have some early credibility. As for possible sons, a scholion at *Odyssey* 11.326, which draws at least in its latter part from the Hesiodic Corpus, describes the special powers of Iphiklos, and makes him a son of Phylakos, son of Deion, by Klymene, daughter of Minyas (= Hes fr 62 MW). From Pausanias, on the other hand, we learn that in the *Nostoi* Kephalos was a son of Deion married to Klymene, daughter of Minyas, who bore to him also a son Iphiklos (fr 5 *PEG*). The same Kephalos, son of Deion, is in another part of the Epic Cycle (the *Epigonoi?*) married to Prokris (*Epig* fr 5 *PEG*), which may seem in conflict with the *Nostoi*, but Pausanias argues that Kephalos married first Prokris and then, after her accidental death at his hands, Klymene (10.29.6). The tale of that death we will return to in chapter 7, when we discuss the daughters of Erechtheus. Apollodoros covers some of this ground by giving to Deion as sons both Phylakos *and* Kephalos, and adds as well Aktor and Ainetos. Quite possibly such sons and the marriage to Diomede go back to the *Ehoiai*, but neither there nor anywhere else are both Phylakos and Kephalos likely to have married Klymene (especially as neither dies an early death), and Iphiklos must be the child of one or the other. Since our consideration of the wooing of Pero later in this chapter will show that Phylakos is the father in all other accounts (including that of Apollodoros), it may be that Pausanias has somehow erred in his citation of the *Nostoi*. As for Kephalos' union with Eos, the Kephalos in question there is almost certainly a separate figure (although the two are later merged: see chapter 7). Apollodoros knows of one last child of Deion, Asterodeia, a daughter, whom the Lykophron scholia (Σ Lyk 939; cf. Σ *Tro* 9 and probably the *Ehoiai*: Hes fr 58 MW) marry off to Phokos, son of Aiakos, producing Krisos and Panopeus, the children who fought in their mother's womb. To Phylakos, meanwhile, Apollonios credits not only Iphiklos, but also Alkimede, the mother of Iason in some accounts (AR 1.45–48).

Line 27 of Hesiodic fragment 10a MW contains just enough space for the name of a seventh son of Aiolos, and the following connective shows that there was, in fact, a name in the gap (either anapaest, spondee, or trochee). "Magnes," the name given by Apollodoros, would fit well enough, but we have seen that in the *Ehoiai* Magnes is, with Makedon, a son of Aiolos' aunt Thuia. Based on the fact that in the *Ehoiai* two daughters of Leukon, son of Athamas, marry grandsons of Orchomenos, son of Minyas, and given that Minyas is without parents of his own, Martin West has suggested that he might be placed here, as the seventh brother.[20] The marriage of his daughter Klymene to a son of what would then be his brother Deion (whether that son is Phylakos or Kephalos) might seem a further argument in favor of such a conclusion, but Minyas, father of Klymene, is regarded by the *Odyssey* scholia at least as a son of Poseidon (Σ Od 11.326). As a final bit of confusion, we find in Apollodoros a Klymene, daughter of Minyas, married neither to Phylakos nor Kephalos, but instead to Iasos, by whom she is the mother of the Arkadian Atalantá (Ap*B*

3.9.2). Whatever Minyas' ancestry, his son Orchomenos is essentially just an eponym (although in Pherekydes he is father of Elara, the mother of Tityos: 3F55); the fate of his three daughters who declined to worship Dionysos we will consider in chapter 18.

The first part of Phrixos' story has already been recounted in dealing with the tribulations of his father Athamas. Whether or not his stepmother really did fall in love with him in the earliest accounts (as at Σ *Py* 4.288a), it seems clear that he was fated to be sacrificed when the crops were ruined, and we know that both the *Ehoiai* and Pherekydes mentioned the golden ram (*Katast* 19 = Hes fr 68 MW; Pher 3F99). We saw, too, that Pindar mentions the woolly golden fleece of the ram who saved Phrixos from the sea and from his stepmother at *Pythian* 4.68 and 159–62; possibly he dealt with the story further in whatever lost hymn named the mother "Demodike." But our real details on the events surrounding Phrixos' flight from his homeland come first from Euripides' lost *Phrixos B,* and Hyginus' account presumably drawn from it (*Fab* 3).

For the journey and Phrixos' subsequent adventures, on the other hand, there is early material. The *Aigimios* related that Phrixos when he arrived in the land of Aietes sacrificed the ram and brought the fleece to Aietes, and that for this reason he was welcomed (Hes fr 299 MW). The *Megalai Ehoiai* apparently had Phineus show Phrixos the way (to Kolchis?) and become blind as a result (Hes fr 254 MW); the same work definitely has Phrixos marry Iophossa, daughter of Aietes, and perhaps (as in Apollonios) beget four children—Argos, Phrontis, Melas, and Kytisoros (Hes fr 255 MW: referent for the children ambiguous). Pherekydes, for his part, says that the Argo was named after this Argos (3F106). Whether the *Ehoiai* also described Phrixos' journey we do not know; in that poem Phineus loses his sight as an exchange for long life (Hes fr 254 MW, as above). Akousilaos agrees on "Iophossa" as the name of Phrixos' wife (2F38), but there must have been variants, for Pherekydes gives "Euenia" as her real name and "Chalkiope" and "Iophossa" as by-names (3F25; in AR 2.1147–56 and Herodoros 31F39 the wife is again Chalkiope). Pherekydes also knows of at least one son, Melas, who marries one Eurykleia and has a son Hyperes (3F101), and "Epimenides" adds another son, Presbon (3B12). Simonides remarks of the journey that the animal was originally white, becoming then purple from the sea (presumably while swimming to Kolchis: 576 *PMG*); Akousilaos agrees (2F37).[21]

Remarkably, there is in all these sources no mention of Helle; we first encounter her in Euripides. However, a scholiast (on Apollonios) credits to Hekataios the idea that the ram by the will of Zeus spoke to Phrixos, encouraging him (1F17), and this in the scholiast's general resume of the situation takes place after Helle has fallen off, so that she appears to be early, even if we cannot say how early; fuller details are in Apollonios (1.256–57; on the ram's speaking to Phrixos *earlier*, at the time of the sacrifice, see above on Athamas).

From Ps-Eratosthenes comes the idea that Poseidon saved Helle when she fell and had by her a son, Paion (*Katast* 19; *Astr* 2.20.1 adds the alternative name "Edonos").

From the later fifth century there is the previously mentioned *Phrixos* of Sophokles with its uncertain plot, and from Euripides the *Phrixos A* and *B;* while the latter of these concerned Phrixos' rescue from the plotting of Ino, the former might have been either a different version of the same events, or the story of Phrixos' subsequent life in Kolchis.[22] Of this existence in Kolchis not much is said, but Hyginus' *fabula* on Phrixos offers an intriguing possibility for drama: Aietes is told that he should beware of death at the hands of a descendant of Aiolos, and therefore kills his own son-in-law (*Fab* 3). Valerius Flaccus at one point (1.41–45) seems to know this same story, though later in his poem (5.224–25) we find Phrixos dead of old age. Hyginus elsewhere says that Hermes brought Phrixos back to Greece in order to convince Athamas of his innocence (*Astr* 2.20). Finally, Apollonios adds one other story, that Phrixos' four sons set off to recover the possessions of their grandfather Athamas, but are shipwrecked and rescued by Iason, who returns them to their mother Chalkiope and is commended to her sister Medeia (AR 2.1093–1156).

The Children of Tyro

NELEUS The *Nekuia* names, as we saw, all five of Tyro's children: Neleus and Pelias by Poseidon, Aison, Pheres, and Amythaon by her uncle Kretheus. Neleus is firmly anchored in Pylos, and his wife Chloris, daughter of Amphion (son of Iasos), is like Tyro one of the women seen by Odysseus in the Underworld (*Od* 11.281–97). Here three sons are named—Nestor, Chromios, and Periklymenos—and a daughter, Pero, whom all men of that time wish to marry; the rest of the tale deals with the task set by her father for prospective suitors, the driving off of the cattle of Iphiklos. Nestor in *Iliad* 11 says that Neleus had in all twelve sons, including himself, but that Herakles slew the other eleven (*Il* 11.692–93). A fragment of the *Ehoiai* offers further details (Hes fr 33a MW): after Zeus causes Neleus to settle in Pylos, the latter marries a daughter of Amphion, son of Iasos (the name is missing but "Chloris" will fit the papyrus gap), and begets twelve children, who are named. Of these, eight names are preserved—Antimenes, Alastor, Asterios, Pylaon, Eurybios, Epilaos, Chromios, and Periklymenos. Nestor of course can be added, and the other three should probably be supplied from Apollodoros' list as Euagoras, Tauros, and Deimachos (ApB 1.9.9). The *Ehoiai* goes on to relate that Poseidon gave to Periklymenos the power to transform himself into all sorts of things, including an eagle, an ant, a bee, and a snake.[23] In the course of Herakles' attack on Pylos this last son slays many men on the battlefield (it is not clear whether this was with the help of his transformations or through his own valor), and then, changed into some animal, perches on the boss of the yoketree of Herakles' chariot and contemplates how to halt his opponent. Athena alerts Herakles to Periklymenos' presence, and he shoots the Neleid with his bow. The fragment, curiously, does not say what animal Periklymenos had become, although this may have been mentioned later. Various scholiasts suggest a bee, a fly, or an eagle; certainly the first two seem unlikely targets for an arrow, but perhaps this was the point. A subsequent fragment of the same poem tells us that while Periklymenos was alive Herakles and his troops were unable to sack Pylos, but that after his death they did so, and Herakles slew eleven children of Neleus; the twelfth, Nestor, escaped because he chanced to be a guest of the Gerenians at the time (Hes fr 35 MW). Conceivably this was the occasion mentioned in *Iliad* 5 (and by Pindar) during which Herakles confronted Hades and perhaps other of the gods, as some scholiasts suppose, but, as we saw earlier, the question remains undecided (see chapter 2, under "Hades"). Apollodoros follows much the same account as the *Ehoiai* (ApB 1.9.9: Periklymenos becomes a lion, a snake, and a bee, but perishes nonetheless). In Hyginus, by contrast, he turns into an eagle and escapes Herakles, who slays his father Neleus together with ten sons (*Fab* 10; Neleus likewise perishes at ApB 2.7.3). Wherever this last notion comes from, it is certainly not what Nestor envisions in *Iliad* 11, where his father is alive to appreciate his later exploits against the Eleans (*Il* 11.682–84). Apollodoros also adds a detail that may be old, namely that Herakles marched on Pylos because Neleus had refused to purify him for the murder of Iphitos (ApB 2.6.2). Isokrates in the *Archidamos* offers another, perhaps more likely, motive, that Neleus and all his sons (save Nestor) tried to make off with the cattle of Geryoneus as Herakles was bringing them back to Eurystheus (6.*Arch* 19). The result—Herakles slays Neleus and the wicked sons and puts Nestor on the throne of Pylos—is, as we shall see, a familiar pattern in Herakles' repertoire of exploits. Aside from what we found in the *Nekuia* and the *Ehoiai*, Pherekydes is the only early source to recount something of Neleus' migration from the north, as a scholion to the *Nekuia* passage tells us: Neleus is driven out of Iolkos by Pelias (so too ApB 1.9.9; Paus 4.2.5) and, going south, receives Pylos from the Messenians and weds Chloris, daughter of Amphion and Persephone (this last one daughter of Minyas) (3F117). All this, of course, may well be taken directly from the *Ehoiai*.

The other important tale involving Neleus is that already found in the *Odyssey*, the courting of his daughter Pero. The *Nekuia* offers one brief account of this story, and *Odyssey* 15 another; in each case it seems clear that the audience was expected to supply missing details. In the *Nekuia*, Neleus refuses to give his daughter to anyone who does not bring back from Phylake (in Thessaly) to Pylos the cattle of Iphiklos (*Od* 11.281–97). An unnamed seer volunteers to do this, but the cowherds keep him in strong bonds (presumably after capturing him), and only at the end of a year does Iphiklos release him, after he has uttered prophecies or wondrous things of some sort. *Odyssey* 15 has its own version, told as part of the tale of the seer Theoklymenos whom Telemachos befriends on his way home from Sparta (*Od* 15.225–56). Theoklymenos is descended from Melampous, who is now specified as the hero of the wooing. We learn that Melampous was a wealthy man of Pylos, but that he left, fleeing Neleus, and that the latter held his possessions by force for a year. He himself was held prisoner in the house of Phylakos during that time, because of the daughter of Neleus and an *atê* sent by the Erinys. But he escaped death, drove the cattle back to Pylos, and paid back Neleus for his "unseemly deeds." He also took the daughter back home as a wife for his brother. None of this exactly conflicts with the version of the *Nekuia*, but it does look like an odd conflation of two separate stories, one in which Melampous leaves Pylos voluntarily in order to win Pero (whether for himself or his brother), and another in which he is exiled and robbed by Neleus, acquires new wealth in the form of cattle, returns to Pylos and avenges himself on Neleus, and then takes the latter's daughter, perhaps only as an afterthought or token of reconciliation. But in either storyline it is very hard to see what role an Erinys would play; as discussed in chapter 1, the primary role of these goddesses in Homer seems the avenging of acts of disrespect by children against their parents.

At further details of the exile story we can only guess, because the wooing of Pero is the storyline followed in all subsequent accounts. The *Ehoiai* related the tale, as did the Hesiodic *Melampodia;* unfortunately, very little survives. A papyrus fragment from the *Ehoiai* says, between gaps, something about accomplishing a task, having unseemly bonds, courting on behalf of his brother Bias (here named for the first time), accomplishing a marriage, cows, and Pero as the prize, after which she bears to Bias Talaos (Hes fr 37 MW). Admittedly this is not much, but it does seem to exclude any possibility of an exile-revenge theme. No doubt, the *Melampodia* described the whole sequence of events in some detail; all that remains are four lines mentioning Melampous, Iphiklos, and Phylakos. Our fullest Archaic account is that of Pherekydes, as given in a long summary in a scholion to the *Nekuia* (3F33). As before, Neleus will give his daughter Pero only to whoever can bring the cattle of his mother Tyro back from Iphiklos in Phylake. Bias alone volunteers, then persuades his brother Melampous to do the task for him; Melampous agrees, though as a seer he knows he will be imprisoned for a year. As anticipated, he is captured by the cowherds while trying to steal the cattle and turned over to Iphiklos. As his year of imprisonment draws to a close, he hears two woodworms saying that a beam in the ceiling of his prison is almost gnawed through. Upon his request his guards carry him out (bed and all) and the ceiling collapses (killing the female guard, who had treated him badly). Her colleague reports all this to Phylakos, and Phylakos in turn to Iphiklos, and the two of them contract to give the sought-for cattle to Melampous if he can cure Iphiklos' inability to beget children. Melampous sacrifices to Zeus and distributes portions to all the birds, whom he then asks for help. They bring to him a vulture, who tells him that when Iphiklos was very small Phylakos chased him with a knife, because he (Phylakos, it seems) had seen him doing something improper (*atopon*: mischievous, probably). Failing to catch the child, he then fixed the knife in a wild pear tree, and the bark grew over it; fear of this knife has caused Iphiklos' childlessness. The vulture's solution is to recover the knife, scrape the rust from it, mix that rust with wine, and let Iphiklos drink the mixture for ten days. In due time a child, Podarkes, is born, the cattle are handed over to Melampous, he brings them to Neleus as the bride price for Pero, and gives her to Bias to wife; children are Perialkes, Aretos, and Alphesiboia. In the course of this account, Pherekydes also adds a point not mentioned by Homer or what we have of the *Ehoiai*: Melampous and Bias are the sons of Amythaon, the son of Tyro and half-brother of Neleus (so also Bak fr 4.50–51 SM; *Py* 4.124–26).

Apollodoros gives substantially the same story, but with interesting additions that may be early (ApB 1.9.11–12). Amythaon here marries the daughter of his brother Pheres, one Eidomene, and Melampous and Bias result. Melampous saves the young of some snakes his servants have killed, and they lick his ears, whereupon he understands the speech of animals. The tale of Pero's wooing and the year in Phylake are as in Pherekydes (the cattle here clearly belong to the father Phylakos, not his son Iphiklos), but when we come to the incident that frightened Iphiklos, it is not simply that the father chased his son while holding a knife, but rather that Phylakos was gelding rams, and Iphiklos saw him. The scholia to Theokritos go even further: Iphiklos was present at this gelding and Phylakos wished to frighten him, but in so doing (and implanting the knife in a nearby tree) it happened that the knife actually touched his son's genitals, thus causing the impotence (Σ Theok 3.43c; cf. Eu-*Od* p. 1685, 37). As so often, we cannot say if the scholiast who is our source for Pherekydes might have omitted this detail, or if Pherekydes omitted it after finding it in his sources, or whether it was known to Pherekydes at all. One other variant occurs in scholia to *Odyssey* 11.290, where the knife is used for gelding as in Apollodoros, but the solution is to sacrifice to those gods made angry by the gelding. Finally, the same scholia offer an explanation of Neleus' original request for the cattle: Tyro his mother was supposedly sent to her uncle Deion/Deioneus, who then gave her to his brother Kretheus as above but retained some of her possessions, that is, the cattle. When Iphiklos (here called a son rather than grandson of Deion) refuses to surrender them, Neleus devises the idea of making them the bride price for his daughter. In the usual genealogy, of course, Melampous and Bias are second cousins of Iphiklos as well as of Neleus, since all have grandparents who are sons of Aiolos.

Melampous and Bias' adventures are not quite finished. In the continuation of the *Ehoiai* fragment that touched on the wooing, they move from Pylos over to Argos, where the king Proitos gives them land on which to settle after Melampous has cured his daughters of the madness sent by one of the gods (Hes fr 37 MW: gaps at the line ends prevent us from knowing which god). The story was clearly just alluded to here, since the line of Pelias immediately follows, but it apparently appeared in more detail later on, when the Catalogue Poet discussed the line of Abas (Hes frr 129, 130, 131 MW). One would expect it to play a role also in the *Melampodia*. But once again our best source is Pherekydes, from a scholion to the passage in *Odyssey* 15 (3F114). In his account, the daughters have been mad for ten years (because they had mocked a shrine of Hera, though notions of their transgression vary), and Melampous offers to cure them for an appropriate reward. Proitos promises a share of the kingdom and one of the daughters (Melampous' choice), and Melampous then effects the cure, not oddly enough through magic or his skills with animals, but by prayers and sacrifices to Hera. We will return to the daughters of Proitos later in discussing his own line (see chapter 10), but we should note here that Bakchylides in his version of the story has them cured via Artemis' appeal to Hera after Proitos has prayed to her (11.40–112); Melampous is not involved at all.

We have also seen that in the *Ehoiai* Pero bears to Bias a son Talaos (Hes fr 37 MW). The author does not give any further family or descendants at this point in the poem. But in Pindar (*Nem* 9.14–16; *Ol* 6.15) and Bakchylides (9.19) Talaos is the father of Adrastos, and the Nemean passage notes as well that the sons of Talaos gave their sister Eriphyle to Amphiaraos to wife. Apollodoros adds to these siblings Adrastos and Eriphyle a brother, Parthenopaios (Ap*B* 1.9.13), with Lysimache, daughter of Melampous' son Abas, as mother of all three. We shall see in chapter 14 that this Parthenopaios (or at least the Parthenopaios who marches with Adrastos against Thebes) is usually an Arkadian (so *Hepta* 547), the son of Atalanta. But several other sources before Apollodoros also call him a son of Talaos, beginning as early as Hekataios (1F32).

As for Melampous, the continuation of the story of the wooing of Pero in *Odyssey* 15 brings him to Argos (by himself), it being fated that he rule the Argives (*Od* 15.238–56). He marries (the *Odyssey* simply says "a woman") and begets Antiphates and Mantios. From Antiphates is born Oikles, and from Oikles Amphiaraos. Mantios for his part fathers Polypheides and Kleitos; Kleitos is snatched away by Eos, but Polypheides becomes a famous seer and father of Theoklymenos. The *Ehoiai* must have covered some of the same ground, to judge from a papyrus fragment mentioning Antiphates and Theoklymenos (as well as Manto and Pronoe: Hes fr 136 MW), but the proximity of names (only the middle of each line is preserved) does not seem to square with the *Odyssey*'s version. We should note, too, that the abbreviated account in Hesiod fragment 37 MW does not say that Melampous married a Proitid, and the *Odyssey* appears to be ignorant of that detail, although it is standard in the later tradition. Pherekydes offers his own genealogy (3F115): from Melampous to Mantios to Kleitos to Koiranos (mentioned in Hes fr 136 MW) to Polyidos, who begets Euchenor and Kleitos, allies of the Epigonoi at Thebes and Agamemnon at Troy, where Paris slays Euchenor (this last also at *Il* 13.660–72). Diodoros offers the same main line of descent from Melampous to Amphiaraos as the *Odyssey*, although in his account Melampous marries a granddaughter of Proitos (DS 4.68.4–5). Fortunately, the variation in details is not of any great consequence for the narrative of Greek myth; of all the names mentioned above, only Adrastos, Eriphyle, and Amphiaraos will play any important roles.

From these interlopers in the story of Neleus and his family (albeit justified as the sons of Amythaon) we return to Neleus himself. We have seen that in accounts beginning with Isokrates, Neleus is among those slain by Herakles, in contrast to the notion of the *Iliad*. In Eumelos he seems to have died and been buried near the Isthmos, a story that probably served the needs of Corinthian tradition (fr 6 *PEG*). In any case, the undisputed death of eleven of his sons at Herakles' hands, however regrettable, simplifies the family picture considerably, and we have only to worry about Nestor. As he tells us himself in *Iliad* 11, there was after Herakles' expedition some problem with the Epeians to the north, who tried to take advantage of the Pylians' weakness with a cattle raid (*Il* 11.670–761). Nestor counterattacks, slaying Itymoneus and bringing back large numbers of sheep and cows to Pylos; Neleus takes a good part of these as compensation for horses that Augeias stole from him when they were sent up to Elis to run in a race. The Epeians come to seek vengeance on the third day, bringing with them the Moliones, but Nestor and the Pylians defeat them handily and drive them off. One other combat Nestor refers to is that between Pylians and Arkadians, during which he defeated the Arkadian champion Ereuthalion (*Il* 4.318–19; 7.132–56). Outside of the Peloponnese there is the battle between the Lapithai and the Kentauroi to which he is formally invited (*Il* 1.260–72), even if we suspect that this is a convenient Iliadic invention. Finally, on a more agonistic front, Nestor shines in the funeral games held by the Epeians for Amarynkeus, as he tells us in *Iliad* 23: he wins the boxing, wrestling, running, and spear-throwing contests (*Il* 23.630–42: in running he defeats Iphiklos, presumably the son of Phylakos cured by Melampous). Only in the chariot race does he lose, to the Moliones, having been, as he says, outnumbered (one drove, the other applied the whip). Nestor's children were listed in the *Ehoiai* (Hes frr 35, 36 MW), but we have mostly gaps; Thrasymedes, Perseus, Echephron, Peisidike, and Polykaste survive, and there were probably three or four more, among them Antilochos who dies at Troy at the hands of Memnon while rescuing his father. At *Iliad* 17.378, Antilochos and Thrasymedes appear together on the battlefield. When Telemachos visits Nestor in *Odyssey* 3 he finds Thrasymedes, Perseus, and Echephron, and as well Stratios and Aretos, whose names will fit into the gaps in the *Ehoiai*, and Peisistratos, the youngest, whose name probably will not (*Od* 3.412–15). There is also Polykaste, youngest of all the children, who gives Telemachos a bath, and their mother, Eurydike (daughter of Klymenos), who appears only briefly, when the ox is being sacrificed (*Od* 3.451–52). The bath would appear to have been quite a success, since in the *Ehoiai* Telemachos marries Polykaste and begets a son Persepolis (Hes fr 221 MW).

PELIAS   Pelias, the twin brother of Neleus, is mentioned in the *Iliad* only once, as the father of Alkestis and thus the grandfather of Eumelos, leader of the contingent from Pherai and Iolkos (*Il* 2.711–15); he fares no better in the *Odyssey*, where the account of his birth and residence in sheep-rich Iolkos is the only reference (*Od* 11.253–55). His children were listed in the *Ehoiai* immediately after the account of the race of Neleus, but only the names of Alkes-tis and Pasidike survive (Hes fr 37.16–22 MW), together with an initial letter *M* that probably indicates that we should add here Medousa, as in Hyginus (*Fab* 24). The end of the *Theogony* calls him *hubristês* and *atasthalos*, and one who has imposed great labors upon Iason, son of Aison (*Th* 992–96). Such language already hints at some sort of family dispute (unless it refers to Apol-lodoros' story that Pelias slew his stepmother Sidero in a temenos of Hera: ApB 1.9.8). Mimnermos likewise calls Pelias *hubristês* and the adventure of the Argo a labor (11 W); it would be interesting to know whether he treated the whole story in any detail.

But despite these tantalizing allusions, a proper account of real villainy on the part of Pelias does not appear until Pindar's *Pythian* 4, where we are told that Pelias took by force the throne that belonged rightfully to his half-brother Aison, son of Kretheus (son of Aiolos) (*Py* 4.106–15). Of how this was done there is no explanation, but the father Aison is still alive to welcome Iason when the latter returns from Cheiron's keeping (*Py* 4.120–23). Iason's birth was in this account kept from Pelias (or his death feigned), and the child sent away, out of his uncle's reach. In the interim, Pelias receives a prophecy at Delphi that death will come to him from one of his own race, and that he must beware anyone appearing before him with a single sandal (*Py* 4.71–78). When Iason does appear, Pelias pretends to accede to his demands, but also claims that Phrixos has commanded in a dream the return of the Golden Fleece from Kolchis, and that since he is now too old, Iason must undertake the task (*Py* 4.159–67). Iason accepts without demur, and the rest of the poem concerns the voyage of the Argo, with no account of the final return to Iolkos; only near the end of the ode does Pindar note that Medeia will cause Pelias' death (*Py* 4.250).

By contrast, the scholia to *Pythian* 4 cite Pherekydes for a rather different version of the story. As before, Pelias receives the usual prophecy, and remem-bers this upon encountering the one-sandaled Iason in from the fields (where he has been plowing) for Pelias' sacrifice to Poseidon (3F105). But instead of a dream we find here a different ploy. Pelias asks Iason what he would do if it were prophesied that one of his citizens would kill him. Iason replies that he would send that person to Aia to get the Golden Fleece, and thus seals his own fate. Pherekydes adds that Hera put this idea into Iason's head, so that Medeia might come as a bane to Pelias. These details are all repeated precisely by Apollodoros, including the plowing, which rather suggests that Iason was here a peaceful subject of Pelias with no claim on the throne (ApB 1.9.16); if we go back to the beginning of Apollodoros' account, likely also taken from Phere-kydes, we see that Pelias, rather than Aison, there succeeds Kretheus as ruler of Iolkos. Thus there may well have been a version in which Pelias rightfully held the throne, and feared Iason solely because of the oracle.[24] The opening of Apollonios' *Argonautika* with its explanation of the Argo's voyage is surpris-ingly brief, but here too Iason arrives (with his one sandal) for the ceremony to Poseidon, not to claim the throne, and nowhere does the poem suggest that the quest is for that purpose: Pelias simply remembers the prophecy and sends Iason off (AR 1.5–17, again with mention of hostility between Pelias and Hera). The scholia to *Odyssey* 12.69, by contrast, clearly agree with the Pindaric idea that the throne was rightfully Iason's, but in their version as against that of Pindar Aison dies while his son is still a child, and leaves the throne to Pelias as regent and guardian until Iason should come of age; Iason's mother Alkimede then sends him to Cheiron in fear for his life, and when he grows up to claim his throne Pelias dispatches him to Kolchis as a necessary requirement. The same idea of Aison's early death and Pelias' regency also appears in the scholia to *Theogony* 993, although there Pelias himself sends Iason to Cheiron, and seemingly intends to surrender the throne until the prophecy intervenes. We should remember, of course, that versions in which Aison dies while his son is still a child will not be compatible with those (as in the *Nostoi*) in which Medeia rejuvenates him.

As to Pelias' death, Pindar and Pherekydes (see above) are the earliest literary sources to mention this event; both agree that Medeia was somehow involved. The tale was dramatized in Euripides' lost *Peliades* of 455 B.C.; from a summary we know that after rejuvenating a ram in a cauldron of boiling water and herbs Medeia persuaded the daughters of Pelias to kill their aging father and boil him in similar fashion (pp. 550–51 N²). The same story was also perhaps told in Sophokles' *Rhizotomoi* ("Root-cutters"), given that Medeia there appeared as a cutter of poisonous herbs (p. 410 R). Whether Pelias in earlier times ever died of a different cause, or without Medeia's assistance, we cannot say, or whether the funeral games held for him might suggest in some traditions a more glorious demise.[25] Likewise it is difficult to assess Medeia's motive, since in no preserved account does it win Iason the throne. We will return to this tale in dealing with the conclusion of the Argo's voyage (see chapter 12), and consider as well later sixth-century vases that show some phase of the rejuvenation (with perhaps Pelias) together with two fifth-century Red-Figure examples on which one Alkandre leads her father to his death.

Whatever the earliest cause(s) of Pelias' death, as early as Stesichoros and the Chest of Kypselos we find the notion of lavish funeral games held in his honor, suggesting perhaps again those versions in which he stands as the rightful heir to the throne of Iolkos, rather than an interloper. As we might expect, the affair seems to have been attended by every hero who could be plausibly assigned to that time period (including the Argonautai and Iason himself). Stesichoros composed an entire poem under this title, although the mention of two victors in less than two lines is scarcely as elaborate as we might expect; perhaps this was part of an initial summary before elaboration. The victors named are Amphiaraos in jumping and Meleagros in the javelin throw (179 *PMG*); elsewhere we learn that the Dioskouroi received their horses from Hermes and Hera (178 *PMG*). Pausanias' report of the Chest of Kypselos offers a good deal more in the way of names as he describes for us the lowest band

(5.17.9–11). The chariot race shows Euphemos in the lead, with Polydeukes, Admetos, Asterion, and Pisos also competing. In boxing, Admetos and Mopsos are depicted; the absence of Polydeukes seems surprising here (as is his presence without his brother Kastor in the chariot race). In wrestling we find Iason and Peleus, while Eurybotas throws the discus. Finally, the footrace features Iphiklos in the lead, followed by Argeios, Phalareus, Neotheus, and Melanion. The whole scene is flanked on one side by Herakles, on the other by tripods and women of whom only Alkestis is named. Pausanias goes on to include Iolaos in a chariot as one of the winners, and one might here certainly suppose him mistaken, for an Iolaos at the far edge of this scene would more logically be placed in the adjacent one, where Herakles slays the Hydra, a task traditionally requiring his nephew's help. But Hyginus' list of winners (*Fab* 273: see below) actually specifies Iolaos as winner in the chariot race, so that there may have been a genuine variant tradition to that effect. Pausanias also saw something that he took to represent these games on the Throne of Amyklai (3.18.16); unfortunately in this case he gives no details at all. Admetos and Mopsos as the boxers would appear confirmed by their similar confrontation on a shield-band from Olympia (B 1010). Simonides for his part describes Meleagros as the winner of the javelin contest, as did Stesichoros, and then cites Homer and Stesichoros as his sources (564 *PMG*). Mention of Homer suggests, as we might expect, that there was an epic poem of some sort on the games, but we have no other information about it. Simonides' own poem in which the above information appeared would seem to have been rather about the life of Meleagros, to judge from the remarks of Athenaios, our source for the fragment. In Ion of Chios' lost *Agamemnon* we find mention of a drinking cup that Kastor won in the footrace here, and apparently gave to his sister Klytaimestra (fr 1 Sn). Kallimachos adds Kyrene, daughter of Hypseus, who he claims won something with dogs given to her by Artemis (*H* 2.206–8).

Some further evidence comes from the preserved artistic tradition. On the so-called Amphiaraos krater, a Late Corinthian pot formerly in Berlin and now known only from a drawing (Berlin:Lost F1655), the artist has combined the motif of Amphiaraos' departure for Thebes on one side with a chariot race on the other. The contestants are, in order, Euphemos, Kastor, Admetos, Alastor, Amphiaraos, and Hippasos. Such names, plus the presence of Akastos, Argeios, and Pheres as spectators (or judges) to the left, make it certain that the funeral games for Pelias are portrayed, and once again, as on the Chest of Kypselos, Euphemos (presumably the Argonaut known to Pindar and later writers) has the lead. Again, too, we find one of the Dioskouroi, but this time it is Kastor, as we would expect. A second contest, under the handles of this column krater, offers Peleus wrestling with one Hippalkimos (a son of Pelops, according to *Fab* 14).

The wrestling contest, however, poses more intriguing questions than one might at first suppose, due to the fact that while Peleus is always one of the wrestlers, his opponent is frequently a woman. Fragments of a dinos from the Akropolis show, in addition to Iphitos, Melanion, Amphiaraos, and Kapaneus (who are apparently preparing for the javelin throw), a man and woman facing in the same direction, with their arms around each other (Athens Akr 590). The names, if they were painted in, are now lost but we are again clearly observing scenes from the games for Pelias. On a Chalkidian hydria in Munich, the man and woman wrestling before spectators are identified as Peleus and Atalanta; interestingly enough, a boar's head and hide lie between them (Munich 596). Only two of the spectators, those to the right, are named—Mopsos and Klytios; the man and the woman behind Peleus to the left remain anonymous. It has been proposed that the artist intended Akastos and his wife Astydameia (or Hippolyte), the latter here perhaps falling in love with Peleus as she watches him compete.[26] Similar wrestling couples on other Black-Figure pots (e.g., Munich 2241, Berlin:Ch F1837) presumably illustrate the same scene, and while the connection with Pelias' games may not seem quite proven, we do finally encounter a literary tradition in Apollodoros, who not only tells us that Peleus did wrestle with Atalanta at these games, but adds that Atalanta won (ApB 3.9.2). The boarskin on the Munich hydria remains, however, something of a puzzle. In the versions of Stesichoros and Simonides, at least (together with something in the epic tradition), Meleagros wins the javelin contest, a fact that sets these games prior in time to the Kalydonian Boar Hunt and Meleagros' consequent death. Were it not so, one might be tempted to see the Munich boarskin as a trophy from the Kalydonian Boar, something to help identify Atalanta or remind us of her great exploit. But quite possibly the artist of our Munich hydria has ignored (or overlooked?) the chronological problems and included the hide for just such purposes. Possibly, too, there really was a narrative tradition that placed these games after the Boar Hunt at Kalydon, with Meleagros thus excluded and Atalanta bringing the hide with her to Iolkos, either to show it off or to offer it as a prize to all comers. As a final piece of speculation, since our two oldest sources (the Chest of Kypselos and the Berlin krater) give Peleus other opponents at Iolkos, perhaps in earlier times Atalanta wrestled Peleus for the hide at *Kalydon*. If this was once the case, then the contest might have been subsequently transferred to Pelias' funeral games (by the time of the Akropolis fragments), and Atalanta made to supplant Peleus' previous wrestling partners. Presumably he won against Hippalkimos and perhaps Iason; we cannot say if in all traditions he lost to Atalanta, but in any case he fared better with Thetis.

Regrettably, Apollodoros has nothing else whatever to tell us about the games. At the other extreme, Hyginus provides us with a list of no fewer than seventeen winners in contests that include singing as well as athletics (*Fab* 273). Of these, the most interesting for our purposes are Zetes in the long run, Kalais in the diaulos, Kastor in the stadion, Polydeukes in boxing, Telamon in the discus, Peleus in wrestling, Meleagros with the javelin, Iolaos in the chariot race, and Orpheus with the lyre. As we saw above, the death of Glaukos, son of Sisyphos, by his own mares also took place at these games, if we believe Asklepiades and Hyginus.

One last point in connection with these games is Iason's surprising participation, at least on the Chest of Kypselos where we found him wrestling with Peleus. Possibly the artist here simply painted in the name of a well-known hero, ignoring the anomaly of Iason thus honoring the king he had plotted to kill. But perhaps, too, we see here further evidence of a tradition in which Iason was not hostile to Pelias, and (although any oracle motivating the voyage must obviously be fulfilled) was free of direct complicity in the latter's death (whether or not caused by Medeia) or else brought it about inadvertently. All known later accounts do have him leaving Iolkos after that death, but not always driven out; indeed in Diodoros he hands the throne over to Pelias' son Akastos (so too *Fab* 24) and finds husbands for the daughters before leaving (DS 4.53).

As for these offspring of Pelias, we have seen that the *Iliad* names Alkestis, and the *Ehoiai* Alkestis and Pasidike plus others whose names have been lost. Akastos appears several times in early art as a spectator or arbiter at Pelias' games, but he is not mentioned in literature until Pindar's *Nemean* 4, when he is finally confirmed as Pelias' son (*Nem* 4.57–60); apparently he is the only one. Our only Archaic list of Argonautai, that in Pindar's *Pythian* 4, does not include him, but he does sail in the version of Apollonios (AR 1.321–23), and Valerius Flaccus' account underlines the irony of the son going on a mission designed by his father to be disastrous for all concerned (VF 1.153–83); one wonders whether the Archaic tradition exploited this possibility. Otherwise, the only story concerning Akastos is that of his attempted destruction of Peleus told by Pindar (see chapter 6). There is no preserved early mention of the mother of Pelias' children; both Apollodoros (ApB 1.9.10) and Hyginus (*Fab* 14) make her Anaxibia, daughter of Pelias' nephew Bias (although Apollodoros adds as a variant Phylomache, daughter of Amphion). In the *Ehoiai*, for what it is worth, Talaos seems the only child of Bias and Pero, despite the fact that Pelias' children immediately follow in the text (Hes fr 37.8–9 MW). Apollodoros' version of those offspring adds to the previously attested Akastos, Alkestis, and Peisidike *(sic)* the names of Pelopeia and Hippothoe; we will see evidence in chapter 12 for an Alkandre attested in art alone.

AMYTHAON, AISON, PHERES   Of the other three sons of Tyro, those borne to Kretheus, there is very little to say; their primary role is to become the fathers of more important figures. We have already observed Amythaon as progenitor of Melampous and Bias; only with Apollodoros does he acquire a wife, namely Eidomene, daughter of his brother Pheres (ApB 1.9.11). Aison is in Pindar the deposed ruler of Iolkos; we will see later that in the *Nostoi* Medeia rejuvenates him (fr 7 *PEG*), and he is on hand to greet Iason when the latter first arrives to confront Pelias in Pindar's *Pythian* 4 (120–23). In Diodoros

(4.50–51) and Apollodoros (ApB 1.9.27), on the other hand, Pelias slays him (and Iason's infant brother Promachos) after Iason and the Argonautai are reported dead; one wonders if there was ever a tradition in which this was done earlier, in order to facilitate seizure of the throne. We saw too above that in some scholia Aison simply dies while Iason is still a child. As for his wife, Iason's mother, she has at least four different names; suffice it to say here that she is Polymele in the *Ehoiai* (Hes fr 38 MW), and Alkimede to Pherekydes (3F104c). In the later tradition of Diodoros and Apollodoros she kills herself after Aison's death. Ibykos does give Iason a sister, Hippolyte (301 *PMG*); she does not surface elsewhere.

Pheres and Admetos both appear on the Berlin Amphiaraos krater, Pheres as spectator, Admetos as competitor in the chariot race (Berlin:Lost F1655). But already in *Iliad* 2 they are father and son, and Admetos has married his first cousin Alkestis and begotten a son, Eumelos, who leads a contingent at Troy (*Il* 2.763–64, 713–15). For the fuller account of the wooing, namely that Pelias required Alkestis' suitors to yoke a boar and a lion to a chariot, and that Admetos did so with the help of Apollo, our earliest sources are Apollodoros (ApB 1.9.15) and Hyginus (*Fab* 50, 51). However, Pausanias seems to have seen this yoking on the Amyklai Throne (3.18.16), and we find it perhaps on a Black-Figure lekythos of the early fifth century, with Apollo's help stressed (Yale 1913.111).[27] Apollodoros also gives Pheres a second son, Lykourgos, who will be father of Opheltes (ApB 1.9.14), and the epic *Naupaktia* mentions a daughter Alkimache/Eriope, who will apparently marry Oileus (fr 1 *PEG*). Pindar's *Pythian* 4 includes both Pheres and Admetos as greeters of Iason when he returns home (*Py* 4.125–27), but for the story of Admetos and Alkestis facing death there is nothing preserved before Phrynichos' lost *Alkestis*, Sophokles' lost *Admetos*, and Euripides' extant *Alkestis*. Sophokles' play is a complete blank; from Phrynichos' we know only that Thanatos appeared onstage with a sword with which he cut off a lock of Alkestis' hair as a ritual preparation for her death (fr 3 Sn). Thus we cannot say what Euripides might have borrowed from these or other sources, and what was his own invention. Presumably all versions included the same central core of the situation—that Alkestis was permitted through the intervention of Apollo to die in place of Admetos (so the Erinyes in Aischylos' *Eumenides* accuse Apollo of inebriating the Moirai so that he might make someone in the house of Pheres "immortal": *Eum* 723–28). But a resolution of the tale featuring Herakles wrestling with Thanatos to rescue Alkestis may not have been canonical: in Plato's *Symposion*, Phaidros claims that the gods so admired Alkestis' bravery that they took it upon themselves to send her back from Hades, and this has the look of an older version improved upon by dramatists, although of course Phaidros may simply be adapting the usual story to the spirit of the discussion (*Sym* 179b; cf. ApB 1.9.15).[28] Eumelos is the only offspring of the marriage recorded by name. In the *Iliad* he has the swiftest horses, and he is said to have received these from his father (*Il* 2.763–65); it is thus appropriate that Admetos should appear in the chariot race at the funeral games of Pelias, although on both the Chest of Kypselos and the Berlin krater he finishes third.

As we saw earlier, most of the important descendants of Deukalion spring from the sons of his grandson Aiolos; the one major exception to this pattern involves lines sprung from Agenor, who is a great-great-grandson of Aiolos' daughter Kalyke via Endymion, Aitolos, and Pleuron (Hes fr 10a.58–65 MW and Ap*B* 1.7.5). Agenor has in the *Ehoiai* at least two children, a daughter Demodike and a son Porthaon (Hes frr 22, 10a.50 MW). No mother for these offspring is furnished by the very scant remains at this juncture; in Apollodoros, Agenor marries his first cousin Epikaste, daughter of his father's brother Kalydon (Ap*B* 1.7.7). The *Ehoiai* goes on to tell us that Demodike is much courted by great kings, but that none of them can persuade her (Hes fr 22 MW). The fragment in question breaks off here, and we must turn again to Apollodoros, who offers a likely enough solution: Demodike encounters Ares, to whom she bears Euenos, Molos, Pylos, and Thestios (Ap*B* 1.7.7). "Euenos" is the name of the father of Marpessa for whom Idas and Apollo contend (*Il* 9.557; Sim 563 *PMG*; Bak fr 20A SM), and Apollodoros explicitly makes him this same son of Ares. In Simonides he pursues Idas and Marpessa unsuccessfully, and kills himself when he fails to overtake them. Bakchylides assigns to him as well the nailing up of skulls from defeated suitors for the hand of Marpessa. From the commentaries to the *Iliad* passage (9.557) we acquire various further details. The b and T scholia offer much the same story as in Simonides: Idas abducts Marpessa from her home in Chalkis with the help of horses obtained from his father Poseidon; Euenos pursues as far as the river Lykormas in Aitolia and then commits suicide. The scholia minora to the same passage maintain, however, that Euenos challenged suitors to this race as a bride contest, and cut off the heads of many losers before Idas with horses from Poseidon outran him; his failure led him to slaughter his horses and then throw himself into the Lykormas river, subsequently named the Euenos (cf. Eustathios, who makes the obvious parallel with Pelops and Oinomaos).

As for the other three sons of Demodike, Molos and Pylos seem not to be otherwise recorded (Molos, father of Molione, is written with an omicron, not an omega), but Thestios marries a daughter of his mother's brother Porthaon (Hes fr 26 MW; probably this is Eurythemiste, as in Ap*B* 1.7.10) and begets three famous offspring, Leda, Althaia, and Hypermestra. Leda will wed Tyndareos (from the race of Atlas and Pleione), Althaia her mother's half-brother Oineus (son of Porthaon), and Hypermestra Oikles from the race of Inachos (these last two in Hes fr 25 MW). . There are several variants to be noted: in Asios, Thestios is directly the son of Agenor (fr 6 *PEG*), while Pherekydes has him beget by Laophonte, daughter of Pleuron, at least Leda and Althaia (3F9). Of course, Thestios and his wife must have some sons as well, for otherwise there would be no brothers of Althaia for her son Meleagros to slay in the aftermath of the Kalydonian Boar Hunt. The *Iliad's* account of the story guarantees at least one such brother (*Il* 9.567) and Bakchylides names two (Iphiklos and Aphares: Bak 5.128–29), while Apollodoros knows of four (Iphiklos, Euippos, Plexippos, and Eurypylos: Ap*B* 1.7.10). The death of some or all of them at Meleagros' hands is the only story about them.

While Demodike has been providing Ares with four children, her brother Porthaon has been even busier. We have already seen above this gentleman married to Eureite, a great-granddaughter of Aiolos (via Perimede), and thereby the father of, among others, Oineus (Hes fr 10a.49–54 MW). But the same *Ehoiai* that recounts this union also presents Porthaon as married to one Laothoe, who bears him three daughters, Eurythemiste, Stratonike, and Sterope (Hes fr 26 MW). Of these, Eurythemiste, as just noted, is probably the daughter who marries her first cousin Thestios, son of Demodike. The second, Stratonike, is carried off by Apollo as a wife for the son Melaneus whom a Nymph, Pronoe, bore to him; from this union springs Eurytos, who will be the father of Deion, Klytios, Toxeus, Iphitos, and Iole. Presumably the third daughter also weds, but the relevant fragment breaks off before arriving at her marriage. Apollodoros notes a tradition that she was the mother by Acheloos of the Seirenes (Ap*B* 1.7.10), although his own view assigns that role to the Muse Melpomene (Ap*B* 1.3.4).

With these last heroes we conclude the early stages of the race of Deukalion. Later offspring, such as Meleagros, Iason, the Apharetidai, and the children of Leda, will play major roles in the myths of the generation of heroes before the Trojan War, and we shall encounter them again as those narratives unfold.

6 Other Early Families

From the family of Deukalion in the last chapter we proceed, as Apollodoros and probably the *Ehoiai* did, to the offspring of Inachos, the river god of Argos. Our evidence suggests that the Argive Akousilaos and likely as well the Argive epic *Phoronis* tried to establish Phoroneus, son of Inachos, as a local rival to Prometheus and Deukalion, regarding him as the first man or at least first inhabitant of Argos; the *Phoronis* calls him "father of mortal men" (fr 1 *PEG*). His impact in non-Argive sources, however, is less clear; indeed for many writers no Inachid of any importance surfaces before Io, who is alone responsible for the future generations of Inachos' race with parts to play in Greek myth. Inachos himself, being a river, is usually considered a son of Okeanos (*PD* 635–36; Ap*B* 2.1.1), although the *Theogony* does not include him among the sons it names, and a line that *may* be part of the Hesiodic Corpus makes his father one Oineus (Hes fr 122 MW). In any event, the early generations sprung from him are almost entirely missing in what we have of the *Ehoiai*; save for Phoroneus (in a Deukalionid, not Inachid, context), our preserved references begin only with Io and her father Peiren (Hes fr 124 MW).

For the stages before Io most of our evidence comes from Apollodoros, who seems to have drawn on Akousilaos and other sources as well as the *Ehoiai*. The opening of the second book of his *Bibliotheke* offers the following: Inachos and his sister Melia (thus an Okeanid) produce two sons, Aigialeus and Phoroneus (Ap*B* 2.1.1). Aigialeus dies childless, but Phoroneus begets Apis and Niobe. Apis in his turn also dies childless, but Niobe, as the first mortal woman with whom Zeus mates, bears a son Argos and also (this from Akousilaos) Pelasgos. Argos begets Iasos, and Iasos begets Io. Clearly, this last detail is not taken from either the *Ehoiai* or Akousilaos, since Apollodoros himself goes on to tell us that in both those works Io's father is Peiren, not Iasos. But our other fragments of Akousilaos do show that he mentioned Phoroneus as son of Inachos and first man/ruler of Argos in the time of the flood, and that Niobe was in some way part of his story (2F23). Presumably the union between Zeus and Niobe was also found in his account, given Apollodoros' language, and probably too in the *Ehoiai*, since Apollodoros adds that for "Hesiod" Pelasgos is autochthonous. But even without this evidence, Niobe's seduction would seem necessary to the poem, for this new section of it must begin like the Deukalion line with the mating of a mortal woman and a god (although not impossibly that woman was Io: see below). Phoroneus himself does appear in the *Ehoiai*, but only as the father of the woman who bears (probably to Doros) the five daughters who in their turn are the mothers of the Nymphai, Satyroi, and Kouretes (Hes fr 123 MW: see chapter 3). This woman might, of course, be Niobe bearing children (other than Zeus') to a mortal husband, although we might then wonder why Strabo (the citer of the lines) does not give the name of such a well-known figure. In Bakchylides and Aischylos, matters are much simpler: Io is directly the daughter of Inachos, and no other names are mentioned (Bak 19.18; *PD* 589–90, 663). It would seem that either genealogists expanded and conflated an original schema of modest proportions,[1] or some poets compressed a more complex one. Fortunately, the matter is of limited importance to our purposes, since none of these early figures have any story to tell; mythology proper begins only with Io.

Her tale was clearly included in the *Ehoiai*, as we would expect, and Apollodoros appears to draw primarily from it in his retelling. In his version, Zeus seduces Io (a priestess of Hera), and is caught red-handed by Hera while embracing the girl. He therefore changes her into a white cow and swears to Hera that he has not lain with her (the relationship between these two actions is not very clear). At this point, Apollodoros adds that in "Hesiod" we learn that lovers are generally permitted to swear false oaths because Zeus did so here (Hes fr 124 MW); the *Ehoiai* must therefore have related the events leading up to this declaration. Hera responds by asking Zeus for the cow, and setting Argos to guard it. There follows the death of Argos (as another source confirms for the *Ehoiai*: Hes fr 126 MW), the sending of the gadfly, Io's wanderings, and the birth of her son Epaphos in Egypt, where she recovers her original form (Ap*B* 2.1.3). One presumes that these latter events and the subsequent genealogy (leading to the Danaides, among others) would not have been omitted entirely by the *Ehoiai*, but there are no relevant fragments from the poem regarding them. The Throne of Amyklai included among its scenes Hera gazing at a cow-Io (Paus 3.18.13), and sixth-century vase-painting offers us a number of representations of Hermes, Argos, and the cow (e.g., Munich 585, London B164), so that that part of the story must have been well known at this time. In the *Aigimios* Argos has four eyes, and is made by Hera the watcher of Io (Hes fr 294 MW); the same poem may have made her travel through Euboia (Hes fr 296 MW: hence the island's name), which has led to speculation that this was her final destination at a earlier stage of things, prior to the entry of Egypt.[2]

In the fifth century we have finally a substantial account of Io's story via her role in two plays of Aischylos. In his *Hiketides*, the Danaides themselves relate through choral flashback and interrogation of the Argive king the story of their ancestor. The interrogation offers the most direct evidence: Io held the keys to Hera's shrine in Argos, Zeus mated with her, and Hera, discovering the affair, turned Io into a cow, presumably to discourage her husband (A: *Hik* 291–324). Zeus, however, continued to mate with Io by turning himself into a bull, and therefore Hera sent Argos to guard the cow. Hermes slew Argos, and Hera then sent the gadfly, who drove Io all the way to Egypt. There, although Zeus seems clearly to have had intercourse with her before (both as god and bull), he begets with her a son, Epaphos, by the touch of his hand, thus explaining the child's name. At this point in the play there is a line missing (A: *Hik* 316), but Libya is apparently the daughter of Epaphos, and she bears Belos (by Poseidon in later accounts: Ap*B* 2.1.4; Moschos 2 [cf. Pher 3F21]), who has in turn two children, Danaos and Aigyptos, fathers respectively of fifty daughters and fifty sons. The fifty daughters are naturally the Danaides, who thus trace their ancestry back to Io and Zeus. The lyric portions of the play recount the same material, but with emphasis on Zeus as the rescuer of Io in Egypt, and on his breath and touch as the means of Epaphos' engendering (A: *Hik* 40–57, 531–94).

In the *Prometheus Desmotes*, on the other hand, Io appears in person and narrates with Prometheus' help her own story. Most of what we find here follows the same lines as did the *Hiketides*, but there are some differences, and we must remember that the two plays may not after all be the work of the same author.[3] Io visits the rock (somewhere northwest of the Black Sea) where Prometheus is bound as part of her long journey down to Egypt after being transformed into a cow (*PD* 561–886). Her father in this play is Inachos (no father was specified in the *Hiketides*) and nothing is said of her being a temple priestess. Rather we are told that dreams came to her at night in her father's home, telling her that Zeus desired her, and that she must go to the meadows of Lerna where he might enjoy her (*PD* 645–82). She ignored these at first, but then revealed them to Inachos, who sent messages to Delphi and Dodona seeking an explanation. In response to these, Apollo commanded him to turn his daughter out of the house or face total destruction. He did so, and Io was immediately changed into her cow form and goaded along by the gadfly, with Argos of the many eyes to accompany her. At this point Prometheus picks up the tale, and tells how Io came to Dodona, where she was hailed as wife of Zeus, and then to the Ionian Sea, before swinging around to the northeast and encountering the bound Titan (*PD* 829–41). In this first part of the story we notice the major deviation from the version of the *Hiketides* and most later sources; as far as we can see, Zeus does not mate with Io before or while she is a cow, and Hera's role as jealous wife is far less prominent, although Prometheus does suggest that she has sent the gadfly (*PD* 591–92, 704). The logic of all this is not immediately apparent. Possibly we are to suppose that Hera anticipated Zeus' desire by turning Io into a cow, but such an idea is never stated, and the implication of Io's immediate transformation is really rather that Zeus is responsible, and for reasons other than those usually ascribed. Perhaps, then, the poet means us to view Zeus as the ultimate controller of his own and human destinies, and hence accountable for everything that happens, even if his motives are not yet perceptible in this first play. Whatever those motives may be, they are, however, surely prefigured by the predictions of Io's ultimate fate. In response to the request of the chorus, Prometheus tells us that her wanderings will take her to the Scythians and the Chalybes, then the Amazones and the Crimean Bosporos, then the Graiai, the Arimaspians, the Aithiopes, and finally up to the Nile delta and Kanobos (*PD* 707–35, 790–815). Here Zeus will make her pregnant by the mere touch of his hand (and presumably here as well as in the *Hiketides* restore her to human form, since she is to bear a human child). Her son Epaphos shall rule all the land of the Nile, and the fourth generation of descent from him, fifty females, will come to Argos in flight from their cousins (*PD* 846–69). There follows in brief the story of the Danaides at Argos, to which we shall return shortly.

Thus it *appears* that in the *Desmotes* Zeus never does have intercourse with Io, despite her initial dreams, and that the essential purpose of her exploitation is to bring her to Egypt and produce the child, although we may wonder why such a roundabout route was necessary. In the *Hiketides*, on the other hand, there certainly is a sexual union between god and mortal, but of course the issues of the Daniad trilogy as a whole revolve around such union and its presumed desirability. By the same token, since the purpose of the Danaides is to praise Zeus and his treatment of Io, they naturally blame Hera for the less attractive aspects of her experience. As noted above, this latter version, with Hera perceiving Zeus' infidelity and punishing Io for it, provides a more cogent (and hence traditional?) motivation for the main events of the story. But Aischylos may have done some inventing for both plays. His portrait of Argos, the watcher of Io, remains tantalizingly vague: Argos is born from the earth (A:*Hik* 305; *PD* 567: cf. Akou 2F27), and all-seeing (A:*Hik* 304), with many eyes (*PD* 678–79), but the number and positioning of those eyes is never addressed, and we are not told exactly how Hermes killed him (although in the *Desmotes* sleep-giving pipe-playing seems to have been involved: *PD* 574–75). Io herself in her maddened raving considers the gadfly to be the ghost of Argos, who rises up from the dead to continue her torment. We have seen that the *Aigimios* assigns him four eyes, and in fact one Black-Figure amphora of the late sixth century shows him with a Janus-type head with faces front and back (London B164). In Pherekydes' account (which seems to have been limited to Argos, at least in this particular part of his work), Hera places an eye in the back of his neck and takes sleep away from him, so that he might guard Io more efficiently (3F66). Pherekydes also makes him the son of Arestor, who is the great-grandson of another Argos, a son of Zeus. From about 490 B.C. on, however, numerous Red-Figure pots show him with eyes all over his body (e.g., Hamburg 1966.34, Boston 08.417), although this notion does not appear in our preserved literary tradition until Euripides' *Phoinissai* (1113–18), and not until Ovid is he specifically said to have a hundred eyes (*Met* 1.625). Apollodoros relates of him a number of previous exploits of a useful character, such as slaying a monstrous and destructive bull, and even Echidna (Ap*B* 2.1.2);

whether these are traditional tales, or even tales transferred from another Argos, there is no trace of them in Archaic literature.

Elsewhere in the fifth century we have a possibly complete dithyramb by Bakchylides (19) which celebrates her story and line as the foundation for the house of Kadmos (through Agenor) and thus for Dionysos, with whom the poem culminates. Here Io is again daughter of Inachos, and flees the land of Argos as a cow, by the plans of Zeus (no further details are offered). Hera sets the watcher Argos, who looks in every direction with tireless eyes, and apparently does not sleep, to guard her. As we saw in discussing Hermes' role in this account (see chapter 2), Bakchylides expresses uncertainty as to how the messenger god brought about his death, and gaps at the ends of lines leave us uncertain about his uncertainty: the choice seems one among violence, weariness, and song (vase-painters, where the death is shown, opt for the sword, with Argos still awake). For the rest, Io arrives at the Nile and bears Epaphos without further explanation. More details would certainly have been found in Sophokles' lost *Inachos*, where the title figure is son of Okeanos and (once more) father of Io (frr 270, 284 R). Hermes and Argos appeared, and probably Iris (frr 272, 281a R), there was a blight on the land of Argos (from Hera?: frr 278, 284, 286 R), and at some point in the course of the drama Io actually underwent the metamorphosis from woman to cow (frr 269a [= POxy 2369], 279 R). The papyrus fragments relating this last event refer to a dark stranger, presumably Hermes, as the agent. Seemingly, then, this version of the story dealt head-on with the reasons for the transformation, but we are not even certain whether the work was a satyr play or a tragedy, much less what questions were posed or resolved.[4] Later accounts are of little help in determining how Io's story (in particular the motive for her metamorphosis) might have looked in pre-Aischylean versions. One variant to be noted, though, is Apollodoros' notion that Hermes was originally charged with stealing Io away from Argos (to smuggle her back to Zeus, it seems); when this plot is revealed by one Hierax, Hermes kills Argos with a stone, presumably from long range (ApB 2.1.3; cf. Σ PD 561).

As for Io's progeny, the geographical expanses involved and the purposes that the offspring are made to serve in furnishing a background for Greek colonization must cause us to wonder to what degree her line has been expanded from its original core. Epaphos in Egypt may seem of questionable value before Greeks have settled in at the port of Naukratis, probably in the last quarter of the seventh century, and the same could be said of an eponymous Libya before the emergence of Kyrene at about the same time. Another problem arises when we add in the name of Agenor, who as early as the *Ehoiai* is the father of Phoinix (Hes fr 138 MW), and in Pherekydes the father of both Phoinix and Kadmos (by different mothers: 3F21). We have seen that in the *Hiketides* Libya bears Belos alone, but there exists no reason for the agents of that disclosure (the Danaides) to mention other offspring, given that their sole interest lies in establishing their descent from Io through Belos. Since the woman who bears Phoinix to Agenor in Pherekydes is Damno, daughter of Belos, it seems more likely than not that Pherekydes thought of Agenor and Belos as brothers, with Agenor marrying his niece. At any rate, Apollodoros confirms this idea by making the two men twin sons of Libya (Ap*B* 2.1.4). If this presence of Agenor (and thus the eponymously important Phoinix) in the line of Io is indeed early, then we must suppose Greek activities in Phoinicia as well. West suggests an original Argive-Boiotian division in the immediate descent from Epaphos, with Danaos and offspring Akrisios and Proitos on the Argive side, Agenor and his offspring Kadmos and Europa on the Boiotian side.[5] Subsequently in his hypothesis (which he emphasizes is more for the sake of example than anything else) would come a Euboian version with Abas and Phoinix added in, then a broader expansion placing Phoinix in Phoinicia (with his father Agenor) and Danaos in Egypt (with a father, Belos, contributed by the Greeks of Naukratis). None of this can be directly proved, but it gives a plausible enough picture of the complexity of development in some areas of Archaic myth, especially those in which aetiology takes precedence over narrative.

In any event, by the time of Aischylos we have a basic outline leading us through Epaphos, Libya, and Belos to Danaos and Aigyptos; Libya as daughter of Epaphos is also attested by Pindar's *Pythian* 4 (14–15). Of these five figures the first three are again primarily names, but the last two bring us to the conflict between the Danaides and their first cousins, the Aigyptioi. This story must have been touched upon somewhere in the *Ehoiai*, for there are references to Aigyptos' fifty sons (who came to Argos without their father), to the Danaides' discovery of springs in the area of Argos, and probably to the clash between Danaos and Lynkeus, the one surviving son of Danaos' brother (Hes frr 127–29 MW). Taken together, these might seem to argue for a continuous narrative, but with the *Ehoiai* one can never be certain. A full account must, on the other hand, have been offered by the epic *Danais* (supposedly 6,500 lines in length), but we know nothing beyond the fact that the Danaides armed themselves by the banks of the Nile, presumably to fight the Aigyptioi (fr 1 *PEG*). Phrynichos put some version of the story on stage before Aischylos: two titles, *Aigyptioi* and *Danaides*, survive, and there is no reason why there could not have been a third. But although Phrynichos, like Aischylos, clearly handled the story at some length, we know of his account only that Aigyptos did come to Argos with his sons (Σ *Or* 872 = fr 1 Sn). On the other hand Hekataios agrees with the *Ehoiai* that Aigyptos was not present, but makes the sons fewer than twenty in number (1F19). Thus, there was certainly an extensive tradition detailing this myth before Aischylos; yet here too, as with Io, we cannot say how uniform the tradition might have been, or how much Aischylos might have changed it. Relevant perhaps to that tradition is the fact that in the *Desmotes* Prometheus offers a capsule summary of the Danaid tale which may or may not represent what Aischylos presented in his full-length treatment (see below).

Turning now to that treatment, we have first of all the evidence of Oxyrhynchus fragment 2256.3. This slim scrap of papyrus, first published in 1952, virtually guarantees that Aischylos presented a complete tetralogy relating the problems of the Danaides, with *Hiketides* and *Aigyptioi* the first two titles, *Danaides* presented third, and *Amymone* the satyr play (*test* 70 R).[6] As with the Prometheus group, only one play, the *Hiketides*, survives, but here we are on much safer ground in supposing it to have been the initial play of the group, with *Aigyptioi* second. The action of this extant play is fairly simple: the Danaides, accompanied by their father, arrive in Argos, with their fifty cousins in hot pursuit and eager to marry them. To this proposal the Danaides themselves clearly object, but it is not clear why: their remarks are at times vague, at others obscured by problems in reading the Greek text.[7] They request asylum from the local king Pelasgos, son of Palaichthon, who at first demurs, but then feels he has no choice but to accept them after they have threatened to hang themselves at the city's altars. The Aigyptioi do subsequently arrive, and send a herald and attendants to drag off the women; Pelasgos intervenes, dismisses the herald despite the latter's threats of war, and prepares to lead the Danaides into the city. Here the drama ends, and we must guess at further events. But we can observe already that the women take quite an aggressive role in this play: the revulsion against their cousins is entirely their own, when it might easily have been in obedience to some attitude of their father's, and they skillfully manipulate the king to get what they want, rather than having their father speak for them. Their fear of the Aigyptioi, on the other hand, leads them to passionate, almost hysterical rejection of marriage, as a part of which they frequently call upon Zeus to protect them in the name of his love for Io. This somewhat paradoxical appeal to a god's lust as grounds for preserving females from further lust is perhaps the irony that Aischylos meant us to use in interpreting the trilogy: what the Danaides seem to fear most is a usurpation over which they have no control, and if this leads them to reject marriage altogether, we must remember that the impetuous (not to say high-handed) approach of their cousins constitutes their only experience in such matters.[8]

The second play, entitled *Aigyptioi*, might seem to warrant a chorus composed of such cousins, as the suppliant Danaides composed the chorus of the first play. This arrangement would also permit the Aigyptioi to state their side of the case, and perhaps put their seemingly arrogant lust in a better light. But technical considerations weigh against such an idea. Assuming that the Danaides' slaying of their cousins on the wedding night takes place between the second and the third plays (it can hardly take place on stage, nor can a whole night pass while it takes place offstage during a play), we must surely see in the course of the second play the process of reasoning by which the Danaides decide on such action, and this can only happen if they form the chorus.[9] In that case, the play's title is based on the role of the Aigyptioi as prime agents in the drama and on the difficulty of finding yet a third title (in addition to *Hiketides* and *Danaides*) that could refer to the same chorus. The play's action will then be set in the town of Argos, and present the Danaides as somehow forced to agree to marry their cousins, but determining (either at the same time or later) to resort to murder to avert the consummation of those marriages. Other traditions on these events are late and often contradictory;[10] according to one, Danaos succeeds Pelasgos as king (Σ *Or* 932; cf. Ap*B* 2.1.4, Paus 2.19.3–4), perhaps after Pelasgos dies fighting the Aigyptioi. But we have seen the strong role played by the daughters in *Hiketides*, and we might suppose that they continue to make their own decisions as the trilogy progresses. The herald of the Aigyptioi does threaten military force at the end of the first play; presumably this is applied, or at least threatened more forcibly, in *Aigyptioi*, and the Argives, with or without Pelasgos, begin to feel that their situation is hopeless. In such circumstances the Danaides might be forced to capitulate, but then perceive that an apparent surrender can be converted into victory, once they have their new husbands at their mercy. The second play would thus conclude with marriage hymns and cheerful expectations for the future, while the audience would perceive the darker realities of the forthcoming night.

The third play, *Danaides*, must reveal the slaughter of the bridegrooms and find some sort of resolution to the resulting dilemmas. The plot will also have dealt with the one Danaid, Hypermestra, who does not kill her husband, as evidenced by the *Desmotes* and virtually all later sources. The *Desmotes* seemingly ascribes Hypermestra's motives to desire (*PD* 865–67),[11] and this development may well have been used to create a contrast between her and her sisters; we should note, however, that in Apollodoros Lynkeus is said to have preserved her virginity, and been spared for that reason (Ap*B* 2.1.5).[12] If Danaos is king of Argos at this point, he may have wished to chastise his daughter for alone failing to obey him, as later authors, including Ovid (*Her* 14), Apollodoros, and Pausanias (2.19.6), suggest. On the other hand, the Danaides' slaying of their husbands while the latter are their guests and guests of the city of Argos is certainly a violation of rights protected by Zeus Xenios, to whom the Danaides themselves prayed in the first play, and the Argives might well wish to separate themselves from such people through some form of punishment. In all events Hypermestra has found love, or at least some favorable feeling for her new partner, while her sisters still experience only distaste. That she alone has chosen the more appropriate course, and indeed becomes the more appropriate successor to Io, seems indicated by our one substantial fragment from the play, a fragment spoken by Aphrodite herself (fr 44 R). In these seven lines the goddess establishes sexual union (typified by the marriage of Ouranos and Gaia) as a cosmic principle by which all life is nurtured and renewed. Her appearance could, of course, be only one side of a debate, with the other part taken by the Danaides or even Artemis. But it seems more likely that she is meant to ratify the playwright's own view, and that Hypermestra's example will gradually have its effect on the other sisters. For a second marriage of the Danaides there is solid early evidence from Pindar's *Pythian* 9 (dated to 474 B.C. by the scholia[13] and thus earlier than this trilogy): here

Danaos arranges a footrace, with the first runner across the finish line to take his pick of the girls, then the second, and so on until all of them have been claimed (*Py* 9.120–26). Pindar alludes to the event briefly, and as something well known; he implies, too, that Danaos is in some hurry to find husbands for his daughters. Such a folkloristic motif is probably a bit undignified as a conclusion to the trilogy we have been discussing, but Aphrodite could well instruct Danaos to choose suitable partners for his daughters from among the young men of Argos, just as any Athenian father would do for his daughter in real life. In this way, though the exact process is admittedly unclear, the Danaides would become reconciled to the rewards of marriage and the need to accept their role in the furtherance of the human race, as did Io, without whom they themselves would not have been born.

The brief account in the *Desmotes* is intended primarily to chart the genealogical descent, via Hypermestra and Lynkeus, from Io to Herakles, the rescuer of Prometheus; thus, unfortunately for our concerns here, nothing is said of the Danaides beyond the fact that all save one killed their husbands, and that one bore a kingly race in Argos (so too Pindar at *Nem* 10.1–6, the earliest source to name Hypermestra). In this the play agrees with what we have supposed for the Danaid trilogy, but one other detail is more troublesome: Prometheus says that a god will begrudge the Aigyptioi the bodies of the Danaides, thus implying some measure of divine support for their actions, in contrast to the resolution proposed above (*PD* 858–59). Perhaps the Titan simply hesitates to put them in too culpable a light when addressing their ancestor; perhaps, too, the truth about the Danaid trilogy involves the gods to a greater extent than I have suggested.

A number of later sources agree that some or all of the Danaides remarried (ApB 2.1.5; Paus 3.12.2; *Fab* 170), but there is also considerable evidence of serious friction between Danaos and Lynkeus (perhaps as early as the *Ehoiai*: Hes fr 129.2 MW) or Danaos and Aigyptos or both, as one might expect after the slaying of forty-nine sons/brothers (Σ *Hek* 886; Paus 2.25.4). In one version Lynkeus actually kills Danaos (and this *may* go back to Archilochos: 305 W); in another he slays not only Danaos but the murderous daughters as well (Σ *Hek* 886).[14] Such a story pattern would well cohere with the basic theme of the father who seeks to prevent the marriage of his daughter lest he be slain by his son-in-law (so ΣA *Il* 1.42 and Σ *PD* 853a, where Danaos receives an oracle that one of Aigyptos' sons will kill him, although the cause of the animosity is his quarrel with his brother). Whatever the truth of the matter, Danaos plays a remarkably central and dominant role in almost all the later accounts, and this may lead us to suspect that he was the dominant figure in the earliest versions as well, with Aischylos alone in restricting his role so as to shift the focus of the dilemma to the daughters. Somehow, in any case, be it by violence or by reconciliation, power passes from Danaos (as king of Argos?) to Lynkeus and his line.

As for the Danaides, who seem on the whole to find satisfactory husbands, there is, of course, one other detail to consider, the motif of their punishment in Hades by being forced to bear water in leaky jars (or to a leaky vat). This all-too-familiar element of their story first survives for certain in the pseudo-Platonic *Axiochos* (first century B.C.?) where they are listed among the familiar transgressors in Tartaros (Tantalos, Tityos, etc.) and assigned the punishment of "useless water-carrying" (*Ax* 371e; the same motif at *Ibis* 177–78, 355–56). In chapter 3 we did find that scenes seeming to represent this activity in the Underworld appear on Attic Black-Figure as early as the late sixth century, but the winged figures there (sometimes male and female) can scarcely have been understood as the Danaides; hence, the punishment is older than its linking with this particular transgression. From the mid-fourth century on, however, such figures become almost entirely young women, as they appear on a series of Apulian Underworld kraters of that time (e.g., Karlsruhe B4; Leningrad St 426; Naples H3222 [the "Altamura Vase," heavily restored]).[15] Whether or not we are to understand these as Danaides in some form, Latin authors—Horace, Tibullus, Ovid—relate the torment of water-carrying just as in the *Axiochos*,[16] and Loukianos refers to it in a manner suggesting that it was well known (*DMar* 8). But its roots as regards the Danaid story remain uncertain. Even if, as suggested above, the daughters bore the moral culpability for their deed in some early versions, their crime is not directly against the gods, and punishment of any sort is hardly mandatory; quite the contrary, their remarriage in Pindar (our only early evidence) suggests a resolution of their conflict. Pindar surely draws that notion of a mass remarriage from some earlier source, but with Phrynichos, the *Ehoiai*, and the *Danais* treating the tale before him he obviously had a variety of materials to choose from, and they may not all have told the same story.

One other Danaid who will, with Hypermestra, in any case escape punishment is Amymone. Her story, that of being surprised and loved by Poseidon while she was fetching water, is preserved only in later sources (Prop 2.26.45–50; *DMar* 8; ApB 2.1.4), but Pherekydes knows of their union (3F4), Pindar (*Py* 9.112–14) and Euripides (*Pho* 185–89) imply it, and it was clearly the subject of Aischylos' satyr play *Amymone* presented with the Danaid trilogy. The two surviving fragments of that play are simply lines from wooing speeches, but Apollodoros and Hyginus offer a very likely plot: Amymone was surprised by a Satyros who tried to rape her (she had aroused him from sleep with an accidental missile, or else fell asleep herself) and saved only by the sudden appearance of Poseidon, who chased the Satyros away and took the maiden for himself (ApB as above; *Fab* 169a). That the Satyros here replicates the role of the Aigyptioi in the tragedies has often been supposed. Likewise one of the play's two preserved lines, "it is fated for me to marry, and for you to be married" (fr 13 R), may have deeper resonances as a paradigm for the acquiescence of Amymone's sisters to marriage when presented with the right suitor. Red-Figure vase-painting also knows the story, beginning probably about 470 B.C., when we see Poseidon accosting a woman with a hydria (PrColl,

Zurich); from *c.* 460 on, the name "Amymone" may be added (VG 20846, etc.). Pherekydes makes the offspring of their union Nauplios; Apollodoros and those other sources that specify the name agree.

Regarding the second marriages of the other sisters, there are rarely names of husbands or children, and no figures of importance emerge. For that matter, the offspring of Hypermestra and Lynkeus are not specified until much later (ApB 2.2.1; Paus 2.16.2). But Bakchylides does call Proitos and Akrisios sons of Abas and descendants of Danaos and Lynkeus (11.64–76), and thus there seems no reason to doubt that the Abas who fathers Akrisios in the *Ehoiai* (Hes fr 129 MW) is there, as in later accounts, Lynkeus' son. Likewise, although the papyrus fragments of the *Ehoiai* do not quite preserve the name of Akrisios' child, she is in that work the mother of Perseus, and certainly Danae, while the brother of Akrisios whose name is lost in a gap marries Stheneboia, and can only be the Proitos who fulfills this dual role in all other accounts. The problems involving these two brothers and their quarrels over power are matters we will return to in chapter 10, when we come to the story of Perseus.

As we saw above, Belos is not actually attested as the son of Libya or the father of Danaos and Aigyptos before Aischylos' *Hiketides*, and quite possibly he represents (given his location) an expansion of the Inachids' original nucleus. Certainly, though, he does appear in the *Ehoiai* in another context, as the father of Thronie, who with Hermes brings to birth Arabos, who in turn has a daughter whose name just misses inclusion in our fragment (Hes fr 137 MW). We also saw before that a second daughter of this same Belos, one Damno, marries in Pherekydes Agenor, son of Poseidon, who is almost certainly her uncle and, like Belos, a son of Poseidon and Libya (3F21). This union of Damno and Agenor produces Phoinix, Isaie, and Melia; Pherekydes then marries off the two girls to Aigyptos and Danaos, their first cousins (and uncles), and the son Phoinix to Kassiepeia, daughter of Arabos, by whom he begets Kilix, Phineus, and Doryklos (this in 3F86). For this last information, however, Pherekydes is not the first source; the same scholion tells us that already in the *Ehoiai* Agenor is the father of Phoinix, who fathers Phineus by Kassiepeia (Hes fr 138 MW).[17] To such a complex of relationships Pherekydes adds that, after his union with Damno, Agenor took Argiope, daughter of Neilos, from whom was born Kadmos (3F21). Bakchylides' notion that Kadmos is a descendant of Agenor and, at some further remove, of Epaphos and Io would thus seem to confirm Agenor himself as a descendant of Io and brother of Belos (Bak 19.46–48, 40–42).

That being the case, we must turn now to examine more closely Agenor's offspring. The son Phoinix attested for the *Ehoiai* appears to have wed in that poem not just Kassiepeia, the mother of Phineus (Hes fr 138 MW), but as well a second wife, Alphesiboia, who bears to him Adonis (apparently the same one loved by Aphrodite; Hes fr 139 MW). So far, the picture is fairly clear, but Kadmos and Europa, the most famous figures in the line of Agenor, will pose more of a problem. We saw above that in Pherekydes Kadmos is a son of Agenor by a second marriage. On this point nothing earlier survives: Hesiod mentions Kadmos only as the husband of Harmonia (*Th* 937, 975–78), and the *Ehoiai* not at all in what we have. Homer, however, while naming neither Kadmos nor this Agenor, makes Europa clearly the daughter of Phoinix (*Il* 14.321–22), an arrangement supported by the *Ehoiai* (almost certainly: Hes frr 141.7 and 140 MW) and by Bakchylides in his dithyramb on Theseus and Minos (17.29–33). Eumelos and Stesichoros in their *Europeia* poems and Aischylos in his drama *Kares/Europa* presumably offered their own opinions, but these are completely lost to us. Europa's parentage is relevant because we might expect that, at least in those narratives where Kadmos is sent out to find her, she will be his sister; thus, since Homer makes Europa the daughter of Phoinix, Kadmos might be supposed his son, while by this logic in Pherekydes Kadmos and Europa would both be children of Agenor.[18] Admittedly, our source for Pherekydes does not list Europa at all among Agenor's children (by either of his wives), but the *lemma* for the scholiast's comment is Kadmos, and he *might* therefore have omitted Kadmos' sister by a second wife (3F21). This comment forms part of a scholion to Apollonios, where the scholiast says quite plainly that some made Kadmos the son of Agenor, others of Phoinix (Σ AR 3.1186). In both Apollodoros and Hyginus, Kadmos and Europa are full sibling offspring of Agenor, in Apollodoros by Telephassa (Agenor's only wife in this author: Ap*B* 3.1.1), in Hyginus by Argiope, the same wife as in Pherekydes (*Fab* 178, 6). Both these authors also add Phoinix as yet another child of Agenor and thus brother to Kadmos and Europa.

Bakchylides for his part calls Kadmos an Agenorides in his dithyramb on Io (19.47), but since the patronymic can mean "descendant" (as Kadmos would be if he were son of Phoinix, son of Agenor) as well as "son," the epithet begs the question. In favor of Kadmos as son of Agenor (with Pherekydes, Apollodoros, and Hyginus) are definitely Sophokles (*OT* 268), Herodotos (4.147), and Euripides (*Bkch* 171 and see below on fr 819 N²). On the other side (with perhaps Homer, the *Ehoiai*, and Bakchylides), a scholion to *Iliad* 2.494 describes at length Kadmos' adventures, in the course of which Europa is called a daughter of Phoinix and a sister of Kadmos; the story as a whole is ascribed to Hellanikos (4F51) and Apollodoros, but while the latter clearly did not provide this genealogy, it is impossible to be sure that the former did either. Whatever the source, this is our first account to make Kadmos explicitly the son of Phoinix, since the others named above speak only of Europa, who was perhaps not Kadmos' brother in every version. One additional point in this connection concerns a fragment from Euripides' lost *Phrixos B*, apparently representing the very beginning of the play (fr 819 N²). Here Kadmos is called a son of Agenor and "born Phoinix, but exchanging his race for that of a Greek." In such a context the Greek word *Phoinix* would seem most naturally to mean "born a Phoinician," but a few lines later in the same fragment we are told that Agenor had three sons, Kilix (eponym of Cilicia), Phoinix (eponym of Phoinicia), and

Thasos (the manuscript breaks off here). Barring manuscript corruption in the word *three* or the names, we would seem to have a Euripidean word play in which Kadmos is not only born a Phoinician but also bears the name "Phoinix," which he changes to "Kadmos" when he becomes a Greek. There is no other trace of such an idea, but if this is what Euripides meant, it would probably represent an attempt to resolve conflicting traditions. In another lost Euripidean play, the *Kretes*, Europa seems to be called daughter of Phoinix (fr 472 N²), but here, too, the word could signify born in Phoinicia, and in any case we should not expect consistency in genealogical matters from such an author. We will return to Kadmos' exploits and family when we consider the legends of Thebes in chapter 14; for the moment, Europa and Phineus will claim our attention.

Whoever her father, all sources agree that Europa was kidnapped by Zeus. The *Iliad* says only that she bore to him Minos and Rhadamanthys (*Il* 14.321–22), but a fragment of the *Ehoiai* (mostly holes) confirms some details of the abduction, and a scholion to a passage in *Iliad* 12 relates a version that it claims is drawn from Hesiod and Bakchylides. In this latter account, Zeus sees Europa in a meadow with other girls gathering flowers and desires her; he therefore changes himself into a bull, lures Europa away, and mates with her once they have arrived on Krete (ΣAb *Il* 12.292 = Hes fr 140 MW = Bak fr 10 SM). The children are Minos, Rhadamanthys, and Sarpedon; Europa herself is given over to Asterion, the king of Krete, as a wife. The *Ehoiai* fragment begins with the crossing of the sea, after Europa has been deceived by Zeus, and proceeds to describe some gift made by Hephaistos and presented by Zeus to Europa (Hes fr 141 MW). Pherekydes also mentions such a present in the form of a necklace given by Zeus to Europa (and by Europa to Kadmos, who gives it to Harmonia: 3F89), and this is surely what the *Ehoiai* intends. Judging by the initial words of the fragment, the gift is proffered after they reach Krete (and Zeus has resumed his own form). The passage goes on to recount her children; only Rhadamanthys is preserved, but there is more than enough room for Minos and Sarpedon, and the remainder of the fragment appears to deal with Sarpedon's role at Troy. Here again we must remember that Eumelos and Stesichoros probably created influential versions of the story, and seventh- and sixth-century vases and architectural reliefs do show Europa (or at least a woman) riding a bull through the sea,[19] but nothing further of a literary nature is preserved until Aischylos' *Kares*. This play seems, remarkably enough, to have delved into Europa's feelings about the whole situation in later years, as we learn from the one real fragment (fr 99 R). In this she complains of the theft performed by Zeus to take her from her father and adds her distress over the fact that her children are no longer with her. A gap here prevents us from knowing what has happened to Minos, but Rhadamanthys has become immortal (probably on the Isles of the Blessed, as in the *Odyssey*), and Sarpedon, for whom she especially fears, is rumored to be fighting at Troy. The play's action almost certainly continued this latter theme, so that we may expect an announcement of Sarpedon's death in battle, and thus a further blow for Europa. How Aischylos resolved this grief, and whether Zeus offered his paramour any consolation, remains uncertain; possibly there are parallels to the sufferings of Io. We should note, as a small variant, the means of abduction specified by Europa: apparently Zeus remained on Krete and sent a real bull to fetch her. Aischylos' language is not totally unambiguous here, but the idea seems also to have been known to Akousilaos, who says that the bull was the Kretan one later captured by Herakles as one of his Labors (2F29). Our summary drawn from the *Ehoiai* and Bakchylides does clearly say, however, that Zeus himself was the bull, and this is also the version of Euripides in an unnamed play (fr 820 N²).[20] On another point, Aischylos is in solid agreement with the *Ehoiai/Bakchylides* version, namely in holding (contrary to the *Iliad*) that Sarpedon is the son of Europa. In the *Iliad*, as we have seen, Europa bears only two children, Minos and Rhadamanthys, and Sarpedon is the son (in quite a detailed genealogy) of Zeus and Laodameia, daughter of Bellerophontes.

Next comes Phineus, whom we saw to be in the *Ehoiai* and Pherekydes the son of Phoinix and Kassiepeia, thus the grandson of Agenor and either the nephew or brother of Kadmos and Europa. But the possibilities are still wider, for Hellanikos makes Phineus instead the son of Agenor (4F95), thus involving him in the same ambiguity we encountered for Europa and Kadmos. And matters become worse: according to Apollodoros, Euripides gave Belos two more sons than we have previously discussed, namely Phineus and Kepheus (Ap*B* 2.1.4 = Eur fr 881 N²), and scholia claiming to draw from the same author assign to Belos not only Phineus, but also Agenor and Phoinix (Σ A:*Hik* 318). We may presume that this Kepheus is the same figure who appears in the *Ehoiai* (Hes fr 135 MW) as Andromeda's father, and in the lost *Andromeda* plays of Sophokles and Euripides as the husband of Kassiepeia as well, although we cannot be sure these works treated the claim of the brother Phineus to Andromeda, a motif that appears first in Ovid and Apollodoros. The *Ehoiai* passage mentions Andromeda only in her role as the mother of Perseus' children; if the story of her wooing was presented at all, it must have been within the context of her own family. Herodotos also makes Kepheus a son of Belos (and father of Andromeda: 7.61), but Hyginus calls him a son of Phoinix, and ascribes this to . . . Euripides (!!: *Astr* 2.9). Like his brother Phineus, Kepheus may have fluctuated between being the son of Agenor and the son of Phoinix, son of Agenor, except in those versions where he was the son of Belos. His marriage to Kassiepeia is, to say the least, a surprise, after the *Ehoiai* and Pherekydes had assured us that she was the wife of Phoinix. Sophokles' play is our first preserved evidence for this union, as it is for the idea that Kassiepeia offended the Nereides by boasting that she was more beautiful (p. 156 R). There exists a possibility that Aischylos had earlier dramatized the story as the middle play of his Perseus trilogy, but he may also have ignored it altogether. Pherekydes, of course, narrated the whole Perseus legend at length, to judge from the detailed summary we are offered, and should certainly have included

Andromeda; oddly enough, she is completely absent from the scholiast's epitome, save as Perseus' wife when he returns to Argos (3F12).

From Kepheus we shift our focus back to Phineus, whose function as rival to Perseus for the hand of the rescued Andromeda seems the only role he has to play in the context of this family. Given that Euripides did mention him somewhere, we might suppose his presence (and lithification) in that playwright's *Andromeda* more likely than not. Elsewhere we find, of course, the Thracian Phineus who was tormented by the Harpuiai and aided by the Argonautai. This unfortunate man's story, or at least the pursuit by the Boreadai of his tormentors (who seem to have snatched him away with them) was related in considerable geographical detail by the *Ehoiai* (Hes fr 151 MW), as was his choice of long life over sight (Hes fr 254 MW). Pherekydes described the extent of his rule (all Thracians in Asia up to the Bosporos: 3F27) and Aischylos presented a *Phineus* (clearly about the Harpuiai's victim) as part of his unconnected production of 472 B.C. But nothing preserved in any of these sources mentions his parents, and given his geographical location there seems no good reason to identify him with the Phineus, son of Phoinix, found in the *Ehoiai* and Pherekydes. Nevertheless, the presence of fragments discussing Europa and the Thracian Phineus in the same *Ehoiai* papyrus (POxy 1358) suggest that the *Ehoiai* may indeed have made the latter an Agenorid.[21] Apollonios definitely calls the Thracian who aided Iason a son of Agenor (AR 2.178), so that even if there were in the beginning two different figures, they have merged by that point at least. The Phineus who married Boreas' daughter Kleopatra and blinded his own sons (as in several lost tragedies) is in any case always the Phineus encountered by the Argonautai; we shall return to this and other of his misfortunes in chapter 12, when we come to the voyage of the Argo.

With Phineus and Kepheus, we reach the end of Agenor's immediate line; Kepheus will reappear later in the tale of Perseus, and Europa's children find their place in chapter 8 (on Minos and Krete), while on Belos' side of the line, Proitos will reemerge in the tale of Bellerophontes (chapter 10), and the grandson of Akrisios will be Perseus himself.

The Daughters of Atlas

The seven women whom Greek mythology comes to identify as the Pleiades give every indication of being a relatively late grouping of originally disparate figures. The *Iliad, Odyssey,* and Hesiod's *Works & Days* are all familiar with the constellation of seven stars by that name; Hephaistos places them on the shield of Achilleus (*Il* 18.486), Odysseus watches them while he steers away from the island of Kalypso (*Od* 5.272), and for Hesiod they signal the beginning of the harvest (*W&D* 383). Hesiod also calls them *Atlageneis,* which might seem to mean "born from Atlas," and was perhaps so understood by Hesiod himself. But the linguistic formation suggests rather the sense that they first appeared above, or were born near, some geographic location indicated by *Atla-,* and that this epithet then led to their connection with the Titan Atlas.[22] That they were in fact women, and not just stars, is first attested by an unattributed hexameter fragment, most likely from the Hesiodic Corpus, which assigns names to them—Taugete, Elektra, Alkyone, Asterope, Kelaino, Maia, and Merope—and adds that Atlas engendered them (Hes fr 169 MW). Here, though, the citer, not the preserved lines, identifies these sisters as the Pleiades; Simonides (555 PMG) is the first datable source to specifically link that term with daughters of Atlas. The names remain largely unchanged throughout their long history, but their association with different geographic regions is in itself an argument against any real family. "Pleiades" as a collective name is also puzzling, since it cannot be a patronymic indicating their father if he is to be Atlas. The solution hit upon by mythographers, at least in later times, was to consider it rather a matronymic referring to one Pleione, an Okeanid unattested in any other context. The first preserved trace of this Pleione is apparently in a lost work of Pindar, where she is the object of Orion's pursuit (fr 74 SM; see Aristarchos' objection below). But we also find her in the A scholia to *Iliad* 18.486, where she and Atlas are together the parents of the seven girls; these latter choose maidenhood and the hunt with Artemis, but find themselves pursued by the amorous Orion and appeal to Zeus, who turns them into stars. The scholion closes with the remark that the story is in the Epic Cycle (Bernabé includes it as fr 14 among the *fragmenta dubia* of the *Titanomachia*), but even should this be so, the scholiast may mean only the very last part of his story (Elektra's defection). Atlas and Pleione also appear as the girls' parents in the first-century B.C. historian Alexandros Polyhistor (so at least Hyginus: *Astr* 2.21.3), and as well Ovid (*Fasti* 5.81–84) and Apollodoros (ApB 3.10.1), among others. In origin, of course, Pleiades might after all be a genuine patronymic, perhaps shifted to a matronymic when the epithet *Atlageneis* was misinterpreted as an indication of their father. "Mousaios" makes the group daughters of Atlas and an Okeanid Aithra (2B18).[23]

Regarding the pursuit of these daughters (or their mother) by Orion, we saw above that in the Epic Cycle he may or may not pursue the daughters as they hunt with Artemis. Elsewhere, the evidence leaves much to be desired. The *constellation* Orion is attested, together with the star group Pleiades, in the *Works & Days*, where the end of the sailing season is indicated by describing how those latter stars fall into the sea, "fleeing powerful Orion" (W&D 619–20). But whether Hesiod here intends anything more than a fanciful conceit based on the proximity of the stars in question we cannot say. Ps-Eratosthenes found somewhere in the Hesiodic Corpus (most likely the *Astronomia*) an account of Orion's birth (from Poseidon and Euryale, daughter of Minos) and various other adventures leading up to his catasterism after being stung by a scorpion on Krete (Hes fr 148 MW). All this is interesting (and we will return to it in more detail in chapter 8), but there is no mention of the Pleiades, whom one might have expected to be a central part of any catasterism (or at least involved in it). Pindar's *Nemean* 2 offers us much the same situation as did the *Works & Days*: we learn that it is fitting for Orion to follow close upon the Pleiades, but not why or whether the poet really knows any story about these figures (*Nem* 2.10–12). Aristarchos (in the scholia to this same passage) is our source for the tale noted above, that elsewhere in Pindar Orion becomes enamored of Pleione and pursues *her*, not (as in *Nemean* 2) the daughters. To resolve this conflict Aristarchos suggested that Pindar meant the name "Pleione" as a collective for all the Pleiades. That is not likely to be correct, but it may indicate that Pindar recounted little more than Aristarchos tells us. Quite possibly, then, the pursuit of both mother *and* daughters credited to Pindar by the ninth-century *Etymologicum Magnum Genuinum* (s.v. "Pleiades") is simply a conflation of two brief Pindaric references as we already know them. Either way, a pursuit of mother and daughters certainly does survive elsewhere, most notably in Hyginus' *Astronomia* (which may draw from a fuller version of Eratosthenes' *Katasterismoi* than what our epitome provides). In Hyginus, Pleione is making her way through Boiotia with her seven children, daughters of Atlas, when Orion attempts to violate her (*not* the daughters: *Astr* 2.21.4). She then takes flight, and Orion pursues for seven years before Zeus, taking pity on the girls, changes them into stars. Obviously something is not quite right here, for the daughters alone are rescued when the mother seems the only one in danger. But something of the same sort appears also in Athenaios (11.490d–e), where the daughters are said to flee too when their mother Pleione is pursued by Orion, and in the scholia at AR 3.225, where Pleione again meets Orion while traveling through Boiotia with her daughters and, falling in love with her, he pursues when she flees. By contrast, the scholia to Aratos' *Phainomena* 254 speak of the daughters as pursued by Orion (who desires to lie with *them*) for five years as they flee through Boiotia with their mother, which is more the sort of emphasis we would expect. But obviously there existed in antiquity some confusion over just whom Orion pursued. Nor does the whole conception of the Pleiades as shy young girls fleeing an undesired suitor easily square with the picture of all seven as seduced by gods (or in one case a mortal) and bearing children to them in unions that are surely early (see below). That they lamented the toils of their father Atlas, even as stars, is a notion preserved in an unplaced fragment of Aischylos (fr 312 R); we do not know if it is a chance remark or something more complicated.

From the Pleiades as a group we turn now to their individual identities and affairs with various gods. Maia has an especially prominent position as Atlas' daughter in both the *Theogony* (*Th* 938) and *Homeric Hymn* 18 (the *Iliad* does not mention her at all, and the *Odyssey* only as Hermes' mother). Perhaps at the time of these works all the Pleiades were thought of as Atlas' daughters, but all accounts of Maia stress how she lived alone in her cave, in an isolated existence apart from others. Her role as Zeus' lover is the only story told of her. For the other sisters, our earliest evidence is the Amyklai Throne, where Pausanias saw Zeus and Poseidon carrying off Atlas' daughters Taugete and Alkyone (3.18.10). A full list then appears in Hellanikos, where we find the following pairings: Maia and Zeus (son Hermes); Taugete and Zeus (son

Lakedaimon); Elektra and Zeus (son Dardanos); Alkyone and Poseidon (son Hyrieus); Kelaino and Poseidon (son Lykos); Sterope and Ares (son Oinomaos); Merope and Sisyphos (son Glaukos) (4F19). Hellanikos adds that, in chagrin at her marriage with a mere mortal, Merope became a dimmer star than her sisters (so too *Katast* 23); an alternative explanation found by scholiasts in Aratos' (now lost) *epikêdeion* to Theopropos makes the fainter star Elektra, who turns her face from the sack of Troy (Σ Arat 254; ΣA *Il* 18.486). The second of these stories also appears in an earlier section of ΣA *Iliad* 18.486, introduced by the words "they say": as such it may be what the scholiast meant to attribute to the Epic Cycle (see above) or a momentary intrusion in a larger citation. Both accounts of the fainter star appear in Ovid (*Fasti* 4.175–78) and Hyginus (*Astr* 2.21.3; *Fab* 192).

As for Elektra's children, a second citation from Hellanikos speaks of them as three in number (all still by Zeus) rather than just one: Dardanos, plus Eetion and Harmonia (4F23). Eetion is here (as probably in the *Ehoiai*: see chapter 2) equated with Demeter's lover Iasion. The remnants of the *Ehoiai*, moreover, mention Elektra, Dardanos, and Eetion at the beginning of consecutive (fragmentary) lines, so that the poem probably anticipated Hellanikos with regard to the two sons (Hes fr 177 MW). On the other hand, our papyrus has no room for a third child, whether Harmonia or anyone else. But Hellanikos' belief in such a child may well deviate from general tradition, since he equates Elektra's daughter Harmonia with the Harmonia, wife of Kadmos, who in the *Theogony* and everywhere else is the child of Ares and Aphrodite. The *Ehoiai* fragment goes on to offer us two sons of Dardanos, Er[. . .] and Ilos. For the first name we can refer to *Iliad* 20, where Dardanos, son of Zeus (no mother is given), fathers Erichthonios (*Il* 20.215–37). The *Iliad* also mentions the tomb of an Ilos Dardanides (*Il* 11.166, 372) who might be the son of Dardanos in question here, but equally the great-grandson of Dardanos (via Erichthonios and Tros) who fathers Laomedon (*Il* 20, as above). Somewhere in the Hesiodic Corpus there was mention of Tros, son of Teukros (Hes fr 179 MW), but this need not have occurred in the *Ehoiai*; Hellanikos seems to think of Teukros as marrying his daughter to Dardanos, an idea that recurs often (4F24). There are no other early references to these figures; we will return to them and the Trojan royal line in general when we look at the Trojan War in chapter 16.

For the children of the remaining five Pleiades we must rely very largely on late sources. Homer names Sisyphos as Glaukos' father at *Iliad* 6.154–55, but with no mention of the mother. We saw earlier that Sisyphos courts wives on behalf of Glaukos in the *Ehoiai* (Hes fr 43a MW; see chapter 5), and here, too, no mother survives. Not until Pherekydes, in fact, is Sisyphos' wife named "Merope" (3F119), and Hellanikos is the first to call her "Merope, daughter of Atlas." Alkyone's child Hyrieus by Poseidon (a name that explains the site of Hyria near Aulis) acquires important children of his own in Apollodoros: by a Nymph Klonie he fathers Lykos and Nykteus, and Nykteus becomes the father of Antiope, who will bear Zethos and Amphion to Zeus (ApB 3.10.1). These last two children will become founders, in one legend at least, of Thebes, and actors in a basic drama of wicked stepmothers and revenge. However, this same Antiope is in the *Nekuia* rather a daughter of Asopos (*Od* 11.260–65; so too Asios fr 1 *PEG*), so that we cannot say for certain if Apollodoros' version is early, or which was utilized by the *Ehoiai*. Later on we will see that a Hyrieus is also the father (in a fashion) of Orion; presumably he is the same figure discussed here (so Pal 51; ΣA *Il* 18.486). In addition to Hyrieus, Alkyone and Poseidon may have had a son, Krinakos, father of Makareus of Lesbos, although the evidence for this falls into the "some say" category (Hes fr 184 MW). More definite is Pausanias' attestation of a son Hyperes, who is mentioned somewhere in the Hesiodic Corpus (although without parentage) as having a daughter Arethousa who lay with Poseidon and was changed into a fountain by Hera (Hes fr 188A MW).

The fifth sister, Kelaino, bears only the one child, Lykos, to Poseidon, and he seems to have no further offspring. As we saw in chapter 3, a papyrus fragment apparently from Hellanikos has Poseidon transfer his child to the Islands of the Blessed, and there make him immortal (4F19b). No other author except Apollodoros repeats this story (Ap*B* 3.10.1), and no reasons for such special treatment are given.

The sixth sister, Taugete, bears Lakedaimon, and here we are clearly in the realm of mythological founders. A fragment of the *Ehoiai* offers us a [. . .]dike as daughter of Lakedaimon and probably wife of Akrisios (Hes fr 129 MW), but we must turn to Apollodoros again to get a full genealogy: Lakedaimon weds Sparte, daughter of Eurotas, and begets Amyklas and Eurydike (Ap*B* 3.10.3). The latter marries Akrisios, the former Diomede, daughter of Lapithes. This marriage of Amyklas is perhaps also attested in the *Ehoiai*, although a good many letters need to be supplied in the relevant fragment (Hes fr 171 MW). In any case the names of the children are lost, and we must turn back to Apollodoros, for whom the offspring are Kynortes and Hyakinthos. That Hyakinthos was a son of Amyklas in the *Ehoiai* is given tantalizing probability by one word preserved at the end of the above fragment: *diskos* in the dative, suggesting the boy's unfortunate death at the hands of his lover Apollo. Kynortes we have already seen as part of a very complex synthesis of different branches bringing together (perhaps as early as Stesichoros) Aphareus and Leukippos, Tyndareos and Ikarios (above, chapter 5). To repeat here briefly, the *Ehoiai* offers no direct information on him, and there are no myths, but Tyndareos is attested as the son of Oibalos in the poem (Hes fr 199 MW), so that very likely it went on as in Pausanias to make Kynortes the father of Oibalos, who in turn marries Gorgophone, daughter of Perseus, and begets Tyndareos (and probably Ikarios, although Pausanias omits him: 3.1.3–4). Apollodoros, who cites several variant possibilities, does list Tyndareos and Ikarios as sons of Oibalos in one of them, and adds as well Hippokoon (Ap*B* 3.10.4); the scholia at *Orestes* 457 assign to the same father Tyndareos, Ikarios, and Arene, with Hippokoon as a bastard son by Nikostrate. Tyndareos and his family we shall return to in chapter 11, after he has married Leda, daughter of Thestios. Ikarios is, by all accounts beginning with the *Odyssey*, the father of Odysseus' wife, Penelope. The third son, Hippokoon, is a more shadowy figure: Diodoros (4.33.5), Pausanias (3.15.3–5), Apollodoros (Ap*B* 3.10.5), and various scholia say that he drove out Tyndareos and Ikarios from Lakedaimonia (or was aided by Ikarios in driving out Tyndareos) but offended Herakles and perished with his ten (twelve? twenty?) sons when the latter attacked. Some form of this story appears to have been told at the start of Alkman's Louvre *Partheneion*, since the names preserved in the fragmentary beginning of that work match with some of those used by Pausanias (1 *PMG*). But the Dioskouroi seem here to have been involved (if early tradition recognized the parentage given by Apollodoros, Hippokoon would be their uncle), and there is also in the poem something about not aspiring to marry above one's station, which might indicate rivalry between the Hippokoontidai and the Dioskouroi. Alkman may therefore have known a somewhat different story from that which our later sources pass on to us. Unfortunately, no other Archaic source even mentions Hippokoon or his sons. Taugete, the Pleiad from whom this whole line begins, is also at times connected with Artemis and the Keryneian Hind pursued by Herakles; indeed, as we shall see in chapter 13, Pindaric scholia recount that she herself became the Hind in an effort to escape Zeus; if so, she was obviously not always successful.

Seventh and last of the Pleiades is Asterope, as the Hesiodic fragment calls her, or Sterope, as she is usually known in other sources. Hellanikos' mating of her with Ares produces Oinomaos. The story of this Elian king's deadly chariot race with suitors for the hand of his daughter Hippodameia is not preserved before Pindar's *Olympian* 1, and full details come only with Pherekydes (3F37), but the *Ehoiai* does list children of Pelops and Hippodameia (Hes frr 190, 191 MW), and both the *Megalai Ehoiai* (Hes fr 259 MW) and "Epimenides" (3B17) speak of the thirteen unsuccessful suitors before Pelops. Presumably Oinomaos was killed in all versions; Hippodameia seems to have been his only child. The race itself and Oinomaos' subsequent line will be covered in chapter 15.

Finally, there is the question of the Pleiades' name. In the *Iliad*, *Odyssey*, and *Works & Days* it is always so spelled, and always appears at the beginning of lines. But already in the Hesiodic *Astronomia* and Simonides (and perhaps also Alkman), the word becomes "Peleiades," presumably to create an association with the Greek word *peleia*, meaning "dove," so that the girls might be compared to weak fluttering creatures (with reference to Orion?). Barring a genuine derivation of "Pleiades" from "Pleione," the otherwise meaningless "Pleiades" represents the *lectio difficilior* and thus should precede "Peleiades." Moreover, the latter form, with its short first syllable, could never occur where "Pleiades" does in Homer and Hesiod, at the beginning of dactylic hexameter lines. If these arguments are cogent, "Pleiades" alone will have an epic pedigree, and "Peleiades" will represent a subsequent respelling effected in order to create a viable etymology. Nonetheless, the association of the sisters with trembling doves as early as the sixth century merely restates our original problem—do they fear only the celestial Orion, or have they already been pursued on earth?

From the Pleiades we turn to their purported sisters, the Hyades. These are mentioned together with the Pleiades as stars in *Iliad* 18.486 and *Works & Days* 615, but once again there is no indication that they were ever considered to have been real people. A quote from the Hesiodic *Astronomia* gives us more help: they are Nymphai like to the Charites, their names are Phaisyle, Koronis, Kleeia, Phaio, and Eudore, and men call them the Hyades (Hes fr 291 MW). "Mousaios," however, seems the first to relate what later becomes the standard explanation of their name: they have a brother, Hyas, who is slain by a boar or lion while out hunting, and they lament him until they perish and are turned into stars (2B18). This same source also makes them five in number, and in addition (like the Pleiades) daughters of Aithra and Atlas. And there is one further novelty: the Hyades are called nurses of Dionysos. Whatever the antiquity of this idea, it is confirmed by Pherekydes, as we saw previously: Semele takes the name "Hye," and the Hyades are the Dodonian Nymphai pursued by Lykourgos while they are attending Dionysos (3F90). They are then turned into stars by Zeus, either in pity over their danger or in gratitude for their having safely conveyed Dionysos into the hands of Ino. In addition, Pherekydes makes them seven in number, and gives names, including all those from the *Astronomia* except Kleeia; to these he adds Ambrosia, Polyxo, and Dione. Their number seems in fact to have been a matter of considerable uncertainty. According to the scholia at *Phainomena* 172, Thales counted two, Euripides three, Achaios four, and Hippias seven. But information from the same scholia to the effect that in Euripides' *Erechtheus* his three daughters actually *became* the Hyades (fr 357 N²) is certainly mistaken; newly found papyrus fragments of the actual lines in question confirm Demosthenes' statement that these daughters after their heroic suicide became Hyakinthides (fr 65.68–74 Aus; Dem 60.27). The Hyades are totally absent from our preserved lyric poetry and early tragedy. Indeed, after the information attributed to "Mousaios," the first author who attests to their parentage appears to be Ovid in the *Fasti*, which agrees with the Hyginus version of "Mousaios" (*Astr* 2.21.2) in making them children of Atlas and an Okeanid Aithra and tells the same tale of a brother Hyas slain by a wild beast (*Fasti* 5.166). Hyginus also cites Alexandros Polyhistor (first century b.c.) as making them daughters of Hyas and Boiotia, in contrast to the Pleiades (*Astr* 2.21.3), although he himself elsewhere calls them (and the Pleiades) daughters of Atlas and Pleione (or Atlas and another Okeanid, name lost: *Fab* 192). One other possibility remains to be noted: the hypothesis to Euripides' *Medeia* tells us that Aischylos in his lost *Trophoi* has Medeia rejuvenate the nurses of Dionysos and their husbands (fr 246a R). But whether Aischylos followed the "Mousaios" account and that of Pherekydes in making these nurses the Hyades we cannot say.

Whatever his responsibility for these two groups of offspring, Atlas does have one other daughter who, like Maia, has a genuine early pedigree: Kalypso on two occasions in the *Odyssey* is addressed as his child (*Od* 1.52; 7.245). In both the *Theogony* (359) and the *Homeric Hymn to Demeter* (422), the name "Kalypso" applies to one of the Okeanides, who may or may not be the same person as Homer's goddess. Homer does not mention any mother; in Hyginus, she is a child of Atlas and Pleione (*Fab praef* 16), while for Apollodoros some-one of that name is a Nereid (*ApB* 1.2.7, but see also below). The very end of the *Theogony* has her bear two children, Nausithoos and Nausinoos, to Odys-seus (*Th* 1017–18), while in the *Ehoiai* she and Hermes produce the race of Kephallenians (Hes fr 150 MW), and Apollodoros gives her (by Odysseus) Latinos, who at the end of the *Theogony* was the child of Odysseus and Kirke (*ApE* 7.24: note that here Kalypso is a daughter of Atlas, not Nereus). Again, there seems to have been no very consistent early story.

The
Daughters
of Asopos

The figure of Asopos represents not one but two or even three different rivers. The *Iliad* knows of the one south of Thebes at which the Argives halted while Tydeus was sent ahead to parlay with Eteokles (*Il* 4.382–84, 10.285–88), and when the *Odyssey* speaks of Asopos as the father of Antiope (who will bear Zethos and Amphion, builders of Thebes: *Od* 11.260), we may presume that the same geography is involved. In neither of these places is Asopos' own ancestry given; we might suppose, as Apollodoros does, that as a river he ought to be a son of Okeanos and Tethys (*ApB* 3.12.6). But Apollodoros also reports that Akousilaos makes him descend from Poseidon and Pero (2F21), while oth-ers say Zeus and Eurynome were the parents. As time goes on, he accumulates quite a number of daughters loved by various gods, not always with his ap-proval. How many of these besides Antiope might be early we cannot say; the name "Asopos" does not survive in any of the fragments of the *Ehoiai*. How-ever, the *Aigimios* does seem to have made Argos (the watcher of Io) a son of Argos *(sic)* and of Ismene, daughter of Asopos (Hes fr 294 MW); Eumelos mentions another daughter, Sinope, probably thinking not of the Theban river but rather of the one in Sikyonian territory near Corinth (fr 10 *PEG*). But Asopos' most famous daughter, Aigina, does not surface until the fifth century, when she appears on a number of Red-Figure pots as the object of Zeus' atten-tion, and in the odes of Pindar, who makes her a twin sister of Thebe and the mother by Zeus of Aiakos (*Nem* 8.6–12; *Is* 8.17–23; *Paian* 6.134–40). In Pindar's account, this romance goes off quite smoothly, but Pherekydes links the affair to the beginning of Sisyphos' problems: after Zeus has taken the girl from Phlious to Oinone/Aigina in the Saronic Gulf, Asopos searches in vain for her until Sisyphos tells him of Zeus' deed (3F119). No consequences of the discovery are reported here; in Apollodoros, Asopos pursues and Zeus must hurl his thunderbolt to discourage him (*ApB* 3.12.6). Already in Kallimachos this last conflict seems alluded to, for we hear of an Asopos who moves slowly, since he has been lamed by a thunderbolt (*H* 4.77–78; cf. Nonnos 7.180–83).

Possibly such an event is also implied by a series of early Red-Figure vases on which Zeus wields his thunderbolt in threatening fashion while pursuing a woman, since on one of them the woman is named as Aigina (NY 96.19.1).[24] One is hard pressed to think that Zeus would need the thunderbolt to compel the maiden, and the composition may be rather a compression of his dealings with daughter and father. Nonnos has Zeus become an eagle to snatch up Aigina, much as we will see in the case of Ganymedes (7.122, 210–14). Of Ovid's notion (mentioned in passing) that Zeus approached her in the form of fire there seems no other trace (*Met* 6.113).

Already in the *Iliad* Aiakos is recorded as a son of Zeus (*Il* 21.189: no mother given), and at the end of the *Theogony* he is wedded to the Nereid Psamathe and sires a child, Phokos (*Th* 1003–5). He also appeared prominently in the *Ehoiai*, since a surviving passage of that work recounts how he found himself alone on the island (presumably Aigina) when he came to manhood, and was grieved; Zeus then transformed all the ants into men and women, and this race was the first to build ships and fit them with sails (Hes fr 205 MW). The passage begins with a line stating Aiakos' conception and birth, but his mother's name is here just a pronoun; given the link with an island, however, it seems certain that she was, as in Pindar and all later traditions, Aigina. We have seen that in the *Theogony* Aiakos already has one son, Phokos. But although he is firmly established in the *Iliad* as the father of Peleus (*Il* 21.189), and Peleus appears immediately after him in the *Theogony* (*Th* 1006–7), the *Theogony* does not call Peleus the child of Aiakos and Psamathe; probably then the author of this section agreed with the later view that Peleus was born of the union of Aiakos and some other woman. Pindar and Bakchylides call her Endeis (*Nem* 5.11–12; Bak 13.96–99); Apollodoros (ApB 3.12.6), Plutarch (*Thes* 10), and Pausanias (2.29.9) concur and assign as her father the Skiron of Megara whom Theseus slew, while for Hyginus (on an emendation: *Fab* 14.8) and several scholiasts (Σ *Nem* 5.12; ΣA *Il* 16.14) this father is Cheiron (Plutarch says that her mother was Chariklo, adding a further note of confusion between Skiron and Cheiron). None of the above sources offers any explanation for the two marriages (or at least matings), although Euripides does claim that Psamathe left the bed of Aiakos (no reason given) and subsequently married Proteus (*Hel* 4–7). That she originally resisted Aiakos' advances, turning herself into a seal to try to escape him, is a story related by Apollodoros (ApB 3.12.6) and the scholia to Euripides' *Andromache* (Σ *And* 687). With a son named Phokos this metamorphosis is scarcely surprising, but it is hard to say which came first.

The tradition that Aiakos was especially upright among mortals may or may not be early; it first surfaces for us, like the name of his mother Aigina, in Pindar. *Nemean* 8 reports that he was "best in deeds of hand and in counsel" (*Nem* 8.7–8); *Isthmian* 8, more surprisingly, says that as the wisest (*kednotatos*) of mortals he rendered judgments in disputes among the gods (*Is* 8.21–24). There is no other reference anywhere to this last idea, but from

Aristophanes onward Aiakos does begin to appear in honored positions in the Underworld. Actually he is nowhere named in the *Batrachoi* as the doorkeeper who confronts Dionysos when the latter descends into Hades, but most of the manuscripts of the play include him among the *personae,* and we may compare Apollodoros (Ap*B* 3.12.6) and Loukianos (*DMor* 6), where he guards the keys of Hades. Plato's *Gorgias* takes that idea further still and makes him one of the three judges of the dead in the Underworld (with Minos and Rhadamanthys: 524a; cf. *Apol* 41a), while in Isokrates' *Euagoras* he shares the greatest honors seated beside Hades and Persephone (9.*Euag* 15). Oddly enough, Pindar does not include him with Peleus, Achilleus, and others on the Isles of the Blessed in *Olympian* 2, but there we are dealing with a poem, after all, not a list. Isokrates is the first to offer another story about Aiakos' life, that when a drought affected the Greeks, representatives from many different cities came to ask him, because of his piety, to pray to Zeus on their behalf; this he did, and Zeus responded by sending rain (9.*Euag* 14–15; cf. Paus 2.29.7–8). We see then that various different traditions point in the same general direction of special qualities for this hero, but not when or how such a concept began to take shape. Perhaps the choral odes of Aischylos' Achilleus or Memnon trilogies contributed something.

The one other tale about Aiakos to be noted appears once again first in Pindar, this time in *Olympian* 8: Apollo and Poseidon share with the mortal the labor of building the walls of Troy (*Ol* 8.31–52). Pindar might easily have characterized this task as a further honor due to Aiakos' excellence, but he says nothing of the sort; instead, the mortal's presence becomes a necessary plot device to explain (and presage) the fall of Troy. As the walls rise, three snakes attempt to leap onto the ramparts; two fail, but the third succeeds, and this prompts Apollo to predict that the city will be taken precisely in that part constructed by Aiakos, and indeed by his very descendants. That this story originated with Pindar is the opinion of the scholia, for whatever that is worth (Σ *Ol* 8.41a). Certainly Homer, who has Poseidon remind Apollo of their efforts for Laomedon in *Iliad* 21 (441–57), says nothing at all about Aiakos there, and indeed implies that Poseidon did all the actual building alone while Apollo tended Laomedon's herds on Ida (he likewise fails to mention Aiakos in a similar context at *Il* 7.452–53). Andromache does refer to a part of the wall where Troy is most easily attacked (near the fig tree: *Il* 6.434–35), but presumably this fact has nothing to do with the city's final destruction.

So far, we have uncovered two sons for Aiakos, Peleus in the *Iliad* and Phokos in the *Theogony.* There is also at times a third child, Telamon (of rather more disputed parentage), and in the Hesiodic Corpus a fourth, Menoitios. Homer speaks of Telamon only as the father of Aias and Teukros, never as the son of anyone; it may or may not be significant that while Achilleus is frequently called *Aiakides,* neither Aias nor Teukros is ever given that epithet. The first author to positively attest Telamon as a son of Aiakos (and Endeis) is Pindar (*Nem* 5.11–12), followed closely by Bakchylides (13.96–99). But the tradition almost certainly is older, since a fragment of the lost epic *Alkmaionis* tells of the joint role of Peleus and Telamon in the slaying of Phokos (fr 1 *PEG*): although the citation (three lines) does not actually say they are brothers, this seems a necessary element if Phokos' death is to have any motive. Pherekydes, on the other hand, says that Telamon is the son of one Aktaios[25] and a Glauke, daughter of Kychreus (3F60: cf. DS 4.72.7, where Glauke is Telamon's *wife*), and is Peleus' friend rather than his brother. Kychreus is not a major figure in Greek myth, but he does seem to have been an important ancestral king/hero on the island of Salamis, and indeed both Diodoros and Apollodoros call him the son of Poseidon and Salamis, daughter of Asopos (DS 4.72.4; ApB 3.12.7). Whatever the merits of this genealogy, we should remember that in both the *Iliad* and the *Ehoiai* Aias comes from Salamis. Banishment for the killing of Phokos would, of course, explain why his father Telamon left Aigina, yet we may wonder if the simpler explanation—that Telamon and Aias were in origin native to Salamis—is not the correct one. In that case, Pherekydes might well reflect an early tradition, even if it is one that links Aias closely to Athens.

The presence of a fourth son of Aiakos, Menoitios, father of Patroklos, is attested only for the Hesiodic Corpus, and that in a summary by Eustathios rather than by a direct quote (Hes fr 212a MW). Eustathios certainly understands the consequences of this genealogy, for he says that it would make Achilleus and Patroklos first cousins. In the *Iliad*, on the other hand, Menoitios is the son of Aktor (*Il* 11.785; 16.14), and in Pindar the same figure (here too the father of Patroklos) is descended from Aktor and Aigina, and thus is Aiakos' half-brother (*Ol* 9.69–70). Presumably, the father Aktor is the one who in Apollodoros (and almost certainly in the *Ehoiai*) descends from Myrmidon and Peisidike, daughter of Aiolos (ApB 1.7.3; Hes fr 10a.99–101 MW). Probably the *Iliad* genealogy represents the older view,[26] with Zeus giving Aigina to Aktor after he has brought her to the island (Σ *Ol* 9.106a comes close to this), much as in some accounts he gives Europa to Asterion after bringing her to Krete. Admittedly, with Menoitios and Aiakos as half-brothers, Menoitios' son Patroklos properly falls in the same generation with Peleus, rather than with Achilleus. But this slight chronological difference between the two friends is not likely to have bothered the author of the *Iliad* or anyone else,[27] and the Catalogue Poet must have had other reasons for grafting Menoitios more closely into the family of Aiakos. We may note in passing that his separation of Myrmidon and Aktor from the line of Aiakos and Menoitios is made possible by the story of Aiakos and the ant-men; thus Myrmidon, although he does appear in the *Ehoiai*, is no longer necessary as an eponym for the Myrmidones of the *Iliad*. But which explanation of that name is actually earlier is another matter.

Returning to the three more certain sons, Peleus, Telamon, and Phokos, we come to the regrettable event alluded to in the fragment of the *Alkmaionis*, namely the death of Phokos at the hands of his two half-brothers. The *Alkmaionis* as quoted by a scholiast simply attests that Telamon struck Phokos on the head with a discus, and that Peleus then completed the deed, hitting him quickly in the back with an axe (fr 1 *PEG*). The context of such a reference is uncertain; probably it was utilized as something already familiar to the poem's audience. Pindar also refers to the murder in *Nemean 5*, but quite obliquely, and as something he does not wish to discuss (*Nem* 5.6–12). No preserved title or even fragment suggests the existence of a tragedy on this promising material. All further details come from scholia and late sources such as Apollodoros and Pausanias; most of these agree that both men plotted the crime together, although there is some variation regarding whether one or the other or both together committed it. In Pausanias, for example, Peleus alone uses the discus to perform the slaying under the guise of training for athletic contests (2.29.9). So too, in the A scholia to *Iliad* 16.14, Peleus does the deed alone and flees to Cheiron, while Telamon's exile is caused by the inadvertent slaying of a fellow hunter during the Kalydonian Boar Hunt. On the other hand, Plutarch (citing one Dorotheos) relates a version—Telamon takes Phokos out hunting and deliberately throws his spear at his brother—which might be intended to exonerate Peleus (*Mor* 311e). Two motives are reported, one that Peleus and Telamon were jealous because Phokos surpassed them in athletic skills (ApB 3.12.6; Σ *And* 687), the other that they wished to please their mother, who was angry at this offspring by another woman (Paus 2.29.9).[28] Some attempt was made to conceal the murder, but Aiakos discovered it, and both his remaining sons went into exile. Telamon indeed did try to defend himself, but his father refused to hear him, and he thus migrated to Salamis (Paus 2.29.10). Only Diodoros claims that the killing (by Peleus) was accidental (DS 4.72.6).

In chapter 5 we saw that Phokos found time before his death to wed Asterodeia, daughter of Deion, and produce Krisos and Panopeus; from this information in late sources (Σ *Tro* 9; Σ *Lyk* 939) we can see that the union was surely related in a mutilated papyrus fragment of the *Ehoiai*, where Phokos and Krisos are certainly mentioned (Hes fr 58 MW). The fragment offers enough additional lines to show that the story of the two brothers fighting in their mother's womb was also related (presumably as an *aition* for historical conflicts between the Phokian cities of Krisa and Panopeus). According to Pausanias, Krisos and Panopeus also appeared as sons of Phokos in the epic poet Asios (fr 5 *PEG*). Pausanias goes on to supply information that may or may not come from the same source, that Panopeus' son was Epeios, the builder of the Wooden Horse (so already in Homer: see below), while Krisos' son Strophios became by Anaxibia (sister of Agamemnon) the father of Pylades (2.29.4). Lykophron likewise tells of the battle in the womb (939–42), but neither he nor any other source speaks of subsequent hostility between the brothers. Instead, he notes that Panopeus once swore falsely by Athena in the matter of flocks, when Amphitryon made his expedition against the city of Komaitho (932–38). The scholia (at 932) rephrase this event but seem to know little more about it. Slightly different is the claim of the T scholia at *Iliad*

23.665 that Panopeus kept back from the common spoils of the Teleboans one Lagaria, presumably a woman and perhaps the mother of Epeios. In any event, in Lykophron the gods punish him by giving him a weakling son (943–45). This son appears conspicuously in the funeral games for Patroklos in *Iliad* 23, where he is called offspring of Panopeus and proclaims his superiority in boxing, at the same time conceding his lack of ability for battle (*Il* 23.664–71). Since he never participates in any of the battle scenes, Homer may mean that he does not fight at all. Stesichoros speaks of him as a watercarrier for the Atreidai (200 *PMG*), and Simonides alludes to the same idea (Athenaios 10.456e-f), so that his lower status seems generally acknowledged, thus perhaps establishing as early the story Lykophron tells.

For the most part, after the incident of Phokos' slaying, Peleus and Telamon go their separate ways, but Pindar on a variety of occasions does make one or both accompany Herakles on two separate ventures, the capture of Laomedon's Troy and the battle with the Amazones (*Nem* 3.36–39; 4.25–30; *Is* 5.34–37; 6.27–30; fr 172 SM). Neither figure has a major role to play in these deeds, but already before Pindar Peisandros sends Telamon to Troy with Herakles (fr 11 *PEG*), and in this connection there is also a child to consider, Teukros. His parentage in the *Iliad* is simply that of a bastard child of Telamon (*Il* 8.281–84), with no mother mentioned and no special reason to do so. But his name naturally suggests that she was somehow a Trojan, and in Sophokles' *Aias* this is indeed the case: he is descended from the royal house of Troy (*Aias* 1299–1303). The playwright obviously expects us to know the story, and he himself may already have told it in more detail, if his lost *Teukros* is earlier than the *Aias*. As matters stand, Xenophon is our first source of explanation (*Kyn* 1.9), followed by Ovid (*Met* 11.211–17) and Apollodoros (Ap*B* 2.6.4): after defeating Laomedon, Herakles gave his daughter Hesione to Telamon as a war prize, and from this woman Teukros was born (so too ΣAb *Il* 8.284). Conceivably this all could be a fifth-century invention, but the tale of Herakles saving Hesione (or someone) from a sea monster is known in sixth-century art, and the rest of the story may well have followed. Telamon's presence at Troy is probably also documented by the pediments of the temple of Aphaia on the island of Aigina. The carvings at the west end appear to show the battle of Greeks and Trojans of Achilleus' time, while those on the east offer a similar battle with an unmistakable Herakles, and thus probably represent his sack of Troy. The east pediment is not likely to date much if at all before 480 B.C., but it had a predecessor of about 500 B.C., which presumably featured the same scene. Nothing guarantees that Telamon is here depicted, but very likely the subject matter was chosen because of the local hero's participation in this exploit.

As for the Amazones, Pindar separately credits both Telamon and Peleus with assisting in the quest for Hippolyte's *zôstêr* (*Nem* 3.38–39; fr 172 SM). Here again Telamon, at least, can make a strong case for being an early part of the story, since a scholiast's citation of lines from a lost hexameter poem (Σ

Nem 3.64a) shows him slaying the sister of the "golden-zoned" queen. On a number of early sixth-century Black-Figure vases, too, he (but not Peleus) is confirmed by name as a companion of Herakles in this battle (e.g., Tarquinia RC 5564; Boston 98.916).[29] Surprisingly, neither brother finds a place in Pindar's abbreviated list of Argonautai in *Pythian* 4, though Peleus is a part of that expedition in fragment 172. Telamon is also missing from the François Krater's roster for the Kalydonian Boar Hunt, where Peleus is paired with Meleagros (Florence 4209; so too on Munich 2243, the Archikles/Glaukytes cup; by contrast, Euripides' *Meleagros* includes him [fr 530 N²]), and from any preserved participation in the funeral games for Pelias.

By all accounts, Telamon's union with Hesione lacks the status of marriage. His legitimate wife, the mother of Aias, is not mentioned in Homer, and indeed not anywhere until Pindar, who makes her Eriboia (*Is* 6.45; so too Bak 13.102–4). In the same poem we learn how Herakles came to Telamon's home to take the hero with him in his expedition to conquer Troy and, holding up his wine cup, prayed to Zeus that Telamon should have a son as hardy and bold as the lion of Nemea; a scholion notes that this event was taken from the *Megalai Ehoiai*, which may have mentioned the mother (Σ *Is* 6.53a = Hes fr 250 MW). In Xenophon, where we learned above of the acquisition of Hesione, this wife is rather Periboia, the daughter of Alkathoos (*Kyn* 1.9); Apollodoros agrees, and adds that Alkathoos was a son of Pelops (ApB 3.12.7). In Pausanias he is located at Megara, and sends his daughter Periboia with Theseus to Krete as one of the victims for the Minotaur (1.42.2). Eriboia is in fact the one maiden named as part of that group in Bakchylides' Ode 17, though we cannot be sure that he equated her with the Eriboia, mother of Aias, in his Ode 13. For his part, Plutarch makes Periboia, mother of Aias, one of Theseus' conquests (*Thes* 29.1). Finally, as we saw above, Diodoros has Telamon wed to Glauke, daughter of Kychreus (king of Salamis); on her death in this author he then marries Eriboia, daughter of Alkathoos (DS 4.72.7).

Telamon's one other deed of interest is the banishing of his bastard son Teukros after the Trojan War, presumably in anger over Aias' death. Sophokles' *Teukros* is our earliest preserved notice of this story (although *Nem* 4.46–47 does put Teukros on Cyprus); it does not appear in Proklos' summary of the *Nostoi*, where we might have expected to find it. The tale may or may not have been dramatized (or at least referred back to) in Aischylos' *Salaminiai* (the third play of his *Aias at Troy* trilogy); we will return to that question and Teukros' fate in chapter 17.

We have seen that Peleus, unlike Telamon, is attested as a son of Aiakos from the *Iliad* onward. Aside from his slaying (with Telamon) of Phokos, participation in various group ventures (Troy, Amazones, Argo, Kalydonian Boar Hunt), and the previously discussed wrestling in the games for Pelias, he has two main adventures: his attempted seduction by the wife of Pelias' son Akastos, and his winning of the Nereid Thetis to be his own wife. The first of these is not mentioned in Homer or Hesiod, but it was recounted at length in the

Ehoiai (Hes fr 208 MW); unfortunately, of this version we know only that <Akastos> decided to hide the sword *(machaira)* made by Hephaistos, so that searching for it alone on Pelion <Peleus> would be overcome by the Kentauroi (Hes fr 209 MW). In Pindar, we learn somewhat more: Hippolyte deceives her husband Akastos with a false tale that Peleus has tried to dishonor her when, in fact, the opposite is the case—Peleus has shunned the wife of his host (*Nem* 5.25–34); Akastos, thus deceived, plots death for Peleus using the sword of Daidalos, but Cheiron wards it off (*Nem* 4.57–61). But for the full story we must turn to Apollodoros, where we learn what circumstances brought Peleus to Akastos' kingdom in Iolkos. In this account, after the death of Phokos, Peleus goes to Eurytion of Phthia for purification (Ap*B* 3.13.1–3). This is carried out, and Peleus then marries Antigone, daughter of Eurytion, who bears him a child, Polydore. But Peleus accidentally kills Eurytion in the course of the Kalydonian Boar Hunt, and he is forced to flee again, this time to the court of Akastos, who provides a second purification. After the funeral games for Pelias, Akastos' wife (here Astydameia) falls in love with him, and when he spurns her advances she accuses him to her husband of improper conduct. Fearing to kill a man he has purified, Akastos takes Peleus hunting on Mount Pelion and, hiding the latter's sword (in cow dung) while he sleeps, abandons him. When Peleus awakes, he searches vainly for the sword as Kentauroi surround him, but Cheiron rescues him and restores the sword (seemingly two separate actions). Scholia add, as a variant, that in some accounts the gods take pity on Peleus in his moment of crisis and send Hephaistos (or Hermes) with the sword, now bestowed for the first time, to help him (Σ *Nem* 4.92a; Σ *Neph* 1063). Still another version makes the abandonment a kind of test: Akastos openly leaves Peleus unarmed in the wilds, announcing that if his actions have indeed been just he will be saved (Σ *Neph* 1063). Already in Anakreon the sword is a gift from the gods because of Peleus' *sôphrosynê* (497 *PMG*; cf. *Neph* 1061–63 and scholia [where the gift is made at the games for Pelias]). That Pindar calls it the sword of Daidalos puzzled the scholiasts, but probably *Daidalos* here is an epithet of Hephaistos.[30] One moment of the tale is illustrated several times on sixth-century Attic pots: Peleus has climbed up into a tree for protection as wild beasts gather below (e.g., NY 46.11.7). On a neck amphora in the Villa Giulia, Cheiron approaches from the other side, thus confirming the interpretation of the scene and repeating the account of the *Ehoiai* and Pindar (VG 24247). Curiously though, Peleus on this pot clearly holds a sword or *machaira* as he crouches in the tree; has Cheiron already given it to him?

The story has in most of our sources an epilogue: Peleus returns to Iolkos on a later occasion with a large force of men and totally destroys it, slaying both Akastos and Hippolyte in the process. The beginning of Hesiod fragment 211 MW seems to guarantee such an action for the *Ehoiai*, and Pindar twice refers to it, once even claiming that Peleus did this all alone, without an army (*Nem* 3.32–34; 4.54–56). But a scholiast shrewdly observes that Pindar may here simply be flattering the Aiginetans for whom the ode was written, and adds that in Pherekydes Peleus has the help of both Iason and the Dioskouroi (3F62). Sophokles and Euripides each wrote a tragedy entitled *Peleus*. That by Euripides probably dealt with these events, though virtually nothing survives. That by Sophokles, on the other hand, apparently related Neoptolemos' rescue of his aged grandfather after the latter had been driven out of his kingdom by Akastos. Thus, in one version at least, Akastos is still alive, although this may after all have been invented by Sophokles for purposes of generating a plot. To the name "Hippolyte" for Akastos' wife, Pindar adds "Kretheis," presumably a patronymic (*Nem* 5.26); we have seen that in Apollodoros (also in some scholia) her name is Astydameia, while other scholia make her Kretheis *or* Hippolyte (Σ AR 1.224), Kretheis, daughter of Hippolyte (Σ *Nem* 4.92), or even Kretheis, daughter of Hippolytos (Σ *Nem* 5.46). Related in some way to these events is perhaps Lykophron 901–2, which speaks of a wolf turned to stone for devouring a compensation. As the scholia explain the lines, this compensation consists of cattle and sheep gathered by Peleus as payment for his accidental killing of Aktor, son of Akastos, while hunting; when the wolf attacks them, Thetis lithifies it. The scholiast also knows, however, of a version in which Psamathe sends the wolf to attack Peleus' herds after he and Telamon have killed Phokos, with the same result.

As for Peleus' stay in the house of Eurytion before migrating to Iolkos, and the marriage to his host's daughter there, evidence prior to Apollodoros is sketchy. The *Iliad* does know of a Polydore, daughter of Peleus, who lay with the river god Spercheios (although she was married to Boros, son of Perieres) and bore the Myrmidon Menesthios (*Il* 16.173–78), and the *Ehoiai* also mentions such a daughter of Peleus (Hes fr 213 MW). Homer never says, however, that this Polydore is Achilleus' sister, and for that reason the scholia (ad loc.: A) prefer to suppose her father a Peleus different from the son of Aiakos. But certainly, later writers take them to be the same person, and no other Peleus is ever attested in Greek myth. Homer likewise does not name his Polydore's mother; Pherekydes is the first (followed by Apollodoros, as we saw above) to call her Antigone, daughter of Eurytion, Peleus' first wife (3F61; 3F1b). Pherekydes also knows the detail of the purification by Eurytion, leading us to wonder if much or all of Apollodoros' account does not derive from him and go back to Homer's time. The scholia's summary of Pherekydes does not extend to Peleus' accidental killing of Eurytion, but from another source we learn that this was definitely to be found in Pindar: Peleus slew his kinsman unwillingly while they were hunting (fr 48 SM). In this source (Aelius Aristeides), however, Peleus is wed to Polymele, daughter of Aktor, while Eurytion is the son of Iros, son of Aktor. Whether this idea is taken from Pindar or some other writer is left unclear; the *Iliad* scholia also suggest as wife Eurydike, daughter of Aktor, or Laodameia, daughter of Alkmaion (ΣA *Il* 16.175). One other point concerns the fate of this wife, since Peleus cannot formally marry Thetis if he is still married to Antigone (or whomever). In Apollodoros, the wife of Akastos falsely informs Antigone that Peleus is preparing to divorce her and marry one of Akastos' daughters; Antigone hangs herself in chagrin (Ap*B* 3.13.3). The hanging at least may be attributable to Pherekydes (3F1b).

We now come to Peleus' winning of Thetis and the birth of their son Achilleus. In *Nemean* 5 Pindar says explicitly that Thetis was given to the Aiakid by Zeus as a reward for his upright behavior in rejecting the advances of Hippolyte, although in *Isthmian* 8 he also informs us of the gods' need to marry Thetis to any mortal rather than a god (*Nem* 5.34–37; *Is* 8.26–47). The *Iliad* only hints at such factors: Thetis complains that she was forced to wed a mortal but never says why, and we may wonder how much Homer knows of her later peculiar destiny. In the *Kypria* (according to Philodemos), Thetis rejected Zeus' advances in order to please Hera, and for that reason (thus not because of any children she might bear) Zeus in anger condemned her to marry a mortal; Philodemos adds that Hesiod tells pretty much the same story (*Kyp* fr 2 PEG). The *Theogony* does note the mating of Peleus and Thetis (together with other unions of goddess and mortal: *Th* 1006–7), but there says only that Achilleus was the offspring, so presumably Philodemos refers to a fuller account of these matters in the *Ehoiai*. *Iliad* 1, of course, casts Thetis as an old ally and confidant of Zeus, rather than one alienated by his anger, but perhaps elsewhere Homer told other stories. In any event, Pindar's *Isthmian* 8 is our earliest preserved source for the notion that Thetis (as revealed by Themis) is fated to bear a son greater than his father, and that in consequence Zeus and Poseidon both curb their amatory inclinations and agree to bestow her on Peleus. The same idea is clearly at the heart of Prometheus' secret in the *Prometheus Desmotes*, when he predicts (wrongly, as events prove) that a woman will bear Zeus a son who will overthrow him (*PD* 755–68); this can only be Thetis, as in fact Philodemos tells us for the *Lyomenos* (p. 306 R). We have already seen that Aischylos conflates Hesiodic genealogy (Gaia = Themis) in this play, and this is presumably to justify, in part, the novelty of transferring the secret to Prometheus. Thus, everywhere except in the *Iliad* (where Homer may simply not care to discuss the matter), Zeus has compelling reasons (not always the same ones) to wed Thetis to some mortal. If we ask why Peleus was chosen, we find once again that the *Iliad* is not as explicit as later accounts. Hera does say that Peleus is exceedingly dear to the gods (*Il* 24.61), and later in the same book Achilleus describes his father as a man to whom "the gods gave glorious gifts from birth. For he surpassed all men in blessings and wealth, and he ruled the Myrmidones, and they made a goddess his wife, though he was a mortal" (*Il* 24.534–37). But the suggestion of these words is surely that the gods' favor toward Peleus was arbitrary, as divine favor tends to be in the *Iliad*, and not based on his *sôphrosynê* or any other accomplishments. Indeed, Achilleus goes on to observe that a god has also given a bad final lot to Peleus, since he is fated to have no children to rule in his halls. Probably the *Ehoiai* had its own version of all this, as would the *Kypria*, but nothing survives; the same holds for the poem Sappho wrote on the wedding (141 LP).

As noted above, Thetis in the *Iliad* is quite clear on the point that the gods forced her, entirely unwilling, to marry Peleus, and that it was a divine command. But for artists (at least) of the following centuries the mortal's winning of his Nereid bride is not that simple.[31] A fragmentary plate from Praisos on Krete dating to the mid-seventh century shows what is very probably Peleus clinging to a fish; the left half of the plate is broken away, but a woman's leg in large scale survives, and may well represent Thetis as woman and fish (Iraklion, no #). In any case, Pausanias claims to have seen the couple wrestling on the Chest of Kypselos (with a snake from Thetis' body threatening Peleus: 5.18.5), so that both the notion of a struggle and Thetis' ability to transform herself would seem to be early. On a late-seventh-century Melian amphora from Kavalla, we see first the series of Nereides from whom Peleus singles out Thetis to grasp (Kavalla A1086),[32] and the same scene reappears on a Late Corinthian column krater from the mid-sixth century where Peleus lies in wait for Thetis as she passes by with other Nereides (Louvre E639). On all three of the Loeb Tripods from Perugia (third quarter of the century), a certain amount of pursuit is necessary, as now a lion, now a snake emerge from Thetis' shoulder (on one example Hermes also follows: Munich SL 66, 67, 68). Attic painting of the same and subsequent periods focuses on the actual seizing and struggle: the would-be groom stands with arms firmly gripped about his bride; lions, panthers, snakes, and other monsters attached to her body in miniature indicate again her capacity for transformation, and Peleus must clearly hang on for dear life (London B215, Louvre CA 2569, etc.). From time to time, Cheiron is shown in attendance, no doubt providing moral support (e.g., Munich 1415). On the literary side, Pindar is the first author to refer to this situation (*Nem* 3.35–36; 4.62–65); as we might imagine, his oblique allusions indicate that it was a well-known story. That Pindar himself should acknowledge it after his insistence that Thetis was a gift from Zeus may seem surprising, but the tale does give Peleus a chance to demonstrate valor, and there is no reason why such a hero should not be asked to prove himself worthy of the gift. Of numerous fifth-century representations, the best known (and surely most charming) is that by Peithinos in the tondo of a Red-Figure cup now in Berlin (Berlin:Ch F2279).

Following Thetis' "acceptance" of her mortal suitor, there was a formal wedding attended by all the gods, and attested already at *Iliad* 24.62–63. The *Kypria* began with this affair, which provided the opportunity for Eris to set in motion the Judgment of Paris, though this may not have been the Homeric concept of the course of events. Sappho also celebrated the occasion in some form, and the Erskine Dinos and François Krater of Sophilos and Kleitias, respectively, commemorate the event in the first half of the sixth century (London 1971.11–1.1; Florence 4209; cf. Athens Akr 587, fragments of a second such pot by Sophilos). Obviously, if all the Olympian gods are to attend there will not be much variation in the guest list, but even so, the choice of figures on these three vases and the order in which they appear are surprisingly similar, and it has been suggested that a detailed literary source such as Stesichoros may be responsible.[33] As these illustrations present the scene, the guests arrive on Mount Pelion to greet Peleus and Thetis, who are at home waiting to receive them, Thetis modestly inside the house, Peleus out in front of it. On the Erskine Dinos, Iris leads the procession, followed by Hestia, Demeter, Chariklo, Leto, and Dionysos; the François Krater begins with Cheiron (who is somewhat further back on the Erskine Dinos), then Iris, Demeter, Hestia, Chariklo, and Dionysos, omitting only Leto. Of the other guests, Zeus and Hera arrive together, as do Poseidon and Amphitrite and Ares and Aphrodite, surrounded by most if not all of the Mousai and all three Moirai. More surprisingly, the procession concludes on both preserved pots and the fragments with Okeanos (shown with a fish tail) and Hephaistos on his donkey. One other figure whom we might have expected to be prominent—Nereus, father of the bride—is rather toward the rear on the François Krater (together with his wife Doris), and absent altogether on the Erskine Dinos. Apollo and Artemis are also in attendance, as is Hermes (Kleitias adds Maia as well). Both Cheirons bring an ash branch, perhaps in allusion to the spear Peleus receives from him in Homer (Il 16.140–44); in the Kypria this was specifically a wedding gift, with Cheiron providing the branch, Athena smoothing it, and Hephaistos fitting it out (fr 3 PEG). Sophilos gives Dionysos only a vine to carry, but in Kleitias' version he bears on his shoulder an elegant amphora. As we discussed in chapter 3, this may be the jar that Thetis contributes to Achilleus' funeral in Odyssey 24, a jar she is said to have received from Dionysos. Stesichoros makes the cause of the gift Thetis' rescue of Dionysos when he was pursued by Lykourgos (234 PMG), but of course it could serve both functions. One hopes in any case that it is filled with wine for the feast. Of a third present mentioned by Homer, the first set of armor made by the gods for this family (i.e., that which Patroklos will lose to Hektor: Il 18.82–85) there is no sign, or any trace of the immortal horses (Balios and Xanthos) contributed by Poseidon in Apollodoros (ApB 3.13.5). Likewise, in contrast to the version of the Kypria, there is no trace of Eris; possibly both artists simply wished to avoid ill-omened overtones, but possibly too Eris' role was not yet canonical at this period. If the guess made earlier about the content of Sophokles' play Eris (probably satyric) is correct, it would have dramatized this wedding and the goddess' intervention.

Peleus and Thetis' subsequent married life and the upbringing of their offspring is a subject of some controversy in our sources. Although the Iliad implies at several points that the couple enjoys a normal home life, with Thetis on hand to witness Achilleus' departure for war or even to welcome him back (e.g., Il 18.57–60, 329–32), the fact remains that on the two occasions when Achilleus calls to his mother (and the one on which Iris summons her in Iliad 24) she is in the depths of the sea with her father and her sister Nereides, having, it seems, abandoned her husband's halls at Phthia. Nothing in Homer suggests when or why. The Iliad scholia claim that in the neôteroi she leaves on the twelfth day after Achilleus' birth, but they also do not say why (ΣΣA Il

16.222; 18.57, 60). Supposedly in Sophokles' *Achilleos Erastai* the cause was that Peleus reviled her (fr 151 R). The source of this information adds that in the *Aigimios* Thetis places each of her children by Peleus in a cauldron of water to see if they are mortal (Hes fr 300 MW; Lyk 177–79 and others make this instead fire); Peleus becomes understandably upset when his children perish (in Lykophron six sons) and prevents his wife from employing the test on Achilleus. Apollonios, by contrast, offers a story similar to that of Demeter and Demophoon: Thetis anoints her child by day and places it in the fire by night to make it immortal (not to test it), but Peleus intervenes and in anger she leaves him (AR 4.869–79). Apollodoros and the Lykophron scholia have the same account (ApB 3.13.6; Σ Lyk 178), and not impossibly it or something like it lay behind the twelfth-day departure.[34] Such an attempt might seem to present distant echoes of Thetis' immersion of Achilleus in the Styx to make him invulnerable, although our earliest sure source for this latter story is Statius in the first century A.D. (*Ach* 1.133–34). For what it is worth, the *Iliad* clearly regards Achilleus as the only child Thetis bore (*Il* 18.436–38; 24.540); Alkaios appears to take the same view (42 LP). In this latter author, Peleus brings his new bride to the home of Cheiron after he has won her. That he also brought Achilleus there to be trained seems implied as early as the *Iliad* (where Achilleus learns medicine from the Kentauros: *Il* 11.830–32), and so too the *Ehoiai*, where Cheiron keeps the lad on Pelion rather than letting him join the other suitors of Helen (Hes fr 204.87–89 MW). The Hesiodic *Precepts of Cheiron* represented, in fact, an entire poem based on this situation, with the advice presumably directed toward Achilleus. In art, the scene of Peleus handing his son over to Cheiron may surface as early as the middle of the Protoattic period, if fragments of a neck-amphora in Berlin are rightly interpreted (Berlin:Ch A9). Even if they are not, such an event is clearly portrayed on a Black-Figure cup by the Heidelberg Painter, with Cheiron followed by his wife and daughters and Peleus by a woman who must be Thetis (Würzburg 452). The scene becomes extremely popular with both Black- and Red-Figure painters; thus by the time we find concrete literary testimony to Cheiron's tendance in Pindar (*Nem* 3.43–49), the story must have been well known. More often than not, Peleus and Cheiron are shown alone with the child, but Oltos on a Red-Figure cup portrays Thetis (named) hurrying away to the right as Cheiron greets the adolescent child; presumably she has been unable to bear the moment of parting (Berlin:Ch F4220). Surprisingly, we hear of no boyhood deeds of Achilleus except for the killing of wild beasts (again in Pindar); his earliest exploits will be those of the Trojan War.

Of Peleus' later life there is little to say. Pindar does place him on the Isles of the Blessed (though with a number of other figures who may also represent Pindaric elevations: *Ol* 2.78), and Euripides expands upon that idea in his preserved *Andromache*, in which Thetis provides the finale by coming to make Peleus immortal and take him down with her to the watery home of Nereus (*And* 1253–58). We have seen that Sophokles wrote a lost play, *Peleus*, apparently about Peleus' difficulties in old age at the hands of Akastos before being rescued by his grandson Neoptolemos (see chapter 17). The plot seems peculiarly suited to the stage; if it is older, no trace has survived.

As noted in the beginning of this section, the *Nekuia* knows yet another daughter of Asopos, Antiope, who is called the mother of Zethos and Amphion, builders of Thebes (*Od* 11.260–65). But the full story of her travails familiar to later writers involves quite a different genealogy, one in which she is the daughter of Nykteus, whose brother Lykos and his wife Dirke torment her until her sons grow to manhood and take vengeance. Euripides' lost *Antiope*, for which our main source is Hyginus (*Fab* 8; cf. ApB 3.5.5), is our first evidence for that tale. The *Ehoiai* mentioned the building accomplishments of Zethos and Amphion, and thus probably discussed their mother's ancestry, but we cannot say what account it might have given (Hes fr 182 MW). Nor is there any way to tell whether Antiope, daughter of Asopos, ever suffered any of the problems of her Nyktean counterpart.

The remaining daughters of Asopos are rarely more than figures designed to provide an ancestry for later generations, and can be dealt with more briefly. Diodoros lists twelve of them (in addition to two sons, Pelasgos and Ismenos), including Aigina, Thebe, and Salamis (4.72.1); later he adds Harpina, mother of Oinomaos by Ares (4.73.1). Salamis, the mother of Kychreus (by Poseidon), we have already encountered above, while Harpina's parentage and offspring appear in Pausanias (5.22.6); in Hellanikos we remember that the mother of Oinomaos is the Atlantid Sterope. The same passage of Pausanias also speaks of a daughter Nemea (perhaps the mother of Archemoros in Aischylos' lost *Nemea*: fr 149a R). Ismene, who married someone named Argos, is known only from Apollodoros (who makes her the mother of Iasos: ApB 2.1.3) and his citation of the *Aigimios*, which makes her the mother of Io's Argos (Hes fr 294 MW). Any or all of these might have found room in the *Ehoiai*, or Bakchylides, or Korinna, but the only name besides those of Aigina, Antiope, and Ismene actually attested in the Archaic period is "Thebe," who appears in both Pindar (*Ol* 6.84–85; *Is* 8.17–20) and Bakchylides (9.53–54). Although Pindar speaks of her metaphorically as his mother, and says that Zeus brought her to the springs of Dirke as he brought Aigina to Oinone, no real child is anywhere recorded, and presumably a desire to create ancestral links with the Aiginetans is the primary agent at work here.

7   The Royal House of Athens

Early Bits and Pieces   Just as the Athenians at Troy receive little notice in the *Iliad*, so references to early Athens and its royal line in general are quite rare, not only in Homer but throughout the Archaic period. In truth, save for the barely attested sixth-century (?) *Theseis*,[1] we have preserved not even the name of an epic that might have dealt with the city's history, and quite probably a series of separate tales about various figures was formed into a coherent whole only at a relatively late date.[2] The genealogy of our tradition is especially confusing, as we shall see, with (more than usual) the fabrication of individuals to create a continuous line of kings for the city. Homer names only one such figure, Erechtheus, who in the *Odyssey* is the owner of a palace in Athens to which Athena retires, perhaps for purposes of being worshipped (*Od* 7.80–81). In the *Iliad*, on the other hand, the Athenians are the "people of great-hearted Erechtheus, whom once Athena daughter of Zeus raised, but the life-giving earth bore him" (*Il* 2.547–48). Since this description fits far better the figure elsewhere known to us as Erichthonios, son of Hephaistos and the earth, it would seem either that the two heroes were originally one person separated into two by variant spellings, or (less probably) that two originally separate figures have become confused.[3] In either case, we can at least say that the tradition of a ruler of Athens who was sprung from the earth and cared for by Athena is as old as the *Iliad*.

Hesiod makes no mention of any early figures from Athens, save for Pandion as the father of the swallow (*W&D* 568). The *Ehoiai* is slightly more helpful: Xouthos, son of Hellen, marries a daughter of Erechtheus whose name begins with *K* and is surely Kreousa as in later tradition (Hes fr 10a.20–24 MW). This passage, however, forms part of the descent from Hellen, and thus has nothing more to say about Athenians. They are surprisingly absent from our other fragments of the poem; West conjectures that they were discussed at length in Book 4,[4] and this may well be right, but what survives (one Sikyon as son of Erechtheus [Hes fr 224 MW] and a further reference to Pandion [Hes fr 180 MW]) is not much help. The late lexicographer Harpokration, in glossing the word *autochthones*, tells us that the epic *Danais* and Pindar both made Erichthonios and Hephaistos born from the earth (fr 2 *PEG*; Pindar fr 253 SM). In Hephaistos' case we may suspect some confusion, since the blacksmith god is always elsewhere Hera's child. But likely the *Danais* (and Pindar) did name Erichthonios, not Erechtheus, as the result of whatever story existed about Hephaistos and Athena[5] (by contrast, Herodotos speaks of "the earth-born Erechtheus": 8.55;[6] for accounts of Hephaistos' pursuit of Athena see chapter 2). Simonides knows of Oreithuia, daughter of Erechtheus, whom Boreas will spirit away (534 *PMG*; so too probably Akou 2F30), and this tale seems to have appeared as well on the Chest of Kypselos (Paus 5.19.1).[7] But this is all we have before the fifth century, and even that period will not add much. Local genealogy is surprisingly absent from the plays of Aischylos and Sophokles (although Aischylos wrote an *Oreithuia*, and Sophokles a *Kreousa* and an *Ion*, all lost); Euripides does rather better in this regard, as we will see, but his versions are anything but consistent. In Herodotos we find only scattered references—to Kekrops, Erechtheus, to Xouthos and his son Ion, and to Pandion and his son Aigeus. Nor does Attic vase-painting exhibit much of the local bias we might have expected, even if Archaic Red-Figure does offer a few scenes of interest.

Of the earliest names, Kekrops, like Erechtheus, was one of the ten eponymous heroes selected (supposedly by Delphi) for Kleisthenes' new tribal system at the end of the sixth century, and both were honored with sacred areas in the later Erechtheion on the Akropolis, but we cannot say what stories Athenians of the time might have known about either of them. The late-fifth-century writer Hellanikos is the first source we can identify as having made any attempt at systematizing earlier material; likely enough his versions were instrumental in shaping the work of the Atthidographers who followed.[8] What remains, however, is disappointingly scant: Kekrops is named as father of the Agraulos (elsewhere often Aglauros)[9] who bore to Poseidon the son Halirrhothios slain by Ares (4F38), and Erichthonios, son of Hephaistos, becomes the first to institute the Panathenaia (4F39; so also Androtion). With so little early material we must descend into the fourth century and later to achieve any sort of coherent picture. Our two most complete sources are the Parian Marble of the third century B.C. (239 *FGrH*) and a list by the first-century B.C. Rhodian Kastor (250F4: probably drawn directly from Eratosthenes); the two offer essentially the same sequence of early Attic kings, although with different comments. The Marble makes Kekrops the first king of Athens (although the autochthonous Aktaios was there before him), and in his reign there occurs the dispute between Ares and Poseidon on the Areopagos (concerning the rape of Ares' daughter Alkippe and the slaying of Halirrhothios). One Kranaos appears next (Kastor calls him "indigenous"), in whose reign the flood takes place and Deukalion flees to Athens. The following ruler, Amphiktyon (apparently a son of Deukalion and son-in-law of Kranaos), sees the founding of Thebes by Kadmos, and his successor Erichthonios the arrival of Danaos and the first Panathenaia. Under Pandion I, the first Minos rules Krete, and in the time of Erichtheus (so the spelling of the Marble) Demeter brings the secret of the grain to Athens. A Pandion II, son of Kekrops II, next appears, then Aigeus, Theseus, and Menestheus. Kastor adds more in the way of genealogical links: in his account, Erichthonios is the son of Hephaistos, while Pandion I becomes the son of Erichthonios, Erechtheus the son of Pandion I, Kekrops II the brother of Erechtheus, and Pandion II the son of Erechtheus. Whatever its source, and despite the fact that Kranaos and Amphiktyon obscure the link between the daughters of Kekrops I and Erichthonios, this line of descent (or at least succession) becomes fairly standard in later times (cf. Ap*B* 3.14–15), with a Pandion I stationed between Erichthonios and Erechtheus, and a Kekrops II between Erechtheus and the Pandion (II) already attested by Bakchylides as the father of Aigeus (Bak 18.15). One must obviously suspect that Kekrops II is a makeshift to fill up space; he is, in fact, omitted by the Herakleides epitome of the lost beginning of the Aristotelian *Athenaion Politeia*, where Pandion is said to have ruled after Erechtheus. The two Pandions might seem to point to the same conclusion, but we should remember that while Athenian tradition made one of them the grandfather of Theseus, as early as Hesiod a Pandion is also the father of the girl who becomes a swallow (i.e., Philomela). Probably, then, there were originally two different figures, though not perhaps in the Athenian scheme of things. As for Erichthonios and Erechtheus, suspicion that they were really a doublet of the same figure began already in later antiquity (e.g., Σ*A Il* 2.547). If we could be absolutely certain that Erichthonios is so named as the child sprung from the earth in the *Danais* we could at least establish the separation between the two as early (if not original), but in the present state of our knowledge it might also (as some think) be a product of fifth-century Athenian restructuring.

Kekrops and His Daughters

We see at any rate that in all our sources Kekrops comes at or very near the beginning. He is best known for two things, a snake-like lower body, and the disaster that befell his daughters (Pandrosos, Herse, and Aglauros, as the later accounts name them). The earliest preserved evidence on these points comes from early fifth-century pottery, but as the scenes there are ambiguous on their own, it may be best to turn first to the literary materials and then work back. From Hermes' prologue and the dialogue between Ion and Kreousa in Euripides' *Ion*, we learn that Erichthonios, child of Gaia, was taken up by Athena from the earth and given over to the daughters of Kekrops and Aglauros to guard unseen (*Ion* 9–26, 260–82). They, however, did open the box or jar in which the child lay, and then leapt to their deaths, presumably from the Akropolis to the place of the Long Rocks, and presumably in fear of what they saw when the box was opened (Athena had set two snakes to guard the child). Later, too, a servant mentions a statue of the snake-tailed Kekrops and his daughters at the entrance of the temple (*Ion* 1163–64). All this is touched on obliquely, as something the audience already knows. As we saw in chapter 2, Ps-Eratosthenes assigns to some play of Euripides as well the events that precede this story, namely the tale of Hephaistos' attempted rape of Athena with

Erichthonios as the result after the god's seed has fallen upon the ground (*Katast* 13); this is our first actual explanation of the birth of Erichthonios mentioned in the *Danais,* and all subsequent narratives agree with it.

As for the artistic evidence from the earlier part of the fifth century, much of our Euripidean material seems in fact anticipated in it.[10] On a Red-Figure cup by the Codrus Painter dating to perhaps 440 B.C. and now in Berlin (Berlin:Ch F2537) the figures are all conveniently named and, taken together with what we know from Euripides, leave no doubt of the story intended. Kekrops, with his body ending in a snake tail, stands to the left; in the center Gaia rises up out of the earth and hands the child Erichthonios to Athena, while to the right Hephaistos and Erse look on (for Kekrops with a snake tail see also the slightly earlier rhyton London E788). The other side of the same cup shows a procession of Attic luminaries: Aglauros, Erechtheus, Pandrosos, Aigeus, and Pallas. This unmistakable pattern of woman with child emerging from the earth enables us to identify the same scene on a number of earlier pots, including a White-Ground lekythos of about 490 B.C. (Mormino Coll 769), which thus constitutes the earliest preserved reference to the birth, aside from the *Danais.* Here Kekrops (now with a fish tail) again watches Gaia emerge from the earth to hand the child to Athena, and is joined by a figure with staff who is probably Hephaistos. From about 470 B.C. we have also a Red-Figure kalpis with the version of the Oinanthe Painter (London E182); surprisingly, Zeus (clear by his thunderbolt) accompanies Gaia and Athena. On a stamnos by Hermonax of only slightly later date (Munich 2413), the figure with staff reappears, looking proudly at the child, but we should keep in mind that we have no certain source for Hephaistos as the father before Hellanikos and the Berlin cup (or Euripides, if the play in which he told the story is earlier). The Palermo lekythos seems also the earliest evidence for Kekrops' snake- or fish-tailed body, which the Kekrops of the Parthenon's west pediment may have featured as well, if fragments of a snake body do in fact belong to Figure B of that group.[11] In literature we might note that the joke at Aristophanes' *Sphekes* 438 presupposes an audience well aware of Kekrops' serpent form (cf. Eur fr 930 N²?). Occasionally, vases do represent him as completely human (see below), but this seems not to have been the dominant tradition.[12]

The second part of the story, the opening of the chest in which Athena has placed the child, almost certainly appears also on several Red-Figure pots.[13] The earliest of these, a cup in Frankfurt in the manner of the Brygos Painter, shows two women racing toward a house and a large snake in pursuit (Frankfurt:Lieb ST V 7);[14] within the house a bearded man and youth sit on chairs, and in front of them another woman reaches out her arms to welcome the two in flight. The bearded man's legs are obscured by the chiton of the woman in front of him, but he does appear to have human feet; nevertheless, he is surely Kekrops (with his son Erysichthon?[15]), watching as one of his daughters moves to the aid of the two who have opened the chest.[16] A pelike in London by the Erichthonios Painter is slightly later but more explicit: we see Athena, the chest, the child, and the pair of snakes that guard him (London E372). Likewise, a lekythos in Basel by the Phiale Painter shows Athena seizing a fleeing woman by the arm, while between them a snake emerges from a box (Basel BS 404). In this way we see that many of the details found in Euripides prove to be part of a previous tradition. Of all of the above vases those that do show the entire child (the Codrus Painter cup and the Oinanthe Painter kalpis) make him quite human (likewise Munich 2413), as later authors also believe; the earliest writer to record that he might have been a snake or (like Kekrops) part snake is apparently Hyginus in the *De Astronomia* (2.13.1–2; cf. *Fab* 166). Probably this is no more than a late confusion of the child and his guardian snake(s), or perhaps a transfer of the chief characteristics of Kekrops.[17]

Regarding the fate of the Kekropides after they opened the chest there are varying accounts. In the *Ion*, all three daughters apparently leapt from the Akropolis (273–74; 496), but on the Frankfurt cup we saw one daughter inside the palace with her father facing the two pursued by the snake. A column krater by the Orchard Painter (Denman Coll, no #) likewise shows Athena pursuing two women while a third moves away calmly to the other side, and the resulting suspicion that not all three are here culpable finds confirmation in later literature. For the fourth-century Athenian Amelesagoras, only Aglauros and Pandrosos are guilty (330F1), while Euphorion names Herse (perhaps not alone) as making the leap after she has opened the chest (fr 9 Pow). In Ovid Aglauros alone does the deed (*Met* 2.552–61), and in Apollodoros and Pausanias it is Aglauros and Herse (ApB 3.14.6; Paus 1.18.2); Hyginus seemingly follows Euripides by including all three (*Fab* 166; *Astr* 2.13). Euripides does not specifically say what was in the chest at *Ion* 271–73, but lines 21–24 of the same play tell us that Erichthonios was guarded by snakes, so the inference of their presence seems pretty certain. Amelesagoras confirms that there were two serpents wrapped around the child, as we had already gathered from the Red-Figure evidence, but both he and Ovid omit the story of the girls' leap, and Kallimachos' version has gaps at all the crucial points (fr 260 Pf). Hence from Euripides we must look to Apollodoros and Pausanias, as cited above. The former says that the sisters were driven mad by Athena because they had opened the chest, and thus jumped from the Akropolis, but he also records a version in which the snake (his chest has only one) destroys them. The latter has them become mad when they see Erichthonios, and says nothing about snakes; possibly, therefore, he agreed with Hyginus on Erichthonios' hybrid form. Amelesagoras, whose primary concern is explaining the absence of rooks from the Akropolis, has no account of their fate at all. In Ovid, Aglauros is turned into a stone by Hermes because she blocked his way to Herse, and while we might consider such a metamorphosis suspiciously Ovidian, a fragment of Philodemos indicates an earlier Greek source, probably Kallimachos (PHerc 243 II = p. 10 Gomperz; the attribution depends upon a partial supplement to the papyrus);[18] in this fragment, metamorphosis (and cause) are the same, although the daughter turned to stone is Pandrosos, not Herse. We should, of course, remember that both Pandrosos and Aglauros had sacred places in Athens, Pandrosos on the Akropolis itself, as part of the precinct with the sacred olive tree just west of the Erechtheion, Aglauros in a cave on the north slope of the same hill, just below the house of the Arrhephoroi (Paus 1.27.2; 1.18.2). Pandrosos, whose name like that of Herse reflects a Greek word for "dew," may well have been linked to the fertility of the tree and the success of the olive harvest in general. But such considerations only lead us away from what we find in our narratives, and we must admit that the cultic associations of the sisters probably mark them out as originally separate entities only later brought together in myth.

The story of the Kekropides does not, however, end with their opening of the chest and demise, for like the Pleiades they are joined in union with several gods and bear children. The fourth-century Atthidographer Androtion tells us that Pandrosos was by Hermes the mother of Keryx, clearly an eponym for the Kerykes clan at Eleusis (324F1). We have seen too that, as early as Hellanikos, Agraulos/Aglauros is by Ares the mother of Alkippe (4F38). Later sources offer some variations: Pausanias relates as the belief of the Kerykes themselves that Hermes and Aglauros were the parents of Keryx (Paus 1.38.3, set against the idea that Keryx was a son of Eumolpos), while a poem of the second century A.D. (Marcellus of Side) assigns the same child to Hermes and Herse (IG 14.1389). Ovid for his part also relates the love of Hermes for Herse, but represents it as thwarted by her sister Aglauros in a fit of jealousy caused by Athena (Met 2.722–835). In Apollodoros, on the other hand, Hermes and Herse are rather the parents of one Kephalos, who is carried off by Eos (ApB 3.14.3). Very likely, this Kephalos is identical with the one abducted by Eos at the end of the Theogony to become the father of a Phaethon, although Hesiod does not name the parents of his abductee (Th 986–87); Apollodoros' idea that the goddess' child by her mortal lover was rather Tithonos (who then fathered Phaethon) is surely the result of some confusion. In Euripides' Hippolytos (954–58) we find again a Kephalos snatched up by Eos to live among the gods, like Semele; the implication would seem that he is still there. The numerous appearances in Red-Figure of a hunter pursued by a winged Eos and sometimes named as Kephalos have been noted in chapter 1, but we should mention here again a cup by Douris in the Getty Museum (84.AE.569) which names not only Eos and Kephalos, but the bystanders Kekrops and Pandion as well (a third such figure has no name). Kekrops would, of course, be appropriate to such a scene as Kephalos' grandfather, Pandion much less so. But likely the artist meant simply to indicate a general Athenian connection for the victim of the abduction. The more famous Kephalos, husband of Prokris, is the son of Deion in virtually all sources, including several early ones. Certainly Ovid and Antoninus Liberalis conflate the two figures by having Kephalos, husband of Prokris, abducted (Met 7.672–862; AntLib 41, perhaps from Nikandros), but their version is very probably late, as we will see below in discussing the daughters of Erechtheus. Hyginus, meanwhile, speaks of a Kephalos as son of Hermes and Kreousa, daughter of Erechtheus (Fab 160); when discussing the husband of Prokris, however, he too insists on descent from Deion, suggesting that even late authors could keep these figures apart when they wished (*Fab* 189; cf. Ap*B* at 3.14.3 and 3.15.1 vs. the conflation at 1.9.4).

For one other offspring of Kekrops—the son Erysichthon possibly to be seen in the Frankfurt cup discussed above (and presumably different from the father of Mestra who insulted Demeter)—our only sources are Apollodoros and Pausanias, who both say that this son died childless (Ap*B* 3.14.2; Paus 1.2.6). Plato also knows the name as that of an Athenian (*Kritias* 110a), and even mentions him in the same breath as Erechtheus and Erichthonios, but says nothing about his parentage or deeds; the same absence of parentage holds also for a brief reference in Athenaios, drawn it seems from the fourth-century writer Phanodemos (Athen 9.392d = 325F2). In any case, this predeceased son paves the way in Pausanias for Kranaos, as the most outstanding of the current Athenians, to succeed Kekrops. Apollodoros adds that Amphiktyon then expelled Kranaos, and Erichthonios Amphiktyon. Such a sequence of events squares perfectly with the succession given by the Parian Marble and Kastor, but less so with the giving of the child Erichthonios to the daughters of Kekrops; the latter story surely reflects a tradition in which Erichthonios succeeds Kekrops directly, and onto which names from other traditions were grafted. While Erysichthon's lack of deeds and childlessness certainly expedites this grafting, we might imagine that at one stage in the tradition he was more important. Our earliest account of the Kranaos version remains the Parian Marble; a reference by Herodotos to the early people of Athens as Kranaoi (8.44) rather suggests that he thought of Kranaos (if he believed in such a person at all) as coming before Kekrops, not after.

Erichthonios and Pandion I

For Erichthonios himself, whether we give him the long or short route to becoming king, there is not much to report beyond Hyginus' picture of him as half-serpent, even if he does introduce chariot racing to Athens on the Parian Marble. The Marble has him succeeded by Pandion I, whom Kastor makes his son (250F4); no earlier source attests this relationship. Euripides' *Ion* may have omitted such a figure altogether, if line 267 means that Erichthonios is the father of Kreousa's father (i.e., Erechtheus), but the sense of *patêr* and *progonos* together here is disputed.[19] In any event, Pandion I's chief claim to fame is as father of Prokne and Philomela. Already in Hesiod and Sappho the swallow is so named as the daughter of Pandion (*W&D* 568; Sappho 135 LP), and somewhere in the Hesiodic Corpus we are told that the nightingale never sleeps, and the swallow only half as much as other birds, in punishment for the lawless feast engineered in Thrace (Hes fr 312 MW). This fits well enough with the tale known from later sources, but the identity of the nightingale who laments her son slain by her own hand seems not always to have been fixed in the tradition: in *Odyssey* 19 we find the story of the daughter of Pandareos, wife of Zethos of Thebes, who kills her own son Itylos by mistake (the scholia add that she meant to kill that of her sister-in-law Niobe) and becomes the nightingale (*Od* 19.518–23). Homer may or may not mean us to understand the word *aêdôn*, "nightingale," as her actual name (the scholia in fact do so). That "Aedon" and "Chelidon" ("swallow") were considered as names in some traditions seems indicated by one of the seventh-century metopes from Thermon on which two women with those names painted in face each other over a child (actually only "Chelidon" plus the *A* of "Aedon" survives: Athens 13410). Chelidon, on the right, has the head of the child held on her lap.[20] Aedon (written as "Aedona") appears again on a Red-Figure cup of about 490 B.C., where the woman in question uses a sword to kill a child (recumbent on his bed) named as Itys (Munich 2638). This certainly looks like an illustration of the Homeric story; whether (without Chelidon) it could also represent the Prokne-Philomela version is harder to say.

In Aischylos' *Hiketides*, we find the name of Tereus mentioned for the first time; his wife, the hawk-pursued nightingale, brings about the death of her child by her own hand, in anger (A:*Hik* 60–68). The child is not here named; *Agamemnon* 1144–45 calls the offspring of the nightingale *Itys*, as on the Munich cup (so too Eur fr 773 N²). As for the *mother's* name, the *Hiketides* may have supplied it, but our text (likely corrupt) leaves the matter quite uncertain; she may have been Aedon, or Metis, or neither.[21] With this much established, we can probably see one phase of the story on a column krater produced shortly before the *Hiketides*: two women move away to the left with hands raised in alarm as a man on a couch to the right raises his still-sheathed sword (VG 3579). The couch is for dining, as the table below it shows, and below that is a chest or basket with a small human leg fragment protruding. Makron may well offer the prelude to this deed on a Red-Figure cup also earlier than the *Hiketides*: his work shows two women with a child held roughly by the arms (Louvre G147). The woman actually holding the child shrinks away right; her companion on the left wears a sword and holds up both hands. Possibly she is reaching for the child, but perhaps too the artist meant us to understand a tongueless Philomela gesturing insistently to Prokne, and taking the initiative in the slaughter of Itys.

Yet despite these hints, any real account of what we know as the tale of Prokne and Philomela, daughters of Pandion, comes only from much later sources, including Konon (26F1.31), Ovid (*Met* 6.424–674), and Apollodoros (ApB 3.14.8). These seem likely to go back to Sophokles' *Tereus*, which must have dramatized the whole story and which gives us the name "Prokne" for the first time (fr 585 R). Indeed, if a recently published Oxyrhynchus papyrus (POxy 42.3013) is the hypothesis to this play, as many scholars believe, we would have sure confirmation of the standard plot found later. In this version of events, Pandion marries his daughter Prokne to Tereus, who takes her off to Thrace where she bears him a son, Itys. Desiring to see her sister Philomela, she sends Tereus back to Athens to fetch her, but Tereus becomes enamored of the girl and rapes her, then cuts out her tongue to ensure her silence. Philomela, however, weaves her fate into a robe (mentioned by Sophokles: fr 586 R) and sends this to Prokne, who grasps its meaning ("the voice of the shuttle": fr 595 R) and manages to liberate her sister. The two of them then kill Prokne's son Itys and serve him to his unwitting father, who on learning the truth pursues the two sisters in order to kill them. On the basis of some divine intervention, Prokne becomes a nightingale, Philomela (with her cut tongue) a swallow, and Tereus a hoopoe (the hoopoe was also definitely a part of Sophokles' play). Aischylos' nephew Philokles presented a *Pandionis* tetralogy at some point in the latter part of the fifth century; this must have told the whole story in considerable detail, but nothing remains, save that Tereus is here again a hoopoe. In Konon's brief account the story is much as in the Oxyrhynchus papyrus hypothesis, although with perhaps greater emphasis on Prokne as the real perpetrator of the revenge; Apollodoros does the same, and adds that Tereus at first told Philomela her sister was dead in order to seduce her.

Turning now to our Roman evidence, we find Ovid preceded by plays of Livius Andronicus and Accius; exactly what they did we cannot say, but by the time the story reaches Ovid, confusion of some sort has caused Prokne to become the swallow and Philomela the nightingale (so too Hyginus and others). This produces, of course, the anomaly that the nightingale now has the cut tongue, while the swallow laments her child mournfully. Some variants found in our later sources may reflect that difficulty: in Apollodoros, for example, Tereus hides his wife Prokne away in the country and, feigning her death, marries Philomela (one might expect that he would here cut out Prokne's tongue, but as usual it is that of Philomela). Hyginus (*Fab* 45) and Servius (Σ *Ecl* 6.78) also know of a version in which Tereus used a false report of Prokne's death to marry Philomela, although neither of them discusses any cutting out of tongues. Eustathios' account seems at first to address this questions of exchanged metamorphosis: his exegesis at *Odyssey* 19.518 reverses the names of the two sisters, so that Tereus marries Philomela and then rapes Prokne and cuts out her tongue as he is bringing her back to visit Philomela. Unfortunately, Eustathios concludes his account with the Greek finale, not the Roman one, and thus Prokne with her cut tongue becomes the nightingale and Philomela the swallow. Hyginus adds to his narrative a brother of Tereus, Dryas, whom Tereus mistakenly kills because of an omen that Itys will die at the hands of a near relative. In all, with so little evidence before Sophokles, it is hard to say when this myth took its precise form, or whether the thematic link in the killing of one's own child between a daughter of Pandareos and a daughter of Pandion is more than coincidence. But at least we have Hesiod's attestation that the swallow is the daughter of Pandion; on the assumption that this is one of the Athenian Pandions, we can say that the tale became associated with Athens (and thus with Prokne and Philomela?) at a fairly early point. If that is right, the Thermon metope may indicate the survival of the story outside of Athens with other, more obvious names.

The Parian Marble makes Erechtheus not only the successor to Pandion I on the throne of Athens, but also his son, and thus if we put separate pieces of information together (not always a good idea), he is the brother of Prokne and Philomela. Apollodoros approves such a link, and adds to it a twin brother of Erechtheus, namely Boutes (ApB 3.14.8: the mother is Zeuxippe). According to the same author the two sons divided Pandion's powers, with Erechtheus receiving the actual rule and Boutes the priesthood of Athena and Poseidon (inherited, of course, by his descendants: ApB 3.15.1). Boutes also marries Chthonia, one of his brother's daughters. Judging from the altar in his honor located somewhere in the Erechtheion (Paus 1.26.5), he must be a figure of some antiquity at Athens, but Apollodoros is the first author to discuss him, and his information is all we have. Erechtheus we have already seen as a name familiar to Homer (albeit in the role of Erichthonios: Il 2.547–48), and as the father of Kreousa in the Ehoiai and of Oreithuia in Simonides (Hes fr 10a.20–21 MW; Sim 534 PMG). The one major myth concerning him is his sacrifice of one or more daughters to save Athens, but we will see that at least some of these daughters, like those of Kekrops, have their own stories as well.

The tale of the sacrifice first survives in Euripides' lost Erechtheus. There, as we know from fragments, the Athenians are at war with Eumolpos of Eleusis, and Delphi predicts that one of Erechtheus' three daughters will have to be killed if the city is to be saved (fr 360 N², as quoted by Lykourgos in his speech against Leokrates [100]). Erechtheus and his wife Praxithea consent (Mor 310d); unfortunately, we know neither the names of the daughters nor which one was selected. As matters turn out, both Erechtheus and Eumolpos die, and all three daughters as well. New fragments now indicate that they took an oath to do so in support of the one chosen, and became Hyakinthides after death (frr 50, 65 Aus). The same fragments also show that although Eumolpos is defeated, Erechtheus is struck down by Poseidon's trident (fr 65.90–94 Aus). In the Ion, on the other hand, we find that Erechtheus sacrificed Kreousa's sisters (more than one) and that she herself was saved because she was only an infant at the time, although here too Erechtheus is slain by Poseidon (and buried in a chasm: Ion 277–82). Demosthenes' Funeral Oration also says that Erechtheus sacrificed more than one daughter (60.27). In Apollodoros, matters are rather as in the Erechtheus: the victim selected is the youngest (no name given) but the other daughters kill themselves, too (ApB 3.15.4). Earlier Apollodoros has named four daughters—Prokris, Kreousa, Chthonia, Oreithuia—but he has also married them all off, and two (Prokris and Oreithuia) are hardly available under any circumstances for a sacrifice or suicide (ApB 3.15.1). For Hyginus, the sacrificed daughter is definitely Chthonia (if we accept an almost certain emendation of a garbled text); the remaining daughters again kill themselves (Fab 46, 238). Possibly, then, Chthonia was not always married to Boutes, and may after all have been the one sacrificed in the Erechtheus. The Souda offers us six names—Protogeneia, Pandora, Prokris, Kreousa, Oreithuia, and Chthonia—but here the first two on the list (the oldest) volunteer and are sacrificed; this information may go back to Phanodemos, who is cited immediately after on a related point (that they were offered up on a Hyakinthos hill: 325F4). We cannot say, of course, that the three daughters from whom the choice was made in the *Erechtheus* (or elsewhere) were intended to represent all the king's daughters; Euripides may have meant us to understand simply the unmarried daughters still at home, with older siblings such as Kreousa and Oreithuia already married. But the persistent notion that all the daughters subsequently died must lead us to suspect that in the beginning the daughters of Erechtheus were simply a set of names, and different from well-known figures such as Prokris, Kreousa, and Oreithuia. As for Erechtheus' own fate, Apollodoros hints and Hyginus explicitly states that Poseidon was angry over the death of Eumolpos, his son by Chione, daughter of Oreithuia and Boreas (*Fab* 46, where Poseidon asks Zeus to kill him); Pausanias says simply that the king fell in battle (1.38.3).

Of the daughters, whether sacrificed, self-immolated, or whatever, we find that in all accounts Oreithuia is abducted by Boreas, Prokris marries Kephalos, the son of Deion, and Kreousa marries Xouthos, the son of Hellen. Oreithuia's story (as we saw in chapter 1) appears first on the Chest of Kypselos and in Simonides (534 *PMG*); Akousilaos adds that Boreas carried her off to Thrace, where she became the mother of Kalais and Zetes (2F30). In the fifth century, we have Choirilos' remark that she was snatched up while gathering flowers on the banks of the Kephissos (fr 7 *PEG*), and we know that Aischylos wrote a satyr play, *Oreithuia*, about the abduction; fragments referring to Boreas' wrath may indicate that he sued formally for the girl's hand and was refused (fr 281 R). Red-Figure pottery offers several good illustrations of the tale, beginning with a late stamnos by the Berlin Painter (Berlin:Lost F2186), and including two pointed amphoras by the Oreithuia Painter of perhaps the third decade of the century. On one of these, also once in Berlin, Boreas and Oreithuia are both named, the god quite striking with his hair frozen into icicles (Berlin:Lost F2165). On the other, in Munich, we see (with inscriptions) the whole family: Herse vainly struggles to aid Oreithuia, while Pandrosos rushes toward Kekrops and Aglauros toward Erechtheus (Munich 2345). Unfortunately, this is not quite the family we might have expected, given that Kekrops should be of a much earlier time, and Herse, Pandrosos, and Aglauros are his daughters. Probably we should allow for artistic license in the composition, unless at this time even a basic genealogy had not yet been agreed upon. The sons Kalais and Zetes appear already in the *Ehoiai* (where their parents may have been mentioned) as pursuers of the Harpuiai (Hes fr 156 MW); we will return to this adventure in chapter 12. Apollodoros adds to the sons two daughters, the Chione noted above as the mother of Eumolpos by Poseidon, and a Kleopatra whom we will likewise encounter in chapter 13 as the wife of the Thracian Phineus (3.15.2–4). The scholia to Apollonios, finally, offer five children: Chione, Chthonia, Kleopatra, Zetes, and Kalais (Σ AR 1.211–15d); since a list of Oreithuia's sisters precedes this one in the same note, we must allow that scribal error might have mislocated the name "Chthonia" to its position here.

As for Eumolpos, Erechtheus' great opponent in Euripides and elsewhere, he is a complex figure who first appears in the *Homeric Hymn to Demeter*, with Triptolemos and others, as one of the leading men of Eleusis (*HDem* 154, 475). In Euripides' *Erechtheus*, however, he has become a Thracian called to help against Athens by his friends the Eleusinians; Lykourgos implies that the parentage from Poseidon and Chione was found in the play (98–100), and the prologue (spoken by Poseidon?) seems to refer to his being saved by the god and taken to Aithiopia (fr 349 N²). Likely enough, then, it detailed the same story told by Apollodoros: Chione cast her child into the sea to save her reputation (perhaps offering it to the god?) and Poseidon rescued it and took it to Aithiopia for his daughter Benthesikyme to rear (Ap*B* 3.15.4); the parallel with Kreousa in the *Ion* is obvious enough. The subsequent peregrinations of Eumolpos—from Aithiopia to Thrace to Eleusis back to Thrace—may well be later elaborations, but somehow he does emerge in Euripides as a foreigner. Yet in later tradition he is often thought of as the initiator of the Eleusinian Mysteries, and this notion may relate to his appearance in the *Hymn to Demeter* as a typical Eleusinian (and his presence on several pots together with Triptolemos). Euripides' play certainly concluded with some sort of heroic or divine honors predicted by Athena for both Erechtheus and Eumolpos, but whether he went this far we cannot say. One solution was to posit two Eumolpoi, the first the Thracian, son of Poseidon, the second an Eleusinian descendant of his and the Mysteries-founder. Thus Andron says that from the first Eumolpos was begotten Keryx, from him another Eumolpos, then Antiphemos, Mousaios, and in the fifth generation Eumolpos, the bringer of the Mysteries (10F13); Istros, for his part, makes this last figure a son rather of Deiope, daughter of Triptolemos (334F22).

Kreousa we have already seen as the mother of Ion (and of Achaios and Diomede) by her husband Xouthos in the *Ehoiai* (Hes fr 10a.20–24 MW).²² In the prologue of Euripides' lost *Melanippe Sophe*, she likewise bears Ion to Xouthos (14 GLP), but in the same poet's *Ion*, matters take quite a different turn: here she has borne Ion to Apollo, who took her by force before her marriage, at the place of the Long Rocks below the Akropolis of Athens. She abandons the child, but Apollo brings him to Delphi where he is brought up to serve in the temple. When, years later, Xouthos and Kreousa come to Delphi to inquire about their childlessness, the god tells Xouthos that Ion is his. Husband and wife both assume that he is therefore the consequence of some youthful indiscretion by Xouthos, and Kreousa tries to poison him; only at the final crisis does Athena enter to reveal the truth of Apollo's parentage. Ion's subsequent role here is to rule Athens, but in Herodotos he is called a general or war leader of the Athenians (8.44; so too Paus 1.31.3 and 2.14.2), which probably reflects a failure to obtain royal status in the general tradition. These authors and others also persist in calling Ion a son of Xouthos, so that his descent from

Apollo might seem a Euripidean aberration. But we noted before the lost Soph-oklean *Kreousa,* which one would imagine covered the same basic situation, since a Kreousa who bears a normal child to her own husband offers little in the way of drama. Sophokles might, of course, have been inspired by Euripides' *Ion,* although that play's percentage of iambic resolution suggests it to be late.[23] About Sophokles' *Ion* we know nothing at all; possibly it was another title for the *Kreousa,* or perhaps it dealt with Ion's military exploits on behalf of Ath-ens. As for the other son, Achaios, he is obviously needed to explain the tribal name of the Achaians; the scholia at *Iliad* 1.2 have him slay a kinsman or fellow-citizen, thus necessitating his exile to Thessaly.

The third sister, Prokris, is a more difficult matter. Odysseus sees her, or at least a Prokris, sandwiched between Phaidra and Ariadne in the *Nekuia* (*Od* 11.321). He offers nothing beyond her name; we shall see that the link with the two daughters of Minos may be significant. The same name also appeared somewhere in the Hesiodic Corpus, but we have no context (Hes fr 332 MW). In the Theban portion of the Epic Cycle (presumably the *Epigonoi*), we are told the tale of the Teumessian fox whom Kephalos, son of Deion, hunted (*Epig* fr 5 *PEG*). He had come to Thebes from Athens to be purified after accidentally killing his wife Prokris, and had with him a dog whom no quarry ever eluded; thus he offered to help in capturing the fox that the gods had sent to torment the Thebans. But as he and the dog closed in on the fox, both dog and fox were turned to stone. This of course is a summary (from Photios and the *Souda*) rather than a quote, and one suspects that some clarifying details have been omitted. From Pherekydes (through a scholiast's epitome), we have the follow-ing story: Kephalos, son of Deioneus, marries Prokris, daughter of Erechtheus (3F34). Wishing to test her, he remains away from home for eight years, then returns in disguise and successfully seduces her. They are however reconciled, but Prokris becomes suspicious of her husband's frequent absences to hunt, and believes him to have a lover; a servant admits hearing him call to one Nephele ("Cloud") to come to him. Jealous, she follows Kephalos one day, and when she hears him make the same appeal leaps out from hiding; he is startled and kills her with the javelin he happens to be holding. Presumably this tale, or at least the latter part of it, formed the plot of Sophokles' lost *Prokris,* but nothing remains of that work, and no other tragedian is known to have dramatized or even referred to the story. A column krater by the Hephaistos Painter dating to the third quarter of the fifth century offers the essential details: Prokris pierced by the javelin in the center, with a dismayed Kephalos on one side and probably Erechtheus on the other (London E477). Hellanikos adds that Ke-phalos, son of Deioneus, was married to Prokris, daughter of Erechtheus, and, after killing her, was tried on the Areopagos (4F169).

Obviously there are still points of plot detail that remain obscure despite Pherekydes, but no further assistance arrives until our usual corps of later mythographers, beginning with Ovid. Here for the first time we find the Ke-phalos, son of Hermes and Herse (whom we saw above carried off by Eos), identified with the Kephalos, son of Deion (or Deioneus), married to Prokris (*Met* 7.672–862). Ovid's use of the abduction is skillful enough: Eos steals away Kephalos but cannot make him love her, and for revenge offers to show him how easily his wife could be tempted by an apparent stranger (so also *Fab* 189). This notion admittedly explains rather better an oddity in Pherekydes' account, namely Kephalos' sudden decision to test his wife, but surely our summary would have included such an event if Pherekydes had related it, and we will see that the abduction does not appear in Apollodoros' account either.[24] The conclusion to be drawn, as I argued earlier, would seem that there are two distinct Kephaloi, one carried off (permanently) by Eos, the other married to Prokris. Apparently Ovid draws from the Hellenistic Nikandros in conflating them into one figure,[25] and then turns the abduction to good advantage in motivating the deception. In postulating this sequence of events we must concede the presence of Red-Figure vases showing Eos with a young man in hunting or traveling garb,[26] but there is after all no reason why the earlier Kephalos should not also be a hunter, and although these representations frequently add a companion hunter, they do not offer anyone who could be Prokris. In Apollodoros' version of the latter's story, she is bribed by one Pteleon with a golden crown to enter his bed, and there discovered by her husband (perhaps then not a test of her virtue), after which she flees to Minos (Ap*B* 3.15.10); in Antoninus, Kephalos suborns a stranger to attempt this bribe, which succeeds after he doubles the amount, and she flees as before (AntLib 41). Neither Pherekydes nor Ovid mentions such a flight, saying simply that the couple was reconciled. But Palaiphatos tells us that Prokris (daughter of Pandion) cured Minos of a genital sickness in return for a dog and a javelin (Pal 2: so too more vaguely *Katast* 33), and Apollodoros and Antoninus explain that, having gone to Krete after the discovery of her infidelity, she helped Minos overcome certain distressing sexual problems (ejaculation of snakes and scorpions), receiving in return a dog and a javelin (Antoninus adds that no quarry ever escaped them). With these (Ovid, Hyginus, and Paus 9.19.1 [dog only] say that she received them from Artemis), she goes back to Athens and Kephalos. Apollodoros says only that they were now reconciled; Antoninus and Hyginus recount that Prokris tricked and seduced her husband in the guise of a boy, so that he became even more guilty than she was. Her death in Apollodoros is a simple hunting accident; Ovid and Hyginus follow Pherekydes' story of her suspicions of another woman (Aura in Ovid), while Antoninus omits her fate altogether. Several of these authors (Ps-Eratosthenes and Apollodoros [Ap*B* 2.4.6–7], as well as Ovid, Hyginus, and Antoninus) also include the tale of the Teumessian fox first seen in the Epic Cycle, with the additional point that the fox was destined never to be caught. In Ovid, the metamorphosis of dog and fox is simply the work of some god who desired that neither side should lose, but Antoninus offers what was surely the original point of the story: a dilemma arose precisely because the fox was fated never to be caught, and the dog never to miss his quarry; to resolve it, Zeus turned both to stone. Hyginus seems to grasp the same idea, and cites for his version Istros (*Astr* 2.35 = 334F65). We might well suppose that this was the intent of the original Epic Cycle account, and that our summary simply failed to report it.

Pandion II and Aigeus   Having now dealt with all the daughters of Erechtheus, it only remains to locate a successor to carry on the family name and occupy the throne. The Parian Marble (239 *FGrH*), Kastor (250F4), and Apollodoros (Ap*B* 3.15.1) all agree that this figure was Kekrops II, although only in Apollodoros is he Erechtheus' son; Kastor makes him a brother (probably so that Pandion II can be a grandson of Pandion I) and for the Marble there is no evidence. There are no myths whatever about him, and clearly his function is just to occupy space in the Attic chronology between Erechtheus and Pandion II. There were, however, other sons of Erechtheus as well, for Pherekydes mentions his siring of a Metion who is by Iphinoe the father of Daidalos (3F146), and Plutarch knows of an Orneus, son of Erechtheus, who will become the grandfather of Menestheus (so too Paus 2.25.6). Though he provides no names, Pausanias tells us that when Erechtheus died, Xouthos (husband of Kreousa) was called upon to decide which of the sons would succeed; having chosen Kekrops (as the eldest), he was driven out by the losers (Paus 7.1.2). Of Orneus we hear no more, although he shows up (apparently misplaced) among the sons of Pandion II on an Attic Red-Figure krater (see below). Metion likewise fades into obscurity, but Apollodoros (Ap*B* 3.15.5) and Pausanias (1.5.3) both attest that his sons drove their cousin Pandion II from Athens and forced him to flee to Megara, where he married the daughter of the local king Pylas.

This Pandion II is, of course, the child of Kekrops II, and presumably the rightful heir to the Attic throne. Sophokles and the Atthidographers name four offspring of his union with Pylas' daughter, according to Strabo, all sons—Aigeus, Pallas, Nisos, and Lykos (9.1.6). Cited in this connection, too, is a fragment from Sophokles' lost *Aigeus*, where the title figure says that to him his father gave the shore and rule of the land, to Pallas the south, to Lykos Euboia, and to Nisos the land next to the coast of Skiron (i.e., Megara: fr 24 R). Subsequently in Strabo's account, Pandion II replaces Pylas as king of Megara, and after his death his sons regain control of Athens (Pausanias has them driving out the Metionidai: 1.5.3). One way or another Aigeus emerges as the land's king, while Nisos controls Megara and Pallas remains dissatisfied; Lykos engages in various travels, founding among other things the Lykian race (in Pausanias he comes to Aphareus in Messenia, having been chased out by Aigeus: 4.2.6). The Parian Marble and Kastor make no mention of the Metionidai; Kastor does include a flight of Pandion II to Megara but follows it immediately with the rule of Aigeus. Of other sons of Metion (besides Daidalos) only Sikyon is ever named; no source suggests that either he or Daidalos claimed the throne of Athens. From this fairly developed tradition, earlier sources preserve only Pandion II's fathering of Aigeus, and that not before the fifth century (Bak 18.15; *Med* 665–66; Hdt 1.173 does add Lykos' exile). But a Red-Figure calyx krater by the Syriskos Painter of about 470 B.C. shows three of the four sons, with scepters, named (right to left) as Lykos, Nisos, and Pallas, and together with them Orneus, a figure more at home as the son of Erechtheus (Athens Akr 735: Pallas alone sits). That of all the brothers Aigeus should be the one omitted seems remarkable; perhaps we must put it down to simple aberration on the part of the painter.

Aigeus, ruler of Athens after Pandion II, owes his fame entirely to tales surrounding the exploits of his son Theseus, and even this child is not always his. As we saw in chapter 2, Poseidon may be the father even when Theseus is described as "Aigeides" (so Il 1.265, possibly interpolated[27]) or "son of Aigeus" (huios Aigeôs), since elsewhere such terms are commonly used to designate the mortal stepfather of a divinely sired child. Perhaps in the beginning Aigeus was the real father, and supplanted by Poseidon only when Theseus' greatness was thought to require more cogent grounds. On the other hand, the hero's uncontested birth in Troizen (from a Troizenian mother) probably indicates a separate origin there, with Poseidon his father in the Troizenian tradition and Aigeus serving that role only in Athens.[28] Evidence before the fifth century, beyond the occasional ambiguous patronymic, is completely lacking. When we turn to the fifth century itself, we find quite a fluctuating parentage, dependent at times on the needs of the story being told. Poseidon is definitely the father in Bakchylides' dithyramb on the voyage of Theseus and Minos to Krete (17); indeed, the tale of the plunge into the depths of the Aegean to recover a ring is meant to prove that very fact. In the same work, however, the force of a different tradition (or epic phrasing) is such that Theseus is also called the offspring of Pandion (Pandionos ekgonos: Bak 17.15–16), something he can only be if Aigeus is his real father. Bakchylides here names his mother as Aithra, daughter of Pittheus of Troizen; we will see that she is already implied as such in the Epic Cycle, since the sons of Theseus go to Troy to rescue her. On Red-Figure pots of the early fifth century we see again and again Poseidon's actual pursuit of Aithra (so Vat 16554, with both names painted in), while the famous Onesimos cup showing Theseus, Athena, and Amphitrite (Louvre G104) illustrates the dive and thus the same parentage. For Aigeus as the real father we have, on the other hand, Euripides' Medeia, where Aigeus in concern over his childlessness has consulted the oracle at Delphi, and been told to beware of unloosing his wineskin before reaching home (Med 665–81). Presumably Medeia withholds the meaning of this oracle in the belief that an Aigeus without heir will be more susceptible to her control;[29] in any case, Euripides certainly expects his audience to perceive that Aigeus' next act of intercourse with a woman will produce a child (perhaps his only one). This, of course, will happen at Troizen, where Pittheus, father of Aithra, will take advantage of his guest's obtuseness. But obviously the story will not work unless Aigeus is the biological father of a child, and that child, conceived at Troizen, must be Theseus. The same situation holds in Euripides' Hiketides, since in the prologue to that work Aithra tells us that her father gave her as wife to Aigeus in accordance with the oracles of Apollo (E:*Hik* 5–7). Probably, too, Aigeus was thought of as the real father in both Sophokles' and Euripides' *Aigeus* plays, where the arrival of Theseus at Athens and his near-poisoning by Aigeus will acquire the appropriate pathos only if father and son are involved. In *Hippolytos*, on the other hand, the theme of Theseus' three wishes more or less requires that Poseidon be his father (*Hipp* 887: elsewhere in the same play he is called son of Aigeus).[30]

As for Theseus' actual begetting, Plutarch says that Pittheus somehow tricked Aigeus into sleeping with his daughter at Troizen (*Thes* 3.3–4), while Pausanias has Aithra wading out to the island of Sphairia, where Poseidon has intercourse with her (2.33.1). Apollodoros and Hyginus are the first preserved sources to bring these two events together in the same night, presumably by having Aithra wade out to the island after she has lain with Aigeus (Ap*B* 3.15.7; *Fab* 37). Plutarch, Apollodoros, and Hyginus all agree that the next morning Aigeus departed, leaving as he did a sword and sandals under a rock; if Aithra should bear a male child, she was to send him to Athens to claim his birthright when he was old enough to lift the rock and recover the items under it. Theseus of course accomplishes this, and sets off by land through the Isthmos to find his father. The hiding of tokens under a rock was clearly a part of Kallimachos' *Hekale*, as the fragments tell us (235, 236 Pf), and we see the lifting of the rock on a series of Attic Red-Figure vases beginning about 450 B.C. (Louvre G423; Stockholm:NM 1701).[31] References to the sword (ivory-hilted?) carried by Theseus as he approaches Athens at Bakchylides 18.48 may possibly foreshadow the event of his recognition, and of course this was dramatized in the *Aigeus* plays mentioned above, where Aigeus must have some means of realizing whom he is about to poison. But for the rest of the above story, that is, Theseus' conception, there are only the late sources cited.

Theseus' Journey around the Isthmos

Theseus' exploits on his land journey from Troizen to Athens are likewise absent from our earliest sources; in literature they do not appear until the same Ode 18 of Bakchylides, where they are briefly catalogued. But we can see most of them in one form or other on a large number of Black- and Red-Figure vases, beginning about 510 B.C., and from the same time or just a little later are the metopes on the south flank of the Athenian Treasury at Delphi (no #), to be joined in the mid-fifth century by the metopes from the Hephaisteion in Athens' Agora.[32] The metopes on the Athenian Treasury were nine in number, but one is completely missing, and at least three others dealt with later exploits (the Minotaur, the Marathonian Bull, and Antiope/Hippolyte), while one simply shows Theseus and Athena standing together. The remaining four metopes display combats, one a wrestling match (no. 3), thus Kerkyon, and a second with a tree (no. 1), thus Sinis. But the other two (nos. 2, 4) offer nothing criterial: in each case, the villain is sprawling backward on the ground, and Skiron, Prokroustes, and Periphetes are all possibilities. The mid-fifth-century metopes on the Hephaisteion number eight, four on the northern and four on the southern return of the east end, and are in rather better condition: here Sinis (tree), Skiron (rock and crab), Kerkyon (wrestling), Bull of Marathon, Sow of Krommyon, and the Minotaur are all clearly recognizable; the remaining two offer the same compositional scheme as the two uncertain metopes from Delphi, and probably represent Periphetes and Prokroustes, thus giving us a complete set of six Saronic Gulf adventures. On vase-paintings in Athens these tales often appear together as a Theseus-cycle around the outside (and occasionally inside) of kylixes.[33] The earliest such cups, all from the beginning of the fifth century, are in London, Florence, and Paris' Cabinet des Médailles. That in the British Museum (London E36) offers the Sow, Kerkyon, Prokroustes, the Bull, and the Minotaur. The cup in Florence (91456) has Sinis, Skiron, Kerkyon, Prokroustes, the Bull, and the Minotaur, while that in Paris shows exactly the same combination as the Florence cup (in pieces: CabMéd 536, 647, et al.). Thus we have five of the six adventures experienced by Theseus before reaching Athens, omitting only Periphetes. Already some of the scenes have begun to exhibit their own distinctive iconography, and we must now consider them individually in conjunction with the literary sources.

The first adventure, taken in sequence after Theseus' departure from Troizen, should properly be Periphetes, whom he encounters at Epidauros. This tale is conspicuously absent from the list in Bakchylides (which includes the other five), but that may be due to the fact that the chorus records his journey from the Isthmos to Athens; conversely, the chorus may have begun at the Isthmos precisely because it knew of no previous deeds. Euripides in his *Hiketides* refers to a fearful Epidaurian club wielded by Theseus against the Thebans (E:*Hik* 714–17), and this gives us a certain *terminus ante quem*. In Diodoros, the villain is named "Korynetes," or "Club-bearer," from the great club that he uses to kill passersby (DS 4.59.2). Ovid simply calls him the club-bearing son of Hephaistos (*Met* 7.436–47; cf. *Ibis* 405–6), and Hyginus makes him Korynetes, son of Poseidon (*Fab* 38) or Hephaistos (*Fab* 158). Only in Plutarch, Pausanias, and Apollodoros do we find the name "Periphetes," with "Korynetes" added on as a surname (*Thes* 8.1; Paus 2.1.4; ApB 3.16.1; in the latter two he is again a son of Hephaistos). Euripides says it was a wooden club, but Pausanias makes it bronze, and Apollodoros iron; the latter also adds the picturesque detail that Periphetes was weak in the feet (like his father?) and therefore carried the club. All sources agree that Theseus killed the brigand and took the club away from him. Certainly this tale seems likely to be the one implied by Euripides' reference to a club in the *Hiketides*, but whether it really is as early as the others is hard to say. There are two possible fifth-century illustrations of it, one a Theseus-cycle cup by the Pistoxenos Painter dating to perhaps 460 B.C. (Munich 2670), the other the first metope on the north side of the Hephaisteion. The cup offers four of Theseus' deeds, including one where the hero attacks his victim with a club. Since Prokroustes and Skiron are already accounted for, and none of the iconography appropriate to Sinis or Kerkyon appears, Periphetes seems the logical choice. In Plutarch, admittedly, the vic-

tory seems accomplished while the miscreant still grasps his club, but this is
not a serious objection. The Hephaisteion metope lacks all traces of the weapon
Theseus held in his right hand, but if we agree that the uncertain metope on
the south side (where there is room for a bed under the victim) depicted Prokroustes, then we have no other brigand to put here.[34] Thus Periphetes (perhaps
under a different name) seems to go back into the first half of the fifth century,
despite his absence in Bakchylides. Yet he remains oddly unpopular compared
with Theseus' other opponents, and may not have as solid a literary pedigree.
As we saw, the Athenian Treasury at Delphi has missing space in which he
might find room, but the more frequently seen Skiron and Prokroustes are
there in competition with him.

With the remaining marauders of the Saronic Gulf there are fewer uncertainties. Sinis is in Bakchylides' poem simply the son of Poseidon and a man
of tremendous strength (18.19–22), but already on one of the Delphic metopes
we see a tree trunk, and numerous vase-paintings offer (beginning with a fine
cup by Douris: London E48) what is clearly a standard iconography. Sinis takes
shelter at the tree, often clinging to it, while Theseus drags him away toward a
branch that he pulls down to him (cf. Munich 8771, where Sinis attempts to
defend himself with a stone). Our later literary sources offer two slightly different accounts of how this villain operated. In Diodoros and Pausanias we find
the familiar tale that he bent two pine trees down to the ground and tied his
victims to them, so that they would be torn apart when the trees sprang up
(DS 4.59.3; Paus 2.1.4). Apollodoros and Hyginus, on the other hand, have
him force or trick passersby into bending down trees which then fling them
into space (ApB 3.16.2; *Fab* 38; *Met* 7.440–42 is harder to decipher). Plutarch
says only that Theseus slew Sinis as Sinis had slain others (*Thes* 8.2). For the
fifth century it is difficult to judge between these variants. Kratinos does speak
of bending down one pine tree, but the fragment is too short to be certain that
he stops with one (fr 328 *PCG*). On a calyx krater by the Dinos Painter from
late in the century Theseus approaches Sinis as the latter pulls down a branch;
possibly he means to ask Theseus to help him with it and then let go unex-
pectedly (Oxford 1937.983). But once the element of surprise is gone, one does
not readily see how Theseus can dispose of Sinis with just one tree, since tying
Sinis to it will neither fling him to his death nor tear him apart. On the Douris
cup we do in fact find two pine trees, with Theseus holding the branches of the
one further away from Sinis, so that this concept was surely also fifth century;
the single pine tree of other artists may then be just a simplification of the
iconography. Apollodoros, Plutarch, Hyginus, and others add the nickname
"Pityokamptes" ("pine-bender"); Plutarch speaks as well of Sinis' daughter
Perigoune, who after some initial shyness in an asparagus patch bears Theseus
a son Melanippos (*Thes* 8.2–3; cf. Paus 10.25.7).

Third of Theseus' exploits is the killing of the Sow of Krommyon, this last
an area just west of Megara. Bakchylides describes the animal (no gender specified) as man-slaying (18.23–24); she is absent from the Athenian Treasury at

Delphi, but may have been on the totally missing metope. In any case, she appears as early as a Red-Figure cup by Skythes of about 510 B.C. (VG 20760). Here she charges at Theseus all by herself, but on the Douris cup in London (E48) she is accompanied by a woman who apparently urges her on, and this becomes very much the standard iconography in subsequent representations (with the woman often shown as quite old). On Madrid 11265 the woman is called "Krommyo" as an eponym of the region, but Apollodoros speaks of one Phaia, the rearer of the Sow, whose name was then transferred to the Sow itself (ApE 1.1). Plutarch suggests that Phaia was really a local female brigand (*Thes* 9.1), but this finds no support in the artistic tradition, and is surely late rationalizing. The representation on one early Red-Figure cup (London E36) does appear to show a boar, not a sow, and in a pose (being dragged off by the hind legs) that suggests live capture; possibly the artist was overly impressed by Herakles' achievement with the Erymanthian Boar; of the literary sources, only Hyginus (*Fab* 38) reflects this idea of a male animal.

From Krommyon, Theseus advances to Megara, and here he encounters Skiron. Again we have a virtually uniform iconography, beginning with the Florence cup (91456), which anticipates and confirms our later literary sources. Theseus has grasped Skiron by one leg, and is in the act of tipping him over; a large rock forms the background. Other depictions add two important elements: a turtle clambering up the rock (so, e.g., Athens Akr 1280, London E48, Berlin:Ch F2288), and a shallow basin (London E48, Louvre G104); on the Codrus Painter cup (London E84), Theseus actually prepares to strike Skiron with this basin, rather than seizing his leg. On the literary side, Bakchylides says only that Skiron was evil (*atasthalos*: 18.24–25), but Diodoros, Plutarch, and Apollodoros all agree that he forced passersby to wash his feet (hence the basin) at a place where the rocks jutted right out to the coast, then kicked them into the sea as they did so (DS 4.59.4; *Thes* 10.1; ApE 1.2–3). Apollodoros (and Pausanias: 1.44.8) adds that a huge turtle then devoured them; probably this last detail occurred already in Kallimachos (Σ *Hipp* 979 = fr 296 Pf), and is obviously anticipated by the vase tradition. Theseus, as he did with Sinis, paid Skiron back in kind by hurling him into the sea. On the Hephaisteion metope, the animal in question appears to be a crab; the basin, if present, has been lost. The story also appeared as a (terracotta) akroterion on the Stoa Basileios (Paus 1.3.1), but Pausanias gives no details, and the decoration, like that showing Eos and Kephalos, could have been placed on the building at any time before his visit. Later pots sometimes show Theseus bringing the basin to Skiron, a scene taken perhaps from a drama where he feigned obeisance to Skiron's demands (Epicharmos and Euripides both wrote plays entitled *Skiron*). We may note, too, although nothing useful survives, that Simonides must have mentioned Skiron in some context, since Plutarch has him note the Megarians' attempt to whitewash the latter's reputation (643 *PMG*).

Fifth in the cycle is Theseus' meeting with Kerkyon at Eleusis. Bakchylides says that he closed Kerkyon's *palaistra* (18.26–27), and the standard portrayal of their encounter on the Cycle vases is simply a wrestling match, with Kerkyon bent forward and Theseus grasping him about the waist. On the Delphi metope they are both upright; on the Hephaisteion Theseus has picked his opponent up by the waist and is about to throw him down. The literary sources supply what we will already have guessed, that Kerkyon forced passersby to wrestle with him, and killed them (DS 4.59.5; ApE 1.3; *Thes* 11.1). In Apollodoros, Theseus slays him by lifting him up and throwing him violently to the ground, and this is perhaps the intention of the Hephaisteion artist's metope. Once again, titles of lost plays (both satyric) suggest a treatment on the stage: Aischylos composed a *Kerkyon*, and Pratinas a *Palaistai* (not certainly on this topic).

In addition to his defeat by Theseus, Kerkyon also appears as the outraged father in a tale regarding his daughter Alope.[35] Pherekydes at least mentioned this pair (3F147), and Hellanikos notes the fact that Alope was by Poseidon the mother of Hippothoon, the eponym of one of Athens' Kleisthenic tribes (4F43; cf. Paus 1.5.2). Whatever else these writers may have said, the story was dramatized in plays entitled *Alope* by Choirilos (who made Kerkyon a half-brother of Triptolemos: Paus 1.14.3) and by Euripides; virtually all our information, however, comes from Hyginus. In his account, Alope is forced by Poseidon and, fearing her father's wrath, exposes the resulting son (*Fab* 187); a mare nurses the child and a shepherd then finds it. This man then gives the child to a second shepherd, but a dispute breaks out over possession of the elegant clothes the child was wearing, and they take the matter to the king; thus Kerkyon discovers what has happened. He then orders his daughter to be locked away to her death and the child exposed a second time, but once again it is saved by shepherds, and this time successfully reared. In due time, Theseus arrives and kills Kerkyon, and at that point the child, whose name is Hippothoos *(sic)*, asks for and receives from Theseus his grandfather's kingdom to rule. We see the nursing of a child by a mare on a Red-Figure oinochoe of the fourth-century (Tübingen 1610), so that probably this detail and others go back at least to Euripides; in the fifth century a Hippothoon also appears (once named) in scenes of the departure of Triptolemos. Pausanias, too, notes Alope's slaying by her father (1.39.3), and Choirilos adds (Paus 1.14.3, as above) that Kerkyon's own father was Poseidon; Hyginus (in a different part of the *Fabulae*: 38) calls this father Hephaistos. Finally, both Athenaios (13.557a: from Istros?) and Plutarch (*Thes* 29) suggest that Theseus was sexually involved with a daughter of Kerkyon, unnamed; if this is not simply a doublet of his escapade with Sinis' daughter Perigoune, he may in some versions have been Hippothoon's father.

Last of Theseus' adventures before reaching Athens is the encounter with Prokroustes. Here we find even more variation of name than in the case of Periphetes. Bakchylides says that "Prokoptes let go the hammer of Polypemon" (18.27–30); "Polypemon" could be the name of the villain and "Prokoptes" an epithet, or (more likely) Prokoptes his name, and Polypemon his father or someone else who gave him the hammer. Diodoros seems the first on the literary side to address him as Prokroustes (DS 4.59.5), and so too Ovid (who once calls him son of Polypemon: *Met* 7.438; *Ibis* 409). But Apollodoros calls him Damastes, surnamed Polypemon (Ap*E* 1.4), Plutarch Damastes, surnamed Prokroustes (*Thes* 11.1), and Pausanias Polypemon, surnamed Prokroustes (1.38.5). Hyginus settles for simply Prokroustes, son of Poseidon (*Fab* 38). Of these names, both "Prokoptes" and "Prokroustes" would seem to mean "beater" or "smiter" (although "Prokoptes" could also be associated with cutting). Early representations on vase-painting uniformly show Theseus advancing toward Prokroustes (so we will call him) with what is either a hammer or double axe. On the early London kylix (E36) the intended victim clings to a rock as Theseus seizes his arm; on the Florence kylix (91456) he reclines on a bed with a capacious wine bowl underneath while Theseus strides forward to grasp his hair. The impression one receives from this latter illustration is that Prokroustes is being assaulted on his own bed. On the Onesimos cup (Louvre G104), we find again a low line of rocks, and Prokroustes so named, as he will be on several other vases of the fifth century (Madrid 11265; Oxford 1937.983). This variation between rock and bed continues throughout the rest of the fifth century, although the bed is ultimately the more popular. There are, however, also quite a few examples, including six Black-Figure pieces from the early part of the century, which show only a tree (three others have just a rock and a tree).[36] Given then that the hammer/axe seems the only necessary element for identifying the scene, one may well wonder if the bed was always a part of the story, and if it is meant to play a central role even when it does appear. Our earliest good narrative source is Diodoros, to whom should perhaps be added a scholion to Euripides' *Hippolytos*. Diodoros says that Prokroustes fitted passersby to a bed; if they proved to be too long he cut off whatever extended beyond the bed's edges, and if they were too short he beat their legs (*proekrouen*, from which verb Diodoros derives "Prokroustes" as a nickname). The *Hippolytos* scholion (at 977) offers essentially the same: Prokroustes (whom it mistakenly calls "Sinis") has a bed in the middle of the road and, after overpowering travelers, measures them on it. Those who are too long have their feet cut off, while those who are too short have their legs beaten with a hammer until they fit (as if flattening them out would lengthen them). Pausanias says nothing about Prokroustes' deeds, and Plutarch only that he made strangers fit the bed. Apollodoros and Hyginus add a new idea, namely that Prokroustes had two beds, one short and one long, and mismatched travelers to them so that some adjustment would always be necessary. Both authors agree that the short were hammered out to greater length and the tall truncated (sawed off, as Apollodoros puts it). Despite some minor differences, this later literary tradition is remarkably uniform, which is all the more reason to ask why the distinctive attributes—a bed, a hammer, *and* a saw or axe—are not uniformly present in fifth-century art. Matters would be simpler if we could tell for certain which Theseus holds, a hammer or an axe. In some cases it certainly looks more like an axe, but Bakchylides does say hammer. Either way, no representation shows both implements at the same time, and I am tempted to suggest that in the beginning Prokroustes simply bashed unsuspecting travelers with one or the other. Possibly he invited them to rest on his bed, and then killed them in their sleep without worrying overly about how they fit.

Theseus
in Athens
With five cutthroats and one sow disposed of, Theseus does finally arrive in Athens, only to find himself further threatened. The story of Medeia's sojourn in Athens after fleeing Corinth does not appear anywhere prior to the mid-fifth century; given our paucity of early sources for Theseus, that does not prove much, but one would certainly like to know if the event was part of Eumelos' *Korinthiaka*. Bakchylides' dithyramb about Theseus' arrival in Athens does not mention a stepmother; perhaps there is no special reason why it should, when the emphasis of the poem is on Theseus' previous deeds and present intentions. But at least by the time of Euripides' *Medeia* in 431 B.C. we have clear hints that Medeia will join Aigeus in Athens, and likely enough she was involved in the *Aigeus* plays of both Sophokles and Euripides dramatizing Theseus' arrival; the former at any rate included the Bull of Marathon (see below), and the latter made mention of a second wife scheming against earlier children (fr 4 N²). These dramas cannot be dated very precisely, but a series of Red-Figure pots starting about 450 B.C. and showing Aigeus, Theseus, the Bull, and a woman who must be Medeia suggest that at least one of them was early.[37] We will see in chapter 9 that other Red-Figure pots, traditionally thought to show Theseus in pursuit (for no very clear reason) of Aithra, may illustrate this same conflict of Theseus and Medeia, in which case it will go back to the time of Makron. The woman on the series with Aigeus and the Bull usually holds a pitcher and cup, and sometimes appears in Oriental costume. In literature the near-poisoning of Theseus actually survives first in the *Hekale* of Kallimachos, where Medeia recognizes the son before his father does (fr 232 Pf) and Aigeus calls out to Theseus not to drink (fr 233 Pf). But the cup and pitcher held by the woman on the above vases surely attest to such a deed as known in the fifth century. For the sequence of attempted poisoning and bull capture there are obviously two possibilities, represented for us by Apollodoros and Plutarch. In that of Apollodoros, Medeia persuades Aigeus to try to destroy Theseus (as yet unrecognized, or at least unacknowledged) by sending him to combat the Marathonian Bull (ApE 1.5–6). He captures it, and so Medeia resorts to a second stratagem, offering him a drink with poison in it. At the last second, however, Aigeus recognizes the sword left for Theseus after his conception and strikes the poison from his son's hand (cf. *Met* 7.404–24). In Plutarch the attempted poisoning by Medeia follows the same lines, but occurs immediately upon Theseus' arrival in Athens (the subsequent capture of the Bull is motivated only by its menace to the countryside: *Thes* 12.2–3, 14). This latter arrangement was also used by Kallimachos (so the *diêgêsis* in fr 230 Pf) and may derive from Philochoros, whom Plutarch mentions at the end of

this section. But while logical in itself, it removes Medeia from the scene before the Bull's capture, and thus cannot be what vase-painters who show her had in mind. Nor is it likely to have been used by Sophokles if Medeia appeared in his *Aigeus*, since the Bull (guaranteed for that play: see below) will serve no purpose once Medeia is defeated. Of Euripides' drama we know (besides the involvement of a stepmother) only that some sort of dangerous task was set (surely the Bull: frr 9–11 N²), but here, too, the near-poisoning of Theseus by Medeia seems the obvious plot. Whether either playwright could have invented this role for Medeia remains an open question. A related issue, that of the child Medos whom Medeia sometimes bears to Aigeus, we will return to at the end of chapter 12.

As for the Bull, he forms, as it were, a coda to this series of Theseus' adventures, and appears not only on the earliest cycle cups, but also on some late Black-Figure pots. On most of these, Theseus is either wrestling with him (usually by gripping a horn) or has already succeeded in taming him (e.g., Florence 91456, London E36, Louvre F271).[38] A smaller number show Theseus with sword or spear, apparently prepared to kill the Bull rather than capture it. But one of the earliest cycle cups, that by the Kleophrades Painter in Paris (CabMéd 536 et al.), presents quite a different scene: Theseus lies supine on the ground, and the Bull is in process of trampling him, while Athena rushes in from the left, presumably to save the hero of her patron city.[39] It is difficult to think of another instance in which a god rescues a major hero from such a predicament, and impossible to say whether this innovation is literary or artistic in origin. Sophokles' *Aigeus* has a clear reference to the capture in a fragment describing the making of a noose or bonds with which to restrain the animal (fr 25 R). Of later sources, Isokrates says that Poseidon let loose the Bull upon the land (10. *Helen* 25), and Diodoros, Apollodoros, and Hyginus claim that this was the same bull that Herakles brought up from Krete (DS 4.59.6; ApE 2.5.7; *Fab* 38). In Plutarch, we saw that Theseus sets out after the creature only after he has been recognized and disposes of Medeia. Whether or not this comes from Philochoros, he is the first named source (apud Plutarch) for another part of the story, that Theseus was overtaken by a storm as he neared Marathon, and sought refuge in the hut of an old woman called Hekale (328F109). She received him kindly, and promised to sacrifice to Zeus in thanksgiving if he should return safely the next day from his encounter with the Bull. Theseus of course did so, but found her dead, whereupon he set up honors for her and created a deme in her name. The existence of a historical Attic deme Hekale may prompt us to ask if this is not a local aetiology popularized by the Atthidographers; certainly such a figure is absent from the artistic tradition. In any case the tale became very popular and forms the basis for Kallimachos' substantial poem *Hekale*, which follows essentially the outline given for Philochoros.

This completes the list of Theseus' early adventures, those prior to the coming of Minos for the tribute and the subsequent voyage to Krete. His encounter with the Minotaur and his other adventures on Krete are discussed in chapter 8, and his later deeds (including his battle with the fifty sons of Aigeus' brother Pallas) in chapter 9.

Before leaving the royal house of Athens we must consider one other story, that involving Aigeus' brother Nisos, the king of Megara, whose city falls to Minos after the machinations of his daughter Skylla. For all its possibilities of representation, this story seems to be unknown in early art, and first surfaces (somewhat elliptically) in Aischylos' *Choephoroi* (613–22). Here the daughter is not named, but she clearly separates her father from his "immortal lock of hair" while he sleeps, and thus destroys him, persuaded by golden chains, the gift of Minos. Clearly too, therefore, Minos connives at this action; what is not clear is whether the girl desires the necklaces for themselves, or whether they are a token of Minos' presumed love. The story does not reappear until Vergil's *Ciris* and the famous account of Ovid's *Metamorphoses*. In the *Ciris* Minos is pursuing (for whatever reason) Polyidos, who has taken refuge at Megara; there the Moirai have decreed that city and country shall be safe as long as the purple lock of the king remains intact. But Skylla, the daughter (here finally named), has in some way offended Hera (apparently by loosening her garments in a temple precinct), and as punishment Eros causes her to fall in love with Minos. She cuts off the lock, and Megara falls to Minos, but the sequel is treated very abruptly: Minos has apparently made some sort of marriage pact with her, and Nisos is dead (whether from the loss of the lock, or during the fall of the city). Skylla herself, however, when we see her again, is being dragged through the Aegean behind Minos' ships, and voices sad complaints until Amphitrite in pity changes her into the bird called the ciris. Zeus then makes Nisos into a sea eagle *(haliaeetos)* so that he might pursue his daughter, and the story ends. In Ovid's version, Minos is on his way to Athens to avenge the death of his son Androgeos, and attacks Megara (*Met* 8.6–151). For six months the city holds out, protected by Nisos' purple lock, until Skylla catches a glimpse of Minos and is lost. She cuts the lock and takes it to Minos, who is immediately horrified; he does remain to take the city, but then leaves, abandoning Skylla, who hurls herself into the sea and swims after the ships until she and her father are transformed. The text also makes it clear that Nisos does not die when the lock is cut; here, as probably in the *Ciris*, the question is one of the city's safety, not the king's. Propertius adds a brief reference in which once again love is the motive, and Skylla is dragged through the sea (3.19.21–28).

The versions of Pausanias and Apollodoros on this myth follow much the same lines as Ovid, with the important difference that there is no metamorphosis, and that Nisos seems fated to die when the lock is lost (Paus 1.19.4, 2.34.7; ApB 3.15.8). Apollodoros provides as well a more comprehensible version of the dragging mentioned in the *Ciris* and Propertius: Minos ties Skylla to the stern of his ship as a punishment and pulls her behind it until she drowns. The scholia to *Hippolytos* 1200 offer the same information, while suggesting like the *Ciris* that Minos had accepted Skylla's offer of the lock and coveted marriage with her; they also make the lock golden (so too Σ Lyk 650). In Pausanias, Skylla is simply thrown from the ship and drowns. Thus we see that there are two quite different versions of Skylla's fate, one in which she is punished by Minos, the other in which he leaves her and she tries to swim after him; in all cases she either drowns or is pursued by her father. Hyginus in *Fabula* 198 adheres closely to Ovid (with Nisos as son of Ares or Deion [Pandion?]), but in 242 the father kills himself after discovering the loss. The fact that Skylla actually brings the lock to Minos in Ovid may be no more than a poetic device, or a proof of what she has done, but perhaps too in some versions possession of the lock (not just the owner's loss of it) is what gives victory or defeat. Such an idea might resolve some of the ambiguity over whether Nisos dies because the city is taken, or the city is taken because he dies, in versions where he does die. Presumably Aischylos had an opinion on these matters, but the *Choephoroi* stops just short of telling us what it was. His words, taken at face value, do suggest that Skylla's motive was greed rather than love, yet the context (a choral ode about intrafamilial bloodshed) *might* be responsible for the suppression of an already existing love motif. The playwright also says, as we saw, that Skylla "destroyed" Nisos, but the Greek word used could perhaps mean that she enabled Minos to kill him as part of the sack of Megara. Oddly enough, Ovid (*AA* 1.331–32) and Vergil (*Ecl* 6.74–77) confuse (or conflate) this Skylla with the Odyssean one, a notion for which there is no early justification (*Ciris* 54–91 even reproaches such a confusion). We will see in chapter 13 that the whole story has a noteworthy parallel in Amphitryon's assault on the cities of the Teleboans. Finally, we have already encountered one other daughter of Nisos in chapter 5, the Eurynome who apparently marries Glaukos, son of Sisyphos, in the *Ehoiai* and becomes the mother of Bellerophontes.

8   Minos and Krete

Rhada-
manthys

When we left Europa in chapter 6, she had arrived on Krete courtesy of Zeus' machinations, and had borne to the god Minos, Rhadamanthys, and Sarpedon (although the *Iliad* puts Sarpedon in the line of Sisyphos, and Kinaithon makes Rhadamanthys rather the son of Hephaistos [Phaistos?], son of Talos [fr 1 *PEG*]). No stories of any sort link these brothers together; they are (as so often) separate figures assigned the same mother. In the case of Rhadamanthys, the early evidence for any narrative tales is especially slim, essentially just a reference in the *Odyssey* to a voyage he once made with sailors to Euboia to see Tityos (*Od* 7.322–24); the poem does not say why he went. Elsewhere, his primary claim to fame is a reputation for wisdom and *sôphrosynê*. Possibly this is already implied in *Odyssey* 4, where he is made an inhabitant of the Isles of the Blessed, and has "the easiest life among mortals" (*Od* 4.564); again, no reason is given. The *Ehoiai* does to be sure give him the epithet *dikaios*, "just," in describing Europa's offspring (Hes fr 141 MW), but his intellectual qualities are first explicitly mentioned by Theognis (701) and Pindar (*Py* 2.73–74; *Ol* 2.74–77). The latter follows the *Odyssey* in putting him on the Isles of the Blessed, where he exercises some sort of counseling function (perhaps together with Kronos; the text is not very clear). *Pythian* 2, for its part, stresses primarily his ability to avoid being deceived, in contrast to Pindar's patron Hieron. Ibykos at some point makes him the lover of one Talos (the Kretan giant? Daidalos' nephew?) and also calls him "just" (309 *PMG*), while in Aischylos' lost play *Kares* Europa describes him as immortal (because he is on the Isles of the Blessed?: fr 99 R). But his role as judge in the Underworld (together with his brother Minos) is not found before Plato's *Gorgias* (523–24), although just possibly some such status lay behind his visit to Tityos.

If we can believe Antoninus Liberalis, Pherekydes recounted that when Alkmene died, Zeus sent Hermes to escort her to the Isles of the Blessed, where she was married to Rhadamanthys (AntLib 33 = Pher 3F84). The end of the story—Alkmene's miraculous disappearance from her coffin—might imply however a Hellenistic source for some of this, perhaps Nikandros. In the Cyzicene Epigrams, Herakles gives his mother to Rhadamanthys in marriage; the introduction adds that this took place in the Elysian Plain, thus after Herakles himself had become a god (*AP* 3.13). Apollodoros relates, more prosaically, that the couple was married while still alive, and lived in Boiotia (Ap*B* 2.4.11; so too Plutarch *Lys* 28.5). He also calls Rhadamanthys an exile from Krete, but does not say for what reason; in the scholia to Lykophron he has killed a brother (Σ Lyk 50: no name given). Possibly such a deed is no more than a stock device to move someone to another area, although we may note that Peleus too went into exile after killing a brother, Phokos, and like Rhadamanthys was known for wisdom and restraint. The play *Rhadamanthys* (attributed to both Euripides and Kritias) appears to have somehow linked its title character to Helen and the deaths of Kastor and Polydeukes (and Rhadamanthys' daughters?); the one substantial fragment, on the vanity of human wishes, suggests something of the title figure's sagacity but nothing of the plot (43 frr 15, 17 Sn).

Minos,
Pasiphae,
and the
Minotaur

For Minos, on the other hand, there is no shortage of tales, some of them odd indeed. In the *Odyssey* he has what we saw to be the strange task of judging among the dead (*Od* 11.568–71); Homer's other remarks about him cover his parentage (by Europa only in the *Iliad*), his fathering of Ariadne (*Od* 11.321–25: Phaidra and Prokris are named just before), and his role as ruler of Knossos (with mention of a regular converse with Zeus, if this passage is rightly interpreted: *Od* 19.178–80).[1] But not until the *Ehoiai* (after the theft of Europa, the deeds of Sarpedon at Troy, and perhaps a section on Rhadamanthys: Hes fr 141 MW) do we get our first glimpses of the familiar family scandal: Androgeos, the sea, a bull, someone (the bull?) falling in love, and Minos' wife bearing to him a great son, like a man toward the feet, but with the head of a bull (Hes fr 145 MW). Whether the poem went on to describe Theseus' conquest of this creature we cannot say. Sappho did refer to the latter event, and the liberation of seven young men and seven maidens (206 LP), but may not have given the background to the story. Despite the tremendous popularity of this saga in seventh- and sixth-century art, there are no other preserved literary sources in that time period, save for Theseus' violation of his oath to Ariadne in the *Aigimios* (Hes fr 298 MW). From the early fifth century, Bakchylides offers us two accounts: in Ode 17 we see Theseus and Minos traveling from Athens to Krete together with the other young Athenians (although there is never any mention of the Minotaur), and Ode 26 (or what is left of it) deals with Pasiphae (here named for the first time) and her instructions to Daidalos to fashion for her something (surely a wooden cow) so that she might mate with the bull. In Pindar, Zeus himself became the bull in desire for Pasiphae, if Porphyry reports this correctly (fr 91 SM), but confusion with Europa or a manuscript error is perhaps at work here. The full story was probably related by Ariadne to Theseus in Sophokles' *Minos*, and actually put on stage by Euripides in his *Kretes*, with the dramatic time of the play being the point at which Pasiphae is about to give birth to the child (Minos is as yet unaware of the father). The result in this latter play is predictably monstrous, as we see from an Oxyrhynchus fragment in which Minos reports on the new delivery to the chorus: the child has a bull's head on a human torso, and a tail, but is at least two-legged (POxy 2461 = fr 81 Aus). There seems to arise at the end of the passage the question of how the infant will be nursed. A parchment in Berlin offers as further evidence an impassioned speech by Pasiphae in which she characterizes herself as maddened by the gods (for what woman would otherwise desire a bull?), rejects blame for her actions, and rebukes Minos as the real culprit for failing to sacrifice the bull to Poseidon (PergBerol 13217 = fr 82 Aus). Minos, unimpressed, orders her led away to prison as the chorus protests. From the tone of all this, it seems likely that the play sided with Pasiphae and the chorus, and that Minos is indeed at fault. There is also mention of hides, which might suggest a more believable ruse than the wooden cow, but it seems on the other hand that in this play Daidalos is punished for *something*.[2]

Later accounts slowly add familiar details to this lacunose picture. Isokrates in the fourth century is the first to actually say that Pasiphae is the daughter of Helios (10. *Helen* 27, where the Minotaur is simply a *teras*), and Palaiphatos the first to describe the wooden cow as the device made by Daidalos to permit the mating of woman and bull (Pal 2). The latter is also the first literary source to employ the word "Minotaur." But already this name appears on the Archikles/Glaukytes Attic Black-Figure cup in Munich (2243), so that the term has at least a sixth-century pedigree (cf. too the Chalkidian hydria now in the Louvre [F18] with the words *Tauros Minoos,* "bull of Minos"). In Philochoros (328F17) and Kallimachos' *Hymn to Delos* (4.311) we first encounter the Labyrinth as the place of the monster's confinement. But only with Diodoros do all the parts fall into place. In his account, Minos keeps the custom of sacrificing to Poseidon each year the fairest bull from his herd, but there comes a year when he cannot bear to do so, and sacrifices a lesser beast instead (DS 4.77.1–4). Poseidon in anger causes Pasiphae to become enamored of the bull, Daidalos creates a device *(mêchanêma)* like to a cow, the mating is accomplished, and the child, a bull from the shoulders up, is born. Daidalos then also builds the maze-like Labyrinth as a place in which to keep this creature. Apollodoros gives exactly the same story, save that in his version Minos prays to Poseidon to send him a bull out of the sea, promising to sacrifice it upon its arrival (ApB 3.1.3–4). This seems likely to be the conception of Euripides (where Pasiphae calls the bull a *phasma:* fr 82.23–24 Aus), and even the *Ehoiai,* where the sea appears to be mentioned (Hes fr 145.10 MW). Apollodoros also tells us that the creature's real name was Asterios. Pausanias and Hyginus offer rather different motives for the misfortune, Pausanias that Poseidon was angry because Minos did not worship him more than the other gods (1.27.9), Hyginus that Pasiphae was punished for neglecting the rites of Aphrodite (*Fab* 40). The artistic evidence for the actual form of the Minotaur we shall consider below.

Daidalos in Athens	From Pasiphae and the Labyrinth we backtrack briefly to the cause of Daidalos' arrival from Athens. We have seen that for Pherekydes this craftsman is a son of Metion, son of Erechtheus (3F146); thus he would be a first cousin of Pandion II, and a first cousin twice removed of Theseus. In Bakchylides' dithyramb on Pasiphae he is, on the contrary, the son of Eupalamos (26.5–7; so too *Fab* 39). Diodoros and Apollodoros (perhaps bothered by the inconsistency and the chronology) both manage to improve on these arrangements: in Diodoros, Daidalos is the son of Metion, son of Eupalamos who is the son of Erechtheus (DS 4.76.1), while in Apollodoros he is the son of Eupalamos, son of Metion who is the son of Erechtheus (Ap*B* 3.15.8, 3.15.1). Clearly, at any rate, by the time of the later mythographers he was solidly ensconced as a member of a cadet branch of the royal house of Athens. Daidalos' reason for leaving Athens seems on all counts to have been the killing of his nephew, the son of his sister. Sophokles apparently called this figure Perdix in his lost *Kamikoi* dealing with Daidalos in Sicily (fr 323 R); we can only guess how much of the story was actually told. It does not resurface until Diodoros, for whom the nephew in question is Talos (DS 4.76.4–7). He is here an apprentice of Daidalos, but fashions all on his own the potter's wheel and iron saw, among other things, and is killed by his master in a fit of jealousy. Daidalos tries to conceal the body, but is discovered by the Areopagos and flees. Apollodoros has him fling his nephew (again Talos, here son of a *sister* Perdix) from the Akropolis, once more in jealousy after the invention of the saw, and with the same result (Ap*B* 3.15.8). Pausanias differs only in calling the child Kalos (1.21.4), a variant also found in Clement of Alexandria (Cl:*Pro* 4.47). Ovid and Hyginus for their part have the same story, but with a reversion to Sophokles' Perdix as the name (*Met* 8.236–59; *Fab* 39). Naturally this enables Ovid to engineer the metamorphosis of the boy into a partridge, although if the name "Perdix" is old, one suspects that the metamorphosis is as well. First in Photios' *Lexicon* do we find preserved the idea that Perdix, sister of Daidalos and mother of the child (here again Kalos), hanged herself in grief at her son's death.
Theseus and the Minotaur	That Theseus' combat with the Minotaur involved the lives of other youths and maidens is clear from the earliest artistic representations (about 650 B.C., see below) and from the reference in Sappho (206 LP); their journey from Athens down to Krete is described by Bakchylides in his Ode 17, and must surely have been recounted by Pherekydes and Sophokles (the latter as background for his lost *Minos*). But nowhere in the remaining evidence for this period do we learn why Athenians are being sent to encounter the Minotaur. Isokrates says that it was in obedience to an oracle (10.*Helen* 27), but only from our usual late sources do we get details. In Diodoros, Minos' son Androgeos comes to Athens for the Panathenaic festival, and in addition to numerous victories acquires the friendship of the sons of Pallas (DS 4.60.4–5). Aigeus, as always fearful of his brother's children and their desire for the throne, has Androgeos in consequence assassinated. Not only does war with Minos ensue,

but also a drought, which forces the Athenians to seek help from Apollo: the god pronounces that only when they have appeased Minos will the drought abate, and the latter's terms are seven youths and seven maidens to feed to the Minotaur every nine years. Plutarch agrees with all of this, although he does not say why Androgeos was killed (*Thes* 15). Apollodoros knows two versions, one that after the youth's victorious performance at the Panathenaia he was sent by Aigeus against the Marathonian Bull, which killed him, the other that his defeated rivals were responsible for the deed (ApB 3.15.7: here as in Diodoros he is on his way to Thebes). Again the rest of the tale follows as before. Pausanias also names the Marathonian Bull as the culprit, but in his account the Athenians are apparently guiltless; Minos however is unpersuaded, and exacts the usual penalty (Paus 1.27.9).

Most of these later versions have the Athenians who are to be sacrificed chosen by lot, with Theseus volunteering. An exception is Hellanikos, who as Plutarch tells us had Minos make the selection himself; Theseus is his first choice (4F164). The adventure on the journey down is told in full detail by Bakchylides (17), and no later writer disagrees with him. Stricken by desire, Minos finds himself unable to keep his hands off one of the young maidens, Eriboia. Theseus in anger confronts him and boasts of his parentage, whereupon Minos proposes a challenge: he will call upon Zeus his father to send a sign proving his own siring by that god, and will throw into the sea a ring that Theseus may easily recover if Poseidon is indeed his father. Zeus duly sends thunder, and Theseus, undaunted, leaps into the sea to get the ring. Dolphins bring him to the home of Poseidon, where he beholds the dancing Nereides and Amphitrite, who gives him a gleaming purple garment and a crown, dark with roses, which Aphrodite had once given her. With these Theseus returns to the ship, which has since moved on toward Krete. There is no further mention of the ring; perhaps Bakchylides takes its recovery for granted, or perhaps he feels that the gifts of Poseidon's wife are sufficiently impressive by themselves. The story, which ends abruptly with Theseus' re-emergence from the sea, finds several illustrations in early fifth-century Red-Figure, most famous of which is a cup by Onesimos in the Louvre showing Theseus, Athena, and Amphitrite (Louvre G104); here too there is no sign of a ring. More imaginative (though perhaps less elegant) is a cup by the Briseis Painter in New York (NY 53.11.4); in the tondo a seated Amphitrite holds out a crown or garland to Theseus, while on the outside Poseidon and assorted females look on while a huge Triton—complete with fish tail—prepares to take Theseus back to his ship. Several other simpler versions agree in giving Amphitrite a crown to hold (Fogg 1960.339; CabMéd 418). According to Pausanias, a painting of the tale by Mikon could be seen in the shrine of Theseus in Athens (1.17.3). Pausanias admits that the scene portrayed does not represent all of the myth, and thus is hard to identify; unfortunately he does not say what part *was* shown. As he himself retells the story, Theseus returns from the sea with both ring and a golden crown from Amphitrite. We have already seen that the crown was not said to be golden in Bakchylides, but rather covered with roses. The question of Theseus, Ariadne, and a crown supplied from some source is one previously discussed in chapter 2; we shall return to it again shortly.

For Theseus' actual exploits against the Minotaur on Krete we do have one good early source, or at least a summary of such, in the form of a scholiast's report on Pherekydes (3F148). From this we learn that Ariadne, daughter of Minos (first named as we saw in the *Nekuia*), falls in love with Theseus on his arrival in Krete, where he has come to be offered to the Minotaur, and gives him a ball of thread which she herself has gotten from Daidalos. She advises him to tie this to a part of the door as he goes in, and unroll it until he arrives at the innermost part (of what is not specified). There, should he find the Minotaur asleep, he is to seize him by the hair and sacrifice him to Poseidon, then follow the thread back (the implication is thus that he has a sword, although this is not stated). Apparently everything evolves as Ariadne has anticipated, for in the following sentence Theseus is boarding ship with her and the youths and maidens not yet given to the Minotaur. Plutarch adds yet another detail from Pherekydes' account, namely that Theseus cut holes in the bottoms of the other ships to prevent pursuit (3F150). Pherekydes went on to relate what happened on the island of Dia, as we will see when we have considered other sources for the slaying of the Minotaur. Among these both Palaiphatos (2) and Philochoros (328F17) attempt to rationalize the exploit into the defeating of some man named Minotauros, but in general the more fantastic version prevails. At some point in the fifth century the story was dramatized, to judge from Oxyrhynchus fragments (POxy fr 2452 = Soph fr 730a-g R). These probably show us a Theseus in verbal confrontation with Minos (or perhaps Ariadne) relating his past exploits, and a dialogue between Eriboia and a sympathetic Ariadne. That Eriboia should appear here as a character (her name and that of Ariadne are given in the margin) is remarkable, but we cannot say more, except to wonder whether Minos' lust for her continued as a theme after the arrival on Krete. Sophokles' *Theseus* and *Minos* (if not the same as his *Kamikoi*) and Euripides' *Theseus* have all been argued as the source of these passages.[3] At some point Euripides does refer to someone carrying a ball of yarn, though our source gives no title (fr 1001 N²).

Later literary sources have surprisingly little to add to what Pherekydes has told us, and often slide over the combat and related events with far less detail than he provides. Certain basic elements are always present—Ariadne's love, the thread, and the Minotaur slain—and what variation there is lies chiefly in the mode of combat: Apollodoros says bare fists and Ovid a club (ApE 1.9; Her 10.101–2). We should recall here the crown that "Epimenides" claims Dionysos gave to Ariadne on Krete, to seduce and perhaps as well deceive her (3B25). Ps-Eratosthenes, our source for this information, goes on to say that according to some writers Hephaistos made the crown of fiery gold and gems from India (so too DS 6.4), and because it gave off light Theseus was saved in the Labyrinth (*Katast* 5; cf. *Astr* 2.5.1). The properties of such a crown, on the one hand, and its source, on the other, may have come from two separate traditions; if not, Ariadne aids Theseus with the love gift given to her by Dionysos. We shall see below, however, that in Pherekydes and other writers, Ariadne receives the crown from Dionysos only after Theseus abandons her on Dia (3F148; in one account of Ps-Eratosthenes it is a gift from Aphrodite and the Horai). Hyginus also cites a version in which Theseus gives to Ariadne the crown that he has received from Amphitrite, but does not say whether in this version the crown gave off light (*Astr* 2.5.4). The idea that the crown did so, or aided Theseus in the Labyrinth, appears in fact only in Ps-Eratosthenes and Hyginus (*Astr* 2.5.1, as above) among literary sources. Bakchylides' description of the crown Amphitrite bestows as "dark with roses" rather suggests that the notion would have been foreign to him. Whether it can be found in the artistic tradition, where Ariadne frequently holds a crown, is a question to which we must now turn.

As early as the eighth century B.C. there are Minotaur-type statuettes (i.e., a man's body with the head of a bull) appearing as cauldron rim ornaments (Louvre C7286; Athens 6678). Similar human statuettes might represent Theseus, but we cannot be absolutely sure that the two types ever appeared on the same cauldron, or that they were meant to be understood as a group.[4] From the end of the century a krater now in London shows a man boarding a ship, and grasping a woman by the wrist as he does so (London 1899.2–19.1). This is an early and controversial piece of evidence which, if it does illustrate a myth, could be Paris and Helen as well as Theseus and Ariadne. In favor of the latter might seem the circlet held in the woman's other hand, a circlet that might serve to identify Ariadne *if* the crown is an early and important feature of the story.[5] In the seventh century we find a clear, albeit unusual, representation on a Tenian-Boiotian relief pithos of about 650 B.C. now in Basel (BS 617). Here the Minotaur has the reverse of his usual form, with the body of a bull and the head (unfortunately missing, but there is long hair) of a man; there are also traces of a horn. Since he has no hands, he naturally holds no weapon; Theseus for his part approaches the monster with a stone in his raised hand, and he is followed by three women and two men in the same position with raised stones. All appear to be holding on to a thread with their other hand; it runs horizontally across the four figures on the upper band of the scene, then drops down to Theseus and the remaining (female) figure on the lower band. This last figure, though directly behind Theseus, seems to be in the same attitude as the others, but possibly she is nonetheless Ariadne. Alternatively, the last figure in the sequence (far left on the upper band) might be so interpreted, with Ariadne here guarding the entrance or holding the end of the thread. In any event, aside from the maverick Minotaur we have also an early illustration of the (logical enough) idea that the other young men and women were sent into the Labyrinth at the same time as Theseus, and aided in the fight. From the same mid-century period comes a stamnos (from Megara Hyblaea?) on which Theseus grasps the Minotaur (now in the familiar bull's head/human body form) by the horn and prepares to strike him with what may be a club (Louvre CA 3837). Behind Theseus stand two women; the Minotaur's feet seem, inexplicably, fettered to each other.

At perhaps only a slightly later date begins a series of relief designs on gold plaques and shield-bands, the latter primarily from Olympia. On these, as on the above stamnos, we see the standard iconography of later times fully developed: the Minotaur has again the same body as on the cauldron ring supports—the head of a bull and the body of a man—and Theseus grasps him by his horn while threatening him with what is now a sword. On one relief plaque a woman, surely Ariadne, stands behind Theseus, perhaps holding the ball of thread in her lowered hand (Berlin:Ch GI 332–36). Her other hand, which is raised, has the fingers spread as if to hold a crown, though none is visible. On a shield-band, a similar female figure is much more curiously represented as a small floating figure squeezed between Theseus and the Minotaur and holding out a crown (Olympia B 1643). Conceivably, this is nothing more than a symbol of victory, but given the arrangement of the figures it is very tempting to regard the scene as evidence for early knowledge of Ps-Eratosthenes' glowing crown.[6] Yet another shield-band, though omitting Ariadne, has a crown with jagged points (rays?) in the upper right corner (Olympia B 1654). This same depiction gives Theseus as a weapon a stone instead of a sword. On one occasion the Minotaur, who is otherwise weaponless, wields a stone, and this will be his standard accoutrement in Attic Black-Figure. An Etruscan Black-Figure pot from the so-called Tomb of Isis at Vulci adds more evidence for the thread, which clearly runs down from Ariadne's hand as Theseus deals with his opponent (London H228: the "Polledrara hydria").[7] From this period we have also Pausanias' mention of illustrations on the Throne of Amyklai and the Chest of Kypselos. On the Throne, Theseus is leading the Minotaur, who is bound; even Pausanias is surprised at such a detail (Paus 3.18.11). It has been taken as confirmation of the fettered Minotaur on the Sicilian stamnos above,[8] but there Theseus prepares to kill his opponent, not lead him out, nor will the latter have been possible, given that the creature's *feet* are bound. On the Chest of Kypselos Theseus and Ariadne alone appear, the former with a lyre, the latter with a wreath (Paus 5.19.1). We should perhaps compare a tripod leg from Olympia where a man hands a lyre to a woman, and both clutch garland or crown (B 3600).[9] From Corinthian painting we have a cup of about 570 B.C. which shows Theseus slaying a Minotaur who is reclining, indeed almost prone (Brussels A1374); this may reflect a tradition similar to that of Pherekydes, where Ariadne anticipated that Theseus would be able to kill the Minotaur in his sleep.

Elsewhere too in the sixth century the combat between Theseus and the Minotaur becomes extremely popular, most notably in Attic vase-painting, but it cannot be said that the highly consistent iconography adds much to our knowledge of the narrative tradition. Theseus virtually always has a sword (occasionally a spear or club), the Minotaur usually a stone, and on the few occasions when Ariadne is present she is simply a flanking figure. Two pieces of some note, however, are the Archikles/Glaukytes cup in Munich (where as we have seen the name "Minotaur" appears for the first time) and the Rayet Skyphos in the Louvre. On the Munich cup, which boasts inscriptions for all the figures, we find Theseus and the Minotaur in the center, flanked by Athena and Ariadne, and then seven more figures (three male, four female) to the left and six more (three male, three female) to the right (Munich 2243). None of these fellow victims takes any part in the combat. Athena for her part holds a lyre; Ariadne in one hand holds out toward Theseus a round object (surely the thread) while in the other hand, down at her side, she has a crown or wreath. The problem of the shield-band thus repeats itself: is Ariadne preparing to garland Theseus in celebration of his victory (for which Athena no doubt readies the lyre on the other side), or is this a reference like the thread to the aid she gives him in the Labyrinth? The number of supernumeraries might seem in any case to be correct, but the figure behind Ariadne (who gestures excitedly, unlike the others) is labeled *trophos*, "nurse." Thus there are seven Athenian males, including Theseus, but only six females. The Rayet Skyphos (Louvre MNC 675), a Boiotian drinking cup of the second quarter of the sixth century, offers Ariadne holding what certainly seems to be a coiled thread (which looks remarkably like a labyrinth) as she stands next to Theseus; he himself grasps the Minotaur by his horn and stabs him with a sword. The other side of the cup again shows Athenian youths and maidens as part of the scene (seven males above, seven females below).

The François Krater, on the other hand, is unusual because it does not show the combat at all (Florence 4209). On the uppermost band of the Hephaistos side we find rather a series of young men and women standing next to a ship whose crewmen throw up their hands in excitement. They move from left to right, hand in hand, seven men and seven women, preceded by Theseus, who holds a lyre. Facing him as if in welcome are a smaller female figure labeled again *trophos* and behind her Ariadne, holding out to Theseus the ball of thread (and possibly in the same hand a wreath, although if this rather than part of the thread was the artist's intention, he has made it very inconspicuous). The other arm is under the himation, and thus not shown. The standard interpretation of this scene is that the rescued Athenians have arrived on Delos and are preparing to celebrate their triumph over the Minotaur. But if they have proceeded as far as Delos, Ariadne ought not to be with them (to say nothing of her nurse). It has therefore also been suggested that they are still on Krete, and not disembarking at all, but rather waiting for the ship, which just now returns to pick them up.[10] This idea does give special meaning to the gestures of the crew, and would explain why Ariadne faces and greets Theseus. Admittedly, there is still the anomaly of Ariadne holding the thread; if Theseus has gone into the Labyrinth without her he ought to have it. But only a scene in which Theseus and the others are arriving on Krete for the first time will really explain this last gesture, and the lyre and crew would seem to put that idea out of the question. Probably we should allow for some artistic license here, with Ariadne displaying the symbol of Theseus' victory.

Late Attic Black-Figure does offer one interesting variant: Theseus drags the Minotaur out of the Labyrinth alive before dispatching him (e.g., Athens 1061, a lekythos by the Beldam Painter; cf. the Red-Figure cup London E84 and column krater NY 56.171.46). These pieces portray the Labyrinth as a kind of *tempietto*, sometimes with a columned porch; perhaps what we see is only the entrance to a more extensive underground structure. The idea that Theseus first captured the Minotaur runs counter to what Pherekydes' account tells us, but it may well be what Bathykles intended on the Throne of Amyklai, since we saw that there the Minotaur is being led off bound. On several other occasions the Minotaur picks up large boulders, rather than small rocks, to hurl at Theseus (so a cup of Epiktetos: London E37); the latter is as before always armed. Otherwise Red-Figure has nothing new to add to what we have seen in Black-Figure, but there are several pieces on which the wreath/crown returns. On a pelike by Hermonax of about 470 B.C., for example, Ariadne holds aloft a circlet over the combatants in a fashion appropriate to one lighting the way for the hero (although the item in question appears definitely intended as a wreath, to judge from its appearance: Hunt Coll, no #). In the same pose, although here she holds the wreath vertically with both hands, we find Ariadne (with Minos behind her) on a calyx krater by the Syriskos Painter (Athens Akr 735), and on a pointed amphora by the Kleophrades Painter (Berlin:Ch Inv 1970.5). On the other hand, Leningrad 804, also by Hermonax, has Ariadne surely stepping forward to crown Theseus with her circlet, since the Minotaur lies already defeated on the ground; perhaps we are to imagine that circlet as serving both purposes. In all, while there is no secure evidence of the illuminating crown before Ps-Eratosthenes, the Olympia shield-band with the floating Ariadne plus the general emphasis on her carrying of a wreath do provide some grounds for suspicion. Yet the story, even if known in Archaic times, would seem a less popular facet of Ariadne's assistance than the thread.

One might suppose that the details of Theseus' escape from Krete would be no less exciting than his struggle in the Labyrinth, but our sources largely ignore the event, although, as we saw, Pherekydes describes the sabotage of the Kretan ships and may have supplied other details. In any event, Ariadne clearly takes ship with Theseus, and there follows the adventure of her death or abandonment on Dia/Naxos. As noted in chapter 2, where Dionysos' relationship with Ariadne was more fully discussed, only the *Nekuia* and a scholion thereon (drawn from Pherekydes?) say that Ariadne died at the hands of Artemis (*Od* 11.321–25); the reasons for that deed, and Theseus' role in it, remain unclear. Presumably, the abandonment is implied by the end of the *Theogony*, where Ariadne rather than perishing weds the god and becomes immortal (*Th* 947–49). The *Ehoiai*, or some part of the Hesiodic Corpus, and also the *Aigimios* make this explicit by narrating that Theseus broke his oath to Ariadne because he fell in love with Aigle, daughter of Panopeus, and/or Hippe (Hes frr 147,

298 MW). One wonders if we are to imagine such an event occurring between Krete and Naxos (in which case Ariadne's rival must have been one of the seven Athenian maidens), or if there was a version in which Theseus left her only later. Ion of Chios, we should note, speaks of actual children born to the couple, if we may believe Plutarch, but of course they could have been conceived between Krete and Naxos, and their names—Oinopion and Staphylos—are suspiciously grape-laden (Ion 29 W, apud *Thes* 20.2: Staphylos' parentage is here not completely clear). That the *Odyssey* scholia should call Ariadne the wife of Theseus and mother of Akamas and Demophon is stranger still, and surely a confusion with the adjacent Phaidra in the text (Σ *Od* 11.321).[11] The scholia to Apollonios assign Oinopion and Staphylos to Ariadne and Dionysos, as we would expect (Σ AR 3.997).

Along with the two references to Theseus' unfaithful behavior in the Hesiodic Corpus, we should also note the cryptic remark of the *Kypria* that when Menelaos goes to Pylos to recruit Nestor for the Trojan War, the latter tells him among other stories "that of Theseus and Ariadne." As with all these tales, we can only wonder if this was at all relevant to Menelaos' own situation: does Theseus, like Menelaos, lose his beloved? Or could he perhaps have been compared to Paris in taking Ariadne away from her father (or Dionysos)? The next surviving literary source is Pherekydes, where we encounter for the first time the story that Athena appeared to Theseus on Dia and ordered him to leave Ariadne there (3F148). For good measure, Aphrodite then appears to an understandably tearful Ariadne and tells her that she will become the wife of Dionysos. Finally Dionysos himself shows up, the union is consummated, and the god presents his wife with a golden crown. One would scarcely expect Pherekydes to invent this story, and in fact we find it already on several Red-Figure pots of the early part of the century, as noted in chapter 2. On one of these, a lekythos from Taranto, Athena is in the process of waking Theseus; Ariadne still sleeps beside him (Taranto 4545).[12] On another, a hydria by the Syleus Painter in Berlin, Athena leads Theseus away in one direction while Dionysos escorts Ariadne in the other (Berlin:PM F2179). The marriage of Dionysos and Ariadne is of course established at the end of the *Theogony* (947–48), and so cannot be simply an Athenian invention to save Theseus' reputation in this matter. Still, it might have been supposed by earlier writers that Dionysos found Ariadne only after Theseus had of his own accord abandoned her, as the *Ehoiai* says (always assuming that a god would be willing to acquire his wife on the rebound). In that case it might well be too that Athena's role in commanding Theseus to leave the island is the work of Athens in the sixth or early fifth century, when Theseus was beginning to take on increased importance as a local hero. Either Sophokles' *Minos* or Euripides' *Theseus* or both might have dealt with this situation in a divine epiphany predicting the future of Theseus and Ariadne, but we have no actual evidence that such was the case. One other point, as discussed in chapter 2, involves the idea that Artemis slew Ariadne because she had lost her virginity. This appears at the end of the *Odyssey* scholia to 11.322, our source for Pherekydes, but with the word *phasin*, "they say," in one manuscript. Most likely then it is the scholiast's addition rather than a Pherekydean original, and in either case, it sounds much like a later attempt to clarify Homer's puzzling account.[13] Theseus' further deeds, including his return to Athens and the death of his father Aigeus, we will return to in chapter 9, after we have dealt with the remainder of Minos' career.

The Children of Minos

Of Minos' children, Ariadne is so named as early as the *Nekuia* (*Od* 11.321–22) and the *Theogony* (947–48); Phaidra (without parentage) is mentioned in the same line of the *Nekuia* (Prokris intervening), but does not appear again anywhere until the dramas of Sophokles and Euripides, so that we cannot say for certain if she was always Ariadne's sister. Elsewhere the *Iliad* knows of a son Deukalion who will become the father of the Achaian hero Idomeneus (*Il* 13.451–52), and so too Pherekydes (3F85). The Hesiodic Corpus adds a daughter, Euryale, who by Poseidon was the mother of Orion (Hes fr 148a MW: see below), and Pindar and Bakchylides have Minos beget a son Euxantios by Dexithea of Keos (*Pa* 4.35–53; Bak 1.112–28). In the *Ehoiai* we also saw mention of Androgeos (Hes fr 145 MW), whose death in Athens may have been noted in the plays of Sophokles and Euripides, although we do not find it until Diodoros (4.60.4–5).

Two other sons must certainly have been involved in lost plays. Glaukos' disappearance into a vat of honey and subsequent resuscitation by the seer Polyidos was apparently the subject of Aischylos' *Kressai*, Sophokles' *Manteis*, and Euripides' *Polyidos*. The three-colored cow that resembled a mulberry tree was certainly a part of the dramatic tradition (Ais fr 116 R), and Minos as bereaved father may have played a central role (perhaps overly demanding in his treatment of the seer). But as usual full details come only later—the curing of one snake by another in Palaiphatos (26), and the rest of the story, including the finding of the child's body and his ephemeral mantic skills, in Apollodoros and Hyginus (ApB 3.3.1–2; *Fab* 136). These last specify that no one saw Glaukos disappear into the honey vat, and thus his fate was unknown. But Minos learned that the seer who offered the best comparison for the miraculous cow that he possessed would also be able to find the boy. Apollodoros says merely that the cow had three different colors; Hyginus adds that it changed color every four hours, from white to red to black. Polyidos likened this phenomenon to the fruit of the mulberry, and subsequently succeeded in locating the child. But Minos also wanted Glaukos brought back to life, and ordered the seer shut up with the corpse until this was done. In the prison thus created (Palaiphatos says it was the boy's tomb), Polyidos observed a snake approaching the corpse; fearing that it meant harm he killed it, only to see a second snake bring the first back to life with the touch of an herb. He therefore used the same herb on Glaukos, and the boy was likewise restored. Apollodoros adds as a coda to all this that Minos made Polyidos teach his son the art of divination. Upon leaving Krete, however, the seer instructed his pupil to spit in his mouth;

having done so, Glaukos forgot everything he had learned. In art we have one certain illustration of the imprisonment on a White-Ground cup of about 440 B.C. (London D5). Seer and child sit within a beehive-shaped structure, clearly a tomb, while below in the exergue of the cup's tondo the two snakes are visible. One wonders if such a tableau could have been presented on stage, and if so, by which tragedian.

The other son is Katreus, whose problems with his daughter Aerope were at least alluded to in Euripides' *Kressai* of 438 B.C., although he is not attested as Minos' offspring until Diodoros (DS 4.60.4). Euripides' play seems to have concerned Aerope's infidelity in Mykenai,[14] in which case the background to her story was probably related in the prologue. We know at any rate that this play told how Katreus discovered his daughter Aerope to have been seduced by a servant, and gave her to Nauplios to drown; the latter instead gave her to Pleisthenes to wife (Σ *Ai* 1297). In Apollodoros, Katreus hands over two daughters, Aerope and Klymene, to Nauplios to be sold (not drowned); Nauplios gives Aerope to Pleisthenes, as in Euripides, but keeps Klymene for himself, and she becomes the mother of Palamedes and Oiax (Ap*B* 3.2.2). From Diodoros we first hear of Katreus' son Althaimenes, who flees from Krete to Rhodes when he learns that he is fated to kill his father. Years later, Katreus follows with an entourage, desperate to see his son again; Althaimenes and his people suppose themselves to be attacked, there is the predictable scuffle, and Katreus dies (DS 5.59.1–4). Apollodoros also recounts this story, and adds to it that Althaimenes took his sister Apemosyne with him and kicked her to death after she had been seduced by Hermes, not believing her story (Ap*B* 3.2.1–2; cf. Paus 8.53.4).

Orion   About this enigmatic figure there is quite a tangle of odd and sometimes conflicting information, and although we discuss him here as grandson of Minos, it cannot be said that he has any very close link to Krete. The *Iliad* knows him only as a constellation (e.g., *Il* 18.486), but in the *Odyssey* he is noted both as a lover of Eos (thereby incurring the jealousy of the gods, until Artemis slays him with her bow on Ortygia: *Od* 5.121–24) and as a great (and handsome) hunter in the Underworld, as he was on earth (*Od* 11.572–75). His descent from Poseidon and Euryale, daughter of Minos, is attested by Pherekydes (3F52) and by Ps-Eratosthenes, who ascribes it to "Hesiod" (*Katast* 32 = Hes fr 148a MW). The latter author goes on to describe in continuous indirect discourse (hence presumably from the same source) Orion's ability to walk upon (or wade through?) water, just as he would on dry land, and the tale of Orion and Oinopion. It would seem likely, then, if not certain, that the Hesiodic *Astronomia* is the source of these details and what follows. In Ps-Eratosthenes' account, Orion arrives at Chios and, becoming drunk, rapes Merope, Oinopion's daughter. When Oinopion discovers the deed he blinds Orion and casts him out of his land; Orion goes to Lemnos, where Hephaistos takes pity on him and donates his servant Kedalion to act as guide. With Kedalion perched on his shoulders he then proceeds east until his blindness is cured, apparently by the rays of the rising sun. His vision restored, he plots revenge against Oinopion, but the latter's own people hide him under the earth. At this point Orion goes to Krete, where he spends his time hunting wild animals in the company of Artemis and Leto, until he boasts that he is a match for any animal on earth; Gaia in anger sends against him a giant scorpion, which slays him. At the request of Artemis and Leto, Zeus places him in the sky, but also the scorpion, as a memento of the event.

Of this tale as given by Ps-Eratosthenes the first part (Orion's drunkenness and assault) seems to have been mentioned by Pindar (although the scant note has him [on Chios] attacking another man's wife, not daughter: fr 72 SM). The blinding and recovery was probably the subject of Sophokles' lost (satyric) *Kedalion* (although that play has also been thought to describe Hephaistos' instruction by a blacksmith Kedalion[15]), and of the *Kataplous* of Korinna (who in any case spoke of the hero in flattering terms as one who cleared many places of wild beasts: 673 *PMG*). Of later authors, Parthenios relates the rape and blinding alone, adding that Oinopion had promised his daughter to Orion (who cleared Chios of wild beasts for him) but then regretted it and delayed the marriage until Orion took matters into his own hands (20). Apollodoros and Hyginus tell the whole of the Oinopion-Merope-Kedalion story in much the same form as Ps-Eratosthenes, including the ability to walk on water (Ap*B* 1.4.3; *Astr* 2.34.1–2), but Servius adds that Oinopion calls on his father Dionysos for help after Orion has offered violence to his daughter, and that the god sends Satyroi who put Orion to sleep and bind him (after which Oinopion puts out his eyes: Σ *Aen* 10.763).

As for Orion's death in other sources, the fatal boast to Gaia which brings the scorpion is found also in Ovid (*Fasti* 5.537–44: here the creature attacks Leto, and Orion intervenes at the cost of his own life) and Hyginus (*Astr* 2.26). But already before Ps-Eratosthenes we have a rather different version of this event: in Palaiphatos, Orion becomes enamored of Artemis and tries to assault her, and she herself then sends the scorpion against him (Pal 51). Whatever its ancestry, this version becomes quite popular, even appearing in Ps-Eratosthenes (*Katast* 7, in contrast to the version of 32), as well as Kallimachos (here Artemis herself shoots him: fr 570 Pf and cf. *H* 3.265), Aratos (634–46), Euphorion (fr 101 Pow = Σ*A Il* 18.486), Nikandros (*Ther* 13–20), and Hyginus (*Fab* 195); as a slight variant, Orion in Apollodoros attacks the maiden Opis, and Artemis again resorts to her arrows, or else he dares to challenge the goddess in throwing the discus (Ap*B* 1.4.5). Of all these sources, only Apollodoros mentions the abduction by Eos, and he relates no version that connects it at all with Orion's death. Strictly speaking, of course, not even *Odyssey* 5 definitely makes that connection: Kalypso simply complains that gods begrudge goddesses their beddings with mortal lovers, as in the case of Eos until Artemis slew Orion. Kalypso here clearly means that the *male* gods of Olympos begrudge such unions, and while the logical sequence of ideas might seem to imply that Artemis kills Orion for that reason, it remains possible that she does so instead for an unrelated personal motive, such as those reported by Palaiphatos and others above. We must note, however, that in Homer the slaying takes place on Ortygia, not Krete, and then too it is difficult to imagine Orion in the company of Artemis (or even coming upon her by chance) once kidnapped by Eos. Conceivably, Artemis acts in some accounts because Orion abandons her company for that of Eos, but more likely his relationships with these two goddesses were originally separate stories, perhaps even doublets of each other. Only Istros relates that Artemis was actually in love with Orion, and intended to marry him, but that Apollo in alarm caused her to shoot him unintentionally (334F64). Nevertheless she does seem to expect loyalty from those who follow her, and just possibly there was a conflict between her and Eos in which his abduction was regarded as punishable desertion.

Other late-appearing stories about Orion include a strained aetiological explanation of his birth and a previous marriage to one Side. The birth myth, found first in (once again) Palaiphatos (51), and then in the *Iliad* scholia (ΣA *Il* 18.486 as above, this too perhaps from Euphorion), Ovid (*Fasti* 5.493–536), and Hyginus (*Fab* 195; *Astr* 2.34.1), has Hyrieus, son of Poseidon and Alkyone, entertaining Zeus, Poseidon, and Hermes in his home. Pleased with their entertainment, the gods ask him what he would like, and are told that though he has no wife, he desires a son. They therefore spread out the hide of the animal slaughtered for dinner and cover it with their semen, then order Hyrieus to bury the hide in the ground for ten months; the child Orion is the result. Strabo tells us that Pindar spoke of Orion's birth in a dithyramb, but says nothing to indicate whether there was a real story, and if so, this one (9.2.12). The wife Side is said by Apollodoros to have compared herself to Hera in beauty, and to have been thrown down into Hades by the goddess as a result (ApB 1.4.3); Ovid, the only other author to mention her, says simply that Orion pined for her (*AA* 1.731). As for Orion and the Pleiades, none of the above sources ever mentions that tale in connection with any of the stories we have considered here; Orion in this role remains completely isolated from all his other roles, probably because it involves a version of his catasterism incompatible with that provided by the others. The sources for his pursuit of Pleione and/or her daughters are few, as we saw in chapter 6: possibly the Epic Cycle; Pindar (for the mother Pleione); and then, for the full story, Hyginus, Athenaios, and various scholia.

Minos and Daidalos

Although the earlier evidence is woefully incomplete, we have seen Daidalos as constructor of the device by which Pasiphae mates with the bull (Bakchylides, Palaiphatos) and as the builder of the Labyrinth (Diodoros). The famous reference from the Shield of Achilleus in *Iliad* 18 notes him rather as the maker of the *choros*, or dancing floor, for fair-haired Ariadne at Knossos (*Il* 18.590–92). As early as Pherekydes we also learn that Ariadne got the thread she gave to Theseus from Daidalos, so that we might well imagine Minos to have several reasons for displeasure with his master-builder. There is, however, no trace at all preserved from the Archaic period for the escape of Daidalos and Ikaros. Indeed, were it not for a fragment of a Black-Figure hydria (?) from about the middle of the sixth century with Ikaros' name clearly written on it, he would be missing from the early period altogether (Athens Akr 601 frr).[16] Here the name occurs under the feet of a figure with winged footgear, and we may presume, although only the feet are preserved, that the artist intended Ikaros to be flying. Daidalos and Ikaros may also have appeared in Euripides' lost *Kretes*, since a scholion to Aristophanes speaks of a monody of Ikaros in that play (Σ *Batr* 849 = p. 505 N²), and later vase-paintings show Daidalos supplicating Minos. But the recently discovered fragments of the play discussed above establish clearly that the action was set at the time of the Minotaur's birth (frr 81–82 Aus). As someone implicated in that event Daidalos might well have become, like Pasiphae, an object of Minos' wrath, but whether the flight from Krete could have ensued here, before the arrival of Theseus, is less certain. A mid-fifth-century chous by the Ikaros Painter shows us what is probably a winged Ikaros falling into the sea (Vlastos Coll, no #; cf. NY 24.97.37); for any details of that story we must turn to the fourth century.

Oddly enough, our first account of the flight of Daidalos and Ikaros occurs in Palaiphatos, who has also been our first source for a number of other features in the story of Pasiphae and the bull. But Palaiphatos' primary purpose in presenting his stories is, after all, to rationalize them, and so his emphasis on this material is probably due to the fact that there is a great deal of the fantastic in the legends of Krete. What he tells us as the received version of his time is that Minos imprisoned Daidalos and Ikaros for some reason, and that Daidalos made wings to attach to himself and his son and flew away (Pal 12). This is all, but since in Palaiphatos' improved rational version Ikaros falls overboard from the ship in which they are fleeing and drowns (becoming an *aitia* for the naming of the Ikarian Sea), we may suppose the familiar story of his watery demise in the original. Vase-paintings from the fourth century represent the moment of attaching the wings to Ikaros, as on an Apulian krater of *c.* 300 B.C., where Athena stands by (Naples 1767).

Sketchy though this outline is, it seems to suggest that the tale of Ikaros' flight as we know it was standard storytelling material in the sixth and fifth centuries, and perhaps even before that. But not before Strabo and Diodoros do we hear that the child's wings melted because he flew too close to the sun; Diodoros adds that Daidalos stayed close to the surface of the sea to keep his wings moist (Str 14.1.19; DS 4.77.5–9). Hyginus also presents the version in which escape is by flight (*Fab* 40), and we find it elaborated at some length in both Ovid and Apollodoros (*Met* 8.183–235; ApE 1.12–13). Yet other writers like Palaiphatos opt for more mundane means. In Kleidemos we find Daidalos traveling by ship to Athens, where Theseus protects him from Minos' son Deukalion (323F17), while in Xenophon he is enslaved by Minos, flees with Ikaros, somehow loses Ikaros, and is re-enslaved by barbarians (*Mem* 4.2.33).

Even Diodoros has a rational version (Pasiphae procures a ship for Daidalos) alongside that of the flight, and in Pausanias the artesan uses small boats with sails (his invention) like wings (9.11.4–5). In a variant in Hyginus, Theseus himself takes Daidalos back to Athens (*Fab* 40). Whether any of these more conventional means of departure have early roots is difficult to say.

As for Minos' own demise, his pursuit of Daidalos and subsequent death in Sicily is noted by Herodotos (without details: 7.170.1), and it was apparently the subject of Sophokles' lost *Kamikoi*, where we find reference to the conch shell (fr 324 R). In Diodoros' version, Minos journeys to the land of Akragas in Sicily, and proceeding to the court of Kokalos demands that Daidalos be handed over to him (DS 4.79.1–3). Kokalos receives him in a friendly fashion, but causes him to be scalded to death in the bath prepared for him. Apollodoros offers the same story with more details: Kokalos' court is at Kamikos (hence presumably the name of Sophokles' play) and Minos arrives without sure knowledge that Daidalos is there (ApE 1.14–15). He brings with him a conch shell (a sort of Labyrinth in miniature, it seems) and offers a great prize to anyone who can pass a thread through it. Kokalos claims to have done this by sending an ant through the shell with the thread attached to him, but Minos perceives that only Daidalos could have devised such a solution, and demands his surrender. There follows as in Diodoros his death in boiling water, and at the hands of Kokalos' daughters (who presumably bathed him). Zenobios (where pitch is substituted for the water: 4.92 [perhaps already in tragedy, if Ades fr 226a Sn is relevant]) and several scholiasts give a similar account; in one of these last Daidalos persuades the daughters to put a pipe down through the roof above the bath, and Minos is inundated with water in that fashion (Σ *Nem* 4.95a; cf. *Ibis* 289–90). In any case, all sources seem agreed that he met a most inglorious end. The event is quite possibly portrayed on a terracotta relief in Basel (from Sicily?) on which a man sits in a lebes while a woman stands beside him with a pitcher (Basel BS 318), and perhaps too on a controversial metope from Foce del Sele (no #) where only the right side of the scene (man and lebes) is preserved.[17] If either of these do indeed portray Minos' death they would take that death back into the sixth century, but other possibilities (Pelias, Iason, Aison, Pelops, Agamemnon) have also been suggested, as we will see in subsequent chapters. At one point in his life of Theseus, Plutarch remarks that Minos suffered all kinds of abuse on the Athenian stage, where he was portrayed as harsh and violent, in contrast to his image in Homer and Hesiod (*Thes* 16.3). Possibly we should take this to mean that Athenian playwrights invented some of the less reputable details about his life. But between Homer and fifth-century Athens there were surely lost sources that gave the Athenians some of their inspiration, even if we concede that Athenian bias would naturally regard Minos as fair game.

9 Theseus' Later Exploits

The Death
of Aigeus
and
the Sons of
Pallas

When we left Theseus in the last chapter, he had abandoned Ariadne (for whatever reasons) on Naxos (or Dia) and was returning to Athens. Perhaps no story in the saga of Theseus is more familiar than his failure to change the sails on his ship, and the consequent death of his father, but were it not for a chance remark by Plutarch we would not have any source for this event before Diodoros. As it is, we know that Simonides mentioned the replacement sail, and made it red, not white as in subsequent accounts (550 *PMG*); how much more of the story he might have told is not stated. Diodoros and our later mythographers all explain this sail in the same way: Theseus sailed from Athens to Krete under a black sail, but had a white one ready as a replacement should he survive the ordeal of the Minotaur and return home safely (DS 4.61.4, 6–7). Because of his grief for the loss of Ariadne (or, in Plutarch, joy at returning to Athens) the change is forgotten and Aigeus, keeping watch from the Akropolis, casts himself down to his death when he sees the black sail. Pausanias specifies that he was on the southwest corner, by the temple of Athena Nike (1.22.5); Plutarch just says "from the rock" (*Thes* 22.1), and the epitome of Apollodoros nothing at all about place (ApE 1.10). Given that the Akropolis is a good four to five miles from any part of the Aegean Sea, it would seem that in these accounts the story does not include any aetiology of the name of that sea via Aigeus' plunge into it. Hyginus is in fact the first preserved writer to claim that Aigeus threw himself into the Aegean, which was then named after him; we are not told where this was thought to have happened (*Fab* 43, 242; so too Σ *Aen* 3.74). Not impossibly the whole idea is a Roman notion, prompted by the fact that the names of king and sea possess greater similarity of appearance in Latin *(Aegeus, Aegaeus)* than they do in Greek *(Aigeus, Aigaios)* (Strabo for his part suggests that the sea is named after the site of Aigai on Euboia: 8.7.4).

With his father dead, Theseus would seem the logical choice to inherit the kingship of Athens. But Aigeus' own claim to the throne was not without dispute from his brother Pallas. There is no reference to this conflict before Euripides' *Hippolytos*, where Aphrodite says in passing that Theseus has come to Troizen (with Phaidra) for purification of the *miasma* incurred from the spilled blood of the Pallantidai (*Hipp* 35). At this point, the scholia offer the following account from Philochoros, that Pallas and his sons intended to launch an attack on Athens, and that while Pallas and his troops approached from Sphettos, his sons arranged themselves in ambush at Gargettos just to the northeast of Mount Hymettos (328F108). The ambush was betrayed to Theseus, who destroyed those participating in it. We last saw Pallas himself in a fragment of Sophokles' *Aigeus*, in which Aigeus says that his brother has the part to the south (presumably of Attika), calls him harsh, and speaks of his nourishing of *gigantes* (fr 24 R). Admittedly, there is a Pallas among the Gigantes who battle the gods in Apollodoros (Ap*B* 1.6.3), but it is hard to see how a member of the royal line of Athens (or his sons) could lay claim to that term. It has long been supposed that the battle scene on the frieze of the pronaos of the Hephaisteion in Athens represents the combat between Theseus and the Pallantidai, with Theseus (figure no. 15 near the center) advancing against four naked men who hurl boulders at him.[1] However likely, this identification is not certain, and even if it were, we should not know a great deal more about the story. Details as so often come late: from Diodoros we learn that Aigeus feared an alliance between Androgeos, son of Minos, and the sons of Pallas (4.60.4–5), while in Pausanias, Theseus kills Pallas and his sons and defends himself at the Delphinion (1.22.2, 1.28.10). Plutarch and Apollodoros both offer as a motive for the conflict the idea that Aigeus was only an adopted son of Pandion II (*Thes* 13; Ap*B* 3.15.5: here his real father is Skyrios), and it may be that in some accounts Theseus' descent from Aigeus was disputed as well. Apollodoros seems the only source to say that the sons were fifty in number (Ap*E* 1.11). Plutarch, who essentially repeats what we found in Philochoros, puts the incident before Theseus' departure for Krete, when his cousins were outraged at his initial appearance and recognition by Aigeus; most others put it after his return from Krete and installation as king (indeed, Pausanias even speaks of a rebellion). A more subdued version offered by the above-noted scholia at *Hippolytos* 35 claims that Theseus slew just one of Pallas' sons, in a dispute over the throne, and then exiled himself for a year because the victim was a relative. In any case, Euripides is the only source to put the event as late as Theseus' marriage to Phaidra, long after he has succeeded his father on the throne.

Peirithoos and the Lapithai

Theseus' friendship with Peirithoos of Thessaly involves him in a number of adventures, notably the battle with the Kentauroi, the attempted abductions of Helen and Persephone, and the carrying-off of the Amazon queen Antiope/Hippolyte. The descent to the Underworld is noted briefly in the *Nekuia* (*Od* 11.631: both heroes mentioned) and illustrated on a shield-band relief from Olympia of about 580 B.C. (B 2198: names included), so that there seems no doubt that the link between the two men is early. Nevertheless, Theseus' original participation in the battle between the Lapithai and the Kentauroi has been questioned. Granted, he is named by Nestor in *Iliad* 1 as taking part, but the reference is confined to a single line that could easily have been interpolated (*Il*

1.265).[2] Elsewhere, the *Iliad* tells us that Peirithoos is the son of Zeus by the wife of Ixion (*Il* 14.317–18 [in later accounts her name is Dia, and Eustathios says that Zeus mated with her in the form of a stallion: see chapter 18]), and stresses *his* role (not that of Theseus) in chasing the Kentauroi out of Thessaly (*Il* 2.740–44). So too in *Odyssey* 21, there is again no mention of Theseus in the clash with the Kentauroi (*Od* 21.295–303). To be strictly fair, it is not certain that the *Iliad* and *Odyssey* describe here exactly the same event. In *Iliad* 1 Nestor simply alludes to a battle between Peirithoos, Kaineus, and their comrades on one side and "mountain beasts" on the other; in *Iliad* 2 Peirithoos drives the "shaggy beasts" from Pelion on that day when his wife Hippodameia *teketo* their son Polypoites. Normally the verb *tiktô* means "to give birth" when used of a woman, and "to beget" when used of a man; if the driving-off of the beasts is to take place at Peirithoos' wedding, as in later accounts, then it must here have (unusually) the sense of "conceive" as applied to Hippodameia.[3] But Nestor's account suggests a long campaign (since there was time to summon him), and not impossibly nine months were required from the time of the original hostilities. Certainly the *Odyssey* (which, unlike the *Iliad*, speaks specifically in this context of "Kentauroi") knows something of that sort, for it tells us that the Kentauros Eurytion was a guest in the home of Peirithoos (here for the first time called a Lapith) and, becoming drunk (no wedding is actually mentioned), did "evil things." As a result the heroes were angered, and after dragging him outside cut off his ears and nostrils; this, the poet tells us, was the beginning of the trouble between men and Kentauroi. Thus there would seem to have been an initial isolated incident (whether or not at the wedding) leading to general hostilities and finally to an all-out war, which the Kentauroi lose. It does, however, seem unlikely that the *Odyssey* conceived of a battle *at* the wedding, and quite possibly the *Iliad* did not either. The same is true of the depiction on the shield in the Hesiodic *Aspis:* Lapithai (and Theseus, with the same line used to include him as at *Iliad* 1) and Kentauroi are represented most elegantly in silver and gold, the Lapithai with armor and spears, the Kentauroi with pine trees for weapons (*Aspis* 178–90). This first appearance of what will become a canonical contrast in weaponry between the two groups, and the fact that the Lapithai do wear armor, would seem to suggest a nondomestic context, while there is no mention at all of women or other noncombatants.

Our first preserved artistic illustration,[4] the François Krater, offers precisely the same elements as the *Aspis:* fully armed Lapithai with spears and shields (and helmets), Kentauroi with pine branches and boulders, no other figures. To the far left, though the relevant figure is lost in a gap, we can also read the name "Theseus," and since this cannot be an interpolation, we can say that Theseus' connection with the battle is at least this early, if not as old as the *Iliad*. His position off to the side might, however, be seen as confirming an early adjunct status, much as in the *Iliad* and the *Aspis*. Such a conclusion would be reinforced if Peirithoos were shown in the center of the struggle, but in fact the Lapith king is not preserved at all; either he was to be found in the large gap on the far right (thus balancing Theseus), or he is not present.

Other examples from Attic Black-Figure are often impossible to identify as this particular Kentauromachy, and in any case show the same basic details already discussed.[5] Only when we turn to the fifth century do we find, in Pindar, the specific idea that Peirithoos' wedding was the source of the trouble (fr 166 SM). Actually, even this fragment from one of his poems, cited by Athenaios in a discussion of words for drinking cups, fails to mention a wedding. But we are told that when the Kentauroi smelled the power of the man-conquering wine, they pushed aside the milk from the tables; it seems obvious that a number of them (not just Eurytion) have been served milk at some social event, and this is surely the nuptial feast. Red-Figure vase-painting follows suit from the 460s B.C. by introducing women into the scene as intended victims of the Kentauroi, and even bits and pieces of the banquet furnishings (e.g., Florence 81268; Berlin:Ch F2403).[6] Clearest is a volute krater now in New York with a long banquet couch behind the combatants (no women visible), who wield spits and cushions, among other items (NY 07.286.84). Lapith women also appear on the west pediment of the Temple of Zeus at Olympia (470–57 B.C.), where they form a prominent part of the struggle; none of the Lapith males has armor (although several wield small weapons), indicating again a banquet. Earlier than either vase-paintings or the sculptures will have been the Theseion in Athens, put up in the 470s and decorated with murals by Mikon and perhaps Polygnotos. Pausanias says only that one wall showed the battle of the Lapithai and the Kentauroi (1.17.2), but it has been plausibly argued that certain idiosyncrasies in some vase-paintings and the Olympia pediments point back to a common source, which may well have been this mural.[7] If that is so, the muralist might have been the first to introduce the idea of violence at the wedding in art. But surely Pindar's picturesque detail of milk pushed aside in favor of the more fragrant wine argues for an already developed literary tradition, although whether it is very much earlier than Pindar we cannot say. In the Olympia pediment two figures stand in the center back to back, with only Apollo (naturally not perceived by the combatants) between them; one of the two raises a sword, the other an axe. Pausanias supposed the two to be Kaineus and Theseus, but that was because he erroneously took the central figure to be Peirithoos (5.10.8). Once that error is corrected, it seems likely enough that we are meant to see Peirithoos and Theseus on either side of Apollo. The lack of weapons found here and elsewhere reappears in the metopes on the south flank of the Parthenon: women are portrayed as being carried off, the men are largely unarmed (two have shields), and several pieces of drinking equipment (such as cups and bowls) are shown. Some Red-Figure representations may also perhaps combine indoor and outdoor aspects of the conflict, as if the fight had started in the midst of the banquet and spilled over into the outdoors,[8] and possibly such depictions do spring from a genuine narrative tradition in which the combatants not unreasonably decide to step outside and settle their differences (as in Ovid: see below). But perhaps some artists took it upon themselves to conflate the wedding battle with the original pitched combat involving weapons, armor, pine trees, and boulders. That this latter version had not fallen completely out of favor is indicated by the west frieze of the Hephaisteion, where there are no women or drinking accoutrements, and at least some of the men are fully armed. In considering the likelihood of artistic innovation for dramatic effect we should remember too the frieze from the Temple of Apollo at Bassai, on which several of the women actually hold small children as they fend off the Kentauroi.

For the full story of the conflict, with Theseus present at Peirithoos' wedding, the Kentauroi becoming drunk and unruly, and the Lapithai defeating them in the ensuing battle, we must look to Diodoros, Ovid, and Plutarch; Apollodoros' account is, like everything else for this part of Theseus' career, only epitomized (ApE 1.21, conjectured from Zenobios). Plutarch's version, perhaps the most straightforward, has two battles, one on the spot at the wedding, the other a formal war (*Thes* 30.3). He notes, however, that Herodoros (end of the fifth century B.C.) does not quite agree with this, since he says that Theseus came to help the Lapithai after the hostilities had already started (31F27); we are left to wonder if for Herodoros those hostilities still began at a wedding, or in some other fashion. Isokrates seems to follow the same tradition in remarking that Theseus became an ally of the Lapithai and marched against the Kentauroi, who were in the process of sacking cities (10. *Helen* 26). Here, as in Homer, the emphasis seems to be on a long-term military conflict between Peirithoos and the Kentauroi, with Theseus like Nestor invited to participate only at an intermediate stage in the proceedings. Diodoros is our first source to specifically mention Peirithoos' wedding to Hippodameia as the cause of the trouble, even if it seems reasonable, as we have done, to suppose such an event implicit in the fragment of Pindar and the numerous artistic depictions of assaulted Lapith women (DS 4.70.3–4: this passage also makes the Kentauroi the victors, but something has happened to the text). On balance Peirithoos was surely the original hero of this tale, but whether his wedding always formed its initial stage is less clear; Eurytion's maltreatment in the *Odyssey* may well represent an early, simpler version of that idea. Either way, the notion of a definitive battle at (or immediately after) the wedding is probably a subsequent development, perhaps fostered by the desire of artists to show the entire story in one scene, and with Theseus of course present.

Not yet considered—partly to simplify discussion of the above questions—is the most striking feature of the actual combat, the overwhelming of the Lapith Kaineus. The story of his unusual demise—being hammered into the ground by the Kentauroi because he was invulnerable and could not otherwise be defeated—makes its preserved literary debut in Akousilaos (see below), but already on a bronze relief from Olympia of about 630 B.C. we find an unmistakable illustration: two Kentauroi (human type) pound an armed warrior down into the ground with tree trunks, while he stabs at them vainly with a sword in each hand (Olympia BE 11a). The François Krater shows the same scene as part of its Kentauromachy, with Kaineus here named and three Kentauroi using tree trunks and boulders; their victim now holds a shield and sword, and is already halfway into the ground. In early literature Homer's Nestor names Kaineus together with Peirithoos and three others (Dryas, Exadios, Polyphemos) as those who fought against the mountain beasts (*Il* 1.263–64), and the *Ehoiai* seems to have told the earlier part of his strange story, namely that he was originally Kainis, daughter of the Lapith king Elatos, and in this form forced by Poseidon (Hes fr 87 MW). The aftermath of the union is that Poseidon offers the girl whatever she may wish; she chooses to become male and invulnerable. We might suppose that this choice is made out of a desire not to repeat her unfortunate experience with other males (so in fact *Met* 12.201–3), but our summary of the *Ehoiai* offers no particular explanation. Akousilaos recounts these same events, save that in his version the girl is named Kaine, and she is converted to a man because it is not permitted that she (or he?: given the gender shift the pronouns are not quite clear here) have children (2F22). In addition to invulnerability, she/he also acquires great strength, and becomes the most powerful hero of his time, as well as king of the Lapithai. But having set up his spear, he does something (in later accounts worshipping it as a god, or ordering others to do so: ΣA *Il* 1.264; Σ AR 1.57) that angers the gods, and Zeus sends against him the Kentauroi, who beat him straight down under the earth and seal him in with a rock. A line of Pindar is here cited (= fr 128f SM), so that he mentioned at least Kaineus' fate, if not more. In any case, this sequence of events, plus Kaineus' kingship of the Lapithai, might lead us to suppose his story separate from the general battle of the Lapithai of Peirithoos with the Kentauroi; the Olympia relief for its part shows only his own combat. On the other hand, he is mentioned by Nestor as participating in the general war, so that if he was originally separate there has been an early move toward incorporation, and his fate is specifically linked to the overall battle as early as the François Krater. Not surprisingly, it is absent from the pediment at Olympia, where it would have spoiled the symmetry of the design. Subsequently it reappears on several temple friezes from the latter part of the century, those on the Hephaisteion, at Bassai, and at Sounion; for the Parthenon metopes with their more limited field it was probably too ambitious. Of later literary accounts the most vivid is certainly that of Ovid, who spends most of *Metamorphoses* 12 on a description of Kainis' transformation, the wedding, and the ensuing battle, with Kaineus' destruction forming the climax (*Met* 12.189–535). But there must after all be a metamorphosis with which to conclude, and thus from the mass of tree trunks piled over the body a yellow bird flies upward, surely a Hellenistic (if not Ovidian) inspiration.

In concluding this section we might note one other story found only in Plutarch: Peirithoos, hearing of Theseus' reputation for courage and great deeds, decides to make a test of him by driving off certain cattle of his at Marathon (*Thes* 30.1). When Theseus comes after him he turns back and meets his pursuer face to face, offering to pay for his act with whatever penalty Theseus may deem appropriate. Theseus is, of course, charmed by this gesture, and they become fast friends. The method of bringing these heroes together seems probable enough as an early tale, and we noted before that the link between them surfaces as early as the Olympia shield-bands. In any case, whatever the antiquity of this particular story, it represents the only preserved attempt to explain the origin of their friendship.

The Abduction of Antiope
Theseus' fondness for women is well documented in our sources. We have seen that the Hesiodic Corpus makes him abandon Ariadne for one Aigle, daughter of Panopeus, and mentions as well a Hippe; to these we should perhaps add from Istros (334F10) and Plutarch (*Thes* 29.1) the daughters of Sinis and Kerkyon. There is also at times the notion of a union between Theseus and Eriboia (or Periboia, or Meliboia) the future mother of Aias, to say nothing of Anaxo, or of Iope, daughter of Iphikles (*Thes* 29.1–2). But these latter names have no early backing, and in any case we have no further details whatever. Matters are different when we turn to the tale of Theseus' Amazon queen, Antiope as she is named in our earliest accounts, Hippolyte in some later ones. In literature the first appearance of the story is in Pindar and Pherekydes, and Simonides must also have referred to it, since Apollodoros tells us that he called the queen Hippolyte (ApE 1.16). One possible artistic representation is as early as 600 B.C.: on a tripod leg from Olympia a man wrestles with a woman while another female (Aphrodite?) looks on (M 77).[9] In any case, by about 520 B.C. the scene of the abduction is certainly found on vase-painting, and it seems to have formed the subject matter of the west pediment of the Temple of Apollo in Eretria, to be dated to perhaps 515.[10] The vase-paintings include both late Black- and early Red-Figure (Oltos, Myson), and generally show Theseus running with the Amazon toward a chariot, or else already with her in the chariot. On four occasions Theseus and Antiope are specifically named, and on three of these one of the helpers is Peirithoos (London E41; Louvre G197; NY 12.198.3; the fourth is Munich 1414). That Peirithoos accompanies Theseus on this venture is also attested by Pindar (fr 175 SM), and so was probably a standard part of the story. Why Pindar should, however, make Demophon the child of Theseus and Antiope is less clear (fr 176 SM: Plutarch, our source, certainly understood Demophon as an *alternative* to Hippolytos, but perhaps he read more into Pindar's words than was meant [*Thes* 28.2]). Of Pherekydes' account we are told by Plutarch that here, as in Hellanikos, Theseus made an independent expedition, and took the Amazon as a spear-captive (*Thes* 26.1 = 3F151), much as the vase-paintings would suggest. By contrast, Plutarch adds, Philochoros has him sail with Herakles and win Antiope on that occasion (i.e., when the latter sets out to acquire an Amazon *zôstêr*: 328F110). The idea of a joint expedition also occurs in Pausanias, who credits it to the uncertain Hegias of Troizen (1.2.1).[11] In this account, however, we find quite a different course of events: Herakles has besieged Themiskyra but is unable to capture it until

Antiope falls in love with Theseus and surrenders. Apart from this reference, Isokrates (12.*Panath* 3193) is the earliest source to cite love as the motive for her transfer to Athens. Closer to Philochoros' notion of a shared venture in which the Amazon is Theseus' prize is the version of Hyginus, for whom Hippolyte is the queen and Antiope some other Amazon given to Theseus (*Fab* 30), and apparently that of Euripides (*Hkld* 215–17). It must be noted, however, that nowhere in the numerous early illustrations of Herakles' combat with the Amazones is Theseus ever shown. Sophokles' *Phaidra* or Euripides' first *Hippolytos* might have offered further information on these matters, but there are no relevant remains, and the latter's preserved *Hippolytos* is no help at all, failing as it does to even name Hippolytos' mother as anything but "the Amazon." When Theseus is not a companion of Herakles we have no real explanation of the purpose of his venture, and whether the Amazones were the original goal of it, or just a happenstance.

As for the Amazon's name, we have seen that in late sixth-century vase-painting she is uniformly "Antiope," and probably so too in Pindar, since Plutarch, who mentions Pindar's unusual name for the son, would surely have noted one for the mother (he himself uses "Antiope"). "Antiope" is likewise the name in Diodoros (4.28.1: he reports both but uses "Antiope"), Pausanias (1.2.1), and Hyginus (*Fab* 30, 241). But we also found "Hippolyte" as the preferred form in Simonides, and he is followed by Isokrates (12.*Panath* 193) and Kleidemos (323F18). Pausanias shrewdly suggests as a way of resolving the conflict that the two might have been sisters (1.41.7), but Apollodoros adds yet another possibility, the name "Melanippe" (ApE 1.16). To complicate matters further in deciding the name of the mother, there is the question of Theseus' sons. Epic tradition outside the *Iliad* knew of two of these who came to Troy with the Achaians; one the *Little Iliad* names as Demophon (fr 20 *PEG*), while the other surfaces in the *Chrestomathia* account of the *Ilioupersis* as Akamas. These will go on to rescue their grandmother Aithra at Troy and have various other adventures. But not until the time of Apollodoros are they specifically named as the children of Theseus and *Phaidra* (ApE 1.18, although of course Phaidra does have [unnamed] children in Euripides' *Hippolytos*), and we have meanwhile seen that for Pindar Demophon at least is a child of Theseus and Antiope. Hippolytos, remarkably enough, is mentioned only once before Sophokles and Euripides, as the beneficiary of Asklepios' skills in the (sixth-century?) epic *Naupaktia* (fr 10 *PEG*); thus Euripides is actually our first evidence for his mother as an Amazon. Under these circumstances we should not be surprised if there has been some shifting around of children from earlier times, or that in the beginning there was no fixed tradition of mothers. Even the idea that Theseus' Amazon was the original mother of Hippolytos has been questioned, with Hippolyte on this reasoning a name supplanting that of Antiope for greater plausibility after said Amazon had been imported into Athenian genealogy.[12] Conceivably too (following Pindar's lead) Demophon and Akamas belonged to Antiope (or someone else) in an older tradition, and were transferred to Phaidra at a later point.[13] That the *Ehoiai*'s arrangement of wives and children survives on none of these points is truly unfortunate. As a result, all we can really say for certain is that by the end of the sixth century there is a tale in which Theseus carries off an Amazon (probably in origin Antiope) by force, and that Peirithoos assists him.

The abduction is, of course, not the end of the matter; the Amazones repay the favor of Theseus' visit to their country and come to Athens. Their assault on the city was depicted in the paintings of the Theseion and those (by Mikon) of the Stoa Poikile (Paus 1.17.2; Σ Ar:*Lys* 679); possibly too on the metopes of the Athenian Treasury at Delphi (no #) and the west façade of the Parthenon, and certainly on the outer surface of the shield of Pheidias' Athena Parthenos (*Per* 31.4). In literature we have a clear reference from Aischylos' *Eumenides* of 458 B.C., in which we are told that the Areopagos is so named because the Amazones sacrificed to Ares there when they used that rock as a base from which to besiege the Akropolis (*Eum* 685–90). Athena says that they carried out this attack because of a grudge against Theseus, but we are left to guess (or already know) what the grudge was. Earlier than the fifth century there are no certain illustrations of the story; Black-Figure Amazonomachies generally seem to show rather the combat with Herakles, or that between Achilleus and Penthesileia.[14] Nevertheless, the tale would seem to go back into the sixth, for aside from Simonides on Hippolyte's name and the love motif in "Hegias" we have Plutarch's claim that the story formed part of the epic *Theseis* (*Thes* 28.1–2). But here matters took quite a remarkable turn, if Plutarch can be trusted: Antiope and the Amazones together attack Athens when Theseus is preparing to marry Phaidra. Judging by the participle modifying their actions (the verb *amunomai*, usually "defend oneself" but also "avenge oneself"), Theseus has thrown over Antiope in order to marry Phaidra, with the Amazon feeling herself insulted by such treatment; thus we would have a second reference in epic to her love for Theseus as a crucial theme of the story. A similar picture is offered by Apollodoros, who relates that she attempted to disrupt the wedding of Theseus and Phaidra and was killed then, or else slain by Theseus in battle (ApE 1.17).

From the fifth century, other than the previously mentioned allusion in the *Eumenides*, there is nothing literary. Isokrates in the following century mentions, as we saw, Antiope's love for Theseus, and adds what we would expect, that her betrayal of the Amazones' laws motivated their expedition against Athens (12.193). But though he mentions the Athenian victory often enough in his speeches, he says nothing of Antiope's fate. Nor is it clear whether in any account the Amazones came to rescue rather than punish her, and whether she ever desired to return to her former life. Diodoros comes close to this idea in conveying the Amazones' opinion that Theseus had enslaved her, but then we learn (here for the first time) that she fell in battle fighting bravely at the side of Theseus (4.28.1–4). Plutarch and Pausanias also know this story, and add that she was slain by Molpadia, one of the Amazones, as she and

Theseus fought against them (*Thes* 27.4; Paus 1.2.1). At the same time, however, Plutarch cites Kleidemos for another version in which Antiope (or rather,
Hippolyte, but certainly the wife of Theseus) mediates a resolution of the conflict between the two sides. Unfortunately, we do not learn the terms of the
resolution, that is, whether Hippolyte remained with Theseus or returned to
the Amazones. On the Roman side there is yet another possibility: in Phaidra's
letter in Ovid's *Heroides* she notes that Theseus slew the Amazon (no name
given) with his own hand, although she was the mother of Hippolytos (*Her*
4.119–20); the accusatory context probably removes any possibility that she
means slain in battle. The reference also seems too brief to be Ovid's invention,
and it appears too in Hyginus, where we are told that Theseus killed his wife
Antiope in response to an oracle from Apollo (*Fab* 241). One wonders if her
death could have been necessary to save Athens.

Turning from the literary evidence back to fifth-century art, we receive
no help from descriptions of the lost large-scale versions of the battle, but there
is a series of Red-Figure depictions, beginning about 460 B.C., and these probably derive in some measure from the mural paintings of the Theseion and the
Stoa Poikile.[15] They show various aspects of the combat, with Theseus specifically named thirteen times, Peirithoos two, Antiope four, and Hippolyte five.[16]
Yet in none of these illustrations is there any sign of either Amazon fighting
side by side with Theseus, and although over sixty different Amazones are
named on these pots, there is no sign of Molpadia. In support of the Hegias/
Isokrates version of an Antiope enamored of Theseus, it should be said that
there are several vases on which an unnamed Amazon might be helping Greeks
against the Amazones. On the other side of the coin, Hippolyte is four times
and Antiope twice shown fighting against Theseus (e.g., Boston 95.48 [Hip-
polyte]; Ferrara 2890 [Antiope]): such a confrontation would seem to reflect
the version of the *Theseis* and Apollodoros in which the jilted queen leads the
attack against Theseus and the Athenians. But not impossibly the paintings
with Hippolyte supposed Antiope to be the abductee, and those with Antiope
the reverse, so that in each case Theseus does battle with the successor of the
Amazon he carried off; in five other cases, different names altogether are used.
Whatever we decide, all versions of the story must of course find some way to
eliminate the abductee so that Theseus may marry Phaidra, and we have seen
numerous methods of accomplishing this: she is slain fighting with Theseus,
slain fighting against him, slain on Apollo's advice, and perhaps even returned
to her own people.

Phaidra and   That Theseus should come to marry Phaidra after his treatment of Ariadne
Hippolytos   certainly seems strange, and has the look of a political union fostered by Athenian mythographers. One might wonder too if she was always Minos' daugh-
ter. Before the tragedies of Sophokles and Euripides she surfaces only once, in
a single line of the *Nekuia*, where she is simply named together with Prokris
and Ariadne (*Od* 11.321). That she is named at all by Odysseus means of

course that the audience was expected to know some story about her, and her mention in the same line with Ariadne may well denote that they are already sisters. On the other hand, the Athenian Prokris rather oddly intervenes between the two, and paves the way for the suspicion that the whole line (or perhaps the whole five lines at *Od* 11.321–25 with their tale of Ariadne) is an Athenian interpolation of the sixth century. But, as noted before in considering Ariadne, the time difference between the *Nekuia* and such interpolations is not likely to be great, and the interpolations may themselves represent reasonably old traditions. In the case of Phaidra, we have too some additional evidence from Plutarch who, after noting the discrepancy between the *Theseis* and other traditions as to the battle with the Amazones, says that regarding the misfortunes of Phaidra and Hippolytos there is no such conflict between historians and tragic poets (*Thes* 28.2). While the assurance that Sophokles and Euripides offer us a more-or-less canonical version of the story is certainly welcome, Plutarch's words might also be taken to suggest that he did not find the story of Phaidra in the *Theseis* or any other epic.

As to what we do have, we know that Sophokles wrote a *Phaidra*, and Euripides two dramas entitled *Hippolytos*, the second a rewrite of the same events presented in the (apparently quite poorly received) first. Of the three, only the *Hippolytos II*, produced in 428 B.C., survives; the *Hippolytos I* was presumably offered just a few years earlier. For Sophokles' *Phaidra* there is no evidence at all as to date; it may have been written before, between, or even after Euripides' two plays. The hypothesis to the surviving play and various other references establish that the Phaidra of *Hippolytos I* was a shameless woman very much on the model of Stheneboia or Akastos' wife or Amyntor's concubine (all women whose stories were, we think, dramatized by Euripides in the 430s B.C.).[17] We have as well a summary taken from one or more tragedians by the fourth-century Asklepiades (12F28), and a Latin version by Seneca (called both *Phaedra* and *Hippolytus*) which, since it follows the above characterization of Phaidra rather than the one we find in *Hippolytos II*, no doubt draws from *Phaidra* or *Hippolytos I* or both.

Presumably, in the traditional form of the story Phaidra was very much the villain, seeking to engage in an adulterous affair with her own stepson behind her husband's back, and propositioning him in her own person for that purpose, as she does in Seneca. As such, her behavior is even more culpable than that of Stheneboia and Astydameia, since both of these select houseguests rather than stepsons as the object of their passion. From the evidence of Asklepiades and Seneca we may suppose that when her proposition is rejected she goes to Theseus personally and lodges a charge of rape by Hippolytos; in Seneca she offers as evidence the sword that Hippolytos first drew to keep her away, then dropped in horror. Theseus calls upon Poseidon to destroy his son, and in answer a bull comes out of the sea as Hippolytos is driving along the coast; his horses bolt, and he himself is dragged to his death. In Asklepiades Phaidra's slander is finally discovered and she hangs herself; in Seneca she repents when she sees Hippolytos' mangled body, clears his name to Theseus, and falls upon a sword. Obviously, such a tale differs from those of Stheneboia and Astydameia also in the fact that here the hero is overcome by the machinations of the lecherous wife; thus his vengeance must come by some other means than his own hand. In his *Nekuia* for the Knidian Lesche at Delphi, Polygnotos painted among other mythological figures a Phaidra seated in a swing; Pausanias, our source for the scene, assumed this to be an allusion to her suicide by hanging, and he may well be right (10.29.3).

Of Sophokles' play in particular we know only that in its course Theseus comes back from Hades, having been thought dead by those he left behind in Athens (frr 686, 687 R). Seneca also uses this idea, and its effect is surely to exonerate Phaidra somewhat; since she believes her husband deceased, her passion for Hippolytos no longer constitutes adultery, and might even be seen as a form of devotion to Theseus. There are as well brief fragments mentioning the necessity of enduring god-sent diseases and the overwhelming power of love (frr 680, 684 R). These might conceivably prefigure or reflect Euripides' treatment of the passion, but they may also be simply rationalizations of her own behavior by Phaidra (or by the nurse); what changes the situation in *Hippolytos II* is the presence of Aphrodite to assure us that Phaidra is indeed in the grip of a higher power. But at least we can assume that Sophokles offers some softening of her character; quite possibly her repentance in Seneca's version is drawn from this play.

For Euripides' *Hippolytos I*, beyond what it presumably shared with Sophokles' version as outlined by Asklepiades above, we have only the obvious fact that it differed in significant ways from his *Hippolytos II*. The revised version features a number of subtle innovations designed, without changing the basic facts of the situation, to alter our response to them. Phaidra's passion is now a genuine sickness, as guaranteed by Aphrodite, and one against which she cannot hope to fight; she is already at the play's opening doomed to be a helpless victim of the goddess' vengeance against Hippolytos. Theseus' son is here characterized as totally chaste, not just abhorrent of union with his stepmother, and thus in conflict with the laws of Aphrodite. Whether he was so presented in the other plays, or in the earlier tradition, we cannot say, although aspects of his cult at Troizen (maidens dedicating locks of hair to him) would seem to indicate that this was the case. Even so, perpetual chastity is not always viewed as an affront to Aphrodite, and we cannot be sure how Hippolytos would have been characterized by other authors (or even by the *Hippolytos I*). But certainly in this play he is judged harshly for his intolerance of women, while Phaidra struggles vainly with the passion she knows will bring disgrace upon herself and her children. Ultimately she resolves to die, and the nurse in order to avoid this acts as go-between without her mistress' knowledge. The outrage of Hippolytos' response is all the more unfortunate because the target of it is essentially innocent; when he adds the suggestion (probably overheard by Phaidra) that he will reveal all to Theseus, we may well feel that she must defend herself. Her slander is perhaps no less excusable, but at least in this play it is undertaken only to protect her children; she herself confides the accusation to a note and commits suicide immediately. The remainder of the play follows the usual course: Hippolytos does not after all violate his oath of secrecy, receives Theseus' curse in person, and leaves Troizen, only to be killed in the wreckage of his chariot after the bull appears. One curious point in the final scenes is the means by which Theseus pronounces his curse: rather than simply call upon the gods for justice (as parents so often do), he appeals to Poseidon to fulfill a promise that he would have from that god three wishes (*Hipp* 887–90). It seems that Euripides wishes him to be uncertain of the validity of this promise, and thus the wish in question is the first. The scholiast to the passage thinks of it as the third, but his suggestion—that Theseus used one wish to escape from Hades and another to emerge from the Labyrinth—is inherently improbable in itself (what roles need Ariadne and Herakles play if Theseus can simply wish himself out of danger?) and not confirmed by any other source; most likely he is guessing. We might presume that Euripides' retention of three wishes when only one is here needed means that the number three was traditional, and possibly Theseus used one such wish to find his way down to Poseidon on his way to Krete. But more likely, the three wishes are a stock formula of which only the third (or in this case the first) is ever used in an actual situation.[18]

Somewhat surprisingly, there seem to be no preserved artistic representations of any part of the story before the fourth century, and even then nothing that varies at all from the literary tradition already established. The same consistency is to be found in later writers, as we perhaps should have expected after Plutarch's remarks. Remembering from the opening of this section that Hippolytos is named in the epic *Naupaktia* as the deceased brought back to life by Asklepios, it would be interesting to know whether Archaic narratives regarded him as unfairly destroyed and hence meriting this resurrection. Certainly such was the view of later writers, who usually include Hippolytos in their list of possible candidates raised by Asklepios; in Ovid he is healed rather by Paion, taken to Italy, and becomes Virbius, the twice-born (*Met* 15.497–546).

The Abduction of Helen

Theseus' carrying off of Helen (with the aid of Peirithoos) and his consequent assistance to Peirithoos in the attempt to abduct Persephone are obviously closely related events, and in any systematized chronology must occur either before or after their respective marriages (although we have seen that Sophokles blurs this point in his timing of the descent to Hades). The simplest solution is to put both events after Peirithoos' marriage to Hippodameia (and that of Theseus to Phaidra), and this seems borne out by our one preserved fragment from a poem on the descent (probably either the *Minyas* or the Hesiodic account: see below) in which Meleagros asks Theseus if Hippodameia (or Deidameia: beginning of line lost) is not still married to Peirithoos (Hes fr 280

MW). Likewise Hellanikos, according to Plutarch, makes Theseus fifty years of age at the time of the taking of Helen (4F168a). Her abduction is not mentioned by Homer, but in *Iliad* 3 we see that she is accompanied by Aithra, daughter of Pittheus, as a servant (*Il* 3.143–44), which can scarcely be the consequence of anything but the story we know. From Pausanias we learn that Alkman, Stesichoros, and Pindar all treated the exploit, although we cannot say in how much detail. Alkman clearly narrated at least the aftermath, in which Kastor and Polydeukes come to Athens (or Aphidna), capture the city, and take back with them the mother of Theseus as well as Helen, Theseus himself being away at the time (21 *PMG*). According to the *Iliad* scholia that are the source on this point, some part of the Cycle (or the *Polemonia?*) told the same story, with Kastor being wounded in the thigh by Aphidnos, the local king (although this detail may also have been found in Alkman: ΣA *Il* 3.242). From Pausanias we learn that in Stesichoros Helen gives birth to a child by Theseus, Iphigeneia, the same girl usually thought to be the daughter of Agamemnon and Klytaimestra (191 *PMG*). Pindar completes the picture from our Archaic sources by suggesting that Theseus' motive for the abduction was the desire to be a relation by marriage to the Dioskouroi (fr 258 SM).

Later authors generally confirm and amplify this narrative, save for the parentage of Iphigeneia, but even this detail does have its supporters, including the fourth/third-century Douris of Samos and others (see below). We must admit, though, that it is contradicted by the usual notion of Helen's age at the time of the abduction. According to Hellanikos, Theseus and Peirithoos both wish to marry daughters of Zeus (4F134). They therefore carry off the seven-year-old Helen (4F168b) and leave her in the village of Aphidna with Theseus' mother Aithra while they go down into Hades to get Persephone. In their absence the Dioskouroi come and, not receiving back their sister, sack Attika and take Aithra prisoner. Herodotos also notes the expedition of the Dioskouroi into Attika to recover Helen, with the added detail that the men of Dekeleia directed them to Aphidna (9.73.2), and Isokrates refers to the abduction briefly as a further credit to Helen's beauty (10. *Helen* 18–19). But once again our first full account is that of Diodoros (4.63.1–3). As he tells the story, Peirithoos' wife has died, and he comes to Athens only to find that Theseus is in the same situation. Accordingly he suggests that they should carry off Helen (now ten years of age). This done, they agree to cast lots to determine who will marry her, with the winner helping the loser to secure another wife of his choosing. After Theseus has won the draw, Peirithoos decides upon Persephone. Theseus cannot dissuade him and so, leaving Helen with Aithra in Aphidna, they make the attempt. In their absence the Dioskouroi raze Aphidna, recover Helen (still a virgin), and take Aithra back to Sparta as a slave. Plutarch has much the same tale, including the allotment, and much additional aetiological material relating to the reception of the Dioskouroi in Athens (*Thes* 31–34). But he also knows of some major variants which he himself supposes were designed to exonerate Theseus: in one of these the Athenian king receives Helen (presumably for safekeeping) from Idas and Lynkeus, who are the ones responsible for the abduction; in another Tyndareos himself hides her with Theseus in order to protect her from the sons of Hippokoon. But most incredible, as he says, is the story reported by Istros, that Hektor carried Aithra off to Troy after a raid on Troizen (334F7). Apollodoros, though his account of the abduction is contained in the preserved part of the *Bibliotheke* (in the story of Helen), gives only the barest details (Ap*B* 3.10.7); Hyginus says that Zeus, marveling at the audacity of the two heroes, ordered them both in a dream to seek Persephone as a wife for Peirithoos (*Fab* 79: his motive for this strange act is not made clear). This latter author reports too that the Dioskouroi carried off on their raid not only Aithra, but also a sister of Peirithoos, one Phisadie or Thisadie, who likewise went to Troy (*Fab* 79, 92).

In art we have a few certain representations of the story, but not many, and only in one case is there any possibility of new information. Pausanias claims to have seen the tale on both the Throne of Amyklai and the Chest of Kypselos. At Amyklai the abduction itself, with Peirithoos, Theseus, and Helen, was represented (3.18.15); at Olympia the scene was rather that of the rescue, with the Dioskouroi (one of them beardless), Helen between them, and Aithra thrown down at Helen's feet (5.19.2–3). Earlier there are several scenes of abductions of some sort on vases which might conceivably depict our story. A particularly likely candidate is a Protocorinthian aryballos in the Louvre (CA 617): a woman faces left with both arms raised; behind her a warrior with spear seizes her by the wrist while another warrior behind him brandishes a sword.[19] To the left are two horsemen riding toward her, quite possibly the Dioskouroi coming to the rescue in a pardonable compression of the tale. A similar scene is shown on a bronze cuirass from Olympia of about the same date, *c*. 670 B.C. (M 397). Two warriors on the left are balanced by two on the right, with an elegantly dressed woman wearing a polos in the middle. The nearest warrior on each side grasps her by the hand or wrist, but she looks toward the two on the left, so that these would presumably be the Dioskouroi. Several different patterns on shield-bands from Olympia have also been interpreted as Theseus (with or without Peirithoos) leading off Helen, but there are obviously other possibilities as well.[20] Certain, on the other hand, is an early Red-Figure amphora by Euthymides, but it also poses a problem; Theseus (so named here) lifts up a woman to carry her off, while another woman running in from the left reaches out to restrain him and Peirithoos acts as rear guard (Munich 2309: two other women are rushing up on the reverse side). So far, so good, but the abducted woman is inscribed as Korone, and the one trying to help her as Helen. Possibly we are meant to suppose that when Helen refused to go with Theseus, he threatened to take her companion instead. Alternatively, the artist may have accidentally exchanged the names[21] (perhaps an assistant put these in) or intended some sort of contemporary joke or allusion that is lost to us.[22] Of later illustrations of this tale the one of real interest for our purposes is a Megarian bowl on which Theseus and Peirithoos bring Helen to Athens

(Athens 2104).[23] Inscriptions identify all the figures, but they also tell us that Theseus took Helen to Korinth first, then to Athens; the reasons for such a stopover are completely unknown. In addition to scenes of Helen's abduction, art also offers depictions, certainly as early as Myson and perhaps also in late Black-Figure, of Aithra being rescued at Troy; these will be discussed together with the rest of that story in chapter 16.

Before concluding this section it may be well to consider more closely Stesichoros' unusual idea that Iphigeneia was the daughter of Theseus and Helen. Homer avoids all mention of this child in any context, unless (which I strongly doubt) she is the same as the Iphianassa of *Iliad* 9. But certainly she is known to both the *Kypria* and the *Ehoiai* as the girl sacrificed at Aulis to aid Agamemnon's expedition, and the latter of these works calls her specifically the child of Agamemnon and Klytaimestra (Hes fr 23a MW). Indeed, one is hard put to imagine any other parentage in the context of this story, for if Iphigeneia is not Agamemnon's real daughter, then Artemis' demand for her death will surely lose much of its impact. Pausanias, our source for Stesichoros, adds as supporters of his version the names of Euphorion and Alexandros Aitolos (2.22.6). In the same passage, having established for these three writers Theseus and Helen as the parents, he goes on to relate that Helen bore the child at Argos on the way back to Sparta, and that she gave her to Klytaimestra, who was already married to Agamemnon. Obviously this last detail is necessary if Iphigeneia is ever to get to Aulis, and it may well go back to Stesichoros. But even so it seems unlikely that an adopted daughter would be demanded for sacrifice when Agamemnon has flesh-and-blood offspring; surely Iphigeneia was counted among those real offspring when she was originally chosen for such a fate. That Agamemnon is indeed married to Klytaimestra at the time of Helen's wooing is, by the way, the situation already in the *Ehoiai* (Hes fr 197.4–5 MW). Douris of Samos also seems to have adhered to Stesichoros' view in later times (76F92), while Lykophron, speaking at one point of Helen's marriage to Theseus (Lyk 143–47) and at another of her *two* daughters (Lyk 102–3), may allude to the same idea.

The Descent into Hades   Whether or not the taking of Helen always led to or motivated the mad attempt to go down into Hades and carry off Persephone, this latter story is among our earliest attested examples of a Theseus exploit. In fact, if Odysseus' previously noted desire to see Theseus and Peirithoos is a genuine part of the *Nekuia* (*Od* 11.630–31),[24] their descent would be a familiar element in the epic tradition, albeit not quite Homeric. Strictly speaking, too, if by anyone's reckoning they are still in the Underworld in Odysseus' time (i.e., after Herakles' death), then they must be supposed to sit there forever; perhaps that is to push a casual reference (or interpolation) too far, perhaps not. Whatever the date of this passage, and the truth of that conception, there is elsewhere ample evidence of at least a seventh- or early sixth-century date for the journey to Hades. We have already seen in chapter 3 that the epic *Minyas* mentioned by Pausanias puts Theseus and Peirithoos on the banks of the Styx (or Acheron), waiting for Charon and his boat, and thus probably described their entire mission (10.28.2). Pausanias also cites a poem about the descent of Theseus and Peirithoos in his list of works by Hesiod, presumably therefore a poem distinct from the *Minyas* (9.31.5). To one of these two poems, surely, belongs a papyrus fragment in epic hexameters from the collection of Hugo Ibscher in which Theseus explains the purpose of the descent to the shade of Meleagros (Hes fr 280 MW). There are gaps as usual, but we do have the whole run of the speech, which occupies fourteen (or perhaps fifteen) lines; the motive (seemingly the only one) it offers is that Peirithoos believes that Zeus will approve a union between himself and Persephone because both have Zeus as a father, and because Peirithoos as a half-brother is closer in kinship to the prospective bride than her present husband Hades, who is only her uncle. Meleagros shudders at this line of reasoning, as well he might, and asks if Peirithoos is not already married. Here the papyrus breaks off; probably Theseus related the death of his friend's previous wife, although perhaps too Peirithoos put her aside as unworthy of a son of Zeus. Throughout the explanation the notion of such a marriage is attributed strictly to Peirithoos, as if Theseus meant to disavow anything more than his reluctant acquiescence.

More firmly datable than either of these shadowy epics is a shield-band relief from Olympia of about 560 B.C. (B 2198). Here two figures labeled "Theseus" and "Peirithoos" sit together on a chair, hands held out in supplication, while a third figure approaches and prepares to draw his sword. The name is worn away, but this is certainly Herakles. What is less clear is whether he draws his sword to confront Hades by force as he prepares to rescue his friends, or imagines that he can cut them free with it, or wields it merely because the artist wished to add this embellishment to an otherwise static scene. Neither can we be sure that he succeeded in rescuing both heroes, although the artist's failure to distinguish between them might be thought to imply that result.[25] Herakles' clear entry into the story at this early point may also prompt us to wonder if the rescue of Theseus did not play a role in Stesichoros' utterly lost *Kerberos*, and if so, how much that poet might have contributed toward the formation of such a version. The story is disappointingly absent from the rest of the sixth century, and does not reappear until Polygnotos' *Nekuia* painting for the Knidian Lesche at Delphi. As Pausanias describes the scene, both Theseus and Peirithoos sit upon chairs, and Theseus holds his sword and that of Peirithoos while Peirithoos looks at them (10.29.9). Pausanias supposes that Peirithoos is angry about the uselessness of the swords, but such a interpretation seems strained and would not in any case explain why Theseus must hold both swords. More likely the painting refers to some means by which Hades tricked or captured the two, though I cannot guess what. Pausanias also cites the fifth-century epic poet Panyasis to the effect that no chains hold the heroes to their thrones (as apparently in other accounts), but rather that the rock (a stone bench?) attached itself to their flesh (fr 14 *PEG*). From later in the century we have Hellanikos, who as we saw before assigns to both Theseus and Peirithoos a desire to marry daughters of Zeus; as a consequence, he says, they go down to Hades, but our summary of his account does not tell how he handled their fate (4F134). In Euripides' *Herakles* Theseus mentions in passing that Herakles saved him from Hades, and this is the first preserved literary reference to a rescue (*HF* 1169–70). The same poet treated the story in much greater detail in the lost *Peirithoos*, if that play is in fact his; Athenaios (who observes that the author may be Euripides or Kritias: 11.496b) and the Euripidean *Vita* express doubts. Modern opinion remains quite divided on the matter, but for our purposes the date will be the same in any case.[26] Byzantine commentators tell us that in this play Peirithoos sits on a rocky seat guarded by snakes, that Theseus accepts a life in Hades because he believes it shameful to abandon his friend, and that both Theseus and Peirithoos are released (this last from Tzetzes: pp. 546–47 N²). Seemingly then Theseus is not bound, but feels the need to remain in the Underworld anyway (cf. *Mor* 96c = 43 fr 6 Sn). A new papyrus fragment adds the beginning of Peirithoos' first speech to Herakles, and *may* suggest that he emerges from a stupor of some sort (POxy 3531).[27] Theseus' voluntary residence in Hades finds no echo in later sources;[28] we will see below, however, that both stupor (if this is correct) and dual release are of importance.

Later sources are clearer on the means by which the two men were imprisoned. In one of his *Odes* Horace notes that "three hundred chains restrain the lover Peirithoos" (3.4.79–80) but in another we find that Theseus "was not able to break the Lethaean chains from his friend Peirithoos" (4.7.27–28); Apollodoros resolves the cryptic aspect of this latter picture by speaking of a "chair of forgetfulness" upon which Hades invites the heroes to sit (Ap*E* 1.24). But he seems uncomfortable with just this explanation, for immediately after in the same sentence the chair attaches itself to them and snakes bind them fast; thus we have all three versions of their confinement. Whether this motif of forgetfulness could go back to the Attic drama discussed above is harder to say; certainly there Peirithoos is in some sort of mental confusion, but one does not immediately see why he should emerge from it on Herakles' arrival, the more so as a conscious Theseus has long been present. Artistic representations of the mid-fifth century further intensify this uncertainty, as we will see below. Regarding the Olympia shield-band, no bonds are visible; it might be argued that the gesture of the two heroes reaching out to Herakles presupposes memory, but that line of logic probably imposes too great a restriction on the artistic need to convey the essence of their predicament.

In vase-painting we find nothing until the middle of the century, when a lekythos by the Alkimachos Painter now in Berlin shows us Herakles reaching out to grasp the hand of a bearded man in traveler's cloak and petasos seated on a rock and holding two spears (Berlin:PM Inv 30035). In this time period, Theseus is usually beardless, and since two other slightly later representations offer the same figure in the same dress with the inscription "Peirithoos," it seems clear that the latter must be intended here as well. He has in any case a somewhat blank expression, or at least a look directed straight ahead rather than up toward Herakles' face. Of the other representations just mentioned, one, a cup in Boston, has Peirithoos alone in the tondo sitting in a chair, his head slumped down, seemingly lost in thought (Boston 99.539). The other, a calyx krater in New York, presents all three figures—Peirithoos and Theseus sitting peacefully on their rock, Herakles alongside but not engaged in any action (NY 08.258.21).[29] Such evidence can, and has been, interpreted in opposite ways. Peirithoos all by himself on the Boston cup might suggest that he is thought to remain in his chair for all time, or only the isolation of his predicament (given that he is after all the real transgressor). For the Berlin lekythos, on the other hand, we must ask why a release of Peirithoos would not include Theseus as well, and hence whether (despite appearances) Herakles' gesture might be one of farewell to a hero he cannot save.[30] The New York krater flanks the three heroes with Hades (to the left of Peirithoos) and Hermes (to the right of Herakles); the obvious assumption, unless a different version of the story was firmly entrenched, is that Herakles will secure Hades' permission and release both men. As for the means of imprisonment, on these pieces too there are no signs of bonds, so that, unless they are invisible, we are left to choose between Panyasis' clinging rock and Horace's chair of forgetfulness. Both cup and lekythos do, as we saw, give Peirithoos a certain blank or unaware quality that might justify assigning the idea of forgetfulness (or something close to it) to a point this early. In support of that interpretation we might also cite the casualness of Herakles' gesture on the lekythos, since he would need only to lift the unbound Peirithoos from the rock/chair in order to free him. But this is very much a guess, and presumes that a release is meant. Conceivably at one time the rock was associated with being stuck fast, and the chair with forgetfulness; our surviving evidence does not, however, do much to support this idea. In the earliest versions of the tale, perhaps, neither clinging rock nor bonds nor forgetfulness was necessary to hold the heroes in their prison, but only the will of the lord of the Underworld.

Following the fifth century we have a number of South Italian pots, several of which show bonds and snakes,[31] and one Apulian volute krater in particular which clearly depicts Peirithoos left behind as Herakles and Theseus depart (Naples Stg 709), our first certain evidence for this version. In Isokrates we read that Theseus was grateful to Peirithoos for helping him acquire Helen and thus ready to do anything in return (10. *Helen* 20), but there are no other sources until Diodoros. In his account we have already seen that Theseus and Peirithoos draw lots for Helen, and that Peirithoos as the loser then chooses to seek Persephone, with Theseus forced to follow (4.63.4–5). Of their imprisonment we are told only that because of their impiety they are bound; subsequently Theseus is released because of the good will of Herakles, but Peirithoos remains bound forever. Yet even on this point Diodoros is not entirely sure, for earlier in Book 4 he has said that Herakles by the good will of Persephone brings both men back from the Underworld, and he also cites unnamed sources for a version in which neither of the two return (4.26.1). Apollodoros, who is the first to state that Hades by a pretense of friendship tricked the heroes into taking their places on the chair, agrees that Herakles took back Theseus but not Peirithoos (Ap*E* 1.24, as above, and cf. Ap*B* 2.5.12, where the two stretch out their hands as at Olympia; here again Herakles rescues Theseus, but the earth quakes when he reaches for Peirithoos and he desists). In Hyginus, where they are tormented by Furies, both are rescued (*Fab* 79). Book 6 of the *Aeneid*, on the other hand, has both Theseus and Peirithoos still in Tartaros when Aineias arrives (*Aen* 6.610, 617–18), but Vergil's purpose here (transgressors as an object lesson) is an incentive to find room for as many people as possible. We saw above too that this is the reading of the *Nekuia* passage as we have it, and quite possibly the *Aeneid* reference is modeled after that. But whether there was in fact ever a serious early tradition in which Theseus as well as Peirithoos remained permanently in Hades' trap is a more difficult question. While the Olympia shield-band indicates a release as early as sixth century, we may well ask if Theseus' and Herakles' stories could have been so intertwined from the very beginning. Then too, the version of Panyasis in which the rock grows to the heroes' bodies may intend us to understand their punishment as irreversible (though in the First Vatican Mythographer Herakles manages by brute force, leaving part of Theseus' posterior on the rock: VM I 48). But clearly we cannot be certain on this issue.

It remains only to note a version in which Peirithoos is not bound at all, but eaten by Kerberos. Tzetzes tells us this (Σ *Batr* 142a), and adds that Euripides has Theseus explain to Herakles the various sights of the Underworld, so that conceivably Peirithoos' devouring derives from that playwright as well. We saw, though, that reference to Euripides in this context may indicate rather a play by Kritias, and we also saw that in some work attributed to Euripides the two are both freed. A possible rationalizing of the devouring occurs in Plutarch, where our two heroes head not to Hades but to Epirus, so that Peirithoos might carry off the daughter of the Molossians' king, one Aidoneus (*Thes* 31.4, 35.1). This Aidoneus, Plutarch assures us, called his wife Persephone, his daughter Kore, and his dog Kerberos. Kerberos consumes Peirithoos and Theseus is imprisoned; when Herakles on a visit to Aidoneus learns of this he asks for and obtains his friend's release. Plutarch mentions Philochoros only at the end of this account, and seemingly for just one small detail, but other references make it probable that the latter is in fact the source for the whole story (323F18). Tzetzes may of course have drawn his reference from that same version, but I suspect in any case that Philochoros has reshaped his tale from a traditional one in which Peirithoos is eaten in Hades by the real Kerberos.

Theseus and Thebes In contrast to the situation for the previous adventures, Theseus' two acts of statesmanship with regard to Thebes are attested no earlier than fifth-century Attic drama, and conceivably they began there. The Athenian king's reception of Oidipous (in the district of Kolonos north of the city) first appears in Euripides' *Phoinissai* (1705-7) and Sophokles' *Oidipous at Kolonos,* both from the last decade of the fifth century. Euripides' play contains just a casual allusion to the death at Kolonos, and is earlier than Sophokles' full dramatization of the event, which would seem to indicate that the story was already well known to Athenians. But many scholars (including those who defend as Euripidean the controversial ending of the *Phoinissai*) concede that the lines on Kolonos are probably an addition,[32] so that Sophokles' version (with no allusions but rather a complete exposition) may well be our first account. As we shall see in chapter 14, all our early material on Oidipous suggests that he remained in Thebes after the discovery of what he had done; indeed the *Oidipous Tyrannos* is the first source to broach even the possibility of exile. Among this material we should note especially, as did Pausanias when confronted with the tomb of Oidipous at Athens (1.28.7), *Iliad* 23, where the Achaian hero Mekisteus is said to have participated in the funeral games for Oidipous at Thebes (*Il* 23.677-80); one naturally infers that the poet believed Oidipous to have died there. In using this reference to refute Sophokles' version, Pausanias implies that he does not know of anything else earlier than the *Kolonos* in which Oidipous does come to Athens. Whether some sort of hero cult actually did exist for the Theban king at Kolonos in earlier times we cannot say, nor are there any artistic representations to help us.

The second act of statesmanship, Theseus' assistance to Adrastos in recovering the bodies of the Seven against Thebes, is dramatized for us in Euripides' preserved *Hiketides,* a play dating somewhere in the vicinity of 420 B.C. Plutarch, however, tells us that Aischylos had already presented the same tale, with Theseus as a character, in his play *Eleusinioi* (*Thes* 29.4-5). Plutarch's primary concern here is to contrast the version of Aischylos, in which the Thebans are persuaded by diplomacy to return the bodies for burial, with that of Euripides, in which Theseus and the Athenians must actually defeat the Thebans in battle in order to accomplish their aim. Isokrates for his part refers to both versions, and asks who has not heard of these events from the tragic poets, with never a mention of any epic or other early source (12. *Panath* 168-71). We should also observe that Pindar, in an ode dating probably to 476 or 474 B.C., speaks of the fallen commanders at Thebes as feeding seven funeral pyres by the banks of the Ismenos, that is, at Thebes, as if there was no question of the bodies ever being denied burial or reclaimed by relatives (*Nem* 9.22-24). It is not out of the question that Pindar here compresses events in order to heighten the contrast with the fate of Amphiaraos, but it is also possible that he reflects a non-Attic epic tradition. Pausanias tells us that the campaign of the Seven was recounted in the *Thebais,* a poem that he praises highly (9.9.5); unfortunately, his own brief account of the battle does not include any mention of burials. Earlier, in the chapter on Attika, he notes the tombs of the fallen on the road leading out of Eleusis to Megara, but there says nothing of the *Thebais* (1.39.2). As in the case of Oidipous, the presence of venerated funeral monuments poses a problem: could these have been transferred as a result of fifth-century literary invention, or do they reflect an older tradition? Likewise, as for Oidipous, there are no artistic representations.

The Pursuit
of Aithra

As we near the end of Theseus' career we must consider one dubious incident not known at all in the preserved literature but seemingly illustrated in Attic Red-Figure. The series of representations begins with a cup by Makron now in Leningrad whose tondo shows a young unbearded man in cloak and petasos in the act of drawing his sword; he does so while face to face with a woman who holds out both arms to him and in fact cups his chin with her right hand (Leningrad 649). The youth is inscribed as Theseus, the woman as Aithra. There follow in the Early Classical period quite a number of vases—over thirty—which offer what would appear to be a related scheme, namely a similar youth actually pursuing a woman with drawn sword; on none of them are there any names.[33] Since the poses on the Makron cup are not as explicit as those that follow, it is possible that this one inscribed scene represents something quite different from the others, such as perhaps Theseus drawing his sword to show it to his mother after finding it under the rock at Troizen. Admittedly, the gesture of Aithra is one more normally connected with supplication, especially when the supplicated individual is threatening physical harm; just so, for example, Nessos reaches out to Herakles on the early Black-Figure Nettos amphora (Athens 1002). But possibly Theseus means to demonstrate his intention to set forth into the world in search of his father, and Aithra seeks to hold him back from the dangers involved. If this or some similar explanation is the case, then the other vases with an actual pursuit will represent a different tale, likely enough that of Theseus and Medeia. But if Makron really does intend his Theseus to threaten the woman opposite him, then we are left with one of two explanations: either there is indeed a lost tale in which Theseus for some reason pursues his mother with intent to kill, or else Makron has made a mental slip and written "Aithra" when he intended "Medeia." Such slips are not uncommon, though in a case like this certainly surprising. The fact remains, however, that Theseus pursuing Medeia (sometimes marked out by her Oriental dress) *is* a common motif in Attic art,[34] and if there had been a tale of a second, very similar pursuit, we might have expected the painters of these thirty-odd vases to have taken more care in telling us which of the two they intended. On balance there is not enough evidence to postulate that Theseus ever designed to kill any woman except Medeia, and perhaps a few Amazones.

Theseus'
Death

At the last, Diodoros, our source for so much else about Theseus, is once more our earliest reference, with the information that Theseus found himself embroiled in political stasis and went into exile, dying in a foreign land (4.62.4). Plutarch is more explicit: Menestheus had already stirred up the people of Athens against Theseus when the Dioskouroi had come to recover Helen and now, in his old age, the king finds that he can no longer control his subjects (*Thes* 35). Accordingly, he sends his children to Euboia and goes himself to Skyros, where he has ancestral land holdings. But here he meets his death, either because Lykomedes, king of Skyros, pushes him from a high cliff, or through an accidental fall; Plutarch offers as Lykomedes' motive fear of Theseus' reputation, or else a desire to please Menestheus. Pausanias and Apollodoros simply state that Lykomedes caused his death (in Apollodoros again by being thrown from a high place: Paus 1.17.6; ApE 1.24). The absence of any earlier preserved tradition may cause us to wonder if Diodoros' notion of a version of the *katabasis* in which both heroes remain in Hades might not after all have early roots. But not all heroes have a death tale (consider Perseus). That Theseus should need to die in any unusual way at all is perhaps primarily due to his exile, and that we might suppose is itself due to the need to explain Menestheus' presence in the *Iliad*'s Catalogue of Ships, where he is leader of the Athenian contingent (with Peteos as father: *Il* 2.552) and there is no mention of the sons of Theseus. The *Ehoiai* also knows of Menestheus (or at least someone from Athens whose father's name begins with *P*) as a suitor of Helen (Hes fr 200 MW), but one would expect to find him here in any case, after his inclusion in the *Iliad*. Diodoros offers a tradition in which Peteos is an immigrant from Egypt (1.28.6–7), while both Plutarch and Pausanias record him as descended from Orneus, the son of Erechtheus whom we encountered in chapter 7 (Paus 2.25.6; *Thes* 32.1). This latter version would make Aigeus and Menestheus second cousins, and Menestheus like Pallas could thus lay some claim to Aigeus' throne. Possibly all this does reflect an early tradition simply not explained by Homer. More likely, though, the *Iliad* draws on a rival version of the state of affairs in Athens, a version in which Theseus' importance to the city is either ignored or as yet undeveloped. When later Athenian writers then wished to bring Theseus and his line into greater prominence, they would have found the *Iliad*'s insistence on Menestheus awkward, and done their best to incorporate him into the Erechtheid clan while at the same time using a tale of Theseus' death as a means to explain his rival's presence as king: Menestheus expels Theseus from Athens, and perhaps even helps to engineer his demise. The children naturally flee as well, leaving this Homeric interloper to usurp the throne. But his rule of course does not endure; Homer does not give him any children, and thus the way is clear for the sons of Theseus to resume the throne (and the royal line) after his death. As we have seen, the epic tradition, albeit not the *Iliad*, does speak of these sons: they are Akamas and Demophon, and in both the *Little Iliad* and the *Ilioupersis* they have come to Troy with the other Achaians in the hope of rescuing their grandmother Aithra. In this venture (oddly left to them by Theseus) they will, of course, succeed once Troy has fallen.

10   Perseus and Bellerophontes

In chapter 6 we saw that the line of Io led us through Belos to his children Danaos and Aigyptos; by the time of the *Prometheus Desmotes,* certainly, the union of their respective offspring—Hypermestra and Lynkeus—points to the future birth of Herakles. All known accounts, however, also make Herakles descend from Perseus, so that very likely in earlier tradition, as in Apollodoros, the child of Hypermestra and Lynkeus is Abas, Perseus' great-grandfather (ApB 2.2.1; cf. Σ *Pho* 180). This Abas is actually documented in a fragment of the *Ehoiai,* but unfortunately the names of his parents are lost at the beginning of the papyrus (although mention of a "great insult" might refer to the slaughter of the Aigyptioi: Hes fr 129 MW). In any case, Abas in the *Ehoiai* marries someone (again the name is lost; Apollodoros suggests Aglaia), and the offspring are two sons, of whom one is Akrisios and the other missing but (since he marries Stheneboia) surely Proitos (first attested as a son of Abas and brother of Akrisios at Bak 11.40, 64–69). The *Ehoiai's* sole concern (here at least) is genealogy; thus there are no stories of the two brothers beyond their marriages and children. Akrisios weds Eurydike, daughter of Lakedaimon; there is room for one child, whose name is lost but who must be, as in the *Iliad,* Danae (*Il* 14.319–20). Proitos has, meanwhile, several children by Stheneboia, three daughters, in fact, though only one name, "Iphianassa," survives. These daughters are destined to a long madness (for varying reasons) and a cure at the hands of Melampous, while their mother will cast covetous eyes on Bellerophontes when he becomes a guest in their home; we will return to both these tales in the second half of the present chapter.

Before leaving the family, however, we should note that Bakchylides recognizes a quarrel between the two brothers over some slight cause, a quarrel that induces the people to suggest that Proitos, here named as the younger brother, leave Akrisios and Argos and found a new city at Tiryns (Bak 11.59–72). Apollodoros adds to this that the brothers quarreled already in their mother's womb (much as did the sons of Phokos in the *Ehoiai*), and continued that argument as grown men, with the kingdom of Argos at stake (ApB 2.2.1). In this latter account, Akrisios succeeds in expelling Proitos from the Argolid altogether; the latter retires to Lykia, where he marries Stheneboia, daughter of the king Iobates. With his new father-in-law's help he then succeeds in returning to the Argolid and installing himself at Tiryns. Pausanias seems to reflect something of the same idea in saying that there was a pitched battle that was inconclusive, and then a reconciliation (2.25.7).

We hear again of Akrisios in one other fragment of the *Ehoiai*, where despite gaps we find Danae bearing Perseus to Zeus and being thrown into the sea in a *larnax* or chest (perhaps before she has actually delivered the child); the word "golden" appears next to Zeus here, but without its last letters we cannot tell whether it referred to him (as a shower of gold?) or something else (Hes fr 135 MW). We can, however, say that the story was not told in any greater detail than this. Otherwise we have nothing until the fifth century, but at that point Pherekydes offers (even in a scholiast's summary) a very full account that largely obviates the need to resort to later sources. As he relates the story, Akrisios marries Eurydike, daughter of Lakedaimon, just as in the *Ehoiai*, and a daughter Danae is born to them (3F10). But when the new father goes to Delphi to inquire about the prospects for a son, he is told that he will have none, but that Danae will bear a son by whom he will die. Accordingly, he returns to Argos and has an underground chamber of bronze constructed in the courtyard of his house to serve as a prison for Danae and her nurse. It seems that we must suppose an aperture in the roof of this chamber to let in light and air, for Zeus, desiring Danae, flows down into her lap like gold; when he has revealed himself the union takes place. Perseus is of course the result, and his mother and the nurse raise him without Akrisios' knowledge until he is three or four years old; at that point, Akrisios hears his shouts as he plays, and the secret is discovered. Akrisios executes the nurse and, taking Danae to the altar of Zeus, demands to know who has fathered the child. Danae's claim that it was Zeus is disbelieved, and both she and the child are placed in a chest, which is then locked and thrown into the sea. Carried through the sea, the chest comes to the island of Seriphos and catches in the nets of the fisherman Diktys, son of Peristhenes. When he discovers the contents, he takes Danae and Perseus home, and treats them as his own family.

This version of the beginning of the story is accepted in its general lines by later writers and becomes the standard account; indeed already in Pindar's *Pythian* 12.17–18 we find reference to the shower of gold by which Zeus came to Danae. There is, however, one surprising deviation recorded by an *Iliad* scholion and ascribed likewise to Pindar among others: the scholiast says that Danae was seduced (or forced) by her own uncle Proitos, and that for this reason Proitos and Akrisios quarreled (ΣAb *Il* 14.319 = fr 284 SM). The scholiast does not actually say that Perseus was therefore Proitos' child, but his language and order of events make clear that he supposes Proitos to be an alternative to Zeus as Danae's lover. Apollodoros offers the same information without naming Pindar, and again as a variant on the usual tale of Zeus and the shower of gold, suggesting that he too thought Perseus might in some accounts be Proitos' child (ApB 2.4.1). We have seen that in both the *Iliad* and the *Ehoiai* Zeus is clearly the father, and elsewhere too (*Nem* 10.11) Pindar mentions his visit to Danae. Consistency in Pindar's use of myths from one poem to the next we need not expect, so that possibly Proitos was in some work of his the father of Perseus. But perhaps too our scholiast and Apollodoros misread their sources, and Akrisios imprisoned his daughter as a punishment for her seduction, leaving Zeus free even at this point to visit her and father her child (compare Aithra, who spends the same night with Aigeus and Poseidon). If this is correct, then the seduction by Proitos substitutes for the oracle (as cause of Danae's imprisonment), rather than for Zeus as Perseus' father. Admittedly, however, if there is no oracle Akrisios' treatment of his daughter will be curious—mere imprisonment after her seduction, but attempted execution after she bears a child. On the whole, Proitos as seducer suggests a familial conflict in which one brother challenges the other's authority by usurping his right to give away his own daughter, but when this idea might have arisen and to what extent it challenged Zeus' role in the matter remain questions.

From Pindar's slightly earlier contemporary Simonides, we have the famous lament of Danae as she watches her son sleep peacefully in the (open?) chest in which they have been placed (543 *PMG*). Although the poem is undeniably elegant, and ends with a poignant appeal to Zeus, it offers us nothing beyond the obvious difficulties of their situation, and does not even name Zeus as the father, though the implication is very strong. Turning to tragedy, we find that all three of the major tragedians dealt with Danae's plight, but very little remains. Aischylos almost certainly dedicated an entire trilogy to Perseus, of which two of the tragedies were *Phorkides* and *Polydektes*, while the satyr play was the *Diktyoulkoi*.[1] This last (in English, *Net-drawers*), treated Danae's arrival on Seriphos and her rescue from the Satyroi, who in a satyr play are naturally the ones to find her.[2] At one point in the preserved fragments, Danae does refer to some blame on the part of Zeus for which she has paid the penalty (fr 47a.18–20 R), so we can probably assume Zeus' complicity. As for the tragedies, in the absence of the third title we must admit some uncertainty. Presumably the middle play was the *Phorkides* and related the conquest of Medousa, while the final drama *(Polydektes?)* probably depicted Perseus' return to Seriphos. But the opening play could equally have dramatized the causes of Danae's predicament or the conflict with Polydektes that forced Perseus to seek the Gorgon's head. In any case, Danae probably provided an Aischylean version of this first part of the story in the course of the *Diktyoulkoi*, since she surely explained her presence in the chest to Diktys, if not to the Satyroi. Judging by the titles *Danae*, *Akrisios*, and *Larisaioi*, Sophokles may also have composed a connected group. Whether this was the case or not, he seems to have dealt quite fully with Akrisios' dilemma, since both the *Danae* and the *Akrisios* are probably set in Argos; perhaps one play dealt with his decision to imprison his daughter and the other with his casting her into the sea after the child is discovered.[3] Nothing useful remains from these plays, save Akrisios' conviction that if the child lives he must die (fr 165 R), but a chorus from the same poet's *Antigone* reminds us that Danae "exchanged the light of the sun for bronze-bound halls," and "honored in her conceiving guarded the gold-poured offspring of Zeus" (*Ant* 944–50). Euripides' *Danae* seems to have followed the same pattern, with Akrisios desiring to have a son, an oracle, Zeus in the form of gold, and Danae pleading for the safety of her child; the imprisonment in the chest may have represented an alternative to his instant death.[4] For the very popular later notion that Danae was imprisoned in a tower rather than underground, the earliest ancient source appears to be Horace (*Odes* 3.16.1–4), followed by Ovid (*AA* 3.415–16 *inter alios*); possibly this is a misconstruction of the Greek word *pyrgos*, usually translated as "tower" but often just an out-building (though admittedly never underground).

In art there is nothing before the early fifth century, and nothing even in that period which suggests any variant traditions.[5] A Red-Figure calyx krater by the Triptolemos Painter (Leningrad 637) shows two phases of the story: on one side Danae (so named) sits on a couch adjusting her headdress while drops of liquid descend into her lap from above; on the other a carpenter adds the final touches to a chest in which Danae and child stand while Akrisios (also named) looks on. Both these scenes repeat themselves often in the remainder of the century (with Danae frequently holding up her skirts to catch the rain), but the motif of the chest's preparation (or Danae seated in it with her child) is perhaps the more popular. Two of the earliest examples, a stamnos by the Eucharides Painter (Leningrad 642) and a hydria by the Gallatin Painter (Boston 13.200) deviate from the representation of the Triptolemos Painter in showing Danae beside the chest while a nurse holds the child, but both also feature the carpenter fitting the chest, as do several later pieces. Such agreement on a rather incidental detail has prompted the suggestion that all these painters have been inspired by a play, most likely one by Aischylos for his trilogy.[6] But of course a wall painting is also a possible source, and then too, the other side of the Leningrad krater is not likely to have been inspired (at least visually) by a stage work. A Red-Figure lekythos by the Providence Painter (Toledo 69.369) presents the chest already finished; Perseus from inside reaches up to his mother, while Akrisios gestures to Danae, presumably ordering that she too must enter. Still other examples show mother and child seated in the chest as Akrisios watches (e.g., Ferrara 818, Boston 03.792). Later vases usually offer just variations on this basic tableau, although on a lekythos by the Ikaros Painter in Providence we see Danae and Perseus actually floating in the chest while birds flutter around overhead (Providence 25.084), and several Red-Figure vases from the 450s show Diktys and his fellow fishermen opening the lid of the chest (on one piece snarled in their nets) to find the mother and child inside (e.g., Clairmont Coll, no #; Agora P29612; Syracuse 23910).[7]

One other quite problematic illustration appears on a White-Ground lekythos of about 450 B.C., also now in Bern (Jucker Coll). An old man, grieving or lost in thought and labeled as Akrisios, sits on the middle step of a three-tiered monument that certainly looks like a tomb; on that middle tier is the name "Perseus" in the genitive, marking the monument as his, and below the letter *s*, perhaps the last letter of Danae's name in the genitive. It has been thought that this is Danae's underground prison, but since Akrisios is at this point in the story unaware of Perseus' existence it becomes hard to see why the child's name should be given. Perhaps, though, he has just now learned of that unwanted birth and sits pondering what to do.[8] Alternatively, there is the suggestion that Akrisios in remorse has built a cenotaph (empty tomb) to honor his lost daughter and grandson after their presumed demise.[9] In any event, a play would seem a likely source for this singular tableau, although if the object is a cenotaph we will be hard-pressed to devise a plot, given that no preserved version brings Perseus back to Argos to find Akrisios. Just possibly Akrisios might have built such a cenotaph at Larissa (for Sophokles' *Larisaioi?*).

Danae and Polydektes

Again Pherekydes is our fullest source, and here our earliest source of any kind. Diktys has a half-brother Polydektes (by the same mother, Androthoe, daughter of Perikastor: 3F4), who is king of Seriphos (3F11). When Perseus has grown to manhood in the house of Diktys, Polydektes chances to see Danae and becomes enamored of her, but is at a loss how to win her. Preparing a feast, he invites Perseus together with many others. At this point, the scholiast's summary of Pherekydes becomes slightly unclear, and we must seek help from Apollodoros, who gives every indication of using Pherekydes as a source (ApB 2.4.2). The feast is actually an *eranos*, that is, an affair designed to solicit contributions; Apollodoros says that Polydektes pretended he was in need of gifts for the wedding of Hippodameia, daughter of Oinomaos.[10] In Pherekydes, Perseus then asks what contribution is needed; Polydektes replies, "a horse," and Perseus answers, "the head of the Gorgon." Our scholiast does not give any reason for this strange retort, but Polydektes chooses to take it at face value, so that when Perseus on the following day brings his horse with the others, the king rejects it and insists on the head. Rather illogically, Polydektes adds that if the head is not supplied, he will claim Perseus' mother. Apollodoros for his part presents the remark as a piece of foolish bravado in which Perseus claims in the spirit of the moment that no request by Polydektes is too great, not even the head of Medousa. This makes fair enough sense, but it could scarcely have been predicted by Polydektes, and so does not explain his purpose in offering the feast to begin with, any more than it explains why Danae should be forfeit. Aischylos may have dramatized the whole situation, if the first play of his Perseus trilogy, like the third, took place on Seriphos. The plot is admittedly not what one normally thinks of as Aischylean drama, but then neither are the plots we believe to have been used for the second and third plays (the beheading of Medousa and lithification of Polydektes). Euripides seems pretty certainly to have used the threat to Danae as the basis for his *Diktys*, in which Danae takes refuge at an altar when Polydektes tries to seize her by force; probably there was some explanation here too of why Perseus had to secure the Gorgon's head. From Pindar's *Pythian* 12 we have only the briefest reference, but he does say that Perseus made bitter Polydektes' *eranos* and the continual slavery and forced marriage bed of his own mother (*Py* 12.14–15). Such language clearly implies that Polydektes had in fact married Danae in some accounts, and we find the same detail in one of the Cyzicene temple epigrams from the second century B.C. (*AP* 3.11). Likely enough the king did not expect Perseus to return, and saw no point in waiting to claim his forfeit. Neither art nor later literature has anything more to contribute to this part of the story, save for the odd tale of Hyginus that upon finding Danae Diktys took her immediately to Polydektes, who married her and caused Perseus to be raised in the temple of Athena (*Fab* 63). The sequel to this has Akrisios come directly to Seriphos, where Polydektes intercedes with him on behalf of Perseus and Danae, then dies. In such a version, Polydektes seems Perseus' protector rather than his enemy, and the marriage to Danae appears amicable; the expedition for Medousa's head is not mentioned. For one other idea, that Polydektes asked Perseus for a horse because he knew the boy could not afford one, I have not found any ancient source. Pherekydes and Apollodoros both state clearly that he did in fact bring one.

Perseus and the Gorgons As we saw in chapter 1, Homer mentions a Gorgon's head in both the *Iliad* and the *Odyssey*, but never Medousa by name, nor Perseus in connection with such an adventure. Indeed, we cannot be entirely certain that Homer knew or thought of Gorgons as complete creatures, suitable for decapitating. At one point we do find the Gorgon head on Athena's aigis (*Il* 5.738–42), but perhaps that detail is older than the explanation of how the head got there (or perhaps Homer knew rather Euripides' tale of Athena's slaying of a Gorgon at Phlegrai [*Ion* 989–96]). Our earliest sure reference to Perseus and the Gorgons is the *Theogony*, where Perseus cuts off Medousa's head (all three sisters are named here), and Chrysaor and Pegasos emerge from her neck (*Th* 270–81). The scene is somewhere toward the edge of night, beyond Okeanos near the Hesperides; no motive or further details are given. In the *Aspis* we see Perseus on Herakles' shield, flying through the air, with winged sandals, a sword slung about his shoulders, a tasseled *kibisis* on his back with the head of the Gorgon in it, and the cap of Hades on his head (*Aspis* 216–37). Other Gorgons (the text does not say how many) pursue. In art the earliest representations appear to be the act of decapitation on two Boiotian relief pithoi (Louvre CA 795, CA 937),[11] and the subsequent flight on the Protoattic Eleusis amphora, all dating probably to the second quarter of the seventh century. On only one of the two relief pithoi is Medousa preserved (as a female Kentauros), but in both cases Perseus averts his gaze, thus attesting to the power of the Gorgon's face. The Eleusis amphora features Medousa's decapitated body stretched out horizontally while her sisters pursue Perseus; already here we find Athena intervening as a rear guard between Perseus and the Gorgons, a detail that will become standard in a good many later representations. Hermes seems first to appear on the Gorgon Painter dinos in the Louvre, where he and Athena bring up the rear, behind the Gorgons (E874). The better preserved Boiotian pithos shows clearly the sandals, *kibisis*, a petasos, and a straight sword; likewise on a clay metope of the later seventh century from Thermon (which shows only Perseus: Athens 13401) and a spouted krater by the Nettos Painter (Berlin:Lost F1682), as well as the Louvre dinos. On the Samos ivory relief Perseus' lower body is missing and the *kibisis*, if present, is hidden; only the pointed cap and sword survive (Samos:VM E 1). The artistic tradition grows progressively richer as we move down into the sixth and fifth centuries, showing sometimes the beheading (as on the Olympia shield-band B 975), more often the pursuit, but rarely adding any new narrative detail to the story. But we do find one exception on a Chalkidian amphora dating to about 520 B.C. (London B155). Here three women, inscribed as Neides, approach Perseus with the gifts he needs: the first holds the winged sandals, the second a broad-brimmed cap, and the third a *kibisis*. Perseus himself already has a straight sword in scabbard slung round his shoulders, and Athena stands behind him. The bronze temple of Athena in Sparta, dated by pottery to about this same time, displayed a similar scene, if we may trust Pausanias (3.17.3).

For any literary account beyond the brief description in the *Aspis* we must once again be grateful to Pherekydes, although for this part of the story we will have some help from Aischylos as well. As the scholiast continues his summary of Pherekydes' account, Perseus in despair over his dilemma goes to the furthest part of Seriphos (3F11). There Hermes appears to him and asks the cause of his lament; on learning of the problem the god takes him to see the Graiai, Athena leading the way. From these sisters Perseus steals their one eye and tooth as they pass them among themselves, and refuses to give the items back until they tell him where he might find the Nymphai who possess the cap of Hades, the winged sandals, and the *kibisis*. They do so, he returns the eye and tooth, and acquires the assistance he needs under Hermes' escort. He then flies to Okeanos where the Gorgons live, with both Hermes and Athena following. They find the Gorgons sleeping; the two gods warn Perseus that he must look away as he cuts off the head, and tell him which of the three is mortal (in this respect agreeing with the *Theogony*). He secures the head, puts it in the *kibisis*, and flees; the sisters pursue but cannot see him. We should note that this account agrees exactly with the Chalkidian amphora as to the Naiades and their gifts to Perseus (cap, sandals, *kibisis*), although we may well wonder why Hermes could not supply the sandals, and why Hades does not have his own cap. Aischylos' *Phorkides* appears to have been rather different in some details, but we must remember the limitations of his stage: Pherekydes' version requires four separate locales (Seriphos, Graiai, Nymphai, Gorgons), and the playwright can show only one. Apparently he chose to put the Graiai on stage, and to eliminate the Nymphai altogether, for several writers say that in Aischylos Perseus received his sword from Hephaistos (e.g., *Katast* 22), and the play is very likely the source for the immediately adjacent idea that Hermes supplied the sandals and cap (full citations in fr 262 iv, v R).

In any case, Aischylos certainly draws greater attention to the Graiai by making them the guardians of the Gorgons; thus, rather than obtaining information from them, Perseus intercepts the one eye that they use to stand guard and throws it into the Tritonian lake (fr 262 i-v R). The Graiai are in this fashion blinded, and the way cleared for Perseus to steal up on the sleeping Gorgons. Some support for a pre-Aischylean origin of this version might come from Pindar's *Pythian* 12, an early ode (490 B.C.?)[12] in which we are told that Perseus "darkened the wondrous race of Phorkys" (*Py* 12.13). Such a remark could, of course, refer to a temporary seizure of the eye such as Pherekydes describes, but it will have far more point if Pindar envisions the same situation as Aischylos. On the other hand, two separate sources associate the motif of permanent blindness specifically with Aischylos, and we can see why he might have invented it: he wants to make his one scene as important as possible, and if the most crucial part of the mission becomes the disarming of the Graiai, then the actual beheading of Medousa can more easily be remanded to a messenger speech. But whether this element is new or not, the playwright does retain the essential features of the story, that is, magical gifts and the help of the gods without which Perseus cannot succeed, and the Graiai as a somehow necessary stepping-stone to the Gorgons. A Red-Figure pyxis lid and a krater fragment, both about 425 B.C., represent the first preserved attempts to show the theft in art. On the lid Perseus creeps in on hands and knees and reaches up as the transfer of the eye is about to be made (Athens 1291); the krater fragment shows him moving away from one of the sisters as she sits eyeless (Delos B7263). But we cannot say for either of these artists whether Perseus keeps the eye or gives it back.[13]

To the few details noted above we can add that Pindar's *Pythian* 10 sends Perseus to the far north, to the land of the Hyperboreans (*Py* 10.29–36). Pindar does not, however, say that Perseus actually found the Gorgons (or the Graiai) there; possibly he was looking for the Nymphai. In Aischylos' *Prometheus Desmotes*, we have already seen that the Graiai and Gorgons live near each other, and somewhere to the far east where Io can encounter them (*PD* 791–800). Prometheus, perhaps exaggerating for effect, says that no mortal can look on any of them and live. In Apollodoros we do find several new features that may or may not go back to Pherekydes' original account. For one thing, the sword (not mentioned at all in our scholiast's summary) is a present from Hermes; for another, we find here the idea that Athena holds up a polished shield so that Perseus may guide his hand when striking the blow (ApB 2.4.2).[14] The first preserved literary appearance of this shield is in Ovid (*Met* 4.782–83; cf. Lucan 9.669–70, *DMar* 14), but several South Italian pots have already illustrated the decapitation in such a way (e.g., Boston 1970.237, an Apulian bell krater). Quite a number of South Italian vases and Etruscan mirrors offer a variant on this, with Perseus and Athena calmly viewing the decapitated head's reflection in a pool of water, presumably to satisfy Perseus' curiosity once the deed has been accomplished (so, e.g., London B620 [mirror]).[15] The idea of that reflection as a defense against her power is by contrast conspicuously absent in sixth- and fifth-century representations, where Perseus simply looks away as he cuts off the head (so Olympia B 975, NY 45.11.1), or even presumes to look at it (Richmond 62.1.1). The birth of Pegasos and Chrysaor from the neck of Medousa, noted as early as the *Theogony* and frequently shown in art, has already been discussed in chapter 1. One other tale, that Perseus visited Atlas on his way back from the isle of the Gorgons, we have likewise discussed in chapter 1, in dealing with Atlas' fate. A dithyrambist Polyidos apparently told an early form of this story (Σ Lyk 879 = 837 *PMG*), but we know it best from Ovid's preserved account (*Met* 4.627–62). In both versions Perseus and the Gorgon's head are simply a device to transform Atlas into a mountain that subsequently supports the sky; Perseus' justification for the deed is that Atlas has threatened him or rudely refused shelter, recalling as he does a warning that a son of Zeus will steal his apples. Perseus is not the son meant, of course, and the tale is probably late in its inception.

Andromeda   Curiously enough, our summary of Pherekydes passes over this adventure altogether and takes us directly back to Seriphos to deal with Polydektes. Later, however, it does acknowledge Andromeda's presence, for Perseus brings her with him when he sails back to Argos (3F12). We should consider too that the purpose of the scholion that gives us this part of the story (the decapitation) is to explain the origin of the Libyan snakes in the *Argonautika* as springing from drops of Medousa's blood; thus there is really no reason for the scholiast to report an unrelated *parergon*. The tale of Andromeda *is*, on the other hand, recounted by Apollodoros, in all probability using material from Pherekydes which the scholiast omitted. As we saw in chapter 6, the *Ehoiai* notes the marriage of Perseus and Andromeda (Hes fr 135 MW), and while the fragment in question says nothing about deeds of heroism to bring about that union, these are guaranteed at least for the sixth century by a Corinthian amphora now in Berlin to which we shall return shortly.

In chapter 6 we found Kepheus provided with two contrasting pedigrees, both ascribed to Euripides: Apollodoros said that the playwright made him and Phineus sons of Belos (Ap*B* 2.1.4; so too Hdt 7.61), while Hyginus claimed that Euripides and others gave him to Phoinix as offspring (*Astr* 2.9). Whichever side of the line of Inachos he falls upon, the literary account of his misfortunes surfaces first in the lost *Andromeda* plays of Sophokles and Euripides. From Sophokles we get only one piece of real information, but an important one: Kassiepeia, wife of Kepheus, dares to compare herself to the Nereides in beauty, and Poseidon sends a sea monster *(kêtos)* to destroy the land; therefore Andromeda is offered up to the monster (p. 156 R apud *Katast* 16, 36). Of Euripides' play we know that Andromeda speaks the prologue from her place of confinement and is then visited by Perseus, who secures promises from her in return for his proposal to slay the beast (fr 132 N[2]). Probably he also frees her at this time; in any case, the latter part of the drama seems to have revolved around Perseus' subsequent difficulties in establishing himself to Kepheus (or Kassiepeia?) as a suitable husband.[16] If we can believe Hyginus (*Astr* 2.10), the original cause of the trouble, Kassiepeia's boast, was here the same as in Sophokles. Ovid and Apollodoros likewise agree with that explanation and add that Kepheus was forced to offer up his daughter after Ammon had pronounced that he could thus appease the monster (*Met* 4.668–71; Ap*B* 2.4.3). Perseus here arrives, contracts a bargain directly with Kepheus for Andromeda's hand, and slays the monster. But Kepheus' brother Phineus, the former betrothed of the girl, objects, and in Apollodoros concocts some sort of plot to kill Perseus, who uses the Gorgon head to turn him and his friends to stone; in Ovid there is simply a pitched battle after Phineus has interrupted the nuptial feast, with similar results (*Met* 5.1–235). On this whole development as an aftermath of the rescue (i.e., Phineus' claim to his niece and Perseus' use of the Gorgon head to lithify his rival), Ovid is our earliest preserved source, followed by Apollodoros and Hyginus (*Fab* 64), but we saw that Euripides in some drama makes Kepheus and Phineus brothers. That being the case, and given that Perseus in the *Andromeda* does encounter difficulties of an uncertain nature in claiming his bride, it seems quite possible that Phineus was a character in the play;[17] if Apollodoros has drawn on Pherekydes for this part of his account the story would be older still. Hyginus' version follows the same lines as the others but makes the former suitor Agenor, not Phineus. As so often with this author, it is impossible to say whether he here records a genuine variant, or has simply confused members of the same family. Herodotos adds that Perseus and Andromeda remained with Kepheus for a time, and left their first-born child Perses with him when they departed, as he had no offspring of his own (Hdt 7.61).

Later literary sources follow closely this general outline, and thus have little to contribute. In art we do find, however, some small points of interest. The Corinthian amphora in Berlin mentioned above is certainly the earliest representation of the tale (Berlin:PM F1652); it may well be joined later in the sixth century by a Caeretan hydria (Hirschmann Coll, no #).[18] The amphora shows Perseus advancing toward the *kêtos* with a stone in each hand, while behind him Andromeda waves her arms in excitement; all three figures are named. On the hydria only Perseus (if it is he) and the *kêtos* are shown; the hero holds a stone in one hand and a *harpê* in the other as he prepares to do battle. The story does not reappear until the third quarter of the fifth century, and we may thus suspect that Sophokles' play is responsible for a renewal of interest (Euripides' version is surely later[19]). In fact, a whole series of Red-Figure vases in this period depict Andromeda as tied between two poles or posts to await her fate; on one, Perseus contemplates her while holding the *harpê* (Basel BS 403).[20] No early source says how Perseus dealt with the monster, although the stones used on the Corinthian amphora might suggest that it was simply driven off. Later writers all have Perseus destroy him, with Ovid in particular describing his use of his sword to do so (*Met* 4.706–34). In the later artistic tradition he likewise employs a sword (so, e.g., Berlin:Ch VI 3238, a Campanian hydria); not until Loukianos do we find it suggested that the head of Medousa came into play (*DMar* 14, but note that here he uses both *harpê* and head). The illustration of Andromeda's imprisonment and rescue is especially abundant in Apulian pottery of the fourth century B.C.. In these examples Andromeda is sometimes still tied to posts (Naples Stg 708), but sometimes also bound to the entrance of a rocky overhanging grotto (Würzburg 855), and finally just chained to a solid outcrop of rock (Halle, no #); this last option will carry the day in subsequent centuries. One other point to be considered is the role of Kassiepeia. She is entirely absent from the fifth-century representations, although she may be the casually seated woman on some fourth-century ones. The astronomical tradition is in solid agreement that her constellation shows her sitting in a chair, and Ps-Eratosthenes says she is presented as being near her daughter (*Katast* 16). But this is absolutely all the literary tradition gives us. Of the Apulian vases, one shows an elaborate empty throne placed under the two posts to which Andromeda is tied (Matera 12538); Kassiepeia is probably the woman standing to the right looking up at Perseus and her daughter. On another, an oinochoe in Bari (1016), Perseus converses with a woman who is seated on a similarly elaborate throne and clearly tied to it. This figure is usually considered to be Andromeda, but given the empty throne on the previous example (with Andromeda already accounted for) we should probably recognize Kassiepeia; Perseus will then be negotiating with her for a promise of marriage to her daughter. Such an interpretation receives some slight support from its recurrence in illustrated medieval manuscripts, with both Kassiepeia (in her chair) and Andromeda (between two trees) shown bound.[21] Why Kassiepeia should be thus treated we will never know: possibly it is to restrain her from going to the aid of her daughter, but possibly too to ensure that she remain to watch the destruction of Andromeda by the monster.

The Death of Polydektes

All accounts (save for that of Hyginus in which Polydektes plays the role of protector) agree that after rescuing Andromeda Perseus returns to Seriphos where he also uses the head of Medousa to lithify the king of that island; our earliest sources are Pindar's *Pythian* 10 and Pherekydes. Pindar's reference is brief, but makes it clear that all the people of Seriphos were turned to stone (*Py* 10.46–48); so too Pherekydes, where Perseus asks Polydektes to gather all the islanders together, and then shows them all the head at one time, averting his own gaze (3F11). Nothing in these writers or others explains why Perseus' vengeance should be so extensive; we must, I suppose, presume that the whole island supported the king's claim to Danae. Aischylos will have dramatized the story in his *Polydektes* (or else a play of lost title, if *Polydektes* was about the *eranos*), and we have already seen how Euripides arranged Perseus' return and rescue of Danae in his *Diktys*, although unfortunately we have no information about that play's denouement. In art the earliest preserved representation is an Attic Red-Figure pelike by Hermonax on which Perseus shows the head of

Medousa to standing and seated men who remain seemingly unaffected (VG, no #).[22] But any doubts about the head's efficacy are removed by a Red-Figure bell krater of about 440 B.C. (Bologna 325): here Perseus holds up the head as Polydektes reaches for it, and we see the lower part of the king's body already turning to stone. Pherekydes goes on to say that Perseus then gives Medousa's head to Athena, who puts it on her aigis, and the *kibisis*, cap, and sandals to Hermes, who returns them to the Nymphai. He himself makes Diktys king of the island, and leaves for Argos with Danae, Andromeda, and the Kyklopes (here inexplicably mentioned for the first time, at least in the scholiast's summary). Subsequently, these Kyklopes will have some role to play in the continuation of the story as the builders of the walls of Tiryns and Mykenai (Bak 11.77–81; Paus 2.16.5), but what they would be doing on Seriphos remains a mystery. Apollodoros, who agrees with Pherekydes in other points of this narrative, does not mention them at all. Finally, no ancient source even hints that Perseus ever gave his mother to Diktys in marriage, as one might have expected.

The Death of Akrisios and Perseus' Children

Continuing with our scholiast's summary of Pherekydes (3F12), we find that Perseus arrives at Argos only to discover that Akrisios in fear has fled north to Larissa. Leaving Andromeda and the Kyklopes and Danae behind with the latter's mother Eurydike, he sets out in pursuit. When he locates Akrisios in Larissa he persuades his grandfather to return with him to Argos. But as they are about to depart, Perseus allows himself to be enticed by athletic games that are taking place; he throws the discus, which rolling strikes his grandfather's foot, and Akrisios subsequently dies of the wound. The people bury him before the city, and Perseus returns to Argos. Apollodoros differs from this narrative only in suggesting that Perseus came to Larissa precisely to compete (and thus perhaps did not know his grandfather was present until he struck him: ApB 2.4.4). As noted, Sophokles wrote a play, *Larisaioi*, on this subject; about all we can deduce of it is that Akrisios himself gave the games (to celebrate his reconciliation with his grandson?) and that Perseus in making his throw was bothered by another competitor. Hyginus' version transfers all this to Seriphos, but the result is much the same: funeral games are given for Polydektes, and in the course of these Perseus' discus throw is carried off line by the wind and strikes Akrisios on the head (*Fab* 63).

Ovid, on the other hand, does not relate the death at all, but offers the novel idea that before returning to Seriphos to deal with Polydektes Perseus went back to Argos, where Proitos had now chased out Akrisios, and turned his great-uncle to stone in revenge (*Met* 5.236–41: Ovid admits that Akrisios scarcely deserved this show of support). Hyginus in a different *fabula* from those we have been considering says, even more oddly, that Megapenthes, son of Proitos, slew Perseus in revenge for his father (*Fab* 244), and possibly Ovid's story is what he is referring to. In Apollodoros, where continuous genealogical narrative is more of a concern, Perseus declines to rule Argos, given the manner of Akrisios' death, and invites the same Megapenthes to exchange with him Tiryns for Argos (Ap*B* 2.4.4). Pausanias tells the same story, and adds the foundation by Perseus of Mykenai, with the name derived either from the cap of his sword or a mushroom (2.16.3).

As for the children of Perseus and Andromeda, Homer notes only Sthenelos, future father of Eurystheus (*Il* 19.116–24). The same fragment of the *Ehoiai* that tells us that Andromeda was the daughter of Kepheus goes on to list her three sons, but here too only Sthenelos survives, in the central part of the line in question (Hes fr 135 MW). Still, the names "Alkaios" and "Elektryon," crucial for all later tradition, will fit the gaps, and what follows seems to have dealt with the death of Elektryon's sons at the hands of the Teleboans. In another (very) fragmentary Hesiodic papyrus, their marriages to three daughters of Pelops are discussed, although only the names of Astydameia and (in part) Nikippe and Sthenelos survive (Hes fr 190 MW). But we surely need not doubt that here as later Alkaios receives Astydameia (and becomes as early as the *Ehoie* of Alkmene the father of Amphitryon: Hes fr 195 MW), while scholia do attest as Hesiodic that Sthenelos takes Nikippe (Hes fr 191 MW; in Pherekydes, *Amphibia* [3F68]). To this second couple, later tradition like Homer assigns a son Eurystheus; the *Ehoiai* may have added a daughter, probably the same as the Astymedousa, daughter of Sthenelos, named by Pherekydes as the third wife of Oidipous (3F95).[23] Regarding the last son of Perseus, the papyrus under discussion fails completely, but a second one confirms that this son, Elektryon, also married a daughter of Pelops (name missing, supplied as "Lysidike" by Plutarch [*Thes* 7] and various scholia) to produce a substantial series of sons and, of course, a daughter Alkmene (Hes fr 193 MW), who has this father also in her own *Ehoie* (cf. *Hkld* 210–11: Alkmene child of a daughter of Pelops). As noted, the names in these unions vary at times, and Apollodoros even has Elektryon marry his own niece Anaxo, daughter of Alkaios, to produce the necessary offspring (Ap*B* 2.4.5),[24] but the basic elements—three sons of Perseus (Alkaios, Sthenelos, Elektryon) generating three first cousins (Amphitryon, Eurystheus, Alkmene)—remain constant. Apollodoros also includes for Perseus a daughter Gorgophone, whose difficulties as a genealogical figure we observed in chapter 5. The *Ehoiai* does not mention her immediately after Perseus' sons, but possibly her introduction was delayed until after the tale of the death of Elektryon's sons.

**Proitos'
Daughters**

At the close of the first section of this chapter Proitos, son of Abas, had made his way from Argos and his brother Akrisios to Tiryns, according to Apollodoros via Lykia (Ap*B* 2.2.1). Whether or not this is an early notion, in Homer Proitos is certainly married to Anteia, daughter of the king of Lykia (*Il* 6.160). The *Ehoiai*, Euripides, and most other sources call his wife instead Stheneboia, but whereas in the *Ehoiai* she is the daughter of <Apheidas> son of Arkas (Hes fr 129 MW), by the time of Euripides' play *Stheneboia* she has apparently become equated with Anteia, and her father specifically named as Iobates (a name that also serves as title for a lost play of Sophokles).²⁵ Whether the Stheneboia of the *Ehoiai* (with her non-Lykian ancestry) also tried to seduce Bellerophon is a difficult question, since that ancestry forms the basis of Proitos' attempt to avenge himself; possibly the Lykian king was in some early versions merely his friend. The lost epic poem *Melampodia*, concerned as it was in part with Proitos' daughters, might or might not have taken a position on this issue. We have seen in Apollodoros, Pausanias, and Hyginus (above) the existence of a son Megapenthes who is either the slayer of Perseus or exchanger of kingdoms with him, and we will meet him again shortly. But far more famous are the daughters, whom the *Ehoiai* names as Iphinoe, Iphianassa, and (probably) Lysippe (Hes fr 129 MW);²⁶ Pherekydes mentions just two daughters, Lysippe and Iphianassa (3F114). Many men courted them (Hes fr 130 MW), yet it was their fate to run afoul of the gods. In the *Ehoiai*, their transgression is to fail to receive the rites of Dionysos (Hes fr 131 MW). Akousilaos, on the other hand, says that they disparaged a statue of Hera (2F28), and Bakchylides that they boasted their father to be wealthier than Hera (11.47–52); Pherekydes agrees with this last version and explains that they compared the wealth of Hera's temple with that of their father's house. Their punishment was by all accounts madness. In the *Ehoiai* this is somehow connected with or leads to *machlosynê* (Hes fr 132 MW), a word used of Paris in the *Iliad* (*Il* 24.30) and seemingly referring to lewd or improper behavior. Very likely we should see in this term a connection with one of the Thermon metopes (Athens 13413) and a carved ivory group in New York (NY 17.190.73), both dating to about 630 B.C.²⁷ Each shows a set of two women who bare part of their bodies; on the Thermon metope they expose their breasts while on the ivory carving their clothes (in at least one case) are falling away altogether. Presumably, then, the madness leads them to fail to cover themselves properly. Beyond this the *Ehoiai* speaks of their beauty being destroyed and their hair falling out (Hes fr 133 MW). In Bakchylides' version we hear simply of their running madly through forests and hills for thirteen months (11.53–58, 92–95); Pherekydes without specifying even this much about their malady says that it lasted ten years. From Vergil's *Eclogues* we get the detail that the girls believed themselves to be cows (*Ecl* 6.48–51). Probus explains the point of this remark immediately after he has given the parentage of the Proitides from Hesiod, so that possibly these pseudo-cows are also from the *Ehoiai*. But the divinity cited as the cause of the problem is Hera, not (as in the *Ehoiai*) Dionysos, and more likely Vergil's source is something later (or his own imagination). In Aelianus, finally, we find specific confirmation that, in some accounts at least, the daughters divested themselves of their clothes (although their names here are Elege and Kelaine: *VH* 3.42).

Definitely from the *Ehoiai* is the fact that Melampous cured the girls through his mantic skills and received for himself and his brother Bias from Proitos a share of land (Hes fr 37 MW). Pherekydes is more explicit here: Proitos promised Melampous a share of the kingdom and his choice of the daughters to wife in return for his services (3F114). Through supplications and sacrifices to Hera the seer succeeds, and chooses Iphianassa. In Bakchylides, oddly enough, there is no trace of Melampous at all; instead, in a very unusual arrangement, Proitos effects the cure himself by offering Artemis twenty red cattle if she will intercede with Hera (11.95–109). Artemis does so, and is allowed by Hera to remove the madness. As we saw in chapter 5, the *Odyssey* brings Melampous to Argos because it is fated that he shall rule over the Argives (*Od* 15.238–42). But Homer simply says that he marries a woman of the Argives; thus we cannot tell if the poet is actually acquainted with the curing of Proitos' daughters but omits it, or knows only what he relates. In Herodotos quite a number of the women of Argos are raving (nothing is said of Proitos or his daughters); Melampous cures them for a share of the kingdom (9.34). Diodoros likewise speaks of the women of Argos (stricken by the anger of Dionysos), but Melampous here receives his prize from Anaxagoras, son of Megapenthes (hence grandson of Proitos), and that prize is Anaxagoras' sister Iphianeira (DS 4.68.45). In Apollodoros the madness begins with the daughters of Proitos, but spreads to the other women, so that Proitos is forced to agree to terms (ApB 2.2.2). Melampous demands a third of the king's land and sovereignty for himself, and a third for Bias (as in other sources). The cure involves chasing the maidens from the mountains with shouting and an inspired dance. Iphinoe somehow dies in the process (we remember that she is missing from Pherekydes) but the other two survive and are married to Melampous and Bias (the latter's previous wife Pero, daughter of Neleus, for whom Melampous labored so much, being conveniently forgotten). Melampous' descendants have already been discussed in chapter 5. Proitos' son Megapenthes begets, as we saw above, Anaxagoras; the same is found in several scholia which make this Anaxagoras the father of Hipponoos, whose son is Kapaneus, whose son in turn is Sthenelos (Σ *Il* 2.564; Σ *Pho* 180). We will find the last two again, in the assaults on Thebes in chapter 14.

*Bellero-
phontes*

Glaukos' long speech to Diomedes in *Iliad* 6 gives us early evidence for both the pedigree of Bellerophontes and his story. As related there, Sisyphos, son of Aiolos, once dwelt in Ephyra in the Argolid, and his son Glaukos becomes the father of Bellerophontes (*Il* 6.152–206). This last incurs the enmity of Proitos, then the ruler of the Argives, after rejecting the amorous advances of Proitos' wife Anteia and being accused by her of attempted rape. Proitos hesitates nonetheless to kill a guest, and instead sends Bellerophontes to his father-in-law in Lykia with a written message instructing the father-in-law to do the deed. The ruler of Lykia (not named in this account) first orders him to slay the Chimaira, which he does, obeying portents sent to him by the gods. Next the king sends him to fight the Solymoi, and finally to destroy the Amazones. When none of these tests succeeds in effecting the death of his guest, the king picks out the finest men of Lykia and places them in ambush, but Bellerophontes slays them all, and the king, now recognizing the special qualities of this adversary, offers him his daughter in marriage and a portion of land to farm. In all this there is no mention of Pegasos.[28]

By contrast, the *Theogony* in its one brief reference to the story specifically says that Pegasos and Bellerophontes together slew the Chimaira (*Th* 319–25). As for the *Ehoiai*, we have already seen there some deviation from Glaukos' version in the *Iliad*: Glaukos, son of Sisyphos, after his ill-fated attempt with Mestra marries a daughter of Nisos (son of Pandion), apparently one Eurynome, if we can trust Hyginus (Hes fr 43a MW; *Fab* 157; in ApB 1.9.3, she is Eurymede). But Zeus seems to have planned that the line of Sisyphos shall have no children of its own, and thus the only offspring of the union, Bellerophontes, is actually the child of Poseidon and Glaukos' wife (by contrast, ΣT *Il* 6.191 says that he is the child of Poseidon and Mestra, daughter of Erysichthon). The *Ehoiai* fragment breaks off badly at this point, although we can see that Poseidon gives to his son Pegasos, whose qualities are described in two lines before the pair dispose of the Chimaira (one line) and Bellerophontes marries the daughter of a king. For the rest of the Archaic period we have only Pindar, whose typically selective treatment omits Proitos and Stheneboia (as we saw her to be named in the *Ehoiai*: Hes fr 129 MW) altogether and begins with Bellerophontes sleeping in a shrine of Athena, where the goddess herself appears to him (*Ol* 13.63–92). She addresses him as Aiolides and son of Poseidon (thus apparently agreeing with the *Ehoiai* as to his father) and bestows upon him a bridle with which he may catch and tame the winged Pegasos. From the latter's back, armed with spear or (more likely) bow and arrows, he does battle with the same three foes—Chimaira, Amazones, Solymoi—as in the *Iliad*. Here Pindar halts, with only an oblique allusion to Bellerophontes' ultimate fate, and no mention at all of how he profited from his exploits. As to that ultimate fate Pindar is more explicit in *Isthmian* 7: Bellerophontes attempted to ride Pegasos up to Olympos to join the company of the gods, and the horse threw him (*Is* 7.43–48). Not surprisingly, since he has already omitted Pegasos earlier, Homer ignores this tale also, but the *Iliad* does say in concluding Bellerophontes' story that he became hateful to all the gods and wandered alone in bitterness, avoiding the paths of men (*Il* 6.200–202), and probably such a fate, like his previous deeds in Homer, presupposes knowledge of the winged horse.[29] We have already found him in Hesiod as helper of Bellerophontes, and he will play that role consistently in Greek art from the early decades of the seventh century (see below). Likely the *Iliad* here, as elsewhere, finds certain fantastical elements ill-suited to the kind of heroic atmosphere it wishes to create, and passes over them as quietly as it can.[30]

From the later fifth century there are three plays, the *Iobates* of Sophokles and the *Stheneboia* and *Bellerophontes* of Euripides, all lost. The *Iobates* presumably dramatized the Lykian king's dilemma when confronted with a guest whom his son-in-law expects him to kill, but we do not know anything more than that. For the *Stheneboia* we have a plot summary (from a Byzantine scholion) that begins with essentially the same story given by Glaukos in the

Iliad (pp. 567–68 N²). In addition, we learn that Bellerophontes comes to Proitos to be purified of a murder he has committed in Korinth, and that when he has slain the Chimaira at the behest of Iobates he returns to Tiryns to deal with Stheneboia. Apparently the play's action, or most of it, centered around this time period, with Stheneboia plotting new treachery against Bellerophontes in order to protect herself. Somehow (perhaps by pretending that he wishes to carry her off as his wife) Bellerophontes persuades her to mount Pegasos with him, and when they are out over the sea, near Melos, he throws her down to her death. Subsequently, he returns to Tiryns and justifies his deed to Proitos as fishermen bring her body on stage. Euripides' second play, *Bellerophontes,* dealt with the ill-fated attempt to reach Olympos. But in contrast to Pindar's brief account, in which Bellerophontes' excessive pride in his own accomplishments is the motivating factor, we find here a sense of extreme disillusionment after some turn of fortune, possibly caused by the slaying of Stheneboia. At any rate, the hero seems to have dwelt on a lament for the lack of divine justice in the world (fr 286 N²) and then to have mounted Pegasos with the intention of riding to Olympos to confront the gods with their inequities. Pegasos seems also to have incurred some blame for yielding to his master's request (fr 309 N², together with Plutarch's remarks introducing the line at *Mor* 807e). Bellerophontes falls, of course, and at the end of the play is brought on crippled to philosophize about his former state of happiness (fr 311 N²). Aelianus, who is our source for this last fragment, seems to think that he is on the point of death (*NA* 5.34); one wonders to what extent Euripides sympathized with his actions. As for Pegasos, someone announces at play's end that he will henceforth draw Zeus' chariot with its thunderbolts (fr 312 N²).

From tragedy as well, one assumes, comes the general summary of Bellerophontes' story preserved by the *Iliad* scholia and cited as from Asklepiades (12F13). This account tells us that Bellerophontes was originally named Hipponous, but slew Belleros, the ruler of Korinth, and had to go into exile. He thus came to Argos and its king Proitos, who purified him. The rest of the tale proceeds as in Homer, with Bellerophontes finally marrying Iobates' daughter Kasandra (or Pasandra) and buoyed sufficiently by his successes to attempt the ride skyward to see Olympos. Zeus in anger sends a gadfly to attack Pegasos (so too Σ *Ol* 13.130c; Σ Lyk 17), and Bellerophontes' fall leaves him to wander a cripple, again as in Homer. Pegasos here is requested and received as a gift from Zeus to Eos, so that he might assist her in her celestial duties. It seems therefore that at a number of points—specifically Bellerophontes' motive and his and Pegasos' ultimate fates—Asklepiades diverges from Euripides, leaving us to wonder from where he drew these details.

Later sources do add a little to this picture. Scholia to the *Batrachoi* suggest that Bellerophontes somehow proves guiltless when he reaches the home of Proitos' father-in-law, and that in shame at her discovery Stheneboia takes poison (Σ *Batr* 1043, 1051; in Hyginus, she kills herself on learning that Bellerophontes will marry her sister [*Fab* 57]). The Cyzicene temple epigrams

offer the intriguing idea that Glaukos (the grandson of the *Iliad*?) saves Bellerophontes from Megapenthes after Bellerophontes has fallen from Pegasos (*AP*
3.15). We have seen that this son of Proitos harbors a grudge against Perseus
in Hyginus (for expelling his father from Argos?), but one is hard put to discern any motive for anger against Bellerophontes, unless it is the death of his
mother, who scarcely deserved less. In Apollodoros, Bellerophontes has slain
his brother Deliades, or perhaps Peiren, or Alkimenes (Ap*B* 2.3.1). The rest of
this account follows the usual lines but ends when Iobates has given Bellerophontes his daughter (here and at Σ Lyk 17 Philonoe, at Σ *Ol* 13.82e Antikleia),
and thus there is no mention of the return to Tiryns or the fall from Pegasos
(Ap*B* 2.3.2). In Pausanias, we find that Bellerophontes is a suitor for the hand
of Aithra, daughter of Pittheus (2.31.9); fortunately for Theseus, he is banished from Korinth (presumably for murder) before the marriage can take
place. Hyginus, in addition to Stheneboia's suicide noted above, claims that
Bellerophontes fell from Pegasos when he looked down and became frightened
(*Astr* 2.18.1: here too as in Euripides he dies from the fall).

As noted, the artistic tradition begins early in the seventh century, with a
Protocorinthian cup and aryballos (Aigina, no #; Boston 95.10), followed by a
Cycladic plate found on Thasos (Thasos, no #). On all these and (almost) everything else in the Archaic period we find the same scene, namely Bellerophontes attacking the Chimaira from the back of Pegasos. Of his other two
exploits, the battles against the Amazones and the Solymoi, there seem to be
no representations of any sort, but later Attic Red-Figure and South Italian
vases do become fond of showing him arriving or taking his leave of Proitos
and/or Iobates. Sometimes the fateful letter (being received or delivered), or
even Stheneboia, are also present (e.g., Boston 00.349; Naples H2418). Stheneboia's fall makes its appearance on an Early Apulian amphora by the Gravina
Painter, with the treacherous hostess plunging headlong into the sea and Bellerophontes and Pegasos watching from above (Taranto I/96; the Lucanian krater in Leningrad with the same scene now seems more likely to be a modern
forgery [St 427]). Finally, a seventh-century Kretan relief pithos now in the
Louvre shows a man who may well be Bellerophontes falling from a winged
horse (Louvre CA 4523);[31] if this is correct, it would constitute valuable early
evidence for the existence of that story.

To conclude this chapter, there are the children of Bellerophontes as Glaukos names them in *Iliad* 6. These are three, Isandros, who dies fighting against
the Solymoi, Laodameia, who bears Sarpedon to Zeus and is later slain by an
angry Artemis (no reason given), and Hippolochos, who becomes the father of
Glaukos himself (*Il* 6.196–206). No later writer adds any other children, save
that Diodoros does call the daughter Deidameia (DS 5.79.3). We have, of
course, seen that in the *Ehoiai* and Aischylos Sarpedon is the son of Zeus and
Europa, and thus not descended from Bellerophontes at all.

11　The Daughters of Thestios

Thestios　In chapter 5, we saw that Agenor, the great-great-grandson of Kalyke (daughter of Aiolos of the line of Deukalion), has two children, a daughter Demodike and a son Porthaon, both attested by the *Ehoiai* (Hes frr 22, 10a.50 MW). Demodike was just on the verge of rejecting all mortal suitors when the papyrus that constitutes Hesiod fragment 22 broke off, leaving us to conjecture that here, as in Apollodoros, she unites with Ares and has four sons (ApB 1.7.7). Of these the fourth is Thestios, who in the *Ehoiai* certainly marries one of the daughters of his uncle Porthaon (probably Eurythemiste) and begets three daughters of his own (Hes fr 26.34–37 MW). An extremely scrappy papyrus fragment on that subject guarantees only the name of Leda (Hes fr 23a MW), but Althaia and Hypermestra are recounted in closely linked fragments, and are surely the other two, as elsewhere. Of sons there is no trace here, but they may have been postponed until all the offspring of the daughters had been discussed. As noted before, we must assume that there were some male offspring (whether or not the *Ehoiai* recognizes them), for otherwise Althaia will have no brothers for Meleagros to kill, a deed he performs already in the *Iliad* (Il 9.566–67) and in Bakchylides (where two are named, Iphiklos and Aphares: 5.127–29). Stesichoros apparently furnished two different names, Prokaon and Klytios (222 *PMG*; so too ΣT *Il* 9.567),[1] while ΣA *Iliad* 9.567 lists five (Iphiklos, Eurypylos, Plexippos, plus Polyphantes and Phanes) and Apollodoros four (the first three of the above plus Euippos: ApB 1.7.10).[2] In Apollonios this same Iphiklos is an Argonaut, accompanying his nephew Meleagros (AR 1.201). As to the mother of these children of Thestios, Pherekydes must know a slightly different tradition, for he makes her one Laophonte, daughter of Pleuron (3F9); he also lists no sons and only two daughters, Leda and Althaia, but they are after all the most important children. Eumelos, as we saw in chapter 5, offers a much more radical variant: in his work, Sisyphos' son Glaukos is the real father of Leda by one Panteiduia, who only subsequently marries Thestios (fr 7 *PEG*). Presumably this is an innovation designed to link Helen and Leda's other children with Korinth, and does not represent general belief. Thestios is never mentioned in Homer, and there seem to be few stories about him personally, although he must, of course, give Leda away to Tyndareos. In Strabo and Apollodoros this is accomplished by having him receive Tyndareos and Ikarios when the latter are driven out of Lakedaimonia by their brother Hippokoon; they offer to expand his territory westward beyond the river Acheloos in exchange for a share of what they acquire (Str 10.2.24; Ap*B* 3.10.5–6). The bargain is made, and carried out, but while Ikarios stays on, marrying Polykaste, daughter of one Lygdaios (Ap*B* says Periboia, a Naiad) after a time, Tyndareos takes his wife Leda, daughter of Thestios, and returns to Sparta. Strabo also calls Thestios the leader of the Kouretes, to whom we shall return shortly in considering the war between Pleuron and Kalydon.

Hypermestra In chapter 5, we saw that Theoklymenos' account of his family in *Odyssey* 15 included a son of Melampous, Antiphates, who in turn begat Oikles, father of the seer Amphiaraos (*Od* 15.241–44). No mother is mentioned, but in the *Ehoiai* Oikles weds Hypermestra, and she bears to him Amphiaraos, together with lovely Iphianeira and Endeos (Hes fr 25.34–40 MW). The papyrus breaks off just at this point, and thus we cannot tell whether there were any additional children. Apollodoros for his part does not even mention the marriage, and of the three children only Amphiaraos (Ap*B* 1.8.2: here as elsewhere named son of Iokles, apparently a variant on Oikles[3]). For Diodoros the children of Oikles and Hypermestra were Amphiaraos, Iphianeira, and Polyboia, but he has no stories to tell about anyone except the seer (DS 4.68.5). Amphiaraos is, of course, a major figure in the tale of the Seven against Thebes; we shall return to his story in chapter 14, where his fate will be intertwined with those of Polyneikes, Adrastos, and his first cousin Tydeus.

Leda Neither Leda nor Tyndareos is mentioned in the *Iliad*, although Helen does tell us that one mother bore Kastor, Polydeukes, and herself (*Il* 3.236–38); her father in both the *Iliad* and the *Odyssey* is clearly Zeus (*Il* 3.199, 418, 426; *Od* 4.184, 219; 23.218). Elsewhere the *Odyssey* makes Tyndareos the father of Klytaimestra (*Od* 24.199), and in the *Nekuia*, Leda is the mother of Kastor and Polydeukes by Tyndareos (*Od* 11.298–300). In the *Ehoiai*, although Tyndareos' name must be supplied in the main papyrus fragment, he is clearly (from other references to the poem) the husband intended in that fragment's account of Leda's marriage and the resulting daughters Timandra, Klytaimestra, and Phylonoe (Hes fr 23a MW). The text goes on to describe the fortunes of these three daughters without mention of other children by Leda, and this is surely indicative. We have seen before that the *Ehoiai* usually discusses all the children of one gender in a family before returning to the other gender, but that procedure will not explain the omission here of Helen when all her sisters are named; presumably she is separated from them because she is not Leda's child by Tyndareos, much as happens with Althaia's children by Ares and Oineus.[4] This conclusion assumes, of course, that Helen *is* Leda's child in the *Ehoiai*; certainly in a later fragment of the poem heroes come to Tyndareos' house to sue for her hand (Hes frr 199, 204.61–62 MW), and elsewhere she is grouped with Timandra and Klytaimestra as victims of Aphrodite's anger (Hes fr 176

MW). Dissenting, however, is one scholiast (on Pindar's *Nem* 10) who says that in "Hesiod" Helen is born from Zeus and an Okeanid (Hes fr 24 MW); conceivably then, in the *Ehoiai* (as in the *Kypria*: see below) she is only adopted by Tyndareos and Leda. But this seems dubious, given the genealogical principle (gods and mortal women) on which the *Ehoiai* operates; likely the scholiast's words (oddly phrased) have become garbled,[5] or perhaps a different poem of the Hesiodic Corpus was intended. The same scholiast also notes that in "Hesiod" both Kastor and Polydeukes are Zeus' sons, in contrast to the situation in Pindar. Likely enough, then, Helen and the Dioskouroi were considered together after the offspring of Leda's other daughters because for the Catalogue Poet all three were children of Leda and Zeus, not Tyndareos. Two short *Homeric Hymns* likewise call the Dioskouroi "Tyndaridai," but then specify that Leda bore them secretly to Zeus (*HomH* 17, 33). Adding to this the arrangement in Pindar, we seem to have in the Archaic period all three possibilities for the Dioskouroi, that they are both sons of Tyndareos *(Nekuia)*, both sons of Zeus *(Ehoiai)*, and that Kastor is the son of Tyndareos and Polydeukes the son of Zeus (*Nem* 10.80–82: no source ever argues the reverse of this split parentage). We will see below that this last arrangement is almost certainly true also for the *Kypria*, where Kastor is mortal but Polydeukes immortal (fr 8 *PEG*).

As for Helen, we saw above that as early as the *Iliad* she has the same mother as the Dioskouroi (thus Leda, even if she is not named), while (in other parts of the poem) her father is Zeus. Indeed, no subsequent source ever suggests that this father could be anyone but Zeus, Tyndareos' role in bringing her up notwithstanding. But for her mother there is in contrast to Homer (and probably to the *Ehoiai*) a direct quote from the *Kypria* in which Helen is the daughter of Zeus and Nemesis (fr 9 *PEG*). As we saw in discussing Nemesis in chapter 1, our source for this twelve-line citation is Athenaios, whose sole purpose in offering it is to establish that Nemesis turned herself into a fish (Athen 8.334b-d). The quote begins by saying that after these (something masculine, presumably the Dioskouroi) Zeus begat thirdly Helen, whom Nemesis bore in union with the ruler of the gods under compulsion.[6] These last words refer to the fact that, for reasons that are not made clear, Nemesis does not wish to mate with Zeus; when simple flight does not avail her she takes the form of a fish and swims through the sea and Okeanos, then travels over dry land while becoming various beasts. Athenaios stops here, before we have reached the conclusion of the story, because his point about fish has been made. But Philodemos adds (between the usual holes in our text of his work) that in the *Kypria* Zeus too turned himself into a goose and pursued Nemesis and that, mingling, they produced an egg from which Helen was born (fr 10 *PEG*).[7] Seemingly, then, both Zeus and Nemesis became geese, with the resulting egg only what we should expect. Of subsequent authors with this tale Asklepiades makes Zeus take the form of a swan for the mating (12F11), while in Ps-Eratosthenes Nemesis turns herself into a swan to escape Zeus, and he follows her lead, swooping down to her at Rhamnous, after which she gives birth to the egg containing Helen (*Katast* 25).[8] For this last detail at least Ps-Eratosthenes cites Kratinos, the fifth-century comic poet who in fact wrote a play called *Nemesis*. In light of the above accounts, certain fragments from that work begin to make sense: in one, Zeus has apparently been metamorphosed into a bird (fr 114 *PCG*), while in another someone tells Leda that she must sit on the egg so that it will hatch (fr 115 *PCG*). The play's title shows that Nemesis is here still the mother of the egg, but somehow it has come into Leda's possession. Since Perikles and Aspasia were caricatured as Zeus and Nemesis (or Leda?), one presumes that Kratinos draws on a familiar myth, and in fact a fragment of Sappho says that Leda once found an egg, surely this one (166 LP). In Apollodoros (where Nemesis becomes a goose and Zeus [perhaps] a swan),[9] a shepherd comes upon her egg and brings it to Leda (Ap*B* 3.10.7); in Hyginus, Hermes himself deposits it in her lap (*Astr* 2.8). Presumably, some form of this transfer goes back to the *Kypria,* and is always a part of the story when Nemesis is Helen's mother; the alternative is to postulate a tradition in which Helen is essentially severed from Sparta.[10]

In art the egg (plus the legs of a woman who could be Nemesis or Leda) first appears on Red-Figure pyxis fragments of about 450 B.C. (Reggio Calabria, no #), while from about 430 a series of vase-paintings, probably inspired by Kratinos' play, show Leda looking at that same egg on a pedestal or altar. That Leda rather than Nemesis is here meant emerges clearly from the presence on some examples of Tyndareos and the Dioskouroi (so Bonn 78). Present, too, at times is an eagle next to or perched on the egg as Leda shrinks back in astonishment (Boston 99.539; Athens 19447); on the latter vase, the egg has cracked and Helen begins to emerge, so that the bird (Zeus?) possibly assisted the process. According to Pausanias, the base of Pheidias' cult statue of Nemesis at Rhamnous portrayed what we may suppose to be a later scene from the story, Leda bringing Helen to Nemesis (1.33.8).

Having now established the existence of versions in which Leda is (1) the natural mother of Helen by Zeus *(Iliad, Ehoiai)* and (2) the stepmother of Helen, child of Zeus and Nemesis as geese *(Kypria)* or swans (Ps-Eratosthenes), we turn to the third and most familiar account of the story, that Zeus' dalliance in the form of a swan is with Leda herself, and that she, not Nemesis, is the mother of the egg. Strictly speaking, of course, we cannot guarantee that Homer and other early sources in which Leda is the real mother did not know this story, but its unusual nature is surely better explained as a later conflation of two separate traditions, one in which Leda is the mother, the other in which two divinities mate as birds. Our earliest actual reference of any sort to Zeus becoming a swan to engage Leda's attention is Euripides' *Helen:* the title character in speaking the prologue calls herself a daughter of Tyndareos, but then relates the report of men that Zeus as a swan sought shelter with Leda when pursued by an eagle, and thus won her affection (*Hel* 16–21). Shortly after, the same play asserts that Leda did indeed produce from this union an egg from which Helen was born (*Hel* 257–59).[11] The dual tradition thus created is well illustrated by Isokrates, who asserts (in his *Helen*, of all places) that Zeus as swan came to both Nemesis and Leda, this despite the fact that only one of them (he does not say which) could bear Helen (10.*Helen* 59).[12] Subsequently, we find a rash of artistic representations, many of them actually portraying Leda in sexual congress with the swan. But whether such a union is older than Euripides, and if so when it originated, we cannot say.[13] In Pausanias, too, Leda herself produces the egg, which can be seen in the sanctuary of the Leukippides at Sparta (3.16.1). After a time, even the Dioskouroi become enmeshed: in Lykophron, eggshells cover their heads (Lyk 506–7; so too *DD* 25), while the scholia at *Odyssey* 11.298 have all three children (as Zeus') emerge from the egg. Apollodoros, although he tells of Nemesis' egg brought to Leda, also reports a version in which Leda consorts with Zeus/swan (to produce Helen and Polydeukes) and Tyndareos (to produce Kastor and Klytaimestra) on the same night (Ap*B* 3.10.7; the same arrangement of children in *Fab* 77). In Servius, we find again the notion (as in the *Odyssey* scholia) that the three children were born from one egg after the mating of Zeus/swan and Leda (Σ *Aen* 3.328; cf. VM I 78; III 3.6). Yet the First Vatican Mythographer adds to this a second version in which two eggs are produced, one bearing Kastor and Polydeukes, the other Helen and Klytaimestra (VM I 204; the implication is certainly that all four are Zeus' children).[14] We shall see too in the next section that the question of immortality for Polydeukes and Kastor complicates the matter of their parentage. On the whole, then, we have considerable uncertainty on a number of points, but at least Helen and Polydeukes seem always to be off-spring of Zeus, while Kastor has that role on many occasions; Klytaimestra claims it only in the last variant cited.

Of Leda there are no other stories beyond this complicated tale of the bringing forth of her children. Of her four daughters one, Phylonoe, is dismissed in just three lines of the *Ehoiai* with a large gap in the middle (Hes fr 23.10–12 MW). But Artemis is involved, and in the third line we find the words "all her days," so that Apollodoros' statement that Artemis made this Phylonoe immortal is surely what was written here (Ap*B* 3.10.6). Unfortunately, Apollodoros does not give a motive, and no one else mentions her at all. The other three daughters, Timandra, Klytaimestra, and Helen, remain behind to marry and become victims of the above-mentioned anger of Aphrodite. The *Ehoiai* and Stesichoros both told this story, as a scholion informs us. The quote from the *Ehoiai* does not include Aphrodite's reason (Hes fr 176 MW); in Stesichoros, it is because Tyndareos omitted her inadvertently when he was sacrificing to all the other gods (223 *PMG*). Stesichoros' memorable version of the punishment is that she made the daughters "twice-married and thrice-married" (presumably thinking in Helen's case of Deiphobos [or Theseus] as well as Menelaos and Paris). The *Ehoiai* says, more concretely, that Timandra left Echemos for Phyleus (presumably the same as the father of Meges in the *Iliad*), Klytaimestra lay with Aigisthos, and Helen shamed her marriage bed. Previously, in the section on Leda's daughters, the *Ehoiai* has already told us that Timandra married Echemos and bore to him Laodokos (perhaps others), while Klytaimestra wed Agamemnon and bore three children, Iphimede, Elektra, and Orestes (Hes fr 23 MW). The passage goes on to describe the sacrifice of Iphimede at Aulis, so that her name is clearly a variant for "Iphigeneia." But the text leaves no room for more than these three children—Orestes and his matricidal deed are immediately followed by Timandra—and thus no room for any of the three daughters, Chrysothemis, Laodike, and Iphianassa, whom Agamemnon offers to Achilleus in the *Iliad* (*Il* 9.144–47). Given that there are neither stories nor offspring from any of these daughters, their omission from the *Ehoiai* is probably not surprising, but they do not disappear entirely from our sources; Chrysothemis (and apparently Iphianassa: S:*El* 157) will resurface in Sophokles' *Elektra*, while the *Kypria* will suggest that Agamemnon had four daughters, including both Iphigeneia and Iphianassa (fr 24 *PEG*).[15]

To the number of Leda's children we must add one more: in Euripides' *Iphigeneia at Aulis* Agamemnon makes the surprising statement that Leda bore three daughters, Klytaimestra, Helen, and Phoibe. We might suppose the last a Euripidean aberration, or confusion with Phoibe, daughter of Leukippos, but a Phoibe of this family does appear named on several Attic vases: so on a Black-Figure hydria of the mid-sixth century where with Helen she flanks the mounted Dioskouroi (Basel, loan) and on a Red-Figure stamnos by Polygnotos where she stands by as Helen is carried off by Theseus and Peirithoos (Athens 18063). Thus the idea has some pre-Euripidean support; it appears once again in Ovid (*Her* 8.77).

The section of the *Ehoiai* relating the wooing of Helen makes clear that Agamemnon has already married Klytaimestra at this point (Hes fr 197 MW). He champions his brother's suit, and Menelaos it seems also offers the most, so that, in the absence of Achilleus, he defeats the other aspirants and wins Helen, who bears to him Hermione (Hes fr 204.85–95). The poem then begins to relate Zeus' machinations for the Trojan War, and there are presumably no further children named here. But a two-line fragment of the same poem cited elsewhere seems to say that Helen after Hermione also bore Nikostratos as the youngest of her children (Hes fr 175 MW). The fragment stops before we can be sure that Menelaos is the father, although this seems the understanding of the epic poet Kinaithon (fr 3 *PEG*) and the Alexandrian Lysimachos (382F12) who with others also attest the child.[16] Somewhere, of course, Helen will have borne at least one more child, to justify the superlative "youngest"; since our source for this fragment implies that Menelaos and Helen beget *only* these two children in the *Ehoiai*, she presumably bore the other(s) to Paris.[17] Several traditions for such offspring will be considered in chapter 16. The *Kypria* appears to have known yet another child of Helen and Menelaos, one Pleisthenes (fr 12 *PEG*); the implication of our scholiast source is that this child was in lieu of Nikostratos, since he juxtaposes the information to that from Lysimachos.

We will return to Helen's wooing in more detail, and the oath extracted from her suitors, in chapter 16.

<table>
<tr><td>

*The
Dioskouroi*

</td><td>

Turning to Leda's two sons, we have seen that they are first mentioned in *Iliad* 3, where they are named as Kastor, tamer of horses, and Polydeukes, good with his fists (*Il* 3.237–38). This is their only appearance in the *Iliad*, and in the *Odyssey* they are restricted to the *Nekuia*, where the same names and epithets are used and they are explicitly the sons of Leda and Tyndareos (*Od* 11.298–300). The *Iliad*, which says nothing about their father, adds that they are covered over by earth in their own land of Sparta (*Il* 3.243–44); such a fate would seem to indicate that they have died a normal death, and perhaps tip the scales toward Tyndareos as their sire. But in the *Nekuia* passage we find that the earth holds them living, and that they have equal honor from Zeus under the earth, being alive one day and dead the next (*Od* 11.301–4). Conceivably, these difficult lines are an interpolation, for such a favor, whatever it means, will be easier to understand in a context where Zeus, not Tyndareos, is the twins' father. That the same notion might be implicit in the *Iliad* (where it is never specifically said that the two are dead or in Hades) seems excluded by the intended pathos of the context, and by the fact that *Odyssey* 11.301 subtly modifies part of *Iliad* 3.243 to make them alive under the earth. Indeed, we might wonder if this location of their honored afterlife did not spring in part from a desire to correct the *Iliad* without openly contradicting it. But whether or not that is true, the twins would seem in the *Iliad* to be entirely mortal, and thus probably sons of Tyndareos. In the *Ehoiai*, we did find both children to be the sons of Zeus (Hes fr 24 MW). Possibly the Catalogue Poet called them the Dioskouroi (as the *Odyssey* at least clearly cannot do), but our first preserved use of that term is in *Homeric Hymn* 33. Both here and in *Homeric Hymn* 17 they are, as in the *Ehoiai*, sons of Zeus and Leda, although addressed by virtue of their stepfather also as the Tyndaridai. So too in a poem of Alkaios they have this parentage (34a LP). As such, with a mortal mother, we would expect they themselves to be mortal, despite their descent from Zeus. In the *Kypria*, however, we are assured by a two-line quote that Kastor is mortal and subject to death, while Polydeukes is immortal; nothing alas is said here about their father (fr 8 *PEG*). Proklos' summary of the *Kypria* further tells us that the poem related their combat with Idas and Lynkeus, and that after Kastor was killed in this encounter Zeus awarded "alternate-day" immortality to them. From this evidence we can only conjecture, and of course a son of Zeus and Leda *ought* to be every bit as mortal as a son of Leda and Tyndareos, but very likely the poet of the *Kypria* has abandoned the usual rules and supposes that Kastor and Polydeukes have different destinies because they have different fathers, as in Pindar (although Pindar in *Nem* 10 may mean rather that Zeus will *give* Polydeukes immortality because the latter is his son, not that it was automatically Polydeukes' birthright). If so, then this poem will represent the first preserved appearance of such a split parentage.[18]

</td></tr>
</table>

We have seen that already in Homer Kastor and Polydeukes are linked to boxing and chariot-driving, and both *Homeric Hymn* 33 and Alkaios (34a LP) stress their special patronage of sailors. They are also standard figures to include in the major group exploits of their time, the Kalydonian Boar Hunt (they are paired on the François Krater) and the voyage of the Argo (they appear on one of the metopes from the sixth-century Sikyonian *monopteros* at Delphi [Sikyonian Treasury, no #], although Polydeukes' combat with Amykos does not surface before the fifth century). They help as well in the *Ehoiai* to supervise the courting of their sister Helen (Hes frr 197, 198, 199 MW). But real stories about them are essentially limited to three: their recovery of Helen from Athens (or Aphidna) after Theseus has abducted her, their own abduction of the Leukippides Phoibe and Hilaeira, daughters of their (sometimes) uncle Leukippos, and their battle with Idas and Lynkeus, sons of Leukippos' brother Aphareus.[19] The first tale, unadorned as it is in the preserved tradition, has already been related in chapter 9. As for the second, the *Kypria* does mention Phoibe and Hilaeira, though as daughters of Apollo (according to Pausanias: fr 11 *PEG*); if they could be stepdaughters of Leukippos here then they might have been carried off in this poem at some point before the conflict over cattle (see below). We know too that Alkman spoke of them, since a scrap of papyrus mentions Phoibe's name (8 *PMG*). But all our preserved literary accounts of parentage, and abduction, and the promised marriage to the Apharetidai, are late. In these we find on the whole that the Leukippides were engaged to their other cousins, the Apharetidai, when the Dioskouroi carried them off (so Theok 22.137–66; Fasti 5.699–702; *Fab* 80; ΣA *Il* 3.243; Σ *Nem* 10.112). In Theokritos Lynkeus delivers a lengthy (and not unreasonable) protest against their actions, claiming that Leukippos had pledged his daughters to himself and his brother on oath before the Dioskouroi bribed him with cattle and other property to change his mind; unfortunately, the first part of Kastor's reply is lost, and we do not know how he dealt with such accusations. In the *Iliad* and Pindar scholia the Dioskouroi are actually invited to the wedding feast of their cousins and carry off the girls there.[20] Lykophron puts the primary blame on Zeus, who inspired a quarrel among the cousins, apparently over the failure to pay a bride-price for the Leukippides, when they are at a feast together (Lyk 512–49; Zeus' motive seems that of ensuring that Troy, which could not resist these four, will not fall to the Greeks too soon). The Lykophron scholia add some other possibilities. In one the quarrel starts at about the time when the Dioskouroi are entertaining Paris, and (unless the scholiast is confused) Lynkeus and Idas steal the girls promised to the Dioskouroi (Σ Lyk 538). Another has the daughters safely in the hands of the Dioskouroi, who are then mocked by the Apharetidai for failing to pay a bride-price (rather than reviled for stealing those promised to others: Σ Lyk 547); the Dioskouroi respond by stealing cattle from their cousins and giving the herd to Leukippos as payment. Apollodoros says simply that the girls were carried off, without reference to the Apharetidai; Hilaeira bears Anogon to Kastor and Phoibe Mnesileos to

Polydeukes (Ap*B* 3.11.2). The scholia at Lykophron 511 also report these off-spring, but add as variants Anaxis and Mnesinoos; those latter two names are the ones given by Pausanias when describing an Argive ebony-wood sculptural group of the Dioskouroi, the Leukippides, and the two sons (2.22.5). He names the same two again as mounted riders on the Amyklai Throne, but offers no myth or other reason for their inclusion there (3.18.13).

In art we find quite a number of scenes of the abduction, but little to further our knowledge of the story, even on the one vase that includes the Apharetidai. Pausanias reports that the abduction appeared on both the Amy-klai Throne (3.18.11) and the Bronze House of Athena (3.17.2), while a lid fragment from a Chalkidian pot shows Polydeukes lifting Phoibe (both named) into his chariot (Reggio Calabria 1027–28). In the following century, Polyg-notos painted the "marriage" of the girls (clearly to the Dioskouroi) on the walls of the Anakeion in Athens (Paus 1.18.1), and the carrying-off (often by chariot, sometimes from a temple) appears several times in Red-Figure.[21] The Meidias Painter toward the end of the century calls the girls Helera and Eri-phyle on a hydria in London (London E224), but the second of these has no other confirmation, and may represent artistic indifference to precision when the story is well known. Metopes from Heraion I at Foce del Sele showing two women fleeing and two men running, and the very fragmentary south frieze from the Siphnian Treasury at Delphi (no #),[22] are also commonly supposed to represent the abduction scene, but we must admit that in both cases the identification has little to support it (Theseus and Peirithoos pursuing Helen is just one alternate possibility). The one artifact that does add the Apharetidai is an Apulian lekythos of the fourth century: on the one side the twins drive off in triumph with the maidens (each in a separate chariot); on the other Idas engages Polydeukes in combat at the tomb of his father after Kastor and Lyn-keus have both been slain (Richmond 80.162). Presumably the two events are meant to be linked, as we see to what fatal point the passion of these brothers has brought them.

In all cases where the Leukippides were originally promised to the Apha-retidai, the combat with those cousins follows close upon the abduction. But the abduction does not always precede the combat. The *Kypria*, Pindar's *Nemean* 10, and Apollodoros ignore the Leukippides in this context, offering a (seem-ingly) quite different reason for the conflict: a dispute over cattle. In the *Kypria* these cattle are apparently stolen by the Dioskouroi from Idas and Lynkeus (*Kyp* p. 40 *PEG*); Pindar is considerably vaguer on the subject (*Nem* 10.60). It is not in fact clear why the *Kypria* relates the story at all, as it takes place after Helen has been carried off by Paris; perhaps the motive was as in Lykophron, where Zeus is said to arrange the quarrel between the two sets of brothers, lest they bring about Troy's fall too quickly (Lyk 512–43). A much fuller account of the cattle version is offered by Apollodoros, who says that the Dioskouroi and Apharetidai went off together on a cattle raid in Arkadia (Ap*B* 3.11.2). Cattle having in fact been taken, the two sets of brothers then proceed to an unusual allotment of the booty, for Idas divides one of the cows into four parts and proposes that he who finishes eating his part first shall receive half the cattle, and he who finishes second the other half. Unfortunately for the Dioskouroi, Idas proves a prodigious eater, finishing both his share and that of his brother before either of the other two have managed theirs; thus, the Apharetidai claim all of the cattle and drive them to Messene. But there the Dioskouroi steal the herd away, and set up an ambush for their foes. This version, with its elements of folktale and fantasy, is often regarded as that of the *Kypria*,[23] and it may well be; evidence in support of a joint cattle venture at least is a metope from the Sikyonian *monopteros* at Delphi showing three men named as Idas, Kastor, and Polydeukes (Lynkeus is lost to the left) driving cattle. Less likely as an early version, but not to be excluded, is the Lykophron scholia's combining of Leukippides and cattle by having the Dioskouroi steal some of the latter from the Apharetidai to pay Leukippos for the former (Σ Lyk 547); if this is not a late attempt to bring conflicting narratives together it might conceivably represent what the *Kypria* and/or Pindar had in mind.

As for the actual battle, although the end result in early accounts is always the same—Idas, Lynkeus, and Kastor dead—there are some variations. In the *Kypria* Lynkeus runs to the top of Mount Taugetos and scans the entire Peloponnesos, finally locating both Kastor and Polydeukes hiding within a hollow oak (fr 15 *PEG:* presumably this is the ambush mentioned by Apollodoros). Idas then somehow kills Kastor with his spear, and Polydeukes (who is immortal) kills both Idas and Lynkeus. In Pindar we have clear if allusive references to the same account: Lynkeus, gazing from Taugetos, sees the Dioskouroi in the hollow oak, apparently with vision that can penetrate through solid objects (*Nem* 10.60–72). Idas then wounds Kastor with his spear (by stabbing through the tree and taking the Dioskouroi by surprise) and Polydeukes pursues both Idas and Lynkeus to the tomb of their father Aphareus. Here they make a stand, and attempt to throw the polished tombstone at Polydeukes. This fails to daunt him, however, and he slays Lynkeus with his spear while Zeus hurls a thunderbolt at Idas. Judging from the scholia to *Nemean* 10, the seeing through solid objects and stabbing through the tree go back to the *Kypria*, and so perhaps too other of Pindar's details. Theokritos' version places more emphasis on Kastor, but likely this is a Theokritean innovation to balance Polydeukes' victory over Amykos in the first half of the same poem. He omits hollow oak and ambush, and instead brings all four combatants to Aphareus' tomb, where the protest over the stolen brides is lodged and Kastor challenges Lynkeus to a duel, leaving aside Polydeukes and Idas (22.137–213). After some sparring Lynkeus is wounded; he drops his sword and flees to Idas at the tomb, but Kastor runs after him and stabs him fatally. Idas then picks up the tombstone all by himself, and is about to hurl it at Kastor when Zeus again intervenes with his thunderbolt (here alone it seems Kastor survives). In Ovid's *Fasti* there is a pitched combat: Lynkeus kills Kastor, Polydeukes kills Lynkeus, and the thunderbolt kills Idas (*Fasti* 5.707–14). For Hyginus, Kastor kills Lyn-

keus, Idas Kastor (when the latter interferes with Lynkeus' burial), and Polydeukes Idas (*Fab* 80); in the Lykophron scholia, Polydeukes kills Idas and Zeus
Lynkeus. Apollodoros follows Pindar, but with the one new detail that Polydeukes is struck unconscious by a stone as he throws the fatal spear at Lynkeus;
Zeus disposes of Idas and takes his son up to Olympos where he recovers (Ap*B*
3.11.2). Why the hollow oak should be missing from these later versions (although it is half-implied in Apollodoros) is not clear. It does seem that Lynkeus' penetrating vision, like Idas' voracious appetite, belongs to a world where
magical powers are more in order, and perhaps for that reason the ambush
(which reflects little credit on the Dioskouroi in any case) was suppressed. Only
the First Vatican Mythographer preserves the idea that as Lynkeus was helped
by his special vision, so Idas had a spear that never missed its mark (VM I 77).
In art we should note again the Apulian lekythos with the Leukippides and the
battle: Kastor and Lynkeus lie already fallen, while Idas raises the vertical part
of the tomb monument over his head in order to hurl it at Polydeukes, and a
thunderbolt closes in on him from above (Richmond 80.162).

Finally, we come to the ultimate fate of these brothers. In the *Iliad*, as we
saw, the earth simply covers them (*Il* 3.243–44), but in the *Odyssey*, after the
earth has again done so, they "although under the earth have honor from Zeus,
and on alternate days they are alive, and on other days they are dead. And they
have received as their lot honor equal to that of the gods" (*Od* 11.301–4). This
surprising passage seems to mean that they remain under the earth always,
though alternately dead (i.e., shades in Hades?) and enjoying some kind of
blessed existence (like that of the mortals of Hesiod's Golden Age?). Something
of the same sort may be intended in a poem of Alkman, where a "coma of the
gods" is mentioned and Menelaos appears to be living with the Dioskouroi
under the earth at Therapnai in an existence in which they delight (7 *PMG*).
Our *Kypria* summary for its part simply says that Zeus granted to the Dioskouroi immortality on alternate days, and thus is not much help; possibly the
original poem was more explicit. Pindar takes us a step further, for in both his
Nemean 10 and *Pythian* 11 it is clear that the two brothers spend alternate
days under the earth at Therapnai and with Zeus on Olympos (*Nem* 10.55–59,
85–88; *Py* 11.61–64). But this concept involves new uncertainties, for now the
brothers are under the earth only half the time, and that period seems to represent their time of death, in contrast to what the *Nekuia* and Alkman might
be thought to imply. And there is a further problem. Nothing in Homer's
words, or Proklos' summary of the *Kypria*, or Pindar enables us to say for
certain whether Kastor and Polydeukes alternate with each other, or alternate
together; the Greek compound "alternate-day" can surely mean both. Even
Polydeukes' impassioned plea to Zeus in *Nemean* 10 does not contain any
appeal that he remain together with his brother, but only that he not have a
better lot than Kastor. On balance, Homer's language, with its plural verbs,
seems to lean to the view that they remain together, while two words in a row
for exchanging in Pindar might suggest just the opposite (*Nem* 10.55). This

latter notion, of rotating with each other, *may* be present in Vergil's phrase *alterna morte* at *Aeneid* 6.121; without question it is the basis of one of Loukianos' *Dialogues of the Gods* (25), a dialogue in which Apollo asks Hermes how one tells the Dioskouroi apart when they look just alike and are never present at the same time. Hermes advises him to check for Polydeukes' boxing scars, and explains that they alternate with each other on Olympos as a way of sharing one immortality. Whether Loukianos found such an idea explicitly stated somewhere, or whether it is his own (perhaps mistaken) interpretation of Homer and others, is difficult to say. Naturally the two brothers are appealed to jointly as gods who protect sailors, and appear together to mortals, or even on stage at the end of Euripides' *Helen*, but clearly their role as divinities is not in any case really compatible with the myth of their shared fate, save perhaps in the beginning when they were heroes under the earth.

Althaia   As early as *Iliad* 9, Althaia is the mother of Meleagros, who is there called the son of Oineus, ruler of Kalydon and (in *Iliad* 14) son of Portheus (*Il* 9.543; 14.115–18). In the *Ehoiai*, this latter figure is Porthaon, son of Agenor, whose union with Eureite produces Oineus while that of his sister Demodike with Ares produces Thestios (Hes frr 10a.49–54, 22 MW). Oineus and Thestios are thus first cousins, and Althaia Oineus' first cousin once removed (essentially a standard uncle-niece mating). The *Ehoiai*'s account of Thestios' daughters seems to have proceeded from the families of the children of Leda (Klytaimestra and Timandra,[24] then presumably Kastor and Polydeukes and Helen) to the offspring of Althaia and Oineus (both named) and then those of Hypermestra and Echemos. But the beginning of the fragment in question, the part describing the fate of Meleagros (Hes fr 25 MW), is mostly lost, which creates a question as to his origins. Following the tale of Meleagros and his death, the text says that "dark-eyed Althaia bore these other children to Oineus" and goes on to list Phereus, Agelaos, Toxeus, Klymenos, Gorge, and Deianeira. The emphasis of word order here, plus the deictic "these" together with *allous*, "other," seems to imply that previous offspring were borne to someone else, and while such phrasing is not paralleled in what remains of the *Ehoiai*, in the *Nekuia* we find almost exactly the same expression (*heterous* for *allous*) for the sons Tyro bears to Kretheus after having borne Neleus and Pelias to Poseidon (*Od* 11.258). The inference to be made is thus probably that Meleagros is not Oineus' son in the *Ehoiai*; certainly Euripides seems to have made him the offspring of Ares and Althaia in his *Meleagros* (*Mor* 312a), and Apollodoros (*ApB* 1.8.2) and Ovid (*Met* 8.437) definitely do so. Hyginus concedes that Althaia lay with Ares and Oineus on the same night, but seems uncertain whom to name as father (*Fab* 171); elsewhere he gives the child to Oineus (*Fab* 174). As we just saw, the *Iliad* does clearly call him a son of Oineus, but there his link to Oineus (who has begun the tale by forgetting to sacrifice to Artemis) is his introduction into the story, and it would make no sense to identify his real father. Likewise, when Meleagros himself calls Oineus his father in Bakchylides' Ode 5 (97–102), it is to establish his own role in the story as the son of the king (earlier in that poem he *is* called a descendant of Porthaon: 5.70). In all, as we found with Theseus, it is very hard to say what the general tradition might have been, or how widespread the notion of a divine parentage for this hero.

The familiar tale of Meleagros' death by means of a burning brand is told in detail by Bakchylides in the same Ode 5, and was probably dramatized by Phrynichos in his lost *Pleuroniai;*[25] there is also a clear enough allusion in the second stasimon of Aischylos' *Choephoroi.* But our two earliest preserved sources, the *Iliad* and the *Ehoiai,* offer a rather different picture, and Pausanias, who cites the *Minyas* as aligned with them, specifies that Phrynichos' is the earliest account of the brand known to him (although he concedes that the playwright does not seem to be innovating: 10.31.3–4). The *Iliad's* version raises here as elsewhere the question of possible Homeric reshaping to create parallels, since Phoinix tells the tale to Achilleus to make a point about the latter's own situation (*Il* 9.529–99).[26] We start out on what will become familiar ground, with Artemis angry at Oineus of Kalydon because he failed to sacrifice to her when he remembered all the other gods. As a result, the Kalydonian Boar is dispatched to ravage the countryside, Meleagros, son of Oineus, gathers together many hunters, and after much loss of life the Boar is slain. But Artemis then causes a war to break out between the Aitolians of Kalydon and the Kouretes (apparently the people of Thestios' city of Pleuron[27]) over the hide. As long as Meleagros fights, the Kouretes dare not remain outside their walls (or Kalydon's walls?). But after a time he withdraws from the fighting, angered because his mother Althaia in grief over the death of one or more of her brothers has cursed him;[28] we are left to presume that these as sons of Thestios fought on the side of the other Pleuronians and were slain by Meleagros in battle. Althaia asks Hades and Persephone for death for her son, and we are told that an Erinys hears her. Subsequently, as the Kouretes storm the walls of Kalydon, the elders plead with Meleagros to come out and defend them, promising many gifts, and then Oineus and the sisters and even Althaia add their voices to the general prayers. But Meleagros will not yield until his wife Kleopatra reminds him of the horrors of a captured city and thus, although he saves Kalydon, he forfeits the gifts. In all this account there is no mention at all of Atalanta, and no indication of Meleagros' ultimate fate. Pausanias assumed, as have others, that the Erinys destroyed him (10.31.3; so too Ap*B* 1.8.3), but if he is irrevocably doomed his intransigence will become all too reasonable, and the loss of the proffered gifts scarcely of any consequence.[29] Perhaps this point is simply to be overlooked for the sake of the story, but more likely (I think) we are meant to understand that when Althaia appeals to her son she recalls her curse (as she surely can); otherwise her appeal will have little point.[30] If that is the situation, then Phoinix envisions a long-lived but giftless hero as an appropriate object lesson for Achilleus. Meleagros is recorded as dead in the *Iliad's* Catalogue of Ships (*Il* 2.642), but by the time of the fall of Troy we would expect him to be deceased in any case. One other point to be noted is the means of attempted vengeance by Althaia; clearly she does not possess the familiar brand in Homer or she would not have resorted to chthonian deities. But of course the brand will scarcely serve Phoinix's purpose, and the curse here may spring from nothing more than Homer's need for an action by Althaia which will trigger her son's anger rather than his death. In all, the notion that Meleagros survives the war with Pleuron is unique to the *Iliad*; on that fact alone we are probably justified in regarding this version (beginning from the withdrawal at least) as a temporary reshaping of a simpler tradition.

In the *Ehoiai* we have preserved only the end of the story, after which the narrative moves on to Althaia's other children (Hes fr 25.1–13 MW). Enough survives, however, to show that Meleagros' qualities as a warrior were stressed, and that he was fighting against the Kouretes before the walls of Pleuron when Apollo struck him down. The wording of the text does not seem to leave room for any special explanation of this action, or cause of anger against Meleagros; Pausanias, who cites both the *Ehoiai* and the *Minyas* for his account, says that Apollo was supporting the Kouretes (10.31.3). If that is the whole cause, then Meleagros' death is not here connected with the Boar Hunt at all, save to the extent that the Hunt may have triggered the war. Apollo seems also to be the culprit in the Ibscher Papyrus fragment, whether this is from the *Minyas* or some other poem; here too alas the text begins just as the story is ending (Hes fr 280.1–2 MW). Moving through the sixth century, which in literature is a blank (although Stesichoros' lost *Suotherai* surely narrated the tale at length), we come back to Phrynichos' *Pleuroniai*, for which Pausanias' comments are really our only information. He asserts that in this play the Moirai have given the fatal log to Althaia with the stipulation that her son will not die until it is consumed, and that she in anger does burn it, causing her son to burn up as well. This is all as we would expect, but Pausanias stops short of linking the event with the Boar Hunt, or anything else. In Bakchylides, Meleagros tells his own story to Herakles: Artemis became angry at his father Oineus, would not heed his sacrifices, and sent the Boar to destroy Kalydon (5.93–154). The best of the Greeks fight against it for six days; Ankaios and the bravest of Meleagros' brothers, Agelaos, are lost,[31] but finally they overcome it, only to have a war break out with the Kouretes over the hide. Althaia's brothers Iphiklos and Aphares are on the opposing side, and Meleagros slays them, not intentionally, but thus the god directs his missiles. So far this is all virtually as in the *Iliad*, but now Althaia, rather than pray to Hades, resorts to the brand hidden away in a chest, the brand that *moira* set as the end of her son's life, and he falls while fighting before the walls of Pleuron. Aischylos' highly abbreviated picture of Althaia destroying her own son by kindling the coeval brand offers just about the same picture, although the motive is never mentioned (*Cho* 602–11). An *Atalanta* play also appears among the titles in the Medicean Catalogue of Aischylos' works, so that he may have written a complete drama on these events, but such a play (we have no references) might also have dealt with the race of suitors for the Boiotian Atalanta, or even (as a satyr play) a struggle with Silenoi (for a likely illustration of this last there is a Red-Figure cup in the University of Giessen of about 460 B.C. [Giessen 46]). Sophokles' *Meleagros* is likewise completely lost, although we know that the Boar as sent by Artemis was a factor (fr 401 R). From the further detail that the chorus consisted of priests (ΣA *Il* 9.575) it has been conjectured that Sophokles here followed the account of Homer.[32] For Euripides' *Meleagros* with its involvement of Atalanta, see below.

Summing up at this point, we appear to have two main traditions. In one, represented by the *Iliad* and Bakchylides, the Kalydonian Boar Hunt leads to a squabble between the Kalydonians and Pleuronians over the hide, and this causes a war in which Meleagros kills his two uncles, who are naturally fighting on the Pleuronian side. Here the *Iliad* and Bakchylides diverge, with the *Iliad* favoring a curse (probably not fulfilled) by Althaia, and Bakchylides finishing off Meleagros by means of the brand burned by his mother. In the other, represented it appears by the *Ehoiai* and the *Minyas*, the Kalydonians and Pleuronians are again fighting (perhaps for the same reason, perhaps not) but now there seems no question of slain uncles (or at least angry mothers), and Apollo kills Meleagros much as he kills Patroklos and Achilleus at Troy, to protect his chosen side.[33] As suggested above, the question then becomes whether the brand motif was a part of the story early enough for Homer to know of it (and replace it). I suspect this was the case (since Althaia's *anger* is certainly this early), but the matter has been argued several ways.[34] In any event, we should note that both these traditions are built around a local war between neighboring cities, an element that might seem to exclude any gathering of famous heroes from all over Greece (who would in any case try to claim the hide for themselves). Our first actual glimpse of that tradition is on the François Krater, where among other hunters we find Melanion and Atalanta (paired), Peleus and Meleagros, Kastor and Polydeukes, and Akastos (Florence 4209).[35] Conceivably this was a device of Kleitias to add greater resonance to his composition, but no doubt the same could be said for Stesichoros' *Suotherai*, where a list of the hunters was certainly supplied;[36] we must admit that we do not know when this shift of direction took place. Many of the same names reappear on the Archikles/Glaukytes cup in Munich, including Iason, Meleagros, Peleus, and Melanion (Munich 2243); Atalanta is here omitted, as she is on Tübingen S/12 2452, a Tyrrhenian amphora that features Meleagros, Melanion, Peleus, and Telamon. But she resurfaces often on other representations of the Hunt (so, e.g., Vat 306) and on a Caeretan hydria tackles the Boar all by herself (Copenhagen 13567). The question we must ask is, at what point does she become the center of the story, by claiming or being given the hide and thus causing a quarrel, not between Kalydonians and Pleuronians, but rather between Meleagros and his uncles. On the literary side our first evidence of Atalanta as femme fatale is Euripides' *Meleagros*, where the remains although gap-filled seem to guarantee that Meleagros does give her the hide and falls in (unrequited) love with her, thus leading him to kill his uncles and bring about his own doom (27 GLP, plus the remains of Accius' *Meleager*); the story subsequently finds its way into Diodoros, Apollodoros, and others (DS 4.34.4–5; Ap*B* 1.8.2; *Met* 8.324–27, 425–44). Its romanticism and melodramatic possibilities may well mark it as a Euripidean invention, one of his more charming, if so.[37] Against such a conclusion (speculative in any case) may or may not be the fact that, as we saw in chapter 5, a Chalkidian hydria in Munich shows Atalanta wrestling Peleus with a boar hide between them (Munich 596). If this hide is that of the Kalydonian Boar, then possibly the whole story of Atalanta's special relationship with Meleagros and her acquisition of the hide was known in the sixth century. But possibly too the artist wished nothing more than to remind us that these two combatants participated in the Hunt. Somewhere the *Kypria* gives Meleagros a daughter Polydore, who marries Protesilaos (fr 26 *PEG*); one would certainly like to know who the mother was, and when Meleagros' union with her took place. We shall see in the next section evidence for an even more puzzling offspring: Parthenopaios as the son of Meleagros and Atalanta.

Two other victims of the Boar Hunt remain to be discussed: Ankaios and Thersites. As we saw above, Ankaios is one of those named in Bakchylides' Ode 5 (together with Meleagros' brother Agelaos: 5.115–20) as slain by the Boar, and this is likewise his fate in the numerous other literary and artistic accounts that include him. But his original identity, and as well perhaps the persistence of this role, pose some problems. Homer knows of an Agapenor, son of Ankaios, who leads the Arkadians at Troy (*Il* 2.609–10), and this Ankaios, in Apollodoros and Pausanias a son of Lykourgos, son of Aleos of the line of Arkas, is the figure whom all later tradition associates with the Kalydonian Boar Hunt and the Argo (Ap*B* 1.8.2, 3.9.1; Paus 8.4.1–10; for an Ankaios of this lineage on the Argo see also AR 1.161–71). But elsewhere in the *Iliad*, Homer has Nestor speak of one Ankaios of Pleuron as the man he defeated in wrestling at the games for Amarynkeus (*Il* 23.634–35), so that not impossibly an originally local victim of the Boar is in time replaced by a (more famous) Arkadian of the same name. With that in mind, we may well wonder if Bakchylides does not follow the earlier tradition, with Agelaos and Ankaios paired at 5.117 precisely because *both* are sons of Althaia (and both, rather than strictly *adelpheôn*, the referent of the supplemented *hous* at 119). As for the artistic tradition, Ankaios (named) is shown sprawled out under the Boar as early as the François Krater (Florence 4209),[38] and he becomes a traditional feature of the scene from that point on, appearing on a number of other Black-Figure vases (e.g., Berlin:Ch F1705; Blatter Coll, no #) and collapsing in the arms of his brother Epochos in Skopas' portrayal of the Hunt for the pediment of the temple of Athena Alea at Tegea (Paus 8.45.5–7; Ankaios and Epochos are brothers at Σ AR 1.164). Apparently the Arkadians took pride in his part in the Hunt, despite the outcome (so Paus 8.45.2), and he does have several impressive moments on the Argo, equipped with bearskin and axe and sharing the middle rowing-bench with Herakles (AR 1.396–400, 2.118–21). Of later authors describing his goring (in the groin) we might note in particular Lykophron (479–93) and Ovid (*Met* 8.391–402).[39]

Thersites, by contrast, is not slain by the Boar, but he too comes to grief. Here again there is a Homeric figure of the same name, and here again there exists some doubt as to his equation with the participant in the Hunt. Homer himself says nothing about the parentage of the deformed Achaian who reviles Agamemnon in *Iliad* 2 and suffers Odysseus' rebuke (*Il* 2.211–77). For the scholia, however, he is the son of Agrios, brother of Oineus, and thus the first cousin of Diomedes' father Tydeus. The exegetical scholia go on to recount as from Pherekydes a tale in which this Thersites shirks his role in the Hunt out of fear, and in consequence Meleagros hurls him from a cliff, thus bringing about the deformities described by Homer (ΣbT *Il* 2.212 = 3F123). The A scholia offer a similar version, but ascribed to Euphorion, in which Thersites abandons his watch-place for safer ground and is then pursued by an angry Meleagros until he falls from a cliff, with the same result (ΣA *Il* 2.212 = fr 106 Pow). Clearly the point of both tales is to account for the Homeric Thersites' condition, but whether Homer would have agreed with this explanation (the scholiasts themselves seem dubious) we cannot say. In Apollodoros, Thersites is specifically named with the other sons of Agrios who wrest the kingdom of Kalydon from Oineus in order to give it to their father; in restoring the kingdom to Oineus, Diomedes kills all of these, save for Thersites and Onchestos, who manage to escape to the Peloponnese (and later kill Oineus in Arkadia: see chapter 17) (ApB 1.8.6). One normally places this exploit of Diomedes *after* the Trojan War (so, e.g., AntLib 37), in which case his cousin would not be the same Thersites slain by Achilleus, but nothing compels such an order of events. In Quintus, as we will see later, Diomedes is actually angry over the slaying of his cousin at Troy, so we may presume that author ignorant of (or choosing to ignore) any quarrel between the two men.

As for the aftermath of Meleagros' death, Diodoros, Ovid, and Apollodoros all say that Althaia killed herself in chagrin at what she had done (DS 4.34.7; *Met* 8.531–32; ApB 1.8.3). Neither Bakchylides nor Aischylos mentions this, but there is no special reason why they should. One is hard put, however, to imagine a full dramatization of the story which did not end with her death, and surely Phrynichos, Sophokles, and Euripides all brought this about, although perhaps not always by suicide (Oineus might have ordered her demise). A fragment of a lost poem by Bakchylides does refer to a wife of someone who apparently commits suicide from a high place, and the last line ends with the letters *Oin-* (fr 20D SM); this could well be the wife of Oineus, but Oinone, first wife of Paris, is also a possibility. Antoninus Liberalis relates to us from Nikandros the tale that Meleagros' sisters mourned for him until Artemis turned them into guinea hens *(meleagrides)*; on the request of Dionysos, Gorge and Deianeira were spared (AntLib 2). Pliny seems to indicate that this transformation goes back to Sophokles, and possibly it formed part of his

Meleagros (fr 830a R). Presumably the sparing of two daughters in Antoninus represents an attempt to bring the story into line with those in which Deianeira at least is otherwise spoken for (in the *Ehoiai*, we might note, Gorge and Deianeira are Oineus' only daughters). Ovid also relates such a metamorphosis, as we would expect (*Met* 8.533–46). We will return to Deianeira in chapter 13, in the context of her marriage to Herakles, but we should remember here the tradition, found in Apollodoros and Hyginus, that she is actually a daughter of Dionysos and Althaia (ApB 1.8.1; *Fab* 129). The *Ehoiai* clearly excludes any father but Oineus, and so too Sophokles' *Trachiniai*. Her marriage is, as we shall see, also guaranteed as early as the *Ehoiai*. But the Catalogue Poet proceeded directly from Deianeira to Hypermestra, sister of Althaia, and thus no marriage was recorded (here at least) for Gorge; in Apollodoros and Pausanias she is wed to Andraimon (ApB 1.8.1; Paus 10.38.5). Of the other sons (when not slain by the Boar) nothing is heard save for the odd story in Apollodoros (as above) that Oineus himself slew Toxeus when the latter jumped over a ditch. In the *Iliad's* Catalogue of Ships we do find that one Thoas, son of Andraimon, commands the Aitolian contingent because no sons are left to Oineus (*Il* 2.638).

Whether in repentance for the death of Meleagros or through other causes, Althaia does seem to die as a part of the early tradition, for already in the *Ehoiai* Oineus takes a second wife (or at least a concubine), Periboia, daughter of Hipponoos (Hes fr 12 MW). In this account, she had apparently been seduced by Hippostratos, son of Amarynkeus, and her father then sent her to Oineus to be killed; in the *Thebais*, she becomes spoils of war after the capture of the city of Olenos (St:*Theb* fr 5 *PEG*). Either way, she bears to Oineus his youngest son Tydeus. The one variant on this arrangement, as noted by Apollodoros, is that of the third/second-century B.C. mythographer Peisandros, who says that Tydeus was Oineus' son by his own daughter Gorge, by the will of Zeus (16F1). In chapter 5 we saw that the *Ehoiai's* account of the daughters of Aiolos led to Eureite and her husband Porthaon, who produced five sons, including Agrios and Oineus; Diomedes at one point in the *Iliad* mentions these two plus Melas, who must be the one name missing in the *Ehoiai* (*Il* 14.113–18). The *Ehoiai* goes on to say that Tydeus kills these (apparently all four of his uncles) because they tried to wrest power away from Oineus (Hes fr 10a.55–57 MW). In the *Alkmaionis* those whom he kills are the *sons* of Melas, but the motive is the same, plotting against his father (fr 4 *PEG*). Similar too is the report of Pherekydes, although here the victims are the sons of Agrios, and the motive for the usurpation Oineus' advancing years (3F122). But in this same author Tydeus accidentally slays his brother (or cousin) Olenias as well, and must flee Kalydon. He comes to Argos, where the king Adrastos purifies him and marries him to his daughter Deipyle. Such a migration is attested already by Diomedes in the *Iliad*, although without naming its cause (*Il* 14.119–21); Tydeus' further career and death at Thebes we will return to in chapter 14. Oineus remains behind in Kalydon, and as we saw suffers in

Apollodoros further problems with the sons of Agrios, at whose hands he finally dies (Ap*B* 1.8.6); possibly this was the plot of Euripides' lost *Oineus*, where Diomedes apparently returned to Kalydon to help his grandfather.

Atalanta   Though the Arkadian Atalanta who participates in the Kalydonian Boar Hunt is obviously not a member of the family of Thestios, the close of this chapter still seems the best place to note her further exploits, as well as those of her Boiotian counterpart. The existence of two essentially separate figures by this name has long been suspected, rightly I think;[40] in what follows, however, I shall try to let the evidence speak for itself. We have seen that an Atalanta wrestles with Peleus at the funeral games for Pelias; at times, too, she even sails with the Argo (Apollonios does not permit her on board because Iason fears problems, but Diodoros and Apollodoros are more accommodating: AR 1.769–73; DS 4.41.2; Ap*B* 1.9.16). Kallimachos also speaks of two Kentauroi who rashly attack her and are shot for their trouble (*H* 3.222–24). But the most famous adventure attached to her name is that which we first encounter in the *Ehoiai*, when such a maiden races with her suitors to avoid marriage (Hes frr 72–76 MW). In what remains of this story she is the daughter of Schoineus (son of Athamas and Themisto in Apollodoros), who himself announces to the assembled multitude the terms on which his daughter will race against Hippomenes. Despite the mutilated text, it is clear that marriage and death are the prizes for victory and defeat. Atalanta is plainly the faster, but Hippomenes has his three apples (apparently a gift from Aphrodite) and by throwing them to the ground so that Atalanta will stop to pick them up he gains the time he needs. In Theognis we also encounter an Atalanta who wishes to avoid marriage. But this one is the daughter of Iasios, and abandons her father's house (taking to the mountains) in order to accomplish her purpose; the poet says nothing about a race, but does concede that she comes in time to fall in love (1287–94). This account is cited as an illustration of the speaker's desire to wound the addressee; since it illustrates nothing of the sort it may be an interpolation, but presumably one reflecting a valid version of some story told about Atalanta.[41] Apollodoros tells of a somewhat similar figure, the Arkadian Atalanta, daughter of Iasos of the line of Arkas, who is exposed by her father because he wants only sons; she is nursed by bears and grows up as a huntress/virgin (Ap*B* 3.9.2). The same writer makes this Iasos a brother of Amphidamas, father of Melanion, so that Melanion and Atalanta become first cousins. An Atalanta is we saw paired with Melanion (or Meilanion) on the François Krater, and Pausanias claims to have seen the two of them together on the Chest of Kypselos, with Atalanta holding a fawn (5.19.2). But this figure, linked as she is to hunting and Iasos/Iasios, is very likely different from the runner of the race.

The later literary accounts of that race offer little variation. The one interesting detail is furnished by Hyginus, who has Atalanta give her suitors a head start and then pursue them with a weapon and kill them if she overtakes them before they reach the finish line (*Fab* 185; so Theognis?). Apollodoros may intend the same, since he says that she races in arms, but his meaning is not quite clear (*ApB* 3.9.2). There is just enough missing in the relevant papyrus fragment of the *Ehoiai* to make it possible that there, too, the race was of such a nature, although probability is against it, given that no word referring to weapons survives in the text (Hes fr 76 MW). In Ovid's account, Atalanta's aversion to men stems not from her own nature but from an oracle that warns her to shun marriage (*Met* 10.564–66). The unfortunate final fate attributed to her name, namely the conversion of herself and her husband into lions, survives first in Palaiphatos, who says no more than that (Pal 13). As Aphrodite tells the story in Ovid, Hippomenes forgets to thank her for providing the apples, and in anger she sends upon him the sudden erotic passion that causes him and Atalanta to comport themselves so indecorously in Kybele's shrine (*Met* 10.681–704). Kybele, in her turn understandably angry, changes them into lions who draw her chariot. Apollodoros says simply that they made love in a temple of Zeus, and were then changed; Hyginus, like Ovid, makes Aphrodite the cause, but with Zeus the agent. Hyginus is also the first to suggest (following Pliny?) that as lion and lioness they are no longer able to mate.

Atalanta's double identity becomes further complicated when we consider her one child, who is sometimes hers by Melanion, sometimes hers by Ares, and sometimes someone else's altogether. As early as Aischylos, an Atalanta has a son Parthenopaios who marches with Adrastos as one of the Seven against Thebes (*Hepta* 532–33, 547). Sophokles and Euripides agree on this point but, like Aischylos, fail to specify the father (*OK* 1320–22; *Pho* 150, E: *Hik* 888–89). Pausanias, however, calls this opponent of Thebes the son of Talaos, and then proceeds to cite a variant tradition as to his killer in the *Thebais*, which perhaps implies the same parentage in that epic (fr 6 *PEG* apud Paus 9.18.6). In any case, we find Talaos as the father of Parthenopaios also in Hekataios (1F32), subsequently followed by Antimachos (fr 29 Wyss) and by the fifth-century tragedians Aristarchos and Philokles (Σ *OK* 1320). In Antimachos the mother is Lysimache (a daughter of Kerkyon, elsewhere Talaos' legitimate wife); our source for the two tragedians does not name this mother, but does specify that she was not Atalanta. A Parthenopaios, son of Talaos, would, of course, be the brother of Adrastos, thus amply motivating his participation in the attack on Thebes. But likewise at the end of the fifth century we find Hellanikos in support of a Parthenopaios sprung from Atalanta (daughter of Iasos), with the father (here for the first time) named as Melanion (son of Amphidamas: 4F99). Apollodoros embraces both these ancestries, for at one point he makes the attacker of Thebes a son of Talaos and the wife Lysimache (daughter of Abas) who bears Talaos' other children (*ApB* 1.9.13), while at another the same attacker is the offspring of Atalanta and Melanion or Ares (*ApB* 3.9.2). Indeed, Pausanias comes close to doing the same, for elsewhere in his work he notes a Parthenopaios, son of Melanion, although he does not name the mother and does not say that this Parthenopaios fought at Thebes (3.12.9).

From such an array of conflicting opinions we turn to Hyginus, who several times calls Parthenopaios the son of Atalanta and Meleagros and states that Atalanta exposed him (*Fab* 70, 99, 270). How old this idea might be depends, of course, in part on when Meleagros first falls in love with Atalanta. Conceivably such a child might have appeared in Euripides' *Meleagros*, for at the end of that play there is a prophecy about Tydeus (and thus Parthenopaios?) at Thebes (fr 537 N²). We must remember though that there Atalanta seems not to care for Meleagros. Suetonius tells us in his life of Tiberius that the emperor was given a painting by one Parrhasios showing Atalanta and Meleagros engaged in a highly intimate act (*Tib* 44.2); if this was the fifth- or fourth-century B.C. painter, then the actual consummation of their relationship would be at least that old, but of course we cannot be sure that Suetonius (or his times) identified the figures correctly, and then too, the painter may have been indulging in a bit of fancy. Since Hellanikos, Apollodoros, and Pausanias do make Parthenopaios the son of Melanion (or Ares) when he is not the son of Talaos, the notion of a brief encounter at Kalydon is probably late. But where Hyginus might have found it remains a puzzling question; fourth-century vases of the Meleager Painter do show Atalanta in the company of Meleagros, for what that is worth (e.g., Athens 15113).

The above survey has for the most part simply related, in no particular order, what our sources have to say about figures named Atalanta, figures whom Apollodoros, for example, would have us believe are one and the same. But what we have seen suggests, I think, two separate individuals (so Σ *Pho* 150, Σ *Theok* 3.42, and surely too Σ *AR* 1.769, despite the loss of a word).⁴² The first will be a Boiotian, daughter of Schoineus (son of Athamas), who does not wish to marry and who with her father's help sets up the fatal race to discourage suitors. The second is an Arkadian, daughter of Iasios (or Iasos, or Iasion), whose father abandons her and who becomes a great huntress, participating in the Kalydonian Boar Hunt and wrestling with Peleus at the funeral games for Pelias. Such a separation would also explain very effectively the two quite different names for the successful suitor: Hippomenes is, for the most part, found only as winner of the footrace, while Melanion is he who woos the Arkadian huntress with whom he is paired on the François Krater. How this second youth actually won his beloved is often overlooked, but there is ample evidence for it in the less familiar sources. As early as Xenophon we find that Melanion succeeded through *philoponia*, that is, great labor (*Kyn* 1.7), while in the same vein Propertius speaks of *labores* (1.1.9–10), and Ovid, whose *Metamorphoses* has described in breathless detail Hippomenes' race, in the *Ars Amatoria* relates how Milanion (Latinized from Meilanion?) follows Atalanta while she hunts, carrying her nets and so forth in an effort to win her (*AA* 2.185–92). Thus it appears that a Melanion distinct from Hippomenes wins the love of this Arkadian Atalanta by sheer devotion, rather than speed or the wiles of Aphrodite. Indeed, we cannot exclude the possibility that Kleitias on his François Krater thought of the couple as already married at the time of the Kalydonian Boar Hunt, and for that reason paired them. Thus the Atalanta spoken of by Theognis (or his interpolator) as daughter of Iasios and fleeing her father's house to avoid marriage will be the Arkadian one, who as huntress shares only this quality with her Boiotian counterpart. The child Parthenopaios seems always to be born to the Arkadian; as we have seen, when his father is not Melanion, he is Meleagros or Ares (or Talaos, by a different mother altogether); Hippomenes never plays this role.

Granted the concept of two originally distinct figures, we should, of course, like to know at what point the exploits of one begin to be attributed to the other. Apollodoros, in concluding his account of the unified heroine, notes that in Euripides she marries Hippomenes (ApB 3.9.2); if this were prophesied at the end of the *Meleagros* we would have the Arkadian Atalanta wed to the Boiotian suitor. But no play title is given, and Euripides may have offered this information in a completely different context dealing with the Boiotian Atalanta. Apollodoros also says, however, that the playwright called her the daughter of one Mainolos, who for Pausanias is the founder of a city of that name in Arkadia (8.3.4; at AR 1.769–70 Atalanta resides in Mainolos). We must wonder then whether he took these two adjacent bits of information from the same source; if so, Euripides will be guilty of at least some degree of conflation. Palaiphatos' account of the changing into lions names Atalanta and Meilanion, so that the same would be true for him if this were the fate of the Boiotian runner (see below). Kallimachos' *Hymn* 3 calls his Atalanta a warder-off of marauding Kentauroi, a huntress, Arkadian, daughter of Iasios, *and* swift-footed (*H* 3.215–16). The epithet could, of course, be generic, but it might also refer to the race, and we have as well Diodoros' statement that Parthenopaios was the son of Atalanta, daughter of Schoineus. Art offers one possible example, fragments of an Attic Red-Figure volute krater by the Peleus Painter (*c.* 440–30 B.C.) on which Atalanta and Hippomenes (both named) prepare for some athletic endeavor in the presence of a boxer (Ferrara 2893); since organized games are involved (the other side in fact probably makes these the games for Pelias), we have here surely the Arkadian Atalanta. But very likely the artist has engaged in an inadvertent confusion.[43] Only in Statius' *Thebais* (6.563–65) do we finally find runner and huntress parent of Parthenopaios identified, and Apollodoros seems the first to call the winner of the race Melanion, rather than Hippomenes (ApB 3.9.2). Further evidence of attempts to link together geographically separate stories occurs in Book 8 of Pausanias, where we hear of an Arkadian plain called Schoinous after the Boiotian Schoineus whom the author assumes migrated there; he mentions too an adjoining site called the *dromoi* (race courses) of Atalanta (8.35.10). But despite all this material, the finale of Atalanta's story—the metamorphosis into lions—is difficult to assign to one maiden or the other: Melanion and the Arkadian Atalanta are after all the hunters (and seemingly backed by Palaiphatos), but Hippomenes and the Boiotian Atalanta would appear to have the more obvious motive, since they are the ones aided by Aphrodite, and they leave behind no children. We must remember, however, that we really know very little of the early form of the tale of Schoineus' daughter and the race, other than what the scraps of the *Ehoiai* tell us, and even if the metamorphosis does belong to her, her fate in the Archaic period may have been quite different.

12   Iason and the Argo

Both the *Odyssey* and the *Theogony* recognize the union of Helios and the Okeanid Perseis, with Kirke and Aietes as offspring (*Od* 10.135–39; *Th* 956–62). The *Theogony* further assigns to Aietes an Okeanid wife of his own, Iduia, who bears to him Medeia. Neither work, however, gives any indication of where Aietes is to be located, save that in the *Odyssey* he seems clearly not to be on the island of Aiaia with his sister Kirke, and our remains of the *Ehoiai* do not mention him at all. In Mimnermos, on the other hand, he does live on Aia, where the sun's rays are stored, at the brink of Okeanos (Mim 11, 11a W). Elsewhere we find him prominently featured in Eumelos' *Korinthiaka*, apparently as a consequence of Greek exploration in the Black Sea and the desire to assign to Korinth ancestral claims in that area.[1] Thus we are told, in a direct quote, that Helios and Antiope (identity unclear) beget two sons, Aietes and Aloeus (Eumelos fr 3 *PEG*). To these Helios apportions out land, that through which the Asopos flows (i.e., between Sikyon and Stymphalos) to Aloeus, and that of the Okeanid Ephyra (i.e., Korinth) to Aietes. But Aietes gives his share voluntarily to Bounos (who is in the quoting source and Apollodoros a son of Hermes) until he or his son or grandson should return, and himself goes to Kolchis. Presumably this is all Eumelian invention designed to link Korinth and Kolchis. Subsequently, Bounos dies, and Korinth passes to Epopeus, son of Aloeus, and thence to Epopeus' son Marathon and Marathon's son Korinthos before Medeia returns to claim it. We have seen that in Apollodoros Aloeus and Epopeus are both sons of Kanake and Poseidon (Ap*B* 1.7.4), and perhaps Eumelos also thought of his Aloeus, son of Helios, as the one who weds Iphimedeia and becomes in both *Odyssey* and *Ehoiai* the nominal father of the Aloadai. In any case an Aloeus (of whatever sort) as child of Helios and brother of Aietes is unique here. "Epimenides" simplifies the whole matter of a connection between Korinth and Kolchis by making Aietes' mother Ephyra herself (3B13). The one myth involving Aietes, other than his dealings with Iason and the Argonautai, is the prologue to that story, his reception of Phrixos after the latter and his sister have fled Orchomenos on the golden ram. As we saw in chapter 5, the *Aigimios* and *Megalai Ehoiai* are the earliest sources to refer to this event; the latter adds that Phrixos married a daughter of Aietes (Hes fr 255 MW), and the same scholion confirms this for "Epimenides" (3B12) and

Akousilaos (2F38; so too Pherekydes 3F25). Given that Euripides wrote two *Phrixos* plays, one of them may well have been set in Kolchis, and perhaps dealt with Phrixos' death at his host's hand, as in Hyginus (see below). In any case, the theme of a prophecy to Aietes to fear danger recurs again and again in later literature. As early as Herodoros, the king is warned against destruction *(apolesthai)* from one of his offspring (31F9), while in Diodoros it is death from strangers carrying off the Fleece (4.47.2), and in Hyginus the loss of his kingdom if the Fleece is taken (*Fab* 22). A separate *fabula* then has Aietes slaying Phrixos after he has received a prophecy bidding him beware death at the hands of a stranger from the race of Aiolos (*Fab* 3). Valerius Flaccus alludes to that same deed at 1.41–45 of his *Argonautica* without mentioning the prophecy; at 5.224–58 Phrixos instead dies of old age, and in a dream tells Aietes to marry off Medeia as quickly as possible, as the Fleece is in danger of being stolen and ruin will follow. Presumably, in these latter accounts where Phrixos is killed, Aietes has misinterpreted the prophecy, which refers not to Phrixos or the daughter who married him, but to Iason and Medeia. But such prophecies in whatever form present us with difficulties, since in no preserved ending of the story does Aietes lose his throne, much less die at the hands of Iason or Medeia or anyone else; the only consequences of Iason's coming are the loss of the Fleece (scarcely catastrophic) and eventually Medeia's brother Apsyrtos. Apollonios, who includes a prophecy much like that of Herodoros (i.e., danger from offspring) avoids the problem by permitting said prophecy to threaten only treachery and disaster (AR 3.594–600), but even here Aietes certainly takes the words to signify the loss of his throne (thus he encourages the sons of Phrixos, his grandchildren, to journey to Greece). Perhaps in some versions the tasks set Iason—harnessing of bulls, fighting sown men—were as in so many other task tales designed to test (or destroy) prospective suitors.

The Argo and Its Crew The *Iliad* mentions on several occasions Euneos, son of Iason and Hypsipyle of Lemnos, which obviously implies the voyage of the Argo, but this is all the poem offers (e.g., *Il* 7.467–71). The *Odyssey* is more explicit: Kirke, in advising Odysseus on the proper negotiation of the Planktai, tells him that only one ship, the Argo on its way back from the land of Aietes, with Iason its captain, has ever escaped them (*Od* 12.69–72). The *Theogony*, as noted, records Iason's union with Medeia, and stresses as well that by the will of the gods he brought her back to Iolkos from Aietes' side, having accomplished the many labors imposed upon him by the lordly king Pelias, he who was *hubristês* and *atasthalos* (*Th* 992-1002). Medeios is the result of their union, but it is never quite clear whether this, or Pelias' death, or something else is to be understood as the gods' purpose in bringing Medeia to Greece; likewise, although Pelias may set difficult tasks for Iason, we cannot say for certain that his hybristic qualities are directed at his nephew rather than the gods. The same holds for a brief quote from Mimnermos, where Pelias is again *hubristês* and again sets a difficult task (11 W). The *Ehoiai* recounted Iason's birth from Aison and Polymele and upbringing by Cheiron (Hes frr 38, 40 MW), and there was also a long section on the pursuit of the Harpuiai (Hes fr 150 MW), but we do not know what, if anything else, might have been narrated. The existence of an early epic *Argonautika* or the relevance of the *Minyas* remains conjectural; on the other hand, the events of the voyage certainly played a considerable part in both Eumelos' *Korinthiaka* and the *Naupaktia* of Karkinos (?). Mimnermos, "Epimenides" (a 6,500-line poem?: DL 1.111), and Simonides also appear to have discussed it in detail, there is valuable material in Pherekydes, and of course the description in Pindar's 300-line *Pythian* 4, not to mention Aischylos' trilogy on the stopover at Lemnos and toward the end of the fifth century a prose *Argonautika* by Herodoros. Nevertheless (given that most of these works are lost), for many details we shall find ourselves forced to resort to Apollonios' third-century epic version. Art in the Archaic period will be of some help, but primarily for just two stories, those of Phineus' torment by the Harpuiai and Iason with the serpent.

The beginning stages of the adventure we have already considered in chapter 5 in dealing with Pelias. We saw there that Pelias sometimes usurps the throne of his half-brother Aison (or Aison's son Iason), but that in other versions he appears the lawful king (so perhaps in the *Theogony*, where he is called *megas basileus*), and Iason merely one of his subjects. The prophecy of the one-sandaled man obviously will have more impact in this latter situation, alerting Pelias as it does to danger from someone he would normally not fear; in the former case he scarcely needs to be warned of a rightful heir who intends to reclaim his kingdom. But our early accounts of both versions (Pindar for the first, Pherekydes for the second) nevertheless include the motif of the lost sandal. Both times, however, the sandal is simply lost or forgotten by Iason under no special circumstances, and so too Apollonios in Book 1 says that it came loose as he was crossing the Anauros river (AR 1.8–14); only much later, in Book 3, does Hera reveal how she tested men, disguised as an old woman, on the banks of the Anauros, and how Iason carried her through the river in flood (AR 3.66–73). In point of fact Hera does not say here that Iason lost his sandal on this particular occasion; it is left to our manuscript introduction to the poem[2] to make that connection (so too Σ *Th* 993). Hera's partisanship of Iason in Apollonios derives partly, of course, from his act of kindness toward her, but earlier in the poem we also learn that Pelias (here too as in Pherekydes the legitimate king) has ignored her in his sacrifices (AR 1.12–14); thus the voyage of the Argo becomes an elaborate means of bringing about his punishment (via Medeia: AR 4.241–43). Pherekydes, although the scholiast source gives no reason for Hera's anger, also spoke of the goddess' revenge through Medeia (3F105), while Hyginus (who includes both omitted sacrifices and Medeia as agent) adds that Hera deliberately caused Iason to lose his sandal, thus (it would seem) making him the person of the prophecy (*Fab* 12, 13). In all versions Pelias notes the missing sandal, remembers the prophecy, and plots Iason's destruction via the Fleece, whether his motive is to save his ill-gotten throne or simply his own life. What Aischylos' play *Argo* or any other early source might have contained on these questions we do not know. But certainly in none of the above versions does Pelias expect Iason to come back.

Of the actual building of the Argo Pindar says nothing in *Pythian* 4, although Hyginus' citing of him for the information that the ship was constructed at Demetrias may mean that he spoke of it elsewhere (*Astr* 2.37). Pherekydes maintains that the ship was named after Argos, son of Phrixos, in which case he and his brothers will have reached the Greek mainland (3F106: for the more usual version see below). In Aischylos' *Argo*, Athena contributes a speaking timber to be a part of the vessel (frr 20, 20a R), and this too appears in Pherekydes (3F111) and Apollonios, where however the ship is constructed by Argos, son of Arestor, under Athena's guidance (AR 1.111–12). The scholiast who is our source for Pherekydes specifically says that in Apollonios the Argo is named for Argos the builder of it as opposed to Pherekydes' notion of Phrixos' son, which implies that Pherekydes did not make his Argos the builder. Yet Apollodoros' Argos, son of Phrixos, does do the building (ApB 1.9.16), so that he would here seem to have conflated two different versions. Apollonios makes the speaking beam come from Dodona, which is logical enough, but the beam plays a surprisingly limited role in his poem, encouraging the crew when they first board the ship, and telling them of Zeus' anger after the slaying of Apsyrtos (AR 1.524–27; 4.580–91). Again we can only regret the near-total loss of Aischylos' play, even if it was (as has been suggested) satyric.[3]

As for the crew, Pindar offers the following: Herakles, Kastor and Polydeukes, Euphemos, Periklymenos, Orpheus, Echion and Eurytos (both sons of Hermes), and Kalais and Zetes (*Py* 4.171–83: Mopsos should probably also be added, since he gives the signal to start). Pindar is rarely one for full details, but still the list is briefer than we might have expected, and he emphasizes several times that these heroes are all sons of gods; possibly a desire to maintain that criterion caused him to exclude others. Elsewhere, in *Olympian* 4, he concedes the presence of a son of Klymenos (*Ol* 4.19–20); in Pausanias this son is Erginos, and the father Klymenos is himself a son of Presbon, son of Phrixos (9.37.1). The *Naupaktia* and Pherekydes seem to have added the seer Idmon (in Pherekydes the son of Apollo and Asteria: *Nau* fr 5 *PEG*, Pher 3F108; Herodoros [31F44] makes him son of Abas), and possibly so did Eumelos (Σ AR 3.1354). Pherekydes also mentions Tiphys (3F107; in Aischylos Iphys [fr 21 R])—who for Apollonios is the helmsman of the Argo (AR 1.400–401)—and says that Philammon (son of Apollo and Philonis), rather than Orpheus, sailed (3F26). He adds as well (or at least knows of) Aithalides, who had received as a gift from Hermes that his *psychê* should be part of the time in Hades, part of the time above ground (3F109; cf. AR 1.640–48, where this tale is repeated and he functions as herald). But Pherekydes (like "Homer" and "Hesiod") omits the Iphiklos, uncle of Iason, taken along by Apollonios (3F110), and together with the *Wedding of Keyx*, Hellanikos, and many other sources has Herakles leave the crew after originally signing on. We will see below that this event takes place at various times and for various reasons; Pherekydes, like some others, places it at Aphetai in Thessaly, and offers as explanation that the Argo herself proclaimed she could not carry Herakles' weight (3F111; so too Antimachos [58 W]). These are all, of course, chance references, usually drawn from scholia to Apollonios and Pindar; one such does tell us that Aischylos in his *Kabeiroi* and Sophokles in his *Lemniai* provided complete lists (Ais fr 97a R; Soph fr 385 R), but the names of Admetos and the Lapith Koronos alone survive (from Sophokles only: fr 386 R).

In art we have for the Argo and its crew only one certain early item of interest, the ship metope from the Sikyonian *monopteros* at Delphi (Sikyonian Treasury, no #); the date will be somewhere about the middle of the sixth century. Here, amid the fragmentary remains, we see the bow of a ship.[4] On deck were apparently three figures, although the left-hand one is lost in a gap; the center and right-hand figures both hold lyres. Flanking them, and in front of the ship, are two horsemen, facing to the front like the musicians. Inscriptions identify the left horseman as Polydeukes and the central figure on deck as Orpheus; thus we assume the ship to be the Argo, and the right horseman to be Kastor. At one time the name "Orpheus" was thought to belong to the right-hand figure on deck, and attempts were made to read a third inscription as "Philammon," thus naming the other musician. But it seems now that the name of the right-hand figure (although he may still be Philammon) was broken away to the right, Orpheus is in the center, and this third inscription, whatever it says (Peleus?), belongs to the missing figure (probably a warrior) on the left.[5] Yet another metope fragment with part of a similar ship confirms that the stern of the ship was represented on the adjacent metope to the right, with more Argonautai and perhaps even some scene from their adventures.[6] The loss of these is unfortunate, but at least we have solid evidence of an early tradition that bards (and two at that) were part of the expedition. In Athens there was also Mikon's painting of the Argonautai for the Anakeion on the north slope of the Akropolis (with its focus on Akastos and his horses), but we have no other information (Paus 1.18.1).

As for later sources, Theokritos seems at one point to imply thirty rowing benches (13.75). Apollonios, being less restrained than Pindar in these matters, lists fifty-three Argonautai, including all those in Pindar (AR 1.23–227). Apollodoros for his part has forty-four (ApB 1.9.16), but the overlap in names between the two writers, twenty-eight, is less than we might have expected, and seems to indicate an absence of any extensive canonical catalogue in the early tradition. We should note that most of Pindar's participants have either areas of specialization—Kastor's skill with horses, Polydeukes' in boxing, Herakles' great strength—or actual magical powers—Euphemos' ability to run across the sea, Periklymenos' to change into any shape, that of the Boreadai to fly, and of Orpheus to move even inanimate objects with his music—not to mention the seer Mopsos. One suspects that most if not all of the original crew had some such special abilities, and that in the course of the voyage each made his own particular contribution in some appropriate crisis where only his skills would avail.[7] Yet by the time of Apollonios most of this tradition, if it did exist, has disappeared, and only Polydeukes and the Boreadai remain to share center stage with a not very impressive Iason. We should note too an odd tendency toward pairs throughout the tradition—the Dioskouroi, the Boreadai, two sons of Hermes, two seers (if Mopsos and Idmon both go) and two bards. In Apollonios and Apollodoros we find among others the Apharetidai, Idas and Lynkeus, whose special skills noted in chapter 11 (eating and the ability to see through solid objects) might well make them worthy members of the first crews.

The Women of Lemnos　First in the list of adventures of the Argonautai is, in almost all accounts, their putting-in at Lemnos, where they find that the women of the island have killed all the men except one. We have seen that the *Iliad* knows at least of the visit, since Euneos of Lemnos is in that poem a son borne to Iason by Hypsipyle, the leader of the women (*Il* 7.467–71). Two of the plays in what I am assuming to have been Aischylos' *Argo* tetralogy were entitled *Hypsipyle* and *Lemniai* (or *Lemnioi*) and must have dealt with the events in question, but nothing survives beyond the fact that in *Hypsipyle* the title figure and the other women refuse to allow the crew to land until they have promised themselves in sexual union (p. 352 R, apud Σ AR 1.769). In the second stasimon of the *Choephoroi* we find simply a reference to the Lemnian horror as something known and loathed by all, and this, following the examples of Skylla and Althaia in the same ode, is surely the same deed familiar elsewhere (*Cho* 631–36). Pindar in *Pythian* 4 treats the matter briefly but explicitly: the Lemnian women are "husband-slayers"; Iason and his men arrive, engage in athletic contests (so also in *Ol* 4), and share the women's beds (*Py* 4.251–54). Herodotos claims that they killed all the men previously on the island, including Hypsipyle's father Thoas (6.138.4). Of the plays written by Sophokles *(Lemniai)* and Euripides *(Hypsipyle)* dramatizing this material or referring back to it nothing useful remains (save that there was a battle with the Argonautai in the Sophoklean version [p. 337 R]), and we must wait for Apollonios to get an account of the murders. As he tells the story, the Lemnian women have long failed to pay appropriate honors to Aphrodite, and she therefore causes their husbands to spurn them and prefer instead Thracian women whom they have captured on raids (AR 1.609–26). The Lemnian women retaliate by slaying their husbands and the concubines, and then in fear of retribution all the other men on the island as well; only Thoas, father of Hypsipyle, is spared, because his daughter puts him in a chest and sends it forth into the sea. Apollodoros tells the same story, adding only that Aphrodite caused the women to emit an evil smell, and for this reason their husbands rejected them (ApB 1.9.17). Other authors agree, and thus presumably this was the tradition known in earlier times. One interesting touch in Apollonios is that Hypsipyle glosses over the full truth of the matter, telling Iason that the menfolk have all been exiled to Thrace; the deception is never discovered. Conceivably, this device had already been used by Aischylos and/or Sophokles, in which case the revelation of the actual chain of events might have prompted the Argo's departure. Without something of this sort it is difficult to see how either play could have generated much drama.

We have already seen that in Pindar the Argonautai engage in athletic contests on the island, apparently with garments woven by the women as prizes; Erginos wins the footrace (*Ol* 4.19–27; *Py* 4.253). Pindar alludes to these games as something familiar, and a scholion on the question of the prizes may indicate that they were recounted also by Simonides (547 *PMG*). Pindar does not, however, say why such games should be held (other than, of course, to show off the heroes), and they do not appear in the poems of either Apollonios or Valerius, nor in Apollodoros. The scholia to Pindar offer two possibilities found supposedly in sources, one that the games were to honor the deceased Lemnian males, the other that they honored Hypsipyle's father Thoas (Σ *Py* 4.450a). Obviously, the first of these explanations will not square with Apollonios, although the second might. How long the Argonautai were thought to remain on Lemnos is also unclear. In Apollonios the women wish to make them permanent husbands, and accept their departure (spurred on by Herakles) only with reluctance (AR 1.861–98). Something of the same sort no doubt motivated the action in Aischylos' *Hypsipyle*, where sex/procreation are on the women's minds from the outset. As suggested above, duplicity over the fate of the husbands may have followed, or perhaps the women plotted to kill these new bedpartners as well, after conceiving children. In any event, the union of Iason and Hypsipyle produces at least one child, Euneos, and usually a second, who is variously Thoas (Euripides, see below), or Nebrophonos (ApB 1.9.17), or Deipylos (*Fab* 15). Hypsipyle's own subsequent adventures after fleeing Lemnos (her saving of her father having been discovered) and being captured by pirates form the basis of Euripides' typically melodramatic play bearing her name as title; we will return to her fate in chapter 14, when we consider the expedition of the Seven against Thebes.

In all, this first exploit of the Argonautai gives surprisingly little opportunity for our heroes to show off their abilities, save in the games staged after their arrival. Probably the incident is best taken as a parallel to Odysseus' time spent in the land of the Lotos Eaters and with Kirke, with Lemnos too a place of ease and comfort which tempts heroes away from the goals that will make them greater heroes. The immediately following adventure, that of the stopover on Samothrace in order to be initiated into the mysteries there (on Orpheus' request), is recorded only by Apollonios (AR 1.915–21). We know, however, that these rites were those of the Kabeiroi, and that in Aischylos' play *Kabeiroi* Iason's crew appeared on stage inebriated (p. 214 R, apud Athen 10.428f); thus the tradition of the visit (but possibly on Lemnos rather than Samothrace) is at least this old. In giving us this information Athenaios says that Aischylos was the first to bring characters onstage drunk in tragedy. If he means by that tragedy proper, and not just the tragic stage (where satyr plays were also produced), then we might reasonably suppose a *Lemniai-Hypsipyle-Kabeiroi* (or *Hypsipyle-Lemniai-Kabeiroi*) trilogy in which the third play would somehow resolve or bring to a close the problems involved in the first two. But if this was the case (Athenaios' remark does not *prove* that the *Kabeiroi* was not satyric), it has left virtually no trace in subsequent accounts.

The
Propontis:
Kyzikos
and Amykos

From Samothrace the Argo proceeds through the Hellespont and into the Propontis, in the narratives of Apollonios and Apollodoros; in Diodoros and Valerius there is first, however, a stop at Troy, so that Herakles may save Hesione from the sea monster and bargain with her father Laomedon (DS 4.42; VF 2.451–578). Generally, though (and more logically), this tale is considered a *parergon* to the Labor of the Amazon queen's *zôstêr*, and we shall reserve it to that place in chapter 13. In the Propontis the heroes make three stops: on the island of Dindymon, where they are welcomed by Kyzikos king of the Doliones, in the land of the Mysoi, where Hylas and Herakles are lost, and in the country of the Bebrykes, whose king Amykos challenges all comers to a boxing match. The first of these stories (or at least the battle part) was apparently told by Herodoros (31F7) before Apollonios; the second is recounted briefly by Theokritos in his *Idyll* 13 and then by Apollonios in more detail (although the *Wedding of Keyx* already contained a form of it). As for Amykos, Epicharmos at least mentioned his defeat by the Argonautai, and Sophokles made him the title figure of a lost satyr play of which we know nothing; there are also a number of artistic representations, the earliest about 440 B.C. But here again Theokritos and Apollonios are the earliest surviving versions we can read.

The tale of Kyzikos remains consistent in all accounts, and can be briefly summarized from Apollonios (AR 1.936-1077). He is the son of Aineus and Ainete, and he and his Doliones greet the Argonautai enthusiastically when the latter put in at Dindymon, an "island" actually linked to the mainland by an isthmus. The other side of the peninsula harbors the Gegeneis, earthborn monsters with six arms; these eventually attack the Argo, but Herakles and the others slaughter them easily (this told also by Herodoros). Having feasted with the Doliones, the Argonautai cast off; after a day of sailing adverse winds arise, and without knowing it they are blown back at nightfall to the very harbor they left. This time the Doliones suppose the arrivals to be enemies, and attack, led by Kyzikos. In the battle that follows, Iason himself slays Kyzikos, and many other Doliones also die. When with morning the mistake is discovered there is a general lament and funeral; Kyzikos' young wife Kleite, daughter of Merops, hangs herself. For twelve days after the battle storms prevent the Argo from setting forth again (AR 1.1078–1152); finally, Mopsos receives a sign, and tells Iason that they must climb the Mountain of the Bears and sacrifice to Rheia. This done, the winds cease, and they are permitted to leave.

From Dindymon they follow the southern coast of the Propontis to the point at Kios where it turns north. Here they are welcomed by the Mysoi and make preparations for a feast, while Herakles wanders into the woods to look for a tree from which he can make a new oar, having broken his (AR 1.1172–1357). Hylas, whom Herakles has carried off in childhood after slaying his father, the Dryopian Theiodamas, goes to a spring to fetch water, whereupon a Nymph of the place becomes enamored of him and draws him down into the spring as he reaches out with his pitcher. Polyphemos, son of Elatos, alone hears the cry; when he cannot find the boy he tells Herakles, who forgets all else and goes himself to look. With morning, Tiphys urges the other Argonautai to seize the wind; they do so, and only when they are underway do they realize whom they have left behind. Telamon immediately accuses Iason of having planned this deliberately, so as to increase his own honor, but the Boreadai restrain him, and then Glaukos appears from the waves to confirm that the loss of Herakles and Polyphemos is indeed the will of the gods. Such is the version of Apollonios; in Theokritos 13 there are three Nymphai, Polyphemos is omitted altogether, and Herakles finally does reach Kolchis on foot. In other accounts, Polyphemos is a standard element, and the idea that Herakles might arrive in Kolchis after all is surprising; one imagines that the whole story of his disappearance was concocted to remove him from a tale in which he would otherwise remove obstacles and difficulties too easily. But we have preserved from scholia quite a range of opinions on this matter. The Hesiodic *Wedding of Keyx* has the hero leave the expedition almost immediately after the original sailing, at Aphetai in Thessaly, here too with the explanation that he went to fetch water (Hes fr 263 MW; so too Hdt 7.193). We saw above that Pherekydes sets him down in the same place, but because the Argo complains about his weight (3F111). Pindar, who includes him among his select original company, says nothing about his loss, but has really no reason to. Herodoros solves the problem by claiming that he never went at all, being in service to Omphale at the time (31F41); by contrast Demaratos (42F2) and Dionysios of Mitylene (or Miletos: 32F6) both suppose that he sailed all the way to Kolchis with the Argo. Apollodoros offers the same account as Apollonios, although he does also cite most of the above variants (ApB 1.9.19).

After the loss of Herakles and Polyphemos, the Argonautai proceed toward the Bosporos, and with a day and night of good wind come to the land of the Bebrykes. Here, as Apollonios tells the story, no stranger who lands is permitted to depart until he has engaged in a boxing match with the local king Amykos, a son of Poseidon (AR 2.1–163). In Theokritos the ensuing combat between Amykos and Polydeukes forms the first half of his hymn to the Dioskouroi (22: the second half, as we have seen, is devoted to the battle between Kastor and Lynkeus). Here Kastor and Polydeukes come across Amykos, pictured more as a crude bully than a king, beside a spring from which he refuses to let them drink until they have boxed with him. Terms are then set such that the winner may do what he likes with the loser, but after Amykos has received a beating and surrenders, Polydeukes contents himself with extracting a promise that Amykos will never again abuse strangers. In Apollonios, matters take a more violent turn: Polydeukes kills Amykos in the course of the bout, and there follows a general melee as the Bebrykes seek revenge. They are, of course, routed and at the same time suffer the indignity of having their farms and lands ravaged by hostile neighbors, the Mariandynoi. So too in Valerius Flaccus Amykos dies in the combat, as in Apollodoros and Hyginus (VF 4.99–343; Ap*B* 1.9.20; *Fab* 17).

This general agreement as to Amykos' fate (Theokritos [and the Hellenistic mythographer Peisandros: 16F5] excepted) is the more surprising in that it stands against what little we know from the fifth century. We had seen at the beginning of this section that Epicharmos composed a comedy, and Sophokles a satyr play, about Amykos; evidence is slim, but in Epicharmos we know that Polydeukes bound his rival, rather than killing him (and that Kastor warned him not to revile his brother: frr 6, 7 Kaibel). The same situation—Polydeukes tying Amykos to a tree or, in one case, a rock—subsequently appears in quite a number of artistic representations beginning with a Lucanian hydria of *c.* 420 B.C. (CabMéd 442: here alone the rock) and finding its most elegant expression in the Ficoroni Cista of about 320 B.C. (VG 24787). In both these examples and others, hydriai are frequently an element of the scene; thus Theokritos' presentation of Amykos as one who barred access to a spring has early roots. But the binding is more difficult to explain. Probably the best answer is that it reflects a useful, almost necessary device of the stage: the defeated Amykos is tied up (in a vertical position) so that he may remain an onstage character, perhaps in Sophokles serving as the butt of the jokes and insults of the Satyroi. Perhaps, too, the Argonautai extracted some information for their voyage from him or, as in Theokritos, persuaded him to mend his ways. In any case, this tableau seems to have exercised a remarkable impact on the artistic tradition. The supposition that Sophokles' play inspired a monumental painting (by Mikon, in the Anakeion) which in turn inspired minor works may help to explain that impact,[8] but there still seems something about this binding scene which we do not quite understand. Whatever the truth, our preserved later tradition clearly opts for a more final resolution of Amykos' challenge. His death may or may not be an early feature of the story altered to meet dramatic needs.

One other representation involving Amykos must at least be mentioned. Fragments of an Attic Red-Figure volute krater now in Ferrara appear to show the boxer at the funeral games for Pelias (Ferrara 2865). Most likely, as Beazley suggests, the artist has made a small mistake in locating the bout between Polydeukes and Amykos here, rather than during the course of the Argo's voyage.[9] Perhaps, though, there were alternate versions in which Amykos presented himself at those games after the quest for the Fleece was over in order to challenge Polydeukes and be defeated.

Phineus and Leaving the land of the Bebrykes, the Argo finally passes through the Bosporos
the Harpuiai and into the Black Sea proper. Here the Argonautai encounter first the blind

prophet Phineus. Apollonios places this meeting in Bithynia, on the south coast, while in Apollodoros it takes place at Salmydessos on the western shore (indicating that the ship had strayed off course). The Phineus who is grandson of Agenor (so the *Ehoiai* and Pherekydes) or son of Agenor (so Hellanikos) or son (with Kepheus) of Agenor's brother Belos (so Euripides) we have already met in chapter 6. Despite the fact that Apollonios calls our Thracian Phineus of the present story "Agenorides" (AR 2.178, etc.), there would seem no logical connection between a king of Thrace and the descendants of Io in Egypt or the Levant, so that Apollonios may have conflated two different figures. On the other hand, we also saw in chapter 6 that the Phineus of the Argo was probably to be found in the Inachid portion of the *Ehoiai*, so that that poem may well have believed in the identity of the two. Admittedly, too, the scholiast who supplies our information on the Levant Phineus' descent in the *Ehoiai*, Pherekydes, Hellanikos, and other sources, does so in reference to the Thracian one (Σ AR 2.178), so that he certainly supposed those sources to describe the blind helper of the Argonautai. For the record, no source earlier than the *Argonautika* specifies any parentage when clearly speaking of the Thracian Phineus. Apollodoros calls this last a son of Agenor or Poseidon; possibly the latter name represents an earlier ancestry (Ap*B* 1.9.21). Elsewhere the same mythographer also records a Phineus as one of the fifty sons of Lykaon, but as these are all destroyed by Zeus' thunderbolt the chances of our Phineus coming from that stock are slim (Ap*B* 3.8.1).

The Phineus of the Argo legend is in any case an atrociously complicated figure, blinded for a variety of reasons and both aided and (in one story at least) punished by the Argonautai. We have seen that in the *Ehoiai* he chooses long life in preference to his sight (Hes fr 157 MW); this is an abbreviated comment from a scholion (the same just discussed above, in fact), and leaves us quite uncertain whether the choice is between two gifts (as we might at first think) or two punishments. In the *Megalai Ehoiai* the blindness is in fact inflicted because Phineus has shown Phrixos the way (to Kolchis? Hes fr 254 MW), but not impossibly he was here given a choice between early death and blindness as the form of the punishment. No agent is mentioned by our source; one might guess Poseidon, lest men travel too freely on the sea. Frequently cited in this regard is the (unattributed) opinion of the *Etymologicum Genuinum* that Phineus chose between being blind (literally, "maimed") with prophetic skills on the one hand and a short but healthy life on the other; [10] here gifts do seem to be involved, if the source is sound, and we may wonder if prophecy could also have been offered in the *Ehoiai*. Puzzling in any case is the further remark that Apollo [Helios?] in anger then blinded him. [11] For Asklepiades, Zeus is angry at Phineus' treatment of his own sons: the punishment is a choice between death and blindness (12F31). Phineus naturally chooses the latter but in expressing his choice asks to no longer see the light of the sun; Helios is offended and sends the Harpuiai to destroy his food. This is, in fact, the first clear statement that the Harpuiai (present already in the *Ehoiai*) are a divinely sent punishment rather than casual marauders. Apollonios combines the two ideas of gift and transgression by having Apollo grant Phineus the gift of prophecy, but Zeus then blind him because he prophesies too clearly Zeus' intentions; for the same reason the god sends the Harpuiai as above (AR 2.178–93).[12]

Turning to tragedy, we know that Aischylos' play *Phineus* (part of the 472 B.C. production, thus *not* from his Argo tetralogy) dramatized Phineus' problems with the Harpuiai, but we cannot say what cause Aischylos gave there for his suffering of these torments, and *Eumenides* 50–51 makes only the briefest of allusions to the winged creatures who steal Phineus' food. With Sophokles we acquire much richer information and more problems. The poet wrote two *Phineus* plays, one like that of Aischylos about the Argo adventure, the other offering a previously unpreserved tale in which Phineus has married Kleopatra, a daughter of Boreas, and has two children (there is some textual corruption in the names, which in any case vary). These he blinds, persuaded by the slander of their stepmother Idaia (fr 704 R). A choral allusion in *Antigone*, however, has the stepmother herself commit the deed, blinding the sons with a shuttle (*Ant* 966–87), while the scholia to the same passage (at *Ant* 981) note Eidothea, sister of Kadmos, "whom Sophokles mentions in his *Tympanistai*" as an alternate possibility for the second wife, together with Idaia, daughter of Dardanos. Other fragments attributed to this lost work of Sophokles *may* mean that the entire play (satyric?) dealt with Phineus, and the scholiast's subsequent words, where the stepmother blinds the children and imprisons them in a tomb, might then well come from it (frr 636–38 R, together with fr 645 [the scholion]). Thus (if *Tympanistai* is not a second title for one of the *Phineus* plays) we would have three Sophoklean efforts, two of them directly about Phineus' family problems. The blinding by Phineus on the slander of the stepmother would then be the version of one of the two entitled *Phineus* (with the mother Idaia, as noted), and that found further on in the *Etymologicum Genuinum*—where Sophokles in a play entitled *Phineus* shows Phineus blinded because he *killed* his sons (fr 705 R)—would constitute the other. From a Sophoklean *Phineus* as well is a fragment suggesting that someone is cured of blindness by Asklepios, possibly one of the two sons (to be followed by the other), possibly of Phineus himself in the play in which he is blinded (fr 710 R). For what it is worth, Phylarchos, although not citing Sophokles, has Asklepios heal the sons as a favor to their mother Kleopatra; his own death by thunderbolt follows as a result (81F18).[13]

To sum up, the evidence for tragedy *seems* to suggest three Sophoklean plays: *Phineus A* (Phineus blinds his sons by Kleopatra after the stepmother Idaia accuses them); *Tympanistai* (the stepmother Eidothea blinds them and imprisons them); and *Phineus B* (Phineus himself is blinded after killing them). Of the two *Phineus* plays, on the principle that blinded sons offer much more scope for onstage dramatics, I would guess that *Phineus B*, where the sons are instead killed, dealt with Phineus and the Argonautai, with those deaths simply part of the exposition. But all this is very largely hypothesis, and even if it is right, it does not tell us whether Phineus was blinded in the first two plays as well, or whether the sons were ever healed. Still, it gives us a possible framework within which to consider other bits of information not specifically assigned to Sophokles. The above-mentioned scholia to the *Antigone* suggest, for example, that in one version of the story the stepmother accused her stepchildren of rape to make Phineus blind them (so too Apollodoros), while in another Phineus put aside his first wife Kleopatra to marry Idaia and Kleopatra in anger then blinded her own children. As for the entombment of the children in the same scholia, we meet it again in Diodoros, who says that the Argonautai found Phineus' sons thus imprisoned and being continually beaten with whips, but not, it seems, blinded (they have here too been accused of attempted rape by their stepmother, who is Idaia: DS 4.43.3–44.4). Despite Phineus' protests, the Boreadai insist on liberating their sister's children, and Phineus himself is slain (by Herakles) when he attempts to stop them.[14] In the Cyzicene Epigrams the sons slay their Phrygian stepmother (i.e., Idaia?) as their mother Kleopatra rejoices (*AP* 3.4); the cause of the deed is again Phineus' unjustified setting-aside of his first wife, but in contrast to the *Antigone* scholia, the mother has certainly not blinded sons who can defend her. The *Odyssey* scholia offer the account noted above drawn from Asklepiades: here Phineus with children from Kleopatra marries Eurytia, and hands them over to their stepmother to be killed after hearing slander against them (Σ *Od* 12.69 = 12F31; we are surely to understand that she made the accusation). Zeus in anger at Phineus for this then gives him the choice of death or blindness cited before, with Helios in anger at the choice dispatching the Harpuiai. Such an version could be Sophoklean, for the children are apparently killed, the stepmother has a name not that found in *Phineus A* or the *Tympanistai,* and the story explains Phineus' full plight at the time the Argonautai find him—just what we would expect, in other words, of our presumed *Phineus B.* But we must remember that Aischylos wrote a similar play, and almost certainly earlier than Sophokles'. Different altogether from any of these versions is that of Diodoros, who says that in some writers Boreas blinds Phineus (DS 4.44.4). To this Apollodoros adds (twice, though not as his main version) that Boreas sailed with the Argonautai, and with their help blinded Phineus as punishment for his treatment of Boreas' grandchildren (Ap*B* 1.9.21; 3.15.3). Slightly different is the account of the *Orphic Argonautika,* where the Boreadai rescue and cure the sons whom Phineus has blinded and exposed to wild beasts, then blind Phineus himself as a punishment; Phineus' deed was here too motivated by an unfortunate marriage and desire for a woman (*OA* 671–76). No other sources besides these two ever suggest that the Argonautai did not help Phineus and he them.

With the above survey, we might seem to have exhausted the possibilities for Phineus' blindness, but two later sources, Istros and Apollodoros, return to the idea found in the *Megalai Ehoiai* and Apollonios, that the blinding was for reasons other than maltreatment of one's sons. Istros maintains that Phineus lost his sight for assistance given not to Phrixos but rather Phrixos' sons, presumably when they were on their way to Greece (334F67). Aietes curses him for that deed, and the father Helios blinds the seer. Behind this tale would seem to lie Aietes' fear of ruin from his own descendants, a motif that in Apollonios caused the king to send his own grandchildren off to Greece (see above); as a pupil of Kallimachos, Istros would have known the *Argonautika* well, but of course both might have drawn from still earlier sources. Apollodoros offers both Apollonios' notion of the gods' anger because Phineus prophesied too skillfully, and an alternative that essentially repeats Istros, save that here it is Poseidon who is angry with Phineus for helping the sons of Phrixos reach Greece and hence blinds him (ApB 1.9.21); possibly this clarifies our reference to the *Megalai Ehoiai,* and Poseidon in both cases resents too free a passage over his domain.

In any event, when the Argonautai arrive at Salmydessos, according to the usual tradition, they find Phineus both blind and tormented by the Harpuiai. Presumably the purpose of their visit is in origin to acquire information from the seer in exchange for a service—the driving off of the Harpuiai—which only the Boreadai can accomplish. That the Harpuiai tormented Phineus by causing him to starve is guaranteed by what little remains of Aischylos' *Phineus* (so too *Eum* 50–51); from Apollonios and Apollodoros we learn that they snatched up some of the food and left a loathsome stench over the rest (AR 2.187–93; ApB 1.9.21). All this may have been a part of the earlier tradition as well. But apparently the *Ehoiai* included a detail that has not survived elsewhere: a line quoted by Ephoros has the Harpuiai take Phineus to the land of the Glaktophagoi, a people of Thrace (Hes fr 151 MW). Perhaps the poet means simply that Phineus' tormentors brought him to Thrace in the first place, but more likely they here snatch him up bodily and carry him around the world, with the Boreadai in pursuit. Unfortunately, we cannot say how he might have been rescued; all we know is that Hermes intervened, and the Harpuiai were not killed (Hes fr 156 MW). Presumably the messenger god promised that they would in future leave Phineus alone, as Iris does in Apollonios (AR 2.273–300). This same resolution seems to have been used by Antimachos, but the scholiast's comment to that effect implies that there were other versions in which the Boreadai did catch the Harpuiai and kill them (Σ AR 2.296a). On that evidence we are probably right to fill in the gaps in a fragment of Philodemos so as to say that this was the result in the accounts of Ibykos (292 *PMG*), Aischylos (fr 260 R), and Telestes (812 *PMG*); certainly Philodemos is in the midst of talking about mythological figures who die. Apollodoros makes mention of a *moira* according to which the Harpuiai are in fact fated to die at the hands of the Boreadai, while the Boreadai will die whenever they fail to catch their quarry (ApB 1.9.21). In the account that then follows, the first Harpuia, Nikothoe (or Aellopous), falls into the river Tigres in the Peloponnesos; the other, Okypete, collapses of weariness at the Strophades Islands, "together with her pursuer." What this means is not entirely clear, but since later in his work Apollodoros speaks of the Boreadai as dying while chasing the Harpuiai (ApB 3.15.2), it would appear that both parts of the moira are fulfilled, with Okypete outrunning the Boreadai but perishing in the process. Apollonios, who as we have seen declares a truce between the two sides, also brings in the Strophades (formerly Plotai) Islands, but here as the place where the Boreadai were turned back from their pursuit; the scholiast attributes this detail to Antimachos and to "Hesiod." Both the *Naupaktia* and Pherekydes are cited as sources for the idea that the Harpuiai went to Krete, to a cave under a ridge called Arginous (*Nau* fr 3 *PEG*; Pher 3F29, apud Σ AR 2.299); thus one would suppose, if one can suppose anything in this story, that in those works too they survived. Finally, we find Akousilaos as the first source for the idea, repeated by Apollonios and others, that Herakles killed the Boreadai at Tenos (2F31). From Akousilaos we do not get a motive; in Apollonios it is because they restrained Telamon when he would have turned the Argo back to find Herakles (AR 1.1289–1309). Given that Herakles was seeking Hylas at that time and no longer cared about the expedition, such a reason seems explanation after the fact, but at least we can array Akousilaos with those other writers who say that the Boreadai did not perish in their pursuit of the Harpuiai.

In art, the earliest representation (identified by inscription) is that on a spouted krater by the Nettos Painter formerly in Berlin and now lost.[15] The panel with the fleeing Harpuiai survives, but not the (presumed) complement with the Boreadai (Berlin:Lost F1682). Subsequently, we find them both on a Lakonian cup in the Villa Giulia (106335): as the two pairs dash across the tondo of the cup, each of the Boreadai reaches out and seizes one of the Harpuiai by the neck. In their other hands the Boreadai hold drawn swords, and we thus have perhaps a precursor of the Ibykos/Aischylos version, unless here too Hermes intervened in time. The cup is by the Boreads Painter and dates somewhere around 570–60 B.C.[16] From about the same time are the ivory fragments of perhaps a throne or chest found in the Halos Deposit at Delphi. Here we see (almost completely preserved) the Boreadai and Harpuiai running right; one of the Harpuiai holds the food just stolen from Phineus, and one of the Boreadai grasps her by the hair while the other draws his sword. To the left is a woman gesturing right but turning her head back left, and in front of her a table with a hand resting on it. The hand must belong to Phineus, who perhaps reclines on a *klinê*; the woman obviously turns to describe to him what is happening. But everything else is lost, and we cannot tell whether other Argonautai were portrayed. Clearly, though, we have once again a situation in which the death of the Harpuiai *may* be indicated. Pausanias tells us that Phineus, the Boreadai, and the Harpuiai were also shown on the Chest of Kypselos and the Throne of Amyklai (5.17.11; 3.18.15); one wonders if the composition of those pieces was similar.

Perhaps just a bit earlier, and only recently published, are fragments of a Corinthian column krater showing complementary aspects of this general scene

(Andreadis Coll, no #).[17] The fragments sort themselves into two groups. On one we see a seated figure identified by inscription as Phineus; beside him is a woman, Vidai————, presumably his second wife Idaia, as in Sophokles. Two men stride forward toward him, and one of these, identified as Polydeukes, clasps his hand. Behind him, to the left, is Iason; he reaches forward and places his hands over Phineus' eyes. The interpretation of this tableau is obviously problematic; since Phineus is blind, there seems no point in covering his eyes, even if one could think of a reason to do so. The first publisher of this material has thus suggested that Iason here heals Phineus' blindness through a laying-on of hands. She also points out, as we saw above, that Aristophanes' reference to Phineus and the recovery of eyesight in one of Sophokles' *Phineus* plays (fr 710 R) could signify Phineus' recovery rather than that of his sons. Iason, of course, like other of Cheiron's pupils, may be thought to have acquired some healing skills, but whether he could heal blindness is another question; in Sophokles' play (whichever *Phineus* it was) the healer appears to have been Asklepios. Conceivably, though, that is a fifth-century modification of the original story for greater plausibility (and in honor of Athens' newly received Asklepios cult).[18] In all, if Iason does not here cure Phineus, we are left at a loss, and the theory would explain as well Polydeukes' gesture of helping the old man to his feet as he recovers his eyesight and can begin to walk. But if the healing is an early tradition, it has left no trace in what we have from later times. The presence of Idaia may also be thought surprising if she has blinded or brought about the blinding of her stepsons, and quite possibly our artist does not know this story. The second group of fragments shows, as we might expect, parts of the winged figures of the Boreadai as they pursue the Harpuiai. Not impossibly the Delphi ivory also included a scene between Iason and Phineus on its missing left-hand side. The same might be true for the Chest of Kypselos and the Amyklai Throne, although Pausanias' failure to mention Iason tells against it, assuming that the scene in question really is of narrative importance.

Of other representations we must at least note the delicate Chalkidian kylix in Würzburg, dating to about 530 B.C., on which elegantly drawn Boreadai, swords in hand, pursue equally elegant Harpuiai over a fish-infested sea (Würzburg 164). Left behind by the pursuit two women observe; behind them Phineus reclines on his couch, a table for food at his side. His closed eyes indicate his blindness; the table is of course empty, and the Harpuiai each hold a dish. Behind Phineus, at the head of his couch, stands a third woman, named Erichtho and perhaps his wife (no other source preserves this name for any figure in Greek mythology). More surprising is the name "Horai" attached to the two women in front of Phineus. Their presence here is a mystery; perhaps they supply the delicacies that the Harpuiai steal. In the early fifth century, emphasis shifts to the stealing of the food, as on a White-Ground lekythos by the Sappho Painter in Basel (PrColl) where Phineus stretches out his arms in vain and the Boreadai are nowhere to be seen;[19] so too the Red-Figure hydria of the Kleophrades Painter (Getty 85.AE.316). Subsequent versions omit also the Harpuiai (as on London E291, a neck-amphora with Phineus praying), and were perhaps inspired by a prologue from the dramas of Aischylos or Sophokles in which Phineus was alone on stage.[20] The same might be said of a Red-Figure pelike of c. 450 B.C. showing a blind Phineus reaching out while two bearded figures, clearly the Boreadai, stand calmly to either side (Boston 1979.40). But strange by all accounts is a Red-Figure column krater by the Leningrad Painter, now in the Louvre, on which Phineus sits stretching one hand toward a table laden with food while a bearded and winged figure comes toward him, both arms also extended down toward the table (Louvre G364). Phineus' gesture (palm upward) *might* be taken as offering the food to the newcomer, rather than reaching for it himself; certainly the winged figure seems intent on taking it. Behind Phineus an unwinged youth raises a spear, apparently in defense. If the winged figure is Boreas, come to take revenge on Phineus for the treatment of his grandsons, we have no easy explanation for his interest in the food (nor the fact that Phineus is already blind); if the figure is a Boread the first objection still applies, and the youth with spear becomes more difficult still. Possibly the artist knows a tale of which we are unaware, but more likely he has combined elements of different stories. Even so, if the winged figure is Boreas, rather than a Boread, we would have some early evidence for Apollodoros' claim that he accompanied the Argo.

Onward to Kolchis

The next stage of the Argo's journey lies along the southern shore of the Black Sea, as Phineus prophesies in detail in exchange for his release from the Harpuiai. The events in queston are mostly minor, and only Homer, in the *Odyssey*'s allusion to the Planktai, offers any kind of early reference;[21] for the rest of what follows, until the ship reaches Kolchis, we can only summarize from Apollonios. The first adventure in this series, which is in fact that of the Clashing Rocks, offers some seeming differences of conception. Kirke in the *Odyssey*, though she names the Planktai as rocks traversed by the Argo, never says that they come together, and speaks rather of terrible waves and blasts of fire that destroy ships (*Od* 12.59–72). Admittedly she also mentions doves who are unable to pass through, which is closer to what we expect (and may be conflated from a different tradition), but otherwise the problem seems entirely one of fighting high waves, caused presumably by the wandering around of these "wandering" rocks. As an alternative to this peril Kirke offers two other rocks, one the abode of Skylla, the other next to the whirlpool Charybdis. This latter possibility is then described at much greater length, and by the time Kirke has finished there seems no question that Odysseus will choose that route, as he in fact does, with the result that there is no further description of the Planktai. Neither do we learn where exactly they are located (save for their proximity to Skylla and Charybdis) nor whether the Argo confronted them on the outward journey or the return. Simonides seems to have called them the Synormades (546 *PMG*), which certainly sounds as if they rushed together, and Pindar, in narrating the Argo's negotiation of them (no formal name given), describes them as living rocks that come together more swiftly than the winds, giving us concrete early proof that they did clash; the Argonautai pray to Poseidon for help in escaping them on their way *to* Kolchis (*Py* 4.207–11). The first actual mention of them as the Symplegades (Clashers) occurs at the beginning of Euripides' *Medeia*, where again they are on the way to Kolchis and seem to be something well known (*Med* 1–2: the scholia here are our source for the idea that Simonides called the same rocks Synormades). The text also calls them *kyaneai*, "dark blue," and this may be either a simple adjective or an actual name used in apposition to Symplegades. In Herodotos, Dareios goes to see these islands (or historical ones equated with them) in the Black Sea, and here they are called the Kyaneai which for the Greeks were once the Planktai (*Hdt* 4.85); presumably the latter name will no longer do because real rocks do not after all wander. Thus, by the latter fifth century all four names—Symplegades, Synormades, Kyaneai, and Planktai—have been linked together. No more information surfaces until Apollonios, who also calls the rocks the Kyaneai (his Planktai come later) and gives us the standard account (AR 2.317–40, 549–610): Phineus advises the Argonautai to secure a dove and release her when they approach the rocks; if it flies through safely they may attempt the passage themselves, but if not it will indicate that the gods' favor is against them. Euphemos releases the dove as instructed; the rocks clashing together catch only its tailfeathers. Accordingly, the Argo itself begins to sail through, but the surf pushes the ship back twice as fast as it surges forward. Finally Athena intervenes, holding back one rock with her left hand and propelling the Argo through the strait with her right. Apollodoros tells the same story of a dove sent through in advance and the rocks coming together, although in his account, as in Homer, the helper is Hera, not Athena (Ap*B* 1.9.22). In Pindar, Apollonios, and Apollodoros the rocks remain fixed together, once the Argo has passed; in the latter two authors this is because the gods have so ordained, if any ship should survive the ordeal.

Next in Apollonios' narrative, the Argo passes the shrine of Dipsakos, who once entertained Phrixos, and at the island of Thynias the crew experiences an epiphany of Apollo, who silently appears to them as he makes his way from Lykia to the land of the Hyperboreans (AR 2.648–719). Sacrifices are of course offered; they set sail again and come to the land of the Mariandynoi and their king Lykos, the enemies of Amykos and the Bebrykes (AR 2.720–898). Naturally the Argonautai are welcomed with great enthusiasm; Lykos tells stories of Herakles' exploits when he came previously to fetch the *zôstêr* of the Amazon, and offers to send his son Daskylos to join the expedition. But there is a darker side to this visit. First the seer Idmon is killed by a boar as he walks along a river bank, and then the helmsman Tiphys falls sick and dies. Two barrows are raised next to each other. At this point, Ankaios volunteers to take the helm, and the Argo sets forth again. They pass the barrow of Sthenelos Aktorides, Herakles' companion, and see his shade standing upon it watching them (AR 2.911–29). Then comes Sinope, named for the daughter of Asopos (so too Eumelos: fr 10 *PEG*) who won from Zeus a promise of perpetual virginity (AR 2.946–54). Next is the land of the Amazones, where Herakles captured Melanippe and won her sister Hippolyte's *zôstêr*; the Argonautai desire to stop here and test themselves in battle, but Zeus sends winds from the northwest to drive them onward (AR 2.964–95). Passing the iron-producing Chalybes, they arrive at Aretias, the island of Ares, where Phineus has bid them anchor so that they might acquire unexpected help. First, however, they are assaulted by birds similar to (or perhaps the same as) those of the Stymphalian Lake, with wings (of iron, according to the scholia) whose feathers can be used as missiles (so already Euripides in the *Phrixos*: fr 838 N²). After Oileus is wounded by such a missile, they roof over the ship with their shields and make sufficient noise to scare the birds away (AR 2.1030–89). They then encounter the promised assistance in the form of four sons of Phrixos (Argos, Kytissoros, Phrontis, Melas) who, having set out for Orchomenos after the death of their father to seek the possessions of Athamas, have been shipwrecked to just this island. Iason explains his mission and asks for their help; they are dubious that Aietes will ever surrender the Fleece, but finally agree to return to Kolchis with the Argo (AR 2.1093–1225). Sacrifices are made at the temple of Ares built by the Amazones, and the Argonautai, after passing many other peoples, finally come to the Phasis River, and the land of Kolchis.

Medeia and the Golden Fleece

Medeia is not mentioned by Homer in any context. We saw that at the end of the *Theogony* Iason, after performing great labors placed upon him by Pelias, takes Medeia from her father Aietes and brings her to Iolkos as his wife; she bears him a child, Medeios, and the intent of Zeus is accomplished (*Th* 992–1002). As the words stand, she seems almost the major goal of Iason's voyage, but what exactly Zeus' intent was, if any, eludes us; possibly the emphasis here given her is simply part of the poem's general focus on matrimony at this point (so too she appears together with Iason on the Chest of Kypselos, where Aphrodite orders them to marry: Paus 5.18.3). She does not surface in our remnants of the *Ehoiai* or elsewhere in the Hesiodic Corpus. A four-line quote from Mimnermos says that Iason would not have carried off the Fleece (our first source to name it); presumably he means "without Medeia's help," although the quote ends before the sentence is completed (11 W). One can scarcely doubt in any case that she is an early part of the story, assisting Iason in an otherwise impossible task as Ariadne does for Theseus, although there are some indications that she may originally have been a less dominant figure. From the fifth century we have the brief description of Pindar and a few references to Pherekydes. The whole story of the events at the court of Aietes was dramatized by Sophokles in his *Kolchides* (which may have been a major source for Apollonios); once again, little of use survives. Pindar begins with an allusion to some sort of violence between the Argonautai and the Kolchians, but then the emphasis quickly shifts to Aphrodite, who creates the first *iunx* wheel and at the same time teaches Iason how to plead his cause, with prayers and even charms (*Py* 4.211–19). Thus, Medeia emerges rather as the victim of Iason and his divine helpers, robbed of her respect for her parents so that she might follow her lover to Greece (cf. *Ol* 13.53–54, where she seems far more responsible for her choice). Vows are exchanged, promises made, and she mixes together an oil with which Iason may anoint himself as a protection. The task consists clearly of yoking a pair of fire-breathing, brazen-hooved bulls and with them plowing a field. Aietes performs this task first, by way of example, and then challenges Iason to do the same, with the Fleece as the prize; Iason does so, much to Aietes' chagrin (*Py* 4.220–42). The latter then sends Iason to where the Fleece is, hoping he will not be able to overcome the snake (as large as a fifty-oared ship) that guards it. Neither before nor after the harnessing of the bulls is anything said about sowing dragon's teeth, but Pindar may simply have omitted this part of an already lengthy tale. Eumelos did tell of them, according to the Apollonios scholia, for Apollonios himself apparently copied lines from his predecessor (Σ AR 3.1354 = fr 19 *PEG* [*dubium*]); which exact lines the scholiast means are not certain, but this whole section of the *Argonautika* deals with the battle, so that the conclusion that teeth were included seems reasonable. Pherekydes too related the story, for he tells us that Athena and Ares took the teeth from the dragon that Kadmos slew and gave half to Kadmos, half to Aietes (3F22). Even the little that remains of Sophokles' *Kolchides* seems to have contained it, since there warriors come out of the ground (fr 341 R). But a full narration of events as we know them comes, as often, only in Apollonios (see below). Exactly how Iason dealt with the serpent warder is another subject left unexplained in *Pythian* 4: we hear that he killed the snake, and by "devices" (*technai: Py* 4.249), but we do not learn whose devices they were. In addition to the mention of the dragon's teeth and bulls of fiery breath and brazen hooves, Pherekydes agrees that Iason killed the serpent (3F112, 3F31). It seems likely that he narrated a good part of these events, although the above is all that remains.

For the bulls and dragon's teeth the artistic tradition will give us no help, but we do somewhat better with the serpent. Best known, and most important, is a cup by Douris in the Vatican dating to perhaps 480 B.C. (Vat 16545). In the upper left part of the tondo a sheep's fleece hung on a tree guarantees the scene, as does the inscription "Iason"; below, the hero emerges from the serpent's mouth, head and arms held downward as if making a dive. To the right Athena looks on. Presumably we have here a primitive form of the story in which Iason has tackled the monster barehanded, and although swallowed manages to fight his way back out, or else tricks the creature into disgorging him. Alternatively he may have allowed himself to be swallowed in order to attack his opponent's unprotected innards, much as we shall see Herakles do in combating the sea monster at Troy. Whatever its exact meaning, this intriguing variation seems definitely older than Douris in art, for it appears on two Early Corinthian pots in a form that, though less clear, can probably be identified thanks to Douris' version: Fleece and divine helper are missing, but on both examples

a man does emerge from the mouth of a snake (Bonn 860; Samos: VM frr).[22]
Thus, this account of Iason's seizing of the Fleece would go back to at least the
late seventh century. Douris' scheme and the shape of the tondo leave no room
for additional figures; that he should choose under such conditions to represent
Athena rather than Medeia might seem to preclude any major role for Medeia's
arts. Possibly this is no more than favoritism toward Athens' patron goddess.
But perhaps, too, in the oldest accounts Iason was a more aggressive figure,
capable of heroic deeds on his own, and Medeia's prominence at the end of the
Theogony a result primarily of her status as a beautiful woman to be won;
Mimnermos (if rightly interpreted: 11 W, as above) is our earliest source to
guarantee her help. Slightly later than Douris is a column krater by the Orchard Painter in New York. Here Iason tiptoes up to the Fleece very cautiously,
as if hoping to abscond with it despite the snake rearing up above (NY 34.11.7).
Behind him stands again Athena; behind her is another Argonaut, by the stern
of the Argo (which has a small head on it, apparently to indicate the speaking
beam). Medeia does not appear, though room could have been found for her in
the place of the unnamed Argonaut. She does become a standard element in
the scene from about 425 B.C. on, which may or may not represent the influence of tragedy. In Euripides' *Medeia*, she claims that she (rather than Iason,
as in Pindar) killed the snake, and possibly such a role is a Euripidean invention. Three earlier Black-Figure lekythoi do show her head framed between
snakes, but perhaps these are simply to illustrate her skills as a sorceress
(Thebes 31.166, 31.166a; London 1926.4–17.1). In Apollonios as other later
accounts she puts the snake to sleep rather than killing it, and indeed shows
great affection for it (AR 4.123–82; VF 8.64–108). Oddly enough, Lykophron
appears to suggest that Iason is cut up and rejuvenated in Kolchis, *before* he
gets the Fleece (Lyk 1315); the scholia have no useful suggestions.

With or without Medeia, the juxtaposition of snake, Fleece, and ship
makes it obvious that for the Orchard Painter, as elsewhere, Iason intends to
take the Fleece and run. In Pindar, however, we saw that this feat was a new
task set for Iason by Aietes, rather than a theft to be committed behind the
king's back. And references to the epic *Naupaktia* suggest that there, too, theft
from the snake was not the only way the plot might develop. Our source, the
scholia to Apollonios, tells that in the *Naupaktia* Aietes plans to murder the
Argonautai after, wined and dined by him, they have fallen asleep, and to burn
the Argo (*Nau* frr 6, 7, 8 PEG). Fortunately, Aphrodite inspires him with an
overpowering desire to make love to his wife, Eurylyte, in order that Iason and
his men might escape back to the ship. On Idmon's advice they leave; Medeia
hears the noise of their departure and follows them, taking with her the Fleece,
which was in the house. Possibly the scholiast means that in this epic version
the Fleece was stored in the house all the time, and thus not guarded by any
snake. But he also cites Herodoros as agreeing with the *Naupaktia* on these
points (31F53), and then adds further that, in Herodoros, after the yoking of

the bulls Aietes sends Iason to fetch the Fleece (31F52). Iason does so (killing the snake in the process) and brings the Fleece back to Aietes, who then issues his treacherous dinner invitation. Very likely, though, if the scholiast had also found this additional information in the *Naupaktia* he would have said so, and a version in which the Fleece is originally in the palace would explain better why the Argonautai do not take it with them when they steal away. Either way, we seem to have in Herodoros, at least, a literary version that squares well enough with the artistic evidence just discussed and with Pindar: after Iason has plowed the field (with or without sowing dragon's teeth), Aietes points out that there is a second task to be accomplished, for someone must get the Fleece away from the snake. Accordingly, Iason kills the snake (for Medeia to openly assist under these circumstances would be impossible) and brings the Fleece to Aietes who, unable to dispose of Iason by the usual means, resolves to do the job himself. The Orchard Painter's rather different conception, that is, a direct flight from the snake's grove to the ship, might be the result of compression by an artist who wished to include the Argo to aid identification; we might also consider such a version the result of presentation on stage, where the extra time needed for a banquet and discovery of Aietes' plot would be more than Sophokles or others could manage. But whether the direct flight ever was an Archaic element in the story, it certainly becomes the standard in later times.

These later versions follow pretty uniformly the tale of Apollonios, whom we have already anticipated in many points. Here Aietes' reluctance to surrender the Fleece stems at least in part from the prophecy that his own offspring will plot against him and bring disaster (AR 3.597–600); when he sees the sons of his daughter Chalkiope returning with the Argonautai he assumes this to be the plot mentioned. His response to the request for the Fleece is thus entirely negative, and his setting of tasks only a device to rid himself permanently of his guests. Medeia, fired by love for Iason (never vice versa), offers an ointment that will protect him from fire and weapons for a single day. With this Iason has no trouble harnessing the bulls and sowing the field, although it takes the better part of a day (AR 3.1246–1345). After resting, he perceives that the earth-born warriors are beginning to spring up everywhere; on Medeia's instructions he casts a large rock into their midst, so that they begin fighting among themselves. But Iason personally does most of the damage in Apollonios' account, rushing among them and mowing them down while they are still in the ground, as if he were a harvester. At the end of the day all are dead; as Book 4 begins, Aietes goes back to his palace to plot how he might yet destroy these strangers, while Medeia plots her escape with Iason. There follows the drugging of the serpent, thanks to Medeia, and the immediate absconding with the Fleece (AR 4.83–182). With morning the deed is discovered; Aietes and his son Apsyrtos (by a previous union with the Nymph Asterodeia) arm for battle and lead the Kolchians in pursuit.

As the geographical knowledge of the Greek world expanded, so did the routes taken by the Argonautai on their way home. The process of expansion was made easier by the fact that most of their adventures had taken place on the outbound journey; hence there were few narratively connected landmarks to hinder the enterprising storyteller. It was, of course, not impossible for the Argonautai to follow their outward route back, and apparently Sophokles (in his *Skythai*: fr 547 R) and Herodoros (31F10) made them do this. But already in the *Ehoiai* they have chosen a different itinerary, sailing up the Phasis River until they reach Okeanos, then following Okeanos around to the south until they come to Libya (i.e., some part of Africa: Hes fr 241 MW). Here they carry the Argo overland to the Mediterranean, and thus sail back to Iolkos. Hekataios follows this same general route, except for having them come down the Nile (1F18), and so too Pindar, who does not mention the Phasis but does include Okeanos and Libya (where Euphemos will meet Eurypylos/Triton) and specifies a twelve-day journey across Africa (*Py* 4.19–27). It is not likely that any Archaic source was more ambitious than this. Apollonios for his part takes the ship across the Black Sea to the west shore and up the Ister (i.e., Danube: AR 4.282–96); the scholiast tells us that in this he follows the Hellenistic geographer Timagetos, who was the first to devise such a route (Σ AR 4.282). Apollonios then brings the Argo down to the top of the Adriatic, where the dogged pursuit of the Kolchians is finally discouraged by the treacherous murder of Apsyrtos and the slaughter of his crew (AR 4.305–521). But Zeus is angry at this deed, and ordains that the Argonautai must cut across Italy via the Eridanus (Po) to the Rhone, and thence down into the Tyrrhenian Sea (AR 4.557–658). At this point they are conveniently located to repeat some of the adventures of Odysseus, and Apollonios takes full advantage of the situation: they visit Kirke, hear the Seirenes (Orpheus outsings them), see Skylla and Charybdis (Thetis assists) and the Planktai (obviously Apollonios separates these from his Clashing Rocks), pass the Island of the Sun, and come to the Phaiacians (AR 4.659–981). Here the Kolchians make one last attempt to recover Medeia; Alkinoos replies that he will not intervene if Iason and Medeia are married, and they prudently devise a hasty ceremony (AR 4.982-1223). One might think that from here they could proceed home, but a determination to include the African part of the journey draws them down to Libya, from whence they sail up to Krete and then to Iolkos (AR 4.1223–1781). A fourth route, even more ambitious, is ascribed by the scholia to Skymnos, a geographer of the second century B.C., and involves sailing up the Tanais River in the northeast corner of the Sea of Azov (Σ AR 4.282). Skymnos says that this brought them to the "great sea," and thence to the Mediterranean; by "great sea" he presumably meant the Atlantic Ocean, so that eventually their route probably involved the Don, the Volga, and even the Baltic or White Sea, with then a return to the Mediterranean via the Atlantic and the Straits of Gibraltar (so too *OA*). Again, none of this can have much to do with early versions of the story, and we shall leave the Argo's peregrinations here.

At some point on the return voyage Medeia's brother Apsyrtos must be disposed of. Apparently Sophokles in his *Kolchides* placed this event in the house of Aietes, before Medeia fled (fr 343 R), but probably such an idea springs from dramatic convenience (although Euripides [*Med* 1334–35] agrees with it when there is no similar compulsion to do so). Our oldest mention of the story occurs in Pherekydes, who recounts it in the form now familiar: on the suggestion of Iason Medeia takes Apsyrtos, who is a small child, when they flee her father's house (3F32). As they see themselves pursued, they kill the child and, cutting up his corpse, throw the pieces into the river; we presume that here as in later accounts Aietes stopped to gather up the pieces. Unfortunately, the scholia to Apollonios which give us this information do not say which river. The lines to which they are a gloss represent the point in Book 4 of the *Argonautika* when the Argonautai are trying to exit from the Phasis into the Black Sea, so that we might think the Phasis is what is intended. But the scholiast's point is really Apsyrtos, and the radical difference between his role in Pherekydes and Apollonios; thus this is the logical place in the poem, when Apsyrtos joins his father for battle, to mention Pherekydes, even if the river is not the same. Apollodoros, who follows Pherekydes in making Apsyrtos a young child abducted by Medeia, has the murder accomplished at Tomoi, thus while the Argo is sailing up the Ister (Ap*B* 1.9.24). But Apollodoros can hardly have taken this last point from Pherekydes, for in that case the Apollonios scholia, which constantly cite from that mythographer, would never have insisted on the Hellenistic Timagetos as the first to send the Argo back via the Danube. Most likely the river that, in Pherekydes, receives the chopped-up body of Apsyrtos is in fact the Phasis, and Pherekydes employs the same route as the *Ehoiai*, Hekataios, and Pindar, although we cannot prove this. It also seems likely that in these early accounts the pursuit by the Kolchians was successfully averted by Medeia's stratagem, and did not constitute a continuing motif on the return.

By contrast, Apollonios has a different idea of the murder altogether. We saw at the end of the previous section that Apsyrtos is here a full-grown man who is not kidnapped by Medeia but rather takes charge of the pursuit while his father Aietes apparently remains at home. He leads his party into the Ister and manages to intercept the quarry at a point where the river divides around several islands. A temporary truce is then made so that the question of Medeia's return to Kolchis can be discussed; during this truce she lures Apsyrtos to one of the islands with promises that she will return with him, and there Iason kills him from ambush (AR 4.305–481). Hyginus gives a roughly similar account, although in his narrative the event takes place much later, after the visit to the Phaiacians, and Apsyrtos is guilty of failing to abide by Alkinoos' settlement (*Fab* 23). Ovid, however, agrees with Pherekydes and Apollodoros: Medeia takes the child Apsyrtos with her and dismembers him (*Her* 6.129–30; 12.113–16). We come next to another difficult question, the content of Sophokles' *Skythai*. His *Kolchides*, as noted, dealt with events at Kolchis, and placed the murder of Apsyrtos there, probably as the climax of the play. But the *Skythai* also dealt with the Argonautai, and specifically with their return, since we are told that in this play they follow their outward route back. Presumably, then, the play is set in Scythia, even though the Argo will not sail up the Ister. Our one substantial fragment relates that Medeia and Apsyrtos were not born of the same mother (fr 546 R). This need not, of course, mean that Apsyrtos played any role in the story itself, and could simply refer to his murder at Kolchis before Medeia fled. On the other hand, if his death is not the subject of the *Skythai*, then that play's content is a total mystery. In support of the death of a full-grown Apsyrtos in Sophokles is perhaps Accius' play *Medea*, which does appear to have dramatized that event (fr 9 Rib). We cannot say for certain that the *Skythai* was Accius' model, but if he drew from any Greek tragedy of the fifth century (rather than Apollonios) the chronological conclusion will be the same. One other version comes from Dionysios of Miletos/Mytilene, in whose account Aietes seems to have caught up with the Argo and engaged its crew in a pitched battle in which he slew Iphis and others; ultimately, however, the Kolchians were routed (32F10).

Returning at this point to the *Ehoiai*-Hekataios-Pindar route of the return (with Apsyrtos slain, if at all, presumably in the palace or on the Phasis), we come to Pindar's recounting of the meeting with Triton in Libya. Probably this was not found in Hekataios, since he takes the Argo into the Mediterranean via the Nile, and may have bypassed Libya altogether. For the *Ehoiai* we cannot say, though here, as in Pindar, the Argonautai would seem to have penetrated into Africa. *Pythian* 4 was composed for Arkesilas of Kyrene, and uses the story of the meeting as aetiology for the city's ancestral founder Battos and his Argonaut ancestor Euphemos; thus the tale can hardly go back past the creation of Kyrene and its short-lived predecessors of about 635 B.C. In this poem the Argonautai, after twelve days of portage, have reached Lake Tritonis in Libya (*Py* 4.19–56). Here they encounter a *daimôn* (Pindar does not name him) in mortal form who claims to be Eurypylos, son of Poseidon, and offers to Euphemos a clod of earth as a token of friendship. This clod, accepted by Euphemos, will bring his descendants back to Libya as colonizers of a glorious city. Unfortunately the clod is lost, washed from the deck of the Argo at Thera; thus the descendants in question become not his legal issue back in his homeland, but rather the race he will beget on Lemnos (future tense: *Py* 4.50–51), who will in time come to Thera, and thence to Kyrene. The logic of this development is not entirely clear, and requires it would seem a visit to Lemnos at the end of the voyage, not the beginning, in contrast to all other accounts. Apollonios supplies the name of Triton as the *daimôn* who calls himself Eurypylos; he also adds a dream in which Euphemos is advised to throw the clod into the sea, so that it may itself become the island of Thera (AR 4.1551–61, 1731–64).

One final adventure remains before the arrival in Iolkos, the confrontation with the bronze Talos on Krete. Simonides seems to have described this figure as made of bronze by Hephaistos and given to Minos as a guard for Krete; he destroys those approaching by burning them up, perhaps after becoming very hot himself (568 *PMG*). We cannot say, however, whether Simonides linked him to the Argonautai. Sophokles gave much the same account in his lost *Daidalos*, according to our source, and also said that Talos was fated to die (frr 160, 161 R). But we have no idea whether Talos' death was the subject of the *Daidalos*, or just a casual reference; certainly there are many other possibilities for the plot of that play.[23] Apollonios makes him the last of Hesiod's race of bronze, the men sprung from ash trees (or Meliai). Zeus here gives him to Europa to guard Krete, and he completes a circuit of the island three times each day on his untiring feet (AR 4.1638–88). Made entirely of bronze, his only weakness is a vein at his ankle, covered by a thin membrane. As the Argonautai attempt to land on Krete he throws boulders at them, and they are forced to retreat. Medeia, however, utters prayers and imprecations and enchantments until Talos grazes the ankle on a sharp rock; this results in the ichor within him pouring out like molten lead, and he finally topples over, lifeless. Something of this sort seems definitely intended on several Red-Figure kraters from the last third of the fifth century. The more famous, a volute krater in Ruvo (1501), shows Talos (named) already in a swoon, as the Dioskouroi seize or support him from either side. Farther to the left stands Medeia, holding an empty bowl and presumably uttering her imprecations. Here no one is near Talos' foot, but on an earlier (*c.* 430 B.C.) column krater now in Salerno much the same scene is repeated with a kneeling figure performing some sort of operation on Talos' ankle and a small mannikin (Thanatos?) hovering in attendance.[24] Apollodoros reports the origins given by both Simonides and Apollonios for Talos, but his bronze man has a single vein running from neck to ankle, and sealed by a nail (ApB 1.9.26). Like Apollonios' warder, he throws rocks at the Argonautai to keep them away. Here we find three alternative versions of his demise: (1) Medeia causes him to go mad by employing certain drugs (perhaps this is what the Ruvo krater intends); (2) she promises to make him immortal and then pulls out the nail, so that the ichor escapes; (3) Poias shoots him in the ankle. Neither in these sources nor anywhere else is it actually said that he was gigantic in size. There does seem to be a general uncertainty about the application of the name "Talos" in the context of Krete: Pausanias cites a Kres-Talos-Hephaistos-Rhadamanthys line of descent (8.53.5, from Kinaithon), and we have seen that Diodoros makes the name that of the nephew of Daidalos (DS 4.76). Of the fiery monster of Simonides and Sophokles there is no later trace.

Medeia and Iason in Greece

Pindar remains our only author to make the rule of Iolkos (here illegally seized by Pelias) Iason's promised reward should he bring back the Fleece (Py 4.138–67). Unfortunately *Pythian* 4, with its focus on Cyrenean tradition, stops short of recounting the end of the Argo's voyage; we do learn that Medeia was to bring about Pelias' death (Py 4.249–50), but not whether in fact Iason ever gained the throne. In Pherekydes and Apollonios, matters are partly the same, for there too Medeia comes to Greece as the agent of Pelias' death, and (in Apollonios at least) that death is not described (3F105; AR 4.241–43). But in contrast to Pindar, as we have seen, the Iason of these versions makes no claim on the throne; rather Hera's anger will be the cause of the deed, because Pelias has slighted her. In Diodoros and Apollodoros, too, Pelias is the rightful king and Iason merely a subject who undertakes the quest of the Fleece for glory (DS 4.40.1–3) or on Pelias' command, in view of the prophecy (ApB 1.9.16). Here, however, we find a new motive for the king's death: in Iason's absence Pelias, still fearing for his throne (he has no male children) or else his life, executes Aison and his wife (together with an infant son); thus, Iason's vengeance upon his return is all too understandable (DS 4.50.1–3; ApB 1.9.27). All our literary accounts seem in fact to justify Pelias' demise, while none of them explain why Iason should in consequence be exiled from Iolkos. From fifth-century drama we have two titles, Sophokles' *Rhizotomoi* ("Root-cutters"), which very likely presented this story, and Euripides' 455 b.c. *Peliades*, which certainly did. Either would have had much to say about Medeia's motive, but on this point nothing survives.

The question whether Iason (and Medeia) always committed this deed is a still more difficult issue. The *Theogony* passage (*Th* 992-1002), when pressed very hard for clues, *might* be thought to yield the following:[25] (1) Pelias is probably the rightful king, since he is called *megas basileus* and imposes tasks on Iason; (2) his less than desirable qualities (as one who is *hubristês* and *atasthalos*) point to a divinely ordained downfall; (3) Pelias and Iason are scarcely on amiable terms, since Iason is forced to accomplish "groaning labors"; (4) Medeia's acquisition is a triumph for Iason, and one approved by the gods; (5) their life together would seem to be without further problems; (6) Medeia is properly, like her aunt Kirke, immortal, and owes her place at this point in the *Theogony* to that fact. Whether all this adds up to a killing of Pelias on their return (at the behest of the gods, or for some other reason) I do not know; possibly the winning of the Fleece and Medeia was glory enough for Iason. Much the same situation holds for Mimnermos, where we have less information but do know that Medeia assisted Iason in accomplishing his task, and that this was again set by the *hubristês* Pelias (11 W). In any case, neither of these characterizations of Pelias will square very well with the notion of elaborate funeral games in his honor, to say nothing of Iason's participation in them (see below). The earliest actual evidence we have of Pelias' untimely death (and of Medeia as its agent) comes not before about 530 b.c., when a series of Attic vases with the ram and the cauldron begins.[26] Thus for those who wish to believe the killing no earlier than the mid-sixth century the field is (relatively) open.[27]

As for the deed itself, the first Attic vases in question (Black-Figure) all show as their central element a ram emerging from a cauldron; flanking the scene are usually several women of uncertain identification and on two occasions an old man seated off to the side (London B328, B221).[28] In all respects this tableau agrees with the tradition known from the *Peliades* and many later sources: Medeia persuades the daughters of Pelias to attempt the rejuvenation of their father by cutting up a ram and bringing it back to life in a cauldron (pp. 150–51 N²; DS 4.52.1–2; Ap*B* 1.9.27; *Met* 7.297–321; *Fab* 24); the daughters then perform this same operation on Pelias, unwittingly causing his death. In fifth-century Red-Figure we find more flexible compositions. A stamnos in Munich spreads the scene around both sides, with five women in all, an unbearded male (Iason?), and the seated old man as above (Munich 2408). Several other vases eliminate the cauldron (or at least the ram) but give one of the women a sword; so on a calyx krater this daughter (named as Alkandre) leads Pelias (also named) to a second woman (Tarquinia RC 685), while in the tondo of a cup she waits before the cauldron as Pelias approaches in some apprehension (PrColl:Basel). Such scenes seem to guarantee a consistent account of the means by which Pelias dies, at least from the latter sixth century on in Athens; on a number of examples, too, Medeia is probably recognizable next to the cauldron from the *polos* she wears or the small box she holds.

In the same period, however, Medeia is also credited with rejuvenating a real person, not just a ram. Indeed, as early as the *Nostoi* she is said to do this for Aison, boiling *pharmaka* in a golden lebes (fr 7 *PEG*: direct quote with Aison's name), while in both Simonides (548 *PMG*) and Pherekydes (3F113) the person made young again (by boiling) is Iason. The idea that Iason should need or want to become younger might well lead us to suppose a mistake here, especially as a reversal of just two letters will, after all, enable Iason to become Aison. But the two scholia constituting our evidence specifically contrast Simonides and Pherekydes with the *Nostoi* on this point, so that, although the scholiasts themselves may have drawn on an erroneous source, they did clearly mean to suggest two separate beneficiaries of Medeia's skills. That being the case, we should probably accept Iason as one of them, though with some puzzlement. In support of this account, an early fifth-century Red-Figure hydria shows Medeia (named) with a cup, the ram emerging from the cauldron, and an old man whose name is inscribed as "Iason" (London E163).[29] Lykophron, too, seems to know something of such a story, for he says that Iason had his body cut to pieces in a cauldron (Lyk 1315).[30] In any case, we are left to wonder which use of Medeia's powers is older, that to slay her husband's enemy or to benefit him and his family. If not an intrusion from the former story, the ram on the London hydria should mean that Aison and Iason, like Pelias' daughters, needed a demonstration before being persuaded. As a final query, we might also wonder whether in an earlier tradition the rejuvenation of Aison or Iason (rather than the ram) was the means by which Pelias' daughters were so persuaded.[31]

As for the aftermath of Pelias' death, there seems no firm evidence at all before Euripides' *Peliades*, where Iason apparently (this from the preserved last line of a hypothesis) gave the kingdom to [Pelias' son] Akastos and departed with Medeia for Korinth. Perhaps in this play he had no further desire to remain in Iolkos, having gained his revenge, or perhaps he, like Pelias' daughters, was a victim of Medeia's plan, failing to realize her intentions until too late. For earlier times the issue of his fate depends inevitably on the question of when Iason (or at least Medeia) first kills Pelias, and as we saw above that is a most uncertain matter, even if the *Theogony* passage seems to imply that the couple finds a blissful life in Iolkos. Puzzling too, as we saw, is Iason's participation in the wrestling at the games for Pelias on the Chest of Kypselos (Paus 5.17.10), implying as it does a tradition with nephew and uncle on favorable terms. Here at least, assuming Pausanias has not erred (and the artist not indulged in a bit of fancy), we seem to be dealing with a narrative in which Iason is quite guiltless of Pelias' fate. Of later sources, Diodoros like Euripides presents Iason as handing the throne over to Akastos, and even finding husbands for the latter's sisters before departing the land (4.53). So too Hyginus has Iason take possession of the kingdom after Medeia has eliminated Pelias, but then pass it to Akastos because the latter sailed to Kolchos with him (as in Apollonios: *Fab* 24). In Apollodoros, however, after the burial of Pelias Akastos expels Iason and Medeia from Iolkos (ApB 1.9.27). As we will see below, Eumelos has Medeia invited to Korinth to assume the rule because of her family background. But not impossibly other writers found other ways to effect her transfer to Korinth, where she occupied an important place in Korinthian traditions, and it has even been suggested that the murder of Pelias was among them, serving as it did to separate Medeia and her husband from a life in Iolkos.[32]

In all events, Medeia's action fails to do more than remove Pelias, and the way is paved for the couple's departure. Pausanias says that in the epic *Naupaktia* they went to Kerkyra, where the elder son Mermeros was killed by a lion (2.3.9 = fr 9 *PEG*). But he also records that in Eumelos' *Korinthiaka* they were summoned to Korinth, where Medeia, through her father Aietes, was declared queen, and Iason co-ruler with her (2.3.10–11 = Eum fr 5 *PEG*; so too in Simonides [545 *PMG*] Medeia is queen of Korinth). Still from Eumelos, perhaps, is Pausanias' further tale that Medeia, as each of her children was born, took it to the sanctuary of Hera and left it there in the expectation that it would become immortal. Apparently the children die, because Iason refuses to forgive her and returns to Iolkos; she in turn leaves the kingship to Sisyphos. Some clarification of Pausanias' rather bald summary survives in the same Pindaric scholia that cited the lines from Eumelos on Medeia's ancestral link to Korinth (Σ *Ol* 13.74g); no author is named, but very likely these further details have been taken from the *Korinthiaka* as well. Here we learn that Medeia averts a famine in Korinth by sacrificing to Demeter and the Lemnian Nymphai. Zeus then falls in love with her, but like the *Kypria*'s Thetis she refuses him out of regard for Hera, and Hera in gratitude promises to make her children immortal. When they die, the Korinthians honor them with a cult. Obviously this account has oddities of its own, but if we combine it with that told by Pausanias, many of the problems disappear; what we would still like to know is how the children died, and why Hera's promise was not kept.

That Medeia destroyed her children unintentionally would seem then to have been the version of Eumelos. But the scholia to Euripides' *Medeia* allude to a very different tradition in which the Korinthians themselves are responsible for those deaths (Σ *Med* 264). The note in question offers two variations on this idea. The first, which is ascribed to Parmeniskos (apparently a grammarian of the second/first century B.C. drawing from earlier sources), presents the Korinthians as unhappy at being ruled by a foreigner, and a woman skilled in drugs to boot. Accordingly, they concoct a plot against her and plan to kill her children, seven males and seven females. These take shelter in the precinct of Hera Akraia, but the Korinthians do not respect the goddess; the children are butchered at the altar. A plague ensues and propitiation must be made; nothing more is said about Medeia. The other story is ascribed (via Didymos) to Kreophylos, who might be either the seventh-century epic poet of Samos (see fr 9 *PEG* [*dubium*]) or the fourth-century historian of Ephesos (417F3). Whichever he was, his version has Medeia (as simply a resident of Korinth) kill Kreon, the ruler of the city, by means of drugs. Fearing vengeance at the hands of his friends, she flees to Athens, but leaves her children behind because they are too young to go with her. To protect them, she places them on the altar of Hera Akraia, thinking too that their father will contrive for their safety. Friends of Kreon do, however, kill them, and then spread the rumor that Medeia did the deed before she left. This last detail (whether or not of a piece with the rest of the story) was obviously concocted by someone familiar with the alternative, namely that Medeia did the deed herself, and interested in accounting for the existence of both versions, the one blaming the Korinthians, the other Medeia. As to the date of this latter version, we have evidence from another story cited by the scholia (and ascribed also to Parmeniskos) in which the Korinthians are said to have paid Euripides five talents to shift the blame from their ancestors to Medeia (Σ *Med* 9). However doubtful this tale may seem as a historical fact, it could not have been plausibly fabricated if there was any sort of well-known pre-Euripidean tradition in which Medeia was the culprit. Most likely then (whatever his motive), Euripides is the inventor of the idea that Medea knowingly killed her children. If we could be sure that Kreophylos' version included the detail of the Korinthian slander we would then be well on the way to inferring that this Kreophylos must have written after Euripides. But such a point could well have been added to a seventh-century Kreophylean account by Didymos or some other well-meaning synthesizer, and even if the whole were from a fourth-century author the beginning of it might still be taken from pre-Euripidean sources. In any case, since at least one of the versions in which the Korinthians are responsible must, like that of Medeia's complicity, pre-date Euripides (else Parmeniskos' bribe story will again make no sense), the Archaic period would seem to have offered two distinct traditions, one in which Medeia inadvertently kills her children, the other in which the Korinthians do it deliberately. To these Euripides would then add as a third possibility the slaying of them by their mother for revenge on Iason. Less clear is how the two so very different archaic traditions came about, and why in the one where the Korinthians are guilty it is sometimes Medeia (so Parmeniskos and perhaps Eumelos) and sometimes Kreon (so Kreophylos) who rules Korinth.

Unfortunately, we are never told why in Kreophylos' version Medeia chooses to kill Kreon. The means used, *pharmaka*, could indicate the same device as in Euripides, and Pausanias' reference to a Spring of Glauke into which Kreon's daughter threw herself, seeking relief from the poison, would seem to suggest an early origin for her death (2.3.6). On the other hand, the summary of Kreophylos puts all the emphasis on the death of Kreon, as if the daughter was not involved and Kreon was the main target. But the scholiast has perhaps not done justice to his source; all we can really say is that Medeia may in Kreophylos have used the same means to slay Kreon as she does in Euripides. Even so, this will not guarantee that her motive was the same; possibly she hoped by killing Kreon to secure the throne for Iason, much as she may have done at Iolkos. If we knew for certain when Glauke's death became a part of the story we could probably resolve this question, for when she becomes the target (unless her death is an accidental consequence of Kreon's) the motive is surely jealousy, as in Euripides. But Pausanias' spring might have acquired its aetiology in a post-Euripidean period; Euripides himself never names Kreon's daughter, making it easy enough for the Korinthians to link her to a previously unrelated landmark. In all, there seems nothing to tilt the scales much either way: Kreophylos may have anticipated (or reflected) Euripides' notion of jealousy as the root of the problem or concentrated rather on some more direct conflict between Medeia and Kreon. The fact remains though that, as matters stand, we have no sure evidence for Iason's abandoning Medeia for another woman before Euripides, even if "Kreophylos" represents only one place in which such a story might have been earlier told without surviving.

Such conclusions will, however, depend to some degree on our handling of another problem, namely the statement of the *Medeia's* hypothesis that Aristotle and Dikaiarchos believed Euripides to have derived his drama very closely from a similar one by Neophron. According to Diogenes Laertius this Neophron came from Sikyon (DL 2.134), and the *Souda* credits him with more than one hundred plays, but *Medeia* is the only title to survive. Apparently there was such a play, for several quotations survive from it; one tells us that Aigeus has come to Korinth precisely to ask Medeia about his mysterious oracle (15 fr 1 Sn). Given that this is an improvement plotwise over Euripides' rather aimless Aigeus, we may well wonder who has copied from whom; Denys Page has marshalled this and other points of comparison to suggest that the work (by a later Neophron?) is probably fourth-century B.C.[33] What follows will proceed on that assumption; even if it is wrong, Neophron would have to be close in time to Euripides, and therefore authorship will not greatly affect our present purposes.

Euripides' treatment of the story, whether his own invention or not, is too familiar to need more than a brief summary here. Iason and Medeia are foreigners to Korinth, not rulers, and their weakened status as such is frequently stressed. Iason proposes to abandon Medeia for Kreon's daughter in an attempt to secure his own future; her displeasure at this prospect is sufficiently vocal that Kreon orders her banishment from the city. Feigning concern for their two children, she persuades Iason to let the children bring gifts to the new bride, who will then intercede for their safety with Kreon. The gifts, a robe and crown, are of course poisoned; when the daughter puts them on, the drugs eat into her flesh, much like the poison that will destroy Herakles. Kreon then enters and embraces her corpse, only to be caught fast against it and killed in the same way. Naturally Medeia fears vengeance against her children as agents of the deed. Her own way lies to Athens, where she will consort with Aigeus; unable to take the children with her, she kills them as a means of further punishing Iason. As the play closes, she departs the stage in a chariot given to her by her grandfather Helios (the scholia at *Med* 1320 say that it was drawn by dragons) while Iason threatens helplessly from below. She adds in parting the information that Iason will die a base death, killed by a falling beam of the Argo. The scholia know two versions of this, (1) that Iason dedicated the prow of the ship in a sanctuary of Hera, and died when it fell on him one day, and (2) that he fell asleep under the ship, and a part of it, being now rotten, broke away (Σ *Med* 1386). We also learn that in Neophron's play Iason is told he will kill himself by hanging (= 15 fr 3 Sn); no further details of this version are known, though Diodoros also says that he killed himself (DS 4.55.1).

In art there is nothing at all on this story until after the date of Euripides' play, which clearly inspired vase-painters: the fourth-century tradition seems to draw on him to the exclusion of any other source, although there are naturally small artistic variations. On the most famous example, an Apulian volute krater in Munich (3296), we find Kreon's daughter called "Kreonteia"; Ovid, Seneca, and Hyginus will all use "Kreousa" (*Her* 12.53; Sen: *Med* 495; *Fab* 25), but Hyginus also records "Glauke," as do the hypothesis to Euripides' *Medeia* and Apollodoros (ApB 1.9.28). As for other literary variations on the story, in Diodoros Medeia accomplishes her purpose by stealing into the palace and setting it on fire (DS 4.54.5), a plan that Euripides' Medeia at one point considers. Hyginus speaks only of the crown, not the robe; its poison seems to create a fire that burns up the daughter, Kreon, and Iason, and the palace as well (*Fab* 25). The same result is briefly alluded to by Apuleius, though without Iason (Apl: *Met* 1.10), and so too perhaps Ovid (*Met* 7.394–95) and Seneca's *Medea* (883–87). Finally, in the scholia to Euripides' *Medeia* we find a variant in which Iason marries not the daughter of Kreon, but rather the daughter of Hippotes, son of Kreon, who has succeeded his father on the throne (Σ *Med* 19). In Diodoros this same Hippotes demands Medeia's return after she has fled to Athens; apparently the Athenians give her a trial and acquit her (DS 4.55.5). The above-mentioned scholion also calls Kreon a son of that Lykaithos who assumed the rule on Bellerophontes' departure from Korinth; the scholiast may mean, but certainly does not say, that Lykaithos is descended from Bellerophontes. No other source appears to mention this name. Kreon was also a major character in Euripides' *Alkmaion in Korinth*, and perhaps his ancestry was discussed there. Both Ovid and Seneca seem to regard him as descended from Sisyphos (*Her* 12.204; Sen: *Med* 512); presumably they are making that link through Bellerophontes and perhaps (whether correctly or not) via Lykaithos. Hyginus, not surprisingly, confuses this Kreon with Iokaste's brother at Thebes, the son of Menoikeus (*Fab* 25).

Medeia's sojourn in Athens with Aigeus has already been treated in chapter 7, with Theseus' arrival at the court of his father; we saw there that this part of her story first appears in the *Aigeus* plays of Sophokles and Euripides, although it may be illustrated as early as the time of Makron. The attempt to poison Theseus in an effort to maintain her influence over Aigeus is the only event recorded for this last phase of her career, but before closing accounts we must glance briefly at the matter of her children. The end of the *Theogony* notes one, Medeios, as her son by Iason, showing perhaps an early interest in linking her name with that of the Medes (*Th* 1000–1002). How early we should date this is hard to say, perhaps not before the sixth century, but in any case we have a tradition which (of necessity) allows at least one of her children to live. Pausanias reports that the epic poet Kinaithon also gave this son to Iason and Medeia, plus a daughter Eriopis; he adds that Kinaithon says nothing else about them (2.3.9 = fr 2 *PEG*). We saw earlier that the *Naupaktia* provides another son, Mermeros, who is killed on the mainland opposite Kerkyra while hunting (fr 9 *PEG*). In Euripides' *Medeia*, there are specifically two sons, unnamed (*Med* 1026–27, 1136); the scholia, plus Pausanias, Apollodoros, and others agree in calling them Mermeros and Pheres (Paus 2.3.6; Ap*B* 1.9.28). Hellanikos offers one Polyxenos by Iason, who in his account is the child Medeia takes with her back to Asia Minor (4F132; elsewhere this is Medos/ Medeios: see below). No source other than Parmeniskos speaks of fourteen children (this number is clearly chosen to explain a ritual at Korinth), but Diodoros does find room for three, the twins Thessalos and Alkimenes and a younger son Tisandros (DS 4.54.1, 7; 4.55.2). In his account, Thessalos escapes when the other two are slain, and makes his way to Iolkos, where he succeeds the deceased Akastos. As for Medeios, or Medos as he is more often known, at some point he becomes the son of Aigeus rather than of Iason. Our first source to actually speak of this transfer is Diodoros, but he ascribes it to tragedy and indeed we should certainly expect it to have occurred in the fifth century B.C. A child Medos could have been used in either Sophokles' or Euripides' *Aigeus* (or both) as an additional reason for Medeia's desire to dispose of Theseus, although we cannot prove this. Diodoros also says that the tragedians allowed Medeia to flee Athens and return safely to Kolchis, where Medos killed Perses, a (previously unsuspected) brother of Aietes who had usurped the latter's throne (so too Ap*B* 1.9.28, save that Medeia commits the deed). Such a tale could derive from a prophecy at the end of one of the *Aigeus* plays, but when we turn to Hyginus we find a similar story, told in great detail with false identities (Medos impersonating Hippotes) and recognitions and Medeia almost killing her own son, which sounds very much like a tragedy in its own right (*Fab* 27). Here too Medos slays Perses (there is no mention of Aietes) and gives his name to the land of the Medes. Clearly the shift of parentage brings with it a narrative convenience, for if Medos is not the son of Iason, storytellers need not explain how he survived the events at Korinth. We should expect, however, that the more important reason was a desire on the part of Athenians to link their race to that of Persia, though why is harder to say. Conceivably, Athenian mythographers added the stay in Athens to her list of adventures for just this purpose, before sending her on to Kolchis.

13 Herakles

Alkmene and Amphitryon

In contrast to the heroes we have so far been considering, tales of Herakles are liberally referred to in the *Iliad* and *Odyssey*, thus assuring us that many of his exploits developed quite early. The *Iliad* knows of his birth in Thebes to Alkmene and Zeus, of his subordination to Eurystheus, his wounding of several gods, sack of Troy, battle with the sons of Neleus, and fetching of Kerberos. In the *Odyssey* we hear of his stepfather Amphitryon and wife Megara, of his treacherous slaying of Iphitos, and again of the descent into Hades. These are all just brief chance references, and Homer no doubt knew other stories as well. But quite a number of Herakles' adventures take him to the ends of the earth, and we must expect that some of these adventures evolved (or at least expanded) as the Greeks' geographical horizons widened in the Archaic period.

Zeus' affair with Alkmene is one of those he mentions to Hera in *Iliad* 14, with Herakles born in Thebes as a result (*Il* 14.323–24). Agamemnon in *Iliad* 19 improves upon this by telling the tale of Zeus' deception by Hera at the time of the birth: after Zeus has sworn that whoever is born that day will rule all those around him, Hera delays the birth of Herakles and accelerates that of Eurystheus, son of Sthenelos of Argos (*Il* 19.95–125). The *Nekuia* adds that Amphitryon was the husband of Alkmene (although here as always Herakles is Zeus' son: *Od* 11.266–68). In chapter 10 we reviewed the evidence, probably as early as the *Ehoiai*, which relates all these figures: Sthenelos, Alkaios, and Elektryon are sons of Perseus and Andromeda; Sthenelos begets Eurystheus, Alkaios Amphitryon, and Elektryon Alkmene. The beginning of the Hesiodic *Aspis*, which we know constituted in origin part of the *Ehoiai*,[1] narrates in detail the circumstances surrounding the conception: in a fit of anger over some cattle, Amphitryon has slain his father-in-law Elektryon, and must go into exile (Hes fr 195 MW: presumably this event occurs somewhere in the Argolid). Accordingly he migrates to Thebes to be purified, and his wife Alkmene, the daughter of Elektryon, goes with him. She does not, however, permit him to enter her bed, and while we might expect that this is in anger or grief over the death of her father, her motive is rather a desire that Amphitryon first avenge the death of her brothers at the hands of the Taphians and Teleboans. Accompanied by Boiotians, Lokrians, and Phokians, he accomplishes this task, making a raid and burning villages. But meanwhile Zeus has decided to beget a son to be a helper and defender of men and gods; he descends from Olympos to Thebes, and there lies with Alkmene. Surprisingly, the text does not say that he took the form of Amphitryon; all we are told is that he went down "plotting deception in his heart." If this means deception of Alkmene, as would seem most likely, it surely refers to some sort of disguise. But perhaps the lines intend simply a deception of Amphitryon through the seduction of his wife in his absence. The question is further complicated by a scene of Alkmene and Zeus together on the Chest of Kypselos. The relevant panel showed Alkmene (apparently named) receiving a cup and necklace from an unnamed man whom Pausanias took to be Zeus transformed into Amphitryon (5.18.3). That Phere-kydes knew about this cup emerges from two sources that seem not entirely in agreement with each other. The first, Athenaios, says that according to Phere-kydes and Herodoros, when Zeus lay with Alkmene, he gave her a cup as a gift in exchange for their union (11.474f = 3F13a, 31F16). The second, a scho-lion to *Odyssey* 11, has Zeus in the guise of Amphitryon present the cup to Alkmene as a war prize and proof that he has slain the Teleboans (Σ *Od* 11.266 = 3F13b). Perhaps this is what Athenaios means too, but his words certainly sound as if Pherekydes had Zeus in his own form win Alkmene's affections with the gift. The scholiast's story, though it must come from somewhere, is also a trifle odd, for the cup is not much proof, and what will the real Amphit-ryon think when he sees it? The scholiast himself seems to realize the awk-wardness of this last point, for he tells us that Alkmene "put the cup away."

Neither of these sources mentions a necklace, although in the case of Ath-eniaos that is not surprising, since the context of his remark is a discussion of cups. But if a necklace was part of the early tradition, it would point again to a seduction rather than deception of Alkmene, since a necklace is even less plau-sible than a cup as proof of a military success. We should remember, of course, that Zeus used the same device—the gift of a necklace—in the seduction of Europa. There, however, the gift came after he had brought her to Krete, and we must allow that something of the same sort may be intended here: Zeus first lies with Alkmene in the guise of her husband, then resumes his own form, reveals the truth, predicts the birth of a son, and offers her the gifts. As a final complication in this uncertain picture, Athenaios some pages later cites the fourth-century writer Anaximandros to the effect that the Teleboans pos-sessed an ancestral cup originally given by Poseidon to his son Teleboas, and that Amphitryon selected this cup for himself as his part of the spoils (Athen 11.498c = 9F1). On the surface, this might seem to explain the cup's use as proof of Amphitryon's accomplishment: if it is a famous Teleboan heirloom, it could well persuade Alkmene. But if Amphitryon has it, how can Zeus give it to Alkmene? Perhaps he appropriates it from Amphitryon, but more likely several different stories have become confused. Regarding one other detail of this whole encounter, Pherekydes is our first attested source for the idea that Zeus persuaded Helios not to rise for three days, so that his night with Alk-mene would be three times the usual length; the story is found in the scholia to *Iliad* 14.324 (3F13c: credited to Pherekydes only in Vratislaviensis)[2] and recurs in Plautus' *Amphitryon* (112–14) and Diodoros (4.9.2), among other sources.

Leaving such questions, we return to the account of the *Ehoiai*. Seduction or deception, Zeus visits Alkmene, and on the same night Amphitryon returns from the campaign. The result is twins of a very different temper, Herakles born to Zeus, Iphikles to Amphitryon, and here the *Ehoiai* ends (so too 3F13b). The poem appended to these lines and known as the *Aspis* offers a few further details: Amphitryon comes from Tiryns to Thebes, where he is welcomed by Kreon and Henioche, and Iphikles has a son, Iolaos, who accompanies Herakles on the venture against Kyknos as his charioteer (*Aspis* 79–89). There is also a strange mention of Iphikles as one who abandoned his home and parents to honor Eurystheus and later regretted it; nothing in our later sources elucidates this situation. Some help with the initial events in the Argolid which caused Amphitryon to migrate to Thebes does, however, come from Apollodoros. In his account Hippothoe, daughter of Mestor, is carried off by Poseidon to the Echinades Islands (off the west coast of Aitolia); their son Taphios creates a settlement of people whom he calls Teleboans (ApB 2.4.5–8). Taphios' son Pterelaos is made immortal by Poseidon via a golden lock of hair on his head, and begets six sons. Since Mestor is here a child of Perseus, these sons return to Mykenai and claim Elektryon's kingdom from him as rightfully theirs. When he refuses the claim, they drive off his cattle. They are pursued and challenged by Elektryon's sons; a fight ensues and all but one on each side are killed. The cattle end up with Polyxenos, king of Elis, and Amphitryon brings them back to Mykenai. Here a fluke accident occurs: one of the cows goes berserk, Amphitryon throws his club at it, and the weapon, bouncing off the horns, kills Elektryon. As in the *Ehoiai*, Amphitryon goes to Thebes for purification. There follows the campaign against the Teleboans to placate Alkmene; like Minos with Nisos' Megara, Amphitryon cannot take Taphos while Pterelaos has his lock of hair, but (like Nisos' daughter Skylla) Komaitho, daughter of Pterelaos, falls in love with the besieger and cuts the lock. Taphos falls, Amphitryon slays Komaitho, and returns home. Obviously this does not all square exactly with the *Ehoiai*, for here the death of Elektryon is involuntary, whereas in the *Ehoiai* it clearly results from a quarrel (probably over the division of the recovered cattle). But the general outline of Apollodoros' story is surely what the *Ehoiai* knows and expects us to supply. Pherekydes also may have told it, or at least the part about Teleboans driving off cattle and killing the sons of Elektryon, if the whole of the scholiast's long note at *Odyssey* 11.266 is derived from him (3F13b).

Herodoros, too, related a genealogy of the Teleboans/Taphians as part of his *Herakleia*, though with some differences: Mestor, son of Perseus, begets Hippothoe, who bears to Poseidon Pterelaos; Pterelaos' sons are Taphios and Teleboas, and from the latter arise the children who demand Elektryon's kingdom and slay his sons (31F15). The story of Pterelaos' golden lock survives only in Apollodoros (who may or may not have found it in Pherekydes) and Tzetzes (Σ Lyk 932), plus a passing allusion in Ovid's *Ibis* (361–62). Tzetzes too tells the story as above, and perhaps takes it from Apollodoros, but he adds that the children surviving the battle were Elektryon's son Likymnios and Pterelaos' son Eueres. He also suggests that the object of Komaitho's passion may have been Amphitryon's ally Kephalos (son of Deion: so too the scholia at Lyk 934).

In Archaic art, Zeus/Amphitryon and Alkmene on the Chest of Kypselos constitutes the sum total of our evidence for this story. Neither is there any reference in the lyric poets until Pindar's *Nemean* 10.13–18, where we learn specifically that Zeus came to Alkmene as Amphitryon; this is our first sure reference to the disguise. In a different poem, *Isthmian* 7, the poet advances the odd idea that Zeus came as or was accompanied by (the Greek will allow either) a golden snowfall (borrowed from the story of Danae?: *Is* 7.5–7).[3] Yet another Pindaric ode, *Nemean* 1, recounts for the first time the tale of the snakes sent into the nursery by Hera to slay Herakles, and his throttling of them (*Nem* 1.33–72). The date of this poem is perhaps 476 or 472 B.C.; as it celebrates Hieron's friend Chromios "of Aitna" (Hieron's refounding of Katane) it can hardly be earlier. Probably, though not certainly, it postdates the beginning of the artistic representations, which lead off with a fine stamnos by the Berlin Painter of about 480 B.C. (Louvre G192). Pindar's treatment of the story does not, in any case, sound like an innovation. As his version of the tale continues, both parents rush to the nursery, only to find the snakes dead; Amphitryon summons Teiresias, who prophesies Herakles' future deeds and final apotheosis. That Hera sent the snakes is logical enough, and that notion remains the standard one. But Pherekydes offers an account in which Amphitryon himself introduces them into the nursery in order to discover which child is his and which is Zeus' (3F69). Either Alkmene has revealed to him that someone else visited her in his form, or he has found the cup.

Turning to tragedy, we are told by Hesychios that Aischylos wrote an *Alkmene* (p. 130 R). Since that title does not appear in the Medicean Catalogue (though others are missing as well), and there are no other references, Hesychios may be mistaken. In any case, there is no indication of plot. The same is true of Sophokles' *Amphitryon*, which could deal with the slaying of Elektryon, or the deception by Zeus, or something else. Euripides' *Alkmene* is more promising: though here again we have no certain evidence of plot, South Italian vase-painting presents on several occasions a tableau with obvious Euripidean potential.[4] On the vases in question Alkmene has taken refuge at an altar around which Amphitryon has then piled wood for a fire which he is in process of lighting (e.g., Taranto 4600, London F149, London F193). Fortunately, Zeus intervenes, sending a thunderbolt to discourage Amphitryon and two clouds to put out the fire. Presumably Amphitryon had come to believe that his rival was some mortal lover of Alkmene, and sought to punish her. The story seems tailor-made for the stage, and especially for Euripides, who uses so well the possibilities for conflict arising out of misunderstanding.

One other story of Herakles' infancy surfaces first in Ps-Eratosthenes and Lykophron, with elaboration by Diodoros, Pausanias, and Hyginus. Lykophron simply alludes to the fact that Herakles once nursed at the breast of Hera (twice: Lyk 38–39, 1327–28), but Ps-Eratosthenes explains that it was ordained that no son of Zeus might obtain heavenly honors unless he had so nursed (*Katast* 44). Accordingly, in the latter account, Hermes takes the newborn Herakles up to Olympos and quietly places him in an appropriate position in the goddess' lap. When Hera notices the child she immediately pushes him away; the milk that is spilled becomes the Milky Way. Hyginus adds that Hera was asleep at the time, thus making the tale a bit more plausible (*Astr* 2.43). In Pausanias' brief notice, Zeus takes the place of Hermes, but we are not told his motive (Paus 9.25.2). Diodoros has a somewhat different version in which Alkmene abandons her child from fear of Hera's anger (DS 4.9.6). Hera and Athena come upon it, and Athena persuades Hera to nurse it. But the infant sucks at Hera's breast too violently; in pain she throws it down, and Athena takes it back to its mother. There are several South Italian scenes showing the nursing (e.g., London F107), and these together with the Lykophron passage indicate an origin before the Hellenistic era, but how much earlier we cannot say. Some vases and Etruscan mirrors even present Hera willingly offering her breast to a grown Herakles (Florence 72740: mirror), which may signify the transferal of the event to the time of the hero's entry into Olympos. In all, it seems probable that the original point of this story was to justify Herakles' outstanding qualities and eventual divine status, as Ps-Eratosthenes says, even if on other occasions sharing of nectar and ambrosia is the usual means of bestowing immortality.

Last, from Pindar, according to Probus (or rather the Vergilian commentaries ascribed to him), comes the notion that Hera gave Herakles his name (originally it was "Alkides") because the glory he acquired was after all the result of her harassment (fr 291 SM); Apollodoros attributes the renaming rather to the Delphic Sibyl (ApB 2.4.12). Delphi as the cause appears as well in an *Iliad* scholion that gives, however, an etymology unrelated to Hera and says that Herakles' original name was (like that of his grandfather) Alkaios (ΣT *Il* 14.324; cf. Σ *Ol* 6.115d); alternatively, the name is said to derive from his assistance to Hera when she was threatened by Pyrphorion. In Diodoros, the change is rather the work of the Argive people (DS 4.10.1); here too the original name is Alkaios.

Theban Exploits

A late sixth-century Black-Figure amphora shows Hermes taking Herakles off to Cheiron (Munich 1615A; Herakles named); one suspects this is merely assimilation to the standard education of other heroes. Later sources assign him a number of teachers in different specialties, as we might expect. But the only real deed of his youth, after the strangling of the snakes, is his unfortunate slaying of his music teacher Linos. Already in the time of Douris we find this illustrated in Red-Figure, with Herakles swinging part of a stool at the helpless musician (Munich 2646). The story recurs on a number of pots as the fifth century progresses, and may have been the subject of Achaios' satyr play *Linos* (20 fr 26 Sn: Herakles is mentioned), but it seems not to survive in literature until Diodoros and Apollodoros. Both tell the same story, that Linos struck Herakles for being a poor pupil, and that in a rage the hero retaliated (DS 3.67.2; ApB 2.4.9). Most sources suppose this Linos to have been the commonly attested son of one of the Mousai; Pausanias, however, makes him a more earthly figure, the son of one Ismenios (9.29.2). Vase-paintings of Herakles (grown) with a lyre are quite common in Black-Figure; only one example is known from Red-Figure.

On reaching young manhood, Herakles deals with several local challenges before enlarging his sphere of activity. The first of these is to slay the lion of Kithairon, which has been destroying livestock. Apollodoros is our only source for the lion itself (ApB 2.4.9–10), but the task involves a *parergon* of considerable notoriety: Herakles comes to Thespiai, west of Thebes, where he is entertained by the king, Thespios, and his daughters. In all accounts these are fifty in number, and Herakles has intercourse with all fifty or else forty-nine. Herodoros says this was done in seven nights (31F20), Pausanias in a single night (9.27.6–7), and Apollodoros in fifty separate nights (with Herakles unaware that his partner changes each night). Apollodoros and Diodoros agree on the motive for this unusual event, namely that Thespios wished to have as many grandchildren as possible by such a hero (DS 4.29.2–3). Pausanias is the author who makes the total number of girls forty-nine; in his account, one daughter refuses Herakles and is punished by being made a priestess with perpetual virginity. After all this, the lion seems a rather simple matter; Herakles slays it and dresses himself in the skin and head, according to Apollodoros. Such a detail strongly suggests what we might already have suspected, that the Kithairon lion is a Theban doublet of the Nemean one. Depending on the relationship we assign to Herakles' Theban and Argolid roots, the Kithairon venture could be the earlier one, but as early as Peisandros we find (probably) that the skin worn by Herakles was taken from the Nemean Lion (fr 1 *PEG*).

The other Theban exploit involves a conflict with the neighboring city of Orchomenos. The story seems alluded to by Pindar (Erginos warned by Apollo?: *Pa* 8.102–4), Euripides (mention of Herakles' victory over the Minyans: *HF* 48–50, 220–21), and Isokrates (tribute paid to the Orchomenians: 14.*Plataikos* 10), but details come primarily from Diodoros, Apollodoros, and (more vaguely) Pausanias. This last tells us that Klymenos, son of Presbon (son of Phrixos), received the rule at Orchomenos (9.37.1–3). Both Pausanias and Apollodoros (ApB 2.4.11) then relate that certain Thebans murdered this man at Onchestos, and that when he was carried back home dying he made his son Erginos swear to avenge him. Accordingly, Erginos marches on Thebes, defeats its people, and imposes a tribute (Apollodoros says one hundred cattle a year for twenty years). When the heralds come for the tribute in this particular year, they find Herakles less than disposed to pay it. In Apollodoros (Diodoros at 4.10.3–5 is less specific) he cuts off their noses and ears, hangs them around their necks, and sends them back to Erginos. Naturally, the Orchomenian king mobilizes for war, but with Herakles at their head the Thebans are victorious. It has been suggested that this story formed the subject of Aischylos' lost (and satyric) *Kerykes*, a play that does seem to have featured Herakles.[5]

As early as the *Nekuia* we find mention of Megara, daughter of Kreon, whom Herakles married; Odysseus says nothing else (*Od* 11.269–70). Not unreasonably, Diodoros and Apollodoros suggest that Kreon gave Herakles his daughter as a reward for the defeat of Erginos (DS 4.10.6; Ap*B* 2.4.11); Apollodoros throws in a younger daughter for Iphikles (already the father of Iolaos) as well, and so too *Megara* (the fourth poem ascribed to Moschos), where she is Pyrrha. Herakles' subsequent madness appeared as early as the *Kypria* (in a digression of Nestor), although we do not know in how much detail (p. 40 *PEG*). Both Stesichoros (230 *PMG*) and Panyasis (fr 1 *PEG*) told of the deaths of his children by Megara; Pausanias' further remarks, after providing this information, imply that in those authors as elsewhere Herakles committed the deed, and while mad (9.11.2). Pindar numbers the children (here too of Megara, daughter of Kreon) as eight, and speaks of sacrifices and games held regularly by the Thebans for them (*Is* 4.61–64); presumably then the grandfather Kreon was thought of as the Theban son of Menoikeus. It must be said, though, that Pindar includes nothing about Herakles' involvement, only that the offspring died and that they were *chalkoarai*, "fitted out with bronze." Had we not more explicit sources elsewhere, we would, I think, have assumed that the sons grew to manhood and were slain in battle, a not altogether unheard of notion (see below).[6]

Pherekydes, for his part, speaks of five children, all thrown into the fire by their father (3F14). The tale is fully dramatized by Euripides in his preserved *Herakles Mainomenos*, where Lykos (descendant of the husband of Dirke) has slain Kreon and Megara's brothers and usurped the throne; Herakles has no difficulty in dealing with him, but Iris and Lyssa (Madness) then enter on the orders of Hera to cause him to slay both his three children *and* Megara. This is our first sure reference to Hera as the cause of the deed; she will become a standard element of the story in later writers, but our earlier sources are not complete enough to ascertain whether her role was found there as well. The Pindaric scholia offer some variants: Lysimachos records the tradition that the children were treacherously slain by strangers, and the Argive historian Sokrates that Augeias was responsible, while an unascribed version names Lykos (Σ *Is* 4.104g). But all other late sources agree on Herakles' complicity; only the number (between two and eight) and the identity (in Apollodoros, two of Iphikles' children are included) of the victims vary. Asklepiades adds Iphikles as someone else who would have been slain, had not Athena intervened

(12F27); in Euripides' play this near victim is Amphitryon; Athena here halts Herakles by throwing a stone that strikes him unconscious (*HF* 1001–8). The only artistic representations are South Italian: on a Paestan calyx krater of the fourth century, for example, Herakles carries a child to his doom on a burning pyre, while Iolaos, Alkmene, and Mania watch from a gallery above, perhaps part of a stage setting (Madrid 11094). The exact placing of this lamentable event in Herakles' career is a problem that we will consider in the next section.

The Twelve Labors Already we have seen from *Iliad* 19 and the birth of Eurystheus that at an early stage of the tradition Herakles was destined to be subordinate to his cousin. Two other passages in the *Iliad* mention labors that Herakles had to perform for Eurystheus (*Il* 8.362–69; 15.639–40); the first of these, in *Iliad* 8, specifies the fetching of Kerberos as one of them. In the *Odyssey*, too, Herakles in the Underworld speaks of how a lesser man enjoined harsh labors on him, including Kerberos (*Od* 11.620–26). Subsequent to Homer, the *Theogony* notes the slaying of the Nemean Lion and the Lernaian Hydra, and the driving-off of the cattle of Geryoneus (*Th* 326–32, 313–18, 289–94), and to these Peisandros adds the Keryneian Hind and the Stymphalian Birds (frr 3, 4 *PEG*); neither poet mentions Eurystheus or actually says that the deeds were done under compulsion. Eurystheus does reappear in *Homeric Hymn* 15, where as in Homer he is the setter of the tasks that take his cousin over land and sea. But none of these sources ever says why Herakles had to perform the tasks, or how many there were, although Peisandros probably provided a (for his own time) complete set. The total from literary sources prior to 500 B.C. is thus six; Black-Figure painting of the sixth century adds the Erymanthian Boar (brought back to Eurystheus), the Kretan Bull, the Mares of Diomedes, a combat with Amazones, and the quest for the Hesperides' Apples. Only the Stables of Augeias must wait until the fifth century to surface. Of the eleven attested prior to that point, only two, Kerberos and the Boar, are specifically linked to Eurystheus, and some of the remainder may originally have been undertaken for profit or other reasons. The Athenian Treasury at Delphi metopes show the Lion and the Hind and Geryoneus, and no doubt others too fragmentary to identify (the Herakles metopes on this building were not, however, all Labors). On the east façade of the Hephaisteion temple in Athens, where the architects had ten metopes at their disposal, Geryoneus was allowed to occupy two metopes, and thus only nine Labors were represented; omitted were the Birds, the Stables, and the Bull.[7]

Slightly earlier in the century, the sculptors at Olympia had found themselves with twelve metopes to carve, since it had been decided to decorate only those over the inner porches at the two ends. Given the influence such metopes would have had over the Greek world as a whole, there is a good possibility that twelve became the canonical number of Labors because there were twelve spaces to fill. In particular, it has been questioned if the Stables of Augeias—which from their very first appearance in Pindar include the mention of *pay* withheld—have not been added in as a sop to local pride. On the other hand, perhaps the number of metopes suggested the choice of the Labors as subject, and in any case there is always the chance that the Stables have replaced some other task. Sophokles' *Trachiniai* (1089–1100) and Euripides' *Herakles* (359–424) both give partial lists, and Aischylos may well have offered his own version in the *Prometheus Lyomenos*, but not until Diodoros do we have a preserved literary account of the twelve Labors as we know them, all ordained by Eurystheus (DS 4.11–26). Admittedly, there are no preserved instances where a source claims any additional Labors or offers anything other than the known ones. But when the twelve we do have all became canonical we can only guess.[8]

As for Herakles' motivation to perform the Labors, there are two main lines of thought. Euripides, who is the first surviving author to commit himself on the matter, says that Herakles wished to return with his family and his father to Tiryns, and promised Eurystheus in return for that permission that he would tame the earth (*HF* 17–21). Certainly this seems a bit weak, especially when compared with Apollodoros' notion that Delphi advised him to serve Eurystheus for twelve years as a penance for killing his own children (ApB 2.4.12). We should note, too, that Euripides' play revolves around the tack of placing the murders late in Herakles' career, after the Labors have been completed, so that earlier triumphs can be followed by tragedy. Most likely, then, the version of Apollodoros, that the Labors are an expiation, is the older one, and Euripides has worked a change to better dramatize Herakles' sense of despair. A third motivation, that Herakles was instructed by Delphi to undertake the Labors as a means to apotheosis, appears first in Diodoros (4.10.7), and is repeated by Apollodoros as a secondary motif after the major one of penance. Obviously this idea cannot be older than the apotheosis itself, and the apotheosis is very likely a sixth-century invention (see below). In any case, the emphasis in Homer is entirely on Herakles' travails and sufferings (and in one instance his death), which would be rather anomalous if he were laboring toward any ultimate reward. Finally, Athenaios' remark—that in the *Herakleia* of the late epic poet Diotimos, Herakles and Eurystheus were lovers—shows that for some writers anything is possible (Athen 13.603d).

On the order of the Twelve Labors there is surprising agreement in our two main sources, Diodoros and Apollodoros. It has long been noted that six of the twelve are located in the Peloponnesos, and both writers separate these off as a group performed before the other six. At Olympia the arrangement was admittedly different: the Augeian Stables, as the local contribution, occupied the place of honor in the last position over the front porch; joining it were the Mares of Diomedes, Geryoneus, the Apples, Kerberos, and one other Peloponnesian exploit, the Erymanthian Boar (so Paus 5.10.9, although he forgets Kerberos). Over the rear porch were the four remaining Peloponnesian tales, plus the Kretan Bull and the Amazones. The presumed decision to elevate the Stables perhaps disrupted the more traditional arrangement, if there as yet was one, and then too the artists may have been guided by considerations of compositional juxtaposition. The Hephaisteion presents, as noted, nine Labors, in the order Lion, Hydra, Hind, Boar, Mares, Kerberos, Amazones, Geryoneus, Apples. In Diodoros we find the following: (1) Lion, (2) Hydra, (3) Boar, (4) Hind, (5) Birds, (6) Stables, (7) Bull, (8) Mares, (9) Amazones, (10) Geryoneus, (11) Kerberos, (12) Apples. Apollodoros' only changes in this order are to invert (3) and (4), (5) and (6), and (11) and (12). Of these three separate inversions of neighboring pairs only the last is really of any interest, for we would like to know which Labor was considered the last and most difficult. As one might expect, different narrators seem to have had different opinions on that question, and here again the loss of Peisandros' work is unfortunate.

Labor I: The Nemean Lion

Since the great majority of our sources make the Nemean Lion the source of Herakles' distinctive costume, they not surprisingly put this Labor first, presumably to outfit him as soon as possible. In Hesiod there is no mention of leonine invulnerability, only the creature's descent from Orthos and the Chimaira (or Echidna?[9]), his fostering by Hera, terrorizing of Nemea, and defeat by Herakles (*Th* 326–32). Peisandros says that the latter wore the skin as a memento of the occasion (fr 1 *PEG*); elsewhere we are told that Stesichoros was the first to represent him as a brigand, with club, lionskin, and bow, in contrast to Homer and the lyric poet Xanthos (229 *PMG*). In Homer, of course, Herakles does have a bow, and little else is said about his equipment or attire; perhaps the comment means that before Stesichoros he was portrayed more as a battlefield warrior. The motif of the Lion's invulnerable hide is hinted at by Pindar and stated clearly by Bakchylides, both in poems dating to about 480 B.C. (*Is* 6.47–48; Bak 13.46–54). Bakchylides then draws the obvious conclusion that Herakles was forced to kill the beast with his bare hands; elsewhere he repeats Hesiod's statement that Hera raised the creature (Bak 9.6–9).

The artistic tradition could begin at any time, since there are numerous early representations of a man and a lion, including a likely instance on a Boiotian fibula (the left side shows a man and birds: London 3204).[10] Definite illustrations emerge toward the end of the seventh century with the shield-band reliefs from Olympia. On some of these, Herakles is clearly engaged in wrestling with the Lion, as they stand or kneel in various positions. But on several others, Herakles holds a sword and, as he grasps the Lion with one hand, either threatens him with the sword (B 1650) or actually plunges it into his body (B 1654).[11] The same scene occasionally surfaces in Korinthian and Attic painting of the sixth century, and quite strikingly on a Chalkidian (or pseudo-Chalkidian) neck-amphora of about 530 B.C. (Louvre E812). Clearly then, though the wrestling version is old, we must ask if there was not also a version in which the Lion was vulnerable, and could be slain with bronze and iron. One suggested solution to such conflict is to suppose that some scenes portray Herakles attempting to kill the Lion with weapons before comprehending that strangulation is the only means; in support of this notion we can point to at least one Black-Figure version of the scene with a bent sword on the ground, no doubt thrown away by Herakles (VG 50406). But it must be admitted that the scenes in which the sword appears to penetrate the Lion look very convincing. The Nemean Lion is the most popular of all Herakles' exploits in art, with hundreds of representations, almost always displaying variations on basic wrestling poses. There are also several examples of Herakles skinning the Lion (so Munich 2085), and the metopes at Olympia offer a wonderfully weary Herakles resting after the conquest. Obviously he cannot (or should not) in any of these portrayals actually wear the lionskin. The first sure example of this dress in art dates to about 600 B.C., on a bronze pectoral (Samos: VM B 2518),[12] after which such costuming remains standard until we reach the early fifth century.

Later literary accounts uniformly adhere to the tale of the invulnerable lion strangled by Herakles. Theokritos, or rather a poem sometimes ascribed to him, adds that Herakles stunned the animal with his club, and used the creature's own claws to cut the skin so that he could take it off and wear it (Theok 25.153–281). The story of his stay with Molorchos while battling the Lion is alluded to by the Tibullan corpus (3.7.12–13) and other Latin works, and given in detail by Apollodoros, who says that he instructed his host to sacrifice a victim to Zeus if he was successful, but to himself as a hero if he did not return in thirty days; he makes it back with the Lion on the last day (ApB 2.5.1). The hypothesis to Pindar's *Nemean Odes* suggests, as we might expect, that Herakles reorganized the Nemean games on this occasion and dedicated them to Zeus.

Labor II: The Lernaian Hydra

In the *Theogony* the Hydra of Lerna is the offspring of Echidna and Typhaon (*Th* 313–18). Hesiod says that Hera raised her in anger at Herakles, and that Herakles slew her with his sword (or something of bronze) with the help of Iolaos and the counsels of Athena. No mention is made of heads, but as in the case of the Nemean Lion it is a very brief reference. In any event, we have quite a series of representations to assure the general form of opponent and combat.[13] On a Boiotian bow fibula from Thebes now in London we see Herakles with sword in hand attacking a snake that he grasps by the neck; six heads spring therefrom (London 3205). Below him a smaller figure, presumably Iolaos, attacks the tail of the creature with a jagged-toothed *harpê*. Already, too, the crab of later written tradition is in place, nibbling at Herakles' feet. Another fibula of about the same period, *c.* 700 B.C., this time with rectangular catchplate, is in the University Museum in Philadelphia (75-35-1). Here Herakles and Iolaos stand on either side of the Hydra; only two of her heads remain, but several necks droop, and there are severed bits and pieces floating about. Iolaos grasps his *harpê* as before, and the crab is again present. Of a bronze tripod leg from Olympia dating to perhaps 620 B.C. only a small part remains, showing the legs of the two assailants, the lower part of the Hydra, and the *harpê* (Olympia B 5800).

At the end of the seventh and beginning of the sixth century Korinthian versions begin to appear.[14] On an aryballos once in Breslau, where Herakles and Iolaos are identified by inscriptions, Herakles clearly drives his sword through the body of a multiheaded snake (I count ten, including severed necks), while on the other side Iolaos prepares to lop off three more heads with his *harpê* (Lost: Breslau, no #). The crab threatens as usual. A cup in Jena (137), an aryballos in Basel (Basel BS 425), and a kotyle (Lost: from Argos) offer almost exactly the same arrangement. On a fragmentary skyphos in the Louvre, however, Herakles wields a more typical weapon, his club, while Iolaos continues the assault with his *harpê* (Louvre CA 3004). On the Chest of Kypselos, by contrast, Herakles shoots at the Hydra with a bow (Paus 5.17.11); the combat also formed part of the Amyklai Throne, but Pausanias there gives no details (3.18.13). In Athens, the first preserved illustration is that on a limestone gable from the Akropolis, where Herakles once again brandishes a club, but Iolaos now stands behind him in the chariot (Akropolis 1). Although Iolaos could be preparing to dismount, it seems more likely that he intends to let Herakles have all the glory. Herakles is likewise isolated against the Hydra (now *he* holds the *harpê*) on a Little Master cup in Berlin (once Berlin F1801; now lost). The presence of the two heroes (in appropriate poses) on a Tyrrhenian amphora in Rome is probably sufficient to assure that the one-headed snake between them is also a Hydra (VG 74989). In all these representations and others, it seems implied that cutting off the heads, or clubbing, or even at times shooting arrows, will be sufficient to dispatch the monster. Not until the latter part of the sixth century do we find traces of the fire used (presumably) to sear the necks and prevent regrowth. A Caeretan hydria of about 530 shows Iolaos still armed with his *harpê*, but between his legs burns a fire (meant to be thought of perhaps as in the background) (Getty 83.AE.346). Subsequently, in Attic Black-Figure toward the end of the century he actually applies a torch to the necks of the creature (VG 106465; Louvre CA 598) or (in Red-Figure of the same period) holds a torch in each hand (White-Levy Coll, no #). But of an immortal head there is as yet no sign.

In literature after Hesiod we have Peisandros, who Pausanias claims invented the idea of a Hydra with many heads to make his account more impressive (2.37.4 = fr 2 *PEG*); we have seen that the artistic evidence guarantees this detail as much older, but Pausanias' remark may indicate that it was not easily to be found in early literary accounts. A scholion to the *Theogony* adds that Alkaios gave her nine heads (443 LP), and that Simonides made the number fifty (569 *PMG*). Already in Stesichoros' *Geryoneis* there is a hint that the creature's blood was poisonous (15 *SLG*), and this is confirmed by Sophokles' *Trachiniai*, where we are told explicitly that Herakles dipped his arrows therein, thus creating the possibility for his own death when he shot Nessos (*Tr* 573–74). Euripides' *Herakles* offers the first literary reference to the searing of the necks (*HF* 419–24); later in the same play the creature is called "the many-headed growing-back-again *(palimblastês)* dog, the Hydra" (*HF* 1274–75), giving us as well our first hint in literature of her regenerative capacities. Sickle and torch reappear in the same playwright's *Ion* (*Ion* 191–200). From the end of the fifth century we have the agreement of Hellanikos (4F103) and Herodoros (31F23) that Hera sent the crab, for which reason Herakles then needed the help of Iolaos. In the fourth century Palaiphatos first states explicitly what vase-painting and Euripides have implied, that a head—two heads, in fact—will grow back for every one cut off (Pal 38). Naturally, the crab reappears in Ps-Eratosthenes, where (of its own accord) it alone of all creatures sides with the Hydra against Herakles and pinches his foot (*Katast* 11). Herakles dispenses with the crab by stepping on it, but Hera is so pleased with its effort that she makes it a constellation. Palaiphatos ascribes at least the pinching of the foot to Panyasis, and the other details may come from that source also.

Subsequent writers, including Diodoros (with one hundred heads: 4.11.5–6), Ovid (*Met* 9.69–76), Apollodoros (Ap*B* 2.5.2), and Hyginus (*Fab* 30: poisonous breath) confirm most of these details. But first (and only) in Apollodoros do we find the idea that one of the nine heads is immortal. After dealing with the crab and the other heads in the usual way, Herakles somewhat surprisingly cuts off the immortal head as well and buries it under a rock; apparently the neck was considerably more vulnerable. The same writer has earlier spoken of ten, not twelve, Labors as ordained by Delphi, and now he explains that variation in number by having Eurystheus refuse to count this task because Iolaos has helped. The other Labor to be excluded, as we shall see, is the Augeian Stables, on the grounds that Herakles hired himself out for pay. Possibly a rival version of ten Labors (not necessarily Apollodoros' remaining ten) suggested this story, but we cannot say.

Labor III: The Keryneian/ Kerynitian Hind

Following the order of Apollodoros we come to the hind with the golden horns. The scholia to the brief account of the Labor in Pindar's *Olympian* 3 tell us that Peisandros (fr 3 *PEG*), the *Theseis,* and Pherekydes (3F71) all agreed with Pindar in making the creature female and golden-horned, and this is in fact the sum total of our Archaic literary sources. Pindar regards the Hind as a creature that Taugete has dedicated to Artemis and inscribed in some way; Herakles pursues her from Arkadia to the river Ister and the land of the Hyperboreans. The scholia explain the allusion to Taugete by relating that she is the same daughter of Atlas whom Zeus desired (Σ *Ol* 3.53). To help her escape his pursuit Artemis turns her into a deer, and when she is finally returned to human form she dedicates the deer (now apparently a separate entity) to Artemis. Either the deer already possesses golden horns, or Taugete gilds them for the occasion, or she attaches such horns. She also writes on the animal's neck her dedication to Artemis. We have seen in chapter 6 that Zeus successfully consorts with Taugete as early as the Amyklai Throne, and probably too in the *Ehoiai*; one note in these same scholia likewise concedes their mating (Σ *Ol* 3.53d), which fits oddly with a tale of escape. But Pindar's allusion seems to expect that his audience knows the whole story, and probably in the fuller original version Zeus somehow outwitted Artemis. As for the Hind's topo-graphical associations, we hear nothing beyond Arkadia until Kallimachos, who links her with that region's Mount Keryneia, the source of the river Kerynites (*H* 3.107–9). Apollodoros, on the other hand, names her after the river rather than the mountain (Ap*B* 2.5.3), which explains the variation between Kery-neian and Kerynitian.

Among other post-Archaic sources we find Euripides, who offers several puzzling bits of information. In his *Helen*, the title character indulges in a brief exposition on the evils of beauty and the solaces of metamorphoses (*Hel* 381–83). She cites first Kallisto, forgetful of her Zeus-caused travails after be-coming a bear, and the "daughter of the Titaness Merops, the golden-horned, whom Artemis expelled from her dances because of her beauty." Conceivably Euripides means what the words say, that Artemis was simply jealous of a rival's good looks. But "because of her beauty" could well be a compressed expression for what her beauty caused, the seduction by Zeus, in which case we would have a very close parallel to the story of Kallisto. At any rate, we seem meant to infer that Artemis changes this daughter of the otherwise un-known Merops (Taugete does have a sister Merope) into a deer as part of the punishment. It is, of course, quite possible that Euripides invented this whole variant whereby Artemis punishes rather than protects the girl for the sake of the parallel with Kallisto. In the *Herakles* we find something altogether differ-ent: here, in the context of Herakles' many accomplishments against various opponents, the Hind is a marauder who steals from the surrounding populace, and Herakles kills her (*HF* 375–79). He also thus "honors the huntress Arte-mis," perhaps by dedicating the horns to her. Once again the relationship be-tween Artemis and the deer is the opposite of what we would normally expect, and again there is a strong possibility of Euripidean innovation. In a lost play, the *Temenidai*, he described the tracking of the Hind (fr 740 N²), but we learn nothing from what little survives. Kallimachos for his part dispenses with any notion of metamorphosis; in his *Hymn to Artemis* the goddess comes upon five golden-horned hinds at Parrhasia in southern Arkadia (*H* 3.98–109). Four of these she captures and harnesses to her chariot, but the fifth escapes by the will of Hera, to become a task for Herakles. The chariot is clearly the rationale for the story, which may have been invented by Kallimachos to provide suitable beasts to draw it, working from the model of the original Hind.

Diodoros tells us simply that the Hind was golden-horned and very swift, and that Herakles either ran her down, or captured her while asleep or with nets (DS 4.13.1). More details come from Apollodoros, whose version provides the now-familiar account (Ap*B* 2.5.3). Though he says nothing of how she came into being, he does specify that the Hind is sacred to Artemis. Herakles therefore hesitates to harm her, and pursues her for an entire year, beginning at Oinoe on the border between Arkadia and the Argolid. When he perceives that this is of no avail, he wounds her with his bow as she is swimming across the river Ladon in central Arkadia, and thus captures her. Artemis and Apollo then arrive and remonstrate with him; by pleading Eurystheus' role in the matter and his own helplessness he mollifies them, and is permitted to take the animal, still alive, back to Tiryns. At no point, here or elsewhere, does the literary tradition say that the Labor required bringing the Hind back alive, but in all cases including the artistic tradition that seems to be the result, save only for Euripides, whose Hind is we have seen uniquely malevolent (Hyg *Fab* 30 does call her *ferox*). Whether in the original telling this notion of a live capture was intended to make the task more difficult, or was always in deference to Artemis, remains open.

Given the simplicity of the pictorial aspects of the story, the surviving artistic representations do not have much to tell us, but they do start quite early, as early in fact as the Boiotian catch-plate fibula in Philadelphia on which we saw the Hydra (75-35-1). The reverse of the same catch-plate shows a deer with horns nursing a fawn, and a man grasping one of the horns while threatening the deer (or fawn?) with a spear. No other source mentions or shows a fawn, but the artist may well have included it here for the sole purpose of establishing that the deer is actually a hind with horns, and thus the mythical creature captured by Herakles.[15] The spear is unexpected, but perhaps serves the same purpose of wounding as in Apollodoros, or marks out the deer as a quarry to be hunted.[16] From this fibula we move down to Attic Black-Figure of the sixth century and a neck-amphora of the Timiades Painter (about 560 B.C.): here Herakles runs beside the Hind, one hand clasping its antlers and the other its neck, as it rushes left toward an enthroned Aphrodite; to the far right stand Apollo and Artemis (Cerveteri, no #). Of the same time period is an Attic Black-Figure plate in Oxford dating to about 560 B.C. on which we see the story fully developed: Herakles and Apollo square off against each other with drawn bows, while the Hind (no horns; probably the artist feared they would obscure the other figures) stands in the center between them; behind her is a woman who may be Artemis or Athena (Oxford 1934.333). I suspect the former, but in any case the presence of Apollo guarantees Artemis' interest in and protection of the Hind as an early element in the tale, as it does too Apollodoros' account of a conflict between hero and goddess after the capture.

From the circle of the Antimenes Painter comes a neck-amphora now in Würzburg which shows much the same scene, except that Herakles now carries the captured Hind on his shoulder, and Apollo tries to wrest it away (Würzburg 199). Behind Apollo stands Artemis; behind Herakles, Athena. Certainly in this representation the Hind itself is what Herakles needs to bring back to Eurystheus. But a neck-amphora near Group E in London may offer another possibility: now Herakles, flanked by Athena and probably Artemis, grasps the two horns of the Hind with his bare hands, and has actually broken off one of them (London B231). Either the artist wishes to capture a moment of frustration, as Herakles loses the most easily grasped part of the animal, or he means to suggest that Herakles' task is to bring back just the horns, not the whole animal. Athena to the left holds up a sheathed sword, obviously that of Herakles; the equally complacent woman to the right holds a bow. If, as we might expect, the bow is also that of Herakles, then she may be just filler; if not, she is a remarkably calm Artemis. Conceivably, the same figure appears on a Red-Figure cup by the Antiphon Painter in the Louvre where Herakles places one knee on the Hind's back and grasps one of the horns with both hands (Louvre G263); a similar pose is used for the Hind metope on the Athenian Treasury at Delphi (no #). But in neither case can we say with any certainty whether Herakles' intention is to break the horn, or simply exert leverage on the animal in order to subdue it. Thus the problem posed by the London amphora remains a dilemma, although we might have expected a tradition in which just the horns are required to have left a greater mark in the literary sources.

Labor IV: The Erymanthian Boar
In no account is there anything especially remarkable about this boar, aside from its predictable ferocity, and perhaps for that reason it almost escapes mention in Archaic literature; its one appearance is in Hekataios, who notes the harm it did to the people of Psophis (1F6). From that reference we proceed to Sophokles' *Trachiniai*, where Herakles can think of nothing to say about it save that it came from Erymanthos (*Tr* 1097). Euripides in the *Herakles'* list of exploits does not even include it. But the artistic tradition, with its special fondness for the Boar's presentation to Eurystheus, provides again a rich series of representations for the sixth century, and may even extend back to the end of the seventh, if a fragment of a metope from Kalydon showing Herakles and the Boar is rightly interpreted.[17] In any case, the sixth century offers us unmistakable examples, beginning with an iron shield-strap from Olympia (E 161) and a metope of Heraion I at Foce del Sele. Both pieces illustrate the same point of action, Eurystheus hiding in his pithos and Herakles raising up the Boar and preparing to ram it down snout-first into the jar. In vase-painting we begin toward the middle of the century, with a neck-amphora near Group E now in London: again Eurystheus from within the pithos waves his hands in horror as a most unfriendly looking Boar held by Herakles looms overhead (London B213). The scene becomes especially popular in the latter part of the sixth century, always with the same essential features (in one instance the Boar descends upon Eurystheus stern first: NY 41.162.190). As this period progresses, however, we also find phases of the capture: one very attractive example by the Lysippides Painter depicts Herakles grasping a hind leg and trying to raise it (London B492), while on others he uses his club or forces the boar to his knees (so Madrid 10915). No evidence remains for the portrayal of this Labor on the Athenian Treasury at Delphi, but enough fragments survive to guarantee that the metopes of both the Zeus temple at Olympia and the Hephaisteion, like their predecessor at Foce del Sele, told the story of Eurystheus and the pithos.

Turning to later literature, we find that in Apollonios Herakles was in the very act of bringing the Boar back to Eurystheus when he heard of Iason's quest for the Golden Fleece and headed for Iolkos (AR 1.122–32). Diodoros specifies that Eurystheus ordered the Boar to be brought back alive, and that when Herakles did so he hid himself in a bronze pithos in terror (DS 4.12.1–2). Apollodoros agrees with Hekataios that the Boar came down from Erymanthos and did much damage to Psophis; here Herakles drives the animal into deep snow and thus traps it (ApB 2.5.4). Though the Boar is then brought back to Mykenai, Apollodoros omits the detail of Eurystheus and the pithos. Earlier he has already recounted how Eurystheus had the bronze pithos prepared for himself after Herakles returned from slaying the Nemean Lion, apparently in order to hide from the hero himself (ApB 2.5.1). We might expect such a story to have its origin rather in this present Labor, on the first occasion when Herakles brings back a live and dangerous creature. Just possibly this cowardice on the part of Eurystheus, and even his pithos, is what Homer alludes to when he says in *Iliad* 15:639–40 that Kopreus conveyed the assignment of each Labor from Eurystheus to Herakles. Hyginus seems the only writer to claim that Herakles slew the Boar (*Fab* 30).

Pholos   Mount Pholoe is just south of Mount Erymanthos, and while Herakles' visit to the Kentauros Pholos there may have begun as an independent adventure, it inevitably becomes in time a stop on his way to obtain the Boar. In the course of his career Herakles has several violent encounters with Kentauroi, including Eurytion and Nessos, but this appears the only occasion on which he fights more than one of them, so presumably the many representations pitting him in battle against a number of them refer to this story. Fortunately some of the earliest artistic examples show the cave or wine jar or both, thus guaranteeing the antiquity of the account familiar from later writers, and we have also a fragment of Stesichoros' *Geryoneis* in which Pholos serves wine to Herakles (181 *PMG*). The early existence of that detail, the presumed cause of the quarrel, seems also to guarantee that this exploit, though often listed as one of Herakles' major accomplishments, was never actually thought of as a Labor. Rather it arose accidentally from a dispute over a jar of wine. Why it should have played a part in a poem about the Geryoneus Labor is uncertain; perhaps Stesichoros added it to Herakles' other adventures in bringing the cattle back from Spain, or perhaps it was part of a reminiscence about past times. The first literary sources referring to the battle are Sophokles (*Tr* 1095–6) and Euripides (*HF* 364–74), but with no details beyond Herakles' defeat of the Kentauroi (Euripides, perhaps by convention, places the whole affair in Thessaly). Sophokles also notes elsewhere in the *Trachiniai* that Cheiron was once wounded by Herakles' arrows (*Tr* 714–15), and Theokritos mentions that same Kentauros as serving Herakles a bowl of wonderful wine in Pholos' cave (7.149–50), but the full story of the confrontation with all the Kentauroi will come only with our later sources.

   In art the earliest evidence is a Protocorinthian aryballos, now in Berlin, which shows Herakles firing arrows at a group of Kentauroi, all of whom have been wounded (Berlin:PM F336).[18] A pyxis lid from Perachora of the same period may show Pholos and his drinking cup together with a branch-swinging Kentauros; certainly his name is preserved on a fragmentary metope from Thermon.[19] When we move down into the sixth century, a Middle Corinthian kotyle in the Louvre brings all the pieces together (Louvre MNC 677).[20] Pholos stands in his cave, cup in hand, next to a large krater and a kindled fire. Meanwhile, Herakles has picked up brands from the fire and uses them to chase other Kentauroi out of the cave. His weapons hang on the wall behind Pholos, indicating that he and his host have been disturbed in the middle of their visit. To the far side of the fleeing Kentauroi stand Athena and Hermes, observing. The story also seems to have occupied all six metopes along the east façade of Heraion I at Foce del Sele; the first two show Pholos (with human forelegs) and Herakles with his bow, the other four Kentauroi charging at him or collapsing from wounds. Pausanias saw the battle on both the Chest of Kypselos and the Amyklai Throne (5.19.9; 3.18.10); in the latter instance he says that it is the battle by the cave of Pholos, but of course he may be supplying this detail from his own memory. The frieze from the Temple of Athena at Assos in Asia Minor also showed the combat, with Pholos and cup clearly visible as Herakles drives off the intruders. Attic Black-Figure takes rather late to the story, or at least to the phases of it involving Pholos, beginning only with the Antimenes Painter and his circle, where we see Pholos welcoming Herakles (London B226), or the Kentauroi beginning to quarrel around the wine jar (Bologna PU 195); a particularly fine example of this last occurs on a neck-amphora in the Vatican, where hostilities have already commenced (Vat 388). The subject also becomes surprisingly popular on lekythoi, both Black-Figure and White-Ground, but for the finale of the tale we must turn again to the literary sources.

Diodoros offers a full account (DS 4.12.3–8). Herakles stops to visit Pholos at a place near Mount Pholoe, and is naturally offered some refreshment. Pholos has in fact a jar of wine sunk down in the earth which has been given to the Kentauroi by Dionysos, with orders to open it only when Herakles should come. Four generations later the day arrives; the wine, by now quite fragrant, attracts the other Kentauroi, who storm the cave in order to obtain it. Pholos hides in alarm, but Herakles stands his ground. The Kentauroi attack with trees and firebrands and axes, and even a rainstorm sent by their mother Nephele (this last detail drawing surely from Pindar's *Pythian* 2, where a cloud-Hera is the grandmother of the Kentauroi). Nevertheless Herakles kills the greater part of them and routs the others. But Pholos in burying the dead happens to be wounded by an arrow he is extracting and dies as well. Diodoros also notes that Herakles accidentally wounds Cheiron during the battle, but says nothing about the consequences of that misfortune.

In Apollodoros, Herakles is likewise visiting Pholos (a son of Silenos!) near Mount Pholoe, and as they are dining (Pholos on raw meat, Herakles on cooked), Herakles calls for wine (ApB 2.5.4). Pholos hesitates to open the jar that belongs to all the Kentauroi in common, but finally does so, and the Kentauroi rush the cave as in Diodoros. Herakles puts them to flight, here using (as on the Middle Corinthian Louvre kotyle) firebrands to do so, then turning to his bow and arrows. With these he hunts the remaining Kentauroi as far as Cape Maleia, where Cheiron dwells and with whom they seek refuge. In this way Cheiron is accidentally wounded by one of Herakles' arrows, which strikes him in the knee. We have already discussed in chapter 3 the resolution of this situation in Apollodoros: the wound proves incurable, and Cheiron being immortal cannot die. Through Prometheus' intervention he exchanges his immortality for someone's mortality, almost surely that of Herakles himself; some form of the story may or may not have been utilized in Aischylos' Prometheus trilogy. As for Pholos, he draws an arrow from one of his comrades, asks how such a small thing could kill a Kentauros, and promptly drops it on his foot; when Herakles returns he finds him dead. One presumes that this is an old story, but it is missing altogether from the artistic tradition, and not found in literature before Diodoros. The same is true of the wounding of Cheiron, although Pindar's *Pythian* 3 does acknowledge that he is dead (*Py* 3.1–5). Only Hyginus reports versions in which the arrow falls accidentally on Cheiron's foot, not that of Pholos (*Astr* 2.38.1–2).

Labor V:
The Stables
of Augeias

As we saw above, this most unglamorous of the Labors does not find any certain reference before the fifth century, when a veiled reference in Pindar and the metope of the Zeus temple at Olympia introduce it. Pindar's *Olympian* 10 speaks of how Herakles slew Kteatos and Eurytos, the Moliones, so that he might be able to force Augeias to pay him for the hired service he had performed (*Ol* 10.26–30). The task itself is not mentioned, nor is Eurystheus, and one is left to suspect that Pindar may not have regarded it as a Labor. Whatever its status, we must allow that it may have been known to the *Iliad,* since that poem is aware of a quarrel between Phyleus and his father Augeias, which in later accounts at least is caused by the failure to pay Herakles (*Il* 2.628–29). Otherwise, Augeias appears in Homer only as part of the dispute between the Epeians and the Pylians, whose racing team he has appropriated (*Il* 11.698–702). No other literary source adds anything to this picture until the third century B.C., when Theokritos has Herakles visit Augeias and take a tour of his herds; as the poem progresses, Herakles reveals that he has great need of Augeias, whose vast herds are a gift to him from his father Helios, but we are never told what that need is (Theok 25). Kallimachos' *Aitia* furnished more detail; what survives are two separate Iliadic scholia summarizing the story and assigning it to this source (ΣΣA *Il* 2.629, 11.700). As they tell of the incident, Herakles has gone to Elis on Eurystheus' order and cleaned out the dung from the stables of Augeias. On requesting pay he is refused by Augeias, who argues that the deed was performed to fulfill a command. Phyleus the son is made arbiter, rules against his father, and is banished by Augeias, who ignores the decision.

Of our standard later authors, Diodoros says nothing about any dispute (or pay), only that Herakles had to clean the stables for Eurystheus by himself (DS 4.13.3). But he is the first source to say that Herakles, deeming it unworthy of him to carry out the dung, diverted the river Alpheios to do the job. Turning to Apollodoros, we find a detailed narrative that pulls all the previous evidence together and adds some new material (ApB 2.5.5). In his version, Eurystheus commands that the stables be cleaned in a single day. Herakles then approaches Augeias and, without telling him of the command, offers to perform the task for a tenth of the herd. Augeias agrees, and Herakles diverts two rivers, the Alpheios and the Peneios. But Augeias subsequently learns that Herakles had to do the cleaning anyway; thus he reneges on his agreement. Phyleus is appointed to settle the matter, and testifies for Herakles; he is banished as in Kallimachos, and Herakles leaves without his pay. Consistent in all but Diodoros, then, is the fact that Augeias refuses to give Herakles some agreed-upon or expected compensation. Perhaps this was always for the reasons provided in Kallimachos and Apollodoros, but more likely in the beginning the Stables were not a Labor, and Augeias' motive was simple meanness, for which he pays dearly. If this conclusion is correct, then somewhere the tradition has effected an ingenious conflation, best seen in Apollodoros, which credits Herakles with working both sides of the street; thus the task becomes a Labor, but loses none of its original consequences.

Unfortunately, the condition of the metope at Olympia does not permit us to say exactly what Herakles is doing there. Pausanias, who saw the frieze intact, tells us that the cleaning of the stables is what is represented (5.10.9), and there is no reason to disbelieve him, but how this is accomplished is less clear. Herakles holds a long pole or handle, of which the bottom part is missing. A shovel or pitchfork or even a broom has been suggested, yet the position of the hands and the angle of the pole (its lower end cannot touch the ground) seem wrong. Probably (though not certainly) he wields a crowbar or something he can use to open a water channel or clear a path into the stables for the water.[21] In that case, the motif of using water as the device for carrying out the cleaning will go back at least to the fifth century. One other possible representation is the colossal statue made by Lysippos for the city of Tarentum and taken to Rome in 209 B.C. (Str 6.3.1; *NH* 34.40). Subsequently it made its way to Constantinople, and descriptions of it there plus Byzantine ivories indicate that it showed a world-weary Herakles sitting on a basket that was perhaps used to carry out the dung.[22] If this is correct, there may actually have been a tradition in which Herakles handled matters the hard way, or at least started to do so before hitting on a less laborious solution.

Labor VI:
The
Stymphalian
Birds

Last of the Peloponnesian Labors is the clearing from the Stymphalian Lake, in the northeast corner of Arkadia near Mount Kyllene, of the birds that infested it. Here our earliest preserved literary source is Peisandros, who as Pausanias tells us had Herakles drive the birds away by means of the noise of rattles rather than by killing them (Paus 8.22.4 = fr 4 *PEG*). This is also the account given by Diodoros, who says that Herakles contrived to make a bronze rattle with which he frightened them off (DS 4.13.2). On the other hand, Pherekydes (3F72) and Hellanikos (4F104), while acknowledging the use of the rattle, have Herakles slay the birds as they fly upward; in Pherekydes someone gives him the rattle, while in Hellanikos as in Diodoros he makes it for himself. Apollodoros agrees with this notion of frightening the birds, then shooting them; in his version Athena supplies the rattle, which Herakles strikes against the side of a mountain to create noise (ApB 2.5.6). Neither Diodoros nor Apollodoros gives any description of the birds, merely suggesting that their sheer numbers made them a nuisance. Pausanias says they were maneaters but for this detail he does not specify any source. We saw in chapter 12 that Euripides and Apollonios both invest the birds that inhabit the Island of Ares in the Black Sea with feathers that can be fired like arrows; whether any author actually equated those birds with the Stymphalian ones is uncertain.

The artistic tradition, slim though it is, follows uniformly the version in which the birds are slain, with no sign anywhere of a rattle. For the very earliest examples we encounter the same problem as with the Nemean Lion: birds, like lions, may be hunted by ordinary people, and such scenes do not necessarily represent Herakles. The problem is compounded, as noted earlier, by the existence of a Late Geometric fibula in London on which appear both a man killing a lion and a man holding up dead birds (London 3204), leaving us to wonder how far we can stretch coincidence. Even earlier is a jug in Copenhagen on which a man chases birds, and has already caught one which he throttles by the neck (PrColl).[23] Obviously there comes a point at which a decision is impossible, and for our purposes even a favorable verdict would not matter much, save as evidence for the antiquity of the story. Quite certain on the other hand are a number of mid-sixth-century Attic Black-Figure portrayals, since Herakles now has his lionskin. The most famous of these, a belly amphora in London (B163), shows him moving to the attack with a stone and sling; on other examples he uses a bow or even a club (Vienna 1841; Munich 1842). Presumably Pherekydes and Hellanikos imagined him with a bow, after he had flushed the creatures from cover. The tale seems to lose interest for vase-painters by the end of the sixth century, for there are no Red-Figure representations at all. On the appropriate metope at Olympia, Herakles simply hands Athena several birds as evidence of the completed Labor. As we saw before, neither the Stables of Augeias nor the Stymphalian Birds appear on the metopes of the Hephaisteion.

Labor VII: The Kretan Bull

Scenes of this Labor appear on Attic Black-Figure painting beginning about 525 B.C. (e.g., Munich 1407); if several Lakonian cups intend the same scene, we may take it back to 550 (e.g., NY 59.15).[24] On the literary side we find it first mentioned by Akousilaos, who says (via Apollodoros) that the bull in question was the one who brought Europa to Krete (thus not in this version Zeus himself: 2F29). Apollodoros also knows, however, another account, in which the bull was the one sent by Poseidon to Minos and loved by Pasiphae (Ap*B* 2.5.7); so too the versions of Diodoros (4.13.4) and Pausanias (1.27.10). Presumably, in Akousilaos, Herakles travels to Krete to capture this bull, as he does in Apollodoros and Diodoros (the latter specifies that he rode the creature across the sea back to the Peloponnesos). Both of these later writers also attest that after showing the bull to Eurystheus at Tiryns Herakles released it, and that it made its way to Attika where it became the Bull of Marathon captured and sacrificed by Theseus. Pausanias varies this account only slightly by having the bull swim of his own accord from Krete to the Peloponnesos and be captured by Herakles there; here too it moves on to Marathon afterward. We saw in chapter 7 that the story of Theseus and the Marathonian Bull does not surface until the earliest cycle cups,[25] about the time of the Kleophrades Painter in the early fifth century. It is therefore often assumed that Theseus' exploit was modeled on that of Herakles, in time leading even to the appropriation of the same bull as victim. But the sparsity of early Theseus literature, together with the overwhelming popularity of the Minotaur combat in early sixth-century art, dictates caution on such a point. The vase-paintings of Herakles' deed all show some stage of the capture, with bare hands or club, and occasionally the driving back to Tiryns (so too the metope from the Zeus temple at Olympia, where the bull tries to break out of its fetters). Thus all available evidence seems to agree that the bull had to be taken alive. For this rather straightforward Labor, our sources have nothing else of interest.

Labor VIII:
The Mares
of Diomedes

For this Labor there is no source at all before the Amyklai Throne, and no literary source prior to Pindar. Pausanias says simply that the Throne shows Herakles paying back Diomedes the Thracian (3.18.12). For the horses the first evidence is a cup by Psiax, now in Leningrad (9270), whose tondo shows Herakles, club in hand, with his right arm thrown around the neck of a stallion.[26] From the horse's mouth, grimly enough, project an arm and a head. Much the same scene appears on a fragmentary Red-Figure cup by Oltos, although here all that remains undevoured is an arm (Florence 1 B 32). On the other side of this latter cup stands Diomedes himself, looking on in some alarm. A third probable example occurs on a Black-Figure lekythos of about 490 B.C., where Herakles grapples with four winged horses (Syracuse 14569). The evidence from Pindar consists of an Oxyrhynchus papyrus published in 1961 which has holes everywhere (fr 169a SM). But Diomedes, king of the Kikones and son of Ares, is mentioned, as well as Herakles' raid to take his horses, here clearly mares by the gender of the modifying words. Eurystheus and Hera are also named as the motivating factors, together with the requirement that Herakles accomplish the task alone; thus, Iolaos has remained in Thebes. The narration may have focused on only a small part of the story, but we can see that Herakles picks up someone and throws him to the horses, and then apparently harnesses them while they are thus engaged. The first part of the fragment also seems to say that Diomedes defended his property bravely, and probably he dies in the process.

Later in the same century we find the story alluded to in Euripides' *Alkestis*: Herakles' visit to the house of Admetos here occurs on his way to the land of the Bistones in Thrace, where Eurystheus has ordered him to seize the four maneating horses of Diomedes; the chorus warns him that Diomedes will not let the horses go without a fight to the death (*Alk* 481–98). In the same poet's *Herakles*, the chorus details among his Labors how he harnessed to a chariot maneating mares who were before unbridled, that is, apparently they had never yet drawn a chariot (*HF* 380–86). Hellanikos says that they tore apart one Abderos, a son of Hermes and lover of Herakles (4F105).

From these bits and pieces we turn to Diodoros, who gives a colorful picture—bronze mangers, iron chains, and a diet of men (DS 4.15.3–4). In order to tame the creatures, Herakles gives them their master Diomedes to eat. The latter has, it seems, taught them their unfortunate habits, and when they devour him they are cured. Herakles then takes them back to Eurystheus, who dedicates them to Hera and breeds them. Apollodoros also, like Pindar, makes Diomedes a son of Ares, and ruler of the Bistones of Thrace (ApB 2.5.8). Herakles comes against him with a band of men and launches a proper raid, overpowering those in charge of the maneating horses and driving the latter off to the coast. The Bistones pursue; Herakles entrusts the horses to Abderos, but they tear him apart in some way, perhaps by dragging (and perhaps in the same fashion as in Hellanikos: the verb—*epispaô*—is almost the same). Subsequently, Herakles makes a stand against the Bistones and slays Diomedes. The horses are then taken to Eurystheus, who lets them go; they come to Mount Olympos, and are destroyed by wild beasts. The divergences between these two accounts of Diodoros and Apollodoros are surprising, the more so as for once it is Diodoros who admits the more fantastic elements. Apollodoros' version contains numerous peculiarities, and we must suspect that he has compressed a very detailed narrative. Nor does it help that Ovid (*Met* 9.196) and Hyginus (*Fab* 30) make Herakles kill the horses as well as Diomedes (Hyginus adds a groom Abderos). About the only thing in common in all these accounts is that the horses are maneaters and that Diomedes somehow dies defending them. The cups by Psiax and Oltos may illustrate Pindar's story of the groom thrown to the mares to distract them, or even Diodoros' story of Diomedes being fed to them himself. But both works might also constitute artistic attempts to make the scene more recognizable by a generic demonstration of the horses' special qualities. Presumably, the story of the eponym Abderos' death, however it occurs, would not have taken shape before the refounding of Abdera by Greeks from Teos after the fall of the Lydian Empire in the middle of the sixth century.

We should note before concluding this section that Herakles' previously noted stopover in the house of Admetos on his way north to seek the mares in

Euripides' *Alkestis* is for that work the occasion of his wrestling match with Thanatos and consequent rescue of Alkestis. As we saw in chapter 5, Euripides' play is the first preserved account of this tale, although Alkestis' story was dramatized earlier in the fifth century by Phrynichos *(Alkestis)* and Sophokles *(Admetos)*, each of whom may or may not have used Herakles in the same fashion to resolve the crisis. As Euripides tells the story, Herakles has come to seek hospitality from his friend Admetos on the very day of Alkestis' death; Admetos hides that fact from him and sends him off to separate quarters to be wined and dined. A somewhat inebriated Herakles then learns the truth from a reluctant servant and sets off to wait for Thanatos by Alkestis' tomb, where he vanquishes his opponent and brings Admetos' wife back to the living. A Black-Figure neck-amphora of about 540 B.C. *may* attest Herakles' earlier participation in this exploit: Hermes accompanies the hero as he leads an unnamed woman (Louvre F60), but to call this figure "Alkestis" obviously involves some risk. An alternative to his role does appear in Plato and Apollodoros, where the gods or Persephone send Alkestis back of their own accord (the gods: *Sym* 179b; Persephone: Ap*B* 1.9.15, which also reports the version with Herakles).

Labor IX:
The Belt of
Hippolyte

Herakles (and friends) battling the Amazones would be a tale with roots in the early to mid-seventh century, if the combat is indeed pictured on a terracotta votive shield from Tiryns showing male and female warriors (Nauplia 4509); more commonly, though, the scene intended is thought to be that of Achilleus and Penthesileia at Troy.[27] But in any case Herakles' exploit is attested for the later part of the same century by an Early Corinthian alabastron from Samothrace, now lost. Here inscriptions confirm Herakles, Iolaos, and a third warrior (Menoitas? Pasimelon?) moving to the attack against Andromeda and two other Amazones (names uncertain).[28] More significant for the narrative is perhaps a Lakonian cup by the Arkesilas Painter, dating to about 560 B.C., which shows a warrior, sword in hand, pursuing two women clad in armor (VG, no #: the Stefani Cup). With his free left hand the warrior certainly appears to reach out and grasp the nearer woman by the belt.[29] In Attic Black-Figure the combat enjoys tremendous popularity from the second quarter of the sixth century on, as Herakles and friends cut their way through masses of Amazones; Herakles' own special opponent, when named, is usually Andromache.[30] But among dozens of examples of this theme, not one attempts to represent any special item of apparel sought by Herakles;[31] what we see is simply a battle between certain Greek heroes and Amazones, and just possibly that is how Attic tradition of this time thought of the story. From the sixth century there is, however, one (casual) reference to the belt: the scholia to Apollonios tell us that in Ibykos alone the *zôstêr* was the property of one Oiolyke, daughter of Briareus, in contrast to other writers who made the owner Hippolyte or Deilyke (299 *PMG*). Although the scholiast adds that there are many stories about this belt, he presumably means that in Ibykos as elsewhere the belt was the object of Herakles' quest.

In the fifth century we find a comedy of Epicharmos entitled *Herakles Ho Epi Ton Zostera* ("Herakles in quest of the *zôstêr*") (fr 76 Kaibel); nothing survives. Pindar related in a lost work how Peleus participated in the expedition "for the *zôstêr* [actually plural] of the Amazon" (fr 172 SM: direct quote). In *Nemean* 3 he refers to the same event in general terms (*Nem* 3.38–39); the scholia quote in explanation four lines of a lost, unidentified epic poem in which Telamon slays Melanippe, sister of the gold-zoned queen (Σ *Nem* 3.64). Obviously we cannot date this reference, but it suggests again that the belt as goal of the mission is older than Attic art would have us believe.[32] The adjective *chrusozônos* here is unusual, since elsewhere the sought-after item is almost always called a *zôstêr*. For Homer the *zôstêr* is a war belt, something worn outside other clothing as part of one's defensive armor, as we see in the case of Menelaos when Pandaros wounds him in the *Iliad* (*Il* 4.132–39). Certainly it is never part of a woman's intimate apparel, and the common English translation "girdle" is grossly misleading. Dion of Prusa (8.32), who has the Amazon queen seduce Herakles, is in fact the first to suggest that the quest lay in that direction; Apollodoros may imply the same with the remark that Eurystheus' daughter Admete wanted the item (still a *zôstêr*), but just previously he has called it a gift from Ares to Hippolyte in token of her primacy (Ap*B* 2.5.9).[33] In earlier times the purpose of Herakles' mission was surely to defeat the Amazones in battle, and the belt was demanded by Eurystheus as the proof of his success.

Monumental art of the fifth century provides several clear examples of the story, but the state of preservation prevents us from drawing much in the way of conclusions. Amazones were prominently featured on the metopes of the Athenian Treasury at Delphi (no #); the battle illustrated, however, is probably that with Theseus and the Athenians, since Herakles already has two sides of the building to himself. On a famous metope from Temple E at Selinous (3921A), Herakles (identified by his lionskin) reaches out and grasps the Amazon's cap while she tries to defend herself with an axe. She does wear a belt, though a very modest and unassuming one. The fragmentary metopes from Olympia and the Hephaisteion both show Herakles standing over a kneeling or fallen Amazon. Reconstructions in each case depict Herakles as reaching down for something, that is, the belt, but there seems to be no actual evidence for this arrangement, other than Pausanias' statement that at Olympia Herakles is "depriving the Amazon of the *zôstêr*" (5.10.9). Whether he saw this, or only inferred it, we are left to guess.

From the later fifth century there is the description in Euripides' *Herakles Mainomenos*; unfortunately the text, which appears to speak of a gold-spangled robe as well as the *zôstêr* (or are they the same?), is partially corrupt (*HF* 408–18).[34] The *Ion* also mentions some sort of garment embroidered with figured scenes, part of the spoils from the expedition, which was dedicated by Herakles at Delphi (*Ion* 1143–45). Hellanikos for his part claims that all those who sailed on the Argo participated in this adventure as well (4F106); it is not clear if he means as part of the Argo's voyage or on a separate occasion. Yet another Euripidean notion, that of Iolaos who in the *Herakleidai* boasts that he went with Herakles to get the *zôstêr* for *Theseus* (*Hkld* 215–17), is presumably an invention of the moment, designed to put Demophon and his people further in Herakles' debt. Theseus (in Herakles' company) carrying off the *zôstêr* (plus an Amazon) recurs in Lykophron (1329–31), probably here too as a slight exaggeration of Theseus' role; the scholia claim that the Amazon was the one who became his bride, and that the *zôstêr* was given to Herakles. A much more important body of evidence surfaces on Red-Figure vases from South Italy, beginning in the latter part of the fifth century.[35] On some eight of these we find a peaceful parley between Herakles and the Amazones, with three in particular showing an Amazon handing over a belt to a seated Herakles (so, e.g., the shoulder of Naples H3241) and the others presumably representing the same event. We have seen that the mainland tradition as so far surveyed uniformly insists on a battle and the apparent killing of the Amazon queen, presumably in order to get the belt. Conceivably, Epicharmos' previously mentioned comedy, where such violence might be out of place, served as one source for this quite different version in which matters are resolved amiably.

From later periods we acquire a variety of details. Apollonios says that Herakles captured Melanippe, sister of the queen, by lying in ambush, and that Hippolyte ransomed her back with her glittering *zôstêr* (AR 2.966–69). Here again bloodshed is avoided, and possibly this is the plot line envisioned by the South Italian painters. Apollonios is also our first source to call the queen Hippolyte; this name does appear on sixth-century Black-Figure, but not as Herakles' opponent. We have seen that thus far our written sources, save for Ibykos, manage to avoid naming her. Melanippe as the sister of the queen, we encountered earlier, in our unplaced epic fragment; since she was there slain by Telamon, we may presume that Apollonios draws on a different tradition. Diodoros also calls the queen Hippolyte (DS 4.16.1). In his account Herakles asks for the *zôstêr* but is refused, and thus turns to battle. After killing numerous Amazones he captures Melanippe, their war leader, and as in Apollonios obtains the belt as ransom for her; another captive, Antiope, is given as a gift to Theseus (so too *Fab* 30). As discussed in chapter 9, Philochoros is the first known writer to regard Theseus as simply an adjunct to Herakles' expedition; Pindar and Pherekydes, among others, plus Attic Black-Figure, make the Athenian's exploit an independent venture, with Peirithoos in tow.

Finally we come to Apollodoros, who provides the account most familiar to modern readers (ApB 2.5.9). Here, as we saw above, Hippolyte possesses the belt by virtue of being leader of the Amazones, and Herakles is sent to obtain it as a Labor because Admete, the daughter of Eurystheus, desires to have it. Herakles' request for the belt is actually well received by Hippolyte, who promises it to him. But Hera, disguised as an Amazon, stirs up the others with a rumor that the queen herself is to be carried off. The Amazones therefore assault the ship, Herakles supposes treachery, and kills Hippolyte, subsequently routing the rest. Since this version does result in the death of the queen and a battle, it could conceivably lie behind the hostilities so uniformly present in sixth-century Black-Figure. But more likely there was in the beginning no question of a parley when battle took place, and Apollodoros or his source has conflated two originally different traditions.[36]

Laomedon,
Hesione,
and Troy

In *Iliad* 5 Sarpedon, son of Zeus, and Tlepolemos, son of Herakles, exchange a few boasts prior to their combat, and in the course of his remarks Tlepolemos notes the previous sack of Troy by his father, when he came with six ships for the sake of the horses (*Il* 5.628–51). Sarpedon concedes Laomedon's folly on that occasion, specifically his failure to keep his word to Herakles after the latter had helped him, thus leading to the sack. Later, in *Iliad* 8, we will find that Telamon's son Teukros is a bastard (with a Trojan name: *Il* 8.283–84), and in *Iliad* 20 that Athena and the Trojans once made a wall for Herakles to hide behind when the *kêtos* (sea monster) pursued him from the shore to the plain (*Il* 20.144–48). Homer clearly alludes to pieces of a story that he expects his audience to know, and although Hesione is never mentioned there seems no reason to doubt that this story involves her rescue and slaying of the sea monster by Herakles in return for the horses of Laomedon. At first glance we might suppose Herakles to have made a single expedition during which he asked for the horses, found Laomedon in some difficulty, struck his bargain, slew the monster, was refused the horses, and destroyed the city. But our fuller accounts always break up the adventure into two visits, and probably this is also what Homer means us to understand. The first visit takes place simply in passing, when Herakles is with the Argonautai (so Diodoros) or on his way to (or from) the land of the Amazones (so Apollodoros). On this occasion he observes Hesione's predicament by chance, offers to eliminate the *kêtos* for the horses, does so, and then sails away, Laomedon having agreed to deliver up the horses when he returns. The second visit, that referred to by Tlepolemos, is then made expressly to receive the horses; when Laomedon reneges, Herakles sacks Troy. Both Diodoros and Apollodoros place this denouement at a considerable remove in time, after Herakles has spent his year in Lydia serving Omphale.

After Homer we find also mention in the *Ehoiai* of Herakles' voyage to Troy to get the horses (Hes fr 165 MW), and Peisandros pairs Telamon and Herakles together on this venture: Herakles gives Telamon a special cup as a prize (fr 11 *PEG*). The sixth century offers only two bits of evidence, both pots with scenes of the rescue of Hesione. On one, a Late Corinthian krater in Boston, Herakles shoots arrows at a huge sea monster while a young woman looks on (Boston 63.420). The other, an Attic Black-Figure cup in Taranto, has the same three figures, but here Herakles holds a *harpê* in one hand and clutches the monster's tongue with the other (Taranto 52155). In the fifth century, Pindar also mentions the second voyage (*Nem* 4.25–26) and, like Peisandros, includes Telamon (*Is* 6.26–30). Sophokles' *Aias* naturally does the same, with references to Telamon's success at Troy and the Trojan princess who became Teukros' mother (*Ai* 434–36, 1299–1303). But only with a summary of Hellanikos, preserved in a scholion to the *Iliad*, do we get a continuous account: the *kêtos* appears at Troy, devouring men and ruining crops, because of Poseidon's anger (already noted in *Iliad* 21) over Laomedon's failure to pay for the building of the walls of Troy by himself and Apollo (4F26b). Laomedon consults the oracle, and is told that his daughter Hesione must be fed to the monster if he wishes to be rid of it. He sets his daughter out as instructed, but also announces his immortal horses, the gift of Zeus to Tros, as the prize for anyone who can kill the monster. Herakles volunteers to undertake the task, with Athena building a protective wall for him. He then enters into the belly of the monster through its mouth and destroys it from within. But Laomedon substitutes other, mortal horses at the time of the payment, a trick that Herakles discovers only later, causing him to mobilize the second expedition. The entry into the monster recalls the possibly similar motif in the combat between Iason and the serpent guarding the Golden Fleece; it may also be the intention of the Taranto cup, showing as it does Herakles grasping the monster's tongue. The idea of destroying the creature from inside recurs in Lykophron, who says that Herakles carved up his liver and that in the intense heat of his innards the hero's hair fell out (Lyk 33–37). In Palaiphatos, the notion of human sacrifice to placate the monster is expanded to the point where the *kêtos* destroys the land if the people in general do not give him their daughters to eat (Pal 37).

From these sources we proceed to Diodoros, whose account is in most respects that of Hellanikos. Here Herakles is on his way to Kolchis with the Argo, Hesione is chosen from all the children of Troy by lot, and Herakles himself proposes the bargain of the horses to her father after releasing her (DS 4.42). Of the monster we are told only that Herakles kills it, and of the horses that they are very fast (no word about immortality). Hesione decides of her own accord to go with Herakles, but she and the horses are left behind with Laomedon until Herakles can return from Kolchis. Likewise, Apollodoros in every respect agrees with either Hellanikos or Diodoros: here again there are no details of the combat with the monster, and Laomedon simply refuses to hand over the horses (ApB 2.5.9). Thus Hellanikos remains the only source to tell of mortal horses substituted for immortal ones. Hyginus claims that the horses could walk over water and ears of grain, and that Herakles asked for them and Hesione as well; he also has a whole series of Trojan maidens fed to the monster before the lot falls to Hesione (*Fab* 89). Much later, the First Vatican Mythographer (136) presents a version without any horses in which Herakles performs the task for Hesione herself (although in no account does he marry her).

As for the placating of the *kêtos*, Servius suggests at one point that Apollo decreed the feeding of well-born Trojan maidens to him, leading many to send or sell their daughters overseas (Σ *Aen* 1.550); elsewhere in the *Aeneid* scholia Apollo asks specifically for Laomedon's daughter (or daughters), and the king instead tries to placate the beast with the children of others (Σ *Aen* 5.30).

Something of this same sort is clearly behind Lykophron's tale of Phoinodamas, a Trojan whose daughters were sent to the far west. Apparently he proposed (in full assembly of the Trojans) that Hesione be offered to the *kêtos* (Lyk 470–75), and Laomedon in revenge gave his three daughters to sailors traveling to the land of the Laistrygones, so that they might be exposed as food for wild beasts (Lyk 951–77). They survived (thanks, we gather, to Aphrodite), and Aigesta bore to the river god Krimisos (who approached her in the form of a dog) a son Aigestes. Dionysios reports this same story in very general terms, adding that the Trojan father was killed, but gives no names (DH 1.52.2–3). Likewise Servius at *Aeneid* 5.30, although he seems to prefer the version in which Aigesta is the daughter of one Hippotes who sends her off to Sicily himself to save her from the *kêtos* (according to some, she later returns to marry Kapys and produce Anchises). Whatever we make of this, all our accounts agree that Hesione was sooner or later exposed, and that Herakles saved her, only to run afoul of Laomedon. The second, punitive expedition during which he finally acquired both daughter and horses we will consider in more detail in its proper place, after the sojourn in Lydia.

Labor X: The Cattle of Geryoneus

This is one of three Labors mentioned by Hesiod in the *Theogony*, although not described as such. Geryoneus is there the three-headed offspring of Chrysaor and the Okeanid Kallirhoe, and slain on sea-girt Erytheia on that day when Herakles drives his cows back across Okeanos to Tiryns; in the process Herakles also kills the cowherd Eurytion and the dog Orthos (*Th* 287–94, 981–83). The details of the story thus seem fairly well developed, including the location of the cattle stalls at the ends of the earth. The description of these as misty probably means that we should already understand, as later, the far west, near the realm of the dead. In art, the earliest representation is certainly a Protocorinthian pyxis of the seventh century, now in London, on which a crudely drawn figure with bow advances toward three warriors with weapons and shields; these last overlap behind the shields (with only four legs), and may be thought to be joined (London A487).[37] Behind them (him?) are what we may take to be cattle, behind Herakles either another cow or a dog. All elements of the story are fully illustrated on a bronze relief from Samos of about 600 B.C.: to the left the cattle, then Herakles closing in on Geryoneus with underneath a two-headed dog and to the right the prostrate herdsman, both slain by arrows (Samos:VM B 2518).[38] Herakles here fights with a sword; Geryoneus has, it seems, one pair of legs but three (helmeted) heads appearing above three shields, with the third head and shield falling back as if mortally wounded. Slightly later, perhaps second quarter of the sixth century, are shield-band reliefs from Olympia (B 1975) and Delphi (4479). Both show Herakles closing in with a sword against a fully armed triple-bodied figure with three distinct torsos and three pairs of legs, closely overlapped. In each case, one of the upper bodies, with head and arms limp, falls backward, dropping his spear and shield. The other two shields cover the waists, and the posture of the six legs—totally unaffected by the decease of one member of the trio—must lead us to suppose a join at the waist. It seems clear too that Herakles must slay each of the three individually in order to defeat the whole. Pausanias saw this same scene on the Chest of Kypselos, where he says that the three forms of Geryoneus were joined together (5.19.1); on the Amyklai Throne he found rather Herakles driving off the cattle (3.18.13).

In the mid-sixth century (presumably later than the shield-bands and hence not their source) Stesichoros' *Geryoneis* recounted the exploit at some length.[39] In this, we are told, Geryoneus had six hands and feet (as on the reliefs) and wings (186 *PMG*). Wings as an attribute, if ever employed by such a creature, would make him an extremely formidable opponent, and perhaps for that reason, or the difficulty of finding room for them, they do not surface at all in the Attic Black-Figure tradition. They do, however, appear on two Chalkidian pots of the latter part of the century, pots surely with a provenience, like that of Stesichoros, in the west. The first, an amphora now in the British Museum, is the other side of the vase on which we saw Nymphai bringing the cap, sandals, and *kibisis* to Perseus (London B155). Here Geryoneus is portrayed as on the shield-band reliefs, but with a set of wings (i.e., one pair) in addition to his triple body and only one pair of legs; thus the tripling is (as on the Samos relief) from the waist up only. Another small change is that while one of the three torsos falls backward, as before, another falls forward, so that Herakles has only the middle one left to deal with (so too on an Attic version by the Swing Painter: CabMéd 223). The second Chalkidian pot, a neck-amphora in Paris, shows the same single pair of wings and legs, but here all three torsos are erect and ready for battle (CabMéd 202). Here we find again an already slain dog and the herdsman Eurytion (name inscribed). On the reverse, in addition to Herakles' chariot, are the cattle, looking a bit bemused.

The very numerous Attic Black-Figure examples begin with a hydria by Lydos (VG 50683), and find special popularity in the work of Group E. The pattern is almost always what we have already seen, with only minor variations: Herakles attacking with bow or sword on the left,[40] a fully tripled-bodied Geryoneus in full armor with helmets and shields and one torso falling back on the right, and either Orthos or Eurytion underneath. In Red-Figure the scene is far less frequent, but we should note a particularly fine cup by Euphronios in Munich, with a two-headed Orthos belly-up in the center, a slumping Eurytion off to the left, and a female figure (Geryoneus' mother?) holding out her hands in alarm (Munich 2620). The reverse shows armed men driving off the cattle; possibly these are helpers of Herakles, but they might also be Neleus and his sons attempting to steal the cattle during Herakles' return journey.[41]

From the actual combat in sixth-century art, we turn to the narrative details of the story as a whole. We have seen that as early as the *Theogony* Geryoneus dwells somewhere beyond Okeanos, thus creating problems in the logistics of finding him and bringing back the cattle. Stesichoros seems to have placed Erytheia opposite the Tartessos River in Spain (184 *PMG*); Strabo, who quotes the lines and presumably knew the whole poem, takes this to mean opposite the mouth of the Tartessos (now the Guadalquiver) near Gades (Cadiz), just outside the Straits of Gibraltar (Str 3.2.11). Obviously such a location will involve considerable overlap with the next Labor, that to acquire apples from the Garden of the Hesperides, and some of the travel procedures used and *parerga* performed appear in now one Labor, now the other. Already in Peisandros we find reference to the cup of Helios, which Herakles receives not from Helios himself but from Okeanos (fr 5 *PEG*). Peisandros also says that Herakles crosses Okeanos in it, but not where he is going when he does so. In Stesichoros, the cup is clearly used to journey to Erytheia, since a fragment from the *Geryoneis* relates how Helios gets into the cup, now restored to him, in order to be taken to the depths of night, while Herakles proceeds into a laurel grove (185 *PMG* = 17 *SLG*). Either the hero has just arrived on Erytheia or (more likely) he has come back across Okeanos to the Tartessos with the cattle before returning the cup. We will see below that in many of our sources this journey begins in the far east at the sun's risings, and follows the stream of Okeanos round some part of the earth much as Odysseus in the *Odyssey* and Iason in the *Ehoiai* seem to have done. In Apollodoros, however, the voyage in the cup takes place only after the journey (on foot) is well advanced (probably in fact not before Herakles has reached Tartessos: Ap*B* 2.5.10), and not impossibly some early accounts had Herakles making the bulk of the trip on foot and borrowing the cup solely for the last leg, the crossing of Okeanos to Erytheia (which might explain too why in Peisandros he obtains the cup from Okeanos).

Pherekydes offers his own version of these events, although our summary, courtesy of Athenaios, begins rather ambiguously. After telling us that Pherekydes speaks of Okeanos, Athenaios quotes as follows: "And Herakles took aim at him with his bow, in order to shoot him, but Helios commanded him to stop, and he in fear did so" (3F18a). By this juxtaposition of paraphrase and quote we are left uncertain whether Herakles means to threaten Okeanos or Helios. Given the wording, one might more naturally assume the former, but as the quote continues Helios gives Herakles the cup that carries him and his horses in exchange for the latter's forbearance, and Herakles uses it to reach Erytheia. In the course of the voyage Okeanos then makes trial of him by sending high waves to rock the cup; Herakles again threatens with his bow, and a fearful Okeanos desists. Since Herakles is not likely to have threatened the same god twice, we should probably take the opening of all this to mean that in the first instance he threatened Helios, not Okeanos, in order to secure transport. Strabo adds that in Pherekydes Gadeira itself, not the island opposite, is the site for the encounter with Geryoneus (Str 3.5.4). If he has understood his source properly, Herakles' voyage is here not across Okeanos from Spain to an island, but rather along the great river stream from a point far away, very likely in the east where he can most readily confront Helios and bargain for the cup. Such a scene definitely appears on Attic Black-Figure pots from the end of the sixth century, with Herakles crouching in wait for Helios and the god rising up in his chariot from the sea (e.g., the lekythoi Athens 513 and NY 41.162.29 [with Herakles roasting meat]).[42] On the New York example the (departing) figures of Nyx and Eos are named, thus further confirming the place and time of day.[43] Presumably Herakles asks for the cup here, at the point where Helios customarily leaves it to mount his chariot for the journey across the sky, so that he may reverse the god's nightly passage back along Okeanos to the west. On only one of these vases does Herakles offer violence by threatening with his club (Cambridge G100); there is, however, a curious Black-Figure skyphos by the Theseus Painter (*c.* 495 B.C.) on which Herakles (armed with bow and club) moves hastily away from a figure in chariot who is rising up from the sea (Taranto 7029). The god looks calmly over at Herakles, seemingly surprised; from his shoulder (or the neck of one of the horses) protrude two arrows. The other side of the cup repeats the same scene, but with Herakles now seated, club in his left hand, right hand extended out toward the god, as if wishing to talk with him.[44] Possibly the artist means to suggest that Herakles has fired several arrows at some part of Helios' chariot in order to frighten the god, and that Helios (as in Pherekydes) then warns Herakles to desist, whereupon the hero explains his need and the cup is given to him.[45] We will certainly see that, in early accounts of the quest for Kerberos, force is combined with negotiation to achieve the desired result. Several other vases of this period show the actual voyage, with Herakles, club and bow in hand, sitting in the cup as it travels along the waves (e.g., Vat 16563; Boston 03.783).

By contrast to all this, it seems that in Panyasis (again courtesy of Athenaios) Herakles obtains the cup of Helios from *Nereus* in order to sail to Erytheia (fr 9 *PEG*). Thus we have a definite link between Nereus and the Geryoneus Labor, but the motif of acquiring assistance from a sea god in order to reach some distant land is one that fluctuates back and forth between this exploit and the journey to the Garden of the Hesperides: in Pherekydes the Nymphai of the Eridanos send Herakles to Nereus to learn the location of the Garden (3F16a; naturally he must hold on while Nereus changes into fire and water). By strictly arbitrary choice we will consider artistic representations of the struggle with Nereus here, although they are clearly applicable to both Labors. As a sea god Nereus is (like Proteus in the *Odyssey*) endowed with special wisdom (so *Th* 233–36), and the need for his knowledge seems especially appropriate in these two instances, since Herakles must travel long distances over water to reach both Erytheia and the land of the Hesperides. An early Attic Black-Figure lekythos in the manner of the Gorgon Painter shows the hero grappling with a large creature, human from the waist up and possessed of a fish's tail from the waist down (Louvre CA 823). Though more commonly the means of portraying Triton, son of Poseidon and Amphitrite, such a creature is presumably here Nereus; his powers of transformation are (as for his daughter Thetis) represented by a snake and lion emerging from his fish tail. On an Olympia shield-band where Herakles seizes a very similar creature we find the inscription *Aliios Gerôn* ("Old Man of the Sea") (B 1881),[46] while full confirmation of Nereus as the opponent appears on a Komast hydria fragment in Samos where he is given a receding hairline and so named.[47]

In fact, the literary tradition as we have it uniformly names Nereus as the god with whom Herakles must wrestle for the needed assistance. Admittedly, though, somewhere in the mid-sixth-century artistic tradition Triton supplants Nereus, for the receding hairline and extra animal protomes disappear, Triton is several times so named as the fish/man with whom Herakles grapples,[48] and Nereus is occasionally added in as a (completely human) spectator (e.g., NY 06.1021.48; NY 16.70). So too perhaps the three-bodied figure on the famous limestone pediment from the Akropolis is Nereus, gazing across (although there is some figure in front of him) to the other corner of the pediment where Herakles wrestles with Triton (or Nereus?: Akropolis 35). As a complication of this picture, from about 560 B.C. on, Nereus also appears here and there in human form as Herakles' elderly opponent (e.g., CabMéd 255; VG 106462, where he is named).[49] After the earliest Red-Figure the combat largely disappears, but we do have several pots showing Herakles' entry into the house of Nereus, and on one example by Myson attacked by a Nereid (Munich 8762; cf. VG 106462, Louvre G155). Surprisingly, none of our Herakles dramas mention any part of this exploit, and Diodoros too fails to include either Nereus or cup as a means to accomplish either Labor. Apollodoros follows Pherekydes in linking Nereus to the Hesperides Labor (here too the Nymphai of the Eridanos send Herakles to him: Ap*B* 2.5.11) and the cup to Geryoneus (Ap*B* 2.5.10), although the cup appears briefly and rather illogically in the Hesperides Labor as well. As to Herakles' acquisition of the cup when seeking Geryoneus, he says that the hero became too hot on his journey, and for this reason aimed his bow at Helios; the latter admired his courage and gave him the cup. Such a story may also go back to Pherekydes (our information from Athenaios is not in conflict, since he begins his account just after this point), but it is certainly not what vase-painters who show Herakles waiting at dawn had in mind, and Apollodoros may have found it rather in some later source.[50] We must add that Hekataios avoids all such questions by placing Geryoneus on the Greek mainland between Ambracia and the Amphilochoi (1F26). Such a version, with a more familiar and accessible goal, could indicate an early form of the story, before trade ventures brought the Greeks knowledge of the far west. But it could also reflect Hekataios' rationalizing tendencies and an attempt to make the story more believable.

One way or another, then, on advice from Nereus or his own initiative, by threats or simple request, at Tartessos in the west or where the sun comes up in the east, Herakles acquires the cup and arrives on Erytheia. Other *parerga*, such as the battles with Antaios and Alkyoneus, which have no direct connection with this or other tasks, we will consider later, after we have finished the Labors. On Erytheia he finds Orthos, Eurytion, and Geryoneus and kills them all. Stesichoros seems to have narrated the fight in some detail, as we would expect, but also to have visualized the situation from Geryoneus' point of view: new Oxyrhynchus fragments offer bits and pieces of conversations between himself and friends, probably in one case his mother, who pleads with him not to risk his life (12, 13 *SLG*). In another fragment he appears to reject such a plea with the argument that if he is destined to be immortal and ageless among the gods there is nothing to fear, and if not, it is better to die gloriously than to await old age (11 *SLG*). Such a humanizing touch may suggest that Stesichoros' account sympathized with Geryoneus, monster though he is. There is also a fragment describing the battle in which Herakles employs his arrows dipped in the Hydra's blood, and having disposed of at least one body shoots a second in the top of the head (15 *SLG*). In the few lines that survive there is a great deal of gore, even by epic standards; Geryoneus himself seems to have little or no chance.

In the fifth century Klytaimestra offers her famous conceit of her husband as a second Geryoneus, taking on a triple coffin of earth, in Aischylos' *Agamemnon* (869–73). The same poet's *Herakleidai* also described the exploit, with Herakles crossing Okeanos (here again in a golden cup) to the ends of the earth to take the cattle from unjust herdsmen and the triple-bodied lord (fr 74 R). The latter is pictured with his three spears and shields and helmet crests; whether the account extended beyond our fragment we cannot say. Pindar's Nomos poem treated this same Labor briefly at the very beginning, before moving on to Diomedes and his mares (fr 169a SM). The emphasis here is on the fact that Herakles took the cattle by force, without paying for them; again we are reminded that this Labor alone involves depriving a seemingly innocent person of his property, and we may wonder on what grounds Aischylos calls the cowherds unjust. In another fragment (which may or may not be from the same poem) Pindar speaks of Geryoneus as praiseworthy compared to others (fr 81 SM); our source, Aristeides, suggests as the poet's reason that Geryoneus defended his property when it was threatened, which is much the way in which the Nomos poem characterized Diomedes. Pindar's one other reference to Geryoneus, in *Isthmian* 1, simply says that his dogs (plural) shuddered before Herakles (*Is* 1.13). Later in the fifth century both Herodotos (4.8.1) and Euripides (*HF* 422–24) mention the Labor, but with no new details. The same is true of sculptured portrayals on the Athenian Treasury at Delphi, the Temple of Zeus at Olympia, and the Hephaisteion: Geryoneus appears on the metopes of all three, but in schemes that simply repeat the patterns of Attic Black-Figure.

Of our later sources Diodoros rationalizes too much to be very useful—he would have us believe, for example, that Chrysaor had three separate sons with three separate armies (DS 4.18.2). But Apollodoros offers some new material, and we have already seen that on several points concerning the cup of Helios he agrees with Pherekydes (Ap*B* 2.5.10). In his account, as in that of Pherekydes, Gadeira is the site of the encounter, although he makes it an island, perhaps influenced by the more standard tradition. Here Geryoneus, who is three-bodied above and below the waist, keeps his red cows, herded by Eurytion and the two-headed (as on the Samos relief and the Euphronios cup in Munich) Orthos. Herakles makes his way overland, by way of Libya, and sets up his famous pillars at Tartessos to mark the boundary between Libya and Europe. At some point before reaching Gadeira, presumably here at Tartessos, he aims his bow at Helios because of the heat and receives the cup; the crossing of Okeanos is made and he kills first Orthos and then Eurytion. At this point a new figure, one Menoites, tells Geryoneus that his cattle are being stolen, and he rushes after Herakles, only to be slain by the latter's arrows. Herakles then puts the cattle into the cup and sails back across to Tartessos, where he returns his vessel to Helios. On the whole, our evidence for this Labor is remarkably uniform; the main points of interest remain exactly how Herakles obtains the cup from Helios in different authors, and how Geryoneus as defender of his property was viewed by the Archaic tradition.

The Journey Back from Tartessos

In all accounts Herakles drives the cattle overland from Tartessos to Tiryns, and this trek involves him in numerous additional adventures, some of which involve attempts to steal the cows. Through Spain and France he encounters no special problems, other than Diodoros' marauding Keltoi (DS 4.19). In Liguria, however, the local populace proves harder to rout, and Herakles finally runs out of arrows. Our first source for this predicament is Aischylos: somewhere in the *Prometheus Lyomenos* the title figure predicts such a situation (fr 199 R) as part of Herakles' journey to the Hesperides (so Str 4.1.7) or back from Erytheia (so DH 1.41 and *Astr* 2.6.3). He further prophesies that Zeus, in pity for his helpless son, will send down a shower of small round stones that Herakles may use as missiles, thus extricating himself from difficulty. Strabo notes that the plain, with its myriad leftover stones, still exists in his own day, between Massilia and the mouth of the Rhone; thus the story is primarily aetiological. Neither Diodoros (though he mentions the stoniness of the land) nor Apollodoros tells it. The latter recounts rather that here two sons of Poseidon, Ialebion and Derkymos, tried to rob Herakles and he killed them (ApB 2.5.10).

From Liguria, Apollodoros takes Herakles directly to Rhegion, where a bull escapes and swims over to Sicily (causing the locals there to name Italy after the Latin word *vitulus?*); Dionysios earlier relates the same story, citing as his source Hellanikos (DH 1.35.2–3; Hell 4F111). For Herakles' stopover in Latium at the site of Rome on his way south we have only Roman writers and Greeks heavily concerned with Roman themes. Diodoros tells of a peaceful visit with those people currently settled on the Palatine Hill; among the leading citizens who receive him are Pinarius and Cacius (DS 4.21.1–4). But this account stands alone. Already in Dionysios we find the tale immortalized by Vergil in *Aeneid* 8, of the brigand Cacus who makes off with the cattle while Herakles is sleeping (DH 1.39; *Aen* 8.190–272).[51] Between these two tellings and those of Propertius (4.9.1–20) and Ovid (*Fasti* 1.543–82), there are no essential differences: Cacus drags the cattle backward into his cave to escape detection, and almost fools Herakles, but one of the cows lows, the ruse is discovered, and Cacus killed. Cacus is presumably Roman in origin; Herakles' introduction into the story serves primarily to explain the cult of the Ara Maxima at the western end of the Circus Maximus. Dionysios adds numerous other details of his stay, including his fathering of both Pallas and Latinus (DH 1.43).

Diodoros and Apollodoros agree that from Italy Herakles and the herd passed over to Sicily, and so too Pausanias (DS 4.23; ApB 2.5.10; Paus 3.16.4). All three authors narrate the story of his wrestling match with Eryx, king of the Elymoi at the western end of the island, who either appropriates some of the cows after they have wandered, or simply challenges Herakles for them. Herakles defeats him in three consecutive falls and kills him. Diodoros and Pausanias also include what is obviously the real point of the story, that the stakes of the match were the cattle against the land of the Elymoi; thus the Greeks laid claim to western Sicily in a rivalry with the Carthaginians. At this point, Diodoros and Apollodoros begin to diverge substantially in the aetiological tales they relate, and there is no point in pursuing them in any great detail. Diodoros takes Herakles back through Sicily, founding a series of cults on the way, across to Italy where he slays Lakinios and Kroton (the latter by accident), and then around the Adriatic and so back to Tiryns. Apollodoros brings him more swiftly to the Ionian Sea, where Hera sends a gadfly to torment the cows and drive them all the way to Thrace. For some reason Herakles there finds fault with the river Strymon (because he cannot cross it?) and fills it up with stones before bringing the herd back to Eurystheus.

Two other stories remain to be mentioned. Herodotos takes Herakles all the way to Scythia, where a strange woman with the body of a snake from the buttocks down steals the horses from his chariot (although she is often called Echidna, Herodotos does not name her: 4.8–9). This snake-woman refuses to return the horses until Herakles has lain with her, and in time three sons are produced, of whom the youngest, Skythes, becomes the eponymous king of that land. The other tale, found only in Isokrates, relates how Neleus and all of his sons save Nestor try to abduct the cattle when Herakles passes through Messenia (6.*Arch* 19). The transgressors are all slain for their efforts, and Nestor placed on his father's throne. As we saw in chapter 5, this sequence of events, while plausible in itself, does not square with either the *Iliad* or the *Ehoiai*, where a full-scale military expedition by Herakles is described, nor with Apollodoros, who makes the cause of Herakles' wrath against Neleus the refusal to purify him for the murder of Iphitos. Isokrates himself admits that the story is designed to justify Dorian possession of Messenia, but that is not in itself reason to think the tale a late invention. As noted above, the Euphronios Munich cup might conceivably portray this driving off of the cattle by the Neleidai (Munich 2620).

Labor XI: The Garden of the Hesperides

The *Theogony* portrays the Hesperides, daughters of Nyx, as the guardians of the trees bearing golden apples somewhere beyond Okeanos (*Th* 215–16, 274–75); elsewhere in the same poem we hear of the snake (unnamed), child of Phorkys and Keto, which also guards golden apples at the ends of the earth (*Th* 333–35), and we presume, even if Hesiod does not say, that they are the same apples. There is, however, no word of Herakles coming to obtain any of the fruit. Our first written source to mention the task is Pherekydes, who also tells us that the trees are a wedding gift from Gaia to Hera, and guarded by a snake to protect them from the daughters of Atlas (3F16, 17). Our source here, as so often the scholia to Apollonios, gives a lengthy account of Herakles' efforts to obtain the apples; at times the narrative is confused, and we cannot be sure that all of it comes from Pherekydes (Σ AR 4.1396). But it does appear that Herakles proceeds from the Nymphai of the Eridanos to Nereus, who tells him where to find the apples. Then, rather oddly, he makes his way from Tartessos to Libya (slaying Antaios) and Egypt (slaying Bousiris) and finally in the cup of Helios along Okeanos to Prometheus (presumably near Okeanos to the far north or northeast). In return for his slaying of the eagle, the Titan advises him not to seek the apples from the Hesperides himself, but to have Atlas do it while he holds up the sky. Herakles follows this advice faithfully, taking the sky on his own shoulders so that Atlas may go to acquire the apples. However, on his return Atlas declares his intention to take the apples back to Eurystheus personally. Herakles asks for just a minute to prepare a padded cushion for his head, Atlas acquiesces and takes back the sky, and Herakles seizes the apples and leaves.

Apollodoros offers a very similar version, drawn it would seem, like that of the Apollonios scholiast, from Pherekydes; he begins his account by insisting that in contrast to what some say the apples in question were to be found among the Hyperboreans. Quite possibly this also comes from Pherekydes, and explains why Herakles begins his quest at Tartessos and is seemingly very close to the goal by the time he reaches Prometheus. In any case, we will see below that art guarantees even earlier this familiar version in which Atlas rather than Herakles does the actual fetching of the apples. But there was a second version as well: in Panyasis, Herakles himself confronted the snake, though we do not know the exact outcome (fr 11 *PEG*), and Sophokles' *Trachiniai* clearly refers to the hero's conquest of the serpent guardian of the golden apples at the ends of the earth (*Tr* 1090–91, 1099–1100). So too the chorus in Euripides' *Herakles* speaks of how he visited the songful maidens, killing the snaky guardian and taking away the golden fruit with his own hand (*HF* 394–407). That the very same passage also mentions his holding up the sky in the home of Atlas surely indicates a conflation of mutually exclusive exploits. The killing of the snake returns in Ps-Eratosthenes, after which he (and Herakles) become constellations (*Katast* 3, 4).

While these literary traditions surface only in the fifth century, artistic

representations go back to at least the mid-sixth, and present the same ambi-
guities and divergences seen in the written sources. Beginning first with two
lost works, on the Chest of Kypselos we find Atlas supporting the sky and at
the same time holding the apples of the Hesperides; another figure with a
sword approaches him (Paus 5.18.4). Pausanias also quotes the hexameter inscription, which says that Atlas holds (or retains) the sky, and will give up the
apples. Conceivably, the artist presents here a version in which Atlas already
has the apples, or can obtain them without yielding up the sky. On the other
hand, perhaps the scene merely assembles all the elements of the story—
Herakles coming to ask for the apples and Atlas having obtained them—in one
tableau. Or perhaps Atlas has just now taken the sky back, and Herakles is
preparing to snatch the apples from him. We do not, of course, know whether
the sword Herakles holds is meant to threaten or not, and the inscription is of
remarkably little help. But at least in this presentation Atlas is guaranteed as
Herakles' means of accomplishing the Labor. The second lost work is a carved
cedar-wood group by Theokles for the treasury of the Epidamnians at Olympia; it included Atlas and the sky (on which the sculptor signed his work),
Herakles, the Hesperides, and an apple tree complete with snake coiled around
it (Paus 6.19.8). The question here is why Theokles should choose to represent
both Atlas and the snake, since Herakles cannot outwit the one and defeat the
other in the same story. Either one of the two is meant as local color, or Herakles receives information from Atlas before going on to the Garden, or Theokles like Euripides has combined two separate versions.

As for preserved illustrations of the story, the earliest are two recently
published pieces, one a Black-Figure cup signed by Nearchos and now in Bern,
the other a shield-band relief found in Sicily (now matched by the same Form
at Olympia). The tondo of the cup shows Atlas, one hand on hip, while Herakles moves away swiftly; both figures are named (PrColl).[52] The center of the
tondo including Herakles' hands is missing, but a third inscription by his legs,
melapheres, confirms what we would have guessed, that he is carrying the
apples as he takes his leave of Atlas. The shield-band offers almost exactly the
same scene: Atlas holds up the sky with both hands as Herakles strides away,
apple in his left hand, club in his right (Basel Lu 217; Olympia B 4836 is less
well preserved).[53] Beyond him Athena stands waiting. In neither of these cases
can we be positive that Atlas is the source for the apples, but very likely both
artists intend the story as told by Pherekydes, since there is no reason why
Herakles should visit Atlas after he has acquired what he seeks. The end of the
sixth century brings a full illustration of the tale, for a Black-Figure lekythos
by the Athena Painter shows Herakles in his lionskin bending under the weight
of the sky while a naked figure with long beard and hair hurries toward him
clutching the apples (Athens 1132). The same scene is brought to marble by
the Olympia metopes of the mid-fifth century, where Atlas brings the apples
to Herakles as the latter (with some help from Athena) holds up the sky. Pan-

ainos likewise represented Herakles as preparing to take over the sky from Atlas on the barriers under the throne of the Zeus statue at Olympia (Paus 5.11.5).

But against this artistic tradition of Atlas' role in obtaining the apples we have also from the last quarter of the sixth century scenes of the other version, that found in Panyasis, the *Trachiniai*, and *Herakles*, in which Herakles finds the Garden and tackles the snake himself. On a Black-Figure lekythos in Mainz (PrColl) Herakles moves in with club raised to threaten a snake that has curled itself about a tree. A second lekythos in Berlin shows Herakles, with club still in hand but lowered, moving away cautiously from a two-headed snake that darts out menacingly from its tree (Berlin:PM VI 3261). On a coin type from Kyrene of about 500 B.C. Herakles confronts rather a Hesperis, with tree and snake between them, but here too he clearly visits the Garden in person, and so too on an amphora in Boulogne, if the scene with Herakles, an apple tree, two women, and a deer is rightly interpreted (Boulogne 421).[54] In the early fifth century the Kleophrades Painter adds a Red-Figure version with Herakles tackling a three-headed snake that protects the apples, while Atlas to the other side of the tree holds up the sky (here surely as a geographic indicator: Getty 77.AE.11). In contrast with the general impression of these scenes and with our three fifth-century literary allusions to the conquest of the snake, later fifth-century art stresses a more peaceful resolution of the affair.[55] Herakles now becomes the honored guest of the Hesperides, as on a White-Ground alabastron in Nauplia where he relaxes on a rock to one side of the central tree with its small innocuous-looking snake, while on the other a Hesperis approaches with the apples (Nauplia 136).[56] The same scene reappears later in the century on a frequently published hydria by the Meidias Painter: Herakles, comfortably seated, is being entertained by a number of Hesperides, one of whom plucks apples from the tree (London E224). Presumably in both these cases no confrontation with the guardian is necessary. But we can understand why playwrights would prefer a more heroically violent form of exploit, and a Red-Figure oinochoe suggests that there was even a satyr play on that theme, since it offers a Satyros in place of Herakles attacking the snake and tree (London E539). Finally, we should note a White-Ground lekythos from Gela which seems to chart a middle course between an actual assault and socializing with the owners: Herakles steals up to the tree cautiously and bends over, basket in hand, as if to pick up apples from the ground, all the while keeping a careful eye on the snake (Gela 125/B).[57] Behind him, Hermes, turned away as if ready to leave, gestures to him, perhaps exhorting greater haste.

Later sources simply repeat various aspects of this diverse picture. We saw that Ps-Eratosthenes also has Herakles visit the Garden and kill the snake, which then becomes the constellation Ophis/Draco curling between the two Bears; Herakles himself is found next to the snake with raised club (*Katast* 3, 4). In Apollonios, too, Herakles slays the snake, as the Argonautai discover when they come to the African desert and find the creature dead and the Hesperides lamenting; here for the first time he is called Ladon (AR 4.1396–1407). Diodoros spends most of his account rationalizing, so that the guardian becomes a man named Drakon, and the apples flocks of sheep (DS 4.26). Lucan (9.360–67) records the snake as robbed of his apples by Herakles, Seneca (*HF* 530–32) as put to sleep; Ovid offers the unusual idea that Perseus turns Atlas (who here owns the tree) to stone (meaning that Herakles will need only to deal with the snake?: *Met* 4.631–62).[58] Throughout, Apollodoros seems to follow Pherekydes, and thus reverts to the version in which Atlas procures the apples, but at the end of his account he too notes that according to some Herakles got the apples personally after killing the snake (ApB 2.5.11). Which of these two means of completing the Labor might be older is impossible to say, and probably pointless to ask: each displays Herakles in a moment of great valor or strength, and no doubt storytellers had both in their arsenal. As for the fate of the apples, Apollodoros has Eurystheus give them back to Herakles, who gives them to Athena, who returns them. No author suggests that possession of these apples might convey immortality, or youth, or any special advantage (although Boardman has suggested that Leningrad 640 [a Red-Figure stamnos] shows Herakles holding an apple as he approaches Zeus on Olympos).[59]

Labor XII: Kerberos

As early as the *Iliad* and *Odyssey*, mythic tradition knew that Eurystheus sent Herakles down into the Underworld to fetch "the dog" (*Il* 8.367–68; *Od* 11.623–26), while Hesiod, who says nothing about Herakles in this connection, identifies the dog of Hades as Kerberos of the fifty heads, who prevents the dead from going back up into the light (*Th* 310–12, 769–73). Of Stesichoros' poem *Kerberos* we have only the title, although we presume that it dealt with this adventure (206 *PMG*). Pindar (fr 249a SM) and Bakchylides (5.56–70) both represent Herakles conversing with the shade of Meleagros on his way to obtain the dog.[60] Such is the sum total of our written Archaic sources. In art we first encounter the story on the same (now lost) Korinthian kotyle of the early sixth century which we noted before in connection with the Lernaian Hydra (Lost: from Argos). The artist's conception of the story is somewhat surprising: Herakles holds down the center, with his bow in one outstretched hand and a stone raised in the other. The object of his threat is clearly Hades, who has vacated his throne and moves away rapidly to the left. To the right, behind Herakles, stands Hermes, and behind him further right a snaky Kerberos who also moves away rapidly, as if frightened of Herakles. One uncertain element is the presence of a female figure with arms folded between Herakles and Hades, and facing right as if to confront Herakles. She is similar to the two women who flank the combat with the Hydra, but this would be an odd place to put a filler. Possibly she is Athena restraining Herakles from harming Hades; possibly too she is Persephone, displaying more firmness of character than her husband. In any case, the artist certainly intends us to understand that Herakles threatens force in order to get Kerberos, in contrast to virtually all later presentations of the story. Whether Herakles' notorious wounding of Hades at Pylos (as found in *Il* 5 and perhaps Pindar's *Ol* 9) offers further proof of violence in the course of this Labor is less certain; we will return below to the attempt of the *Iliad* scholia to link the two stories.[61]

In Athens, the earliest artistic examples are from the time of Group E and Exekias, and display the procession of Herakles and his divine helpers back from Hades with Kerberos. On several of these pieces the dog himself is only fragmentary, but a lost Little Master cup by the Xenokles Painter presents a huge and quite fearsome creature (two-headed) from whom Hermes starts back in alarm, even though Herakles has him securely leashed (Hope Coll, no #).[62] The same ferocity also appears on a Lakonian cup: a three-headed Kerberos showing lots of teeth and snarling in all directions occupies almost all the field; only around the edges do we see Herakles' hands holding a raised club and taut leash (Erskine Coll, no #). Thus Herakles' mastery of the beast is not as complete in these examples as it was on the Korinthian kotyle where Kerberos actually seemed afraid of the hero.

From about 530 B.C. on, although the procession theme continues, we find as well a new aspect of the story, namely Herakles' attempt to mollify the animal and win its confidence before slipping the leash over its necks.[63] So, for example, on a Black-Figure amphora by the Lysippides Painter Herakles goes down almost on one knee and reaches forward cautiously to pat one of the heads which Kerberos obligingly lowers (Moscow 70). Behind him Hermes looks on intently, while behind the dog (in a porch representing the entrance to Hades) stands a woman who must be Persephone, arms out in what seems a friendly gesture. Elsewhere too Persephone watches the proceedings with gestures that hardly suggest alarm or disapproval; on a Black-Figure neck amphora in Rome, Hermes explains the situation to her while Herakles ponders how to approach Kerberos (VG 48329). Sometimes Hades joins her, as on an amphora and a hydria of the Leagros Group (in both cases represented as an old man: Vat 372; Amiens 3057.225.47a). The latter vase places Herakles off to the far left, hand to mouth as if in consternation and dismay, while Athena and Hermes both attempt to calm Kerberos, and Hades looks on, uncertain himself how to gentle his dog. Red-Figure adds the most eloquent example of such scenes in the amphora of the Andokides Painter on which Herakles, club put aside and chain concealed, again reaches out toward two (here rather disgruntled-looking) heads while Athena observes from behind him (Louvre F204). Even Hermes lends a direct hand on an early Red-Figure amphora by the Nikoxenos Painter: here he kneels in front of Herakles, chain in one hand, and scratches Kerberos' throat while Herakles standing above him prepares to pat the dog's head (Paestum, no #).

The overall direction of these portrayals from the last third of the century seems clear enough: on the one hand Persephone and Hades have no strong objection to Herakles borrowing Kerberos; on the other, the dog himself has his own ideas on the matter, and it sometimes requires a cautiously joint effort of Herakles and his helpers to win the animal over. A completely different approach to the story appears on two Caeretan hydriai of the latter half of the sixth century, one in the Louvre (E701), the other in the Villa Giulia (50649). On both we see not the capture or even the procession, but rather the arrival at the palace of Eurystheus. Here again, as in the Labor of the Erymanthian Boar, Herakles' nemesis has taken refuge in his pithos as Kerberos, Herakles in tow, bounds toward it to greet him. The dog's size on these pots is suitably appalling, and as on the Lakonian cup three heads are shown. We saw earlier that artistic portrayals of Eurystheus hiding from the Boar go back to the late seventh or early sixth century; these are the only examples for Kerberos. The artist in question may have engineered his own imitation of a well-known motif for another Labor, or he may reflect duplication of this idea in an earlier source.

In later authors this last Labor is frequently mentioned, with three heads becoming the standard form of description, but there are no further details of interest until we come to Diodoros and Apollodoros. In Diodoros Herakles has no problems whatever; Persephone is only too happy to accommodate him, and apparently gives him Kerberos already chained to take back up, as well as Theseus and Peirithoos (DS 4.26.1). Matters are slightly more difficult in Apollodoros: Herakles confronts Meleagros and Medousa, must wrestle with Menoites, and rescues Theseus but not Peirithoos (ApB 2.5.12). This Menoites, son of Keuthonymos, is presumably the same Menoites whom Herakles encounters in Apollodoros' account of the taking of the cattle of Geryoneus, for both there and here he has the same function, to guard the herds of Hades. Before, however, he was on the island of Erytheia, where he could observe Herakles stealing Geryoneus' cows; here he seems to be in the Underworld proper, for Herakles, having already rescued Theseus and wishing to furnish the *psychai* with blood, slaughters one of Hades' cows. Menoites quite naturally objects, a wrestling match ensues, he sustains broken ribs, and is spared only at Persephone's request. One suspects that in earlier versions of these events Herakles, like Odysseus, slaughtered the cow at the entrance to the Underworld (very likely Erytheia) and only then spoke with Meleagros as the first of his encounters with the shades of the dead. Herakles in this account of Apollodoros also removes the stone from on top of Askalaphos, the shade who in Ovid and later writers is punished by Demeter for attesting that Persephone ate part of a pomegranate (*Met* 5.534–50). But only here in Apollodoros is there mention of a rock as the punishment, and Askalaphos does subsequently suffer the chastisement found elsewhere, that is, being turned into an owl.

As for the actual Labor in Apollodoros, Hades tells Herakles that he may take Kerberos provided he uses no weapons. Accordingly, Herakles grabs hold of the dog and, although bitten by the snake tail, refuses to let go until he persuades the creature to obey. No artistic representation (unless we accept a fragmentary metope from Foce del Sele[64]) shows the two wrestling; Herakles certainly does wield his club on many of the vases preserved, and it is therefore hard to say where Apollodoros might have found his version. For another idea in his account, that before the descent Herakles went to Eleusis to be initiated, we have already in the fifth century Euripides, whose *Herakles Mainomenos* credits the hero's success in taming Kerberos to his witnessing of the Mysteries (*HF* 612–13).[65] In all, the little evidence we have suggests a pattern of greater force and violence in the early form of the story and more tact and negotiation as time goes on. As we saw in chapter 2, however, the bT scholia at *Iliad* 5.395 combine these two approaches in one story by suggesting that Dione's tale of the wounding of Hades by Herakles happened only *after* the capture. In their account Hades has permitted Herakles to attempt the dog's capture, provided he use no shield and no iron. Herakles agrees, and succeeds by utilizing a hide in place of his shield and stone-tipped arrows; Hades protests, and Herakles in anger shoots him. This story certainly has traditional motifs, but one does not immediately see how arrows of any sort (or for that matter a shield) will help in taming a dog; perhaps some of it has been transferred from another context to help explain Homer's allusion. With so much uncertainty as to when, where, and why the god was wounded, the locating of that event here can only be one guess among several. Whether Herakles' carrying of Hades on some pots (or his bringing down of the cornucopia in Lactantius) might also be related to this Labor are other difficult questions to which we will return below.[66] Finally, Apollodoros is the first author to state what is perhaps always assumed, that Herakles returns Kerberos to the Underworld when he has shown him to Eurystheus.

Antaios,
Bousiris,
Emathion

These three antagonists are all encountered by Herakles in Africa or Arabia, and can with equal facility be made part of the quest for Geryoneus' cattle or for the golden apples. Antaios and Bousiris are both attested in sixth-century vase-painting (Antaios by name) and early fifth-century literature (Antaios in Pindar and Pherekydes, Bousiris in Pherekydes alone). We know as well that Peisandros called the daughter of an Antaios Alkeis, and thus he may have told the story (fr 6 *PEG*). For Emathion, son of Eos, there is only a brief reference from Pherekydes and authors of a much later period.

Herakles and Antaios are probably represented as early as the Foce del Sele metopes in the second quarter of the sixth century; the metope in question shows two figures wrestling but is unfinished and thus offers no details.[67] Much more certain are a series of Attic Black- and Red-Figure vases beginning in the last quarter of the century. An amphora of the Leagros Group now in Munich clearly names Antaios as Herakles' opponent in a wrestling match: Herakles forces him to one knee with a headlock (the same pose as on the Foce del Sele metope) while Athena looks on (Munich 1417). Other portrayals vary the pose considerably. On a hydria of the same group and also in Munich, for example, each wrestler grasps the other by a foot (Munich 1708). But in virtually all instances Herakles is pushing or attempting to push Antaios toward the ground; not one of some thirty examples makes any effort to show him raised up in the air. The same holds for a bronze shield-band relief from Olympia dating to about 500 B.C. if, despite the club, this does show Antaios: Herakles employs a headlock and hooks his leg around his victim's knee to pull him down, not lift him up (Olympia B 984). Pindar in his *Isthmian* 4 says simply that Herakles went to wrestle with him, so that he might prevent the man from roofing the temple of Poseidon with the skulls of strangers (*Is* 4.52–55). The scholia have little to add, save what we might expect, that Antaios forced passers-by to wrestle with him. From Pherekydes we learn that Herakles engaged Antaios in this contest and killed him, then lay with his wife Iphinoe, begetting a son Palaimon (3F76); the same author elsewhere makes Antaios a son of Poseidon (3F17). Both Phrynichos and Aristias wrote plays entitled *Antaios*, and the satyr play by Aristias' father Pratinas entitled *Palaistai* ("Wrestlers") may have been on the subject, but nothing survives save the possibility that Aristias also made Antaios the son (or grandson) of Poseidon (someone in the play was descended from the god: 9 fr 1 Sn). Thus for the Archaic period, although we can be sure the match took place, we know very little about why, or just how Herakles won.

For later information we have a bit of a wait. The story disappears from Attic vase-painting altogether after about 470 B.C., and neither Sophokles nor Euripides mentions it. A Tarentine coin of the third century B.C. does finally show Herakles starting to lift Antaios off the ground, and the same scene reappears on a Roman wall painting of the following century.[68] But Diodoros says merely that Herakles slew Antaios (DS 4.17.4, 4.27.3), and then too, attempting to lift an opponent prior to throwing him to the ground is a standard device of ancient wrestling, to judge by other representations (compare Theseus and Skiron). The first source to actually state that Antaios drew strength from contact with the earth is Ovid. In his *Ibis* the poet asks that his unnamed enemy be crushed "like the wrestler flattened by the Aonian stranger, a wrestler who was, wondrously, victorious when he fell" (*Ibis* 393–95); the *Metamorphoses* makes this notion a bit clearer by saying that Herakles deprived Antaios of his mother's *alimenta*, or sustenance (*Met* 9.183–84). Subsequently Lucan relates the tale in full, with the obvious expedient of holding Antaios high off the ground in order to defeat him (4.593–653), and there are allusions also in Statius' *Thebais* (6.893–96) and Juvenal (3.88–89). Turning to Apollodoros we find a brief, straightforward account with only the essentials: Herakles is seeking the golden apples when he comes to Libya, where Antaios son of Poseidon forces strangers to wrestle with him and kills them (ApB 2.5.11). Herakles catches him in a hold that suspends him in the air and thus puts an end to him, having discovered that he grows stronger upon touching the earth. Both Lucan and Apollodoros suggest that Antaios is a son of Gaia, as seems natural given his special powers (so too *Fab* 31). Unfortunately Apollodoros says nothing about Antaios' own family, or any wife with whom Herakles might have lain, and thus we cannot with any confidence posit Pherekydes as his source. The antiquity of Antaios' bond with the earth remains a puzzle; the motif itself is surely old, but on our evidence it may have become associated with Antaios in a post-Archaic time. One final exploit in this connection is preserved only by Philostratos, who tells of the Pygmies' attack on the sleeping Herakles after he has defeated Antaios (*Imagines* 2.22).

From Libya we move east to Egypt, where the king Bousiris is accustomed to sacrificing strangers until Herakles arrives. As noted above, our one Archaic literary source is a scholiast's summary, hopefully all taken from Pherekydes (3F17). We are told here that after slaying Antaios Herakles comes to Memphis and Bousiris, who like Antaios is a son of Poseidon. He kills the king himself, his son Iphidamas and the herald Chalbes, and numerous attendants at the altar of Zeus where the slaughter of strangers takes place. Such a scene with its Egyptian iconography is easy enough to spot in sixth-century vase-painting: on a belly amphora by the Swing Painter Herakles grasps one Egyptian by the foot (for throwing purposes) while he throttles another; a figure who is presumably Bousiris slumps face downward on the altar (Cincinnati 1959.1). The presence of several knives indicates that the Egyptians did indeed expect to sacrifice their guest. Outside of this one piece, the story's Black-Figure history is limited to a few small fragments plus a wonderfully lively Caeretan hydria in Vienna on which Herakles terrorizes some ten opponents at one time (Vienna 3576). In Red-Figure, one thinks of several cups by Epiktetos and especially of the pelike by the Pan Painter (Athens 9683). In all cases the main details are the same, Egyptians being flung around or fleeing and Herakles slaying Bousiris at the ever-present altar.

From the later fifth century Herodotos simply reports that Herakles massacred the Egyptians who meant to sacrifice him (2.45; no king is named). Of Euripides' lost satyr play *Bousiris* nothing at all useful remains. Turning to the fourth century, Isokrates' encomium *Bousiris* makes the king a son of Poseidon and Libya, daughter of Epaphos (the place held by Belos in the usual tradition); not surprisingly (given his topic) he denies the incident with Herakles. Diodoros offers nothing beyond the bare event (DS 4.18, 27), but Apollodoros provides some additional details (ApB 2.5.11). Bousiris is here the son of Poseidon by Lysianassa, daughter of Epaphos, and his sacrifice of strangers stems from advice given to him by one Phrasios, a seer from Cyprus. Egypt has suffered a nine-year blight, and Phrasios ordains that to end it they must sacrifice one stranger to Zeus each year; Phrasios himself begins the series. When Herakles arrives, he is bound and taken to the altar, but once there he breaks free and kills both Bousiris and the son Amphidamas. This same situation (caused by a drought) also appears in Ovid's *Ars Amatoria*, where the seer (here Thrasius) likewise pays for his prophecy with his life (*AA* 1.647–52). Various other sources, including Hyginus (*Fab* 56), agree with this account but add nothing new.

Finally we come to Emathion. In the closing section of the *Theogony*, he (and Memnon) are the sons of Eos and Tithonos, but the passage says nothing else about him (*Th* 984–85). The scholia on these lines report that in Pherekydes he is slain by Herakles as the latter is going to obtain the golden apples

(3F73); we do not learn why. In Diodoros he is the king of the Aithiopes, and attacks Herakles without provocation as the latter sails up the Nile (DS 4.27.3). Apollodoros also narrates the event in the course of the quest for the apples, although he locates it in Arabia; about the deed itself he says only that Herakles slew Emathion, son of Tithonos (ApB 2.5.11). There seem to be no artistic illustrations of this tale whatever, as we might expect given the lack of any interesting features to illustrate. The exploit may have arisen primarily to help chart Herakles' wanderings across the fabled borders of an expanding Greek world.

Alkyoneus   In literature, Herakles' battle with the giant figure of Alkyoneus is first attested by Pindar, who twice says (on neither occasion giving a motive) that Herakles and Telamon together subdued him. *Isthmian* 6 lists the exploit after the Trojan sack and the defeat of the Meropes (on Kos), and thus may have connected it with the return from Troy; the two heroes find the herdsman, who is as large as a mountain, at Phlegrai (presumably Thracian Pallene), and Herakles attacks him with bow and arrows (*Is* 6.31–35). In *Nemean* 4 the same three exploits—Troy, the Meropes, and the huge, fearful warrior Alkyoneus—are mentioned, and the battle with this last is of some magnitude, for Alkyoneus destroys twelve chariots and the heroes in them with a rock before he is overcome (*Nem* 4.25–30). So far there is nothing in these accounts unusual for Herakles, since monstrous rivals of one sort or another are always challenging him. But surprising is the link with Phlegrai/Pallene, the very place where the Olympians usually battle the Gigantes. We will see in discussing that battle later in this chapter that huge size is not generally a criterion of the Gigantes. Nevertheless the suspicion arises, given the sameness of locale, that Alkyoneus was in the beginning a Gigas, although Pindar never calls him that. Later sources do certainly rank him among them, as an unascribed lyric fragment attests in calling him "Phlegraian Alkyoneus of Pallene, the eldest of the Gigantes" (985 *PMG*).

The scholia to the two Pindar passages go even further: the one for *Isthmian* 6 tells us that he inhabited the isthmus of Thrace (again Pallene), and that the cows he herded he had driven off from Helios, thus precipitating the war between the gods and Gigantes (Σ *Is* 6.47). The note on *Nemean* 4 claims that he was one of the Gigantes and attacked Herakles at the *Korinthian* isthmus, when Herakles was driving back the cattle of Geryoneus; with his rock he destroyed many chariots, until he threw it at Herakles, who knocked it aside with his club and killed him (Σ *Nem* 4.43). We are also told here that this battle took place by the planning of Zeus, because the Gigantes were his enemies. Both scholiasts appear to regard the combat as an isolated one, as must Pindar, since Telamon and other mortals are involved. But in Apollodoros we get quite a different story: Porphyrion and Alkyoneus together are the most impressive of the Gigantes, and Alkyoneus has as well the special *moira* to be immortal as long as he fights in the land where he was born (ApB 1.6.1). More

confusingly, we are told that Alkyoneus has abducted the cattle of Helios from
Erytheia, where we normally find the cattle of Geryoneus. In any case, Herakles arrives, shoots his adversary, and then on Athena's advice drags him out
of Pallene, so that he dies. It is not clear whether this is a part of the larger
battle between the gods and the Gigantes or a prelude to it, but there is in
Apollodoros a clear connection between the two events. This is basically what
we have on the literary side: a villain who is sometimes huge, sometimes (perhaps always) a Gigas, sometimes at Pallene and sometimes at Korinth, steals
Helios' cattle on occasion, and may be a private entrepreneur or part of a larger
conflict.

In art we find quite a number of instances in which Herakles dispatches an
oversized figure, beginning probably as early as a metope from Heraion I at
Foce del Sele (no #)[69] and several shield-band reliefs from Olympia. The
metope shows Herakles stabbing a large opponent who is turned away from
him (Herakles holds him by the hair), and so too the shield-bands (B 1801, B
1010). But a terracotta frieze of about the same period (Basel BS 318) follows
a different scheme,[70] as does the vase-painting tradition of the latter quarter of
the sixth century:[71] Alkyoneus (guaranteed on several pots by inscription: so
Louvre F208) reclines as Herakles approaches. On some examples he is clearly
sleeping, and there even appears at times a winged Hypnos hovering overhead
or perched upon him, perhaps sent by Athena (who also appears) to assure
Herakles' victory (e.g., Munich 1784, Toledo 52.66). On an Ionian hydria the
giant wakes up as Herakles attacks (perhaps because Herakles plants his foot
against his thigh and right arm: Vat 229), and this may explain the scenes
where the two are fighting. But a reclining Alkyoneus would be difficult to fit
into a metope in any case, while the emphasis on sleep on other pots strongly
suggests that Herakles was thought to take advantage of his opponent's slumber
to dispatch him.

The weapon Herakles uses varies: sometimes it is a sword, sometimes a
club (Alkyoneus often has a club by his side while sleeping), and sometimes he
even attacks with arrows from a safe distance. Five pots also feature on the
reverse a herd of cows who must belong to the story (e.g., Tarquinia RC 2070,
Taranto 7030), although we cannot tell if they are the property of hero or
villain. The obverse of the second of the two pots cited shows Herakles with a
hammerlock on the villain, whom he seems to be dragging. If this is still Alkyoneus, we *might* have as early as 500 B.C. a reference to the dragging out of
Pallene, perhaps after his wounding or otherwise being surprised while sleeping. What else might lie behind the notion of a sleeping giant is hard to guess;
the literary tradition offers us no trace of any such situation, nor would it agree
with what we read in Pindar, where Alkyoneus seems to have attacked Herakles
and his men, not to have been taken unaware himself. Likewise uncertain,
finally, is a Pontic amphora of about 550 B.C. on which two armed men with
raised spears approach a huge, unkempt, reclining man who holds up a large
boulder as if to display it (Cambridge, no #). Neither of the armed men is

distinguished in any way as Herakles, but perhaps we are to think of Herakles and Telamon together, as in Pindar's *Nemean 4* where the two of them appear and a huge rock is Alkyoneus' weapon.

Kyknos   Neither Homer nor Hesiod knows of any Kyknos, but our epitome of the *Kypria* mentions a son of Poseidon by that name whom Achilleus slays at Troy. Presumably this figure, and too Kyknos, son of Poseidon and father of Tennes, were always distinct from the Kyknos, son of Ares, whom Herakles encounters in Thessaly as the main tale of the Hesiodic *Aspis*. This poem is the first preserved mention of the story, and characterizes Kyknos as a fierce warrior, resplendent in armor, who occupies the shrine of Pagasaian Apollo and steals the sacrifices that worshipers bring there. Herakles himself is on his way to visit Keyx of Trachis (to whose daughter Themistonoe Kyknos is married), when Kyknos bars his way, hoping to take his armor. Despite the lengthy build-up, the combat is quite short: Herakles blocks Kyknos' spear-thrust with his shield, and counters with a spear-thrust over the latter's shield into the neck which is instantly fatal. Ares then follows with an attack of his own, despite Athena's warning; Herakles wounds him in the thigh and he limps off. Keyx buries Kyknos' corpse and puts up a memorial that is obliterated by the river Anauros on the command of Apollo.

In the *Aspis*, then, Kyknos is slain at the first encounter, and despite the presence of his father. But Stesichoros in his lost *Kyknos* seems to have made Herakles the defeated party in that first meeting (apparently because of Ares' help), and only subsequently victorious when he returns later, finds Kyknos alone, and kills him (207 *PMG*). Also described here is Kyknos' grim habit of cutting off the heads of wayfarers in order to build a temple to Apollo with them.[72] Pindar notes briefly the same retreat of Herakles without relating the subsequent return (*Ol* 10.15–16), but no doubt we are to assume knowledge of it. When we turn to Apollodoros we find a double version of the whole event. In the first account, Herakles' search for the Garden of the Hesperides brings him to Kyknos, son of Ares and Pyrene, at the river Echedoros (in Makedonia), and the two begin a single combat with Ares as overseer (Ap*B* 2.5.11). However a thunderbolt (hurled presumably by Zeus) lands between them and breaks off the conflict. Apollodoros here says nothing more before sending Herakles onward, so that no further action ensues. On the other hand, at a later point in the account of Herakles' deeds the mythographer has him face a Kyknos, son of Ares and Pelopeia, near Trachis and kill him (Ap*B* 2.7.7). One imagines that this latter figure is the one described in the *Aspis*; harder to see is how a variant in which the combatants are halted might have arisen. Hyginus says that Zeus' thunderbolt separated Herakles and *Ares*, the latter having attacked (as in the *Aspis*) after Kyknos was killed (*Fab* 31). For once (surprisingly), Hyginus has preserved a far more logical account of affairs than Apollodoros, for one does not quite see why Zeus should protect Kyknos from Herakles (or need to protect Herakles from Kyknos), while there is every reason to intervene if his son and a god are involved. But we will see below that there is some precedent for both mythographers' versions.

In art, aside from the *monomachia* of Herakles and Kyknos on the Amyklai Throne (Paus 3.18.10), there are numerous representations on vases from about 560 B.C. on; these emphasize as a whole that Herakles' battle with Kyknos constitutes his one real single combat as a hoplite, where he is (often) fitted out with shield and sword or spear against a fully armed opponent.[73] On about half the vases Ares stands behind Kyknos, preparing like his son for the fight, while Athena less aggressively backs up Herakles. While this scheme remains popular for the rest of the century, on some examples after 550 a new element is added, namely a dignified bearded figure who intervenes between the combatants. On the shoulder of a neck-amphora by the Princeton Painter Kyknos has turned toward his father to flee, but as Herakles starts to pursue, the bearded man interposes himself, pushing down Herakles' shield as he does so (London B212). The scene repeats itself on a number of occasions, often with the bearded figure holding both hands in the air (e.g., London B156 and B197, Munich 1379, probably Louvre F29). The obvious suspicion that this must be Zeus is now confirmed by a tripod pyxis of the Amasis Painter recently discovered in the Temple of Aphaia on Aigina and dating to about 540 B.C.[74] Here Athena, Zeus, Kyknos, and Ares are all named, and Herakles easily recognizable by his lionskin. Unfortunately the center of the composition is gone, but one of Zeus' hands is still visible reaching to seize Kyknos' right wrist as the latter prepares to thrust with his spear (Ares behind him stands poised in the same position). Seemingly, then, Zeus did in a sixth-century tradition halt the fighting before Kyknos was harmed, as Apollodoros says. But *why* Zeus would want to do so remains (to me at least) unclear; possibly Kyknos and Ares are thought to fight in tandem, and thus Herakles is overmatched.

The more expected version, that in which Zeus presents himself only after Kyknos is dead and Herakles and Ares have come to blows, survives on a late oinochoe by Lydos of about 530 B.C. now in Berlin (Berlin:PM F1732). Kyknos (named) is already on the ground dead, and Herakles and Ares close with each other, spears raised, over his body. Behind Herakles, Athena seems also ready to fight, but in the very middle of the picture stands again Zeus, one hand raised. What else he might have done we (here too) cannot say, because most of his upper body is apparently lost (drawings showing him with a thunderbolt calmly held in his other hand depend upon a reconstruction of the vase).[75] Thus Hyginus' version also finds early confirmation, and there was a tradition in which the ruler of the gods intervened to prevent further harm to either of his sons, much as he does on the Siphnian Treasury at Delphi pediment in the case of Herakles and Apollo. The *Aspis* still constitutes our only preserved evidence for the idea that Herakles actually fought *and* defeated Ares on this occasion.

One other brief (but seemingly early) reference I have left to the end because it has so little in common with anything discussed above. According to the *Iliad* scholia, Poseidon, after begetting the horse Areion from an Erinys, gave him to Kopreus, king of Haliartos, and Kopreus in turn gave him to Herakles (ΣA *Il* 23.346). Herakles then used him to win a horse race against Kyknos, son of Ares, at the shrine of Pagasaian Apollo, after which he gave the animal to Adrastos. The summary concludes by crediting the tale to the genre of epic, and we may well believe that the scholiast found it in the *Thebais*, where Adrastos seems to be saved by his horse's swiftness (Bernabé makes it fr 8 of that epic). But how Herakles and Kyknos might proceed from a horse race to armed combat is most unclear.

Eurytion As we saw earlier, Herakles' encounters with Kentauroi are three in number: he confronts them as a group in the cave of Pholos, and singly he defeats Nessos and Eurytion, with this last (bearing the same name as Geryoneus' cowherd) easily the least well-known opponent. The name is also that of the Kentauros thrown out of Peirithoos' house at *Odyssey* 21.295–302, a fact that leads the scholia to remark that Bakchylides' Eurytion by contrast was a guest in the home of Dexamenos of Elis, and tried to force himself upon his host's daughter; Herakles, who fortunately was in the neighborhood, came to the rescue and killed him (fr 44 SM). This otherwise unattested poem of Bakchylides is our earliest reference. In Diodoros the occasion is rather a formal wedding at Olenos in Achaia, with Dexamenos' daughter Hippolyte about to marry one Azan, and Herakles and Eurytion both guests at the feast (DS 4.33.1). The Kentauros' behavior is, however, just as in Bakchylides, and with the same result. Apollodoros offers a slight variant: when Herakles visits Dexamenos in Olenos he finds that his friend is being forced to marry his daughter (Mnesimache) to Eurytion; appealed to for help, Herakles dispatches the bridegroom when he arrives (ApB 2.5.5). So too perhaps the *Ibis*, which says that Herakles slew both Nessos and Dexamenos' son-in-law (403–4). Hyginus shows traces of something similar, but in a more complicated fashion that plays on the obvious similarities between this rescue and that of Deianeira from Acheloos. In his account, the daughter of Dexamenos *is* Deianeira, whom Herakles seduces and promises to marry (*Fab* 33). In his absence, however, Eurytion asks for her, and Dexamenos, fearing violence, agrees; only on the day of the wedding does Herakles return to slay Eurytion and carry off his bride.

In art there is virtually nothing usable regarding this story, since illustrations of Herakles killing a Kentauros while a man and woman look on (as, e.g., London 1898.7–16.5, a Red-Figure stamnos) could always represent Herakles and Nessos, with Oineus as well as his daughter added. Indeed one such grouping, on a Red-Figure stamnos in Naples, names the two flanking figures as Oineus and Deianeira (Naples H3089; this is the only example on which there are any names at all). Disconcerting, however, is the fact that this same pot names the Kentauros as Dexamenos. Either the painter has both confused Eurytion with his would-be father-in-law *and* put him in the wrong story, or the separate narratives (and perhaps the names) have already been brought together in the literary tradition. If the latter is the case, it may be that Hyginus' account has earlier support than we might otherwise have supposed. One further vase meriting our attention is a bell krater of the same period (*c.* 450 B.C.) in Paris on which a Kentauros and a bearded man share a banqueting couch (Louvre G345). To the left, at the foot of the couch, a woman kneels; to the right Herakles looks on, as the Kentauros smiles and gestures broadly back in the woman's direction. Quite possibly we see here the moment in which Eurytion initiates his proposal to become a member of the family.

Augeias and the Moliones

As we saw above, Herakles' cleaning out of the Augeian Stables at Elis, whether or not originally a Labor, seems to have involved from the beginning a question of pay withheld: Pindar tells us that Herakles wished to recover the promised fee, and for that reason ambushed near Kleonai the Moliones—Kteatos and Eurytos, the sons of Poseidon—who had once destroyed his own Tirynthian army at Elis (*Ol* 10.26–34). Pherekydes may also know of this initial defeat at their hands; he certainly agrees with Pindar that their elimination was the key factor in Herakles' revenge upon Augeias (3F79b). Oddly enough the *Iliad*, although it speaks repeatedly of the Pylians' problems with both Augeias and Herakles, never brings the latter two parties together into conflict. What we do learn from that poem is that Kteatos and Eurytos were called the "Aktoriones," that is, the sons of Aktor, and also the "Moliones," presumably a matronymic derived from a mother Molione (*Il* 2.620–21; 11.750).[76] Since Nestor on the latter occasion adds that their father Poseidon once saved them on the battlefield (*Il* 11.750–52), we should probably understand Aktor to be their stepfather, Poseidon having at some point lain with Molione. Nestor's near victory over these two in the battle between Pylians and Epeians is partly explained by the statement that they were then still just boys, and not yet fully skilled in warfare; he is less successful against them in the funeral games for the Epeian Amarynkeus, as he himself admits in *Iliad* 23.638–42. There he wins all the contests in which he has entered, save for the chariot race, where the twin Moliones defeat him, since one holds the reins while the other lashes the horses. At no point here or elsewhere does Nestor say that the Moliones were *Siamese* twins, but of course such a peculiarity would explain why two men were allowed to compete against one, since they would not in that case be able to compete separately.

Leaving aside for the moment the very suggestive early artistic tradition, we turn to the *Ehoiai*, where a fragmentary papyrus and the A scholia to the *Iliad* confirm that Molione was the mother, Aktor the reputed father, and Poseidon the real father (Hes fr 17 MW). More important, the papyrus (between gaps) establishes that there was something noteworthy about the number of feet, heads, and hands they possessed, so we gather (the papyrus breaks off here) that their physical appearance *was* unusual. Scholia to Nestor's account of the funeral games in the *Iliad* also cite Aristarchos as using the *Ehoiai* in support of his view that the word "twins" at *Iliad* 23.641 has an odd sense. What follows in the scholion is muddled, but Aristarchos seems to have meant that the Moliones, unlike the Dioskouroi with their two bodies, were joined together. Regarding the Homeric passage he is, like ourselves, guessing, but of course for the *Ehoiai* he had a fuller text than we do. Ibykos in a fragment quoted by Athenaios may have entertained the same idea, although his wording too leaves much to be desired: Herakles (we suppose) boasts that "I slew the youths of the white horses, the children of Molione, of the same age, an equal number of heads, one in limbs, both born from a silver egg" (285 PMG). The egg (and the white horses) conjure up thoughts of the Dioskouroi, but we have seen that at this early point in time only Helen is likely to have been associated with such a birth. Overlooking this strange coincidence, we seem to have what is thought of as two people, and certainly two heads, but only one body or at least one torso. The Iliadic scholion that notes the ambush of the brothers in Pherekydes also says, just previously, that they were biformed, having each two heads, four hands and feet, but just one body, whereby they defeated enemies and athletic opponents alike (ΣA *Il* 11.709). Read strictly, this would indicate that *each* brother had two heads, four hands, and so on, but our other evidence scarcely supports such a conclusion. Probably the scholiast's linguistic resources were not equal to expressing clearly such an oddity, and he means rather that each brother had one of their two heads and two of their four arms and legs, while sharing one body between them.

Later authors offer much the same picture. Apollodoros, who certainly says that the brothers were joined together but does not elaborate, recounts that Herakles fell sick on the march to Elis, and that the Moliones took advantage of his absence to defeat his army (Ap*B* 2.7.2). He therefore retreated, and on a later occasion at the Isthmian games slew the two of them when they came to represent their city. Here their stepfather Aktor is a brother of Augeias; in Pausanias he is the son of Phorbas, son of Lapithos, and Hyrmine, daughter of Epeios (5.1.11). Pausanias elsewhere adds that in the first battle between Herakles and Augeias, Herakles' brother Iphikles fell at the hands of the sons of Aktor, who were named after their mother Moline (8.14.9). Diodoros' account of the conflict eliminates the Moliones altogether; although Herakles does suffer a defeat by the Eleans, he ultimately slays Eurytos, son of Augeias, near Kleonai, and thus the taking of Elis is assured (DS 4.33.1–4).

Moving finally from literature to art, we encounter a series of very early scenes that should probably be taken as attempts to represent Herakles' combat with this unlikely duo.[77] The earliest in the series are two Late Geometric pots, one a krater from the Kerameikos (Louvre A519), the other an oinochoe from the Athenian Agora (Agora P4885). The krater is actually a fragment of one; at its left edge in the lower band we can distinguish, however, a figure with four legs and two left arms. Unfortunately, the head(s) and right arm(s) are broken away. He seems engaged in battle with a normal combatant to the right, but then most of the figures on this krater are involved in warfare.

The Agora oinochoe has under its pouring side a chariot scene that could represent either a race or hostilities; the opposite side under the handle shows a warrior advancing with raised spear against two figures who stand by a chariot. Of these two the one on the left brandishes a sword against their foe, while the one on the right holds whip and reins and has already placed one foot in the chariot. From waist to shoulder their bodies are covered by rectangular checkerboard shields that join together to form a square. This seeming fusion of the two figures could be an illusion, but the oddly close positioning of the torsos when the two pairs of legs are so widely separated and the heads turned in opposite directions does suggest, here again, Siamese twins. Only slightly later, toward 700 B.C., is a plate fibula from Krete attributed to the Swan Master (Athens 11765). Here the form we are looking for is certain: a warrior with sword attacks another who has a single torso but two heads, four arms, and four legs (in fact, two complete lower bodies; the join comes at the waist). The two left hands each hold a separate spear, while the two right ones clutch the same spear, for a total of three directed at the opponent. We can therefore say that the concept of Siamese twins *was* known and illustrated at this time, and given that much, we may be fairly sure that the Moliones were intended. But we cannot be as certain that Herakles rather than Nestor (or a generic warrior) is the opponent. There are no later representations of this Siamese-twin type; the early seventh century marks the end of its career in preserved Greek art.

As for the narrative, there are few further details. No source offers us any information about the combat with the Moliones beyond the agreed-upon fact that they perished in an ambush. Once this obstacle is removed, the sack of Augeias' city (in revenge for the king's failure to pay the fee for cleaning his stables) poses no problem. Pindar says simply that the "guest-deceiving king of the Epeians" saw his city destroyed by fire and the sword (*Ol* 10.34–38), and so too the summary of Pherekydes (3F79). Pausanias likewise dismisses the event in a sentence, although he tells us that the Epeians in their anger over the ambush at the Isthmian games henceforth boycotted those games (Paus 5.2.1–2). Apollodoros adds that Herakles slew Augeias and his sons, save for the exile Phyleus who had taken Herakles' side and whom he placed on the throne (Ap*B* 2.7.2). In Pindar, as in Apollodoros, the aftermath is the founding by Herakles of the Olympic games.

Neleus and Hippokoon

We have already considered in chapter 5 Herakles' expedition against Neleus and Pylos, an event placed by later mythographers just after the sack of Elis. In the *Iliad*, by contrast, Augeias is still alive after the sack of Pylos (and death of Nestor's brothers), for Nestor at that point launches an expedition against the Eleans and their king in retribution for stolen horses (*Il* 11.671–761). Either Homer does not accept the later chronology, or he does not know of the sack of Elis at all. What he tells us of the assault on Pylos is limited to the death of the Neleidai; we learn nothing of the reasons for the quarrel. Our fragments of the *Ehoiai* show that the death of Periklymenos (despite his ability to transform himself) was there given special attention, and that eleven sons in all were killed, but here again no motives survive (Hes frr 33, 35 MW). Not until Isokrates (who says that Neleus wished to steal the cattle of Geryoneus: 6.*Arch* 19) and Apollodoros (where the problem is Neleus' refusal to purify Herakles for the killing of Iphitos: Ap*B* 2.6.2) do we find any cause for such carnage. We saw, too, some divergence of opinion on whether Neleus survives. In Homer he does, as Nestor tells us, but in Isokrates his demise enables Herakles to place Nestor upon the throne of Pylos. The latter story pattern is curiously like that of Augeias and Phyleus, with son favorable to Herakles replacing father as king; we shall see it again at Troy and (in modified form) at Sparta. Similar too in the sacks of Elis and Pylos is the presence of some formidable defender (in one case the Moliones, in the other Periklymenos) who must be eliminated before the sack can succeed. One other detail to be noted again in this context is the *Aspis'* insistence that Herakles wounded Ares when the latter was defending Pylos (*Aspis* 359–61). For neither this event nor the wounding of Hades at Pylos in the *Iliad* can we guarantee any tie-in with Neleus, but that link is a possibility (and in Hades' case claimed by Apollodoros: 2.7.3). The god whom we should have expected to protect Neleus on this occasion is, of course, his father Poseidon.

Both Diodoros and Apollodoros follow the attacks on Elis and Pylos with a third tale of similar type, the vengeance taken against Hippokoon and his sons at Sparta (DS 4.33.5–6; Ap*B* 2.7.3). We have already met Hippokoon in chapter 6 as a descendant of Taugete (daughter of Atlas) and (at least in later sources) as the brother of Tyndareos and Ikarios. We saw there that Hippokoon exiles Tyndareos (sometimes also Ikarios) from Sparta in these sources and rules that country with his many sons (twenty in Diodoros, twelve in Apollodoros). No source, however, claims that Herakles attacked Hippokoon for this reason; rather Diodoros, Apollodoros, and Pausanias (3.15.4–5) all agree that Herakles was angry over the death of a son of his uncle Likymnios. Diodoros and Pausanias call this son Oionos; Apollodoros does not name him but describes how he was passing by the home of Hippokoon, and being attacked by one of the dogs threw a stone at it. The sons of Hippokoon then rushed out and clubbed him to death. Apollodoros also adds a second motive, that Hippokoon and his sons had sided with Neleus in the previous conflict, while Pausanias says that Hippokoon like Neleus refused to purify Herakles for the murder of Iphitos. By all accounts Herakles slays both Hippokoon and all the sons, thus paving the way for Tyndareos' return to Sparta, although in Pausanias the hero is first wounded and must retreat. Pausanias says too that Herakles actually invited Tyndareos back to rule, thus giving us a kind of parallel with the action of the previous two tales (although here there is no out-of-the-ordinary defender). Something of this whole late narrative must lie behind Alkman's Louvre *Partheneion*, for there (in the fragment that survives) a number of Hippokoon's sons are individually named as slain, and the scholia to Clement, citing Alkman, tell us that Herakles was responsible, receiving in the process a wound to the hand (Σ Cl:*Pro* 36.2). But the *Partheneion* also mentions Polydeukes, and we learn from the same scholia that Euphorion in his *Thrax* made the Hippokoontidai in some way rival suitors of the Dioskouroi (fr 29 Pow). Possibly the conflict had other roots as well, and Kastor and Polydeukes aided Herakles in this venture. The *Partheneion* goes on to talk about obvious dangers to those who aspire to marry Aphrodite or a daughter of Porkos (= Nereus?), which may or may not be relevant.[78] At least we can see that Pausanias preserves an early notion of Herakles' wounding, but for the rest it may be that Alkman relates a rather different tradition from the one we know.

Diodoros and Apollodoros also report one other related story (DS 4.33.6; ApB 2.7.3). In launching his expedition against Sparta, Herakles turns first to Tegea, where he persuades Kepheus, son of Aleos (the latter elsewhere a brother of Stheneboia), to march with him. Diodoros says only that Kepheus brought with him twenty sons (we remember that the same author gives Hippokoon twenty sons) and that seventeen of these together with Kepheus perished in the battle. Apollodoros offers a more interesting story, that Kepheus feared to leave Tegea undefended because of the threat of Argive attack. Herakles therefore gives to Sterope, daughter of Kepheus, a lock of Medousa's hair in a bronze hydria (he has received this from Athena) and tells her that by holding it up three times from the walls of Tegea with face averted she will turn back any army that approaches. Kepheus then agrees to accompany Herakles, and dies together with his twenty sons (and Iphikles, brother of Herakles). Pausanias also mentions the lock of Gorgon hair that protects Tegea, but does not relate the entire tale (8.47.5).

Auge and Telephos

Clearly connected to the story of Hippokoon, at least genealogically, is the tale of Herakles' rape/seduction of Auge, Aleos' daughter and the sister of Kepheus.[79] The *Ehoiai* knows a relatively unfamiliar version of this event, for a fragment of that poem has Teuthras of Mysia receive Auge as a daughter, apparently on direct command from the gods; she is brought up in his home and seduced by Herakles only when he comes to get the horses of Laomedon, with Telephos Arkasides, king of the Mysians, the result (Hes fr 165 MW). All other preserved sources, in contrast, locate the seduction on the mainland of Greece. Hekataios told of it, according to Pausanias, and Pausanias' version may derive from him: Auge gives birth to a child Telephos by Herakles (with whom she has been having a continuing affair); in anger her father locks her and the child in a chest and throws it into the sea (Paus 8.4.9). The chest negotiates the way from Arkadia over to the Kaïkos River in Asia Minor, where the local king, Teuthras, finds it and marries Auge. Aischylos' plays *Mysoi* and *Telephos* appear to have dramatized the hero's exploits in Asia Minor and his journey to Argos following his wounding by Achilleus. Likely enough there was a third Telephos play presented with these two to form a connected trilogy, but we have no appropriate title and no special reason to think that it treated his birth.[80] We have good evidence, though, that Sophokles did write a connected *Telepheia* with such a play, the *Aleadai*, which in turn was almost certainly one of the sources of a plot summary made by the fourth-century Athenian

Alkidamas (pp. 140–41 R). In this summary, Delphi informs Aleos that if his daughter should bear a child, that offspring will bring about the death of Aleos' own children. Accordingly he hastens home and makes his daughter a priestess of Athena, threatening at the same time to kill her if he should find her with a man. Herakles arrives to seek Aleos' aid against Augeias, is lodged in the temple, and matters take their course. When Aleos discovers the pregnancy, he sends for the ferryman Nauplios and gives him his daughter to drown. The latter duly leads her away, but after she has given birth to Telephos near Mount Parthenion he disregards Aleos' orders and sells both mother and child to Teuthras of Mysia. Such a tale is not likely to reflect Sophokles' drama exactly, for a fragment of the *Aleadai* speaks of a horned doe coming down from the hills (fr 89 R), and surely here as in Diodoros, Apollodoros, and numerous later art works[81] the child (abandoned) is nursed by that doe. Moreover, if Telephos is taken to Mysia as a child he will scarcely be in a position to carry out the oracle (a contradiction demonstrating that Alkidamas' story is not likely to come from a single source).[82] But the first part of that story, with the threat to Aleos' sons, would well explain a play with the title *Aleadai*. Unfortunately, we know nothing of exactly how Telephos came to kill his uncles once he had grown up in Arkadia (one presumes this was the plot of the play). Hyginus confirms that he did kill several sons of Aleos and Neaira, including a Hippothoos and at least one other name which has fallen out (*Fab* 244),[83] and Aristotle's mention of a *Mysoi* in which a man arrives in Mysia from Tegea in an unspeaking condition may indicate that he came to Mysia seeking purification from the pollution of those murders (whether in Sophokles' *Mysoi* or that of Aischylos: *Poet* 24.1460a).[84] A Late Corinthian aryballos on which Telephos (named) does attack someone has been taken as an early illustration of the story (Boston 1960.302), but caution is obviously indicated here.[85]

Euripides wrote two relevant dramas for separate occasions, a *Telephos*, set like that of Aischylos in Achaian Argos (with a prologue preserved), and an *Auge*, dealing directly with the plight of the mother. In the *Telephos*, the title character tells us that he was born of Herakles and Auge, daughter of Aleos, near Mount Parthenion, but mother and child were then apparently separated, for he relates that subsequently he was reunited with her in Mysia and received a kingdom from Teuthras (17 GLP); thus in this version, as in Sophokles' *Aleadai*, he is probably abandoned at the time of his birth. On the other hand, Strabo (13.1.69) relates that Euripides (no play named) had Aleos put Auge and her child Telephos (by Herakles) into a chest that Athena brought safely to the Kaïkos and Teuthras—the same story we found in Hekataios (or at least Pausanias)—and this must be the version of the *Auge*. A plot summary from late sources offers what is very likely the story: Herakles (after too much wine) rapes the priestess Auge during a festival of Athena (pp. 436–37 N²). Her father proposes immediate death for both the mother and the resulting child, but Herakles returns and persuades him to relent. It would seem, though, that the punishment is mitigated only slightly, if here as in Strabo the two are instead cast adrift in a chest. The summary does note a closing prediction of Auge's marriage to Teuthras; probably Athena made this to Herakles, thus causing him to accede to Aleos' plan. Despite what would appear promising material (on the model of Danae and Perseus), the scene of the making of the chest finds no preserved illustration in art until the second-century Telephos frieze on the Great Altar at Pergamon.

Our later literary sources provide some fuller accounts of these events. Diodoros makes Aleos disbelieve Auge's claim that Herakles is the father of her child and, as in Alkidamas, sends her off with Nauplios to be drowned (DS 4.33.7–12). Here again she bears the child on the way to Nauplion, but this time the child is abandoned and the mother alone sent with Karians to Mysia and Teuthras. Meanwhile, herdsmen find the child being suckled by a doe, and take it to their king Korythos, who adopts it. Grown to manhood, Telephos desires to find his mother; the oracle at Delphi sends him to Mysia where he is welcomed and adopted by Teuthras. There is no trace of any ill-fated uncles here, but Diodoros' version may well reflect in some of its details Sophokles' *Aleadai* and/or Euripides' *Telephos*. Apollodoros has some slight variants: Herakles does not know that Auge is the daughter of Aleos, and Aleos himself exposes the child, after coming upon it in the temple precinct where Auge has left it (ApB 2.7.4). Again a fawn nurses it and shepherds find it; again too Aleos gives Auge to Nauplios, and he gives her to Teuthras, who marries her. A later section of Apollodoros then describes how the land became barren at Telephos' birth because of Auge's impiety in hiding the child in the temenos of Athena, and how (as in Diodoros) the oracle sent Telephos to Mysia, where he was adopted by Teuthras (ApB 3.9.1).

One might have thought that the reunion of Telephos and his mother would offer more dramatic possibilities than we have so far encountered, and in fact Hyginus supplies such a tale. In his account, Auge herself flees her homeland after the discovery of her child and comes to Mysia, where Teuthras as in the *Ehoiai* adopts her as his daughter (not wife: *Fab* 99, 100). Such a change of detail makes it possible for Teuthras to offer Auge to Telephos as a reward after the latter has arrived and helped defend his kingdom. But Auge (for whatever reasons) wishes to remain unmarried, and plans to kill Telephos in their bridal chamber. After the gods have sent a huge snake to discourage this project, she confesses the plot, and Telephos prepares to execute her, until she calls on Herakles to protect her, and he realizes her identity. Aelian essentially guarantees the tragic roots of this tale, for he complains that in tragedy Oidipous is unwitting enough to lie with his own mother, and that Telephos nearly does so, being saved only by a god-sent snake (NA 3.47). Since we have seen that Euripides' *Telephos* and *Auge* both take place on the Greek mainland, Sophokles' *Mysoi* is usually regarded as the most likely candidate for this plot.[86] Oddly enough, Hyginus concludes his account with the return of both Telephos and Auge to mainland Greece, as if there were no question of his remaining in Mysia to become king and battle Achilleus (contrast *Fab* 101);

the same idea may appear in the Cyzicene Epigrams, where Telephos says at least that he intends to take his mother home (*AP* 3.2).

In art we have mostly late representations, most often on coins or Roman walls, of Telephos and the doe, or of Herakles finding Telephos and the doe.[87] This last scene appears also on the Pergamon frieze, but with no secure sequence of events it becomes difficult in all these cases to say whether Herakles' discovery of his child (not mentioned in literary sources) has any bearing on the narrative or is just a tableau. For the Pergamon frieze in general we have already seen that the making of the chest in which Auge will be imprisoned is shown, but unless Telephos is there abandoned and then found in time to share her fate it would seem that he remains behind. Subsequent panels have been interpreted as showing his arrival in Mysia and even his marriage to Auge and the snake.

Summing up, we seem to have three main strands of narrative, one in which Telephos is born in Mysia after the gods send Auge there, a second in which Aleos places mother and child in a chest and they arrive there (or Nauplios sends them there?), and a third in which Telephos is left behind and finds his mother only when he is grown. The first of these survives only in the *Ehoiai*, the second in Hekataios (presumably, apud Pausanias) and Euripides' *Auge*; if we are wrong in thinking Pausanias to have drawn from Hekataios for this part of his account then the chest with mother and child in it might conceivably be a Euripidean invention. The third approach appears in Sophokles' *Aleadai* (and probably *Mysoi*), Euripides' *Telephos*, the Cyzicene Epigrams, Diodoros, Apollodoros, Hyginus, and almost certainly the Pergamon altar (where the chest is seemingly borrowed from the Hekataios/Euripides version). Telephos' combat with Achilleus and further adventures in Argos we will consider in chapter 16.

Deianeira,
Acheloos,
and Nessos

Up to this point the post-Labor adventures discussed have been loosely connected, with little temporal or causal relationship among them. We come now, however, to the events that will lead, slowly but inexorably, to Herakles' death. On the time of his marriage to Deianeira there is some uncertainty: he and his bride must be together long enough to produce a son (Hyllos) nearly full-grown when his father dies, but there is also the question of Herakles' suit of Iole, if it is that. Either he made an appropriate bid for Iole's hand before marrying Deianeira, and was rejected, or he meant to make her simply a concubine, being already married. The latter sequence gives storytellers a ready motive for Eurytos' rejection of the request, but probably the two wooings took shape without cognizance of each other, and only later were systematized. That the present account treats Deianeira's wooing first is no more than a matter of convenience: the affair at Oichalia will lead more directly to the murder of Iphitos, the exile in Lydia with Omphale, and finally the revenge against Oichalia with its terrible aftermath.

Neither Deianeira nor Nessos is ever mentioned by Homer, but there is no context in which we would expect to find them. The *Ehoiai* lists Deianeira in the appropriate place as that one of the two daughters of Oineus and Althaia who

> joined with mighty Herakles bore Hyllos and Glenos and Ktesippos and Oneites. These she bore and contrived dreadful deeds in the folly (?) of her mind, when anointing a chiton with a drug she gave it to the herald Lichas to convey. And he gave it to lord Herakles son of Amphitryon sacker of cities [Hes fr 25 MW].

Clearly, therefore, the means of his demise is this early, even if the text does not supply all the details. Perhaps even earlier is a lost poem of Archilochos in which, as Nessos attempts to ravish Deianeira, she reminds Herakles of her wooing by Acheloos, and of his combat with that god in the latter's form as a bull (286 W). Our source, Dion of Prusa, dryly remarks that Nessos should have had plenty of time to accomplish his purpose in the course of this narrative (DP 60.1). This observation, taken together with the immediately following criticism of Sophokles for allowing Herakles to shoot before the appropriate time, while Nessos and Deianeira were still in midstream, suggests that in Archilochos Nessos had reached the far bank with his passenger, and there attempted to ravish her, thus providing a suitable occasion (if not length of time) for her lament to Herakles.[88] A scholion to Apollonios further assures us that in this poem of Archilochos Herakles did slay Nessos (at the Euenos River[89]), and adds that he had left Kalydon after killing a servant of Oineus in anger (Σ AR 1.1212 = 288 W; Ap*B* 2.7.6 says that the victim was Eunomos, a relative of Oineus, and that the deed was accidental).

Bakchylides skillfully foreshadows all this at the end of his *Ode* 5, when Herakles on his visit to the Underworld asks Meleagros if he has any sisters still alive at home, and the latter mentions that Deianeira is yet unmarried (Bak 5.165–75). The same poet's dithyramb on Herakles ends by noting how disaster began for her when she received a wondrous thing from Nessos on the banks of the Lykormas (our first guarantee that the fatal *pharmakon* of the *Ehoiai* came from this source: Bak 16.23–35).[90] Pindar also seems to have recounted the combat between Herakles and a bull-Acheloos for Deianeira's hand in a lost work (fr 249a SM: Acheloos loses a horn), but the above is the sum of our Archaic literature. Still, the artistic tradition supports the main events, and Sophokles in his *Trachiniai* very likely drew on a fairly uniform tradition. Deianeira opens that play by relating how Acheloos wooed her in three forms—as a bull, a snake, and a half-man/half-bull—until Herakles arrived and defeated him in combat. Subsequently, she will explain how Nessos attempted to rape her in the midstream of the Euenos River while ferrying her across (*Tr* 555–77). Herakles promptly shot him, and he offered her his blood (mixed with the blood of the Hydra) as a powerful love charm. Later authors have little to add to these stories; Diodoros offers a typical account, with Herakles still on the near bank when Nessos has carried Deianeira to the far bank (DS 4.36.3–4). But both Diodoros and Apollodoros provide the intriguing notion that the Kentauros instructs Deianeira to mix his emitted seed with his blood to form the supposed love charm (ApB 2.7.6; DS 4.36.5). And from Ovid we have a sympathetic narrative of the Acheloos combat from the loser's point of view (*Met* 9.1–100). Here and in Apollodoros (ApB 2.7.5) he again suffers the breaking-off of a horn; its recovery for or conversion into a horn of plenty we have already considered in chapter 1.

In art this wooing combat surfaces on vase-painting as early as the second quarter of the sixth century. A Middle Corinthian cup shows Herakles wrestling a creature with horns and a human torso, but a bull's (or horse's) body joined to the waist in the manner of a Kentauros (Brussels A1374). The earliest Attic versions (from about 570 B.C.) alter this to a complete bull with only a human face and beard (NY 59.64; Boston 99.519), but the Kentauros form does reappear by the time of the Leagros Group (e.g., London B313). In virtually all cases, Herakles grasps Acheloos by his (usually single) horn. An Archaic scarab may show the horn broken off, if this rather than a club is what Herakles holds in his hand (London 489).[91] In any case, that idea is certain by the early fifth century, when a Red-Figure column krater displays the broken-off horn lying on the ground (Louvre G365; Acheloos still has a second horn). In these scenes figures presumably meant to be Deianeira and Oineus are sometimes included, as are Athena and Hermes. Pausanias saw the battle on the Amyklai Throne but gives no details (3.18.16); he also encountered it in a group of carved cedar figures set up in the Megarian Treasury at Olympia which he says depicted Zeus and Athena, Deianeira, Herakles and Acheloos, and Ares helping Acheloos (an idea not found elsewhere: 6.19.12).

As for the slaying of Nessos, in theory any scene showing a man and a Kentauros could illustrate this tale, beginning with the bronze statuette group of about 750 B.C. now in New York (17.190.2072),[92] and there is also a seal of about 700 B.C. in Munich with a Kentauros leading off a small female figure (A1293 [Münzsammlung]). This last example seems especially promising, but there is no Herakles, and Peirithoos' bride may be intended. Our first sure examples are Protoattic of the middle of the seventh century: the so-called New York Nessos amphora and the Argive Heraion stand. On the New York amphora Herakles with drawn sword closes in on a Kentauros who already begins to stumble forward (perhaps shot?) while behind the hero Deianeira sits in a chariot, her feet facing the combat but her body twisted around to hold the reins (NY 11.210.1). Despite the lack of inscriptions, the presence of woman and chariot surely indicates this story. From the Argive stand we have just the smallest fragment, but a woman stands next to or sits on a Kentauros, holding up one hand in alarm while he tries to pull an arrow from his back (Athens, no #). This second example seems to anticipate the conception of Sophokles in which Nessos and Deianeira are some distance away from Herakles when the attempted rape takes place; our interpretation of the New York amphora will depend on whether or not Nessos is already wounded.

Later art (beginning with the Attic Black-Figure Nettos Painter amphora where there are names: Athens 1002) often shows Herakles in hand-to-hand combat with Nessos. Most probably such an arrangement stems from the fact that art and narrative stand somewhat at cross-purposes in this story. For the narrative to work, Nessos must have time to offer Deianeira his poisoned blood, and she to accept it, before Herakles can reach them; his ill-fated lust will also seem more plausible if he can suppose Herakles unable to interfere from the far bank of the river. But few artistic fields will permit a realistic representation of such a situation with the necessary distances; thus the two combatants fighting at close range is only what we should expect. By the time of late Black-Figure and the fifth century, compression of all three figures into one close-knit group has become standard, and at times Herakles even threatens Nessos with his club. The scene remains popular, with a long list of vase-painting representations, but there is nothing pertinent to our understanding of the narrative. In particular, there is no attempt to portray the exchange between Deianeira and Nessos after his wounding. The fight also appeared on the Amyklai Throne (Paus 3.18.12) and probably on the metopes at Foce del Sele (no #). In addition to a hand-to-hand combat scene, these last may have shown Herakles shooting at Nessos across a triglyph.[93] Yet here a woman with raised arms stands behind the kneeling bowman, so that we might also think of Herakles defending Hera from the Silenoi preserved on two other metopes.[94]

Eurytos, *Iphitos,* *and Iole*

At some point in his career, whether before or after the winning of Deianeira, the mythographers bring Herakles to visit Eurytos of Oichalia (variously located, but usually in Euboia[95]) and there a quarrel ensues which leads to bitter enmity on Herakles' part. The Samian epic poet Kreophylos (probably of the seventh century) wrote a *Capture of Oichalia* that must have expounded on the causes, but we have only a single rather uninformative line spoken by Herakles to Iole (fr 1 *PEG*). In the *Ehoiai,* Stratonike (one of the daughters of Porthaon and Laothoe) bears Eurytos to Melaneus; Eurytos in turn becomes the father of Deion, Klytios, Toxeus, Iphitos, and a daughter Iole on account of whom Herakles <sacks> Oichalia (Hes fr 26 MW). A fragmentary preface to Herakles' apotheosis elsewhere in the poem offers something about a refusal and killing (Hes fr 229 MW). Mention of Iphitos leads us back to the *Odyssey,* where we have two references of interest. In *Odyssey* 8, Odysseus notes Herakles and Eurytos as men skilled with the bow, and able to vie with the gods (*Od* 8.223–28). Unfortunately, Eurytos challenges Apollo and is slain by the god in anger before he comes to old age (we do not learn if they actually compete). The second reference involves Odysseus' bow, which *Odyssey* 21 tells us he received as a gift from Iphitos, son of Eurytos, in Lakedaimonia (*Od* 21.13–38). Odysseus had come there to obtain reparation from the Messenians, while Iphitos was searching for twelve mares and their mule colts. These mares have apparently been stolen by Herakles, for he has them, and to keep them slays Iphitos when the latter is his guest. We are further told that Iphitos inherited the bow when his father died. The last detail squares well enough with the notion of Eurytos' (early) death at the hands of Apollo, but such a death seemingly conflicts with the fate of Eurytos attested by later tradition: if Eurytos dies before Herakles kills Iphitos, the hero can hardly take vengeance upon him for the consequent exile in Lydia, or sack his city. Perhaps Homer does not know of this last event; certainly he uses (for no very obvious reason) a form of Eurytos' story which ignores it.

By contrast, both Kreophylos' poem (to judge by the title) and the *Ehoiai* are aware of the sack, as we saw, and probably both of them (certainly the *Ehoiai*) assign Iole as the cause. A tantalizing hint of her role also appears on an Early Corinthian column krater that shows Herakles entertained in the house of Eurytos (Louvre E635). Here six males (all named) recline feasting on four couches. Klytios and Toxos share a couch, followed by Didaion and Eurytios *(sic)*. Then we see Iphitos on a couch by himself, and finally Herakles, with between the two of them a standing Iole. She looks back at her brother, perhaps in modesty, as Herakles stares at her.

Quite different, however, are the scenes we find toward the beginning of the fifth century, when the banquet has given way to an archery contest or a fight or some combination of both. The fight appears most clearly on a Red-Figure cup by Onesimos: here a dispute seems to have broken out in the course of the banquet, and Herakles battles Klytios (named) with his fists while Iphitos (also named) and two others move toward them with bow and club (those of Herakles?: NY 12.231.2). The outcome of the skirmish is regrettably unclear: one is hard pressed to suppose that Herakles kills all of the sons with his bare hands (especially when they have weapons), but hard pressed too to believe the hero defeated and unceremoniously expelled from the house in which he has been a guest. On a Black-Figure belly amphora by the Sappho Painter matters take a grimmer turn, as Herakles armed with his bow and arrows shoots down some of the sons (Madrid 10916). The hero stands to the left with drawn bow; below him Tiono (?: all figures named), also clutching a bow, collapses in death, and similarly further back Iphitos. In the center of the composition is a white-haired Eurytos holding out his hands in alarm, while behind him Antiphonos (Antiphilos?) advances in full armor; Iole stands to the far right, a target with four arrows in it just to the left of her neck. This last detail suggests, of course, that the quarrel broke out in the course of an archery contest, and with that much assured we can discern such a contest similarly on other vases of the period. A Red-Figure stamnos by the Eucharides Painter has one son moving toward Herakles and his drawn bow right while the father looks back toward Iole, who now has a target on her breast with an arrow extending from it (PrColl, Basel Market). Seemingly, then, the proximity of the target to Iole's neck on the Madrid amphora is not a coincidence, although why Eurytos should thus endanger his daughter is not clear; perhaps a drunken Herakles insisted on displaying his skills in such fashion, and Eurytos and his sons are attempting to dissuade him. Red-Figure cup fragments in Athens and Palermo lack crucial areas (especially the upper part of Iole), but the cups when intact clearly presented a shooting Herakles to the far left or right, in the middle the sons (with bows) and Eurytos running toward Herakles but looking back, and to the other side Iole, here again probably the target (Athens Akr 288, Palermo V653). On the Palermo fragment all figures seem intact, but on those in Athens a leg stretched out on the ground indicates that here too Herakles turned his bow against his hosts. If the artists have not compressed different stages of the narrative, we are apparently to think of the death of Eurytos' sons (and perhaps Eurytos himself) as following immediately upon an archery contest at which Iphitos was present.

As for literature of the fifth century, we know that Panyasis treated the taking of Oichalia in some detail (indeed, he was accused of borrowing from Kreophylos) but nothing survives save perhaps some admonitions to a somewhat inebriated guest (frr 16, 17 PEG). If these are from this part of Panyasis' Herakleia, they would seem to support what we will find in Sophokles, with Eurytos the speaker and Herakles clearly married. But of course Herakles was frequently a bit inebriated. We come next to Pherekydes, who relates that Herakles journeyed to Oichalia to seek Iole, for himself in one scholiast's version, for Hyllos in another's, and won some sort of contest set by Eurytos (3F82). Nevertheless, the father refused to hand over his daughter (as in Hes fr 229 MW above?), and thus on a later occasion when Iphitos was seeking his lost horses and came to Tiryns, Herakles in anger lured him to the edge of the walls and cast him over. There follows (in one account) his servitude to Omphale in Lydia; the other omits the killing and its consequences and proceeds directly to the capture of Oichalia and killing of the rest of Eurytos' sons (Eurytos escapes to Euboia). Bakchylides in his Herakles dithyramb specifies that Herakles sends Iole back to her home after the sack of Oichalia, thus triggering Deianeira's jealousy as we should expect (16.25–29). Sophokles' Trachiniai, which represents Deianeira as married to Herakles for a good part of his life, has Lichas first tell her that her husband was insulted by Eurytos, who boasted of his sons' superiority with the bow and then threw a drunken Herakles out of his house, leading to the slaying of Iphitos and servitude with Omphale (Tr 248–80). Subsequently, of course, Lichas admits that Herakles' real motive for the destruction of Eurytos' city was his passion for Iole, whom he had sought unsuccessfully from her father as a concubine (Tr 476–78). Nothing in the play explains how this original passion came about, nor is it clear whether Lichas' recantation completely invalidates his original story, a tale that might seem to be illustrated on the New York Onesimos cup noted above. More complete information arrives with Herodoros, who concedes what the early fifth-century vase tradition and our summary of Pherekydes imply, that Iole is offered by her father to the winner of an archery contest (31F37). Herakles accepts the challenge and triumphs, but is refused nonetheless by Eurytos; he returns later, sacks Oichalia, and slays the sons, while Eurytos again escapes to Euboia (Oichalia is plainly somewhere else).

Of later writers, Diodoros says simply that Herakles asked for Iole's hand,

and that Eurytos demurred because he feared a return of the madness that destroyed Megara's children (DS 4.31.1–2), but Apollodoros, like Pherekydes and Herodoros, relates the tale of the archery contest pitting Herakles against Eurytos and his sons with Iole as prize (ApB 2.6.1). Eurytos here reneges for the same reason he refused in Diodoros, and of all his sons only Iphitos takes Herakles' side. In both authors there is subsequently the usual disappearance of Eurytos' cattle and the death of Iphitos when he goes to look for them. We should note that in both authors, too, Herakles is unmarried at the time of his first visit to Oichalia, and thus his suit is entirely proper; presumably the notion in (one version of) Pherekydes—that he sued on behalf of Hyllos—is an attempt to maintain this propriety in the face of his marriage to Deianeira. Either way, Iphitos' murder seems ironic if he supported Herakles; on the Madrid amphora, as we saw, he dies instead (with the rest of the family?) in a general battle. As one final odd detail, Apollodoros earlier says that Eurytos taught Herakles archery (ApB 2.4.9, 11), which scarcely seems to accord with much of anything else we have encountered, save perhaps *Odyssey* 8. In sum, we have a tale in which Iole plays a central role from at least the late seventh/early sixth century on, and an insult-revenge pattern already familiar from the stories of Augeias, Neleus, and Hippokoon; the difference here is that Herakles does not create a new ruler for the conquered city, but instead slays all the sons and sends his conquered booty Iole back to Trachis. We shall return to the fatal denouement of the story below.

Delphi and the Tripod   Herakles' sack of Oichalia and his own subsequent death do not follow immediately on the murder of Iphitos; first there intervene the exile in Lydia and several other adventures. Iphitos' slaying, a base and cowardly act in itself, also violates the laws of guest-friendship, since Herakles is his host at the time, and Zeus is understandably displeased. Our earliest literary sources for this consequence of the murder are Pherekydes (3F82) and the *Trachiniai*, in both of which the manner of the deed causes Zeus to have Herakles sold abroad to Omphale of Lydia. To this, Diodoros and Apollodoros add that despite Herakles' efforts to be purified (first by Neleus, who refuses, then by Deiphobos, son of Hippolytos) he becomes diseased, and finally goes to Delphi to seek advice (DS 4.31.4–5; ApB 2.6.2). In Diodoros' version, Apollo simply offers a solution—that Herakles sell himself into slavery—and Herakles accepts it. But in Apollodoros the Pythia fails to give any answer, prompting the hero to begin despoiling the temple of its treasures, including the Pythia's tripod, which he proposes to use in setting up his own oracle. Apollo physically intervenes at this point, and Zeus must throw a thunderbolt between the two to separate them.

Pausanias also tells this last story, in a form credited to the Delphians: Xenokleia (the Pythia) at first refuses to respond on the grounds that Herakles is a murderer, but after he seizes the tripod she rethinks her position and capitulates (10.13.8). Pausanias supposes that from this disagreement arose the poets' elaboration of an actual struggle between Herakles and Apollo. That poets did describe the conflict is hardly surprising, given the early artistic evidence (below), and yet nothing survives beyond an uncertain allusion in Pindar; our earliest sure reference to the tale occurs in Cicero (*ND* 3.16.42). Pindar's contribution is in fact the same problematic Herakles-versus-the-gods passage from *Olympian* 9 discussed on several occasions previously (*Ol* 9.32–33). Here again interpretation turns on whether in naming three separate gods—Poseidon, Apollo, and Hades—Pindar means three separate combats at different times, or a pitting of Herakles against all three divinities together. The scholia argue for the former solution, and thus that the combat with Apollo refers to this story of the tripod. But Pindar's words, which speak of Apollo fighting with his silver bow, do not exactly suggest the wrestling match over the tripod familiar from art; possibly, too, the poet meant rather the dispute over the Keryneian Hind. Of other sources only Hyginus adds anything new, supposing as he does that the dispute took place after the death of Megara and the children, not the murder of Iphitos (*Fab* 32). By all accounts the resolution of the conflict requires Herakles' sale and servitude, as we will see below.

In art we find quite a flourishing early tradition, beginning with a bronze tripod leg from Olympia dating to about 700 B.C. (B 1730). Here two figures wearing helmets hold a tripod between them and make threatening gestures with their free hands. A struggle is clearly in progress, and despite the helmets this seems likely to have intended the story of the Delphic tripod.[96] Subsequent representations are not, however, found until almost 150 years later, in the mid-sixth century. The earliest example from this time period is probably a metope from Foce del Sele on which Herakles and Apollo are plainly identified by club and quiver, respectively. Herakles holds the tripod on his shoulder and moves off to the left, while Apollo comes up behind him and seizes the tripod's legs; Herakles turns his head back to see who is impeding his progress and brandishes his club. The same pattern emerges on a shield-band from Olympia in the second half of the century (B 520: earlier such reliefs [B 1889, B 972] sometimes thought to illustrate this myth are probably just boxers competing for a tripod). The Attic examples likewise begin in the second half of the sixth century, with the story becoming steadily more popular as we move into Red-Figure; again, the moment chosen is that of Herakles about to make off with the tripod and Apollo in pursuit.[97] Artemis and Athena are frequently added, so that the scene comes to mirror the composition of the argument over the Keryneian Hind. The flight/pursuit arrangement, with various attendant figures (mostly headless now), also appears in the pediment of the Siphnian Treasury at Delphi (no #). But here, although the two contestants might have adequately filled the central space, there stands between them a bearded figure (again headless; only the tip of the beard remains) whom we may take to be Zeus, come down to Delphi to personally resolve matters.[98] The same composition appears on a hydria by the Antimenes Painter, as a bearded figure with scepter intervenes between Apollo and Herakles (London B316: the figure's hand obscures the top of this scepter, but Hermes is already in the scene to the far right with Athena).[99] Likely, then, all early versions of the story required some action by Zeus to break the impasse between his two sons (Apollodoros, as we saw, uses a thunderbolt). Alternatively, Hermes could fulfill that role, as we see on a neck-amphora by the Amasis Painter (Boston 01.8027): Herakles is to the right with the tripod, Apollo to the left and reaching for it, and Hermes between them, looking back right but moving left. Presumably, he has been sent by Zeus to act as mediator between the combatants. We will see in the next section that he is a standard feature of Herakles' vending into servitude.

Omphale and the Kerkopes

Although Pherekydes and Sophokles' *Trachiniai* omit the tale of the fight over the tripod (perhaps like Hyginus they placed it earlier in Herakles' career), both writers state that the hero is sentenced (by Zeus directly or the oracle) to be sold to Omphale, queen of Lydia. Pherekydes specifies that Hermes undertook the sale, and that the price was three talents (3F82), an amount probably paid over to Eurytos as compensation for the death of his son. In the *Trachiniai* Lichas tells us that Herakles served Omphale as a slave for a full year, after Zeus (in anger at the death of Iphitos) ordered him sold abroad, but offers no other information (*Tr* 248–53, 274–78); Herodoros says the servitude was for three years (31F33). These are our earliest literary sources; art offers before the fourth century just one sure example, a fragmentary amphora from Group E which shows a seated woman wearing a lionskin and holding a bow and arrows (Getty 77.AE.45). Before her stands a man (only partly preserved) with what is apparently a kithara; behind her may have been another man seated, but given the state of the amphora all we can really conclude is that already in the sixth century Omphale had appropriated Herakles' attributes to herself (whether or not she made *him* wear *her* clothes). In the fifth century, both Achaios and Ion of Chios composed satyr plays entitled *Omphale;* we might well imagine these to have emphasized the more comic (and humiliating) aspects of Herakles' predicament, but again we have no solid evidence about them. Although a Boiotian skyphos of the period (*c.* 435 b.c.) with Herakles greeted by a woman who stands in front of a loom has been taken to illustrate one of the hero's tasks, the loom itself is not very prominent, and may simply designate the woman of the household (Berlin: PM VI 3414).[100] Surely definite, however, is a mid-fourth-century Lucanian pelike on which a woman hands to Herakles a spindle as he leans on his club (Louvre K545). One other possibility from the fourth century is an Apulian hydria with a seated woman turned partly away from Herakles and an Eros with crown flying toward him (Berlin: Ch F3291); *perhaps* we see here the first inklings of a romantic relationship between mistress and servant.

Our later sources furnish some further details. In Diodoros, Herakles takes himself voluntarily to Asia Minor at the oracle's command, and has one of his friends sell him to Omphale, daughter of Iardanos (DS 4.31.5–8). The money is paid over to the sons of Iphitos, Herakles' disease is healed, and he sets about ridding the land of local brigands (Syleus, the Kerkopes, the Itonoi) as part of his servitude. Omphale is sufficiently impressed by this that she sets him free, and in addition bears him a child, Lamos. In the *Heroides* Ovid confirms this child Lamos and adds, in Deianeira's taunting words, our first literary reference to Herakles as forced to wear women's clothes and hold a basket of wool while Omphale and her ladies do their spinning (*Her* 9.53–118). Seneca repeats that notion briefly in his *Hercules Oetaeus* and suggests, what is not clear in Ovid, that Herakles willingly submitted to this treatment because he was infatuated with Omphale (371–77). Statius, too, knows of such service, implying perhaps that the hero himself spun wool (*Ach* 1.260–61). Apollodoros' account is surprisingly laconic: as in Pherekydes, Hermes is the one who sells Herakles, and the period of servitude is, as in Herodoros, three years (Ap*B* 2.6.2–3; Eurytos refuses the compensation offered him). Omphale is here the daughter of Iardanes and the widow of Tmolos, from whom she has inherited her rule. But after this we learn only about the overcoming of miscreants, including again Syleus and the Kerkopes; as in Diodoros, there is no mention of any humiliations. Loukianos mentions carding wool, wearing women's clothes, and being beaten with a sandal (*DD* 15); Hyginus records nothing beyond the fact of the sale (*Fab* 32).

As for the useful deeds attested by Diodoros and Apollodoros, the Itonoi are mentioned only by the former, who makes them raiders of the territory of Omphale; Herakles razes their city and enslaves the inhabitants. Both writers make note of Syleus, whom they agree forced passersby to hoe his vineyard until Herakles killed him. Apollodoros adds that Herakles slew Syleus' daughter Xenodike and burned the vineyard as well. Konon's account has Herakles fall in love with the daughter (unnamed) after killing the father; she subsequently dies of longing in his absence (26F1.17) Some form of the story had much earlier been told by Euripides in a satyr play entitled *Syleus*. If we can trust an anonymous commentator, plus some useful fragments, Herakles is sold to Syleus (by Hermes?) to work in the vineyards (p. 575 N²). He proceeds to wreak havoc by hauling away the vines, slaughtering a cow, and breaking into the wine supplies in order to hold a feast for himself; fragment 694 N² may be spoken to a woman with whom he proposes to lie. Attic Red-Figure takes the story back still earlier in the fifth century with a series of representations beginning with the name vase of the Syleus Painter, a stamnos dating probably to the 480s B.C. (Copenhagen 3293).[101] Here Athena stands to the left, Herakles in the center holding a mattock, and Syleus to the right, apparently remonstrating with his new farmhand. Subsequent illustrations carry out the same arrangement, with Herakles having either a mattock or a double axe, and Syleus rushing up (with axe himself, or staff) to see what is happening. A Nolan amphora now in the Louvre puts both these figures together on one side, with a running woman (Syleus' daughter?) on the other (Louvre G210). The whole series of representations seems to fall between 490 and 460 B.C., and hence cannot have been inspired in any way by Euripides' effort, but of course Euripides himself may have drawn from a lost satyr play of earlier date. The pattern of this exploit, which has left no other traces, is curiously similar to some of Theseus' Isthmian adventures, even if the treatment of Syleus' goods is purely Heraklean.

The third task noted is the conquest of the Kerkopes. Apollodoros locates them at Ephesos and says simply that Herakles caught and bound them (Ap*B* 2.6.3); Diodoros records that they plundered and committed other evil deeds, until Herakles killed some of them and brought others alive to Omphale (DS 4.31.7). The more familiar aspects of their story—how their mother warned them against the Melampygos ("black-bottomed one"), how they attempted to rob Herakles of his arms while he was sleeping, and how having been captured and hung up by their heels they recognized too late the crucial feature of Herakles' anatomy—are preserved only in very late sources, primarily "Nonnos" (p. 375 Westermann [*Narrationes* 39]) and the *Souda*, along with various accounts of their names and parentage. But this tale, or some form of it, has unquestionably much earlier roots. We see it first in the early sixth century, perhaps on a Middle Corinthian cup from Perachora,[102] very likely on two Corinthian pinakes of less certain date (Berlin:Ch F766, F767),[103] and quite clearly on a shield-band from Olympia (B 975) and metopes from Foce del Sele (no #) and Temple C at Selinous (3920C). These last four all show Herakles with a pole over his shoulder and the two Kerkopes suspended from it by their feet in the manner of captured hunting quarry, one before, one behind. Harpokration (s. "Kerkopes") tells us that they are shown to be cheats and liars in a poem ascribed to Homer, and the *Souda* cites several verses about their dishonest habits and their wandering over the earth deceiving men.[104] Presumably this poem related their encounter with Herakles, and most likely dates to the seventh century. Scenes in Attic vase-painting begin about 550 B.C. (with the same composition as on the shield-band and metopes) and include some nine Black-Figure examples.[105]

For the fifth century we have the brief comment that in Pherekydes the Kerkopes were turned to stone (3F77). We know, too, that Kratinos at least mentioned them in his lost comedy *Archilochoi* (fr 13 *PCG*), and Hermippos, Plato, and Euboulos all wrote lost comic *Kerkopes* plays. Surprisingly, there is no trace of a satyr play about them. Herodotos locates their activity rather in mainland Greece, near Thermopylai, and seems to know something of the story as we find it in later sources, for he refers to the "rock of the Melampygos and the haunts of the Kerkopes" (7.216). From somewhere between the fourth and first century B.C. we have the statement of Xenagoras in his *Peri Neson* ("About the Islands") that because of their mischievousness they were turned into monkeys *(pithêkoi)* and came to inhabit the island of Pithekoussai (240F28); the idea is repeated by Ovid (*Met* 14.90–100) and perhaps hinted at by Lykophron (688–93). In Zenobios, there is even a suggestion that they tried to cheat Zeus (1.5). The question of their fate is, however, a confused one. In the tradition represented by "Nonnos" and the *Souda*, Herakles lets the Kerkopes go free after laughing at their indelicate jokes about his anatomy; Plutarch suggests something of the same sort when he says that Herakles took delight in them as one would flatterers (*Mor* 60c). In Diodoros their offenses are regarded more seriously, and they are brought to Omphale as captives, but we do not learn what happens to them; the same viewpoint seems indicated by the accounts in which they become stones or monkeys. For what it is worth, the Kerkopes on the Selinous metope are grinning broadly, perhaps indicating that the more comic resolution of the story is an early one.

The Return to Troy and the Detour to Kos

Previously in this chapter we saw that Herakles earlier in his career (whether on route to the Amazones or Kolchis) saves Hesione from a sea monster in response to her father Laomedon's offer of his horses from Zeus. Either at that time or later, Laomedon reneges on the bargain (or, as in Hellanikos, substitutes other horses) and thus Herakles is forced to return on a subsequent occasion to sack the city so that the promise might be made good. We found, too, that this second expedition is recognized as early as the *Iliad*, amid Tlepolemos' ill-fated boasts to Sarpedon (*Il* 5.628–51: Herakles comes with six ships). Later in the same poem we hear of the leave-taking from Troy after the conquest, when Hera stirred up storm winds that blew the hero down to Kos (*Il* 14.249–56; 15.18–30). The *Ehoiai* also knows of the expedition to get the horses (Hes fr 43a MW), and Peisandros attests that Telamon accompanied Herakles (reasonable enough, since we know he will receive Hesione: fr 11 *PEG*). Vase-painting offers nothing on this story; our one sure Archaic illustration is on the east pediment of the Temple of Aphaia, where Athena holds the central position, Herakles kneels off to the right aiming his bow, and other figures engage in a general melee. The magnificent bearded warrior collapsing in the left corner is usually taken to be Laomedon, with Telamon just to the left of Athena and Iolaos the young boy next to Herakles, but of course these are guesses. Although the remains are scanty, the west pediment of the Treasury of the Athenians at Delphi may have displayed the same subject.

Fifth-century literature has likewise little to offer: we hear in Pindar's *Isthmian* 6 of how Herakles came to fetch Telamon when he was preparing to avenge the wrong done by Laomedon (*Is* 6.27–31) and in *Nemean* 3 of Telamon and Iolaos as part of the venture (*Nem* 3.36–37), but otherwise there are only the previously mentioned references in Sophokles' *Aias* to Telamon's participation, plus Hellanikos' account as very briefly noted in our scholia. From these last we learn that Herakles sacked Troy and got the horses (4F26b), and that Telamon anticipated him in tearing down part of the wall but appeased his (consequent) anger by setting up an altar to his name (4F109). If Sophokles did in fact write an *Oikles* (or if the *Iokles* of our sources is a variant on his name), that drama might have presented the exploits of the title figure (father of Amphiaraos) on the occasion of the sack (see below).

Moving to our standard later sources, we find that Diodoros offers two separate accounts of the sack, the first as part of Herakles' adventures after

completing his period of servitude for Omphale (DS 4.32.1–5), the second later
in the same book as part of his description of the Argo's return voyage from
Kolchis (DS 4.49.3–6: both versions suppose that Hesione was saved on the
outward leg of the Argo's journey). In the first of these two narratives, Herakles returns to Troy with eighteen ships for the express purpose of getting the
horses and Hesione (who has exercised her option of going with her rescuer).
Upon landing he sets out for the city with some of his troops, leaving others
with Oikles (here called a son of Amphiaraos) to guard the ships. Laomedon,
however, makes a direct attack on the ships with a smaller group of men, and
succeeds in killing Oikles, while the latter's comrades take the vessels out to
sea. On his way back from the coast, Laomedon is then attacked by Herakles'
army, which after slaying the king and many of his men lays siege to the city
itself. Telamon is the first to breach the walls, and receives Hesione as his prize;
Herakles, who was meanwhile storming the akropolis, completes the slaughter
and gives the kingdom to Priam because the latter was the only one of Laomedon's sons to counsel honoring the original agreement.

Diodoros' second narrative, which involves the whole crew of the Argo,
seems to derive from a different source altogether. Here Herakles, upon reaching the Troad with Iason and the others, sends his brother Iphiklos *(sic)* and
Telamon to request payment of the horses and Hesione. Laomedon's response
is to imprison both men and plot an ambush for the rest of the crew. In this
nefarious scheme he is supported by all his sons except Priam, who argues as
in the first account for handing over what was promised. Being ignored by the
others, Priam smuggles in two swords to Telamon and Iphiklos; these they use
to kill the guards and make their escape back to the Argo. When the Argonautai discover what has happened they mobilize for a pitched battle, in the course
of which Herakles slays Laomedon. The city then falls, those who plotted
treachery are punished, and Priam ascends his father's throne.

Apollodoros, for his part, contents himself with just one account, which
generally follows that of Diodoros' first narrative (Ap*B* 2.6.4). Here again Oikles is slain while guarding the eighteen ships, and again Telamon is the first
to break into the city; there ensues the same tale found in Hellanikos, that
Herakles is jealous of Telamon's success and considers killing his friend until
Telamon gathers stones together for an altar to Herakles the Victor. Elsewhere
in the *Bibliotheke* Apollodoros assigns to Laomedon five sons, including Podarkes (Ap*B* 3.12.3). Four of these Herakles now slays, together with their
father, but Podarkes is spared (no reason given; he does not here side with
Herakles) and freed through a purchase by Hesione, who is as usual the prize
of Telamon. The point of the symbolic purchase is clearly to explain the name
"Priam" (from an aorist root attached to *ôneomai*, "buy") which Podarkes now
assumes. Hyginus repeats the same etymology without attempting to explain
it; the rest of his account merely summarizes the essential events of the story,
including the sack, slaying of Laomedon, and installation of Priam in place of
his father (*Fab* 89). The pattern inevitably recalls that seen before—wrong

done to Herakles, return at a later date with allies, destruction of city, death of king, accession of son who supported Herakles—in the tales of Augeias and Neleus, and (with only some of these elements) those of Hippokoon and Eurytos.

One other minor event must be noted here. Lykophron's account of Teukros' later misfortunes refers to him at one point as "Trambelos' brother, whom Kassandra's sister [that is, Hesione] bore to Telamon" (Lyk 467–69). Though it seems unlikely, the antecedent to "whom" in these lines might possibly be Trambelos rather than Teukros, in which case he would be Teukros' full brother. But the scholia to the passage state that Telamon received one Theaneira as part of the spoils of Troy, citing Istros (= 334F57) for this point, and that she, becoming pregnant by her captor, escaped and made her way to Miletos, where the local king Arion received her and her child Trambelos and brought him up as his own. Presumably, then, this tale (whether all of it comes from Istros or not) is what Lykophron alludes to. Trambelos' subsequent fate at the hands of Achilleus (as further related by these scholia and Euphorion) we will return to in chapter 16.

On leaving Troy, Herakles encounters the wrath of Hera in the form of a storm that blows him southward to Kos, as the *Iliad* twice tells us. Neither Homer nor any other source rationalizes her anger as related to this particular occasion, so that it is apparently just part of her general bitterness toward Zeus' son. In *Iliad* 14, we hear how she had Hypnos put Zeus to sleep while she stirred up the winds; these carried Herakles to Kos, separating him from all his companions (*Il* 14.249–56). The rest of this account concerns only Hypnos, who fled to Nyx for safety after Zeus woke up. The opening scene of *Iliad* 15 adds that Zeus saved Herakles from danger and brought him back to Argos, but we are not told how (*Il* 15.18–30). We do, however, learn that this was the occasion on which Zeus suspended Hera by her wrists from a golden chain, with anvils attached to her feet; whoever came near to help her was thrown out of Olympos, and this was (as we saw in chapter 2) probably the situation that led to the fall of Hephaistos recounted in *Iliad* 1. The brevity of these allusions suggests that the story was well known to Homer's audience. The Catalogue of Ships also tells us that Kos was the city of one Eurypylos, and that the contingent from Kos and the surrounding islands was led by Pheidippos and Antiphos, the sons of Thessalos, son of Herakles (*Il* 2.676–79). In the *Ehoiai*, Poseidon and Mestra beget Eurypylos on Kos; he in turn begets two sons, Chalkon and Antagores, and Herakles sacks his city on the way home from Troy (Hes fr 43a MW).

From epic and the Catalogue Poet we turn to Pherekydes, who says that Herakles' Hera-induced landing on Kos is opposed by the local king Eurypylos, son of Poseidon (3F78). Herakles resorts to force and sacks the countryside, killing Eurypylos and his sons in the process and engendering a son, Thessalos, by the king's daughter Chalkiope. This last point neatly explains the situation in the Catalogue: Antiphos and Pheidippos lead the contingent from Kos because they are great-grandchildren of Eurypylos via his daughter and Herakles. In Pindar, both references to the sack of Troy by Herakles are accompanied by mention of the defeat of the Meropes, and these are clearly the Koans (*Nem* 4.25–26; *Is* 6.31–32; so too Pherekydes). A scholion to the former passage suggests that Herakles took Kos because of his love of Chalkiope (Σ *Nem* 4.42c); no other source records this, and it may well be borrowed from the story of Iole. Diodoros has no report of any stopover on Kos, but Apollodoros offers much the same tale as our summary of Pherekydes, and he may (as elsewhere) have drawn from that author directly. Additional details provided by him include that Herakles is first repelled with stones by Koans believing him to be a pirate, that he assaults the city by night, and that Eurypylos' mother is Astypalaia (ApB 2.7.1). Nothing is said here of any daughter Chalkiope, but she appears later as Eurypylos' child and mother by Herakles of Thessalos in the general list of the hero's offspring (ApB 2.7.8). Apollodoros' account also includes one Chalkedon who wounds Herakles, forcing Zeus to rescue him from the battle. In Book 7 of Ovid's *Metamorphoses*, we find the strange comment that Medeia in her flight from Iolkos passes over "the city of Eurypylos, where the Koan women wore horns when the forces of Herakles withdrew" (*Met* 7.363–64). Presumably this means that they were changed into cows, but for what reason we do not know.

<table>
<tr><td>

*The Battle
of the
Gods and
Gigantes*

</td><td>

Apollodoros concludes his account of Herakles' campaign on Kos by saying that from there the hero came with the help of Athena to Phlegra, where he fought with the gods against the Gigantes (ApB 2.7.1). We have seen that Pindar instead links together Troy, Kos, and Alkyoneus, whom he does not actually call a Gigas but does locate at Phlegrai. The problem is a baffling one; we deduced before that Pindar cannot have equated Alkyoneus' defeat with the larger war, since he includes Telamon here, but the coincidence of place and time is striking. One solution might be that an originally isolated combat between Herakles and Alkyoneus at Phlegrai caused that site to become the locale of the war when Herakles joined the gods in their combat. Such a theory would have more to recommend it if Herakles was not always a part of the war, but we have no convincing evidence one way or the other on that point. Complicating matters further is the fact that the site of the combat is sometimes the Phlegraian Fields in Italy north of Naples rather than Phlegrai/Pallene in Thrace.

</td></tr>
</table>

   In chapter 1 we considered the Gigantes briefly as a race mentioned by both Homer and Hesiod. The *Odyssey* tells us that they were ruled at one time by Eurymedon, "who destroyed his folly-ridden people, and perished himself" (*Od* 7.56–60). Later, Alkinoos refers to them in the same breath with the Kyklopes, since both are close to the gods (*Od* 7.206), and Odysseus himself compares them to the Laistrygones, whom he says "were more like Gigantes than men" (*Od* 10.118–20). What this last remark means is another puzzle. In their visit to the land of the Laistrygones, Odysseus' men first meet the daughter of Antiphates, whose appearance passes without comment; her mother on the other hand is said to be as large as a mountain, and the husband like Polyphemos snatches up one of the men for dinner (*Od* 10.105–24). The two survivors are pursued back to the ships by scores of the local populace, who hurl large boulders at them. In all, the account rather suggests that the huge bulk of Antiphates' wife is not typical of the Laistrygones as a whole. But they are clearly thought of as good-sized, although whether it is in this respect that they are like the Gigantes and unlike men we cannot say; the *Odyssey's* emphasis might be thought to fall more on their uncivilized behavior. This passage from *Odyssey* 10, and the exceptional stature of Alkyoneus in art (if he really is a Gigas), constitute our only evidence that the Gigantes were ever giants in our sense of the word. In Archaic representations of them in the battle with the gods (their only myth), they are always normal-sized hoplites in armor (see below). Hesiod's treatment of them is confined entirely to their birth from the severed testicles of Ouranos, at which point they are called *megaloi* (tall) and equipped with armor and spears (although this detail could be interpolated: *Th* 185–86). Neither in Homer nor Hesiod is anything ever said about their fighting the gods, and we are left to guess at how Eurymedon's subjects perished. Indeed, we cannot even be sure that Homer and Hesiod understood the same thing by the term *Gigantes*.

Nevertheless the mention of glittering armor, whether original or added, does hint at military activity, and the end of the *Theogony* tells us that Herakles performed a "great deed among the gods" (*mega ergon: Th* 954), which seems very likely to be his participation in this war. The *Ehoiai* provides more definite allusions: after the note about Herakles' sack of Kos, the Catalogue Poet adds that he was said to have "slain overbearing Gigantes" (Hes fr 43a.65 MW); the poem then returns immediately to Mestra and Sisyphos, and we hear no more. The beginning of this line is lost; there is room for the words "in Phlegrai," but even if this was the original text, we must admit that the whole line, with no real link to what precedes or follows, might easily be an interpolation. Less specific but better integrated into the text of the *Ehoiai* is the Catalogue Poet's remark elsewhere that Zeus begat Herakles to be a "warder-off of disaster from gods and men" (Hes fr 195.28–29 MW). Herakles does save Hera from amorous Silenoi on one occasion (see the next section), but the reference here is surely to something more substantial, that is, the defending of all the gods from the overthrow threatened by the Gigantes. Thus, we should probably take Herakles' role in the battle as guaranteed from at least this point.

Whether lost works of the epic tradition gave a fuller account of the conflict is more difficult to say. The proem to the *Theogony* tells us that the Mousai delight the mind of Zeus by singing of the race of men and the powerful Gigantes, which might be taken to mean that the epic repertoire contained a story about the latter (*Th* 50–52). Likewise, Xenophanes' preserved diatribe against epic recitations at table includes mention of the Gigantomachy as one of the topics to be avoided (1.21 W), so there was apparently some sort of poem in existence by the latter part of the sixth century. Such a poem is often thought to be attested by the remark of the Apollonios scholia to the effect that in the *Gigantomachia* Kronos begets Cheiron by mating with Phillyra as a horse (Σ AR 1.554). But against this suggestion of an entire epic poem on the combat we must note that (1) Cheiron would not have any very obvious role in a *Gigantomachia*, (2) Clement of Alexandria tells us that Cheiron appeared in the *Titanomachia* (fr 11 *PEG*), and (3) Hellenistic and later writers commonly confuse Titans and Gigantes, merging them together into one set of opponents for the Olympians. [106] That such a conflation could represent any early belief seems totally excluded by the artistic evidence, which never represents the Titanomachy or shows Titans in any of the numerous scenes of the Gigantomachy. We are left to conclude that either the Apollonios scholiast wrote *Gigantomachia* by error, because of the later syncretism of the two groups, or else that a war between gods and Gigantes formed a coda to the *Titanomachia*, thus justifying an alternate title. For this last possibility there is no other evidence, but conceivably there was a version in which Gaia sent the Gigantes to avenge the defeat of the Titans, just as she does in Apollodoros.

One other point of note is the observation, in a scholion to the first *Odyssey* passage (Σ *Od* 7.59), that Homer "does not know the things in the *neôteroi*, neither that <the Gigantes> were monstrous and snake-footed as paintings show them, nor that they inhabited Phlegra, nor that they fought against the gods." If we could be sure that the scholiast found snake-footed Gigantes in these *neôteroi* and not just in paintings, we might have evidence of a *post*-Classical literary account (since the many vase-paintings of the Archaic and Classical periods never show the Gigantes as anything but fully human). But quite possibly he conflates different kinds of sources. Of sixth-century lyric poets, Ibykos may have dealt with the battle, since new papyrus fragments of his work present the words *machai* and *Gigantes* next to each other (192a *SLG*).

Passing over for the moment the sixth century's substantial artistic tradition, we come back to Pindar and his allusions to the battle. *Nemean 7*, from the 480s, briefly apostrophizes Herakles as "you who conquered the Gigantes" (*Nem* 7.90), but our best information comes from *Nemean 1*, where Teiresias predicts that Herakles with his bow shall slay many of the Gigantes when the gods oppose them in battle on the plain of Phlegra (*Nem* 1.67–69). Again, although Phlegra is also the site of Herakles' battle with Alkyoneus in Pindar, the poet must intend two different events, since the Alkyoneus combat forms part of Herakles' expedition with Telamon and other mortal supporters. But *Pythian* 8, the latest of Pindar's preserved odes, does offer us one name, that of Porphyrion, who is said to have provoked Zeus by trying to take more than was his due (*Py* 8.12–18). The fate of Typhoeus intervenes at this point, but Porphyrion is surely to be identified with the king of the Gigantes overcome by Zeus' thunderbolt and Apollo's bow in the subsequent lines.

From Aischylos we learn nothing at all about the battle; he does, however, provide two interesting usages of the term *Gigas* in the singular (the first singular usages, in fact). The *Seven against Thebes* addresses Kapaneus by such a name (*Hepta* 423–25), and the *Agamemnon* employs the same word for the wind Zephyros (*Ag* 692). Admittedly, the messenger in the *Seven*, after calling Kapaneus a Gigas, goes on to say that he is larger than the previous attacker (Tydeus), so that some notion of size may be involved. But this is only one possibility, and in any case Kapaneus is surely never a giant in anything like our sense of the word. Neither has anyone explained what "Gigas" could indicate about Zephyros, save perhaps his strength.[107] Sophokles' *Aigeus* brings us back to a curious notion considered in chapter 9, that Pallas, brother of Aigeus, could be called a "nurser of Gigantes" (fr 24 R); one presumes that these are his sons, awesome in battle no doubt, but scarcely monsters or rivals to the gods. Turning back to the Gigantes in question, we obtain from Euripides some brief glimpses of the combat. In the *Herakles*, Amphitryon boasts of how from a chariot his son fired arrows at the Gigantes, nurslings of earth, and raised a victory cry with the gods (*HF* 177–80); in the *Ion* the chorus sees on the walls of the temple at Delphi Athena battling Enkelados and Zeus destroying Mimas with his thunderbolt (*Ion* 206–18). Dionysos is also here present, although his opponent is simply an unnamed Gigas.

One other reference from later in the *Ion* has already been noted in chapter 1: when the Gigantes meet the gods at Phlegrai, Gaia brings forth as an ally for her sons a Gorgon (*Ion* 989–96). Athena slays the creature, and places its skin upon her breastplate, the aigis. Euripides does not say that the Gorgon was Medousa, and this alternative tale of the Gorgoneion on the aigis could conceivably be old, since Homer has nothing to contradict it; certainly it fits well with the Homeric notion of the Gorgon as a generic monster. On the other hand, it seems suspicious that such a duel between goddess and Gorgon never appears in art, where it would have enlivened the usual iconography. Euripides' purpose in mentioning the event is to provide a source for the poison with which Kreousa proposes to kill Ion; as that plot is likely peculiar to this play, so perhaps is the background for it. Elsewhere Euripides, on not one but two occasions, suggests that Athena's peplos in Athens (newly woven every four years) contained the battle with the Titans rather than the traditional one with the Gigantes (*Hek* 466–74; *IT* 221–24). Why this last event should glorify Athena, or how she could on the usual tradition be supposed to have participated in it, remains unexplained. Whatever Euripides' motive, we probably have here the beginning of the confusion between Titans and Gigantes so prevalent in later times.

Subsequent sources, despite the problems caused by this confusion, do offer additional material of interest, regardless of antiquity. We have already seen that the scholia to *Isthmian* 6 speak of Alkyoneus as stealing the cattle of Helios and thereby initiating the battle between Olympians and Gigantes (Σ *Is* 6.47). Likewise, we found in chapter 2 that the scholia to *Iliad* 14 (where Homer speaks of the first mating of Zeus and Hera) offer a quite different cause for bitterness between the two groups, and ascribe it to Euphorion (presumably the third-century poet of Chalkis: ΣAb *Il* 14.295 = fr 99 Pow). In this account Eurymedon, one of the Gigantes, rapes Hera while she is yet unmarried, and she bears Prometheus. When Zeus subsequently marries his sister and discovers what has happened, he hurls Eurymedon into Tartaros and, on the pretext of the stolen fire, chains up Prometheus. The Townley scholia to the same passage record a slight variant, that Hera being a maiden fell in love with Eurymedon, and thus bore to him Prometheus; the rest follows as above. Not inconceivably, this event is what *Odyssey* 7 refers to when it says that Eurymedon destroyed his people and himself perished, but Homer's wording does not encourage such a conclusion. We may remember, too, that the scholia to the *Odyssey* passage maintain that Homer is ignorant of the war, so they cannot themselves know of any tradition that would make Eurymedon's folly a prelude to it. Of course Euphorion or his source may be inventing a new story to explain Homer's remark. More in keeping with what we find elsewhere is the account of the scholia to *Nemean* 1: "Phlegra is a place and a village in Thrace, where the Gigantes were defeated by the gods. For when these last were engaged in battle with them, and could not obtain the upper hand, they say that Gaia announced that the Gigantes would not be conquered unless two of the *hêmitheoi* should fight as the gods' allies. Herakles and Dionysos therefore joined the battle, and the gods were victorious" (Σ *Nem* 1.101). Whatever we make of Dionysos' role as *hêmitheos* here, this certainly seems the obvious explanation of Herakles' participation as we see it in sixth-century art: the gods need special help from an unexpected source if they are to turn back the challenge of the Gigantes.

Among later accounts of the mythographers we have both Diodoros and Apollodoros. Diodoros posits several battles, one on Krete, one at Pallene, and one on the Phlegraian plain in Italy (DS 5.71.2–6). With his customary toning down of the unusual he makes the Gigantes simply arrogant mortals who, by relying on their power, enslave those around them and challenge the honors of the gods. Apollodoros suggests that Gaia bears to Ouranos the Gigantes because of her anger over the treatment of the Titans; they are large and powerful, with long hair and beards and scaly snakes for lower limbs (Ap*B* 1.6.1–2). From Phlegrai (in Italy?) or Pallene, they hurl boulders and burning torches at the sky, led by Porphyrion and Alkyoneus (the last as we saw immortal as long as he remains in the land where he was born). Here too, as in the *Nemean* 1 scholia, there is a prophecy that the gods cannot slay the Gigantes alone, but may do so if they are aided by a mortal. Gaia attempts to forestall this by securing a special *pharmakon* that will be proof against even the mortal; Zeus counters by forbidding Eos and Selene and Helios to shine, then cutting the *pharmakon* himself. Finally, Herakles is summoned to the gods' assistance by Athena. When he first shoots Alkyoneus, the latter falls to the ground and (like Antaios) recovers his strength; on Athena's bidding, Herakles then drags his adversary out of Pallene and Alkyoneus dies. In the battle proper that follows, Zeus and Herakles together slay Porphyrion after he lustfully attacks Hera. Apollo and Herakles combine to kill Ephialtes, Dionysos dispatches Eurytos with his *thyrsos*, Hekate slays Klytios, Hephaistos Mimas, and Athena Enkelados (by throwing Sicily on him). Athena also disposes of Pallas and, flaying him, uses his skin as a shield. Poseidon has meanwhile broken off that part of Kos which is called Nisyros and throws it at Polybotes (cf. Str 10.5.16). Hermes (in Hades' cap of darkness) kills Hippolytos, Artemis Gration (? *locus corruptus*), and the Moirai (with bronze clubs!) Agrios and Thoon. To be certain of victory, Herakles shoots all of them as they are dying, as the prophecy seems to require. A variety of other authors offer similar details and confirm the snaky feet; Claudian even goes so far as to say that Athena changed her foes to stone with the Gorgon's head (*CarMin* 52.91–103).

Turning finally to the artistic evidence, we must first consider that our starting point will depend on our definition of what constitutes a Gigantomachy. Representations of Zeus battling snake-footed Typhoeus-like creatures are common in Archaic Greek art, and some of these *may* be early attempts at portraying the Gigantes. But on the one example with names (the Chalkidian hydria in Munich: 596), the opponent is inscribed as Typhoeus, and similar figures elsewhere are probably the same adversary. We should remember too that our early written sources clearly differentiate among the various individuals or groups threatening Olympian rule; thus the Titans, the Gigantes, the Aloadai, and Typhoeus all mount separate challenges at separate times, and are defeated in separate combats. With this in mind we may choose to exclude from consideration here individual duels between Zeus and one opponent, such as we see in the corners of the pediment of the Temple of Artemis on Kerkyra. What seems rather to pinpoint a Gigantomachy proper is the presence of a number of gods, including Zeus, and a large number of opponents, usually but not always in hoplite armor. These when identified have names that are at least in part recognized in the literary tradition to be those of Gigantes; on no occasion do we ever find the names of Titans in such a context, and this is our justification for supposing that they are never intended. Conversely, we never find the names of known Gigantes in any context other than that of actual battle with the Olympians (save for Alkyoneus), and thus art has nothing to tell us of the narrative events surrounding the combat.

Using such criteria, our earliest representations of the Gigantomachy are votive pinakes from Korinth and Eleusis, together with Attic Black-Figure pots of the same period, the second quarter of the sixth century.[108] The pinakes are fragmentary and not absolutely certain of interpretation, although the one from Korinth shows an archer (surely Herakles) fighting to the rear of a much larger figure with thunderbolt (Berlin:Ch F768), and that from Eleusis (legs only) names as combatants Ares and Ephialtes (Eleusis 1398). This last example could be drawn from Ares' encounter with the Aloadai as told in *Iliad* 5; on the other hand the piece seems part of a larger battle. We should note here that while Ephialtes will appear again among the Gigantes in art, and is named as such by Apollodoros, Otos is never so identified. Thus we should probably conclude that there were from the beginning two Ephialtes, one a Gigas, the other the twin brother of Otos.

The Attic Black-Figure examples commence with fragments of a very fine dinos by Lydos found on the Akropolis (Athens Akr 607), and to these may be added bits and pieces of three other contemporary Akropolis vases with the same general scene.[109] On all these scenes the central group appears to consist of Zeus, Gaia, Herakles, and Athena. Zeus stands with his thunderbolt poised, while Herakles aims his bow from a chariot and behind the hero's horses Athena wields her spear. Behind Herakles himself is a female figure, barely visible, who reaches out to grasp Zeus' beard in supplication, and this can only be Gaia, pleading in vain for the lives of her children. To the left of Zeus on Lydos' dinos, Hermes (in helmet) and Dionysos (ivy crown) also wield spears against hoplite foes; Dionysos is assisted by a host of wild beasts who overwhelm his opponent. Further still to the left, Aphrodite and Mimos square off against each other, and beyond them Hephaistos (with tongs and spear) is pitted against Aristaios; a crucible stands behind the god's legs. To the right of the central group there are quite a number of Gigantes, plus Artemis and Apollo in animal skins, and then a scene that apparently included the island of Nisyros and hence Poseidon. Two other goddesses remain to be identified, since their attributes are not complete enough to make them recognizable; one is probably Hera, the other perhaps Kybele. The other Akropolis vases are too fragmentary to reconstruct, but offer similar schemes. Athens Akr 1632, for example, shows clearly Hermes (with petasos) and Dionysos (again with animals) to the left of Zeus; beyond is probably Poseidon crushing a Gigas with Nisyros. Athens Akr 2134 adds Dionysos and panther, plus bits of <Eury>medon, Artemis, Ephialtes, and Hephaistos' bellows and crucible. One other Attic vase of this period now in Malibu offers despite its fragmentary condition further names of opponents: Euboios and Euphorbos fallen, Herakles against Pankrates, Zeus against Polybotes, Dionysos against Oranion, Athena, Ares, and Hermes against unknown Gigantes, and finally Ephialtes (Getty 81.AE.211).[110]

Subsequent efforts from later in the century survive only in fragments, like these early pieces, or utilize a smaller field with one or two combats, usually of Athena and Zeus or Hermes. But an (Attic? local?) amphora from Caere of this period gives us a more generous selection, with Zeus taking on Hyperbios, Ephialtes, and Agasthenes, Hera against Harpolykos, Athena against Enkelados, and Poseidon with the mass of Nisyros on his shoulder while he charges at Polybotes (Louvre E732). Herakles, however, seems clearly absent. More informative still is the frieze on the north flank of the Siphnian Treasury at Delphi (no #), where the sculptors have carved more than thirty participants to the action, about one-third of them with names preserved. To the far left are Hephaistos and his bellows observing the battle, then two women of completely uncertain identification fighting two Gigantes. Next are a male with knotted lionskin and a female (Kybele?) in a chariot drawn by lions, both fighting more Gigantes. Though likewise unnamed, Apollo and Artemis make an obvious pair of archers in the following scene; among their opponents are Kantharos, Ephialtes, and Hypertas. The central section, where we might have expected to find Zeus, is unfortunately lost; all that remain are the foreparts of the horses that presumably drew his chariot. If the sculptors here followed the design of earlier Attic painting, then Herakles was probably mounted in the chariot and has been lost as well, in which case the lionskin-clad figure to the far left will be Dionysos.[111] Otherwise, Herakles (assuming he is present) will be that figure, and Dionysos may have been omitted. On the right side of the relief Hera (named) thrusts her spear downward to finish off a fallen Gigas, while Athena (also named) does battle with Berektas and Laertas. Beyond them a figure who is probably Ares strides across the fallen Astartas to fight Biatas and Enaphas. Of the remaining figures only Hermes is recognizable; a large gap probably conceals Poseidon.

The popularity of the story in the sculpture of this time is also attested by its appearance in a number of pediments, those of the Alkmeonid Temple of Apollo and the Athenian Treasury at Delphi, the Megarian Treasury at Olympia, and the Old or Peisistratid Temple of Athena at Athens; we should add as well metopes from Temple F at Selinous (3909A, 3909B). But from the remains we can only say that Athena was present in all cases, and that on the Megarian Treasury Zeus occupied the center, with Athena and possibly Herakles flanking him. In all but one instance the Gigantes are portrayed as armed hoplites, as they are on the Siphnian Treasury; the exception is the Peisistratid Temple in Athens, where they are for the most part naked.

The fifth century continues the series of vase-paintings into Red-Figure, with as before primarily selected vignettes decorating amphoras and the like. But we must certainly note a very fine cup in Berlin by the Brygos Painter (Berlin:Ch F2293). Here the central sequence of the early Black-Figure examples is clearly reproduced, with a magnificent Zeus just stepping into his chariot. Squarely behind the horses (rather than in the chariot) is Herakles aiming his bow, and then Athena behind the horses' front legs. Gaia is replaced in the composition by a column. On the other side, Hephaistos wields two pairs of tongs with pieces of fiery metal, Poseidon attacks with trident and the island fragment Nisyros on his shoulder, and Hermes can be recognized by the petasos pushed back from his head. There are no names, and thus none of the Gigantes can be identified.

In the latter part of the century Pheidias probably employs the story for the east façade metopes of the Parthenon, and certainly for the inside of the shield of Athena Parthenos. Of the metopes there is almost nothing to be said in their present condition, save that there were apparently four chariot groups, and that Eros and Nike seem to have appeared as helpers. The shield has left even fewer traces, but it may well be copied in the series of Red-Figure portrayals of the battle beginning in the 420s B.C. These follow the style of the times in utilizing a rather broader canvas, so that the Olympians aim their spears and missiles downward against the Gigantes; the latter, now more un-couth in appearance and often without armor, pick up huge boulders and seem-ingly attempt to scale Olympos itself, perhaps inspired by the Aloadai (so Naples H2883). Gaia occasionally appears in these examples, rising out of the earth. After such developments there is not much else to report, as vase-paint-ers basically continue to enlarge upon the possibilities for dramatic battle com-positions. An amphora of about 400 B.C. now in the Louvre does show a female among the Gigantes; she is slain by Herakles or Zeus, and has no distinctive attributes (Louvre S1677). Noteworthy too is a squat lekythos of about 380 in Berlin, for here for the first time we see Olympians (Dionysos and Herakles) battling a Gigas with snakes in place of legs (Berlin:PM VI 3375). Such a motif, and indeed the whole theme of the battle, will achieve its fullest expression in the frieze of the Great Altar of Pergamon. But neither this nor other Hellenistic efforts offer anything to further our notions of the story. The one artifact among hundreds of scenes of combat which does purport to show something different is a Red-Figure skyphos dated to 430 B.C.: Athena directs a figure named Gigas as he carries a large boulder, apparently as part of a fortification process (Louvre G372). If there was a real narrative behind this idea, it must have involved forced labor by the survivors of the losing side; more likely, I think, it is just an invention of the moment.

In sum, though the rich artistic tradition for the most part simply confirms the existence of the battle, we may draw one or two conclusions. The repeated appearance of Poseidon with a large mass on his shoulder in the earliest repre-sentations clearly illustrates the tale told by Strabo and Apollodoros of a part of Kos being broken off and hurled at one of the Gigantes. Such a story would hardly ever be comprehensible in artistic terms alone, and thus there must have been some sort of detailed early narrative (such as Xenophanes refers to). Gaia's appearance, so curiously shielded behind Herakles in the three early examples, likewise suggests a well-known appeal to Zeus to spare her children. As for Herakles, his role on these Attic vases is surprisingly central, ensconced as he is in Zeus' chariot. Probably we should expect as much, given the general enthusiasm for Herakles in Athens in the sixth century, but it seems clear too that the notion of his participation as *necessary* to the gods' victory is also this early. The parallel motif of Dionysos' fated participation, known only from the *Nemean* 1 scholia, is harder to evaluate; artists usually include him, but more as an adjunct than a key figure, and since he is a god there is nothing remark-able about his presence. To be sure, there would be nothing remarkable about Herakles' presence either if the battle took place *after* he became a god, and some early narrators and artists may have supposed this to be the case. But obviously his contribution is the more impressive if he is still mortal, and one suspects that most tellers of the tale took advantage of that fact.

Either way, the question of the origins of the conflict between gods and Gigantes remains very much unsolved. Homer's references to the Gigantes and their king Eurymedon in *Odyssey* 7 might seem to suggest the sort of people

Zeus could wipe out with a thunderbolt, rather than having to engage in battle. And the idea of Eurymedon's rape/seduction of Hera, if this is old, puts emphasis on a personal quarrel, not an attempt by an entire race to overthrow the Olympians. If a quarrel is the earlier concept, then the theme of a pitched battle might have been concocted in a post-Homeric era for the express purpose of displaying Herakles' skills. But equally, the battle as we know it (although perhaps without Herakles) may be much older, and simply ignored by Homer in favor of other traditions.

Herakles and the Gods: Minor Tales   It remains, before proceeding to Herakles' final exploits, to note or recall several odd stories, apart from the battle with the Gigantes, which involve him with the gods. In chapter 3 we saw that there was apparently a tale of his rescue of Hera from the attentions of Silenoi, one completely unknown to our literature. Our best evidence comes from a cup by the Brygos Painter in London on which Herakles hastens up from the right as Hera starts away from the Silenoi in alarm and Hermes tries to reason with them; names assure the interpretation (London E65). Here, as for the other side of the cup with Iris actually being attacked by the Silenoi, satyr plays have been suggested as the inspiration. Likely enough that is true, but the supposition that playwrights invent such plots may not hold in this instance, for already on the Foce del Sele metopes we find something suspiciously similar. Two of these metopes show Silenoi charging from right to left, with (probably) stones in their hands poised for throwing; their intended victim may be either a kneeling archer with behind him a woman who throws up her hands, or a man drawing a sword as a woman behind him touches his arm.[112] In either case the man will be understood as protecting the woman, so that (since no other such myth with Silenoi is known) Herakles and Hera become very likely. Unfortunately, this is the sum of our evidence, and thus we can only guess at the circumstances. Perhaps such a rescue by Herakles of his bitter divine antagonist paved the way for his reception on Olympos. Or perhaps it was invented precisely to make that apotheosis more plausible.

The theme of Herakles' dealings with the gods also brings us, one last time, to the stories of his conflicts with or woundings of various Olympians. For the wounding of Hera (with an arrow, in the right breast) *Iliad* 5.392–94 is our primary source; Homer does not say that it was intentional, and a misdirected shot during the battle with the Gigantes might be one possibility. For their part the scholia offer two other ideas, (1) that Hera, Hades, and Poseidon sided with Neleus against Herakles (and Athena and Zeus) at Pylos (the Messenian one, obviously) in the dispute over purification (ΣA *Il* 5.392), and (2) that Herakles wounded Hera (with a bow??) when she refused to nurse him as a small child (ΣbT *Il* 5.392; cf. Σ Lyk 39). Panyasis may have agreed with the first of these theories, since he too located Hera's wounding at "sandy Pylos" (fr 24 *PEG*) and according to Arnobius related Herakles' maltreatment of both Hera and Hades (fr 25 *PEG*). Too, the *Iliad*'s reference to the wounding of the lord of the Underworld immediately after that of Hera might seem to confirm this arrangement, for Hades' misfortune takes place at Pylos "among the dead" (*Il* 5.395–402). But Homer's Greek, with its mention of Pylos here and not before, creates a strong presumption that for him Hera was *not* wounded at Pylos, or at least not the same Pylos at which Hades came to grief, and thus that two separate events were involved. In commenting on Hades' wounding here, the A scholia advance an explanation quite different from the earlier idea that he and Hera were defending Neleus: now the wound is a result of the clash with Herakles over the fetching of Kerberos, a task that Hades opposed (ΣA *Il* 5.397: Pylos is here taken as equivalent to *pylai*, the "gates" to Hades). That this was the occasion is also the view of ΣbT *Iliad* 5.395, as we saw earlier. Possibly, of course, the assault on Elean Pylos and the descent into the Underworld were sometimes linked.

Next we recall that Herakles confronts Apollo, Poseidon (at Pylos), and Hades in Pindar's *Olympian* 9.29–35. If one single occasion is meant, it must be the attack on Messenian Pylos, although Apollo would be an odd substitution for Hera. But again it seems more likely that the confrontations in question were three, as the scholia here emphatically argue, making the first the quarrel over the tripod at Delphi, the second Poseidon's defense of Messenian Pylos in support of his son Neleus, and the third the quest for Kerberos (Σ *Ol* 9.43, 44a: note that Pindar is accused of conflating the three stories). On the other hand, Apollodoros does support in part the A scholia's earlier notion of affairs (at *Il* 5.392), for he claims that Herakles wounded Hades at Messenian Pylos while the god was assisting Neleus; nothing is said about the participation of any other divinities, and certainly nothing about the wounding of Hera (here or elsewhere: ApB 2.7.3). Pausanias placed Hades' misfortune at the Elean Pylos, where Hades supported the Eleans against an attack by Herakles (6.25.2–3). The *Aspis* adds that Herakles wounded *Ares* at sandy Pylos (*Aspis* 359–67), a notion that finds no support elsewhere and may be spur-of-the-moment elaboration. In any case, we should not forget that these explanations of Homer's lines in *Iliad* 5 might all be post-Homeric efforts to flesh out allusions no longer understood.

In art a Pontic amphora shows Herakles squared off in single combat against a woman armed with spear and shield who is clearly not an Amazon, especially since a dignified-looking male with staff stands behind her (London B57). In such circumstances the female is very likely Hera, and that possibility may be strengthened by the goat horn extending up from her cap (or head?); such iconography in Etruscan and early Roman art is later linked with Iuno Sospita. If this interpretation is correct, the artist perhaps intended a story in which Hera challenges her husband's son (the male behind her seems in fact to hinder her spear-thrust). Herakles also confronts Poseidon alone on several pots, including a Black-Figure amphora from Caere now in the Villa Giulia on which he wields Poseidon's trident and seems to be threatening the god with it (VG 20842). Between their feet lie a fallen hydria and drinking cup, which might indicate that the event's origin lay in too much wine. A second amphora, by the Kleophrades Painter, has Herakles aiming his bow while Poseidon (on the other side, holding trident and fish) looks mildly amazed (Berlin:Ch F2164).

There are also a number of Red-Figure vases (first quarter of the fifth century) which show Herakles in the company of, shaking hands with, or, most curiously, carrying on his back a bearded man with a cornucopia.[113] On one of these last we see simply the two figures isolated in a tondo (CabMéd 822), but on the other preserved example, a bell krater, Hermes leads them, and fish below their feet suggest a crossing of water (Berlin:PM Inv 31094).[114] We saw in chapter 2 that Hades is the god usually associated with the cornucopia; not impossibly Herakles, after wounding the lord of the Underworld, takes him up to the earth or Olympos to be cured, with the water crossed perhaps the Acheron or Styx, and Hermes quite appropriately in attendance. If such means of transport seems undignified for a god, the situation might still well suit a satyr play, for which it was perhaps invented. Scenes showing Herakles with the cornucopia have moreover been thought to mean that Hades confers that object upon Herakles, perhaps so that the hero may bring the fruits of the earth back up to mankind. But given the statement of Lactantius noted in chapter 1, that Herakles took the cornucopia down into the Underworld (Σ St:*Theb* 4.106), we might also ask if in some sources Herakles did not present the cornucopia to Hades as a gift or compensation for his wound, thus serving to justify the god's possession of this familiar attribute in fifth-century art. This is, of course, all quite speculative, and even the identity of the figure carried is by no means certain; the Attic Palaimon/Melikertes, for whom a cult place has now been located near the Ilissos River, is one alternative suggestion proposed.[115]

One last tale to be noted here falls into no very clear category at all: the encounter of Herakles and Geras, or Old Age. There is no literary attestation of any kind for this event, and our only evidence consists of (probably) one Black- and four or five Red-Figure vases, all dating to between 490 and 460 B.C. Two of the Red-Figure examples actually name Geras, thus assuring us of his identity. On one of these pots he is a small, naked, emaciated man with a staff whom Herakles clutches by the hair and seems about to strike with his club (Louvre G234); the other makes him about equal to Herakles in size and again naked, but running away while twisting his upper body around and holding out his arms to his pursuer in supplication (or invitation?: London E290). Herakles for his part stretches out one arm of his own as if to halt the fugitive, while his other (lowered) holds the club. To these two sure instances, several others have been added at times, including a number of Olympia and Perachora shield-band reliefs,[116] but they fail to display anything like the necessary criteria (small stature, emaciation, a cane) and surely intend other opponents of our hero (perhaps Alkyoneus or Antaios). Brommer has, however, uncovered a Red-Figure skyphos in Oxford with essentially the same scene as on the London amphora (Oxford 1943.79), and as well a late Black-Figure lekythos on which Herakles pushes down to the ground his smaller, naked antagonist

(Adolphseck 12); we may wish to include as well a pelike in Berlin on which Herakles holds a small, naked, emaciated and *winged* man by the throat and raises his club to strike (Berlin:Ch VI 3317).[117]

The general idea behind these illustrations seems clear enough, even if the story is not: Herakles seeks to catch and perhaps harm Geras. But a fifth example, a Red-Figure pelike in the Villa Giulia, shows Herakles leaning on his club and holding out his arm to gesture, while the small, naked, and extremely emaciated old man opposite him likewise leans on his staff and gestures to Herakles in the same way, as if in vivid conversation (VG 48238). What we are to make of all this I do not know. Herakles does not ever live to experience old age, so that perhaps his defeat of Geras signifies his successful escape from that period of human existence. Admittedly, though, this line of argument would be more convincing if the fate he thus obtained were a glorious one of dying in battle, rather than ignominiously and painfully by a woman's hand. A second alternative, although it faces the same objection, is that he means to extract information from Geras on the nature of old age before deciding if he wishes to experience it. That the encounter could in any way relate to his apotheosis I doubt; old age is a state that most mortals suffer, and has nothing to do with the acquisition of immortality or the fate of death. All we can say, once again, is that there must have been some story, in this case known to fifth-century Athens but not to us.

The Sack of Oichalia and Herakles' Death

We have previously viewed the beginning stages of Herakles' final adventure, with the hero visiting Oichalia in hopes of winning the hand of Eurytos' daughter Iole (for himself or Hyllos) and being somehow mistreated by Eurytos and his sons. In some fashion, the death of Iphitos at Herakles' hands ensues (attested as early as *Od* 21), and then Herakles' servitude in Lydia, thus setting the stage for an expedition of vengeance against the Euboian king. We saw that both Kreophylos' *Capture of Oichalia* and the *Ehoiai* know of the sack; the former poem included Iole as a character and the latter specifically names her as the reason for the assault (Hes fr 26.31–33 MW). But the context of this latter reference is the account of the marriages of Porthaon's daughters (one of whom, Stratonike, begets Eurytos), and thus the poem does not here dwell on the event. In another context, the *Ehoiai* mentions Deianeira and the anointed garment she sends to Herakles (Hes fr 25 MW), so that the Catalogue Poet apparently knew the whole story, whether or not he fully related it (it seems to receive only one line at Hes fr 229 MW). We did find before that *Odyssey* 8, where Eurytos is slain by Apollo for boasting about his archery skills (*Od* 8.223–28), might intend a different story, and so too the Sappho Painter's Madrid amphora, on which wooing, archery contest, and slaughter of the Eurytidai form part of the same visit (Madrid 10916). Iole's capture and Herakles' demise from the poisoned blood of Nessos are never mentioned by Homer or Hesiod. Nevertheless, we must have some means of bringing Herakles to his doom in whatever variant accounts we suppose, and the traditional tale of death through

Deianeira's jealousy is the only one that is ever advanced in any of our surviving sources; presumably it was always the consequence of Herakles' dealings with Eurytos.

After the *Ehoiai's* reference we find fuller details in Bakchylides 16 (a dithyramb), and then the complete story in Sophokles' *Trachiniai*. The *Ehoiai* tells us that Deianeira accomplished terrible things when applying a drug to a chiton that she gave to the herald Lichas to bring to Herakles, for death soon came to him when he had received it (Hes fr 25.20–25 MW). Iole and Deianeira are not actually linked here, but Deianeira must have some motive for her action. In Bakchylides we hear how Herakles left Oichalia to its fiery end and proceeded to a sea-girt cape, apparently that of Zeus Kenaios at modern Lithada (Bak 16.13–35). Here he plans to offer nine bulls to Zeus, and others to Poseidon and Athena. Meanwhile Deianeira learns that he is sending Iole back to his house to be his bedmate, and in jealousy contrives her own undoing by failing to understand the nature of that which she received that day long ago from Nessos on the banks of the Lykormas River. Taken together these two sources give us most of the essential features, and what we would probably have guessed from them is fully confirmed in Sophokles' play. Conceivably his effort was preceded by one of Aischylos', for a fragment thought to be from that poet's *Herakleidai* mentions something burning and a *pharmakon* in successive lines (fr 73b R). Such a reference argues persuasively for Herakles' death as the topic of this particular speech, but of course it might only be a flashback or reminiscence in a play about Herakles' children. In any case, the *Trachiniai* is our first known source to detail how Nessos tricked Deianeira into believing that his blood mixed with the Hydra's venom from Herakles' arrows would constitute a powerful love charm to bind her husband to her. Not surprisingly she employs it on the occasion of the play's action, when Lichas has brought Iole from Oichalia to Trachis and finally confesses that the new captive is to share Herakles' bed. The anointed chiton is duly consigned to Lichas, who brings it to Herakles as the latter prepares to sacrifice on Cape Kenaion (as in Bakchylides). The poison, triggered by the heat of the sacrificial flames, has the same effect as that used by Medeia against Iason's new bride: it clings to its victim's flesh and eats into him like acid. In Herakles' case, the result is not fatal, and he has the strength to throw Lichas into the sea. But the pain proves finally unendurable, and he commands Hyllos to build for him at Oita a funeral pyre on which he can immolate himself. His dying wishes include the request that Hyllos marry Iole, so that no other man shall have her; Deianeira has already killed herself with a sword upon learning of the outcome of her deed (Bakchylides implies the same in saying that Deianeira destroyed herself). There are no useful illustrations of any of this in art (although Herakles is shown lying, still alive, on the pyre in Red-Figure beginning about 460, and on one occasion handing his quiver to a young man who stands beside the pyre: PrColl New York).[118] Likewise nothing is preserved from either the relevant part of Panyasis' *Herakleia* or the work of Kreophylos from which Panyasis supposedly borrowed, so that the above material represents all of our early evidence.

Among our later sources, Diodoros (4.38), Ovid (*Met* 9.101–272), Apollodoros (ApB 2.7.7), and Hyginus (*Fab* 36) all recount these same events in full—including Nessos' deception and the deaths of Lichas and Deianeira—with no substantial variation, and we have as well Seneca's version of the Sophoklean play *(Hercules Oetaeus)*. The one significant addition in these authors is the presence of Philoktetes (or Philoktetes' father Poias in Apollodoros) to light the pyre and receive from Herakles as a gift his bow. The New York psykter noted above surely illustrates this event,[119] so that the notion of Philoktetes possessing the bow goes back to at least the mid-fifth century. Sophokles himself never relates that story in either the *Trachiniai* or the *Philoktetes*, but he seems to expect his audience to know it, for at the end of the *Trachiniai* Iolaos balks at touching the pyre, and throughout the *Philoktetes* we are reminded that the wounded hero's bow once belonged to Herakles and was a gift from the latter. But how early Philoktetes' bow had that origin, and whether it always possessed special relevance to Philoktetes' fate and that of Troy is less certain, even if magic (or quasi-magic) bows sound epic. The *Iliad*'s Catalogue of Ships does call him skilled in the use of the bow, but it goes on to say the same thing of his troops (and to place his territory well northeast of Oita: *Il* 2.718–20). Beyond this the *Iliad* says simply that the Achaians will someday have occasion to remember Philoktetes, whom they left on Lemnos (*Il* 2.721–24). The *Little Iliad*'s narrative went further, bringing the hero back from his exile and allowing him to slay Paris in single combat; the impression, for what it is worth, is that they fought hand to hand, not with bows (but on this point see chapter 16).

Of other fifth-century sources that address these questions, Aischylos (with a mention of the Spercheios River near Mount Oita: fr 249 R) and very probably Euripides preceded Sophokles with their own Philoktetes plays, and Dion of Prusa has thoughtfully left us a comparison of the three dramas (DP 52). But although Dion states at the outset that in all three works the crucial action is the stealing of the bow, the motive for the theft seems in Aischylos and Euripides the forcing of a thereby defenseless Philoktetes to go to Troy; only in Sophokles does the bow itself possess special properties. Likewise Herakles seems to appear only in Sophokles' version, and only in this context (after he has completed his discussion of the other two plays) does Dion say that Philoktetes was fated to help secure the fall of Troy with the bow of Herakles. But of course in all versions where the Achaians retrieve the wounded hero from Lemnos, they must have some reason for their action. Bakchylides, too, told (in a lost dithyramb) of the Greeks' need to bring Philoktetes to Troy, and our scholiast source for that point adds that the bow of Herakles was necessary to Troy's fall (Σ *Py* 1.100 = fr 7 SM); it is not clear whether he actually found this last idea in the poem's text. If he did not, it might conceivably have been concocted by Sophokles for his now lost *Philoktetes at Troy*, a play certainly earlier than the *Philoktetes* that we have.

The Apotheosis

In *Iliad* 18, Achilleus confronts his mother Thetis with his readiness to die, since Patroklos is dead, and observes that he cannot after all live forever: "No, not even mighty Herakles escaped doom, he who was dearest to Zeus Kronion, but *moira* and the strong wrath of Hera overcame him" (*Il* 18.117–19). One is hard put to see much point in this comparison unless the *Iliad*'s audience believed that Herakles did die and remained dead in the Underworld. That Homer here alters a familiar story also seems out of the question, for then Achilleus would have stressed the innovation more pointedly, lest we draw the wrong conclusions from his silence. In the *Odyssey*, Odysseus at the end of the *Nekuia* sees Herakles, or something like him: "After this one [Sisyphos] I perceived mighty Herakles, an *eidôlon*. For he himself delights in feasts among the immortal gods and has fair-ankled Hebe, daughter of great Zeus and golden-sandaled Hera" (*Od* 11.601–4). The words from *eidôlon* to Hera constitute three complete lines. In what follows those lines we hear at length of the striking figure Herakles cuts in the Underworld with his bow and arms, following which he recognizes Odysseus and speaks to him, complaining of the hard labors he endured while alive, including the quest for Kerberos (*Od* 11.605–27). That such an *eidôlon* might appear in a Greek Underworld, and even aim its bow, is (I suppose) possible, but that it should speak to Odysseus with Herakles' *nous* and *phrên* seems extremely farfetched; Loukianos well parodies the absurdities of the situation in his *Dialogues of the Dead* (*DMor* 11). Likewise, there is no point to the *eidôlon*'s lament if Herakles has gone up to Olympos to a life of bliss. Leaving aside for the moment the issue of whether the *Nekuia* is an original part of the *Odyssey*, we have here almost certain proof that an earlier stage of thinking in which Herakles did die (and was seen by Odysseus in Hades) was followed by a subsequent stage in which he ascended to Olympos. This later development then led to an updating of the *Nekuia* episode by the addition of three lines that redefined Herakles' *psychê*, or shade, as an *eidôlon* and thus corrected the previous notion of his mortality. Combined with Achilleus' speech in the *Iliad*, such a situation strongly suggests that the eighth century (or at least that part of it represented by the Homeric poems) was wholly ignorant of the idea of Herakles' apotheosis.

So much seems (for once) clear. But determining just when in subsequent times Herakles acquired his divine status reanimates the usual problems. Like the *Odyssey*, the *Theogony* also mentions Herakles' residence on Olympos and marriage to Hebe, but in the last hundred lines, which are not likely to be the work of Hesiod (*Th* 950–55).[120] And here again, although the run of thought—marriages of Zeus' children—makes the mention of Hebe reasonable enough, the lines could well be an interpolation into the original added text. They stress that after completing his heavy labors Herakles wed Hebe on snowy Olympos;

thus he lives blessed and ageless, having wrought a great deed among the gods
(i.e., defeating the Gigantes?). The implication might thus seem that the apotheosis is a reward for his accomplishments. From Hesiod we pass to the Deianeira fragment of the *Ehoiai;* here we find, after Herakles has put on the
poisoned garment and felt its effect, the following: "And he died and went
down into the <much-groaning> house of Hades. But now he is a god, and
he has escaped all evils. And he lives in the same place as others having homes
on Olympos, immortal and ageless, having fair-ankled Hebe, daughter of great
Zeus and golden-sandaled Hera. Before, the white-armed Hera hated him beyond all other gods and mortals, but now she loves him, and honors him above
all the other gods after mighty Kronion himself" (Hes fr 25.26–33 MW). The
flow of thought is clearly smoother in this passage than it was in the *Nekuia,*
and we cannot advance any real proof of an interpolation. Yet here too that
possibility must be considered, for Herakles' descent into Hades before going
up to Olympos is a trifle odd, and the poem does sound defensive in its presentation of Hera's about-face. Such questions will not, however, make much difference to our efforts at dating, for the artistic evidence will confirm the apotheosis for a time not very much later (perhaps even earlier) than the probable
date of the *Ehoiai.*

That artistic tradition first surfaces in Samos, on present evidence, with an
unpublished Orientalizing krater on which Herakles and Hebe (names inscribed) ride together in a chariot flanked by other gods (Samos, no #, exca-
vation depository). Subsequently, the same scene appears in Corinth at about
600 B.C., on a Middle Corinthian aryballos found at Vulci (VG, no #).[121] Here
again names identify the couple riding in their chariot (Hebe with her veil held
out in a bridal pose) as they are welcomed by the Charites, Athena, and Aphrodite, escorted by Apollo and the Mousai (Kalliope in the lead), and approach
a seated Zeus and Hera on Olympos. No doubt remains, then, that already by
the start of the sixth century Herakles has achieved (at least in some circles)
his deification and divine marriage. As the illustrations of this theme continue
(primarily in Athens), Hebe largely disappears from view, and the scenes fall
into two main categories, Herakles being escorted into the presence of Zeus on
Olympos and Herakles in a chariot led by Athena (sometimes also Hermes).
In Attic Black-Figure the first type is represented by about twenty-five examples, the second by well over a hundred, but of course only the presence of
Zeus (or other assembled gods) will guarantee the meaning of the scene.[122] So,
for instance, on a Siana cup in London dating to the vicinity of 570 B.C.: Zeus
sits to the left, thunderbolt in hand and Hera seated behind him, while a procession consisting of Hermes, Athena, Herakles, Artemis, and Ares approaches
(London B379). Names are lacking but the iconography—kerykeion, aigis,
lionskin and cowl, bow, helmet—assures the identity of the participants.

Of about the same time period is the so-called Introduction Pediment from
one of the early limestone structures on the Athenian Akropolis (Akropolis 9).
Anchored in what is probably the center of the composition is a seated Zeus

turned profile-right; to the right of him is a now headless female, also seated but facing out to the front (as on the Vulci aryballos, where she is as we would expect Hera). Further to the right Herakles, almost completely preserved and with lionskin, advances flanked by two other figures, one preceding and one following. The one in front of him is completely lost but was probably Athena. The one behind is, like Hera, headless and wears some sort of fawn- or other animal skin over a short tunic; Hermes, Iris, Artemis, and Dionysos have been suggested. If this scene did occupy a whole pediment, then Zeus as the largest figure will hold the middle, and there will have been a number of figures behind him; only one suitable candidate survives, a completely draped male with no special attributes (Akropolis 55).

Other notable early illustrations include a lekythos on which Hermes and Athena approach Zeus from the right (Hermes gesticulating vigorously) while Herakles comes up behind Zeus from the left, as if slightly apprehensive about meeting his father (Athens 413). The same idea is surely present on a cup by the Phrynos Painter which reduces the scene to just three figures, Zeus seated on the right, Herakles on the left, and Athena in the center gesturing to Zeus with her left hand while pulling a reluctant Herakles along behind her with the right (London B424). In both these examples, the freshness of the notion that a mortal could become equal to the gods seems very much present. The following decades continue the story in vase-painting, utilizing both this introduction scheme and that of the procession (with or without chariot) in progress to Olympos; there seems no reason to doubt, with the apotheosis now firmly established for the sixth century, that this second type also constitutes part of its iconography. Other types probably to be taken as representing the same story include Herakles reclining on a couch as Athena approaches, and Herakles playing the lyre as Athena or other gods look on. Exekias offers us a relatively rare view of Herakles actually in residence among the gods on Olympos: an amphora in Orvieto shows him seated between Zeus and Athena, with the three of them facing Apollo, Hermes, and Dionysos (Orvieto 78). As noted, there is little sign of Hebe in any of these scenes; the focus remains on Herakles coming to join the gods, or to meet Zeus. But we do see the couple together in a chariot again on a late sixth-century hydria in New York, where the identification is once more guaranteed by inscription (NY 14.105.10), and a woman in chariot with Herakles on several earlier examples might be Hebe. It seems clear, though, that for Athenian artists she is not the most crucial feature of Herakles' new status. Outside of Attika, Pausanias tells us that the journey to Olympos was shown on the Amyklai Throne (Paus 3.18.11), and we have as well a Lakonian bowl (NY 50.11.7) and an Ionian hydria (the "Ricci Hydria": VG, no #); on the latter Athena leads Herakles into a chariot preceded by Iris and Hermes. In Attic Red-Figure the number of examples of any of the above types drops off sharply, but we should note the magnificent cup by the Sosias Painter on which Herakles pronounces the words "Dear Zeus" as he approaches the gathering of the gods (Berlin:Ch F2278).

Neither fifth-century nor later written sources have anything like a description of the entry into Olympos. Pindar mentions the apotheosis and marriage to Hebe briefly on three separate occasions, all without details, although he does stress the marriage more than Attic art might have led us to expect (*Nem* 1.69–72, 10.17–18; *Is* 4.55–60). Perhaps Aischylos had something to say on the subject in the course of Prometheus' predictions to Herakles in the lost *Prometheus Lyomenos*, but we have no relevant fragments. Toward the end of the century we actually see Herakles as a god in Sophokles' *Philoktetes*, when he appears at the close of the play to persuade his friend. Whether the same playwright's earlier *Trachiniai* might have asked its audience to ignore the hero's forthcoming divinity (since the play dramatizes his death with no mention thereof) remains very much a debated question. In Euripides' *Herakleidai* there is an epiphany of Herakles and Hebe to Iolaos (*Hkld* 853–57), and toward the end of the play the chorus reasserts his godhood and divine marriage (*Hkld* 910–18). Of our later mythographers, Diodoros rationalizes the whole event by suggesting that a lightning bolt struck the pyre of Herakles after Philoktetes had lit it, thus destroying all remains and causing Iolaos and the rest to suppose his ascension (DS 4.38.4–5). Apollodoros says rather that a cloud moving (under?) Herakles sent him up into the sky with a crack of thunder (ApB 2.7.7). His reconciliation with Hera follows, and the marriage to Hebe, by whom he has, here alone, two sons, Alexiares and Aniketos. Ovid also tells the tale, with Zeus ordaining Herakles' divinity by fiat and Hera reluctantly agreeing (*Met* 9.242–61).

In all, then, our evidence leans strongly toward the conclusion that the apotheosis took shape no earlier than the late seventh century, and that the relevant materials in the *Odyssey*, the *Theogony*, and the *Ehoiai* are later than that. The hero's death by poisoned robe stands as the earliest (and sole) account of his earthly demise, whether or not followed by immortality; we remain, however, still quite uncertain whether the self-immolation on a pyre always played a role, since our earliest attestation for that element is fifth-century (the vases noted above, the *Trachiniai*, Euripides' *Herakleidai*, possibly a play by Aischylos). As for the purpose of his earthly life, we saw in the last part of the *Theogony* the possible suggestion of divinity as a reward for great labors and sufferings, and this may well have been an underlying assumption for subsequent treatments of his story. But not until Diodoros do we find stated the idea that Herakles was *promised* godhood as recompense for the Labors before undertaking them (DS 4.10.7). There are no myths at all about him after his acquisition of divinity, save for his appearance to Philoktetes in Sophokles and perhaps the defeat of the Gigantes; apparently storytellers did not feel that life on Olympos could ever match his mortal accomplishments.

Eurystheus and the Herakleidai The tale of Eurystheus' pursuit and harassment of Herakles' children by Deianeira after their father's death is best known from Euripides' preserved *Herakleidai*, where the conflict and its resolution receive full dramatic treatment.

One would indeed be tempted to suppose Euripides the creator of this turn of events, with its many possibilities for suppliant drama, had we not the briefest allusion in Pindar and a possible summary from Pherekydes to prove otherwise. As it is, the story must go back beyond the fifth century, but we can say nothing else about its origins. In *Pythian* 9 Pindar tells us that Iolaos, nephew of Herakles, cut off the head of Eurystheus (*Py* 9.79–83); obviously he expects the circumstances to be well known. He does not, however, mention Athens in this context (admittedly there is no reason to do so), and we must allow that he *may* not have recognized her involvement. In the Athenian Pherekydes, matters are different. Our source here is Antoninus Liberalis, who may have used other authors as well (AntLib 33 = 3F84), but the first part of his tale should be Pherekydian, and here we learn that Eurystheus drove the children from their fatherland (Thebes? Tiryns?) and became king himself (elsewhere he is already king of Tiryns, and never of Thebes). When the children flee to Demophon and his brother Akamas, the sons of Theseus, in Athens, he then sends a herald threatening war if they are not surrendered. The Athenians refuse, and in the ensuing battle Eurystheus is killed and his army routed, thus allowing the Herakleidai to return to Thebes. We saw earlier that Aischylos also wrote a *Herakleidai* before that of Euripides, but such a title could denote simply the make-up of the chorus, and we cannot say at all what the plot might have been; Herakles' death is one possibility. To complicate matters further, the Aischylean title *Alkmene* (attested by Hesychios alone and omitted from the Catalogue) may or may not be an alternative title for the Aischylean *Herakleidai*. At any rate, we see that Euripides did have some precedents for his story, whether or not they included a complete play on which to model his own.

As for that Euripidean version, we find his play set at Marathon, where Iolaos and Alkmene have come with Hyllos and the other children of Herakles. As the drama opens, Iolaos explains that Eurystheus has pressured Trachis and every other city to expel their band, threatening war if his demands are refused. The Argive herald Kopreus soon enters, and his debate with Iolaos makes clear that Eurystheus wants the fugitives led back to Argos to be executed, no doubt in fear that the children will grow up to avenge their father. Iolaos appeals to the Athenian king Demophon, son of Theseus, and his brother Akamas for sanctuary, stressing kinship, Herakles' aid to Theseus, and the honor of the gods at whose altar they have sought refuge. Demophon receives the appeal favorably; Kopreus is sent packing, and both sides prepare for war. At first, matters look quite hopeful for the suppliants, but then oracles reveal to Demophon that Persephone requires the sacrifice of a girl of noble ancestry if Athens is to prevail. Herakles' daughter Makaria volunteers and is led away. Next, news arrives that Hyllos has returned from his scouting with a large supporting army. Iolaos is determined that he will fight as well, old though he is, and dons arms. The battle itself follows, reported by messenger speech: Hyllos challenges Eurystheus to single combat but is refused, and there is a protracted engagement. At this point, Iolaos on the battlefield prays to Zeus and Hebe for the return of his youth for just one day, so that he might capture Eurystheus himself. His wish granted, he overtakes his tormentor at Megara and brings him back to Marathon in chains. The end of the play, however, presents the fugitives in a less admirable light, as they debate with Eurystheus whether they should not simply kill him, despite the chorus' misgivings as to this treatment of prisoners of war. Alkmene persists, and as the play closes Eurystheus is led out to his death. Likely enough much of this finale was conditioned by current issues in wartime Athens; presumably Pindar viewed the matter differently when he had Iolaos cut off Eurystheus' head.

Later sources follow this dramatic account without much variation. In Diodoros the children have gone to the court of Keyx, king of Trachis, from whence they depart when Eurystheus threatens war against their host in fear of them (DS 4.57). Athens alone receives them, and settles them at Trikorynthos, a town north of Marathon. Eurystheus' attack is then repelled by the Athenians, led by Theseus, Iolaos, and Hyllos; Eurystheus and his sons all die in battle, Eurystheus himself at the hands of Hyllos after his chariot breaks down in mid-flight. Strabo also says that he died in battle, with his body buried at Gargettos (in central Attika) and his head (here again cut off by Iolaos) at Trikorynthos (Str 8.6.19). Pausanias, like Diodoros, makes the Athenian king in question Theseus; he tells too of the voluntary sacrifice of Makaria, commemorated by a spring of that name at Marathon (Paus 1.32.6). This insistence on Marathon rather than Athens as the place of the fugitives' supplication in most of our sources may suggest that an old local tradition lies behind the story. Further on in his description of Attika, Pausanias notes the tomb of Eurystheus, whom he says Iolaos slew at Skiron's rocks as he was fleeing after the battle (Paus 1.44.9). For his part, Apollodoros has the children, after leaving Keyx, come to Athens itself and the Altar of Pity in the Agora (ApB 2.8.1). Makaria is again omitted, as in Diodoros and Strabo, while Eurystheus here loses five of his sons in battle, and is himself slain by Hyllos at the same Skironian rocks. In a grim coda to this account, Hyllos cuts off the head and brings it back to Alkmene, who gouges out the eyes with shuttle pins. Finally, there are the scholia to the Iolaos reference in *Pythian* 9, which argue that in fact Iolaos had died before Eurystheus' attack on Attika, but prayed to come back to life when he heard what was happening; he did so, slew Eurystheus, and then died again (Σ *Py* 9.137). The same scholia also maintain that the version in which Iolaos is simply rejuvenated is the work of writers who found the original tale too implausible. We cannot, of course, guarantee that this version of the story's development is correct, but it does seem reasonable, and might suggest a greater antiquity for the whole legend than we would otherwise have suspected. Likely, too, Hyllos' role in the death of Eurystheus is a further extension of the same thinking by storytellers who found any military participation by Iolaos at his age improbable.

The final fate of Alkmene has already been treated in chapter 8—marriage to Rhadamanthys either in Boiotia or on the Isles of the Blessed; sources for the former version are Apollodoros and Plutarch, for the latter Pherekydes (or Nikandros?) and the Cyzicene Epigrams. We can only guess as to what Aischylos' *Alkmene* might have contributed on this matter. As for the children, in Herodotos we find the claim that both houses of Spartan kings were descended from Aristodemos, the great-grandson of Hyllos (Hdt 6.52, 7.204, 8.131). Diodoros gives a typical version of events: with Eurystheus dead, the Herakleidai attempt a return to Mykenai to seize power, and are opposed at the Isthmos by Atreus (DS 4.58.1–4). A bargain is made for single combat on the terms that if the Herakleidai champion is defeated the children will all withdraw their claim for a period of fifty years. The Tegean king Echemos then kills Hyllos in the combat, and the Herakleidai return to Trikorynthos. Apollodoros fills out the tale with the return of the Herakleidai to the Peloponnesos three generations later, under Temenos and Aristodemos, Hyllos' descendants (ApB 2.8.2–3). Presumably, much of this developed in Dorian Sparta as a mythologizing of the influx of the Dorians themselves at the end of the Bronze Age.

One other son of Herakles deserving special mention is Tlepolemos, Herakles' child by Astyoche of Ephyra who falls at the hand of Sarpedon in *Iliad* 5.655–59. In the Catalogue of Ships Homer tells us that on coming of age this Tlepolemos slew his father's uncle Likymnios (son of Elektryon and half-brother of Alkmene), and as a result had to flee the family's anger and migrate to Rhodes, where Zeus poured down great wealth (*Il* 2.653–70). In Pindar we find much the same: Tlepolemos in anger strikes Likymnios with his staff as the latter emerges from the chamber of Midea (presumably here as elsewhere Likymnios' mother: *Ol* 7.20–38). The Delphic oracle then advises Tlepolemos to colonize Rhodes, and here in time Zeus sends the golden snowfall. Diodoros also relates events in this manner, specifying that a quarrel was involved (DS 4.58.7), but in Apollodoros the death is accidental, for Tlepolemos is beating a slave, and Likymnios in attempting to intervene is struck (ApB 2.8.2). In various scholia this last idea is taken even further: Tlepolemos sees Likymnios being manhandled by a slave, and strikes at the slave but hits Likymnios (ΣA *Il* 2.662), or accomplishes the same result when aiming at a cow (Σ *Ol* 7.36c). But other parts of the latter scholia speak rather of a dispute over payments or status (Σ *Ol* 7.49a, 54), which would certainly be closer to what Pindar has in mind when he says that Tlepolemos struck in anger. In all cases the flight to Rhodes is the result, so that this tale too would seem to take its impetus from (or at least find its home in) the historical facts of Dorian conquest.

14   Thebes

Kadmos   Most likely when we think of Thebes' earliest history, that is, its founding, we think of Kadmos' trek from Delphi to Boiotia, following the prophesied cow that led him to the city's destined site. As early as the *Iliad*, indeed, the Thebans are called Kadmeioi (the only name the poem ever uses for them), suggesting some awareness of this story. But the *Iliad* never actually mentions Kadmos himself or the founding, and the *Odyssey* names him only once, as the father of Ino (see below). Quite the contrary, *Odyssey* 11, the *Nekuia*, offers a completely different founding legend, that of Antiope who bore to Zeus Amphion and Zethos, builders of the walls of Thebes. The *Ehoiai*, Pherekydes, and Pindar also refer to the efforts of these twins, and thus it seems clear that from some fairly early point in time we have two completely separate foundation myths. Fitting them together obviously posed a problem for mythographers; Pherekydes puts Amphion and Zethos first and then follows with Kadmos (3F41d), but the more usual solution was to suppose Antiope's sons the authors of a refounding of the city during some convenient break in the line of Kadmos. Such an expedient is scarcely what the original stories intended, but since like the mythographers we must begin somewhere, we will follow the lead of this latter arrangement.

In chapter 6 we found, as part of the line of Io from Inachos, quite conflicting traditions about the father of Europa, who is sometimes Agenor and sometimes Phoinix. Presumably Kadmos is always her brother, or at least a relative (why else would he set out to search for her?), but our first actual mention of his lineage is in Pherekydes, where he is the son of Agenor and half-brother of Phoinix (3F21), while our first specific acknowledgment of Europa and Kadmos as sister and brother appears in Hellanikos, if this part of a scholiast's summary does derive from that author (4F51: both siblings are children of Phoinix). To Kadmos' one appearance in the *Odyssey* noted above (as Ino's father: 5.333) we can add that he marries Harmonia at the end of the *Theogony* (937, 975–78: Semele, Ino, and three other children named), and is again Semele's father in *Homeric Hymn* 7. Of his own exploits, however, there is not a word in Hesiod, and he is entirely absent from what remains of the *Ehoiai*. Almost certainly he played a role in Stesichoros' lost *Europeia*, for our one surviving reference says that Athena sowed the dragon's teeth (195 *PMG*). Pausanias also speaks on several occasions of another Europa poem, often ascribed to Eumelos, which must have covered a considerable territory, since Amphion and Zethos are treated, but he never mentions it when discussing Kadmos himself (9.5.8). Of more uncertain origin and date is the remark (by a scholiast) that Mousaios in a *Titanographia* (?) related how Kadmos followed the cow from Delphi (2B1). From these scant crumbs we are, I think, entitled to conclude that the tale of Kadmos' founding of Thebes was probably well known in the seventh and sixth centuries (if not earlier), and has escaped fuller presentation only through chance.

Nevertheless, the full details of the story do not survive before the fifth century and Pherekydes. From three different references we see that the Athenian mythographer must have related most if not all of the familiar events at Thebes preceding the founding: Kadmos slays the dragon with a sword (3F88), whereupon Ares and Athena give him half the teeth (the other half go to Aietes) and he sows the ground with them at Ares' direction (3F22). Armed men then spring up out of the earth, causing Kadmos in fear to throw a stone at them. Thinking to be attacked by each other, they turn to mutual slaughter, until only five—Oudaios, Chthonios, Echion, Pelor, and Hyperenor—remain, and these become the foundation of the city. Such details give us most of the basic story, at least in outline. Pindar, although he mentions Kadmos only in connection with his daughters, does several times name the Spartoi, that is, the sown men (*Py* 9.82–83; *Is* 1.30; 7.10; fr 29 SM), and Aischylos in the *Hepta* calls the Theban defender Melanippos one of these same Spartoi, spared by Ares (*Hepta* 412–13). But the founding seems not to have been dramatized in tragedy—Euripides' *Kadmos* most likely concerned later misfortunes—and our first consecutive account derives from an *Iliad* scholion that claims both Hellanikos and Apollodoros as sources (ΣA *Il* 2.494 = 4F51).[1] Here, suspending for the moment judgment on authorship, we find that after Europa, daughter of Phoinix, has been kidnapped from Sidon, her brother Kadmos is sent out to find her. Failing in this, he goes to Delphi, and is advised not to interfere in the matter of Europa, but rather to make use of the cow-guide and found a city wherever she should stop to rest. He of course follows this advice, and travels through Phokis until he encounters a suitable cow that leads him through all of Boiotia before sinking to the ground. Wishing to sacrifice the cow to Athena, Kadmos sends his men to fetch water from the spring of Aretias, but a dragon guarding the place kills a number of them. Kadmos in his turn kills the dragon, and on Athena's advice sows the teeth, thus producing the earth-born men. The dragon, however, is somehow sacred to Ares, and the god in anger wishes to destroy Kadmos; Zeus intervenes to save him. As a result Kadmos is given Harmonia, daughter of Ares and Aphrodite, to wife, but must first perform menial service for a year as atonement for the dragon's death. All the gods and the Mousai attend the wedding, and each brings to Harmonia a gift.

To this detailed but uncertainly attested account we can add from other scholia the facts (definitely Hellanikian) that Kadmos killed the dragon with a stone (4F96), that he sowed the teeth by the will of Ares, and that five men *alone* (with the same names as in Pherekydes) sprang up out of the ground; thus here there was no combat (4F1). But how much of the *Iliad* 2.494 scholion as a whole might derive from Hellanikos remains uncertain. Apollodoros, the second author cited by that scholion, has in fact the first part of its text in almost the same words (Ap*B* 3.4.1–2), leaving us to suspect that (as often) the scholiast has gone directly to that source for a good deal of his information. But Apollodoros then turns to Pherekydes (whom he names) and other sources for the battle among the Spartoi, a battle not mentioned by the scholiast and explicitly not a part of Hellanikos' version. Since the scholiast has here (if not before) surely utilized a source drawn from Hellanikos, we may well wonder if the subsequent details of his account—Ares' anger, Zeus' intervention, Kadmos' servitude to Ares and marriage to Harmonia—are not likewise derived from that author, even if they also appear (minus Zeus' explicit role) in Apollodoros.[2] Elsewhere in Hellanikos, there is admittedly one small detail seemingly in conflict, namely that Harmonia is a daughter of Elektra and Zeus, rather than Ares and Aphrodite (4F23); but here too we remain uncertain of authorship, since that (unusual) genealogy is in the scholiast source only preceded and followed by references to Hellanikos.

Several plays of Euripides also dealt with pieces of the legend. The prologue to his lost *Phrixos B* (spoken by Ino?) begins with a description of why Kadmos came from Phoinicia to Thebes; alas the quote breaks off before we learn why (fr 819 N[2]). In the *Herakles* we find as in Aischylos the idea that Ares saved a few of the Spartoi to populate Thebes (*HF* 4–7); the same play later suggests that Ares himself sowed the teeth after he had taken them from the dragon's jaws (*HF* 252–53). And in the *Phoinissai* the chorus provides a rapid survey of the major events: Tyrian Kadmos following the cow as the oracle has commanded until it falls to earth and signals the place of settlement; Ares' dragon guarding the spring, and Kadmos slaying it with a rock when he comes for water; then the sowing of the teeth (by Athena's command) and the combat of the resulting warriors (*Pho* 638–44, 657–75). Further on in the drama, Teiresias tells Kreon that his son Menoikeus must die if Thebes is to be saved, and as reason for this cites Ares' continued anger over Kadmos' slaying of the dragon (*Pho* 931–44). Kreon and his sons are the last of the pure line of the Spartoi, the men born of the dragon's teeth, and thus the lot falls to them. Herodotos contributes to all this only the more historical detail that Kadmos stopped at Kalliste/Thera on his journey from Phoinicia, and there left his friend Membliaros and others to colonize the island (Hdt 4.147).

From all these sources we obtain a remarkably consistent tradition; the one major variant is Hellanikos' notion that only five Spartoi were born, and thus that no fight took place. By contrast the combat is clearly recognized in Pherekydes, Aischylos, and Euripides, and the extreme brevity of Aischylos' reference shows that it must be older than his *Hepta*. Still somewhat unclear, however, is Ares' role in the sowing and his response to the death of the dragon. Our summary of Pherekydes shows that there Athena and Ares give Kadmos the teeth together, and Ares directs the sowing. Hellanikos adds that this sowing was by the will of Ares; the attribution in ΣA *Il* 2.494 of it to the advice of Athena might mean (if this is also from Hellanikos) that she conveyed to Kadmos Ares' demands (or proposed to Ares this course of action). But either way the god's participation suggests that the sowing was an atonement for the dragon's death, that is, a way of assuring that Kadmos' new city would not exclude the previous powers inhabiting that site. Puzzling if that is true is the *Iliad* scholia's belief that Ares was angry *after* the sowing and that Zeus had then to intervene. Possibly neither Pherekydes nor Hellanikos included this detail or the subsequent servitude to Ares. But more likely, I think, the scholiast has slightly confused the order of events, and sowing, servitude, and marriage are all part of a single settlement worked out by Athena, if not by Zeus. Euripides' statement in the *Herakles* that Ares himself sows the teeth gives us no real clue to the god's motives; the same is true for Stesichoros, where Athena does the sowing.

In art we have only a little evidence. Our earliest illustration is probably a Lakonian cup of the mid-sixth century now in the Louvre; on it a warrior with helmet, shield, and spear attacks a serpent that has twisted itself around a column of a shrine or fountain house and rears itself up to strike (Louvre E669). Most often this is taken to represent Achilleus at the fountain house where he will ambush Troilos,[3] but without Troilos present it is hard to see how customers would recognize the story, unless a preliminary encounter with a snake was a standard part of the literary tradition. We will see in chapter 16 that a snake does in fact appear with Achilleus in several artistic representations of the ambush, but never as an object of Achilleus' concern. More likely then, our painter intended to show this deed of Kadmos, although in the absence of additional figures (other than animals) our understanding of the story is not much improved. The same must be said for a Red-Figure cup by Apollodoros in Tarquinia where a warrior draws his sword to strike a snake (RC 1123); here, without any fountain house to provide backdrop, even the supposition of a myth is dubious.

More helpful, and clearly showing the story in question, are two vases of the mid-fifth century in New York.[4] On one, a calyx krater near the style of the Niobid Painter, we see Kadmos starting back in alarm, one hand holding a water jug and the other with a stone poised to throw (NY 07.286.66). The object of his apprehension is presumably the snake that rears up before him, but it emerges from behind a seated woman who reclines quite calmly. The scene is flanked to either side by Athena (left, with Kadmos) and Ares; neither looks at all alarmed, although that may be more the style of the painting than a narrative detail. The other pot, a bell krater, has Kadmos approaching cautiously (this time with spears and hydria); the snake now rises up over the head of the woman (NY 22.139.11). The identity of this woman has occasioned some uncertainty. Harmonia is one possibility, but the figure seems too closely linked to the snake for that to be possible, and probably we should imagine some divinity of the spring (or else a proleptic personification of Thebes herself, as on a late-fifth-century hydria where names are given and Thebe is one of several divinities present: Berlin:Lost F2634). In any case, both these kraters reaffirm the idea that Kadmos went to the spring for water, and the rock that he uses as a weapon on the calyx krater is that which we found in Euripides' *Phoinissai*. But the exact role played by the gods continues to be obscure. Given the range of variation in our evidence, it may be that the nature of their participation, beyond helping Kadmos, was not firmly fixed in the earliest versions.

Later literary sources have little to add on this or any other point; Ovid gives the fullest account (with a blood-curdling description of the dragon) but omits Ares altogether, so that Athena alone counsels the sowing (*Met* 3.1–137). A scholion to the *Phoinissai* does offer an eighteen-line hexameter version of the oracle given by Delphi to Kadmos, in which we learn that the cow was to have a white mark like the circle of the moon on each side of its back (Σ *Pho* 638). In general, all our late sources that narrate the story of the founding give the standard details, including the combat among the Spartoi; Hellanikos remains alone in suggesting that there were only five Spartoi to begin with. Likewise, Hellanikos (or at least ΣA *Il* 2.494) and Apollodoros are the only preserved sources to report a period of servitude by Kadmos as penance for killing Ares' dragon.

We saw above that as early as the end of the *Theogony* Kadmos receives Harmonia, daughter of Ares and Aphrodite, to wife (*Th* 937), but no writer ever explains why he was honored in this way (ΣA *Il* 2.494 does suggest that it was somehow part of the reconciliation with Ares). We should note in this regard that Harmonia, although her parentage should make her a full-fledged divinity, never quite achieves the status of Thetis. On the contrary, writers generally seem to imagine her growing old with Kadmos in normal domestic tranquility, her godhood somehow forgotten in the process. Theognis notes that the Mousai and the Charites attended the wedding (15–18), and Pindar compares the two marriages, that of Thetis and that of Harmonia, as occasions on which the gods honored men with their presence (*Py* 3.86–96). In art the wedding was shown on the Amyklai Throne (Paus 3.18.12: the gods bring gifts), and the happy couple appears in a chariot on a fifth-century Black-Figure neck-amphora (Louvre CA 1961: names provided),[5] but regrettably nothing survives to match the splendor of Thetis' wedding as we see it in the works of Sophilos and Kleitias. The *Iliad* scholia state, however, that all the gods brought gifts, and Diodoros provides a list of these, including the necklace that will play such a large role in the future history of the race (DS 5.49.1). Here Diodoros makes it a gift from Athena (together with a peplos); earlier he had described it as a present from Aphrodite (DS 4.65.5). In Apollodoros, Kadmos himself makes the presentation, the necklace having been fashioned by Hephaistos (ApB 3.4.2). But as we saw in chapter 6, Apollodoros found in Pherekydes the idea that Kadmos acquired the necklace not from Hephaistos but from Europa, who got it from Zeus (3F89). Presumably this is the gift referred to as given to Europa by Zeus in the *Ehoiai* after they have arrived on Krete (Hes fr 141 MW). Presumably, too, Pherekydes did not have Europa leave Krete to find her brother, but prevailed upon Zeus or one of the other gods to deliver the present. Whatever the route of transmission, the necklace is clearly always of divine manufacture, and thus a prized heirloom for future generations. Only Statius offers the idea that Hephaistos made the necklace as a source of evils for Harmonia and her descendants, in revenge for Aphrodite's adultery with Ares; in addition to Harmonia herself, he names Semele, Iokaste, Argeia, and of course Eriphyle among those who suffered from it (St: *Theb* 2.265–305, followed by VM I 151 [citing Statius] and VM II 78).

The end of the *Theogony* lists five children of the union of Kadmos and Harmonia, four daughters, Ino, Semele, Agaue, and Autonoe, and a son Polydoros (*Th* 975–78). No later author rejects any of these or makes further additions; we will return to their misfortunes in the following sections. As for Kadmos' final fate, after so much disaster in his family, Pindar places him on the Isles of the Blessed, with Peleus, Achilleus, and others (*Ol* 2.78). Euripides does not contradict this, but does provide via Dionysos (in the *Bakchai*) a startling prediction about his old age: the god ordains that he and Harmonia will be changed into snakes, and that at the head of a vast army (driving an ox-cart) they will sack many cities, until they come to their defeat in assaulting the oracle of Apollo (*Bkch* 1330–39). But Ares will then save them and transport them to the land of the Blessed. This revelation stands in our text immediately after a substantial lacuna (perhaps fifty lines), and thus whatever preceded the metamorphosis (obviously an exile of some sort) has been lost. But both the speech itself and Kadmos' response to it (*Bkch* 1354–60) establish that he and his wife will become snakes *before* they lead barbarian hordes back into Greece, bizarre as this notion may seem. One wonders, too, if they will remain snakes when they go to the land of the Blessed (surely not). The lost *Kadmos* of Euripides might have dealt with these matters, and thus paved the way for the *Bakchai*, although here too such events would probably have to be covered by prediction. Apollonios notes that Kadmos and Harmonia are buried in the country of the Encheleis, in Illyria (AR 4.517–18), and Apollodoros agrees that this was their place of exile (ApB 3.5.4). But Apollodoros is not prepared to accept their snake transformation until after their further deeds are accomplished; thus in human form they are chosen leaders of the Encheleis in their battle against the Illyrioi, and Kadmos even begets another son, Illyrios. Only at the close of their lives do they become serpents before being sent by Zeus to the Elysian Fields.

Ovid, too, makes the metamorphosis the climactic event of their existence, as we might expect; in his account Kadmos, tired after long wandering (no battles or kingship are mentioned) thinks of the snake he slew at Thebes, and prays that if the gods are angry with him for this they might turn him into a snake (*Met* 4.563–603). They do so, and as he curls himself up in Harmonia's lap she also is transformed; they slither off together. Hyginus develops this notion of divine anger further by stating that Ares destroyed Kadmos' children for that reason; the additional point that he and Harmonia become snakes *may* imply the same cause (*Fab* 6). Elsewhere Hyginus offers a story not otherwise known, that Agaue in her wanderings came to Illyria and married the king Lykotherses, then slew him so that she might give the kingdom to her father Kadmos (*Fab* 184, 240, 254). That Kadmos came to Illyria in his old age seems well enough agreed upon by everyone. The snake motif is more puzzling, but may go back to some dimly remembered ancestor worship of our hero himself or his divine wife.[6]

Semele and Ino

Kadmos' most famous daughter Semele, like her sister Ino, is already known to Homer, for Zeus in *Iliad* 14 reminds us that she is the mother of his son Dionysos (*Il* 14.323–25). To be fair, Zeus does not actually call her a daughter of Kadmos, but he does place her with Alkmene in Thebes, and the inference as to her father is very likely. The end of the *Theogony* gives us the first explicit statement of her origins, as we saw above, and also recognizes the unusual circumstances attending the child she conceives: although mortal she gave birth to Dionysos, an immortal, and subsequently obtained divine status herself (*Th* 940–42). In *Homeric Hymn* 1, despite a large gap in the text,[7] we learn first of the different locales where Semele is thought to have delivered the god, and are then informed that these are all erroneous, since Zeus was the one to bring the child to birth (on Mount Nysa). The author of the poem clearly intends to say more on the subject, but unfortunately this is where the lacuna occurs, and when the text resumes Zeus is just finishing a prophecy. In the remains of this Hymn, Dionysos is three times called *eiraphiôtês*, a word debated even in antiquity (see ΣA *Il* 1.39). If it derives from *rhaptô*, "to sew," or could have been thought to do so by our poet, it could refer to the idea that Dionysos was sewn up in Zeus' thigh. On the other hand, we must admit that the whole tale of the sewing might have been invented (at whatever point) to explain an otherwise obscure epithet. What we can say for certain is that as early as this Hymn there is something unusual about Dionysos' birth, and that he does seem to be brought forth from some portion of his father's anatomy. The poem also offers at its close the first occurrence of Semele's other name, Thyone.

Unfortunately little else is said about Semele in the rest of the seventh and sixth centuries. Tyrtaios mentions her, but the fragment is from a papyrus, and there is no usable context (20 W). Sappho in a similar fragment names Thyone, almost certainly as the mother of Dionysos, when the god is being invoked together with Hera and Zeus (17 LP). In art, Semele appears together with Dionysos (both named) on a charming Black-Figure cup by the Kallis Painter in Naples; only the heads are shown, and mother and son look at each other intensely as he holds up a kantharos (Naples Stg 172). The two are also found on a hydria in Berlin, from the Leagros Group, with Dionysos entering a chariot while his mother watches; here she is named both Semele and Thyone (Berlin: Lost F1904). Finally, Dionysos and a woman named only as Thyone stand behind the chariot of Peleus and Thetis on another late sixth-century hydria in Florence (3790). In addition to these three vases, there are quite a number of other Black-Figure examples in which Dionysos is shown with an unnamed woman in a chariot setting or the like, and some of these have even been interpreted as the bringing-up from Hades of Semele. But, of course, any such pairing could as easily represent Dionysos and Ariadne, or perhaps even more likely Dionysos and a goddess, such as Aphrodite: we must remember that the god of wine is a staple feature of generic/metaphoric scenes in art, and his appearance with Aphrodite would well illustrate the pleasures of the grape combined with those of love.[8] In any case, such uncertainty should prevent us from drawing any firm conclusions about stories present or not present in the sixth century.

From the first half of the fifth century we have several useful references in Pindar, and what must have been a very detailed treatment in Aischylos' *Semele*, which was possibly part of a larger connected production. In *Olympian* 2, composed for Theron of Akragas in 476 B.C., we find note of the sufferings of the daughters of Kadmos balanced against the greater blessings that Semele and Ino ultimately obtained (*Ol* 2.22–27). In the case of Semele this means that "dying in the blast of the thunderbolt she lives among the Olympians, and Pallas loves her always, and Zeus the father exceedingly, and her son the ivy-bearer." This is, surprisingly, our first concrete evidence for the manner of Semele's death, although something out of the ordinary has already been guaranteed by the fact that in *Homeric Hymn* 1 Zeus must bear the child. The opening of *Pythian* 11 confirms that Semele is to be found among the gods (*Py* 11.1), while *Pythian* 3, after observing again the misfortunes of Kadmos' daughters, offers the consolation that at least Zeus came to the bed of Thyone, here too clearly Semele (*Py* 3.96–99).

Aischylos' play or plays on the subject are surrounded by intriguing plot possibilities and major controversies.[9] The one certain fragment of any use is a single line: "Zeus, who killed him" (fr 221 R). The context of this sparse quote is a discussion of linguistic forms, so that we derive no help there, and cannot even be sure that the thought is relevant to the action of the play. If it is, then Dionysos himself, mistakenly believed to have perished with his mother, is one candidate for the victim; I believe, however, that there is another likelier figure, to be discussed below. Turning for the moment to a still more crucial problem, we find that Plato in Book 2 of the *Republic* complains of (among other things) playwrights who bring Hera onstage disguised as a temple priestess and collecting alms for the "life-giving children of the Argive river Inachos" (*Rep* 2.381d = fr 168 R). The same line and its predecessor are cited by the scholia to Aristophanes' *Batrachoi* 1344, with the added information that Asklepiades attributed these lines to Aischylos' *Xantriai*. From other sources we know that the *Xantriai* contained at least a reference to the death of Pentheus (fr 172b R), and very likely dramatized that event (see below). That Hera would have a role in such a play is surprising, although there is always the possibility that she stirred up Pentheus or the chorus against the worship of Dionysos. But at this point we encounter a remarkable coincidence: the later sources that recount in full Semele's story—Diodoros, Apollodoros, Ovid, Hyginus—are unanimous in stating that she met her doom because she was deceived by Hera, and Ovid and Hyginus specify that this came about through Hera's transforming of herself into Semele's nurse Beroe (references below). If this last detail is not exactly what we find in Aischylos, it does seem clear that the standard run of the tale made Hera in disguise offer the fatal suggestion to her husband's paramour. Assuming this was the case in Aischylos' *Semele* as well (someone after all must make the suggestion), we can hardly avoid the thought that Asklepiades has miscited the source of his information, and that Aischylos' disguised temple priestess is indeed from the *Semele*.

Furthering this suspicion is an Oxyrhynchus papyrus fragment containing these same lines about Hera and giving us what precedes and follows (POxy 2164; text in Radt's fr 168). We do not learn as much as we would like, but the chorus, in speaking just prior to Hera's entrance, mentions Semele (twice) and Kadmos; thus the play was surely part of a Semele/Thebes trilogy. Hera herself after her opening lines continues to speak of the daughters of Inachos, but in connection with marriage, modest brides, the begetting of children, and the marriage bed, which all sounds like a veiled attack on Semele's adulterous relationship with Zeus rather than a diatribe against Dionysos. On balance I would argue that the motif of a Hera in disguise in order to bring Semele to disaster is probably as early as this play. For the rest of the work we know with certainty only that Aischylos brought Semele on stage pregnant and divinely inspired, and that those women who touched her belly became inspired as well (p. 335 R). The drama's alternate title *Hydrophoroi* ("Watercarriers") might refer to water being brought for the expected delivery, or simply to a general occupation of the chorus.

Sophokles' play *Hydrophoroi* may or may not have dealt with the same topic as that of Aischylos; nothing survives. The latter state of affairs holds as well for a comic *Semele* by Eubolos and a poem, *The Birthpangs of Semele*, by Timotheos, and for several fourth-century tragic efforts. But Euripides does assure us in the prologue to the *Bakchai* (spoken by Dionysos himself) that Semele was consumed by lightning as she gave birth to the god, and that Hera's *hybris* (an odd word here) against her was the cause (*Bkch* 1–9). A fragment of the same playwright's *Antigone* addresses the god as the child of Dione, apparently in a conflation with Thyone (fr 177 N²). And the scholiast who cites the line also suggests that in Panyasis Thyone was Dionysos' nurse, someone distinct from Semele (Σ *Py* 3.117 = fr 8 *PEG*); the line quoted as evidence does not quite prove that (unless a *trophos* could never be one's mother), but of course our citer had access to the rest of the poem.

Of later (and fuller) accounts the earliest is that of Diodoros, who assigns in two separate places two different motives for the misfortune. In the first of these Hera comes to Semele in the guise of one of her friends, and goads her to seek honor equal to that of Zeus' wife (DS 3.64.3–4). In the second version Hera does not appear at all; instead Semele herself becomes distressed because Zeus does not speak to her when he visits, and thinking herself despised she asks him to come to her bed as he does to that of Hera (DS 4.2.2–3). Zeus therefore arrives for their lovemaking with his lightning and thunder. Semele perishes in the fire, having delivered her child prematurely, and Zeus gives the baby to Hermes to convey to the Nymphai of Nysa. This is our first clear explanation of the accidental nature of Semele's death by the thunderbolt; very early accounts *might* have been different. In Ovid, as we noted, Hera initiates the catastrophe in the guise of Semele's Epidaurian nurse Beroe (*Met* 3.256–315). Thus concealed, she causes Semele to doubt that her lover really is Zeus, and encourages her to seek proof. Semele extorts from Zeus an oath to grant her an unnamed request, much as Phaethon does from Helios, then makes the same wish as in Diodoros. Zeus brings his very lightest, tamest bolts, but the effect is still too much for the expectant mother. Apollodoros gives the same general account, but limits himself to noting that Semele was deceived by Hera into making her request, and died of fright when seeing the lightning and thunderbolts being hurled (Ap*B* 3.4.3).

Hyginus, like Ovid, has Hera visit Semele in the form of the nurse Beroe; here, however, the suggested motive for the request is so that Semele may know the greater pleasure of lying in love with a god (*Fab* 167, 179). Hyginus also records as we saw in chapter 2 the idea that Zeus took the pulverized remains of the heart of the god (Liber, i.e., Dionysos/Zagreus) born to him from Persephone and gave them to Semele in a potion, from which she conceived the second Dionysos (*Fab* 167: see Appendix A). Finally, a variant account of Semele's delivery may be preserved on a late-fifth-century Red-Figure hydria now in Berkeley: Semele herself lies (eyes closed) on a bed in the center, while Hermes to the left carries the child away, apparently forestalling Iris (winged cap, kerykeion) who approaches from the right for the same purpose; behind her stands a taller woman with scepter who will surely be Hera, as from above a thunderbolt descends (Berkeley 8.3316). If Zeus' wife did plot to steal away the child herself, the idea has not survived elsewhere. This seemingly normal birth of a viable child might also seem to preclude the second birth from Zeus' thigh, a detail hinted at in *Homeric Hymn* 1 and made fully explicit on several Red-Figure pots of the fifth century (see chapter 2).

We saw at the beginning of this section that both the end of the *Theogony* and Pindar recognize Semele as a mortal woman who becomes immortal and joins the gods on Olympos. Such a development seems obvious enough, given the status of her son; the Cyzicene Epigrams (*AP* 3.1), Diodoros (4.25.4), Apollodoros (Ap*B* 3.5.3), Plutarch (*Mor* 565f-566a), and Pausanias (2.31.2) all report that Dionysos actually went down into Hades and brought his mother up from the dead, an action paralleled only by that of Orpheus, albeit unsuc-cessfully. Diodoros adds that Dionysos renamed his mother Thyone on this occasion. The three Black-Figure cups cited earlier as showing Semele (named) and Dionysos together certainly reflect some such tradition for the sixth cen-tury. One might have hoped to see the actual fetching of Semele in art, but without further appearances of her name nothing presents itself very securely. The best candidate is probably a lip cup by the Xenokles Painter in London on which we see Dionysos and Hermes and women who could be Semele and Persephone (London B425). The other side of the cup shows Zeus, Poseidon, and probably Hades, which might encourage us to see the reverse as an Under-world scene, yet Ariadne or simply undefined goddesses are always possible. If Aischylos' *Semele* (or the trilogy of which it was part) has any kind of resolu-tion flattering to Zeus we must expect Semele's apotheosis to be predicted or narrated there, as compensation for her unhappy treatment by Hera. To me this seems extremely likely, but the question has much to do with one's general view of Aischylos' gods, and opinions will obviously vary.[10]

In all, Semele remains a unique figure, the only mortal woman to become the mother of a god, and a major one at that. She is also a rare example of a continuing sexual affair between god and mortal (as opposed to goddesses and mortals), although Apollo and Koronis might constitute another instance. Of course a continuing affair is necessary if she is to meet her fate as tradition describes it, and probably her destruction by thunderbolt was always an impor-tant part of her image, lending as it does an air of sacrality. The motif of the unwitting request plays its part in this, and has a folktale look about it, but we must still allow that in some early accounts Zeus might have intentionally slain Semele, as indeed Apollo slays Koronis. Diodoros actually cites a Naxian ver-sion to this effect, with Zeus wishing his son to be born from himself and not a mortal woman, so that he would be a god (DS 5.52.2). This seems unlikely to be early, given the close bond between Dionysos and Semele in our Archaic sources, but it does give an idea of the possibilities. Another (and darker) cause for Zeus' potential displeasure will emerge in the next section, when we look at Aktaion's fate. That Semele (like Koronis) miscomported herself and paid the penalty in some versions of the story is, of course, not impossible, and in that case Hera's jealousy might have been added as a later element to shift the blame for her fate. But on present evidence we have no reason to suppose that the goddess' role was not always a part of Semele's tale.

On the artistic side in this connection we should note a number of vases on which Zeus threatens a woman with a thunderbolt poised and ready to throw (e.g., London E313, by the Berlin Painter). Such a tableau has been taken by some to denote Zeus and Semele, and while it could scarcely represent the familiar story (where Zeus brings his thunderbolt only reluctantly), it might conceivably anticipate Diodoros' version noted above. But as we saw in chapter 6, on one such vase the female in question is named Aigina (NY 96.19.1), so that probably all of them represent that object of Zeus' affections.[11]

As for Ino, Semele's sister who in some accounts cares for the infant Dionysos, we have already surveyed the various myths about her and her husband Athamas in chapters 2 and 5. Here it may perhaps be repeated that, although she does appear in the *Odyssey* as the sea goddess Leukothea, Homer says nothing of what brought her to that pass. Pherekydes is our first source to make her a nurse of Dionysos, although Aischylos presumably dramatized a similar situation in his lost *Athamas*, with the consequent madness sent by Hera. For the other tales, of Ino as vanished first wife of Athamas come back to save her children, or second wife bent on destroying her stepchildren, we must await Euripides' *Ino* and two *Phrixos* plays, or rather our reconstruction of them based on Hyginus. The leap into the sea with Melikertes was apparently part of the *Ino*, and is mentioned (*sans* Melikertes) in the *Medeia*; it seems, however, already implied by the *Odyssey*, and Melikertes' death is in Pindar the origin of the Isthmian games. One emerges from these many different stories with a suspicion that Euripides (or perhaps Sophokles before him) took Ino from the basic tale in which she is driven mad by Hera and arbitrarily replaced other names with hers in myths about other wives of the multifaceted Athamas. In origin she would seem a counterpart to Semele in Hera's wrath against Dionysos; indeed Aischylos' *Athamas* and *Semele* may have been part of the same trilogy. Her ultimate fate as a sea goddess is certainly regarded by Pindar (and probably Homer) as a blessing; whether in all accounts it outweighed her suffering is more difficult to say.

Aktaion The fate of Aktaion, son of Autonoe (sister of Semele and Ino), follows logically enough here as part of the fortunes of the family, but we will also see that it is not completely separate from the tale of Semele herself. After Semele's union with Zeus the *Theogony* notes, for Autonoe alone of the three other daughters of Kadmos, a marriage, to Aristaios (*Th* 977); no children are given, and we cannot even be sure who this Aristaios was, although he may be the son of Apollo and Kyrene by that name. Our first encounter with offspring is in the *Ehoiai*, where according to a very fragmentary papyrus summary Aktaion son of Aristaios and Au[. . .] desires to marry someone whose name ends in -le (Hes fr 217A MW).[12] He suffers something at the hands of his grandfather (presumably Kadmos), is turned into a stag by the will of Artemis, and torn apart by his own dogs. The text is part of a series of capsule summaries of mythological figures suffering metamorphosis, with this particular summary attributed specifically to the *Ehoiai*. Unfortunately, given its brevity and the slight gap between Aktaion's desire for someone and his death, the motive behind Artemis' deed remains unclear. But other authors almost certainly help. Although Stesichoros rationalizes the affair slightly by saying that Artemis threw a deerhide over Aktaion to bring about his fate, he also says that she did this to prevent him from marrying Semele, thus giving us (surely) the name missing in the *Ehoiai* (236 PMG). Akousilaos probably completes the picture, for according to Apollodoros he offered as motive that Zeus was angry because

Aktaion was courting Semele (2F33). Possibly there are two different accounts here, with two different divinities holding center stage, but more likely the conflict is the same in both cases, and Zeus sends Artemis to eliminate Aktaion so that he may reserve Semele's favors to himself. Likely too, with so little room in the *Ehoiai* summary for a separate offense to Artemis (and no special reason to mention desire for Semele otherwise), that work also made Aktaion's relationship to his aunt the cause of his troubles.[13]

In the early fifth century, Phrynichos wrote an *Aktaion* attested only by the *Souda*; more intriguing are the remains of Aischylos' *Toxotides*, which dealt with the same subject. To judge by the title, the chorus of that play consisted of huntress attendants of Artemis, who are probably the ones to note that Aktaion never returns from a day's hunt without some quarry (fr 241 R). But other fragments turn us back to the question of maidens and marriage: Aktaion speaks something about glances and marriage beds (the text is very corrupt), then also says, "The blazing gaze of a young girl does not escape me, if she has tasted of a man; for such I have an experienced eye" (frr 242, 243 R). On the assumption that any chorus of huntresses, whether devotees of Artemis or not, will be virgins, we must suppose Aktaion's remark to be directed elsewhere. Nothing will prove that he is thinking of Semele, but if he desires marriage in this play, then here (as in the *Ehoiai*, Stesichoros, and Akousilaos) she is probably the object of his intentions, and we imagine that the affair with Zeus has already begun. Admittedly that is a great deal to assume; on the other hand, if the play revolves around any of the later-attested causes for Aktaion's demise his concern with young women here will be very hard to explain. To take speculation just one step further, the *Toxotides* and *Semele* may also have been part of a connected dramatic production, in which case issues raised in the first play could carry over into the second. In that regard we might then wonder if the line preserved from the *Semele*—"Zeus, who killed him"—does not refer to Aktaion, for whom Semele may or may not have cared. Whatever the case, the brutal removal of a rival would certainly seem to reflect badly on Zeus, as does the treatment of Semele in her play, for though Zeus may not cause her destruction he is ultimately responsible for it. We must remember, however, that Dionysos' birth is in question, and then too Aktaion's interests may have been directed more toward exposing Semele's shame than seeking her hand. In all, though we can say nothing with certainty, Aischylos' handling of this material seems likely to have agreed with that of his predecessors, and to constitute a version quite different from the one made familiar by Kallimachos and Ovid.

We will see shortly that there is an extensive artistic tradition, reaching back into the middle of the sixth century, on the subject of Aktaion's death, with Artemis virtually always in attendance. Certainly this material is of interest, but since it shows only that one phase of the story it does not help us much in establishing the whole narrative. At the end of the fifth century Euripides in the *Bakchai* offers a brief glimpse of other details: Aktaion is here torn apart by his dogs because he boasted to be better in the hunt than Artemis herself (*Bkch* 337–40). Fragment 241 R of the *Toxotides* has already emphasized Aktaion's hunting prowess in that play, and conceivably it was a dramatic issue for Aischylos. But the context of the *Bakchai* reference is Teiresias' advice to Pentheus after the latter has slighted Dionysos, and Euripides might very naturally have reshaped Aktaion's offense to conform to the point required. That the crime exactly parallels that of Agamemnon at Aulis in the *Kypria* could mean equally that it is old or that Euripides thought of the *Kypria* in inventing it.

Our more familiar tradition, that Aktaion (inadvertently) saw Artemis while the goddess was bathing, surfaces first in Kallimachos' *Hymn* 5, on the Bath of Pallas (5.107–18). In this poem Athena, who has just blinded Teiresias for a similar offense against her, tells his mother, Chariklo, to be grateful that he was not treated as Artemis did Aktaion. The parallelism between the two situations raises (obviously) the suspicion that Kallimachos might have invented the one for the sake of the other, but that cannot be proved, and in any case, since Teiresias' deed is related in far more detail, one might reasonably suppose his tale, not that of Aktaion, to be the innovation. For what it is worth, Apollodoros tells us that the bathing motif (rather than the courting of Semele) is the version of most authors (Ap*B* 3.4.4); very probably, then, it is older than the Hellenistic period. Our most famous description of the bath and Aktaion's subsequent fate is, of course, that of Ovid in the *Metamorphoses* (3.138–252). Somewhat different is Diodoros, who suggests that Aktaion actually desired to marry the goddess, having presented her with the fruits of his hunting,[14] or else (as in the *Bakchai*) that he claimed to be a better hunter than she (DS 4.81.4–5). Hyginus combines two of these ideas (or perhaps expands upon what Diodoros meant) by having Aktaion see Artemis while she is bathing and desire to violate her (*Fab* 180). We seem in all to have three main lines of thought: (1) that Aktaion angered Zeus by desiring a woman the god had appropriated to himself; (2) that he behaved outrageously toward Artemis in some way; and (3) that he innocently viewed the naked goddess. I have argued above that (1) is the most likely motif for Aischylos' *Toxotides*, but (2) might conceivably be possible, if the lines on marriage and maidens could refer to Artemis (does Aktaion mean that he wants the one woman who has assuredly tasted of no man?). Such aggressive hybris strikes me as difficult to make plausible on stage, although it would unquestionably be dramatic.

As for the artistic tradition, we find in all early cases the actual rending of Aktaion by his dogs, rather than any other part of the story, and the surrounding elements are less informative than we might expect. The earliest example, an Attic Black-Figure cup of the mid-sixth century, featured a running Aktaion attacked on all parts of his body by dogs; two women flank the scene (Lost: from Bomarzo). Two lekythoi from the end of the century offer the same composition (Athens 488, 489); others vary only in arming Aktaion with a sword or club. Such a detail may be artistic license, since a metamorphosed Aktaion would not hold any weapon. That he is in fact human in these paintings is only to be expected, given the need to make the scene comprehensible (and pathetic). All the same, if we remember that in Stesichoros Artemis envelops the hero in a deerskin, we may ask if there was not a general tradition in which the goddess simply made the dogs believe their master was a stag. A number of Attic Red-Figure pots of the early fifth century do show Aktaion wearing such a covering as the dogs attack, as does the famous metope from Temple E at Selinous (3921C). But it is hard to say whether these artists are expressing a literal mode of thought or simply trying to convey Aktaion's dual nature. Attempts of the latter sort unquestionably appear, beginning with a terracotta plaque of about 470 B.C. now in Reggio Calabria (4337). Here Aktaion actually has a stag's head; later efforts in the same direction will give him just the antlers and sometimes the ears.

One other detail found on occasion from the late fifth century on is the figure of Lyssa (Madness), so named on a bell krater by the Lykaon Painter of about 440 B.C. (Boston 00.346). She may represent either the madness of Aktaion as a stag, or perhaps that of the misguided dogs. Also on this krater is Zeus standing to the side observing. One is tempted to view such a scene as drawn from a tragic production, with Lyssa an onstage character (as in the *Herakles Mainomenos*) and Zeus relating his role in the slaying. It must be admitted, however, that this is a completely isolated instance of Zeus' presence, and if Semele was involved, one might have expected her to be portrayed. Indeed, the central role of Artemis in every representation of Akataion's story, often in complete isolation with her victim, does seem to suggest that she was originally more important to the story than the Stesichoros-Akousilaos version would imply. The bath is completely absent in art before Kallimachos, but it would be a bold artist who undertook to show her nude (or even disrobing) in Archaic or Classical times; thus this absence may not be very significant.[15] We are left, on the whole, with a good many unanswered questions regarding Aktaion's complicity in the events that caused his doom.[16]

Agaue and Pentheus

Neither Agaue's marriage nor her son is mentioned at all in our literary sources prior to the fifth century, although Pentheus and one Galene (named) do appear on a Red-Figure psykter by Euphronios; the subject is, as we might expect, Pentheus' *sparagmos* (Boston 10.221). The earliest known narration of the tale occurs in one or more lost plays of Aischylos—the *Pentheus*, *Xantriai*, and *Bakchai*. Of these titles we know almost nothing, save the claim (in Aristophanes of Byzantium's hypothesis to Euripides' *Bakchai*) that the story had already been told in the *Pentheus*. Strictly speaking, that might seem to eliminate the other two titles from consideration here, but with Aischylos the connected trilogy form is always a likelihood, and a scholion to *Eumenides* 26 notes that in the *Xantriai* Pentheus' death occurred on Mount Kithairon. By itself this might be a chance reference in a play on another topic; yet if the entire story of Pentheus was told in Aischylos' *Pentheus*, we might expect our scholiast to think of and cite that work, not an unrelated one. More likely the chorus of the *Xantriai* ("Carders") "carded" Pentheus by tearing him apart, and we are dealing with a group production whose third element was probably the *Bakchai* (although nothing whatever is known of that play, and *Semele* is frequently included instead).[17] If that is right, then Aristophanes in citing one title really meant a whole trilogy, and Aischylos extended the story of Pentheus to some length. Even so, we understand virtually nothing of how the narrative might have been handled. The remark of the Pythia in the *Eumenides* which gave rise to the scholion is simply to the effect that Dionysos led out *(estratê-gêsen)* the Bakchai, contriving for Pentheus "death as for a rabbit."

From about 510 B.C. comes the Red-Figure psykter by Euphronios with women pulling at the upper body of Pentheus (named); named too as one of the women is Galene (Boston 10.221). Slightly later is a hydria with women holding various limbs and the head (Berlin:Ch Inv 1966.18), and then (perhaps contemporary with Aischylos) several more such Red-Figure pots, including a stamnos by the Berlin Painter (Oxford 1912.1165). As in the case of Aktaion, these and subsequent efforts concentrate almost entirely on the rending, and thus contribute little to our notions of how the story progressed. For what it is worth, however, we should note that nowhere prior to Euripides do we find Agaue and her sisters specifically named or shown as agents of the deed.

Before Euripides' version came certainly that of Xenokles (winner in 415 B.C. with a *Bakchai*), and probably also that of Sophokles' son Iophon. But the preserved *Bakchai* constitutes our first real narration of the story. Here Dionysos returns to the scene of his birth, intent on vengeance against those who besmirched his mother's name, that is, Semele's sisters, who claimed that Zeus' thunderbolt destroyed her for falsely naming him as her child's father. Accordingly, all the Theban women have been driven mad (or inspired, at least) and sent out to the hills, while Dionysos prepares to confront the skepticism of Pentheus. The latter is presented as the son of Agaue and Echion, who already in Pherekydes was one of the original five Spartoi (3F22). What has happened to Echion, or where he has gone, we do not hear; Pentheus is clearly in charge of the city of Thebes, and determined to eradicate completely the presumed perversion of Dionysiac worship. Some of the Theban women are captured, but their bonds do not hold them, and when Pentheus applies the same treatment to Dionysos (who is disguised as one of the god's devotees) the whole palace collapses. More crucial to the drama, in the exchanges between Pentheus and the god we see the emergence of the former's repressed sexual conflicts, now channeled into voyeurism and intense longing for the very licentiousness he has condemned. Playing on his desire to infiltrate the ecstasies of the Theban women (including his own mother), Dionysos entices him into a Mainad's costume, then takes him out to the hills alone so that he might spy on the supposed orgies. But when he has gained his perch high in a fir tree the god betrays him to the women, who surround the tree and uproot it. Agaue here takes the lead in tearing her son apart; in the play's finale she appears on stage with his head, boasting of her hunting of a great lion. Only gradually with Kadmos' help does she perceive the truth, before Dionysos enters to announce final punishments for all those who doubted his divinity. Agaue must go into exile, and even Kadmos, as we saw before, will have to leave Thebes, ultimately to be metamorphosed into a snake. Pentheus' own ill-assumed arrogance, plus the hypocrisy of his professed morality, seems ample justification for his wretched fate, which is after all the heart of the story. But the harsh treatment of other members of the family reveals a surprisingly grim Dionysos; we can only speculate on whether this was Euripides' conception alone, or that of Aischylos or other playwrights before him, just as we must speculate on whether mother and aunts previously participated in the *sparagmos*.

Other evidence of this time or later rarely departs from the narrative line set down by Euripides. A number of pots show Pentheus arrayed for hunting or actually armed for battle as he sets out to capture the raving women. If any of them could be dated to (or soon after) the time of Aischylos we might suspect that this was the version of his plays; as it is, they are end of the century at best, leaving us uncertain of the origin of such an idea. Possibly artists simply developed the logic of the situation into an appropriate scene, with Pentheus' basic hostility thus portrayed. Apollodoros tells the story very briefly, and with nothing new: Pentheus tries to hinder the worship of Dionysos and goes out to Kithairon to spy on the women; Agaue tears him apart thinking him a quarry (ApB 3.5.2). Ovid offers a lengthy account, but the bulk of it is the tale of Dionysos and the sailors as told by the captured Acoctes (Dionysos?); only at the end of *Metamorphoses* 3 does Pentheus charge out to confront the enemy (how we are not told) and meet his usual fate at Agaue's hands while spying on the women (*Met* 3.511–733). Neither of these writers considers at all the plight of Agaue herself. In Hyginus we have already seen that she abandons Thebes for Illyria, where she marries the king Lykotherses and later kills him (to help her father: *Fab* 184, 240, 254). One other story about her surfaces only in the Second Vatican Mythographer, who says that her scorn for Dionysos was such that climbing a tree she lay in ambush for him with a weapon (VM II 83). The text then shifts to Pentheus, and we are left to supply the outcome. In all, it does seem true that Pentheus' transvestitism and deception by Dionysos appears only in Euripides (and much later Nonnos: 46.81–127). With relatively few later accounts, however, this may be mere coincidence.

*Antiope,
Amphion,
and Zethos* On two occasions the *Bakchai* tells us that Kadmos handed over his throne to Pentheus, the son of his daughter Agaue, while at no time does the play ever mention Polydoros, the son of Kadmos attested by the end of the *Theogony*. This Polydoros does, however, reappear toward the end of the fifth century: in Herodotos, Sophokles' *Oidipous Tyrannos*, and Euripides' *Phoinissai* he is son of Kadmos and father of the Labdakos who will father Laios (Hdt 5.59; *OT* 267–68; *Pho* 5–9). Diodoros at one point implies that he accompanied Kadmos into exile, for in that writer he returns to claim the throne after the death of

the Niobidai (DS 19.53.5). But this is as much as we ever hear about the details of his life. Pausanias seems to suggest that he was king when Pentheus met his fate (9.5.3); in Apollodoros he marries Nykteis, daughter of Nykteus, the son of Chthonios (another of the original Spartoi), and the child is again Labdakos (ApB 3.5.5). The father-in-law Nykteus is for Apollodoros the same as the Nykteus who with his brother Lykos provides the background for Euripides' lost *Antiope*, and Antiope in turn will lead us to Amphion and Zethos, the second founders of Thebes.

We saw in chapter 6 that this role of the brothers is as old as the *Nekuia* (*Od* 11.260–65), although in that work Antiope is the daughter of Asopos. Apparently there was a tradition that saw no need to link her to a current ruling house in Thebes (as in Pherekydes, where her children founded Thebes *before* Kadmos?), and which perhaps knew nothing of her problems with her father or uncle. In the *Kypria*, however, we read that Nestor's digressions included the tale of Epopeus' ruin (probably the sack of his city) after he had seduced the daughter of Lykourgos (error for Lykos?: p. 40 *PEG*). We will see shortly that this cryptic summary is probably relevant, the daughter in question being Antiope, although elsewhere her father is always Nykteus. To complicate matters, Apollodoros, having first made Nykteus a son of the sown man Chthonios, later offers a different ancestry in which the father and uncle (Nykteus and Lykos) are *not* descended from the Spartoi, but are the children of Hyrieus, who in turn is the son of Poseidon and the Atlantid Alkyone (ApB 3.10.1). This latter tradition seems also to have invaded the previous one, for even in ApB 3.5.5, where Nykteus is sprung from Chthonios, he and his brother arrive at Thebes (from Euboia [or Boiotia?] by way of Hyria, after killing Phlegyas), and settle there because of the friendship of Pentheus. Apollodoros may mean us to understand that they moved away from Thebes at some earlier point, but more likely he has conflated different traditions. Whatever the case, Lykos is in this first version chosen regent by the Thebans (presumably after the death of Pentheus). As for Labdakos, who might reasonably have been expected to succeed to the throne, Apollodoros tells us that he perished also, thinking the same sort of thoughts as Pentheus. The exact meaning of this sinister phrase is not explained, and no other author clarifies it. Pausanias relates a slightly different story in which Nykteus receives the rule as regent for a very young Labdakos; he then dies in the course of the Antiope story and leaves the office to Lykos, who invests Labdakos with it when the latter comes of age (9.5.4–5). But Labdakos himself dies soon after, and Lykos then becomes regent for the son Laios.

In one manner or other, then, our later sources put the line of Kadmos aside for the moment, and the way is cleared for Antiope and her children to hold center stage. Her tale, or at least its latter phases, was dramatized as we saw by Euripides, and in addition to numerous small fragments we have an *Antiopa* by Pacuvius based on it (Cicero, *De finibus* 1.?) and an avowed summary of the play by Hyginus (*Fab* 8).[18] From these we learn that in Euripides, as in Pausanias, Nykteus is king of Thebes, and that Antiope his daughter, having been embraced by Zeus, flees the anger of her father and comes to Sikyon, where the king Epaphos (probably garbled for Epopeus: see above on the *Kypria* and below *passim*) marries her. One might suppose this would save matters, but Nykteus is not appeased, and on his deathbed asks Lykos the new king to see that she is punished. Lykos does so, killing Epaphos and bringing Antiope back to Thebes in chains; on the way (near Kithairon) she gives birth to twins, who are abandoned. At Thebes Dirke, the wife of Lykos, takes charge of Antiope and keeps her in continual torment until she manages to escape and return to the cave in Eleutherai where she delivered the children. Here the play actually begins, and here she finds the twins, Amphion and Zethos (now grown), without, of course, recognizing them. To her appeals for sanctuary Zethos turns a deaf ear; Amphion was no doubt more amenable, but nothing is decided and after the brothers leave the stage Dirke enters with some Bakchai, sees Antiope, and drags her off to be executed. By this time, however, the herdsman who raised the twins has convinced them that Antiope is their mother, and offstage they rescue her and tie Dirke to a bull.

In the play's denouement, Lykos is also dealt with; summoned by a ruse he is almost slain by Amphion, but Hermes intervenes at the last minute (10 GLP). Naturally the throne is to be handed over to the children, and there is a prediction as well of the role of Amphion's lyre in bringing stones to help the builders; thus we see that his musical powers are as old as this play. Zethos too was given some role, but our papyrus evidence suffers a gap here. The play also contained a theoretical debate between the two brothers, on the active versus the contemplative life—at what point and in what regard we do not know. One other detail, supplied by the sixth-century A.D. Byzantine writer John Malalas, is that in this drama Zeus took the form of a Satyros to rape Antiope (pp. 410–11 N²).[19] In art we see nothing of any of this tale until after the time of Euripides; a Sicilian calyx krater of the early fourth century offers the most complete representation, with the bull trampling Dirke in the background while Amphion and Zethos draw their swords to kill Lykos as Antiope watches and Hermes prepares to intervene (Berlin:Ch F3296).

Pausanias and Apollodoros both know this same basic story, and add some variants for the initial stages of it. In Pausanias, Epopeus of Sikyon carries off Antiope, and her father Nykteus launches a war against Sikyon to get her back (2.6.1–3). The Thebans lose, and Nykteus dies, but not before passing the reign over to his brother Lykos and commanding him to continue the effort, with a view toward chastising Antiope. Why Antiope should be chastised is not here explained. As matters turn out, Epopeus has also received wounds in the battle, and dies; his successor returns Antiope to Lykos, and she delivers her twins on the way back, as in Euripides. That the twins appear even when Zeus has not been mentioned suggests that Pausanias has attempted to minimize the tale of the rape in order to create a more historically plausible motive for Theban-Sikyonian hostilities; obviously, though, Zeus' contribution to the story is going to resurface at points, producing an awkward conflation. Apollodoros follows Euripides more closely, and in fact his one significant new detail, that Nykteus kills himself in shame after a pregnant Antiope has fled to Sikyon, may be taken from the play (ApB 3.5.5). Here too, as against Pausanias, Lykos defeats Epopeus in battle after Nykteus' death, and thus recovers Antiope; the remainder of the story is recounted too briefly to add anything else. The scholia to Apollonios, which offer an account similar to that of Hyginus, also know that Zeus takes the form of a Satyros to rape Antiope (cf. Nonnos 7.123), and that Nykteus, who is grieved/annoyed, then dies (Σ AR 4.1090).

Two other sources supply greater novelties. Book 9 of Pausanias attributes to the oracle Bakis the idea that because Dirke was a devotee of Dionysos the god became angry over her death and sent madness upon Antiope, until Phokos, grandson of Sikyon, cured and married her (9.17.6). On the other hand, Hyginus, who in *Fabula* 8 explicitly follows Euripides, precedes that tale with one in *Fabula* 7 in which Antiope is married to Lykos but raped by Epaphos (again surely a mistake for Epopeus), as a result of which Lykos repudiates her. Zeus then embraces her, while Lykos marries Dirke. The latter, suspicious that her husband still harbors affection for his first wife, imprisons Antiope, but Zeus effects her escape and she delivers the twins on Mount Kithairon; the revenge of her children then follows the normal pattern (although we do not know what happens to Antiope while they are growing up). This is an odd story with a Hellenistic look to it; nevertheless, parts of it may be old, as we shall see below.

Having thus entered the development of Antiope's tale in midstream, via Polydoros, his wife Nykteis, and her father Nykteus, we must turn back to our earliest sources and the tradition that Antiope's ancestors were not originally Thebans, or even lived in Thebes. The *Nekuia*, as we saw, makes her the daughter of Asopos; beyond that it says only that she bore Amphion and Zethos to Zeus, and that they were the first to settle and fortify Thebes (*Od* 11.260–65). Our three-line fragment from the epic poet Asios also makes her the daughter of Asopos and mother of Amphion and Zethos (in language clearly not borrowed from the *Nekuia*: Paus 2.6.4 = fr 1 *PEG*). But the third line adds, surprisingly, that she bore the children after having conceived by both Zeus and Epopeus. Whether such wording could ever be a loose expression for the bearing of children to one's husband in appearance but a god in reality I do not know (cf. Hes fr 17a MW, of the Moliones). If not, then of the two children only one is here Zeus' son. No other author suggests such a split paternity, although our late paraphrases and summaries are not always explicit on the matter. Assuming this is what Asios meant, the three lines as they survive still give no clue as to which son he supposed to be by which father; if one had to guess one would, I suppose, assign Amphion to Zeus, since he possesses wonderful musical skills not matched by anything we can see in Zethos. Indeed, we might hazard that those skills encouraged the notion of separate parentage, although music elsewhere always comes to mortals from Apollo or the Mousai, not Zeus. The *Nekuia* does not mention musical abilities at all; Pausanias notes that the poet of the *Europa* (apparently not Stesichoros' effort, but the epic poem sometimes ascribed to Eumelos) called Amphion the first to play the lyre, with Hermes his teacher, and that Amphion's singing caused animals and stones to follow him (9.5.8 = Eum fr 13 *PEG*). Presumably, this uncertainly dated epic precedes Euripides' play, where we find explicitly stated the fact that the lyre could construct walls (10 GLP, as above).

The *Ehoiai* may also have included such a motif: Palaiphatos, who begins his account of the building of Thebes with the words, "Hesiod and others say that they put up the walls of Thebes with a lyre," then continues, "and some believe that they played the lyre while the stones jumped into place of their own accord" (Pal 41). These last words might seem to cast doubt on the magical properties of the lyre in "Hesiod" as opposed to other writers. Yet it is hard to see what else the words "put up the walls with a lyre" could mean; most likely, the *Ehoiai* was simply not explicit enough to please Palaiphatos, and the tradition of a lyre moving stones does go back to that poem. Pherekydes, incidentally, tells us that the Mousai gave Amphion his lyre (3F41).

We found above that in Pherekydes the Thebes of Amphion and Zethos takes shape long before the time of Kadmos, in defense against the Phlegyes, and is destroyed by that people under the leadership of Eurymachos after Amphion and Zethos have died. In this way Kadmos is free to rebuild the city, and there is no conflict between the two foundations. Since no tradition before Apollodoros is known to have linked Nykteus and Lykos with the Spartoi and thus with Kadmos (and some pointedly do not), Pherekydes' solution may have been the one universally employed in early times, although the *Nekuia's* language does not absolutely exclude that Antiope's children refortified a city once inhabited by Kadmos. Certainly this last is the version of Diodoros and Pausanias: Kadmos builds the upper city, or Kadmeia, and Amphion and Zethos enlarge that with the lower city of Thebes, so that the Kadmeia becomes the citadel (DS 19.53.5; Paus 9.5.6). In Diodoros this happens between the reigns of Kadmos and Polydoros, but Pausanias and Apollodoros probably follow a more canonical line in putting it somewhere between the death of Pentheus and the adulthood of Laios. In Pausanias, we found Lykos as a double regent, first for Labdakos, then for Laios; upon his defeat by Amphion and Zethos, Laios is spirited away by friends until he should be full-grown. In Apollodoros, Lykos apparently usurps the throne from the infant Laios and reigns for twenty years (ApB 3.5.5). When Amphion and Zethos kill or expel him (Apollodoros says both) they also exile Laios, who goes to the Peloponnesos. Hyginus likewise says that they exiled Laios, son of the king Labdakos (by order of Apollo?: *Fab* 9). No very good reason for such high-handed behavior is offered; most likely it arises as a simple narrative necessity when the Antiope-Lykos-Dirke founding of Thebes and the tradition of the Labdakidai come into conflict.

It remains to consider briefly the domestic life of these twins. Amphion is from the time of Aischylos' *Niobe* onward clearly married to the daughter of

Tantalos, and the father of the children whom Apollo and Artemis slay (frr 154a, 160 R). That he is not so named earlier, even in Homer where the death of the children is recounted, is presumably just coincidence; the *Ehoiai* will certainly have specified a father, since we know it gave the number of the children (twenty: Hes fr 183 MW), but from that part of the poem no actual quotes survive. The tale itself, and Amphion's ultimate fate (of which there are several versions), will be discussed in the next chapter, when we deal with the family of Tantalos. As for Zethos, we have already touched upon his marriage in covering the travails of Prokne and Philomela in chapter 7: *Odyssey* 19 tells us that the daughter of Pandareos (Aedon, either the nightingale or a proper name) slew her own child Itylos, the son of Zethos, by mistake (*Od* 19.518–23). Several different scholia agree that she was one of the three daughters of Pandareos, and that in jealousy of the many children of her brother-in-law Amphion and his wife Niobe she plotted to kill one of the latter; unfortunately, she miscalculated the beds and killed her own son, then prayed to be turned into a nightingale. Some or all of this story seems to be ascribed to Pherekydes, who elsewhere is said to have named one Nais as a daughter of Zethos (3F125). The scholia also know a version in which Aedon succeeds in killing one of Amphion's sons, then kills her own to forestall Niobe's vengeance, much as Euripides' Medeia does. Pausanias refers very vaguely to the Homeric story when he says that Zethos' wife killed their son through some sort of error, and that Zethos died of grief (9.5.9). Apollodoros registers nothing of this; he simply notes Zethos' wife as Thebe, eponym of the city, and moves on to the calamity of Niobe without further comment (ApB 3.5.6). There seems no other mention of the misfortune in antiquity.

Laios   At the beginning of the last section we saw Sophokles, Herodotos, and Euripides as guarantors for the direct line of descent from Kadmos (via Polydoros, Labdakos, and Laios) to Oidipous. Labdakos is not, in fact, mentioned as an ancestor of the house (or anything else) before Sophokles' *Antigone* (593), and Laios himself first appears by name in Pindar's *Olympian* 2 of 476 B.C. But presumably this pedigree is of some antiquity, since the epic *Thebais* has Oidipous' sons serve him with the cup of his father and the table of Kadmos, both seemingly family heirlooms; elsewhere, of course, Polyneikes is in possession of the necklace of Harmonia. The previous section showed that in those accounts where Antiope's children intrude into the line, Laios' early manhood is usually the victim, and he must wait for their demise to assume the throne. Fortunately both Amphion and Zethos suffer disaster to themselves and their children, thus paving the way for Laios' return. Meanwhile we may, if we like, follow Apollodoros in assigning his exile to Elis, so that he might meet and carry off Pelops' son Chrysippos.

This story of the first homosexual abduction among mortals is the only tale told of Laios, other than his death at the hands of his own son, and its antiquity is a matter of some question. The earliest sure appearance is the dramatization in Euripides' lost *Chrysippos,* where little survives beyond the title but enough to guarantee the situation. More detail comes down to us from a scholion to the same poet's *Phoinissai,* where we find an extended account of Theban misfortunes, including the idea that Hera sent the Sphinx because the people had failed to punish Laios' unlawful (and contrary to the rites of marriage) passion for Chrysippos (Σ *Pho* 1760 = 16F10). The source cited by the scholiast at the end of his lengthy narrative is one Peisandros; if this could be Peisandros the epic poet of Kameiros, we would have a solid Archaic pedigree for a great many things, but given the long run of the story and some of its details the account surely belongs rather to a Hellenistic mythographer of the same name.[20] What sources he used (including the *Oidipodeia?*) and in what combination we cannot say, nor can we be sure that his Chrysippos material does not depend on Euripides or post-Euripidean sources. One pre-Euripidean work in which attempts have, however, been made to find room for Chrysippos' kidnapping is Aischylos' *Laios,* where the deed would serve to somehow motivate Laios' subsequent problems with Apollo.[21] Personally I find this unlikely in the context of a drama that must have stressed heterosexual passion and/or desire for a son as the cause of Oidipous's birth. We might have expected too that the third play of the group, the *Hepta,* would at least mention such a crime, but the theory of its inclusion here remains possible. Conversely, nothing absolutely forbids us to conjecture that Euripides invented the pederasty for the sake of a play, although it is a lot to invent.[22] Either way, the Peisandros scholion resolves Chrysippos' plight after his abduction by having him kill himself with a sword in shame (a made-for-the-stage ending), and something of the same sort is surely supposed in the oracle to Laios (cited by the hypotheseis for the *Oidipous Tyrannos* and *Phoinissai*) where the king is told that his child will slay him as Zeus' response to the prayers of Pelops, who has cursed Laios for his crime (cf. Σ *Pho* 60).

About this same Chrysippos there is a second tradition, preserved as early as Thoukydides and Hellanikos, that he was slain by his brothers out of jealousy: Thoukydides actually says only that Atreus had to leave Elis because of Chrysippos (1.9.2), but Hellanikos claims that Atreus took the lead in the murder of this offspring of Pelops by a previous marriage because Hippodameia and her children feared that he would inherit his father's throne (4F157). Plato's *Kratylos* offers the same idea, that Atreus foully slew Chrysippos (395b), and thus it would seem to have had considerable currency (for further details see chapter 15). Such a grim fate does not exclude that the boy was earlier carried off by Laios, but it is hard to put the two stories into the same framework. Two authors who do manage to combine Chrysippos' abduction with his death at the hands of his own family are Hyginus and the undated (but late) Dositheos. In Hyginus, Chrysippos is carried off at the Nemean games but recovered by Pelops and then killed by Hippodameia and sons (*Fab* 85). In Dositheos, Laios is caught by Atreus and Thyestes but forgiven by Pelops when he pleads love for the boy (54F1). Apparently this means that Pelops condones the affair, for when Hippodameia steals into her stepson's bedroom to kill him (her sons having refused) he is sleeping next to Laios, with whose sword she commits the deed. Laios is naturally suspected, but Chrysippos lives long enough to name the real killer.

In art we have only an Attic Red-Figure vase of perhaps the last two decades of the fifth century (showing a Chrysippos with Aphrodite, perhaps not relevant: NY 11.213.2), plus several later Apulian ones with Laios carrying off Chrysippos and figures in Persian dress left behind in astonishment (e.g., Berlin:Ch Inv 1968.12; Getty 77.AE.14; the same scene also on a Praenestine cista in the Villa Giulia).

Turning from such misadventures to the matter of Laios' marriage, we find again considerable uncertainty. The *Nekuia* calls Oidipous' mother Epikaste but offers nothing else about her or Laios prior to his death and her fatal remarriage (*Od* 11.271–73). Of the treatment of any of these matters in the *Oidipodeia* (or *Thebais*, if that work had references backward) no trace remains, and likewise for the Peisandros scholion, whatever the date(s) of its information. In the fifth century we do extract something from Pherekydes—the mythographer reports that Kreon gave Laios' wife Iokaste, Oidipous' own mother, to him as wife (3F95)—and from the dramatists.

Aischylos' version of the king's ill-fated end—as recounted in the lost *Laios* and *Oidipous*—we must reconstruct from the third play in that trilogy, the *Hepta*. The chorus there tells us that there was an ancient transgression, a *parbasia* committed by Laios and swiftly punished, although something in this connection has survived to the third generation (*Hepta* 742–49). We also learn that Laios ignored Apollo when the god thrice prophesied from Delphi that dying without issue he would save Thebes. The playwright, of course, supposes us to have seen the first play of the group, the *Laios*; thus he does not specify whether the transgression was the refusal to heed Apollo, or something done earlier for which the prophecy was a kind of punishment. Either way, we must be surprised that Laios' begetting of a child would threaten the city; we expect rather that such an event will threaten Laios, and indeed the chorus' next words relate how, overcome by his own foolish counsels, he brought death to himself in the form of the father-slaying Oidipous. But the son must first grow up, and the killing of Laios many years later does not seem much like the swift punishment claimed. Nor is the failure to observe a warning (*not* a command) from Apollo what we usually mean by a *parbasia*. On balance we will probably do better to regard the *parbasia* as a previous offense leading Apollo to offer Laios a cruel choice: either no children, or possible danger to the city he rules. As we saw, the abduction of Chrysippos could be the original transgression; the chorus does not allude to it, but we must admit that they do not allude to anything else either. The peril to Thebes constitutes yet another problem: if it springs directly from Oidipous' engendering, then Aischylos must mean the danger (though not disaster) brought upon the city by the quarrel between Eteokles and Polyneikes, figures who but for Laios' folly would not have been born. If, on the other hand, the danger is arbitrarily imposed by the gods to balance Oidipous' birth, we could argue for the Sphinx, although Laios would then be providing both the cause of the danger and the agent of its elimination. Throughout this morass of questions the link between crime and punishment persists in escaping us: there seems nowhere any swift retribution for Laios, and no very clear reason for involving the city when Laios' neglect of Apollo's advice seemingly redounds first and foremost on himself.

As for the action of the *Laios*, if (as I think) it did not involve Chrysippos (or certainly not directly, for enacting his story here would force Oidipous' entire life into the middle play), the drama probably began with Laios setting out from Thebes (for Delphi?) and ended with a messenger speech announcing his demise at a crossroads. The intervening space would then describe and reflect upon past events—the *parbasia* (Chrysippos here?) and Apollo's oracle, the child's begetting, and the subsequent abandonment (in a belated effort to save the city?). Again, one does not quite see how Laios' death many years after relates to these happenings. In Sophokles' *Oidipous Tyrannos* there is not the slightest hint of any such prologue to the child's birth; Laios and Iokaste simply receive a prophecy that whatever child is born to them will be the slayer of his father, and Laios understandably seeks to be rid of him; hence his exposure when he is only three days old (*OT* 711–19).[23] The same holds for the prologue of Euripides' *Phoinissai*, where Iokaste relates past events: Laios consults Delphi because of his childlessness, Apollo predicts his own death if a child is born, and events take their course. The one new detail here is the notion that Laios lay with Iokaste, after receiving the oracle, in a fit of lust and drunkenness (*Pho* 21–22). The Sphinx's arrival, as in Sophokles, is fortuitous, that is, not linked to any previous event.

Our later mythographers all follow this simpler Sophoklean/Euripidean version of affairs and offer nothing that would help to explain Aischylos' more complicated arrangement, although as we saw, the Peisandros scholion and the oracle of the *Oidipous* and *Phoinissai* hypotheseis do link the abduction of Chrysippos to the Sphinx or to Laios' death. One other point to be dealt with is the name of Laios' wife, or wives. Homer speaks of only the one wife, Epikaste, who is clearly the natural mother of Oidipous, while Pherekydes and Sophokles agree in calling the same person Iokaste (Aischylos fails to name her in the *Hepta*). Such a modest variant is hardly cause for concern, but our Epimenidean corpus says that Laios married one Eurykleia, daughter of Ekphas, and that she bore to him Oidipous (3B15). Our source for this information, the scholia to the *Phoinissai*, fails to include, however, the most crucial point: did its author suppose Eurykleia to be the woman Oidipous later married, or did Laios take a second wife Epikaste/Iokaste, making Oidipous' bride merely his stepmother? The scholiast's subsequent remark, that some sources did give Laios two wives, suggests that "Epimenides" did not, but the idea that Oidipous and his mother were not joined in marriage does therefore seem to have been known, unless we are to understand that in the unnamed sources the second wife, not the first, bore the child. Of Euryganeia and Astymedousa, wives of Oidipous whom some modern scholars have taken to be still other identities of his mother, we will see more in the next section.

Oidipous   The tale of Oidipous' abandonment is presumably basic to all accounts of his story, but we find it first attested only in Aischylos' trilogy, assuming the verb *chutrizein*, cited as from the *Laios*, does refer to the child's exposure in a pot (fr 122 R). Subsequently the story finds a full narration in Sophokles' *Tyrannos*, where in response to the oracle Oidipous is given over by Iokaste to a shepherd, that he might be exposed on Kithairon with an iron pin through his ankles (*OT* 717–19, 1171–76). The shepherd instead entrusts him to a Korinthian colleague with whom he shares pasturage, and the latter brings him to Polybos, king of Korinth, who with his wife Merope adopts the child as his own. Here again the *Phoinissai* scholia offer us some anonymous variants (Σ *Pho* 26). In one, Oidipous is placed in a chest that floats to Sikyon, from whence he is taken up by Polybos. A Hellenistic relief cup shows the scene of this finding, with Periboia (as the wife of Polybos is also called by Apollodoros and others) taking the infant Oidipous from a basket and handing him to her husband (Louvre MNC 660).[24] The same story of Periboia's discovery (while she is washing clothes) appears in Hyginus (*Fab* 66), and might reflect a situation (and means of recognition) in Euripides' *Oidipous*, if Periboia there came to Thebes in later times to seek her son (as she does in *Fab* 67). Intermediaries in this version may be indicated by the *Odyssey* scholia, where shepherds from Sikyon actually raise Oidipous (Σ *Od* 11.271).

The other variant takes us further afield, to Olympia, for the same *Phoinissai* scholia suggest a version (something is lost at the beginning) in which Hippodameia, daughter of Oinomaos, presents the child to someone (surely Pelops?) as his. Subsequently, Oidipous having grown, Laios appears and abducts his son's presumed brother Chrysippos, and Oidipous in trying to intervene kills his father. When Iokaste arrives to claim the body, he then meets and marries her, thus completing the disaster. Bizarre though this story seems, it does link together the abduction of Chrysippos and Laios' death in an ingenious fashion, and obviates the need for a curse by Pelops. That it could represent the plot of Aischylos' *Laios* seems discounted, given the range of time and place required. If it is not from some other early source, it is certainly a shrewd late attempt to improve on original elements. In this context we should at least note another remark elsewhere in the *Phoinissai* scholia, that Oidipous killed Laios because both men were enamored of Chrysippos (Σ *Pho* 60). Art offers us, besides the Hellenistic cup noted above, only a Red-Figure amphora by the Achilleus Painter: a man with petasos and spear (thus presumably a traveler) named as Euphorbos carries the infant Oidipous (also named); on the reverse is an unnamed bearded man holding a staff, presumably the recipient of the child (CabMéd 372).

For the story of Oidipous' departure from Korinth and arrival at Thebes (that is, when he grows up in Korinth, not Olympia), there is likewise some diversity of narrative. In Sophokles, as Oidipous himself relates the tale, the day came when a Korinthian, overfilled with wine at a banquet, called him a bastard, and taking the words to heart he questioned his father on the matter (*OT* 774–813). Naturally Polybos avowed himself as parent, but doubts gnawed at Oidipous until he resolved to take his questions to Delphi. There Apollo refused to answer his query about real parents; the god did, however, tell him that he was fated to slay his father and marry his mother (this latter detail withheld from Laios and Iokaste). Accordingly he determined to put as much distance as possible between himself and his supposed homeland, and thus set out eastward. At a place where three roads meet he encountered Laios (we may guess, but are not told, that the latter was headed to Delphi, although Kreon does call him a *theôros*) with a party of five men and a wagon. The herald attempted to push him off the road so that the wagon might pass, and he pushed back. Laios then struck him with his goad as the wagon went by; at this Oidipous lost his temper completely and toppled the old man backward out of the wagon, killing him, whereupon he also killed all the rest, no doubt in self-defense. We know, of course, that this account is not precisely right: one attendant, the same man who took Oidipous away at his birth, has escaped and returned to Thebes with a tale fabricated for his own protection, that robbers in great number set upon the king.

Euripides in his *Phoinissai* gives a slightly different version of these events, that Laios and Oidipous were both on their way to Delphi when they met, Oidipous to seek his parents, Laios to ask if his child had survived (*Pho* 32–45). Oidipous is told that he is dealing with a king, but the same altercation ensues, with Laios' horses trampling on Oidipous' feet. After killing his father, Oidipous takes the horses back to Polybos, so that he seems not to have reached Delphi or to have received any prophecy. The scholia note this point and offer as explanation that he felt he could not consult the god in his polluted condition; no source is named, and the scholiast may be guessing (Σ *Pho* 44). A further note suggesting that Oidipous on his return to Korinth obtained purification and then went on to Delphi, as in Sophokles, likewise seems muddled and is not what Euripides' text implies. Iokaste at this juncture in the prologue proceeds to speak of Kreon's offer of her in marriage (*Pho* 45–50), which might seem to imply that Oidipous came directly from Korinth to solve the riddle and claim the prize, not in flight from Polybos. Such a deviation from the Sophoklean norm, if we have correctly understood it, does offer one distinct advantage: if Oidipous has not been warned by the oracle, there is nothing unreasonable in his slaying a man old enough to be his father or marrying a woman old enough to be his mother. Unfortunately, Euripides' lost *Oidipous* has nothing preserved on this point, and neither does Aischylos' *Oidipous* trilogy, although there the killing seems to have taken place near Potniai, slightly over a mile south of Thebes (fr 387a R), which might well indicate for both men intended goals quite different from those in Sophokles, and here too no actual visit to

Delphi.[25] Otherwise, about the encounter in Aischylos we know only that Oidipous spat out the murdered man's blood (fr 122a R).

In Antimachos' *Lyde*, Oidipous also takes the horses back to Polybos, offering them to his father as an appreciation for his rearing (70 W), so that Antimachos (whose poem is perhaps older than the *Phoinissai*) like that work has failed to bring Oidipous to Delphi. Diodoros, too, like Euripides, has Oidipous and Laios meet on the same road *to* Delphi, although he says nothing of what follows the killing (DS 4.64.2). As a sheer bit of speculation, the detail of two men meeting on a road to the same place would explain (as Sophokles' version does not) why the encounter takes place at a point where three roads come together. In Nikolaos of Damascus, like Diodoros a late first-century B.C. writer, Oidipous is on his way to Orchomenos for horses, and Laios has Epikaste with him when they meet (90F8). The killing takes place as usual, Epikaste is spared (the servants come up too late to help), and Oidipous hides in the woods for a while before returning to Korinth (oddly enough, the *Phoinissai* scholia state that Oidipous did kill his mother in some versions: Σ *Pho* 26). Here again the animals (this time mules) are taken back to Korinth to be given to Polybos. Seneca's *Oedipus* offers no problems of any sort, and only the briefest mention of the encounter (*Oed* 768–72), while Hyginus follows for the most part what we considered for the *Phoinissai*—a meeting with Laios on the way to Delphi, and a subsequent journey to Thebes to solve the riddle (*Fab* 67).

By contrast, Apollodoros returns us to the Sophoklean account, with Oidipous told at Delphi specifically what will happen if he does not avoid his homeland (ApB 3.5.7). The same author calls Laios' herald Polyphontes and says that he killed one of Oidipous' horses when the latter refused to make way for him (in Pherekydes there is a herald named Polypoites: 3F94). But in all, given the general lack of emphasis on Oidipous at Delphi, we must ask whether Sophokles could have invented the detail of the second prophecy for his play, where it serves to intensify the irony of a man fleeing toward that which he thinks to escape, and tightens the sequence of events working inexorably toward Oidipous' doom. I myself find this attractive, and we should remember that in Aischylos' *Hepta* not even the first prophecy is as we see it in Sophokles, but for the Archaic period there is really no evidence. A visit to Delphi in some early versions might easily have been altered by later writers for the reasons cited above, to eliminate seeming carelessness of behavior in a man forewarned of his fate.

Either way, in flight from Korinth or lured by the promise of reward for defeating the Sphinx, Oidipous comes to Thebes. His encounter with the Sphinx is not actually attested before Aischylos, who mentions in the *Hepta* that Oidipous overcame her and who presumably dramatized that event in the immediately following satyr play *Sphinx*; for the same period we have the famous cup in the Vatican on which Oidipous contemplates the creature as she perches on a column (Vat 16541). Comparison with this virtually certain presentation (see below) permits us to suppose that a Chalkidian (?[26]) hydria in Stuttgart (65/15), datable to perhaps 530 B.C., also shows the confrontation: here too the Sphinx is on a column, and before her sits a single man on a folding chair, while eight small women heavily swathed in robes look on from various positions. We will see shortly that this type of scene, with numerous men gathered around the column and no single figure identifiable as Oidipous, repeats itself often in the late sixth and early fifth centuries. But the Sphinx's role as a bane of Thebes certainly goes back much farther, to the *Theogony* and the *Oidipodeia*, in fact.[27] The first of these says simply that she (called Phix) brought destruction to the Thebans (*Th* 326–27); in the second she apparently causes the death of the "fairest and most desirable of all, the child of Kreon, glorious Haimon" (fr 1 *PEG*). The *Phoinissai* Peisandros scholion claims, as we saw before, that Hera sent the Sphinx to devour whatever Thebans she came across because they had dishonored her by failing to punish Laios' abduction of Chrysippos (Σ *Pho* 1760). The same source includes Haimon among her victims, thus confirming the incomplete quote from the *Oidipodeia*. From other scholia to the *Phoinissai* we learn that Euripides somewhere (probably in the *Antigone*) has Dionysos send the Sphinx, although the reason remains unclear (Σ *Pho* 1031 = fr 178 N²). Among later sources Apollodoros also says that Hera sent the Sphinx (with a riddle learned from the Mousai) to eat Thebans but gives no motive (Ap*B* 3.5.8). No other source offers any reason at all for her appearance at Thebes; perhaps, since she is a monster, we should not expect one.

The *Theogony* and *Oidipodeia* material cited above constitute our entire stock of literary evidence for the Sphinx in the seventh and sixth centuries. The art of the same period fleshes out her portrait, but often in uncertain ways. As we saw in chapter 1, Sphinxes do populate Corinthian and early Attic Black-Figure vase-painting as generic decoration, and likewise crown Attic grave stelai and dedicatory columns of the sixth century. But our first clear piece of narrative unfolds on a Siana cup by the C Painter which depicts some eight youths running away from a Sphinx while their comrade, a ninth youth, clings to the underside of her chest and belly, much like Odysseus and his ram (Syracuse 25418).[28] This curious pose is repeated on a *c.* 500 B.C. lekythos (Athens 397), and (though on neither vase is the Sphinx flying) might perhaps anticipate the description of Parthenopaios' shield in the *Hepta*, where an apparently airborne Sphinx carries one of the Kadmeans under her as a protection against missiles (*Hepta* 539–44). A Red-Figure lekythos now in Kiel certainly does show a Sphinx in flight, with her paws wrapped around her young victim (Kiel B555), and another lekythos in Athens depicts the moment of takeoff with her prey (Athens 1607; so too now Getty 85.AE.377, where the youth appears to be dead). Such scenes, while striking, are relatively rare; far more common is the moment of capture, with the Sphinx either leaping against the chest of a young man to knock him down, or crouched over him in triumph as he lies supine. But in almost all such examples the victim is, remarkably, a young, naked, unbearded man (on two occasions there are beards). In all, this material, taken together with the *Hepta* shield and that play's later reference to her as a "man-snatching bane" (*Hepta* 776–77), appears to indicate a tradition in which the Sphinx flies off with her quarry (so probably already the intention of the C Painter). What purpose might be served by abducting rather than simply killing her victims is hard to say.[29] That she shunned other possible quarries seems confirmed by a series of similar Black-Figure lekythoi on which she crouches over a boy while grown men on either side make deprecating gestures (e.g., Louvre CA 111; Syracuse 12085).

The above conclusions, if correct, might also suggest a tradition in which there is no riddle, for youths rather than grown men will scarcely have been sent out to try to solve it. What we may have instead is a monster who snatches up young boys (including Haimon) at will, for whatever purpose. In literature the idea of a riddle first surfaces with Pindar, in the barest of fragments quoted as part of a metrical treatise: "the riddle from the savage jaws of a maiden" (fr 177d SM). Presumably this does refer to the Sphinx, and if the expression "savage jaws" (*agrian gnathôn*) is not just poetic coloring for the source of a deadly puzzle, it might imply that here too she ate people (as in the Peisandros scholion and Apollodoros) while adding riddle-posing to her repertoire. That the Sphinx did ask riddles of the Thebans is not absolutely certain until the *Tyrannos* (OT 130–31, 391–94), and not before Asklepiades do we learn what the riddle (quoted in dactylic hexameters) was. Yet the words *kai tri*[. . .], appearing as they do between Oidipous and the Sphinx on the Vatican cup, would seem with their allusion to something three-footed to guarantee that Oidipous' thoughtful pose there is a response to a riddle. With this much granted we must surely take that riddle back at least to the Stuttgart hydria of *c.* 530 B.C. where we found the same pose. Asklepiades' version of the conundrum runs as follows: "Two-footed and four-footed and three-footed upon the earth, it has a single voice, and alone of all those on land or in the air or sea it changes form. And when it goes supported on three [or its most?] feet, then the speed of its limbs is weakest" (12F7a; manuscript uncertainty between three and most). The hexameter form employed could indicate an origin in an epic source such as the *Oidipodeia*, but Asklepiades generally takes his stories from tragedy, and hexameter is the meter used for riddles on the stage.[30] We have seen that the riddle is not specified in Sophokles, and while it was referred to in Euripides' *Oidipous*, the very scant fragment that survives reveals a different wording from that of Asklepiades (fr 83.22–24 Aus). Presumably, then, the latter's quote derives from some other Oidipous play, and Aischylos' *Sphinx* (where the encounter must fill a whole drama) will be a likely possibility (keeping in mind that whatever play Asklepiades drew on could itself have borrowed from epic sources).

Asklepiades' further account of the story may actually provide a bridge between the motif of the riddle and the youth-snatcher so popular in art: he says that the Thebans gathered daily in their assembly to ponder the riddle, since they could not rid themselves of the Sphinx until they had answered it, and whenever they failed to so do she snatched away whomever she wished of the citizens (12F7b). Something of this sort is perhaps indicated by the many Black- and Red-Figure vases which, beginning about 510 B.C., portray the Sphinx on her column surrounded by seated and/or standing men, mostly bearded, all with cloaks and staffs (e.g., Basel BS 411, Louvre G228). Of this group the most suggestive is probably Vienna 3728, a pelike by Hermonax on which the men certainly appear engaged in a fervent discussion. Conceivably this combination of riddling and snatching is the explanation of the apparent split in our earlier evidence, but it may also be a subsequent invention designed to reconcile that split. Sophokles not only fails to give the actual riddle, but also never specifies under what conditions it was posed, or what exact harm befell the Thebans because of it. Euripides in the *Phoinissai* has Iokaste say that the Sphinx burdened Thebes with her snatchings, prompting Kreon to offer the queen to whoever could solve the riddle (*Pho* 45–49). Later in the same play we find that the Sphinx sang a riddle and alighting on the walls snatched up the Thebans and carried them off (*Pho* 806–11; the scholia say that she tore them apart and dropped them), and later still that she snatched up *young* men (*Pho* 1026–31). From the same poet's *Elektra* we may add (ornamenting Achilleus' helmet) "Sphinxes bearing off song-involving quarry with their talons" (E:*El* 470–72: the adjective is perhaps being stretched to indicate the riddle). All this fits well enough with Asklepiades' version, but is too sketchy to be the sole source for it. We must remember of course that many other fifth- and fourth-century tragedians wrote Oidipous plays, including Achaios, Philokles, and Xenokles. As for Aischylos, we really know nothing at all for certain of his *Sphinx*, not even (though few will doubt it) that Oidipous was a character. Possibly some accounts offered a mixed tradition in which the Sphinx carried off young boys but resorted to a riddle contest when forced to contend with a grown, more powerful man. In any case the cause of her downfall is probably always Oidipous; nothing in any of our ancient sources suggests otherwise.

Regarding that downfall, we have surprisingly no good early information. In both Sophokles and Euripides Oidipous destroys the Sphinx in some manner after answering the riddle, but we are not told how; Aischylos says simply that he "removed" her (*Hepta* 775–77). Force as the method might seem indicated by a squat Red-Figure lekythos of the late fifth century on which Oidipous aims a spear at a cowering or collapsed Sphinx, but there is a column in the background, and she has perhaps already fallen from that, or else gives herself up to death by Oidipous' spear because the riddle has been answered (London E696).[31] In any case the use of real force against a resisting Sphinx should be linked to the presence or absence of the riddle, for in versions (if any) where riddles played no part Oidipous can only have resorted to violence, while in versions where the riddle was posed its solution would accomplish nothing if the monster was to be (and could be) overcome by brute strength. Be that as it may, Palaiphatos in the fourth century is our first source to say that she threw herself from a rock and died after the riddle was answered (Pal 4). His account offers as well what most of us probably think of (based on Sophokles) as the standard Sphinxian *modus operandi,* namely her sitting on the Phikion mount outside the city and posing her riddle to all Theban citizens who passed by, with death the penalty for those who could not answer it. This odd notion of a winged being who can commit suicide in such a fashion we have already noted in chapter 1. In Diodoros, too, she throws herself to her death after Oidipous' correct response; Diodoros suggests that this was in accord with some oracle (DS 4.64.4).

Apollodoros appears to conflate a number of these different traditions, for his Sphinx, like that of Palaiphatos, is a riddler who sits on the Phikion mount, and yet the Thebans gather in assembly and suffer the loss of whomever she snatches up when they cannot discover the answer, just as in Asklepiades (ApB 3.5.8). Cohering with the Peisandros scholion is the fact that she here eats her prey, and with Diodoros the oracle that the Thebans will be rid of her when they have solved the riddle (although why she is forced to suicide is less clear). Finally, as in the *Oidipodeia* and the Peisandros scholion, Haimon is here one of her victims, causing Kreon to offer the rule and Iokaste to whoever can deal with the problem. Hyginus has the Sphinx first ravage the Theban land, then strike a bargain with Kreon that she will leave Thebes when her riddle is solved but will devour anyone who fails to solve it (*Fab* 67). Kreon accordingly advertises throughout the Greek world, and Oidipous succeeds only after many other aspirants have been eaten; once again the Sphinx throws herself from a cliff. One final bit of rationalizing comes from Pausanias, who cites an account in which the Sphinx was actually a bastard daughter of Laios to whom he had confided the oracle given to Kadmos by Delphi; when she ruled after her father's death she used this secret as a test to discourage claimants, until Oidipous came, having learned the prophecy in a dream (9.26.3–4). The presence of an oracle here as in Diodoros is suggestive, but what exact role it might have played in the beginning I do not see.

On his arrival at Thebes itself Oidipous invariably marries the queen and assumes the throne. In Sophokles this appears to be the offering of a grateful people after his victory over the Sphinx; in Euripides' *Phoinissai* and other sources it represents the pre-announced reward to anyone who accomplished that task. After the marriage (and in some sources begetting of children: see below), there are no incidents of any sort to record until the discovery of Oidipous' parentage. This most famous point in Oidipous' life is first and most fully preserved in Sophokles; Aischylos' *Oidipous* may have dealt with the same events, but it may also (as I shall argue later) have treated problems of his old age at Thebes. With or without this tragic model, Sophokles will have had at least one epic precursor, the *Oidipodeia;* we have no idea what use he made of such material, or if other dramatizations for the Athenian stage preceded his.

As the *Tyrannos* opens, Thebes is beset by a plague, and this fact will subtly determine all of the subsequent action. Oidipous sends his brother-in-law Kreon to Delphi for help; the city is told in response that it must find the murderer of Laios if the disease is to abate. Oidipous accepts the challenge of this new riddle with confidence, but there are few leads to such an old killing, although the one surviving witness is sent for. Also summoned, meanwhile, is Teiresias, who concedes knowledge of the solution but refuses to divulge it. When Oidipous in natural frustration threatens force, the seer does finally accuse him, using language that gives the king little chance to guess the truth. Suspicion of Teriesias leads to suspicion of Kreon, for Oidipous from the outset supposes his predecessor's death to have been politically motivated. Kreon's protest that he derives greater advantage as the king's brother-in-law is to no avail, and he is about to be exiled (or worse) when Iokaste enters and separates the quarrelers. On hearing of her husband's problems with Teiresias she cites her own experience with a spokesman for Apollo who told her that her son would kill his father; thus the child was abandoned with a pin through his feet, and the father instead met his death in a meeting with bandits at a place where three roads converged. This chance topographical detail undoes all the intended consolation of the story, for Oidipous now realizes that he may after all have slain Laios. Accordingly he tells Iokaste of his own background, beginning with his trip to Delphi and the oracle's pronouncement to him that he would kill his father and marry his mother. These he supposes, despite some previous doubts, to be Polybos and Merope of Korinth, and thus when a messenger now arrives to announce that Polybos has died of old age he allows himself to feel some measure of relief. But the same messenger then admits that Oidipous was adopted, brought to Korinth in fact by the messenger himself. Iokaste, who knows to whom she gave her child and where he was to be exposed, now grasps the truth, and rushes into the palace to hang herself.

For Oidipous there are several gaps still to be filled in, but the eyewitness to Laios' murder proves to be the same man who took the child to Kithairon, and on his admission that he received that child from Thebes' queen all the pieces fall into place. Oidipous hurries after Iokaste, finds her dead, and puts out his eyes with the brooches from her gown; Kreon reassumes power, only to face immediately the knotty question of whether to exile the polluter. Here the play ends, with Oidipous' fate unresolved. Sophokles has stressed primarily the role of the gods and *moira* in springing the trap so cunningly laid, and the ironic distance between what we must assume and what we can know.

By contrast, our few scrappy fragments of Euripides' *Oidipous* reveal a plot with surprising deviations from the Sophoklean account. Most important, Oidipous is blinded by the servants of Laios, presumably at Kreon's command (fr 541 N²). At this point in the play he is called son of Polybos, so that the discovery must have been made in two distinct stages, first that he killed the previous king (for which he is punished), then that he is the king's son. This second revelation probably takes place after Polybos' wife has arrived in Thebes (see above), but we have no certain details. Between the two points of emerging

truth, Iokaste seems to assert her loyalty to her husband, a position she may
or may not have maintained after finding him to be also her son (fr 543 N²).
In general Oidipous is contrasted with Kreon, if certain gnomic utterances are
rightly interpreted (frr 551, 552 N²); mention of the latter's envy may indicate
that he, not Oidipous, took the lead in discovering the murderer, and that the
unfortunate king was here a comparatively passive figure.[32] Obviously we
would give much to have the conclusion, so that we might see exactly what the
play intended with such characters. Of later sources, neither Diodoros nor
Apollodoros says anything beyond the fact that Oidipous' situation did come
to light. The Peisandros scholion offers, however, quite a novel variation on the
means by which the truth is revealed: Oidipous buries Laios and the other dead
with their cloaks, but takes away the sword and zôstêr of Laios (Σ Pho 1760, as
above). Subsequently he finds himself near the same place while traveling back
with Iokaste from the completion of certain sacrifices, and being thus reminded
of the event relates it to his wife while showing her the zôstêr. At this she
recognizes him as the murderer of Laios, but not as her son, and therefore
keeps silent. The second part of the secret is revealed only when a stablehand
arrives from Sikyon to relate how he found Oidipous as a child and took him
to Merope; swaddling clothes and the ankle-pins are produced as evidence, and
a reward sought, thus bringing the parentage into the open. The more leisurely
pace of this version reminds us how intensely dramatic Sophokles' onstage one-
play treatment is, and rouses suspicion that this scholiast's account, or at least
parts of it, are far more likely than Sophokles' to derive from early epic. One
other variant from the Phoinissai scholia, that Polybos blinded Oidipous when
he heard the predictions concerning the slaying of fathers, would seem eccentric
in the extreme, jeopardizing as it would much of the subsequent action (Σ Pho
26); possibly this too arose from the need of some dramatist to create a new
tragic situation, with Polybos subsequently discovering his mistake, although
we may wonder how Oidipous will then manage to fulfill the oracle.

We have seen that in the Nekuia, as in Sophokles, Iokaste (or Epikaste, as
Homer calls her) does indeed commit suicide by hanging, "and she left behind
to him exceedingly many pains, as many as the Erinyes of a mother accomplish" (Od 11.279–80). In Euripides' Phoinissai, on the other hand, she is alive
long after the discovery, and may be also in the recently found Lille fragment
of Stesichoros (see below); for Aischylos' Oidipous trilogy we cannot tell. The
whole problem of her fate is linked to that of Oidipous' blindness and/or subsequent remarriage, to which we must now turn. The Nekuia also says that
after Oidipous killed his father and married his mother "the gods soon made
these things known to men" (Od 11.274). The word used for "soon" here,
aphar, normally means "quite soon," and already in antiquity we find Pausanias arguing that such language precludes the begetting of any children by
Epikaste (9.5.10–11). As further support for such an un-Sophoklean state of
affairs he offers the Oidipodeia, where he says that Euryganeia, daughter of
Hyperphas, was the mother of the four children, and as well a painting by

Onasias at Plataia (of unknown date) in which Euryganeia is the woman bent down with grief while the two sons fight. Whether this was indeed the understanding of the *Nekuia* we cannot say for certain, but that Book's subsequent observation that Oidipous continued to rule Thebes after Epikaste's death does suggest that he was not blind, and thus might well have remarried (*Od* 11.275–76). The central part of the Lille Stesichoros fragment features an address by the mother of Oidipous' two sons as they seek some means to avoid a dire prophecy made by Teiresias about their fate (PLille 76a, b, c; PLille 73).[33] Oidipous' possessions appear to be in dispute, so he is presumably dead, but we have no way of knowing whether the unnamed mother is Iokaste, here not a suicide, or a second wife such as Euryganeia (and consequently no way either of knowing whether the children are here any more than in Homer the product of incest).

In Aischylos' *Hepta* we find for the first time a definite statement that Oidipous begat his children by his own mother, and these children are clearly the usual four, Polyneikes, Eteokles, Antigone, and Ismene (*Hepta* 752–57). Pherekydes offers a more complicated situation: in the continuation of his account previously mentioned Iokaste bears to Oidipous Phrastor and Laonytos, who perish at the hands of the Minyes (3F95). Apparently Iokaste disappears as well, for after a year Oidipous marries Euryganeia, daughter of Periphas, who becomes the mother of the four standard offspring. And to this state of affairs Pherekydes adds, after Euryganeia has died, a third wife as well, one Astymedousa, daughter of Sthenelos. The scholiast source for all this then concludes by noting that, according to some, Euryganeia was a sister of Iokaste. The scholion to *Phoinissai* 1760 also knows of a wife Euryganeia whom Oidipous marries after the death of Iokaste and his blinding and who is the mother of the four children; that information is noted under a "some say" heading and may have been found in that form in the mythographer Peisandros, our supposed source for the entire entry. Finally, although no wives of Oidipous are to be found in the *Ehoiai*, a papyrus fragment of that poem does appear to describe his funeral just before turning to Elektryon and his children (Hes fr 193 MW). Some link with the sons of Perseus must therefore be involved, and as Astymedousa is a daughter of Elektryon's brother Sthenelos, it seems more than likely that his branch immediately preceded, with Astymedousa's marriage to Oidipous concluding it. That his funeral is recorded (in some detail) may or may not mean that she married him in his old age.

From Oidipous' wives we turn finally to his ultimate fate. In *Iliad* 23 Homer remarks that Mekisteus, son of Talaos (thus brother of Adrastos), attended the funeral of the "fallen" Oidipous at Thebes (*Il* 23.677–80). The word for "fallen" used here could be meant figuratively, but it would be very remarkable if it did not imply death in battle or by some sort of violence, that is, not old age. Similarly the holding of a funeral at Thebes (with games, no doubt) suggests that Oidipous was a man of some honor and position there when he died, which would agree with the *Nekuia*'s apparent concept of him as continuing to rule after the discovery. In Hesiod's *Works & Days* we encounter the idea that the conflict of the great heroes of the fourth age at Thebes was over the flocks of Oidipous, again indicating that he possessed considerable wealth on his death (*W&D* 162–63). And as we saw above, the funeral appeared too in the *Ehoiai*, a social event attended, it seems, by all the women of Thebes and accompanied by wonderment at the corpse of much-grieved Oidipous (Hes fr 193 MW); a scholiast to the *Iliad* passage adds that Argeia, daughter of Adrastos (and at some point the wife of Polyneikes), came "with others" (Hes fr 192 MW). The same scholiast too, after noting that Homer does seem to suppose Oidipous dying in his own land, adds, "not as the *neôteroi*" (ΣT *Il* 23.679). In fact, Euripides in *Phoinissai* (if this part of the play is his) and Sophokles in *Oidipous at Kolonos* are the first known sources to take him away from Thebes after the discovery, and the idea may well have been an Attic tradition of relatively recent vintage.[34] We shall find in the next section that the epic *Thebais* certainly knows of quarrels at Thebes between Oidipous and his sons in his old age, when he is weak and dependent upon them (and here seemingly no longer king).[35] As a last point, the A scholia to *Iliad* 4.376 offer an unattributed story to the effect that after Oidipous has put aside Iokaste, his new wife Astymedousa accuses the two sons of attacking her, thus causing her husband to curse them.

None of this amounts to a consensus, but from many quarters we have hints that Oidipous remains in Thebes after the discovery, often with his kingship and perhaps his sight intact, and that he takes one or even two more wives, with his children at times (perhaps always before Aischylos, though I doubt it) the product of a union different from that with his mother. That the *Iliad* implies him to have died in battle remains a puzzle; later sources follow pretty uniformly the Sophoklean account of his death at Athens, and thus offer no clues.

Polyneikes and Eteokles The expedition of the Seven against Thebes, and the quarrel between Oidipous' sons which caused it, appear as early as *Iliad* 4, but we learn nothing beyond the fact of Tydeus' pre-attack embassy into the city and its bloody aftermath (*Il* 4.376–98). Eteokles and Polyneikes are mentioned nowhere else in Homer, and not anywhere in Hesiod, while the *Ehoiai* has only a passing reference to Polyneikes (Hes fr 193 MW). The *Thebais* was an epic devoted entirely to this event, since we know its opening line to have been "Sing, goddess, of thirsty Argos, whence the lords . . ." (fr 1 *PEG*). This might seem to begin the poem with Adrastos, but other fragments show that the poet went back to the source of the conflict, as we would expect. Whether any such origins of the dispute were recounted in the *Oidipodeia* we do not know. What the *Thebais* does tell us about the beginnings is that Oidipous on at least two separate occasions cursed his sons for poor tendance of him. In the first of these incidents, Polyneikes serves his father using the silver table of Kadmos and a golden cup (fr 2 *PEG*). The introductory summary by Athenaios (11.465e), before quoting the lines in question, makes clear that Oidipous has forbidden the use of these heirlooms of his father; when he perceives them lying before him, great pain fills his heart, and he prays that his children will share out their patrimony amidst wars and battles. The Greek cited here rather implies that Oidipous can see, since he recognizes the items for what they are, but possibly the poet meant that he knew by feeling them. The same holds for the second occasion, when the sons, through carelessness or some other reason, send Oidipous not his customary portion from the sacrifice, that is the shoulder, but rather the haunch (fr 3 *PEG*). Oidipous is again angry, believing himself insulted, and prays to Zeus that his sons might die by each other's hand. The two events are clearly doublets of the same motif, but such is the stuff of epic, and the second occasion may be justified too by the greater precision that the curse there acquires. Once more, however, we learn nothing of *why* Polyneikes and Eteokles quarreled, only that they were fated to do so.

From epic we turn to Stesichoros' account of these matters as attested by the new fragment in Lille (PLille 76a, b, c).[36] As we saw, Oidipous is here probably dead, but the boys' mother is not, and she speaks all the lines in question. From her words we gather that Teiresias has just uttered a prophecy concerning their mutual slaughter and the danger to the city. That Teiresias should predict, rather than Oidipous pray for, this result, seems puzzling; possibly the poem's time frame is limited, and for that reason the seer is called upon to state more clearly how the gods intend to implement a curse made earlier by the father. If not, then the prophecy must spring from some cause unrelated to Oidipous (in Aischylos' *Hepta* we will find Apollo's anger [against Laios?] given great emphasis, but there the curse is very much in evidence). In any case, the mother (we remember that she is unnamed) despite her despair thinks to see a way of escape that will still accord with Teiresias' words: she proposes that one son retain the gold and other possessions of their father but leave Thebes, while the other remain behind in the city (and presumably occupy the throne, although this is not stated). The choice will be made by lot, and as the fragment breaks off both sons prepare to obey. Something very similar (minus the lot) is preserved for us by Hellanikos, who says that Eteokles offered Polyneikes his choice, either to rule Thebes or take a share of the property and leave; Polyneikes chose the chiton and necklace of Harmonia, abandoned the throne to his brother, and went to Argos, where he gave those items to Argeia, daughter of Adrastos (4F98). Why such an arrangement in either Stesichoros or Hellanikos should lead to conflict we are left to guess; probably Polyneikes like Esau regretted his bargain, and unlike Esau decided to renegotiate. But our scholiast source for Hellanikos points out that not everyone followed this version: in Pherekydes it seems that Eteokles expels Polyneikes by force, and thus that there is no bargain (3F96; cf. ΣA *Il* 4.376, where Eteokles as the older son expels his brother, and Sophokles' *Oidipous at Kolonos* [see below]).

One might think that at this juncture we could consult Aischylos' version of the quarrel in his *Hepta*, where Polyneikes' assault on Thebes forms the action of the play. Yet that drama is surprisingly reticent on the subject. As the play begins, we find Eteokles at the battlements of Thebes preparing for the attack; the play remains with Eteokles for its entire course, and neither he nor the chorus chooses to discuss what led to such a state of affairs. It is, of course, clear that Eteokles has the kingship and that Polyneikes wants it, but we do not learn the basis of the former's tenure or the latter's claim. At one point, Polyneikes does call his brother (via messenger speech) an exiler (*Hepta* 637–38),[37] which might seem to support Pherekydes' version, and both brothers claim to have Dike on their side. But the larger action of the play suggests, I believe, a background closer to that documented by Stesichoros and Hellanikos. Although Eteokles is, from the beginning, aware of his father's curse on himself and his brother, for much of the play's length he seems to trust that that curse has been deflected. Only when he discovers that Polyneikes will face him at the seventh gate does his hope waver; indeed, it collapses altogether as he abandons himself to the Erinys of his father's imprecation and prepares for battle.

This shift from defiance to utter capitulation is truly abrupt, and has caused some critics to locate responsibility in an Erinys-sent madness that deprives Eteokles of his reason.[38] It may be, however, that we here pay the price of not having the second play, where the curse must have taken place. From what remains, its terms are not quite clear, but it appears that the sons were fated to divide the property by the sword (*Hepta* 785–90). If such a prediction offers little basis for optimism, there was also a dream (to whom we do not know: *Hepta* 709–11) which may have spoken of a foreign mediator coming to allot the shares (*Hepta* 727–33). This dream apparently served the same role as the mother in the Stesichorean version, that is, it held out hope that the most extreme implications of the curse—mutual fratricide—could be avoided. Probably, then, in the *Oidipous* the two brothers worked out an arrangement by lot, thus leading Eteokles to hope that the curse had been averted or at least softened. Instead, when he finds that an *allotment* held by the Argive champions has brought Polyneikes opposite him in battle, he realizes finally the grim truth: the foreign mediator is simply iron, and curse and dream both point to the same inexorable outcome.[39] Thus he arms himself, despite the chorus' protests, and sets out for the last gate in the knowledge that he and Polyneikes are destined to die there, sharing out only whatever land their corpses will occupy.

If this interpretation of the *Hepta's* dramatic action is correct, it leads to a further conclusion, namely that the action of the preceding *Oidipous* was set at a time when the two brothers were old enough to be cursed, that is, when their father Oidipous had become an old man. In that case, the trilogy omitted the staging of his great discovery about himself, relegating it no doubt to choral odes or the audience's previous knowledge, a situation that many scholars are reluctant to suppose. But the alternative is to conclude that Oidipous cursed his sons when they had done nothing to him, and indeed were too young to understand his words. The Second Stasimon of the *Hepta* has seemed to some to imply this, for we learn there that Oidipous, when he became apprised of what he had done, "carried away in pain over his wretched marriage, with maddened heart accomplished a twin evil. With the hand that killed his father he took away his eyes, dearer than children [?]. And wrathful at the fostering/tendance he cast bitter-tongued curses upon his children, that they would someday share out the property with an iron-wielding hand" (*Hepta* 778–90).[40]

The last sentence of this passage begins a new antistrophe, and so might be separated from the rest, yet the apparent meaning of the Greek, with its epexegetic asyndeton and subsequent connective, is that Oidipous after the discovery committed two unfortunate deeds: he blinded himself and cursed his sons. If he did both these things immediately, his motive for the curse will have been that his children were the product of an incestuous union. But the form of that curse is then strange indeed. We might expect that a father would wish such children swallowed up by oblivion as quickly as possible, but not made to incur further pollution through fratricide. And why, if the motive is the children's begetting, is the curse made to address only the sons, not the daughters? What Aischylos shows us is a man who is angry, certainly, but angry *at* his sons; hence the precise shape of his curse. The cause must then somehow be found in the word *trophas*, "care, upbringing, tendance," whatever the meaning of its modifier (if it has one): the sons' care of their father in his old age has in some way been at fault, perhaps for one or both of the reasons given in the *Thebais*, perhaps for something else. The transgression may have been shown or related, but the curse will form the first part of the play, and efforts to avert or soften it the second. As one possibility for the latter, Eteokles may have triumphed in a winner-take-all lottery and thus been able to exile Polyneikes. Such conclusions still leave us, however, with the "twin evil" of *Hepta* 782 to be explained. Either the curse was proclaimed many years after the discovery, or the evil in question was the putting out of one's "twin" eyes, as a scholiast supposed. I am not entirely happy with either of these proposals, straining as they both do the Greek, but I find them preferable to a reconstruction that treats the curse too casually. We should remember, too, that Aischylos' audience knew very well what he meant to say, having just seen the *Oidipous;* thus some obscurity of expression would be more tolerable. In all, our evidence suggests that for the Archaic period Oidipous' old age at Thebes and ill-treatment by his sons was an important part of his story, perhaps even as important as the catastrophe of his earlier days.

For the end of the fifth century we have evidence from both Euripides and Sophokles. Euripides' *Oidipous,* since it treated the discovery, probably had nothing to say about later events, although it might have predicted Oidipous' future. Much more information comes from the same poet's counterpart to the *Hepta,* the *Phoinissai,* especially the prologue spoken by Iokaste. Obviously, in this version Oidipous has only one wife, and she remains alive long after the discovery and his self-blinding. Oidipous himself is, as the play opens, also still alive, but his sons on coming to manhood have shut him up in hopes of causing their shame to be forgotten. For this reason he curses them to divide their inheritance by the sword, and they respond by agreeing to remain apart. But here for the first time we encounter the idea of an exchange of roles, that is, that the two brothers have agreed to alternate between ruling Thebes and staying in exile. Polyneikes takes the first shift of a year away from Thebes, then finds himself permanently ousted when Eteokles fails to adhere to the bargain. As their subsequent debate shows, Eteokles stands throughout this debate as the villain; he acknowledges the injustice of his conduct but holds it of no account when set against the chance to retain power. By contrast, in versions where Polyneikes is compensated for his departure (as in Hellanikos) the subsequent conflict seems entirely his doing as the one abjuring the agreement. Either way, however, we find in this play, as in Stesichoros and Hellanikos (and, I believe, in Aischylos), the idea that the brothers are cursed to kill each other, and seek to avoid that fate by physical separation. In Sophokles' *Oidipous at Kolonos*, our only preserved source of this period to send Oidipous away from Thebes before his sons' death, matters take a different turn, owing probably to the fact that Sophokles wished to present the curse onstage rather than earlier. We learn here that after the initial shock of discovery of his deeds Oidipous repented of his wish to leave Thebes and desired to stay; Kreon, however, turned him out nonetheless, and his sons did nothing to help him. Even so, he held his peace for the time, and his sons fell to quarreling over the throne of their own accord. Eteokles got the upper hand with the people and expelled his brother, who in the course of the play comes to his exiled father for his blessing and receives instead his curse.

Thus we have a variety of possibilities for the quarrel, including that of Aischylos' *Hepta* where the mutual fate (hence mutual transgression?) of the two brothers is stressed rather than anything one did to the other. Later authors such as Diodoros and Apollodoros give us the same version of the dispute as the *Phoinissai*, so that the rotating-year motif, whatever its antiquity, has become far and away the most familiar form of the story (DS 4.65.1; ApB 3.6.1; *Fab* 67 makes Oidipous ordain this alternation of rule after his self-blinding). In all accounts, after leaving Thebes Polyneikes makes his way to Argos, where he marries the daughter of Adrastos and mobilizes the Argives for a military expedition against his homeland. We shall return to his checkered fortunes in the next two sections, after we have considered the larger background of this ill-fated expedition.

Adrastos, Eriphyle, and Amphiaraos In chapter 5 we found that for the *Ehoiai* (although not for Pherekydes) Bias and Pero's marriage is blessed with a son Talaos (Hes fr 37 MW). The *Ehoiai* does not develop the family further at this point in the poem, but in Bakchylides a Talaos is the father of Adrastos of Argos (9.19), and Pindar speaks of Adrastos and the other sons of Talaos who confer their sister Eriphyle on Amphiaraos, son of Oikles (*Nem* 9.9–17). Adrastos (no parentage mentioned) has already appeared in the *Iliad* as ruler of Sikyon (*Il* 2.572), father-in-law of Tydeus (*Il* 14.121), and owner of the divinely fast horse Areion (*Il* 23.346–47). He does not appear in the *Odyssey*, but the *Nekuia* tells of Eriphyle as the woman who took gold for her husband (*Od* 11.326–27), and later we hear of Amphiaraos as the man who died at Thebes "because of gifts to a woman" (*Od* 15.246–47). The details of this latter event, namely Amphiaraos' fatal participation in Polyneikes' expedition, are well known to later writers, and must have been recounted in detail by both the *Thebais* and Stesichoros' *Eriphyle*.

The famous Middle Corinthian krater once in Berlin (and considered in chapter 5 for its illustration of the funeral games for Pelias) shows on its other side Amphiaraos' departure for the battle (Berlin: Lost F1655). As he steps into his chariot he turns his head back to view the crowd of well-wishers waving goodbye from the doors of the palace. To the rear stands Eriphyle (so named); one hand holds a necklace. There are also a half-grown son and another child sitting on a woman's shoulder; unfortunately, these are not named, but we will see that they are important. A Black-Figure lekanis lid offers fragments of a very similar composition (Athens Akr 2112), and Pausanias would appear to have seen much the same scene on the Chest of Kypselos (5.17.7–8), so that perhaps all were inspired by a large-scale composition. On the Chest, if Pausanias is actually reading inscriptions, the group in front of the house waving goodbye to Amphiaraos includes an old woman carrying the infant Amphilochos, Eriphyle with the necklace, her daughters Eurydike and Demonassa, and a naked Alkmaion; Baton stands in the chariot and Amphiaraos again turns around as he steps in. Certain from this group, on a Black-Figure amphora of about 520 B.C., are Eriphyle and Alkmaion, both named as the mother holds up the child to the departing warrior (Chiusi 1794).[41] In Attic Red-Figure beginning about 450 B.C. we actually see Polyneikes handing the necklace to Eriphyle (e.g., Lecce 570). Our later sources will specify that the whole story started with a dispute between the families of Adrastos and Amphiaraos, and indeed Pindar does say that Adrastos once fled Amphiaraos, with Eriphyle's bestowal to the latter becoming the token of reconciliation (*Nem* 9.13–17). But neither Bakchylides nor Pindar discuss Eriphyle's subsequent transaction in what survives of their work (although Pindar seems to have mentioned it: fr 182 SM), and our actual account comes from Amphiaraos himself in Euripides' *Hypsipyle*, plus scholia to Pindar and the *Odyssey*.

As the Pindar scholia relate these matters, there was a quarrel over something (land and power, presumably) between the descendants of Melampous (i.e., Amphiaraos) and those of his brother Bias (Talaos and his family: Σ *Nem* 9.30 *passim*). In a version then cited as from the fourth-century historian Menaichmos of Sikyon, Pronax, son of Talaos, is king of Argos but dies, and his brother Adrastos flees to Sikyon where he inherits the kingdom of his mother Lysimache's father Polybos (Σ *Nem* 9.30 = 131F10; on this last point cf. Hdt 5.67). According to others, however, the dispute leads to Amphiaraos' slaying of Talaos, after which Adrastos flees as before but gets the kingdom of

Sikyon by *marrying* Polybos' daughter (Σ *Nem* 9.30b). Either way, Polybos dies without heirs, and the throne of Sikyon passes to Adrastos. Subsequently there is a reconciliation between the two sides, with as in Pindar the marriage of Eriphyle, sister of Adrastos, to Amphiaraos.

The further developments are offered by the *Odyssey* scholia at 11.326, and since these are credited to Asklepiades they probably reflect one or more Attic tragedies, including Aischylos' *Epigonoi* and Sophokles' *Epigonoi* and *Eriphyle* (these last probably, though not certainly, separate plays). None of these dramas will have presented the actual betrayal, but all of them may have referred to it in exposition; the same is true for numerous *Alkmaion* plays by different authors (including two by Euripides) treating either the matricide or its aftermath. Whether the betrayal could ever be said to have a humorous side I do not know, but Sophokles did write a satyric *Amphiaraos* of unknown content (perhaps culminating in the marriage to Eriphyle). In any event, Asklepiades' account begins on a slightly different note from what we found in Pindar, for here Amphiaraos and Eriphyle are already married when the dispute arises (12F29). Somehow she resolves the argument, and the two men declare that in future they will always abide by her decision in disputes between them. When the expedition for Thebes is taking shape, Amphiaraos tries to warn the Argives of their impending doom, but is himself forced to join them by Eriphyle, who has received from Polyneikes the necklace of Harmonia. Her husband has seen her take the gift, however, and while he has no choice but to go, he does exact from his son Alkmaion a promise to avenge him. Later sources all follow this basic narrative without any significant deviation, save that in one note of the Pindaric scholia Adrastos harbors a grudge against Amphiaraos, and himself uses the necklace to bribe his sister, so that her husband might be destroyed (Σ *Nem* 9.35).[42] The scholiast may have a genuine tradition for this, but he may also be guessing in an effort to explain *Nemean* 9's aphoristic line 15.

Backtracking now from this early attested phase of Polyneikes' recruitment of allies, we must start at the beginning of the affair, his actual arrival in Argos and marriage to Adrastos' daughter. The *Iliad* says nothing on this point, although there must be some reason for Argos' support of a Theban exile in that poem, and Homer does mention Tydeus' similar marriage (*Il* 14.121, as above). All later sources, beginning with Pherekydes (probably), call the daughter whom Tydeus marries Deipyle (3F122), and likewise they agree that Polyneikes' bride was Argeia. Previously in this chapter we saw that an Argeia, daughter of Adrastos, came to the funeral of Oidipous at Thebes in the *Ehoiai* (Hes fr 192 MW). Possibly she was at that time already married to Polyneikes, although our text says simply that she came with others. Alternatively, Polyneikes might still have been living at Thebes, and have met his future bride for the first time on this occasion, subsequently going to Argos to seek her hand (and Adrastos' support). The Lille Stesichoros papyrus provides just enough text (after the brothers have drawn for throne and property) to show that Teiresias predicted Polyneikes' migration to Argos, where Adrastos would offer him his daughter; more details must have been given, but they do not survive, nor do we have any idea what the *Thebais* might have contributed. The first preserved accounts of Polyneikes' wooing are in three plays of Euripides, *Hiketides*, *Hypsipyle*, and *Phoinissai*; Polyneikes himself gives the most complete version in the last of these, but the main details have already been anticipated by Adrastos in the first. In this play Polyneikes comes to Adrastos' door by night, seeking shelter, and apparently finds a bed (or at least porch) available for that purpose (E: *Hik* 131–61). Soon after, another exile, Tydeus, son of Oineus, arrives seeking the same thing, and the two begin to fight over the available space. When Adrastos comes out to investigate the commotion he remembers an oracle given to him by Apollo, that he should marry his daughters to a boar and a lion, and from the manner of their fighting deduces that these two men are what the god intended. Polydeukes and Tydeus thus become his sons-in-law; to each of them he promises restoration to their homeland, beginning with Polyneikes.

With this much as evidence we can understand more clearly a Chalkidian calyx krater of about 530 B.C. on which we see a scene of the arrival: to the right Adrastos (named) reclines on his couch, with a woman standing to one side; both look to the far left where two men are seated on the ground, their mantles wrapped round them, with two more women standing over them talking to each other (Copenhagen VIII 496). One of the two seated men is inscribed as Tydeus, the other (perhaps: the inscription is not immediately beside him) as [Pr]omachos. No other names survive, but it seems a reasonable guess that the female figures are Adrastos' wife (Amphithea?) and two daughters, and that Promachos (or whoever) is meant to be Polyneikes, come like Tydeus in search of shelter. Aischylos' *Hepta* presumably understands the same basic events, since Adrastos, Amphiaraos, and Tydeus are all part of the expedition with Polyneikes (Adrastos in a noncombat role), and no explanation of their presence is considered necessary.

One other question raised by Euripides' detailed account of Adrastos' bestowal of his daughters concerns the role of Apollo in counseling a course of action that leads to disaster. In *Hiketides*, Theseus comes close to exculpating the god by intimating that Adrastos misinterpreted the oracle in marrying his daughters to two total strangers (E: *Hik* 135–45). Polyneikes in relating the same events to Iokaste in *Phoinissai* has no such doubts about its meaning, but we will expect his perspective to be different. The chorus of the lost *Hypsipyle* also recounted the conflict of Tydeus and Polyneikes and their subsequent marriages, perhaps in more detail than either of our preserved Euripidean plays, but only scraps confirming the oracle about animals remain (12 GLP). Our later sources, including Apollodoros (ApB 3.6.1) and the *Iliad* and *Phoinissai* scholia (ΣA *Il* 4.376; Σ *Pho* 409), plus Statius (St: *Theb* 1.390–497) and Hyginus (*Fab* 69), all adhere to the view that Apollo's oracle did command the marriages, and usually add more convincing grounds for Adrastos' reading of it: either the two heroes bear on their shields the insignia of a lion (Polyneikes) and boar (Tydeus: ApB, Σ *Pho*) or they are clad in the skins of those animals (Σ *Pho*, ΣA *Il*, St:*Theb*, Hyg). Sometimes the creatures even become symbols for the lands of those they designate, with the lion indicating the Sphinx and the boar the Kalydonian Boar (Σ *Pho*, Hyg). Conceivably these details are late inventions to make Adrastos' deduction more plausible than it appears in Euripides. Yet the motif of bridegrooms recognized through prophecy does have solid credentials in folklore, and perhaps it is here an early part of the story toned down by Euripides in order to serve the desired characterization of Adrastos as a man who does not use good judgment in dealing with the gods. If that is so, we are left with an Apollo as obscure as ever in his maneuvering of the Argives toward catastrophe. In any event, the result of Polyneikes' marriage is always the same: Adrastos promises his help, Eriphyle is bribed to commit her husband to the endeavor, and an expedition of Argives and their allies sets forth for Thebes to restore the exile to the throne his brother occupies.

The Expedition of the Seven

As we saw above, the *Iliad* knows of the march on Thebes by a generation prior to the one at Troy, and we learn from Sthenelos that his father Kapaneus and Diomedes' father Tydeus joined Polyneikes in his unsuccessful assault (*Il* 4.405–10). Agamemnon adds the tale of Tydeus' embassy to which we will return shortly. The *Works & Days* counts the event together with the siege of Troy as the two great exploits of the age of heroes (*W&D* 161–63), and the epic *Thebais*, as the opening line showed us, began (and no doubt concluded) with it. From this last work we gain the name of another participant, Parthenopaios (fr 6 *PEG*), and perhaps a speech in honor of Amphiaraos (fr 10 *PEG*) but little more (possibly Tydeus' devouring of Melanippos' brains: see below). Pausanias saw Eteokles and Polyneikes actually fighting each other on the Chest of Kypselos (with a Ker: Paus 5.19.6). And Hekataios is named among those who made Parthenopaios a son of Talaos (and thus it would seem a brother of Adrastos: 1F32). But beyond these few scraps we must rely on the fifth century, and in particular Pindar, Bakchylides, and of course Aischylos, to be followed at century's end by Euripides' two plays previously mentioned, the *Hiketides* and *Phoinissai*.

For the preliminaries to the expedition we do, however, have useful information from the *Iliad*: Polyneikes and Tydeus together come to Mykenai to seek assistance, and the citizens there are minded to help them, but Zeus sends contrary omens, and the mission fails (*Il* 4.376–81). Homer then proceeds to the embassy to Thebes (logically enough, since Tydeus is the topic at hand) and omits the stop at Phlious. Our first reference to this second phase of their journey comes from Simonides, who says that they lamented the death of the child [Archemoros] (553 *PMG*). Bakchylides takes matters a step further: at Phlious the Argive heroes set up the Nemean games in honor of Archemoros, whom a snake has slain in his sleep; the event is somehow taken as an omen of Argive failure at Thebes (Bak 9.10–20). Pindar agrees, in *Nemean* 9, that

Adrastos founded the Nemean games on the banks of the Asopos (the river that flows past Phlious and Sikyon) but does not say why (*Nem* 9.9). The hypothesis to the *Nemean Odes* as a whole offers several different versions of the story, including the fact that in Aischylos, among others, this Archemoros is the son of Nemea.[43] Presumably, then, the child's death and the games' founding were the subjects of his lost play *Nemea*. Unfortunately, neither the hypothesis nor any other source tells us anything more about Aischylos' handling of the tale.

The loss of Aischylos' play is the greater because Euripides in his partially preserved *Hypsipyle* offers us quite a different mother for the same child, one Eurydike, wife of Lykourgos, a priest of Nemean Zeus; Hypsipyle, the former paramour of Iason, is involved because she has become the child's nurse, after being exiled from Lemnos and captured by pirates. The child here has as his given name Opheltes, to be changed to Archemoros in the course of the story. As the action of the play opens, Amphiaraos and his companions are on their way north to Thebes, and encounter Hypsipyle while searching for water with which to perform a sacrifice.[44] She takes the seer to a spring guarded by a serpent, and there the serpent somehow manages to kill the child. Eurydike is naturally bent on revenge, but Amphiaraos persuades her that what has happened was destined: the child will be called Archemoros, as signaling the beginning of the expedition's doom, and games will be established. Eurydike yields to this explanation, and the remainder of the play—Hypsipyle's recognition of her sons, who have come to find her—need not concern us here. Apollodoros (Ap*B* 3.6.4), Hyginus (*Fab* 74, with a prophecy that the child is not to be put down until he can walk), and the *Nemean Odes* hypothesis all provide a similar account of Archemoros' parentage and death. The hypothesis' one other significant variation lies in the presenting of a third set of parents, Euphetes and Kreousa. That Aischylos told this same story of Lemnian nurse and snake in his *Nemea* with merely a different name for the mother (and perhaps the father) is possible, but I doubt it: surely neither Aischylos nor anyone else would have named such a play after the child's mother if the plot focused on the misfortunes of the nurse who failed to guard her charge. We must allow, I think, that Aischylos' version may well not have included Hypsipyle at all.

Elsewhere there is some scant evidence that might relate to the Euripidean parents, and which in any case should be noted. Pausanias tells us that on the Amyklai Throne Adrastos and Tydeus halt a fight between Amphiaraos and Lykourgos, son of Pronax (3.18.12). The same scene is apparently represented on the elbow guard of a shield-strap from Olympia where a central figure named as Adrastos stands with raised arm between two warriors closing in battle; other unarmed men to either side forcibly restrain them (B 1654). Other names preserved, though unfortunately incomplete, identify the left-hand combatant as [. . . mph.ar.o . . .]—surely Amphiaraos—and someone on the right side (not necessarily the combatant) as [. . .]orgos—very likely Lykourgos. If this is the Lykourgos of the *Hypsipyle*, and if he was present to witness or hear of his son's death in some accounts (in Euripides, he is out of town), he might well blame Amphiaraos for the tragedy and seek vengeance. But against this possibility is the fact that the shield-relief offers no sign of a woman or child, although there is certainly room for them. We saw, too, that in the *Nemean Odes* scholia Pronax is the son of Talaos and brother of Adrastos, and this arrangement occurs also in Apollodoros (Ap*B* 1.9.13). Thus, if Pausanias' information is right, the Lykourgos of the Throne would be Adrastos' nephew, and more likely a part of the expedition setting out from Argos than someone encountered along the way at Nemea. For what it is worth, Apollodoros himself distinguishes two Lykourgoi in his discussion of these legends, the one a son of Pronax of whom we hear nothing more, the other a son of Pheres (and brother of Admetos) who marries Eurydike and begets Opheltes (Ap*B* 1.9.14). How early this latter figure might be we cannot say; our Archaic sources neither mention nor exclude him. In any case, and with one father or other, the child and his death seem an established part of the tale. Whether Opheltes and Archemoros might ever have been two separate children, with the one usurping the death of the other, remains less certain.

As for the quarrel on the Throne, it is apparently also portrayed on a Lakonian cup by the Hunt Painter of which only a small fragment has been found (Cyrene, no #). The part preserved shows a warrior grasping the wrist of a comrade who has drawn his sword, and the restrainer is clearly named as Parthenopaios; behind him is another figure whose name ends in -os (Adrastos?). This does not help us much, but it does seem to ensure that the quarrel was somehow a part of the story of the Seven (unless Parthenopaios is here in his capacity as a member of Talaos' family). We will see shortly that in Aischylos (and probably earlier) there is bad blood between Amphiaraos and Tydeus, and it has therefore been suggested (since both are present on the Throne) that Pausanias failed to attach the right names to the right figures in making his description. The shield-strap might confirm this view *if* the (restored) name "Lykourgos" there refers to one of the on-lookers, with the name of Tydeus lost over the head of the right-hand warrior.[45] But perhaps there is a dispute alluded to in these works which we have simply lost. Hekataios offers the odd remark that Amphiaraos once fell asleep while standing guard, and suffered the consequences of it (1F33); perhaps this error, whatever its circumstances, was what aroused Lykourgos' (or Tydeus') anger.

The third event preliminary to the actual assault on Thebes is that mentioned several times by the *Iliad*, the sending of Tydeus into the city alone to negotiate with Eteokles. In *Iliad* 4, Agamemnon says that this happened when the forces had come to the Asopos River, and completed a good part of their journey; thus he is thinking, as we would expect, of the Boiotian Asopos that runs south of Thebes, not the Sikyonian Asopos where the Nemean games were founded (*Il* 4.382–400). Tydeus arrives in the city with a message for the Kadmeians, and finds the leaders gathered together in feasting at the home of Eteokles. Undaunted, he challenges them all to contests, and with Athena's help wins everything easily. The losers are sufficiently angered that they send a force of fifty men, led by Maion and Polyphontes, to ambush Tydeus on his way back to the Asopos. He kills forty-nine of these, sparing only Maion, whom he sends back to Thebes on the advice of the gods. Athena and Diomedes both mention this same event more briefly in later parts of the poem (*Il* 5.800–808, 10.285–90); the only new detail is Diomedes' statement that Tydeus was carrying a "gentle message," that is, not just a threat. What we do not learn from any of these passages is how the Kadmeians responded to the message; presumably they rejected any appeal for negotiation, and then too Tydeus' *aristeia*, not his diplomatic skill, is the point of the story. In Diodoros' version, Adrastos sends the hero all the way up to Thebes from Argos to seek Polyneikes' return (DS 4.65.4). Conceivably here the ambush takes place before he reaches Thebes, but in any case he slays all and returns to Argos, and only then is the expedition mobilized. Status devotes most of Book 2 of his *Thebais* to the episode; Tydeus leaves from Argos as in Diodoros, but here there is a lengthy confrontation with Eteokles, who refuses any claims based on justice, and the ambush occurs as usual on the return. Apollodoros returns to the Homeric version, with Tydeus dispatched just south of Thebes and killing all but Maion (ApB 3.6.5). Likely enough the adventure played a major role in the epic *Thebais* or some other early narrative as a foretale to the actual assault; Status' lengthy treatment well shows how easily the story lends itself to elaboration.

Given, then, this likelihood of a substantial early telling of Tydeus' advance exploits at Thebes, we may consider here too the odd tale of Tydeus and Ismene, for the encounter between them must occur either during the embassy or as part of the general attack, and the possibilities for such a story in the earlier context will obviously be greater. Our first evidence comes from Mimnermos: a scholiast says that in his poems Tydeus, on the command of Athena, slew Ismene while she was consorting sexually with one Theoklymenos (21 W). The scholiast concedes the strangeness of this, as he does the version of Ion of Chios in which both Antigone and Ismene are burned to death in a temple of Hera by Laodamas, son of Eteokles (740 *PMG*), but offers no motive for either event. A Late Corinthian amphora now in the Louvre adds pictorial support: Tydeus (all figures named) advances with drawn sword toward a bed on which Ismene reclines, her breasts uncovered, and with his free hand seizes her by the arm; behind him a naked Periklymenos runs away (Louvre E640). Even without Mimnermos, we should not have had much trouble divining the situation presented here; what we are still lacking, however, is any reason for Tydeus' interest in the misbehavior of an unrelated Theban woman. Intriguing, too, is the variant "Periklymenos" for Mimnermos' Theoklymenos, since in the epic *Thebais* Periklymenos is the Theban champion who defeats Parthenopaios. We should also note fragments of an Attic Black-Figure skyphos from the Akropolis: only Ismene (again named) actually survives, and appears to be kneeling on a bed while someone to the right of her grasps her by the wrist;

to the left survives an arm holding a spear vertically (Athens Akr 603). A White-Ground cup in the Louvre (G109: male figure leans over a second [female? center missing] with clearly hostile intent) has also been cited in this connection; I am dubious, but in any case with only the two figures the scene has nothing to tell us.[46] The same is true of a Red-Figure skyphos by the Triptolemos Painter now in Berlin on which a man in armor with drawn sword pursues a (clothed) woman as Athena watches, all in an architectural setting (Berlin:Ch Inv 1970.9).[47] To conclude, we have a reference in Pherekydes: among Oidipous' children is Ismene, whom Tydeus kills by a spring that is then named after her (3F95).

Such is the sum total of our information about the slaying; the story does not appear in any later author, and we are left with one of the more baffling situations in Greek myth. Tydeus' presence in any locale appropriate to intimate activities between Ismene and a lover seems impossible unless he has some claim on her as relative or betrothed. The former, of course, is not the case, and the latter automatically excluded by the fact that he only comes to Thebes by virtue of having married Deipyle, unless we postulate that all this took place before his arrival in Argos. Mimnermos' statement that Athena advised the slaying may help us here, since it implies that the goddess, not the mortal, was the one who was angry. But deducing a cause for Athena's anger at a trysting of lovers is not much easier, and her sending of Tydeus into Ismene's boudoir is almost as unconvincing as his entry there on his own initiative. Pherekydes' transfer of the slaying to a site outside the city removes the latter difficulty, but it may also remove the lover insisted upon by both Mimnermos and the Louvre amphora, and thus might represent a change in motive. Clearly the original story is very well hidden; just possibly its earliest forms involved an Ismene (such as the daughter of Asopos?) other than the Theban offspring of Oidipous.[48] Whatever we conclude, one cannot say that the cause of the expedition seems in any way advanced by her demise.

We come finally to the actual attack on the city, and in this connection must consider the identity of the seven champions who mount the assault. For seven or any specific number in the *Thebais* there is no evidence, unless Asklepiades' comment that Pindar borrowed lines from that work for his *Olympian* 6 refers to 6.15 (with its seven pyres; so too *Nem* 9.22–24) as well as the lament for Amphiaraos which follows (Σ *Ol* 6.26). But even if that were so (and it seems unlikely) we would have to debate for the *Thebais*, as we will for Pindar, what those seven pyres might signify. In *Olympian* 6 and all other preserved accounts, Amphiaraos is swallowed up by the earth and does not require cremation; likewise Adrastos, on all occasions on which he is one of the attackers, survives. In theory, then, Pindar should have just five or six pyres, if there were originally seven champions. Possibly though, as the scholia suggest, he means that there was a pyre for the *armies* of each of the seven champions (Σ *Ol* 6.23d), or perhaps a pyre for the fallen at each of Thebes' seven gates. But we cannot totally exclude the idea that an original group of seven did all perish in some early versions, or the possibility that from a larger group some survived. Indeed, Pausanias specifically claims that Aischylos brought the number down to seven from something larger, including heroes from Messenia and Arkadia (2.20.5). To such a notion we might object that seven champions is the logical number to utilize when one is assaulting a city with seven gates, but nothing before Aischylos pairs off the attackers with the gates, and surprisingly few sources after him, leaving us to wonder whether this motif has any early authority. All that we have then for the period before the fifth century is a group of uncertain size, from which we can guarantee Polyneikes, Tydeus, Kapaneus, Amphiaraos, and Parthenopaios, plus perhaps Lykourgos and of course Adrastos, if he is in early versions a combatant.

For the fifth century itself, there is the famous list/description of Aischylos' *Hepta,* where a band of seven champions (excluding Adrastos) is assigned one by one to each of the city's gates, with Eteokles then appointing seven defenders to oppose them. Later in the century Euripides will offer his own lists (slightly different from each other) in his *Hiketides* and *Phoinissai,* and Sophokles too in *Oidipous at Kolonos.* There is also from the first half of the century an Etruscan gem, now in Berlin, which shows five of the heroes (names inscribed) in conversation or brandishing weapons (Berlin: Ch GI 194).[49] The names provided are Parthenopaios, Amphiaraos, Polyneikes (all sitting), plus Tydeus and Adrastos standing in arms; of those we might definitely have expected to find only Kapaneus is lacking. That only five figures appear is probably not significant, given the difficulty of putting even that many on a gem.

In Aischylos we find the Seven saying a last farewell to Adrastos, who is present but not of their number, and giving him tokens for their loved ones before proceeding to the allotment of the gates (*Hepta* 42–56). That allotment is as follows: (1) Tydeus attacks the Proitid gate, with the moon and stars on his shield (Melanippos defends); (2) Kapaneus stands at the Elektran gate, a man with a torch on his shield (Polyphontes defends); (3) Eteoklos is at the Neistan gate, bearing on his shield a man scaling a siege-ladder (Megareus of the house of Kreon defends); (4) Hippomedon assaults the gate of Athena Onka, with a shield showing Typhon (Hyperbios, son of Oinops, defends); (5) Parthenopaios of Arkadia is at the North gate, a Sphinx on his shield (Aktor, brother of Hyperbios, defends); (6) Amphiaraos at the Homoloid gate bears no device at all on his shield (and engages in verbal abuse of Tydeus, whom he blames for the war; Lasthenes defends); (7) Polyneikes advances to the seventh gate, with Dike on his shield leading him back to his city (Eteokles defends). Such an arrangement lies for the most part along anticipated lines, with five of the six previously named heroes involved, and Adrastos escorting them but held out of battle. The resulting two openings fall to Hippomedon and Eteoklos. Both these names will reappear in later (perhaps also contemporary) lists, thus lessening the possibility that they were invented by Aischylos. Otherwise we might have been inclined to suppose novelty at least for Eteoklos, a name that might seem to represent an omen for Eteokles as the gates are assigned.

We should also note that there is here no sign of Periklymenos as the defender who slays Parthenopaios, in contrast to the account of the *Thebais*. Aischylos' *Epigonoi*, which must in some way have dealt with the sons of the Seven, presumably named some or all of the fathers, and its list might well have differed from that of the *Hepta*, but the play is completely lost, leaving behind no information of any sort.

Sophokles' *Antigone* reiterates the idea of seven champions at seven gates, without however offering names or details (*Ant* 141–43). In Euripides' *Hiketides* we find a list identical to the *Hepta's*; Adrastos is again not an actual attacker, and survives to seek from Theseus and the Athenians the recovery of the bodies of the slain (E:*Hik* 857–931). The only new information advanced here is that Parthenopaios becomes specifically the offspring of Atalanta, and Eteoklos emerges as the son of Iphis, whose daughter Euadne is married to Kapaneus. In the *Phoinissai*, by contrast, although six of the seven champions are the same, the warrior at the seventh and last gate is Adrastos, replacing Eteoklos; he withdraws after witnessing Kapaneus' fate and Zeus' displeasure (*Pho* 1104–38). Sophokles' *Kolonos* dramatizes only the anticipation of the conflict, but a full list is given, matching that of the *Hepta* and *Hiketides*; Eteoklos is here simply Argive-born, but Hippomedon is called a son of Talaos, which ought to make him another brother of Adrastos (*OK* 1311–25). Of later sources, Diodoros agrees with the *Phoinissai* in including Adrastos at the cost of Eteoklos (DS 4.65.4–5), and so too Statius (St:*Theb* 4.32–250), Apollodoros (ApB 3.6.3), and Hyginus (who makes Kapaneus and Hippomedon sons of sisters of Adrastos: *Fab* 70). But Apollodoros in the same place cites a variant according to which Eteoklos and Mekisteus (yet another brother of Adrastos: ApB 1.9.13; so too *Il* 2.566 and 23.678, where we saw him at the funeral of Oidipous) replace Polyneikes and Tydeus in the list of seven. Mekisteus is also a combatant, though not necessarily a leader, in Herodotos, where he is again a brother of Adrastos and a victim (like Tydeus) of Melanippos (Hdt 5.67.3); Pausanias at 9.18.1 says exactly the same. Conceivably, this alternate roster could represent a very old Argive version of the tale before outsiders became involved, but it might also reflect a desire in Argos for an all- (or largely) Argive seven, with less concern for the motivating role played by Polyneikes in the story. Adding Adrastos' two sons-in-law to such a group would give a total of nine, which might in part explain what Pausanias meant in saying that Aischylos *reduced* the number to seven.

One other source of uncertain date to be considered is Pausanias' description of the monument at Delphi showing the Seven, a monument set up by the Argives near the beginning of the Sacred Way to commemorate their victory over the Spartans at Oinoe (10.10.3). The victory, won by the Argives with the help of Athens, does not lend itself to a precise date, but most scholars would now agree on a time somewhere in the 450s B.C.[50] More to the point for our purposes is the source of Pausanias' identification of the various figures, since we do not know if he is working from inscriptions or local tradition, and if the former, whether the inscriptions are as old as the monument. The names given are: Adrastos, son of Talaos; Tydeus, son of Oineus; Kapaneus, son of Hipponoos, and Eteoklos, son of Iphis (these last two both descendants of Proitos); Polyneikes; Hippomedon, son of Adrastos' sister; Amphiaraos (or at least his chariot, in which stands a charioteer Baton); and finally one Alitherses. Thus we would seem to have eight heroes rather than seven. Conspicuously missing is Parthenopaios; the usual explanation, that the sculptors omitted him because he was not Argive (or even married to one) is probably correct. As for the large number, Pausanias' language certainly suggests that he thought all eight figures were participants, but of course he may be wrong; possibly the sculptors conceived of Adrastos, placed as he is at one end, in the escort role he so often plays elsewhere. Or we could drop the totally unknown Alitherses at the other end and consider him like Baton a supernumerary. If we could be sure of a *c.* 450 date for these names we would have a more secure background for Eteoklos, whose antiquity we suspected above as oddly similar in name to Eteokles. Conceivably Aischylos utilized this figure rather than Adrastos as one of his Seven so that all the attackers would perish. But we must admit that in the final analysis we do not know whether Adrastos was ever a combatant in early times. Our one real piece of evidence for that point comes from Pausanias, who says that in the *Thebais* Adrastos flees Thebes on his horse Areion, wearing "mournful clothing" (8.25.8). His flight and torn (?) garments might suggest that he was one of the fighters, but the latter might also signify that he himself tore his clothing when he saw the fate of his friends. For my own part, I do not see why Euripides would have placed Adrastos at the seventh gate (it makes little difference to his play) if he had not found such an idea in earlier works, and then too there is no reason why as one of the instigators of the expedition Adrastos should not fight in the earliest versions of the story. But for all that, he may not have.

We should note in concluding that even among the Argives the list of participants seems not to have been firmly fixed: Pausanias at Argos itself saw an undated Epigonoi group that included sons of Parthenopaios (here the son of Talaos), Hippomedon, Polyneikes, Tydeus, Kapaneus, Amphiaraos, Adrastos, and even Mekisteus, but no son of Eteoklos (2.20.5).[51] I suggested above that Parthenopaios was missing from the Delphi dedication of the Argives because of his Arkadian origin. If so, this Argive claim of parentage from Talaos, first found as we saw in Hekataios, probably represents an attempt to convert him to Argive status and thus justify his participation.

Turning now to details of the combat, we must for the period before 500 B.C. content ourselves with the two small bits of certain information seen above from the *Thebais*, that Periklymenos defeated Parthenopaios and that Adrastos fled the scene on his famous horse. Surprisingly there is nothing preserved from Black-Figure or other Archaic art until the very end of that period (*c.* 460 B.C.), when we find the battle portrayed on the central antepagmentum in the pediment of Temple A at the Etruscan port of Pyrgi.[52] Here two scenes elegantly overlap: from the left Athena approaches, a small jar in her hand, while the center stage shows two warriors sprawled on the ground, the one biting into the skull of the other, and behind them Zeus preparing to hurl his thunderbolt at yet another warrior. Already in the *Hepta* Eteokles has hinted that Zeus will strike down the boaster Kapaneus (*Hepta* 444–46), and this is uniformly the later tradition. As for the remaining figures, both Bakchylides (fr 41 SM) and Pherekydes (3F97) tell us that Athena intended to make Tydeus immortal, and Pherekydes further explains the occasion as the moment of Tydeus' death in battle: he has been wounded by Melanippos, and when Amphiaraos kills the latter and throws Tydeus the head, he begins to gnaw on its brains in his rage. At this critical juncture Athena arrives from *ouranos* bearing immortality, but when she sees Tydeus' savage behavior she throws it away in disgust. Tydeus perceives this before he dies, and exhorts the goddess to bestow the favor on his son instead. The immediate source of this account is the *Iliad* scholia at 5.126 (AbT); all three manuscript traditions credit it to Pherekydes, and we have no reason to doubt them. But much the same account, although in different language, appears in the Geneva scholia to the *Iliad*, with the words "the story is from the Cyclic poets" appended by a later hand.[53] If this is correct, then the tale of Tydeus' lost immortality probably goes back to the *Thebais* (Bernabé includes the scholion as part of his *Thebais* fr 9). The story reappears in Apollodoros (who specifies that Amphiaraos' intention in giving Tydeus the head was precisely to rob him of Athena's gift: Ap*B* 3.6.8), and is clearly what our Etruscan antepagmentum intends. Apollodoros does omit the transfer of the immortality to Diomedes, but Athena's bestowal of that status on the latter is noted by Pindar (*Nem* 10.7) and explained as above by the appended scholia (Σ *Nem* 10.12). In art, we also have a fragmentary Red-Figure bell krater in New York on which a man, presumably Tydeus, is seated on a rock and accompanied by Athena and Athanasia ("Immortality": NY 12.229.14); a now lost bell krater by the Eupolis Painter or his like, showing Athena leading a maiden away from a seated warrior, may intend the same scene (the Rosi Krater).[54] The Pyrgi terracotta contains as well a sixth figure, another warrior, who stands between and behind Zeus and Kapaneus; possibly he represents Kapaneus' original Theban opponent whom Zeus supplants.

For these two of the Seven, then, we have special stories, obviously Archaic in origin, which remain standard in later times. Adrastos is as we saw always saved, combatant or not, and the other attackers are all simply killed by their Theban counterparts, with the exception of Amphiaraos. His fate, to be swallowed up by the ground while still alive, is first preserved in Pindar's *Nemean* 9 and *Nemean* 10. *Nemean* 9 says that Zeus accomplished this, chariot and all, so that he might not be slain by the pursuing Periklymenos (*Nem* 9.25–27); *Nemean* 10 adds that the god split the ground with his thunderbolt (*Nem* 10.8–9). That the seer continues to exist under the earth seems indicated by *Pythian* 8, where he delivers a prophecy as the Epigonoi set out for Thebes (*Py* 8.38–55). Aischylos has, save for the allusion to Kapaneus' fate, none of this; a messenger simply reports back to the chorus that at six of the gates all has gone well, while at the seventh Oidipous' two sons have killed each other. Quite possibly the same poet's *Eleusinioi* or *Argeiai*, although they dealt with the aftermath of the expedition, contained a fuller account of the combats; Kapaneus' fate is mentioned in one fragment of the *Argeiai* (fr 17 R). Sophokles' *Antigone* has nothing relevant about the battle, and Adrastos' funeral speech in Euripides' *Hiketides* merely repeats what we already know of Kapaneus and Amphiaraos while omitting Tydeus' misfortune. But in the *Phoinissai* we get a more unusual sequence of events: after an initial pitched battle in which Kapaneus is struck by a thunderbolt and Parthenopaios is slain by Periklymenos, the Thebans gain the upper hand, and Adrastos pulls his forces back (*Pho* 1141–99, 1219–39). Eteokles then offers to fight Polyneikes in single combat to decide the entire outcome; in the resulting duel, he uses a Thessalian trick to deliver a fatal wound to his brother, but fails to finish him off before taking the spoils (*Pho* 1356–1424). With his dying breath Polyneikes returns the favor, and Iokaste completes the picture by killing herself over the two bodies (*Pho* 1455–59).

One other important detail to be noted in the *Phoinissai* is the prophecy of Teiresias that the city will be saved only if Menoikeus—a hitherto unattested son of Kreon—should throw himself from the walls to the spot where Kadmos slew the dragon, in atonement for that deed (*Pho* 903–1018). Menoikeus tricks his father into leaving the stage, then hurries off to the walls to perform the required sacrifice. Makaria and Iphigeneia are two other examples of Euripides' fondness for voluntary self-immolation, and he may well have invented its appearance here, but we cannot say for certain. Apollodoros includes both the single combat and Menoikeus, and seems by his account to be drawing directly from the tragedian (ApB 3.6.7–8). Statius also presents them, but in the context of a much broader tapestry in which the seven attackers fall one by one over several books until only Eteokles and Polyneikes are left to fight; again we miss the strict symmetry of the seven combats at seven gates found in Aischylos. Art has relatively little to offer, other than those pieces with Tydeus noted above: A volute krater of the mid-fifth century does offer a panorama of all the combatants (Ferrara 3031). But amidst these latter, only Amphiaraos is distinguished in any way, as he and his charioteer and horses sink down into the earth at the bottom of the scene; the other figures are merely stock warriors (for a slightly earlier version of Amphiaraos' fate, shown in isolation, see Athens 1125, a Black-Figure lekythos by the Beldam Painter).

*Antigone
and the
Burial of
the Seven*

Next in the sequence of events following the attack of the Seven comes Kreon's refusal to inter their bodies, and the defiance of this proclamation by Antigone when she buries the corpse of her brother Polyneikes. We have seen that Pausanias strongly implies a knowledge in early epic of Oidipous' children, and presumably the ones known to us, but no source prior to the fifth century ever mentions Antigone, in this context or any other. Both she and Ismene emerge at the end of Aischylos' *Hepta* to lament the loss of their brothers, and this is her first appearance in literature or art (*Hepta* 961-1004). The sisters' dirge is, however, interrupted at line 1005 by a herald bearing Kreon's decree, and Antigone in response to this vows at the play's end that she will bury Polyneikes nonetheless. For a variety of reasons, including stylistic ones, most scholars have come to feel that this last section of the drama cannot have been written by Aischylos, and I believe that to be the case.[55] More likely, the final scene with its hanging conclusion was added onto the *Hepta* to update it for a later revival, when the story of the negated burial had become virtually mandatory due to audience familiarity with it. Harder to say is whether the sisters should be excised from the *Hepta* altogether, or allowed to perform their lament. But they are both mentioned as Oidipous' daughters by Pherekydes (3F95), and thus they have some standing prior to Sophokles.

Nevertheless, if the above conclusion about the *Hepta* is correct, then Sophokles is our first source to say anything about Antigone's act of heroism. As his play *Antigone* opens, she is lamenting the decree prohibiting burial of Polyneikes as the latest in a series of catastrophes afflicting their house. Her sister Ismene sympathizes but feels they are too weak to act; Antigone dismisses her scornfully and prepares to bury the body by herself. Her initial step, the covering of the corpse with earth, is found out by the guards after she has left to fetch offerings, and when she returns she is apprehended. In the confrontation with Kreon, she refuses to concede validity to any position but her own; by the terms of the proclamation she is led off to be imprisoned alive in a cave. Haimon, Kreon's son and her betrothed, then pleads with his father for leniency, but Kreon turns a deaf ear when he finds his son siding against him. Finally Teiresias appears, to announce that the gods are rejecting all Theban sacrifices. At this Kreon yields, but too late: Antigone has hanged herself in her prison, and Haimon, discovering the body, draws his sword to meet the same fate. At the end, even Kreon's wife commits suicide, leaving him to mourn a chain of disaster caused partly by his own folly but partly too by Antigone's martyr-like determination to be proved right at all costs. As we saw in chapter 3, the play does not argue that Polyneikes will be in any way benefited by Antigone's devotion to him, and the gods through Teiresias are the ones who accomplish his burial. The intensely confrontational nature of the whole situation might seem to argue that it was created for drama, and we must certainly allow the possibility that Sophokles did invent it. Leaning in this direction too is the fact that in the *Oidipodeia* Haimon is carried off by the Sphinx long before the present action, and we have also found early sources in which Ismene is killed before the assault of the Seven. On the other hand, neither of these figures is essential to Antigone's situation, and they might be simply dramatic additions to a story that Sophokles did, after all, find in epic.

Complicating further the question of dramatic inventions are the remains of Euripides' lost *Antigone*, a play whose plot has sometimes been linked to Hyginus' *Fabula* 72. In Hyginus' account, Antigone and Polyneikes' wife Argeia carry his body in secret to the same funeral pyre on which Eteokles has been placed. When they are discovered Argeia flees, but Antigone is taken before Kreon, who orders her betrothed Haimon to lead her off to execution. Haimon pretends to do so but actually entrusts her to shepherds, and she bears him a child who comes to Thebes years later to compete in games. Like all the Spartoi he has a birthmark that Kreon recognizes, and thus the parents are discovered; when Herakles' pleas on their behalf are to no avail, Haimon kills both Antigone and himself. Admittedly, all or even part of this would be diffi-cult to stage, and it has been thought, too, that Hyginus is drawing from the fourth-century *Antigone* of Astydamas rather than that of Euripides. As an alternative for the latter, following hints from the Sophoklean hypothesis and the fragments, we might set the play at the time of the burial, with Haimon caught helping Antigone and both of them in trouble until Dionysos arrives to save the situation and bring about their marriage. Certain in any case is the fact that at some time in the story (not necessarily the action) of this play Antigone, though caught burying her brother, is married to Haimon and bears him a son Maion (hypothesis to *Ant*; Σ *Ant* 1350). Conceivably, all this could be made to square with Ion of Chios' notion that both Antigone and Ismene are burned to death in a temple of Hera by Laodamas, son of Eteokles (740 *PMG*), but more likely Ion has found (or invented) yet another tradition. We should note too that a Maion, son of Haimon, has already appeared in *Iliad* 4 as the one ambusher spared by Tydeus on the return leg of his embassy to Thebes; if this is the Haimon we know, he will have been married to Antigone (or someone) long before the attack of the Seven. In Statius, Haimon is omitted altogether; Argeia and Antigone meet by chance while searching for Poly-neikes, and as in Hyginus cremate him on Eteokles' funeral pyre (St:*Theb* 12.177–463, 677–804). But here, in contrast to Hyginus, both are captured, and saved from execution by Kreon only because of Theseus' attack on the city. Apollodoros simply outlines the story in its Sophoklean form (without Hai-mon); the one new feature of his account (manuscript reading not certain) is the notion that Kreon caught Antigone himself (Ap*B* 3.7.1). It has also been suggested that behind the uncertain title of Aischylos' *Argeiai* (sometimes transmitted as *Argeioi*) may actually lie *Argeia*, that is, a play about the joint efforts of Polyneikes' wife and sister to secure his burial. Certainly that is possible, but we might have expected the title to be *Antigone*, unless Argeia plays more of a role than we see in Statius and Hyginus. As matters stand, we must concede Sophokles' primacy, without being able to say whether anything in his version or those of later authors draws from earlier periods. As a final point, the speeches in Euripides' *Hiketides* do seem to imply that there Poly-neikes' corpse is recovered by Theseus along with the others for burial; one would like to know if and how Aischylos' *Eleusinioi* dealt with this matter.

As for those other burials and the fate of the rest of the Seven, we have already seen in chapter 9 that Aischylos' lost play is our first evidence for such a prohibition of burial or Theseus' intervention; the *Iliad*'s statement that Tydeus is buried at Thebes (*Il* 14.114) and Pindar's description of the seven corpse-devouring pyres there (*Nem* 9.24) may or may not imply ignorance of such actions. In Euripides' *Hiketides*, we see Theseus and the Athenians defeating the Athenians in battle to obtain the corpses, but Plutarch tells us that in Aischylos' version the same result was accomplished by diplomacy (*Thes* 29.4). The one significant detail of the funeral in Euripides, once the bodies are recovered, is that Euadne, wife of Kapaneus, throws herself on her husband's pyre. Such events could easily find a place in epic (more easily, I think, than Antigone's heroism) although we must ask how early Theseus and/or the Athenians are likely to have played such a central role. Later accounts offer nothing useful, but Pausanias does mention seeing the tombs on the road out from Eleusis (1.39.2). As noted before, the antiquity of this kind of veneration (or rather, the objects of it) is a question that only adds to our uncertainties.

The Epigonoi From Herodotos we learn that there was also an epic *Epigonoi*, at times attributed to Homer (Hdt 4.32). From this title, and the fact that in the poem Manto, daughter of Teiresias, was sent to Delphi from the spoils by the Epigonoi (there to marry one Rhakios, the first person she met: fr 3 *PEG*), we assume that the work related the sack of Thebes by the children of the Seven, who were known as the Epigonoi, or "After-born." This successful attack is, of course, well known to the *Iliad*: Sthenelos, son of Kapaneus, boasts of how he and the other sons succeeded in assaulting Thebes (with fewer men) where their fathers failed (*Il* 4.405–10). He cites as cause for this their observance of signs from the gods and Zeus' help, suggesting once again that the Olympians opposed (or at least tried to discourage) the original expedition. The *Odyssey*, for its part, names Alkmaion and Amphilochos as sons of Amphiaraos (*Od* 15.248: we saw above that the latter's leave-taking in art often shows two sons, an older and a younger) but Homer has no more to tell us than this, and the term "Epigonoi" does not appear in either *Iliad* or *Odyssey*. The second assault may also have been related (or referred back to) in the epic *Alkmaionis*, but our knowledge of the content of that poem is virtually nonexistent. The same is true of Stesichoros' *Eriphyle*, where the one real fragment apparently shows Alkmaion, son of Amphiaraos, leaving some sort of feast at which Adrastos exhorts him to remain (148 *SLG*).

In the fifth century we have first of all Pindar, whose *Olympian* 2 identifies (in an unrelated context) Thersandros as the son of Polyneikes (*Ol* 2.43–45), and whose *Pythian* 8 offers a prophecy from the dead Amphiaraos while the Epigonoi (so named) approach Thebes on this "second march" (*Py* 8.39–55). The seer discerns Alkmaion as first through the gates, and Adrastos, who was beaten in the previous venture but is now enjoying better fortune, save in his son, who shall be the only one of the attackers to die. One should like to think that this ironic arrangement—Adrastos alone suffering loss here after being the only one to escape in the original expedition—was an early part of the story. From tragedy we have numerous titles but little in the way of facts, even regarding plot. For Aischylos' *Epigonoi* we really know nothing beyond the title, our only reason for thinking that the play even concerned these events. An actual assault on Thebes as part of the dramatic action seems unlikely here (in contrast to the *Hepta*, this attack has no curse and no Eteokles), and we should note, too, that Sophokles' similarly titled play deals with the slaying of Eriphyle. Curiously, in the *Hepta* Aischylos seems to overlook this notion of a second expedition, since that play calls Eteokles and Polyneikes *ateknous* (*Hepta* 828), which would eliminate at least Thersandros. Against this view it has been argued that the chorus specifically refers to the Epigonoi by using that term to refer to those to whom the brothers' property remains (*Hepta* 902–5).[56] But the word *epigonoi* there occurs in a line for which there is no strophic responsion (i.e., we must postulate a lacuna in the matching strophe to save it), and even if it is genuine it will more likely refer to future generations in general.[57] Nor should we wonder that Aischylos takes this course: the tragic impact of the brothers' destruction and the relief over Thebes' safety will be considerably lessened if we are in any way reminded of the sequel, although that does not mean the audience was unaware of it. Either the *Epigonoi* of this same poet resurrected those sons or—not impossibly—his version of the sequel did not require them, since desire for vengeance against Thebes (and Kreon) by the offspring of Amphiaraos, Kapaneus, and others of the Seven could provide ample motive without further help from the house of Oidipous.

With Sophokles we do scarcely better on story lines. As noted above, his *Epigonoi* included the matricide, with a hostile exchange between Adrastos (the deceased's brother) and Alkmaion after the deed (if Radt is correct in his attribution of these lines: fr 187 R); what role the second generation of attackers could have played to merit becoming the title is not clear. Asklepiades' statement that Amphiaraos commanded his son to avenge him *before* marching on Thebes with the Epigonoi (12F29) would seem to suggest that in some dramatic accounts the expedition *followed* the matricide, so that perhaps the other sons here formed a group supportive of Alkmaion. The same poet's *Eriphyle* might be another title for the above; if not, it must have offered another version of the same events or else perhaps the original betrayal of Amphiaraos. Euripides' contribution consists of two Alkmaion plays, both relating adventures after the matricide and thus not directly connected with Thebes' fall. Turning to Thoukydides, we find that Amphilochos, son of Amphiaraos, is responsible for the founding of Amphilochian Argos in Akarnania (2.68); the same information without specification of father has earlier surfaced in Hekataios (1F102c), although we will see later that there is some confusion surrounding personages of this name. As to the other participants, we have from Pausanias an account of the monument of the Epigonoi at Delphi, placed by the Argives next to that of the Seven and commemorating the same event, the victory over the Spartans at Oinoe (10.10.4). Here again he gives names, which again are likely but not necessarily from fifth-century inscriptions: Sthenelos, Alkmaion, Promachos,

Thersandros, Aigialeus, Diomedes, with Euryalos between the last two. Pausanias says in passing that Alkmaion was honored before Amphilochos because he was older, which may mean that the younger brother was also present. That would give us a total of eight figures, but nowhere are we ever told that the sons of the Seven were themselves seven in number. Of those named we have already met Sthenelos, Diomedes, Thersandros, and Alkmaion and Amphilochos (as the offspring of Kapaneus, Tydeus, Polyneikes, and Amphiaraos respectively). Aigialeus we will find identified by Hellanikos as the doomed son of Adrastos (4F100), leaving only two names to be accounted for; these, like their fathers, will vary somewhat in the tradition.

Among later sources Apollodoros offers us the same names read by Pausanias at Delphi, with the additional information that Promachos was the son of Parthenopaios and Euryalos the son of Mekisteus (ApB 3.7.2–3). This Euryalos, son of Mekisteus (son of Talaos), is in fact also one of the Achaians at Troy in the *Iliad* (where his appearance is the occasion for the two places where his father is named: *Il* 2.565–66, 23.677–78). That father, Mekisteus, we recall as a brother of Adrastos and a member of Apollodoros' "all-Argive" seven who march with Polyneikes and Tydeus. Presumably, this was the genealogy followed by the Argive commission at Delphi, although it is curious that neither Parthenopaios nor Mekisteus is included on the companion monument showing the Seven. The undated Epigonoi group that Pausanias saw at Argos offers itself a variation on the Delphi version (2.20.5). Here, in addition to Sthenelos, Diomedes, Thersandros, Aigialeus, Alkmaion, and Amphilochos with the usual fathers, we have Promachos, son of Parthenopaios, and Polydoros, son of Hippomedon; added immediately after are Euryalos, son of Mekisteus, and two other sons of Polyneikes, Adrastos and Timeas. The eight of the first group (with the same fathers) recur in the scholia to Sthenelos' *Iliad* 4 speech, save only that Promachos, son of Parthenopaios, becomes Stratolaos, son of Parthenopaios (Σb *Il* 4.404; ΣT *Il* 4.406); added here as a ninth is Medon, son of Eteoklos, perhaps because Eteoklos rather than Adrastos is here accepted as the seventh in the original party. In fact, any source that does not count Adrastos as one of the Seven but does admit his son will probably wind up with nine Epigonoi, assuming that each of the Seven sends at least one son and Amphiaraos sends two. Hyginus' list also matches that of the group at Argos and the *Iliad* scholia (minus Amphilochos and Medon), with the son of Parthenopaios now Tlesimenes or Biantes (*Fab* 71).

As for the assault itself, both the Townley and b scholia agree that Laodamas, son of Eteokles, was killed and Thebes razed. In Apollodoros, too, Laodamas is slain (by Alkmaion) after himself killing Aigialeus; Pausanias by contrast has Laodamas spared and sent off to Illyria with those Thebans who escaped (9.5.13). Elsewhere he locates the initial battle on the plain of Glisas to the northeast of Thebes, but he also places there the tombs of Promachos and others who fought with Aigialeus, implying a tradition in which the son of Adrastos was not the only one of the leaders to fall fighting. One other facet of the tale of the Epigonoi, found first in Diodoros and subsequently in Apollodoros, presents us with a doublet of Polyneikes' original bribing of Eriphyle (DS 4.66.3; ApB 3.6.2). On that first occasion she receives the necklace of Harmonia, but Polyneikes also possesses (as Hellanikos has guaranteed for the fifth century: 4F98) a robe of Harmonia, and his son Thersandros now uses this to bribe Eriphyle to send her son on the second campaign. Apollodoros adds to this that Alkmaion discovered the deed only after the campaign was over. One is hard put to square this, as Apollodoros tries to do, with the idea we found in Asklepiades that Amphiaraos ordered Alkmaion to avenge him as soon as he should be old enough: if Alkmaion already knows of the original bribery he is not likely to yield to his mother's wishes on this second occasion. But then this doublet even on its own terms is a bit lame: Eriphyle does not send her son to his death as she did his father, but rather toward a glorious enterprise, and neither does she have the special hold over him that she did with his father. On the other hand, Asklepiades' version is not so tightly plotted either, for if Alkmaion kills his mother before going on the expedition, as his father commands, we must ask how he could participate in such a joint venture in his polluted condition, and why the Erinyes did not then pursue him. But either of these motifs could be early, although probably not at the same time. Our scant fragment of Stesichoros' *Eriphyle* sounds much as if Alkmaion is departing hastily from a victory banquet to kill his mother, which might suggest that he has just learned (from a drunk and boastful Thersandros?) of her duplicity in the matter of his father. If this is so, there would certainly be room in that poem for the second bribing, which might have originally developed, like the double offense to Oidipous by his sons, in the congenial confines of epic.

Regarding the final destruction of the city, in Diodoros the Thebans are advised by Teiresias to leave their town before the final assault, and most of them do; captured, however, is the seer's daughter, as she was in the epic *Epigonoi*, although here her name becomes Daphne rather than Manto (DS 4.66.4–6). Again she is sent to Delphi as a thank-offering, but now remains in Apollo's shrine as the first Sibyl. Pausanias matches the *Epigonoi* in the matter of Manto's name and union with Rhakios, even if, as he tells the story, Rhakios is from Klaros, not Kolophon, and Manto meets him when she is sent out with other prisoners to found a colony (9.33.2). Teiresias himself dies soon after the evacuation, as we will see below.

Alkmaion and Eriphyle — Whether conscious of Eriphyle's treachery before the expedition of the Epigonoi or not, and whenever he carries out the deed, Alkmaion does slay his mother for her treachery in sending his father to Thebes. The confrontation between mother and son, so parallel to that of Klytaimestra and Orestes in the *Choephoroi*, must have been narrated by the *Alkmaionis* and Stesichoros' *Eriphyle*, and dramatized in Sophokles' *Epigonoi* and possibly the play of the same title by Aischylos. The end of the epic *Thebais* may also have included it, although we cannot be sure on this point. Nothing survives from any of these works, but the end of our *Odyssey* scholiast summary from Asklepiades says that Alkmaion suffered madness after the matricide, and was subsequently cured by the gods because he had acted in defense of his father (12F29). Our one preserved piece of Archaic evidence from art is a Tyrrhenian amphora from Orvieto (Berlin:PM VI 4841).[58] Here we see a woman collapsed in death over what is probably a grave mound, with blood spurting from her neck. Just to the right an armed warrior steps into a chariot whose charioteer has already whipped up the horses. As the warrior turns to look back over his shoulder, a huge snake rises up from behind the mound and threatens him, fangs bared. Further to the right, in front of the horses, a woman races toward the center of the scene; most of her head is missing, but one raised hand appears to hold a bow or snake. Behind the horses are traces of another (male) figure, and on the left of the mound four women, perhaps mourners. The inscriptions, as so often on Tyrrhenian amphoras, are meaningless; nevertheless, the tableau does surely illustrate the death of Eriphyle. Whether such a snake could represent an Erinys (we will return to this problem with Orestes at Foce del Sele) and whether an Erinys portrayed as a woman would carry a bow are harder questions. But it does seem evident that Alkmaion's deed has stirred up some sort of malignant nether powers, and that he will need to come to terms with these, if possible.

In the Classical period we find, apart from the effort(s) of Sophokles, two plays of Euripides dealing with problems after the matricide, *Alkmaion in Psophis*, presented with *Alkestis* in 438 b.c., and *Alkmaion in Korinth*, part of the posthumous production that included the *Bakchai* and *Iphigeneia at Aulis*. Both plays are lost, but from Pausanias and Apollodoros we derive what must have been their basic plots, and probably that of Sophokles' *Alkmaion* as well. Psophis is a locality in western Arkadia, just south of Mount Erymanthos. In Apollodoros, Alkmaion arrives here to seek purification from the king Phegeus, since his mother's Erinyes are pursuing him (Ap*B* 3.7.5–6). The purification accomplished, he marries the king's daughter Arsinoe and gives her the necklace and robe of Harmonia, which he has taken from his mother. But the land becomes infertile, and Apollo commands him to seek further purification from Acheloos. In Pausanias, the daughter is named Alphesiboia, and it is Alkmaion's own sickness, whether physical or mental, which causes him to seek Apollo's aid (8.24.8–10). The Pythia advises him that he must seek a land not in existence at the time of his mother's death, and he finally understands this to mean the delta recently formed at the mouth of the Acheloos river. This latter part of the story is also found in Thoukydides (2.102.5–6); Apollodoros acknowledges it as well, but clearly is not always drawing from the same source as Pausanias. As Pausanias and Apollodoros continue the story, Alkmaion arrives at the far western shore of Aitolia and marries the daughter of Acheloos, Kallirhoe, by whom he has two sons, Akarnan and Amphoteros. But alas, Kallirhoe has heard of the fame of Harmonia's robe and necklace, and forces Alkmaion to return to Psophis to get them. Alkmaion does so, concocting a story for Phegeus that he needs to take the items to Delphi to complete his purification. Unfortunately, the father and/or his sons discover the truth from a servant, and the sons set an ambush for Alkmaion in which he is killed. Pausanias stops here; in Apollodoros' continuation, Arsinoe accuses her brothers and is sold as a slave by them, while Kallirhoe prays to Zeus that her sons might immediately become old enough to take vengeance on their father's slayers. After Zeus grants this and the vengeance is accomplished, Alkmaion's sons also kill Phegeus and his wife, then return to the far west to colonize Akarnania.

The other story, that of Alkmaion in Korinth, is specifically assigned by Apollodoros to Euripides, and smacks like the former of dramatic elaboration (ApB 3.7.7). Alkmaion has here begotten two children, Amphilochos and Tisiphone, by Manto, daughter of Teiresias. These he has left for safekeeping with Kreon of Korinth when they are very young, but at some point subsequently Kreon's wife gives the girl away into slavery, fearing her beauty, and by an incredible coincidence she is eventually purchased by Alkmaion himself, without recognizing her, as a personal servant. As the play begins, our hero has come back to Korinth to find his children, not realizing that he already has the one and not recognizing the other when he sees him.[59] From fragments we learn in addition to this that Amphilochos has been brought up as Kreon's son, and that Alkmaion undergoes a fit of madness and is nearly killed by the Korinthians, led by Kreon. Somehow, though, the children's identities are established and Kreon's plot defeated, so that Amphilochos may go off to found Amphilochian Argos. Where the Alkmaion of the earlier play would have found time for all this is a question we are probably not supposed to ask; the plot may owe much to Euripidean invention, but we must remember that the epic *Alkmaionis* covered a broad range of material, and likely put considerable emphasis on foundation legends for northwest Greece. If that is true, conflicting stories explaining different events may have crowded together under its aegis. In any case, since Euripides is credited by Apollodoros with this story, Sophokles' *Alkmaion* (where the protagonist suffers from madness) probably dealt with the story of Euripides' Psophis play, whether before or after his colleague. An unassigned fragment mentioning Alphesiboia may indicate that he, like Pausanias, gave Phegeus' daughter this name (fr 880 R). Both Agathon and Achaios also wrote *Alkmaion* plays, to name only two, but we know little of any of them (although Achaios' was satyric). One other activity credited to Alkmaion by Ephoros (apud Str 10.2.25) and reappearing in Apollodoros (ApB 1.8.6) is a journey to Aitolia with Diomedes to help the latter restore the throne to his father Oineus.

Last, we turn to Alkmaion's brother Amphilochos, founder in Thoukydides of Amphilochian Argos, "after the Trojan expedition, having returned home and not being pleased with the situation in Argos" (2.68.3). That Amphilochos went to Troy is certainly not known to the *Iliad*, where he is never mentioned, but an Amphilochos is named as one of the three warriors holding the victim on the Tyrrhenian amphora portraying the sacrifice of Iphigeneia (London 1897.7–27.2). The name also appears in an unascribed hexameter quote where Amphilochos is exhorted by some older person to adapt (like the *polupous*) to whatever land he might come to, and this is sometimes assigned to the *Thebais* (fr 4 *PEG*). In the Hesiodic Corpus, according to Strabo, an Amphilochos dies at the hands of Apollo at Soloi in Cilicia (Hes fr 279 MW). This last Amphilochos, whom Strabo and other late sources show departing from Troy with Kalchas and becoming embroiled in a dispute with Mopsos (son of Apollo and Manto), is generally understood by them to be a relative of Alkmaion, if not his brother. Strabo himself relates the most important of these tales, that Amphilochos and Mopsos together founded Mallos on a site just east of Soloi (Str 14.5.16). Subsequently in this account, Amphilochos goes back to Argos, but then returns to Cilicia to claim a share of the new settlement; Mopsos refuses, and in the ensuing duel both die. We find a veiled allusion to this mutually fatal combat in Lykophron (439–46), and thus it must be older than the Hellenistic era; Amphilochos' death via Apollo in "Hesiod" could well be a variant of it, with Apollo intervening on behalf of his son (or after Mopsos has been killed). Strabo elsewhere knows a story in which Amphilochos makes his way to the southern coast of Spain, where he dies (Str 3.4.3).

In Apollodoros we find Amphilochos and Kalchas traveling down from Troy to Kolophon, where they meet Mopsos and the famous contest of seers ensues (ApE 6.2; for this contest see chapter 17). A later reference by the same author has Amphilochos blown by storm from Troy to the home of Mopsos, thus triggering their combat (ApE 6.19). In most of these cases, our hero is identified as the brother of Alkmaion rather than the latter's similarly named son, but we must allow that some confusion may have existed between the two separate figures (in origin probably the same person with variant parentages). As a hero Amphilochos has a broad-ranging cult, including Athens and Sparta as well as Mallos, Rhodes, and Aitolia, and the need to account for the various locales may explain some of his peregrinations. Apollodoros adds one other interesting note, that according to some he shared in the slaying of his mother Eriphyle (ApB 3.7.5). We hear nothing else of this, or its consequences; Kallistratos' late-fifth-century tragedy *Amphilochos* might have dealt with such a topic, but of course the events surrounding the conflict with Mopsos and/or Apollo are also a possibility.

Teiresias   Last, as a bit of unfinished business in this chapter, we may consider briefly the career of Thebes' illustrious seer. We first see him in death, in the *Odyssey*, for Kirke tells us that to his shade alone Persephone has granted to retain his wits, and that Odysseus must go to the edge of Hades to consult him (*Od* 10.490–95). No reason at all is given for this special privilege, and we find in fact that any shade can speak intelligently to Odysseus once it has drunk the sheep's blood. Teiresias' own remarks include nothing about himself, and Kirke describes him only as the blind Theban prophet. But the Hesiodic Corpus—

probably the *Melampodia*—seems already to have related the odd story of his gift of prophecy with most of the details known to later times. According to the summary (courtesy of Apollodoros), while near Mount Kyllene Teiresias saw two snakes mating; he struck them and was turned into a woman (Hes fr 275 MW). At some later date, on observing the same two snakes mating again, he was changed back into a man. For this reason, when Zeus and Hera fell into dispute over which sex derived more pleasure from the act of love, they turned to Teiresias for an answer. Here something has gone afoul in the account, for Apollodoros first says that, reckoning such pleasure into nineteen parts, man enjoys nine and woman ten, then cites two hexameter lines in which man enjoys one of ten shares and woman all ten. Both confusion in the first version and interpolation of the second have been suspected. But the second version with its hexameter quote and one-to-ten ratio also appears in the scholia to *Odyssey* 10.494, and something very close to it in the scholia to Lykophron 683. This last, however, also brings in something about nine shares, and knows too a version in which the ratio is one to nine out of a total of ten. This slight difference probably reflects uncertainty over whether men and women could be rated separately on the same scale or had to share out the ten parts of it between them; the resulting ten parts for women in the first instance and nine parts in the second may then have led to the erroneous notion of nineteen parts and Apollodoros' probable error. In any case, and whatever the exact response of the *Melampodia*, women were clearly the greater beneficiaries of the sexual act, and thus Zeus won the argument. Hera in anger blinded Teiresias; Zeus in compensation gave him mantic skills and a long life. These last gifts we find lamented by the seer in a quote assigned specifically to the *Melampodia*, and here he claims to have lived through seven normal life-spans (Hes fr 276 MW). One oddity of Apollodoros' version is that he does not make Teiresias strike the snakes on the second viewing, as the seer does in all other accounts. Possibly he omitted this through carelessness, supposing it to be understood by his audience.

As for variations in other versions, the scholia to *Odyssey* 10 say that on seeing the snakes copulating Teiresias struck just one of them, the female, and after killing her became a woman; then, killing the male (on the same occasion? subsequently?), he regained his original form (Σ *Od* 10.494). Tzetzes at Lykophron 683 says much the same, with the implication that the gender of the snake slain controlled the form Teiresias assumed. The second-century A.D. writer Phlegon, drawing (so he says) from Hesiod, Dikaiarchos, Kallimachos, and other sources, has Apollo advise Teiresias on how he might undo the original transformation (257F36). Ovid has both snakes struck on each occasion, with Teiresias testing out the premise that every such act will cause a change from whatever sex one happens to be at the moment (*Met* 3.322–38). A new (for us) detail from the same account is the length of Teiresias' career as a woman: seven years. Sadly, Ovid's version of the dispute merely says that Teiresias sided with Zeus; Hyginus, who mentions trampling on snakes (perhaps a garbling of a Greek source), is equally laconic on the matter of the argument (*Fab* 75).

Turning back to Apollodoros, we find that Teiresias' bisexual experience and ill-fated pronouncement to Hera are not the only possible cause of his blindness. Before relating the events described above, the mythographer concedes that there are other explanations, including the idea that the seer divulged to men what the gods wished kept secret (as in some accounts did Phineus) and Pherekydes' tale that he saw Athena naked (3F92). This unfortunate accident seems somehow to have taken place because Athena and Teiresias' mother Chariklo were friends; probably Teiresias stumbled upon the two of them while they were bathing. In any case, Athena places her hands over Teiresias' eyes, and he becomes blind. To Chariklo's anguished laments the goddess replies that she cannot undo the blindness, but she does allow Teiresias to understand the speech of birds, and she gives him a staff with which he can walk as if sighted. This same version of events is narrated at greater length by Kallimachos in his *Hymn* 5 ("The Bath of Pallas"). Here Chariklo and Athena are in fact bathing, in a spring on Mount Helikon, when Teiresias, fresh from the hunt and thirsty, comes to the same spring to drink. At Athena's mere words he loses his sight; Chariklo's protest prompts the justification that the laws of Kronos require such punishment. Athena adds too that Teiresias may consider himself lucky compared with Aktaion, who will soon lose his life for a similar transgression. But here too there are compensatory gifts—the profession of *mantis*, with the ability to utter prophecies and distinguish between good- and ill-omened birds, the guiding staff, a long life, and the retention of his senses among the dead (this last as we saw given by Persephone in the *Odyssey*). From Athena's address to her victim we learn that his father is one Eueres, and this is supported by Apollodoros and Hyginus as well. In Apollodoros, he is furthermore descended from Oudaios, one of the five original Spartoi. Presumably, this ancestry derives from the father, but we know nothing else about Eueres; indeed, Kallimachos is the first writer to mention either parent. Because of his long life Teiresias makes a suitable foil for a variety of mythic plots: Oidipous' discovery of his birth, the quarrel of Oidipous' sons, the sacrifice of Menoikeus, Kreon and Antigone, even Herakles in his nursery at Thebes. But the seer has no further adventures of his own, and his life does finally come to an end on the flight out of Thebes at the time of its destruction: he dies after drinking from the spring Tilphoussa, near the mountain of the same name in the region of Haliartos (Ap*B* 3.7.3).

15 The Line of Tantalos

Tantalos himself is never mentioned in the *Iliad,* not even when Achilleus relates the tale of Niobe to Priam. In the *Odyssey* he does appear once, but only in the *Nekuia,* among the transgressors whom Odysseus sees at the very end of his visit (*Od* 11.582–92). Here we encounter already the punishment so familiar in later tradition: Tantalos stands in a pool of water up to his chin, but when he attempts to drink, the water disappears into the ground; likewise when he reaches up for the branches of fruit overhead—pears, pomegranates, apples, figs, olives—a breeze blows them beyond his grasp. The lines also call him an old man, but say nothing about the transgression that brought him to this state of affairs. Elsewhere in the epic tradition, in a work referred to by Athenaios as the *Return of the Atreidai* (likely the more familiar *Nostoi* under another name[1]), we find a rather different account of the situation: here Tantalos has been enjoying the freedom of socializing with the gods, and on one such occasion receives from Zeus a promise to have whatever his heart should desire (*Nostoi* fr 4 *PEG*). Displaying a weakness for divine pleasures, he asks to live always the same life as the gods. Naturally Zeus is aghast at this suggestion, yet has no choice but to fulfill it; at the same time, though, so that Tantalos might be unable to enjoy the things set before him, he suspends a rock over the mortal's head. Athenaios closes his account by saying that Tantalos is unable to obtain any of the proffered items, implying that the unlucky banqueter fears the rock will fall if he so much as reaches for them. The items in question are presumably food and drink, in which case the preventive role of the rock will serve a purpose not so very unlike that of the pool and branches in the *Nekuia.* That the rock also played a major role in the versions of other authors is guaranteed by references in Archilochos (91 W), Alkman (79 *PMG*), Alkaios (365 LP), Pindar (*Is* 8.9–10), and Pherekydes (3F38), but although Alkman does mention sitting among pleasant things, and Archilochos and Pindar use "Rock of Tantalos" as a proverbial expression (like "Sword of Damokles"), we do not learn anything else of interest regarding either crime or punishment.

We will see shortly that the Archaic period also offers evidence of another transgression altogether, one involving Tantalos, Pandareos, and a dog, but that seems to be a separate story with its own resolution; for the situation that in

531

most accounts brings Tantalos to his tormented fate we have only the epic cited by Athenaios, plus a variant account described in Pindar's *Olympian* 1. This ode, probably his most famous, we know to have been composed for Hieron of Syracuse in 476 B.C., on the occasion of a victory in the single horse race. Hieron's mythical counterpart in such victory, as the first to triumph with horses at Olympia, is Pelops, and that thought brings with it a narration of events leading up to the hero's winning of his bride. But the story that emerges is not quite what later sources would lead us to expect, and Pindar himself seems conscious that his audience will be surprised at times by his version. Pelops, he tells us, was he whom "Earth-shaker Poseidon fell in love with, when Klotho pulled him forth from a pure cauldron, and he was resplendent with his ivory shoulder" (*Ol* 1.25–27). From this brief reference we are likely to presume the later-attested familiar tale of Pelops' resurrection by the gods after his father has tried to serve him for dinner, and Bakchylides seems to confirm knowledge of some such story for this time, since the scholia tell us that in his work Rheia cured Pelops in a cauldron (fr 42 SM).[2] Problems arise, however, when we consider subsequent developments in Pindar's poem, for the poet (after a warning about novelties) goes on to relate that Tantalos offered the gods a "most lawful/well-arranged" banquet at Sipylos in return for the feasts to which they had invited him. The term "most lawful" would seem designed to counter any notions of a meal at which Pelops becomes the dinner, and in fact it is on the occasion of the banquet that Poseidon carries the boy off to Olympos in a fit of passion. His disappearance then leads neighbors to speculate that the gods have eaten him, and thus arises the familiar but (in this poem at least) mistaken tale of a cannibalistic feast. The difficulty is that nothing in this revision of the facts will explain Pindar's opening scene, for if Pelops has not been cut up for dinner he has no need to be in a cauldron, or reason to possess an ivory shoulder. Attempts to explain the former as part of a birth ritual seem dubious (would Poseidon fall in love with a newborn child?) and still leave the shoulder to be dealt with.[3] Whatever we make of this conundrum, Tantalos is here exonerated of trying to kill his own son, and thus needs a new transgression for which he can be punished. Pindar makes this the sharing with his friends of the nectar and ambrosia with which the gods made him immortal. For such unauthorized extension of their favors, Zeus suspends over him a rock that he constantly desires to keep away from his head, and thus absenting himself from happiness he has a helpless life, a fourth toil with three others (*Ol* 1.54–64). What these "three others" are remains an insoluble problem; if Tantalos and his rock are in the Underworld we might think of other transgressors, or even other torments (hunger, thirst, and ?), but Pindar can hardly have expected his audience to provide a specific meaning for such a terse allusion. More likely the expression is proverbial, indicating something like "toil upon toil," that is, the hopeless eternity of Tantalos' predicament.[4] Whether Pindar himself supposed the additional torment of unreachable food and drink we cannot then say, but he certainly might expect his audience to supply those details from earlier epic, once the rock was mentioned.

As one further response of the gods in *Olympian* 1 Pelops is sent back to earth, to grow into manhood and assume mortality, and apparently this development is the real point of Pindar's story: the gods' experiment in making men immortal has failed, as Tantalos' sharing of his good fortune with others shows, and thus Pelops must work out a new relationship between man and god, in a world of heroes and darkness occasionally irradiated by divine light. To convey that idea Pindar needs a transgression that will illustrate Tantalos' failure as an immortal, not (as in Athenaios) improper aspirations in that direction or any entertaining of gods with human flesh; thus he settles on the redistribution of nectar and ambrosia as the crime. Whether he invented it is harder to say. Whatever we decide, the cauldron and shoulder remain as tangible vestiges of a different tale with which he clearly supposes his audience to be familiar.

From perhaps only slightly later in the fifth century we have Polygnotos' painting of Hades for the Knidian Lesche at Delphi. Here, as Pausanias tells us, Tantalos is made to endure the same torments as in Homer, and in addition that of the rock suspended over him (10.31.12). Pausanias credits the artist's knowledge of the rock to Archilochos, who he says may well have been the first to tell of it. We saw, however, that our own brief Archilochian reference is essentially a proverb ("May the rock of Tantalos not hang over this island") and the poet must have narrated the story at greater length elsewhere if Pausanias' belief has any merit. In any event, the writer clearly believes that no source before Polygnotos thought to combine the punishments of rock and pool. Euripides' *Orestes* begins with Elektra lamenting the fortunes of the house; we are told that Tantalos "hovers in the air, fearing the rock hanging over his head. And he pays this penalty, as they say, because being a man, and having equal honor at the table of the gods, he could not keep his tongue in check" (*Or* 4–10). Elektra also calls Tantalos a son of Zeus, as will most later authors. But why he should float in air remains unexplained, even if the idea apparently reappears later in the play, when the chorus prays to be taken to the place where the rock (the sun?) swings on golden chains, so that it might lament the fortunes of the house to Tantalos (*Or* 982–85). The scholia to the earlier passage suggest that Tantalos was thus placed between heaven and earth so that he might not hear more of the gods' conversation on Olympos or reveal more of it to mortals (Σ *Or* 7).[5] Scholia to the *Odyssey* refer to Zeus as binding Tantalos' hands and suspending him from a high mountain, with Asklepiades given as source (Σ *Od* 11.582). We cannot say, of course, whether Asklepiades had other sources besides this play, or to what extent the *Orestes* scholia might be guessing. It would seem, however, that such a punishment must certainly preclude the pool and probably also the rock. As for the offense, the scholia obviously suppose that it was similar to that of the Thracian Phineus: disclosing too much of the gods' plans to other men. But Euripides' language could allow for other possibilities: excessively arrogant speech at the table of the gods, or boasting of his good fortune to others, or even the same ill-considered request as in Athenaios. But a crime of the tongue will at least eliminate two possibilities, the cooking of his son and sharing out of the food of the gods. We may add that Sophokles and other playwrights are credited with works entitled *Tantalos* of which we know nothing; the usual assumption is that most if not all of these dealt with Pandareos' theft of the dog.

Later sources have very little to add on any of these points. Both Plato (*Kratylos* 395d) and Hypereides (fr 173 Kenyon) in the fourth century mention the rock (Plato, like Polygnotos, locates it in Hades), and this mode of punishment remains consistently popular in subsequent times. But Horace (*Epodes* 17.65–66; *Satires* 1.1.68–69) and Ovid (*Met* 4.458–59) repeat the Homeric version, and Apollodoros (*ApE* 2.1) and Hyginus (*Fab* 82) combine those torments with the rock, again like Polygnotos. Apollodoros also notes that in some accounts Tantalos is punished for revealing the *mustêria* of the gods, and Hyginus says that he divulged the counsels of the gods which Zeus had confided to him. A poem in the *Greek Anthology* stresses too that Tantalos' tongue was what brought him to grief (*AP* 16.131.9), and Loukianos speaks of his babbling (*Sal* 54.3; *De sacrificiis* 9.10), while Cicero quotes a line from an unknown play in which the miscreant is accused of *suberbiloquentia* (*TD* 4.16.35).

As for the crime that Pindar denies, Euripides' Iphigeneia also finds unbelievable the "banquet of Tantalos for the gods, that they would enjoy the taste of a child's flesh" when she is forced by the Tauroi to sacrifice men to Artemis (*IT* 386–88). And Menelaos in the same poet's *Helen* offers the wish that Pelops had perished "when persuaded you made a feast for the gods" (*Hel* 388–89); the oddity of phrasing (to what was Pelops persuaded?) may indicate some corruption. But we learn nothing further until Lykophron, where for the first time we see Demeter devour Pelops' shoulder (152–55), and then Ovid, who knows of the ivory replacement and specifies that Tantalos was the one to cut up his son (*Met* 6.403–11). Hyginus, too, relates this last fact, and adds that Demeter contrived the new shoulder (*Fab* 83). We saw before that Pindar rather implies (in the version he then rejects) the gods as the perpetrators of the feast (so perhaps also Euripides), but as such a version would not explain Pelops' survival (surely mandatory in all accounts), it is not likely to have ever constituted a tradition. Oddly enough, none of these sources says why Tantalos should have wished to serve the gods in such a fashion; various scholia suggest that he was attempting to be hospitable, or to make a significant contribution to the *eranos* to which the gods had invited him (Σ *Lyk* 152; Σ *Ol* 1.40a), while Servius seems the first to suppose that he wished to test the divinity of the gods (Σ *G* 3.7; cf. the motives of Lykaon in chapter 18). Some of these later sources also state that Demeter was upset over the loss of Persephone when she ate the shoulder (Σ *Lyk* 152), and that Zeus ordered Hermes to restore Pelops with the ivory replacement (Σ *Ol* 1.40). The Pindar scholion notes as well that according to some, Themis (or Thetis: manuscripts vary), rather than Demeter, was the inadvertent consumer of the shoulder.

Amid such a range of transgressions and two distinct punishments we might suppose Tantalos free of other misadventures. But there exists yet another tradition, one distinct from everything considered above in that no part of it is ever interchanged with what we have already seen. On a sixth-century Black-Figure cup by the Heidelberg Painter now in the Louvre we find a man in stately dress, followed by a very large dog, a winged figure, another man running up with a leash (?), and two women (Louvre A478). There are alas no names, but the cup presumably illustrates a story found in scholia to the *Odyssey* and *Olympian* 1 and in Antoninus Liberalis. The *Odyssey* scholia are those concerned with the daughters of Pandareos in *Odyssey* 19 and 20: by way of justifying the consignment of these girls to the Erinyes we are told that Zeus' shrine on Krete possessed a live golden dog, and that the Milesian Pandareos, son of Merops, stole it (ΣΣ *Od* 19.518, 20.66). Fearing, however, to take the dog back to Miletos, he left it for safekeeping with Tantalos in Phrygia. When Hermes came to look for the dog, Tantalos swore by all the gods that he did not have it, but Hermes found it anyway; Zeus punished Tantalos by placing Mount Sipylos on top of him. The account of these scholia also relates that Pandareos and his wife Harmothoe first fled to Athens and then to Sicily, where Zeus discovered them and killed them both.

The Pindaric scholia tell the same story, although the dog, which is not here said to be golden, now guards the shrine of Zeus on Krete, and the punishment of Pandareos is omitted (Σ *Ol* 1.91). In Antoninus the dog has been set by Rheia to guard the goat that nourishes Zeus (AntLib 36). Pandareos steals him as before, and deposits him with Tantalos, but here he himself returns to claim the animal, and it is to him that Tantalos swears that he does not have it. Zeus punishes Pandareos for the theft by turning him to stone, and Tantalos for the false oath by (again) burying him under Sipylos. A further variant surfaces at the end of the *Odyssey* 19 scholia: the scholiast says that Tantalos was the stealer of the dog, and that Pandareos, receiving it from him, denied the fact (leading to the punishment of his two younger daughters). Possibly this is a genuine tradition, but the scholiast may well have reversed the roles of the two malefactors.

In all, there seems little likelihood of bringing Tantalos' various offenses and chastisements together into a coherent whole, and in particular making this last misdeed fit with the rest. The one possibility for overlap would seem to lie in the fact that a false oath is a crime of the tongue, which we saw to be one of the transgressions of the rock/pool Tantalos. But our first reference of this sort, Euripides' *Orestes*, pointedly connects the man's "unrestrained" speaking with his access to the gods' table, so that an oath on earth to Hermes or anyone else would seem excluded. Having a mountain fall on one also seems suspiciously close to waiting for a rock to do the same, but the point of the rock is after all that it never falls; in the epic cited by Athenaios, as we saw, its function is much closer to that of the branches and pool. Nor do any of these fates bear much resemblance to a Prometheus-type binding on a mountainside. Surprisingly, there are no preserved artistic representations to help us with any of these matters.[6]

One final entanglement takes us in another direction altogether, though it survives only in late sources. Mnaseas, a third-century B.C. mythographer with Euhemerizing tendencies, apparently had Tantalos rather than Zeus abduct Ganymedes, after which the latter died while hunting (ΣbT Il 20.234).[7] Related to this, it might seem, is the report of Diodoros that Tantalos was driven out of Paphlagonia by Ilos, son of Tros (DS 4.74), and indeed the third-century A.D. historian Herodian makes the connection by stating that Ilos and Tantalos went to war over the abduction of Ganymedes, as brother and lover respectively (1.11; so too Σ Lyk 355). Seemingly this tale is incompatible with that in which Zeus takes Ganymedes up to Olympos, and may well have been created as a rationalizing variant on that one, but why in that case Tantalos should play the part of the miscreant is not immediately clear.[8]

Before concluding this section, we should consider also Tantalos' parentage and wife. Our earliest information on the first of these points is Euripides, where Tantalos is a son of Zeus (Or 5); later sources all agree on that much, save for the scholion to this same passage, which names Tmolos as the father. The mother seems, however, on all occasions when she is named, to be one Plouto (Paus 2.22.3; Σ Od 11.582; Σ Or 4; Fab 82, 155; Nonnos 7.119 [union with Zeus only]). Hyginus calls her the daughter of Himas (Fab 155), but we know nothing else about her. Tantalos' wife and the mother of Pelops is Euryanassa in the scholia to Orestes 4 and Dositheos (54F1), but in the scholia to Orestes 11 Euryanassa, daughter of Paktolos, or Eurythemiste, daughter of Xanthos, or Klytia daughter of Amphidamas, this last credited to Pherekydes (3F40). For Hyginus she is instead Dione, a daughter of Atlas (Fab 9, 83).

Niobe

Tantalos' daughter Niobe (though without parentage) makes her first appearance in Iliad 24, when Achilleus uses her as an example to Priam of the need to eat, even amidst great grief (Il 24.602–17). The resulting suggestion that Niobe does not immediately succumb to her grief clashes in fact with most later accounts, and has roused suspicions that Homer is here innovating (as perhaps also in the case of Meleagros in Iliad 9) to make a point.[9] What Achilleus tells us is that Niobe compared herself to Leto because she had many children and Leto only two; in anger Apollo and Artemis, two though they were, slew her twelve offspring, Apollo the six males and Artemis the six females. The dead lay in their own blood for nine days, since there was no one to bury them, Zeus having turned the people to stone. Finally on the tenth day the gods themselves buried them, and Niobe took thought of food, when she had tired of weeping. But now, he continues, she is among the rocks in the lonely hills of Sipylos, and continues to nourish her grief, although she is stone. The oddities here are of two kinds. On the one hand, Niobe's decision to resume the normal activities of life seems much in conflict with her subsequent metamorphosis, which we presume is in some way caused by her grief, and here Homer may well have added some new material.[10] But the other surprises—for we see no reason why the gods should turn the local populace to stone, or take it upon themselves to bury corpses—are not really necessary to Achilleus' purpose at all, and may form part of an older tradition that has not survived. Based on what we have, the gods would seem to have intensified Niobe's punishment by threatening for a time to keep her children unburied, even though this was not their ultimate intent. Nothing guarantees, however, that Homer has given us all the facts, and the true story may be much more complicated, involving, for example, some transgression on the part of the Thebans (but does Homer mean that they remained stone?).

For the rest of the Archaic period we have virtually no literary evidence beyond what late sources (primarily Aelian, Aulus Gellius, and a *Phoinissai* scholion) tell us about the number of Niobe's children in different early authors. A surprising number of authors are cited, although we do not know for most of them whether they actually narrated the story. More often than not the total figure is divided equally between males and females, as in Homer; after his twelve we have the following: in "Hesiod" nine and ten, or else ten and ten (Hes fr 183 MW); in Alkman ten in all (75 *PMG*), in Mimnermos twenty in all (19 W); in Sappho nine and nine (205 LP); in Lasos seven and seven (706 *PMG*); in Pindar (fr 52n: see *apparatus*) and Bakchylides (fr 20D) ten and ten; in Aischylos, Sophokles, and Euripides seven and seven (Σ *Pho* 159); in Pherekydes six and six (3F126); in Hellanikos four and three (4F21); in Herodoros two and three (31F56). Of these writers we can say that Aischylos and Sophokles wrote *Niobe* plays, and that Euripides apparently did not (the figure attributed to him comes from his *Kresphontes*). We have also a single line from Sappho to the effect that "Leto and Niobe were exceedingly good friends" (142 LP); probably this is meant as a parallel to some current reversal of feeling charted by Sappho, but it may suggest that Niobe's acceptance by the gods as a near-equal brought about her downfall, as it did that of her father. Not before Aischylos do we learn (via a papyrus fragment) that she is the daughter of Tantalos, and married to Amphion (fr 154a R), although no later author ever disputes these points.

Aischylos' dramatization apparently began with Niobe veiled and seated at the tomb of her children, and for some time refusing to speak, so that her boast and the slaying of those children have already taken place. At some point in the play Tantalos will appear (to take his daughter home?) but this is all we know of the action. The fragments do offer some odd statements, most especially the lines quoted by Plato to the effect that "God creates a cause in mortals, whenever he wishes to destroy a house entirely" (*Rep* 2.383b). This would seem to shift the blame from Niobe, but we do not know if the speaker was right; the papyrus fragment mentioned above also includes these lines, and shows that there followed immediately after a caution against mortals speaking too boldly in the midst of their prosperity (fr 154a R). Still, an earlier part of the speech offers an anguished query as to what anger the gods had against Amphion, that they should so strip the leaves from his house; we gather therefore that at least part of the play entertained a questioning of the gods' actions. Tantalos, when he does appear, remarks that his fortune has fallen from *ouranos* to earth, and says, "Learn not to honor too much the things of man" (fr 159 R). That he should already have committed his transgression, as it would seem, and still be free to come to Thebes, is remarkable; perhaps it was necessary for the plot. His own experience with the gods may have put him in a position to help his daughter grasp more clearly the error of her ways, but here we are guessing. The one other fragment of interest says that Amphion's house (i.e., the actual building) will be destroyed by the thunderbolt; we will see possible reasons shortly. In his *Poetics*, Aristotle tells us that Aischylos is to be commended for treating only a part of the story of Niobe; this may mean that her metamorphosis to stone in Lydia was not included, or it may refer simply to the play's commencement after the slaughter (18.1456a.15–19). In Pherekydes' recounting, Niobe goes back to Lydia by herself (thus not as in Aischylos) and sees her city destroyed and the rock suspended over her father; in her grief she prays to Zeus to become stone (3F38; so too in Bak 20D Zeus in pity turns her to stone). Something of this sort could conceivably lie behind Homer's version, with Niobe at first taking courage after her own disaster but then broken by the further misfortunes in her homeland.

In Archaic art we have only one representation, that on a Tyrrhenian amphora of about 560 B.C. showing Apollo and Artemis with between them three fleeing victims (Hamburg 1960.1). The scene does not resurface until the famous calyx krater of the Niobid Painter from about 450 B.C. (Louvre G341). Subsequently it becomes especially popular in sculpture, but the scene represented is always the massacre, and thus we learn nothing further about the story.

In the Classical period we have above all Sophokles' *Niobe,* which seems to have taken quite a different approach in staging from that of Aischylos. Papyrus fragments now make it clear that Artemis and Apollo appeared in person to hunt down the daughters—Apollo even calls his sister's attention to one who is hiding and must not be allowed to escape (fr 441a R). The sons have, it seems, already been killed elsewhere, which is a trifle puzzling because Plutarch tells us that in this play one of the sons when shot calls upon his lover (*Mor* 760d), and Athenaios that the homosexual attachments of the sons were treated in some fashion (13.601a). Presumably this last feature was to increase the pathos of their deaths, and the actual slaughter of them, with whatever appeals were made to loved ones, was reported in a messenger speech. *Iliad* scholia add to all this that Sophokles had the children perish in Thebes, and Niobe then return to Lydia (ΣT *Il* 24.602). Unless we suppose a very unlikely change of scene, a god must have predicted this journey or Niobe announced it herself; we cannot say whether the metamorphosis was foretold. In any case, the overall impact, with the innocent daughters cut down by the gods virtually on stage, must have been considerable.

Later sources do provide some interesting bits of information. We should first note that Telesilla has two of the children, Amyklas and Meliboia, spared (721 *PMG*); of the sources so far considered, only Homer actually states that all were killed (although we should probably assume this in versions where Niobe returns to Lydia, or asks to become a rock). Pausanias adds to the notion of survivors the idea that Meliboia became permanently pale as a result of the ordeal, and was renamed Chloris (2.21.9–10). Apollodoros, our source for Telesilla, has as his own names for the saved pair Amphion and Chloris, which latter he equates with the wife of Neleus (ApB 3.5.6). In fact the *Nekuia* does make Neleus' wife a daughter of Amphion, but that Amphion is said to be the son of Iasos and ruler of Orchomenos, as also in the *Ehoiai* (*Od* 11.281–84; Hes fr 33a MW). Probably then some confusion has taken place between two figures of the same name, and Neleus' wife has in origin nothing to do with Niobe. But how old the tradition of children surviving might be we cannot say (Pausanias, despite his information, rejects it on Homer's authority). One other odd variant to record is that of the Hellenistic (and rationalizing?) Timagoras, who claims that the Thebans themselves slew the children from ambush, being annoyed at treatment received from Amphion and his friends (381F1).

In Ovid, Niobe finds the Theban women worshiping at Leto's altars, and dares (on the basis of lineage, beauty, and fourteen children) to claim Leto's honors as her own (*Met* 6.147–312). The sons are dispatched as they exercise their horses outside the city; Apollo is tempted to spare the last, hearing his appeal, but the arrow has already slipped from his fingers. The father Amphion kills himself at the news. Although Niobe also laments, she cannot help noting that her seven daughters are still more than Leto's brood, and so of course these are killed as well. The metamorphosis then occurs immediately, the result of shock and grief; a whirlwind carries the rock to Lydia to take its accustomed place as a local landmark. Apollodoros, like Homer, has Apollo kill the sons (while hunting on Kithairon) and Artemis the daughters (in their father's house); their mother's crime, as in Ovid, was to boast of her larger family (ApB 3.5.6). We have seen that like Telesilla this author spares two of the children, and like Pherekydes and Sophokles he takes Niobe back to Lydia, where as in Pherekydes her prayer to become stone is granted. Hyginus offers much the same: in his version Apollo slays the sons in a forest while Artemis deals with all the daughters (save Chloris) in the palace; Niobe again turns to rock in Lydia through her weeping (*Fab* 9).

As for Amphion, Telesilla has the two gods slay him also, in contrast to Ovid's notion of suicide. Pausanias says that he pays a penalty in the Underworld (he does not say what, or how the man died) for being among those to mock Leto and her children, and cites the *Minyas* as one source for this idea (9.5.8–9). In Hyginus, who may or may not know the same story as Telesilla, he attempts to attack the temple of Apollo, and dies by the god's arrows. One would like to know whether in this version he was simply angry over the loss of his children (as Hyginus' order of narration implies) or had as in Pausanias already begun to participate in the scorning of divine powers. We remember that in Aischylos' play his palace is destroyed, and perhaps there too he does something personally to merit the gods' wrath.

Pelops and
Hippodameia
In discussing Tantalos we have reviewed the evidence for his son's narrow escape from the banquet of the gods at Sipylos. Pelops' one appearance in Homer occurs in *Iliad* 2, when we learn that Agamemnon has a scepter that has passed from Hephaistos to Zeus to Hermes to Pelops, lasher of horses, to Atreus to Thyestes to Agamemnon (*Il* 2.98–108). I suppose we are to understand that Hephaistos made it for Zeus to give to Pelops (via Hermes) as a symbol of authority, although on our later evidence Hermes presenting a gift to Pelops is a bit odd, and Atreus passing on power peacefully to Thyestes, or Thyestes to Agamemnon, distinctly puzzling. Aristarchos supposed Homer therefore ignorant of the family's problems, but the poet may simply have considered them inappropriate to the point he wanted to make about the scepter. We should also keep in mind that the word used for each transfer, "leave," might indicate that power passed to the successor via the previous holder's demise, rather than his approval. In any case, and whatever Homer knows, we have an early link between Pelops and the house of Atreus. That he is in fact Tantalos' son (not said in Homer) is attested by the *Kypria* (fr 15 *PEG*) and Tyrtaios (12 W), while the feast we found first noted by Pindar in a context that showed it to be well known (in some form). The *Ehoiai* seems (based on a very fragmentary papyrus) to have charted the courting of his daughters by the sons of Perseus, as in later accounts; certainly an Astydameia is mentioned (Hes fr 190 MW).

The most famous myth concerning Pelops is, however, his race with Oinomaos for the hand of the latter's daughter. The *Megalai Ehoiai* mentioned some (perhaps all) of the previous entrants who died in this contest; Pausanias cites the work for Alkathoos as one victim and may have drawn from it for others on his own list, which totals seventeen (6.21.10 = Hes fr 259a MW). The Pindaric scholia for their part assign to "Hesiod" and "Epimenides" a total of thirteen (Σ *Ol* 1.127b), and provide three different lists of names, with thirteen, fifteen, and thirteen respectively (Σ *Ol* 1.127b, c, d); only a few suitors like Alkathoos, Lasios, and Eurymachos figure repeatedly in all of these. Pausanias elsewhere reports seeing the race between Oinomaos and Pelops (the latter with Hippodameia) depicted on the Chest of Kypselos; he notes that each driver has two horses, but that Pelops' are winged (5.17.7). For this chariot race in which Pelops wins his bride our first real narration is again *Olympian* 1, whose mythic portion after telling of Tantalos' fall focuses on his son's earthly life. Here, with his beard growing and his thoughts turned toward marriage, Pelops decides to sue for Oinomaos' daughter, and calls on his own former wooer Poseidon for help. The god bestows upon him a golden chariot and tireless winged horses; with these he defeats strong Oinomaos (thirteen previous suitors were unsuccessful) and takes Hippodameia as his bedmate. As this paraphrase shows, Pindar's account passes rather summarily over the race itself, but we presume that the victory is owed to the gift of the god.

Yet another, darker tradition surfaces as early as Pherekydes, to the effect that Myrtilos the charioteer of Oinomaos played a major role in the victory. Our source for the mythographer here, the scholia to Apollonios, strictly speaking mention Pherekydes only (in mid-stream of their account) for a variant detail (Σ AR 1.752 = 3F37a). But since they do not record him as diverging in other matters, we may assume that they found him in agreement on most details of the story. As they relate the tale, Oinomaos establishes the bride contest for his daughter because an oracle has told him that his son-in-law will kill him. Hippodameia, however, becomes enamored of Pelops when he presents himself, and asks Myrtilos, son of Hermes, to assist his victory. In Pherekydes this is accomplished by omitting to insert the linchpin in Oinomaos' chariot, so that it will fall apart; in other versions, rather more plausibly, a waxen linchpin that will disintegrate as the race progresses is utilized. Whether in Pherekydes Myrtilos was promised anything for this service we do not know, but other scholia report that in the mythographer's account Pelops did throw Myrtilos into the sea one day when the two of them were riding around the Peloponnesos with Hippodameia and the charioteer attempted to kiss her (3F37b). The same reference mentions that the horses pulling the chariot were winged, which seems an odd detail to include in an account stressing other means of victory. Indeed, one might be tempted to suppose the wings a Pindaric invention designed to dignify the triumph, and from there conflated into an older tradition, were it not for Pausanias' report of the same motif on the Chest of Kypselos. As it is, both versions must boast some antiquity, different though their approaches to the winning of victory are.

In fifth-century art we have the famous sculptures from the east pediment of the Temple of Zeus at Olympia. Here Zeus occupies the center, presumably indicating his approval of the outcome. To the left are Oinomaos and his wife Sterope (according to Pausanias), to the right Pelops and Hippodameia, and then toward each corner the chariot teams of the two competitors.[11] No fewer than four different of the crouching figures (B, C, L, N) have been identified as Myrtilos, assuming him to have been present; the one kneeling (by Oinomaos' chariot wheel?: C) is perhaps the most likely, though nothing in his pose makes him especially remarkable. To judge from the remains both sets of horses were unwinged. Perhaps the artist has deliberately suppressed both treachery and divine horses in order that Zeus alone might seem to determine the outcome; but perhaps too he presupposes Myrtilos' role, and seeks with this understatement to heighten the tension between the calm demeanor of the figures and the fatal "accident" to follow. From much later in the century a neck-amphora now in Arezzo shows Pelops and Hippodameia together in his chariot (Arezzo 1460).[12] She stands straight up, unaffected by the action, but he leans well back as he strives to control the horses and looks back over his shoulder. Clearly, then, the race is in progress, and if Hippodameia is already at Pelops' side (here as on the Chest of Kypselos), we might guess that this race is actually a kind of mock bridal-rape, with the suitor taking the prospective bride into his chariot as if to abduct her, and the father setting out after in pursuit. This would explain, too, the grouping at Olympia, with Hippodameia next to Pelops, not her father, as they prepare to start the race. We will see shortly that various later authors confirm this notion.

As for literature in the later fifth century, both Sophokles and Euripides wrote plays entitled *Oinomaos*. Of the first we know only that Hippodameia was passionately fired by Pelops' gaze (fr 474 R), that Oinomaos used the suitors' skulls for some architectural project (fr 473a R), and that the race began onstage, with no doubt a messenger report of the subsequent action. But one would like to think that Myrtilos was involved, and he *is* mentioned by the chorus of Sophokles' *Elektra* as thrown headlong from the chariot into the sea (S: *El* 505–15).[13] For Euripides' version we have nothing at all, save perhaps the possibility that Oinomaos was sympathetically treated; in a choral ode of the *Orestes*, however, we find Myrtilos again thrown into the sea, near Geraistos at the southern end of Euboia, and this is now the origin of a subsequent curse on the family (*Or* 988–96). From the contemporary Hellanikos we have already seen Oinomaos' genealogy as son of Ares and Sterope, daughter of Atlas (4F19).

Our later sources support most of these details and flesh out the story. In Apollonios, Iason's robe, made for him by Athena, shows Pelops and Hippodameia together in flight, while Oinomaos and Myrtilos give chase (AR 1.752–58). Oinomaos holds his spear poised, clearly to throw or thrust into Pelops' back, but before he can do so the axle of his chariot breaks and he falls. Diodoros makes Oinomaos (here too son of Ares) learn from an oracle that he will die when his only daughter marries (DS 4.73.1–6); we saw this motif already in the scholia to Apollonios, which probably draw from Pherekydes among others. Faced with such a prospect, he sets up the race for Hippodameia's suitors, giving them a head-start from Pisa in a four-horse chariot while he sacrifices to Zeus; then he overtakes them before they reach the Isthmos and kills them with his spear. Pelops duly appears and persuades Myrtilos to help him, but we are not given details: his chariot simply beats that of Oinomaos to the Isthmos and Oinomaos kills himself, convinced that the oracle has come true.

Apollodoros relates two separate motives for Oinomaos' treatment of his daughter, first that he was in love with her himself and did not wish another to marry her, and second that he received an oracle of his doom as above (ApE 2.4–9). The notion of an erotic attachment to his daughter we find also in the scholia to the *Orestes*, which credit the idea to the "more accurate of the historiographers" (Σ *Or* 990).[14] Apollodoros continues with the usual account, agreeing in many particulars with the Apollonios scholia: here Myrtilos, son of Hermes, is specifically in love with Hippodameia, and thus agrees to help her when she falls in love with Pelops. The race is again to the Isthmos, with the suitor taking Hippodameia in his chariot and trying to prevent Oinomaos from overtaking him. As in Pherekydes, Myrtilos removes the linchpins from the wheel hubs; Oinomaos becomes entangled in the reins and is dragged to his death. But Apollodoros also cites a rival version in which Pelops kills his opponent himself (we are not told how). Whatever the means of death, Oinomaos has somehow perceived Myrtilos' treachery, and he curses his charioteer to perish by Pelops' hand. In Apollodoros' conclusion to the story, Pelops, Hippodameia, and Myrtilos are subsequently out together on an excursion, in the course of which Myrtilos tries to rape Hippodameia after Pelops has gone to seek water; on Pelops' return he casts Myrtilos into the sea (again by Geraistos), and is himself cursed by his rival on the way down.

Hyginus also uses the motif of the oracle to begin his account, but has Pelops approach Myrtilos directly after seeing the skulls of previous suitors fixed on Oinomaos' palisade (*Fab* 84). In return for his help, Myrtilos is promised half of Oinomaos' kingdom, and the pins are withheld, but Pelops then regrets his offer and hurls Myrtilos to his doom instead. Pausanias gives us a similar narrative, save that here Pelops offers not half the kingdom but rather a night with Hippodameia; again he fails to keep his word (8.14.11). In the Vergil scholia, the result is the same but Hippodameia the one who promises herself to Myrtilos in return for his help (Σ *G* 3.7). The *Orestes* scholia (Σ 990 as above), after establishing Oinomaos as enamored of Hippodameia, follow closely the version of Apollodoros: Myrtilos being also enamored of Hippodameia is persuaded by her to remove the linchpins, and suffers his master's curse as a consequence. But at this point we are offered two possibilities: either Myrtilos tries to rape Hippodameia and is thrown into the sea, or he is falsely accused of rape by her. The latter version also appears in the *Iliad* scholia, where Hippodameia, who has engineered Myrtilos' treachery because of her love for Pelops, now falls in love with Myrtilos as well, and in Pelops' absence (he has again gone to get water) begs the charioteer not to scorn her advances (ΣA *Il* 2.104). He does so, however, and to protect herself she accuses him of rape to Pelops, thus bringing about his doom. We see, therefore, some variation in Myrtilos' role and relationship to Hippodameia, but none at all in his fate; in every account he is thrown to his death.[15] Possibly his status as the son of Hermes means that the race and his part in it was related as early as the *Alkmaionis*, where we know that Hermes for some reason began the quarrel between Atreus and Thyestes (see below), but on present evidence this is a guess.[16] As for Pelops, our summaries never really make clear whether in some versions he might have been ignorant of his intended's machinations to ensure his victory. Both Apollodoros and the *Orestes* scholia send him off to Hephaistos to be purified of the murder, and it seems generally agreed that Myrtilos' curse will fall upon his children rather than himself.

Pindar's *Olympian* 1 assigns to Pelops and Hippodameia six sons but does not name them (*Ol* 1.89). We saw that in the *Iliad* Pelops is said to have left his scepter to Atreus, and Atreus in turn to Thyestes, but there we have no indication of the exact relationship between the three men. In fact, no Archaic source specifies that Atreus and Thyestes were the sons of Pelops; the closest we come is Aischylos' *Choephoroi*, where Orestes calls himself a Pelopid (*Cho* 503); not until Sophokles' *Aias* (1291–94) and the prologue of the *Orestes* is the line of descent made explicit. Given the link established in Homer, however, there seems little reason to doubt that Atreus and Thyestes were always two of the sons. Presumably they were so named in the *Ehoiai*, but the relevant passages have not survived, nor can we say anything about other of Pelops' sons, if any, in that work. Other writers of the Archaic period do offer some suggestions of their own for these sons: a Sikyon is named in Ibykos (308 *PMG*: probably in the *Ehoiai* a son of Erechtheus [Hes fr 224 MW]), Kleonymos and Argeios (husband of Hegesandra, daughter of Amyklas) appear in Pherekydes (3F20, 3F132), and Alkathoos, founder of Megara, in a section of the Theognid Corpus referring to the Persian invasion of 480 B.C. (Theog 773–74). These names are, of course, primarily place eponyms (not surprising, given that Pelops' own name serves as source for the word *Peloponnesos*), and such offspring may be the sort of sons Pindar has in mind. Euripides' *Medeia* and *Herakleidai*, for their part, add a more substantive figure, namely Pittheus of Troizen, the grandfather of Theseus (*Med* 683–84; *Hkld* 207). Whether his link to the house of Pelops stems from Athenian pride in Theseus or goes back to something older we do not know; he does appear frequently in later lists. Apollodoros for example names him (with Atreus, Thyestes, and "others": Ap*E* 2.10) and so too the scholia to *Olympian* 1 (Σ *Ol* 1.144). These last actually offer three slightly different lists, as follows: (1) Atreus, Thyestes, Pittheus, Alkathoos, Pleisthenes, Chrysippos; (2) Atreus, Thyestes, Pittheus, Alkathoos, Hippalkmos, Dias, plus the bastards Chrysippos and Pleisthenes; (3) Atreus, Thyestes, Pittheus, Hippalkmos, Pleisthenes, Pelops the younger. Pindar's six children are all borne by Hippodameia; the scholia's suggestion of sources which included Chrysippos and Pleisthenes in that group might seem then to indicate versions in which they were legitimate. The scholia at *Orestes* 4 name Atreus, Thyestes, and Pittheus, plus ten other legitimate sons (largely eponyms), two daughters, and Chrysippos by one Axioche. Probably Apollodoros, too, had divergent lists from which to draw, and therefore contented himself with the three generally agreed-upon names followed by "others." In Hyginus there are only three legitimate children, Atreus, Thyestes, and Hippalkos *(sic)*, plus the bastard Chrysippos whom Atreus and Thyestes kill (*Fab* 85).

As we saw in chapter 14, Atreus' exile because of the death of Chrysippos occurs as early as Thoukydides (1.9.2), and Hellanikos relates the full story as we might expect it, that Pelops favors this son from a previous liaison, and that Hippodameia and her children plot his death, lest he receive preference for accession to his father's throne (41F57). As the two eldest, Atreus and Thyestes take the lead; when Pelops discovers the deed he exiles them, with a curse that they and their race may die at each other's hands. Plato also mentions the murder in passing (Atreus alone cited as agent, since the point is a play on his name: *Kratylos* 395b). The *Orestes* scholia noted above (at *Or* 4) have a tale similar to that of Hellanikos, with Chrysippos' mother here a certain Axioche, and the other sons together with Hippodameia persuading the two eldest (again Atreus and Thyestes) to do the deed in envy of Chrysippos' favored status. Having killed him, the two brothers throw the body in a well, but Pelops suspects the truth and exiles them with an unspecified curse. Dositheos has an unusual variant that we considered earlier in connection with Laios: here the Theban king is sleeping together with the boy when Hippodameia, having failed to persuade her sons to stain their hands, steals into his room and commits the murder herself with a sword taken from Laios; presumably she hopes that Laios will be blamed, but Chrysippos survives long enough to reveal the truth, and Hippodameia is banished (54F1). Some version of the tale as a whole *may* have been the subject of Sophokles' lost *Hippodameia*, if there really was such a play;[17] possibly, too, it formed the basis of Accius' *Chrysippus* or his *Pelopidae*. Neither of Chrysippos' fates—death at the hands of his family and suicide after his abduction by Laios—claim our attention before the fifth century; how much older than that period either might be is difficult to say. For Hippodameia's fate in those versions where she is involved our earliest sources are silent; Hyginus speaks of suicide (*Fab* 85), Pausanias (6.20.7) as well as Dositheos of exile. The other children we shall deal with in the following sections.

Turning from Pelops and Hippodameia's sons to their daughters, we found in chapter 10 that a papyrus fragment of the *Ehoiai* probably listed three of these, although only the names "Astydameia" and "Nikippe" (the latter from scholia) survive, and that they were there courted by the three sons of Perseus, Alkaios, Sthenelos, and Elektryon; the third name, that of Elektryon's bride, we can supply from later sources as "Lysidike," although these names for the daughters and even Elektryon's marriage to a Pelopis are not universally agreed to.[18] Such unions obviously give the family of Pelops a certain foothold in the Argolis, and we will see shortly how this device (sometimes in conjunction with the murder of Chrysippos) enabled storytellers to justify the transfer of the sons Atreus and Thyestes from Pisa to Mykenai (though in some early versions Oinomaos may already have ruled all the land between Pisa and the Isthmos).

Atreus and Thyestes

Whether cursed by Myrtilos for their father's slaying of him, or by their father himself for the murder of Chrysippos, these two most famous sons of Pelops seem destined to a tragic feud with each other. The *Iliad* stands alone in suggesting, if that is indeed its intention, a peaceful transition of power (via the scepter) from one brother to the other; in every later account they are at each other's throats, vying for the throne of the land to which they have come. Possibly their struggle was recounted in the *Nostoi* as background to Agamemnon's demise, and the *Orestes* scholia record that in the epic *Alkmaionis* a golden lamb sent by Hermes in anger was the initial cause of the trouble, with one Antiochos the shepherd who brought the creature to Atreus (Σ *Or* 995 = fr 6 *PEG*). An epic concerning Alkmaion is not likely to have dealt with the Atreidai at length, and admittedly we find no other trace of their conflict before Aischylos' *Agamemnon*, but Kassandra's dark hints and barely coherent allusions in that drama show that the story was well known, at least in its general outlines. What we learn from her ravings and visions is that Thyestes entered his brother's bed, and that Atreus in turn fed Thyestes the flesh of his own children (*Ag* 1191–93, 1219–22). Aigisthos' entrance late in the play brings further information: Atreus had exiled Thyestes but allowed him back as a suppliant, and under pretext of sacrificing for a feast day served him the dreadful meal (*Ag* 1583–1611). On discovering the nature of the feast Thyestes vomited forth what he had eaten, kicked over the table, and cursed the whole Pleisthenid race. What Aischylos supposed to have happened after this we do not know; we see only Aigisthos, claiming that Agamemnon's death is vengeance for that deed. Pherekydes in this same period apparently gave an account similar to that of the *Alkmaionis*, but with the anger of Artemis, not Hermes, causing the lamb to be produced and the difficulties begun (3F133).

The latter part of the fifth century offered Athenians quite a range of dramatic treatments: Sophokles' lost *Atreus* and *Thyestes in Sikyon*, plus at least one (possibly two) more *Thyestes* plays, and Euripides' similarly lost *Kressai* and perhaps a *Thyestes*; for the latter poet we have as well substantial references in his *Elektra* and *Orestes*. Of the lost plays, both the *Atreus* and the *Kressai* probably related the power struggle preceding the feast, and Dion of Prusa comes close to saying that in both playwrights the golden lamb was again a factor (66.6). Somewhere, too, Sophokles must have dealt with the feast, for we are told that he made the sun abandon its usual course in horror at Atreus' deed (*AP* 9.98), but this might have been in a *Thyestes* play or even a choral ode of an unrelated drama; the same is true of the throwing of Aerope into the sea, which may come from the *Aias* (see below). Euripides' *Kressai* told the story of Aerope's seduction on Krete, and her father's consequent consigning of her to Nauplios to be drowned, but judging from the fragments this was all prologue, and the actual plot concerned the adultery *and* the feast that followed. If the play followed the pattern of Euripides' other dramas on profligate women, the emphasis may have been upon Aerope's seduction of Thyestes for reasons of passion, rather than his seduction of her to gain power. There is also a *slight* hint in the fragments that the children killed may have been born to Thyestes and Aerope, not to Thyestes and a legitimate wife (fr 460 N²). If that is true, we should have to imagine the affair between Thyestes and Aerope as long-term, and the resulting children raised by Atreus in the belief that they were his; his anger on discovering this truth might also be thought to better motivate the terrible vengeance he takes. We know that Agathon and perhaps the younger Karkinos wrote plays entitled *Aerope*, and that in some such play the performance of the actor Theodoros as Aerope supposedly moved Alexander of Pherai to tears (*VH* 14.40); whatever the truth of that story, the implied focus on Aerope (rather than Atreus or Thyestes) as a pathetic figure might mean that there too the children were hers. Certainly she and Thyestes are the parents in Hyginus (*Fab* 246); our one piece of evidence to the contrary is the scholion at *Orestes* 4, where Thyestes marries a Laodameia who bears to him Orchomenos, Aglaos, and Kalaos.

For other details of the story we must rely on what we find in the *Orestes* (and scholia) and Apollodoros. From the *Orestes* itself we see clearly enough that there was a quarrel over the golden lamb (*Or* 812–13, 997-1000). The scholia offer two slightly divergent accounts, but both link the lamb to the kingship. In the one, that lamb, provided by Hermes as a way of causing trouble for those who slew his son Myrtilos, is proclaimed by Atreus as a sign of his right to the throne (Σ *Or* 998; so too Σ *Or* 995, Byz Σ *Or* 812[19]). Thyestes then seduces Aerope, and she gives her lover the lamb that he uses to become king in place of his brother. In the other version, supplied also by Apollodoros and the *Iliad* scholia, Atreus promises to sacrifice to Artemis whatever is most beautiful among his flocks, but when he discovers the golden lamb hides it away in a chest instead (Σ *Or* 811; ApE 2.10–11; ΣA *Il* 2.105). As before, Thyestes seduces Aerope to get the lamb, then proposes to Atreus in an assembly of the people that whoever possesses the lamb should be king; Atreus agrees, thinking himself the possessor, and discovers the truth too late. Since Pherekydes attributes Atreus' problems to Artemis, it seems likely that he presented this latter account, in which case Apollodoros as elsewhere may have drawn from him.

The events following the transfer of power from Atreus to Thyestes seem likewise to order themselves according to several slightly different patterns. In a choral ode of Euripides' *Elektra,* we find that after Thyestes' deception Zeus causes the stars and the sun to change course, so that the sun now moves from east to west, and there are general shifts in the climate (E: *El* 699–736). Apparently this is a permanent reversal of an earlier order, as we find too in Plato's *Politikos,* where the Stranger maintains that Zeus altered the rising and setting places of the sun and stars to their present arrangement in order to assist Atreus (269a). In *Orestes,* however, the alteration consists of turning the sun back from the west toward the dawn, thus just a temporary aberration from the normal state of affairs (*Or* 1001–6). Either way, the reason for this celestial portent is surely that offered by scholia and Apollodoros: after Thyestes' theft of the lamb Zeus sends Hermes to arrange with Atreus a stratagem in which the latter either announces that he will display a portent greater than the lamb, or gets Thyestes to agree to surrender power when the sun changes course (Σ *Or* 811; ΣA *Il* 2.105; ApE 2.12–13). Zeus then brings about the miracle, and Thyestes is forced to step down (cf. Σ *Or* 998, where the sun and Pleiades fail to set because of Thyestes' impiety). One further complication to consider is a Euripidean fragment in which Atreus says, "Demonstrating the opposite path of the stars I saved the people and made myself ruler" (fr 861 N²). The citer,

Achilles Tatius, seems to think that this refers to the sun's retrocession when compared to the stars, as Loukianos (without referring to Euripides) specifically argues was the means by which Atreus recovered his throne, in other words a scientific discovery rather than a miracle (*De astrologia* 12). This is, of course, rationalizing of a myth, but one which Euripides seems to have used somewhere. The same should probably be said of Sophokles, since Achilles cites him in the same context and says that he credited Atreus with the discovery of astronomy (fr 738 R).

By contrast with all this, we saw earlier that somewhere in Sophokles the sun turns backward in the sky of its own accord in revulsion when Atreus serves to Thyestes his own children. That change in motive has some important consequences, for if the portent is a response to Atreus' crimes rather than those of his brother, then it becomes simply a decorative motif and will not explain how Atreus recovered the throne from Thyestes. The Byzantine scholia at *Orestes* 812[20] do seem to suppose such a sequence of events, for in their exegesis, immediately after Thyestes' trick, Atreus "not enduring his misfortune and being angry that he was unjustly deprived of the rule (1) revenged himself on his wife Aerope (both because of her adultery with Thyestes and because she gave away the lamb) by casting her into the sea, as Sophokles says, and (2) killing Aglaos, Orchomenos, and Kaleos the three children of Thyestes served them to their father and later killed him also." Here too the sun in horror travels from west to east for one whole day. Possibly, then, we are to assume that Thyestes abandons the throne after such a horrible experience, but as the king one might expect him rather to seek revenge in his turn. In both Seneca's *Thyestes* and Hyginus (*Fab* 88), where again the sun's motive is a reaction to the feast (as at *Ibis* 429), Thyestes returns from exile for his grim banquet, indicating that Atreus has resecured power long before. Aischylos, we saw, does bring Thyestes back to Mykenai (or Argos) as a suppliant for the feast, but from this alone we cannot tell which version of the story (if either) he intended. On the whole it might seem, given the similarity in the function of the celestial portent, that much of the Byzantine scholia entry is drawn from a play of Sophokles, even allowing that said scholia's specific reference to Sophokles may well derive from an entirely different context (the *Aias*: see below). Atreus as the slayer of Thyestes is in any event surprising; elsewhere Thyestes has the final revenge, and perhaps that is what the scholiast meant.

As for the feast itself, in Seneca's play it forms the centerpiece of the drama, and may have done so in productions by Sophokles and Euripides as well. Seneca gives to Thyestes three sons, Tantalos, Pleisthenes, and a third child unnamed; Atreus slaughters them all for the banquet. At the play's climax Thyestes, having eaten his fill, asks to have his sons brought in, and Atreus presents him with the heads and other remains, advising him that what he does not see he already has. The work closes with laments and protests on the part of Thyestes, but no predictions of any specific vengeance to be taken. Such a treatment of the story seems obvious enough, and could well draw from both

Sophokles and Euripides. In Aischylos' *Agamemnon*, on the other hand, Aigisthos appears to say that he was the thirteenth of Thyestes' children, and the only survivor, being still in swaddling clothes (*Ag* 1605–6). The slaughter (and even partial consumption) of twelve children seems unnecessarily grotesque; more likely there is a corruption here in our single manuscript tradition, with the word for "ten" intruding and converting an original "three" into "thirteen."[21] In that event, two children would constitute the Aischylean meal. Whatever the number, though, Aischylos does attest to an Aigisthos already born at the time of the meal, which we shall see is not always the case.

In Apollodoros three sons are again killed and cooked, and the extremities produced only after Thyestes has finished (*ApE* 2.13); the names—Aglaos, Orchomenos, and Kallileon—are virtually the same as those in the *Orestes* Byzantine scholia at 812 (see above) and scholia vetera at 4 (Aglaos, Orchomenos, Kalaos). Hyginus, on the other hand, reports the same names—Tantalos and Pleisthenes—as did Seneca, although he seems to know of only two children (*Fab* 88, 246, with Aerope the mother); Seneca does not name the third, and may have borrowed the number "three" from the tradition represented by Apollodoros and the *Orestes* scholia. One other story occurs only in Hyginus, namely that after his expulsion Thyestes sends Atreus' son Pleisthenes, whom he has brought up as his own, to Atreus in order to kill the man; Atreus, still believing this to be his brother's son, has him killed instead (*Fab* 86; cf. perhaps the garbled Σ *Or* 16). We will see below that other accounts involving this same son of Atreus do not square well with such a tragedy, even though Pleisthenes does as a rule die young. But Euripides composed a lost work entitled *Pleisthenes* for whose plot there are few candidates other than this one, and thus the story may well be as old as the fifth century, or before. It forms a curious counterweight to the perhaps also Euripidean notion that Atreus for a time believed Thyestes' children by Aerope to be his own.

Regarding Thyestes' children, there is yet one more tale to note, that of Klytaimestra's first husband as alluded to by Klytaimestra herself in Euripides' *Iphigeneia at Aulis* (1149–52), where she says that she was originally married to one Tantalos, and that Agamemnon killed both him and their child. She adds that Agamemnon then married her by force, and the implication is thus that his motive for the murders was to obtain her, although the text does not actually say that. Apollodoros repeats the story, calling the Tantalos in question a son of Thyestes (thus not slain for the feast: *ApE* 2.16), and Pausanias agrees with this genealogy and the marriage, although he omits the child (2.18.2). Subsequently, however, the latter writer calls this same first husband of Klytaimestra Tantalos, son of Thyestes or of Broteas (2.22.3), this last presumably the same Broteas who appears as a son of the original Tantalos at 3.22.4 (and at Σ *Or* 4). Apollodoros does not recognize such a variant, but he does mention a Broteas (between his accounts of Tantalos and Pelops) as scorning Artemis and boasting that not even fire can harm him; he becomes mad and throws himself upon flames (*ApE* 2.2; cf. Ovid *Ibis* 517–18). Clearly then, this Broteas is a member of the family, but certainly the intrigue surrounding Klytaimestra's first marriage will be much greater when her husband is the son of Thyestes. Aischylos' Klytaimestra has ample opportunity to accuse Agamemnon of that husband's murder and does not do so, nor does she mention him in any way; in any case, the slaughter of Iphigeneia to win a war probably suited the playwright's purposes far better than a deed for which Agamemnon could plead passion as an excuse. That the story was known to the Catalogue Poet, in whose *Ehoiai* Agamemnon plays an influential role in persuading the Dioskouroi to give Helen to his brother after he himself has married their sister, may seem unlikely, but hardly impossible.

Thyestes in Sikyon

We know that Sophokles wrote a play of this title, and part of Hyginus' *Fabula* 88 does indeed take Thyestes to Sikyon, where he begets a child by his own daughter; given that he has no other reason to be in such a place, even as an exile, Sophokles' plot surely in some way related that unusual event. Further evidence may well be offered by an Apulian calyx krater of about 340 B.C., the work of the Darius Painter (Boston 1987.53). Here, in what certainly looks like a stage confrontation, we find Thyestes at the center of the scene, looking left to a servant who holds the infant Aigisthos (all figures named). To the right of Aigisthos stands Adrastos, and beyond him Pelopia and Adrastos' wife Amphithea. Adrastos is presumably present as ruler of Sikyon, while the child must belong to the unwed Pelopia. Thyestes, of course, will almost certainly know that he is the father; less certain is whether Pelopia and Adrastos also know this. Either way, as fatherless bastard or the product of incest, the child seems about to be exposed, as Thyestes and his daughter agonize over an action probably mandated by Adrastos.

Whatever we make of this plot, and whatever play it represents, Hyginus' version of Thyestes' stay in Sikyon (no sources credited) would seem to offer no room for such dramatics. As he tells the story, Thyestes after the banquet flees to a certain king Thesprotos, and thence to Sikyon, where he chances upon rites to Athena being conducted by his own daughter Pelopia. Fearing to defile the ceremonies he hides in a grove, and thus happens to see the priestess disrobed when she comes to the same place to wash her bloodstained garment. Face veiled, he leaps out from his hiding place and rapes the girl, who in the process pulls his sword from its scabbard and subsequently hides it in the temple. On the next day, Thyestes departs for Lydia. Meanwhile, barrenness of the land has forced Atreus to seek his brother, and he pays a visit to Thesprotos; although he arrives too late to find Thyestes, he does meet Pelopia, whom he obtains from Thesprotos, thinking her to be the latter's daughter. She then bears Aigisthos from the embrace of her nocturnal assailant; the child is abandoned but shepherds have him nursed by a goat and ultimately Atreus finds and raises him. At some later point, Agamemnon and Menelaos capture Thyestes as he is consulting the Delphic oracle and bring him back to Atreus, who commissions the son he thinks to be his own, Aigisthos, to kill his bitter enemy. Aigisthos is prepared to carry out this order in Thyestes' prison when his victim recognizes the sword he lost on the night of the rape. Pelopia as the person who provided the sword is sent for; realizing now the identity of her child's father she seizes the sword and stabs herself. Aigisthos then returns to Atreus with the bloody weapon as proof of Thyestes' death. Atreus goes down to the beach to sacrifice in thanksgiving and Aigisthos there kills him, thus restoring the throne to his father.

Obviously such a long and contorted story cannot have been dramatized in its entirety, and there are some logical inconsistencies, such as why Atreus finds Pelopia with Thesprotos rather than at Sikyon, and why Thesprotos allows Atreus to suppose the girl his daughter. But the last series of events—arrival of a captive Thyestes in Mykenai, Atreus' order to Aigisthos, Aigisthos' confrontation of Thyestes, Pelopia's entrance and death, and a messenger report of the death of Atreus—would work well enough on stage, with the preceding action related in the prologue (either by Pelopia or a god). Such a play would not, however, be likely to bear the title *Thyestes in Sikyon*, when all the stage action takes place in Mykenai. Since we do have one or even two other Sophoklean *Thyestes* dramas to account for, we should probably apportion the story out between two productions, with *Thyestes in Sikyon* relating the events of the rape itself (or perhaps the conflict shown by the Darius Painter), and another *Thyestes* (or even *Atreus*) presenting the outcome years later when Thyestes is captured. Possibly the two plays were even part of a connected trilogy, although a *Thyestes in Sikyon* presenting the Darius Painter's plot will not have been compatible with any subsequent story in which Atreus believes the child to be his.

One other aspect of the union between father and daughter which may shed light on Sophokles' dramas is the question of Thyestes' motivation. In Hyginus' *Fabula* 88 we see Thyestes stumbling upon the sacrifice by chance and being tempted to his deed by the priestess' state of undress, which rather suggests that he does not recognize his daughter and is simply overcome by the passion of the moment. But the same writer's *Fabula* 87 tells us that Thyestes had been advised by an oracle to beget a son by Pelopia to avenge him, and we find a compressed version of that story also in Apollodoros and the Euripides scholia (ApE 2.14; Σ *Or* 15).[22] The emotional pressures on a man advised to violate his own daughter might seem to offer much to a tragedian, especially if the father is then threatened with the exposure of the child he has so terribly desired. On the other hand, Sophokles may well have preferred a version in which Thyestes is ignorant of his deed, and condemns his daughter as severely as Adrastos (or more so) until the truth and his own complicity are revealed. Either way, it does seem that in the situation presented by the Darius Painter Thyestes must know the truth about Aigisthos' birth, or come to learn it soon after the child is born.

Apollodoros goes on to say that Agamemnon and Menelaos eventually seized power from Thyestes and exiled him again, this time to Kythera; we have no evidence as to his ultimate fate. Aischylos' *Agamemnon,* as we noted above, has Aigisthos alive at the time of the banquet, which would seem to exclude the more scandalous account of the child's conception. That Aischylos knew that tale is not impossible; clearly, though, he would have no use for it here if he did, since an Aigisthos who has already avenged his brothers' death on Atreus will have no plausible claim to the life of Agamemnon on the same grounds (quite the opposite). Presumably, those accounts that did acknowledge the tale of Pelopia presented Aigisthos' later act of bloodshed as an attempt to regain his father's power or (as Homer implies) to appropriate Klytaimestra for himself. That Pelopia's travails could on the other hand be simply an invention of Sophokles or his time must also be allowed, although it seems unlikely. Of Euripides' *Thyestes* mentioned before, we know virtually nothing, save that Atreus was a character. The capture of Thyestes and death of Atreus *could* conceivably have been the subject, and such a play might even have preceded that (or those) of Sophokles.

Pleisthenes We come last of all in this chapter to the most perplexing member of the house of Tantalos. Homer never mentions him, either in *Iliad* 2's succession account or elsewhere, and while the standard epithet *Atreidês* can mean simply "descendant of Atreus," both the *Iliad* and *Odyssey* on occasion call Agamemnon or Menelaos specifically a *son* of Atreus. But the Hesiodic Corpus saw matters differently: *Iliad* scholia tell us that while Homer makes Agamemnon the son of Atreus and Aerope (she is not mentioned in the *Iliad* or *Odyssey*; presumably the scholiast gets this from the Epic Cycle), in Hesiod he and his brother are the sons of Pleisthenes (ΣA *Il* 1.7 = Hes fr 194 MW). Another *Iliad* scholion repeats this idea, although *without* mentioning Hesiod; it does cite Porphyrios and "many others" for it, and adds that Pleisthenes died young, having done nothing of note, whereupon his sons were raised by Atreus (ΣA *Il* 2.249). Tzetzes (in his *Exegesis in Iliadem*) explains further what we will have already guessed, that in this version Pleisthenes is the son of Atreus. He goes on to say that for Hesiod, Aischylos, and others, Pleisthenes is born of Aerope, and that this Pleisthenes, wed to Kleola, daughter of Atreus' brother Dias (she is thus his own first cousin), begets Agamemnon, Menelaos, and Anaxibia (pp. 68–69 Hermann, reproduced in part as Hes fr 194 MW).[23] Here too we find the father dying young, so that the grandfather Atreus raises the sons who come to be thought of as his. Whether the "Hesiodic" source for all this could be the *Ehoiai* is unclear, for fragmentary lines of that poem just preceding the tale of Alkmene appear to attest that Aerope (not Kleola) is the mother of Agamemnon and Menelaos (and a third son: Anaxibios?), although whether by Atreus or Pleisthenes we cannot tell (Hes fr 195 MW). If that is correct, then either Tzetzes has drawn some of his information from his other named sources alone, or his reference to "Hesiod" intends another part of the Hesiodic Corpus.

We should note here (as likely happens in Euripides) that a father adopting his deceased sons' children might plausibly marry the mother as well; thus it would be no surprise to find Aerope (or even Kleola) in some accounts married to first Pleisthenes and then Atreus. But in the scholia to the *Orestes* (where Dias is again a brother of Atreus), we find just the opposite: here Atreus marries Kleola, daughter of Dias, she who was the wife of Pleisthenes in Tzetzes, and the two of them become the parents of the (infirm of body) Pleisthenes (Σ *Or* 4). We might suppose that the roles of Aerope and Kleola have simply been reversed, were it not that Pleisthenes marries someone quite new, one Eriphyle by whom he becomes the father of Agamemnon, Menelaos, and Anaxibia. But it remains possible that Atreus was wed to Kleola and Pleisthenes to Aerope in the *Ehoiai*, and that Tzetzes' account of "Hesiod" inadvertently reversed those two women. As noted above, Euripides seems likely to have passed Pleisthenes' wife Aerope on to Atreus (in the *Kressai:* see below).

Tzetzes offers one other curious bit of information, not in his *Exegesis* but in his scholia to that work: while in Homer Agamemnon and Menelaos are the sons of Atreus, son of Pelops, in Hesiod they are the sons of Pleisthenes, the hermaphrodite or lame one, who wore a woman's mantle (addendum to Hes fr 194 MW).[24] What the first of these terms might imply about Pleisthenes' actual physical condition is hard to say, nor is it clear whether one item of feminine dress is sufficient to categorize him as desirous of a gender change. But the lameness concurs with the elsewhere reiterated idea that he was weak or sickly, and we find it supported in particular by Loukianos in his play *Podagra*, where the title character (Gout) is humorously credited with afflicting various mythical figures (*Podagra* 250–57). Among these are Achilleus, Philoktetes, and Oidipous, people with foot afflictions, to be sure, but not gout, so that when Pleisthenes is also included his lameness is probably meant.

The remainder of the Archaic period provides some further references, if not help. Stesichoros uses the name "Pleisthenides" of someone, probably Menelaos, in a fragment showing Helen conversing with Telemachos (209 *PMG*). From the same poet's *Oresteia*, we have two lines relating a dream of Klytaimestra in which she sees a snake with bloody head which becomes or from which springs or after which appears "a king Pleisthenides" (219 *PMG*). We will be obliged to consider the exact identity of this king more fully in chapter 17; for present purposes it will suffice to note that the Pleisthenid ought to be some member of Agamemnon's rather than Aigisthos' line, most likely Agamemnon himself or his son Orestes, as a Pleisthenes son of Atreus would certainly guarantee. With Ibykos, however, matters take a more confusing turn, for in his poem to Polykrates on the heroes at Troy he speaks of Agamemnon as "the king Pleisthenides, leader of men, son of a noble father Atreus" (282 *PMG*). Either the poet here heedlessly combines two conflicting descriptions (from different epic traditions?), or he knows of a genealogy other than those we have found so far.

For the fifth century we have first of all Bakchylides, who calls Menelaos "Atreides" and "Pleisthenides" in the same poem (15.6, 48), and then Aischylos. The *Agamemnon* shows us Klytaimestra after the murder of her husband offering to bargain with the *daimôn* of the Pleisthenidai for acceptance of the present situation if he will leave to afflict some other house (*Ag* 1568–73). One would suppose she means to include all the misfortunes of the family, in which case Pleisthenes ought to be at least an ancestor of Atreus and Thyestes. But perhaps that is to press a generic epithet too closely in a situation where the audience cannot mistake the meaning. Further on in the drama Aigisthos appears, and in relating the grim feast of Atreus describes how Thyestes on learning the truth kicked over the table and prayed that all the race of Pleisthenes might thus perish (*Ag* 1598–1602). Whom Thyestes means by that designation is again unclear, especially as just previously at line 1600 he has called down destruction upon the Pelopidai. This last wish would, of course, include himself and his line, and perhaps at this moment he indeed wishes to see the entire race blotted out. But Aigisthos cites the curse primarily as proof of the justice of Agamemnon's death, so he seems to understand it as an appeal for vengeance against Atreus, not total obliteration of everyone in the family. If that is the case, then Pleisthenes must in some way indicate Atreus' branch of the family but not Thyestes', and this condition will again be satisfied if Pleisthenes intervenes between Atreus and Agamemnon. Against such a conclusion, however, we must admit that the play elsewhere and Aigisthos himself in this very speech call Agamemnon the son of Atreus (*Ag* 60, 1583). We saw above that Tzetzes credited the Pleisthenes son of Atreus who died young to Aischylos as well as to "Hesiod," but we do not know whether Tzetzes drew that conclusion from *Agamemnon* 1598–1602 alone, or whether he found more detailed, certain information in a lost play (the *Iphigeneia?*). On balance, all we can really say is that Aischylos has here conflated Homeric and non-Homeric tradition, with Homer holding sway most of the time but Pleisthenes thrown in at one point for good measure. What he did elsewhere may or may not have been quite different.

Scholars also equate at times the Pleisthenes under discussion with the Pleisthenes named by the *Olympian* 1 scholia as a son (not always legitimate) of Pelops. But making this brother of Atreus the important Pleisthenes (rather than a separate figure of the same name) will not resolve any of our previous difficulties, for he would still have to be the father of Agamemnon and Menelaos if the patronymics we have encountered are to make sense, and his children still adopted by Atreus, who would remain only their stepfather. If Agamemnon (or Menelaos) was ever truly both "son of Atreus" and "Pleisthenides," then Pleisthenes must at some time have been a direct ancestor of Atreus, and for this our tradition would *seem* to leave no room.

Turning to Sophokles' *Aias*, we find on the part of Teukros in that play total adherence to Homer: Pelops begets Atreus who begets Agamemnon (*Ai* 1291–97). He adds too (by way of insult to Agamemnon) Thyestes' feast, and then Agamemnon's Kretan mother, "in whose bed finding an alien man the father enjoined that she be quarry for the fishes." As those words stand the reference would seem to be to Katreus, Aerope's father, who found her with a slave and gave her to Nauplios to kill. But the word here translated as "alien" *(epaktos)* would more naturally refer to an adulterer, since in the bed of an unmarried woman any man would be inappropriate, and only a small adjustment to the text (involving the word *father*) would produce rather a reference to Aerope and Thyestes. Either way, Aerope must be the Kretan mother, married to Atreus, but if the manuscript correction is accepted we would have here our first reference to Aerope being thrown from a cliff as punishment for her adultery. The account of the Byzantine *Orestes* scholia at line 812, where Sophokles is said to attest that fate for Aerope, seems to guarantee that it appeared somewhere in his work, but of course the scholiast might be referring to this same passage of the *Aias*, where the meaning is as we have seen controversial.

No later source says anything at all about Aerope's death, although Atreus would be expected to put aside such an adulteress, and those versions involving a new marriage to Pelopia must suppose some such action. The scholia for the *Aias* passage tell us that in Euripides' *Kressai* Nauplios (as usual disobeying Katreus' order to drown Aerope) gave her to Pleisthenes in marriage (Σ *Ai* 1297). Beyond this information we are left to speculate about Euripides' drama, but if, as Apollonios of Alexandria suggests, Aerope's further wantonness was the topic (Σ *Batr* 849), we might reasonably conjecture that by the time of the play's opening Pleisthenes has died, leaving his father Atreus to both adopt the children and marry his son's wife. Indeed, in all versions where Pleisthenes intervenes between Atreus and Agamemnon, this would seem the logical means of bringing Atreus and Aerope together, unless Tzetzes' notion that Atreus was originally married to Aerope and Pleisthenes to Kleola has some basis after all.

We saw before that a play entitled *Pleisthenes* is also attributed to Euripides, and that the only conceivable plot for it, unless a story has been completely lost, is Hyginus' *Fabula* 86, where Atreus unwittingly kills his own son Pleisthenes sent to him by the foster-father Thyestes. Such a tale could certainly be dramatized, and it would explain Pleisthenes' early death. But nowhere else is it suggested that Pleisthenes is not known to be Atreus' son from birth, and by the time he dies, the traditional Pleisthenes is a grown man with a wife and several children. When we add these difficulties to the inherent improbability of such parental confusion, we may well feel that Euripides has here given us a new story, perhaps a twist on the confusion over Aigisthos. Whatever the exact genealogy in these lost plays, Euripides is in our preserved dramas quite ready to follow Homer: both the *Helen* and the *Orestes* present a direct Pelops-Atreus-Agamemnon line of descent, with no possibility of intervening members and in both cases Aerope as Agamemnon's mother (*Hel* 390–92; *Or* 11–18).

Later sources have virtually nothing to record on these matters. Apollodoros does confirm Aerope's rescue by Nauplios and betrothal to Pleisthenes, to whom she bears Agamemnon and Menelaos (Ap*B* 3.2.2), but we hear nothing more of him, nor does the mythographer say how Aerope later comes to be married to Atreus when he relates the tale of her infidelity with Thyestes (Ap*E* 2.10). Hyginus' only reference to Pleisthenes is the story just discussed; at no point does he name him as father of Agamemnon and Menelaos. In concluding our look at this odd figure, we may be tempted to ask why storytellers bothered to create or preserve him, since with or without him the Atreidai remain effectively the sons of Atreus. There are, of course, his mysteriously bisexual tendencies in the Hesiodic Corpus (if Tzetzes' allusions are accurate), but the one real instance in which he appears to serve a purpose is the story we postulated for Euripides' *Kressai*, with a young Aerope married to a (perhaps) much older Atreus after her first husband has died, and for that reason attracted to the (perhaps) much younger Thyestes. Admittedly, such a reconstruction sounds archetypally Euripidean, especially when we note that the play was written in his "fallen women" period of the 430s B.C.. But given the need to explain Pleisthenes' presence much earlier, in the *Ehoiai* and other early sources, it may be that this plot of unhappy younger wife is quite old, and forms an important starting point for the conflict between Atreus and Thyestes.

16 The Trojan War

In *Iliad* 20 the Trojan Aineias comes face to face with Achilleus, and in response to the latter's taunts provides a capsule history of the race of Troy (*Il* 20.215–41). First among the rulers is Dardanos, son of Zeus, who founds a settlement on the slopes of Mount Ida, Troy itself not having yet been built. Dardanos' son is Erichthonios, whose wealth includes three thousand mares, and with some of these Boreas consorts in the form of a horse, producing twelve colts who run across blades of asphodel and sport above the breakers of the sea. To Erichthonios is born Tros, and to Tros three sons, Ilos, Assarakos, and Ganymedes. The last of these, because of his beauty, is snatched up by the gods to become wine-pourer for Zeus, but Ilos begets Laomedon and Assarakos Kapys. Laomedon in turn has five sons—Tithonos, Priam, Lampos, Klytios, and Hiketaon—while Kapys produces just one, Anchises who will father Aineias, the point of this whole recitation.

Lampos, Klytios, and Hiketaon all appear briefly with Priam in *Iliad* 3, as elders sitting on the wall of Troy (together with Panthoos, Thymoites, Oukalegon, and Antenor: *Il* 3.146–48); Tithonos we will naturally not expect to find, since he has been abducted by Eos. Homer never elsewhere alters any part of the above genealogy, but he does at *Iliad* 6.23–24 add a sixth son for Laomedon, one Boukolion who is the eldest and apparently illegitimate. And Diomedes in *Iliad* 5 varies the tale of the acquisition of the horses a bit by having Zeus give them to Tros as compensation for the loss of his son Ganymedes (*Il* 5.260–72: nothing else is here said about the abduction). The same speech adds that after the horses had passed to Laomedon Anchises bred foals from them by his own mares without the owner's knowledge. That Herakles bargained with Laomedon for some or all of the horses is established by *Iliad* 6, as we saw in chapter 13. From a number of references throughout the poem we also discover that Aineias is Anchises' son by Aphrodite, although the circumstances of such a mating are never explained. Against this overall picture, the use of "Dardanides" as a patronymic elsewhere in the *Iliad* has been thought to betray an earlier, less developed family line, with the patriarch Dardanos originally much closer to the generation involved in the Trojan War.[1] In particular there is the application of that adjective (ten times) to denote Priam (*Il* 3.303, etc.), but also the presence at several points of a tomb of Ilos Dardanides in the middle of the Trojan plain (*Il* 11.166, 371–72; tomb without the patronymic also at 10.415, 24.349). Possibly in both these cases the patronymic's range has simply been (remarkably) extended. But possibly too Ilos, son of Tros, was in earlier times viewed as a brother of Erichthonios and son of Dardanos, and came to occupy a different niche only as the family expanded.

The *Ehoiai* for its part offers one small bit of evidence to support this last conclusion in the form of a papyrus fragment with only the left edge preserved (Hes fr 177 MW). From what survives we see that Dardanos' mother was apparently Elektra, and we should probably make this figure as in Hellanikos (where she bears Dardanos to Zeus: 4F19a) a daughter of Atlas. The fragment further gives Dardanos a brother Eetion (Hellanikos [4F23] calls him both Eetion and Iasion), and like the *Iliad* a son Erichthonios. But here there is also a second son Ilos, after whom the papyrus breaks off, so that we cannot tell through which of the two sons the royal line continued. If through Ilos, there might have been a tradition rival to Homer, perhaps reflected by Ilos' tomb even within the *Iliad*. But the *Ehoiai* probably supposes (as perhaps the *Iliad* in its use of Ilos Dardanides) a cadet brother of Erichthonios. One other brief reference assigned to the *Ehoiai* calls Tros the son of Teukros (Hes fr 179 MW); nothing, however, indicates how these two figures would relate to any of the others. The *Little Iliad* (or a similar poem) also mentioned Ganymedes' abduction in some unknown context (probably the arrival of Eurypylos at Troy), and here we do find a significant change in the line, for the abductee is now the son of Laomedon, not of Tros, while Zeus' gift to the bereaved father becomes the vine, in some way ornamented by Hephaistos (*IlMik* fr 29 *PEG*).

In the *Homeric Hymn to Aphrodite*, the goddess' allusion to Ganymedes follows the same general outline presented by Diomedes in the *Iliad*: the youth is again the son of Tros, who finds considerable consolation in the news of his son's fate (as revealed by Hermes) and the present (from Zeus) of the horses (*HAph* 202–17). Here though, in contrast to *Iliad* 20, it is Zeus alone, not the gods as a whole, who does the abducting, "on account of his [Ganymedes'] beauty, so that he might be among the immortals and pour for the gods in the house of Zeus, a wonder to see, honored by all the immortals, drawing off red nectar from a golden krater." Admittedly, Aphrodite's point in telling this story (and that of Tithonos which follows) is to excuse her own descent into Anchises' bed by stressing the undoubted good looks of the race of Troy. But while the attraction in Eos' case and her own is sexual, we are not entitled on that account to assume the same for Zeus and Ganymedes. On the contrary, emphasis here as in the *Iliad* remains on Ganymedes' beauty as something admired and shared by all the gods as they watch him serve them; quite possibly, then, the sexual element in this relationship has not yet taken shape. Whatever Zeus' motive, the boy does seem in the Hymn to have been carried off to Olympos by a whirlwind, much as Penelope envisions happening to her in the *Odyssey*.

The main body of the *Hymn to Aphrodite* tells, of course, how the goddess, by the contrivance of Zeus himself lest she boast of sending other gods to bed with mortals, conceived a desperate passion for Anchises, and how she came to him claiming to be the daughter of the Phrygian king Otreus. Her tale—of being snatched up by Hermes and brought to Mount Ida to become Anchises' wife—is not perhaps overly plausible, but it allays his fears that she is a goddess, and on that assumption he is only too willing to take her to bed. Only afterward does she reveal her true identity and announce the child who is to be born to them, a child who will be cared for by the Nymphai until he is old enough to come to his father. Anchises' subsequent fate—perhaps alluded to here by the goddess but not confirmed until Sophokles' *Laokoon* and then, of course, the *Aeneid*—has already been considered in chapter 2, under the heading of Aphrodite's amours. The end of the *Theogony* also notes briefly this mortal-immortal union (*Th* 1008–10), while the *Iliad* makes mention of daughters of Anchises by an unnamed mother (seemingly his wife) of whom the eldest and most-admired—Hippodameia—is wed to the ill-fated Alkathoos (*Il* 13.427–35). We should keep in mind, of course, that the *Kypria* and other poems of the Epic Cycle may have offered their own background on the royal house of Troy, even if nothing survives.

What little there is from the later Archaic period all relates to Ganymedes, save for the previously discussed tale of Herakles and Laomedon. In literature we find a brief mention by Theognis, who is our first source to specify that Zeus' interest in Ganymedes was erotic (*Theog* 1345–48) and then Pindar, who concedes the same point as a precedent for Poseidon's abduction of Pelops (*Ol* 1.43–45). Ibykos, too, seems to have related the tale, but we have no details beyond the fact of the abduction (289 *PMG*). In chapter 15 we considered the evidence (from *Iliad* scholia and the historian Herodian) for Tantalos rather than Zeus as the abductor; the same scholia also know of a version in which Minos played that role (ΣbT *Il* 20.234, credited to Dosiadas [458F5]). In art, the earliest sure rendering of the gods' intervention is the Red-Figure cup by Oltos in Tarquinia (RC 6848) on which Ganymedes (named and portrayed as a naked young male) pours nectar for Zeus and the other gods. Soon after, however, Zeus begins to appear as perpetrator of the kidnapping, as on a (lost) White-Ground alabastron by the Diosphos Painter with Zeus (prodded by Eros) pursuing Ganymedes while Tros looks on (Berlin:Lost F2032: names again furnished), and then a whole series of Red-Figure pots.[2] The final sequence of this action, the actual abduction, appears on a cup by Douris (Louvre G123) and a terracotta group at Olympia (T 2), both dating to about 475–70 B.C. In the case of the cup, the scene could possibly be one of human activity (despite the presence of a scepter), but a statue dedication of this type at a sanctuary of Zeus must surely represent the god. Both the statue and many of the pots include a cock as love gift, either clutched or pursued by Ganymedes. In a number of cases the child seems indifferent or unwilling, and Zeus must resort to a certain amount of tugging (e.g., Ferrara 9351). On no occasion, however, do we see any sign of an eagle, either as agent of the abduction or in any other capacity.

From the literature of the time we might have expected at least a satyr play, but there is no record of any drama bearing the title *Ganymedes*, and only the briefest mention of him in one of our preserved tragedies (*Tro* 820–24). The middle of the fourth century brings us our first traces of the eagle as abductor, most notably in a lost work of Leochares described by Pliny (*NH* 34.79). The later literary tradition offers two explanations of this form of the tale: Ps-Eratosthenes (*Katast* 30), Vergil (*Aen* 5.254–55), Apollodoros (*ApB* 3.12.2), and Pliny himself suppose the eagle to be a servant of Zeus bringing Ganymedes to his master, while the (Hellenistic?) *Peri Apiston* of one Herakleitos (28) as well as Ovid (*Met* 10.155–61) and Loukianos (*DD* 10) make the eagle Zeus in disguise. Under such circumstances, we cannot tell what most artists intended in representing the eagle in this role, although one Hellenistic sculptural group in Naples portrays an unmistakable exchange of looks between eagle and boy (Naples 6351). For the more important issue here, namely how early the eagle became a part of the story, we are likewise at a loss. We have seen that in the *Hymn to Aphrodite* a whirlwind is the instrument of abduction, but of course this may not have been the only early form of the story. Admittedly, though, a whirlwind as the standard device in the Archaic period would explain why we never see for that period an artistic portrayal of the abduction, in contrast to the ever-popular Europa and her bull.

As for other members of the Trojan line in our late sources, Lykophron has a cryptic reference to a Trojan ancestor who swims (with the help of some sort of craft) from Samothrace to the Troad during the great flood (Lyk 72–80). Konon and other writers establish that this was Dardanos himself, although in Konon's version the motif for the migration is grief over the death of his brother Iasion, killed for desiring Demeter (26F1.21). In this account, as in Hellanikos (and probably the *Ehoiai*), the brothers are sons of Zeus and Elektra, daughter of Atlas; Konon adds that, having left Samothrace on a raft, Dardanos comes to the mainland, and there, after a covenant with Teukros, son of Skamandros (the local king), founds a city Dardania at the place where he first arrived safely. Upon Teukros' death, he then comes into possession of the entire kingdom. Hellanikos may well have related all of this, since we know that in his *Troika* Dardanos marries Bateia, daughter of Teukros (4F24). The same writer also appears to have said that Dardanos was advised by Apollo against settling on the site of Troy, and for this reason made his way to Mount Ida where he founded Dardania (4F25). Possibly this last detail is meant to explain why Dardanos settles so very far away from what would be the most natural landfall for one arriving from Samothrace. Diodoros too, though he says nothing about a journey from Samothrace, has Dardanos marry Bateia, daughter of Teukros Skamandrides, ruler of the land, and found a city named after himself (DS 4.75). In Lykophron this daughter is Arisbe, and her father Teukros comes originally from Krete, having journeyed to the Troad with his father Skamandros on a raid (Lyk 1301–8).[3] As for Troy, Lykophron calls its site "the hill founded by the wandering cow" (Lyk 29), and both Apollodoros and the Lykophron scholia explain that Ilos followed this cow to find the site for his city. Apollodoros makes the cow a gift from the king of Phrygia (ApB 3.12.3); in the scholia Ilos has a herd of cows, and he is told to watch for the one who will lie down. But in each account he clearly acts on instructions from an oracle, so that this tale is a virtual doublet of the founding of Thebes. Diodoros likewise says that Ilos founded the new city of Ilion out on the plain, and both he and Konon agree on one other point, that Assarakos ruled Dardania (26F1.12). This is what we might expect, at least after Assarakos' brother Ilos has moved north to found his new city, and such a division probably means that Assarakos' line was believed to remain near Mount Ida. Certainly in the *Iliad* we see the great-grandson Aineias bitter toward Priam over his lack of status at Troy (*Il* 13.459–61), and Achilleus in his speech to Aineias boasts that he once chased his opponent from Ida to Lyrnessos (*Il* 20.188–94). The remainder of Apollodoros' account repeats much of what is found in Konon and Diodoros, saving only the rulership of Dardania, and adds (as in the *Ehoiai*) an Ilos, son of Dardanos, who here dies without issue (ApB 3.12.1–3). Subsequently he includes also Ilos, son of Tros, as a second figure of that name; possibly the *Iliad* had already supposed such a doublet. To Laomedon's family (sons alone named in Homer) Apollodoros assigns as well three daughters, Hesione, Killa, and Astyoche, and of the sons as given by Homer makes Boukolion offspring of the Nymph Kalybe, thus clearly illegitimate. Purely Latin is presumably the tradition in which Dardanos and Iasion have their original home in Italy (*Aen* 3.163–68), and Dardanos at least makes his way from there to both Samothrace and the Troad (*Aen* 7.205–8).[4]

**The Birth
and
Childhood
of Paris**

Priam's parentage, his alternate name Podarkes, and his accession to his father's throne after the affair with Herakles and the horses we have already considered in chapter 13. In all accounts he is the son of Laomedon, with his mother Zeuxippe according to Alkman (71 *PMG*) and Strymo according to Hellanikos (4F139). Of his wife Hekabe, the *Iliad* says that her father was Dymas (and her brother Asios: *Il* 16.717–18), and Pherekydes agrees on this point (3F136); Euripides on the other hand makes the father Kisseus (*Hek* 3), and later tradition offers still other names. The *Iliad* also makes clear that Priam has fifty sons (twenty-two are named, among them Hektor, Paris, Helenos, Deiphobos, and Troilos) and twelve married daughters living with him (most notably Laodike); the unwed Kassandra and Polyxena (the latter never mentioned by Homer) must be added to these last, plus perhaps other unmarried daughters or married ones living elsewhere. Some of these offspring are specifically Hekabe's and some are not; Priam at *Iliad* 24.496 finally discloses the actual number of sons (not daughters) which she has borne to him—nineteen—but Homer offers no other details of their marriage or life together, and we must wait till

Apollodoros to hear of Priam's previous union with one Arisbe, daughter of Merops, who bears him a son Aisakos, or of Kreousa as his daughter by Hekabe (ApB 3.12.5; cf. Σ Lyk 1232 on the latter). Already in Stesichoros, however, we find the idea that Hektor was Apollo's son, not Priam's (224 *PMG*), and so too Ibykos (295 *PMG*), Lykophron (Lyk 265), and Euphorion (fr 56 Pow); Homer clearly knows nothing of this. That Troilos was also a son of Apollo has no preserved authority earlier than Lykophron, as we will see later in this chapter.

In any case, there is no hint in the *Iliad* of any problem or decision at the time of Paris' birth, despite the numerous insults and imprecations leveled at him in the course of the poem. Our first trace of such a story comes from Pindar, whose *Paian* 8a (from a papyrus) tells of a dream or vision vouchsafed to Hekabe while she was pregnant with Paris: she seemed to give birth to a fire-breathing Hundred-Hander, and he with harsh strength destroyed the whole of the city of Ilion. Another figure (a *mantis?*) then replies, mentioning something about forethought, and here the papyrus breaks off. The obvious implication, that Priam and Hekabe were warned of Paris' future before he was born, is confirmed by the A scholia at *Iliad* 3.325, where Hekabe dreams that she gives birth to a flaming torch that burns down both Troy and the forests of Mount Ida; seers then advise that the child be abandoned on Ida as food for wild beasts, and this is done, only to be thwarted by a shepherd who finds Paris and raises him. A similar story formed the prologue of Sophokles' and Euripides' *Alexandros* plays, both of which dealt with Paris' return to Troy as a young man. For the reconstruction of those plays we have a few fragments, plus a papyrus hypothesis of Euripides' version (POxy 3650),[5] but our primary knowledge of plot comes from Hyginus, so that we cannot say which details belong to which playwright, much less whether any might have been added from other sources. As Hyginus tells the story, Hekabe in her dream gives birth to a blazing torch from which numerous serpents issue (*Fab* 91). Diviners therefore advise that whatever offspring she is carrying should be destroyed when she delivers it, and the infant Alexandros is handed over to servants to be killed. The servants, however, in pity expose the child, and of course shepherds discover him and bring him up as their own, calling him Paris. Grown to young manhood, he finds one day that men sent by the king are leading off his prize bull to be used as an award for games to be celebrated in honor of Alexandros. With no other way to recover his property he follows them to Troy and enters the contests, where he defeats all comers including his own brothers. Such a defeat prompts Deiphobos to draw his sword against the unknown upstart; Paris flees to an altar of Zeus for sanctuary, and Kassandra then reveals his true identity as son of Priam. Priam himself acknowledges this lost child, and apparently no more is said about the omen of his future.

Of this eminently dramatic plot we can assign for certain to Sophokles only the context in which a herdsman defeats men of the city (fr 93 R), but this seems enough to guarantee the playwright's use of the whole Hyginian tale in some form. For Euripides we have more substantial fragments showing that Kassandra appeared, that Deiphobos took his defeat extremely hard, in contrast to Hektor, and that Hekabe, finding the victory of a supposed slave over free men intolerable, proposed that her sons should kill the newcomer (9 GLP).[6] Briefer fragments from Stobaios seem to indicate that wealth and poverty, slave and free man, and the illusory difference between them, were key issues, as we see reflected in the same poet's *Elektra*. From the preserved *Troades*, produced together with the *Alexandros*, we have an allusion to the dream and Paris as a torch (*Tro* 920–22); presumably, the *Alexandros* itself did not contradict this. In a separate play altogether, the later *Andromache*, the chorus relates how Kassandra called upon everyone in the city to destroy the infant Paris, to no avail (*And* 293–300). Varro tells us that Ennius used Euripides' etymologizing of the name "Alexandros" for his own play of that title (*LL* 7.82), which has led some scholars to suppose the whole of Ennius' play drawn from Euripides, but obviously he could have conflated different plays, and in any case we do not have much of his effort either. What does survive from it includes a prologue spoken by Kassandra (in which Hekabe again dreams that she is delivered of a burning torch, and Apollo interprets the omen: *Ex incertis* fr V Rib), the fact that the shepherds gave Paris the name "Alexandros" (*Alexander* fr V Rib), and a call by Kassandra to the populace to come quench the brand, that is, Paris (*Alexander* fr VI Rib). This last detail suggests a different means of recognition than in Hyginus, for Kassandra is not likely to stop her brothers from killing Paris by revealing his name and then incite them to kill him anyway. Servius knows a version in which the identification is made by means of a rattle or amulet *(crepundia)* given to him as an infant (Σ *Aen* 5.370); it has also been proposed that Hekabe might observe the resemblance between her sons and the stranger, or Paris make some chance remark about his origins which could lead to the discovery. In either case the servant who failed to kill the child may be called upon as well, much as in Sophokles' *Oidipous*.

The story was also quite popular on late Etruscan urns, where Paris in his Phrygian cap crouches on an altar and a Trojan (presumably Deiphobos) tries to kill him; Aphrodite generally intervenes. Other figures include Priam and Hekabe and also Kassandra, who holds an axe and wishes for reasons of her own prescience to dispatch her brother. That Aphrodite appeared in tragedy as well to identify Paris and/or resolve the crisis is certainly possible, but we would then expect her (or any *deus ex machina*) to repeat the initial warning about Paris, which would leave Priam in a difficult position. More likely, Kassandra is disbelieved, as usual, and the omen is forgotten in the joy of the moment. Surprisingly, there is no record of the story in vase-painting. Although he omits any details of the recognition, Apollodoros tells much the same tale as Hyginus, with the dream of the torch (as in Ennius no snakes) and an interpretation by Priam's son Aisakos, after which the child is exposed on Mount Ida and nursed by a bear for five days (Ap*B* 3.12.5). Here too, as in

Ennius, shepherds name the child Alexandros, in contrast to the *Troades* and Hyginus, where his parents give him that name. Already in Homer we find both appellations used, though with no explanation of their source; conceivably, Sophokles used one version of the dual naming and Euripides the other. We should note in that connection that while Varro has Ennius borrow Euripides' etymology for Alexandros he does not quite attest that the circumstances—shepherds bestowing the title—were also the same, even if that seems likely. On the whole we must admit, as so often, that though the motif of prophecy and abandonment is certainly old, we cannot say how old it is in the particular case of Paris. Proklos' summary of the *Kypria*, where we might have expected to find it, has nothing on Paris' early life at all, and one does not immediately see where else it might have been told. The problems involved in fitting it together with the judgment of the goddesses we will return to below.

One additional tale of Paris' birth, alluded to quite obscurely in Lykophron and explained in the relevant scholia, suggests that Hekabe had a sister Killa, married to Thymoites, with whom Priam secretly lay; she bore a child Mounippos, and when an oracle advised Priam to kill both the woman who had just given birth and her child he slew Killa and Mounippos rather than Hekabe and Paris (Σ Lyk 319). Earlier, however, the same scholia make the father of the child Thymoites himself; here too the child is killed with his mother after Aisakos has advised slaying the offspring born on that day (Σ Lyk 224). We have seen above that in Apollodoros Killa is the sister of Priam, not Hekabe (ApB 3.12.3), and that Homer mentions Thymoites once, as one of the elders sitting with Priam and his brothers (*Il* 3.146). Diodoros calls Thymoites a son of Laomedon, although he does not relate any part of the above story (DS 3.67.5). In Vergil, meanwhile, we find the remark that Thymoites "is the first to encourage our bringing the horse within the walls and placing it on the *arx*, whether through treachery or because the fates so now ordained" (*Aen* 2.32–34). The mention here of treachery seems really too casual to have more sinister overtones, but Servius after relating the same tale of Priam's killing of the wife and son of Thymoites in response to an oracle (again the utterance of his son by Arisbe) argues that Vergil may be alluding to a grudge on the part of the angered father (Σ *Aen* 2.32); it does seem clear, though, that he has no independent source for such an idea.

Tyndareos and the Wooing of Helen

We have seen that in Homer Helen is consistently a stepdaughter of Tyndareos, and a half-sister of the Dioskouroi (since they share a common mother). About her wooing and bestowal upon Menelaos, neither the *Iliad* nor the *Odyssey* has anything to say, despite Menelaos' seeming lack of stature for such a role. Likewise, neither poem makes mention of any oath taken by suitors to defend the eventual bridegroom's rights; we are presented rather with heroes who have come to Troy for glory and spoils.[7] Possibly such obligations on the part of the suitors have been omitted from the *Iliad* because they would inevitably affect our response to Achilleus' withdrawal from battle, but other sources solve that problem by dropping Achilleus from the list of suitors, and Homer could have done the same. If he has heard of the oath, perhaps his motive for its exclusion is the hope of imparting greater effectiveness to those scenes in which the Achaians, Agamemnon included, contemplate abandoning the war. But, of course, Homer may not have known the story at all. The *Kypria*, or rather our summary of it, also ignores all aspects of the wooing, beginning rather with the wedding of Peleus and Thetis and the Judgment of Paris, after which Paris sails to Sparta, where Menelaos and Helen are already married. The same summary does, however, relate subsequently the incident of Odysseus' feigned madness to avoid participating in the expedition, behavior that might lead one to suppose that he is under some commitment to Menelaos.

In the *Ehoiai*, at any rate, there was an extremely detailed report of the wooing, in part preserved, with a catalogue of all the suitors who sent gifts to Sparta (Hes frr 196–204 MW). That they sent gifts rather than coming in person seems to have been the standard procedure, at least at first, for the Berlin papyrus that is our main source of information notes that one suitor (name lost) knew of Helen only by hearsay, and that in contrast to the others Idomeneus did come himself to plead his case. Yet ten lines later in the same fragment, after a most inconvenient gap in the papyrus, we find someone extracting a clear oath from the suitors to pursue anyone carrying off Helen by force. From this event it might seem that all the suitors are now present in Sparta, but given the brevity of the missing space in which they would have to assemble it may be that the oath is administered severally via messenger, and that there never is an actual gathering of wooers. As to the names of the aspirants, the fragments offer the following: Odysseus; Thoas, son of Andraimon; Podarkes, son of Iphiklos; Protesilaos, son of Aktor; someone from Athens who is very likely Menestheus; Aias; Elephenor, son of Chalkodon; Idomeneus; and the two sons of Amphiaraos. Of these all but the last are familiar figures in the *Iliad*. Unfortunately, we have no idea of the original length of the list or of how many names were included. We do, however, find Kastor and Polydeukes mentioned repeatedly as recipients of the various envoys, and at one point the poem says that the two brothers would have given Helen to (name lost, alas), had their brother-in-law Agamemnon not interceded on behalf of Menelaos (Hes fr 197 MW). From this passage we see that (1) the Dioskouroi, rather than Tyndareos, seem to have the decisionmaking role, and (2) Agamemnon is not among the suitors, being already married to Klytaimestra. Why Klytaimestra should have been married before Helen is something of a puzzle; perhaps we are to understand that she was older, or perhaps storytellers wished to avoid explaining Agamemnon's defeat in the wooing by his own brother. Other fragments tell us that Odysseus sued but sent no gifts (knowing that Menelaos would win as the wealthiest of the Achaians: Hes fr 198 MW), that the Athenian contestant believed himself the wealthiest (Hes fr 200 MW), and that Aias of Salamis offered sheep and cattle from Troizen, Epidauros, Aigina, Megara, etc. (Hes fr 204 MW). Finally the oath is sworn by all, after which we are told very simply that Menelaos is chosen because he has furnished the most goods. All the same, the poet adds, he would not have won had Achilleus been among the suitors; the latter's absence is here ascribed to the fact that he is still with Cheiron on Mount Pelion, and perhaps that he is still very young. Beyond this we have only a reference from scholia which adds the Kretan Lykomedes to the list of suitors (Hes fr 202 MW).

In the mid-sixth century, Stesichoros seems also to have recounted the wooing, almost certainly in his lost *Helene*. Our one reference to his treatment of the occasion (a scholiast's summary) regards the oath: Tyndareos fears to make enemies of the other Greek leaders by preferring one of them, and so extracts a common oath that they will all defend the rights of whoever should win her; this done, he gives her to Menelaos (190 *PMG*). The same general rationale appears in the fifth century in Euripides' *Iphigeneia in Aulis,* where Agamemnon describes the oath as conceived by Tyndareos to preserve order after the suitors (here clearly assembled) begin to threaten each other (*IA* 49–71). But when they have all agreed to protect Helen from any sort of abduction, he allows her to choose her own husband according to the whims of her heart. Of later sources our best accounts are from Apollodoros and Hyginus, both of whom give lists of the suitors. That of Apollodoros contains thirty-one names, familiar as Achaian leaders in the Catalogue of Ships and elsewhere in the *Iliad* with the exception of Amphilochos, son of Amphiaraos (ApB 3.10.8). Among those mentioned, there are thus few surprises, save perhaps for the inclusion of Patroklos and the absence of Idomeneus and Meriones. The omission of Idomeneus in particular, combined with those of Podarkes and Lykomedes, would seem to show that Apollodoros is not here basing himself directly on the *Ehoiai*, unless he is reciting (fallibly) from memory. The one other notable detail in this account (in which the suitors are again clearly together at Sparta) is the claim that the idea for the oath comes from Odysseus, after Tyndareos has expressed fears about anger among the losers. Odysseus makes this offer of help in exchange for Tyndareos' assistance in securing the hand of Penelope from Ikarios. Tyndareos then chooses Menelaos; we are not told why. Hyginus' list of thirty-six suitors is a bit more chaotic, as we might expect, and also omits Podarkes and Lykomedes (as well as any son of Amphiaraos), so that the same conclusion applies as for Apollodoros (*Fab* 81). Regarding the selection of the winner he says that Tyndareos "fearing lest Agamemnon repudiate Klytaimestra and lest discord arise out of the matter, on the advice of Odysseus bound himself by oath and made Helen the selector of her own husband" (*Fab* 78). Thus Odysseus is again the instigator, but there is (unless something has been misunderstood) no suitors' oath, and Helen here as in Euripides makes her own choice, although Hyginus does not say why she should prefer Menelaos. Our one other bit of evidence comes from Pausanias, who points out the Tomb of the Horse on the road out of Sparta toward Arkadia and says that Tyndareos here sacrificed a horse and took the suitors' oaths over it (3.20.9). One emerges from this survey with the impression that storytellers found Helen and Menelaos irrevocably linked, despite the presence of seemingly more attractive suitors, and made the best of the situation.

The *Iliad* has just one solitary reference to the event that formed the cause of the Trojan War, and even that is couched in terms vague enough to be controversial. Hera and Athena several times in the course of the poem state their bitter enmity toward Troy and their determination that it be destroyed, but only in Book 24 is any cause stated for this anger. When the poet tells us that all the other gods urged Hermes to steal back the body of Hektor from Achilleus he excepts three—Hera, Poseidon, and Athena—and adds that Troy and Priam and the people were hateful to these "because of the folly of Alexandros, who created contention with the two goddesses, when they came to his courtyard, but approved the one who furnished to him an object of grievous lust" (or "made him desirable in a way which caused grief": *Il* 24.28–30). If we cannot get the exact sense of these last words, we have still enough to say that this is the Judgment as we know it: two goddesses are disappointed, while the entire *Iliad* proclaims that the third, here chosen by Paris, has provided him with Helen.[8] That Homer does not mention the story elsewhere may seem surprising, but the anger of such goddesses must have some origin, and we will understand that Homer does not wish to stress too strongly divine responsibility for the war. Nor should Poseidon's inadvertent involvement in this passage be an issue: the poet knows that his audience will not confuse the god with the real contestants, and they have already heard Poseidon's own reason for wrath, namely his ill-treatment by Laomedon at the time of the building of Troy's walls (*Il* 21.441–57). Thus, nothing really supports Aristarchos' athetizing of these lines; their allusive quality indicates rather the familiar nature of the tale, as so often in Pindar.

What details we miss in Homer are certainly atoned for by the *Kypria*, where Paris' famous decision seems to have been fully narrated, to judge by Proklos' summary. There Eris, being present at the wedding of Thetis, starts the quarrel among Hera, Athena, and Aphrodite as to beauty, and Zeus orders Hermes to take them to Paris on Mount Ida to resolve the matter. Paris, swayed by the promise of a marriage with Helen, chooses Aphrodite; we are not told what if anything Hera and Athena offered. Prior to all this the *Kypria* has begun with Zeus and Themis plotting together to bring about the Trojan War; our summary says no more than that, but the *Iliad* scholia offer a quote from the poem showing that Zeus' motive was to relieve the earth of the weight of so many mortals, in an act of pity (ΣA *Il* 1.5–6 = fr 1 *PEG*). The quote is preceded by a more general narrative of the situation which is probably also drawn, at least in large part, from the *Kypria*. This tells us that Gaia is burdened not only by the number of men, but also by their impiety, and that she makes an appeal to Zeus to lighten the weight. His first response to her request is the war at Thebes. Subsequently he plans to employ thunderbolts and great floods as well, but Momos prevents him, and advises Thetis' marriage to a mortal and his own engendering of a beautiful daughter, from which two events will arise a great war. That either Helen's birth or Thetis' union with Peleus was a preplanned device to trigger the Trojan conflict is not an idea found elsewhere, and then too another source reports that in the *Kypria* Zeus gave Thetis to a mortal out of anger, because she rejected him (Philodemos: fr 2 *PEG*). But however we take these details, the central theme of overpopulation and large-scale war as a solution is obviously early, although Paris' ultimate responsibility as a cog in this plan remains uncertain. The Berlin fragments of the *Ehoiai* appear to know something of the same story, for immediately after Helen's marriage and the birth of Hermione (unexpected, for some reason) they tell us that the gods were divided in strife, as Zeus continued to set the earth in turmoil and to blot out much (or all?) of the race of men (Hes fr 204 MW). The problems of this passage, with its mention of *hêmitheoi* and a life of the blessed ones apart, we have already discussed in part in chapter 3. An event involving heroes falling in strife, as the text says at one point, and following so closely upon Helen's appearance, must surely be the Trojan War. Yet the motive, whatever it is exactly, obviously differs from that of the *Kypria*, and what we see next in the fragments of the *Ehoiai* is some sort of natural disaster with high winds (after which the papyrus breaks off), rather than any of the usual preludes to the war. Possibly we are to understand, as in the *Kypria*, Momos' intervention and a change of plan, but certain words do suggest that war and natural devastation are both part of Zeus' plan from the very beginning. In any case, we cannot say whether the Judgment of Paris appeared in the *Ehoiai* at all, or just how the war there began. Our one other literary source of the Archaic period on this point is Akousilaos: apparently in his version Aphrodite somehow arranged the war, so that Aineias' house might become the ruling one (2F39).

In art we have a substantial number of early representations, the Judgment of Paris being a favorite subject of the Archaic period.[9] The very earliest are an ivory comb from Sparta, of uncertain date but usually regarded as seventh-century, and the Protocorinthian Chigi Olpe of about 640 B.C. The comb shows Paris seated to the left on an elaborate chair or throne, and the three goddesses approaching him, Hera with a cuckoo, Aphrodite with a goose (presumably these are attributes, not bribes: Athens 16368).[10] On the Chigi Olpe in the Villa Giulia much of the lower part of the scene is broken away, but here there are in recompense names to guarantee the artist's intention (VG 22679). Alexandros now stands to the left, greeting a missing figure who by the tip of his kerykeion must be Hermes; behind the latter are the three goddesses, of whom, since the second and third are Athena and Aphrodite, the first must be Hera. Neither of these depictions adds much to our knowledge of the story, but they do attest it for the seventh century, and much as we see it in the *Kypria*. For the sixth century we have first of all the Chest of Kypselos, where an inscription quoted by Pausanias assures us that here again Hermes is leading the three goddesses to Alexandros, who is to resolve the issue of their beauty

(5.19.5); our guide saw the same scene also on the Amyklai Throne (3.18.12). Unfortunately, in neither case does he note any indication of the prospective judge's attitude toward this contest. It is a question of some interest because from about 570 B.C. onward Attic Black-Figure representations often show Zeus' designated arbiter displaying a certain reluctance to assume his assigned role. On a tripod kothon by the C Painter in the Louvre Paris steps away gingerly to the right as Hermes (looking back) and his charges approach (Louvre CA 616). Between the two men a female figure faces Paris with a garland in each hand; she may be one of the contestants sneaking ahead for a private interview, although (since there *are* three females behind Hermes) she may also be Paris' lover, Oinone. A neck-amphora and column krater by Lydos develop this reluctance still further: Paris now vigorously strides away, virtually running, while Hermes increases his own pace and raises his arm as if to halt his quarry (Florence 70995; London 1948.10–15.1). Such attempted discretion might seem to accord ill with the subsequent acceptance of Aphrodite's bribe, but this last feature of the story was no doubt locked in, leaving us with a Judgment in which Paris is prudent enough to foresee the dangers of his task, but not prudent enough to avoid them. Whether this attractively dubious characterization derives from a literary source or represents an artistic innovation of the sixth century remains open.

In non-Attic art of the period we have a Pontic amphora from Vulci now in Munich (837), and the British Museum's Boccanera slabs from the cemeteries of Caere (no #). Both works display a Paris waiting calmly for the divine procession to reach him, as on the Chigi vase; the Munich amphora has as well cows behind the Trojan, our first concrete reference to his herding activity. The Attic pieces so far considered (and others of the same time) show him rather in long chiton (and himation on occasion) and sometimes carrying a scepter (or at least an elegant staff) which gives him quite the look of a royal personage. Not until around 520 B.C. do the trappings of a shepherd begin to appear: a dog, animals from the herd, and Paris himself seated on a rock, often with a lyre for entertainment. At the same time, or a little later, the fleeing Paris motif begins to become less common, in part perhaps because Hermes and the goddesses alone, without Paris, emerge as the most popular type. In Red-Figure, Paris on his rock resurfaces as the standard mode of representation, and as the century progresses emphasis shifts from the procession to the goddesses crowded around the handsome, youthful Trojan. In two such cases from the early part of the century one goddess offers to Paris what certainly looks like an apple (a piece of fruit, in any case), so that we see here for the first time the prize to be awarded (London E178, E257).[11] Oddly enough, Hermes in the earlier representations is never given custody of this item; as we saw in chapter 1, its first literary appearance is quite late (ApE 3.2; *Fab* 92; *Sal* 45).

The artistic evidence thus suggests that the Archaic period for most of its length chose to portray Paris as a prince of the house of Troy, rather than a shepherd tending his livestock. Indeed, we might suppose his role as herdsman to begin as late as the latter sixth century, were it not that the *Kypria* does place him on Mount Ida for the goddesses' visit. But since *Iliad* 20 speaks of Aineias as herding cattle on Mount Ida when he is unlucky enough to encounter Achilleus, it seems clear that livestock-tending is not inappropriate for royalty. More problematic is the relationship of Paris' abandonment to the Judgment: one would like to know whether in the *Kypria* and other early accounts the goddesses agreed to be judged by a shepherd of no supposed birth or distinction, or whether they came to him after his restoration to royal status at Troy, when he had become a royal shepherd rather than a common one. Both solutions seem slightly anomalous (although I suppose Zeus could have revealed Paris' identity to his wife and daughters), and not impossibly the visit to Paris on his hillside was originally conceived in a world where he was always a royal shepherd, never an abandoned waif. If that were true we might suppose the tale of prophecy and abandonment a later elaboration, one inspired by his shepherding duties but never quite accounting for the honor of his role in the Judgment.[12]

For the fifth century our evidence comes from a variety of dramatic sources, and serves on the whole to reinforce what we have already seen. Aischylos does not mention the Judgment in the *Oresteia* (scarcely surprising since human responsibility is such a primary issue) and there is no trace of it elsewhere in his work, or any hint among the lost titles. Sophokles did write a satyric *Krisis* which dramatized the conflict; our source, Athenaios, suggests that Athena's intellectual nature and athletic prowess may have been contrasted to Aphrodite's hedonism in a kind of philosophical allegory (fr 361 R). Presumably the Satyric chorus had in mind rather a physical display of the goddesses' charms. In the *Dionysalexandros* of Kratinos (430 or 429 B.C.), the Judgment was caricatured, with Dionysos (i.e., Perikles) disguised as Paris rendering the verdict and causing the war. Here for the first time, if our summary of the play is accurate, do we hear of three bribes: Hera promises an unshaken *tyrannis*, Athena success in battle, and Aphrodite that Paris will be most handsome and desirable (POxy 663 = vol. 4, p. 140 *PCG*). The particular form of Aphrodite's offer *may* reflect what *Iliad* 24 meant, or was thought to mean, if it does not arise from something in the Periklean comparison intended; in any case, it leads to the usual result, Paris' seduction of Helen. Only shortly after this comedy comes Euripides' version of the same events, as related by Helen in the *Troades*: Pallas begins the contest by promising that as general of the Phrygians Paris will destroy Hellas, and Hera in her turn offers a tyranny over all Asia and Europe (*Tro* 924–37). Finally Aphrodite extols the marvels of Helen, and Paris makes his choice. Helen then adds that as a consequence of that choice the Greeks have been saved from Eastern domination, as would have happened had Paris taken either of the other offers; probably the poet has exaggerated those offers for the sake of just this argument (which Hekabe not surprisingly ridicules as absurd, since Hera and Athena would never abandon their favorite Greek cities). Likely Kratinos has not invented the three bribes, given that they become a standard part of the later tradition. But we have seen that only Aphrodite's appears in our brief evidence from the *Iliad* and the *Kypria*, and whether the others were always present must remain uncertain; conceivably in the earliest accounts Hera and Athena merely flaunted their charms, while Aphrodite alone presented an additional inducement for Paris' consideration, her rivals' attempts to do likewise representing a post-*Kypria* development.

Elsewhere, Euripides' references to the Judgment come from choral odes and other allusions in a variety of plays. From the *Andromache* we have an ode lamenting that Paris ever survived, or judged the contest (*And* 274–92). Here as before Hermes brings the goddesses—a triple-yoked team—to Mount Ida, where the emphasis is very much on the solitary nature of Paris' existence among his livestock. The goddesses pause to wash in a nearby spring before actually arriving, and then "pushing themselves forward past each other with the going beyond of their hostile words they came to Paris"; the awkwardness of the translation reflects the ambiguity of these words, which may mean simply that the goddesses tried to outdo each other in disparaging the allurements of their rivals. Briefer mentions in the *Helen* (23–30) and *Iphigeneia at Aulis* (1283–1309) also establish Paris as a shepherd on Ida at the time of the Judgment, and seem to imply that he has set up permanent housekeeping there, as we saw before.

In the fourth century the story finds a place in Isokrates, whose encomium to Helen likewise includes mention of the three offers made to Paris (10. *Helen* 41–44). Here Athena promises victory in battles, Hera rule over all of Asia, and Aphrodite Helen. The author also adds a surprising defense of Paris' choice, namely that he preferred Helen not for the sake of pleasure but in order to become a son-in-law of Zeus, with the consequent advantages to his future children. The very earnestness of this last argument suggests it is new, nor does it ever reappear. For the bribes in essentially this form we have also Apollodoros (ApE 3.2), Loukianos (the *Dearum Iudicium*), and Hyginus (*Fab* 92), the latter adding from Hera unsurpassed riches and from Athena knowledge of all skills. Later artistic representations continue the trend of the latter fifth century, with the goddesses grouped around Paris and Eros sometimes in attendance. Obviously, they are seeking to cajole or influence him, but a painting cannot tell us by what means. Regarding one other aspect of Paris' early career, his lover Oinone whom he abandons for Helen, we find nothing until Hellanikos, who knows of their child who came to Troy to find his father; we will return to that story and her fate later in this chapter, when we come to the death of Paris.

The
Abduction
of Helen

The *Iliad* twice mentions Paris' journey from Sparta back to Troy with Helen, once when he himself reminds Helen how they made love on the island of Kranae (presumably for the first time: *Il* 3.443–45), and again when the poem mentions the elegantly woven robes brought back by Paris from Sidon on his return (*Il* 6.289–92). The location of Kranae is a mystery, and even the name itself, which means "rocky," may be nothing more than an epithet. Pausanias identifies the island as one just off Gythion south of Sparta on the coast, which is perhaps the most logical guess (3.22.1); Strabo says rather the island of Helene off Sounion (9.1.22), and so too Lykophron (110–11). The terms of the single combat in *Iliad* 3 also establish that Helen brought with her substantial property belonging to Menelaos (*Il* 3.67–72, etc.), and Paris confirms this in *Iliad* 7 when he announces to the assembled Trojans that he is willing to give back those possessions but not Helen (*Il* 7.362–64).

For anything beyond these sparse details we must turn to the *Kypria*, where Aphrodite tells Paris to build ships for his voyage to Greece and to take Aineias with him, while Helenos and Kassandra (in apparently two separate scenes) foretell the future. On his arrival in Lakedaimonia he is greeted first by the Dioskouroi, and then at Sparta by Menelaos, who entertains him in his home; Paris for his part reciprocates by giving gifts to Helen. For reasons unstated, Menelaos then sails off to Krete, after instructing Helen to make sure that the visitors have everything they need. Aphrodite now takes a hand in bringing Paris and Helen to bed together, after which they take a good deal of property and sail away during the night. Hera sends a storm that drives them to Sidon, where Paris captures the city. On reaching Troy they are then formally married. So runs Proklos' summary, with the same theft of possessions and stopover at Sidon found in the *Iliad*; scholia add for the *Kypria* that Helen also takes her child Pleisthenes with her to Cyprus, and bears to Paris one Aganos (fr 12 *PEG*). Puzzling in comparison with all this is Herodotos' remark that in the *Kypria* Paris with a fair wind and a calm sea reaches Troy on the third day (counting the one on which he set out), as opposed to Homer where he visits Sidon and generally wanders around (Hdt 2.117). Various explanations have found support, among them that Herodotos was mistaken, that Proklos' summary is contaminated by material from the *Iliad*, that *Kypria* poems by two different authors existed, and that the version of Herodotos' time was subsequently expanded (to better conform to Homer?) into the one known to Proklos.[13] It should be added here that we also do not know why the *Kypria* bears the title it does; reference to a stopover on Cyprus and an acknowledgment of Aphrodite as the Kyprian goddess are two possibilities (neither very convincing).

Of other authors relating the flight from Sparta, Diktys of Krete has Paris welcomed by the king of Sidon, whom he murders once inside the palace (Dik 1.5). Such a sequence of events—certainly more plausible than an assault on the city with the few men Paris should have with him coming from Sparta—is perhaps what Proklos found in his *Kypria* as well, if not an attempt to rationalize that account. In Apollodoros as in the *Kypria* Menelaos departs for Krete while Paris is his guest, here in order to bury his grandfather Katreus, whereupon Helen abandons her nine-year-old daughter Hermione and sets sail with Paris by night (ApE 3.3–4). Again she takes much of her husband's property with her, and again Hera's storm forces them to Sidon. But of a capture of the city Apollodoros has no word; Paris simply delays in Phoinicia and Cyprus to throw off pursuit. Homer, as we saw, does not actually attest more than a visit to that area. Regarding offspring of the adulterous pair, *Odyssey* 4 begins by noting that the gods granted to Helen only one child, Hermione (*Od* 4.12–14); given the context this might mean only one child from Menelaos, but the wording suggests otherwise. As we saw in chapter 11 Kinaithon and the *Ehoiai* mention a son Nikostratos (fr 3 *PEG*; Hes fr 175 MW), and the Lakedaimonians are cited for two sons, Nikostratos and Aithiolas (ΣA *Il* 3.175); the *Kypria's* Pleisthenes seems nowhere else mentioned. Helen in later sources will bear a number of sons to Paris (32F11; Σ Lyk 851), none of them very important unless Korythos is in fact hers (see below). As a variant to Paris' usual motive for visiting Sparta we should also note the Antheus whom Lykophron says was loved (in a sexual sense) by Paris (Lyk 134). The scholia thereto relate that this Antheus was a son of Antenor whom both Paris and Deiphobos desired; after accidently killing him Paris fled Troy in fear, sailing with Menelaos to Sparta where he met Helen. Of this story, too, there is no other trace, and seemingly when it was told it replaced the Judgment of Paris.

In art, though the abduction is frequently represented, especially in Attic Red-Figure, the nature of the scene is not such as to provide narrative detail.[14] Possibly it surfaces as early as the Geometric period, if the famous departure/abduction on the Late Geometric krater from Thebes now in London does show this couple, rather than Theseus and Ariadne or Iason and Medeia (London 1899.2–19.1), but for our purposes nothing will really be gained by a positive identification when the *Iliad* already guarantees the event. The same is true of a number of shield-bands from Olympia on which a warrior seizes the wrist of a woman. But a Middle Corinthian krater does offer names, as Paris and Helen (cloak held out modestly to shield her face) arrive at Troy in a chariot; Hektor is named among the couples flanking them (NY 27.116). In Attic Red-Figure we have Makron's cup in Boston on which Paris, now armed with helmet and spear, leads away by the wrist a downward-gazing Helen; Aineias, Aphrodite, and Peitho are also present while overhead hovers a small Eros (Boston 13.186). Another cup by the same painter in Berlin offers much the same general scene, but without the divine figures. Here instead Aineias seems to be fending off Timandra, Helen's sister, who hastens toward him imploringly while one Euopis informs Ikarios and Tyndareos of the event (Berlin:Ch F2291). Both cups do suggest a certain reluctance on the part of Helen, who must be led along by her would-be lover. We have already seen Helen in *Iliad* 3 as a woman who has under Aphrodite's persuasion made her choice, for better or worse, and blames no one else for her decision, however much she may regret it (cf. too *Od* 4.259–64). Yet we have also seen that both the *Ehoiai* and Stesichoros cite Aphrodite's anger as the cause of the Tyndareides' adulterous comportment, because (in Stesichoros at least) Tyndareos once neglected to sacrifice to her (Hes fr 176 MW; Stes 223 *PMG*). Thus there may well have been a tradition that attempted to mitigate Helen's behavior in leaving Menelaos. No source, however, goes so far as to argue that she is actually kidnapped against her will, although this may be implied in some of the versions in which she never arrives at Troy (see below). From Homer's picture of her as lured away from a better husband by the cajoling of Paris we turn to the similar portrait in the choral odes of Aischylos' *Agamemnon*, where she trips lightly through the gates of Troy, bringing death as a dowry to her new in-laws (*Ag* 403–8); the poor figure she cuts in Euripides' *Troades* as she seeks to excuse her actions we have already noted. That tragedy should judge her in these harsh terms is perhaps to be expected; with the war itself frequently weighed and found wanting, as it was not in epic, she becomes a natural scapegoat. Vase-painting of the later fifth century generally concentrates on her first meeting with Paris and his attempts to seduce her; Eros is again frequently present to assist in overcoming her reservations.

There was, however, also an early tradition that exonerated Helen altogether by the simple expedient of denying that she ever ran off with Paris. Our first evidence for this version is the so-called Palinode of Stesichoros, written, according to Plato and others, because the poet had lost his eyesight after telling the generally known tale of Helen's flight to Troy in a previous poem (probably the one implicating Tyndareos). His solution was to compose a new poem in which he recanted that account, saying instead (as Plato quotes the lines): "That was not a true tale; you did not sail in the well-benched ships, nor did you come to the towers of Troy" (192 *PMG*). Thus it seems that in the Palinode Helen never leaves Sparta, or at least not in the normal fashion. But Stesichoros can hardly have recanted the whole Trojan War, and Plato elsewhere discloses the device used by the poet to generate the conflict without her: Paris has taken an *eidôlon* of Menelaos' wife to Troy, and over this the two sides fight in ignorance of the truth (*Rep* 9.586c). Plato does not actually say that Stesichoros invented such an idea, but he does seem to suppose that, and so too later authors who discuss this radical variant. The one exception is a paraphrase of Lykophron which gives "Hesiod" priority in the matter of the *eidôlon* (Hes fr 358 MW [*dubium*]); probably it is mistaken, or else means by Hesiod a very late part of the Hesiodic Corpus. Admittedly, though, we cannot say how the Trojan War began in the *Ehoiai*, or what role Helen played.

Another issue regarding the Palinode on which we should like to be better informed involves where Helen resided while her *eidôlon* was at Troy. From our one quote we have seen that she did not sail away with Paris, and (if she in fact did not enter "well-benched ships") not with anyone else either, although of course a god (as below in Euripides) could presumably take her wherever he liked. More specific on the matter is Dion of Prusa's Egyptian informant in his Trojan discourse, who states that in Stesichoros Helen does not sail anywhere, while other writers have Paris carry her off to Egypt, where she remains (DP 11.41). The implication of the Greek here is, I think, that Helen neither sails nor goes anywhere, in which case Stesichoros would seem to have made her spend the war at home. But other sources claim just the opposite, that is, that

Stesichoros did somehow bring her to Egypt: in particular, a papyrus commentary on the melic poets says quite directly that when in Stesichoros the *eidôlon* went to Troy, Helen was lodged with Proteus (193 *PMG*). The scholia to Aristeides (at 13.131) go still further with the statement that Stesichoros had Paris take her to Egypt where Proteus rescued her (cf. Σ Lyk 113). This last is not impossible, for even in a version which exonerated Helen she might have been taken as far as Egypt by force, but given the lines quoted by Plato it seems best to suppose the attribution of this account to Stesichoros as in error. If we agree on the other hand that Helen can hardly remain in plain sight in Sparta for the whole length of the war we may feel inclined to side with the commentary, and to suppose that a god in fact brought her to Proteus so that the war might take place. Our earliest sources, the *Odyssey* and the *Nostoi*, both show Menelaos driven down to Egypt after the sack of Troy by a divine storm, with the real Helen already at his side; perhaps this well-established stopover gave Stesichoros (or whoever) the idea of hiding Helen with Proteus until Menelaos, who was scheduled to put in there anyway, could come to pick her up. Our fragments of Hekataios also show Helen in Egypt, but no more than that, and here as in Homer she may have come with Menelaos (1F308, 309).

For the Archaic period Stesichoros' probable translation of Helen to Egypt during the Trojan War is in fact the only appearance we have of that story. The later fifth century brings us to Euripides' *Helen* of 412 B.C., which fully dramatizes the reunion of Menelaos and his wife after he has unwittingly traveled down to Egypt with the *eidôlon*. Much of this drama is likely to be Euripidean invention, but the basic situation—Helen's stay in the house of Proteus—is also referred to in Euripides' *Elektra* (1280–83: Zeus creates the *eidôlon* to start the war), the metrics of which appear to guarantee an earlier date than that of the *Helen*;[15] thus Helen in Egypt, even if not Stesichorean, would precede this telling of the tale. As Helen herself explains matters at the beginning of the latter play, the *eidôlon* was the work of Hera, who angry over her loss in the Judgment begrudged Paris his prize. The Trojan received the *eidôlon* when he came to Sparta, while Zeus sent Hermes to transport Helen though the air to Egypt where Proteus might guard her until the war was over. The play's dramatic conflict arises from the fact that Proteus has since died, and his son Theoklymenos wishes to keep Helen for himself. We shall come back to this delicate situation in chapter 17 when we consider the returns from Troy. Existence of this version prior to Euripides is also indicated by its appearance (in a far more rationalizing form) in Herodotos, who says that according to the priests of Egypt Paris brought Helen there when he stopped with Proteus, the current king, for a rest on his way back to Troy (Hdt 2.113–19). On discovering his guest's treatment of his previous host Proteus was suitably shocked, and announced that he would keep Helen and the stolen property in his palace until the rightful owner should come to claim them. In this account, Helen is not completely exonerated, but she is presented as a woman temporarily seduced and deceived by Paris' charms, while Paris as the seducer must shoulder most of the blame. As for the *eidôlon*, it never materializes here, for Paris returns to Troy without Helen, and the Greeks attack, refusing to believe that she is not in the city. Only when Troy is sacked do they at last realize the truth, and Menelaos sails down to Egypt to find his wife safe and sound.

Apollodoros has the same version of these events as Euripides, citing unnamed writers for whom Hermes brings Helen from Sparta to Egypt while Paris and the *eidôlon* go to Troy (ApE 3.5). Philostratos, on the other hand, repeats Herodotos' version faithfully in his life of Apollonios of Tyana, where Achilleus, granting a rare interview, adds that the Greeks did learn the truth before Troy's fall but would have been ashamed to leave without accomplishing some deed of note (*ApTy* 4.16). Accounts of Menelaos' wandering after the sack may in some cases have had him aware of the *eidôlon's* true nature, and thus searching for his wife when he reaches Egypt; in Euripides, as we saw, this is not the case, and the *eidôlon* reveals itself (by disappearing) only after Menelaos has encountered the real Helen. In any case, those versions in which Paris (rather than Hermes) brings Helen to Egypt and leaves her there leave room for the possibility that she was abducted against her will, so that this form of the story, like that in which she never goes away with him, may have served to exculpate her.

The First Mobilization at Aulis   At this point in the account of preparations for the expedition against Troy, the *Kypria* digresses to record the fate of Kastor and Polydeukes, so that listeners will understand why they do not mobilize with the other Achaians to seek out their sister's abductor. Iris then informs Menelaos of his loss, and he begins plans for the expedition with Agamemnon. They go first to Nestor, who accompanies them on their recruiting efforts elsewhere, including Ithaka where Odysseus feigns madness until the leaders threaten recriminations against his son on the advice of Palamedes. Subsequently the heroes all gather at Aulis and observe the omen of the snake and the sparrows (interpreted by Kalchas) before setting sail. But when they come to the shore of Asia Minor they mistake Teuthrania in the land of Mysia for Troy and attack. The local king Telephos slays Thersandros, son of Polyneikes, but is himself wounded by Achilleus. As they depart, the Achaians encounter a storm that disperses them and takes Achilleus to Skyros, where he marries Lykomedes' daughter Deidameia. From here, without further explanation, the action shifts to Argos and Telephos' arrival to seek from Achilleus a cure for his wound in exchange for guiding the army to Troy. So the summary of Proklos; there are no fragments or quotes touching on this part of the story, and we can only guess at what the original poem contained by way of detail.

Homer relates nothing of such a prologue, save for the omen of snake and sparrows recalled by Odysseus in *Iliad* 2, after the troops have been summoned back from the ships (*Il* 2.299–330); aside from this passage and a listing in the Catalogue of Ships (*Il* 2.496), Aulis is not mentioned in either *Iliad* or *Odyssey*. What Homer does tell us about the omen is that while the Achaians were sacrificing at Aulis a snake came out from under the altar and devoured eight baby sparrows plus their mother, after which Zeus turned him to stone. Kalchas then predicted that the Greeks would fight at Troy for so many years before capturing the city. The reference in the *Kypria*, where the Greeks are also sacrificing, is too brief for us to say whether the full version would have agreed with the *Iliad*'s, and whether it was simply derived from that poem. More crucial is the question of the two mobilizations found in the *Kypria*; nothing in Odysseus' words in *Iliad* 2 suggests such a situation, or a mistaken landing in Mysia, but his purpose in speaking is to stress the foretold victory, not past hardships. We therefore cannot really say how much Homer did or did not know of the *Kypria*'s complicated chain of events prior to the arrival at Troy. One of those events in particular might seem necessary to any account of the war, for if Achilleus does not come to Skyros he will not beget a son Neoptolemos, who will be vital to the final taking of Troy. But we will see that there is an alternative to the *Kypria*'s means of bringing him there: in quite a number of later sources Achilleus arrives on Skyros in flight from the original mobilization, sent by his mother to hide. In fact, very little in the *Kypria*'s prelude is essential to the war as conceived by the *Iliad*, and may or may not be post-Homeric elaboration. One point perhaps in conflict between the two poems is the fact that Kalchas (rather than Telephos) is credited at *Iliad* 1.71–72 with leading the Greeks to Troy by means of his prophetic skills, but this may just be characterization of the moment.

One other event not mentioned at all by Proklos but apparently part of the *Kypria* concerns the daughters of Anios. Diodoros makes Anios a son of Apollo and Rhoio, daughter of Staphylos, and locates him on Delos (DS 5.62.1–2). Lykophron alludes to the fact that he invited the Achaians to stay with him, and that his daughters somehow provisioned the army at Troy (see below), but for details we must turn to the scholia. These attest that one Dorippe bears to Anios (same parentage as in Diodoros) the Oinotrophoi,[16] that is, Oino, Spermo, and Elais (Σ Lyk 570). Dionysos gives these daughters the power to take (? *lambanein*) grain whenever they wish, and Pherekydes is then cited for the idea that Anios persuaded (tried to persuade?[17]) the Achaians to remain with him for nine years until the time of Troy's fated fall should arrive, with his daughters supplying all their needs for that period (3F140). The note concludes with the claim that this material is also to be found in the *Kypria*. Some lines later, the same scholia assert that Oino made wine, Spermo seed, and Elais oil, and that these girls saved the Greeks from starvation by going to Troy (Σ Lyk 580); Palamedes, in fact, goes to fetch them when the troops find themselves short of food (Σ Lyk 581).

The *Odyssey* has what may be a reference to such a story, for Odysseus tells Nausikaa that he once visited Delos in connection with the war, and the scholia to the passage claim that he had gone there with Menelaos to fetch the Oinotrophoi, citing Simonides' *Kateuchai* as a source for the tale (Σ *Od* 6.164); the scene is illustrated, with Menelaos alone appealing to Anios at an altar and the three girls holding respectively a grapevine, stalks of grain, and an olive branch, on an Apulian calyx krater by the Darius Painter [PrColl, Miami]).[18] One wonders if Odysseus and Palamedes were here rivals trying to accomplish the same task in competition with each other (in Servius' comment at *Aen* 2.81, Palamedes does succeed in obtaining grain for the army after Odysseus has failed to do so, though Servius says that they [or at least Odysseus] went to Thrace). What we find in Lykophron's version itself is the same invitation by Anios to the Achaians to remain on Delos for nine years, and the daughters again somehow capable of creating provisions—grain, wine, and oil (Lyk 569–83). But though the offer is refused by the Achaians, here too, as in the scholia, those daughters journey to Troy to provide for the needs of the Greeks, suggesting that Agamemnon in time thought better of his refusal. In Ovid, Dionysos' gift is the power of the daughters to turn whatever they touch into wine, grain, and oil (*Met* 13.632–74). On learning of this capability, Agamemnon sends armed forces to claim them for his expedition. Two of the (here four) daughters flee to Euboia while the other two seek their brother Andros on the island of the same name (seemingly they were at or on their way to Aulis). Andros yields to pressure and surrenders them, but Dionysos saves them by turning them into white doves. Lest we suppose that this metamorphosis is Ovid's own invention, we should note that Lykophron at one point also calls the sisters *phabes* ("doves" or "pigeons"); admittedly, though, the scholia offer no explanation of this word, and it can hardly allude to precisely the same story told by Ovid if in Lykophron the girls do go to Troy (willingly or unwillingly). For Apollodoros, the special power of the Oinotrophoi consists of the ability to produce the wine, grain, and oil from the earth (ApE 3.10). He mentions them amid the preparations for the first mobilization but without connecting them in any way to the narrative; apparently their role was lost in the course of epitomizing. Finally, from Diktys we have the statement that Anios and his daughters provided the Greeks with supplies before they left Aulis; how they generated the supplies he does not say (Dik 1.23).

From this digression we return to Telephos. In the fifth century, Pindar refers briefly to Achilleus' heroism in wounding him and to Mysia with its many vines (*Is* 8.49–50). His travails were also the subject of plays by all three of the major tragedians, although none have survived. In the case of Aischylos certainly and Sophokles probably, the works in question were connected trilogies covering (one assumes) both the attack on Mysia and the healing in Argos, with in Sophokles, perhaps, Telephos' birth and/or the fate of his son Eurypylos as well. Euripides' effort, entitled *Telephos* and part of his production of 438 B.C., showed Telephos' appeal to the Achaians at Argos to cure his wound; we know that the hero appeared as a beggar in rags (mercilessly parodied by Aristophanes) and that he seized the infant Orestes as a hostage after his disguise was penetrated. Subsequently, the Achaians were mollified by the discovery that he really was a Greek by birth, and he agreed to guide them to Troy in exchange for Achilleus' aid to heal the wound. Aischylos' *Telephos* must have dealt with the same situation, but we know only that he *may* have anticipated Euripides in the use of Orestes as a hostage (Σ *Acharnes* 332 says so, but has been questioned[19]). Red-Figure, however, certainly begins to illustrate that detail in the second quarter of the fifth century (e.g., London E382). If Sophokles, too, dramatized this part of the story, he must have done so in the *Syllogos Achaiôn*, which obviously dealt with some phase of the mobilization. Both Aischylos and Sophokles also wrote plays entitled *Mysoi*, which may or may not have treated the attack and wounding. For the third Aischylean title nothing presents itself; that completing Sophokles' group may have been the *Aleadai* or the *Eurypylos*. In neither case can we say what the overall pattern of the story was.

Later sources of information include Apollodoros (Ap*B* 3.17–20) and the A scholia to *Iliad* 1.59, which agree that Telephos after killing many Greeks came face to face with Achilleus and fled; becoming entangled in vines (the scholia say that Dionysos was angry with him because he had deprived the god of honors) he was wounded in the thigh by his opponent. On being advised by an oracle that the wound could be cured only by he who caused it, he journeyed to Argos, and after promising to show the Achaians the way to Troy and not to help the Trojans himself (so the scholia) he was healed by Achilleus. Apollodoros adds that Achilleus used the rust from his spear to effect the cure, a motif we find first in Propertius (2.1.63–64), Ovid (*Ex ponto* 2.2.26), and an undated painting seen by Pliny (*NH* 25.42; 34.152); in all likelihood, this folktale-laden motif goes back to the *Kypria*. Indeed, the general similarity (including the absence of Orestes) between the *Iliad* scholia (citing the *neôteroi*) and Apollodoros on the one side and the *Kypria* on the other has prompted the belief that these later sources are drawing directly from the Epic Cycle,[20] although Apollodoros' rags should come from Euripides if Aristophanes' jabs are to have any point. In Hyginus' version there is the wound and the oracle, but no rags; Telephos seizes Orestes on the advice of Klytaimestra and the Achaians capitulate when they receive a prophecy that they will not take Troy without his help (*Fab* 101). Achilleus arrives and denies any knowledge of healing, but Odysseus points out that Apollo means the spear, not the man wielding it. Again Telephos points the way to Troy, although he declines to fight himself, being married to Priam's daughter Laodike. All this sounds like a play, but without the rags it may be that of Aischylos or Sophokles, or a melding of different sources.

From Diktys, finally, comes the seemingly innocuous detail that Diomedes carried the body of the slain Thersandros out of the battle in Mysia (Dik 2.2). Such elaboration is typical of Diktys, but in this case it leads us back to the early fifth century and a Red-Figure calyx krater by Phintias of which only fragments survive (Leningrad St 1275).[21] What remains are Patroklos (named), Diomedes (also named, and bent forward under the weight of something, surely a fallen comrade), plus the inscription "Dionysos" (figure not preserved). Seemingly, then, the main part of the krater represented Achilleus and

Telephos, with the god's role in the latter's wounding thus guaranteed as at least this early.

For further information on the other events of this first mobilization we must generally look again to the later mythographers. Odysseus' attempt to avoid service by feigning madness may be hinted at in the *Odyssey*, for Agamemnon in the Underworld states that he and Menelaos persuaded their comrade with some difficulty (*Od* 24.115–19). More likely, though, mention of persuasion means that they had no real claim on his services, and had to talk him into fighting at Troy. On the other hand, one might reasonably expect to find his ruse described in the *Palamedes* plays of all three major tragedians, and Sophokles put the tale on stage in his *Odysseus Mainomenos*, but in no case are useful fragments or references preserved. As we saw above, Proklos' report of the *Kypria* simply mentions the assumed madness and Palamedes' threat to kill Telemachos without specifying what form the stratagem took. In Lykophron, Kassandra wishes that Odysseus had stayed home, "hitching up a lustful ass to the yoke in the counterfeit contrivances of madness" (Lyk 815–19), which gives us some suggestion of the familiar story of plowing. In describing a painting of unknown date Loukianos mentions a wagon, a team of two different animals, and Palamedes threatening to kill Telemachos with his sword unless Odysseus ceases his pretense (*Oik* 30).

But the full story does not survive before Hyginus, who says that when the envoy came to Ithaka Odysseus, knowing from a prophecy that his absence would be for twenty years, donned a rough cap and yoked a horse and an ox together to his plow (*Fab* 95). Here Palamedes, rather than personally menacing the child, puts him directly in front of the plow, and Odysseus is forced to turn aside, thus conceding his sanity. The *Kypria*'s version, although Proklos' language is vague, seems rather to agree with Loukianos on this last point, and so too Apollodoros, who has Palamedes take Telemachos from his mother's arms and brandish his sword until Odysseus relents (ApE 3.7). Beyond this, Apollodoros like Proklos simply says that Odysseus behaves as one mad, which may mean that he is drawing from a summary of the *Kypria* no more detailed than ours. He does seem to put all the actors in Odysseus' house, not out in a field, and this could mean that in the *Kypria* no plow was involved, but he could also be guessing. Both Servius and the Lykophron scholia follow the account of Hyginus, with the plow, different animals, and Palamedes placing the child in harm's way; Servius adds that Odysseus sowed salt (Σ *Aen* 2.81), the scholia that he yoked a horse and an ox or an ox and an ass (ΣΣ Lyk 384, 815). The one constant feature of the story in all forms is Palamedes' role as the unmasker of Odysseus' deception, thus setting the stage for Odysseus' subsequent plot against him at Troy.

Last, there is the matter of Achilleus' recruitment. The *Kypria*'s notion that he came to Skyros as part of the return from the first expedition is unique to that poem, the *Little Iliad* (fr 24 *PEG*, probably as background to the fetching of Neoptolemos to Troy), and possibly the *Iliad*, where Patroklos' bedmate

Iphis is said to have been provided by Achilleus on conquering Skyros (*Il* 9.666–68).[22] In all later sources the situation is quite different: Thetis determines to hide the youthful Achilleus when the mobilization first begins, and takes him to Skyros to conceal him among the women of King Lykomedes' court. It has been argued (Proklos notwithstanding) that this was actually the version of the *Kypria*, since the *Iliad* scholia (see below) credit it to the Cycle.[23] Otherwise, our earliest evidence is a painting by Polygnotos, showing Achilleus among the women, which Pausanias refers to in describing works in the Propylaia in Athens (1.22.6).[24] Sophokles' play *Skyrioi*, once thought to have dramatized the hero's discovery by Odysseus and Diomedes, is now believed to have presented (probably) the summoning of Neoptolemos. But a papyrus hypothesis tells us that Euripides' *Skyrioi* was definitely about these events, with Lykomedes at first unaware that his young charge is not a girl (PSI 1286).[25]

As the play opens, it seems that Deidameia is already pregnant, having been raped or at least surprised by Achilleus, and Lykomedes is soon to be informed of the situation. Thus, when Odysseus and Diomedes arrive, Achilleus will find himself torn between his new family and the military needs of the Greeks. Nothing, however, shows us exactly how Odysseus made the identification, and we must look to later sources for that part of the story. Bion's (or an imitator's) poem on the subject breaks off in midstream, while Achilleus is still persuading Deidameia to share his bed (Bion 2), but in Ovid Odysseus himself explains the trick: he placed weapons among the feminine goods he had set forth, and waited to see who would pick them up to admire (*Met* 13.162–70). When Achilleus alone of all the women of the household did so, he had his man (so too Σ Lyk 277). The version of Apollodoros has a slightly different notion, that Achilleus was discovered by means of a trumpet (ApB 3.13.8). This same trumpet appears in Statius' account of the event, but only as an afterthought following Achilleus' betrayal of himself with the arms (*Ach* 1.750–920). Not until Hyginus do we see what must have been its original purpose: here Achilleus is not so foolish as to commit himself on first seeing the weapons, but Odysseus orders a trumpet to be sounded, whereupon the disguised hero supposes the city under attack, and rushes to the arms (*Fab* 96). Possibly this device is taken from Euripides, although we must note that Hyginus in contrast to the Euripidean hypothesis has Lykomedes aware of the deception from the beginning, and then, too, what we know of Euripides' play suggests perhaps that Achilleus will have to make his own decision whether or not to fight. One other detail of interest in Hyginus is Achilleus' name: the maidens of the palace call him Pyrrha from his reddish hair. Presumably this explains the son's name; the *Kypria* says that Lykomedes called that son Pyrrhos, and Phoinix Neoptolemos (fr 21 *PEG*).

As a final problem, the story of Achilleus' concealment is told in the scholia to *Iliad* 19, after Achilleus has mentioned his son Neoptolemos on Skyros. In these scholia (crediting the Cycle), Peleus rather than Thetis becomes the one to hide his son with Lykomedes, who as in Hyginus is party to the deception and provides the women's clothes (Σb *Il* 19.326). On receiving an oracle that Troy will not fall without Achilleus, the Achaians send Odysseus, Phoinix, and Nestor to visit the old man, and subsequently they make their way to Skyros where Achilleus is entrapped exactly as in Ovid. The scholiast then notes the birth of Neoptolemos to Deidameia and his participation at Troy, and concludes with the ascription to the Cyclic poets, in contrast with our evidence for both the *Kypria* (Proklos) and the *Little Iliad* (direct quote). That the scholiast could mean just the material immediately preceding his comment, that is, the birth of Neoptolemos and his deeds, seems unlikely, and hence the uncertainty about the epic tradition(s) must remain.

Iphigeneia   In *Iliad* 9 Agamemnon speaks of three daughters who are available for Achil-
and the   leus to wed, Chrysothemis, Laodike, and Iphianassa (*Il* 9.144–45). Neither
Second   here nor elsewhere does Homer ever mention Iphigeneia or any difficulty in
Mobilization departing from Aulis. That Iphianassa should have a name so similar to that of
at Aulis   Iphigeneia has been taken by some as a signal that Homer means to reject the
tale of the sacrifice,[26] but this is dangerous ground, and the use of a slightly different name is surely too subtle a touch to make the intended point. Rather, I think, the poet is concerned to avoid imbuing Agamemnon with the sort of tragic depth which might well accrue to him if he has sacrificed his own daughter for the expedition, on the grounds that such depth would be ill-suited to his general character in the *Iliad*. The poet of the *Kypria* seems to have agreed at least with the notion of distinct persons for the names in question, for in his work there are four daughters, including both Iphigeneia and Iphianassa (fr 24 PEG). The scholiast who tells us this does not give the other two names, although his wording implies that the *Kypria* has simply added Iphigeneia to the three names supplied by Homer.

    Our first actual sources for the sacrifice at Aulis are the *Kypria* and the *Ehoiai*. In Proklos' summary of the former, Artemis becomes angry because Agamemnon upon shooting a deer boasts that not even the goddess is his equal in the hunt, and in her rage sends winds that keep the fleet at Aulis from sailing. Kalchas then informs the leaders that they must offer up Iphigeneia if they are to appease Artemis, and they undertake to do so, after bringing her to Aulis with the promise of marriage to Achilleus. The sacrifice, however, is not carried out, for the goddess substitutes a deer on the altar in place of Iphigeneia, who is taken off to the Tauroi and becomes immortal. For the *Ehoiai*, our evidence consists of the same passage in which we have previously seen Leda's children and grandchildren described (Hes fr 23a MW). The text, which has some major gaps, runs as follows: "Agamemnon <lord of men> married the dark-eyed daughter <of Tyndareos, Klytaimestra, for the sake of her beauty (?)>. And she in his halls <bore slim-ankled Iphimede> and Elektra who rivaled the goddesses in beauty. Iphimede the well-greaved Achaians slaughtered on the altar of famed <Artemis of the golden arrows> on that day <when they sailed in their ships> to Ilion <to exact> a penalty for the <slim-

ankled> Argive woman, an *eidôlon*, that is. For <Iphimede herself the huntress> showerer of arrows easily saved, and poured down upon her head <lovely ambrosia, so that her flesh might be unchanging>, and she made her immortal and ageless all her days. And now the races of men upon the earth call her Artemis of the wayside, <the attendant of the famous> showerer of arrows." As if this narrative were not remarkable enough, Pausanias asserts that in the *Ehoiai* Iphigeneia does not die, but becomes Hekate by the will of Artemis (1.43.1 = Hes fr 23b MW), and that same notion (with the same attribution to "Hesiod") also appears in Philodemos (*Peri Eusebeias* p. 24 Gomperz).

That "Iphimede" is here simply a variant name for "Iphigeneia" seems an inevitable conclusion, even if we did not allow the same for the Homeric Iphianassa. More troubling is the equation with Hekate, an equation for which there seems no room in our present text (the lines immediately following deal with the birth of Klytaimestra's third child Orestes). Possibly she is hidden in the supplemented gaps, or perhaps the equation was made elsewhere in the poem. But perhaps, too, these authors (or their sources) took it upon themselves to interpret the preserved words "Artemis *einodia*" ("Artemis of the wayside") as indicating Hekate, whether correctly or not. We saw in chapter 1 that *einodia* is used of Hekate as early as Sophokles (fr 535 R), but it is also used of Demeter and Persephone. We saw as well that Hekate (Iphigeneia or not) is not elsewhere attested in early Greek thinking as closely linked to Artemis, certainly not so closely linked that she should become simply an aspect of Artemis bearing the goddess' name. On the other hand, Philodemos says that Stesichoros in his *Oresteia* followed "Hesiod" in making Iphigeneia Hekate (= fr 215 *PMG*); unless Stesichoros used exactly the same (ambiguous) phrasing as the Catalogue Poet, we must suppose that he at least made explicit an idea that may or may not have been in the *Ehoiai*.

Whatever we make of this problem of Artemis and Hekate, it does seem at first glance that all three of our earliest sources—the *Kypria*, the *Ehoiai*, and Stesichoros—agree on the essential outcome of the sacrifice, namely that Iphigeneia/Iphimede is saved by Artemis and becomes an immortal of some sort. But it has been argued that our text of the *Ehoiai* contains an interpolation of much the same sort as that generally supposed for Herakles' "appearance" in the *Nekuia*, for here too a narrative seemingly headed in a different direction is corrected by a line beginning with an *eidôlon*.[27] In line 17 of the fragment we are told that the Achaians "butchered" Agamemnon's daughter, not just that they intended to (aorist tense), and the Greek verb *sphazô* surely conjures up images of bloodshed and iron cutting into flesh. But four lines later we are assured that the maiden only appears to die, for what is sacrificed is an *eidôlon* (which dies convincingly in her place?) while the girl herself is rescued. That this version requires such an improbable replica of Iphigeneia when the *Kypria*'s deer was available can only mean that its author knew a tradition in which Iphigeneia did die, and wished to modify that; almost certainly this was the *Ehoiai* in its original form. Dating the six lines of the addition is another matter; for all we know, they may have been supplied well before the end of the Archaic period, and been part of the text read by Aischylos and others. In any event, if the lines are an interpolation, then both rescue and slaughter versions will have been known in early times, and there seems no criterion by which we could even begin to guess at the priority of one over the other. One further consequence of conceding an interpolation here would be the reordering of our time sequence in the matter of Iphigeneia-Hekate: while the *Ehoiai* is probably earlier than Stesichoros, the interpolation could well be later, and thus inspired by a Stesichorean innovation rather than vice versa.

In art the tragic story, which might seem to lend itself to illustration, is barely known. For the seventh and sixth centuries our one possibility is a Protoattic krater by the New York Nessos Painter preserved only in fragments (Boston 6.67). On one of these we see two men carrying a woman horizontally; only her feet and the skirt of her garment are visible. On the other piece, a bearded man turns his head to look back over his shoulder. Possibly this is Agamemnon averting his gaze as he prepares for the sacrifice, but there are no names to guarantee the interpretation, and no way to tell whether Artemis' intervention was anticipated or not. Certain on the other hand is a whiteground lekythos of the fifth century by Douris now in Palermo (Palermo NI 1886). A warrior identified by inscription as Teukros and wielding a drawn sword gently leads Iphigeneia (also inscribed) toward an altar. To the rear another sword-bearing warrior (name lost, if there was one) follows. Iphigeneia here seems resigned, but scarcely enthusiastic, while the presence of Teukros in a commanding role suggests that the sacrifice was supported by the entire army. One other pot to be mentioned is a Red-Figure pyxis in the British Museum on which Iphigeneia stands in the doorway of her house, seemingly preparing for her wedding (London E773). Danae approaches to offer her something from a chest, and other figures in various domestic scenes labeled as Helen, Klytaimestra, and Kassandra confirm that the artist has conflated heroines from different stories to produce a series of unrelated vignettes. Once again there is no sign of Artemis, and thus no clue to Iphigeneia's actual fate.

Turning to the fifth century in literature, we find Pindar and Aischylos in agreement that the girl did die at Aulis, both authors using this fact as part of the motivation for Klytaimestra's subsequent wrath against her husband. Pindar alludes to the event in the course of his *Pythian* 11 (written probably in 474 B.C.),[28] asking whether Iphigeneia slaughtered far from her homeland or the pleasures of a stranger's bed did more to turn her mother to murder (*Py* 11.17–25). The verb employed for the slaying of Iphigeneia is again *sphazô*, as it was in the *Ehoiai*, and of course Klytaimestra's response shows her to believe her daughter dead, as she would not if Artemis had been seen to intervene at Aulis. The same holds true for Aischylos' *Agamemnon*, where a description of the sacrifice occupies much of the parodos, and the elders, who were present at Aulis ten years before, certainly suppose the victim dead (*Ag* 228–49). Probably we should expect no less, for the chain of transgression and revenge with which the *Oresteia* is concerned will lose a very important element if Iphigeneia is saved. But Aischylos' presentation of the sacrifice via the elders remains problematic all the same, and both Artemis' motive and Agamemnon's freedom of choice have triggered controversy. In contrast to the account of the *Kypria*, there is here no initial offense against the goddess, no boast or anything else to which the chorus can point as cause of the disaster. Instead we find at Aulis a new omen, two eagles that appear to the assembled army and proceed to devour a pregnant hare (*Ag* 109–20). Kalchas pronounces that Artemis is angry at this feast of the "hounds of the father," who are clearly Agamemnon and Menelaos, and prays that she will not block the expedition. Despite his appeal, the constraining winds do arise, and finally the seer is forced to reveal the one solution that will allow the fleet to sail. Agamemnon, after some hesitation and a speech that the chorus reports verbatim, consents; Iphigeneia is then slain (we are not told how she was brought to Aulis) in a most pitiable description, and the expedition's success is assured.

This lack of clear motivation on the part of Artemis has been quite variously explained: for some scholars the crux of the matter is a conflict between Artemis and her father, with Agamemnon a helpless victim caught in the middle, while for others the eagles' consumption of burgeoning new life symbolizes the indiscriminate destruction that Agamemnon will visit on Troy, and the goddess, anticipating his intent, commands him to begin the slaughter with his own child, if he can.[29] Artemis' purpose would thus be dissuasive, rather than vengeful, but not prohibitive; Agamemnon has the choice left open to him. Aischylos also composed a lost play entitled *Iphigeneia* about which we know absolutely nothing. Unless some other story concerning her has been lost, we must choose for the plot between a full-length treatment of the sacrifice and the Euripidean tale of Iphigeneia among the Tauroi, with her recovery by her brother Orestes. In the former case, we cannot even say whether Iphigeneia would have been killed or rescued by Artemis, since Aischylos' treatment of the myth in one play need not preclude a totally different version in another. Neither do we know whether the *Iphigeneia* was an independent play or part of a connected trilogy; similarly "orphaned" Aischylean titles such as the *Hiereiai* ("Priestesses") and *Thalamopoioi* ("Marriage-chamber Builders") might be brought together with it to form a continuous narrative of sacrifice and transfer to the Crimea,[30] but this is speculation of an extreme sort.

From later in the century we have a similarly lost *Iphigeneia* of Sophokles (where fragments do seem to guarantee that the subject was the sacrifice), plus references to the event in the same poet's *Elektra*, and then a description of both sacrifice and rescue in the parodos of Euripides' *Iphigeneia among the Tauroi* followed by a full dramatization of these events in the *Iphigeneia at Aulis* (produced posthumously). Of Sophokles' lost play we know for certain only that the stratagem of a marriage with Achilleus was employed to lure Iphigeneia to Aulis, since we have a line (almost certainly addressed to Klytaimestra, who must therefore have been a major character) mentioning the acquisition of a great son-in-law (fr 305 R). In his *Elektra*, the title figure attempts to justify her father's actions in a debate with Klytaimestra by recalling the crisis at Aulis (S: *El* 563–76). We are told here that Agamemnon was amusing himself in a precinct of Artemis and surprised a deer, which he succeeded in shooting, whereupon he uttered some sort of boast. The goddess, becoming extremely angry, determined that he should not leave until he had sacrificed his daughter, and so made it impossible for himself or the army to go anywhere, either to Troy or homeward, before the deed was carried out. Obviously, both these details are designed to exculpate Agamemnon by making the goddess seem unnecessarily vindictive and by giving the mortal no choice whatever, in contrast to Aischylos' *Agamemnon*. That Agamemnon was in a sanctuary of Artemis when he shot the deer may or may not have been a detail of the *Kypria* skipped over by Proklos' summary. The same holds for the notion that the army was totally trapped at Aulis, although I very much suspect that this is a Sophoklean invention of the moment to aid Elektra's argument. That Iphigeneia here actually dies, or is believed to die, is of course (as in Aischylos) necessary if Klytaimestra is to have any defense at all for her own actions.

In Euripides' *Iphigeneia among the Tauroi*, to take his earlier play first, yet another device is found to trigger the crisis as the army prepares to sail. The winds arise without explanation, and Kalchas then reveals that by failing to sacrifice Iphigeneia long before, Agamemnon has neglected to fulfill a vow once made to Artemis, that he would give her the most beautiful thing the year should bring forth, which for the year in question happens to have been his daughter, now long overdue (*IT* 15–25). Odysseus is dispatched to Argos with the ruse of a marriage to Achilleus, and Iphigeneia arrives at Aulis where the sacrifice is prepared. But Artemis takes her away and substitutes a deer without the knowledge of her father or any of those watching; thus Orestes, when he arrives in the land of the Tauroi to fetch the image of Artemis, has no notion that he will find his sister there, and the surprise is the greater. The effect of the new motivation is again to exonerate Agamemnon, since a vow once made to a god must be fulfilled, whether or not one wishes to sail to Troy. But it is of course a folktale motif, seen as well in the homecoming of Idomeneus, and may have been part of the story in some earlier version. Odysseus' role will become standard, as we might expect, since the bringing of Iphigeneia involves deception, and might be early, although here again Proklos' summary of the *Kypria* is not specific. We should note, too, that while Iphigeneia's stay among the Tauroi certainly goes back to the *Kypria*, she is in that work a goddess; Euripides' conception of her as a priestess sacrificing strangers to Artemis is surely a different matter, and not attested before this play (although it *may* have appeared in Aischylos).

In *Iphigeneia at Aulis* the situation is somewhat different, for now as in Aischylos the winds arise without any provocation, and Agamemnon may clearly (if he chooses) disband the expedition (*IA* 87–107, 352–53). But vanity and the promptings of his brother cause him to heed Kalchas' call for the offering of Iphigeneia to the goddess to whom that place is sacred, and thus he has informed Klytaimestra by letter of the supposed betrothal to Achilleus. Subsequently he repents of this deception and sends a second letter repudiating the first, but it is intercepted by Menelaos, who strongly rebukes Agamemnon for his weakness and lack of patriotism. Iphigeneia does then arrive, accompanied by Klytaimestra, and Menelaos weakens in his resolve; Agamemnon perceives, however, that with his daughter actually in camp Odysseus will surely reveal the prophecy to the troops, and they will then demand her death so that they might sail. He hopes to keep his wife ignorant of this until after the deed is done, but Achilleus, impatient for action and ignorant of the promise made in his name, comes to the tent when only Klytaimestra is there, and at her mention of the marriage the whole deception comes out. In his indignation, Achilleus at first declares that he will protect the girl single-handedly; his attempts to persuade the army, however, are unsuccessful, and he even risks being stoned as they clamor for war and Troy. Finally Iphigeneia herself resolves the situation by deciding that she will voluntarily surrender her life for the good of all concerned. She exits, and a messenger returns with a final speech describing to Klytaimestra the deer substituted for her daughter (some of this last material may have been rewritten from fragments in later times).[31] There is also a line of a speech by Artemis, concerning the deer, which has been attributed by Aelian to this play (*NA* 7.39); if that is correct, then (in a section now lost) the goddess appeared to Klytaimestra before the messenger came back and revealed to her the whole truth about her daughter's fate. Naturally there have also been suspicions that the whole ending is a post-Euripidean addition, and that the play as he wrote it did send Iphigeneia to her death. But with such a playwright we are never likely to be very sure of anything.

Our sources subsequent to the fifth century are, as usual, Apollodoros and Hyginus. The former offers the same reason for Artemis' anger as the *Kypria,* that on shooting a deer Agamemnon had boasted to be her equal, but also a curious variant on the *Iphigeneia among the Tauroi,* namely that Atreus had failed to give the goddess the golden lamb after promising her the finest thing in his flocks (*ApE* 3.21–22). Agamemnon here sends Odysseus and Talthybios to Argos with the fabricated betrothal, and they bring back Iphigeneia. Sacrifice and rescue also follow the lines of the *Kypria,* but while that work had Artemis take the girl to the Tauroi and make her immortal, Apollodoros has Iphigeneia either among the Tauroi (as a priestess) *or* immortal. Probably this reflects influence from Euripides, who as we saw has a different idea of Iphigeneia's life among the Tauroi from that of the *Kypria.* Hyginus, too, gives the motive of the slain deer and consequent boast as the cause of the trouble (*Fab* 98). At Kalchas' subsequent prophecy Agamemnon himself wavers, but Odysseus comes up with the scheme of the marriage deception, and he and Diomedes here make the journey to Argos for the girl. She is again rescued with a deer as substitute and taken to the Taurian land to become a priestess. Given the presence of deer and Odysseus as executor of the ruse, Hyginus cannot here be drawing from either of Euripides' plays exclusively, or even both together. Odysseus as creator of the marriage deception *might* go back to Sophokles' *Iphigeneia,* where Odysseus is a character, but in that work Klytaimestra seems to have come to Aulis, as she does not in Hyginus; perhaps we should think instead of Aischylos or even the *Kypria.* A quite different outcome of the sacrifice appears in Diktys, who bypasses the miraculous by having Achilleus save Iphigeneia and entrust her to the conveniently present king of the Scythians (Dik 1.22). What more might have passed between rescuer and rescuee in such an account we cannot say, but for the third-century (?) B.C. historian Douris (76F88 apud ΣbT *Il* 19.326) and Lykophron (324), Neoptolemos is the son of Iphigeneia; Douris appears to add that she was taken (by Achilleus) to Skyros and left there. Her career as a priestess in the Crimea, and her return to Greece with Orestes, we will return to in chapter 17.

As one final curiosity to mention in connection with the Achaians' departure for Troy, Odysseus' impersonation of Aithon (a younger brother of Idomeneus) during his interview with Penelope in *Odyssey* 19 brings with it the tale that the real Odysseus was on his way to Troy when he was blown off course at Cape Maleia and driven to Krete (*Od* 19.172–202). There, "Aithon" says, Odysseus found Idomeneus already departed for Troy some ten days before, and left himself after he had enjoyed the local hospitality and the north winds had diminished. Conceivably, the *Odyssey* means that both men were on their way to Aulis in order to mobilize for Troy, but that is not really what the text (twice) says. More likely, Aulis has been forgotten for the moment in order to make this tale of an encounter with Odysseus plausible, but we must admit the possibility of a version in which the Achaians first assembled at Troy, or somewhere nearby.

The Journey to Troy: Philoktetes and Tennes

With the expedition finally launched (for a second time), the Achaians now make their way over to Troy with relatively little trouble or incident. The *Kypria* (or rather, as always, our epitome) notes only two stopovers, Tenedos, where Philoktetes is bitten by the snake while the troops are feasting, and Lemnos, where he is left behind because of the smell of the wound; there is also a quarrel between Agamemnon and Achilleus, the latter "having been invited late," but the summary does not make absolutely clear at which of the two stops this took place. If "invited late" means (as one would assume) to a feast, we might logically suppose it to be the one on Tenedos during which Philoktetes is bitten. On the other hand, Agamemnon's speech of reproach to the troops in *Iliad* 8, when he reminds them of their boasts of military valor while they ate and drank on Lemnos (*Il* 8.228–34), would seem to indicate a feast here too. But Aristotle in the *Rhetoric* makes reference to Achilleus' anger at not being invited to dinner on Tenedos (*Rhet* 2.24), and he of course will be drawing from some complete work, not an ambiguous summary. Of any further details of the quarrel Proklos says nothing, and even the *Iliad* has no allusion to it. Possibly relevant, however, is a passage in *Odyssey* 8, when the Phaiacians' singer Demodokos offers the tale of a quarrel between Achilleus and Odysseus (at a banquet) at which Agamemnon rejoices, having been told something by Apollo at Delphi which leads him to believe that this signals the beginning of disaster for the Trojans (*Od* 8.75–82).

On the surface these would seem to be two separate quarrels, and the scholia agree, making this latter tale one of an Achaian discussion at Troy, after Hektor's death, on how best to take the city. But in Plutarch's *Moralia*, we read that in Sophokles Odysseus once incited Achilleus by claiming that the latter's professed anger over a dinner was really a ruse to conceal his fear of battle and Hektor, now that he had seen the walls of Troy (*Mor* 74a). Possibly this is still another dinner, but it sounds very much as if the Achaians have just arrived at (or near) Troy, and Hektor is clearly still alive. Perhaps then, at the feast on Tenedos, Achilleus is originally angry with Agamemnon because of the late invitation and threatens to leave, but then becomes embroiled in an argument with Odysseus when the latter tries (successfully, as matters prove) to taunt him into staying with accusations of cowardice. Unfortunately, Plutarch does not name the play of Sophokles from which he quotes; it may have been the *Syndeipnoi* (probably satyric) or the *Syllogos Achaiôn*, if these are not two titles for the same play. To this whole reconstruction one might, I suppose, object that Agamemnon has little reason to rejoice in the first year of the war. But it is technically the beginning of troubles for the Trojans, and then too Agamemnon may have misinterpreted an oracle referring in fact to his own dispute with Achilleus nine years later.

From quarrels we turn to the unfortunate Philoktetes. In the *Iliad's* Catalogue of Ships we find much the same story given by the *Kypria*, that the hero, son of Poias and here leader of a contingent of seven ships from the territories around Mount Pelion, was bitten by a snake and consequently abandoned by the Achaians on the island of Lemnos in great pain (*Il* 2.716–25). But Homer does not say anything about where he was bitten, or why, only that the Achaians will eventually come back to get him. This same passage plus a reference by Odysseus in the *Odyssey* (8.219–20) also establishes Philoktetes' skills as an archer, and we have seen in chapter 13 the tradition that he or his father Poias received the bow of Herakles upon the latter's death. But we have no other information at all about him until the fifth century, when Pindar gives him a brief mention (as one whom great heroes will bring back from Lemnos to sack Troy: *Py* 1.50–55), and Aischylos, Sophokles, and Euripides all write plays about the Achaians' return to Lemnos to fetch him. Of these only Sophokles' effort survives, and since it was produced in 409 b.c. it was probably the latest of the three. All three gave some background regarding the cause of the abandonment, to judge from Dion of Prusa's discussion of their plots (DP 52), but of Aischylos' version of these events he offers nothing. For Euripides, thanks to his paraphrase of the prologue, we know that Philoktetes was bitten when he showed the other Greeks the altar of Chryse, where it was necessary that they sacrifice if they were to win the war (DP 59). In Sophokles we find that Philoktetes has been bitten on/at Chryse (*Ph* 263–70), and Neoptolemos later adds that the snake in question was a sacred one guarding the unroofed shrine of the divinity Chryse (*Ph* 1326–28).

Already in about 460 B.C., Hermonax shows this moment on a stamnos, with Philoktetes lying on the ground, Achilleus, Agamemnon, and Diomedes looking on in alarm, and the statue of Chryse (named) off to one side (Louvre G413). The location of the Homeric Chryse has always been a problem, but Pausanias speaks of the wounding taking place on a small island named Chryse near Lemnos which had sunk into the sea before his own time (8.33.4). As to the cause of such a change in geography from that of the *Kypria* we can only speculate, but if Euripides and Sophokles do mean the same place as Pausanias, they (or an earlier tradition) might have been motivated by the seeming illogicality of taking a man wounded on Tenedos all the way back to Lemnos in order to abandon him. The A scholia at *Iliad* 2.722 solve this problem more simply by locating the incident on Lemnos itself; here Philoktetes is cleansing the sacred precinct (again of Chryse) when the snake strikes. For Hyginus, who also places the wounding on Lemnos, the cause is rather Hera's anger because Philoktetes aided in the cremation of Herakles; thus she sends the snake expressly to bite him (*Fab* 102). Apollodoros seems considerably closer to the *Kypria* (as often) in his account, for there the attack is again on Tenedos, with the snake crawling out from the altar while the heroes are sacrificing to Apollo (ApE 3.27). Both the stench of the wound and Philoktetes' cries are cited as the reason for the abandonment, as in Sophokles; Odysseus takes him to Lemnos on orders of Agamemnon.

For another quite different version of the wound we have Servius and the Vatican Mythographers (Σ *Aen* 3.402; VM I 59, II 165). These all relate the same story, that Herakles wished no one to know where his mortal remains lay, and extracted a promise from Philoktetes to that effect. When the other Achaians pressed Philoktetes for that information later, not believing Herakles dead, he stamped on the ground with his foot to indicate the place, hoping thus to maintain his oath. But on the way to Troy an arrow (poisoned with the Hydra's blood) accidentally fell from his quiver and struck the offending foot as payment for the transgression. The Lykophron scholia repeat the tale of the *Iliad* scholia that Philoktetes was cleaning an altar (of Athena), but they also know one in which Chryse is a Nymph who falls in love with Philoktetes and has him bitten by the snake when he rebuffs her advances (Σ Lyk 911). Whether any of these stories are early we cannot say, although they perhaps show a developing pattern of attempts to find clearer reasons for Philoktetes' misfortune. His subsequent rescue and deeds at Troy we shall return to toward the end of this chapter.

One other tale that must be placed in this time frame of the voyage to Troy survives only in Lykophron (allusive as usual) and later authors—Konon, Diodoros, Apollodoros, Plutarch, Pausanias, and scholia. Lykophron tells us that two children died together with their father, who was killed by a millstone; he then adds that these children had narrowly escaped death before when they were cast adrift in a chest by a gull-reared father who believed the lies of a flute-player (Lyk 232–42). There follows mention of someone who forgot to declare the commands of a goddess mother, and died by the sword. As Konon tells this story, one Kyknos ruler in the Troad (as we will see, probably not the ally of the Trojans slain by Achilleus) has two children, Tennes and Hemithea, but upon the death of their mother he remarries, and the new wife, becoming enamored of Tennes and being rejected, falsely accuses him (26F1.28). As in all such stories the father is convinced, and locks both Tennes and Hemithea (when she sides with her brother) in a chest that is thrown into the sea. It drifts to an island known as Leukophrys where the inhabitants rescue it and make Tennes their king, renaming the place Tenedos in his honor. Subsequently Kyknos arrives to ask forgiveness, but as he speaks from his ship Tennes takes an axe and cuts the hawser cables to prevent him from landing.

Diodoros confirms most of this except the last, adding that a flute-player had supported the slanders of Tennes' stepmother and that Tennes himself was killed by Achilleus when the Achaians sacked Tenedos on their way to Troy (DS 5.83.4–5). Apollodoros gives the name of the first wife as Prokleia (daughter of Laomedon) and the second as Philonome; the flute-player is identified as Eumolpos (ApE 3.25–26). The story then proceeds as in Konon, save that instead of coming to Tenedos after he learns the truth Kyknos puts both wife and flute-player to death. More to the point for present purposes, we hear that Thetis has warned Achilleus not to slay Tennes (actually the son of Apollo according to some) lest he himself die by Apollo's hand. But as the Achaians approach the island Tennes tries to ward them off with stones, and Achilleus kills him with his sword. Plutarch offers an elaboration of this same motif: Thetis not only warns Achilleus, but charges a servant to remind him of the warning should the occasion arise (*Mor* 297d-f). As the Achaians are ravaging Tenedos, Achilleus comes upon Tennes' sister, who is extremely beautiful, but Tennes interposes himself to save her and is slain. When Achilleus realizes what he has done, and the fact that the servant though present failed to stop him, he kills the man, and buries his fallen opponent. The first part of the story is here only briefly told, but the flute-player is called Molpos. Pausanias gives us almost exactly the same tale as Konon, with the addition of the names of the two wives as given by Apollodoros, and Poseidon claimed as Kyknos' father (10.14.1–4).

In the Lykophron scholia, Kyknos is the son of Poseidon and one Skamandrodike, who abandons her child near the shore, to be found by a swan and then kindly fisherman (Σ Lyk 232). Here too when grown he marries Prokleia, daughter of Laomedon, and then a second wife Phylonome, leading to the story of the chest and the arrival of the children on Leukophrys. But as we have seen, none of the versions recounted so far will allow Achilleus to slay father and both children in the same place, as Lykophron implies. Whether from other sources or just guessing, the scholia on this point maintain that upon discovering the truth about his children Kyknos came to Tenedos and lived with them, and that Hemithea died when the earth swallowed her up as Achilleus was pursuing her. One other novelty is that the servant who fails to advise Achilleus is called Mnemon, and his crime is the greater because it is fated that Achilleus die soon after he has killed a son of Apollo, as Tennes here is. One wonders if Apollo's sometime paternity of Hektor and Troilos was used to activate the same motif. As for Kyknos himself, we will see below that the Kyknos whom Achilleus slays at Troy is sometimes killed with a stone, but that hero has intimations of invulnerability about him, and Lykophron has probably conflated aspects of the two (although they may well go back to a single original).

How early this story of children cast adrift and arriving on Tenedos might be is, as usual, uncertain. The absence of any reference to the killing of Tennes in Proklos' summary could indicate that it was not a part of the *Kypria*, but we really have very little means of controlling how complete that summary is. Several uncertain references suggest that Euripides or Kritias (fr 21 Aus = 43 fr 20 Sn), and perhaps as well Aischylos,[32] may have written plays entitled *Tennes*. The first of these works, for which a fragmentary hypothesis does exist, apparently recounted the Potiphar's wife adventure in the home of Kyknos, with the stepmother finally put to death and Apollo ordering the island to be called Tenedos; the second, far less certain, is conjectured to have related rather the hero's defense of his island.

To the tale of Tennes we should add briefly that of Trambelos, whom we saw in chapter 13 to have been a son of Telamon and a Trojan captive Theaneira. Istros, who with Lykophron (467) is the earliest to mention him, says that he was slain by Achilleus during a raid on Miletos, and that Achilleus on discovering his identity built a tumulus for him (334F57). Parthenios relates in addition to this a story from Euphorion that Trambelos fell in love with one Apriate on Lesbos; she resisted and died either at his hands or while trying to flee him; his own subsequent death is here seen as punishment for that deed (Par 26 = fr 27 Pow).

The Landing: Protesilaos, Kyknos, and the Embassy to Troy

At this point in our epitome of the *Kypria* we are told simply that the Greeks attempted to land on the shores of Troy, that the Trojans opposed them, with Hektor killing Protesilaos, and that Achilleus then took charge of the situation, slaying Kyknos, son of Poseidon, and routing the Trojans. As in the case of Philoktetes, the Catalogue of Ships has an entry for Protesilaos, son of Iphiklos and thus first cousin to Philoktetes, even though he is no longer alive to lead his contingent: the poet tells us that he died at the hands of a "Dardanian man," being the first to leap down from the ships, and that he left behind a wife tearing both cheeks and a home only half-completed (*Il* 2.698–702). There is no trace here of either a prophecy or a wife whose husband visits her one last time after his death. Pausanias does tell us that in the *Kypria* the wife's name is Polydore, daughter of Meleagros (4.2.7), so that poem may have told something of her story, but on the other hand in all those later accounts where we do find the tale of Protesilaos' last visit she is called Laodameia. Sophokles wrote a (lost) *Poimenes* that recounted in some way the events of the landing and the death of Protesilaos at the hands of Hektor, but this seems to have been told from the viewpoint of the Trojans, and to have included as well the exploits of Kyknos (frr 497, 500, 501 R). The earliest preserved trace of the tale of what followed his death is Euripides' lost *Protesilaos*, in which, as a scholiast tells us, the protagonist after just one day of marriage is summoned to join the expedition for Troy (p. 563 N²). He is the first to touch shore, as in the *Kypria*, and dies, but appeals to the gods of the Underworld and is allowed one more day to spend with his wife. Fragments of the play seem to indicate that this is prologue, and that the drama showed the actual day of his return, with probably (as we shall see below) Laodameia's suicide when he finally departs. Laodameia's father Akastos would also seem to have been a character, perhaps trying to exhort his daughter to remarry.

After the fifth century we have Ovid's *Heroides* with a letter from Laodameia to her husband after he has departed for Aulis (*Her* 13), and Loukianos' version of Protesilaos' overtures to Hades in the Underworld (*DMor* 28), but no further information until Apollodoros. Here we learn for the first time that Thetis has warned Achilleus not to be the first to disembark at Troy, since the first to land will be the first to die (Ap*E* 3.29–30). Instead, Protesilaos (who, it would seem, does not know the oracle) is the first, and after killing a number of Trojans is slain by Hektor. His wife Laodameia in grief then has a statue made in his likeness with which she "associates" (*prosomileô*, often used in a sexual sense). The gods observing this behavior take pity on her, and Hermes brings Protesilaos back from Hades. Laodameia believes him restored to her alive from Troy; when Hermes comes for him and she realizes the truth she kills herself. Obviously the last part of this is a bit unclear, perhaps because the epitomator of Apollodoros has omitted something. Hyginus also relates the prophecy that whoever landed first at Troy would die, but in his account this fact is clearly general knowledge, for when all the others hesitate Protesilaos takes the initiative, paying with his life at Hektor's hands (*Fab* 103). The strange notion here that Protesilaos was actually Iolaos, son of Iphiklos, and renamed only after his valorous sacrifice, presumably means that the mythographer has confused two figures of similar parentage (Iphiklos, Iphikles) who both receive favors from the gods regarding their mortality (resurrection, rejuvenation). He goes on to relate that Laodameia requested the return of her husband for a period of three hours. When Hermes finally led him away, she despaired and caused a bronze (or waxen?) statue in his image to be made, which she embraced and took with her to bed (*Fab* 104). After this fact was discovered by a servant, who mistakenly believed he had caught her with a lover, her father learned the truth and ordered the statue burned to spare her further pain, but she threw herself on the pyre constructed for it and died.

Following close upon the death of Protesilaos in the *Kypria*, as we saw above, comes the death of Kyknos on the Trojan side, slain by Achilleus; our epitome notes nothing unusual about this seemingly normal battlefield event. Homer does not mention Kyknos, while Pindar, who does, simply reiterates that Achilleus killed him (*Ol* 2.82; *Is* 5.39). To judge from a remark by the character of Euripides in Aristophanes' *Batrachoi* (962–63), Aischylos may have brought him on stage, but we do not know in what play, or if his whole story was dramatized. Sophokles included him in his *Poimenes* (as a rather brash character: fr 501 R), and that play may actually have focused on his arrogance and death. One curious fragment says that "neither bronze nor iron takes hold of (someone's) flesh" (fr 500 R), so that probably we have already here the idea of Kyknos' invulnerability. In any case, such an idea, whether Sophoklean or not, is confirmed by a chance remark of Aristotle, who tells us in the *Rhetoric* that Kyknos prevented the whole army of the Achaians from landing, and was unwoundable (*Rhet* 2.22.12). How he was nevertheless slain is perhaps explained by Ovid, who has him strangled by Achilleus with the straps from his own helmet after attempts to pierce him with spear or sword have failed (*Met* 12.72–144). But in Apollodoros (where nothing is said of invulnerability) Achilleus slays Kyknos with the cast of a stone (ApE 3.31), so that perhaps in early versions the latter's protection against harm covered only bronze and iron (keeping in mind fr 500 R above), or else objects that cut. Either way, the magical element would be quite appropriate for the Epic Cycle, but with no help at all from Proklos we cannot say more than that. Another rather unusual detail seems to have been provided by Hellanikos, who according to a scholiast related that Kyknos was white with respect to his skin from birth (i.e., an albino?: 4F148); the same scholiast notes that somewhere in the Hesiodic Corpus it is simply his head (*kephalê*: hair?) which is white (Hes fr 237 MW). All sources seem to agree that Kyknos was a son of Poseidon, although there is nothing to link him with the similarly named son of Poseidon whom we have met as father of Tennes.

With the Achaians now successfully in command of the beach at Troy, the *Kypria* proceeds to the sending of an embassy into the city to demand the return of Helen. Some later accounts (including Apollodoros: see below) place this request earlier, when the Greeks are still at Tenedos, but the event remains essentially the same. Antenor mentions it in *Iliad* 3, when he supports Helen's assessment of Odysseus by recalling how that hero and Menelaos had come and stayed in his house when they addressed all the Trojans on the question of Helen's return (*Il* 3.205–24). The mission apparently involved some danger, for we learn in *Iliad* 11 that Antimachos, having been bribed by Paris' gold to oppose their request, urged the assembled Trojans to slay Menelaos on the spot rather than allowing him to return to the Greek camp (*Il* 11.122–42). Neither the *Iliad* nor our *Kypria* epitome assigns to Antenor any special role in preventing this action, but we will see below that the Epic Cycle was probably familiar with that detail. A Late Corinthian krater of the early sixth century now in the Vatican offers us a tableau of the embassy: Menelaos, Odysseus, and Talthybios sit to the left on a gradated tier of seats while Theano (Antenor's wife) and attendants come to meet them (Vat K40099). Horsemen follow, some named, but there is surprisingly no sign of Antenor himself. In any case, these are obviously formalities of welcome preliminary to the actual request for Helen.

Turning to the fifth century, we find in the corpus of Bakchylides a fragmentary dithyramb entitled "The Antenoridai, or the Demand for Helen" (Bak 15). Here too Theano is prominently positioned, for the poem begins (somewhat abruptly) by speaking of her as a priestess of Athena who does something (edges of text missing) for Odysseus and Menelaos. There are then apparently speeches by one or more of these parties in a lacuna, after which the sons of Antenor must have led the embassy to the Trojans' agora; Antenor himself proceeds to alert Priam to the proposal about to be offered, while heralds summon the people to the assembly. These as they gather pray to the gods, and it seems that they desire respite from their sufferings, but the final section of the poem (if it is complete) is devoted entirely to Menelaos' speech, in which he contrasts Dike with Hybris, the ruin of the Gigantes, and suggests that it is open to the Trojans to save themselves from their sufferings. Obviously they fail to do so, and the poem was probably meant to draw impact from the contrast between what we see and what we know will follow, as often in Bakchylides.

Sophokles' lost drama *Helenes Apaitesis* ("The Request for Helen") seems likely to have brought on stage the whole story, including perhaps the proposal to murder Menelaos, but we have no real evidence for any part of its plot, and just possibly it dramatized instead the attempt to recover Helen from Egypt. On the other hand, in the same poet's *Aias Lokros*, there is certainly a reference to a leopardskin placed on the door of Antenor's house (fr 11 R; cf. Str 13.1.53). The bT scholia to *Iliad* 3.205–6, where the embassy comes from Tenedos, say that Antenor not only offered hospitality but actually saved the ambassadors when they were about to be treacherously slain, and that in gratitude Agamemnon placed a leopardskin on his door during the sack of Troy in token that this house should be spared; we find this same idea of leopardskin and safety for the family in Polygnotos' painting of the Trojan Sack for the Knidian Lesche at Delphi (Paus 10.27.3), so that it is very likely older than the fifth century. This last conclusion is perhaps reinforced by the fact that in the *Little Iliad* Odysseus carries a wounded Helikaon, son of Antenor, out of danger during the night assault (Paus 10.26.8), although such an action might conceivably have been motivated simply by bonds of guest-friendship. The safeguarding of Antenor's family is a theme that appears again, although in the altered form that the Greeks spared these people because they supported the return of Helen, at the very beginning of Livy's history of Rome. Apollodoros, like the *Iliad* scholia, deviates from the *Kypria* in having the embassy set out from Tenedos, before the Greeks have landed on the shores of Troy; like the *Iliad* scholia, too, he has Antenor save Menelaos and Odysseus when they are threatened with death

(ApE 3.28–29). He does not in the epitomator's account of the sack report any formal amnesty for Antenor, but we are told that Odysseus and Menelaos saved Antenor's son Glaukos (ApE 5.21), so that some such theme may have appeared in the full version.

Achilleus and the Early Years of the War

Next in the *Kypria* comes Achilleus' desire to actually see Helen (suggesting here again that epic tradition did not think of him as one of the original suitors). We are told simply that Aphrodite and Thetis brought them into the same place, with no further detail. Presumably, Aphrodite led Helen secretly out of Troy to a place where Thetis was waiting (in equal secrecy) with her son, but this is a guess. No other source so much as mentions this story, but we do have a curious remark in Lykophron, where Kassandra prophesies that Helen shall have five husbands—Theseus, Menelaos, Paris, Deiphobos, and Achilleus, whom she causes to toss and turn upon his bed at Troy as he sees her in his dreams (Lyk 139–74). Since the same lines also describe Achilleus as the future husband of Medeia, Lykophron cannot be thinking here of a union with Helen in Elysion (such as we find in Pausanias). Whether in that case he supposed a rendezvous as in the *Kypria*, with erotic consequences, I do not know; both the scholia to this passage (Σ Lyk 143) and those to the *Iliad* at 3.140 (b only) claim that Achilleus was Helen's fifth husband "in a dream," surely a strange notion. At *Iliad* 19.325, for what it is worth, Achilleus calls Helen *rhigedanê*, "chilling," but of course the whole situation of the *Iliad* requires from him a certain lack of enthusiasm for the goals of the war.

After this encounter, the *Kypria* presents an otherwise totally unrecorded event, namely that the army revolted and wished to return home, but was held back by Achilleus. That this particular hero, who had himself earlier threatened to leave, should play such a role may seem odd; perhaps we are to think that his viewing of Helen has inspired him to remain and win her back. No reason is given for the army's action; possibly supplies were short, and this was the point at which Agamemnon decided to send for the daughters of Anios, if in fact the *Kypria* contained that story. On the other hand, the arrival of those daughters now would eliminate all difficulties in finding provisions, and the next event in the poem is Achilleus' seizure of the cattle of Aineias, followed by the sack of Lyrnessos (both incidents alluded to in *Il* 21), plus Pedasos and other of the nearby cities. From *Iliad* 2 we learn that Briseis was acquired at Lyrnessos, where Mynes and Epistrophos, the sons of Euenos Selepiades, were slain (*Il* 2.688–93). Briseis' own speech in *Iliad* 19 adds that Mynes was the king of Lyrnessos, and that her husband (perhaps this same Mynes) was also one of Achilleus' victims (*Il* 19.295–96).

The other city that we know from the *Iliad* to have been sacked is Thebe, the home of Andromache's father Eetion, who perished on that day with his seven sons, although Achilleus allowed Andromache's mother to be ransomed back (*Il* 1.366–67; 6.414–28). From somewhere in this general raid Chryseis too emerges as part of the booty; the scholia suggest that the people of Chryse had all fled to the better-defended Thebe because of the war (ΣA *Il* 3.366), or else that Chryseis was visiting Iphinoe, sister of Eetion, on the occasion of a sacrifice to Artemis and thus was captured (bT scholia ad loc.). Whatever the *Iliad* in fact supposed, Eustathios tells us that the visit-and-sacrifice version appeared in the *Kypria* (although he also notes that in other accounts she was a native of Thebe: *Kyp* fr 28 *PEG*). Achilleus himself in *Iliad* 9 refers to a total of eleven cities that he has captured on land, in addition to twelve by sea (*Il* 9.328–29); he gives no names, although earlier in the same book Agamemnon mentions Lesbos in this latter category (*Il* 9.128–30), and further on we find Skyros as well (if this is, in fact, the island: *Il* 9.666–68); we have already seen possibilities for Tenedos and perhaps Lemnos. Pedasos is a site occupied by Trojan allies at *Iliad* 6.33–35; the scholia assign to the Hesiodic Corpus the tale that Achilleus besieged this town, aided by a maiden of the community who became enamored of him and sent a message advising that water supplies were low (Hes fr 214 MW). The taking of Lesbos presumably preceded Odysseus' wrestling contest with someone there at *Odyssey* 4.324, if the two poems know the same story. In later times the list and range of territory covered was predictably expanded; thus in Apollodoros we find such places as Smyrna, Klazomenai, and Kolophon.

Troilos and Lykaon   Our *Kypria* summary closes its one sentence noting all the places that Achilleus sacked with the laconic remark that Achilleus also "slew Troilos," as if it were of little consequence in itself and, moreover, somehow related to the raids of surrounding territory. From our other sources this seems not the case, but the fact remains that our epitomator was not very interested in this episode, or else wished to pass over it quickly. The *Iliad* does speak of Troilos, but just barely: Priam in Book 24 lists him among those of his sons who have perished, and calls him "delighting in horses," but this is all we learn. For the entire remainder of the Archaic period our only certain literary evidence is a casual reference in Ibykos' Polykrates poem, where Troilos' beauty is stressed (282a.40–45 *PMG*), and a line from an unnamed play of Phrynichos speaking of the "light of love glowing on his reddening cheeks" (3 fr 13 Sn). But Ibykos probably told elsewhere of Troilos' slaying outside the city walls, to judge from the commentary in an Oxyrhynchus papyrus scrap (224 *SLG*). To the citation with the above information the commentator adds that [Achilleus] lay in wait for Troilos and slew him outside the walls of Troy, in the Thymbraion precinct; it is not clear, however, whether this detail might be drawn from Ibykos' poem, or simply appended to it as a clarification from other sources. In any case, the Thymbraion we know from other authors to have been an area sacred to Apollo,[33] since Thymbra in the Troad formed the basis for one of his cult titles, and we will see later that this detail may be significant.

Early vase-painting and other artwork presents quite a wealth of material covering several different phases of the exploit, although of course this evidence cannot speak to the most important question of all, Achilleus' motive in slaying an essentially helpless and unoffending opponent. The earliest of these illustrations is conceivably a Protocorinthian aryballos of the seventh century on which a warrior in armor walks behind an unarmed man on horseback, but there is no certainty that pursuit is involved here (London 1969.12–15.1). The contrary is, however, the case on a subsequent Protocorinthian aryballos of about 650 B.C. where the name "Troilos" and part of the name "Achilleus" are painted in (Kanellopoulos Coll 1319). Here Troilos (spear or sword in hand) rides off rapidly to the left as Achilleus behind him pursues on foot. In metalworking, we have a bronze tripod-leg relief from the end of the seventh century and two shield-band reliefs from the first quarter of the sixth century at Olympia. On the tripod leg, although the upper right corner is missing, a large, fully armed warrior seizes the hair of a much smaller figure, as the latter seeks to climb a set of stairs, and menaces him with a sword (Olympia B 3600). On the first of the shield-bands we see a young boy, naked, crouching on a raised platform with his left arm around a slender tree (B 988). His right arm is caught by the wrist and raised high in the air by the figure to his left, an armed warrior with helmet and breastplate who seems (once again) intent on dispatching the boy with his sword. Conceivably, both these scenes could represent the death of Astyanax, or indeed any young Trojan victim on the night of Troy's fall, but the child is rather old for our usual understanding of Hektor's son, and the platform would seem likely meant as an altar, an element that will emerge as central to Troilos' story. The second shield-relief offers much the same picture, but the tree is gone, the boy now faces his assailant, and the platform has clearly become a formal altar; moreover, there is a cock sitting upon it (B 1912). This last element inevitably causes one to think of the tradition (preserved only very much later) of Achilleus' sexual passion for Troilos, with the cock here as love gift; to dismiss it as nothing more than a coincidence here is difficult, to accept such a theme this early perhaps equally so.[34]

Of Attic vase-paintings there are quite a number beginning about this same time, c. 575 B.C., with the earliest also the most famous, the band directly below the Wedding of Peleus and Thetis on the François Krater. To the left in this band is a fountain house behind which stand Apollo and a young Trojan who is collecting water in a hydria. Before the same fountain, to the right, are one Rhodia and Thetis, then Hermes with his head turned back toward Thetis, then Athena. This last figure has her left hand held out at her side as if in encouragement, and indeed in the center of the band a running figure (upper body and name lost) is pursuing a mounted Troilos, who is beardless, clad in tunic, and riding one of two horses galloping in tandem. Below these horses is a hydria on its side; to the right, in front of them, a running woman, for whom the upper body and name are again lost, save for two letters of the latter which are probably enough to guarantee her as Polyxena. The object of their haste, as pictured on the far right, is Troy; before the walls we see Antenor turning back and gesturing to a seated Priam, while emerging from a gate in the walls are Hektor and Polites in hoplite armor. A simpler form of the same scene appears on a Siana cup by the C Painter dating to about 570 B.C.: to the left the fountain house, then the armed Achilleus in pursuit of Troilos and the two horses, the fallen hydria (here between Achilleus' legs), and to the far right Polyxena (NY 01.8.6; no names given). A second Siana cup by the same artist shows a slightly earlier moment: although Troilos has already wheeled his horse around to flee and Polyxena starts away in fright, Achilleus is crouched behind the fountain house, demonstrating that he has hidden there to ambush his prey (Louvre CA 6113).

As the century progresses, we see these same basic elements over and over again on numerous Attic Black-Figure pots and a few non-Attic examples, including a Middle Corinthian bottle with ambush and fountain house (signed by Timonidas: Athens 277) and a Late Corinthian amphora on which Troilos turns to aim a bow at Achilleus while the latter prepares to hurl his spear (Zurich ETH 4).[35] Since the fountain house is not the same as an altar (and Troilos runs *away* from it in any case), these scenes would appear to indicate that Achilleus here catches Troilos and pulls him off his horse, in contrast to the version of the Olympia bronze reliefs (and other depictions noted below) where the slaying and altar are joined. Illustrations of the actual moment of overtaking are rare, but this phase of the action does appear on one of the Etruscan Loeb Tripods now in Munich (SL 66: tripod B), as well as on a Pontic amphora in the Louvre (E703). In both cases, Achilleus seizes the hapless Troilos by the hair to drag him down to his doom. On another Pontic amphora, however, he has Troilos slung over his shoulder, and appears to be carrying him toward an altar while mounted warriors pursue (Reading 47 VI 1). Possibly, therefore, the full form of the story had Troilos taken from his horse to the Thymbraion to be killed there (as a deliberate insult to Apollo?); perhaps he was even riding toward that precinct in hope of sanctuary, and Achilleus, catching him just before he got there, took him into the precinct to demonstrate his contempt for Troy's gods. But we cannot exclude the possibility that altar and fountain house represent two quite different versions of the story that have (on the Reading amphora) become confused.

As for the more precise details of these scenes, some of the above-mentioned examples show Troilos holding several spears, and wearing a cloak or tunic or both, but on only one occasion does he have any kind of defensive armor (a helmet and shield, plus a sword, on a cup by Oltos: Louvre G18). In the great majority of cases we see two horses, as on the François Krater, rather than just one; we will return to this point shortly. Achilleus waiting in ambush behind the fountain house (rather than in pursuit) is shown on quite a number of the pots, on a metope from Heraion I at Foce del Sele (no #) (Troilos lacking, but see below), and possibly on one of the poros pediments from the sixth-century Athenian Akropolis (Akropolis 52). The vase-paintings present quite a consistent picture: Achilleus in armor crouching behind the vertical façade of the fountain (which is usually fitted out with a lion waterspout) while on the other side Polyxena prepares to fill her jug as a mounted and undefended Troilos waits with the two horses. A bird often perches on top of the fountain, but whether he was a traditional decorative element or a part of the narrative we cannot say. One additional detail on two Lakonian representations is the presence of a snake at Achilleus' feet (VG 106349, Troilos and Polyxena in exergue; the second, from Samos, lost);[36] in neither instance does it seem to concern him, and it is probably a guardian of the spring. We have already considered yet a third such cup on which the warrior actually aims his spear at the snake as more likely part of the story of Kadmos (Louvre E669; see chapter 14).

Of the manner of Troilos' death there is also some sixth-century information via Attic Black-Figure. Two Tyrrhenian amphoras of about 570 B.C. agree on the grimmest detail, that Achilleus has decapitated his victim, and done so at what is again unmistakably an altar. On the tamer of these, Achilleus holds the severed head by the hair, as if to hurl it at the Trojans (Hektor, Aineias, Agenor) who approach from the other side of the altar; the headless corpse slumps on the ground (Florence 70993). The second amphora offers essentially the same scene: Troilos' head now appears to be impaled on the point of Achilleus' spear as he aims it at the advancing Trojans, but perhaps we are to understand that it is in midair, having already been thrown by Achilleus (Munich 1426). Here Hermes and Athena stand behind Achilleus; Hektor is now joined by Aineias and Deithynos. Nor is this a notion confined to the Tyrrhenian series of Attic pots: a band cup of about 560 B.C. shows Achilleus holding Troilos by the leg with one hand while he raises the head in the other as if to throw it at his opponents (PrColl, Basel), and a memorable hydria of the Leagros group offers Troilos' corpse beginning to fall to the ground as Achilleus strides upward on the altar to brandish the head at the attacking Trojans (London B326). A Middle Corinthian column krater may illustrate the stage just prior to this, for Achilleus here holds up the intact body by the foot (over an altar) as Hektor, Aineias, and other Trojans close in (Louvre E638). Attic Red-Figure has none of this; the emphasis falls entirely on the pursuit of the horse, with a cup by the Brygos Painter showing once again Achilleus seizing Troilos' hair in order to pull him from his mount (Louvre G154); on numerous other examples the Achaian's outstretched hand has Troilos almost within reach. The sequel is illustrated on a cup by Makron where the horse is lying on the ground, and Troilos, still clinging to his neck, finds himself in the grasp of his pursuer, who plunges a sword into his shoulder (Palermo V659). In a great many (though not all) of these scenes, we continue to find Troilos with two horses, although the second plays no useful part in the story once its master has turned to flee; that artists persisted in including such a detail may suggest a literary (or artistic?) predecessor of remarkable impact. The original motive for these horses we will return to below. Before leaving the artistic evidence altogether we should also note a second metope from Foce del Sele (no #) showing a figure clinging to a column with one arm while another figure with drawn sword tries to pull him away. If this is a further stage of the Troilos story (after the metope with Achilleus hiding behind the fountain), we would have additional evidence for the version first seen in the Olympia shield-reliefs, but the scene is perhaps better interpreted as Orestes and Aigisthos.[37]

Turning back to literature in the fifth century, we find rather less than we might have expected. Neither Aischylos, Pindar, nor Bakchylides mention Troilos at all in what is preserved of their work; in the case of Pindar this is perhaps significant, since Achilleus' other exploits are noted with approval on several occasions in his *epinikia*. In fact the only fifth-century writer (other than Phrynichos) known to have dealt with Troilos at all is Sophokles, who wrote a play of that title. Scholia to the *Iliad* tell us that in this drama Troilos was ambushed[38] while exercising his horses near the Thymbraion (ΣT *Il* 24.257); otherwise we know only that the city itself was the setting, a eunuch spoke some lines, and that Polyxena and Troilos' mutilation may have been involved. We have already encountered the Thymbraion as the site of the slaughter in the Ibykos commentary (perhaps drawing from just this play), but the more specific detail that the *ambush* took place there, plus the presence of horses being exercised, brings us back to a previous uncertainty, whether the fountain house, Polyxena, and the flight are always part of the same story as the slaying at an altar. For although Sophokles (and even Ibykos before him?) might quite reasonably put the fountain house near the Thymbraion, and bring Troilos there after exercising to water his horses, such a sequence leaves no plausible reason for Polyxena's presence; one expects, I think, that in the beginning Troilos came with her directly from Troy, perhaps as an escort. Then too, in the fountain house version, Troilos is clearly run down by Achilleus, a feat that loses much of its point if the Thymbraion where he is killed is essentially adjacent to the point of ambush; on the François Krater, we may remember, he seems to be fleeing back toward the city. Nevertheless, Troilos' watering of his horses (somewhere) does seem to have been a part of the play, since one of the few fragments preserved mentions an approach to spring drinking water (fr 621 R). Whatever we conclude, the mention here of the Thymbraion, together with the numerous altars in the artistic tradition, certainly suggests an early account in which that precinct was the site of the slaying.

From this intriguing state of affairs we move to Lykophron, where in just seven lines we find two entirely new details, first that Achilleus had fallen in love with Troilos, who remained "unwounded" by the one he conquered, and second that the Trojan was in fact a son of Apollo, at whose altar he was decapitated (Lyk 307–13). Lykophron's language is highly obscure, as usual, and one would be surprised if this motif of Achilleus' passion was something that he had invented. Presumably we are to understand from the word "unwounded" that Troilos did not return Achilleus' affections and was slain for that reason. This last, at any rate, is the version of the scholia, in which Troilos takes refuge in the precinct of Apollo to avoid Achilleus' advances; when the latter is unable to persuade him to come out, he goes in and kills him at the altar (Σ Lyk 307). The erotic motif occurs too in Servius, where Achilleus in his desire lures Troilos to him by offering doves; on trying to take them the boy is seized, and dies in Achilleus' embrace (how or why not said: Σ *Aen* 1.474).

A quite different (and more honorable) motive for his demise first survives in Plautus, who tells us that Troilos' death was one of the events necessary to the fall of Troy, like the stealing of the Palladion (*Bacchides* 953–55). If this notion could go back to the *Kypria* it would explain much; as matters stand, however, our epitome of Apollodoros, where we might hope to find it in that case, says only that Achilleus ambushed Troilos in the sanctuary of Thymbraion Apollo (Ap*E* 3.32), much as he appears to do in Sophokles. Apollodoros' one other contribution is to reiterate the idea that Troilos might have been a son of Apollo (by Hekabe: Ap*B* 3.12.5). Hyginus is even less help; although he mentions Troilos' death in several lists he never narrates it in any form. By contrast the First Vatican Mythographer elaborates on what we found in Plautus by claiming that Troy was destined never to fall if Troilos reached the age of twenty, and thus that Achilleus killed him from ambush as he was exercising outside the walls of the city (VM I 210). His very brief narrative adds that Troilos' lifeless body was dragged back to Troy still tied to his horses. In Dares we find for the first time Troilos as warrior (of the first rank), leading the Trojans after the death of Hektor and even wounding Diomedes and Agamemnon, until his horse is brought down and Achilleus seizes his opportunity (Dar 33).[39] That he or any warrior should fight (even briefly) from horseback seems very much a post-epic invention, one no doubt designed to accommodate to a military context the long-established tradition of a mounted Troilos meeting his fate.

On the whole, the only respectable motive for Achilleus' deed emerging from this survey is that of the prophecy that guarantees Troy's safety if the boy should live, late though that is in our sources. The brutal death of Rhesos (to keep his horses from watering at the Skamandros) considered below would be then an obvious parallel, and one missing even in Homer. But we cannot in either instance be sure that the device of a prophecy has not been imported into the story to palliate unseemly actions. The versions in which Troilos' killing is at an altar must surely involve desecration of a precinct, especially if the altar is the Thymbraion of Apollo, and no prophecy will explain the brutality (to say nothing of insensitivity) with which Achilleus decapitates the body and throws the head at the boy's brothers in sixth-century art. We will see below that in some accounts Achilleus is slain in this same precinct, indicating perhaps Apollo's revenge.

Before leaving Troilos altogether, we should perhaps note briefly the later, post-Classical developments that bring (heterosexual) romance into his life. No such motif appears in Dares, but his elevation of Troilos to a fully grown adult appearing on one occasion in combat with Diomedes, plus the telling of the familiar tale of Briseis, perhaps opened the door to a more innovative approach by the twelfth-century Benoit de Sainte-Maure in his *Le Roman de Troie*, a poem of some thirty thousand lines which includes an account of the love of

Troilos for the Trojan Briseida, here daughter of Kalchas. Benoit claims to have drawn much of his poem from Dares, and possibly he had a fuller version of that author than we do. In any case, Troilos and Briseida are lovers, but her father Kalchas, having gone over to the Greek side, asks Priam to send her to him, and the latter does so. She then falls prey to Diomedes' entreaties and forgets Troilos, and although she reproaches herself later, she feels she cannot return to Troy; the tale ends somewhat abruptly with Achilleus as usual dispatching the unhappy Troilos. Subsequently the same tale appears in the *Florita* of the early fourteenth-century Armannino and the *Filostrato* of Boccaccio slightly later in the same century, both (perhaps independently) substituting the name "Criseida" for that of Briseida. The change may or may not have arisen from a confusion between Kalchas and Chryses, the fathers, possibly aided by a misreading of Ovid's *Remedia Amoris* 467–74. Whatever the truth of the matter, Boccaccio's lengthy poem served as the source for Chaucer's even longer work some fifty years later, and from thence to Shakespeare's play, so that for better or worse Cressida has become in Western literature the object of Troilos' affections.

One other exploit of Achilleus to be discussed in this same general context is the capture of Lykaon, whom we meet in a memorable scene in *Iliad* 21. There Achilleus accosts this son of Priam as the latter is escaping from the river, and discovers him to be the same youth whom he had once before ambushed by night while the latter was cutting fig branches in an orchard in order to make chariot rails (*Il* 21.34–48). On that occasion Achilleus sold him to Euneos of Lemnos, but Euneos in turn allowed him to be ransomed by one Eetion of Imbros, apparently a family friend, and this last sent him to Arisbe, north of Troy on the Hellespont. The intention seems to have been that he remain there, but he escapes, and has been enjoying his return to Troy for eleven days when he falls into Achilleus' hands again, only to meet his death this time. *Iliad* 23 adds that Euneos gave Patroklos a splendid silver krater as the price for the captive (*Il* 23.740–47); otherwise we learn from the *Iliad* only that he was Priam's child by Laothoe, daughter of Altes, with no explanation of why he should risk so much by going out at night, or why Achilleus should have been waiting for him. But the Townley scholia remind us here that Achilleus does earlier claim to have spent "many sleepless nights" in prosecuting the war (*Il* 9.325), and this present incident taken together with the death of Troilos may suggest that there was a period at Troy during which open hostilities were less in evidence, and warriors gained fame and booty by more devious means. The *Kypria* also knows of this story, although our summary mentions it only in a roundabout fashion in noting that Patroklos takes Lykaon off to Lemnos and sells him; nothing is said of his capture. Possibly, of course, the *Kypria* included this event based simply on what was recorded about it in the *Iliad*.

Palamedes   Homer never mentions this figure, not even in the Catalogue of Ships, although we have seen that the abandoned Philoktetes and the deceased Protesilaos found room there. Earlier in this chapter we encountered him in the *Kypria*'s account of the recruitment of Odysseus, when at his suggestion the Achaians somehow threatened the infant Telemachos and thus discovered the father's ruse. Proklos (near the close of his summary) says only that Palamedes died, but Pausanias cites the poem to the effect that he drowned while fishing, and that Diomedes and Odysseus were responsible. Why they should want to do this is not stated. Otherwise, our only references to this hero before the fifth century occur in the *Nostoi*, Stesichoros, and (probably) the *Aigimios* of the Hesiodic Corpus, for Apollodoros says that according to Kerkops (one reputed author of the latter work) Nauplios and Hesione begat Palamedes, Oiax, and Nausimedon, while in the *Nostoi* his mother was instead Philyra, and for the tragedians Klymene, daughter of Katreus (Ap*B* 2.1.5). We have met this Nauplios already before, in chapter 6, as the offspring of Poseidon and the Danaid Amymone; we will see shortly that as father of Palamedes he plays a crucial role in the aftermath of his son's demise, and probably did so from an early date, given that he is mentioned in the *Nostoi*. Stesichoros is our first source for the idea that Palamedes discovered or invented something (*stoicheia* [letters?]: 213 *PMG*); for more exact details we must turn to the fifth century.

From that time period we have Pindar's remark that Palamedes surpassed Odysseus in some fashion regarding *sophia* (fr 260 SM) plus *Palamedes* plays (all lost) by each of the three major tragedians; to these last should perhaps be added as well Sophokles' *Nauplios Katapleon*, if in that play Palamedes' father defended his departed son (see below). For Aischylos we know (from a scholion to the *Desmotes*) that the playwright elsewhere assigned many of Prometheus' cultural improvements to Palamedes (Σ PD 457–59a), while an actual Aischylean quote says that Palamedes organized the army into units, and determined the proper times for meals (fr 182 R). Stobaios adds to this another citation, unattributed, which shows Palamedes describing his invention of arithmetic for a confused and muddled Greek world (fr 181a R). Sophokles somewhere had Nauplios credit his son with a similar range of discoveries, weights, numbers, measures, military tactics, and how to read the movement of the stars (fr 432 R), and another fragment adds dice and draughts (fr 429 R).[40] That Euripides followed suit is guaranteed by a quote expressly from his play in which we hear again of writing as a new skill, the "drug of forgetfulness, voiceless yet speaking" (fr 578 N²). Seemingly, then, all three poets shared this characterization of Palamedes as benefactor of the Greeks through gifts in some respects similar to those proffered by the Aischylean Prometheus. Other traces of this tradition appear in Gorgias' rhetorical defense speech for Palamedes, where military tactics, writing, written laws, weights and measures, counting, beacon fires, and draughts are listed (82B11a), and in Plato's *Republic*, where Sokrates remarks on how foolish Agamemnon looks time and again in tragedy, given that prior to Palamedes' discoveries the Achaian general was seemingly unable to count the number of his ships or even his feet (*Rep* 7.522d).

As for the plot of these plays, the *Orestes*' title character attests Oiax's desire for revenge against Agamemnon for Palamedes' death (*Or* 432–33), while (according to Dion of Prusa) Euripides' *Philoktetes* made Odysseus claim to have destroyed Palamedes by a false charge of trafficking with Priam's sons (DP 59). But for any continuous narration of the story of his downfall we must look to later sources, beginning with the *Orestes* scholia.[41] These tell us that while the Achaians were becalmed at Aulis, Palamedes solved difficulties with the rationing of food by showing them the use of Phoinician letters, that is, writing, and that to distract them he invented as well games using dice, adding in the bargain measures and arithmetic (Σ *Or* 432). For these innovations he acquired a great reputation, and in jealousy of his fame Agamemnon, Odysseus, and Diomedes plotted his downfall, suborning a servant to hide gold that they had intercepted from a Trojan messenger under his bed. To complete the trap the same messenger was forced to write a letter linking Palamedes in a scheme with Priam to betray the Greeks, and thus when the plotters demanded a search of his tent the incriminating evidence resulted in his being stoned to death by the army. In Hyginus, by contrast, Odysseus alone plots against Palamedes, because he has been "deceived by the ruse of the latter," a reference surely to the feigned madness on Ithaka (*Fab* 105; cf. *Fab* 95 and *Met* 13.56–60). Toward this end the Ithakan convinces Agamemnon that a dream has advised the moving of the Greek camp for a single day. Agamemnon does so, and in the interim Odysseus buries the gold in the spot where Palamedes' tent has been pitched. After the camp is moved back and Palamedes repitches his tent in the same place, Agamemnon receives a letter purportedly from Priam to Palamedes noting this hidden gold; its discovery seems to confirm all charges, and Palamedes is again stoned.

Apollodoros' version is too brief to add much to this, although here too, as in Hyginus, Odysseus acts alone, and we find the letter of the Phrygian captive, planted gold, and the death by stoning at the hands of the army (Ap*E* 3.8). Servius' account likewise follows much the lines of Hyginus, save that the camp is not moved (Odysseus somehow buries the gold in the dead of night with the help of a bribed slave) and that Odysseus pretends to support Palamedes after the letter is found, calling on the Greeks to exonerate Palamedes by searching his tent. And the second-century A.D. Polyainos in his *Stratege-mata* notes that in the tragedians Odysseus' stratagem of hiding the gold in the tent results in Palamedes, the wisest of all the Greeks, being convicted of treason; there is a hint here too that the trial may have been viewed as a battle of wits between the two rivals (1 *prooem* 12).

Taken as a whole, this body of post-*Kypria* material is remarkably consistent. The variations that do exist would seem to reflect perhaps two basic versions, one in which jealousy of Palamedes' accomplishments (by Odysseus, Agamemnon, and Diomedes) is the motive for his death, with letter and gold found together in his tent and perhaps summary execution, and a second in which Odysseus carries out solitary vengeance, with the letter produced first and a trial or at least debate held, followed by the discovery of the gold which convinces Agamemnon and the troops. For our purposes it will not matter a great deal which version was used by which tragedians, but a fragment of Aischylos' play (asking for what cause the speaker's son was killed: fr 181 R) does seem to indicate that Nauplios appeared in that play, and thus that the action was either *all* set after Palamedes' death or else very briefly dramatized in its opening phases.[42] By contrast, a fragment defending Palamedes in Sophokles' play of that name (fr 479 R) will surely not have been spoken by the father if, as seems likely, his trip to Troy to protest his son's death was dramatized by that same poet's *Nauplios Katapleon*. In that case, Odysseus may well be the defender, pretending as in Servius to side with Palamedes in order to more effectively (and maliciously) spring his trap.[43] Finally, in Euripides' play someone addresses Agamemnon with the remark that all men, those who are friends of music and those who are not, strive for money (fr 580 N[2]). Presumably this is Odysseus speaking, there is a debate, and Agamemnon is as in Servius and Hyginus an uninvolved arbiter whom Odysseus must convince. These points being so, it has not unreasonably been proposed that Servius has followed Sophokles, Hyginus Euripides, and the *Orestes* scholia (which, in fact, conclude with Nauplios' visit) Aischylos, although of course we cannot say how much contamination of different authors these later sources may contain.[44]

Notable in any case is the agreement of said sources that Palamedes was judged guilty of treason and executed by the army, in marked contrast to the *Kypria* where his death is a private matter at the hands of Odysseus and Diomedes and there is presumably no question of treason. The reason for their deed in that early work remains a mystery. Certainly the *Kypria* contained Palamedes' uncloaking of Odysseus' madness on Ithaka, but if revenge is the sole motive here it is difficult to see why Diomedes should help, so that we should perhaps suppose rather jealousy the cause as in the *Orestes* scholia. Conceivably, in fact, something like the *Kypria's* account survives in Diktys, the only other retelling we have in which Palamedes suffers a similar death: here he becomes envied because an oracle of Apollo has selected him to perform a great sacrifice, and because he is generally popular with the troops (Dik 2.14–15). Accordingly, Diomedes and Odysseus persuade him to go with them to a well where they claim to have found gold, and lower him down to retrieve it. When he reaches the bottom they throw stones down on top of him and thus kill him. Relevant, too, may be Servius, where as we saw in discussing the daughters of Anios Palamedes succeeds in securing grain for the army at Troy after Odysseus has failed, thus increasing the latter's enmity (Σ *Aen* 2.81, followed by VM I 35, II 200).

There is finally the above-noted coda to the tale of Palamedes, the wrath of his father Nauplios and journey to Troy to accuse those responsible for his son's death. The *Orestes* scholia constitute our clearest source for this event, stating as they do that Nauplios came to Troy after his son's death to protest, but received little attention because the army wished to please the leaders (Σ *Or* 432: we remember that a number of heroes including Agamemnon conspire toward Palamedes' death in this account). We saw above that this voyage was almost certainly part of Aischylos' *Palamedes*, and probably too Sophokles' *Nauplios Katapleon*, assuming that play is not the same as his *Nauplios Pyrkaeus*. In any case, the one fragment of protest specifically assigned to a Sophoklean Nauplios (fr 432 R) indicates that the poet dramatized the story in some work. In Euripides, matters were handled a bit differently: here after the trial and execution of Palamedes his brother Oiax ponders how to inform their father of what has happened. With commendable ingenuity, if not plausibility, he decides to inscribe the story on oars that will then float back to Greece; the device is brutally parodied by Aristophanes in the *Thesmophoriazousai* (768–84; see scholia at 771). Given this emphasis on a painfully slow method of transmitting events, it seems impossible that Nauplios could have arrived at Troy in the play; if we hear anything more of him, it will be of his final vengeance, via a *deus ex machina*.

That vengeance involved, to judge by our later sources, two different actions. Lykophron hints pointedly at the first of these, making Kassandra prophesy that the Greeks shall not be happy in their return from Troy, for the "hedgehog ruining homes by such devices shall deceive the roosters' hens who keep the roosts, so that they become hostile" (Lyk 1093–5). What he means is surely explained by Apollodoros, who says that after Nauplios returned from his unsuccessful voyage to Troy he visited the homes of a number of the Greek leaders and managed to turn their wives to adultery (we are not told how; perhaps by tales, true or not, of their husbands' paramours at Troy: ApE 6.9). Included in the list are Klytaimestra's affair with Aigisthos, that of Aigialeia, wife of Diomedes, with Sthenelos' son Kometes, and that of Meda, wife of Idomeneus, with Leukos. But this last liaison turns sour, for Leukos kills Meda and her daughter Kleisithyra (after they have taken refuge in a temple) and seizes possession of part of Krete, repelling even Idomeneus when the latter returns. That tale is in fact also alluded to by Lykophron, and with Apollodoros' help we now see that there too Nauplios is implicated:

> Not calmly does the fisherman with his net row his two-oared craft, meaning to cause confusion for Leukos guardian of the throne and weaving his hatred into deceitful devices. And that one, savage in his mind, will spare neither the children nor the wife Meda, nor the daughter Kleisithera, whose hand her father will promise with bitter consequences to the nursling snake. And with unholy hands he will kill them all in the temple [Lyk 1216–24].

It would seem, then, that Leukos is a foster child brought up in the home of Idomeneus, and that he was betrothed to the latter's daughter before his regrettable loss of restraint, although there is no clear mention here of adultery with the mother; we will return to these problems in chapter 17, when we consider the returns of the Achaians. One other detail is reported by the *Odyssey* scholia, that Nauplios persuaded Antikleia of Odysseus' death, whereupon the grieving mother hanged herself (Σ *Od* 11.197, 202, credited to the *neôteroi*). On this phase of Nauplios' vengeance we have no other information; just possibly it (rather than the debate at Troy) was the subject of Sophokles' *Nauplios Katapleon*, if that play was distinct from the *Pyrkaeus*. The matter of this latter drama was certainly the second phase of the retribution, a phase surely in the *Nostoi* and indicated by both Apollodoros and the *Orestes* scholia: as the Achaians prepared for their return from Troy, Nauplios proceeded to the promontory of Kaphereus at the southern end of Euboia and lit deceptive fires that lured the ships to destruction. Again, this is an event to which we shall return in chapter 17.

The Actors
of the Iliad

Before turning to the *Iliad* itself, whose plot forms the next sequence of action in the war, we might pause here to consider the main figures encountered in that work, as found primarily in Book 2's Catalogue of Ships. Homer's list of Achaians in this catalogue is arranged geographically, rather than by importance, but the various councils held, plus valorous deeds in battle, show us clearly whom to regard as the major figures. From Mykenai and Sparta, respectively, come Agamemnon and Menelaos, the sons of Atreus and chief prosecutors of the war, Agamemnon with a hundred ships, Menelaos with sixty (*Il* 2.569–90). Pylos sends the aged Nestor, son of Neleus, whose reminiscences on problems with Herakles and Augeias have been mentioned already in chapter 13; ninety ships follow him (*Il* 2.591–602), plus his sons Antilochos and Thrasymedes. From Krete arrives Idomeneus, son of Deukalion, the son of Minos (*Il* 13.448–53), accompanied by Meriones, son of one Molos (*Il* 10.269–70), and eighty ships. From Argos and Tiryns are the two sons of the Seven against Thebes already encountered in chapter 14, Diomedes, son of Tydeus, and Sthenelos, son of Kapaneus; with them is Euryalos, son of Mekisteus, the son of Talaos, and eighty ships again follow (*Il* 2.559–68). Aias, son of Telamon, comes from Salamis with just twelve ships (*Il* 2.557–58); his half-brother Teukros (for whom see Herakles' sack of Troy in chapter 13) is not mentioned in the Catalogue but appears frequently elsewhere. The other Aias, this one the son of Oileus (*Il* 2.527–35), comes from Lokris with forty ships.

From Athens arrives Menestheus, son of Peteos, a marshaller of men and horses second only to Nestor, with fifty ships (*Il* 2.546–56); we have seen in chapter 9 that Theseus' sons Demophon and Akamas are not named in the *Iliad* but are present in the closing stages of the Cycle to recover their grandmother Aithra. Ithaka and the surrounding islands (Kephallenia, Samos, Zakinthos, etc.) are led by Odysseus, of course, but with only twelve ships (*Il* 2.631–37); the nearby islands of Doulichion and the Echinades are led by Meges, son of Phyleus, with forty (*Il* 2.625–30). Finally, there is from Phthia and Pelasgikon Argos Achilleus with his Myrmidones (*Il* 2.681–84) and close friend Patroklos, son of Menoitios. This last is also not mentioned in the Catalogue; we learn about him from various other parts of the poem, including the fact that, angered over some game, he killed a companion when very young and was compelled to go into exile (*Il* 23.84–90). Fifty ships follow Achilleus

Iliad 1 suggests rather that Zeus' plan mentioned here is nothing more than the plan to accommodate Thetis' request, and springs from no personal motive at all, however much he might favor the Trojans. But seemingly the poet of the *Kypria* differed with this view, or else Proklos has introduced a motive of his own for the action in concluding his summary.

In any case, the next event in our preserved picture of the Trojan War is certainly the quarrel between Achilleus and Agamemnon, brought about by the fact that Chryses, father of Agamemnon's war prize Chryseis and priest of Apollo, is (unusually) still alive. His request for the return of his daughter, accompanied as it is by an offer of ransom, might seem nothing more than an exchange of goods, but Agamemnon chooses to regard the loss of the girl (low though slave women generally are in the Iliadic scale of values) as a serious loss of status, and thus rejects the offer. Chryses in his anger appeals to Apollo as the god's loyal priest, and Apollo acknowledges that responsibility by sending plague to ravage the army. When the troops finally assemble at Achilleus' summons, Kalchas reveals the cause of the problem, but Agamemnon is still unwilling to acquiesce without an immediate replacement for Chryseis. Achilleus not unreasonably points out that this is impossible at the moment, and adds some remarks about Agamemnon's general greed; the upshot is that Agamemnon finds himself compelled to forcibly appropriate Achilleus' own war prize, Briseis, in order to save face. At this threat Achilleus nearly dispatches Agamemnon on the spot, but with Athena's encouragement settles for a few more insults and the pronouncement that he himself will no longer fight for such a leader, nor will his men. The loss is clearly more than the Achaian side will be able to support (Nestor hints at as much), but to make sure of Agamemnon's humiliation without him, Achilleus asks his mother Thetis to intercede with Zeus, requesting victory for the Trojans until Agamemnon should apologize. Zeus foresees problems with Hera over this course of action, even though it will not affect the eventual outcome of the war, but finally succumbs to Thetis' pressure. Meanwhile, Odysseus has been delegated to return Chryseis to her father, and Briseis is removed from Achilleus' tent by heralds sent by Agamemnon.

Thus the action of *Iliad* 1. From this point on, the course of events proceeds forward in a more desultory fashion, and for the purposes of this book we need only mention the more critical moments. In Book 2, Zeus sends a false dream to encourage Agamemnon; the latter's failure to recount this to the troops combined with an odd sense of the appropriate time to test their loyalty leads to a rush for the ships, halted only by Odysseus and Athena. We meet also in this book Thersites, the ugliest and most unpleasant man in the army, who reviles Agamemnon for his lack of leadership, until chastised by Odysseus. After the leaders on both sides have been itemized with their contingents (the Catalogue of Ships) we proceed to Book 3 and a single combat between Paris and Menelaos designed to resolve the war for good (the Achaians to leave if Paris wins, the Trojans to hand back Helen and all stolen goods and pay a penalty in the opposite event). But though Menelaos has no problems with the unwarlike Paris, Aphrodite intervenes as her favorite is being dragged back to the Achaian side by his helmet, breaking the strap and carrying him back to Troy where she induces Helen to indulge in lovemaking with him. As Book 3 closes, Menelaos and the Achaians are claiming victory over the vanished Paris, but in Book 4 Hera protests this too-peaceful result and, after offering to abandon Argos or Sparta or Mykenai when their time comes, obtains Zeus' permission to send Athena down to earth to restart hostilities. This Athena does, in the guise of Laodokos, son of Antenor, by tempting one Pandaros to fire a shot at Menelaos during the current truce so that the Trojans will not have to admit defeat; she also assures, however, that the arrow so fired only wounds Menelaos. Both sides rush back to arms, the truce is forgotten, and battle joined. As Agamemnon exhorts his men, at times with criticism, we find the memorable exchange with Diomedes and Sthenelos concerning their fathers and the expedition of the Seven against Thebes.

In Book 5 Diomedes occupies center stage, creating havoc in the Trojan ranks and wounding two of the gods supporting their cause. First he scratches Aphrodite on the wrist as she seeks to protect her son Aineias, felled by a stone; she drops him and flees in Ares' chariot up to Olympos where her mother Dione comforts her (Apollo accomplishes the actual rescue of Aineias). At the close of the same book, with Athena's special permission, he wounds Ares, who has been literally fighting for the Trojans, in the belly; this departure from approved methods of support for one's chosen side is apparently the reason for Zeus' approval of such harsh treatment, as Ares goes bellowing and complaining back to his father's palace. Book 5 also brings the death of the treacherous Pandaros at Diomedes' hands, having failed to obtain any of the gifts that Athena/Laodokos promised.

In Book 6 Hektor returns to Troy to advise Hekabe to appeal to Athena for relief from the devastations of Diomedes; Hekabe offers a robe, which Athena refuses. Hektor also visits the house of Paris to bring his brother back to battle, and engages in a poignant meeting with Andromache and his son Astyanax on the walls of the city, where they have been watching the war. The manner in which the child here shrinks back from the image of his father in full armor as the latter stoops to pick him up surely encourages us to suppose an allusion to Astyanax's ultimate fate, and thus strengthens the notion that Homer was generally familiar with events outside the compass of his poems. In Book 7, for no very clear reason, we are treated to a single combat between Telemonian Aias and Hektor; night intervenes before any serious damage can be done, although Aias more than holds his own. At a subsequent assembly of the Trojans, Paris agrees to give back Menelaos' stolen property but not Helen, and a burial truce is arranged during which the Achaians construct a wall and trench to protect their ships. In Book 8 Zeus sets about fulfilling his promise to Thetis, and thus forbids the other gods to descend to the battlefield. The Achaians are accordingly pushed back, and by the end of the book have conceded the entire plain to the Trojans, who are (for the first time?) camped upon it, their many fires like to the stars above.

Accordingly, in Book 9 Nestor and the other Achaian leaders pressure Agamemnon to offer Achilleus the necessary apology, that is, the return of Briseis (untouched) together with numerous other handsome gifts. Odysseus, Aias, and Achilleus' old tutor Phoinix bring this offer to Achilleus, but he is adamant in his refusal, stressing the extent of his pain and the hurt of the insult. Phoinix here tells the story of Meleagros discussed in Chapter 11, seemingly to no avail though Achilleus does recant his announced intention to leave immediately. In Book 10 the Achaians, depressed over this failure, feel the need to scout out Trojan intentions, and Odysseus and Diomedes volunteer for the mission. At the same time Hektor has sent out one Dolon, son of Eumedes, to scout the Greek side, promising him the horses of Achilleus if he should succeed. He is, however, captured by his Greek counterparts and killed after revealing the location of a new contingent of Trojan allies, that of the Thracian Rhesos, who has splendid white horses. Odysseus and Diomedes then raid this camp while its occupants are sleeping; Odysseus takes the horses while Diomedes butchers thirteen men, including Rhesos himself, and they make their escape back to their own side. In Book 11 various Achaians are wounded—Agamemnon by Koon Antenorides, Diomedes by Paris, Odysseus by Sokos Hippasides, Machaon by Paris, Eurypylos by Paris. Nestor brings Machaon back to the ships, and Achilleus seeing them pass by sends Patroklos to confirm the wounded man's identity—a fatal act of concern. Nestor offers Patroklos the story of his family's conflict with Herakles and with the Epeians of Augeias, and then suggests that Patroklos might enter the battle in Achilleus' place. At the book's close, on his way back to the tents of the Myrmidones, Patroklos is intercepted by Eurypylos, who asks for help in tending his wound. Book 12 opens with the tale of how Poseidon and Apollo later destroyed the wall of the Achaians, after the war was over, and then proceeds to the Trojans' successes before the wall. These last are somewhat negated by an omen sent by Zeus—an eagle whose prey of a snake twists around in his captor's clutches to bite him and escape. The seer Poulydamas quite properly interprets this portent to mean that the Greeks will similarly escape the Trojans' grasp, though Hektor is unable to accept that fact. As this book closes Hektor smashes the gates of the Achaians' wall with a stone, and calls upon his allies to follow him through to the ships.

Book 13 brings Poseidon onto the battlefield to encourage the Achaians as they struggle to hold back Hektor, and we see the death of Alkathoos, husband of Hippodameia, Aineias' half-sister. Also dying in this book is Euchenor, son of Polyidos, who upon being told by his father that he will die either in battle or of a painful sickness chooses the former. In Book 14 Agamemnon once again proposes returning to Greece, but Odysseus, Nestor, and Diomedes rebuke him, and suggest lending their presence, albeit wounded, to the battle without actually fighting. Hera also assists by concocting a story (of a planned visit to the quarreling Okeanos and Tethys) which allows her to request from Aphrodite the latter's embroidered *himas*, or strap, source of all desire, and with this she has no trouble luring Zeus away from the battle and to bed, hidden away in the clouds on Mount Ida. For good measure she bribes Hypnos—with the gift of Pasithea, one of the Charites, to wife—to put Zeus to sleep after their lovemaking, and Poseidon is left free to further aid the Achaian side.

Book 15 features Zeus' awakening and command to Poseidon to abandon the battlefield, accompanied by the first prediction of Patroklos' fate and Hektor's doom following close upon it. Apollo on his father's command then shakes the aigis, and the Achaians are panicked into running for the ships, where Aias virtually alone is forced to hold off Hektor and the Trojans. At this most critical point of danger, Book 16 brings Patroklos back from his tendance of Eurypylos to Achilleus with the suggestion that he lead the Myrmidones out in the latter's place to save their comrades from total destruction. Achilleus agrees, but only to the extent that Patroklos push the Trojans away from the ships, lest he win too much glory for himself or come to grief at Apollo's hands. Patroklos thus takes all of his friend's armor except the spear that only Achilleus can wield and, with Automedon as charioteer and the horses Xanthos and Balios, sets out for battle. After notable successes he comes face to face with Sarpedon, and here Zeus makes his famous suggestion to Hera that he might avert fate and save his son. Hera expresses appropriate alarm that *aisa* and the laws of mortality should be thus flouted, and Zeus relents, agreeing instead to her proposal that Hypnos and Thanatos carry the body back to Lykia, after he has sent Apollo to rescue it from the battlefield. Hektor in fear now turns back to Troy, where Patroklos in pursuit assaults the walls three times, to be turned back each time by Apollo with his bare hands. On the fourth attempt, Apollo calls out that Troy is not fated to fall to Patroklos or even Achilleus, and Patroklos desists. But his own death is now near, for as he continues fighting Apollo comes up behind him in a mist and strikes him on the back, causing his helmet and breastplate to fall away and his spear to shatter in his hand. Euphorbos takes advantage of his defenseless condition to wound him with a throw of his spear, but does not dare confront him, and it remains for Hektor to dispatch the hero with a sword-thrust. Patroklos' dying words predict death in turn for Hektor at Achilleus' hands, but the Trojan boldly suggests that Achilleus, not he, might die in such an encounter.

Book 17 deals with the battle over Patroklos' body, after Hektor has returned from his vain pursuit of Achilleus' horses to strip off the armor. Menelaos sends Antilochos to announce the death to Achilleus, and as the book closes he and Meriones shoulder the corpse while the two Aiantes hold off Hektor and Aineias. In Book 18 Achilleus does finally hear of Patroklos' fate, and in response to his lament Thetis once again rises up out of the sea. To his insistence that he will now return to battle to fight Hektor she accedes, but proposes that she first obtain new armor from Hephaistos to replace that which Hektor has taken. After her departure Iris arrives, sent by Hera, and suggests that Achilleus go out to the ditch and shout, so that the Trojans might be frightened and the Achaians given a chance to bring back the body. This is done, and as night falls Poulydamas (whom we now learn was born on the same night as Hektor, and is better in counsel) advises retreat to safety within the walls, a plan rashly rejected by Hektor and the other Trojans. Meanwhile, Hephaistos produces the armor requested by Thetis, and as Book 19 begins she brings these items, including the wondrous shield, back to her son. Agamemnon then tells the story of Zeus and Ate as part of a reiteration of his apology, and the same gifts offered the day before are taken to Achilleus' tent, together with Briseis. But Achilleus himself has little thought for anything except Hektor, and refuses even the food that Odysseus suggests the army needs. In this book we also see Briseis' lament over Patroklos (with the remarkable claim that he would have persuaded Achilleus to marry her had he lived), and Achilleus' only reference in the *Iliad* to his son Neoptolemos on Skyros. Finally, there is the most fanciful moment of the poem: Achilleus' call to his horses not to leave him to die as they did Patroklos, and Xanthos' reply (inspired by Hera) that *moira* and Apollo slew his friend, while he himself will soon fall to a mortal and a god.

Book 20 brings us to Achilleus' entrance into battle, while the gods themselves are given leave by Zeus to go down and help their favorites (Hera, Athena, Poseidon, Hermes, and Hephaistos to the Achaians, Ares, Apollo, Artemis, Aphrodite, Leto, and Xanthos the river to the Trojans). Aineias now confronts Achilleus, but after each have missed with their spears Poseidon proposes to the other gods that they should save Aineias from a certain death, since he is fated to carry on the line of Dardanos, dearest of Zeus' sons, and rule over future generations of Trojans. Hera remains indifferent, but Aineias is duly carried out of battle to safety. Achilleus then loses Hektor as well, for Apollo wraps the Trojan in a mist and carries him away as they prepare to fight. By the beginning of Book 21 the Trojans are in full flight to the Xanthos, where Achilleus proceeds to slaughter them, filling up the river with carnage and slaying, among others, his former captive Lykaon. At this glutting of its waters the river itself protests, and rises up in pursuit of the hero to drown him, in the process calling to the Simoeis for aid. Poseidon and Athena come to Achilleus in his flight to promise support, but it is Hera who appeals to Hephaistos to take action; he responds by setting fire to the banks of the Xanthos, and the river quickly yields. From this first encounter between rival gods the narrative proceeds to other confrontations. Athena has no difficulty knocking Ares down with a stone after he has tried to stab her; Aphrodite helps the defeated war god away, but is herself struck to the ground by a blow of Athena's hand at Hera's urging. Poseidon challenges Apollo, chiding him for supporting the Trojans after their own ill-treatment by Laomedon, but Apollo will not fight with a god his senior and yields the victory, much to the disgust of Artemis. She, however, fares little better against Hera, who strips her of her bow and boxes her ears. Finally, Hermes and Leto find themselves face to face.

Hermes, like Apollo, declines such a match, and offers Leto the chance to boast of her superiority; she prefers to pick up her daughter's fallen arrows and head back to Olympos. At this book's close Apollo buys the Trojans time to retreat by snatching Agenor, son of Antenor, out of battle as he prepares to face Achilleus and, in the guise of Agenor, leads Achilleus away from the battle by feigned flight.

Book 22 brings finally the death of Hektor, whose time has run out. Apollo reveals his true form to Achilleus, and the latter turns back to the walls where Hektor is waiting for him, determined to atone for his folly in keeping the Trojans out on the plain by a showdown with his rival. Yet this long-awaited duel is hardly climactic: Hektor's courage fails before they have even begun to fight, and Achilleus must chase him back and forth before the walls as he looks for help from his comrades above. As the two come back around by the hot and cold springs of Skamandros for the fourth time, Zeus sets up his golden scales, placing in one the *kêr* of death for Achilleus, in the other that of Hektor. Hektor's sinks down, and Apollo abandons him. To further his destruction Athena in the guise of Deiphobos gives him encouragement to make a stand; after both Achaian and Trojan have thrown their spears and missed, she brings back Achilleus' spear but not Hektor's. Seeing himself deceived and with no second spear, Hektor launches a desperate rush with his sword and is easily slain by Achilleus' spear cast, the latter aiming at an opening in the neck of the armor he knows so well. Hektor, like the horse Xanthos, has a prophecy to deliver, naming Paris and Apollo as the mortal and god who will contrive Achilleus' own death. Unimpressed, Achilleus drags the body behind his horses before the walls and then takes it back to the ships in the same fashion, as Hektor's parents and wife look on.

Book 23 offers the funeral of Patroklos and the games, after twelve Trojan prisoners have been slaughtered in his honor. The chariot race brings Diomedes home first, since his prayer to Athena results in an accident to the chariot of Eumelos, whose horses were fastest. Antilochos is second, followed by Menelaos, Meriones, and Eumelos, but Menelaos questions Antilochos' dangerous tactics at a narrow part of the course and their order of finish is reversed. Even so, when Antilochos yields, Menelaos is appeased and passes back to his opponent the mare that is second prize. For Eumelos there is a special prize, in recognition of his misfortune, and the phiale originally intended for the fifth-place finisher is given to Nestor. In boxing Epeios drops Euryalos with one punch, while in wrestling Odysseus and Aias after a long struggle are called upon by Achilleus to accept a draw. The footrace features Odysseus, Antilochos, and Aias, son of Oileus; Odysseus is just behind this last in the final stage of the course when, like Diomedes in the chariot race, he prays to Athena. As a result, Aias slips in the blood and dung near the finish line and must settle for second. The general amusement greeting his fate, combined with his contentious attitude during the viewing of the chariot race, reminds us of his generally unpopular character and perhaps his ultimate folly. For the duel in armor, Diomedes and Aias are the opponents, and while the combat is soon halted for fear of harm, Achilleus judges Diomedes to have had the better of it. In the throwing of a huge iron weight (which is the prize), Polypoites far outstrips Aias, Leonteus, and Epeios. In archery, Teukros and Meriones compete; the latter wins when Teukros fails to pray to Apollo for success. Finally, there is the spear throw; Agamemnon and Meriones present themselves, but Achilleus declares Agamemnon the winner by common consent, without an actual competition.

Book 24 then concludes the *Iliad* with the real climax of the poem, the confrontation between Achilleus and Priam when the latter comes to the Achaian camp to ransom the body of Hektor, which is still being maltreated by Achilleus. After some discussion among the gods, Zeus sends Thetis to tell Achilleus that he must release the corpse to Priam, asserting that the rights of the dead cannot be ignored. At the same time Iris is sent to Priam with instructions for the ransom, including the assurance that Hermes will meet him on the way for protection. Priam accordingly sets out, although when Hermes does appear it is in the guise of a young Myrmidon who offers to take Priam secretly into Achilleus' compound. This done, Priam slips into the latter's quarters and takes his hands in supplication, reminding him of his own father Peleus soon to be bereaved of his son. The two share a mutual lamentation and food, Achilleus arranges the body for the journey, and contracts with Priam for an eleven-day period of mourning during which he shall hold back the Achaians from battle. When Priam returns to Troy with the body there are formal eulogies from Andromache, Hekabe, and Helen, and then the building of the pyre and the final rites, and here the *Iliad* ends (although the Townley scholia tell us that in some versions the last line was altered so as to create a link with the first line of the *Aithiopis*).

Of other or later versions of all these events there is not much to say; the monumental form of the *Iliad* as we have it seems to have become highly canonical, and while lyric poets might refer to the events of the war in general as a model of heroic times, no literary source deals with the story again in any detail until Aischylos, whose lost Achilleus trilogy (*Myrmidones, Nereides,* and *Phryges*) clearly dramatized the entire central action from original abandonment of the war to reconciliation with Priam. Unfortunately, we know very little of the particulars, much less how Aischylos viewed the overall situation. In the first play, a chorus of Myrmidones seems to have visited Achilleus in his tent, exhorting him to return to battle. From these, or Phoinix, or someone, there may also be a threat of stoning by the army, and finally the report of the ships' peril which induces Achilleus to send out Patroklos. Before the play ends news will come back of the latter's death, and fragments preserved at this point do indicate a sexual element in the two friends' relationship, in contrast to the *Iliad* (frr 134a-136 R). The second play brings on the Nereides (probably with Achilleus' new armor), and he then appears to have gone out to face Hektor, returning subsequently with the corpse. In the third play, Achilleus once again sits brooding in his tent, until Hermes comes to tell him that the body must be returned, and Priam follows with the ransom, apparently weighed out pound for pound against Hektor's body (ΣAT *Il* 22.351). Aside from the sexual attachment and the threat of stoning, this all might be nothing more than Homer's tale put on stage just as he wrote it, with an *Oresteia*-like reconciliation at the end, but we may underestimate the poet's originality.

Sophokles too *may* have dramatized the last part of the *Iliad* in his *Priamos* (or *Phryges?*),[45] but otherwise neither he nor Euripides appears to have dealt with any part of the poem's *narrative,* and the same is by and large true of other tragedians as well, save of course for Rhesos' death in the play of that name (see below).[46] But we should note the comment of Tekmessa in the *Aias* to the effect that Hektor was dragged to his death by means of the belt he received from Aias, while Aias died by the sword he got from Hektor (*Ai* 1026–33); presumably this is Sophoklean invention.

There were also *Phoinix* plays by Sophokles, Euripides, and Ion, among others; of these, Sophokles' perhaps and Euripides' certainly told of Phoinix's conflict with his father. In Euripides' version we have reason to suspect that the mother is dead, that the concubine attempts to seduce Phoinix, rather than vice versa, and that Amyntor, believing her subsequent slander, orders his son blinded.[47] Apollodoros gives a similar account, adding that Peleus brought Phoinix to Cheiron, who restored his sight (Ap*B* 3.13.8; this may all have been drawn from Euripides). The Cyzicene Epigrams, on the other hand, seem to assume the same story of mother and concubine as in the *Iliad,* with the mother (here Alkimede) still alive and in the relief described trying to prevent Amyntor from blinding his son with a torch (*AP* 3.3). The same is true of Lykophron, where Phoinix is blinded for entering the concubine's bed (Lyk 421–23); the scholia call the mother who requested this favor from her son Kleoboule and the concubine Klytie or Phthia (she is Phthia also for Apollodoros). In the A scholia at *Iliad* 9.448, the mother is Hippodameia and the concubine again Klytie; the rest of the comment simply repeats Homer's version, in which, as we have seen, Amyntor's punishment of his son is rather a curse of childlessness.

As for the preserved Greek tragedy entitled *Rhesos* handed down to us under Euripides' name, scholars remain dubious of the attribution and therefore completely uncertain as to date (early fourth century?).[48] Nevertheless, the play offers some interesting variations (one might even say improvements) on the account in *Iliad* 10. As the drama opens, the Trojans are in some alarm at seeing the many fires lit in the Achaian camp, and the army gathered around Agamemnon's hut. Hektor, fearing that they mean to leave by night, calls for a volunteer to spy out the situation, and here as in the *Iliad* Dolon comes forward, naming on his own initiative the horses of Achilleus as the desired reward. Dolon then departs, clad in a wolfskin and promising to bring back the head of some Achaian—Odysseus, say, or Diomedes—as proof of his venture. Next a shepherd announces the arrival of Rhesos, son of the river Strymon and a Muse, from Thrace together with a huge force, and Rhesos himself follows, pleading war with the Scythians at home as excuse for his late appearance. The chorus is much impressed, and Rhesos is confident that his forces can defeat the Greeks in a single day. All exit the stage, and Diomedes and Odysseus now enter, carrying the spoils they have taken from Dolon, who is already dead. Their original intent seems to have been to kill Hektor in his sleep, but Athena appears and steers them to Rhesos, whom she says no Achaian will be able to withstand if he survives that night. As in the *Iliad*, Diomedes does the killing while Odysseus takes the beautiful white horses; Athena assists with an imitation of Aphrodite when Paris arrives suspecting trouble. The play then closes with the Trojans' discovery of the deed, bitter accusations by the surviving Thracians against Hektor, and the coming of the Muse (unnamed) to take her son away. All this does not perhaps have a great deal of bite, but treachery is countered by treachery, and the Achaian sortie now has some real purpose and consequence.

If we may trust the *Iliad* scholia, Pindar too gave the story better motivation: in his version, Rhesos actually fought at Troy for a day, and wreaked such havoc among the Achaians that Hera and Athena advised Diomedes and others to undertake the night raid (ΣbT *Il* 10.435 = fr 262 SM; ΣA *Il* 10.435). The remarks in the latter of these two scholia go further still, and cite an account of "others" (Eustathios says the *neôteroi*) in which Rhesos arrived at Troy during the night, and died before he could taste the water there. For it was fated, the scholia continue, that if he should taste the water, or his horses drink from the Skamandros and feed on its banks, that he would become invincible. Vergil seems to know something of the same story, since the *Aeneid*, too, has Diomedes take the horses of Rhesos before they have grazed at Troy or drunk the water of the Skamandros (*Aen* 1.469–73); Servius at 469 reports this to mean that there was a prophecy of *Troy's* invincibility should the horses thus feed or drink. Thus we find in this version (whether it is the warrior or the city at risk) much the same notion attached to Troilos by the *Bacchides* of Plautus (although the latter's list of three such prophecies does not include Rhesos).

In art there is a rich collection of representations from the *Iliad*, beginning with scenes of the embassy and final ransom on shield-bands from Olympia and continuing on to Corinthian and Attic Black-Figure pots, but the events of the poem have nothing like the popularity accorded to Herakles or even Perseus, and the illustrations that survive do not offer much that differs from Homer's account.[49] On a fragment of a dinos by Sophilos, for example, we see the funeral games for Patroklos (so labeled): there are the stands with cheering crowds and the first horses coming into view, but we cannot tell to whom they belonged, save that his name ended in *-os* (Athens 15499). An inscription also tells us that Achilleus was portrayed on the other side of the stands, but he is entirely lost. The François Krater offers as part of its second band precisely the same event: Achilleus stands to the far right next to a tripod, waiting for the arrival of the competitors, who are (in order) Olyteus (i.e., Odysseus), Automedon, Diomedes, Damasippos, Hypothoon (*sic*) (Florence 4209). Diomedes is, as we saw, the winner of the race in the Homeric version, and Automedon, although he does not compete there, is at least a charioteer of Achilleus and Patroklos. But Odysseus, here the winner, is likewise not a competitor in the *Iliad*, where nothing is ever said of his horses, Damasippos does not appear in the poem at all, and Hippothoon (as close as we can get to the last contestant) fights only on the Trojan side. That this scene could represent an alternate version of the race remains a possibility of course, but when both of the otherwise unfamiliar names contain the root *hippos*, or "horse" (Damasippos, "horse-tamer"; Hippothoon, "swift-horsed"), we may be forgiven for suspecting that the painter has done some inventing to augment a less-than-perfect memory of the Homeric version.

From about the same time is a metope of the Heraion I temple at Foce del Sele (no #): here, a figure who is surely Patroklos reaches up for what is apparently his breast-plate while another warrior (Hektor? Euphorbos?) stabs him in the back with a spear.[50] In *Iliad* 16 we saw that Patroklos' armor falls off from the force of Apollo's slap to the back; here the armor seems almost to be flying away, and conceivably the artist envisioned (or knew from variant epic accounts) something more magical than simply a god's intervention in battle. Other metopes from the same structure *may* show Helen and Andromache with infant Astyanax (on one section) and Hekabe with the corpse of Hektor (on another) in a general mourning scene.[51] From Korinth about 570 B.C. comes an olpe with Thetis' visit to a prostrate Achilleus, apparently engrossed in his grief for Patroklos and unwilling to eat (Brussels A4). For the rest of this century, and extending on through the fifth century, we have quite a number of Attic Black- and Red-Figure vases with scenes from the epic, including the leading away of Briseis, the duel between Aias and Hektor, the embassy to Achilleus, the carrying away of the corpses of Sarpedon and Patroklos, the making of the new armor and its consignment to Achilleus, the combat between Achilleus and Hektor, the slaughter of Trojan prisoners, and the ransoming of Hektor's body. Especially noteworthy from an artistic point of view are the New York Euphronios krater with Hypnos and Thanatos carrying off the body of Sarpedon as Hermes supervises (NY 1972.11.10), the Sosias Painter's intimate portrait of Achilleus bandaging Patroklos' arm in the tondo of a kylix (Berlin:Ch 2278), and the ransoming scenes on cups by Oltos (Munich 2618) and the Brygos Painter (Vienna 3710). But all these show simply expected elements of Homer's story, or details (such as Patroklos' wound) which can easily be extrapolated from it.[52]

The same is true of the relief panels from the east frieze of the Siphnian Treasury at Delphi (no #): to the left sit the gods, Trojan allies (Ares, Aphrodite, probably Artemis, and Apollo) on one side of Zeus, Achaian allies (possibly a kneeling Thetis and Poseidon, certainly Athena, Hera, and Demeter) on the other. On the right a battle rages over a fallen corpse, either that of Sarpedon or Patroklos, with Glaukos, Aineias, and Hektor on one side, Menelaos, ?, and Automedon on the other. From all this we learn that someone put Demeter (not named as a participant in the *Iliad*) on the Greek side, but otherwise the frieze's (considerable) values are entirely artistic.

The additional last line of the *Iliad* quoted from the Townley scholia above shows that the following poem in the Cycle, the *Aithiopis*, began with the arrival of the Amazon Penthesileia to help the Trojans, and so too Proklos in his summary of that work. What Proklos tells us beyond that is simply that Penthesileia was a daughter of Ares, Thracian in origin, and that after displaying great valor on the battlefield she was slain by Achilleus and buried by the Trojans. Thersites then reviled Achilleus for supposedly being in love with the Amazon, and Achilleus in anger slew him as well, creating dissension among the Greeks and necessitating a trip to Lesbos where he was purified by Odysseus. Subsequent to this account there are no literary references at all until Hellanikos, for whom we learn, courtesy of Tzetzes, that the Amazon was thought to have come to Troy to win glory in battle against men so that she might marry, since it was forbidden to Amazones to consort with men before they had done so (4F149). I have no explanation for such an idea. Lykophron alludes to the death of Thersites as due to Achilleus' wrath after Thersites had struck a blow to the eye of Penthesileia as she was dying (Lyk 999-1001; on this blow to the eye see also Σ *Ph* 445). The scholia relate that in fact the Aitolian gouged out her eye, but they know as well the versions in which Thersites' tongue is his undoing, and in which his accusation against Achilleus seems in fact one of necrophilia. Diodoros remarks briefly that Penthesileia came to Troy because she had killed a relative, and although she was queen of the Amazones she had to go into exile (DS 2.46.5). In Apollodoros, too, she has killed someone, namely Hippolyte, bride of Theseus, but inadvertently, while they were fighting together at the wedding of Theseus and Phaidra; here she is the daughter of Ares and one Otrere, and is purified at Troy by Priam, after which she slays Machaon and falls to Achilleus (ApE 5.1–2). Apollodoros also includes the death of Thersites as in the *Aithiopis* (he seems to regard Thersites' revilements as true, as does Propertius: 3.11.15–16) but says nothing about Achilleus' purification. In Eustathios, Achilleus accomplishes the slaying with a blow to the face, and as the *neôteroi* are cited, this may go back to the Cycle (Eu-*Il* 2.219, p. 208; cf. Σ *Ph* 445, Σ Lyk 999).

Of other authors, Quintus makes Penthesileia's accidental victim her own sister Hippolyte, slain by her while casting at a deer (QS 1.18–25). Here she brings with her twelve other Amazones, and after her death Achilleus falls in love with her when he has removed her helmet; Thersites dies as in the *Aithiopis* (his criticism is of Achilleus' weakness in loving a woman) and the corpse of Penthesileia is given back to the Trojans for burial. As for the aftermath in Quintus, as sole kinsman of Thersites (son of Agrios, Oineus' brother) Diomedes is alone among the Achaians in protesting his cousin's murder, and nearly comes to blows with Achilleus until the other Greeks reconcile them. In chapter 11 we saw that long before this Pherekydes (or someone) makes Thersites the son of Agrios and Dia, daughter of Porthaon (3F123: slight manuscript uncertainty), and thus such a conflict between Diomedes and Achilleus may be what Proklos refers to in saying that at this point in the *Aithiopis* there is stasis over the killing. Only in Diktys of Krete does Achilleus fail to completely dispatch Penthesileia (who here comes solely for glory and spoils); after some discussion Diomedes drags her nearly lifeless body to the Skamandros and throws it in (Dik 4.3). The Lykophron scholia (at 999) report the same deed, but there she is already quite dead and Diomedes' motive is specifically the fact that she brought about the death of his cousin.

Art offers a number of representations of Achilleus slaying the Amazon, beginning with shield-band reliefs from Olympia and elsewhere dating as early as perhaps 625 B.C. (Olympia B 112; name included on the later B 1555). In painting there is the famous neck-amphora by Exekias in the British Museum (London B210) and of course the name-piece of the Penthesileia Painter from about 455 B.C. (Munich 2688); one Black-Figure hydria of the Leagros Group even shows Achilleus carrying the body of his opponent out of battle (London B323). But otherwise our examples are straightforward combat scenes; nothing survives of any other part of the story (save Thersites' death: Boston 03.804, an Apulian volute krater), so that here as largely for the *Iliad* we learn nothing new from the artistic tradition, not even whether Achilleus' love for his fallen foe was generally credited.

After the death of Penthesileia and Achilleus' purification, the *Aithiopis* turns to yet another new ally of the Trojans, this time Memnon, son of Eos, who also wears armor forged by Hephaistos; the *Theogony* names Tithonos as his father, as we might expect (*Th* 984–85). Thetis tells Achilleus something about this next opponent, and in the ensuing battle Achilleus defeats him after Antilochos has fallen to him. Eos then obtains immortality for her son from Zeus. The *Odyssey* twice refers to the death of Antilochos, on the second occasion specifying that he was slain by the son of Eos, so that the author of that poem clearly knew much the same story (*Od* 3.108–12, 4.186–88). The only other Homeric reference is that of the *Nekuia*, where in speaking to Achilleus Odysseus asserts that Neoptolemos was the most beautiful of all those at Troy after Memnon (*Od* 11.522). For the seventh and sixth centuries there are just two brief allusions, a line of Alkman in which "Aias rages with his polished spear, and Memnon lusts for blood" (exact meaning of this last verb uncertain: 68 *PMG*), and Strabo's assertion that Simonides wrote a dithyramb *Memnon* in which the hero was buried in Syria (on the coast, near Paltos: 539 *PMG*).

In art there is the well-known amphora from (probably) Melos with Apollo in chariot greeted by Artemis which dates to about 640 B.C.; on the neck are two warriors confronting each other with armor stacked up between them, and in panels to either side a concerned woman looking on (Athens 3961). In the absence of names the armor (rather than a corpse) between the combatants has been taken to signify the duel between Aias and Diomedes at the funeral games for Patroklos (where the armor of Sarpedon was in fact the prize), or perhaps the conflict between Aias and Odysseus for the armor of Achilleus. But such scenes will not in any way explain the women, and more likely we do have here our first look at Achilleus and Memnon, accompanied by their mothers.[53]

Subsequently, a Middle Corinthian column krater of about 580 offers the two warriors (names inscribed; there is nothing between them) flanked by horses (Berlin:PM F1147) and a second krater of perhaps twenty years later has sons, mothers, and corpse of Antilochos, all named (Korinth C 72–149; so too a Chalkidian amphora in Florence [4210], among others). From Athens a Black-Figure amphora shows all five figures of the group, but while the warriors and their mothers are named as we would expect, the corpse in the center is Phokos, not Antilochos (PrColl, Athens). The presence of Hektor behind Eos (when he should be long since dead) suggests that the artist did not take his identifications as seriously as we might like. The combat also appeared on the Amyklai Throne (Paus 3.18.12: only the two fighters are mentioned) and the Chest of Kypselos (Paus 5.19.1, here definitely with the mothers), and even perhaps on a small terracotta altar from Agrigento on which one mother (Eos?) holds a second spear for her son.

In the fifth century we have several Pindaric allusions to Achilleus' victory over Memnon, but no details of interest beyond the fact itself (*Ol* 2.83; *Nem* 3.61–63, 6.51–55). In *Pythian* 6, however, we learn that Antilochos' father Nestor risked falling to Memnon after one of his horses (struck by Paris' arrows) hindered his chariot from flight; he called for his son, and Antilochos "purchased with death the safe return of his father" (*Py* 6.39). Admittedly this is remarkably like the moment early in *Iliad* 9 when Nestor's horse is similarly wounded by Paris, and the old man, busy trying to cut the traces, is saved by Diomedes as Hektor threatens (*Il* 8.80–91). Pindar's version is not a story found elsewhere, but as his point is the rather strained one of a comparison with Thrasyboulos, son of Xenokrates, who drove his father's chariot to victory, he is probably drawing on something already known to his audience. Even more enlightening, if only we had it, would certainly have been Aischylos' lost Memnon trilogy, consisting of *Memnon, Psychostasia*, and perhaps *Phrygioi*. The first of these, though there is little hard evidence, brought Memnon onstage from Aithiopia and probably included the death of Antilochos. In the second, as Plutarch tells us, Aischylos reshapes the weighing of the *kêres* (of Achilleus and Hektor) in *Iliad* 22 into a weighing of the *psychai* of Achilleus and Memnon, with beside the scales of Zeus Thetis and Eos, one to each side pleading for the life of her son (*Mor* 17a). What difference there might be between *kêres* and *psychai* remains a matter for dispute. Other evidence for the play comes from Pollux, who says that the *theologeion* was a platform above the *skênê* used for example for Zeus and those with him in the *Psychostasia* (4.130 = pp. 375–76 R). From such information it would seem that Zeus himself appeared onstage, and that there was an elaborate weighing scene, with perhaps actors playing Achilleus and Memnon actually standing in a pair of giant scales. It has, however, been objected that the technical requirements of that kind of tableau were probably quite beyond the capabilities of the Aischylean stage, and that Pollux's information may refer to some much later performance (or rewrite) of the play (nor does Plutarch actually say that in Aischylos Zeus held the scales).[54]

Vase-painting of the sixth and fifth centuries offers us a number of representations of this weighing, and while one of the earliest of these, an Ionian hydria in the Villa Giulia (the Ricci Hydria, no #), does show Zeus seated on his throne holding scales (Eos and Thetis kneel/stand before him, Achilleus and Memnon square off to the right), the others agree in portraying rather Hermes with the scales. The earliest of all (c. 540 B.C.) is an Attic Black-Figure dinos on which a seated Zeus and Hermes with scales are flanked by Thetis and Eos, thus establishing that Hermes performs the weighing as an agent of Zeus (Vienna 3619). Here too we see on each tray of the scales an *eidôlon* or miniature image of one of the contestants. Subsequently we have a Black-Figure lekythos of about 500 B.C. which omits Zeus and the mothers but again shows the two small images of the real warriors on the scales, while Achilleus and Memnon themselves are shown lifesize (London B639: no names). Other representations are all Red-Figure, including a very fine cup by Epiktetos on which Thetis and Eos both appeal to Zeus while looking back at Hermes, who stands between their sons holding the scales (VG 57912). But in all, the evidence is clearly sufficient to tell us that the motif of a weighing of the *psychai* (or *kêres* or whatever) of Achilleus and Memnon is older than Aischylos' trilogy, in contrast to what Plutarch seems to believe. The question has, of course, special importance because his remarks about Aischylos reshaping the *Iliad* would otherwise have led us to the conclusion that such a weighing did not appear in the *Aithiopis*. Sixth-century representations will not by themselves establish that the weighing was a part of that epic, but it seems likely, in which case Plutarch was not as familiar with the poems of the Cycle as he ought to have been.

As for Aischylos, we should probably conclude that Eos and Thetis appealed to a Zeus not physically present, and that Hermes as his representative (silent, if the play was two-actor) performed the onstage weighing in the *Psychostasia*. A further comment by Pollux (not mentioning this play by name) says that Eos came by means of the *geranos* to fetch the body of her son, again probably part of a later staging or version. We have no evidence as to how Aischylos' drama ended; possibly Eos' loss here was thematically related to the action of the third play of the trilogy, where Thetis probably lost her son Achilleus (see below). In any case, art represented also this sad mourning by the dawn goddess of her mortal son, perhaps on the Black-Figure name vase of the Vatican Mourner Painter (Vat 350), certainly on the fine Red-Figure cup by Douris, where the poses of Eos and Memnon resemble a pre-Christian pietà (Louvre G115). Of later literature there is little to say; Sophokles' *Aithiopes*

may have treated this story or it may not, and subsequent authors have nothing
new to add to the basic events.

*The Death
of Achilleus*

As we saw in our brief look at the *Iliad*, not only does Thetis several times
prophesy Achilleus' imminent death if he should slay Hektor, but Hektor himself as he lies dying in *Iliad* 22 predicts that Paris and Apollo shall bring death
to the hero beside the Skaian gates. Earlier, Achilleus' horse Xanthos has said
much the same thing in Book 19 by speaking of a mortal and a god as the
agents, although Achilleus in Book 21 uses the phrase "arrows of *Apollo*" in
recalling his mother's words (*Il* 21.276–78). The *Aithiopis* adds to this that
Achilleus put the Trojans to flight and was actually pursuing them into the city
when he was killed by Paris and Apollo. We have no other literary references
until the fifth century, when Pindar's *Paian* 6 appears to tell us (the relevant
section of papyrus has many gaps) that Apollo in the mortal form of Paris kept
back the day of Troy's destruction and restrained Achilleus with death, casting/
shooting (something) at him (*Pa* 6.75–86). The implication of the adjective
opsiteros, used to define "taking (of Troy)," would seem that Apollo here acts
to protect *moira*, much as he does in *Iliad* 16 when Patroklos tries to assault
the walls, or as Poseidon does in *Iliad* 20 when he rescues Aineias. From somewhere in Aischylos' work comes the quote given to us by Plato in which Thetis
takes the god of prophecy to task for telling her that her children would live
long lives, then slaying her only child (fr 350 R). I suspect this occurs in the
third play of the Memnon trilogy, in a play specifically about the death of
Achilleus and perhaps titled *Phrygioi*,[55] but even if that is true it does not help
us much; the statement that Apollo killed her son should not in the circumstances be taken to mean that Paris played no part. The same holds for Neoptolemos' description of his father's death in Sophokles' *Philoktetes* (334–35:
"no mortal destroyed him, but the god Apollo"), since the point here is the
hero's invincibility under normal circumstances and the god's maliciousness.
On the other side of the coin, Euripides twice has characters suggest that Paris
was responsible (*Hek* 387–88; *And* 655); again, where the point is the culpability of the Trojans, the failure to mention Apollo is probably not significant.
Vergil's *Aeneid* is, remarkably, the first work to state what the *Iliad* implies,
that Paris shot the arrow and Apollo guided it to its mark (the "body" of
Achilleus: *Aen* 6.56–58; cf. *Met* 12.598–606).

Nevertheless, despite such a wealth of sources, nothing in them (or in
what is preserved, at least) ever speaks of a uniquely vulnerable foot, or of
Achilleus' being struck there. Our first known author to even touch on such
an idea is Statius, in whose *Achilleis* Thetis recalls a dream in which she seems
a second time to be dipping her son in the Styx (*Ach* 1.133–34). The brevity
of the reference shows that Statius alludes to some story already familiar to his
audience; further clues appear at *Achilleis* 1.268–70, where Thetis laments that
she did not arm her child completely in the waters of the Styx, and *Achilleis*
1.480–81, where she says that carrying him in secret through the Styx she

made his fair limbs impervious to iron. Lactantius' commentary adds to this picture that Thetis, fearing death for her son, dipped him in the Styx, and that he became invulnerable in his whole body save for that part by which he was held (ΣΣ *Ach* 1.134, 296, 480; so too Servius at *Aen* 6.57, in virtually the same words). But none of these writers ever say that the part held was the foot, much less what particular part of the foot might be involved. Apollodoros, who with Hyginus is in fact the first to mention feet, says that Achilleus was struck in the *ankle (sphuron)* by an arrow shot by Paris and Apollo (ApE 5.3); the epitomator does not specify if he was vulnerable only there or not. We are, however, surely meant to understand that Achilleus dies (on the battlefield) from this wound (were it only incapacitating, the actual slayer would surely be credited). Hyginus, like Pindar, has Apollo operate in the guise of Paris, angered because Achilleus has boasted that he will sack Troy all by himself (*Fab* 107). He adds to this that Apollo struck and killed Achilleus with an arrow to the ankle *(talum)* "which alone mortal he is said to have had," thus giving us our first specific reference to the foot (and ankle) as the vulnerable part alluded to by Statius.

On the artistic side, we have some important early evidence which may anticipate details of the literary tradition. First is a Protocorinthian lekythos of about 670 B.C. with no names but a number of warriors in a battle scene (Athens, no #). To the left of the four main combatants an archer kneels, and an arrow he has just fired is about to strike the shin of the first of the opposing figures. Next comes a Pontic amphora from Copenhagen dating to perhaps 540 B.C.; again there are no names, but as two warriors square off against each other a third in Phrygian dress moves in from the right, aiming an arrow down toward the buttock or thigh of the man in front of him (Copenhagen 14066).[56] The third piece is a lost Chalkidian amphora, formerly in the Pembroke-Hope collection, of about the same date. Here we have quite a vigorous battle scene, with names for most of the figures. At the center lies Achilleus' corpse, with an arrow through one ankle (or more accurately the part of the foot just above the ankle) and seemingly another in his back. Over him Aias plunges his spear into Glykos (i.e., Glaukos: cf. ApE 5.4, where Aias slays this Lykian over the corpse), who had tied a rope around that same foot of Achilleus and was in process of dragging away the body. To the left Athena supervises (and Sthenelos binds up a wound of Diomedes); to the right Paris moving away in flight turns back to fire an arrow, while Aineias and other Trojans come up to help. Fourth is an Attic Red-Figure pelike by the Niobid Painter on which Paris to the left takes aim at a casually standing Achilleus to the right (Bochum S1060). Neither figure is named, but the clear presence of Apollo in the center of the composition with one hand held palm open toward Achilleus surely guarantees the moment in question (rather than for example that of *Iliad* 11 where Paris wounds Diomedes in the foot), and Paris here even wears a laurel crown like his divine patron. Though he draws back an arrow to fire again, one has already been released, and drops downward ominously toward Achilleus' foot (perhaps guided by the god?).

Taken together, these four pots would seem to leave little doubt that Achilleus was wounded in the foot (and that Glaukos was slain by Aias in the fight over the corpse) at an early point in the tradition. That being the case, we might well hypothesize that Apollodoros' account with its references to Glaukos and Achilleus' ankle is taken more or less directly from the *Aithiopis*. But it should then follow (given that in the *Aithiopis* as in the *Iliad* Apollo helps) that the wound to the foot is deliberate, rather than (as when Paris wounds Diomedes) an off-center shot to a peripheral part of the body.[57] In other words, if Paris did in the *Aithiopis* strike Achilleus' ankle with divine aid, he did so surely because only there could Achilleus be slain, and only with Apollo's assistance could he hope to hit such a difficult target. Seemingly then, at least one early version did know of Thetis' attempt to make her son physically invulnerable. As an alternative, certain points in the *Iliad* have been thought to support the theory that in some accounts it was Achilleus' armor, the work of the gods, which was invulnerable (thus explaining Patroklos' necessary loss of it before his defeat).[58] In that case we might suppose that Apollo simply guided Paris' arrow to one small part of Achilleus' (very vulnerable) body not covered by his invulnerable armor, and that this arrangement was somehow transformed into or replaced by the concept of the (almost) invulnerable body.

Complicating both these views, however, and all other accounts of Achilleus' death, there stands the puzzling fact that a vulnerable ankle ought not to be the cause of a *fatal* wound, as opposed to a disabling one; we need only to compare Diomedes, who simply limps off the field of battle after Paris puts an arrow through his foot in *Iliad* 11. True, Quintus of Smyrna does have Achilleus expire from such an ankle wound (after fighting on bravely for a considerable time: QS 3.60–185), but such overblown rhetorical elaboration is probably the result of accepting a long-standing tradition without the magic behind it. What we really need, if this fatal blow to the ankle is to make sense, is a story in which the hero's vital organs are displaced to a part of his body where his opponents will not expect to find them, or against which they will have difficulty mounting an assault. Perhaps in such a story the obtaining of personal invulnerability required as a tradeoff that one vulnerable spot be left in which all the recipient's vitality could be concentrated, with of course fatal results if anyone learned the location of that spot. But this kind of motif, if it did exist for Achilleus, has clearly been lost, and could never have been accounted for by the bath in the Styx, which will at best explain only the child's quasi-invulnerability. I suspect then that already at an early point the full magical ramifications of Achilleus' peculiar situation have dropped out of the tradition, leaving behind a vulnerable ankle that somewhat implausibly remains the cause of his death. If that is so, then the bath may have been invented quite a bit later, perhaps even (as has been suggested) under the influence of Christian baptism.[59] One final point concerns the hero's better-known invulnerable *heel*. We have seen that all our evidence, both Greek and Latin, specifies the ankle, and this holds even for the Second and Third Vatican Mythographers, where the part not impregnated is the *talus* (VM II 205; VM III 11.24; VM I 178 says the *planta*, or sole of the foot). But seemingly the referent of *talus* shifted downward in the later Latin form *talone*, as the modern French *(talon)* and Italian *(tallone)* words for "heel" would indicate.

Added to this uncertain picture is the fact that late authors also offer quite a different version of Achilleus' death, one based on his desire for Priam's daughter Polyxena. Our best sources for this story are the scholia to the *Hekabe*, Hyginus, Servius, and Lactantius, plus the uncertainly dated Diktys and Dares. The *Hekabe* scholia suggest that, according to some, Achilleus died in the precinct of Thymbraian Apollo while he was negotiating with Priam for the hand of Polyxena in marriage (Σ *Hek* 41). Servius adds that Achilleus first saw her when she came with her father to ransom Hektor's body, was falsely promised her hand if he would stop the war, and on coming to the precinct of Apollo for the treaty was slain by Paris from ambush (with an arrow: Σ *Aen* 3.322); Lactantius has Paris hiding behind a statue in the precinct when he commits the deed (aiming, as we saw, at the vulnerable ankle: Σ *Ach* 1.134). Hyginus' very brief note (given only as an explanation of Polyxena's sacrifice) is vaguer, but Achilleus is here again slain by Paris (and Deiphobos) when he comes (somewhere) to discuss a union with their sister (*Fab* 110). In Diktys' pro-Greek version, Achilleus first sees Polyxena by chance at a religious festival and offers to bring the war to an end if he might marry her (Dik 3.2). Nothing comes of this, but Priam later brings Polyxena with him when he arrives to fetch his son's body, and asks Achilleus to keep her with him (Dik 3.27). Achilleus defers that decision for the moment, and Priam subsequently sends some sort of message to him on the subject in the Thymbraion via the herald Idaios. Paris and Deiphobos take advantage of the situation to approach Achilleus in the same precinct as if bringing a further communication; Deiphobos seizes and immobilizes him in an embrace so that Paris coming forward may stab him in the side (Dik 4.10–11). Dares' pro-Trojan version begins in much the same way, with Achilleus first seeing Polyxena when she and her parents come to pay honor at the tomb of Hektor. He proposes that he will personally abandon the war in return for her hand; Priam counters that only a complete cessation of hostilities will suffice. The issue is then dropped, but later Hekabe, angered at the death of Lykaon and Troilos, sends a message in Priam's name asking Achilleus to come to the same precinct of Apollo to discuss the marriage (Dar 34). When he and Anticholos arrive, they are overwhelmed by superior forces and cut down by Paris in person. Conceivably this variant mode of death was created to explain the otherwise rather unusual sacrifice of Priam's daughter at the tomb of Achilleus, an event found already in the *Iliou Persis*; certainly such a demise was not part of the *Aithiopis*, where Proklos' summary guarantees that Achilleus died on the battlefield.[60]

With Achilleus now dead, however that event was brought about, the *Aithiopis* proceeds to the struggle over his body and the wondrous armor. We are told by Proklos that after a considerable battle Aias, shouldering the corpse, brought it back to the ships, with Odysseus holding off the Trojans to the rear (this last also at *Od* 5.308–10). Antilochos was then buried and Achilleus laid in state for the mourning of Thetis, the other Nereides, and the Mousai, after which Thetis snatched her son from the funeral pyre and took him away to the White Island (or perhaps in the original an island named Leuke). The Achaians piled up a mound nonetheless and held funeral games, and then Odysseus and Aias disputed the disposition of his armor. Proklos' summary of the *Aithiopis* ends here, but a Pindaric scholion, if trustworthy, would have the poem include the suicide of Aias (toward dawn: *Aith* fr 5 *PEG*). We know in any case that the following poem, the *Little Iliad* of Lesches, began with the contest for the arms and that same suicide. Here Odysseus wins by the contriving of Athena, and being maddened Aias outrages the herds of the Achaians and then kills himself. Scholia add that in the poem Nestor recommended the sending of spies to listen under the walls of Troy to Trojan opinions of the disputing heroes; these heard one maiden comment on Aias' valor in carrying back Achilleus when Odysseus was unwilling to do so, but heard another (inspired by Athena) respond that even women can carry burdens, but not everyone can fight (*IlMik* fr 2 *PEG*, with *apparatus*). We learn elsewhere that because of the anger of the king, Aias' body was buried in a coffin rather than being cremated (*IlMik* fr 3 *PEG*). Interestingly enough, a papyrus fragment from what is apparently early epic suggests that in at least one account Odysseus actually was the one to carry back the body (*IlMik* fr 32 [*dubium*] *PEG*; cf. Σ *Od* 5.310).

The *Odyssey* has its own version of a few of these events, for Odysseus on seeing Aias in the Underworld notes the latter's continued anger over the contest for Achilleus' arms, which Thetis proposed and *paides Trôôn* plus Athena judged (*Od* 11.543–60).[61] His further words make it clear that Aias perished on account of those arms, but he does not say how, nor is there any mention of madness. Scholia to this passage expand Odysseus' account a bit by suggesting that Agamemnon specifically asked Trojan prisoners which hero had harmed them most; with no source given we might perhaps suspect this to be the version of the *Aithiopis* (Σ *Od* 11.547). *Odyssey* 24 also contains a description of Achilleus' burial by Agamemnon, who tells us that after a whole day of contending over the body Zeus sent a storm, and the Achaians brought the corpse back to the ships (*Od* 24.36–92). There they washed it, and (as in the *Aithiopis*) Thetis, the Nereides, and the nine Mousai arrived, here lamenting for seventeen days. On the eighteenth, the Achaians cremated the body and placed the bones together with those of Patroklos in a golden jar contributed by Thetis, and after the mound had been piled up Thetis obtained prizes from the gods for funeral games. That Thetis does not then snatch the body off the pyre, as she does in the *Aithiopis*, is only to be expected, given that for both *Odyssey* 11 and 24, Achilleus' shade is in the Underworld like that of any other mortal. Apollodoros' epitomator says, rather oddly, that the *Achaians* buried Achilleus and Patroklos together on the White Island (possibly compression is responsible for this) and that in the games in his honor Eumelos won the chariot race, Diomedes the stadion, Aias the diskos throw, and Teukros the archery contest (ApE 5.5). We have already noted the evidence from other Archaic authors (Ibykos 291 *PMG*; Simonides 558 *PMG*) concerning Achilleus' life with Medeia after death, and likewise in Pindar he has a blessed existence (*Ol* 2.79–80; *Nem* 4.49–50; cf. *IlMik* fr 32 [*dubium*] *PEG*).

Aias' downfall continues as an important theme in the fifth century, when both Aischylos and Sophokles compose plays on his fate and Pindar offers some strong comments in his defense. Once again Aischylos seems to have composed a trilogy, consisting of *Hoplôn Krisis* ("Judgment of Arms"), *Threissai*, and *Salaminiai*. The first play certainly presented the dispute, with Aias casting aspersions on Odysseus' ancestry (fr 175 R) and the Nereides *perhaps* serving as judges (someone does call upon them to do so: fr 174 R). In the second occurred the suicide, with Athena or some other female divinity showing Aias the one place where he was vulnerable (the armpit: fr 83 R). For the third drama we do not even know the location, much less the plot; it may have been at Troy, on the island of Salamis when Teukros returned home, or even on Cyprus, and (depending in part on location) Aias' burial, or Teukros' concern for him, may or may not have been issues. Pindar speaks of the vote in two odes written for Aiginetans: *Nemean* 7.23–30 asserts that the Achaians were blind to the truth when they valued Odysseus above Aias, causing the latter to commit suicide, while *Nemean* 8.21–32 suggests that lies were told, to make the Danaans favor Odysseus with their secret vote when Aias clearly did more to win back Achilleus' body. Both in these poems and in *Isthmian* 4, where Aias' suicide in the night (by throwing himself on his sword) is said to have brought reproach to the Greeks at Troy, Pindar seems to suppose that the Achaians themselves made the decision (although since he criticizes that decision, we can hardly expect him to stress Athena's role).

Sophokles' preserved *Aias* (produced in the 440s B.C.?) gives us our first full account of the story. The play begins with Odysseus gingerly approaching the tent of Aias, after the army has become alarmed over the slaughter of some of their flocks. It is thus the night after the judgment, and Athena comes to inform her favorite hero of the situation. We learn from this and other parts of the play that here too, as in Pindar, the Achaian leaders themselves voted (as they may have done in the *Aithiopis*, the *Hoplôn Krisis*, and even perhaps in the *Odyssey* and *Little Iliad*, if the Trojan opinions there were simply advisory), and that Aias believes Odysseus and the Atreidai to have unfairly influenced the result against him. Accordingly, he has plotted to strike at the leaders that night in their sleep, and only here has Athena intervened, sending madness to turn him instead against the flocks, which he mistakenly believes are the Achaians. At the height of this folly he has dragged a particularly large ram back to his tent in the belief that it is Odysseus, and proceeds to lash it with a whip. Athena invites Odysseus to exult at his enemy's ruin, but he is more horrified at the downfall of a comrade and fellow mortal. Aias' delusion now ends, and realizing what he has done he determines on suicide, despite the appeals of his concubine Tekmessa, by whom he has a son Eurysakes. The deed is carried out at the beach, where he throws himself on his sword, and the second half of the play revolves around a conflict between the Atreidai, who have forbidden burial, and Teukros. The dispute is only resolved when Odysseus reappears and asks burial for his fallen opponent as a personal favor, arguing that it is not right to carry hatred past the limit of death.

The play thus emerges as something of a contrast between Aias' steadfast intransigence and Odysseus' flexibility, with the latter's viewpoint seemingly more effective. For Athena's treatment of Aias, moreover, the one defense offered is that Aias once dismissed her offer of help on the battlefield, claiming that he by himself would be sufficient (*Ai* 770–77). We saw above that madness and the issue of burial were also elements of the *Little Iliad*, but we do not know if the madness there was of the same type (Proklos does not say what Aias supposed himself to be doing when he attacked the herds), nor whether there was any protest at the proposal for inhumation. Apollodoros is here again too brief to be of much help, and what he does offer is as in Sophokles, but we do find repeated as well the detail of the *Little Iliad* that on Agamemnon's order Aias (alone of all the Achaians) was buried in a coffin (ApE 5.7).

As for Aias' near invulnerability, no writer before the fifth century preserves any trace of it (although it may be hinted at in art: see below), and Homer certainly excludes it (*Il* 23.820–23). Aischylos thus is our first certain source for the idea. But in Pindar's *Isthmian* 6, Herakles comes to the house of Telamon and prays that his friend might have a child as unbreakable in form as the hide of the Nemean Lion (*Is* 6.42–49). Possibly such words are simply a request for strength, and the scholia do not elaborate, but under the circumstances they should probably be taken as an allusion to the impenetrability of the Lion's hide and that of the child. That Herakles' visit was the occasion on which Aias became invulnerable is at any rate the view of Lykophron, who says that Herakles' prayer was made after Aias was already born, that he held the child in his arms, that the lionskin conferred the invulnerability, and that the one place where Aias could be killed was the part covered by Herakles' quiver (Lyk 455–61). The scholia clarify this somewhat by adding that Herakles wrapped the child in the skin, and that the part not covered was either by the ribs or the collarbone (cf. ΣAb *Il* 23.821). Scholia to the *Isthmian* 6 passage add that the story of Herakles' prayer as Pindar tells it is taken from the *Megalai Ehoiai* (Σ *Is* 6.53 = Hes fr 250 MW), so that the whole tale probably goes back that far; whether it was found in the *Aithiopis* or the *Little Iliad* we cannot say.[62] Aischylean in any event might still be the curious appearance of a goddess to Aias to tell him where he is vulnerable, since that information is something he might well know by himself in earlier accounts.

For these events in art we have a fine Late Corinthian hydria with Thetis and the Nereides gathered around the body of Achilleus (Louvre E643), while a problematic Athenian Black-Figure amphora of the Leagros Group with a large warrior running across the sea (there is a ship below) *may* mean to suggest Achilleus' journey to the White Island (London B240). Beyond these two pots there are a good number of representations of three other scenes, the rescue of Achilleus' body, the dispute over the arms, and Aias' suicide. For the first of these, illustrations may begin as early as the end of the eighth century, if we accept scenes of a man being carried on an ivory seal from Perachora (Athens, no #) and the repeated seal impressions on a clay vessel from Samos (T 416). Toward the middle of the seventh century we start to find more detailed, and hence more convincing, recreations of this motif: a terracotta relief from Tarentum offers us on the top band of a woman's skirt a male figure carrying on his shoulder another man (in helmet and almost twice the bearer's size) (Naples, no #). The same disproportion appears even more vividly on several slightly varying shield-band reliefs from Olympia, where the bearer wears corselet and greaves, the corpse a chain-link corselet and helmet (B 1921, B 1911), and on a terracotta mold from Lemnos (1205), both of the second half of the century. In no case are there names, but nothing at any point in our tradition assigns this role to anyone but Aias, while the large size of the deceased (in the absence of any known story involving the porting of oversized opponents; Alkyoneus would not be armed) seems an early attempt to convey Achilleus' stature as a fighter.

By the sixth century Thetis' son assumes more normal dimensions in this scene, as we see on both handles of the François Krater, where the names of the two men are included (Florence 4209). Here Aias is in the *knielauf* position (looking quite elegant) and Achilleus without arms; probably Kleitias wished by this latter device to increase the pathos of his death. Subsequently, Exekias produced a powerful version of his own, with a fully armed Aias bent under the weight of a fully armed and very heavy-looking Achilleus (Munich 1470: both sides). The face of Aias is all but hidden by his shield in each version, and the effort involved, in contrast to the opinion of Lesches' Trojan maidens, is very pointed. The same artist assayed yet another version of this tableau for a lost amphora once in Berlin (Berlin:Lost F1718); his general compositional scheme seems to have set the fashion for virtually all future illustrations of the story. In later Black-Figure portrayals, there are supporting figures, including at times one who might be Odysseus, but it cannot be said that his role is at all emphasized. The only other figural scheme illustrating this story is that of Aias beginning to lift the body of Achilleus from the ground, or supporting him on one arm, as on an odd late sixth-century amphora in Munich on which the dead Achilleus is shown full face, looking more like a Satyros than a human (Munich 1415).

The dispute over Achilleus' arms, while obviously known to epic tradition and possibly illustrated as early as the Melos amphora discussed above (Athens 3961), cannot be identified with absolute certainty in art until the Red-Figure period, when several Attic cups offer the spectacle of partially armed warriors drawing swords against each other while their comrades (including a bearded man in the center) try to restrain them (Douris: Vienna 3695; Brygos Painter: Getty 86.AE.286; London E69). By themselves these representations could intend as well combats in funeral games for Patroklos or Achilleus, but in each case we see on the other side of the cup the voting for the arms, thus virtually guaranteeing that at some point the dispute between Aias and Odysseus threatened to resolve itself by force. Conceivably this notion was suggested by the dramatic trilogy of Aischylos, but against such a theory are a small number of Black-Figure pots where we find the same sort of scheme, albeit without an accompanying vote. In this category are a lekythos from the third quarter of the sixth century (two naked men oppose each other with swords, a third stands between with a spear or staff; armor on the ground: Berlin:Lost F2000), an amphora of the last quarter (two old men restraining in the center, while younger men to each side pull on the sword arms of the disputants, who are fully armed: Munich 1411), and an oinochoe of the same period (combatants again naked except for swords, and numerous restrainers: Louvre F340). In neither of the last two cases are any arms shown as prizes or spoils, but it seems a reasonable conjecture that all three pots represent the conflict, an event that perhaps led the Achaian leaders to agree to decide the disposition of the arms.

A first stage of that disposition appears on a late (*c.* 500 B.C.) Black-Figure pelike with Odysseus (named) standing on a platform and arguing his case while Aias (also named) listens (arms between them: Naples 81083). The vote itself then follows on several Red-Figure cups, including the above-mentioned pieces by Douris and the Brygos Painter: on all of these a platform or low block stands in the center, and at one end or the other the Greeks place their pebbles as ballots, approaching from both sides. At least three examples feature Athena in the center, supervising the process; Aias stands off to the side and puts his head in his hand as he sees the vote going against him. I suggested above that the threat of decision by combat probably preceded the resort to a vote, but of course it could also have come afterward, with Aias attacking Odysseus in his frustration at losing.

Finally, we turn to artistic versions of the suicide. Aias is the only figure in mythology known to have thrown himself on his sword, so that the surprisingly large corpus of such representations all presumably illustrate this story (on a steatite intaglio from the latter seventh century he is in fact named: NY 42.11.13). Oldest in time is certainly a Protocorinthian aryballos of about 700 B.C. which shows Aias slanting across a vertical sword amid a general parade of unrelated figures (Berlin:PM VI 3319). Subsequently, there are quite a number of Corinthian offerings, including the "Eurytios" krater of about 600 B.C. on which warriors in poses of astonishment stand to either side of the transfixed Aias (Louvre E635); the sword point here seems split in two, perhaps suggesting early knowledge of the (almost) invulnerable hero found in Aischylos. A Middle Corinthian cup of the early sixth century also shows a number of Greeks (named) flanking the prostrate corpse: Phoinix and Nestor are closest, seeming almost to remonstrate with each other, then Odysseus and Diomedes to the left and Agamemnon, Teukros, and Aias (obviously the son of Oileus) to the right (Basel, Loan). Meanwhile, the scheme of the krater resurfaces on shield-band reliefs from Olympia, with again warriors facing each other over the corpse, hands held out (Aias himself has his face touchingly buried in his hands: B 1636, B 1654). The death even appears on an unfinished metope from Foce del Sele (no #), where Aias, here all alone, leans awkwardly over the upright sword. From Athens there is above all the amphora by Exekias showing not the fact of death but rather Aias carefully planting the sword in the ground, his whole attention wrapped up in that one deliberate act (Boulogne 558). Less poignant but still affecting is a Red-Figure lekythos of about 460 B.C. on which, the sword now planted, the intended suicide kneels and holds both hands up to the sky (Basel, Loan). In a masterful tondo by the Brygos Painter, on the other hand, we see Aias lying on his back, with the sword protruding upwards from his chest, while a woman (surely Tekmessa) prepares to spread a cloak over him (Getty 86.AE.286). The entry of the sword from the back is here clearly more appropriate to a murder than a suicide, thus prompting some scholars to think rather of Klytaimestra and Agamemnon.[63] But the woman's gesture seems one of tenderness, an empty scabbard to upper right suggests that the sword was the man's own, and (as we have already seen) the outside of this cup presented the quarrel over the arms and the vote. Finally, an Etruscan mirror of the early fourth century depicts the moment of suicide (and Aias' invulnerability): the sword clearly bends back against his chest as Athena appears, her hand outstretched to indicate (one presumes) the correct spot (Boston 99.494).

One other story (if it is that), to be mentioned here for want of a better place, is the game of dice or draughts between Aias and Achilleus. The confrontation appears only in art, beginning about 550 B.C. with a Black-Figure cup now in the Vatican (343). The scene of fully armed warriors seated or crouching with a small gaming table between them appears on both sides; on one of these, other warriors and older men look on, while on the reverse the warriors turn away, as if heading out to battle. Only nonsense inscriptions appear here, but the famous Vatican amphora by Exekias, which shows the two men alone, leaning intently over the table on which their tokens lie, provides the names of Aias and Achilleus (Vat 344). By the 520s B.C. a central Athena has been added to the composition (overseeing the game or calling the warriors to battle?) and knucklebones are sometimes in use. In all, there are over 125 vase-paintings of the scene, plus Olympia shield-band reliefs (B 4810) and probably a statue group (including Athena) on the Akropolis in the last decade of the sixth century.[64] Most likely, the moment intended is that before Achilleus' last battle, but it is difficult to think of a literary plot line in which such an event could hold much importance, unless Achilleus and Aias played for some stakes (such as Achilleus' armor after he died?). The sudden spate of illustrations in the latter part of the sixth century may argue rather for a fanciful invention by a sculptor or monumental painter.

Next in the sequence of events charted for us by the *Little Iliad* comes the capture by Odysseus of the Trojan Helenos, son of Priam, "from ambush." Already in the *Kypria* Helenos possessed prophetic skills (mentioned only once by Homer: *Il* 6.76), and so too here, for he predicts something that leads Diomedes to sail back to Lemnos for Philoktetes. Returning to Troy, Philoktetes is healed of his wound by Machaon and slays Paris in a single combat; Paris' corpse is then maltreated in some way by Menelaos but recovered by the Trojans for burial. We saw above that the *Iliad* too knows of this return, although without offering any details (*Il* 2.721–25). No other treatments of the story surface until the fifth century, when Pindar uses it as an exhortation to Hieron in his *Pythian* 1, and all three of the major tragedians dramatize the envoy to Lemnos. Pindar's allusion, in an ode composed for a chariot victory in 470 B.C., presents us with the surprising idea that Philoktetes is not healed when he fights at Troy: "But now he [Hieron] has gone to war in the fashion of Philoktetes. For even the proud courted that man under necessity, and they say that godlike heroes went to bring him from Lemnos, worn out though he was from his wound. And he sacked Troy and brought an end to the Achaians' labors, plying a strengthless frame, for so it was fated" (*Py* 1.50–55). The scholia note here that Hieron was at the time suffering from some form of stones, and probably Pindar has himself changed the myth on this one occasion for the sake of the analogy, since his purpose is to encourage Hieron to endure his malady. The same scholia also tell us that a dithyramb by Bakchylides contained this story, and that there Philoktetes was brought back because Helenos had prophesied that Troy would not fall without the bow of Herakles (fr 7 SM).

Of the three dramatic versions of the tale only that of Sophokles survives, but we do have the two discourses by Dion of Prusa noted above, one comparing the three plays, the other reproducing in dialogue form material almost certainly from the prologue of Euripides' effort (DP 52, 59). From the comparison we learn less about the plays than we might have hoped, but we can say that in Aischylos the chorus consisted of men of Lemnos, and that Odysseus himself played the primary role in separating Philoktetes from his weapons and so persuading him to come back. This he was able to accomplish because Philoktetes failed to recognize him after so much time, and he took advantage of the fact to fabricate a story in which Agamemnon was dead, Odysseus charged with some sort of base deed, and the army in general in a wretched condition. Such deception apparently served the purpose of cheering up Philoktetes and making him more trusting of his visitor, but we do not know anything else of Aischylos' plot, in particular how reluctant Philoktetes was or was not to return and how Odysseus managed to persuade him. Dion's failure to mention any other characters does suggest that the play had only two

actors, and perhaps only two main roles. Euripides' drama was probably written before that of Sophokles, given the late (409 B.C.) date of the latter, and
took advantage of the third actor to have Odysseus and Diomedes come together. Odysseus has here been disguised by Athena so that Philoktetes will
not recognize him, and the chorus again consists of Lemnians, who apologize
at some point for having ignored Philoktetes for so many years. Discourse 59
adds to this picture a dialogue between Odysseus and Philoktetes which reproduces closely four of the fragments actually attributed to Euripides' play, and
is thus surely modeled on the prologue of that work, which we know to have
been spoken by Odysseus.

In this discourse, Odysseus muses on the difficulties that a reputation for
wisdom brings, since such men are always embroiled in difficult situations as
the most likely to succeed. As in Bakchylides, Helenos has named Herakles'
bow (and apparently Philoktetes as well) as necessary to the taking of Troy, and
while Odysseus at first refuses the mission because he himself abandoned the
wounded hero, Athena persuades him to change his mind. The situation is
complicated, however, by the fact that the Trojans are themselves in process of
sending a delegation to Lemnos, hoping to persuade Philoktetes to come back
with them so that Troy will never fall (Dion attests this to be a Euripidean
innovation). Odysseus' story to Philoktetes is that he is an Achaian driven
from the Greek camp by Odysseus because he was a friend of Palamedes,
whom Odysseus has destroyed. Somehow he has managed to arrive alone on
Lemnos in his flight, and Philoktetes calls upon him to share his own lot for
the moment. Philoktetes adds that the pain from his foot is not as great as it
once was, but here the dialogue ends, and once again we know nothing about
the resolution of the play, save that a Lemnian named Aktor who was known
to Philoktetes made an appearance.

In Sophokles' drama, Odysseus is again the leader of the expedition, but
here he has brought with him Neoptolemos rather than Diomedes. As we will
see in the next section, the summoning of Neoptolemos from Skyros to Troy
happens in the *Little Iliad* only *after* Philoktetes' return, so that Sophokles has
altered the epic chronology. A second innovation concerns the island of Lemnos, now completely deserted save for Philoktetes; the chorus consists of the
Achaian sailors who came with Odysseus and Neoptolemos. But as before,
Philoktetes hates the Greeks who abandoned him, and Odysseus' plan is that
Neoptolemos carry out the necessary deception by acknowledging his identity
but claiming to have left Troy in anger after the Atreidai and Odysseus refused
to give him his father's armor. Although Odysseus does not say what precisely
he thinks this tale will accomplish, Philoktetes' response is to ask to be taken
back to Greece on Neoptolemos' ship, a wish intensified by the arrival of a
sailor from Odysseus with the news that the Greeks are coming for Philoktetes.
So far this is as we might expect, but Philoktetes then gives Neoptolemos his
bow to hold while he rests after an attack of pain, and Odysseus, finding the
bow in Neoptolemos' hands, declares that the weapon alone will suffice, if Phi-

loktetes refuses to come to Troy with it. Whether he believes this or is simply bluffing to frighten Philoktetes we never learn, for Neoptolemos balks at depriving a crippled man of his only means of support and gives the bow back, over Odysseus' protests. He does also, however, try to persuade Philoktetes that it will be in his own interest to come back to Troy, citing Helenos' prophecy and the glory he will win there and revealing now for the first time, toward the close of the play, that Philoktetes can be cured of his terrible wound if he will consent to come. Yet Philoktetes still refuses, and only the appearance of the divine Herakles at the play's close convinces him that what is fated must after all be carried out. As such, the drama is as much a study of Neoptolemos' character under pressure and temptation as it is of Philoktetes, and Sophokles is likely to have invented a good many of the details of his plot to serve that purpose. We should note, though, that other playwrights of the fifth century (e.g., Achaios, Philokles) also wrote dramas entitled *Philoktetes*, and we cannot say what they may have added to the tradition. Later writers offer us nothing of any interest on the matter of the actual fetching, adhering as they do to one or other of the above authors; for what it is worth, Apollodoros sends Odysseus and Diomedes to fetch the bow and wounded hero.

As for the events following Philoktetes' return, namely his physical recovery and the death of Paris, we know that Sophokles wrote a *Philoktetes at Troy* that must have covered some of this material. The scanty fragments show that the hero still suffered from the excruciating pain of his wound for at least part of the play, and it seems to have been a matter of some concern to him. Given the difficulties in finding much tragedy in this situation if he knows he is to be cured, we might conjecture that he does not know (in contrast to the later Sophoklean play set on Lemnos), and that he spends much of the drama lamenting his condition. If so, the work will have had a difficult time finding room for the combat with Paris, save as a prophecy, and perhaps that was how matters were handled. But equally, the combat may have held center stage as the primary event. Either way, the confrontation between Philoktetes and Paris offers one puzzle. The language of our summary of the *Little Iliad* certainly implies that these two noted archers fought a duel, which one would expect to be a traditional combat with sword and spear (*monomachia* as found here is the term used in the Alexandrian book headings of the *Iliad* for the single combats between Menelaos and Paris and Aias and Hektor, i.e., combats fought while the rest of the army watched). In that case, it seems certainly odd that both men should change weapons (especially when Philoktetes' bow is the presumed key to his success) and that these two in particular should be chosen to meet. Diktys, however, does present a single combat with bows (Dik 4.19), and conceivably this was after all the epic version as well; Paris is here wounded in the left hand, then the right eye, and finally both feet (cf. Σ Lyk 911). On the *Tabula Iliaca Capitolina*, a pictorial relief from Augustan times with scenes supposedly drawn from the *Little Iliad* (as well as from Homer, Arktinos, and Stesichoros), we do see a figure who must be Paris falling backward in death with a bow in his hand,[65] but we cannot say how precisely the artist (or his pictorial sources) would have followed the original text. Lykophron and Apollodoros report simply that Philoktetes did shoot Paris with an arrow (Lyk 914–15; ApE 5.8).

Other differences between Apollodoros' version and epic are the curing of Philoktetes by Podaleirios, not his brother Machaon (necessary because in Apollodoros Machaon is by this point already dead, having been killed by Penthesileia) and the delivery of the prophecy about Philoktetes and the taking of Troy by Kalchas, not Helenos. This last change probably stems from the incorporation of an event (related first by Konon and then Apollodoros) which requires Helenos' presence in Troy at this moment (and for some time after): following Paris' death he and Deiphobos contend for Helen's hand, and when Deiphobos is chosen (Konon says by force and intriguing, although he was younger), Helenos leaves Troy for Ida in anger (26F1.34; ApE 5.9). He is, however, captured by Odysseus on Kalchas' recommendation, and delivers various prophecies about Troy's fall to which we shall return in the next section. Servius at *Aeneid* 2.166 gives much the same account, adding that Priam assigned Helen to Deiphobos, and that once captured Helenos revealed the secret of the Palladion out of hatred. Obviously, the *Little Iliad* cannot have told this story of a dispute over Helen, for there Helenos is captured by the Greeks before Paris dies; where Konon and Apollodoros might have found such a tale we do not know.

One other sequence of events connected with Paris' death can likewise not have come from the *Little Iliad*, where he clearly dies on the battlefield and his corpse is disfigured by Menelaos before its recovery for burial. The key figure in this sequence is Oinone, daughter of Kebren, about whom Parthenios tells two tales. In the first, which he credits to Hellanikos and Kephalon (i.e., the Hellenistic Hegesianax[66]), Korythos, Paris' son by Oinone, comes to Troy to fight and is much taken by Helen, who receives him quite kindly, since he is very attractive (Par 34 = 4F29, 45F6). On discovering this fact, Paris kills him. The author then adds that according to Nikandros Korythos was instead the son of Paris and Helen, and offers a quote to prove it. In the second tale, credited to Kephalon and Nikandros, Paris is actually married to Oinone before he abducts Helen (Par 4 = 45F2). This former love possesses for whatever reason the gift of prophecy, and foretells to Paris that he will leave her to find a bride in Europe, thus bringing war to his people and to himself a wound in battle which only she can heal. Matters proceed as she predicts, he is wounded by Philoktetes' arrows and, remembering her words, sends a messenger to ask for her help. She replies that he would do better to seek help from Helen, whom he preferred to her, and hearing this refusal from the messenger he dies. When she sees that he is indeed dead she laments bitterly and kills herself.

Konon has a fuller version (or combination) of these two tales, as perhaps Hegesianax before him, with Paris and Oinone parents of a child Korythos who surpasses his father in beauty (26F1.23). His mother deliberately sends him to

Helen at Troy, hoping to make Paris jealous and create trouble with his new wife. This in fact happens, for Paris, entering their bedroom one day, sees Korythos sitting next to Helen and, inflamed by suspicion, kills him. On hearing of her son's death, Oinone proclaims that Paris will one day need her when he is wounded by the Greeks. The rest of the story proceeds as in Parthenios, with Paris carried toward Mount Ida in a wagon and the messenger going on ahead. Here, however, Oinone has a change of heart after sending the messenger away and arrives with the necessary herbs too late, hanging herself when she learns of Paris' death. The latter part of this story is certainly as early as Lykophron, who speaks of the jealous bride, skilled in healing, who threw herself from a high tower to share the death of her bedmate Paris, although Lykophron deviates from Parthenios in making Oinone send her son "to inform about the land," apparently telling the Greeks how they may find Troy (Lyk 57–68). The scholia to this passage offer nothing not found in Konon and Parthenios, save that Oinone was hindered by her father when she wished to heal Paris.

Apollodoros gives much the same version as Konon, but without mention of any son; Oinone, daughter of Kebren (the river), having learned the art of prophecy from Rheia, warns Paris against abducting Helen; he fails to heed her, is wounded by Philoktetes, and appeal, death, and repentant suicide follow (ApB 3.12.6). In Ovid's *Heroides,* too, the son is absent; Oinone speaks of a marriage with Paris while he was still an unknown shepherd, and laments his abandonment of her for Helen (*Her* 5). The tale as a whole has an obvious overlay of Hellenistic romanticism, but although it cannot have been told in the *Little Iliad,* we cannot say for certain that it is not in some form as old as the Archaic period.[67] If Hellanikos on the evidence guarantees for us only a son of Paris by Oinone whom his father rashly kills, at least this means that the union of Paris and Oinone was known in his time.

*The Last
Events
before
the Sack*

By all accounts, whether there was a dispute or not, Helen does marry Deiphobos after the death of Paris; probably this was known even to the author of the *Odyssey,* for the story of Helen's attempt to reveal the secret of the Wooden Horse includes the fact that Deiphobos accompanied her there, although Menelaos does not call him her husband, and when the Achaians emerge from the Horse Odysseus and Menelaos proceed to Deiphobos' house (*Od* 4.274–76, 8.517–20).[68] Next in the *Little Iliad* comes the bringing of Neoptolemos from Skyros to Troy by Odysseus, a maneuver that may or may not have been required by Helenos for the taking of Troy. In the *Nekuia,* Odysseus tells Achilleus exactly the same story, that he himself went to Skyros to bring back the latter's son to the war (*Od* 11.508–9). The event does not surface again until Pindar's *Paian 6* (which simply confirms the summoning: *Pa* 6.98–104) and Sophokles' *Skyrioi,* for which our few fragments indicate only that someone (Lykomedes and/or Deidameia?) tries to discourage Neoptolemos from the possible dangers of following in the footsteps of his father (fr 555 R, possibly also 554 R).[69] In the same poet's *Philoktetes*, Neoptolemos himself mentions that Odysseus and Phoinix came to fetch him, offering the argument that with his father dead it would not be *themis* for Troy to fall to anyone but him (*Ph* 343–47). The timing of his arrival here, right after his father's death, is probably due to the need to make plausible the false quarrel with Odysseus over the arms. Apollodoros also has Odysseus and Phoinix undertake the mission, adding that they had to persuade Lykomedes to let his grandson go (*ApE* 5.11), and the same two Achaians are named on a Red-Figure volute krater of about 470 B.C. where they appear together with Lykomedes and his (unnamed) daughter and grandson (Ferrara 44701). In Quintus, on the other hand, the envoys are Odysseus and Diomedes, the same two who induced Achilleus to leave Skyros for the war, and the reminder of the loss of her husband does much to influence Deidameia's feelings toward this new request (*QS* 6.56–113, 7.169–393. Among other details in Quintus' lengthy account, there is a warning by Lykomedes of the dangers of the sea which matches closely the content of Sophokles' fragment 555 Radt, and scholars have suggested that his version may draw heavily from the *Skyrioi*.

To the same sentence of Proklos' summary of the *Little Iliad* relating Neoptolemos' arrival and receiving of the arms of his father from Odysseus are added the words "and Achilleus appeared as a *phantasma* to him." Presumably this means that Achilleus' ghost somehow manifested itself to Neoptolemos (rather than to Odysseus), but for what purpose we do not learn. PRylands 22 may have placed the event at Achilleus' tomb, if a substantial supplement is correct;[70] perhaps Neoptolemos went there in hopes of receiving encouragement from his dead father. In any case, Neoptolemos requires some sort of formidable opponent if he is to display his military skills; thus Eurypylos, son of Telephos, arrives to assist the Trojans, performs various heroic deeds (including in this poem, according to Pausanias, the killing of Machaon: 3.26.9 = fr 30 *PEG*[71]), and is then slain by the son of Achilleus. His defeat is recounted by Odysseus to the shade of Achilleus in the *Nekuia*, speaking of Eurypylos' magnificence and beauty (second only to Memnon), and of how many Keteians perished with him because of "womanly gifts" (*Od* 11.519–21). Homer does not explain that last phrase; the scholia credit Akousilaos with the story that Eurypylos was the son of Telephos and Astyoche, and that when Priam sought his help as the inheritor of the kingdom of Mysia his mother at first refused, until Priam sent her a golden vine (Σ *Od* 11.520 = 2F40). One line later, other *Odyssey* scholia repeat this tale, adding that the vine was a gift from Zeus to Tros in recompense for Ganymedes, that Priam had inherited it, and that Astyoche was his sister (Σ *Od* 11.521). They also, however, cite an alternative explanation for Homer's words, namely that Priam had promised Eurypylos one of his daughters in marriage, much as Kassandra was betrothed to the foreigner Othryoneus.[72] Neither of these persuasive devices is mentioned by Proklos in his summary of the *Little Iliad*, but we saw earlier in this chapter that a fragment of that poem (or similar epic: *IlMik* fr 29 *PEG*) does speak of a golden vine (the work of Hephaistos) given by Zeus to Laomedon in compensation for Ganymedes, so that Priam's gift to Eurypylos' mother was very likely the version used by Lesches.

Sophokles seems also to have treated the story of the combat, probably in a play entitled *Eurypylos* that would have brought the hero to Troy and included his death and the lamentation of his mother.[73] Elements of this drama apparently included frequent references to Telephos and his healing by the spear of Achilleus, pointed emphasis on the irony of that same spear being used by Achilleus' son to slay Telephos' son, and reproaches by Astyoche against Priam, who persuaded her (fr 211 R). Unfortunately, this last section is quite mutilated in the papyrus source, and does not quite allow us to say for certain whether her acceptance of gold in return for her son was included here.

In art we have only one early illustration, a Black-Figure hydria of about 510 B.C. on which Eurypylos already lies dead, the spear protruding from his chest, while Neoptolemos pursues his chariot (slaying the charioteer) and Apollo with drawn bow closes in from the right (Basel BS 498). Before Apollo lies the dead body of Helikaon (in the *Iliad* son of Antenor and husband of Priam's daughter Laodike [*Il* 3.121–24]); we have seen and will see again that in the *Little Iliad* Helikaon is rescued by Odysseus on the night of Troy's fall. If Apollo and the son of Achilleus did engage in a confrontation after Eurypylos' death, no literary source preserves it; Apollodoros via our epitomator says no more than we learned from Proklos (although, as we saw, he reassigns Machaon's death to Penthesileia).

Next in the *Little Iliad* we find the Trojans in desperate straits, being now truly besieged, and at this point Athena suggests to Epeios the building of the Wooden Horse. Such at least seems to be the sense of the Greek word *proairesis*, that the stratagem was at Athena's choosing. In the *Odyssey* we hear on two occasions of how Epeios built the horse, once with Athena's help, and we are told as well that Odysseus took the lead in the matter, opening and closing the hidden door and generally showing courage when other Achaians were frightened, but nowhere does Homer go so far as to say that the idea was his (*Od* 8.492–95, 11.523–27). No doubt Arktinos' *Iliou Persis* and that of Stesichoros had something to say on the subject, but we do not know what, though Arktinos does seem to have given the Horse a movable tail, knees, and eyes (fr 2 *PEG*). In Konon, the instigator is Helenos, who after his capture says that it is fated that Troy be captured by a wooden horse (26F1.34); Apollodoros on the other hand makes the conception entirely that of Odysseus, who persuades Epeios to do the building (Ap*E* 5.14). Likely his growing reputation for deceit, not just strategy, led to this shift of responsibility, but we cannot say when.

From the building of the Horse one might expect Lesches to proceed to the abandonment of the camp by the bulk of the Achaians so that the Trojans might come out to claim their trophy, but instead the *Little Iliad* offers two final adventures, both involving the infiltration of the city. In the first, Odysseus enters the city alone, disguised as a beggar, in order to spy (he has been in some way wounded or mutilated by Thoas as part of the deception); when Helen recognizes him they plot together for the destruction of the city and he returns to his own camp, after killing a number of Trojans. The second concerns the return of Odysseus with Diomedes in order to steal the Palladion, an image of Athena housed in the city. Why Odysseus should need to spy, or what he hopes to learn, is not clear. But two such similar adventures side by side might well seem tedious if they were not connected; possibly, therefore, Odysseus learned from Helen only after he had entered the city that the Palladion must be stolen, and being unable to accomplish that alone went back to camp to fetch Diomedes, with whom he returned in the dead of night. Alternatively, Odysseus may have known already from Helenos of the need to secure the Palladion and ventured into the city in disguise to scout out its location or otherwise plan the theft, with Helen offering assistance after she recognized him.[74] Apollodoros follows at least the logic of this latter proposal, for he compresses matters into one foray in which Odysseus leaves Diomedes outside the walls while he goes in with his disguise, steals the Palladion with the aid of Helen, and uses Diomedes' aid to get it back to the ships (ApE 5.13).[75]

In *Odyssey* 4, Helen relates the story of the visit (not the theft), but tells us little more than Lesches, namely that Odysseus entered the city disguised, was recognized by her alone, admitted his identity after she had washed and anointed him and sworn not to betray him, and then revealed to her the *nous* of the Achaians (Od 4.242–64). Here too as in Lesches he kills Trojans before departing, and when he has left, Helen is pleased at the thought of rejoining her husband. This claim by her, combined with the word *nous*, which should properly mean here a plan, strongly suggests that Odysseus has told her about the Horse, as Lesches' account also leads us to suppose. Such a conclusion may seem contradicted for the *Odyssey* by Menelaos' subsequent story of how Helen and Deiphobos tried to trick the Greeks inside the Horse into giving themselves away. But this contradiction is already inherent in *Odyssey* 4, to whatever end, given that Helen herself claims she was longing at that point to return to her first husband. That she says nothing of the Palladion may indicate that even as early as the *Odyssey* Odysseus' role in that venture was not entirely glorious (see below).

Euripides' *Hekabe* provides the next bit of evidence about the first mission: Hekabe there asserts that when Odysseus came to spy, Helen did reveal his identity to her, and that he was thus forced to supplicate her for his life, which she granted (Hek 239–50). Why the Trojan queen should be so charitable is not explained, and since she here mentions the incident in order to reproach Odysseus pointedly for failing to save Polyxena in return, we may well suspect that Euripides invented the whole idea. The (interpolated) list of plays drawn from the *Little Iliad* in Aristotle's *Poetics* includes *Ptocheia (Begging)* that must have been based on the spy mission, but we know nothing about it (Poet 23.1459b6). The list also cites a *Lakainai*, and this we do know to have been composed by Sophokles, and to have dealt with the theft of the

Palladion. Our one really informative fragment reveals that two people entered Troy together through a sewer (fr 367 R), while the title of the play can only mean that they contacted or were found by Helen after they got in, since her attendants must have been the chorus. A second fragment justifying the Greek position in the war might, however, more logically be addressed to a Trojan (fr 368 R), and later sources (e.g., Σb *Il* 6.311) do make Theano the one to hand the image over, after Diomedes and Odysseus have purportedly come on an embassy to Priam (cf. Σ Lyk 658, where Antenor serves as middle-man). Finally, an unplaced fragment in which Odysseus reviles the ancestry of Diomedes (fr 799 R) has caused some scholars to suppose the subsequent quarrel over the Palladion took place here as well, but of course such a speech might appear in a number of contexts.

Servius at *Aeneid* 2.166 confirms the fact that in some accounts Diomedes and Odysseus were thought to have entered the city through a sewer, while Aristophanes in the *Sphekes* probably refers to the same idea (so the scholia) in describing one of Philokleon's attempts to break out of his house, dressed like Odysseus in rags (*Sph* 350–51). That rags and sewer should be part of the same venture here might seem to agree with Apollodoros' account of just one raid, but given the oddity (clearer than in Apollodoros) of someone donning rags and then stealing surreptitiously into Troy we should probably suppose conflation of two separate expeditions for the sake of the parody. Yet the version of Aristophanes' contemporary Antisthenes, in whose *Aias* Odysseus allows slaves to beat him in the face and back and then, clad in rags, infiltrates Troy at night to steal the statue (*Aias* 6), poses the same problem in a more serious context, so that perhaps we might after all think of an earlier (if not very logical) literary source. The *Rhesos* envisions a more plausible sequence in which Odysseus' foray to get the Palladion is followed later by a completely separate mission in rags, one presumably carried out in broad daylight (*Rh* 499–507). As we noted above, though, the two separate devices for infiltrating the city can be made to work together if only Odysseus is allowed to enter first in the daytime in his rags and then again at night for the actual theft. Lykophron follows Lesches in having Thoas disfigure Odysseus for his disguise but says nothing about the Palladion; he does state that Odysseus fooled even Troy's leader, presumably Priam, with his tears (Lyk 779–85). The scholia argue that he blamed these on Agamemnon, so that he was presumably recognized as a Greek, but what sort of Greek he claimed to be we do not know.

As for the quarrel between Odysseus and Diomedes which forms the aftermath of the theft of the Palladion, the *Little Iliad* must have recounted this part of the story in some form, since Hesychios makes the poem the source of the proverbial phrase "Diomedean compulsion" which he says arose from the theft (fr 25 *PEG*).[76] But for any explanation of that expression we must turn to later sources, most explicitly the account of Konon in which we find (in complete contrast to what we have seen so far) that Diomedes stood on the shoulders of Odysseus in order to climb over the city wall, and then failed to pull his comrade up after him although Odysseus stretched up his hands (26F1.34). Thus he was able to secure the Palladion all by himself; to Odysseus' queries as they went back across the plain to the ships, knowing the trickery of the man, he replied that he had not taken the Palladion specified by Helenos, but another one instead. The statue itself, however, moved or stirred in some way (by the will of a god) so that Odysseus knew it to be the proper one, and being behind Diomedes he drew his sword to kill the man and bring the image back himself. But Diomedes saw his sword glitter in the moonlight and forestalled him; for the rest of the journey he made Odysseus walk ahead of him, striking him with the flat of his sword to keep him moving, and hence the origin of the proverb. Presumably we are to understand this summary account to mean that from the outset of the venture Diomedes feared treachery on Odysseus' part, and concocted the story of a second, false Palladion in hopes of discouraging any attempt to kill him for it. But we must admit that the invention is not very plausible (why has Diomedes taken the statue at all if it is not the right one?) and curious too is the statue's identification of itself, for if Athena is responsible she only exposes Odysseus to humiliation thereby.[77] Numerous later writers gloss the saying with a more or less similar story, and Servius specifies, as we assumed, that Odysseus tries to kill Diomedes because he wants all the credit for himself (Σ *Aen* 2.166).

We must note, however, that while in this tradition the second Palladion seems simply an invention of one of the characters, we *may* have literary evidence for a false Palladion already in epic: Dionysios reports that in Arktinos the real Palladion was a statue given by Zeus to Dardanos, and hidden away in an *abaton* for safekeeping while an exact duplicate was put on display; this latter image was what the Achaians stole (DH 1.69.3). Obviously such a story cuts against the run of Lesches' tale and is not entirely logical, either, for if Troy falls despite the Achaians' failure to obtain the right statue, then Helenos' prophecy is wrong. Indeed, the concept of a genuine Palladion not stolen by the Greeks serves only one real need, namely the Roman claim that the statue had been brought to Italy by Aineias, and one would normally suppose that the Romans themselves invented the story to support that claim. We must therefore consider the possibility that Dionysios is somehow mistaken in ascribing this tale to Archaic epic; perhaps he was working from an interpolated text.[78] In any case, we see that such a version requires the Achaians to be fooled by the stratagem, in contrast to Konon's account in which Diomedes claims to have taken a false Palladion but actually has the genuine article.[79]

Art has, however, a concept of this tale surprisingly different from what we have found so far.[80] On a Red-Figure cup by Makron in Leningrad Diomedes and Odysseus, at the far left and right of the scene respectively, are engaged in a vigorous dispute with drawn swords; between them, acting as peacemakers, stand Demophon, Agamemnon, Phoinix, and Akamas (Leningrad 649: all figures named). What is here remarkable is that both Diomedes and Odysseus hold a Palladion in their free arms. That Makron has not simply indulged in a bit of whimsy seems guaranteed by a similar scene on a belly amphora by the Tyszkiewicz Painter: Athena now substitutes for the restraining Achaians, and the Palladion held by the right-hand figure is just barely visible (the top of her helmet appears just above his shoulder), but there are again two such statues (Stockholm:Med 1963.1). The idea resurfaces on an Apulian oinochoe of about a hundred years later, with Athena now pointing at something, either the Palladion carried by Diomedes or (beyond him) an unidentified woman with (probably) a torch (Louvre K36). One might guess that she in some way resolves the dispute between the two warriors, for a dispute there must have been (as the Leningrad cup shows) if both Diomedes and Odysseus returned to camp with a Palladion that they claimed was the one necessary to the taking of the city. Literary support for a double theft is not entirely lacking: Ptolemaios Chennos (whom we should certainly otherwise have thought to be fabricating) says that Odysseus and Diomedes stole two of them (3.8 [p. 24 Chatzis]). Unfortunately we know nothing more about what story he recounted.

Although Theseus' sons might plausibly be added to any Attic scene of the Achaians at Troy, their special presence on the Leningrad cup (as arbiters?) has led some scholars to suppose the tale of two Palladia an Athenian invention, with Akamas and Demophon given the real image (in gratitude for their intervention?) and bringing it back to Athens to become enshrined at the court/ precinct of the Palladion southeast of the Athenian Akropolis. Were that true, however, we should expect these sons to be present also on the Stockholm amphora; Athena in the role of arbiter there suggests that it was the quarrel itself, not who resolved it, that mattered. Likewise the idea of inventing a second Palladion in order to justify the awarding of the first to the Theseidai seems unnecessarily complex; Dionysios of Samos says simply that the statue was entrusted to Demophon (15F3, apud Cl:*Pro* 4.47.6), while Pausanias reports (specifically in connection with the Palladion court) that Demophon made off with it after an inadvertent clash between his people and Diomedes' Argives as the latter returned from Troy (1.28.9).[81] Perhaps, though, the two statues represented an Athenian response to claims by other cites (such as Argos) that they possessed the true Palladion.[82] But all this is definitely speculation. Makron's tableau (and for that matter the story itself) does not seem the sort of thing easily handled by the two-actor tragedy mandatory in his time, so that his source will probably have been another medium.

We should add finally the account in the b scholia to *Iliad* 6.311, where after Odysseus and Diomedes have brought the Palladion (handed over to them by Theano) back to camp a dispute arises between Aias and Odysseus over who shall take the image home. As the hour becomes late, the statue is left with Diomedes for safekeeping until morning, but during the night Aias dies mysteriously and Odysseus is suspected. In Diktys we find many of the same details: Antenor brings the Palladion to the Achaians and after the sack Aias Telamonides (still alive), Diomedes, and Odysseus dispute ownership; Diomedes eventually withdraws, but Aias persists, and when the leaders have voted,

Odysseus is the winner. Enraged, Aias makes threats; the next morning he is found dead, with suspicion falling primarily on Odysseus. For his part, Quintus ignores the incident of the Palladion altogether.

One other requirement before Troy may fall surfaces in Lykophron and Apollodoros. Lykophron's cryptic remark says only that the city's destruction was aided by the remnants of the son of Tantalos (Lyk 52–55), but Apollodoros explains (what we would have guessed) that the Achaians were required to fetch the bones of Pelops (ApE 5.10; so too the Lykophron scholia). In this latter author, the prophecy of this need is made by Helenos, who adds to it the further tasks of the fetching of Neoptolemos and the theft of the Palladion. Conceivably, Pelops' Lydian origins have something to do with the notion of his presence if the Achaians are to capture an Asian town, but neither of these authors (nor the scholia) offers any further explanation.

*The Fall
of Troy*

In *Odyssey* 8 the blind singer Demodokos tells how the Greeks set fire to their camp and sailed away, while Odysseus and others remained hidden in the Horse (*Od* 8.499–510). The Trojans pulled this object as far as their acropolis and then debated what to do next, some arguing that it should be cut open, some that it should be thrown down from a high place, and others that it should be left intact as an offering to the gods; this last opinion of course prevailed. Nothing is here said of Sinon or Laokoon, but in such a brief summary we should not expect to find them, and then, too, Demodokos' song is about Odysseus. Lesches for his part relates that the Greeks caused the leaders to enter into the Horse and then set fire to their camp, taking the fleet out to Tenedos. The Trojans, thinking to be released from their difficulties, received the Horse into the city (destroying a part of their wall to do so) and celebrated in the belief that they had won the war. A reference to the *Little Iliad* in the Lykophron scholia adds to this epitome that Sinon did appear in Lesches' version, lighting a beacon as a signal to the other Greeks in the dead of night, when the moon was just rising (fr 9 *PEG*, with *apparatus*); we are told too by Aristotle that a *Sinon* play (probably by Sophokles: see below) was drawn from the epic (*Poet* 23.1459b). There is, however, no word in Proklos of Laokoon, and we cannot tell if he formed part of the *Little Iliad* or not.[83] Our first certain appearance of this latter figure is in the *Iliou Persis* of Arktinos, which begins (in our epitome) at the point where the Trojans are uncertain what to do about the Horse. As in the *Odyssey* there is a debate, with some wishing to push it from a cliff or burn it and others to dedicate it to Athena. When this last opinion gains the upper hand the Trojans turn back to their celebration, supposing that they are rid of the war. But at this point two serpents appear and destroy Laokoon and one of his two children. "Bearing badly" *(dusphorêsantes)* such a portent, Aineias and his followers abandon the city for Ida; Sinon then lights the signal fires, having before gotten into Troy by claiming for himself (or pretending) something. As we should expect, Proklos' summary of the narrative does not entirely square with the best-known ancient account of these events, that of Vergil's *Aeneid* 2. But Arktinos' Sinon (and that of Lesches?) may well have played much the same role as he does in Vergil, for the Greek word *prospoiêtos* can certainly mean a fabrication (or "taking a new identity to oneself") such as the *Aeneid* offers when Sinon claims to have been destined for human sacrifice by Odysseus and to have barely escaped with his life (*Aen* 2.77–144).

Vergil's epic makes Sinon go on to state that the Horse is a present to Athena, made large so that the Trojans might not bring it into the city; that idea is contested by Laokoon, who casts his spear at the wooden creature, nearly exposing it before the serpents put an end to him (and his two sons). All this seems entirely logical: Laokoon is removed by the gods because he endangers the success of the Greeks. In Arktinos, by contrast, Laokoon's fate plays no direct role in the decision of the Trojans to accept the Horse because it happens only after the fact. Possibly he was nonetheless an advocate of the Horse's destruction, and perished (albeit late) so that the Trojans might believe they had done the right thing, but as Proklos presents the situation the primary result of his demise is to stir Aineias to flight. We cannot, however, be certain that Proklos reproduces accurately the cause and effect sequences of his original, and then, too, the word used of Aineias' response properly suggests that he is angry or vexed about something; perhaps the other Trojans were not sufficiently grieved at the death of his sometime (*Fab* 135) uncle. It has even been suggested that Arktinos' portent signifies the fall of Troy and the elder line of the ruling house (as Laokoon and one son perish) but the survival of the cadet branch as represented by Aineias.[84] In any case, the latter is here not available to help with the final defense of the city as he is in Vergil, and his escape is more plausibly (though less heroically) explained (for other versions of his fate see below). To all this we can add that Bakchylides somewhere made the serpents come from the Kalydnai Islands (Kalymnos and Leros?) and had them changed into humans; he also involved Laokoon's wife in some way (fr 9 SM).

Such represents the sum total of our evidence for either Sinon or Laokoon in the Archaic period. Sophokles composed both a *Sinon* and a *Laokoon*; from the former (where the emphasis was surely on the duplicity of the title figure) nothing whatever remains, but of the latter we know that here, too, Aineias leaves before the fall of the city, carrying his father, and that he does so on his father's advice, for the latter recalls warnings from Aphrodite and also recent signs concerning the sons of Laokoon (fr 373 R). If used precisely (our source is Dionysios), this last phrase should mean that two (or more) children are killed, but that Laokoon himself survives. Sophokles also gave the names of the snakes (fr 372 R), which might suggest that they became human as in Bakchylides. In Apollodoros' version both Kassandra and Laokoon object to the Horse on the grounds that there are armed men inside; what follows—diverse support for hurling it from a cliff, burning it, and making it a dedication, with the latter prevailing, then feasting and the snakes sent by Apollo as a "sign" *(sêmeion)*—is remarkably close to the version of Arktinos (ApE 5.16–19). Here, though, it is the two sons alone who die (devoured, in fact), as perhaps in Sophokles, and Sinon (who may or may not have gained access to the city) lights the beacon fire outside Troy, at the tomb of Achilleus. What exactly the death of Laokoon's sons is a sign of is not clear, at least not in the epitome. The Lykophron scholia follow Sophokles in giving names to the snakes (Porkis and Chariboia—one male and one female) and Bakchylides in bringing them from the Kalydnai Islands (although with the odd expression that they sailed); they add that Laokoon was a son of Antenor, and that his child or children were killed in the precinct of Thymbraian Apollo (ΣΣ Lyk 344, 347).

First in Hyginus do we find the notion that a previous transgression was the motive for the snakes' assault. Laokoon is here the brother of Anchises and a priest of Apollo; although the god does not wish him to marry and beget children this is done, and as a consequence Apollo sends the snakes (from Tenedos) to kill the sons Antiphas and Thymbraios (*Fab* 135). Laokoon is at the moment sacrificing to Poseidon, having been drawn by lot to do so (exactly as in Vergil); when he tries to help his sons he perishes as well. Servius, on the other hand, cites as the transgression Laokoon's intercourse with his wife Antiope in the precinct of Thymbraian Apollo, before the images of the gods (Σ *Aen* 2.201). Earlier in the same note he has mentioned Euphorion (as the source for the Trojans' killing their priest of Poseidon when he failed to prevent the arrival of the Greeks), but what follows is probably drawn from elsewhere. We should remember that Bakchylides made Laokoon's wife a significant character in his version, so that one of these two accounts *might* go back to him (although see below). Just possibly in some versions where Laokoon has committed a previous offense the attack of the snakes takes place at a time quite removed from that of Troy's fall. For Vergil, on the other hand, his demise is the key factor in persuading the Trojans to bring the Horse within the walls, and we assume that the snakes are sent by the gods for just such a purpose. A previous offense might also have played a part in Sophokles, given tragedy's fondness for guilt themes, although there the reference to Aineias' flight makes clear the time frame.

Against this literary tradition, art has surprisingly little to offer. But almost certainly depicting the story in some form is a Lucanian bell krater of the late fifth century now in Basel: a woman raises an axe and rushes at two snakes that coil themselves around a cult statue of a beardless male crowned with and holding laurel; on the ground before the statue is a child in pieces, behind the woman a distraught bearded male cloaked in a mantle and behind him Apollo himself (Basel, Slg Ludwig, no #). A very similar scene appears on an Apulian vase fragment found at the end of the last century: here Apollo is to the left, turned away toward Artemis, while the snakes coil around the cult statue as before and the woman rushes in (something raised over her head) from the right (Ruvo, no #). As before, pieces (legs) of a child lie on the ground, but in contrast to the Basel krater one of the snakes here has an arm in his mouth (the head of the second snake is lacking); new also is the tripod next to the statue, while Laokoon (if he was present further right) has been broken away. Seemingly then, we have a version in which the attack takes place in the precinct of Thymbraian Apollo, only the children (or one child?) are killed, and Laokoon's wife makes a (vain?) attempt to avenge them, perhaps perishing in the process. Conceivably this act of daring on her part is what our sources refer to when they place her in Bakchylides' version, and constitutes the limit of her involvement. On the other hand, such a role in the climax of the story may indicate a greater complicity in its causes, that is, a forbidden procreation version such as Hyginus and Servius attest. By comparison with such tantalizing hints, the famous Hellenistic (or Roman) sculpture unearthed in the Golden House of Nero in the early sixteenth century tells us only that its sculptors preferred to show all three males of the family as victims.[85]

From the preliminaries we pass to the actual night of the Sack. The Greeks hiding in the Horse (three thousand according to Lesches, if Apollodoros is correct, but something smaller has surely been garbled in transmission[86]) are referred to three times in the *Odyssey*, first in Book 4 when Menelaos tells the tale of Helen's attempt to disclose their presence (4.271–89), second in Book 8 when Demodokos sings of the Sack (8.499–520), and third in Book 11 when Odysseus describes Neoptolemos' bravery to the shade of Achilleus (11.523–32). The first of these brief notices remains a puzzle even in its own context, since the notion that Helen imitated the voices of the leaders' wives in hopes of surprising them into speech contradicts her own just finished claim that she longed to return home.[87] The event is not mentioned elsewhere until Apollodoros (who surely takes it from the *Odyssey*), and the name of the Achaian whom Odysseus must restrain from calling out, Antiklos, is one not found in the *Iliad*; if the *Odyssey* poet has not here indulged in a bit of invention to praise Odysseus, he at least draws on an epic tradition not entirely in line with the *Iliad*'s cast. Whatever the truth of the matter, Helen's gambit fails, and the Achaians within the Horse are left to emerge at their leisure, presumably after the Trojans have gone to sleep. In Proklos' summary of Lesches we saw that a part of the city wall was destroyed to bring in the Horse, leaving one to wonder whether the risk of hiding men inside it was really necessary. The summary of Arktinos says nothing on this point; Apollodoros, who *may* be following him, since he quotes Lesches' number of men as a variant, reports that the (fifty) stowaways open the gates, as we might expect. Eustathios adds that in Stesichoros the number of men was one hundred, but elsewhere twelve, whom he names as Menelaos, Diomedes, Philoktetes, Meriones, Neoptolemos, Eurypylos, Eurydamas, Pheidippos, Leonteus, Meges, Odysseus, and Eumelos (Eu-Od 11.522, p. 1698). Conspicuously absent are Agamemnon and Idomeneus, but of course someone must command the fleet. Sinon's role in these events is less clear. In the *Little Iliad* we know only that he lit a fire; in the *Iliou Persis*, where he pretends to something, we presume that he is taken into the city, and lights the fire from there, but conceivably he left the city to do so. We saw that he is certainly outside the walls (at the tomb of Achilleus, in fact) in Apollodoros' version, perhaps because the fire was meant not only as a signal but also as a guide to ships attempting a landing in the dark. In Vergil, Sinon's primary function is to persuade the Trojans to admit the Horse; here he lights no fire at all, but rather opens the panel that lets the Greeks out of the Horse. At any rate the beacon brings back the army from Tenedos, and they join forces with those already inside the city to carry out the massacre of the inhabitants. To all this the second *Odyssey* reference adds that Odysseus and Menelaos went together to the house of Deiphobos, where there seems to have been an actual combat won by Odysseus (*Od* 8.517–20).

From other evidence we know that the *Little Iliad* contained a description of the massacre, despite Proklos' (or an epitomator's) failure to record the fact. For the battle itself in this poem our best source is Pausanias, who recounts in detail the points at which Polygnotos' painting of the Sack for the Knidians at Delphi recalls the version of Lesches (10.25–27). Among the parallels are the wounding of Meges in the arm by Admetos, son of Augeias, and a similar wounding of Lykomedes, son of Kreon, in the wrist by Agenor. A Trojan Astynoos was also mentioned, as was the Helikaon (son of Antenor) rescued from the fighting as we saw before by Odysseus, presumably because of his family's support of the Greek cause (see above). Of other Trojans or their allies, Axion, son of Priam, is here slain by Eurypylos, Agenor and Eioneus are dispatched by Neoptolemos, and Admetos falls to Philoktetes. Priam himself also dies at Neoptolemos' hands, but only after having been dragged away from the altar of Zeus Herkeios to the doorway of his house. One figure slain here by Diomedes but elsewhere by Neoptolemos is Koroibos; his appearance (as a corpse) in Polygnotos' painting prompts Pausanias to note that he was a son of Mygdon of Phrygia, and that he came to Troy to wed Kassandra, but we are not given any source for this tale.[88] Mygdon is mentioned by Priam in *Iliad* 3 as a leader of the Phrygians (*Il* 3.186); Homer never speaks of any son at Troy. In *Iliad* 13 we find Kassandra betrothed to Othryoneus, but as he dies in that book, I suppose she might have been promised to yet another foreigner. As for Astyanax, both Pausanias and specific lines from the *Little Iliad* quoted by Tzetzes make Neoptolemos responsible for throwing him from a tower, but this (the quote says) is done on Neoptolemos' own authority, not because the Greeks as a whole voted on or approved such an action (fr 21 *PEG*). The quote, which describes the deed in just three lines, may imply that Neoptolemos performed it in his capacity as the winner of Andromache. Finally, in both the *Little Iliad* and Ibykos, according to Aristophanes scholia, Menelaos dropped the sword with which he proposed to kill Helen when he saw her disrobed (Σ Ar:*Lys* 155 = fr 19 *PEG*). We will see below that such a tableau is also attested in seventh-century Greek art; certainly, though, it does not accord very well with the earlier suggestion (from Proklos' summary) that in this poem Helen and Odysseus somehow came to an agreement or plan for the fall of the city.

Compared with these bits and pieces of the carnage in the *Little Iliad* we have Proklos' full summary of the assault as found in Arktinos' *Iliou Persis*. Presumably, though, this has been compressed a good bit, for the only events recorded are Neoptolemos' slaying of Priam after the latter had fled to the altar of Zeus Herkeios, Menelaos' slaying of Deiphobos and leading away of Helen to the ships, and Aias Oileiades' accidental dragging away of a statue of Athena while trying to separate Kassandra from it. This last bit of tactlessness so enrages the other Greeks that they attempt to stone him, and are only thwarted by his seeking of refuge at an altar of Athena. There follows after the burning of the city the death of Astyanax, here at Odysseus' hands, and as well the sacrifice of Polyxena and recovery of Aithra, to be discussed below. The summary closes with the statement that Athena contrived destruction for the Greeks after they had put to sea, an unexplained action given that they have done their best to punish Aias. The few fragments we can add to this picture note only that Astyanax was thrown from the walls (fr 5 *PEG*), as Andromache at *Iliad* 24.734–38 predicts with the reasoning that some Greek will be angry over the many deaths brought about by Hektor. Here too, as before, we know nothing of the versions presented by the *Little Iliad* poems of Kinaithon and Diodoros of Erythrai, if these are different from the one ascribed to Lesches.

As for Stesichoros' *Iliou Persis*, the scholion telling us of Astyanax's fate in Arktinos may or may not say that he met a different fate in this lyric work (202 *PMG*); we know for certain about the poem only that those wishing to stone Helen dropped their stones at the sight of her (201 *PMG*). Some further information might appear on the *Tabula Iliaca Capitolina*, which claims for its representation of the Sack to illustrate Stesichoros' poem.[89] But whatever the exact truth of this statement, Vergil has also clearly been used,[90] and the scenes offered (aside from that of Aineias' departure, for which see chapter 17) are essentially standard repertoire (Aias and Kassandra, Neoptolemos and Priam, Menelaos and Helen, Demophon and Aithra, sacrifice of Polyxena, etc.) which tell us nothing new. From recent papyrus finds, we know that Alkaios also dealt with Aias' impiety, probably as part of an attack on Pittakos; nothing survives but the fact that an insane Aias tore Kassandra away from Athena's protection, and thus caused hardships at sea for the other Greeks because they failed to punish him (262 *SLG*).

From the fifth century and later in literature, there is not a great deal of interest. Neither Pindar nor Bakchylides has anything to offer, and in tragedy only Sophokles' lost *Aias Lokros*, with presumably a description of the dragging forth of Kassandra (presented as background to a trial?), seems to have dealt with any of these events. Euripides' *Troades*, which one might think would review the horrors of the city's taking, concerns itself entirely with the happenings of the morning after (including the decision of the Greeks as a whole to hurl Astyanax from the walls at Odysseus' insistence). Lykophron assigns part of Sinon's task to Antenor, calling him a traitor who opened up the Horse to let out the Greeks (Lyk 340–43); the scholia claim that he had made a pact with the Greeks in exchange for the rule of the city afterwards. In the epitome of Apollodoros, we hear of one Echion, son of Portheus, who dies attempting to leap down from the Horse; the others more prudently lower themselves by means of a rope (ApE 5.20). They then open the gates to those coming back from Tenedos. Neoptolemos slays Priam at the altar of Zeus Herkeios as before, Menelaos slays Deiphobos and takes Helen away, Odysseus and Menelaos intervene to save Glaukos, son of Antenor, and Aias offers some sort of violence to Kassandra when she has wrapped herself around an image of Athena; the Greek verb used, *biazomai*, is a standard term for sexual assault but can also denote the simple application of force. In the A scholia to the *Iliad*, however, all doubt is removed: Aias rapes Kassandra in the very precinct of Athena, so that the statue of the goddess turns its eyes upward toward the roof; here too, as in Alkaios, the deed serves as the root cause of the Greeks' subsequent difficulties at sea (ΣA *Il* 13.66). The portent of the statue turning its eyes upward at Kassandra's plight also appears in Lykophron (361–64) and, as we shall find below, in Quintus.

Aineias, we have seen, always survives the Sack, as Poseidon predicts at *Iliad* 20.300–305, but the means by which he does so vary considerably. In both the *Iliou Persis* of Arktinos and the *Laokoon* of Sophokles he leaves Troy well before the city's destruction, warned, it seems, by the fate of Laokoon and carrying (in Sophokles at least) his father on his back. Xenophon, however, speaks of him as among those defeated by the Greeks, for he says that by saving the ancestral gods of his parents, and as well his father, he gained a reputation for piety *(eusebeia)* that caused the Greeks to leave him undespoiled (*Kyn* 1.15); Apollodoros seems to understand something similar, for he places Aineias' departure (carrying his father) squarely in the middle of the Sack, and says that the Greeks allowed him to depart, again because of his piety (ApE 5.21). That the Greeks should leave any male Trojans alive, other than their benefactor Antenor, may sound surprising, but perhaps Aineias' mother Aphrodite contributed to his safety in some versions. Nevertheless, the notion of his piety recurs again and again. In Lykophron he is said to have abandoned wife, children, and property, selecting rather the household gods and his father when the Greeks permitted to him alone to choose out something from his house (Lyk 1261–69); no reason is given for this favor. Diodoros suggests that the Greeks made a truce with Aineias and others who still held a part of the city and allowed each to take away as much as he could carry; while others chose their valuables Aineias lifted up his father, and on being given for that reason a second choice took the household gods (DS 7.4). In Aelian, the option is one item alone; here Aineias' first choice is the gods, the second his father, whereupon the Greeks vote to abstain from his property altogether (*VH* 3.22). Neither account, however, says anything about a wife or children. In contrast to this notion of choice, Dionysios, who claims that his entire narrative here derives from Hellanikos, has Aineias mobilize a mass withdrawal from the city during the Sack, sending out first women, children, and the aged to Mount Ida, then defending the citadel, and finally retreating in good order with his father, gods, wife, children, and others as the situation becomes hopeless (DH 1.46.2–4 = 4F31). There is no suggestion in any of this that Aineias sacrificed family or property, or that he gave any preference to gods or father. Finally, although the Lykophron scholia simply paraphrase what the *Alexandra* contains, they do give Kreousa as the name of the wife and Askanios and Euryleon as the two children to whom Aineias prefer gods and father (Σ Lyk 1263). The subsequent quote from Lesches in these same scholia to the effect that Aineias is taken away from Troy in Neoptolemos' ships as a captive is quite doubtful (especially as the same lines are elsewhere ascribed to one Simias); we will consider the problem more fully in chapter 17. Likewise the extensive artistic tradition on Aineias' departure is here postponed to chapter 17, since it inevitably involves the question of where he goes after Troy.

Turning from these Greek sources to Vergil we find a continuous and detailed narrative of events, although of course the capture of Troy is seen entirely through Aineias' eyes, and he departs before the night is entirely over. Prior to that point, however, he provides a vivid account, with Kassandra (here first, followed by Apollodoros[91]) joining Laokoon in predicting Troy's demise, and Sinon opening the Horse for the Greeks inside. The ghost of Hektor appears to Aineias in a dream, warning him to flee; Panthoos, the priest of Apollo, running away with conquered gods and a grandchild, offers the same message. We meet again Koroibos, son of Mygdon, betrothed to Kassandra as he is in Pausanias (from Lesches?); when he sees his intended dragged away from Athena's precinct by her hair, he dashes to her aid and is cut down by Peneleos (a leader of the Boiotians in Homer). Even Panthoos dies, and Aineias finds himself by a secret door in the palace, where he witnesses first the slaughter of Polites by Neoptolemos before Priam's eyes, then the death of the old man himself, impiously butchered at the courtyard altar where his family has taken refuge. Such atrocities put Aineias in mind of the danger to his own family, but before he gains his house he sees Helen lurking in the shadows of the shrine of Vesta, and must be dissuaded by his mother from killing her. When he does arrive home, he faces objections to flight on the part of his father Anchises; these having been surmounted by an omen, the party sets forth, Aineias carrying Anchises and the household gods and leading Askanios, with Kreousa following behind. On finding her subsequently missing Aineias turns back, but her ghost advises him that Aphrodite has protected her from the Greeks. To all this *Aeneid* 6 adds a brief report from the shade of Deiphobos in the Underworld, who stresses Helen's treachery in leading the women of Troy in Bacchic revelry while she planned the city's destruction, and her removal of his sword while he slept so that Menelaos might enter the house and mutilate him. Some of these details obviously serve Vergil's own special purposes and may have been invented by him; about others, such as Helen's assistance to the Greeks, we cannot say. The Polites who appears at *Iliad* 2.791–94, for example, seems to be a grown warrior, although we will see shortly that the question of a child slain by Greeks during the Sack is a controversial matter in early Greek art.

As for Diktys and Dares, both writers bring about quite different resolutions of the siege: in the former, Antenor and Aineias negotiate a peace that the Greeks break (the walls having been breached to bring in the Horse), while in the latter Antenor, Aineias, and the rest of the Trojan peace faction betray the city after Priam insists on further fighting. We should note too that Diktys, like Vergil, has Menelaos cut off portions of Deiphobos' anatomy. In Quintus' version, Sinon is tortured by the Trojans but maintains his story (the same as in Vergil); Laokoon's protests against the Horse lead Athena to blind him, and when he continues to object she sends the serpents (swimming again from Kalydne) to destroy his children. Kassandra's predictions are simply ignored, and Odysseus leads the Greeks out of the Horse at Sinon's summons. For the rest (although Diomedes, here as in Pausanias, is the one to slay Kassandra's fiancé Koroibos, who seems to have offered his aid to Troy in return for her hand), matters proceed much as in the *Aeneid*. Of interest, however, are Priam's prayer that Neoptolemos kill him, and the clear rape of Kassandra by Aias, who cannot restrain himself despite the warning given by the statue, which turns away its eyes as in Lykophron and the *Iliad* scholia at 13.66.

In art we have an assortment of scenes, beginning with the Horse itself on a bow fibula (from Thebes?) dating to perhaps 700 B.C.: only the Horse itself is shown, but the presence of wheels instead of hooves (and what are perhaps windows) makes its identity certain (London 3205). A pithos from Mykonos dating to the second quarter of the seventh century elaborates on this theme, with again wheels for the Horse and windows (seven in all) from which the heads of the Greeks inside can be seen as they peer out, handing down their weapons; other warriors (Trojans? Greeks?) parade around outside (Mykonos 69).[92] On the body of the same vessel in three rows is a series of nineteen panels, at least six of which show bleeding children or warriors actually stabbing children with swords while their mothers watch (one warrior has no weapon and dashes his child down to the ground head-first); seven other panels have women supplicating warriors who threaten them or (in one case) a woman brutally stabbed by her assailant. In no case do any Trojan warriors seem to be present. One specific scene is very likely identifiable, that in which the woman's conspicuously exposed breast identifies her as Helen, mounting her own defense against Menelaos and his drawn sword (panel 7); a second, the warrior throwing his child to the ground, may be Neoptolemos (panel 17), but the atrocity of Astyanax's death would be rather lost in the general carnage shown here (indeed the two stabbings of children [panels 14, 19] are far more horrific). Such emphasis on the slaughter of innocents seems strange to be sure when set against a literary tradition in which the women and children were largely spared, in accordance with the usual practice of war. But it cannot be denied that even in the subsequent vase-painting tradition of Athens the accent is heavily on the less attractive aspects of the Sack—the slaughter of Astyanax (or Polites?), the death of Priam, and the dragging away of Kassandra from the statue of Athena.

This last was illustrated on the Chest of Kypselos (Paus 5.19.5 gives no useful details) but our first preserved evidence is a series of shield-bands from Olympia starting at about the same time, in the first quarter of the sixth century. On all of these the general composition remains the same: Aias moves in from the left, seizing Kassandra's arm with his left hand while the right holds a threatening sword (B 1801, B 1654, B 975, etc.). She herself seems to clutch at the dress of the Athena to the right, a figure with raised spear and shield which has been interpreted as both the goddess and a statue (would a live goddess permit the impending impiety?). The girl's apparent nudity on the oldest example might be taken as no more than an indication of youthfulness, but when later pieces clearly delineate her breasts we must assume that the artist wished to emphasize her nakedness. The same situation holds for a good many of the illustrations in vase-painting, where the other Trojan women are fully clothed; seemingly then, Aias' lust for and rape of Kassandra was a part of the early tradition, although the ever-present sword (surely unnecessary to force such a victim) remains curious, as does her subsequent presentation to Agamemnon as a prize.[93] In Attic Black-Figure the earliest known example is a Siana cup in the manner of the C Painter: Kassandra is half-hidden as she crouches behind Athena (the latter again in something approaching a Promachos pose: London B379). Numerous later Black-Figure paintings repeat this exact same composition: heavily armed Aias with sword, crouching Kassandra (sometimes half-draped or dressed), and Athena with shield held out and spear horizontal. On some examples the tip of the sword is dangerously close to Kassandra's neck, and did we not know better we would surely assume that she was executed on the spot. In Red-Figure versions the Athena becomes more clearly a statue on a pedestal, sometimes in the Promachos position, sometimes not; the most elegant account forms part of the Kleophrades Painter's general representation of the Sack on a hydria from Nola wherein Aias seizes by the hair a quite alluring Kassandra who is fully naked, save for a cloak knotted around her neck (Naples H2422). As Red-Figure progresses, Kassandra is more often running toward the statue than crouching beside it, and Aias holds a spear rather than a sword; sometimes, too, the statue is turned away from Aias, as in Lykophron, but the basic narrative shows no signs of having changed. Noteworthy are several caricatures, including one of the fourth century on which Aias clings to the statue while Kassandra grasps him by the helmet (VG 50279); perhaps the reference is in part to his seeking of shelter (as we saw in Arktinos) when the other Greeks wished to stone him.

Next in the artistic repertoire of the sack comes the death of Priam, which we find again and again linked with the death of a child whom we usually take to be Astyanax. This latter event is perhaps first seen on a Late Geometric pot fragment, where a man holds an upright child by the lower leg (Agora P10201),[94] and perhaps also as we saw above on the Mykonos pithos, where one of the panels shows a warrior holding a child by his ankles and striking him against the ground (Mykonos 69). Possible, too, is an Olympia shield-band relief where a warrior with raised sword holds a child off the ground by the wrist (B 847). Both these latter poses will return in vase-painting in scenes that appear connected with the death of Astyanax; that with the sword may or may not reflect a version of the death by means other than falling from the battlements. Priam's own death first appears on an Olympia shield-band (where the prostrate figure lying upon an altar can be no one else: B 160) and perhaps the left corner of the Artemis temple pediment on Kerkyra (although here the victim is on a throne).[95] In each case the method of execution is a spear, in contrast to what we will see below. On a Black-Figure lekane cover of about 565 B.C. by the C Painter, a warrior swings a child by the ankle back over his head and dashes toward an altar behind which stand an old man and woman, their hands raised in alarm; behind the warrior a mounted figure gallops toward the altar, and behind him are warriors on foot (Naples, no #). If this is Neoptolemos, we will have the deaths of a Trojan child (whatever we call him) and Priam brought together for the first time. Such a link is in any case certain on a slightly later Black-Figure lekythos where the warrior holds the child (dangling by a leg) over a corpse stretched out upon an altar and threatens him with drawn sword (Syracuse 21894). Subsequently, however, this sword gives way to a much more popular composition, beginning with Lydos in the 550s and perhaps prefigured by the C Painter lekane: the pose found there (child brandished above head like a club) is now combined with the old man on the altar, so that Neoptolemos appears to be dashing the child down upon the body of Priam (Louvre F29; so too Berlin:Ch F3988, a tripod kothon). The same arrangement appears too on an Olympia shield-band of the last quarter of the century (B 4810). In these instances Priam seems to be dead, but in several Black-Figure examples of the latter half of the century he is clearly alive, and raises his hands to protect himself as the child is swung toward him (e.g., Louvre F222; Bonn 39). On none of these vases is the child identified as Astyanax (although he will be in Red-Figure: see below). More uncertain is a hydria of the Leagros Group on which the child is about to be dashed against an altar while an old man crouches behind the warrior rather than in the line of fire (Munich 1700; battlements on the shoulder). In this instance (and perhaps also that of the C Painter lekane), we *may* want to think of Troilos, or at least of confusion between the details of his story and that of Astyanax.

In Red-Figure there are fewer occurrences of the scene, but on at least one of those the child is identified as Astyanax (Athens Akr 212). On the Brygos Painter cup in Paris, meanwhile, a young boy named as Astyanax flees the slaughter, while on the other side Priam on his altar is as usual threatened by a warrior with a similar but unnamed youth, leading us to wonder if the child could appear twice on the same pot (Louvre G152). This cup provides in any case a vivid picture of the Trojan women's desperate struggle against the Greeks, for while their men lie dying on the ground Andromache has picked up a pestle or the like and rushes into battle; Astyanax stands behind her, starting away in fear. One other curious detail of this cup is the pair to the left of Priam and Neoptolemos: Akamas leads away Polyxena, who looks back gently at the death of her father. A mistake in the names has been suggested, but after all someone must take the girl captive, even if this is not recorded in what little survives of the literary versions. Finally, we have the hydria of the Kleophrades Painter in Naples, where Priam sits on the altar with his already dead child (numerous stab wounds) in his lap as a Greek prepares to deliver the final blow (Naples H2422). To the left is the previously mentioned scene of Kassandra's seizing, with beyond that Aineias carrying off Anchises; to the right is another Greek menaced by a woman with a pestle, and then the rescue of Aithra by her grandsons (see below). On none of these pots is Neoptolemos named, but with the manner of executing the child so impiously conceived he is the obvious candidate; certainly we will not think of Odysseus here. Whether the killing of child and grandfather together is an artistic compression by painters disinclined to show battlements, or whether it really does derive from a literary tradition, is a more difficult question. Likewise, we cannot say whether an early story of Polites slaughtered in his father's arms might be illustrated here (or drawn upon to furnish iconography for a death of Astyanax), as opposed to being a late invention of someone like Vergil, perhaps inspired by that very death of Astyanax in Greek art.

One other quite popular scene, Menelaos' recovery of Helen, we have seen illustrated as early as the Mykonos relief amphora of the seventh century. Subsequently, the same theme, or at least a man in armor leading off a woman or threatening her with a sword (or both) appears on a sixth-century grave relief from Sparta (Sparta 1), on the Chest of Kypselos (Paus 5.18.3: Menelaos advances on Helen with sword drawn), and then in Attic Black-Figure from the time of Lydos (Berlin:PM F1685, where the juxtaposition with the death of Priam guarantees the scene).[96] But only in Red-Figure does the encounter take on any emotion: in the late work of the Berlin Painter we see Menelaos for the first time fling away his sword and run toward Helen with (presumably) something other than murder on his mind (Vienna 741; Naples 126053). Subsequently, this form of representation becomes quite popular, with an Eros sometimes added overhead. In no instance does Deiphobos ever appear. As a final point, Helen is again in a state of undress (naked to the waist, in fact) on the *Tabula Iliaca Capitolina*, in the part supposedly drawn from Stesichoros' *Iliou Persis*. In that poem we saw that the Achaians as a group threaten Helen with stones (fr 201 *PMG*); here Menelaos stands alone with his sword.

Aftermath: The Recovery of Aithra and Sacrifice of Polyxena

The first of these two events certainly appeared in both the *Little Iliad* and the *Iliou Persis*. In Lesches, Aithra made her way out of Troy at its fall to the Greek camp, where Demophon sought formal possession of her from Agamemnon; the latter consulted Helen, as the proper owner of the woman, and when she consented, grandmother and grandchildren were reunited. Of Arktinos' version we are told only that Demophon and Akamas found Aithra and took her away with them. We have seen the recovery illustrated above as part of the general sack of Troy by the Kleophrades Painter (Naples H2422; so too London E458, a calyx krater by Myson), and it appears as well on the *Tabula Iliaca Capitolina*. From Euripidean scholia (at *Hek* 123) we learn that in some writers the sons of Theseus came to Troy for this purpose alone, presumably providing a convenient excuse for their failure to appear in the *Iliad*, where Menestheus leads the Athenians. The same scholia add that in Hellanikos they come hoping to get Aithra as spoils if Troy falls, and to ransom her with gifts otherwise; they have been in exile in Euboia, not wishing to be ruled by Menestheus (4F142). That they first tried diplomacy in recovering their grandmother might be indicated too by Lykophron's claim that Laodike, daughter of Priam, stole into the bed of one of them and bore to him Mounitos, who was later killed by the bite of a snake to his heel (Lyk 494–500). Parthenios attests that the son of Theseus in question was Akamas; he adds, however, that Diomedes and Akamas had come to Troy to seek the return of Helen, and that this was the occasion on which the unmarried Laodike conceived a passion for him (Par 16; we have seen that in the *Iliad* Laodike is married to Helikaon, son of Antenor). With the help of friends, both visit the town of Dardanos (further north, on the coast of the Hellespont) at the same time, and there the mating is accomplished; the child Mounitos is brought up by Aithra until Troy falls, and then given over to Akamas, only to be slain by the snake while hunting in Thrace. Parthenios credits all this to one Hegesippos of Mekyberna (east of Olynthos), of perhaps the fourth or third century B.C. The scholia at Lykophron 447 and 495 relate much the same details of the affair, with Euphorion cited for at least Mounitos' death.

The fate of Polyxena, however, like the fall of Troy itself, is missing from our summary of the *Little Iliad*, and we do not know whether Lesches related it. Surprisingly, it does appear in a place we would not expect to find it, namely the *Kypria*, and in a totally unique form: Polyxena is wounded by Odysseus and Diomedes in the course of the Sack, and dies of her wounds (*Kyp* fr 34 PEG). The problem of fitting such an event into a poem whose narrative ends long before the Sack has generated suspicion that something is misattributed here, although the device of a prophecy might provide a solution.[97] In Arktinos we first encounter the familiar form of her death, that she was slaughtered at the tomb of Achilleus; Proklos' summary gives no further details. The scene is clearly illustrated on a Tyrrhenian amphora of about 570 B.C., where three Greeks—Amphilochos, Antiphates, and Aias (Oileiades, we presume)—hold Polyxena horizontal while Neoptolemos cuts her throat so that the blood runs down upon a tomb or mound (London 1897.7–27.2). Behind Neoptolemos to the left stand Diomedes and Nestor in attendance; behind Aias to the right is Phoinix, but with his back turned as if disapproving or unable to watch. Dramatic though this scene is, we are once more left without explanation of the reason for such brutality, and the tale reappears on only one other occasion in Archaic literature, when Ibykos confirms that Neoptolemos was the slayer.

In the later fifth century, however, Polyxena finds a place in plays by

Sophokles and Euripides, and as well in one of the paintings of Polygnotos displayed in the Athenian Propylaia. The painting, according to Pausanias, simply showed her about to be killed beside the tomb of Achilleus, and is thus not much help (1.22.6). Sophokles' play about her was the *Polyxena*, which featured someone's ghost or shade, a second sacrifice to placate Athena, and grim predictions about the Achaians' future; the tomb appears to have been onstage, and both ghost and sacrifice may have been vividly presented (although probably not actually shown). But here again we do not see why a human sacrifice was necessary. Only with Euripides' preserved *Hekabe* is a purpose for the deed revealed: Achilleus' ghost has appeared above his tomb as the Greeks prepared to sail, and demanded the life of Polyxena as the price of their departure (*Hek* 35–44). The language used (by Polydoros' ghost) in recounting this fact, as well as the words of Hekabe, the chorus, and Odysseus later in the play, suggest that the matter is one of honor to the departed hero, a distribution to him of his share of the spoils (*Hek* 93–95, 113–15, 309–10). Neoptolemos' remarks at the sacrifice itself (reported) convey in addition the notion of a blood offering to the dead (*Hek* 534–38). There is to be sure debate in the Greek camp: Agamemnon opposes the idea (out of sympathy for Kassandra, his own prize), but the sons of Theseus support it and Odysseus finally carries the day. At no point in the play, however, do we ever hear of any amorous passion for Polyxena on the part of Achilleus; she is simply valued because she is among the most beautiful of the captives, and is therefore an appropriate gift for Achilleus to choose. The same playwright's later *Troades* also touches on the event, with Talthybios there telling Hekabe that Polyxena will "tend" the tomb of Achilleus (*Tro* 264). That Achilleus actually desires her as an object of love is first hinted in Lykophron, if the words "savage bridal rites and marriage sacrifices" can be taken with that sense (*Lyk* 323–24). Subsequently, as we have seen in Diktys and Dares, Achilleus falls in love with the girl while he is still alive, and dies in the precinct of Thymbraian Apollo while trying to negotiate for her (so too *Fab* 110). Ovid follows Euripides in stressing Achilleus' honor as the cause of his demand (*Met* 13.445–48), but in Seneca's *Troades* Achilleus requests Polyxena's death so that he might become her "husband" in Elysion; she seems not displeased by the prospect (Sen: *Tro* 938–48). Philostratos takes matters even further, for in his account Polyxena reciprocates Achilleus' love, and commits suicide at his tomb in order to be with him (*ApTy* 4.16). The evidence thus seems to suggest that Achilleus' feelings of passion for Polyxena arise at some point after the fifth century, but we must admit that the Archaic period is largely a blank here.

Hekabe and Polydoros

The tale of Polydoros' murder by the treacherous Polymestor of Thrace, and Hekabe's subsequent revenge against him, is not mentioned anywhere in our remains of the Epic Cycle. If, as in Euripides' *Hekabe*, the whole series of events took place in the Thracian Chersonese, where the Greeks were encamped prior to departure, we might expect it to have been related at the beginning of the *Nostoi*, as part of the difficulties with that departure. But Proklos says nothing of it in his summary, and neither does the *Odyssey*, which ought to have told of it if it was part of an Odyssean stopover further on in Thrace. In point of fact, Euripides' play is our very first trace of the story, and that circumstance, combined with the presence in the *Iliad* of a Polydoros, son of Priam, slain by Achilleus on the field of battle (*Il* 20.407–18), must make us suspect Euripidean innovation on a substantial scale. Admittedly, this Iliadic Polydoros is not the child of Hekabe, but rather of Laothoe (and thus brother of the twice-captured Lykaon of *Iliad* 21); nevertheless, Homer calls him the youngest of Priam's children, as does the *Hekabe*, and Euripides' character probably has no other counterpart in epic. In the *Hekabe*, Polydoros himself speaks the prologue as a ghost, relating how toward the end of the war Priam sent him out of Troy with a certain sum of gold to his friend Polymestor, king of Thrace, so that the line might be preserved in case of disaster to the city. With the city's fall, however, Polymestor has slain his guest and cast the body into the sea, to be found washed up on shore by Hekabe's servant in the opening part of the play. Hekabe appeals to Agamemnon for justice, and he allows her to summon Polymestor and his sons. Lured by a promise of hidden Trojan gold, he enters Hekabe's tent, where his sons are killed by the women and he himself blinded. With his appeals to Agamemnon denied, the play closes on his strange prediction that Hekabe will climb the mast of the ship taking her to Greece and be changed into a dog, with her final resting place commemorated by the name "Kynossema." An unascribed lyric fragment that may well be earlier than this play also shows her becoming a dog, although we learn nothing of the circumstances (965 *PMG*).

The story of treachery by this king of Thrace is further improved upon in Pacuvius and Hyginus by the presence of one Iliona, eldest daughter of Priam and Hekabe, who has married Polymestor and borne him a son Deipylos at about the same time that Hekabe bears Polydoros (Pac *Iliona* frr I–XVIII, plus [probably] *Ex incertis* fr XLII Rib; *Fab* 109). Priam thus sends Polydoros to his daughter to be raised together with her son, for the same reasons as in Euripides. She, however, from suspicions not explained, raises her own son Deipylos as Polydoros and her brother Polydoros as Deipylos. In time, Polydoros (the real one) finds his own reasons to suspect the situation and goes off to an oracle of Apollo to seek his true identity. Meanwhile, Troy falls, and the Greeks, not wishing to leave any of Priam's sons alive (save Helenos), inform Polymestor that they will give him Elektra, Agamemnon's daughter, to wife if he kills Polydoros for them. He of course then kills his own son Deipylos by mistake, thinking him to be Polydoros. At the oracle, the real Polydoros receives an ambiguous answer to the effect that his mother is a slave and his homeland is in ashes. Hastening home in alarm, he learns the whole truth from his mother, and persuades her to bring about the blinding and subsequently the death of Polymestor. She then kills herself. Much of this is worthy of Euripides; since it seems not to derive from him, however, it may stem from the Alexandrian era (like the tale of Atreus and Aigisthos?). Surprisingly, Apollodoros has no mention of any version of Polydoros' fate, but Vergil creates an unforgettable picture of his betrayal with the thicket of cornel wood which speaks to Aineias from above his grave in *Aeneid* 3 (22–68). The nature of the scene requires (as against Euripides' version) a burial, but otherwise Vergil's few details are in accord with the *Hekabe;* he clearly expected his Roman audience to know the story.

As to Hekabe's ultimate fate, dog or not, there are some other points to note. Most often we think of her as assigned to Odysseus, but in truth our preserved bits of the Epic Cycle say nothing about her allotting, and she never appears as a companion or shipmate of Odysseus at any point in the *Odyssey*. Her despair at such a future is most memorably portrayed in the *Troades* of Euripides, who seems once again the first to mention it. Earlier, in the *Hekabe*, nothing at all is said of whose slave she will be; the plot rather implies that Agamemnon controls her destiny. In any case, there is an early variant of all this in the *Iliou Persis* of Stesichoros, where she is taken to Lykia by Apollo (198 *PMG:* we should remember that in some traditions she is the mother of Troilos [or Hektor] by the god). Dares, on the other hand, takes her across to the Chersonese with Helenos, Kassandra, and Andromache (Dar 43). Nikandros retains her canine conversion, although apparently at Troy, after she sees the city in ruins and dashes into the sea (Σ *Hek* 3). In Lykophron the setting is also Troy: Hekabe curses the Achaians and is stoned by them, becoming a dog at some point in the process (Odysseus casts the first stone: Lyk 330–34, 1174–88). The scholia at 1176 seem to suppose that she turns into a dog first and is stoned in that form. Either way, she goes down to Hades, where Lykophron says that she serves as the hound of Hekate. In Diktys she is again stoned by the Achaians for her curses, but this author omits any transformation (Dik 4.16); Quintus, by contrast, omits the stoning, but has her turned into a dog by the gods (no stated reason) and then turned to stone (QS 14.347–51). In Ovid, she is stoned by the Thracians immediately after she has blinded their king (*Met* 13.565–71).

Last, we find first in Lykophron the idea that Laodike is swallowed up by the earth and goes down to Hades alive (Lyk 316–18, 496–98). Although Apollodoros too mentions a chasm that opens up and swallows her (ApE 5.23), only Quintus offers the explanation that she requests this fate, lest she become a slave, and some unspecified god fulfills it (QS 13.544–53). One might suppose that as the wife of Helikaon, son of Antenor (*Il* 3.121–24), who is saved in the *Little Iliad* by Odysseus, or at any rate as the mother of Akamas' child Mounitos (see above), she would have reason to expect a better fate than slavery, but her role as one of Priam's more beautiful daughters may have dictated the situation here.

17   The Return from Troy

Menelaos and Nestor

Proklos' summary of Arktinos' *Iliou Persis* concludes with the laconic remark that following the division of booty the Greeks sailed away, and Athena contrived their destruction at sea. Both the epic *Nostoi* and Nestor in the *Odyssey* speak more specifically of a quarrel between Agamemnon and Menelaos after the taking of Troy, when the ships were preparing to leave. If our epitome is correct, in the *Nostoi* Athena created the quarrel (concerning something about the leave-taking), and Agamemnon remained behind, offering sacrifices to appease her anger, while Diomedes, Nestor, and after them Menelaos, among others, departed immediately. Hermes in *Odyssey* 5 (speaking to Kalypso) claims that the Achaians on the return "transgressed" against Athena, causing her to send a storm from which Odysseus survived to reach Kalypso's island (*Od* 5.108–11). This last detail—that Odysseus was involved in the general catastrophe—is not supported by the rest of the *Odyssey* or any other source, and is probably an oversimplification of the moment. Likewise the phrase "on the return" is presumably short for "during preparations for the return," if as we would guess the transgression involved some lack of proper behavior to the gods before departing.

Nestor in *Odyssey* 3 is more loquacious, but he too will not say exactly what caused Athena's anger; we are told only that some of the Achaians were not prudent or just, and thus Athena's wrath was visited upon them via Zeus (*Od* 3.130–36). Possibly this means simply Aias' violation of Kassandra's sanctuary during the Sack (which it seems the Achaians failed to punish), but Nestor may also be alluding to the more general lack of gratitude to Athena advanced by later authors, or to something else that has not survived. In any case, the dispute between the Atreidai caused by Athena results in a general assembly called near sundown, at which Menelaos (following, it seems, the view of Nestor and Odysseus) advises all to leave as quickly as possible, while Agamemnon wishes to stay and carry out sacrifices in the hope of appeasing the goddess. As Nestor sees the situation, and as events prove, this last is a vain effort. Nevertheless, about half the army determines to stay. At dawn the other half departs, Nestor, Diomedes, and Odysseus among them, but when they reach Tenedos, doubt reassails Odysseus' crews, and they and Odysseus turn back (thus explaining why Nestor knows nothing more of their fate). At

Lesbos, where Nestor and Diomedes have stopped to consider their best route across the Aegean, Menelaos catches up with them; they sacrifice to the gods, who advise them to sail above rather than below Chios. At Euboia they put in at Geraistos and sacrifice to Poseidon in thanks for their safety. The fourth day from their departure sees Diomedes safe at Argos, and Nestor continues on to Pylos without incident.

So runs Nestor's first account of the return in *Odyssey* 3. But when Telemachos quite properly wonders what has happened to Menelaos, if Agamemnon's death on his return went so long unpunished, his host concedes that at Sounion Apollo shot the pilot of Menelaos' ship, one Phrontis, son of Onetor, and that Menelaos remained behind there to bury him (*Od* 3.276–302). The rest we must assume he learned from Menelaos after the latter's return: the storm sent by Zeus at Cape Maleia which drove his fleet to Gortyn on Krete, where many ships foundered; the passage of five of them down to Egypt; and Menelaos' sojourn there (collecting provisions and gold), with a successful voyage back to Sparta only in the eighth year, after Orestes had avenged Agamemnon. Further details of the stay in Egypt are then provided by Menelaos himself in *Odyssey* 4, when it is his turn to entertain Telemachos. He speaks of time spent in Cyprus and Phoinicia (Sidon), in Aithiopia and Libya and among the Eremboi, as well as in Egypt (*Od* 4.81–85). Seemingly he was in no great hurry to return to Sparta, for his actual becalming on the island of Pharos at the mouth of the Nile occupies only twenty days out of the eight-year period. At the end of those twenty days Eidothea, daughter of Proteus, approaches him with a solution to his dilemma (*Od* 4.351–569): she tells him that he and three of his crew must hide among the seals in the cave where her father comes to rest each day at noon. She herself provides the sealskins to cover them, and ambrosia for their nostrils so that they may withstand the smell. When Proteus arrives and settles down, having failed to notice them, they spring forth and seize him, holding on despite his transformations (lion, serpent, panther, boar, water, tree) until he agrees to reveal the source of their becalming: they have failed to sacrifice to Zeus and the other gods before setting out and must return to the Nile to do so properly. At the same time, the old man also discloses information about other events (Aias Oileiades' fate, Agamemnon's death, and the whereabouts of Odysseus) to which we will come in due course. The pronounced cure for the lack of wind is, of course, successful; Menelaos sets up a barrow for his dead brother after completing the sacrifices at the Nile and sets sail for home, arriving just in time for the funeral of Aigisthos, whom Orestes has slain. The *Nostoi* epitome's account of all this is much more limited, but there too Menelaos reaches Egypt with five ships after the rest are lost at sea, and his return to Sparta is effected only after Orestes and Pylades have taken vengeance for Agamemnon.

In the *Odyssey* certainly and the *Nostoi* presumably, Helen really was at Troy, so that there was no need to retrieve her in Egypt. In Stesichoros, where the *eidôlon* first takes her place, matters proceed rather differently, but we still do not know for certain that Helen stayed with Proteus in his Palinode,[1] and we cannot say much about Menelaos' return voyage in that work; it may not even have been included. Moving down to the fifth century, we have a full dramatization of the encounter with Proteus in Aischylos' lost satyr play *Proteus*, the fourth drama in his *Oresteia* production of 458 B.C. Presumably there were thematic connections between Menelaos' problems here (adverse winds) and those of his brother at Aulis in the opening play of the production, the *Agamemnon*.[2] Presumably too, after the chorus' attack against Helen in that play, the *Proteus* continued to represent her as a genuine runaway rather than an innocent victim. But we do not know at all what else this satyr play might have contained. Only with the *Helen* of Euripides (preceded as we saw in chapter 16 by a brief allusion in his *Elektra*) do we find clearly told the story of Menelaos' finding of Helen in Egypt after he has departed from Troy. In both plays she has spent the war in the house of Proteus (here more king than sea god), but in the *Helen* Proteus has since died, and his son Theoklymenos wishes to keep Helen in Egypt permanently as his wife. At this point Menelaos arrives, thinking the *eidôlon* that accompanies him to be Helen, and is thus understandably confused at seeing the genuine article. Matters are eventually straightened out, aided by a report of the miraculous disappearance of the *eidôlon*, but Theoklymenos (who kills all Greek visitors on the chance that they might be Menelaos) remains to be dealt with. Helen solves this problem by announcing that messengers have come with news of her husband's death, and that to mourn him properly she must be sent out on a ship into the harbor for a special Greek ritual. Too eager to claim his bride, Theoklymenos falls for the ruse, and Helen and a disguised Menelaos make their escape, aided by the *deus ex machina* appearance of the Dioskouroi to halt pursuit. Their subsequent life together, as we see it in *Odyssey* 4, seems unmarred by any conflict or controversy; even the marriage of Menelaos' bastard son Megapenthes (on the same day that Hermione is being sent to Neoptolemos) causes no difficulties.

Agamemnon   Not surprisingly, the *Iliad* tells us nothing of Agamemnon's forthcoming death when he reaches the plain of Argos. But the *Odyssey* has a good deal to say about that event, much of it in the context of an unfavorable comparison between Klytaimestra and Penelope as model wives and a likening of Aigisthos to the suitors.[3] Indeed, in the opening passage of the epic, Zeus observes that Hermes was sent down to earth by the gods to tell Aigisthos not to kill Agamemnon and take his wife, lest he suffer the consequences, as he subsequently did (*Od* 1.35–43). Nestor in Book 3 adds details of Klytaimestra's seduction by Aigisthos: at first it seems she was unwilling to accede to his blandishments, and then too she was attended by a singer left behind by Agamemnon to guard/ protect her (*Od* 3.263–75). But presently, "when the *moira* of the gods constrained her to succumb" (whatever that means), the singer was taken to a deserted island to become prey for birds, and she went willingly to Aigisthos' house. This last phrase may simply be a carryover of the normal Greek idiom for marriage, and Nestor later states that Aigisthos for seven years ruled golden Mykenai, having subdued the people (*Od* 3.304–5). All the same, we will see shortly that there is some reason to believe that the *Odyssey*'s Klytaimestra took up residence with Aigisthos, rather than vice versa. Aigisthos' residence, by the way, is here located by Nestor "in a nook/recess of horse-pasturing Argos," that is, somewhere in the Argolid. Nestor's further statement that after the successful seduction Aigisthos made many costly sacrifices and dedications to the gods (*Od* 3.273–75) might seem to indicate that his motive was primarily one of passion, rather than a desire for power or revenge against Agamemnon's side of the family. The same conclusion is probably what we should understand from Zeus' words in *Odyssey* 1, although in both cases such a coloring of the event may be influenced by a desire for contrast with the faithful Penelope and the lustful suitors. Zeus also emphasizes Aigisthos' part in initiating both seduction and murder, but Athena (as Mentor) attributes the latter to the deceit of lover *and* wife (*Od* 3.232–35); we will see Klytaimestra's role given more prominence as the poem progresses.

In *Odyssey* 4 Telemachos acquires further information on the killing via details given by Proteus to Menelaos in Egypt (*Od* 4.496–537). A storm, it seems, caught the ships of Aias and Agamemnon at the Gyrian rocks (Tenos? Mykonos?); Aias was drowned, but Hera saw Agamemnon safely through and he found himself almost about to put in at Cape Maleia when a wind carried him back out onto the open sea. At this point the text becomes somewhat puzzling, and must be quoted: "to that far edge of land, where Thyestes had his home before, and then Aigisthos son of Thyestes lived. But when also from that place a safe return was in view, the gods turned back the wind, and they came to their homeland." Here Agamemnon kisses the ground in his joy, but he has been spotted by a lookout, paid by Aigisthos, who has been watching for a whole year and now reports the return to his master. Aigisthos takes twenty men and sets up an ambush; "on the other side" (of the megaron?) he orders a feast prepared and sallies forth in his chariot to invite Agamemnon to dinner. Unwitting, the latter comes, and after the meal, is cut down "like an ox in his stall." There is, moreover, a general struggle of forces, for none of Agamemnon's companions survive, and none of Aigisthos' either.

Some obvious questions arise here. Specific mention of Aigisthos residing where his father Thyestes used to live strongly implies that he is in fact there at the moment, not in Agamemnon's palace. Certain in any case, I think, is the fact that he invites Agamemnon to his own house, where the murder takes place, for how on any logic can he invite his cousin to dinner in the cousin's house without making it obvious that he has moved in? Textual emendation has been proposed at various points,[4] but it seems simpler to try to interpret the narrative on its own terms, and to assume that Aigisthos remains in his own house, to which he invites and in which he slays Agamemnon. Homer's text will then have intended something like the following: because of the winds Agamemnon nearly lands near Aigisthos' home (somewhere further east in the Argolid?) where he is not expected and no lookout is posted; from there he would have been able to make his way, either to Aigisthos' house where he would have found his wife and cousin together, or homeward to Mykenai where rumors of the truth (and Klytaimestra's absence) would have alerted him to his danger. Instead with a change of wind he comes to Nauplia, where he is seen, and thus Aigisthos' invitation intercepts him before he can reach his (wifeless) home; he detours instead to Aigisthos' house where the ambush has been prepared. This is admittedly a cumbersome chain of events, but logical; presumably the audience was familiar with it from more detailed versions. Alternatively, given Nestor's earlier reference to ruling at Mykenai (Od 3.304), we might suppose Aigisthos and Klytaimestra there, from which point, when the warning arrives, Aigisthos sends men to arrange the banquet and ambush back at his house (could this be the meaning of heterôthi?) and rides out as if from that house to intercept Agamemnon. Either way, the locale of the murder gives greater point to the need for advance warning: Agamemnon must not simply be prepared for, but diverted from his natural goal, namely his own palace. Such an arrangement also allows for a more realistic treatment of Agamemnon's political power: as a king he returns from Troy with subjects and retainers, men who will contest his murder and with whom Aigisthos can deal far better on his own territory. Klytaimestra for her part will be hidden until the trap is sprung (Proteus in fact never mentions her, either as motive or agent). Admittedly, such a role does not give her quite the duplicity we might have imagined from the words of Athena/Mentor in Book 3, or those of Menelaos at 4.91–92 (when he laments his brother's demise at Aigisthos' hands through the treachery of an accursed wife), but perhaps this notion of treachery refers simply to her adultery, or else to the planning of her husband's death in advance of the actual event. That she did participate in the killing may or may not be supposed in these first accounts; certainly it is the case in two later ones to which we must now turn.

The first of these later narrations is in the Nekuia, where Agamemnon's shade describes the scene of the murder to Odysseus (Od 11.405–34). We hear nothing about where the victim puts into harbor, but here as in Book 4 he has been invited to dinner by Aigisthos (the term oikonde surely refers to the latter's house), and there having feasted he and his men are slaughtered. His contrasting the scene with a battlefield suggests that there is no real combat with Aigisthos' forces, but only a massacre, with much blood running over the floor. As he raises his hands and (apparently) beats the ground in an appeal for vengeance he hears the cries of Kassandra, killed near him by Klytaimestra, who turns away and does not even close his eyes or mouth. The text here offers some slight ambiguity: either Agamemnon dies pierced by someone else's sword (presumably that of Aigisthos), or he throws his hands about Klytaimestra's in a vain attempt to prevent her from killing Kassandra. Kassandra's presence with Agamemnon in Aigisthos' house should mean (as we would expect) that he is still en route from Troy to his own home; presumably, Klytaimestra has been in hiding until the trap is sprung. Odysseus' response to this account does specifically link the notion of her deception with planning the deed in Agamemnon's absence at Troy. The second passage, the *nekuia* of *Odyssey* 24, brings back the shade of Agamemnon to lament again his ill-fortune. At one point here he says that Aigisthos and Klytaimestra performed the deed together (*Od* 24.96–97); at another he seems to credit his wife alone, perhaps because of the contrast with Penelope (*Od* 24.199–202). Either way, the beginning of this Book states once again that the murder occurred in the house of Aigisthos, with Aigisthos thus surely the host (*Od* 24.21–22). Such is precisely the opposite of the situation in Aischylos' *Agamemnon,* but Homer's arrangement allows him to emphasize the role (and transgression) of either lover or wife as uppermost, depending upon the current situation. On the other hand, we should note that the poet never mentions Orestes' killing of his mother, and probably has no desire to do so, or even suggest it, given the favorable parallel he wishes to establish between Orestes and Telemachos; for this reason it is in his interests to minimize Klytaimestra's direct complicity as party to a homicide, however much he may stress her infidelity.

In the *Nostoi* epitome, too, Agamemnon is said to have been slain by Aigisthos and Klytaimestra (see below for a possible illustration on a "Homeric" bowl); no other details are given. One additional event of interest in this poem is the appearance of the ghost of Achilleus (as in the *Little Iliad*) to the ships of Agamemnon as they are leaving Troy, in an attempt to dissuade their departure by predicting what will happen. What follows in the summary is the storm at the Kapherides rocks and the death of Aias, a disaster that may or may not have coinvolved Agamemnon; we will return to that problem too below, in discussing Aias and Nauplios. Stesichoros' lyric *Nostoi* may also have included an accounting of Agamemnon's travails, but we have no idea at exactly what point his *Oresteia* begins, and thus cannot say what part of the return and slaughter was covered in either of those poems, although we assume that the story was told in one or the other (if not both). Philodemos, as we saw in chapter 16, attests that the *Oresteia* spoke of Iphigeneia's transformation into Hekate, so that this poem may well have treated in detail the background to Orestes' vengeance. One detail that did appear somewhere was the placement of Agamemnon's kingdom in Sparta rather than Mykenai; our source, a Euripidean scholiast, notes that Simonides also located it there (216 *PMG*). Scholars have naturally seen such a variant as politically motivated: Agamemnon as a Spartan ruler would give the kings of that city an Achaian as well as a Dorian ancestry, thus allowing them to claim whichever was more advantageous for a given moment.[5] Whether this is true or not, the change of venue means that Stesichoros may well have contrived a completely different logistical situation for Agamemnon's death than that seen in Homer. But in the absence of any notion of where Aigisthos would have lived when Agamemnon ruled Sparta we cannot say more, and we have no other information for this poet or for Simonides. The same is true of Xanthos, the obscure older poet on whom

Stesichoros is supposed to have drawn. One other detail from Stesichoros seen earlier regards the cause of the Tyndareides' problems: a wrathful Aphrodite causes their infidelity after their father forgets her sacrifices (223 *PMG*). In the *Ehoiai*, too, the goddess' anger (at Tyndareos?) is the root of the difficulty; a direct quote offers the picture of Klytaimestra leaving glorious Agamemnon to bed with Aigisthos, thus choosing an inferior husband (Hes fr 176 MW). Elsewhere in the latter poem the Catalogue Poet tells us that after two daughters (Iphimede and Elektra) Klytaimestra bore Orestes, who "coming to full youth avenged himself on the *patrophoneus* and killed his own mother" (Hes fr 23a MW). *Patrophoneus* is properly a male agent noun, and is used of Aigisthos with this exact same wording at *Odyssey* 3.197. All the same, the Catalogue Poet must have envisioned Klytaimestra as closely involved in the murder, if Orestes is to be at all justified in killing her.

From the early literary tradition we now turn to art of the same period, before considering the abundant evidence of the fifth century.[6] The theme of Agamemnon's death is probably illustrated as early as a terracotta relief plaque from Gortyn of the late seventh century on which we see a woman and a man flanking a seated figure and seemingly engaged in a struggle with him (Iraklion 11512). Given a less-than-perfect pressing, the details of the scene are fuzzy and arguable, but the woman (on the left) does appear to be bending over the seated man and grasping his right wrist (as he raises his arm) with her right hand, while her left arm passes behind his body and is obscured. The man to the right catches the seated figure's spear just below the blade with his left hand and presses down on the top of the man's head with his right. The victim (if he is that) has something over his head which may be either his hair or part of a garment. On the whole, this seems likely to be the event in question, with both Klytaimestra and Aigisthos participating, but given the murkiness of the representation in its present condition it is hazardous to go further; we cannot really say with any certainty that the enveloping cloak is here shown, or even that Klytaimestra rather than Aigisthos is meant to be striking the fatal blow.[7]

Much clearer is the next item, a shield-band relief from Olympia, dating to the second quarter of the sixth century, with a woman and two men in a deadly struggle (B 1654).[8] Here the men grapple with each other as if wrestling; the one in the center of the composition aims a blow of his hand at the one on the right, who has him caught in a headlock. Behind him, to the left, the woman seizes his drawn-back elbow to impede him and plunges a sword/knife into his back or side. Behind the right-hand figure a spear stands upright: Agamemnon's weapon, perhaps, put aside incautiously, or a symbol of his rule. A very similar composition on a fragmentary shield-band from Aigina (no #) probably illustrates the same scene, although the left-hand figure here is not definitely a woman.[9] In any case, we finally have an early version in which Klytaimestra plainly does the killing herself, treacherously striking from behind while Agamemnon is engaged with Aigisthos. Earlier than any of these pieces, however, is a fragment of bronze sheathing from the Argive Heraion, of the mid-seventh century, which probably shows Klytaimestra slaying Kassandra: one woman seizes a second by a lock of her hair and stabs her in the side with a short sword or dagger (Athens, no #).[10] Obviously we cannot guarantee this interpretation, but one is hard pressed to think of any other story or situation involving two women in such a pose.

Having surveyed this much, we must now consider several less certain examples which, if they do represent the death of Agamemnon, would, like the Olympia shield-band, give Klytaimestra quite a central role. The first, a steatite gem from Krete known already in the last century and dating to perhaps 700 B.C. (NY 42.11.1), shows just two figures, a seated man and a woman bending over him.[11] The woman's right hand (gem, not impression) holds or rests over a water jug; her left is extended out toward the man's midsection. He in turn has his right arm extended out toward the woman's waist, while his right leg is raised almost to the same point and his left arm placed back behind him for support. If this is Klytaimestra and Agamemnon, it is not only the earliest illustration of their story, but assigns Klytaimestra a primacy in the killing we might not have expected. But given the limitations of space on such a gem, it may be that the scene as we see it has been cut down from a fuller representation like that on the Olympia relief: Klytaimestra strikes from ambush in Aigisthos' house while Aigisthos himself (not shown) distracts the victim. On the other hand, the interpretation of the scene in question as the death of Agamemnon (when we cannot even be sure a murder is in question) is very far from certain. The alternative suggestion of Eurykleia washing the feet of Odysseus seems equally plausible, if not more so, leaving us (as so often for the earliest stages of Greek art) without the sort of evidence on which we can base any really sound conclusions.

A second category of tantalizing representations involves the device of Agamemnon's bath, a detail not firmly attested until Aischylos' *Oresteia*. On a relief amphora from Thebes of the seventh century a damaged (and quite uncertain) scene offers a totally different composition from what we have seen so far (Boston 99.505).[12] Aigisthos (if it is he) now stands to the left, his left hand clutching the wrist of the man in the center, his right outstretched and perhaps holding a weapon. Of the central figure all except the head and one hand are lost, but toward the bottom are what appear to be the legs of a stool, or perhaps a tripod. The woman in the scene stands to the right, not directly involved, but her right hand may hold the hilt of a lost sword. Such a tableau has generated other interpretations, including Apollo and Herakles struggling for the Delphic tripod, or even Orestes and Aigisthos,[13] but the fact that the central figure is behind (or *in*) the tripod might suggest that the missing section showed the lebes used to heat water for a bath. That there was a lebes, as opposed to just a tripod (in which, for example, Herakles might be sitting, to establish his own oracle), has been argued on the parallel of the previously discussed metope from Foce del Sele where a man is definitely so sitting in such a vessel.[14] Unfortunately, the left side of this metope, where another figure must have been positioned, has been broken away, as has the final surface of what remains. But the man in the lebes does have his left hand raised (the right is missing) in a gesture that looks like alarm. We saw in chapters 8 and 12, however, that there are several other possibilities for this metope, including Minos slain by the daughters of Kokalos, Pelias slain by Medeia (although there the daughters do the actual deed before putting the pieces in water), Aison or Iason rejuvenated, or even the resurrection of Pelops. Relevant to this scene also is the small terracotta relief band (reputedly from Sicily), now in Basel, on which a quite similar figure sits in a lebes, with the left side of the scene now completed by a woman who holds a water jug in her right hand and a weapon (or the man's upraised right arm?) in her left (Basel BS 318).[15] To the far right stands a figure with a long cloak who is probably male and who seems relatively uninvolved in the action. Certainly bathing appears to be involved in this last example (even if no one ever actually bathed in a lebes—probably tub and cauldron for heating water have been combined for reasons of space), but even so, Minos is perhaps as likely as Agamemnon here, with a daughter of Kokalos on one side (pouring in the fatal hot water) and Kokalos himself on the other. In that case the parallels offer no sure early evidence for Agamemnon's bath, and we must reserve judgment on the Boston amphora as well. If the Foce del Sele metope *could* represent the death of Agamemnon, it might provide further evidence for versions in which Klytaimestra takes the leading role (assuming Aigisthos was not in a lost metope to the right), but we are in dangerous waters here.

Two last, still more uncertain pieces remain to be mentioned. One is a Protoattic vase, the so-called Oresteia Krater formerly in Berlin (Berlin:Lost A32) and known at present primarily from drawings.[16] A male with drawn sword follows another male and, reaching around his body, grasps a long strand of something that seems to attach to the latter's forehead. The latter in turn reaches back in a supplicating gesture, so that he seems about to be killed. Beyond him to the far right a woman stands turned away, her hand to her cheek. The strand in question has recently been interpreted as a schematic representation of the net or garment pulled over Agamemnon's head,[17] but it cannot be said to be very convincing, nor does one quite see why the woman would look distressed at (or at least uninterested in) the proceedings. We shall return to this vase below in the context of its more familiar interpretation, Orestes slaying Aigisthos.

The other piece is a "Homeric" bowl of the second century B.C. now preserved in Berlin (Berlin:PM 4996).[18] Here we have without question the death of Agamemnon and Kassandra (as proved by inscriptions) and some indication of the artist's source. To the left Klytaimestra reaches out with drawn sword and grasps the hair of the helpless Kassandra. To the right a male figure in long cloak over one shoulder charges (with similarly drawn sword) at a reclining Agamemnon, the latter with a garland on his head and drinking cup in hand; a robe or blanket covers his lower body. Similarly dressed are three men behind him in various stages of starting up to flee. Their way, however, is blocked by

two armed warriors who poise their spears for the kill. Of these three companions of Agamemnon, two have names that can be read: Alkmeon, and Mestor,
son of Aias; the henchmen of Aigisthos are Antiochos and Argeios. To this
primary mold design, the potter casting the actual bowl has made two clear
additions: using the segments of the mold to overstamp, he has added the upper
torso of Agamemnon at the feet of Klytaimestra in her scene, and represented
Kassandra as falling onto the legs of Agamemnon in his. Most important, in
the area between the arms of the original Kassandra and Aigisthos, there is an
inscription that identifies the scene as the death of Agamemnon and probably
specifies before that the source of the story. Not all the letters are preserved,
but what remains seems to indicate the *Nostoi of the Achaians* as responsible,
in which case we would have a valuable illustration from that lost epic. What
is here shown, even without the overstamping to bring Agamemnon and Kassandra into closer proximity, is essentially what the *Nekuia* tells us. Agamemnon and his men are having dinner when they are surprised by the ambush
launched by Aigisthos and his band; the latter deals with Agamemnon while
Klytaimestra dispatches Kassandra, and there is no sign of any bath. Either
then the *Nekuia* and the *Nostoi* were very similar in their account of this event,
or the artist drew his inspiration from the more familiar *Odyssey* but credited
the work to which the story narratively belongs.

In all, the only certain thing we can conclude from all of our artistic evidence prior to the fifth century is that Klytaimestra (based primarily on the
Olympia shield-band) did at times assume an active role in killing her husband.
Seemingly, Homer brings her out from ambush in Aigisthos' house, where
Agamemnon has been invited to dinner; the conflicting notion of a bath during
which he was killed may or may not have developed prior to the fifth century,
and may or may not indicate at the same time a shift of the scene of action to
the palace at Mykenai (since Agamemnon might as well expect to be bathed in
Aigisthos' house after a long journey as he would in his own). More definite
conclusions seem to me undesirable, although the possibilities for different
early versions are unquestionably intriguing.

For the first half of the fifth century we have in literature Aischylos' *Agamemnon* plus allusions in Pindar's *Pythian* 11, and in art the detailed representation of the Dokimasia Painter on an Attic Red-Figure krater in Boston (Boston 63.1246).[19] Complicating the deductive process here is the uncertainty of
relative dating, for while the *Agamemnon* is firmly fixed by its hypothesis to
the spring of 458 B.C., *Pythian* 11 could (from its scholia) celebrate a victory
in either 474 or 454, and the krater is dated between 470 and 460, too close to
assure that it precedes Aischylos. Nevertheless, with the reader warned, we
will take Pindar first, then the krater, and finally the *Oresteia*.[20] *Pythian* 11,
written for Thrasydaios of Thebes, moves from the land of Pylades to the tale
of his Lakonian comrade Orestes, who, his father slain, was saved from the
strong hands and grim treachery of Klytaimestra by his nurse Arsinoe, when
his mother dispatched Kassandra and Agamemnon to the shores of Acheron

with the flashing bronze (*Py* 11.15–22). The poet then asks, pointedly, whether Iphigeneia's slaughter at the Euripos stirred her hand, or rather was it nights spent in another's bed. Subsequently he locates the murder at Amyklai, where Agamemnon perished himself and brought about the death of Kassandra as well. These few lines offer a number of important points. As noted in chapter 16, Pindar stands as the first extant author (depending on date) to specifically link Iphigeneia's death with Klytaimestra's betrayal (as well as the first, for that matter, to attest unambiguously that Iphigeneia did die). He suggests, again for the first time, that Orestes was in some danger from his mother, who might have killed him had he not been rescued. He follows Stesichoros in moving Agamemnon's home to Sparta, or rather nearby Amyklai, instead of the Argolid. And he is our first literary source to move Klytaimestra fully to center stage, making the initiative and control of the situation hers (as well as the deed?), with Aigisthos reduced to a supporting role.

The first and fourth of these points are crucial to Aischylos' treatment of the story, and thus our interest in knowing whether he or Pindar has prior claim to them. But one might well be skeptical that either poet has introduced wholly new themes here; Klytaimestra's motivation and role in the murder are obvious areas for exploration, and we cannot be sure that the *Nostoi* and Stesichoros (among others) did not explore them.[21] We should note too that in treating this whole story Pindar is, like Aischylos, concerned with its proper completion, the matricide; thus, like Aischylos (and unlike Homer), we should expect him to underline what justified that extreme measure by a greater emphasis on Klytaimestra's role.

Moving from Pindar to the Dokimasia Painter, we find a scene not entirely in line with these observations. His krater shows without any question both events, the death of Agamemnon on one side and the death of Aigisthos on the other, and the second probably dictated his treatment of the first. What we see on this first side is Aigisthos striding forward from the left, drawn sword in right hand, to seize Agamemnon by the hair as his victim shrinks backward in alarm. Aigisthos is here fully dressed; Agamemnon's body is entirely covered (head and hands included) by a diaphanous bordered garment under which he is completely naked, and there is already a stab wound in his chest. The garment clings in a peculiarly web-like fashion around his right hand, as if failing to provide an expected exit. To each side of this central group a woman runs forward, hand outstretched; that on the left holds an axe in her other hand. Beyond these, two other women run away from the scene in terror, virtually colliding with the columns that form the frame of the whole composition. Obviously we have here at last indisputable evidence for an entangling cloth of some sort, and probably for the bath as well, since Agamemnon is naked (although see below on Seneca and Apollodoros). The woman behind Aigisthos must by virtue of the axe be Klytaimestra running up to help (or to slay Kassandra); that behind Agamemnon might be Kassandra or a daughter of the house, with Kassandra the simply clad slave figure running away right. On the principle of better compositional symmetry, I would favor Klytaimestra and Kassandra balancing each other as the two major figures flanking the men, but it does not much matter for our purposes. Since we have here again, as for Pindar, elements new and vital to Aischylos' presentation of the story, it might seem crucial in this case also to establish priority, and to that end it is frequently argued that Aigisthos would not take the leading role if the painter had drawn from Aischylos. That argument assumes, however, that a painter cannot conflate ideas from different sources, and it also ignores the problem of the other side: if a painter has doubts about showing the death of Klytaimestra in the sequel, he will naturally focus on Aigisthos in the original act, so that slayer and object of vengeance will be the same person. Aischylos could afford to focus on the matricide because he had two full plays in which to explore and justify the deed; the Dokimasia Painter had no such luxury. Nevertheless, I do believe that he illustrates a tradition older than the *Oresteia*, regardless of the date of his work, for reasons explained below.

With Aischylos' great trilogy of 458 B.C. we find ourselves in the presence of the most famous and influential version of the fortunes of the house of Atreus. The *Agamemnon* opens at Mykenai, or rather Argos (a shift usually thought to be prompted by the political realities of the time), but certainly in any case Agamemnon's home. There is here as in Homer a lookout, but on the roof of the palace, posted there by Klytaimestra to watch not for Agamemnon himself but rather for a beacon relay that will announce Troy's taking. The watchman confides that all is not well within, which we take to mean the presence of Aigisthos in the proper owner's place; nevertheless he seems confident that with his master's return the problem will resolve itself. The beacon does now appear, Klytaimestra explains its significance to the elders as they ponder the long-ago death of Iphigeneia, and a herald enters to confirm the expedition's success. We learn from him that Troy was razed to the ground, temples and all; Klytaimestra has already suggested the dangers in such an act, and it develops that the fleet did encounter a catastrophic storm on the way home. But Agamemnon is safe enough, and soon arrives, bringing with him Kassandra, whom he flaunts in front of his wife. She has for her part strewn the path to the palace with purple garments, and persuades Agamemnon to walk on these, hoping to make him even more guilty in the eyes of the gods. His entry into the palace to perform sacrifices of thanksgiving is followed by that of Kassandra, but only after she has delayed some time to predict Agamemnon's imminent demise, and her own, to the chorus. The impact of this scene arises in part from the chorus' inability to grasp darkly worded hints which the audience, based on prior knowledge, understands only too well. In particular, we must suppose that the truncated references to the fatal bath and net, not fully explained on stage until much later, will have little point if they do not refer to a tradition older than the play. In the same way, the net imagery used of Troy's capture earlier by the chorus in the First Stasimon will have no larger implications if the motif of the net is not already known.

In any event, Kassandra like Agamemnon goes to her doom. We hear two cries from Agamemnon himself within the palace, then see Klytaimestra coming out, with the bodies of husband and war prize on some sort of platform, to recount her deed. Kassandra has already implied that he was in the bath (standing up to get out of it, I suppose) and amid garments (*peploi*) when he was struck (*Ag* 1126–29). Klytaimestra speaks now of how she threw a robe (or robes) about him so that he might not escape, and struck him three times, the third as he was going down (*Ag* 1382–92). The implement used is not here in any way specified; at *Choephoroi* 1011 it seems to have been the sword of Aigisthos (borrowed by Klytaimestra?), while in the *Nekuia* we saw a sword to be either the murder weapon of Aigisthos (slaying Agamemnon) or Klytaimestra (slaying Kassandra), depending on how we read a difficult text (*Od* 11.421–24). The Dokimasia Painter is the first known source to give Klytaimestra an axe in this particular situation. We shall see below, however, that for the confrontation with Orestes she is so equipped as early as the Foce del Sele metopes, and in several Red-Figure vases before the time of the *Oresteia*. Thus, her call for an axe in the *Choephoroi* with which to defend herself is not an Aischylean invention, but rather an element of earlier tradition which might have influenced storytellers' choice of her weapon for the slaying of Agamemnon (at whatever point, although we have seen her twice with a sword/dagger in the seventh and sixth centuries). Likewise, of course, the influence might have gone the other way, with an axe first used against Agamemnon subsequently adopted for the confrontation with Orestes (although an artistic corpus of some quantity does not show it before now). In the latter part of the fifth century this axe will become a standard feature (see below).

Two other points need to be made before leaving Aischylos. The one concerns Orestes, whom Klytaimestra has herself sent away to Strophios of Phokis, unlike her counterpart in Pindar (and in Euripides and Sophokles); thus there can be no question of her planning to kill him (*Ag* 877–85). The second point involves Aigisthos, who emerges from the palace long after the killing is over and makes no protest when the chorus suggests that he took no part at all in the deed, but only in the planning. His task, he insists, was to remain hidden, lest he arouse the suspicion of a man who was his enemy. It is clear that he remained hidden longer than was necessary, but his premise is sound: he has been living in Agamemnon's house, and his appearance too soon would have given away Klytaimestra's deception. This whole balance of responsibility, with Klytaimestra playing very much the man's part and Aigisthos the woman's, probably owes a good deal to the trilogy's overall theme of perversion in male-female relationships, a theme adumbrated in the watchman's opening characterization of his queen and worked out only in the *Eumenides*. To what extent Aischylos might have found such a feminine-slanted imbalance in earlier versions of the story remains uncertain. But we can say that Aischylos' setting of the murder in Agamemnon's own home, where the work of deception will fall to Klytaimestra, has effaced general awareness of earlier accounts in which Aigisthos probably played that role.

Subsequently in the fifth century there are several dramatic allusions, although they do not add a great deal. At no point does Klytaimestra yield the status found in Pindar and Aischylos; either the deed is all hers, or she shares it with her lover. Euripides' *Orestes* says that "casting a piece of weaving without exit over her husband she slew him" (*Or* 25–26), and later, that he "lies dead, having fallen in the very last bath offered by his wife" (*Or* 366–67). In the same poet's *Elektra*, Agamemnon dies "in his own home, by the deceit of his wife Klytaimestra and the hand of Aigisthos, son of Thyestes" (E:*El* 8–10); his old tutor here rescues Orestes, as he does in Sophokles' *Elektra*. Three different plays of Euripides, plus this same drama of Sophokles, mention an axe as the murder weapon (*Hek* 1279; *Tro* 361–62; E:*El* 279; S:*El* 96–99), and we see it as well on a cup of the same general period by the Marlay Painter on which Klytaimestra uses it to dispatch Kassandra (Ferrara 2482). There are, surprisingly, no more representations of the death of Agamemnon after the Dokimasia Painter's krater. In Pherekydes we hear that Aigisthos slew the child of Orestes' nurse Laodameia, thinking it to be Orestes himself (3F134); one suspects, even if our scholiast source does not say, that the nurse deliberately sacrificed her own son to facilitate her charge's escape.

Of later sources, Pausanias offers the famous information used to such good effect by Schliemann, that within the ruins of Mykenai were the graves of Agamemnon and all those coming back with him from Troy, whom Aigisthos slaughtered after having given them a feast (2.16.6). Probably this reflects a fusion of the Homeric feast in Aigisthos' house with the rival view that Agamemnon died in his own house at Mykenai. Pausanias' further information, that Agamemnon had one grave, his charioteer Eurymedon another, and his twins Teledemos and Pelops by Kassandra another, may come from local tradition. The notion that Kassandra had time to conceive and bear twins after the fall of Troy is puzzling to say the least; its only other occurrence is in the *Odyssey* scholia, where we are told (in the context of the slaughter, although for no discernible reason) that Teledemos was the son of Agamemnon and Kassandra (Σ *Od* 11.420).

In Lykophron, as in Aischylos and Euripides, there is a bath, and here too as in Euripides a piece of material from which Agamemnon seemingly expects to find some exit for his head, and does not (Lyk 1099–1102). Seneca's *Agamemnon*, which follows the general narrative line of Aischylos' version, also has this feature: Agamemnon is feasting in his palace upon his return when his wife calls upon him to take off his Trojan spoils and put on instead a cloak (*amictus*) that she herself has made for him (Sen:*Ag* 875–905). The cloak does not offer easy exit for his head and hands, and while he is struggling with it, Aigisthos stabs him and Klytaimestra then finishes him off with her axe. Apollodoros, too, puts the murder at Mykenai, and in his version we see more clearly what Seneca, and Euripides and Lykophron before him, must have meant, for here Klytaimestra gives her husband a chiton without places for his hands and without a neck; he is, as in Seneca, killed while trying to put it on (ApE 6.23; so too Σ *Il* 1.7, VM I 147, ΣΣ Lyk 1099, 1375).[22] Such a trick garment sounds remarkably like what Agamemnon is wearing in the Dokimasia Painter's version of the tale, where we saw the entangling material clinging oddly to head and hand. Presumably this device will have been part of the story only in versions where Agamemnon is in his own home and greeted by his wife (i.e., not feasting with Aigisthos). It does not, however, seem what Aischylos intended, for although Klytaimestra does mention robes that she threw over her quarry like a net, she says nothing about any special deviousness in this ploy, as she surely would have had she made a special garment. We might indeed wonder if the bath was not originally an alternative to the garment (only Euripides and Lykophron combine the two), but of course a bath is certainly logical before changing clothes after a journey, and the failure of Apollodoros to mention it means little in an epitome. One other detail of note in Apollodoros is the crediting of the infant Orestes' rescue to Elektra.

We conclude this section with several more curious variants. Diktys, followed by Hyginus, offers a novel but not illogical version in which Oiax, the brother of Palamedes, falsely informs Klytaimestra that her husband is bringing home a concubine whom he prefers to her, hoping to get revenge for his family's wrongs (Dik 6.2). In Hyginus, Oiax's slander consists simply of stating that Kassandra is being brought back as a concubine (which in all other accounts is true); Klytaimestra consults with Aigisthos, and the two kill Agamemnon (and Kassandra) with an axe while he is sacrificing (*Fab* 117). The story, which rather exonerates Klytaimestra, may be based in part on Agamemnon's claim in *Iliad* 1 that he prefers Chryseis to his own wife. Finally, we should note Pausanias' remark that in Kinaithon Orestes has a bastard son by Erigone, daughter of Aigisthos (fr 4 *PEG*). Presumably (although Pausanias does not say), this Erigone is a child of Aigisthos and Klytaimestra; we shall learn more of her later.

Orestes' | As discussed above, neither *Iliad* nor *Odyssey* ever says exactly that Orestes
Revenge | killed his own mother Klytaimestra, but the *Odyssey*, after stressing on several occasions that he slew the killer of his father Aigisthos (with the gods' express approval: *Od* 1.40–47), strongly implies a matricide by telling us that Menelaos returned from Egypt on the very day when Orestes was giving a funeral feast for both Aigisthos (whom he had killed) and his own "hateful mother" (*Od* 3.306–12). The lines with this last information (309–10) do not appear in all manuscripts, and have been thought by some an interpolation (even if a funeral for Aigisthos at least is confirmed by *Od* 4.546–47). But Homer never suggests any other form of punishment or future for Klytaimestra, and since she is clearly guilty in his scheme of things, we can only suppose him aware of her death, whatever we do with the questioned lines. On the other hand, there

is nothing in *Iliad* or *Odyssey* to help us decide whether that era was aware of Orestes' problems after killing his mother; again, this is the sort of coda that the *Odyssey* (given Orestes' role there) might be expected to suppress, if it did know of it. One other puzzling detail is the notion at *Odyssey* 3.307 that Orestes returned to his homeland for his revenge from Athens, rather than the Phokis of his friend Pylades (admittedly never mentioned by Homer). Zenodotos actually proposed to read "Phokis" for "Athens" here, in keeping with later tradition, and Aristarchos suggested "Athena," Orestes being thus under her protection (at Tegea?) during his exile (Σ *Od* 3.307).

Following Homer we have the *Nostoi*, where Proklos remarks simply that the murder by Aigisthos and Klytaimestra is followed by the vengeance of Orestes and Pylades. What this vengeance consists of is not said, although mention of Klytaimestra's role in the crime might be thought to imply her sharing the punishment. In the *Ehoiai*, as noted earlier, when Orestes comes of age he avenges his father's death on the slayer and also kills his "overbearing [?] mother with the pitiless [bronze]" (Hes fr 23a.30 MW). The matricide is thus simply mentioned in passing, as part of a two-line characterization of Orestes whom Klytaimestra bore as one of a number of children; we cannot say if the poem returned to it elsewhere. Stesichoros' *Oresteia* must have grappled with it, although our only real evidence for that fact is the information that in his poem Apollo gave to Orestes a bow with which he might defend himself from the Erinyes (who would hardly pursue him for the death of Aigisthos: 217 *PMG*). The work's most famous quote, that concerning the dream of Klytaimestra, shows that Aischylos in the *Choephoroi* borrowed this device (although not, it seems, the exact same dream). As our source Plutarch recites the lines, "a serpent seemed to come to her, the top of its head covered with blood, and from it [or after this?] a king Pleisthenides appeared" (*Mor* 555a = 219 *PMG*). We have already considered in chapter 15 the difficulties involved in ascertaining who this Pleisthenes is and hence who his descendant might be. But the snake with its bloodied head must certainly be Agamemnon, and the king either the same person in human form or (more likely) his son Orestes, whose appearance as king indicates that Aigisthos' line will not retain the throne. Either way, we learn little more than we would naturally have guessed about Stesichoros' version.[23] The presence of Erinyes from whom Orestes must defend himself presumably indicates that the matricide was an issue, but how treated, or even how resolved, we cannot say.

In art the earliest presumed representation of the revenge is the abovementioned Protoattic krater from Berlin sometimes taken to show rather the death of Agamemnon (Berlin:Lost A32). Since that is unlikely, given the pose of the woman with one hand to her face, we might well imagine the scene to present Orestes (backed by Elektra: hand visible) leading the two culprits to their deaths, although it would require a very subdued and resigned Klytaimestra.[24] From the same period, or perhaps a bit later in the century, comes a Kretan bronze mitra found at Olympia on which a young man approaches a woman on an elaborate throne (B 4900).[25] Above the woman arches a piece of cloth, which she grasps; the youth may or may not be drawing a sword (the crucial left edge of the mitra is broken away). If the woman is pulling the cloth away to reveal herself (rather than using it in an attempt to hide) we might look rather to Menelaos' recovery of Helen.[26]

Of the early sixth century are several bronze reliefs from Olympia. The shield-band pattern usually taken to present this story shows an elegantly dressed man seated in an equally elegant chair, struggling to unsheathe his sword, while another man, unbearded and perhaps naked except for a sword-strap over his shoulder, seizes his antagonist by the forelock and prepares to stab him with a spear (Olympia B 988 and others).[27] Orestes is an obvious guess here, but there are other possibilities, such as Neoptolemos and Priam or even Zeus and Kronos. The same holds for the sculptures previously considered under those headings in the left corner of the pediment of the Temple of Artemis on Kerkyra (Museum, no #: only the seated figure fully preserved).[28] Much more dramatic is the other Olympia relief, on a bronze strip probably from a tripod: a man seizes the woman facing him by the throat with his left hand while his right drives his sword completely through her body (M 77).[29] To the left, behind the attacker, stands another female, one hand raised with her cloak as if in encouragement; to the right, behind the dying woman, a man moves away hurriedly, reaching out toward a stepped structure (an altar?) while looking back at the scene behind him. Such a scene is almost certainly a rare view of the death of Klytaimestra, one picture making up for all of Homer's reticence (although objections have been raised[30]), and the man moving away to the right becomes then Aigisthos seeking refuge from Orestes.

Of the mid-sixth century also are several problematic metopes from Foce del Sele. On one of these we have a clear illustration of a woman with an axe being restrained by another woman;[31] from the intensity with which the restrainee advances to the right we should probably imagine at least one additional metope linked to this one with her intended victim on it. Conceivably these women are Klytaimestra and Kassandra in an otherwise unattested pose, but the two available candidates for the second metope both suggest rather the death of Aigisthos. On the first of these possibilities a man facing right (Orestes?) draws a sword while a woman behind (Elektra? Laodameia?) appears to encourage him; if that is correct, Aigisthos must have occupied yet a third (lost) metope.[32] On the second example one man stabs another in a pose similar to what we saw on the tripod leg, with the victim grasping a column at the top of a stepped platform while he turns back to supplicate for his life.[33] This last piece comes dangerously close in its composition to shield-bands discussed in chapter 16 where the small size of the victim seemed to justify his identification as Troilos, cut down at the altar to which he had fled.[34] Here, by contrast, with two figures of equal size and insufficient detail to be sure of beards, we have a more difficult problem. But the gesture of supplication appears nowhere else in Troilos iconography, and another part of that story (Achilleus behind the foun-

tain house) is present at Foce del Sele. Quite possibly, therefore, the man clinging to the column is Aigisthos, about to be slain by Orestes while either Elektra
or Laodameia restrains Klytaimestra from intervening with her axe. We must
admit, however, that the other reconstruction, with Orestes and sister threatening a lost Aigisthos (or Klytaimestra herself?), is also possible.

One other metope from Foce del Sele believed by many to portray Orestes
focuses on an entirely different part of the story. We see a man with drawn
sword preparing to strike at a snake that has coiled itself around him and rears
up menacingly: supposedly this is an Erinys threatening Orestes after he has
killed his mother.[35] I would not exclude the possibility, but I confess to some
skepticism in the absence of better parallels than we have. The whole question
of the portrayal of Erinyes re-embroils us in the problems of the Tyrrhenian
amphora with the possible matricide of Alkmaion discussed in chapter 14 (Ber-
lin:PM VI 4841). On that vase a snake certainly rears up over the corpse of the
dead woman (and the tomb on which she lies); at the same time the murderer
prepares for a rapid exit right, suggesting that the snake threatens him and is
thus some sort of avenger of the deceased, regardless of how we interpret the
woman running in from the right with bow/snake. But lacking certainty that
the woman is not an Erinys, and with no literary support of any kind for an
Erinys in purely snake form, I am dubious about the painter's intentions. One
should note in this connection two efforts by the Cactus Painter toward the end
of the sixth century, on each of which two large snakes threaten an unarmed
man (Athens 12821; PrColl, Athens [lost?]).[36] In the second of these a tomb is
indicated, and thus both sets of snakes *may* be tomb guardians, but scarcely
the Erinyes; the context is much too general, and Erinyes are never thought to
protect (or avenge) *all* the dead. Of course they have snaky hair in the *Oresteia*
and other literary works, and they frequently hold snakes with which to
threaten Orestes in fifth-century Red-Figure. But from Homer and Hesiod
onward we understand these divinities (I think) as anthropomorphic. If this
view is correct the Foce del Sele metope will better represent some other hero,
Iason with the serpent guarding the Golden Fleece, perhaps, or Herakles challenging the snake who guards the Hesperides' apples.[37] The context (that is, the
other metopes flanking this one) may well have helped viewers to a correct
understanding of the artist's intentions.

For the fifth century we have the versions of Pindar (Orestes comes back
from his stay with Strophios and Pylades near Parnassos to kill both mother
and Aigisthos: *Py* 11.15–16, 34–37) and Aischylos; the latter's *Choephoroi* is
in fact the first continuous preserved account of the matricide, to be followed
by the *Elektra* plays of Sophokles and Euripides. In Aischylos, Orestes returns
from the exile in Phokis to which Klytaimestra sent him accompanied by Pylades and determined to recover his patrimony. He has also visited Delphi,
where Apollo instructed him to kill both Aigisthos and his mother, or else
experience dire torments. Accordingly he proceeds to his father's tomb to seek
support. There he meets Elektra, his sister who remained with her mother, and

hears of Klytaimestra's dream wherein she gave birth to a snake; nursing this, she was bitten by its fangs, which drew out blood as well as milk. Orestes naturally recognizes himself as the snake and is further encouraged. The plot devised by the two friends is to present themselves at the palace door, claiming knowledge of Orestes' death (as told to them by Strophios). Klytaimestra is the first to hear this news, and seems (despite her protestations of grief) quite eager for Aigisthos, the master of the house, to hear it as well. In the meantime, she retreats to her own quarters, but is summoned out again by a servant announcing that those supposedly dead have come to life and killed Aigisthos. At this point she calls for the famous axe, but then bares her breast (when she sees Orestes with Aigisthos' corpse) and summons up a child's feelings for his mother. She also attempts some justification of her deed; Orestes wavers, but on appeal to Pylades is reminded of the god's command, and leads her offstage to her death. As he returns to the stage with the fatal garment used to trap his father (it is here called a *pharos*), he sees for the first time the Erinyes, dark-robed women entwined with snakes, eyes dripping blood; their pursuit will send him back to Delphi, where Apollo instructed him to return for protection.

This narrative line of the *Choephoroi*, whatever the source of individual details, likely follows in its general shape the run of the story familiar to most Athenians by the time of Aischylos. When we turn to the third play of the trilogy, however, there is much less to be sure about. In fact, we have seen that well before Aischylos Stesichoros preserves for us the notion of a mother's Erinyes tormenting Orestes (217 *PMG*), but we know nothing about the outcome of the problem in his account, nor what early artists (whether or not the snakes discussed above are Erinyes) thought of the matter. As Aischylos presents the story, Orestes' fate is closely tied to civic developments in Athens, and one might be forgiven for guessing that this and even the flight to Athens itself were the inventions of an Athenian (not necessarily Aischylos). In any event, as the *Eumenides* opens Orestes is back in Delphi, but although Apollo delays his pursuers for a while the god cannot deter them altogether. His advice is that Orestes should go to Athens and seek Athena's help; Hermes escorts him off as Klytaimestra's ghost rouses the Erinyes and they and Apollo exchange reproaches. In Athens both parties, Orestes and the Erinyes, appeal to Athena for justice, agreeing to abide by her decision. She, however, declines to take sole responsibility, and instead turns the case over to a panel of twelve impartial Athenians, the first jury. Apollo arrives to speak for Orestes; the Erinyes present their own case. Their concern is with the fact of matricide and the precedent it creates for disrespect by children to parents. Orestes' claims of the necessity of his revenge are for the most part lost on them, for the deed creating that necessity, a wife's killing of her husband, does not involve any link by blood, and is thus outside their jurisdiction.

As we saw in chapter 1, there is not much effort to secure a consistent theology here; the Erinyes maintain that they protect all blood relationships from harm (*Eum* 605), but they have nothing to say (indeed they are never asked) about Agamemnon's sacrifice of his daughter Iphigeneia. Against their view that a simple admission of the deed by Orestes is sufficient for conviction, Apollo counters with the claim that the father supplies all the genetic input for offspring, the mother being merely an incubator and therefore not related by blood. The Erinyes in turn argue that the whole order of civilization, and the status of the older gods within it, will collapse if such things are permitted. What the audience (or the jury) made of all this we do not know; the entire debate seems inconclusive, with the jury in fact dividing their twelve votes evenly between the two parties. Scholars are not agreed on whether Athena now votes for Orestes to break the tie (because she herself has no mother) or acquits him on the general principle of innocent until proven guilty.[38] Either way the narrative problem of Orestes' future after matricide is resolved, and the jury system has been created. True, the Erinyes remain behind to threaten Athens with crop failure and the like, but once Athena assures them of their place in the new order (as guarantors of punishment decreed by the state) they yield to her persuasion and take up residence under the Areopagos. In such a dramatic treatment Orestes and the merits of his case have not, one may feel, held center stage; he is acquitted and summarily dismissed while the playwright assures us that a method of dispensing justice useful for all situations has been devised.

Following Aischylos in the preserved literary record of the fifth century are the *Elektra* plays of Sophokles and Euripides (both probably from its last twenty years, although we have no way of determining which effort came first). Sophokles adds to the cast Chrysothemis, a child of Agamemnon and Klytaimestra whom we have not seen since her father's casual reference to her in *Iliad* 9 and her (probable) inclusion as one of four daughters in the *Kypria*. In that connection we may remember that she is clearly excluded from the *Ehoiai*, where Agamemnon and Klytaimestra have only two daughters (Iphimede and Elektra: Hes fr 23a MW). Her role in Sophokles is to serve as a foil for Elektra's greater aggressiveness, urging prudence when action might seem required; considering Sophokles' use of Ismene for much the same purpose in *Antigone* (and the existence of tales about Ismene's death at a much earlier point) we might suspect that this daughter too has been resurrected from obscurity by the playwright, were it not for her appearance on a Red-Figure pelike that must be earlier than this play (see below). The play itself focuses primarily on the conflict between Klytaimestra and Elektra, the mother attempting to justify her actions, the daughter (aided by Agamemnon's genuine lack of choice at Aulis) refusing to listen. Orestes, who has returned with both Pylades and his childhood tutor, sends the tutor on ahead to announce to the household his death in a chariot mishap. Elektra then resolves to kill Aigisthos herself, however much Chrysothemis might denounce the plan as folly. At just this moment Orestes appears, with an urn supposed to contain his ashes, and reveals himself to Elektra as soon as he perceives it safe to do so. Aigisthos is for the time being away; with the tutor's help they enter the palace and kill

Klytaimestra as she prepares the urn for burial. When Aigisthos finally appears, having been summoned by the news of Orestes' death, he is shown his lover's corpse and then led in to his own death.

Throughout this play there is a total avoidance of any overt reservations about the justness of matricide. Orestes has here again been to Delphi, but he seems to have asked only about the manner of his revenge, not whom he should kill, and is told only that it must be done by stealth, not direct force. Elektra's plot involves Aigisthos alone; Orestes never discusses his, but simply walks into the palace and slays his mother as Elektra approves. Matters are thus very much in the offspring's hands, with no indications of the sort of future that they or Pylades (a completely silent character) might expect. At one point in the play Elektra does accuse her mother of "engendering children" with Aigisthos, which may be meant to acknowledge existence of a daughter Erigone (S: *El* 587–89); quite possibly she was the subject of the *Erigone* plays by Sophokles, Philokles, and others of which we know nothing (see below for later tales).

Euripides' interpretation brings us to a more surprising (and surely novel) rethinking of some situations. Elektra is here married to a peasant, Aigisthos reasoning that neither husband nor the children thus produced will be a danger to him. Although this husband has not touched her, she feels bitterly her exclusion from the palace and even laments the lack of decent clothes which prevents her from participating in Hera's festival. Orestes on his return comes to her husband's house to find her, and they plot the murders together. Once again Orestes has been to Delphi, or at least in contact with the god. But he says nothing at first about the nature of the response, and it appears for a while that the advisability of matricide is not to be an overt issue in the play. In their opening exchanges Orestes simply asks his sister if she is prepared to kill their mother as well as Aigisthos, and she affirms that she is. Because the intended victims are too well guarded in the palace, however, a stratagem different from those we have seen before must be devised. Orestes will approach Aigisthos down in the meadows, where he is at the moment readying a sacrifice for the Nymphai, while Elektra will send for her mother on the pretext that she has given birth to a child. All goes as planned: Orestes is invited to the sacrifice by the unwitting Aigisthos, and strikes as the latter turns his back to inspect the entrails. Klytaimestra for her part hastens to the hut, where Orestes, seeing her, begins to waver in his resolve. Here for the first time we learn that Apollo did after all command the matricide; when Orestes still hesitates, Elektra takes the lead. At this crucial moment, Euripides offers us an *agôn* in which Klytaimestra's wrongs are more sympathetically treated than they were in Aischylos or Sophokles; she has come too, it seems, to regret the treatment of her children and to be little in control of her own life. Nevertheless Elektra perseveres, luring her mother into the hut where Orestes strikes the blow, his sister urging him on. Both are quite shaken when they re-emerge, as the full horror of the deed sinks in. But before they can reflect further, the Dioskouroi appear, to lament their sister's death, denounce (tactfully) Apollo's oracle as false, and predict Orestes' future as it is played out in the *Eumenides*, complete with Erinyes and a judgment at Athens. The only new details here are Orestes' ultimate settlement near the Alpheios River in southern Arkadia, and the command that Elektra marry Pylades; this union is also predicted in the *Iphigeneia among the Tauroi*, where Pylades is a grandson of Atreus and cousin to Elektra (*IT* 912–19). In Pausanias and several scholia, that relationship is explained as due to a marriage between Pylades' father Strophios and Agamemnon's sister Anaxibia (Paus 2.29.4, perhaps drawn from Asios; ΣΣ *Or* 765, 1233). Anaxibia is certainly the name of Agamemnon's one sister in the *Ehoiai*, although her marriage in that poem is not preserved; elsewhere in the *Orestes* scholia this same sister and wife of Strophios is Kydragora (Σ *Or* 33; cf. Σ *Or* 1233), while Hyginus calls her Astyoche (*Fab* 117).

The same poet's *Orestes*, securely dated to 408 B.C., treats the aftermath of the matricide in different fashion: Elektra and an Orestes driven mad by his mother's Erinyes face stoning by the Argives, unless Menelaos can arrive to save them. He does arrive, but is dissuaded by an angry Tyndareos from taking any action in his nephew's defense. Orestes' subsequent attempt to address the Argive people directly gains nothing more than a concession of suicide, and at Pylades' prompting he determines to gain some measure of vengeance against Menelaos by killing Helen before he dies. Elektra for her part adds the thought that they might escape their own doom by taking Hermione hostage. In the course of their takeover of the palace Helen mysteriously disappears, but they are about to slay Hermione and fire the whole structure when Apollo appears to resolve matters. Helen, he announces, has been taken up to Olympos to sit with her brothers and the gods; Menelaos should remarry. Orestes shall spend a year in exile in the Parrhasian plain (the same part of Arkadia indicated in the *Elektra*) and then journey to Athens for his trial (here with the gods seemingly as jurors on the Areopagos). Ultimately he (not Neoptolemos, who is fated to die at Delphi before he can do so) shall wed Hermione, and Pylades shall have Elektra (the latter already so promised by Orestes).

The art of the period meanwhile offers us a number of Red-Figure representations of the death of Aigisthos, many of them prior to the production of the *Oresteia* and nearly all of them featuring as a common element Klytaimestra and her axe. Admittedly, it is absent from the earliest pieces, two fragmentary cups of the late sixth century in Florence (4B19 etc.) and Oxford (1973.1032), on which Aigisthos is sprawled helplessly on the ground as Orestes seizes his hair.[39] But on these Klytaimestra herself is missing, probably not preserved. When she does finally appear, in a memorable role on an early pelike by the Berlin Painter (*c.* 500 B.C.), we find a tableau with Aigisthos now on a throne, but again hopelessly unbalanced and ineffective as Orestes grasps his hair (Vienna 3725). Both Orestes and Chrysothemis behind him (named) look back to the left, as if at something approaching, and this we see on the other side of the vase: Klytaimestra charges forward with an axe while an older figure (labeled "Talthybios") seizes the blade in order to restrain her. We have already encountered the axe (plus restraining female figure) on the Foce del Sele metopes, but only now can we be certain that Klytaimestra means to use it to defend Aigisthos rather than (as in the *Choephoroi*) herself. The presence of Chrysothemis, not Elektra, is a surprise so clearly in advance of Sophokles, and we must wonder if (despite her role as a mere foil in his drama) she played some more important part in an Archaic version of the revenge. Subsequently we have a Red-Figure lekythos with similar scene (although there is no sister, and the restraining figure is one Telamedes: Boston 1977.713) and then among others a column krater probably by the Harrow Painter with just Klytaimestra, Talthybios, and the axe (Vienna 1103). On a stamnos by the Copenhagen Painter (*c.* 475 B.C.) Orestes seems in considerable peril as he stabs Aigisthos, for his attention is wholly on his victim and there is no restraining figure as Klytaimestra closes in from the left, axe raised (Berlin:PM F2184). To the other side of Aigisthos' chair Elektra (named) stands, hand outstretched in alarm. The same composition (including both female figures) reappears on a column krater by the Aegisthus Painter, although now a semi-naked young male (Pylades?) grasps the axe blade and Orestes looks back (Bologna 230). A newly published calyx krater by the same painter brings back the older bearded man as restrainer, while between Klytaimestra and Orestes comes a woman holding a small child; to the right the "Elektra" figure now holds one hand up to her forehead (Getty 88.AE.66).[40] The woman with child is a surprise here; most likely she represents a nurse holding Erigone or another of Aigisthos' children by Klytaimestra (see below). Finally, a stamnos by the Berlin Painter (Boston 91.227a, 91.226b) and the other side of our Boston calyx krater by the Dokimasia Painter (Boston 63.1246) introduce yet another new element, a lyre clutched in the left hand of Aigisthos as he is killed. On both of these, as in the Copenhagen Painter's version, Orestes is unaware of his mother's threat, and on both, the "Elektra" figure again runs up in alarm from the other side (the stamnos has a restrainer, the calyx krater none).

Even allowing for the possibility that many of these illustrations derive from a single monumental painting, we seem to have evidence of a highly dramatic version of the story in which Klytaimestra did almost dispatch her son while he was occupied with Aigisthos, and was prevented from doing so only by some third party. Such a version, with Orestes perhaps acting in self-defense to save his life, might also have been designed to mitigate the stigma of a deliberate matricide. Aischylos' more theatrically pointed confrontation of words between mother and son finds no such counterpart in art; indeed, the shield-band from Olympia discussed above is the only direct illustration of her death; other scenes showing a woman fleeing a man *might* be taken for this story (rather than that of Menelaos and Helen), but nowhere do we ever see the telltale axe. Thus the account in which Klytaimestra battles to protect her lover may have been the predominant (or only) version prior to Aischylos. Common to all these representations is the haplessness of Aigisthos; his costume (banqueting dress) suggests that he was taken by surprise, and at no time does he put up a convincing fight. Compared with this generally uniform artistic tradition we may be surprised to find that according to Pausanias a Polygnotos painting of the revenge in the Athenian Pinakotheke showed Pylades dispatching the sons of Nauplios who had come to aid Aigisthos (1.22.6). No other literary or artistic version that we know of includes such allies, although their presence (as enemies of Agamemnon, one of the slayers of their brother Palamedes) is not without some logic.

Later literary sources bring us nothing new on the subject of the deaths of Aigisthos and Klytaimestra, but they do offer new details about offspring of their union. According to the Parian Marble it was [Erig]on[e], daughter of Aigisthos, who brought Orestes to trial on the Areopagos, where the latter was victorious (239F25). Apollodoros knows of this trial (prosecuted by Erigone or perhaps Tyndareos), and adds that Klytaimestra was the girl's mother (ApE 6.25). In Diktys this Erigone hangs herself in disappointment after Orestes is acquitted at Athens (Dik 6.4); the same result appears in the account of the *Etymologicum Magnum* (s. *Aiôra*) after Erigone and Tyndareos have come together to Athens to prosecute the unsuccessful trial. Given that much, we might well suppose the story to have been told by Hellanikos, where the Athenians agree to judge the dispute between Orestes and "those coming from Lakedaimon" (4F169a). Yet the denouement at least is suspiciously close to the tale (claimed for Eratosthenes, whose poem about her is attested) of Erigone, daughter of Ikarios, who hanged herself after she found that her father had been killed by the cowherds to whom he gave wine (ΣAb *Il* 22.29). This latter figure has been thought a Hellenistic conception, but the fact remains that we cannot say for certain whether Sophokles' attested *Erigone* (or similar plays by Philokles, Kleophon, Phrynichos II) concerned the daughter of Aigisthos.[41] Apollodoros also states that Orestes married either Hermione or Erigone (ApE 6.28), drawing perhaps for this latter idea on the same tradition we found ascribed (by Pausanias) to Kinaithon (fr 4 *PEG*): Erigone, daughter of Aigisthos, bears to Orestes a bastard child Penthilos. That the same woman is in one tale Orestes' bitter enemy and in another his lover is to say the least puzzling.

Finally, in Hyginus alone we find the story of a *son* of Aigisthos, Aletes (*Fab* 122). Hyginus does not say that his mother was Klytaimestra, and some of the wording might be taken to mean that she was not, although with Hyginus any such conclusions are perilous. The tale itself is quite simple and smacks of tragedy: Aletes has seized the throne of Mykenai amid false reports that Orestes has been killed by the Tauroi. Elektra, however, goes off to Delphi for confirmation of his death, and there finds her brother and Iphigeneia (nearly killing the latter through ignorance). Reunited, the three return to Mykenai where Orestes kills Aletes and would have killed Erigone as well, had not Artemis snatched her away and made her a priestess in Athens. The last detail seems again to betray confusion with Erigone, daughter of Ikarios, and even a doublet of Iphigeneia's original fate. Sophokles (or a namesake) may have written a play *Aletes*; we know nothing about it.[42] The rescue of Iphigeneia is discussed below, as are Orestes' further deeds, including the slaying of Neoptolemos.

Iphigeneia among the Tauroi

We saw in chapter 16 that as early as the *Kypria* Iphigeneia is rescued at Aulis by Artemis and taken to the Tauroi, where she is made immortal. The implication of this is, I suppose, that she is to be worshipped by the Tauroi, but something may have been lost in the summation. In the *Ehoiai* (or rather, what we took to be an interpolation in that work) there is the same notion of apotheosis but no mention of the Tauroi; rather, Iphigeneia becomes an attendant of the goddess under the name "Artemis *einodia*" or (possibly) "Hekate" (Hes fr 23a MW). This last version seems to have been found also in Stesichoros' *Oresteia* (215 *PMG*), and strengthens our impression of a tradition in which, whatever the differences in detail, Iphigeneia is taken away to a blessed existence of immortality from which she most certainly does not need to be rescued. That she is nonetheless brought back by Orestes and Pylades in Euripides' *Iphigeneia among the Tauroi* probably stems from a variety of factors relating more to the needs of cultic aetiology than narrative considerations. For one thing, she herself had become linked (or fused) with Artemis at both Brauron and Halai Araphenides (north of Brauron), where the Athenians had a cult of Artemis Tauropolos (Str 9.1.22) and kept one version of the statue of her claimed to have been brought back from the Crimea (*IT* 1448–57).[43] For another, the historical Tauroi of that peninsula were described already by Herodotos as sacrificing all foreign sailors to a maiden goddess whom they identified with Iphigeneia, daughter of Agamemnon (Hdt 4.103). How this idea was concocted we cannot say, but certainly it must go back to the time of the *Kypria*; in Euripides, Athena proclaims the cult title "Tauropolos" as derived from the Taurian land, and that derivation (taken in reverse, of course) might well be the truth of the matter.[44] From the land of the Tauroi, at any rate, a desire to bring Iphigeneia narratively into contact with Brauron and Halai, so as to better explain the cults there, might have generated the impetus for Euripides' play. His drama is our first source to say that she was rescued from the Crimea; whoever invented this story invented as well perhaps her shift back to mortal status, making her a priestess rather than the divinity herself.[45]

As the play opens, Iphigeneia describes her situation, brought to these people and their king Thoas after the sacrifice at Aulis and made to consecrate foreigners to the goddess. Orestes and Pylades then appear, seeking just this shrine of Artemis in order that they might carry off the statue within, for Apollo has told them that only thus, when they have conveyed it back to Athens, will Orestes' madness end. They are, however, spotted by herdsmen and captured, so that they come before Iphigeneia as prospective victims, in ignorance of her real identity and she of theirs. But they are Greeks, of course, and she conceives the plan of saving one of them so that he might take back to Orestes a letter from her; when its contents are revealed as a safeguard against loss the whole truth comes out. Iphigeneia then proposes that Orestes' pollution as a matricide may be turned to their advantage; much as in the *Helen*, she tells the king that such a victim must be purified at sea before the sacrifice, and the statue as well, thus acquiring an avenue of escape. The king's forces pursue when they discover statue and victims making for open water, but Athena appears to Thoas and instructs him to desist: Orestes will take the statue to Halai Araphenides in Attika, where he will establish a cult in Artemis' honor, while Iphigeneia shall become keeper of a second shrine at Brauron, where she shall be buried when she dies. These last details patently justify Athenian cult practice, and are much strained to fit the circumstances of a royal family of Argos, but no doubt Athenian audiences enjoyed them.

Later accounts of the rescue follow Euripides without serious deviation, save in the fact that the statue often winds up elsewhere; Pausanias, for example, found the Spartans convinced that Iphigeneia had brought it there, to be the image of Artemis Orthia (3.16.7). But Hyginus adds to the successful return an interlude that we must here consider. In this tale, as Orestes and Iphigeneia make their way back from the Crimea, they have stopped in at the island of Sminthe where they find the priest of Apollo—Chryses—and his daughter Chryseis, who years before on her return from Troy bore a child conceived by Agamemnon whom she named Chryses after her father. Fearing to admit the truth, however, she has claimed that the child is Apollo's. At this point the text shows some obscurity (or rather, reference back to *Fab* 120), with Chryses (the younger) apparently planning to return Orestes and Iphigeneia to Thoas, who is perhaps an ally. The elder Chryses then learns (from his daughter, presumably) the truth, which he reveals to his grandson, namely that these refugees are the latter's half-siblings. The refugees are therefore assisted as they kill Thoas (newly arrived to claim his victims?) and reach Mykenai safely with the statue. Obviously this sounds like a standard recognition play of the later fifth century, and in fact Sophokles is credited with a *Chryses* (of uncertain content) which might then anticipate the rescue in the *Iphigeneia among the Tauroi*. But such a play (if it concerns this Chryses) might also deal with his problems at Troy or elsewhere.

Neoptolemos Of Neoptolemos, Nestor in *Odyssey* 3 says that he brought the Myrmidones back safely, one presumes by sea and to their homeland of Phthia (*Od* 3.188–89). Admittedly, Homer is concerned here to contrast the blissful condition of the many who did return home gloriously with the special pain of those few (Agamemnon, Odysseus) who did not; when concerned with other stories of the war's aftermath he may have seen matters differently. Whatever the case, Neoptolemos' subsequent misfortunes give special relevance to the issue of his Trojan prisoners. We saw in chapter 16 that the *Little Iliad* made the son of Achilleus responsible (on his own initiative) for the death of Astyanax, while the *Iliou Persis* gave that role to Odysseus. Either way, both works agree that Neoptolemos received as a special prize Andromache, wife of Hektor.

But there is a complication, for Tzetzes, our source for the *Little Iliad* on this point, insists that the hero took on board his ship not only Andromache but also Aineias, and offers an eleven-line quote from Lesches to that effect (Σ Lyk 1268 = fr 21 *PEG*). Of these eleven lines, however, the last six, where Aineias is actually mentioned, are also quoted by the scholia to the *Andromache*, which ascribe them to Simias of Rhodes, a shadowy figure known from the *Souda* and certainly of Hellenistic times (Σ *And* 14). Elsewhere, Tzetzes adds that Aineias was freed after Neoptolemos' death at Delphi, which may also come from Simias (Σ Lyk 1232). Certainly the idea of such a captivity is strange, and would serve little purpose before Aineias has become linked to Rome, for by himself he is (unlike Helenos, who is a seer) of no use to Neoptolemos. In all other versions he either escapes during Troy's fall or is freed by the Greeks.

The *Nostoi* has nothing on this matter; what it does say is that Thetis warned Neoptolemos of the dangers awaiting the Greeks at sea, and that in consequence he journeyed overland, meeting Odysseus at Maroneia in the land of the Kikones. Subsequently he buried Phoinix, who had died, and in the land of the Molossoi was recognized by Peleus (who of course had never seen his grandson). The genuine part of Tzetzes' quote of the *Little Iliad*, with its talk of boarding ships, might seem to contradict this, but perhaps the warning came after he had departed Troy, and he put back in to shore when convenient. Something similar is recorded by Eustathios, who says that Neoptolemos burned his ships at Thessaly by the advice of Thetis after traveling there by sea, and then journeyed to Epeiros, recognizing his destination from a portent given by Helenos (Eu-*Od* p. 1463; cf. Σ *Od* 3.188).[46] Nothing in our summaries of the three epics suggests that Helenos accompanied him; such a detail might not have struck epitomators as especially important.

No other Archaic source mentions the return until Pindar, who notes in *Nemean 7* that on leaving Troy Neoptolemos missed Skyros and ultimately found himself at Ephyra in Molossia, where he ruled a short time (*Nem* 7.36–39). The earlier *Paian 6* of the same poet identifies the site as near Mount Tomaros, apparently thinking of the same location. This latter poem also implies that Apollo may have been responsible for the hero's failure to arrive at Phthia, for we are told that the god in his anger vowed that the slayer of Priam would never arrive at his home (*Pa* 6.112–17). But other versions may have chosen to regard the Molossian land as somehow Neoptolemos' proper home, for we have seen that in the *Nostoi* he finds his grandfather Peleus there (though this might be an improperly stated compression of the epitomator). The *Odyssey* hints at one point of a Peleus under some pressure from neighbors in Achilleus' absence (*Od* 12.494–504), and the notion of a recognition in the *Nostoi* might suggest that he was, like Odysseus' family, in difficulty when his grandson arrived, wherever that was. Such a story *might* also have formed the basis of the lost *Peleus* by Sophokles. As often, we have no details of the work, although it must be earlier than Aristophanes' *Hippes* (424 B.C.) and the account in Diktys (see below) may be drawn from it. Euripides offers a likely reference to it at the close of his *Troades*, where Talthybios tells Hekabe that Neoptolemos has already departed for Phthia, having heard news that Peleus has been cast out of the land by Akastos, son of Pelias (*Tro* 1123–28). The scholia add that in some accounts the expellers are rather the *sons* of Akastos, Archandros and Architeles, and that Peleus' setting forth in search of his grandson came after a storm to Kos (or Ikos?) where he was entertained by Molon and died. Kos seems rather too far away to be likely here, but poem 7.2 of the *Palatine Anthology* agrees with the idea that he is buried on Ikos (modern Alonissos), one of the Northern Sporades.

In the version of Diktys noted, Neoptolemos comes first to the Molossian land, but then, while repairing his ships, the hero receives a report that Peleus has been expelled from his kingdom in Thessaly by Akastos (Dik 6.7–9). After sending subordinates to assess the situation, he finally resolves to go himself, but has further troubles at sea, and barely puts to shore on the Sepiades Islands. Presumably by these Diktys means the islands next to the Cape of Sepias in Magnesia, that is, the same Northern Sporades off the entrance to the Gulf of Iolkos. There Neoptolemos finds Peleus hidden in a cave. By chance the sons of Akastos (here Menalippos and Pleisthenes) are coming to hunt on the island, and Neoptolemos takes advantage of the situation to ambush and kill them. Next, disguising himself as a Trojan prisoner, he encounters Akastos and lures him to the cave with a tale of an unguarded Neoptolemos sleeping there. Caught in the trap, Akastos comes close to losing his life, but Thetis appears to appeal for him after berating him severely. He concedes the kingdom to Peleus, and the Aiakidai return to their rightful land. Certainly this sounds like a play, and the *Troades* shows that the premise for it was known in the fifth century; its Sophoklean pedigree remains a guess, if an attractive one.

As for other versions of the return, Apollodoros says that Neoptolemos remained behind on Tenedos for two days (again on Thetis' advice), then set out with Helenos by land, and came to the Molossoi (burying Phoinix on the way), where after a battle he ruled the country (ApE 6.12–13). Andromache bears him a son, Molossos, and Helenos founds his own city, having been given to wife Neoptolemos' mother, Deidameia. Only after Peleus has been driven out of Phthia by the sons of Akastos and dies does Neoptolemos obtain his rightful kingdom of Phthia; we are not told how. Much of the first part of this agrees with our epitome of the *Nostoi*, but there is here no recognition by Peleus, unless we assume that he comes to the Molossian land after his expulsion (which is not impossible) and tells his grandson what has happened. Pausanias, like Eustathios, speaks of prophecies of Helenos which guide Neoptolemos to Epeiros, where he has three sons by Andromache—Molossos, Pielos, and Pergamos; after his death at Delphi, Helenos receives Andromache and they have a son, Kestrinos (1.11.1). That Helenos and Andromache should thus wed is an idea first preserved in Euripides, as we shall see below. It reappears, of course, in Book 3 of the *Aeneid*, although with no very convincing explanation; according to Servius it was Helenos (not as elsewhere Thetis) who gave Neoptolemos the initial warning not to sail to Greece by sea, and for this reason he was favored with Hektor's bride after her new master's death (Σ *Aen* 3.297). Hyginus records as the one child of Neoptolemos and Andromache the name "Amphialos" (*Fab* 123).

Regarding Neoptolemos' death itself, Pindar's *Paian* 6 and *Nemean* 7 are in fact our earliest references; both poems place the event at Delphi, but neither involves Orestes in any way, nor says anything about a quarrel over Hermione, daughter of Helen and Menelaos. That Neoptolemos married Hermione is told as early as the *Odyssey*, where Telemachos' arrival at Sparta coincides with the day on which she is to be sent off to Achilleus' son as a bride, having been promised while both father and prospective groom were still at Troy. Homer mentions this event as part of a definite context, a portrait of the domestic felicity not yet vouchsafed to Odysseus and Penelope; he can scarcely here mean us to think of any subsequent assault on the marriage bond by Orestes (who in the *Odyssey* is very much the defender of the home) and perhaps does not know that story.

Pindar's account in *Paian* 6 makes Apollo the cause of death; he is angry with the slayer of Priam, and thus ordains that Neoptolemos shall never return home nor reach old age (*Pa* 6.117–20). Death here comes by the god's hand while the hero is arguing with attendants over fees (presumably for consultation). This apparently too negative characterization is ameliorated in *Nemean* 7 by eliminating all mention of Apollo's wrath and having Neoptolemos journey to Delphi precisely to offer trophies to the god. At the temple he enters into a quarrel over sacrificial victims, not fees, and is slain by "a man," to the great distress of the local populace (*Nem* 7.40–43). Pindar stresses, however, that higher purposes are served by this death, for Neoptolemos thus remains within the sanctuary, to be a watcher for all time over the ceremonies, as *moira* intended.

In Pherekydes there is likewise no mention of Orestes; instead we are told that having married Hermione Neoptolemos goes to Delphi to inquire about their prospects for children (3F64a). There he sees men of Delphi carrying off meat from the sanctuary, and takes it away from them. At this point our text, from a Euripidean scholion (Σ *Or* 1655), adds that he kills himself with a knife *(machaira)* and is buried by the priest under the threshold of the temple. Such an ill-motivated suicide has obviously been questioned; we will see in a moment that textual corruption is probably involved here. The *Odyssey* scholia (and Eustathios) give us the plot of Sophokles' lost *Hermione*, a play offering some version of these same events. The drama centered on a conflict in the girl's betrothing: Menelaos had promised her to Neoptolemos while the two were at Troy, but at the same time Tyndareos back in Sparta gave her to Orestes (Σ *Od* 4.4). Upon his return Menelaos took her away from Orestes in order to maintain his promise; Neoptolemos, however, met his death at Delphi, slain there by a man named Machaireus when he tried to seek satisfaction from the god for the death of his father (this motive only in Eustathios), and thus Hermione was able to return to Orestes, to whom she bore Tisamenos.

Given the basic similarity between the name of the killer here and the *machaira* employed as the murder weapon in our text of Pherekydes, scholars have not unreasonably supposed that such a name (as murderer) stood originally in the latter text, but was mistakenly taken by someone to be a weapon, leading to the change of "him" *(auton)* to "himself" *(heauton)* and the erroneous notion of a suicide.[47] Such a conclusion, with Machaireus in Pherekydes as in Sophokles the killer, seems on the whole likely, the more so as something must be done about that suicide. Curiously though, in Pindar's *Nemean 7*, where we found a murder and a dispute over meat, the name of the killer is omitted but not the murder weapon, which is a *machaira* (*Nem* 7.42). Possibly this is a play on the killer's name, but since a *machaira* was commonly a butcher knife (and "Delphic *machaira*" a proverbial expression for the priests' share of the victims), the idea may in origin have been that Neoptolemos was killed with such a weapon because it was ready at hand when the dispute broke out, said weapon subsequently evolving into a person named after it. Machaireus as killer is also the version of Asklepiades, who says that nearly all the poets agree that Neoptolemos was slain by him, and that although first buried under the threshold he was later removed by Menelaos and buried in the temenos (12F15). As to who Machaireus was (a priest?), or exactly why he committed the deed, we have no other information, nor can we say to what extent Orestes is involved as a character in the *Hermione* (he and Neoptolemos do confront each other at Delphi in Pacuvius' *Hermiona*). But at least there seems some common adherence to a tradition in which someone other than Orestes is the murderer. Further testimony on this point is probably to be found in the *Andromache* scholia: we are told there that in (name has fallen out) Neoptolemos is slain by Machaireus, but that in other writers such as Euripides he is slain by Orestes (Σ *And* 53). If such a remark will not quite prove that Euripides invented the idea, it does link him rather than earlier poets with it.

Regarding Neoptolemos' motive for being at Delphi, Pherekydes' notion of childlessness stands (rather more respectably) against the idea that Neoptolemos wished to lay a claim against Apollo for the death of his father. We saw that this latter motif may have appeared in Sophokles' *Hermione* (if Eustathios is drawing from that source); certainly it is part of both Euripides' *Andromache*, where Neoptolemos makes a second trip to Delphi to apologize for his previous behavior (*And* 49–53), and his *Orestes* (*Or* 1653–57). Quite a number of later writers do report children of Neoptolemos and Hermione, and the tragedians Philokles and Theognis even claim that Hermione was pregnant by Orestes when she was taken by her new husband (Σ *And* 32; the child is Amphiktyon). This last detail may indicate that in some versions Neoptolemos was the villain, taking Hermione away by force from a man she loved and whose child she was carrying.

In any case, we find from this brief survey that Sophokles is the first preserved source to have Orestes marry Hermione, and that prior to the end of the fifth century there is a substantial tradition making Apollo (or Machaireus or some other Delphian) the cause of Neoptolemos' death. That Orestes himself did the deed (or rather, caused it to be done) first survives in Euripides' *Andromache*. That work also introduces another complicating factor, the presence of the concubine Andromache, who emerges as a reluctant rival for Neoptolemos' affections. The play opens with Andromache seeking refuge at the shrine of Thetis, fearing the anger of Neoptolemos' wife Hermione in his absence, for she herself has unwillingly borne to him a child (never named in the play, "Molottos" in some cast lists) while Hermione remains barren. The reason for Neoptolemos' absence is, as we saw above, a second trip to Delphi, undertaken in an attempt to atone for an earlier visit there when he demanded justice from Apollo for the death of his father. Hermione for her part has been joined by her father Menelaos, and accuses Andromache of causing her childlessness through spells or potions. The play's action turns around attempts to extricate Andromache from her refuge. When she refuses to leave the altar her child (seized by Menelaos) is threatened, and although she surrenders on the promise of his safety, her captors announce their intention to execute both. Fortunately, Peleus arrives to save the situation, with Menelaos wilting totally before the latter's anger and deciding he will be safer back in Sparta.

Thus abandoned, Hermione begins to fear the reproach of her husband when he returns and learns of her failed plot, and at just this moment Orestes enters, in passage to Dodona. Seeing Hermione's plight, he recalls the fact that she was promised to him by Menelaos but repromised to Neoptolemos at Troy, his subsequent pleas to Neoptolemos being rebuffed because of his matricide and maddened condition. When Hermione explains her now precarious position, he announces that Neoptolemos is doomed, fated to die by the god and his own slanders already planted at Delphi. The two then make their escape to Sparta, while a messenger enters to report to Peleus the death of Neoptolemos. He had, it seems, on his previous visit despoiled the shrine, and Orestes (somehow present) has spread the rumor that he has returned for the same purpose. Accordingly he is ambushed and killed by the Delphians, despite a noble and heroic resistance. The play concludes with a theophany by Thetis, who consoles the distraught Peleus and orders him to bury the body at Delphi as a reproach to Orestes. She further decrees that Andromache shall marry Helenos (not previously mentioned in the play) in Molossia, and that from her child by Neoptolemos will spring future rulers of that land. Peleus himself will henceforth live with her as a god in Nereus' home beneath the sea; thus the work closes.

The somewhat later *Orestes* of the same writer adheres instead to what might seem a more canonical version of Neoptolemos' death at Delphi: only one visit is made (as in the *Andromache* and perhaps Sophokles' *Hermione* to reproach Apollo for slaying his father) and he dies by a "Delphic sword" (*Or*

1653–57). Since Apollo predicts this outcome to Orestes it seems clear that the latter will not be involved, and that Neoptolemos pays rather the price of his own hybris. By contrast, the *Andromache's* unique notion of a double visit allows Euripides to include Neoptolemos' claim against Apollo while at the same time (since Neoptolemos repents) creating room for Orestes, not Apollo, to be the cause of his death. Again, I think, we see grounds for supposing that Euripides himself concocted Orestes' role in the killing.[48] One other novel element in the *Orestes*, the idea that Hermione has not actually been wed to Neoptolemos, may have arisen from the need to explain why she is with her mother in Mykenai and thus available for Orestes and Pylades to threaten.

Subsequent evidence includes an Apulian krater of about 370 B.C. on which we see a wounded Neoptolemos, sword drawn, in a desperate struggle for his life ("H.A." Coll 239). Above him are the temple, Apollo, and the Pythia, to the left an unnamed attacker with poised spear, to the right the omphalos and behind it Orestes (named). This last crouches cautiously, as if fearing to confront his rival directly, but he too has a drawn sword. Although his role here is more aggressive than that described in the *Andromache*, one has the impression that the artist has taken his scene directly from that play. Much more circumspect is the part Orestes plays in Diktys, who hedges on the critical details. Here Neoptolemos goes to Delphi to give thanks to Apollo (because he has been vindicated against Paris for the death of his father), leaving behind Hermione, Andromache, and the latter's one surviving son by Hektor (Laodamas: Dik 6.12). The action then proceeds as in Euripides' *Andromache*, with the exception that Orestes plans to kill his rival after the latter's return and is apparently forestalled by the death at Delphi, attributed by rumor to Orestes but actually of unknown cause. The first writer to claim that Orestes himself actually slew Neoptolemos seems then Vergil, who in *Aeneid* 3 makes good use of the parallel between Neoptolemos' butchering of Priam at an altar in Troy and being himself killed (from ambush) at an altar by another Greek (*Aen* 3.325–32: the phrase *patrias aras* at 332 [Servius attempts various explanations] remains obscure). Orestes' reason is, as usual, desire for Hermione, the "wife snatched away" from him, with a contributing nod to his mother's Erinyes; Neoptolemos has meanwhile abandoned Andromache to Helenos in order to pursue this marriage. The appropriateness of fate here might tempt us to think that Vergil himself improved upon the account of Euripides by making Orestes the slayer, but a lost intermediary between them has probably already taken that step (see below). The alternative version with Machaireus was not forgotten, however: it appears in Strabo, for example, with again the motif of a demand for redress from the god (Str 9.3.9), and so too in Apollodoros (Ap*E* 6.14). Strabo, like those before him, does not quite say that Machaireus slew Neoptolemos *because* the latter demanded redress, but that is the natural conclusion, as it is for Pausanias, who has a priest of Apollo do the killing at one point (10.24.4), and Delphians on orders from the Pythia at another (1.13.9). Apollodoros makes the connection more explicit by stating that Neoptolemos' hostile actions (taking of meat, looting the shrine) are the result of his failure to obtain satisfaction, with Machaireus acting to protect the sanctuary. The same writer, however, also reports the story that Orestes struck the blow out of jealousy, thus lessening the chances that Vergil innovated here. Hyginus adds his support to this latter version with the detail that Orestes killed Neoptolemos while the latter was sacrificing at Delphi (*Fab* 123). In all, we seem to have two separate strands of thought, the one blaming Neoptolemos for his rash challenge to Apollo and desecration of the latter's shrine, the other shifting much of the guilt to a jealous Orestes. Yet in the first case the greed of the shrine's priests is also sometimes a factor, and in the second Neoptolemos' usurpation of an already betrothed woman often the source of the trouble.

Teukros   Of the son of Telamon our *Nostoi* summary says nothing, and likewise the *Odyssey*. Both Pindar (*Nem* 4.46–47) and Aischylos (*Persai* 894–95) speak of his eventual settlement of Cyprus from Salamis, but the problems in his homeland which motivated this event are first recorded by Euripides' *Helen*, and then by Lykophron. Conceivably they formed part of Aischylos' lost *Salaminioi* (or *Salaminiai*) as the final play of his Aias trilogy, although nothing of the plot survives, and for such a title there are many other possibilities, including events at Troy (since a chorus of Salaminians need not be on Salamis). More certain evidence comes from Sophokles, for as early as the *Aias* Teukros anticipates his father's anger, and even possible exile, should he return home without his half-brother (1006–21). Sophokles also wrote a (lost) *Teukros*, which from the remains would definitely seem to have dramatized this homecoming of Telamon's bastard son. One or both of these lost plays were probably a source for Pacuvius' *Teucer*, whose fragments in turn add some details.

   Of Sophokles' play we know (virtually for certain) that it was set on Salamis, where Telamon and his visitor Oileus waited for news of their children. Oileus apparently consoled his friend when Teukros arrived with the news of Telamonian Aias' death, but subsequently found himself in the same position when news came of the death of his own son in the storm (fr 576 R and *TD* 3.71). The bearer of this news may have been Odysseus; certainly he is present at some point and accuses the half-Trojan Teukros of likely treachery against the Greeks (frr 579a, b R). We have nothing of the outcome of the debate, although we will naturally suppose Teukros banished for failure to assure his brother's return. Pacuvius' version seems to have included Teukros' mother Hesione, who grieved (for her child's exile?), and an accusation that Teukros has somehow lost (perhaps only for the moment) his brother's son. There was certainly here a detailed description of the return voyage and storm, but whether this means that Lokrian Aias' death was again an issue, or represents Teukros' defense for losing the child, we do not know.

   At the beginning of the *Helen* Teukros makes a very brief appearance, stopping off in Egypt on his way to Cyprus, so that Helen may be apprised of the outcome of the Trojan War before Menelaos arrives (*Hel* 68–163). Of himself he tells Helen simply that after he was expelled by his father in anger over Aias' death Apollo ordered him to Cyprus so that he might found a new Salamis. Lykophron says, more precisely, that Telamon banished Teukros because he blamed him for Aias' death, not believing the story of the suicide at Troy (Lyk 450–69). Apollodoros has, surprisingly, no word of this event (although the *Epitome* does say that some Greeks settled on Cyprus), and neither does Hyginus. But in *Aeneid* 1 Dido comments that Teukros came to Sidon, and that her father Belus helped him find a home on Cyprus, having recently conquered it (*Aen* 1.619–26). Servius adds that according to some Telamon was angry because Teukros appeared without Tekmessa and Eurysakes, who had been placed on a ship not yet arrived in port (Σ *Aen* 1.619). Likely enough this is the explanation of the allusion seen above in Pacuvius; it may or may not go back to Sophokles. The Lykophron scholia offer nothing new, save that Teukros on Cyprus married Eue, daughter of Kypros, and had a daughter Asterie (Σ Lyk 450).

One other story of Teukros is preserved only in Justin's epitome of Pompeius Trogus, but could perhaps incorporate early elements: we are told that on learning of his father's death Teukros attempted to return to Salamis from Cyprus, but that his nephew Eurysakes prevented him, and that he then went on to the site of New Carthage in Spain (44.3). New Carthage itself goes back no further than the late third century B.C., but the rest of the tale (with a less ambitious final destination) might be earlier: we know in fact that Sophokles wrote a *Eurysakes*, and this seems the likeliest plot for it. The same story was probably dramatized in Accius' *Eurysaces*, for which fragments show that a homeless, wretched-looking exile was a major character. The Athenians for their part were ready to maintain that Eurysakes and his brother Philaios had given over the island of Salamis to Athens and taken out Athenian citizenship, the one at Melite, the other at Brauron (*Sol* 10).

*Aias
Oileiades
and
Nauplios'
Revenge*

We saw that Homer mentions neither Palamedes nor the vengeance of his father Nauplios against the Achaians returning from Troy. The *Odyssey* does note the disaster at Gyrai and the death of Aias (described briefly by Proteus to Menelaos): here Aias and Agamemnon are seemingly together when the storm strikes, thus both part of the second departure from Troy, after Menelaos and Nestor have led away the first group (*Od* 4.499–513). But what caused the storm is not said, only that Poseidon drove Aias' ship against the rocks. The location of Gyrai is likewise uncertain: Mykonos, Tenos, and Cape Kaphereus (on the southeast tip of Euboia) are variously claimed by later sources; only the last-named site would immediately suggest Nauplios as part of the story. In many later accounts the reason for the storm is the gods' anger after the sacrilege of Aias (or other Achaian misdeeds), with the ships then driven to Kaphereus. Possibly this was always the sequence of events, but perhaps too Nauplios' role in causing the disaster was originally independent, and fused together with Olympian intervention in a later syncretism. What Proteus does tell us in the *Odyssey* is that Aias was saved by Poseidon when his ship went down, and that he would have avoided death, even though he was hateful to Athena, had he not boasted that he had escaped the sea despite the gods. Upon hearing him, Poseidon broke off the section of rock on which he was sitting with his trident, and Aias drowned. Agamemnon himself was somehow saved by Hera and made his way to the Argolid, where he met his usual fate.

Proklos' summary of the *Nostoi* says for this part of the story simply that there was a storm at the Kapherides rocks and that Lokrian Aias perished. The choice of this site for the storm probably means that Nauplios' part was related also, although Proklos does not speak of him and there is no proof that he was always linked to Euboia. In his favor, however, is the fact that he *was* mentioned in some context in the poem, for Apollodoros tells us that his wife in that work was Philyra (ApB 2.1.5). To be perfectly strict, Proklos' wording also does not guarantee that the Kapherean storm and Aias' death were part of the same sequence of events, although this would seem a reasonable assumption.

From epic we turn briefly to lyric and then tragedy. Judging from papyrus fragments, Alkaios dealt with the desecration of Athena's statue by Aias and seems also to have described the storm (the fragments end at just this point: 262 SLG). Aischylos' memorable account of this storm in *Agamemnon* gives no particulars of place or victims (*Ag* 646–73); Sophokles' *Aias Lokros*, set almost certainly at Troy after the desecration (since Athena addresses the Argives: fr 10c R), probably concluded with a prediction of divine punishment, now totally lost. The same poet's *Teukros* we have seen to combine Telamon's wait for his son's return with that of Oileus, so that there will have been here at least a messenger speech describing the storm and Aias' death (perhaps without Nauplios). But Sophokles' *Nauplios Pyrkaeus* must have dramatized the actual vengeance as we know it from later sources, with the old man lighting beacons near the rocks of Cape Kaphereus to lure the Achaian ships to destruction, in our first sure appearance of that story; no details of the plot survive. Not impossibly *Nauplios Katapleon*, *Aias Lokros*, and *Nauplios Pyrkaeus* were linked together as a connected trilogy, with the first two plays bringing Nauplios and Athena to Troy to protest unjust deeds, and the third dramatizing the combined vengeance of the two plaintiffs when their appeals are not heard.

Euripides' *Troades* begins with a prologue shared between Poseidon and Athena in which the goddess asks Poseidon to assist her in vengeance upon the Greeks for the desecration of her shrine (*Tro* 48–97). With the emphasis entirely on her own anger nothing is said here of Nauplios, but Euboia and the Kaphereian promontory are mentioned as site of the disaster (along with other points scattered across the Aegean); here too we encounter the unusual idea that Zeus has promised his daughter that *she* may throw the thunderbolt (*Tro* 80–81). More specific is the same poet's *Helen*, where two brief references confirm the general run of Nauplios' deed (the false fires and ships crashing on the rocks: *Hel* 766–67, 1126–31, with Menelaos' presence at the time perhaps poetic license). In the latter of these passages Nauplios is called *monokôpos*, "rowing alone," suggesting that he rowed out in a small boat to the point where he lit the fires; clearly at any rate Euripides refers to a well-known (and detailed) version of the story. Oddly enough, in describing Nauplios' efforts to corrupt the wives of the Achaians Lykophron calls him a fisherman with a *dikôpon selma*, "two-oared craft," as if he spent a great deal of time in that boat (Lyk 1217). The same work features Kassandra predicting the storm, with cryptic references to Nauplios' fires and Aias' drowning, after which Thetis buries his washed-up corpse on Delos (Lyk 373–407). This last detail is also found in the *Iliad* scholia (ΣA *Il* 13.66) and may, like other parts of that account, be drawn from Kallimachos' *Aitia*.

Of later writers, Vergil follows Euripides' *Troades* in the idea that Athena herself wielded the thunderbolt, for he has her personally hurl one at Aias' ship (*Aen* 1.39–45). The same image reappears (vividly) in Seneca's *Agamemnon* (470–578) and later in Apollodoros, Hyginus, and Quintus (ApE 6.6; *Fab* 116; QS 14.449–589). These last four all present a similar sequence of events: Zeus and/or Athena sends the storm, with Aias' consequent death (Poseidon's doing in Seneca, Apollodoros, and Quintus), and the surviving ships make their way through the night to Euboia, where Nauplios is waiting with his beacons. Apollodoros adds as the place of Aias' burial by Thetis Mykonos (not, as above, Delos), and Hyginus has the further grim detail that Nauplios killed any Greeks who were able to swim to shore. The other part of Nauplios' vengeance, the leading of Achaian wives to betray their husbands, we have already considered in chapter 16. Apollodoros also has one odd variant on all this, that Nauplios made a general practice of luring ships to destruction with beacon fires (presumably for their cargoes), and that he somehow died in the same fashion (ApB 2.1.5).

Idomeneus, The just-mentioned second part of Nauplios' revenge on the Greek leaders, the
Diomedes, corrupting of their wives with false tales, involved in particular Idomeneus and
Philoktetes, Diomedes. Like Neoptolemos, both men are said by Nestor in the *Odyssey* to
and Others have gotten home without incident, the implication being that their homecomings were thus happy ones (*Od* 3.180–82, 191–92). Our *Nostoi* summary says only that Diomedes left Troy with Nestor and came safely home; there is no mention of what he found there, and no mention of Idomeneus at all. If Sophokles' *Nauplios Katapleon* did concern one or more of these corrupted wives there may have been some sort of prediction of their fate at the play's end. Otherwise our first source to treat the consequences of the infidelities (other than that of Klytaimestra) is Lykophron, who presents as we saw in chapter 16 a surprising sequence of events: Leukos, the guardian of Idomeneus' kingdom, is stirred by Nauplios' lies and deceptions to kill in a temple precinct both Idomeneus' wife Meda and her children, including a daughter, Kleisithera, to whom he himself is married (Lyk 1214–25). The apparent deduction to be

made here is that Leukos, far from seducing Meda, is falsely led to believe her infidelity with someone else, in contrast to Nauplios' machinations with Klytaimestra and Aigialeia.

Apollodoros, however, tells us that as a result of Nauplios' schemes Leukos does become the lover of Meda, whom he kills together with her daughter Kleisithyra *(sic)* in a temple; nothing is said of any marriage to the latter (ApE 6.10). When Idomeneus returns Leukos drives him out, having taken control of ten cities on Krete. This mention of ten cities apparently springs from attempts to explain why *Iliad* 2.649 calls Krete a land of a hundred cities when *Odyssey* 19.174 speaks of it as having only ninety. The scholia to these two passages both suggest a conflict between Idomeneus and Leukos which somehow resulted in the sacking or seizure of ten cities; both also make Leukos a son of Talos who has been adopted by Idomeneus and left in charge of things. But neither scholion says anything about wives, daughters, or adultery, real or imagined. The Lykophron scholia at 386 simply repeat Apollodoros, although his version conflicts with their text. At 1218 they recount instead that Nauplios persuades Leukos to aim at the throne, and the latter then kills Meda and Kleisythera (to whom he was engaged), as well as several male children; Idomeneus on his return blinds him.

Most later sources do agreee with Apollodoros that Idomeneus vacates Krete, for whatever reason. In *Aeneid* 3, for example, his abandonment of the island permits Aineias to attempt a settlement there (3.121–23: no mention of Leukos). Later in the same Book we hear of him settled at Sallentinum (the very tip of the heel of Italy: 3.400–401), while in *Aeneid* 11 we find a cryptic reference to the "overturned household gods" of Idomeneus (11.264–65). Commenting on the first and third of these passages, Servius produces an entirely new (or at least unsuspected) tale, that on his return from Troy, after surviving a storm, Idomeneus promised that he would sacrifice to Poseidon whatever first met him on Krete. This proved to be his son, whom he either did sacrifice or tried to; the people in alarm at his cruelty (or because of the consequent plague) banished their king. The First Vatican Mythographer makes this a daughter rather than a son, but otherwise the details are the same (VM I 195; VM II 210 retains the son). The story seems not to survive elsewhere; one might have thought it or Meda's adultery or both to be the stuff of tragedy, yet suitable titles by any playwright *(Idomeneus, Leukos, Meda)* are entirely lacking. Surprisingly, Diktys, although his narrator is nominally a companion of Idomeneus, has no special story to tell of his leader's return: Idomeneus here dies peacefully and passes on the rule to Meriones. Lykophron has him buried instead at Colophon in Asia Minor (Lyk 424–32), perhaps without returning to Krete (so the scholia, with strong objections to such a version), while Servius claims that he went to somewhere in Asia after having journeyed to Italy (Σ *Aen* 3.401). Like so many others of the Greeks, his travels seemed designed above all to allow various Greek settlements to claim him as founder.

With Diomedes we encounter a similar situation, the more so as he is much more involved in the process of settling the Greek West. After his wounding of Aphrodite in *Iliad* 5, Dione is heard to reflect that his wife Aigialeia (daughter of Adrastos and thus also his aunt) may yet lament his loss; she envisions, it seems, no more than his possible death in battle (*Il* 5.406–15). But later sources, beginning with Lykophron and the scholia thereto, offer us quite a different outcome, namely that Aphrodite in revenge for her wound will cause Aigialeia to become unfaithful. Lykophron's long account of the hero's travails is filled with the usual obscurities, but shows that a detailed version of the story was familiar to his audience (Lyk 592–632). In the first part of this tale we can discern that his wife did indeed madly desire another, and that he narrowly escaped death thanks to an altar of Hera. Subsequently he comes to the Daunian lands in Italy, where he founds Argyrippa (Arpi, near the Garganus promontory). His men are for some reason transformed into birds who roost on the island (off said promontory) which comes to be called after him. There is also in Lykophron a dispute over land, settled in a way that disappoints him by his brother Alainos; he therefore pronounces a curse that only one of his own race shall successfully till it. The scholia explain this dispute as arising from a division of the spoils won in battle when Diomedes helped the local king Daunos: his half-brother Alainos, in love with the king's daughter Euippe and serving as judge, gave Daunos the land taken and Diomedes only the booty, thus the latter's curse (Σ Lyk 592). The scholia further add that Daunos later killed Diomedes, but the motive is not clear; lamenting him, his men are changed into birds. Predating this account is a work loosely ascribed to Aristotle, the *Peri Thaumasiôn Akousmatôn*, in which birds who guard the shrine of Diomedes on Diomedeia are descended from the companions of Diomedes, who were shipwrecked off the island at the time when Diomedes himself was slain by the local king, one Aineas (*Mir* 836a).

The scholia to *Iliad* 5 describe more fully Aigialeia's adultery, saying that at first she missed her husband greatly, but that subsequently because of Aphrodite's anger she carried on with all the young men, and especially with Kometes, son of Sthenelos, to whom Diomedes had entrusted the affairs of the house (ΣbT *Il* 5.412). Upon returning, he himself was almost killed and escaped only because he sought refuge at an altar of Athena. In this account he proceeds to Italy, where he is treacherously killed by the king Daunos, or else by a son of Daunos while they are hunting; Athena then makes him immortal and turns his companions into herons. Apollodoros also knows of Aigialeia's affair with this same Kometes, but attributes it rather to the work of Nauplios, who leads her into temptation as he did Meda and Klytaimestra (ApE 6.9). Unfortunately the epitome says nothing whatever about the events following Diomedes' return to Argos; this is the *Bibliotheke*'s last mention of him. Earlier Apollodoros does speak of the help rendered to his grandfather Oineus in Kalydon (see above, chapter 11), but without making its time-frame clear.

For his part, Diktys offers a version of Diomedes' domestic problems which seems to acquit Aigialeia, for in his account Oiax, son of Nauplios, is the one who falsely reports her husband's amours at Troy, and rather than taking a lover of her own she enlists the help of the citizens to shut him out of Argos (Dik 6.2). He then proceeds to Kalydon to assist Oineus as above. Hyginus, like Diktys, makes this conflict with Agrios, brother of Oineus, an adventure after Troy, but says nothing of wives or exile (*Fab* 175). Vergil in *Aeneid* 11 has messengers report back to Turnus and Latinus from Diomedes at Arpi: he refuses to aid their cause, and in so doing declares that the gods, hating him since the day he wounded Aphrodite, have kept him from seeing his beloved wife and fair Kalydon (*Aen* 11.269–77). The mention of a "beloved" wife would seem at odds with her usual adultery; probably this is just exaggeration for effect (but see below on Antoninus Liberalis). Diomedes also refers cryptically to his companions' metamorphosis into birds, which must have been a story generally familiar to Romans; Servius objects that they ought not to have been transformed while their master was still alive, since the cause is grief for his death, but poetic license and a bit of compression is likely at work here. In the *Aeneid* Daunos is, of course, the aged father of Turnus; Vergil does not, however, say more of him than that, and clearly does not regard Turnus and Diomedes as linked by marriage.

Adultery as the starting point for Diomedes' troubles reappears in Antoninus Liberalis in a story that may come from Nikandros (AntLib 37). Here, too, after leaving Argos Diomedes journeys to Kalydon to help his grandfather, but then intends to return to Argos and is foiled only by a storm that brings him to the Daunioi in Italy, where the king Daunios *(sic)* promises him land and his daughter in return for aid against the Messapioi. This is done, and Diomedes lives out his life there, being buried on the island Diomedeia. In all, there were clearly some variants regarding the nature of Diomedes' relationship with Daunos and the Italians, although all sources who consider the matter agree that he made his way to Italy after leaving Argos.

Philoktetes we saw was also attested by Nestor at *Odyssey* 3.190 as safely reaching home (Meliboia and environs, south of Mount Ossa, according to *Il* 2.716–18), but he too, like Diomedes, seems subsequently destined for Italian shores. Our first hint is again in the Aristotelian *Thaumasiôn*, where we find him settled at a place called Mykalla (or Makalla) in the territory of Kroton, and honored by the Sybarites (*Mir* 840a). He has dedicated his bow to Apollo, and he lies buried near the river Sybaris where he aided the Rhodians who came with Tlepolemos (the death of Tlepolemos in *Iliad* 5 is apparently no impediment to this tale). Lykophron knows something of the same story, for he speaks of Philoktetes received by Krimissa, and buried near Sybaris after his death at the hands of the Pellenioi (from the town near Sikyon) whom he was fighting to aid people from Rhodes (Lyk 911–29). Strabo adds to this that he was driven out of Meliboia following some sort of political stasis, and thus came to southern Italy, where he founded several cities between Kroton and Thourioi, including Krimissa and Petelia (Str 6.1.3). Some of this account he says he has found in Apollodoros (the second-century B.C. Athenian), whom he elsewhere credits with drawing heavily on Demetrios of Skepsis from earlier in the same century (Str 8.3.6), but we cannot trace the development of these wanderings with any precision. From the *Epitome* of our mythographer Apollodoros we learn only that Phikoktetes went to Campania (ApE 6.15), but Tzetzes (presumably working from a more complete version of the *Bibliotheke*) quotes him to the effect that the hero was driven to Campania, and from there, after warring against the Lucanians, he settled in Krimissa and dedicated his bow (Σ Lyk 911 = ApE 6.15b). In Vergil, Helenos' warnings to Aineias likewise include the information that Philoktetes has settled Petelia (*Aen* 3.401–2).

From Lykophron too first comes a story that a Trojan captive named Setaia burned ships of the Greeks near Sybaris, and as punishment was chained to a rock to die of exposure (Lyk 1075–82). Strabo sets his version of the tale at the river Neaithos (modern Neto) in this same area, between the promontory of Krimissa and Kroton: here certain Trojan women fired the ships of their Greek captors because they were weary of traveling; the men accordingly created a settlement, and the river was named after the incident (Str 6.1.12). Apollodoros (apud Tzetzes), although he calls the river "Nauaithos," knows the same story, with the captives here led by the sisters of Priam, Aithylla, Astyoche, and Medesikaste, and acting from a desire not to be taken to slavery in Greece (Σ Lyk 921 = ApE 6.15c). In Vergil the event is transferred to Sicily, where some of the Trojan women in Aineias' party burn ships in order not to continue their journey (*Aen* 5.604–718: they are settled at Segesta). Presumably Vergil borrowed this device from its older setting in Italy, although we cannot be certain.

Other returnees of whom Apollodoros (or Tzetzes citing him) speaks include Gouneus (who went to Libya; so too Lyk 897–98), Antiphos (to Thessaly), Pheidippos (to Andros and then to Cyprus), Agapenor (to Cyprus), Menestheus (to Melos), Podaleirios (to Caria by way of Delphi), and Demophon (to Thrace and then Cyprus). This last, however, is said by Apollodoros to have first married Phyllis, the daughter of the king of Thrace (ApE 6.16–17). When he then wished to leave she gave him a chest with instructions not to open it unless he decided not to return to her. He went to Cyprus and did open it, seeing something that caused him to fall from his horse in fear and die; Phyllis herself had already committed suicide. The orator Aischines knows at least some part of this, for he tells his audience that a son of Theseus (here Akamas, not Demophon) received the place called Ennea Hodoi in Thrace as a dowry (2.31). Loukianos likewise mentions Akamas and Phyllis (perhaps not as part of the same story: *Sal* 40) while the Lykophron scholia relate the tale as in Apollodoros, with Akamas (here too in place of Demophon) frightened by a *phasma* when he opens the chest and impaled on his own sword as his horse falls (Σ Lyk 495). In Hyginus the faithless lover is, as in Apollodoros, Demophon, but there is no word of his death; Phyllis hangs herself, and her grave is shaded by trees that mourn her (*Fab* 59, 243). In Servius, after her suicide she turns into an almond tree that puts out leaves when Demophon embraces it (Σ *Ecl* 5.10). One searches Ovid's *Metamorphoses* in vain for this tale; Phyllis' lament over her abandonment by Demophon does form part of the *Heroides* (2). Two other heroes—Meges and Prothoos—Apollodoros tells us were drowned at Kaphereus (Σ Lyk 902 = Ap*E* 6.15a), and the Aristotelian *Peplos* concurs with this (although it assigns to Gouneus the same fate: fr 640 [pp. 400–401 Rose). Prothoos is mentioned only in the *Iliad*'s Catalogue, but Meges is a figure of some weight in that poem whom we might have expected to survive.

Last we come to Kalchas, the seer of the Achaian expedition. In Apollodoros he, together with Amphilochos, Leonteus, Podaleirios, and Polypoites, does not take ship at all from Troy, but travels by land down to Kolophon where he dies, defeated in a contest of prophecy by Mopsos, son of Apollo and Manto (Ap*E* 6.2–4). Strabo like Apollodoros relates the two riddles involved, and cites lines from the Hesiodic Corpus for the first of them: Mopsos being asked by Kalchas how many figs a certain tree holds replies ten thousand, with one of those left over after the rest have filled the measure of a *medimnos* (Str 14.1.27 = Hes fr 278 MW). When this count proves to be correct, Kalchas dies, so that there was here presumably no second riddle. The same seems true of the version Strabo reports from Pherekydes: here Kalchas asks how many piglets a pregnant sow will bear, and Mopsos replies three, of which one a female, whereupon Kalchas dies of grief (3F142). His death was not always simply a matter of chagrin, however, for Strabo notes that in Sophokles' *Apaitesis Helenes* it was fated for the seer to die when he should encounter a better seer (the contest takes place in Kilikia). At some point both riddles were incorporated into a single story; thus in Lykophron, Kalchas asks Mopsos about the fig tree, and Mopsos having successfully responded counters with the question about the sow (Lyk 426–30). Apollodoros follows the same arrangement, with Kalchas replying that eight piglets will be born and Mopsos declaring that the true number is nine, all male. In the Lykophron scholia, Mopsos asks both riddles, and Kalchas has no answers to offer; the number of piglets is here ten, one male, and recognizing the truth of the oracle Kalchas kills himself (Σ Lyk 427; cf. Σ Lyk 980). Strabo also knows of versions in which Kalchas asks about the sow and Mopsos the fig tree, but in all cases Mopsos prevails. The contest takes on a rather different look in Konon, where the two seers are unable to resolve their dispute until Amphimachos, king of the Lykians, intervenes; Kalchas prophesies to him victory in battle, but Mopsos defeat; when the king is in fact defeated, Mopsos is honored and Kalchas again commits suicide (26F1.6). His fate has one other variant, found at a later point in Lykophron and explained by the scholia: here he is in southern Italy, near the river Siris, and dies when struck by Herakles after announcing the number of figs on a tree (Lyk 979–83). If we can trust the scholia, Herakles tried in vain to fit the leftover fig into the *medimnos*; when Kalchas laughed at his efforts he was killed.

Odysseus   At the beginning of this chapter we found that in Nestor's account of the return Odysseus and his crews for some reason turned back at Tenedos and rejoined Agamemnon, leaving Nestor and Diomedes to go on alone (*Od* 3.159–64). Odysseus in his own accounting to the Phaiakians omits this, saying only that the winds brought him to Ismaros, a town of the Kikones in Thrace. A raid is launched and spoils divided, but Odysseus' men overindulge in wine and do not heed his command to retreat. As a result they are overmatched by a Kikonian counterattack and must flee; nothing is here said of Maron, priest of Apollo, whom Odysseus spares and who gives him in consequence the powerful wine used on Polyphemos. After Thrace there is a storm, and the crews are forced to row to land. Possibly this is the disaster at Kaphereus, but we may wonder that Odysseus does not say so. At Cape Maleia there is more bad weather, winds that blow the ships past Kythera and on for nine days, until they reach the land of the Lotus-Eaters. Three men alone of the crew are sent out to reconnoiter; the locals give them the lotus, causing them to lose all desire for home, and Odysseus must drag them back weeping to the ships.

Next is the island of the Kyklopes, giants lacking most of the trappings of communal life or the civilization brought by fixed agriculture. Odysseus' ship alone goes to explore, and he and twelve others approach Polyphemos' cave (seemingly with half a mind to steal his sheep). There they are trapped when their host proves inclined to eat them (two at a time); because of the huge stone blocking the doorway they cannot even kill him as he sleeps. With the Ismarian wine of Maron—mixed with twenty parts water for most men, but Polyphemos takes it straight—the Kyklops is therefore drugged, leaving Odysseus free to put out his eye with a stake hardened in the fire. At his cry of pain the other Kyklopes come to inquire, but when Polyphemos repeats the name Odysseus has told him ("Outis" ["No one"]), they assume his misfortune to be the work of the gods, and leave. The actual escape is effected by means of Polyphemos' sheep: each member of the crew clings to the underside of three of them tied together as they exit the cave (Odysseus takes one large one), and their master, feeling only their backs, fails to detect the men. From the seeming safety of the ships Odysseus shouts back news of the escape to Polyphemos, and narrowly misses being sunk by a huge rock the Kyklops hurls. His second announcement is his true identity, which gives his victim a name to use in calling on his father Poseidon for vengeance (the failure of Polyphemos to observe the laws of guest-friendship, though often remarked, seems not to be a consideration here).

Book 10, the second of Odysseus' narrative, begins with the arrival on Aiolia, the floating home of Aiolos Hippotades, whose six sons are married to his six daughters (see chapter 5). After a month of hospitality the crews are sent off with a bag in which all the winds except Zephyros are tied up, so that that one will bring them the more speedily to Ithaka. The desired land is actually in sight when Odysseus drifts off to sleep; thinking the bag to contain riches his men open it and a storm ensues. Driven back to Aiolia, they find that Aiolos will not help them a second time, as he supposes them hateful to the gods. In their wanderings they then come to the land of the Laistrygones (named "Telepylos," if this is not an epithet). Here, through no fault of their own, the reconnoiterers are attacked (and one eaten) by Antiphates, whose wife is as large as a mountain. Other Laistrygones then assault the harbor, throwing huge stones and spearing the crews for dinner. Odysseus' ship alone escapes, and makes its way to Aiaia, the island of Kirke, who is like her brother Aietes a child of Helios and the Okeanid Perse.

Unaccountably determined to investigate the inhabitants of this land as well, Odysseus divides his men up into two groups, led by Eurylochos and himself, and they draw lots. Eurylochos, clearly the loser, goes off with twenty-two others to find Kirke in her halls, surrounded by tame wolves and lions and spinning at her loom. A drink of cheese, barley, honey, and wine is offered; all but Eurylochos (who has stayed outside) drink and at the touch of her wand are changed into swine. He reports this back to Odysseus, who sets forth alone on a rescue mission and is intercepted by Hermes in the guise of a young man. The god gives him a root called *moly* that will protect him from Kirke's enchantments. He is warned, however, that while he must accede to her request to share her bed, he must also extract an oath of safety first, lest she unman him when he is naked. All things then proceed as predicted (although we are never told how the *moly* functions): on failing in her enchantment Kirke grasps the identity of her would-be victim, for Hermes had once foretold his coming. She then tries her second ploy, but Odysseus extracts the oath as instructed. There are no more deceptions; at his insistence she returns his men to human form (by rubbing a salve on them) and, returning to the ship, he summons the remainder of his crew (including a most reluctant Eurylochos). They are sufficiently well entertained that they spend a year with the enchantress, until the men, becoming restless, ask Odysseus to think of their departure. He consults Kirke, who makes no protest but tells him that they must first journey to the realm of Persephone to consult the seer Teiresias on how best to reach Ithaka. Nor do all of them leave her house unscathed: Elpenor has apparently gone up to the roof for some cool air after drinking heavily, and on waking and forgetting where he is falls off, breaking his neck.

Book 11 of the *Odyssey* deals entirely with the visit to the Underworld; the details of his journey there we have mostly considered in chapter 3. Odysseus encounters not only Teiresias, but also Elpenor, his mother Antikleia, companions from Troy (Agamemnon, Patroklos, Antilochos, Achilleus, Aias Telamonides), a host of famous women (Tyro, Antiope, Alkmene, Megara, Epikaste, Chloris, Leda, Iphimedeia, Phaidra, Prokris, Ariadne, Maira, Klymene, Eriphyle), Minos, Orion, three transgressors (Tityos, Tantalos, Sisyphos), and finally Herakles, or rather the *eidôlon* of his shade in the poem as we have it. From Teiresias he learns very little of his return, but something of his old age, when he will carry an oar inland until he finds a people who think it a winnowing shovel. There he will sacrifice to placate Poseidon and then go back to Ithaka, where a gentle death will come to him from the sea (or perhaps "far from the sea," that is, when he is long retired from sailing) in his old age (*Od* 11.134–36 for this last).

In Book 12 the wanderers return to Aiaia to bury Elpenor, and are given by Kirke the specific sailing advice we expected them to get from Teiresias. From her island they proceed past that of the Seirenes, Odysseus stopping the ears of his men with wax and ordering them to tie him to the mast. When he hears the song he does indeed wish to be released (signaling so with his eyebrows), but Eurylochos and Perimedes further secure his bonds. On Kirke's recommendation they have avoided the Planktai in favor of the strait between Skylla and Charybdis. The former dwells in a cave turned toward Erebos, barking like a puppy; she has twelve feet, six necks, and three rows of teeth in each head. Only the upper part of her body extends out from the cave, as she snatches up sea creatures and whatever sailors pass by. Kirke's advice is to bear toward her side and probably lose some of the crew rather than come too close to the whirlpool of Charybdis and risk the entire ship; she in fact gets six, and eats them immediately.

Next comes Thrinakia, the island of the Sun, which Odysseus wishes to avoid on the warning of both Teiresias and Kirke. Eurylochos and the others overrule him, however, and they land to spend the night. At first they have the provisions given them by Kirke, but a storm arises and the winds Notos and Euros becalm them for an entire month. At last even hunting fails, and when Odysseus goes off by himself to pray to the gods for help, Eurylochos persuades the others to solve their problem by slaughtering the cattle of the Sun. They feast for a week on the spoils, even as Helios extracts a promise from Zeus that they will be punished. At last the winds shift and they leave, only to be drowned when Zeus strikes the ship with a thunderbolt. Odysseus alone survives, clinging to mast and keel; he is borne back to Charybdis where he must cling to a fig tree while his makeshift craft is sucked under, waiting for it to reemerge. When it finally does so, he is carried to the island of Ogygia, where Kalypso, daughter of Atlas, keeps him as her lover for seven years, until Hermes comes from Zeus to order his release. We see his departure at the beginning of Book 5, the narrative to the Phaiakians having now ended: although Kalypso offers him a permanent life with her, and immortality as well, he is determined to leave, building a raft to do so. At this juncture, however, Poseidon vents his wrath for the blinding of his son Polyphemos (he had been among the Aithiopes when the other gods approved Hermes' mission) by sending a storm. Ino Leukothea intervenes to bid Odysseus abandon the raft and his garments and trust in her veil; he is reluctant to do so, but the raft finally shatters and he has no choice.

The veil aids him to arrive in Scheria, the land of the Phaiakians, where naked and exhausted he meets Nausikaa, daughter of the king, who has come down to the river (as Book 6 opens) to do laundry. With her advice and some new clothes he makes his way into the city, seeks shelter with Alkinoos and Arete, weeps at the tales of the bard Demodokos, reveals his identity, tells of his wanderings, and is promised safe passage to Ithaka by the king. Meanwhile, as the poem has already recounted in Books 1–4, Athena disguised as the Taphian Mentes encourages Telemachos to set off on a journey to Pylos, that he may question Nestor about his lost father. Penelope's suitors, who have encamped in the palace, refuse him aid, but he manages nonetheless, aided by Athena in a new disguise as Odysseus' old companion Mentor. From Pylos, having heard Nestor's account, he proceeds with Nestor's son Peisistratos overland to Sparta to see Menelaos. Nothing essential to the plot results from either of these visits, but the various reminiscences characterize Odysseus and set the stage for his return. The suitors for their part plot to ambush Telemachos on his return voyage; they are of course foiled by Athena, who sends the ship a different way. Telemachos on leaving Pylos has also picked up a new passenger, Theoklymenos of the race of Melampous, who is fleeing a homicide. They arrive back in Ithaka just after Odysseus, who has been set on shore (with many gifts) by a Phaiakian ship. Poseidon cannot prevent this, but he turns the ship to stone on its return. He intends also to surround the Phaiakians with a great mountain; as we leave them for the last time they are sacrificing to him in the hope of averting such a fate.

The second half of the *Odyssey* treats Odysseus' successful reclaiming of his role as ruler of Ithaka, helped as always by Athena. Having hidden his gifts from the Phaiakians he goes first to the hut of the swineherd Eumaios, whose loyalty he tests before revealing his identity. There he is also reunited with Telemachos, who brings him up to the palace disguised as a beggar, so that he might assess the situation and formulate a plan of attack against the suitors. In the course of Books 17–18 he is predictably ill-treated by them, especially Antinoos and Eurymachos; at one point he must fight and defeat a rival beggar, Iros, to maintain his place. In Book 19 he is interviewed by Penelope, to whom he speaks of Odysseus' return, and recognized by his old nurse Eurykleia, who finds a scar on his leg when she washes his feet; in a digression we are told that he received the wound as a boy when hunting with the sons of his maternal grandfather Autolykos on Parnassos. As the book closes Penelope announces to him her intention of holding a competition the following day to settle the matter of her disposition; whichever suitor can string Odysseus' bow and shoot an arrow through twelve axe blades (or handles?)[49] will become her husband. Thus the stage is set for Odysseus' triumph. Telemachos begins the contest in Book 21, and we are told would have finally strung the bow had Odysseus not signaled him to desist; the others all fail miserably. On Telemachos' insistence the beggar is also given a try: he both strings the bow and shoots the arrow through all twelve targets without difficulty, then with his next arrow slays

Antinoos. At this a general combat breaks out, Odysseus and Telemachos aided by their thoughtful previous removal of weapons from the hall, the suitors by the treacherous goatherd Melanthios who recovers some of those arms for them. In the end all are killed except the herald Medon and the singer Phemios, who are absolved by Telemachos of guilt. Twelve serving women of the house who slept with the suitors are then hanged, and Melanthios executed. The final two books of the poem relate Odysseus' recognition by Penelope (only after he reveals the secret of their bed, carved out of a live olive tree) and his father Laertes. Last in the series of reintegrations with his former world is that with the people of his island: the parents of the suitors threaten an armed attack to recover the bodies of their sons, but the ever-watchful Athena intervenes to make peace between the two sides, and the *Odyssey* comes to a close.

As with the *Iliad*, there is little if anything in this account which art or subsequent literary versions present much differently. The *Nostoi* seems, as we would expect, to have ignored his wanderings (although it did note the meeting with Neoptolemos in Thracian Maroneia). Stesichoros' *Nostoi* may or may not have included something of his adventures; certainly the same poet's *Skylla* must have dealt with a part of them. The very end of the *Theogony* mentions the hero's dalliances with Kirke and Kalypso, resulting in (by the first) Agrios, Latinos, and Telegonos, and (by the second) Nausithoos and Nausinoos (*Th* 1011–18). Of these we will return to Telegonos below. In the fifth century we know that Aischylos recounted some phases of the wanderings and return, probably in a connected trilogy with as titles *Psychagogoi, Penelope, Ostologoi*, and *Kirke* as the satyr play. The *Psychagogoi* seems to have dramatized the *Nekuia*, with a chorus of spellweavers summoning up the shades of the dead; our only useful fragment concerns Teiresias' prediction of Odysseus' death (fr 275 R). In the *Penelope* Odysseus confronted his wife, repeating from the *Odyssey* his disguise as a Kretan (fr 187 R). The *Ostologoi* ("Bone-Gatherers") has been taken to refer to both a chorus of beggars in the palace and the relatives coming to collect the remains of the dead suitors. The latter is, I think, the more probable, in which case the end of the *Penelope* probably featured a messenger speech with the account of the suitors' defeat (and the recognition by Penelope?).[50] But in all, we know virtually nothing of the interpretive direction these plays took. *Kirke* (guaranteed as satyric) is a total blank.

Sophokles contributes two titles of his own, *Nausikaa*, or *Plyntriai*, and *Niptra*. Had it not been for the alternate title of the first of these (referring to a chorus of young girls doing the washing) we should probably have assumed the play satyric; as it is, it would seem a tragedy, although one is hard pressed to divine the conflicts at work. There may have been a fair amount of retelling of previous adventures, as seems also the case in the *Niptra*, where Eurykleia washes Odysseus' feet. For this last play we have a version by Pacuvius which includes Odysseus' death; probably he has conflated the *Niptra* with Sophokles' *Odysseus Akanthoplex*, which did deal with that subject. A play *Skylla* involving Odysseus is mentioned by Aristotle, who does not name the author

(*Poet* 15.1454a). We will return to Skylla and the misfortune which in some cases made her a monster in chapter 18.

The earliest artistic representations of the *Odyssey* date from the mid-seventh century, and show Odysseus and his men blinding Polyphemos.[51] On a fragment of a krater from Argos we see the Kyklops stretched out in repose while two much smaller men (the others are missing to the right) from a considerable distance direct the stake toward his eye; he reaches up with one hand to push it away (Argos, no #). On the more famous Protoattic amphora from Eleusis, Polyphemos is seated to the right holding a wine cup; from the left Odysseus (here distinguished from his men by being in reserve) drives the stake into his eye from close range (Eleusis, no #). Once again the victim reaches up with his hand as he awakes from his stupor. The same scene reappears in Italy on the Aristonothos krater, made apparently by a Greek living in Caere; Polyphemos is smaller here, and the men hold the stake at waist level as they move forward (Rome: Conservatori, no #). The last of them pushes off with his foot from the wall behind him for extra power, while behind the Kyklops to the right is a platform on a pole holding six cross-hatched objects, perhaps a drying rack for cheeses. Of about the same time is a Black-and-White-style pitcher from Aigina, the so-called Ram Jug on which we see three of the men clinging to the underside of their sheep (Aigina 566). To these we may wish to add the Melian amphora of the end of the century with a neck panel showing Hermes (clear from his kerykeion and winged sandals) and a woman who may or may not be Kalypso (Athens 354).

In the sixth century Polyphemos continues to be popular. A Lakonian cup of about 550 B.C. portrays him sitting up, a human leg (from the knee down) in each hand (CabMéd 190). Four men approach with the stake on their shoulders; the leader holds out a kantharos to the Kyklops and he starts to drink from it as the stake pierces his eye. On an Attic cup of the same time we see Polyphemos (head missing) surrounded by Odysseus' men with a huge wineskin; those further away have their swords drawn, and Athena has been added to the scene (Boston 99.518). From the end of the century, still in Black-Figure, comes an oinochoe showing two phases of the action: the stake being hardened in the fire and then mobilized against the slumbering Kyklops (his eye now closed in sleep: Louvre F342). Likewise the escape from the cave surfaces frequently, with an Attic krater fragment of *c.* 560 offering us a quite hairy Polyphemos feeling over the back of the very ram under which Odysseus (named) is concealed (Cahn Coll, no #). In all, Attic Black-Figure preserves some forty examples, with among others a krater by the Sappho Painter featuring Odysseus still under his ram but with drawn sword, as if prepared for discovery (Karlsruhe 167).

The sixth century also saw the emergence of two other Odyssean tales in art, those of the Seirenes and Kirke. Portrayals of the first of these might possibly begin about 600 B.C. with a Corinthian aryballos in Basel (Basel BS 425), but on this example the captain of the ship seems busy with the sail, rather than being tied to the mast, and the one Seiren shown is well off to the side (beyond a totally irrelevant chariot, in fact) while a real bird hovers over the vessel.[52] Of the same time period is a small Black-Figure fragment from Naukratis which shows five men sitting in a boat and part of a wing overhead (London B103.19); although this seems a more likely illustration of the story in question, it tells us little in the absence of Odysseus. The first preserved representation with useful detail is that on the Boston aryballos of the mid-sixth century, where the Seirenes are fully in evidence and Odysseus clearly under restraints (Boston 01.8100; curiously enough, two birds also appear here, seemingly about to attack the crew). All further scenes of this type, from the late-sixth-century Attic Black-Figure oinochoe (Stockholm:Med, no #) and White-Ground lekythos (Athens 1130) with flute/lyre-playing Seirenes to the famous Red-Figure stamnos with a (dying?) Seiren plunging down to the ship (London E440), show Seirenes alone (no birds), and a bound Odysseus seemingly lured by their music, as we would expect from the *Odyssey*.[53]

For Kirke, the earliest representation is perhaps that on a pot fragment from the end of the Geometric period found on Ithaka: a man stands before a woman with what may be a branch in his hand while the woman has one hand raised as if in astonishment. Odysseus revealing the *moly* to Kirke is obviously only one possible interpretation, but does have the fragment's find-spot in its favor.[54] Certain illustrations begin about 560 B.C., when we see Kirke with Odysseus' transformed men. On a Black-Figure kylix now in Boston the sorceress stands in the center pouring a drink for one of the men while three others to either side of her are shown with their heads alone changed (into lions, dogs, roosters, etc.: Boston 99.519). From the far left Odysseus approaches, sword in hand. A second cup in Boston (that with Polyphemos on the other side) offers much the same scene, although now Kirke is nude, and three of the men have animal forelegs as well as heads (of sheep, dogs, and boars: Boston 99.518). Again Odysseus appears with drawn sword on the left, but now he raises his arms and draws back a bit, as if in astonishment; behind a lion-man runs off terrified. This method of portraying the transformed men becomes standard in later vases, none of which add anything of note to our literary narrative; most dramatic is perhaps the Red-Figure krater of the mid-fifth century on which Odysseus leaps up from his chair, sword in hand, as Kirke starts back in alarm and the cup falls to the floor (NY 41.83). The crewmen here have tails as well, possibly because the scene was inspired by a satyr play in which Satyroi played their roles (i.e., Aischylos' *Kirke*).

Among less certain scenes to be noted is that of the metope from Foce del Sele on which we see a man astride a large turtle and peering ahead (no #).[55] The idea is unknown to any literary tradition, and the guess that the rider might be Odysseus is based largely on the fact that he spends far more time in (as opposed to on) the sea than any other hero. But it is helped perhaps by a second such rider on a Black-Figure skyphos from the end of the sixth century: this time the man lies flat on his stomach on the back of the turtle in order to see ahead, and behind him is clearly a fig tree such as Odysseus in the *Odyssey* mentions near Charybdis (Palermo P335). There Odysseus uses the fig tree to hang from until the whirlpool sends back up the flotsam on which he has been riding; here we are perhaps to think that he finds instead a turtle that serves to bring him to Ogygia and Kalypso. Admittedly the evidence for such a conclusion is slim, and would require some non- (or variant) Homeric version otherwise completely unsuspected. I am not myself convinced, but the artists of these pieces surely had some myth in mind.[56] Nausikaa may perhaps be shown on a mid-sixth-century Black-Figure exaleiptron now in Baltimore (WAG 48.198). Around the shoulder a series of women move away in alarm, with the last of them turning back to gesture at a couple who seem lost in animated conversation. Peleus and Thetis have been suggested, but there is no hint of wrestling or transformation, so that Odysseus and Nausikaa seem at least possible. Pausanias claims the scene of the journey to the shore for the Chest of Kypselos, where two women (one veiled) were shown in a mule-cart (5.19.9); he seems however clearly without the aid of inscriptions here, and may or may not be correct.[57]

Fifth-century Red-Figure adds to this modest corpus a number of additional scenes, though most of them not before the middle of the century. Odysseus naked before Nausikaa (Athena stands between) is now definitely portrayed on an amphora in Munich (Munich 2322) and again on a lid of a pyxis in Boston (Boston 04.18: Athena here seems to insist that Odysseus accost the girl). Also in Boston (Boston 34.79) is a pelike by the Lykaon Painter with Odysseus, head on hand and sword drawn, sitting before the slaughtered sheep as the shade of a young man, surely Elpenor, rises up from the Underworld to converse; Hermes stands to the right. Other illustrations of this period are all taken from that part of the epic dealing with Odysseus on Ithaka: we see the reunion with Eumaios (probably: Tübingen S/10 1605), Penelope grieving and Eurykleia washing her master's feet (both on the same skyphos, Chiusi 1831), the suitors bringing gifts to their intended bride (Syracuse 2408), and Odysseus dealing out death to his adversaries who seem in the midst of banqueting (Berlin:PM F2588). Surprisingly there is no sign of other stories, such as Skylla, or the Laistrygones, or the death of the dog Argos; for these we must await later centuries.

Last there remains to be considered Odysseus' old age, and his son by Kirke. We saw that the end of the *Theogony* speaks simply of the birth of this son, Telegonos, together with two others, Agrios and Latinos (*Th* 1011–16). All three are said to rule over the Tyrsenoi (presumably Etruscans), but probably only the latter two are meant; their names (Agrios = Silvius? Faunus?) would seem to reflect a hazy fusion of Latins and Etruscans in the early Greek West.[58] Telegonos, on the other hand, is the protagonist of a clearly Greek epic, the *Telegoneia* credited to Eugammon of Cyrene as the closing part of the Epic Cycle. Proklos' summary of this work begins with the burial of the suitors, then sacrifices to the Nymphai and a business trip to Elis, where Odysseus is entertained by Polyxenos and tales of Trophonios, Agamedes, and Augeias are recounted. After a return to Ithaka he journeys north to the land of the Thesprotoi, where he marries the queen Kallidike. When war arises between the Thesprotoi and the Brygoi (Odysseus leading the former), Ares gives victory to the Brygoi until Athena intervenes; the two gods apparently come to blows, and are halted only by Apollo. On Kallidike's death Odysseus' son Polypoites (presumably by Kallidike) succeeds her and Odysseus returns to Ithaka. Now Telegonos appears, searching for his father, and not knowing that he has found him ravages the island; Odysseus in attempting to defend his homeland is fatally wounded by this son. On discovering his error, Telegonos takes the corpse, Penelope, and Telemachos back to his mother. There Kirke makes all three of them immortal; Telegonos marries Penelope, and Telemachos Kirke.

Homer, or at least the *Nekuia*, knows too of some later adventures of Odysseus, and his death, for at *Odyssey* 11.134–36 we saw Teiresias prophesy of a journey inland with an oar, and of a gentle death from (or away from) the sea in old age. The events of Eugammon's poem may also have been described in some fashion in an epic called *Thesprotis*, since Pausanias tells us that there Odysseus has a second son Ptoliporthes by Penelope after returning from Troy (8.12.6). For that matter, Clement seems to think that Eugammon borrowed heavily from a work about the Thesprotians which might be this poem (see *Tel test 3 PEG*), but of course he will not have had reliable information on which was earlier. Apollodoros' version of Odysseus' later life is close enough to that of Proklos that it might have been drawn directly from Eugammon: sacrifices (to Hades, Persephone, and Teiresias) are followed by the trip to Thesprotia and placating of Poseidon (Ap*E* 7.34). Then comes the union with the queen Kallidike (who offers him her kingdom) and the birth of their son Polypoites, the defeat of neighboring peoples, and the giving up of the kingdom to his son when he leaves. On returning to Ithaka he finds a son Poliporthes borne to him by Penelope. Finally Telegonos comes to the island, searching as before for his father, and in the course of a cattle raid kills Odysseus with a spear having as its point a *kentron*; something has fallen out here which is surely (as in Lykophron [795–96] and many other sources) the *trugôn*, "sting ray," whose tail forms the spear point (cf. Σ *Od* 11.134 and Oppianos, *Halieutika* 2.497–505).[59] Afterwards Telegonos takes the corpse and Penelope back to Kirke; when he has married his stepmother, Kirke sends them both to the Isles of the Blessed. No mention is made here of Telemachos and Kirke, but quite possibly we should combine this summary with that of Proklos (which it nowhere contradicts) to get the gist of the *Telegoneia*.

From the *Odyssey* scholia we have also other kinds of information, including a curious quote from Aischylos' *Psychagogoi*. In that play, as in the *Odyssey*, Teiresias seems to have prophesied Odysseus' death, but with the statement that a heron flying overhead would deposit a load of excrement upon him, including an *akantha* (anything thornlike or spiny) which would cause his aged skin to rot (fr 275 R). Such an unusual notion might prompt us to suspect the text, but Sextus Empiricus confirms that he at least understood the words as we have them (*AdvMath* 1.276).[60] Whether Aischylos invented this bizarre fate we cannot say; whoever did so would seem to have desired a different demise for Odysseus than that brought by Telegonos, and hence concocted a new version that, like that of the *Telegoneia*, conformed with Teiresias' words in the *Odyssey*. Conceivably the encounter with the heron might even be what the *Nekuia* alludes to, assuming it does envision a death *from* the sea, although in that case most of us (with the scholia ad loc.) will probably prefer Telegonos. Sophokles treated the death in his lost *Odysseus Akanthoplex*, but such a title (with the same word *akantha* as in Aischylos) leaves us unable to say for certain even if Telegonos was involved. Yet very likely he was, for Aristotle speaks of the patricide as occurring somewhere in Greek tragedy (*Poet* 14.1453), Pacuvius includes him in his *Niptra* modeled in part (we think) on this play, and the few surviving lines speak of a prophecy from Zeus at Dodona which Odysseus seems to believe false. The content of that prophecy we probably find in Diktys, Hyginus, and a hypothesis to the *Odyssey*, all of which refer to a prediction that Odysseus will die by his son's hand. In Diktys and the hypothesis this not unnaturally causes him to fear Telemachos, against whom he takes precautions (in Diktys Telemachos is actually sent away to Kephallenia: 6.14–15). When Telegonos arrives, Odysseus thus faces him confidently and only after his fatal wounding learns the truth. Likely much of this goes back to Sophokles' play; whether it might also go back to Eugammon (there is nothing about a prophecy in either Proklos or Apollodoros) is another matter. Hyginus does deviate from this proposed plot a bit by having Telemachos accompany his father to face Telegonos; he also has Athena advise the survivors to take the corpse to Kirke, and arrange the two marriages (*Fab* 127). Kirke and Telemachos here beget Latinus, while Penelope and Telegonos beget Italus.

That the two couples thus formed following Odysseus' death live happily ever after (perhaps forever) seems certainly the notion of all the writers so far surveyed. But in Lykophron we encounter veiled allusions to Telemachos' slaying of his wife, and his being slain in turn by her daughter, his own sister the cousin of Glaukon and Apsyrtos (Lyk 807–11). Such a cousin can only be a daughter of Kirke, so that the wife of Telemachos referred to must be Kirke herself, and the avenger who is his own sister a daughter of Odysseus and Kirke. The scholia name this daughter as Kassiphone, but their explanations have Telemachos married to Kassiphone and killing his mother-in-law Kirke (being unwilling to take orders from her), after which his wife exacts revenge (Σ Lyk 808). Another entry in the scholia then recounts a version in which Kirke brings Odysseus back to life with a potion and marries off Telegonos to Penelope and Telemachos to Kassiphone in the Isles of the Blessed (Σ Lyk 805); the purpose of these arrangements is presumably so that, having satisfied everyone else, she might keep Odysseus for herself. Much of this sounds late, but Lykophron's story of Telemachos, wife, sister, and two killings was clearly known to his audience.

One other story of this period is preserved only in Parthenios, who ascribes to Sophokles an otherwise virtually unknown play entitled *Euryalos* (Par 3). He tells us that after the death of the suitors Odysseus went to Epeiros because of certain oracles, and that there he seduced Euippe, the daughter of his host Tyrimmas. The offspring Euryalos, when he grew to manhood, was sent off by his mother with certain sealed tokens to find his father, but when the boy arrived on Ithaka Odysseus was away, and Penelope guessing the truth persuaded her husband on his return to kill the new arrival as a conspirator of some sort. Only afterwards, having shown a lack of self-control and appropriate behavior in this action, did he learn the truth. Parthenios adds to this account his death from the sting of a ray wielded by one of his own race; possibly the play contained a prophecy of such. Our one other reference to this drama is from Eustathios, who says that in Sophokles' *Euryalos* Telemachos kills the boy (Eu-*Od* p. 1796). If this is not a mistake, we must suppose that Odysseus causes his son to be the agent of the deed.

Last there are some other variants cited by Apollodoros (Ap*E* 7.38–40). According to some, he says, Penelope was seduced by Antinoos and thus sent back by Odysseus to her father Ikarios, where she bore Pan as a result of a union with Hermes. We saw in chapter 2 that Penelope as mother of Pan is at least as old as Herodotos, perhaps even Hekataios; only in Douris of Samos, however, does she lustfully consort with all the suitors to produce the child (76F21). Pausanias too reports (as a Mantinean tradition) the notion that Penelope was expelled from Ithaka for inchastity (8.12.6). Apollodoros' second variant is an account in which Odysseus personally kills his wife for adultery with Amphinomos, another of her suitors in the *Odyssey*. He then concludes his *Bibliotheke* (at least in our epitome) with a version in which Odysseus is judged by Neoptolemos for the deaths of the suitors. Convicted by the latter (who hopes to get Kephallenia) he goes to Thoas, son of Andraimon, in Aitolia and, marrying his daughter, begets a son Leontophonos, after which he dies. Plutarch also tells of Neoptolemos' judgment against Odysseus; he does not, however, mention any selfish motives for the exclusion from Ithaka, Kephallenia, and Zakynthos, and Odysseus here retires to Italy (*Mor* 294c-d). Of the union in Aitolia and a final son there is no other word. That he has also in the *Telegoneia* a son by Kalypso, one Teledamos, is perhaps indicated by a somewhat confused comment of Eustathios (fr 3 *PEG*). As for Telemachos, we saw earlier that in the *Ehoiai* he weds Polykaste, daughter of Nestor (Hes fr 221 MW), thus presumably excluding his marriage to Kirke in that poem; in Hellanikos, by contrast, he is married to Nausikaa (4F156).

Aineias

Strictly speaking, Aineias is not one of those who returns from Troy, and much of his story is Roman invention. But this seems the most appropriate place, now that we have dealt with the Achaians, to document what early Greeks supposed about his wanderings after Troy fell. In *Iliad* 20 we found him saved from death at Achilleus' hands by Poseidon, otherwise an Achaian supporter, because it was fated that he should survive, lest the line of Dardanos, the favorite son of Zeus, be snuffed out; in so doing Poseidon noted Zeus' anger with the house of Priam as the reason why Aineias' branch of the family and his children's children were henceforth to rule the Trojans (*Il* 20.300–308). Just what Trojans Poseidon imagines will be left to rule is not clear, nor is the logic entirely sound if Aineias already has children (but perhaps he does not: none are ever mentioned in Homer, and Askanios is the name of a Phrygian ally of Troy). In any case the god's words are most naturally taken to mean that Aineias' line will flourish in a new settlement at Troy, or else somewhere close by. Aphrodite too in her *Homeric Hymn* predicts to Anchises that Aineias and his children after him shall rule the Trojans, but gives no details (*HAph* 196–97). We saw in chapter 16 that Arktinos' *Iliou Persis* solved the problem of Aineias' survival by having him abandon Troy for Mount Ida with many of his people after the death of Laokoon, being for some reason displeased at that event. Our summary does not, however, say that these people remained or settled there. From Lesches, assuming the lines of Tzetzes' quote putting Aineias on board ship with Neoptolemos are by Simias of Rhodes (see above), we have nothing; Proklos' epitome of this poem does not even mention him.

Moving down into the sixth century, we must consider again the controversy surrounding Stesichoros and the Augustan limestone relief known as the *Tabula Iliaca Capitolina*.[61] In the panoramic central section of this version of Troy's fall Aineias appears three times: (1) inside the walls, receiving a large round box or other object from a kneeling figure; (2) issuing forth from a gate, with Anchises (and the box) on his shoulder, Askanios led by the hand, and an unnamed woman behind (Hermes precedes); (3) with Anchises, child, and Misenos boarding a ship. In this last scene we find the inscriptions *Anchisês kai ta hiera* ("Anchises and the sacred things"; he is in fact handing a box to a crewman) and *Aineias sun tois idiois apairôn eis tên hesperian* ("Aineias with his people setting out for Hesperia"), while just above to the left, in part of the space between (2) and (3), largest of all, are the words *Iliou Persis kata Stêsichoron* ("The Fall of Troy according to Stesichoros"). If the artist of the relief (one Theodoros) did in fact derive all this from the source named we would have important evidence that Aineias' migration toward western lands was known as early as Stesichoros' treatment of the Sack. But even if everything else in these scenes should be from Stesichoros, the artist might easily have intruded the one word *Hesperia* and the figure of Misenos from later Roman tradition to make the departure more significant. There is, moreover, no reason to think that the other elements are all Stesichorean: the kneeling figure in (1) seems suspiciously like Vergil's priest Panthoos, the woman of (2) has disappeared by the time we get to (3), and not only the *hiera* but the whole tale of Aineias' escape is here given uncommon attention in a poem about a Greek victory. Misenos himself, we should note, is not known as a Trojan before Vergil, and here as he prepares to board he holds something very much like a trumpet (cf. *Aen* 6.164–67). Probably then, as we might have suspected, Theodoros has claimed Stesichoros (along with several epic poems) as sources for his work, but not scrupled to give his Roman audience touches of the *Aeneid* (or its predecessors) at points where that version would be more familiar (and palatable) to them. In that case we have no real evidence at all for what Stesichoros did with Aineias; if the ship can be trusted, the Trojans did at least put out to sea, but perhaps even that is too much to say for certain.

From actual sixth-century art, as opposed to illustrations of later times, comes a substantial series of Attic Black-Figure vases showing Aineias carrying his father away.[62] All date to the second half of the century, and most cluster in the last decade. On the earliest complete scene, from an eye cup in Paris, Aineias strides right while Anchises perches on his shoulder (or upper back) and faces back to the left (Louvre F122). The latter's left hand holds a staff; the right is empty. Below are just visible the legs of a child striding along beside his father. Subsequent examples alter the pose so that Anchises faces forward and clings to the neck and back of Aineias. The child is sometimes but not always present, most memorably on a neck-amphora in Würzburg where Aineias seems to coax him to abandon a dog on which his attention is fixed (Würzburg 218). A woman also frequently accompanies the group, leading the way (e.g., Berlin:Ch F1862), and another sometimes follows (Würzburg 212). The son when present on these occasions usually runs between the leading woman and Aineias; in three instances there are two sons, one to either side (e.g., Munich 1546). In contrast to this figural scheme one vase presents the preceding woman with a small child on her shoulder (Tarquinia RC 976); thus we can say that here at least Aineias' wife is intended (whether Eurydike or Kreousa), but neither she nor any of the children are ever named on these pots.

As the series progresses toward the end of the century the women become more and more just stock filler elements. In many cases, Anchises grasps a pair of spears, reasonable enough since Aineias must use at least one hand to reach back and support his father's legs. But these spears are his total baggage; nowhere can he be said to hold anything like sacred objects or a container for them. We first see such objects for certain on an Etruscan gem of the early fifth century, where Anchises with his free hand pointedly exhibits a flattish pixis or cista (CabMéd 276). An Etruscan Red-Figure amphora of the same period shows the woman in front of Aineias with a long oval container on her head which has also been taken to be a receptacle for such objects, but the straps suggest perhaps rather a piece of luggage (Munich 3185);[63] in any case this woman, like the one on the Tarquinia neck-amphora, must be Aineias' wife. The same is true of the figure seen accompanying Aineias on a silver tetradrachm of about 500 B.C. from the Greek town of Aineia (in the northwest corner of the Chalkidike): Aineias carries a male figure of adult size while the woman walking before him and looking back carries a smaller figure, seemingly female from her long chiton.[64] Since this scene represents not just the departure from Troy but the founding of a new city, we may assume that the artist of the coin (and the people of the city) supposed both husband and wife to have made that departure successfully. On the other hand, there is no sign of any wife in the Kleophrades Painter's version of the Sack in Naples; we see only Aineias with his father on his back and his young son following along. The Parthenon's north metope 28, if correctly interpreted, placed the emphasis rather on the escape of father and son, with Anchises and a woman standing alongside.[65]

It would appear, then, that Athenians of the sixth and fifth centuries were quite familiar with Aineias' rescue of his father from Troy, and with the son who usually accompanied the two of them. As in the later literary sources surveyed in chapter 16, his wife was a less essential element who might be omitted, but she too made her escape at times. What the pots do not tell us is where Aineias is going (in no case is there any sign of a ship). To be sure, the coin type from Aineia offers one answer already in circulation in the sixth century, but we cannot say how widespread an idea this might have been. Virtually all the Black-Figure examples were found in Italy, and while that is not a highly unusual situation, it may indicate already at this time a special interest in Aineias on the part of the Etruscans, possibly as a founder hero who came to their land.

Turning back to literature, we have quite a number of casual references from Dionysios, who surveys as part of his history various traditions on Aineias' departure from Troy and subsequent exploits (1.46–59). In such a context he is our source for the previously noted fragment of Sophokles' lost *Laokoon* in which, as in Arktinos, Aineias takes his father to Mount Ida after the Laokoon affair (fr 373 R). In the fragment itself we see the two of them (Anchises on Aineias' shoulders) preparing to exit the city and surrounded not only by their slaves but also by a "crowd such as you would not believe, who are eager for this colony of Phrygioi." The use of the word *apoikia* ("colony"), plus Dionysios' failure to discuss (here or later) their destination, might suggest that in Sophokles' play the departees intended to take up residence on Ida. But the quote will have been from the end of a play not primarily about Aineias, and the playwright may not have committed himself.

From the end of the fifth century we have (via Dionysios' summary) Hellanikos' *Troika*, offering as we saw in chapter 16 a more militarily oriented account with Aineias in charge of Troy's defense (4F31). As the Achaians begin their successful assault on the city and are engrossed in plunder, he directs an exodus of the Trojans, women, children, and aged first, to Mount Ida, following himself with the troops and his father and native gods in chariots. From Ida, having gathered a large force from the surrounding areas, they hope to return to Troy after the Greeks have left, but the latter instead plan to assault the mountain as well. Finally a settlement is negotiated in which the Trojans agree to vacate the Troad, taking with them their valuables, and the Greeks promise safe conduct. Askanios is sent off to rule the land around Daskylion (southeast of Kyzikos), but the rest sail to Pallene (in the Chalkidike, and not so very far from Aineia). Here Hellanikos' contribution to Dionysios' inquiry presumably ends, as the latter turns to later writers who make Aineias die in Thrace or move from there to Arkadia. As evidence for the journey to the far west and Italy he then cites various aspects of Roman culture, as well as monuments still extant in Greek territories. From these he proceeds to a brief sketch of wanderings after Thrace, from Pallene to Aineia to Delos, Kythera, Zakynthos, Leukas, Actium, Dodona, Bouthroton, and so over to Italy. No sources are given for this part of the story, and while some scholars have supposed that Hellanikos is responsible for all of it, Dionysios' occasional vague references to writers in general suggests just the opposite. At 1.72.2, however, he certainly does say that the compiler of the accounts of the priestesses at Argos, who should be Hellanikos, has Aineias arrive in Italy from the land of the Molossians with Odysseus (!) and found Rome, naming it after a Trojan woman Rhome, who burned the ships to halt their wandering (4F84). The motif is one we have seen earlier in this chapter, when Trojan women in the hands of unnamed Greeks took similar measures in southern Italy; it seems to be a recurring theme of the migration west. To what extent this whole narrative might be in conflict with the *Troika*, and whether Hellanikos really is the author of it, remains uncertain.[66] If it is rightly ascribed to him (Dionysios also names his pupil Damastes of Sigeion as relating something of the same sort) he would become the first known writer to link Aineias with Italy or Rome. In that case, one might guess that there was influence from Italian legends back to Greece.

At any rate, in the following centuries there grew up among the Greeks a vast corpus of tales about Rome's origins, with Aineias becoming the father of sons Romulus and Remus, or Rhome marrying Latinus and bearing these children, or Askanios begetting Romus, or even Odysseus and Kirke doing so (DH 1.72.5, supposedly from Xenagoras). This last suggestion, together with Odysseus' children by Kirke (Latinos and Agrios) at the end of the *Theogony*, shows that there was an effort on the part of some Greeks to derive native peoples in the west from a Greek ancestor rather than a Trojan one. But none of this material, Greek or Italian, can have been formulated much before the fourth century, and as such, like the rest of Aineias' later adventures, it lies beyond the scope of the present book. We should note however that, on the whole, Askanios plays a surprisingly limited role in the Italian adventure; indeed, Dionysios leaves him behind in Asia to settle at Daskylion in Mysia and subsequently return to Troy (DH 1.47.5; cf. the Alexandrian historian Lysimachos at 382F9, where Askanios is given over into Akamas' care for this purpose). In the west Aineias' ancestor role depends almost always on his fathering of other children, if not Romulus and Remus themselves, then perhaps their mother Ilia, as in Naevius and Ennius, so that the twins become his grandchildren. In this respect, as often, what looks traditional in Vergil, Askanios' engendering of the line of Alba Longa, may in fact have been relatively novel.

18   Other Myths

Ixion

Important and well-known though Ixion's tale is, we have not dealt with it before now because his parentage does not link him into any of the major mythological families discussed in earlier chapters. Homer says of him only that Zeus lay with his wife (unnamed) and begat Peirithoos (*Il* 14.317–18); from this point on our literary sources are completely silent until the fifth century, when Pindar incorporates his exploits into *Pythian* 2, and Aischylos uses them for a production that included the plays *Ixion* and *Perrhaibides*. *Pythian* 2 has long posed problems of dating, and probably does not even commemorate a victory at Delphi.[1] But it is dedicated to Hieron of Syracuse, and thus falls somewhere between 480 and 468 B.C. The mythic section begins with Ixion's punishment, bound as he is to a winged wheel that rolls everywhere while he proclaims the need to honor benefactors. As the cause of this fate unravels, we learn that he was welcomed by the gods (apparently on Olympos) but then in the madness of his mind conceived a passion for Hera, adding this transgression to that of being the first mortal to slay a kinsman. What he lay with when he tested Hera's honor, however, was a cloud in her form fashioned by Zeus (as we saw in chapter 3), and that cloud produced from the union a child Kentauros, "bearing honor neither among men nor in the laws of the gods" (*Py* 2.42–43). Kentauros in his turn mingled with Magnesian mares on the slopes of Mount Pelion, and thus the Kentauroi were born, a dreadful progeny for Ixion to boast of.

Pindar obviously speaks to an audience already familiar with this story, or at least with the first part of it. The scholia explain the murder as that of his father-in-law Deioneus, who expected gifts when he gave away his daughter Dia and was invited by Ixion to come to collect them (Σ *Py* 2.40b). When he arrived he fell into a pit of fire prepared by Ixion and died, and of this murder no one wished to purify Ixion, not even the gods. Finally Zeus took pity on him and not only performed the purification but brought him up to *ouranos* to share the gods' hearth; there he became enamored of Hera. Diodoros tells almost exactly the same story (the father-in-law is Eioneus, the bride Dia: 4.69.3–4), and it is surely what Pindar had in mind, for we see brief glimpses of it also in Aischylos' *Perrhaibides* (a work that might or might not be earlier than *Pythian* 2). Here some character demands gifts belonging to him (including gold and silver cups: fr 184 R), and there is talk of a man who has perished pitiably, cheated of his property (fr 186 R), while someone else spits out the blood of a murder victim (fr 186a R). There are no other details, but Deioneus/ Eioneus' death seems clearly the subject matter. Of the *Ixion*, from presumably the same trilogy, nothing survives, leaving us to speculate that it concerned Ixion's purification on Olympos and his passion for Hera, if that was not re- served for a third play. From the preserved *Eumenides* comes the (curious) insistence of Apollo that Zeus did not err in receiving the supplications of the primal murderer Ixion (*Eum* 717–18).

The Pindar scholia comment as well on the name of Ixion's father, which was a matter of some controversy: Aischylos, they say, made him one Antion, Pherekydes made him Peision, others Ares, and still others Phlegyas (so too ΣA *Il* 1.268; almost certainly this is Phlegyas, father of Koronis). In scholia to Apollonios we find Phlegyas as the father credited to Euripides (with a quote) but Pherekydes' choice now becomes Antion (unless something has fallen out: Σ AR 3.62). Diodoros also gives as the name "Antion," who in his account is the son of Periphas (son of Lapithes) and marries Perimele, daughter of Amy- thaon, to produce Ixion. The scholia to *Odyssey* 21.303 claim that Ixion is a son of Zeus; nothing daunted, Hyginus adds yet another possibility, Leonteus (*Fab* 62). Apollodoros (in the *Epitome* section: see below) does not specify a father. Euripides' preference for Phlegyas probably occurs in his lost *Ixion*, a play of which we know only that it included the punishment of the wheel. The *Ixion* play of Sophokles, if it existed, is a total blank;[2] the chorus of the *Philok- tetes* remarks at one point that Ixion dared approach Zeus' bed and was bound to a wheel (*Ph* 676–79).

Later sources concentrate mostly on the attempted seduction of Hera, of- ten ignoring the homicide altogether. Apollodoros' epitomator simply repeats the essentials of that part of Pindar's story, including cloud, wheel (borne through the air), and offspring Kentauros (Ap*E* 1.20). Of interest, though (and making more sense of the cloud than Pindar does), is the detail that Zeus fash- ioned that cloud in order to see whether Ixion was actually guilty. The same idea appears in the *Odyssey* scholia, where as we saw Ixion is a son of Zeus, and the father suspects that Hera is slandering his children (Σ *Od* 21.303). In addition, this scholion has Ixion partake of nectar and ambrosia on Olympos: hence the punishment of the winged wheel, because he cannot be killed. The scholia to *Phoinissai* 1185 include both homicide and passion for Hera, briefly told, with request for bride gifts, a pit of fire (the father-in-law is again Ei- oneus), purification by Zeus, the cloud, child, and wheel. Here again Ixion is made immortal, and the cloud is designed to test Hera's accusation against him. New in these scholia, however, are the reports that Zeus sends Ixion down to Tartaros, and that the wheel is fiery. In the Apollonios scholia we find our most precise details about the murder: when Eioneus came to collect his gifts Ixion prepared his pit and then covered it over with thin pieces of wood and fine dust, so that his father-in-law fell in (Σ AR 3.62, as above). Subsequently Ixion went mad because of this (a detail seemingly from Pherekydes), until Zeus cured him. Madness is also an ingredient of the A scholia at *Iliad* 1.268, where Ixion suffers this fate after treacherously burning Deioneus, father of his bride Dia, when the latter comes for the gifts. Purification and dalliance with the cloud follow as usual, but here punishment is said to take place only after death, and the wheel to which Ixion is bound rolls around in the Underworld. Our first datable source for this last idea is Apollonios, who has Hera say that she will protect Iason even if he should descend into Hades to free Ixion from his bronze chains (AR 3.61–63). Hades is his place of torment in Vergil as well, both in the *Georgics* (3.37–39 [where the wheel has snakes]; 4.484) and the *Aeneid* (6.601). The latter passage goes on to describe for both Ixion and Peirithoos the fate normally associated with Tantalos—a rock teetering over their heads and food they cannot eat; either a line with Tantalos' name has fallen out, or Vergil here takes some liberties with the normal tradition. Lactantius Placidus and the Second Vatican Mythographer seem the only sources to say that Zeus struck Ixion with his thunderbolt before the binding to the wheel (Σ St: *Theb* 4.539; VM II 106). His reason, they add, was not simply that Ixion desired Hera, but that after returning to earth he boasted of lying with her (so too, perhaps, ApE 1.20).

Finally, as we saw at the beginning of this section, Zeus in *Iliad* 14 claims that Peirithoos is his son by the wife of Ixion (317–18). Both the A and bT scholia hasten to assure us that this was before her marriage to Ixion, when she was still a maiden. Such a sequence of events is not likely to have been supported by the storytellers who made her father claim bride gifts for his daughter, and the scholiasts may be improvising, but at least they appear ignorant of any story in which Zeus' affair with Dia might have been linked (as motive or revenge) to Ixion's attempt upon Hera. Nonnos has a brief reference to Zeus, Dia, and an equine mating (7.125), and Eustathios cites a tale in which Zeus does in fact mate with Dia in the form of a stallion (as a way of explaining the offspring's name: Eu-*Il* p. 101); perhaps the story of Kentauros has influenced matters here.

In art we have a few illustrations, but nothing earlier than the fifth century and little that does more than confirm details already known. Earliest are two Red-Figure cup fragments from the beginning of that century showing the central portion of Ixion's body tied to the wheel (Agora P26228; Rome: Forum, no #). From the middle of the same century comes a kantharos by the Amphitrite Painter with a naked Ixion led before Hera by Ares and Hermes while Athena rolls in a wheel with wings attached to it (London E155); the presence of these wings probably guarantees that Ixion and the wheel were here thought to remain in the upper world. The other side of the same kantharos, with a similar figure seeking refuge at an altar as his victim slumps to the ground and is received by Thanatos, has been thought to show the death of Eioneus, the more so as the killer is in the coils of a snake who threatens to bite him.[3] No literary source ever suggests that Ixion was pursued by the Erinyes (although the notion of his madness could, I suppose, imply this), and as we have seen elsewhere an Erinys as snake is a questionable concept. But still more difficult are other details: the supposed father-in-law is young and beardless, while the supposed son-in-law does have a beard and holds a drawn sword with which he has clearly wounded his victim (no sign of a fiery pit). This is the same scene that we have previously found interpreted as Laokoon and his sons (or Orestes and Neoptolemos), and its meaning remains a problem.

The end of the century brings us a skyphos on which Hephaistos is finishing construction of the wheel (again winged) while Hera converses with a seated Zeus (Cahn Coll 541). Unfortunately, the rest of the scene is broken away. Still later, a Campanian amphora of the late fourth century shows Ixion (as on the two cup fragments) already bound to the wheel, while Hermes and Hephaistos look on from below (Berlin:PM F3023). Tongues of fire seem to be indicated on the wheel, while coiling around Ixion are several snakes, clearly older in the tradition than their appearance in Vergil; whether their pedigree is originally literary or artistic is hard to say. Likewise unclear is the point at which Ixion and his wheel are brought down into the Underworld. On present evidence this would seem to take place in Hellenistic times and probably represents a simple assimilation to the fate of other transgressors. In any case the shift must involve the loss of his function as an admonisher to others of the dangers of ingratitude.

Last, and in utter contrast to any of the above material, is a tale preserved only in the Cyzicene Epigrams, namely that Ixion slew Phorbas and Polymelos in retribution for the penalty enacted against his mother (*AP* 3.12). The introduction explains that her name was Megara, and that she had chosen to marry neither of them, whereupon they killed her. We can only presume that this is the Ixion familiar to us; despite the many authorities for his father's name, Diodoros alone identifies his mother, calling her Perimele (DS 4.69.3, as above).

Orpheus
: The name "Orpheus" is not found anywhere in Homer, or the *Hymns*, or Hesiod or the Hesiodic Corpus. The earliest appearance of this figure seems to be, in fact, on the metopes of the Sikyonian *monopteros* at Delphi, where his name painted in guarantees him to have been one of the Argonautai (see chapter 12). One would guess that at some point his musical skills were of special use to the expedition, and indeed in Apollonios he saves the crew by drowning out the song of the Seirenes which would have lured them to their deaths (AR 4.891–911); scholia take this tale back to Herodoros, and add that Cheiron advised Orpheus' inclusion on the voyage for just this purpose (Σ AR 1.23 = 31F43b). The obvious idea that his song could charm savage beasts is first preserved in Simonides, where birds fly overhead and fish leap from the sea in time to the music (567 *PMG*). It resurfaces probably in Bakchylides 28 (trees and the sea may be involved) and certainly in Aischylos' *Agamemnon* (1629–32). With Euripides at the end of the century we find both trees (*Bkch* 560–64)

and rocks (*IA* 1211–14) following the singer as well, and one suspects that by this time such magical powers were commonplace for Orpheus.

For the most famous part of his story, however—the descent into Hades to recover his wife and his subsequent tearing apart by Thracian women—the evidence is less plentiful. Nothing whatever survives of either of these tales prior to the fifth century, and even then there is surprisingly little. Difficult in particular is the matter of his appearance in Aischylos' Lykourgos production, a set of plays attested as consisting of *Edonoi*, *Bassarides*, *Neaniskoi*, and *Lykourgos*. For the most part these dramas must have related Lykourgos' refusal to accept the worship of the newly arrived Dionysos, as *Iliad* 6 recounts (see chapter 2). But Ps-Eratosthenes' discussion of the Lyre constellation opens up other possibilities: after recounting the passage of the lyre from Hermes to Apollo to Orpheus, who won great renown with it, he says,

> But having gone down into Hades because of his wife and seeing what sort of things were there, he did not continue to worship Dionysos, because of whom he was famous, but he thought Helios to be the greatest of the gods, Helios whom he also addressed as Apollo. Rousing himself up each night toward dawn and climbing the mountain called Pangaion he would await the sun's rising, so that he might see it first. Therefore Dionysos, being angry with him, sent the Bassarides, as Aischylos the tragedian says; they tore him apart and scattered the limbs [*Katast* 24].

If nothing else we can at least say that Orpheus' death was mentioned in the *Bassarides* of Aischylos, and that Dionysos was there responsible. But most likely this was in a choral ode, something recalled by the Bassarides briefly as an exemplum or warning to Lykourgos not to make the same mistake, rather than in a full dramatization of Orpheus' fate in what was otherwise a tetralogy about Lykourgos. If that is the case, we are left to decide how much of Ps-Eratosthenes' account might have been found in such a choral ode. The placement of Aischylos' name, where it is, after specific mention of the Bassarides, makes it perhaps more likely that only their role in the story comes from his work, with the rest—descent into Hades, worship of Helios, equation of Helios and Apollo—deriving from elsewhere. But this is just one possibility, and even if correct will not alter the fact that Aischylos and his audience must have known a myth about Orpheus and Dionysos (and Helios?), whether or not he tells all of it. The narrative logic of Ps-Eratosthenes' tale poses another problem, for it is not immediately clear why that which Orpheus sees in the Underworld should turn him away from Dionysos and toward the sun; does the darkness of Hades cause him to appreciate better the sun's light? Hyginus, who in his *De Astrologia* cites Eratosthenes at this juncture, suggests that Orpheus simply forgot Dionysos in his praise of the gods (rather, it would seem, than consciously determining to ignore him: *Astr* 2.7.1).

If the initial part of Ps-Eratosthenes' narrative does come from Aischylos it would mark our first trace of the tale of Eurydike. Otherwise, that honor goes to Euripides' *Alkestis*, where Admetos boasts that if he had the tongue and voice of Orpheus he would descend to Hades so that having charmed Demeter's daughter and her husband with songs he might take his wife back (*Alk* 357–62). Strictly speaking he does not here say that Orpheus ever did such a thing, only that he could do it if anyone could, but to suppose the audience ignorant of Eurydike would involve a remarkable coincidence. More troubling to some has seemed the fact that Orpheus did not ultimately rescue his wife, so that the parallel is a bit ill-omened. Perhaps Euripides knows a version in which that wife was successfully reclaimed, but Admetos may well mean simply that he would not repeat Orpheus' crucial mistake. Orpheus also formed part of Polygnotos' Nekyia painting at Delphi, as described by Pausanias (10.30.6); here, however, he sits next to a willow tree holding his harp, seemingly one of the shades rather than a visitor, and there is no mention of Eurydike at all. In Plato's *Symposion* the speech of Phaidros includes the claim that the gods, while admiring Alkestis who died for her husband, were not so impressed with Orpheus, who did not die for his wife but contrived to enter Hades while still alive; thus they showed him a *phasma* of his wife but did not allow her to leave (*Sym* 179b-d). The gods' logic here fits the situation too well not to arouse suspicions of Platonic revision, but at least we see a familiarity with the story we know. The first actual mention of the wife's name occurs in the *Lament for Bion* ascribed to Moschos, where the singer hopes that Persephone will restore to him the dead Bion as she once granted to Orpheus Eurydike because of his music (3.123–24). Hermesianax of Kolophon (in a poem to his mistress Leontion) is, by contrast, alone in calling this same wife Agriope (or perhaps Argiope), and has been thought by some to imply that Orpheus succeeds in bringing her back (fr 7 Pow).

Of other Hellenistic and later works, Phanokles' poem *Kaloi* speaks of Orpheus' love for Kalais, son of Boreas, and his death (with his head torn off) at the hands of women who objected to his introduction of homosexuality into Thrace (fr 1 Pow); the poem seems generally devoted to homosexual relationships of Greek heroes, but for Orpheus as so inclined there is supporting evidence elsewhere. In Konon we find first the familiar explanation of Orpheus' failure, that after winning Eurydike back from Plouton and Persephone by his songs he forgot their instructions concerning her and so lost her (26F1.45). The account continues with his death at the hands of Thracian women, either because he now hated all women or because he refused to admit them to certain rites. Diodoros will perhaps have been among those believing that the wife is successfully restored, for he suggests that Orpheus is to be compared with Dionysos, who had brought his mother Semele up from the Underworld (DS 4.25.4). In the *Culex* of the *Appendix Vergiliana*, Eurydike keeps her part of the bargain with Hades and Persephone on the journey upward by looking ahead and maintaining silence, but Orpheus breaks his by turning to seek kisses from her (*Cu* 268–95). Vergil's famous treatment of the star-crossed lovers in the *Georgics* puts much of the blame on Aristaios, son of Apollo and Kyrene, who by pursuing Eurydike with lustful intent caused her to step on a snake (G 4.453–503). Orpheus' descent into Hades to rescue her proceeds as we would expect, but Persephone (no reason given) requires Eurydike to follow her husband up into the light; when he turns at the very edge of the upper world and looks back in his desire she is lost to him. From this point on he does nothing but lament, with no thought of remarriage, and the Thracian women, thinking themselves despised, tear him apart, casting his head in particular into the Hebros River, where it continues to lament.

Ovid's *Metamorphoses* omits any assault on Eurydike, but in his account also she is bitten by a snake (while taking a walk after her marriage: *Met* 10.1–85). The rest evolves as before, with the novelty of a vow by Orpheus that he will remain in the Underworld himself if his prayer is not granted. As in Vergil he is not allowed to look back until he has reached the upper air, but in concern and desire to assure himself that she is there he falters, an error rather more sympathetically treated by Ovid. Subsequently he returns to Thrace, where although avoiding women he does not shun the love of young boys. After several digressions the women of Thrace again dispatch him for his scorn of them, and here too his head thrown into the Hebros retains the power of song (*Met* 11.1–66).

In Apollodoros, who also makes a snake the cause of Eurydike's death (so too Σ *Alk* 357), there is the novel idea that Orpheus was instructed not to look back at his wife until he had reached his own house (Ap*B* 1.3.2). He founds the mysteries of Dionysos, and is again torn apart by women (no reason given). Pausanias says simply that the women of Thrace in a drunken state killed him because he had persuaded their husbands to follow him in his rovings; he also adds a version in which the death is by thunderbolt, because Orpheus has revealed the mysteries to the uninitiated (9.30.5). In Hyginus the cause of his death is no fault or act of his own, but rather Aphrodite's anger over his mother Kalliope's decision in the matter of Adonis (*Astr* 2.7.3: see below).

Thus literature offers virtually no early evidence for the story of Eurydike, and the same is true for art. Attic Black-Figure ignores her and the descent to Hades altogether, while Red-Figure does not discover her until the fourth century (in southern Italy); we have already seen that Polygnotos omits her. But the question of the antiquity of Orpheus' journey to the Underworld is a complex one, the more so as later "Orphic" tradition claimed the existence of a *Katabasis* poem describing the event.[4] For Orpheus, far more than for most of the figures in this book, mythic hero becomes subsumed to claimed ancestor of a wide variety of mysteries and cults, while the descent into Hades serves as a crucial proof of his shamanistic powers. Under such circumstances we must be even more cautious than usual in assessing what stories were current (and how widespread) in the Archaic period.

What Red-Figure art of the fifth century does show us vividly, beginning with a cup in Cincinnati (1979.1) and a stamnos (by Hermonax) now in the Louvre (G416), is the death of Orpheus. In all cases women attack the helpless musician, sometimes simply with their bare hands or boulders, other times with swords and axes. Even the severed head is shown on occasion, clearly with prophetic powers from the intensity with which the bystanders gaze at it (e.g., Basel BS 481). With this much of the later tradition represented in fifth-century art we might suppose the event that led to it—the loss of Eurydike—guaranteed as well. But we have seen that in some sources there is no direct connection between Eurydike and the Thracian women, the cause of Orpheus' death being rather his refusal to share with them mysteries that he had introduced, his scorn of them, or other such reasons.

One final point of concern is Orpheus' parentage. Pindar in *Pythian* 4 appears to say that he is the son of Apollo, but the scholia claim that the poet elsewhere calls Orpheus the son of Oiagros; they then cite Ammonios' suggestion that the preposition *ek* used in *Pythian* 4 means only "drawing inspiration from," for which there are parallels (Σ *Py* 4.313a). Whatever Pindar did mean in this case, Oiagros is clearly one early father, and Asklepiades gives us additional fifth-century authority for Apollo (and Kalliope) as the parents (12F6). Subsequent accounts keep almost entirely to these two options, with Oiagros seemingly representing the majority opinion (Bakchylides, Plato, Apollonios, Diodoros, etc.); the Apollonios scholia specify Oiagros and Polymnia (so "others," in contrast to Asklepiades' view: Σ AR 1.23). The late Pergamean historian Charax and the *Certamen Homeri et Hesiodi* do offer a genealogy for this Oiagros: from Aithousa and Apollo was born Linos, from Linos Pieros, from Pieros and Methone Oiagros, from Oiagros and Kalliope Orpheus (103F62; *Cert* 46–48 [Allen 1912]). The name of Pieros reappears in Pausanias, who maintains that a daughter (unnamed) of his was Orpheus' mother (9.30.4). Apollodoros acknowledges the tradition of both fathers, but adds the odd idea that Oiagros was the real father and Apollo the reputed one, when from a mythographer we might expect just the reverse (Ap*B* 1.3.2).

Lykaon and Kallisto   The tales of Lykaon and his daughter Kallisto and their respective encounters with Zeus are best known to us from Ovid's *Metamorphoses*, where the narratives appear as completely separate stories, linked only by the family relationship of the two protagonists. Both tales can be traced back to Eratosthenes, however, and from there, at least in part, to the Hesiodic Corpus in what is a very tangled development. What we know for certain of the Archaic period is that the relationship of the two as father and daughter did appear in Eumelos (fr 14 *PEG*) but was not uniformly agreed upon: according to Apollodoros, "Hesiod" made her one of the Nymphai (Hes fr 163 MW), Asios a daughter of Nykteus (fr 9 *PEG*), and Pherekydes a daughter of Keteus (3F157). What Ps-Eratosthenes claims to draw from the Hesiodic Corpus (not necessarily from the same poem referred to by Apollodoros) is a story in which the daughter of Lykaon (presumably Kallisto) follows Artemis in the hunt, and having been made pregnant by Zeus hides the fact from the goddess as long as she can (*Katast* 1: *Arktos Megalê*). Finally, though, her pregnancy is discovered while she is bathing, and Artemis in anger changes her into a bear, in which form she gives birth to a son Arkas. Both bear and child are then captured by shepherds and turned over to Lykaon, after which the bear unknowingly wanders into a forbidden sanctuary of Zeus, pursued by her son and the Arkadians. At this point she is about to be put to death, but in consideration of their union Zeus rescues her and makes her a constellation. The text here seems to indicate that Arkas (and others) pursued her only after she had entered the sanctuary, and only because she had done so; we will see a slightly different version shortly. Presumably, the mating with Zeus and birth of Arkas appeared in the *Ehoiai*, and probably some version of Kallisto's final fate, but we will see that this last was subject to some variation.[5] If the catasterism was as early as the Archaic period it could perhaps have formed part of the Hesiodic *Astronomia*. The union of Zeus and Kallisto was also mentioned in the corpus attributed to "Epimenides," where they beget twins, Arkas and Pan (3B16).

In the fifth century Aischylos composed a *Kallisto* from which we probably would have learned a great deal more, but absolutely nothing of it survives. Euripides' *Helen* mentions the girl by name as bride of Zeus and a bear, a metamorphosis that Helen oddly considers as bringing relief from woes, and a happy lot compared to that of her own mother Leda (*Hel* 375–80); this whole passage is difficult, but on the surface it might seem that Euripides is ignorant of or ignores any danger to Kallisto in her bear form. The fourth-century comic poet Amphis offers more detail on the seduction: Zeus here takes the form of Artemis herself to deceive Kallisto, and when Artemis later demands the identity of the guilty party the seducee can only name the goddess (fr 47 Kock); the latter's consequent rage and Kallisto's transformation are thus only too understandable. In Kallimachos, however the seduction was accomplished, it seems that Hera discovered it and herself transformed Kallisto, following which she instructed Artemis to shoot the bear; Zeus saved Kallisto by catasterism, but nothing in the brief account that survives says anything about a child (fr 632 Pf).

Ovid too relates Zeus' disguise as Artemis, although with a bit more verisimilitude: Kallisto realizes the identity (or at least the gender) of her seducer, if to no avail, and thus does not implicate Artemis (*Met* 2.409–530). When her pregnancy is discovered at the bath she is simply banished from the company of the maidens and in human form delivers a human child; only subsequently does she suffer Hera's anger, as in Kallimachos. Arkas grows to manhood, goes out hunting, and nearly kills his own mother; Zeus intervenes to take them up to the heavens. Hera, however, has the final word, for she secures from Tethys the promise that Kallisto and her child shall be debarred from the sea (a detail not found in any of the sources drawn from Eratosthenes). Hyginus in *Fabula* 177 has a very abbreviated version of this, saying simply that Kallisto, daughter of Lykaon, was changed into a bear by Hera in anger at Zeus' affair with her, and that after the catasterism Hera obtained from Tethys the same request as above.

Turning to Apollodoros, we find a somewhat different account; after his discussion of the varied genealogies for Kallisto he proceeds (without naming a source) to relate that Zeus approached her in the guise of Artemis or perhaps Apollo, and then, wishing to conceal the matter from Hera, himself turned her into a bear (ApB 3.8.2). Hera, not fooled, persuades Artemis to shoot the bear (as a wild beast: thus unwittingly) or else Artemis commits the deed of her own volition in anger over Kallisto's lost virginity. Quite probably this last version implies a variant in which Kallisto does not become a bear at all, for Artemis is not likely to transform her *and* shoot her, or to slay her for her own reasons after Hera has accomplished the transformation (cf. *Cert* 117–18, where Artemis again slays Kallisto because she succumbed to marriage, and no bear is mentioned).[6] After her death in Apollodoros Kallisto is changed into a constellation, while Arkas is rescued from her womb, much as Dionysos and Asklepios were taken from their mothers. Apollodoros' last reference before beginning this tale is a favorite source, Pherekydes, and that mythographer may have been responsible for the version he offers. Pausanias returns to Hera as the cause of the transformation, but here too Artemis shoots the bear "as a favor" to her, and the child is taken (by Hermes rather than Zeus himself) from the dying mother soon to be placed among the stars (8.3.6–7).

Hyginus in the *De Astronomia* gives slightly varying versions of most of the above. In the first part of his discussion of the "Arktos Megalê" he follows the same account as *Katasterismoi* 1, save that after Arkas has followed Kallisto into the precinct the Arkadians wish to kill both of them (*Astr* 2.1.2). In the chapter on the "Arktophylax," however, after Arkas is served by Lykaon to Zeus for dinner (see below) he is restored and given to foster parents (*Astr* 2.4.1). When he grows up and goes out to the hunt he sees a bear (his mother, of course, here *not* a pet of Lykaon) and gives chase for the purpose of killing her. The pursuit leads into the forbidden shrine of Zeus, so that here too both mother and child incur the death penalty and must be saved by Zeus (cf. the Germanicus scholia at 27). Later sections under the "Arktos Megalê" heading report that according to others Hera changed Kallisto into a bear and caused her to encounter Artemis, who killed her before realizing who she was (*Astr* 2.1.3: catasterism follows), or that Zeus changed her into the bear to avoid Hera's anger, but that Hera perceived the trick and had Artemis kill her (*Astr* 2.1.4, as in Apollodoros).

We would seem to have then two distinct strands of narrative. In the first, Artemis' anger includes (when she does not shoot the girl on the spot) the metamorphosis of Kallisto into a bear after her pregnancy is discovered; subsequently the bear is threatened by an unwitting son, or both are threatened by the Arkadians (or some combination of the two), and Zeus must intervene to take her/them up to the heavens (possibly Eratosthenes recounted both versions). In the second, Artemis merely expels Kallisto from her company, and Hera enters as jealous wife to accomplish the metamorphosis and then deceive (or perhaps order) Artemis to kill the animal, which she does. In this latter account no catasterism is strictly necessary (although always possible) and the child Arkas is seemingly not involved. For the first of these two narratives our earliest source is Eratosthenes, for the second Kallimachos followed by Apollodoros (perhaps drawing on Pherekydes).

Art offers for certain in the fifth century only the lost painting of the Underworld by Polygnotos in the Knidian Lesche at Delphi: Kallisto is with Nomia and Pero, and sits or reclines on a bearskin (Paus 10.31.10). The skin surely alludes to her transformation; whether her very presence here could be said to exclude a catasterism is a more difficult question. A Red-Figure amphora of about the same time has been taken to show Artemis in the act of shooting a (human) Kallisto as she clutches her child (Seill Coll, no #). There is no sign of any metamorphosis here, and the child's garment does seem to indicate a girl, but the more usual interpretation, that of Artemis and Niobe, would make Artemis' victim grotesquely small. In the fourth century we do find coins from Arkadia showing the shooting of a girl (clearly Kallisto, with Arkas beside her) by Artemis, and on several Apulian pots we see the unfortunate woman beginning to turn into a bear (so Boston 13.206, Getty 72.AE.128). On this latter example Hermes picks up the child; likewise on an Apulian calyx krater in Cremona where Hermes, Arkas, Kallisto, Apollo, Artemis, and Lyssa are all named, and Hermes moves off, surely to take Arkas to new parents (Cremona, no #). Whether Artemis' presence is sufficient to guarantee that she rather than Hera has caused the transformation I do not know, so that we are left quite uncertain of Aischylos' (or earlier) treatments of the story.

Lykaon's story as we find it in Ps-Eratosthenes and most other authors remains on the whole isolated from these events. The Vatican fragments of the Eratosthenes epitome do come close to suggesting that Lykaon invited Zeus to dinner and served him a child because he knew of his daughter's seduction; the account is attributed to "Hesiod" (*Katast* 8R = Hes fr 163 MW). Our other version of this epitome, while ignoring such a motive (and making no mention of "Hesiod"), calls the slaughtered child Arkas himself, who is thus served (unwittingly or not) to his own father (*Katast* 8D). In both accounts destruction of the house and restoration of Arkas follow, plus Lykaon's transformation into a wolf in 8R. That Lykaon should have such access to his grandson may seem surprising, given the boy's birth in the wilds, but we must remember that one version of Kallisto's story (that found elsewhere in Ps-Eratosthenes) has both her and Arkas captured by goatherds and given to Lykaon (who may or may not recognize them: *Katast* 1). Possibly, then, these two stories were part of a single narrative, whether or not part of the Hesiodic Corpus. Arkas as the victim served to Zeus also appears in the scholia to Germanicus' translation of Aratus and in Hyginus' *Astronomia*, the latter stressing that Lykaon wished to test his guest (*Astr* 2.4.1; we are again uncertain whether Lykaon realizes the paternity of the child).

Of other authors, Ovid has Zeus in his own form carry out the visit to Arkadia, wishing, we are told, to investigate rumors of human wickedness (*Met* 1.199–243). His host, who entertains some doubts about his guest's identity, serves him the flesh of a hostage whom he has slaughtered for the occasion. As in Ps-Eratosthenes, Zeus strikes the house with a thunderbolt and turns Lykaon into a wolf as punishment. Apollodoros offers much the same account, with the difference that here Zeus visits the house incognito to test the reputed impiety of the fifty sons of Lykaon, who serve him the intestines of a child (Ap*B* 3.8.1: no motive other than said impiety is cited). Zeus upsets the table and destroys Lykaon and his sons with the thunderbolt, all but Nyktimos the youngest, whom Gaia saves (cf. *Mor* 300b, where two children [the only innocent ones] escape). In the *Fabulae*, Hyginus too makes the sons the primary culprits, serving human flesh to see if their guest is a god, but keeps the changing of Lykaon into a wolf (*Fab* 176). He also begins his brief account with the rape of Kallisto, conveying the impression that that deed took place at the start of this same visit. Lykophron calls the victim served Nyktimos, presumably here as elsewhere Lykaon's own child (Lyk 480–81); in the scholia the other sons are again responsible (and again as a test of divinity), with all those not killed by the thunderbolt turned into wolves. Pausanias reports what may be the core of the myth, or else its rationalization: Lykaon brings a child to the altar of Lykaian Zeus and sacrifices it, thus leading to his metamorphosis into a wolf (8.2.3); subsequently Pausanias speaks of Nyktimos as the eldest of Lykaon's children, and the one who inherits his father's rule (8.3.1).

It only remains to note briefly the line of descent from Arkas, who is the ancestor of a number of figures already treated elsewhere in this book. Apollodoros gives the most complete account: Arkas is the father of Elatos and Apheidas (Ap*B* 3.9.1–2). Of these, Apheidas begets Stheneboia, who will marry Proitos, and Aleos, who fathers Kepheus, Lykourgos, and Auge. Auge we have seen as the mother of Telephos by Herakles, and Kepheus as the ruler of Tegea who perishes with his sons while aiding Herakles against Hippokoon. Lykourgos becomes the father of the Ankaios slain by the Kalydonian Boar, and as well of Iasos and Amphidamas; Iasos will become the father of the Arkadian Atalanta and Amphidamas the father of her consort Melanion. Pausanias has most of this same information (with more geographical details: 8.4.1–5.2) and adds that from Elatos sprang Ischys, the same figure who as early as Pindar's *Pythian* 3 consorts with Koronis as she carries Apollo's child (*Py* 3.31–32).

Smyrna/ Myrrha and Adonis

In chapter 2 we looked briefly at the parentage of Adonis in the context of his affair with Aphrodite. The earliest known reference to such a person proved to be in the Hesiodic Corpus, where we learned that he was the offspring of Phoinix, son of Agenor, and Alphesiboia (Hes fr 139 MW). Nothing guarantees that this Adonis is the same one loved by Aphrodite, but Apollodoros, who gives us the information, thought so, and he presumably had the whole "Hesiodic" original or something based on it to look at. In any case no later writer supports this parentage; we next find Adonis in the fifth century, where for Panyasis he is the child of Theias, king of the Assyrians, and his own daughter Smyrna (fr 27 *PEG*). In this version it seems that Smyrna is punished for not honoring Aphrodite by being made to fall in love with her father, whose bed she enters for twelve consecutive nights (with the help of her nurse) before he discovers the truth. When he draws his sword to make an end of her she prays she might disappear, and the gods pitying her turn her into a myrrh tree; in the tenth month after, the child Adonis is born from the tree.

Antoninus Liberalis has essentially the same story, although Adonis is born before the transformation and Theias kills himself (AntLib 34). Nor does Ovid's account deviate much from Panyasis, save that father and daughter are now Kinyras and Myrrha; the nurse as in Antoninus persuades the father that a young girl wishes to share his bed, and thus Myrrha accomplishes her desire (*Met* 10.298–514). Kinyras is also the name of Adonis' father at ΣbT *Il* 5.385 and other late sources; the daughter is sometimes Smyrna (so Hyginus and Cinna's lost *Zmyrna*), sometimes Myrrha. In Hyginus the mother of Smyrna is Kenchreis, who causes all the trouble by boasting that her daughter is more beautiful than Aphrodite (*Fab* 58). The goddess responds by instigating the unspeakable desire, but here there is apparently no discovery; Smyrna instead hides in the woods to conceal her pregnancy, and Aphrodite in pity turns her into the myrrh tree. Servius reverts to the more usual pattern, but with the detail that the anger of Helios was responsible for Myrrha's love (Σ *Ecl* 10.18); no further explanation is given.

As for the tale of Aphrodite's dispute with Persephone for custody of the child, Apollodoros and Hyginus are our only real sources. In Apollodoros, Aphrodite takes Adonis while he is still very young and hides him in a chest, apparently to conceal him from the other gods (Ap*B* 3.14.4). The chest is then given to Persephone for safekeeping, but on seeing the child she does not wish to give him back, and thus a conflict arises which Zeus must resolve. His solution is to give Adonis to each of the two goddesses for a third of the year, the remaining third to be at Adonis' own disposition. Adonis gives that third in fact to Aphrodite, so that he is with her for eight months and Persephone for four. Soon after, however, he is slain by the boar (seemingly this would mean that Persephone gained total custody of him, but Apollodoros does not say so). In Hyginus matters are much the same, save that there is no mention of how the dispute arose, and Zeus assigns Kalliope to make the decision (*Astr* 2.7.3). Her award is for six months to each goddess, but Aphrodite, enraged at having to share Adonis, causes in the women of Thrace such passion for Kalliope's son Orpheus that they tear him apart in their eagerness to possess him; nothing more is said of Adonis.

In art we see what is probably the first part of the story on a series of terracotta reliefs from Lokroi in southern Italy dating to about 450 B.C.: a seated woman lifts the lid of a chest or basket in which a small child is sitting, hands on knee (Reggio Calabria, no #). The sanctuary in which these plaques were found has been assigned to both Aphrodite and Persephone; doves on some examples make the goddess shown more probably Aphrodite, but either way we would seem to have a fifth-century attestation of the clash over the child. About a hundred years later come several representations of the decision itself in Apulian vase-painting. Most notable is a pelike in Naples with on the shoulder Zeus seated between a standing Persephone to the left and an Aphrodite kneeling in supplication to the right (Naples Stg 702). Aphrodite clutches in her free hand a small winged Eros, while to the left with Persephone (as we should expect since she has custody at the time of the judgment) a small Adonis grasps the lower part of Zeus' scepter. That he should be awarded, even in part, to Persephone is surely a doublet of his death on the tusks of a boar, whatever the immediate cause, and although there are no specific accounts of Aphrodite bringing him back to life, the essence of his story and the religious practices surrounding it remains his participation in two worlds, and his return from the dead.

Skylla and Glaukos

We saw in chapter 7 that both Vergil and Ovid identified the Skylla, daughter of Nisos and betrayer of her father, with the monster Skylla who threatened sailors attempting the strait between herself and Charybdis. But in fact there is no basis for such an identification, and Ovid himself later reveals knowledge of a completely different story about the monster Skylla's origins. The *Odyssey* tells us that her mother was Krataiis, who "bore her as an evil for men" (*Od* 12.124–25) and assigns to her twelve feet, six heads, and three rows of teeth in each head; we also learn that she barks like a dog and extends the upper part of her body out of her cave to grab sailors, whom she eats (*Od* 12.80–100). Such scant information would seem to suggest that she has had this form from birth. The same conclusion might be drawn for the *Megalai Ehoiai*, where she is the child of Phorbas and Hekate (Hes fr 262 MW), and even more so for Akousilaos, who makes her the daughter of Phorkys (famous progenitor of monsters) and Hekate (2F42; so too Σ *Od* 12.85). Stesichoros apparently wrote an entire poem entitled *Skylla* from which we have only one piece of information, that the mother was Lamia (220 *PMG*); this may or may not be the Lamia, daughter of Poseidon, who became by Zeus the mother of the first Sibyl (*Mor* 398c; Paus 10.12.1). Of the dithyramb (by Timotheos?) *Skylla* referred to by Aristotle, nothing has survived (although it involved a lament by Odysseus: 793, 794 *PMG*), and the rest of the fifth and fourth centuries offer nothing. But the monster returns to play a role in Apollonios' *Argonautika*, where she threatens the homeward journey of the Argo until Thetis lends a hand. Here again she is the daughter of Phorkys (or Phorkos) and Hekate, with "Krataiis" another name for the latter (perhaps correctly: AR 4.825–31). Apollodoros also gives Krataiis as the mother, and Phorkos or Trienos (Triton?) as the father (ApE 7.20). To this picture the *Odyssey* scholia add some further details, namely that she had dogs (or dogs' heads) attached to her flanks, and that the lower part of her body remained in her cave because it was rooted to the rock (Σ *Od* 12.85).

So far, then, we have a female monster who has from all appearances always been such. But in the Roman authors the situation is quite different, and to judge from the comments of the Vergilian corpus' *Ciris* the concept of Skylla as a beautiful young girl probably goes back at least to Alexandrian times. The *Ciris* says in fact that many poets have turned Skylla, daughter of Nisos, into the Odyssean sea monster, but while it rejects this conflation it reports several origins for said monster, including the idea that Skylla was embraced by Poseidon, and hence changed into a monster by Amphitrite out of jealousy (with poison spread about) or, as a second choice, changed by Aphrodite after flaunting her beauty too outrageously (*Ciris* 54–88). Ovid also attests the transformation of Skylla, daughter of Krataiis (*Met* 13.749), but for other reasons: Glaukos, the half-fish god of the sea, has fallen in love with her, and when she rejects his advances he turns to Kirke for help (*Met* 13.900–14.74). Kirke, however, becomes enamored of Glaukos, and when he spurns her for Skylla she takes revenge against her rival by pouring poisons into the water at the place where Skylla regularly bathes; on entering the pool the girl's lower body turns into the foreparts of dogs. Probably all or most of this can be traced back at least to the third century B.C., for Athenaios tells us that the Samian (?) poetess Hedyle composed a *Skylla* in which Glaukos was in love with the title figure (Athen 7.297b).

Of still other authors, Hyginus follows the Ovidian account precisely (*Fab* 199); likewise Servius, but with alongside it the *Ciris* version (Σ *Ecl* 6.74: Amphitrite uses the poisons of Kirke). Amphitrite is as well the villain in the Lykophron scholia, where she like Kirke in Ovid pours the poison directly into the place where Skylla bathes (Σ *Lyk* 46). One other story, that the monster Skylla was slain by Herakles when she tried to take some of the cattle of Geryoneus and was brought back to life by her father by means of fire, survives only in Lykophron (44–49 and scholia [where the father is Phorkys]) and the previously mentioned *Odyssey* scholia at 12.85, the latter crediting a Dionysios of uncertain identity.

Before leaving this section we must consider also the transformation of Skylla's would-be lover Glaukos. Pausanias tells us that both Pindar and Aischylos spoke of the fisherman who ate grass and became a god of the sea with prophetic powers, Pindar briefly, Aischylos in an entire play (9.22.7). From Pindar nothing else survives, but we have a number of fragments from Aischylos' *Glaukos Pontios* confirming the miracle and the eating of the "undying" grass, with the location of the event at the northern end of Euboia (frr 25c–29 R). His prophetic skills are affirmed by Euripides in the *Orestes* (where he announces to Menelaos the death of Agamemnon: *Or* 362–67), and Palaiphatos like most later sources gives as his homeland the town of Anthedon across from Euboia on the Boiotian coast (Pal 27). Various scholia recount that having caught a fish he cast it upon some grass, which it proceeded to eat, thus reviving itself; when he ate the same grass he became immortal and leapt into the sea (Σ *Or* 364; Σ *G* 1.437; Σ *Lyk* 754). This is also the version that Ovid's Glaukos recites to Skylla when he attempts to win her; on eating the grass he here has an irresistible urge to cast himself into the sea, where his fellow divinities pour the waters of rivers and seas upon him to give him his new form (*Met* 13.917–65). With such consistency in all these accounts and no other details it is a bit surprising to find in Athenaios allusions to numerous additional stories by little-known Hellenistic writers, such as that of Theolytos in which Glaukos falls in love with Ariadne on Dia but is defeated and bound by Dionysos (Athen 7.296–97c). Other tales include his identification with Melikertes, or his love for Melikertes, or even being loved by Nereus (this from Nikandros); there are also quite a variety of parentages to choose from. Neither Apollodoros nor Hyginus tells his story.

Maira In chapter 5 we considered the evidence from Pausanias for one Thersandros, son of Sisyphos, who in turn has a son Proitos (9.30.5). Pausanias, who is looking at the figure of Maira in Polygnotos' Nekuia for the Knidians, makes this Proitos Maira's father, and tells us that in the *Nostoi* (with this descent) she dies while still a maiden (*parthenos*: fr 6 *PEG*). Since Proitos of Tiryns, brother of Akrisios, is elsewhere always of the line of Io (his father being Abas, son of Lynkeus and Hypermestra), one would normally expect the present Proitos to be a separate individual. But the *Odyssey* scholia insist that Maira is the daughter of Proitos and Anteia, the latter as early as *Iliad* 6 the wife of the Tirynthian (Σ *Od* 11.326), so that somewhere a conflation has probably occurred. The *Odyssey* itself at 11.326 simply names Maira as one of the women seen by Odysseus in Hades, expecting, it seems, that we will know her story. The scholia cite Pherekydes as source for their account: although Maira is a devotee of Artemis and the hunt and guards her virginity, Zeus approaches and somehow deceives *(lanthanôn)* her, with the child Lokros the result (3F170). When she no longer comes to the hunt she is shot by Artemis. Proitos and Anteia as her parents appear at the very beginning of this note, and may also derive from Pherekydes. No other writer mentions her save for Eustathios, who adds nothing new; he does, however, regard this story as separate from that in which she dies a maiden (Eu-*Od* p. 1688). Unfortunately, he does not tell us whether he really knows of a second, distinct story, or whether he is simply guessing on the principle that a *parthenos* will not have a child. Strictly speaking, the term *parthenos* does not always indicate a virgin; at *Pythian* 3.34, for example, it denotes Koronis at a time long after she has lain with Apollo, and elsewhere too sometimes means no more than "young" or "unmarried." But whether Pausanias (and other parts of the *Od* 11.326 scholia) would so emphasize the word as characterizing Maira when she had borne a child to Zeus is difficult to say. One wonders too if Pherekydes had Zeus simply abandon the girl to Artemis' anger when elsewhere he usually provides some sort of (quite late) assistance. On the whole we seem unlikely to have the complete story; sadly, the preserved parts of the *Ehoiai* fail to mention Maira at all.

Melanippe   Prior to Euripides the only trace of this figure is in a line of Asios, where she bears Boiotos in the halls of Dios (fr 2 *PEG*); Strabo, who quotes the line, seems convinced that Dios is the father. Euripides himself makes her in the first of his two plays about her *(Melanippe Sophe)* a daughter of Aiolos, son of Hellen, and Hippo, daughter of Cheiron. Melanippe speaks the prologue in person, claiming that her mother, because her charms and cures released men from pain, was turned into a horse by Zeus (14 GLP). Several sources attest that this speech (or at least its beginning) is indeed from the *Sophe*; by contrast, Ps-Eratosthenes offers a somewhat different version of the mother's fortunes which he cites as from a Euripidean *Melanippe*. Here the daughter of Cheiron (now Hippe) is seduced by Aiolos and as the time of her delivery nears flees into the forest (*Katast* 18). Her father comes in search of her while she is in labor, but as he is about to discover her secret she prays that the gods might hide her from him by turning her into a horse. Out of respect for the piety of father and daughter, Artemis then places her among the stars, in a part of the sky not visible to the Kentauros (her father), as the constellation called Hippos. Hyginus (*Astr* 2.18.2) and the Germanicus scholia support this summary, so that it seems a genuine account of Eratosthenes' original; possibly Euripides used such material at some point in his *Melanippe Desmotis*. Hyginus goes on to relate as well a story similar to that of the *Sophe*, that Hippe had prophetic powers and was changed into a horse lest she reveal the intentions of the gods (*Astr* 2.18.3), then says that in Kallimachos she ceased to follow Artemis in the hunt, and was transformed by the goddess for that reason (= fr 569 Pf). Hippe's motive for leaving Artemis is not here stated, but surely the cause, as with Kallisto and Maira, was her seduction and consequent pregnancy. Ovid calls his daughter of Cheiron (and Chariklo) Okyrhoe; she too learns the art of prophecy, and after predicting the fate of the child Asklepios and her own father finds herself becoming a horse, apparently at Zeus' command (*Met* 2.635–79).

Returning from this preface to the actual plot of Euripides' *Sophe*, it seems that Hippo/Hippe's daughter Melanippe is herself pregnant, having been forced by the god Poseidon, and that she has borne twins, by name Aiolos and Boiotos.[7] If we can trust Ennius' Latin version of the play, the children are placed in a cowshed, leading to the mistaken notion that they are the unnatural offspring of one of the cows. Hellen (Melanippe's grandfather) persuades her father Aiolos to have them burned; Melanippe tries to defend them without revealing her own complicity, but in the end her secret comes out, putting her no doubt in worse difficulties than before. According to Pollux, there was a special mask for Hippo (as a horse?) in Euripides (4.141); presumably, then, she appeared at the end to declare the gods' will and rescue her daughter. The only illustration of this play (or for that matter any part of Melanippe's travails) is an Apulian volute krater of the later fourth century: a cowherd presents the two infants to a grim Hellen (all characters named), while to one side Aiolos stands observing and to the other Melanippe and her nurse do the same (Sciclounoff Coll, no #). To the far left a young Kretheus (Aiolos' son) crowns a horse with a wreath; whether this detail could be meant to indicate Hippo is uncertain.

The plot of the second play, the *Melanippe Desmotis*, is considerably more complicated, and not entirely compatible with the *Sophe*. The scene is set in Metapontion in southern Italy, where Metapontos is apparently king, and to which place Melanippe has been brought (Str 6.1.15). Athenaios adds that there was a woman in the play named Siris (12.523d), and this was presumably Metapontos' wife. The rest of the story is harder to reconstruct, for Hyginus gives a rather jumbled version of it (*Fab* 186), and Diodoros a historical narrative that includes Melanippe but makes her granddaughter Arne the woman who bears Aiolos and Boiotos to Poseidon and is exiled with them to Metapontion by her outraged father (DS 4.67.3–6). The one useful fragment of the play is a messenger speech in which the queen hears of an abortive attempt by her brothers to slay Aiolos and Boiotos, whose birth and (probably) right to the throne they contest (fr 495 N^2 = 13b GLP). Adding this to what we find in Hyginus, it would seem that Melanippe's children were brought up by the queen as her own, while Melanippe herself, unaware of their identity, served in the palace in some menial capacity. The queen's brothers at this point obviously know the children's true origins, but whether Siris also wishes them dead is not clear; in Hyginus (where she is Theano) she finally produces children of her own, and thus her feelings for Melanippe's sons change. In any case, in the *Desmotis* the queen's brothers are slain, Melanippe threatened (perhaps by the children themselves, if they still do not recognize her), and everything finally revealed, as we would expect; the queen probably commits suicide, leaving Metapontos free to marry Melanippe. Hyginus deviates from this reconstruction slightly by having the children he has assigned the queen (now grown) attempt the ambush in order to eliminate their rivals. He also has Melanippe's father (Desmontes, from a misunderstanding of the subtitle *Desmotis*) blind her; eventually Poseidon restores her sight and the father is killed by his grandchildren. The Cyzicene Epigrams tell us that Aiolos and Boiotos saved their mother from death; the introduction adds that they rescued Melanippe from the bonds in which her father had placed her because of her seduction (*AP* 3.16). Obviously, much of the above is similar in kind to the stories of Tyro, Hypsipyle, and Antiope, and whether it had an early existence of its own may be questioned. In Pausanias, Melanippe is the mother of Boiotos by one Itonos son of Amphiktyon; nothing else is said of her story (9.1.1).

Kresphontes Kresphontes the elder is a quasi-historical figure, known primarily as the Herakleides who obtained Messenia by using a token of damp earth (or fired clay) when the allotment was made (ApB 2.8.4; Paus 4.3.4–5). Of his subsequent career the usual account is that Messenians or rivals to the throne slew him and perhaps some of his sons (so first Isokrates 6. *Arch* 22–23). But Euripides produced a play *Kresphontes* whose plot can probably be recovered from Hyginus' *Fabula* 137 with help from an Oxyrhynchus papyrus (POxy 2458); some fragments survive also of Ennius' version of the same story. As Euripides' drama begins, the elder Kresphontes has long since been murdered by one Polyphontes, who has taken his wife Merope and seized the throne, killing two of his children in the bargain. Merope, however, has managed to conceal a third infant child, also named Kresphontes, and send him away to Aitolia. In the course of the play he naturally returns, but Merope (aided by Polyphontes) has somehow arrived at the idea that he has killed her son, and his own death at her hands (onstage, with an axe) is barely averted (this from Plutarch: *Mor* 998e = fr 456 N²). She then returns to Polyphontes, pretending to be reconciled to the death of her son, and suggests a sacrifice to which the young stranger will be invited. This stratagem puts a weapon in the son's hands, he kills the usurper, and justice triumphs. Hyginus adds to this bare outline the idea that Polyphontes had advertised a reward for the death of Kresphontes, with as usual the intended victim then presenting himself at the palace claiming to have done the deed; such a standard plot device may well come from Euripides. The Cyzicene Epigrams also celebrate the tale (Kresphontes fixes a spear in Polyphontes' back while Merope strikes the miscreant on the head with a staff: *AP* 3.5), and Apollodoros very briefly recounts Polyphontes' crime and the son's revenge, although he calls that son Aipytos (Ap*B* 2.8.5; cf. Paus 4.3.6–8).

The Daughters of Minyas

Of these ill-fated daughters our first preserved account is in Ovid, but Antoninus Liberalis credits his own version to Nikandros and Korinna, and so we will begin with it (AntLib 10). Minyas, son of Orchomenos, has in fact three daughters, Leukippe, Arsippe, and Alkathoe, who are extremely industrious. For this reason they find fault with all those women who leave the city for the mountains to engage in Bakchic revels, even when Dionysos himself in the form of a young girl advises them not to neglect the rites of the god. Upon their continued refusal he turns himself into a bull, a lion, and a leopard, while milk and nectar flow from their looms. At this they become frightened and draw lots; when that of Leukippe emerges first, she takes her own son Hippasos and with her sisters tears him apart as a sacrifice to Dionysos. They then go out to the hills and join the revels, until Hermes with his *rhabdos* turns them into a bat and two different kinds of owls. Ovid's version follows much the same lines, with Alkithoe *(sic)* and her sisters determined to remain at their weaving while the others run off to the festival (*Met* 4.1–42, 389–415). Here, however, there is no appearance by the god and no sacrifice; their looms are simply overrun by vine tendrils and all three turn into bats. In Aelianus, their motive for refusing the god is a desire not to leave their husbands (*VH* 3.42). Vines, ivy, snakes, and the like appear as they tend their looms, but even this does not impress them, and so they become maddened and slay the young child of Leukippe. When they then try to join the other Mainades they are rejected, and become a crow, a bat, and an owl. For his part Plutarch (where Arsippe becomes Arsinoe) simply comments that they conceived a mad desire for human flesh (apparently to eat) and thus drew lots, killing as before Leukippe's child Hippasos (*Mor* 229e). Among the plays of Aischylos about which little or nothing is known there are two, *Bakchai* and *Xantriai*, which have been thought by some to relate this myth.[8] *Xantriai* (the title means "Carders") might seem especially appropriate, given the girls' attachment to their weaving, but we have seen in chapter 14 that a reference to Pentheus in that play is probably reason enough to assign it to his story. For the *Bakchai*, on the other hand, there is really no evidence one way or another, and thus a fifth-century account of this story is certainly a possibility.

Appendix A

Some "Deviant" Cosmogonies

The choice of what material to include in this section is of necessity arbitrary and subjective. But most scholars would agree, I think, that in our corpus of Greek myths there exist versions of the creation and first beginnings which of their own volition remain outside the mainstream of Greek thought, versions that address a small clique of believers and represent decidedly personal views about the nature of humans and the destiny of the soul. We have touched on some of these in chapters 1 and 2, since it seemed inappropriate to omit them from the main discussion altogether, but I should like at this point to review what we know of their beliefs in a more systematic fashion. The material in question falls into two main categories, that ascribed to the undoubtedly historical Pherekydes of Syros and that ascribed to Orpheus. Had we more of "Mousaios" and the "Epimenides Theogony" they might have been included here as well, since the ideas attributed to them seem cut from much the same cloth. But what survives of their cosmogonies is too scant to make a summary feasible, or even to be sure that their intentions were as "deviant" as they sometimes appear, and their remnants have therefore been incorporated into the main text as variants on our more "canonical" traditions.

Pherekydes of Syros

Pherekydes of the island of Syros west of Mykonos we know to have lived in the sixth century, probably writing in the middle of it, and there are no grounds to suppose him not the source of the ideas attributed to him.[1] He was sometimes regarded as the first writer of narrative prose (or else prose about the gods), and Diogenes Laertios preserves the opening lines of his work, which announce that Zas and Chronos always existed, and Chthonie, she whose name became Ge when Zas gave her the earth as a prize (*geras:* 7B1). Subsequently we learn that Chronos produces from his own seed fire, water, and *pneuma;* these are in some way deposited in five recesses (*muchoi*) where (perhaps in different combinations) they become a second (and numerous) generation of gods (7A8). Meanwhile, Zas is preparing a marriage with Chthonie, and on the third day of the ceremonies gives her a robe or cloth (*pharos*) on which are embroidered Ge and Ogenos and the dwellings of Ogenos; he perhaps indicates as well that marriages will be under her care (text damaged: 7B2). Apparently we are to understand this cloth as the prize mentioned by Diogenes: Zas creates the earth and sea, as symbolized by the cloth with those entities embroidered upon it, and Chthonie receiving the cloth becomes Ge, the earth. The cloth is also associated in Pherekydes with a winged oak tree on which it hangs, according to Isidoros (7B2 again), and we find mention as well of "the oak and the robe" (*peplos:* 7A11), the tree being in some way a support or foundation for earth and sea. This last source mentions too as from Pherekydes the birth of Ophioneus and the battle of the gods. Such a battle proves to have been between Kronos (not Chronos) and Ophioneus, each with their forces (the latter's including his children) drawn up for combat; an agreement is struck whereby whichever should be driven out and fall into Ogenos shall be the loser, the winner to hold *ouranos* (7B4). At another point we learn that Zeus (so spelled) casts down into Tartaros whomever of the gods shows hybris, and that the daughters of Boreas and the Harpuiai and Thyella guard the place (7B5).

Not attested as from Pherekydes, but showing obvious affinities, is a part (not all) of the song sung by Orpheus in Book 1 of Apollonios' *Argonautika:* "how Ophion and Eurynome daughter of Okeanos held the rule on snowy Olympos, and how Ophion yielded his power to the might and force of Kronos, and Eurynome to Rheia, and they fell into the waves of Okeanos" (AR 1.503–6; there follow lines in which Kronos and Rheia rule the Titans until such time as Zeus is born, probably not relevant here).

This is all, leaving us with mostly questions. Scholars have generally assumed that at some point Chronos becomes Kronos, and Zas Zeus, and perhaps Ge Rheia. Such an assumption seems likely to be right, but poses some problems for our understanding of the relationship between Zeus and Kronos: do they clash as in Hesiod after the fall of Ophioneus, or are they allies in that battle and subsequently, with Zeus simply assuming a more prominent role toward the end of the poem? Those holding the first view must confront the difficulty that for Ophioneus to fall into Ogenos the latter must first have been created by Zas, in which case his wedding to Chthonie/Ge will precede Kronos' defeat of Ophioneus. No doubt this obstacle can be circumvented, but there still remains the fact that Zeus (as Zas) and Kronos (as Chronos) have both existed forever, in contrast to Ophioneus, and there seems no good reason why either of them should suddenly engage in conflict with the other. Significant too, as recently pointed out, is the passage of Aristotle placing Pherekydes with those mythographers for whom the initial principles of the world reflect the Good (*Metaphysics* 1091a29–b12). Conceivably this could mean only Zas, but when we consider Chronos' role in the creation of things it seems impossible to regard him as an opposing force of evil. On the whole, then, I think it best to assume that Zas and Chronos work together in harmony from beginning (of which there is none) to end, and that the battle with Ophioneus (from his name clearly a Typhoeus counterpart) and his brood is the only conflict which Pherekydes envisioned.

The Orphic Theogonies

In the case of Pherekydes we have some reason to hope that we are dealing with the ideas of a single individual, conceived, expressed, and preserved in a coherent and consistent fashion. The situation with "Orpheus" is quite different. It has long been argued, rightly I think, that so-called Orphic texts, as collected in Otto Kern's *Orphicorum Fragmenta* (Berlin 1922), are simply works that their authors chose to attribute to Orpheus rather than themselves; by so doing they hoped to achieve for their ideas greater prestige and a more willing reception. Since this option was open to anyone, regardless of the nature of his ideas, we will be hard-pressed to speak of any consistent "Orphic" beliefs; every such text may well be an individual entity with little or no allegiance to others sharing the same claim of authorship. Nevertheless, certain kinds of ideas coming from Thrace and the Near East do seem to have been found more suitable for ascription to the shamanistic Orpheus who had been to the Underworld and returned, and some scholars do still believe in a single unified Orphic religious movement, with corresponding texts, as early as the fifth century B.C. Whatever the truth of the matter, we will certainly see some common threads at work in the different stories designated as "Orphic."

These texts have recently been restudied by Martin West in his book *The Orphic Poems* (Oxford 1983), which is essential reading on the subject, even for those who do not accept his basic premises. Beginning with the end-point of our knowledge, the so-called Rhapsodic Theogony assembled in the first (?) century B.C., West constructs a stemma of the relationships between various texts that were eventually combined to form the Rhapsodic version. His results depend to a considerable extent on material from a newly published papyrus, discovered at Derveni near Thessalonica in 1962. This papyrus, which dates to the later part of the fourth century B.C. or perhaps even earlier, includes a commentary on certain passages of an Orphic text concerned with the beginnings of things. Comparison of this version with that of the Rhapsodic Theogony and several others known to have been in circulation in antiquity leads West to the conclusion that originally two separate lines of tradition existed, both of which go back to the fifth century B.C.; the one is represented in his view by the so-called Protogonos Theogony of which the Derveni version is an abridgement, the other by the Eudemian Theogony (named for its mention in the work of the Peripatetic Eudemos). Both works were then drawn upon for the composition of the Cyclic Theogony, a poem that West believes stood at the head of the Epic Cycle when that entity was organized in the third century B.C. From there the trail leads to Apollodoros, whom West thinks used a prose summary of this material as he did the rest of the Cycle, and to the Rhapsodic Theogony, which combined material from the Eudemian, the Cyclic, and the Hieronyman (Stoic) redaction of the Protogonos Theogony to form its own version.

West's arguments are obviously strongest at the beginning (the Protogonos Theogony, *c.* 500 B.C.) and the end (the Rhapsodic Theogony) of this process because at those two points he has some solid evidence; in between there is a certain amount of guesswork, along with deductions based on very slim testimony. Nevertheless, he manages to suggest some order in what is an immensely complicated body of material, and the overall picture has much to recommend it. Since a reasonably clear presentation of that material is all that is needed here, what follows will adhere to his basic arrangement of the tales, with sources noted from Kern's edition of the fragments and hypotheses distinguished from firm evidence.

In the Protogonos Theogony (as represented by the Derveni papyrus), it is certain that Zeus was preceded by Ouranos and Kronos, as in Hesiod, and that Kronos committed a "great deed" against Ouranos (surely the castration). But in contrast to Hesiod we find that Ouranos is the son of Nyx, and that Zeus becoming ruler swallows (on her advice) the *daimôn* "who first sprang forth into the aither" (West here rearranges lines on what I believe are valid textual grounds to produce this sense, but see below). Said *daimôn* is subsequently named Protogonos (elsewhere known as Phanes), and after Zeus has swallowed him all the immortals and rivers and springs and all other things "attach themselves" *(prosephun)* to Zeus. Apparently he then brings them forth again from his mouth, save for Aphrodite who is a product of his seed. As the Derveni citations end he has created Okeanos and Acheloos (and probably everything else) and desires to lie in love with his mother.

To all this West adds from the Hieronyman and Rhapsodic Theogonies the following material, which he believes goes back to the Protogonos. Chronos creates an egg from Aither (fr 70 Kern), and from that egg springs forth Protogonos (fr 60), four-eyed (fr 76), four-horned (fr 77), with golden wings (fr 78), many animal heads (frr 79, 81), and both male and female sexual organs (fr 81), which he uses to mate with himself (fr 80). At his emergence Chaos and Aither are split (fr 72). His offspring include Nyx (fr 98), who is the mother by him of Ouranos and Gaia (fr 109). Gaia gives the Titans to Nyx to hide and nurse (frr 129, 131), after her first two sets of offspring have been imprisoned by Ouranos. Events (castration of Ouranos, etc.) follow as above and in Hesiod, with Okeanos perhaps reluctant (fr 135). Somehow Zeus replaces Kronos in power and recreates the world through the swallowing of Protogonos (frr 129, 167, 168). Zeus then mates with his mother Rheia who is also Demeter (frr 153, 145); their union in the form of snakes produces Persephone, who may have two faces and horns (fr 58). Zeus in the same snake form mates with Persephone, and the child Dionysos is born (fr 58). Apollo and Persephone produce the Eumenides (fr 194), and probably there is a battle between the Olympians and the Titans. Protogonos creates a golden race and Kronos a silver one (fr 140); Zeus adds a third race, hapless men who know nothing of the avoiding of evils or seizing upon the good (fr 233). The poem as a whole would date to about 500 B.C., composed perhaps for a "Bacchic" society in Ionia.

By contrast, for the second branch of tradition, that called the Eudemian, we know for certain only that Nyx had absolute primacy, appearing first of all (fr 28 Kern). West proceeds on the assumption that Plato's *Timaios* order of succession, in which Okeanos occupies an intermediate genealogy between Ouranos and Kronos (*Tim* 40e), comes from this poem, and that we need only put Nyx at the head of it. Phorkys' mention as a brother of Kronos there may mean that he and Dione (a thirteenth Titan in Apollodoros) assume the places of Okeanos and Tethys to make up the canonical twelve Titans, in which case Dione is probably Aphrodite's mother as in the *Iliad*; the castration of Ouranos is omitted. Zeus is nursed by Adrastea and Ida and guarded by the Kouretes on Krete (ApB 1.1.6; frr 105, 151 Kern). Metis gives Kronos an emetic to swallow (ApB 1.2.1); he is perhaps also intoxicated with honey and castrated by Zeus (frr 148–9, 154, 137 Kern). Zeus and Persephone produce Dionysos on Krete. Spurred on by Hera (or their own jealousy) the Titans tempt the child with toys, tear him apart, and roast and eat the remains (frr 34, 35, 214). Athena, however, rescues the heart (fr 35), and Zeus uses it in some fashion to create a new Dionysos (probably by placing the heart in a body of gypsum: fr 214). As for the Titans, they are destroyed by Zeus' thunderbolt, and a new race of men is fashioned from the ashes (fr 220). Persephone is guarded by the Kouretes but nonetheless abducted by Plouton, to whom she bears the Eumenides (frr 151, 197); at the time of her abduction she is weaving a robe with a skorpion (frr 192, 196). West assigns this poem to the last third of the fifth century at Athens.

I would add here only that in other hands the chronological assessment of these myths can look quite different, and even too the sense. The second edition of Kirk, Raven, and Schofield's *The Presocratic Philosophers*, for example, holds to the originally presented order of lines in the Derveni papyrus, with the result that Zeus swallows not the revered Phanes (as he certainly does in the Rhapsodic tradition), but instead a phallus, apparently that severed from his grandfather Ouranos (Phanes is thus not mentioned at all). The myth in consequence offers a much closer parallel to the Hurrian-Hittite tale of Kumarbi, who cuts off the weather god's phallus and swallows it. Indeed, the authors suggest that Hesiod deliberately eschewed this form of the castration and swallowing motifs in favor of something tamer. They also argue for a single line of Orphic tradition in the fifth century, one that included Chronos but not Nyx as a first principle, and an egg but perhaps Eros (in his Hesiodic role) rather than Phanes as its contents. On the other hand, the tale of Zeus and his daughter Persephone as parents of an original Dionysos torn apart by Titans and reborn does seem to be accepted by most scholars as early Orphic belief, and this is perhaps that body of tradition's most distinctive contribution to the Greek myths as we know them.

Appendix B

Editions of Ancient Texts Cited

Accius
Tragicorum Romanorum Fragmenta, ed. O. Ribbeck. *Scaenicae Romanorum Poesis Fragmenta* 1. Leipzig 1897.

Aelianus
De Natura Animalium: Claudii Aeliani De Natura Animalium libri xvii, ed. R. Hercher. Leipzig 1864.
Varia Historia: Claudii Aeliani Varia Historia, ed. M. R. Dilts. Leipzig 1974.

Aischylos
Fragments: *Tragicorum Graecorum Fragmenta* 3, ed. S. L. Radt. Göttingen 1985.
Plays: *Aeschyli Tragoediae,* ed. D. L. Page. Oxford 1972.

Aithiopis
Poetae Epici Graeci 1, ed. A. Bernabé. Leipzig 1987.

Akousilaos
Die Fragmente der griechischen Historiker 1, ed. F. Jacoby. 2d ed. Leiden 1957.

Alkaios
Poetarum Lesbiorum Fragmenta, ed. E. Lobel and D. L. Page. Oxford 1955.

Alkmaionis
Poetae Epici Graeci 1, ed. A. Bernabé. Leipzig 1987.

Alkman
Poetae Melici Graeci, ed. D. L. Page. Oxford 1962.

Anakreon
Poetae Melici Graeci, ed. D. L. Page. Oxford 1962.

Antimachos
Antimachi Colophonii reliquiae, ed. B. Wyss. Berlin 1936.

Antisthenes
Antisthenis Fragmenta, ed. F. Caizzi. Milan 1966.

Antoninus Liberalis
Mythographi Graeci 2.1, ed. E. Martini. Leipzig 1896.

Apollodoros
Apollodorus, ed. J. G. Frazier. 2 vols. Cambridge, Mass., 1921.
Mythographi Graeci 1, ed. R. Wagner. Leipzig 1894.

Apollonios of Rhodes
Apollonii Rhodii Argonautica, ed. H. Fränkel. Oxford 1961.

Apuleius
Apuleius I: Metamorphoseon libri xi, ed. R. Helm. Leipzig 1931.

Aratos
Arati Phaenomena, ed. E. Maass. Berlin 1893.

Archilochos
Iambi et Elegi Graeci 1, ed. M. L. West. Oxford 1971.

Aristophanes
Fragments: *Poetae Comici Graeci* 3.2, ed. R. Kassel and C. Austin. Berlin 1984.
Plays: *Aristophanis Comoediae*, F. W. Hall and W. M. Geldart. 2 vols. Oxford 1906–7.

Aristotle
Constitution of Athens: Aristotelis Atheniensium Respublica, ed. F. G. Kenyon. Oxford 1920.
Peplos: Aristotelis qui ferebantur librorum fragmenta, ed. V. Rose. Stuttgart 1886.
Peri Thaumasiôn Akousmatôn: Aristotle: Minor Works, ed. W. S. Hett. Cambridge, Mass., 1936.
Poetics: Aristotelis de Arte Poetica Liber, ed. R. Kassel. Oxford 1965.
Rhetoric: Aristotelis Ars Rhetorica, ed. W. D. Ross. Oxford 1959.

Asklepiades
Die Fragmente der griechischen Historiker 1, ed. F. Jacoby. 2d ed. Leiden 1957.

Aspis
Hesiodi Theogonia, Opera et Dies, Scutum, ed. F. Solmsen. 3d ed. Oxford 1990.

Athenaios
Athenaei Naucratitae Dipnosophistarum libri xv, ed. G. Kaibel. 3 vols. Leipzig 1887–90.

Bakchylides
Bacchylidis Carmina cum fragmentis, ed. B. Snell and H. Maehler. Leipzig 1970.

Bion
Bucolici Graeci, ed. A. S. F. Gow. Oxford 1952.

Certamen Homeri et Hesiodi
Homeri Opera 5, ed. T. W. Allen. Oxford 1912.

Cicero
De Divinatione: M. Tulli Ciceronis scripta quae manserunt omnia, fasc. 46, ed. R. Giomini. Leipzig 1975.
De Natura Deorum: M. Tulli Ciceronis scripta quae manserunt omnia, fasc. 45., ed. W. Ax. 2d ed. Stuttgart 1933.
Tusculan Disputations: M. Tulli Ciceronis scripta quae manserunt omnia, fasc. 44, ed. M. Pohlenz. Stuttgart 1918.

Claudian
Claudii Claudiani Carmina, ed. J. B. Hall. Leipzig 1985.

Clement of Alexandria
Clément d'Alexandre: Le Protreptique, ed. C. Mondésert. 2d ed. Paris 1949.

Editions of Ancient
Texts Cited

Dares

A. J. Valpy, ed. *Dictys Cretensis et Dares Phrygius: De Bello Trojano*. London 1825.

Demosthenes

Demosthenis Orationes, ed. S. H. Butcher and W. Rennie. 3 vols. Oxford 1903–31.

Diktys

Dictys Cretensis, ed. W. Eisenhut. Leipzig 1973.

Diodoros Siculus

Diodorus Siculus: Library of History, ed. C. H. Oldfather et al. 12 vols. Cambridge, Mass., 1933–67.

Diogenes Laertius

Diogenes Laertius: Lives of Eminent Philosophers, ed. R. D. Hicks. 2 vols. Cambridge, Mass., 1925.

Dion of Prusa

Dionis Prusaensis quem vocant Chrysostomum quae exstant omnia, ed. J. de Arnim. 2 vols. Berlin 1893–96.

Dionysios of Halikarnassos

Dionysius of Halicarnassus: Roman Antiquities, ed. E. Cary. 7 vols. Cambridge, Mass., 1937–50.

Dionysios Skytobrachion

Die Fragmente der griechischen Historiker 1, ed. F. Jacoby. 2d ed. Leiden 1957.

Ennius

Annales: The Annals of Q. Ennius, ed. O. Skutsch. Oxford 1985.

Epigonoi: Poetae Epici Graeci 1, ed. A. Bernabé. Leipzig 1987.

Epimenides

Die Fragmente der Vorsokratiker 1, ed. H. Diels and W. Kranz. 6th ed. Berlin 1951.

Etymologicum Magnum

Etymologicum Magnum seu verius Lexicon, ed. T. Gaisford. Oxford 1848.

Euphorion

Collectanea Alexandrina, ed. J. U. Powell. Oxford 1925.

Euripides

Fragments: A. Nauck, *Tragicorum Graecorum Fragmenta*. 2d ed. Leipzig 1889.

Plays: *Euripidis Fabulae*, ed. J. Diggle and G. Murray: vol. 1 (Diggle): *Kyklops, Alkestis, Medeia, Herakleidai, Hippolytos, Andromache, Hekabe*. Oxford 1984; vol. 2 (Diggle): *Hiketides, Elektra, Herakles Mainomenos, Troades, Iphigeneia among the Taurians, Ion*. Oxford 1981; vol. 3 (Murray): *Helen, Phoinissai, Orestes, Bakchai, Iphigeneia at Aulis, Rhesos*, 2d ed. Oxford 1913.

Eustathios

Eustathii Commentarii ad Homeri Iliadem. 4 vols. Leipzig 1827–30.

Eustathii Commentarii ad Homeri Odysseam. 2 vols. Leipzig 1825–26.

Hekataios

Die Fragmente der griechischen Historiker 1, ed. F. Jacoby. 2d ed. Leiden 1957.

Hellanikos

Die Fragmente der griechischen Historiker 1, ed. F. Jacoby. 2d ed. Leiden 1957.

Herakleitos
Peri Apistôn: Mythographi Graeci 3.2, ed. N. Festa. Leipzig 1902.

Herodoros
Die Fragmente der griechischen Historiker 1, ed. F. Jacoby. 2d ed. Leiden 1957.

Herodotos
Herodoti Historiae, ed. C. Hude. Oxford 1927.

Hesiod
Fragments: R. Merkelbach and M. L. West, *Fragmenta Hesiodea.* Oxford 1967.
Poems: *Hesiodi Theogonia, Opera et Dies, Scutum,* ed. F. Solmsen. 3d ed. Oxford
1990.

Homer
Iliad: Homeri Opera 1–2, ed. D. B. Munro and T. W. Allen. 3d ed. Oxford 1920.
Odyssey: Homeri Opera 3–4, ed. T. W. Allen. 2d ed. Oxford 1917–19.

Homeric Hymns: Homeri Opera 5, ed. T. W. Allen. Oxford 1912.

Hyginus
De Astronomia: Hygin: L'Astronomie, ed. A. Le Boeuffle. Paris 1983.
Fabulae: Hygini Fabulae, ed. H. J. Rose. Leiden 1933.

Hypereides
Hyperidis Orationes sex, ed. C. Jensen. Stuttgart 1917.

Ibykos
Poetae Melici Graeci, ed. D. L. Page. Oxford 1962.

Isokrates
Isocrate: Discours, ed. G. Mathieu and É. Brémond. 4 vols. Paris 1962–67.

Istros
Die Fragmente der griechischen Historiker 3B, ed. F. Jacoby. Leiden 1950.

Kallimachos
Callimachus, ed. R. Pfeiffer. 2 vols. Oxford 1949–53.

Konon
Die Fragmente der griechischen Historiker 1, ed. F. Jacoby. 2d ed. Leiden 1957.

Kypria
Poetae Epici Graeci 1, ed. A. Bernabé. Leipzig 1987.

Little Iliad
Poetae Epici Graeci 1, ed. A. Bernabé. Leipzig 1987.

Loukianos
Luciani Opera, ed. M. D. Macleod. 4 vols. Oxford 1972–87.

Lykophron
Lycophronis Alexandra, ed. L. Mascialino. Leipzig 1964.

Lykourgos
Lycurgi Oratio in Leocratem, ed. N. C. Conomis. Leipzig 1970.

Macrobius
Saturnalia: Macrobius 1, ed. J. Willis. Leipzig 1970.

Menandros
Menandri Reliquiae Selectae, ed. F. H. Sandbach. Oxford 1972.

Mimnermos
Iambi et Elegi Greci 2, ed. M. L. West. Oxford 1972.

Moschos
Bucolici Graeci, ed. A. S. F. Gow. Oxford 1952.

Mousaios
Die Fragmente der Vorsokratiker 1, ed. H. Diels and W. Kranz. 6th ed. Berlin 1951.

Naupaktia
Poetae Epici Graeci 1, ed. A. Bernabé. Leipzig 1987.

Nikandros
Nikander: The Poems and Poetical Fragments, ed. A. S. F. Gow and A. F. Scholfield.
　　Cambridge 1953.

Nonnos
Nonni Panopolitani Dionysiaca, ed. A. Ludwich. 2 vols. Leipzig 1909–11.

Oidipodeia
Poetae Epici Graeci 1, ed. A. Bernabé. Leipzig 1987.

Orphic Argonautika
Les argonautiques d'Orphée, ed. G. Dottin. Paris 1930.

Ovid
Ars Amatoria: P. Ovidi Nasonis Amores, Medicamina Faciei Femineae, Ars Amatoria,
　　Remedia Amoris, ed. E. J. Kenney. Oxford 1961.
Fasti: P. Ovidi Nasonis Fastorum libri sex, ed. E. H. Alton, D. E. W. Wormell, and
　　E. Courtney. Leipzig 1978.
Heroides: P. Ovidii Nasonis Epistulae Heroidum, ed. H. Dörrie. Berlin 1971.
Metamorphoses: Ovidius: Metamorphoses, ed. W. S. Anderson. Leipzig 1977.
Remedia Amoris: P. Ovidi Nasonis Amores, Medicamina Faciei Femineae, Ars Amato-
　　ria, Remedia Amoris, ed. E. J. Kenney. Oxford 1961.

Pacuvius
Tragicorum Romanorum Fragmenta, ed. O. Ribbeck. *Scaenicae Romanorum Poesis*
　　Fragmenta 1. Leipzig 1897.

Palaiphatos
Mythographi Graeci 3.2, ed. N. Festa. Leipzig 1902.

Palatine Anthology
The Greek Anthology, ed. W. R. Paton. 5 vols. Cambridge, Mass., 1916–18.

Parian Marble
Die Fragmente der griechischen Historiker 2B, pt. 3, ed. F. Jacoby. Berlin 1929.

Parthenios
Mythographi Graeci 2.1, ed. P. Sakolowski. Leipzig 1896.

Pausanias
Pausaniae Graeciae Descriptio, ed. F. Spiro. 3 vols. Stuttgart 1903.

Pherekydes of Athens
Die Fragmente der griechischen Historiker 1, ed. F. Jacoby. 2d ed. Leiden 1957.

Pherekydes of Syros
Die Fragmente der Vorsokratiker 1, ed. H. Diels and W. Kranz. 6th ed. Berlin 1951.

Philochoros
Die Fragmente der griechischen Historiker 3B, ed. F. Jacoby. Leiden 1950.

Philodemos
Philodem: Über Frömmigkeit, ed. T. Gomperz. Leipzig 1866.

Philostratos (Flavius)
Flavii Philostrati Opera 1, ed. C. L. Kayser. Leipzig 1870.

Philostratos the Younger
Flavii Philostrati Opera 2, ed. C. L. Kayser. Leipzig 1871.

Phrynichos
Tragicorum Graecorum Fragmenta 1, ed. B. Snell. Göttingen 1971.

Pindar
Fragments: *Pindarus* 2, ed. B. Snell and H. Maehler. Leipzig 1975.
Odes: *Pindarus* 1, ed. B. Snell and H. Maehler. Leipzig 1971.

Plato
Platonis Opera, ed. J. Burnet. 5 vols. Oxford 1905–10.

Plautus
T. Macci Plauti Comoediae, ed. W. M. Lindsay. 2 vols. Oxford 1904–5.

Pliny the Elder
Pliny: Natural History, ed. H. Rackham et al. 10 vols. Cambridge, Mass., 1938–63.

Plutarch
Lives: Plutarchi Vitae Parallelae 1 and 3, ed. K. Ziegler. Leipzig 1960–73.
Moralia: Plutarch: Moralia, ed. F. C. Babbitt et al. 15 vols. Cambridge, Mass.,
   1927–69.

Polyainos
Polyaeni Strategematôn libri viii, ed. E. Woelfflin and J. Melber. Stuttgart 1887–1901.

Pratinas
Tragicorum Graecorum Fragmenta 1, ed. B. Snell. Göttingen 1971.

Propertius
Sexti Properti Carmina, ed. E. A. Barber. Oxford 1960.

Pseudo-Eratosthenes
Mythographi Graeci 3.1, ed. A. Olivieri. Leipzig 1897.

Ptolemaios Chennos
Der Philosoph und Grammatiker Ptolemaios Chennos, ed. A. Chatzis. Paderborn
   1914.

Quintus of Smyrna
Quintus de Smyrne: La suite d'Homère, ed. F. Vian. 3 vols. Paris 1963–69.

Sappho
Poetarum Lesbiorum Fragmenta, ed. E. Lobel and D. L. Page. Oxford 1955.

Σ Apollonios of Rhodes
Scholia in Apollonium Rhodium vetera, ed. C. Wendel. Berlin 1935.

Σ Aratos
Scholia in Aratum vetera, ed. J. Martin. Stuttgart 1974.

Σ Aristophanes
Scholia Graeca in Aristophanem, ed. F. Dübner. Paris 1877.

Σ Euripides
Scholia in Euripidem, ed. E. Schwartz. 2 vols. Berlin 1887–91.

Σ Germanicus
Eratosthenis Catasterismorum Reliquiae, ed. C. Robert. Berlin 1878.

Σ Hesiod
Theogony: Scholia vetera in Hesiodi Theogoniam, ed. L. Di Gregorio. Milan 1975.
Works & Days: Scholia vetera in Hesiodi Opera et Dies, ed. A. Pertusi. Milan 1955.

Σ Homer
Iliad: Scholia Graeca in Homeri Iliadem, ed. W. Dindorf and E. Maass. 6 vols. Oxford
    1875–88.
Odyssey: Scholia Graeca in Homeri Odysseam, ed. W. Dindorf. 2 vols. Oxford 1855.

Σ Lykophron
Lycophronis Alexandra 2, ed. E. Scheer. Berlin 1908.

Σ Pindar
Scholia vetera in Pindari carmina, ed. A. B. Drachmann. 3 vols. Leipzig 1903–27.

Σ Sophokles
Scholia in Sophoclis Tragoedias vetera, ed. P. N. Papageorgius. Leipzig 1888.

Σ Statius
*Lactantii Placidi qui dicitur commentarios in Statii Thebaida et commentarium in
    Achilleida*, ed. R. Jahnke. *P. Papinius Statius* 3. Leipzig 1898.

Σ Theokritos
Scholia in Theocritum vetera, ed. C. Wendel. Stuttgart 1914.

Σ Vergil
Aeneid: Servii Grammatici qui feruntur in Vergilii carmina commentarii: Aeneis,
    ed. G. Thilo and H. Hagen. 2 vols. Leipzig 1881–84.
Eclogues: Servii Grammatici qui feruntur in Vergilii Bucolica et Georgica commentarii,
    ed. G. Thilo. Leipzig 1887.
Georgics: Servii Grammatici qui feruntur in Vergilii Bucolica et Georgica commentarii,
    ed. G. Thilo. Leipzig 1887.

Seneca the Younger
L. Annaei Senecae Tragoediae, ed. O. Zwierlein. Oxford 1986.

Sextus Empiricus
Sextus Empiricus, ed. R. G. Bury. 4 vols. Cambridge, Mass., 1933–49.

Simonides
Poetae Melici Graeci, ed. D. L. Page. Oxford 1962.

Sophokles
Fragments: *Tragicorum Graecorum Fragmenta* 4, ed. S. Radt. Göttingen 1977.

Plays: *Sophoclis Fabulae*, ed. A. C. Pearson. Oxford 1924.

Statius
Achilleis: P. Papini Stati Achilleis, ed. A. Marastoni. Leipzig 1974.
Thebais: P. Papini Stati Thebais, ed. A. Klotz. 2d ed. Leipzig 1973.

Stesichoros
Poetae Melici Graeci, ed. D. L. Page. Oxford 1962.

Strabo
Strabo: Geography, ed. H. L. Jones. 8 vols. Cambridge, Mass., 1917–32.

Suetonius
C. Suetoni Tranquilli Opera 1, ed. M. Ihm. Stuttgart 1908.

Thebais
Poetae Epici Graeci 1, ed. A. Bernabé. Leipzig 1987.

Theognis
Iambi et Elegi Graeci 1, ed. M. L. West. Oxford 1971.

Theokritos
Bucolici Graeci, ed. A. S. F. Gow. Oxford 1952.

Thoukydides
Thucydidis Historiae, ed. H. S. Jones and J. E. Powell. 2 vols. Oxford 1942.

Titanomachia
Poetae Epici Graeci 1, ed. A. Bernabé. Leipzig 1987.

Tzetzes, John
Exegesis in Homeri Iliadem: Draconis Stratonicensis Liber de Metricis Poeticis; Ioannis Tzetzae Exegesis in Homeri Iliadem, ed. G. Hermann. Leipzig 1812.

Valerius Flaccus
C. Valeri Flacci Argonauticon, ed. E. Courtney. Leipzig 1970.

Vatican Mythographers
Scriptores rerum mythicarum Latini tres Romae nuper reperti, ed. G. H. Bode. 2 vols. Celle 1834.

Varro
M. Terenti Varronis De Lingua Latina quae supersunt, ed. G. Goetz and F. Schoell. Leipzig 1910.

Vergil
Aeneid: P. Vergili Maronis Opera, ed. F. A. Hirtzel. Oxford 1900.
Eclogues: P. Vergili Maronis Opera, ed. F. A. Hirtzel. Oxford 1900.
Georgics: P. Vergili Maronis Opera, ed. F. A. Hirtzel. Oxford 1900.
Minor works (*Ciris, Culex*, etc.): *Appendix Vergiliana*, ed. W. V. Clausen, F. R. D. Goodyear, E. J. Kenney, and J. A. Richmond. Oxford 1966.

Xenophon
Kynegetikos: Xenophontis Opuscula, ed. E. C. Marchant. Oxford 1920.

Zenobios
Corpus Paroemiographorum Graecorum 1, ed. E. L. Leutsch and F. G. Schneidewin. Göttingen 1839.

Appendix C

Catalogue of Artistic Representations

Abbreviations

BF	Attic Black-Figure	MC	Middle Corinthian
EC	Early Corinthian	PA	Protoattic
LC	Late Corinthian	RF	Attic Red-Figure
LG	Late Geometric	WG	Attic White-Ground

ABL   C. H. E. Haspels, *Attic Black-Figured Lekythoi* (Paris 1936)

ABV   J. D. Beazley, *Attic Black-Figure Vase-Painters* (Oxford 1956)

ARV²   J. D. Beazley, *Attic Red-Figure Vase-Painters*, 2d ed. (Oxford 1963)

CH   J. M. Hemelrijk, *Caeretan Hydriae* (Mainz am Rhein 1984)

ChV   A. Rumpf, *Chalkidische Vasen* (Berlin 1927)

CorVP   D. A. Amyx, *Corinthian Vase-Painting of the Archaic Period* (Berkeley 1988)

DL 1   F. Brommer and A. Peschlow-Bindokat, *Denkmälerlisten zur griechischen Heldensage* 1 (Marburg 1971)

FS   K. Schefold, *Frühgriechische Sagenbilder* (Munich 1964)

LCS   A. D. Trendall, *The Red-Figured Vases of Lucania, Campania and Sicily* (Oxford 1967)

LIMC   *Lexicon Iconographicum Mythologiae Classicae* 1–5

LV   C. M. Stibbe, *Lakonische Vasenmaler des sechsten Jahrhunderts vor Chr.* (Amsterdam 1972)

OF II   E. Kunze, *Olympische Forschungen* II (Berlin 1950)

OF XVII   P. Bol, *Olympische Forschungen* XVII (Berlin 1989)

Para   J. D. Beazley, *Paralipomena* (Oxford 1971)

RVAp   A. D. Trendall and A. Cambitoglou, *The Red-Figured Vases of Apulia* 1–2 (Oxford 1978–82)

RVP   A. D. Trendall, *The Red-Figured Vases of Paestum* (Rome 1987)

SB II   K. Schefold, *Götter- und Heldensagen der Griechen in der spätarchaischen Kunst* (Munich 1978)

SB III   K. Schefold, *Die Göttersage in der klassichen und hellenistischen Kunst* (Munich 1981)

SB IV   K. Schefold and F. Jung, *Die Urkönige, Perseus, Bellerophon, Herakles und Theseus in der klassischen und hellenistischen Kunst* (Munich 1988)

SB V   K. Schefold and F. Jung, *Die Sagen von den Argonauten, von Theben und Troia in der klassischen und hellenistischen Kunst* (Munich 1989)

VL   F. Brommer, *Vasenlisten zur griechischen Heldensage* (Marburg 1973)

The catalogue is divided into six sections, as follows:

Vases:
> Painted
> Relief

Painted Clay Artifacts (other than vases)
Small Reliefs (ivories, terracottas, bronze fibulas, tripods, shield-bands, gems, etc.)
Architectural Sculpture
Free-standing Sculpture

Numbers in the bibliographic references refer to *page* numbers in the case of basic reference works (Beazley, Trendall, Amyx, Brommer, etc.), but *catalogue* numbers in Stibbe and *plate* numbers in Schefold's five *Sagenbilder* volumes (save where figures are specified). *LIMC* numbers refer to catalogue entries in the *Lexicon* articles cited; I follow that work's usage in appending an asterisk to those entries for which an illustration is included in the respective plate volume, and a bullet (°) for those in which a drawing accompanies the entry in the text volume. For references to the many illustrations of Attic Black- and Red-Figure vases published since Beazley's catalogue volumes the reader should consult the second edition of the *Beazley Addenda* (ed. T. H. Carpenter et al., Oxford 1989), using the page numbers to *ABV* and *ARV²* given below.

Vases

PAINTED

Adolphseck: Schloss Fasanerie

			Herakles and Geras
12	BF lekythos		
	ABV 491	*Para* 223	*LIMC:* Geras 3*

Agora Museum (Athens)

P334	BF dinos frr		"Silenos"
	ABV 23		Kalydonian Boar Hunt
			LIMC: Atalante 1*
P4885	LG oinochoe		Herakles and Moliones
		FS 7a	*LIMC:* Aktorione 3*
P10201a	LG fr		Death of Astyanax?
			LIMC: Astyanax I 26*°
P26228	RF cup fr		Ixion and wheel
	ARV² 110	SB III 203	*LIMC:* Ixion 8
P29612	RF bell krater fr		Danae on Seriphos
			LIMC: Danae 57

Aigina: Museum

566	PA oinochoe		Odysseus and ram
		FS 37	
no #	PC skyphos		Bellerophontes and Pegasos
		FS 22	

Aigina: Excavations

no #	BF tripod pyxis		Herakles and Kyknos

Amiens: Musée de Picardie
| 3057.225.47a | BF hydria | | Herakles and Kerberos |
| | *ABV* 384 | | *LIMC:* Hades 143 |

Andreadis Collection (Thessalonike)
no #	MC column krater		Phineus
			LIMC: Iason 7*
			LIMC: Boreadai 4*

Arezzo: Museo Civico
| 1460 | RF neck-amphora | | Pelops and Hippodameia |
| | *ARV*² 1157 | SB IV 9 | *LIMC:* Hippoda-meia I 23* |

Argos
| no # | Argive krater | | Odysseus and Polyphemos |
| | | *FS* fig. 15 | |

Athens: National Museum
277	MC bottle		Ambush of Troilos
	CorVP 201		*LIMC:* Achilleus 251
354	Melian amphora		Hermes and Kalypso?
		FS fig. 45	*LIMC:* Hermes 689
397	BF lekythos		Sphinx
	ABV 505	*ABL* 19	
413	BF lekythos		Herakles on Olympos
	ABV 75	SB II 33–34	*LIMC:* Herakles 2848
	ABL 7		
488	WG lekythos		Death of Aktaion
	ABV 586	*ABL* 266	*LIMC:* Aktaion 3*
489	BF lekythos		Death of Aktaion
	ABV 500		*LIMC:* Aktaion 2*
513	BF lekythos		Herakles and Helios
	ABV 380	*ABL* 196	*LIMC:* Helios 95*
			LIMC: Herakles 2545°
664	MC amphoriskos		Return of Hephaistos?
			LIMC: Hephaistos 129*
1002	BF neck-amphora		Herakles and Nessos
	ABV 4		Gorgons
		FS 59	*LIMC:* Gorgo 313*
1061	BF lekythos		Labyrinth
	ABL 268		
1125	BF lekythos		Death of Amphiaraos
	ABL 266		*LIMC:* Amphiaraos 37*
1130	WG lekythos		Seirenes
	ABV 476	*ABL* 217	
1132	WG lekythos		Herakles and Atlas
	ABV 522	*ABL* 256	*LIMC:* Atlas 7*
1291	RF pyxis lid		Perseus and the Graiai
	VL 287	SB IV 119	*LIMC:* Graiai 2*

1607	RF lekythos		Sphinx and youth
	ARV² 1172		
1926	WG lekythos		Charon
	ARV² 846		*LIMC*: Charon I 5*
3961 (911)	Melian amphora		Achilleus and Memnon?
		FS 10	*LIMC*: Achilleus 846
9683	RF pelike		Herakles and Bousiris
	ARV² 554	SB IV 214	*LIMC*: Aithiopes 13*
12821	BF lekythos		Snakes and man
	ABV 505	*ABL* 198	
13910	Lakonian cup		Zeus and Kronos?
	LV #103		
15113	RF neck-amphora		Atalanta and Meleagros
	ARV² 1411		
15375	RF aryballos		Eros with whip
		SB III 258	*LIMC*: Eros 365a
15499	BF dinos frr		Games for Patroklos
	ABV 39		*LIMC*: Achilleus 491*
16346	RF pelike		Hades with cornucopia
	ARV² 1113		*LIMC*: Hades 25
16384	BF skyphos krater		Herakles and Prometheus
	ABV 6	*FS* 57a	
18063	RF stamnos		Helen and Phoibe
	ARV² 1028	SB II 227	*LIMC*: Helene 35*
19447	Lakonian olpe?		Leda and egg
			LIMC: Helene 4*
19765	BF lekythos		Hekate in Hades?
			LIMC: Erinys 7*
Akr 212	RF cup		Sack of Troy
	VL 384		*LIMC*: Astyanax I 17*
Akr 288	RF cup frr		Herakles and Eurytos
	ARV² 370		*LIMC*: Eurytos I 5*
Akr 587	BF dinos frr		Wedding of Peleus and Thetis
	ABV 39		*LIMC*: Chariklo I 1*
Akr 590	BF dinos fr		Games for Pelias
		FS 65	*LIMC*: Alkestis 52*
			LIMC: Amphiaraos 2*
Akr 601	BF hydria frr		Ikaros
	ABV 80		*LIMC*: Daidalos 14°
Akr 603	BF skyphos frr		Tydeus and Ismene
	VL 488		*LIMC*: Ismene I 4*
Akr 607	BF dinos		Gigantomachy
	ABV 107	SB II 60–64	*LIMC*: Gigantes 105
Akr 735	RF calyx krater		Brothers of Aigeus
	ARV² 259		Theseus and Minotaur
		SB IV 46–47	*LIMC*: Ariadne 30
Akr 1280	BF skyphos		Theseus and Skiron
	ABL 249		

Akr 1632	BF cup frr		Gigantomachy
	VL 65		*LIMC*: Ge 4*
Akr 2112	BF lekanis lid frr		Departure of Amphiaraos
	ABV 58		*LIMC*: Amphiaraos 8*
Akr 2134	BF kantharos frr		Gigantomachy
	ABV 347		*LIMC*: Gigantes 106*
no #	stand (Heraion)		Nessos and Deianeira
no #	PC pyxis lid fr		Herakles and Kentauroi
	VL 88		
no #	PC lekythos		Death of Achilleus?
		FS fig. 14	*LIMC*: Achilleus 848°
no #	RF cup		Boy on swan
	*ARV*² 17	SB II 53	*LIMC*: Hyakinthos 5

Bari: Museo Archeologico

1016	Apulian oinochoe		Kassiepeia?
	RVAp 874		*LIMC*: Andromeda I 16*
1535	Lucanian hydria		Makareus and Kanake
	LCS 45	SB IV 34	*LIMC*: Aiolos 1*

Basel: Antikenmuseum and Ludwig Collection

BS 403	RF calyx krater		Perseus and Andromeda
	Para 456	SB IV 132	*LIMC*: Andromeda I 6*
BS 404	RF lekythos		Athena and Kekropid
	VL 258		*LIMC*: Aglauros 19*
BS 411	BF hydria		Sphinx on column
BS 425	MC aryballos		Odysseus and Seiren?
	CorVP 180	SB II 360	Herakles and Hydra
			LIMC: Herakles 1992*
BS 428	BF cup		Herakles and Kyknos
	ABV 60		Neleidai and cattle?
BS 481	RF hydria		Head of Orpheus
		SB IV 98	
BS 498	BF hydria		Herakles and Kyknos
	Para 119		Neoptolemos and Eurypylos
		SB II 339–40	*LIMC*: Eurypylos I 1*
Kä 404	RF bell krater		Aloadai and Artemis
	*ARV*² 1067	SB III 193	*LIMC*: Aloadai 1*
Kä 420	BF amphora		Silenoi making wine
	Para 65		*LIMC*: Dionysos 408*
Slg Ludwig	Lucanian bell krater		Laokoon
	LCS	SB III 202	*LIMC*: Apollon 273*
	Supp 154		
Loan (PrColl)	MC cup		Death of Aias
	CorVP 562	SB II 337	*LIMC*: Aias I 122*
Loan (PrColl)	RF lekythos		Death of Aias
			LIMC: Aias I 105*
Loan (PrColl)	BF hydria		Helen and Phoibe
		SB II 227	*LIMC*: Dioskouroi 180*

Berkeley: University of California			
8.3316	RF hydria		Semele in child-birth
	ARV² 1343	SB III 19	LIMC: Dionysos 664*
Berlin: Charlottenburg (Antikenmuseum)			
A9	PA neck-amphora		Achilleus and Cheiron
		FS 29a	LIMC: Achilleus 21*
WS 4	Lakonian cup		Capture of Silenos
	LV #292		
F1704	BF amphora		Birth of Athena
	ABV 96	SB II 1	LIMC: Athena 346*
F1705	BF neck-amphora		Kalydonian Boar Hunt
	ABV 96		
F1722	BF column krater		Herakles and Prometheus
	ABV 104		
F1753	BF cup		Birth of Pegasos
	ABV 56		LIMC: Gorgo 319
F1775	BF cup		Eris
		SB II 246	LIMC: Eris 1*
F1837	BF amphora		Zeus and Pandora?
	ABV 509	SB II 21	LIMC: Artemis 1264*
			Peleus and Atalanta
			LIMC: Atalante 71*
F1862	BF neck-amphora		Aineias and Anchises
	Para 141		
F2163	RF amphora		Iris
	ARV² 409		LIMC: Iris I 27*
F2164	RF amphora		Herakles and Poseidon
	ARV² 183	SB III 150–51	LIMC: Herakles 3370*
F2278	RF cup		Herakles on Olympos
	ARV² 21	SB II 42–43	LIMC: Hestia 8*
			Achilleus and Patroklos
		SB II 277	LIMC: Achilleus 468*
F2279	RF cup		Peleus and Thetis
	ARV² 115	SB II 257	
F2288	RF cup		Theseus and Skiron
	ARV² 438		
F2291	RF cup		Paris and Helen
	ARV² 459		LIMC: Alexandros 63*
F2293	RF cup		Selene
	ARV² 370	SB III 121	LIMC: Astra 39*
			Gigantomachy
		SB III 122	LIMC: Gigantes 303*
F2403	RF volute krater		Wedding of Peirithoos
	ARV² 599		
F2455	WG lekythos		Hermes and Charon
	ARV² 846		LIMC: Charon I 7a*

F2524	RF cup		Nyx?
	ARV² 931		*LIMC: Astra* 5*
F2537	RF cup		Gaia and Erichthonios
	ARV² 1268–69	SB III 65–66	*LIMC: Ge* 17
			Eos and Kephalos
		SB III 457	*LIMC: Eos* 274*
F3291	Apulian hydria		Omphale in love?
	RVAp 426		
F3296	Sicilian calyx krater		Amphion, Zethos, Lykos
	LCS 203		*LIMC: Antiope I* 6*
F3988	BF tripod kothon		Death of Priam
			LIMC: Astyanax I 10*
F4220	RF cup		Thetis and Cheiron
	ARV² 61		*LIMC: Achilleus* 39*
VI 3151	BF cup		Silenos captured
	ABV 79		
VI 3238	Campanian hydria		Perseus and Andromeda
	LCS 227		*LIMC: Andromeda I* 19*
VI 3283	BF skyphos		Seirenes
	Para 259		
VI 3317	RF pelike		Herakles and Geras?
		SB IV 212	*LIMC: Geras* 7
Inv 1966.1	BF neck-amphora		Three Silenoi
	ABV 285		
Inv 1966.18	RF hydria		Death of Pentheus
Inv 1968.12	Apulian bell krater		Laios and Chrysippos
	RVAp 501		*LIMC: Chrysippos I* 2*
Inv 1970.5	RF amphora		Theseus and Minotaur
			LIMC: Ariadne 29
Inv 1970.9	RF skyphos		Tydeus and Ismene?
Berlin: Pergamon-Museum			
F336	PC aryballos		Herakles and Pholos
	CorVP 37	FS 24a	
F1147	MC krater		Achilleus and Memnon
	CorVP 234	FS 76c	*LIMC: Achilleus* 808*
F1652	LC amphora		Perseus and Andromeda
	CorVP 268	FS 44b	*LIMC: Andromeda I* 1*
F1685	BF amphora		Menelaos and Helen
	ABV 109		*LIMC: Astyanax I* 9*
F1697	BF amphora		Silenoi
	ABV 297		
F1732	BF oinochoe		Herakles and Kyknos
	ABV 110	SB II 176	*LIMC: Ares* 42*
F1895	BF hydria		Hermes and Iris
	ABV 268		*LIMC: Iris I* 127*
F2179	RF hydria		Dionysos and Ariadne
	ARV² 252	SB III 379	*LIMC: Ariadne* 93

F2184	RF stamnos ARV² 257		Death of Aigisthos LIMC: Aigisthos 11*
F2264	RF cup ARV² 60	SB II 307	Iris LIMC: Antilochos I 4*
F2588	RF skyphos ARV² 1300		Odysseus and suitors LIMC: Amphialos II 1*
F2591	RF skyphos ARV² 888		Iris and Silenoi LIMC: Iris I 113*
F3023	Campanian amphora LCS 338	SB III 207	Ixion and wheel LIMC: Ixion 15*
VI 3261	BF lekythos ABV 472	ABL 198	Herakles and Ophis LIMC: Herakles 2692*
VI 3289	RF cup VL 502		Phrixos and ram
VI 3319	PC aryballos VL 380		Death of Aias LIMC: Aias I 118
VI 3375	RF lekythos	SB III 135	Gigantomachy LIMC: Gigantes 389*
VI 3414	Boiotian skyphos VL 174		Omphale?
VI 4841	BF amphora ABV 97	FS fig. 30	Alkmaion and Eriphyle LIMC: Alkmaion 3*
Inv 30035	RF lekythos ARV² 532	SB IV 224–25	Peirithoos in Hades LIMC: Herakles 3515
Inv 31094	RF bell krater ARV² 1446		Herakles carries Hades? LIMC: Hades 71

Berlin: Lost or Unknown

A32	PA krater FS 36a		Death of Aigisthos? LIMC: Aigisthos 36*
F1655	LC krater CorVP 263		Departure of Amphiaraos LIMC: Ainippe II 1* LIMC: Baton I 3* Funeral Games of Pelias
		SB II 233	LIMC: Amphiaraos 3* LIMC: Argeios II 1*
F1682	BF bowl ABV 5	FS 44a	Perseus and Athena LIMC: Athena 6* Harpuiai
		FS 64a	LIMC: Harpyiai 1*
F1718	BF amphora ABV 144	SB II 334	Aias and dead Achilleus LIMC: Achilleus 871
F1801	BF cup ABV 159		Herakles and Hydra LIMC: Herakles 2029
F1904	BF hydria ABV 364		Dionysos and Semele
F2000	BF lekythos ABL 258		Aias and the arms LIMC: Aias I 75°

Catalogue of Artistic
Representations

F2032	WG alabastron		Zeus and Ganymedes
	ABL 237	SB III 289–90	*LIMC:* Ganymedes 10
F2165	RF amphora		Boreas and Oreithuia
	ARV² 496		*LIMC:* Boreas 62a
F2186	RF stamnos		Boreas and Oreithuia
	ARV² 208		*LIMC:* Boreas 19
F2273	RF cup		Hephaistos in chariot
	ARV² 174	SB II 30	*LIMC:* Hephaistos 43*
F2634	RF hydria		Kadmos and snake
	ARV² 1187		*LIMC:* Kadmos I 19*
VI 3275	RF calyx krater		Persephone and Silenoi
	ARV² 1276		

Blatter Collection (Bollingen)

no #	BF dinos frr		Kalydonian Boar Hunt
			LIMC: Atalante 5*

Bochum: Ruhr Universität

S1060	RF pelike		Death of Achilleus
			LIMC: Alexandros 92*

Bologna: Museo Civico

230	RF column krater		Death of Aigisthos
	ARV² 504		*LIMC:* Aigisthos 12*
236	RF column krater		Hermes and Persephone?
	ARV² 532	SB III 435	or daughter of Dryops?
			LIMC: Hermes 886*
288 bis	RF calyx krater		Aphrodite and Phaon
	ARV² 1056	SB III 400–402	*LIMC:* Aphrodite 1549*
325	RF bell krater		Perseus and Polydektes
	ARV² 1069	SB IV 137	*LIMC:* Gorgo 337*
PU 195	BF neck-amphora		Herakles and Pholos
	ABV 288	SB II 159	

Bonn: Akademisches Kunstmuseum

39	BF neck-amphora		Death of Priam
	VL 394		*LIMC:* Astyanax I 13*
78	RF bell krater		Leda and the egg
	ARV² 1171	SB III 342	*LIMC:* Dioskouroi 185*
860	EC alabastron		Iason and serpent?
			LIMC: Iason 30*
2661	RF pelike		Erysichthon
	Para 448	SB III 251	*LIMC:* Erysichthon I 1*
2674	Ionian hydria		Wedding of Peirithoos
		SB II 206	*LIMC:* Kaineus 70*

Boston: Museum of Fine Arts

00.346	RF bell krater		Aktaion
	ARV² 1045	SB III 187	*LIMC:* Aktaion 81*
00.348	Apulian bell krater		Athena and Marsyas
	RVAp 267		*LIMC:* Athena 620*

00.349	Apulian stamnos		Bellerophontes and Proitos
	RVAp 24		
01.8027	BF neck-amphora		Herakles and Apollo
	ABV 152	SB II 189	*LIMC:* Hermes 538*
01.8100	LC aryballos		Seirenes
		FS fig. 46	
03.783	BF olpe		Herakles in Helios' cup
	ABV 378	*ABL* 197	*LIMC:* Herakles 2550*
03.792	RF hydria		Danae, Perseus, and chest
	*ARV*² 1076		*LIMC:* Akrisios 7*
03.804	Apulian volute krater		Death of Thersites
	RVAp 472		*LIMC:* Achilleus 794*
04.18	RF pyxis lid		Odysseus and Nausikaa
	*ARV*² 1177		
6.67	PA krater		Sacrifice of Iphigeneia?
	VL 413		*LIMC:* Iphigeneia 2°
08.30a	RF cup		Iris and Silenoi
	*ARV*² 135		*LIMC:* Iris I 110
08.417	RF hydria		Argos, Io, Hermes
	Para 391	SB III 135	*LIMC:* Hera 486*
10.177	RF stamnos		Hermes with scales
	*ARV*² 518		*LIMC:* Achilleus 800*
10.185	RF krater		Pan
	*ARV*² 550	SB III 436	*LIMC:* Daphnis 1*
10.221	RF psykter		Death of Pentheus
	*ARV*² 16	SB II 92	*LIMC:* Galene II 1*
13.186	RF cup		Paris and Helen
	*ARV*² 458		*LIMC:* Helene 166*
13.200	RF hydria		Danae, Perseus, and chest
	*ARV*² 247		*LIMC:* Akrisios 2*
13.206	Apulian fragment		Kallisto
	RVAp 166	SB III 322	*LIMC:* Kallisto 5*
34.79	RF pelike		Odysseus and Elpenor
	*ARV*² 1045		*LIMC:* Elpenor 6
63.420	LC krater		Herakles and Hesione
	CorVP 507		
63.952	BF amphora		Silenoi making wine
	Para 62	SB II 230	
63.1246	RF calyx krater		Death of Agamemnon
	Para 373		*LIMC:* Agamemnon 89*
			Death of Aigisthos
			LIMC: Aigisthos 10*
91.227a and			
91.226b	RF stamnos		Death of Aigisthos
	*ARV*² 208		*LIMC:* Aigisthos 13*
93.99	WG lekythos		Helios
	ABL 206		*LIMC:* Helios 2*
93.100			Pholos

95.10	PC aryballos		Bellerophontes and Pegasos
95.12	PC aryballos		Zeus and Typhoeus?
		FS fig. 4	
95.31	RF cup		Zephyros and Hyakinthos
	*ARV*² 443		*LIMC:* Hyakinthos 45*
95.39	RF lekythos		Birth of Dionysos
	*ARV*² 533	SB III 25	*LIMC:* Dionysos 666*
95.48	RF squat lekythos		Theseus and Hippolyte
	*ARV*² 1248		*LIMC:* Amazones 240*
97.374	lekythos (forgery)		Oidipous and Sphinx
98.916	BF neck-amphora		Telamon and Amazones
	ABV 98		*LIMC:* Amazones 9*
99.518	BF cup	SB II 354	Odysseus and Polyphemos
	ABV 198	SB II 359	Odysseus and Kirke
99.519	BF cup		Odysseus and Kirke
	ABV 69		Herakles and Acheloos
			LIMC: Acheloos 215*
99.539	RF cup		Peirithoos
	*ARV*² 1142		Leda and the egg
1960.302	LC aryballos		Telephos and Aleadai?
1970.237	Apulian bell krater		Perseus and Medousa
	RVAp 48		
1977.713	RF lekythos		Death of Aigisthos
			LIMC: Aigisthos 6a°
1979.40	RF pelike		Phineus and the Boreadai
			LIMC: Boreadai 17
1987.53	Apulian calyx krater		Birth of Aigisthos
Boulogne			
421	BF amphora		Herakles and the Hesperides
			LIMC: Herakles 2700*
558	BF amphora		Death of Aias
	ABV 145	SB II 338	*LIMC:* Aias I 104*
Breslau (now Wrocław)			
lost	EC aryballos		Herakles and Hydra
	CorVP 557		*LIMC:* Herakles 1991°
Brommer Collection (Mainz)			
Mainz	BF lekythos		Herakles and Ophis
	ABV 499	SB II 155	*LIMC:* Herakles 2691
Brussels: Musées Royaux			
A4	LC olpe		Achilleus and Thetis
	CorVP 581	*FS* 73b	
A130	BF neck-amphora		Triptolemos
	ABV 308		
A1374	MC cup		Herakles and Acheloos
	CorVP 203	*FS* 58b	*LIMC:* Acheloos 246*
			Theseus and Minotaur

Cabinet des Médailles (Paris)

174	BF amphora		Theseus and Bull?
	ABV 315		*LIMC*: Aigeus 2*
190	Lakonian cup		Odysseus and Polyphemos
	LV #289	SB II 353	
202	Chalkidian neck-amphora		Herakles and Geryoneus
	ChV 8	SB II 146	*LIMC*: Herakles 2464*
219	BF neck-amphora		Birth of Dionysos?
	ABV 509	SB III 20	
222	BF neck-amphora		Dionysos and Mainades?
	ABV 152		*LIMC*: Dionysos 294*
223	BF neck-amphora		Herakles and Geryoneus
	ABV 308		*LIMC*: Herakles 2467
255	BF hydria		Herakles and Nereus
	ABV 361	SB II 168	
278	BF lekythos		Sphinx
298	BF lekythos		Persephone and Silenoi
	ABV 522	SB III 82	
	ABL 258		
306	WG lekythos		Apollo and Python
	ABV 572		*LIMC*: Apollon 993*
372	RF amphora		Euphorbos and Oidipous
	*ARV*² 987		
418	RF calyx krater		Theseus and Poseidon
	*ARV*² 260		
423	RF bell krater		Eos and Kephalos
	*ARV*² 1055		*LIMC*: Kallimachos 1*
442	Lucanian hydria		Amykos
	LCS 36		*LIMC*: Amykos 11*
536, 647 et al.	RF cup		Theseus' exploits
	*ARV*² 191	SB IV 294–96	*LIMC*: Athena 537*
542	RF cup		Hera and Prometheus
	*ARV*² 438	SB III 111	*LIMC*: Hera 347*
822	RF cup		Herakles carries Hades?
	*ARV*² 1521		*LIMC*: Herakles 3497*
846	RF skyphos		Eos and Tithonos
	*ARV*² 1050		*LIMC*: Eos 182*

Cahn Collection (Basel)

?	BF krater		Odysseus and ram
191	RF column krater frr		Capture of Silenos
		SB III 228	
541	RF skyphos		Ixion and wheel
		SB III 206	*LIMC*: Bia 1*
912	BF oinochoe frr		Abduction of Persephone?
		SB III 370	
921	BF amphora		Departure of Amphiaraos
			LIMC: Amphiaraos 10*

1173	LC krater fr *CorVP* 582		Herakles and Nereus
Cambridge: Fitzwilliam Museum			
G100	BF lekythos *ABL* 120		Herakles and Helios *LIMC:* Helios 96*
no #	Pontic amphora		Herakles and Alkyoneus? *LIMC:* Alkyoneus 34*
Cerveteri: Museo Nazionale Cerite			
no #	BF neck-amphora		Herakles and Hind *LIMC:* Herakles 2181*
Chicago: University			
89.16	RF column krater *ARV*² 585	SB III 211	Salmoneus *LIMC:* Iris I 155*
Chiusi: Museo Civico			
1794	BF amphora *ABV* 330		Departure of Amphiaraos *LIMC:* Amphiaraos 13*
1831	RF skyphos *ARV*² 1300		Odysseus and Eurykleia *LIMC:* Antiphata I*
Cincinnati: Art Museum			
1959.1	BF amphora *Para* 134		Herakles and Bousiris *LIMC:* Bousiris 10*
1979.1	RF cup *ARV*² 416	SB IV 93–95	Death of Orpheus
Clairmont Collection (Princeton)			
no #	RF pyxis	SB IV 114–17	Diktys and Danae *LIMC:* Danae 57
Copenhagen: National Museum			
3293	RF stamnos *ARV*² 251		Herakles and Syleus
13567	Caeretan hydria *CH* 29		Atalanta and Boar *LIMC:* Atalante 12
14066	Pontic amphora *VL* 357		Death of Achilleus *LIMC:* Alexandros 97*
VIII 496	Pontic calyx krater *ChV* 15	SB II 240	Adrastos and suitors *LIMC:* Amphithea 1°
Cracow: Czartoryski Museum			
1225	RF hydria *ARV*² 1121	SB IV 247	Lykourgos
Cremona			
no #	Apulian calyx krater *RVAp* 263		Kallisto *LIMC:* Arkas 2*
Cyrene			
no #	Lakonian cup fr *LV* #221	SB II 244	Amphiaraos and Tydeus? *LIMC:* Amphiaraos 79

Delos
 B7263 RF krater fr   Perseus and the Graiai
       *ARV*² 1019 SB IV 118   *LIMC:* Graiai 3*

Denman Collection (San Antonio)
 no #   RF column krater   Athena and Kekropides
                     LIMC: Erechtheus 29*

Dresden: Albertinum
 350   RF calyx krater   Hermes and Persephone
       *ARV*² 1056   *LIMC:* Hermes 639

Eleusis
 1231   BF sieve   Silenos captured
                      LIMC: Hermes 887
 1804   RF skyphos   Hades and Persephone
              SB III 372 *LIMC:* Hades 110*
 no #   PA amphora   Odysseus and Polyphemos
                    Gorgons
              FS 16   *LIMC:* Gorgo 312*

Erskine Collection (London)
 no #   Lakonian cup   Kerberos
       LV #217   *LIMC:* Herakles 2605

Ferrara: Museo Nazionale di Spina
 818   RF cup   Danae, Perseus, and chest
       *ARV*² 231   *LIMC:* Akrisios 4*
 2482   RF cup   Death of Kassandra
       *ARV*² 1280   *LIMC:* Aias II 75
 2737   RF volute krater   Zeus and child Dionysos
       *ARV*² 589   SB III 23   *LIMC:* Dionysos 702*
 2865   RF volute krater   Amykos
       *ARV*² 1039   *LIMC:* Amykos 14*
 2890   RF calyx krater   Theseus and Antiope
       *ARV*² 991   *LIMC:* Amazones 232*
 2893   RF volute krater   Atalanta and Hippomenes
 3031   RF volute krater   Persephone and Silenoi
       *ARV*² 612   SB III 85–86

                    Seven against Thebes
                    LIMC: Amphiaraos 38*
 9351   RF cup   Zeus and Ganymedes
       *ARV*² 880   SB III 297 *LIMC:* Ganymedes 44*
 44701 RF volute krater   Embassy to Skyros
       *ARV*² 536

Florence: Museo Archeologico
 3790   BF hydria   Dionysos and Thyone
       ABV 260   *LIMC:* Apollon 844*
 4209   BF volute krater   Wedding of Peleus and
                    Thetis

	ABV 76		Ambush of Troilos
			LIMC: Achilleus 292*
			Return of Hephaistos
			LIMC: Hera 309*
			Wedding of Peirithoos
			LIMC: Kaineus 67*
			Games for Patroklos
			Theseus on Delos
			LIMC: Ariadne 48*
			Kalydonian Boar Hunt
			LIMC: Atalante 2*
4210	Chalkidian neck-amphora		Achilleus and Memnon
	ChV 7		*LIMC:* Achilleus 809
4218	RF skyphos		Iris and Kentauroi
	ARV² 191	SB III 157	*LIMC:* Iris I 167*
70993	BF amphora		Death of Troilos
	ABV 95		*LIMC:* Achilleus 360*
70995	BF neck-amphora		Judgment of Paris
	ABV 110		
76359	BF amphora		Herakles and Prometheus
	ABV 97		*LIMC:* Demeter 471*
81268 (3997)	RF column krater		Wedding of Peirithoos
	ARV² 541		
81600	RF cup		Hephaistos in chariot
			LIMC: Hephaistos 44*
81948	RF hydria		Aphrodite and Adonis
	ARV² 1312	SB III 399	*LIMC:* Adonis 10*
91456	RF cup		Theseus' exploits
	ARV² 108	SB III 255	
1 B 32	RF cup		Herakles and Mares
	ARV² 58		*LIMC:* Herakles 2415
4 B 19 et al.	RF cup frr		Death of Aigisthos
	ARV² 108		*LIMC:* Aigisthos 41
Fogg Museum (Cambridge, Mass.)			
1960.339	RF column krater		Theseus and Amphitrite
(60.339)	*ARV²* 274		*LIMC:* Amphitrite 78*
Foggia			
132723	Apulian amphora		Hera in throne
	RVAp 925		*LIMC:* Hephaistos 126*
Frankfurt: Liebieghaus			
560	BF eschara		Charon
			LIMC: Charon I 1*
ST V 7	RF cup		Kekropides
	ARV² 386	SB III 57–58	*LIMC:* Aglauros 15*

Gela: Museo Archeologico
125/B	WG lekythos		Herakles and the apples
	ABV 476	*ABL* 218	*LIMC:* Herakles 2716

Getty Museum (Malibu)
72.AE.128	Apulian oinochoe		Kallisto
	RVAp 167	SB III 319–21	*LIMC:* Kallisto 6*
77.AE.11	RF volute krater		Herakles and Ophis
	ARV² 186		*LIMC:* Herakles 1702*
77.AE.14	Apulian volute krater		Laios and Chrysippos
	RVAp 866		*LIMC:* Chrysippos I 4b*
77.AE.44.1	RF calyx krater fr		Athena and Philoktetes
			LIMC: Herakles 2915*
77.AE.45	BF amphora		Omphale
81.AE.211	BF dinos		Gigantomachy
			LIMC: Gigantes 171°
83.AE.346	Caeretan hydria		Herakles and Hydra
	CH 41		*LIMC:* Herakles 2016*
84.AE.569	RF cup		Eos and Kephalos
			LIMC: Eos 48
85.AE.316	RF hydria		Phineus
			LIMC: Harpyiai 9*
85.AE.377	RF cup		Sphinx and youth
86.AE.18.1–9 et al.	RF cup		Plouton
86.AE.286	RF calyx krater		Death of Aigisthos
88.AE.66	RF cup		Aias and the arms
(formerly NY 69.11.35 L)	*Para* 367		*LIMC:* Aias I 72*, 83*
			Death of Aias
			LIMC: Aias I 140*

Giessen: University
46	RF cup		Atalanta and Silenoi
	ARV² 768		*LIMC:* Atalante 96*

Göttingen: University
J14	BF neck-amphora		Triptolemos
	ABV 309	SB II 28	
R23	BF oinochoe		Kadmos and Harmonia?
	Para 185		*LIMC:* Harmonia 10*

"H.A." Collection (Milan)
239	Apulian volute krater		Orestes and Neoptolemos
	RVAp 193		*LIMC:* Apollon 890*

Halle: University
214	Apulian amphora frr		Andromeda
	RVAp 504		*LIMC:* Andromeda I 12

Catalogue of Artistic
Representations

Hamburg: Museum für Kunst und Gewerbe
    1960.1   BF amphora   Niobidai
                        Para 40   *FS* 53   *LIMC:* Apollon 1077*
                                                      LIMC: Artemis 1346*
    1966.34   RF amphora   Argos
                        Para 347   SB III 173   *LIMC:* Io I 4*

Hirschmann Collection (Zurich)
    no #   Caeretan hydria   Perseus and *kêtos?*
                        CH 45

Hope Collection (Deepdene)
    lost   BF cup   Herakles and Kerberos
                        ABV 184   *LIMC:* Herakles 2606
    lost   Chalkidian amph   Death of Achilleus
                        ChV 9   SB II 297   *LIMC:* Achilleus 850*

Hunt Collection (Dallas)
    no #   RF pelike   Theseus and Minotaur

Iraklion
    no #   plate   Peleus and Thetis?
                                 FS figs. 11, 12

Ithaka
    no #   LG handle   Odysseus and Kirke?
                                 FS fig. 3

Jena: University
    137   MC cup   Herakles and Hydra
                        CorVP 204   *LIMC:* Herakles 1995*

Jucker Collection (Bern)
    no #   WG lekythos   Akrisios at tomb
                                   SB III 337   *LIMC:* Akrisios 10*

Kanellopoulos Collection (Athens)
    1319   PC aryballos   Ambush of Troilos
                        VL 364   *LIMC:* Chimaira 115°

Karlsruhe: Badisches Landesmuseum
    167   BF krater   Odysseus and ram
                        ABV 507   SB II 358
    B4   Apulian krater   Danaides?
                        RVAp 431   *LIMC:* Danaides 8*
    B2591   BF amphora   Herakles and Prometheus
                        ABV 97

Kassel: Staatliche Kunstsammlungen
    S 49b (lost)   Lakonian cup frr   Sisyphos?
                        LV #210

Kavalla
    A1086   Melian amphora   Peleus and Thetis

Kerameikos Museum (Athens)

154	BF krater		Chimaira
	ABV 3		
658	BF amphora		Kentauroi
	ABV 3		

Kiel: University

| B555 | RF lekythos | | Sphinx |

Kimbell Museum (Fort Worth)

| 84.16 | RF lekythos | | Eros with bow |
| | | | LIMC: Eros 332* |

Korinth

| C 72–149 | LC krater | | Achilleus and Memnon |
| | CorVP 582 | | LIMC: Achilleus 811 |

Kyrou Collection (Athens)

| no # | RF hydria | | Hermes and child Dionysos |
| | | SB III 31 | LIMC: Ino 10* |

Lecce: Museo Provinciale

| 570 | RF pelike | | Polyneikes and Eriphyle |
| | ARV² 629 | | LIMC: Eriphyle I 2* |

Leningrad/St. Petersburg: Hermitage Museum

637 (St 1733)	RF calyx krater		Danae and golden rain
	ARV² 360		LIMC: Danae 1*
			Danae, Perseus, and chest
			LIMC: Danae 48*
640 (St 1641)	RF stamnos		Herakles on Olympos
	ARV² 639		LIMC: Herakles 2875
642 (St 1357)	RF stamnos		Danae, Perseus, and chest
	ARV² 228		LIMC: Danae 41*
649 (St 830)	RF cup		Theseus and Aithra
	ARV² 460		LIMC: Aithra I 25*
			Odysseus and Diomedes
			LIMC: Akamas 6*
			LIMC: Athena 104*
804 (St 1711)	RF stamnos		Theseus and Minotaur
	ARV² 484	SB IV 305	
988 (St 355)	Lucanian volute krater		Release of Hera
	LCS 161		LIMC: Hera 318*
St 426	Apulian volute krater		Danaides?
	RVAp 864		LIMC: Danaides 13*
St 427	Lucanian krater (forgery)		Bellerophontes and
			Stheneboia
St 1807	RF calyx krater		Eris and Themis
	ARV² 1185		LIMC: Eris 7*
St 1275	RF calyx krater		Achilleus and Telephos
	ARV² 23		LIMC: Diomedes I 7*

Inv 9270	BF cup		Herakles and Mares
	ABV 294	SB II 130	*LIMC:* Herakles 2414*
London: British Museum			
A487	PC pyxis		Herakles and Geryoneus
	VL 63		*LIMC:* Geryoneus 11*
B57	Pontic amphora		Herakles and Hera?
			LIMC: Hercle 362*
B103.19	BF fragment		Seirenes?
B147	BF amphora		Birth of Athena
	ABV 135	SB II 6	*LIMC:* Athena 349*
B155	Chalkidian amphora		Perseus and Nymphai
	ChV 10	SB II 93	Herakles and Geryoneus
			LIMC: Herakles 2479*
B156	BF amphora		Herakles and Kyknos
	VL 103		
B163	BF belly amphora		Herakles and Birds
	ABV 134	SB II 126	*LIMC:* Herakles 2241*
B164	BF amphora		Argos, Io, Hermes
	ABV 148	SB II 20	*LIMC:* Hera 485*
B168	BF amphora		Dionysos and Ariadne?
	ABV 142		*LIMC:* Ariadne 156*
B197	BF amphora		Herakles and Kyknos
	ABV 296		*LIMC:* Ares 36*
B210	BF neck-amphora		Dionysos and Oinopion
	ABV 144	SB II 13	*LIMC:* Dionysos 785*
			Achilleus and Penthesileia
		SB II 320	*LIMC:* Achilleus 723*
B212	BF neck-amphora		Herakles and Kyknos
	ABV 297		
B213	BF neck-amphora		Herakles and Boar
	ABV 143		*LIMC:* Herakles 2115*
B215	BF neck-amphora		Peleus and Thetis
	ABV 286	SB II 255	
B221	BF neck-amphora		Medeia and ram
	ABV 321		
B226	BF neck-amphora		Herakles and Pholos
	ABV 273	SB II 158	*LIMC:* Hermes 545a*
B231	BF neck-amphora		Herakles and Hind
	ABV 139		*LIMC:* Athena 511*
B240	BF neck-amphora		Achilleus' *psychê?*
	VL 347	SB II 335	*LIMC:* Achilleus 901*
B261	BF neck-amphora		Hades, Persephone,
	ABV 373		Sisyphos
			LIMC: Hades 148*

B313	BF hydria		Herakles and Acheloos
	ABV 360		*LIMC:* Acheloos 248*
B316	BF hydria		Herakles and tripod
	ABV 268		*LIMC:* Apollon 1034*
B323	BF hydria		Achilleus and Penthesileia
	ABV 362		*LIMC:* Achilleus 725*
B326	BF hydria		Death of Troilos
	ABV 363		*LIMC:* Achilleus 363*
B328	BF hydria		Medeia and ram
	ABV 363		
B379	BF cup		Herakles on Olympos
	ABV 60		*LIMC:* Herakles 2847*
			Aias and Kassandra
			LIMC: Aias II 16*
B380	BF cup		Birth of Pegasos
	ABV 55		*LIMC:* Gorgo 320*
B424	BF cup		Herakles on Olympos
	ABV 168–69	SB II 35	*LIMC:* Athena 429*
B425	BF cup		Dionysos and Semele?
	ABV 184		
B492	BF oinochoe		Herakles and Boar
	ABV 256	SB II 119	*LIMC:* Herakles 2103*
B533	BF lekythos		Herakles and Amazones
	ABV 489		*LIMC:* Amazones 70*
B639	WG lekythos		Achilleus and Memnon
	ABL 227		*LIMC:* Achilleus 798
D4	WG cup		Anesidora
	*ARV*² 869	SB II 89	*LIMC:* Anesidora 1*
D5	WG cup		Polyidos and Glaukos
		SB IV 51	*LIMC:* Glaukos II 1*
E3	RF cup		Silenoi
	*ARV*² 45, 70–71	SB II 74–75	
E12	RF cup		Iris with corpse of Memnon
	*ARV*² 126	SB II 329	*LIMC:* Iris I 146*
E36	RF cup		Theseus' exploits
	*ARV*² 115	SB II 218–19	Theseus and Bull
E37	RF cup		Theseus and Minotaur
	*ARV*² 72	SB II 202	
E41	RF amphora		Theseus and Antiope
	*ARV*² 58		*LIMC:* Antiope II 8*
E45	RF cup		Herakles and Amazones
	*ARV*² 316		*LIMC:* 67*
E48	RF cup		Theseus and Sinis
	*ARV*² 426, 431		Theseus and Skiron
		SB II 198	
E64	RF cup		Apollo pursuing girl
	*ARV*² 455	SB III 278	*LIMC:* Apollon 1085*

E65	RF cup		Iris and Silenoi
	ARV² 370	SB III 156	LIMC: Dromis 1*
			Hera and Silenoi
		SB III 155	LIMC: Babakchos 1*
E69	RF cup		Aias and the arms
	ARV² 369		LIMC: Aias I 73
E82	RF cup		Hades with cornucopia
	ARV² 1269	SB III 304	LIMC: Hades 44*
E84	RF cup		Theseus and Minotaur
	ARV² 1269	SB IV 301	Theseus' exploits
E140	RF skyphos		Triptolemos
	ARV² 459	SB III 71	LIMC: Demeter 344*
E155	RF kantharos		Laokoon and snake?
	ARV² 832	SB III 205	
			Ixion and wheel
		SB III 204	LIMC: Ares 86*
			LIMC: Ixion 1*
E163	RF hydria		Medeia and the ram
	ARV² 258		LIMC: Iason 62*
E178	RF hydria		Judgment of Paris
	ARV² 503		
E182	RF hydria		Gaia and Erichthonios
	ARV² 580		LIMC: Athena 477*
E224	RF hydria		Herakles and Hesperides
	ARV² 1313	SB IV 19	LIMC: Akamas 26*
			Leukippides
		SB IV 19	LIMC: Dioskouroi 201*
E257	RF amphora		Judgment of Paris
	ARV² 604		
E290	RF neck-amphora		Herakles and Geras
	ARV² 653		LIMC: Geras 1*
E291	RF neck-amphora		Phineus
	ARV² 662		
E313	RF neck-amphora		Zeus and Aigina
	ARV² 202		LIMC: Aigina 3*
E372	RF pelike		Erichthonios in the chest
	ARV² 1218		LIMC: Athena 480*
E382	RF pelike		Telephos and Orestes
	ARV² 632		LIMC: Agamemnon 11*
E440	RF stamnos		Seirenes
	ARV² 289		
E447	RF stamnos		Capture of Silenos
	ARV² 1035		
E458	RF calyx krater		Recovery of Aithra
	ARV² 239		LIMC: Aithra I 66*
E467	RF calyx krater		Pandora
	ARV² 601		LIMC: Anesidora 2*

E477	RF column krater		Prokris and Kephalos
	*ARV*² 1114–15	SB IV 84	*LIMC*: Erechtheus 55*
E539	RF oinochoe		Satyros and Ophis
	*ARV*² 776		
E696	RF lekythos		Oidipous and Sphinx
	*ARV*² 1325		
E699	RF lekythos		Aphrodite and Adonis
	*ARV*² 1324		
E773	RF pyxis		Iphigeneia
	*ARV*² 805–6		*LIMC*: Helene 380*
E788	RF rhyton		Kekrops
	*ARV*² 764	SB IV 69	*LIMC*: Aglauros 28*
F107	Apulian lekythos		Hera nursing Herakles
	RVAp 395	SB IV 157	*LIMC*: Herakles 3344*
F149	Paestan bell krater		Alkmene at the altar
	RVP 139		*LIMC*: Amphitryon 2*
F193	Campanian neck-amphora		Alkmene at the altar
	LCS 231		*LIMC*: Alkmene 6*
F269	Apulian calyx krater		Hephaistos and Ares?
	RVAp 339	SB III 161	*LIMC*: Ares 73*
F271	Apulian calyx krater		Lykourgos
	RVAp 415		
H228	Etruscan hydria		Theseus and Minotaur
			LIMC: Ariatha 1°
1897.7–27.2	BF amphora		Death of Polyxena
	ABV 97		*LIMC*: Amphilochos 3*
1898.7–16.5	RF stamnos		Herakles and Eurytion
	*ARV*² 1027	SB IV 230	*LIMC*: Deianeira II 3*
1899.2–19.1	LG krater		Paris and Helen?
		FS 5c	*LIMC*: Alexandros 56°
1910.2–12.1	WG lekythos		Capture of Silenos
	ABL 227		
1926.4–17.1	BF lekythos		Medeia
	ABL 68		
1948.10–15.1	BF column krater		Judgment of Paris
	ABV 108		*LIMC*: Hermes 455b*
1969.12–15.1	PC aryballos		Troilos?
1971.11–1.1	BF dinos		Wedding of Peleus and Thetis
	Para 19		*LIMC*: Chariklo I 2*

Lost Vases (other than those once assigned to museums or collections)
From:

Argos	MC kotyle		Herakles and Hydra
	CorVP 185	FS fig. 23	*LIMC*: Herakles 1990*
			Herakles and Kerberos
			LIMC: Athena 11°

Bomarzo	BF cup		Aktaion
		FS fig. 19	*LIMC:* Aktaion 1°
Samos	Lakonian cup		Achilleus and snake
	LV #294		*LIMC:* Achilleus 264*
Samothrace	EC alabastron		Herakles and Amazones
	CorVP 557		*LIMC:* Amazones 1°
?	Apulian(?) amphora		Leto with children and snake
			LIMC: Apollon 995°
Louvre (Paris)			
A478	BF cup		Tantalos and Pandareos
	ABV 66	SB II 84	*LIMC:* Kameiro 2*
A519	LG krater		Herakles and the Moliones
CA 111	WG lekythos		Sphinx
	ABL 241		
CA 598	WG lekythos		Herakles and Hydra
	ABL 233		*LIMC:* Herakles 2004*
CA 616	BF pyxis		Birth of Athena
	ABV 58	SB II 2	*LIMC:* Athena 345*
			Judgment of Paris
CA 617	PC aryballos		Helen and Dioskouroi
	CorVP 23	*FS* fig. 9	*LIMC:* Helene 28*°
CA 823	BF lekythos		Herakles and Nereus
	ABL 1–2		
CA 1961	BF neck-amphora		Kadmos and Harmonia
	Para 248	SB IV 27	*LIMC:* Harmonia 9*
			LIMC: Kadmos 45*
CA 2569	BF plate		Peleus and Thetis
CA 3004	MC skyphos		Herakles and Hydra
	CorVP 190	*FS* 54c	*LIMC:* Iolaos 26*
CA 3837	Sicilian stamnos		Theseus and Minotaur
CA 6113	BF cup		Ambush of Troilos
			LIMC: Achilleus 310*
C10228	Caeretan hydria		Herakles and Nessos
	CH 31	SB II 197	
E635	EC column krater		Herakles and Eurytos
	CorVP 147	*FS* 60a	*LIMC:* Eurytos I 1*
			LIMC: Iole I 1*
			Death of Aias
		FS 78a	*LIMC:* Aias I 120*
E638 bis	MC column krater		Death of Troilos
	CorVP 567		*LIMC:* Hippichos 1°
E639	LC column krater		Peleus and Thetis
	CorVP 266	*FS* 70b	
E640	LC amphora		Tydeus and Ismene
	CorVP 270		*LIMC:* Ismene I 3*

E643	LC hydria		Thetis mourning
	CorVP 264		*LIMC*: Achilleus 897*
E662	Lakonian dinos		Herakles and Pholos
	LV #313	SB II 157	
E669	Lakonian cup		Kadmos and snake
	LV #303	SB II 91	*LIMC*: Gorgo 167*
E701	Caeretan hydria		Herakles and Kerberos
	CH 14	SB II 150	*LIMC*: Herakles 2616*
E703	Pontic neck-amphora		Death of Troilos
	VL 363		*LIMC*: Achle 17
E732	Caeretan amphora		Gigantomachy
			LIMC: Gigantes 170*
E812	Chalkidian? neck-amphora		Herakles and Lion
	ChV 162		*LIMC*: Herakles 1809*
E852	BF neck-amphora		Birth of Athena
	ABV 96		*LIMC*: Athena 334*
E857	BF neck-amphora		Birth of Chrysaor?
	ABV 97		
E864	BF neck-amphora		Tityos
	ABV 97	SB II 78	*LIMC*: Apollon 1066*
E874	BF dinos		Gorgons
	ABV 8	*FS* 45	*LIMC*: Gorgo 314*
E876	BF dinos		Silenoi
	ABV 90		*LIMC*: Hephaistos 138b*
F18	Chalkidian hydria		Theseus and Minotaur
	ChV 13		*LIMC*: Ariadne 25*
F29	BF amphora		Herakles and Kyknos
	ABV 109		Sack of Troy
		SB II 343	*LIMC*: Astyanax I 8*
F60	BF neck-amphora		Herakles and Alkestis?
	ABV 308	SB II 180	*LIMC*: Alkestis 58*
F122	BF cup		Aineias and Anchises
	ABV 231		*LIMC*: Aineias 60*
F204	RF amphora		Herakles and Kerberos
	ARV² 4	SB II 152	*LIMC*: Herakles 2554*
F208	BF amphora		Herakles and Alkyoneus
			LIMC: Alkyoneus 3*
F222	BF neck-amphora		Sack of Troy
	ABV 316		*LIMC*: Astyanax I 12*
F271	BF neck-amphora		Theseus and Bull
	ARV² 194		
F340	BF oinochoe		Aias and the arms
	ABV 176		*LIMC*: Aias I 77*
F342	BF oinochoe		Odysseus and Polyphemos
	ABV 433	SB II 355–56	
G18	RF cup		Death of Troilos
	ARV² 61		*LIMC*: Achilleus 369*

G42	RF amphora		Tityos
	*ARV*² 23	SB II 82	*LIMC*: Apollon 1069*
G104	RF cup		Theseus and Skiron
	*ARV*² 318		Theseus and Amphitrite
		SB IV 290	*LIMC*: Amphitrite 75*
G109	WG cup		Tydeus and Ismene?
		SB V 58	*LIMC*: Ismene I 6*
G115	RF cup		Eos and Memnon
	*ARV*² 434		*LIMC*: Eos 324*
G123	RF cup		Zeus and Ganymedes
	*ARV*² 435	SB III 296	*LIMC*: Ganymedes 52*
G147	RF cup		Prokne and Philomela
	*ARV*² 472	SB IV 79	
G152	RF cup		Sack of Troy
	*ARV*² 369		*LIMC*: Akamas 11*
			LIMC: Astyanax I 18*
G154	RF cup		Ambush of Troilos
	*ARV*² 369		*LIMC*: Achilleus 344*
G155	RF cup fr		Herakles in house of
	*ARV*² 347		Nereus
G164	RF calyx krater		Tityos
	*ARV*² 504	SB III 196	*LIMC*: Ge 44*
G192	RF stamnos		Herakles and snakes
	*ARV*² 208	SB IV 156	*LIMC*: Alkmene 8*
G197	RF amphora		Theseus and Antiope
	*ARV*² 238		*LIMC*: Antiope II 10*
G209	RF amphora		Hades with cornucopia
	*ARV*² 648		*LIMC*: Hades 20*
G210	RF amphora		Herakles and Syleus
	*ARV*² 647		
G228	RF pelike		Sphinx on column
	*ARV*² 250		
G234	RF pelike		Herakles and Geras
	*ARV*² 286		*LIMC*: Geras 4*
G263	RF cup		Herakles and Hind
	*ARV*² 341		*LIMC*: Herakles 2189*
G341	RF calyx krater		Niobidai
	*ARV*² 601	SB III 212	*LIMC*: Apollon 1079*
			Theseus and Peirithoos in
			Hades?
			LIMC: Herakles 3520*
G345	RF bell krater		Herakles and Eurytion
	*ARV*² 1108		*LIMC*: Deianeira II 1*
G364	RF column krater		Phineus
	*ARV*² 569		*LIMC*: Boreadai 18*
G365	RF column krater		Herakles and Acheloos
	VL 3	SB IV 227	*LIMC*: Acheloos 218*

G366	RF column krater		Kronos and Rheia
	ARV² 585		
G372	RF skyphos		Athena and Gigas
	ARV² 1300	SB III 116	LIMC: Athena 50*
G413	RF stamnos		Wounding of Philoktetes
	ARV² 484		LIMC: Agamemnon 43*
G416	RF stamnos		Death of Orpheus
	ARV² 484		
G423	RF bell krater		Theseus and the rock
	ARV² 1064		
K36	Apulian oinochoe		Odysseus and Diomedes
	RVAp 206		LIMC: Diomedes I 25*
K545	Lucanian pelike		Omphale and spindle
	LCS 184		
MNC 675	Boiotian skyphos		Theseus and Minotaur
	VL 242		LIMC: Ariadne 35*
MNC 677	MC kotyle		Herakles and Pholos
	CorVP 184		
S1677	RF amphora		Gigantomachy
	ARV² 1344		LIMC: Gigantes 322*

Lugt Collection (The Haag)

no #	BF lekythos		Herakles and Kyknos
	VL 105		

Macinagrossa Collection (Bari)

26	Apulian hydria		Abduction of Persephone
	RVAp 871		LIMC: Hades 113*

Madrid: Museo Arqueológico Nacional

10915	BF neck-amphora		Herakles and Boar
	ABV 602		LIMC: Herakles 2098*
10916	BF amphora		Herakles and Eurytos
	ABV 508	SB II 199	LIMC: Antiphonos 1*
11017	RF bell krater		Hades with cornucopia
	ARV² 1440		LIMC: Hades 70
11094	Paestan calyx krater		Madness of Herakles
	RVP 84	SB IV 162	LIMC: Herakles 1684°
11097	RF amphora		Eos and Kephalos
	ARV² 1043		
11265	RF cup		Theseus and Prokroustes
	ARV² 1174		Theseus and Sow

Matera: Museo Ridola

12538	Apulian calyx krater		Perseus and Andromeda
	RVAp 501		LIMC: Andromeda I 64*

Metaponto

20145	RF column krater		Graiai
			LIMC: Graiai 1*

Milan (formerly Vidoni Collection)
  no #

                                            Herakles and Prometheus

Mormino Collection (Palermo)
  769   WG lekythos   Gaia and Erichthonios
                            SB IV 64–65   *LIMC:* Ge 13*

Moscow: State Historical Museum
  70   BF amphora   Herakles and Kerberos
                   ABV 255   *LIMC:* Herakles 2555

Munich: Antikensammlungen
  585   Ionian amphora   Argos, Io, Hermes
                           SB II 19   *LIMC:* Io I 31*
  596   Chalkidian hydria   Zeus and Typhoeus
                   ChV 12   *FS* 66

                                            Peleus and Atalanta
                                            LIMC: Atalante 74*
  837   Pontic amphora   Judgment of Paris
                           SB II 249   *LIMC:* Alexandros 14*
  1379   BF amphora   Herakles and Kyknos
                   ABV 303
  1407   BF amphora   Herakles and Bull
                   ABV 290   *LIMC:* Herakles 2329*
  1411   BF amphora   Aias and the arms
                   ABV 311   SB II 298   *LIMC:* Aias I 76*
  1414   BF amphora   Theseus and Antiope
                   ABV 367   *LIMC:* Antiope II 4*
  1415   BF amphora   Peleus and Thetis
                   VL 322, 376   Aias and dead Achilleus
                                              LIMC: Achilleus 877*
  1417   BF amphora   Herakles and Antaios
                   ABV 367   *LIMC:* Antaios I 1*
  1426   BF neck-amphora   Death of Troilos
                   ABV 95   *FS* 73a   *LIMC:* Achilleus 364*
  1470   BF neck-amphora   Aias and dead Achilleus
                   ABV 144   *LIMC:* Achilleus 876*
  1493   BF neck-amphora   Sisyphos
                   ABV 316   *LIMC:* Amyetoi 2*
  1494   BF neck-amphora   Sisyphos
                   ABV 308   *LIMC:* Aias I 145*
  1546   BF neck-amphora   Aineias and Anchises
                   ABV 392 (as Munich   *LIMC:* Askanios 3*
                   1554)
  1549   BF neck-amphora   Sisyphos
                   ABV 383   *LIMC:* Hades 121*
  1615A   BF neck-amphora   Herakles and Cheiron
                   ABV 484   *LIMC:* Herakles 1665°
  1700   BF hydria   Sack of Troy
                   ABV 362   SB II 285   *LIMC:* Astyanax I 29*

1708	BF hydria		Herakles and Antaios
	ABV 360	SB II 169	*LIMC*: Antaios I 5*
1784	BF oinochoe		Herakles and Alkyoneus
	Para 183		*LIMC*: Alkyoneus 10*
1842	BF lekythos		Herakles and Birds
	ABV 455		*LIMC*: Herakles 2275
2085	BF cup		Herakles and Lion
			LIMC: Herakles 1916*
2241	BF band cup		Peleus and Atalanta
2243	BF band cup		Sphinx
	ABV 163	SB II 238	Kalydonian Boar Hunt
			LIMC: Iason 76
			Theseus and Minotaur
			LIMC: Ariadne 28*
2304	RF amphora		Iris as cup-bearer
	*ARV*² 220		*LIMC*: Iris I 142*
2309	RF amphora		Theseus and Helen
	*ARV*² 27	SB II 209	*LIMC*: Helene 41*
2322	RF neck-amphora		Odysseus and Nausikaa
	*ARV*² 1107		*LIMC*: Athena 566
2345	RF amphora		Boreas and Oreithuia
	*ARV*² 496	SB III 461–62	*LIMC*: Boreas 62b*
			LIMC: Aglauros 30*
2408	RF stamnos		Medeia and ram
	*ARV*² 257		
2413	RF stamnos		Gaia and Erichthonios
	*ARV*² 495	SB III 63	*LIMC*: Hephaistos 217*
2417	RF psykter		Idas, Marpessa, Apollo
	*ARV*² 556	SB III 253–54	*LIMC*: Artemis 1433
2426	RF hydria		Iris and infant Hermes
	*ARV*² 189	SB III 54	*LIMC*: Hermes 734*
2618	RF cup		Achilleus and Priam
	*ARV*² 61	SB II 317	*LIMC*: Achilleus 656*
2620	RF cup		Herakles and Geryoneus
	*ARV*² 16	SB II 147–48	*LIMC*: Herakles 2501*
2638	RF cup		Aedon and Itys
	*ARV*² 456	SB IV 32	
2646	RF cup		Herakles and Linos
	*ARV*² 437		*LIMC*: Herakles 1671*
2670	RF cup		Theseus' exploits
	*ARV*² 861		
2686	WG cup		Europa and bull
		SB III 329	*LIMC*: Europe I 44*
2688	RF cup		Achilleus and Penthesileia
	*ARV*² 879		*LIMC*: Achilleus 733*
2777	WG lekythos		Hermes and Charon
	*ARV*² 1228		*LIMC*: Charon I 10*

3185	Etruscan RF amphora		Aineias and Anchises
	VL 389		LIMC: Aineias 94*
3268	Apulian volute krater		Laertes and Antikleia
	RVAp 16	SB III 209	LIMC: Antikleia 1*
3296	Apulian volute krater		Medeia and Kreon's
	RVAp 533		daughter
			LIMC: Hippotes 1*
3300	Apulian amphora		Lykourgos
	RVAp 535		
8762	RF pelike		Herakles in house of
	ARV² 1638	SB IV 210	Nereus
8771	RF cup		Theseus and Sinis
		SB IV 287	

Münster: University
673	Apulian dish		Phrixos and Helle
	RVAp 530		

Naples: Museo Nazionale

("H" preceding numbers indicates vases included in Heydemann's 1872 catalogue of the museum
[Heydemann 1872]; subsequent inventory numbers are given in parentheses. "Stg" indicates vases
in the Niccola Santangelo collection, which is also included in that catalogue.)

H1767	Apulian krater		Daidalos and Ikaros
			LIMC: Daidalos 20
H2418 (82263)	Lucanian amphora		Bellerophontes and Proitos
	LCS 44	SB IV 147	
H2422 (81669)	RF hydria		Sack of Troy
	ARV² 189		LIMC: Aias II 44*
			LIMC: Astyanax I 19*
			LIMC: Andromache I 47*
H2883 (2045)	RF calyx krater		Gigantomachy
	ARV² 1338	SB III 132	LIMC: Gigantes 316*
H3089	RF stamnos		Herakles and Eurytion?
	ARV² 1050	SB IV 229	LIMC: Deianeira II 2°
H3091	RF amphora		Hades and Persephone
	ARV² 647		LIMC: Hades 77*
H3222 (81666)	Apulian volute krater		Triptolemos in Hades
	RVAp 431		Danaides?
			LIMC: Danaides 9*
H3237	Lucanian volute krater		Lykourgos
	LCS 114		
H3241	Lucanian hydria		Herakles and Amazones
	LCS 36		LIMC: Amazones 777*
H3358 (81038)	BF pelike		Aias and the arms
	ABV 338	SB II 336	LIMC: Aias I 80*
H3412 (82411)	Paestan calyx krater		Phrixos and Helle
	RVAp 84		

126053	RF amphora		Menelaos and Helen
	*ARV*² 202		*LIMC*: Helen 261
Stg 31	Apulian volute krater		Aktaion and Artemis
	RVAp 203		*LIMC*: Aktaion 110*
Stg 172	BF cup		Dionysos and Semele
	ABV 203	SB II 50	*LIMC*: Dionysos 55*
Stg 270	RF neck-amphora		Ino and Phrixos
	*ARV*² 1161		*LIMC*: Ino 13*
Stg 702	Apulian pelike		Aphrodite, Adonis, Persephone
	RVAp 490		*LIMC*: Adonis 5*
Stg 708	Apulian pelike		Andromeda
	RVAp 536		*LIMC*: Andromeda I 14
Stg 709	Apulian volute krater		Theseus and Peirithoos
	RVAp 533		in Hades
no #	BF lid		Sack of Troy
	ABV 58	FS 78b	*LIMC*: Astyanax I 28*

Nauplia
| 136 | WG alabastron (forgery?) | | Herakles and Hesperides |
| | *VL* 72 | | *LIMC* Vol. 5, p. 103 |

Naxos
| no # | Cycladic amphora | | Aphrodite and Ares |
| | | FS 9 | *LIMC*: Aphrodite 1285* |

New York: Metropolitan Museum of Art
01.8.6	BF cup		Ambush of Troilos
	ABV 51	SB II 282	*LIMC*: Achilleus 307*
06.1021.48	BF hydria		Herakles and Triton
06.1021.144	RF pelike		Kronos, Rheia, and stone
	*ARV*² 1107	SB III 11	
06.1070	BF lekythos		Medousa and Pegasos
	ABV 702	*ABL* 235	*LIMC*: Gorgo 309*
		SB IV 123	
07.286.66	RF calyx krater		Kadmos and snake
	*ARV*² 617	SB IV 24	*LIMC*: Harmonia 1*
07.286.84	RF volute krater		Wedding of Peirithoos
	*ARV*² 613		
08.258.21	RF calyx krater		Peirithoos in Hades
	*ARV*² 1086	SB IV 223	*LIMC*: Hades 151*
11.210.1	PA amphora		Herakles and Nessos
		FS 23	
11.213.2	RF lekythos		Laios and Chrysippos
	*ARV*² 1324		*LIMC*: Chrysippos III 1*
12.198.3	RF hydria		Theseus and Antiope
			LIMC: Antiope II 6*
12.229.14	RF bell krater fr		Athena and Tydeus
	VL 489		*LIMC*: Athanasia 2*

12.231.2	RF cup		Herakles and Eurytos
	*ARV*² 319		*LIMC:* Iphitos I 2*
12.235.4	RF skyphos fr		Marsyas
		SB III 234	*LIMC:* Artemis 1430*
14.105.10	BF hydria		Herakles and Hebe
	ABV 261		*LIMC:* Apollon 840*
14.130.15	LG krater		Herakles and the Moliones
16.70	BF hydria		Herakles and Triton
22.139.11	RF bell krater		Kadmos and snake
	*ARV*² 1083		*LIMC:* Harmonia 4*
24.97.37	RF lekythos		Ikaros
	*ARV*² 696	*ABL* 270	*LIMC:* Daidalos 47*
27.116	MC krater		Paris and Helen
	CorVP 196	*FS* 70a	*LIMC:* Alexandros 67*
28.57.23	RF bell krater		Hekate and Persephone
	*ARV*² 1012		*LIMC:* Hermes 637*
31.11.11	BF krater		Return of Hephaistos
	ABV 108	SB II 23–24	*LIMC:* Dionysos 563*
34.11.7	RF column krater		Iason and serpent
	*ARV*² 524		*LIMC:* Iason 36*
41.83	RF calyx krater		Odysseus and Kirke
	*ARV*² 1012		
41.162.29	WG lekythos		Helios
	ABV 507	*ABL* 226	*LIMC:* Astra 3*
41.162.190	BF neck-amphora		Herakles and Boar
	ABV 287		
45.11.1	RF pelike		Perseus and Medousa
	*ARV*² 1032	SB IV 126	*LIMC:* Gorgo 301*
46.11.7	WG oinochoe		Peleus in a tree
	ABV 434	SB II 224	
49.11.1	BF pelike		Silenos
	ABV 384		
50.11.7	Lakonian bowl		Herakles going to Olympos
	LV #140	SB II 52	*LIMC:* Hera 459*
53.11.4	RF cup		Theseus and Amphitrite
	*ARV*² 406	SB IV 292	*LIMC:* Amphitrite 76*
56.171.33	BF lekythos		Herakles fishing
	ABL 54		*LIMC:* Herakles 3369
56.171.46	RF column krater		Theseus and Minotaur
59.15	Lakonian cup		Herakles and Bull?
	LV #300		*LIMC:* Herakles 2317*
59.64	BF neck-amphora		Herakles and Acheloos
	Para 31		*LIMC:* Acheloos 214*
88.AE.66	RF cup		Aias and the arms
	Para 367		*LIMC:* Aias I 72*, 83*
			Death of Aias
			LIMC: Aias I 140*

96.19.1	RF column krater *ARV*² 536		Zeus and Aigina *LIMC*: Aigina 15*
98.8.11	BF neck-amphora *ABV* 308		Judgment of Paris
1972.11.10	RF krater	SB II 303	Death of Sarpedon *LIMC*: Hermes 593*

Ortiz Collection (Geneva)

Orvieto: Museo Civico (Faina Collection)

78	BF amphora *ABV* 144	SB II 39	Herakles on Olympos *LIMC*: Apollon 828*

Oxford: Ashmolean Musuem

G275 (525)	RF volute krater *ARV*² 1562	SB III 90	Epimetheus and Pandora *LIMC*: Hermes 643
G291 (530)	RF hydria *ARV*² 1061		Blinding of Thamyris *LIMC*: Argiope 1*
1912.1165	RF stamnos *ARV*² 208	SB III 243	Death of Pentheus
1934.333	BF plate *ABV* 115	SB II 123	Herakles and Hind *LIMC*: Artemis 1315*
1937.983	RF calyx krater *ARV*² 1153		Theseus and Sinis
1943.79	RF skyphos *ARV*² 889		Herakles and Geras *LIMC*: Geras 2*
1973.1032	RF cup frr		Death of Aigisthos *LIMC*: Aigisthos 23

Paestum

no #	RF amphora *ARV*² 220		Herakles and Kerberos *LIMC*: Herakles 2564*

Palermo: Museo Nazionale

45	BF lekythos *ABL* 208		Pholos
996	BF lekythos *ABL* 66		Water-carriers *LIMC*: Amyetoi 3*
NI 1886	WG lekythos *ARV*² 446		Sacrifice of Iphigeneia *LIMC*: Iphigeneia 3*°
P335	BF skyphos		Turtle-rider
V653	RF cup frr *ARV*² 73		Herakles and Eurytos LIMC: Eurytos I 4*
V659	RF cup *ARV*² 480		Death of Troilos *LIMC*: Achilleus 368*
no #	RF skyphos	SB III 284	Apollo and raven *LIMC*: Apollon 352*

Policoro

38462	Apulian hydria *RVAp* 407		Danaides? *LIMC*: Danaides 7*

Private Collections (Unnamed)

Athens	BF amphora		Achilleus and Memnon
			LIMC: Achilleus 822*
Athens (lost?)	BF lekythos		Snake and tomb
	ABL 198		
Basel	WG lekythos		Phineus
			LIMC: Harpyiai 8*
Basel	BF cup		Death of Troilos
		SB II 278	LIMC: Achilleus 359a*
Basel	RF cup		Death of Pelias
			LIMC: Alkandre 2*
Basel (Market)	RF stamnos		Herakles and Eurytos
			LIMC: Eurytos I 7*
Bern	BF cup		Herakles and Atlas
			LIMC: Atlas 2*
Copenhagen	LG jug		Herakles and Birds?
		FS 5b	LIMC: Herakles 2275
Miami	Apulian krater		Daughters of Anios
New York	RF psykter		Herakles and Philoktetes
			LIMC: Herakles 2910
New York (Market)	RF cup		Iris with sacrifice
Rome (Market)	RF bell krater		Athena and Tydeus
	ARV² 1073		LIMC: Athanasia 1°
Zurich	RF lekythos		Poseidon and Amymone
	ARV² 656		LIMC: Amymone 17

Providence: Rhode Island School of Design

25.084	RF lekythos		Danae, Perseus, and chest
	ARV² 697		LIMC: Danae 53*

Reading: University

47 VI 1	Pontic amphora		Abduction of Troilos
		SB II 279–80	LIMC: Achle 18*

Reggio Calabria: Museo Nazionale

1027–28	Chalkidian lid		Leukippides
	ChV 14	SB II 225	LIMC: Dioskouroi 194*
4001	BF amphora		Triptolemos
	ABV 147	SB II 38	
no #	RF pyxis frr		Nemesis/Leda and egg
			LIMC: Helene 3*

Richmond, Va.: Virginia Museum of Fine Arts

62.1.1	RF hydria		Perseus and Medousa
	ARV² 1683		LIMC: Gorgo 299*
80.162	Apulian lekythos		Polydeukes and Idas
	RVAp	SB IV 20	LIMC: Dioskouroi 217
	Supp 1, 84		Leukippides
			LIMC: Dioskouroi 203*

Rome: Museo dei Conservatori			
no #	Italic krater		Odysseus and Polyphemos
Rome: Forum Antiquarium			
no #	RF cup fr		Ixion and wheel
	*ARV*² 178		*LIMC:* Ixion 11*
Ruvo: Museo Jatta			
1097	Apulian volute krater		Hesperides and snake
	RVAp 417		*LIMC:* Hesperides 2*
1501	RF volute krater		Talos
	*ARV*² 1338	SB V 17	*LIMC:* Argonautai 15ʲ
no #	Apulian fr		Laokoon
	VL 533		
Samos: Excavations			
no #	Orientalizing krater		Herakles and Hebe
			LIMC: Herakles 3330
Samos: Vathy Museum			
1540	Lakonian cup		Boreadai and Harpuiai
	LV #119		
no #	Cor aryballos frr		Iason and serpent?
no #	BF hydria fr		Herakles and Nereus
	ABV 25	FS 55a	
Sciclounoff Collection (Geneva)			
no #	Apulian volute krater		Melanippe
		SB IV 36a	
Seillière Collection (Paris)			
no #	RF amphora		Artemis and Kallisto?
	*ARV*² 604	SB III 316	*LIMC:* Artemis 1347ʲ
Stockholm: National Museum			
6	RF bell krater		Persephone and Silenoi
	*ARV*² 1053		*LIMC:* Erysichthon I
1701	RF lekythos		Theseus and the rock
	*ARV*² 844		*LIMC:* Aithra I 19*
Stockholm: Medelhavsmuseum			
1963.1	RF amphora		Odysseus and Diomedes
	*ARV*² 1643		*LIMC:* Athena 103*
no #	BF oinochoe		Seirenes
	Para 183		
Stuttgart: Württembergisches Landesmuseum			
65/15	Chalkidian amphora		Oidipous and Sphinx
		SB II 104	
Syracuse: Museo Archeologico			
2408	RF column krater		Penelope and suitors
	*ARV*² 537		

12085	WG lekythos		Sphinx and youth
	ABL 241		
14569	BF lekythos		Herakles and Mares?
	ABV 487	*ABL* 222	*LIMC:* Herakles 2416*
21894	BF lekythos		Sack of Troy
	Para 201	*ABL* 15?	*LIMC:* Astyanax I 7*
23910	RF bell krater		Danae on Seriphos
			LIMC: Danae 55
25418	BF Siana cup		Sphinx and youths
	ABV 53	*FS* fig. 29	

Taranto: Museo Archeologico

I/96	Apulian amphora		Fall of Stheneboia
	RVAp 32		*LIMC:* Aphrodite 1531*
4545	RF lekythos		Theseus and Ariadne
	*ARV*² 560		*LIMC:* Ariadne 52*
4600	Sicilian calyx krater		Alkmene at the altar
	RVAp 36		*LIMC:* Amphitryon 1*
4991	Lakonian cup		Kyrene and lion
	LV #358	SB II 22	
7029	BF skyphos		Herakles and Helios
	ABV 518	*ABL* 120	*LIMC:* Herakles 2546*
		SB IV 197	
7030	BF skyphos		Herakles and Alkyoneus
	ABV 518		*LIMC:* Alkyoneus 17*
52155	BF cup		Herakles and Hesione
	VL 70	SB II 182	

Tarquinia: Museo Nazionale

RC 685	RF calyx krater		Alkandre and Pelias
	*ARV*² 864		LIMC: Alkandre 1*
RC 976	BF neck-amphora		Aineias and Anchises
	ABV 269		*LIMC:* Aineias 70
RC 1043	BF amphora		Tityos
	ABV 97	*Para* 37	*LIMC:* Ge 11
RC 1123	RF cup		Kadmos and snake?
	*ARV*² 120		*LIMC:* Kadmos I 56
RC 2070	BF cup		Herakles and Alkyoneus
	ABV 654		*LIMC:* Alkyoneus 16
RC 5291	RF cup		Theseus and Ariadne
	*ARV*² 405		*LIMC:* Ariadne 53*
RC 5564	BF neck-amphora		Telamon and Amazones
	ABV 84		*LIMC:* Amazones 5
RC 6848	RF cup		Assembly of gods
	*ARV*² 60	SB II 21	*LIMC:* Ganymedes 60*

Thasos

no #	plate		Bellerophontes and Pegasos

Thebes

31.166	BF lekythos		Medeia
	ABL 68		
31.166a	BF lekythos		Medeia
	ABL 68		

Toledo: Museum of Art

52.66	BF lekythos		Herakles and Alkyoneus
			LIMC: Alkyoneus 7*
69.369	RF lekythos		Danae, Perseus, and chest
			LIMC: Akrisios 5*
82.134	Etruscan BF kalpis		Men into dolphins

Tübingen: University

S/10 1605 (E120)	RF oinochoe		Eumaios
			LIMC: Eumaios 4*
S/10 1610	RF oinochoe		Hippothoon
		SB IV 334	*LIMC:* Alope 1*
S/12 2452 (D2)	BF amphora		Kalydonian Boar Hunt
	ABV 96		

Vatican Museums

229	Ionian hydria		Herakles and Alkyoneus
			LIMC: Alkyoneus 31*
306	BF dinos		Kalydonian Boar Hunt
			LIMC: Atalante 4*
343	BF cup		Achilleus and Aias
		SB II 330–31	*LIMC:* Achilleus 398*
344	BF amphora		Achilleus and Aias
	ABV 145	SB II 332	*LIMC:* Achilleus 397*
350	BF amphora		Eos mourning
	ABV 140	SB II 328	*LIMC:* Eos 327*
372	BF amphora		Herakles and Kerberos
	ABV 368	SB II 153	*LIMC:* Hades 137*
388	BF neck-amphora		Herakles and Pholos
	ABV 283		
16541 (H569)	RF cup		Oidipous and Sphinx
	*ARV*² 451		
16545	RF cup		Iason and serpent
	*ARV*² 437		*LIMC:* Iason 32*
16554	RF hydria		Poseidon and Aithra
	*ARV*² 252		*LIMC:* Aithra I 2*
16563 (H545)	RF cup		Herakles in Helios' cup
	*ARV*² 449	SB IV 198	*LIMC:* Herakles 2552*
16592	Lakonian cup		Atlas and Prometheus?
	LV #196	SB II 56	*LIMC:* Atlas 1*
K40099	LC krater		Embassy to Troy
	CorVP 264	*FS* 72	*LIMC:* Harmatidas 1*

Vienna: Kunsthistorisches Museum

741	RF amphora		Menelaos and Helen
	*ARV*² 203		*LIMC:* Helene 260*

1103	RF column krater		Death of Aigisthos
	ARV² 277		
1773	RF skyphos		Ariadne and children?
	ARV² 972	SB IV 342	LIMC: Akamas 1*
1841	WG lekythos		Herakles and Birds
	ABV 522	ABL 256	LIMC: Herakles 2245*
3576	Caeretan hydria		Herakles and Bousiris
	CH 50	SB II 171	LIMC: Bousiris 9*
3619	BF dinos		Eos and Thetis
	ABV 140		LIMC: Achilleus 799*
3695	RF cup		Aias and the arms
	ARV² 429		LIMC: Aias I 71*
3710	RF cup		Achilleus and Priam
	ARV² 380		LIMC: Achilleus 659*
3725	RF pelike		Death of Aigisthos
	ARV² 204	SB II 351–52	LIMC: Aigisthos 6*
3728	RF pelike		Sphinx and elders

Villa Giulia (Rome)

3579	RF column krater		Tereus and the Pandionides
	ARV² 514	SB IV 80	
11688	RF bell krater frr		Herakles on pyre
			LIMC: Herakles 2909*
20760	RF cup		Theseus and sow
	ARV² 83	SB II 216	
20842	BF amphora		Herakles and Poseidon
	ABV 381		
20846	RF pelike		Poseidon and Amymone
	ARV² 494		LIMC: Amymone 20a
22679	PC olpe		Judgment of Paris
	CorVP 32	FS 29b	LIMC: Alexandros 5*
24247	BF neck-amphora		Peleus in a tree
	VL 318		LIMC: Cheiron 15*
48238	RF pelike		Herakles and Geras
	ARV² 284	SB IV 211	LIMC: Geras 5*
48329	BF neck-amphora		Herakles and Kerberos
	ABV 370		LIMC: Herakles 2560*
50279	Paestan calyx krater		Aias and Kassandra
	RVP 85		LIMC: Aias II 107*
50406 (M472)	BF amphora		Herakles and Lion
	ABV 291		LIMC: Herakles 1882*
50649	Caeretan hydria		Herakles and Kerberos
	CH 23		
50626	BF neck-amphora		Pholos
	ABV 270		
50683 (M430)	BF hydria		Geryoneus
	ABV 108	SB II 142	LIMC: Herakles 2463*
57231	Lakonian cup		Capture of Silenos
	LV #342		

57912	RF cup		Eos and Thetis
	ARV² 72	SB II 322	LIMC: Achilleus 804*
74989	BF amphora		Herakles and Hydra?
			LIMC: Herakles 2822*
106335	Lakonian cup		Boreadai and Harpuiai
	LV #122	SB II 231	LIMC: Boreadai 6*
106341	BF neck-amphora		Tityos
	ABV 121	FS 54b	LIMC: Ge 12*
106349	Lakonian cup		Achilleus and snake
	LV #291		LIMC: Achilleus 261*
106462	RF cup		Herakles and Nereus
	ARV² 1623		
106465	BF amphora		Herakles and Hydra
no #	MC aryballos		Herakles and Hebe
			LIMC: Herakles 3331°
no # (Ricci	Ionian hydria		Eos and Thetis
Hydria)	VL 166	SB II 324–25	LIMC: Achilleus 797
			Herakles going to Olympos
		SB II 44	LIMC: Herakles 2908*
no # (Stefani	Lakonian cup		Herakles and Amazones
Cup)	LV #193	SB II 131	LIMC: Amazones 2*
no #	RF pelike		Perseus and Polydektes

Vlastos Collection (Athens)

no #	RF chous		Ikaros
	ARV² 700	SB IV 55	

Walters Art Gallery (Baltimore)

48.198	BF exaleiptron		Odysseus and Nausikaa?

Weimar (once Preller Collection)

no #	RF cup		Herakles carries Hades?
	ARV² 1511		LIMC: Hades 71b

White-Levy Collection (New York)

no #	RF amphora		Herakles and Hydra

Würzburg: University (Martin von Wagner Museum)

164	Chalkidian cup		Silenoi
	ChV 15	SB II 17	LIMC: Dionysos 763
			Phineus
		SB II 232	LIMC: Boreadai 7*
			LIMC: Harpyiai 14*
199	BF neck-amphora		Herakles and Hind
	ABV 287		LIMC: Herakles 2177*
212	BF neck-amphora		Aineias and Anchises
	ABV 371		
218	BF neck-amphora		Aineias and Anchises
	ABV 316		LIMC: Aineias 69*
252	BF amphora		Silenoi
	ABV 315		

391	BF mastos cup		Dionysos and child
	ABV 262	SB II 12	*LIMC:* Ariadne 159*
452	BF cup		Achilleus and Cheiron
	ABV 63	SB II 262	*LIMC:* Achilleus 35*
474	RF cup		Silenos
	*ARV*² 173		
855	Apulian pelike fr		Andromeda
	RVAp 174		*LIMC:* Andromeda I 10*

Yale University
| 1913.111 | BF lekythos | | Admetos' chariot |
| | *ABL* 221 | | *LIMC:* Admetos I 15* |

Zurich
| ETH 4 | LC amphora | | Ambush of Troilos |
| | *CorVP* 268 | | *LIMC:* Achilleus 336 |

RELIEF

Athens: National Museum
2104	"Megarian" bowl		Theseus and Helen at Korinth
		SB IV 313	*LIMC:* Helene 37*°
5898	relief amphora		Leto in childbirth?
		FS 12	*LIMC:* Eileithyia 58*
11798	"Megarian" bowl		Zeus and Antiope
			LIMC: Antiope I 2*

Basel: Antikenmuseum and Ludwig Collection
| BS 617 | pithos | | Minotaur and Athenians |
| | | *FS* 25a | *LIMC:* Ariadne 36 |

Berlin: Pergamon-Museum
| 4996 | "Megarian" bowl | | Death of Agamemnon |
| | | | *LIMC:* Alkmeon 1° |

Berlin: Lost or Unknown
| 3161a | "Megarian" bowl | | Sisyphos and Autolykos |
| | | SB III 210 | *LIMC:* Antikleia 2° |

Boston: Museum of Fine Arts
98.828	Arretine bowl		Death of Phaethon
		SB IV 42	
99.505	amphora		Agamemnon in bath?
			LIMC: Aigisthos 1*

Cabinet des Médailles (Paris)
| 3003 | relief pithos | | Europa and bull |
| | | *FS* 11b | *LIMC:* Europe I 91* |

Louvre (Paris)
| CA 795 | amphora | | Medousa as Kentauros |
| | | *FS* 15b | *LIMC:* Gorgo 290* |

CA 937	amphora fr		Perseus
CA 4523	Cretan relief pithos		Fall of Bellerophontes
MNC 660	"Megarian" bowl		Oidipous as foundling

Mykonos

69	pithos		Trojan Horse
		FS 35a	LIMC: Equus Troianus 23*
			Death of Astyanax?
			LIMC: Astyanax I 27*
			Menelaos and Helen
		FS 35b	LIMC: Helene 225*

Tenos

| no # | relief amphora | | Birth of Athena |
| | | FS 13 | LIMC: Athena 360* |

Painted Clay Artifacts (other than vases)

Berlin

F766	Corinthian pinax		Herakles and the Kerkopes
F767	Corinthian pinax		Herakles and the Kerkopes
	DL 97		
F768	Corinthian pinax		Gigantomachy
			LIMC: Gigantes 98

Eleusis

| 1398 | pinax | | Gigantomachy |
| | | SB II 54 | LIMC: Gigantes 99 |

Nauplia

| 4509 | clay shield | | Achilleus and Penthesileia? |
| | | FS 7b | LIMC: Amazones 168* |

London: British Museum

| no # | Boccanera slab | | Judgment of Paris |

Small Reliefs (ivories, terracottas, bronze fibulas, tripods, shield-bands, gems, etc.)

Agrigento: Museo Civico

| no # | terracotta arula | | Achilleus and Memnon? |
| | | | LIMC: Achilleus 825* |

Aigina: Museum

| no # | shield-band | | Death of Agamemnon |

Athens: National Museum

4196	Melian relief		Phrixos and ram
11765	Kretan fibula		Herakles and the Moliones
		FS 6b	LIMC: Aktorione 7*
15350	ivory		Kentauros
15354	ivory		Prometheus and eagle
		FS 11a	

16368	ivory comb		Judgment of Paris
			LIMC: Alexandros 6*
no #	ivory seal		Aias and corpse of
			Achilleus
			LIMC: Achilleus 864
no #	bronze sheathing		Death of Kassandra
		FS 32c	

Basel: Antikenmuseum and Ludwig Collection

BS 318	terracotta frieze		Herakles and Alkyoneus
			LIMC: Hermes 537*
			Agamemnon in bath?
Lu 217	shield-band		Tityos
	Form CI: *OF* XVII		*LIMC:* Apollon 1076
	142	SB II 79	
			Herakles and Atlas
		SB II 154	*LIMC:* Atlas 3*

Berlin: Charlottenburg (Antikenmuseum)

GI 194	Etruscan gem		Seven against Thebes
			LIMC: Amphiaraos 29*
GI 332–36	gold plaques		Theseus and Minotaur
		FS fig. 7	*LIMC:* Ariadne 37

Berlin: Pergamon-Museum

| TC 6281 | Melian relief | | Gaia and Erichthonios |
| | | | *LIMC:* Erechtheus 23 |

Boston: Museum of Fine Arts

| 99.494 | Etruscan mirror | | Suicide of Aias |
| | | | *LIMC:* Aias I 135* |

Cabinet des Médailles (Paris)

276	Etruscan gem		Aineias and Anchises
			LIMC: Aineias 95
M5837	Cycladic sealstone		Kentauros

Delphi

4479	shield-band		Herakles and Geryoneus
	Form XXIV: *OF* II 25		*LIMC:* Geryoneus 9*
no #	ivory		Phineus and the Harpuiai
		FS 64b	*LIMC:* Boreadai 13*
no #	ivory		Departure of Amphiaraos
			LIMC: Amphiaraos 16*

Florence: Museo Archeologico

| 72740 | Etruscan mirror | | Hera nursing Herakles |
| | | | *LIMC:* Hercle 404* |

Iraklion

| 11512 | terracotta plaque | | Death of Agamemnon? |
| | | FS 33 | *LIMC:* Agamemnon 91* |

Lemnos			
1205	terracotta mold		Aias and corpse of Achilleus *LIMC*: Achilleus 860*
London: British Museum			
489	scarab		Herakles and Acheloos *LIMC*: Acheloos 222*
3204	Boiotian fibula		Man and lion *LIMC*: Herakles 1913 Man and birds *LIMC*: Herakles 2280
3205	Boiotian fibula	*FS* 6a	Herakles and Hydra *LIMC*: Herakles 2019* Trojan Horse *LIMC*: Equus Troianus 22*
B620	Etruscan mirror	SB IV 134	Perseus and Medousa
no #	Cretan gem (impression)		Prometheus
Munich: Antikensammlungen			
A1293	seal *DL* 124	*FS* 6c	Nessos and Deianeira?
SL 66	tripod (Loeb B)		Peleus and Thetis (as lion) Achilleus and Troilos *LIMC*: Achle 63 *
SL 67	tripod (Loeb A)		Peleus and Thetis (as snake)
SL 68	tripod (Loeb C)		Peleus and Thetis (as lion)
Naples: Museo Nazionale			
no #	terracotta	*FS* 32b	Aias and corpse of Achilleus *LIMC*: Achilleus 861°
New York: Metropolitan Museum of Art			
17.190.73	ivory	*FS* 14	Proitides
42.11.1	steatite gem		Death of Agamemnon *LIMC*: Agamemnon 94*
42.11.13	steatite gem	*FS* 32a	Suicide of Aias *LIMC*: Aias I 110*
58.11.6	tripod leg (forgery?)		Peleus and Thetis
Olympia			
B 103	bronze relief		Departure of Amphiaraos *LIMC*: Baton I 5°
B 112	shield-band Form V: *OF* II 11	*FS* fig. 38	Achilleus and Penthesileia *LIMC*: Amazones 171°

B 160	shield-band Form XXXV: *OF* II 35		Death of Priam
B 520	shield-band Form XXV: *OF* II 26		Herakles, Apollo, tripod *LIMC:* Herakles 2984
B 847	shield-band Form IX: *OF* II 14		Birth of Athena *LIMC:* Eileithyia 2e° Death of Polites? Troilos?
		FS fig. 40	*LIMC:* Astyanax I 34a°
B 975	shield-band Form XXIX: *OF* II 29		Aias and Kassandra Herakles and Kerkopes Perseus and Medousa *LIMC:* Athena 502°
B 984	shield-band Form XLVI: *OF* II 39		Herakles and Antaios? *LIMC:* Antaios I 33°
B 988	shield-band Form I: *OF* II 7	*FS* fig. 35	Death of Troilos *LIMC:* Achilleus 376*° Zeus and Typhoeus
		FS fig. 17	
		FS fig. 44	Death of Aigisthos *LIMC:* Aigisthos 2°
B 1010	shield-band Form III: *OF* II 9		Herakles and Alkyoneus Admetos and Mopsos boxing *LIMC:* Admetos I 8°
B 1555	shield-band Form XXXII: *OF* II 33		Achilleus and Penthesileia *LIMC:* Achilleus 721°
B 1636	shield-band Form XXVI: *OF* II 27		Zeus and Typhoeus Suicide of Aias *LIMC:* Aias I 127°
B 1643	shield-band Form VII: *OF* II 12		Zeus and Typhoeus Theseus and Minotaur *LIMC:* Ariadne 34°
B 1650	shield-band Form XXVIII: *OF* II 29		Herakles and Lion *LIMC:* Herakles 1847
B 1654	shield-band Form IV: *OF* II 10		Herakles and Lion *LIMC:* Herakles 1846° Theseus and Minotaur Amphiaraos and Lykourgos
		FS fig. 31	*LIMC:* Amphiaraos 33° Suicide of Aias Aias and Kassandra Death of Agamemnon
		FS fig. 43	*LIMC:* Agamemnon 92*

B 1687	shield-band		Medousa, Pegasos, Chrysaor
	Form XIV: *OF* II 18		*LIMC*: Gorgo 273°
			Birth of Athena
		FS fig. 20	*LIMC*: Athena 361°
B 1730	tripod leg		Herakles, Apollo, tripod
			LIMC: Apollon 1011
B 1801	shield-band		Herakles and Alkyoneus
	Form I: *OF* II 7		Aias and Kassandra
		FS fig. 42	*LIMC*: Aias II 48°
B 1881	shield-band		Herakles and Nereus?
	Form XXX: *OF* II 31		*LIMC*: Halios Geron 2°
B 1911	shield-band		Aias and corpse of Achilleus
	Form XIV: *OF* II 18		*LIMC*: Achilleus 862°
B 1912	shield-band		Death of Troilos
	Form XV: *OF* II 19	*FS* fig. 34	*LIMC*: Achilleus 377°
B 1921	shield-band		Aias and corpse of Achilleus
	Form XIII: *OF* II 17		*LIMC*: Achilleus 862°
B 1975	shield-band		Herakles and Geryoneus
	Form X: *OF* II 15	*FS* fig. 25	*LIMC*: Herakles 2478°
B 2198	shield-band		Theseus and Peirithoos in Hades
	Form XXIX bis: *OF* II 30	*FS* fig. 24	*LIMC*: Herakles 3519°
B 3600	tripod leg		Theseus and Ariadne?
		FS fig. 28	*LIMC*: Ariadne
			Death of Troilos
		FS fig. 28	*LIMC*: Achilleus 375°
B 4475	shield-band		Menelaos and Helen
	Form CXVIII: *OF* XVII 153		*LIMC*: Helena 69a*
B 4810	shield-band		Achilleus and Aias at dice
	Form CXXIX: *OF* XVII 156		Death of Priam
B 4836	shield-band		Herakles and Atlas
	Form CI: *OF* XVII 142		*LIMC*: Atlas 4
			Tityos
B 4900	mitra		Death of Klytaimestra?
			LIMC: Alexandros 52°
B 4964	shield-band		Man in cauldron
	Form CXXVII: *OF* XVII 155		
B 4992	shield-band		Prometheus and eagle
	Form XLV: *OF* XVII 149	*FS* 41a	

B 5800	tripod leg		Herakles and Hydra
			LIMC: Herakles 2025
B 8402	shield-band		Release of Hera
	Form CXX: *OF* XVII		*LIMC:* Hera 321
	154		
BE 11a	bronze plaque		Kaineus and Kentauroi
		FS 27c	*LIMC:* Kaineus 61*
E 161	shield-band (iron)		Herakles and Boar
	Form XXXVIII: *OF* II		*LIMC:* Herakles 2118
	36		
M 77	tripod leg		Theseus and Amazon?
		FS 80	*LIMC:* Antiope II 1*
			Death of Klytaimestra
		FS 80	*LIMC:* Aigisthos 19*
M 397	cuirass		Helen and the Dioskouroi
		FS 26	*LIMC:* Helene 58*

Philadelphia: University Museum

75-35-1	fibula		Herakles and Hydra
			LIMC: Herakles 2020
			Herakles and Hind
			LIMC: Herakles 2205

Reggio Calabria: Museo Nazionale

4337	terracotta plaque		Artemis and Aktaion
			LIMC: Aktaion 76*
no #	terracotta plaque		Persephone opening chest
			LIMC: Aphrodite
			1365b*

Samos: Vathy Museum

B 2518	bronze pectoral		Herakles and Geryoneus
			LIMC: Herakles 2476°
E 1	ivory		Perseus and Medousa
		FS 17	*LIMC:* Gorgo 291*
T 416	stamped clay		Aias carrying Achilleus
			LIMC: Achilleus 865

Sparta

| 1 | grave relief | | Menelaos and Helen |
| | | *FS* 69 | *LIMC:* Helene 230* |

Villa Giulia

13199	Etruscan cista		Laios and Chrysippos
			LIMC: Chrysippos I 7*
24787	Etruscan cista		Amykos
	(Ficoroni Cista)		*LIMC:* Amykos 5*

Architectural Sculpture

Akropolis Museum (Athens)

| 1 | pediment | | Herakles and Hydra |
| | | | *LIMC:* Herakles 2021* |

9	pediment		Herakles on Olympos
			LIMC: Hera 458*
35	pediment		Bluebeard group
52	pediment		Ambush of Troilos?
			LIMC: Achilleus 276*
55	pediment		Herakles on Olympos?
631	pediment		Athena and Gigantes
			LIMC: Athena 125°

Athens: National Museum

2870	metope fr		Sphinxes?
13401	Thermon metope		Perseus fleeing
		FS 18	
13410	Thermon metope		Aedon and Chelidon
		FS 20	
13413	Thermon metope		Proitides
		FS fig. 6	
no #	Kalydon metope		Herakles and Boar
			LIMC: Herakles 2135

Delphi (in museum)
    Sikyonian Treasury

no #	metope		Europa and bull
			LIMC: Europe I 77*
no #	metope		Idas, Kastor, Polydeukes
		FS 63b	*LIMC:* Apharetidai 4*
no #	metope		Argo and crew
		FS 63a	*LIMC:* Argonautai 2*

    Siphnian Treasury

no #	pediment		Apollo, Herakles, tripod
			LIMC: Herakles 3026*
no #	north frieze		Gigantomachy
		SB II 67–69	*LIMC:* Gigantes 2*°
no #	east frieze		Trojan War
		SB II 291–92	*LIMC:* Apollon 861a*
			LIMC: Hera 298*
no #	south frieze		Leukippides?
			LIMC: Dioskouroi 207*

    Athenian Treasury

no #	pediment		Gigantomachy
no #	metopes		Theseus' exploits
no #	metope		Herakles and Hind
			LIMC: Herakles 1703°
no #	metopes		Herakles and Geryoneus
			LIMC: Herakles 1703°

    Temple of Apollo

no #	pediment		Gigantomachy
		SB II 70	*LIMC:* Gigantes 3°

Glyptothek (Munich)
   no #   Aigina: East   Fall of Laomedon's Troy
                                  SB II 183–84   *LIMC:* Athena 129°

Hephaisteion (Athens: in situ)
   no #   metopes   SB IV 299   Theseus' exploits
   no #   metope   Herakles and Boar
                                                      LIMC: Herakles 1706*°
   no #   metope   Herakles and Amazon
                                                      LIMC: Herakles 1706*°
   no #   metope   Herakles and Geryoneus
                                                      LIMC: Herakles 1706*°
   no #   pediment   Theseus and sons of Pallas

Kerkyra/Corfu
   no #   pediment   Medousa, Pegasos,
                                                      Chrysaor
                           FS fig. 16   *LIMC:* Gorgo 289*°
   no #   pediment   Death of Aigisthos?
                           FS 42

Olympia (in museum)
   Temple of Zeus
   no #   east pediment   SB IV 2–5
   no #   west pediment   SB IV 315   Pelops and Oinomaos
   no #   metope   Wedding of Peirithoos
                                                  Herakles and Lion
   no #   metope   *LIMC:* Herakles 1705*°
                                                  Herakles and Boar
   no #   metope   *LIMC:* Herakles 1705*°
                                               Herakles and the Stables
   no #   metope   *LIMC:* Herakles 1705*°
                                               Herakles and Birds
   no #   metope   *LIMC:* Herakles 1705*°
                                               Herakles and Bull
   no #   metope   *LIMC:* Herakles 1705*°
                                               Herakles and Amazon
   no #   metope   *LIMC:* Herakles 1705*°
                                               Herakles and Geryoneus
   no #   metope   *LIMC:* Herakles 1705*°
                                               Herakles and Atlas
                                               LIMC: Herakles 1705*°

   Megarian Treasury
   no #   pediment   Gigantomachy
                                                      LIMC: Gigantes 6*°

Paestum (in museum)

   Foce del Sele temples
   no #   metope   SB II 350   Man and snake
   no #   metope   Tityos
                                SB II 76–77   *LIMC:* Apollon 1075*

no #	metope		Silenoi
		SB II 89	LIMC: Hera 328*
no #	metope		Herakles and Pholos
no #	metope	SB II 85	Sisyphos
no #	metope	SB II 226	Leukippides?
no #	metope		Man in cauldron
no #	metope		Herakles and Boar
			LIMC: Herakles 1698*
no #	metope		Herakles and Alkyoneus?
			LIMC: Herakles 1698*
no #	metope		Herakles and Deianeira
			(Hera?)
			LIMC: Herakles 1698*
no #	metope		Herakles, Apollo, tripod
		SB II 190	LIMC: Herakles 1698*
no #	metope		Herakles and the Kerkopes
		SB II 174	LIMC: Herakles 1698*
no #	metope		Achilleus at fountain house
			LIMC: Achilleus 279*
no #	metope		Achilleus and Troilos?
			Orestes and Aigisthos?
		SB II 349	LIMC: Aigisthos 20*
no #	metope	SB II 348	Klytaimestra
no #	metope	SB II 302	Hektor and Patroklos
no #	metope		Suicide of Aias
			LIMC: Aias I 128*
no #	metope	SB II 361	Man on turtle

Palermo: Museo Nazionale

Selinous Temple C

no #	pediment		Gorgon
			LIMC: Gorgo 61
3920B	metope		Perseus and Medousa
			LIMC: Athena 12*
3920C	metope		Herakles and the Kerkopes

Selinous Temple E

3921A	metope		Herakles and Amazon
			LIMC: Amazones 96*
3921C	metope		Death of Aktaion
			LIMC: Aktaion 31*

Selinous Temple F

3909A	metope		Gigantomachy
			LIMC: Gigantes 13*
3909B	metope		Gigantomachy
			LIMC: Gigantes 13*

Selinous Temple Y

3915	metope		Europa and bull
		SB II 15	LIMC: Europe I 78*

Parthenon (in situ)
    no #   metopes (east)   Gigantomachy
                                                                              LIMC: Gigantes 18*

Syracuse: Museo Archeologico
    no #   Gela pediment   Gorgon

Thermon
    no #   metope   Herakles and Kentauroi
                       DL 140

Villa Giulia (Rome)

Pyrgi Temple A
    no #   antepagmentum   Seven against Thebes
                                                                     LIMC: Athena/Menerva
                                                                      239*

Free-standing Sculpture

Athens: National Museum
    6678   cauldron rim figure   Minotaur
    7544   bronze statuette   Silenos

Lefkandi
    no #   terracotta   Kentauros

Louvre (Paris)
    C7286   cauldron rim figure   Minotaur

Naples: Museo Nazionale
    6351   marble   Ganymedes and eagle
                                                            LIMC: Ganymedes 130*

New York: Metropolitan Museum of Art
    17.190.2072   bronze group   Man and Kentauros
                                    FS 4a

Olympia
    T 2   terracotta   Zeus and Ganymedes
                                    SB III 295   *LIMC*: Ganymedes 56*

Appendix D

Genealogical Tables

TABLE 1: THE FIRST GODS

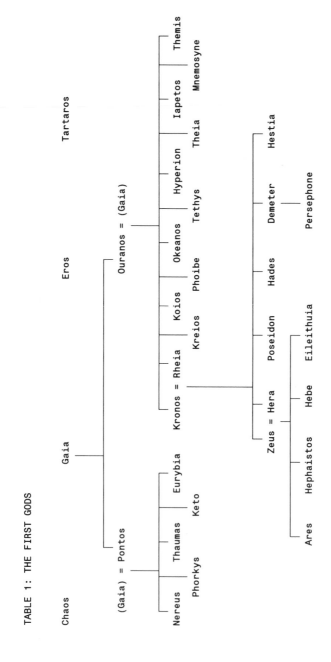

TABLE 2: THE CHILDREN OF PONTOS

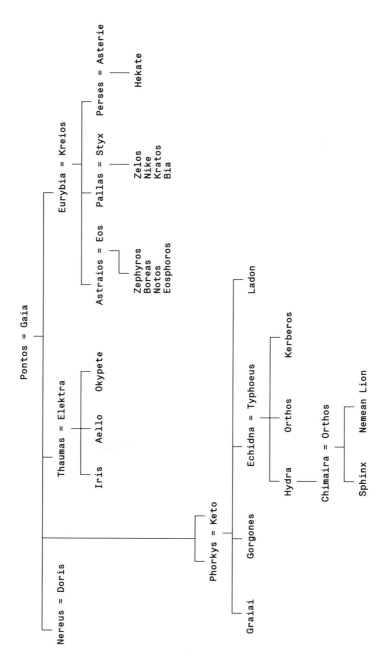

TABLE 3: THE LINE OF DEUKALION

Iapetos = Klymene
├── Prometheus = ?
│   └── Deukalion = Pyrrha = Zeus
│   └── Hellen
│   ├── Doros
│   ├── Aiolos
│   │   ├── Sisyphos
│   │   ├── Salmoneus
│   │   │   └── (Five Daughters) = Hermes
│   │   │   └── Nymphai Satyroi Kouretes
│   │   ├── Kretheus
│   │   ├── Athamas
│   │   ├── Perieres
│   │   ├── Deion
│   │   ├── Minyas
│   │   ├── Peisidike
│   │   ├── Alkyone
│   │   ├── Kalyke
│   │   ├── Kanake
│   │   └── Perimede
│   └── Xouthos = Kreousa
│   ├── Achaios
│   └── Ion
└── Epimetheus = Pandora

806

TABLE 4: THE DAUGHTERS OF AIOLOS

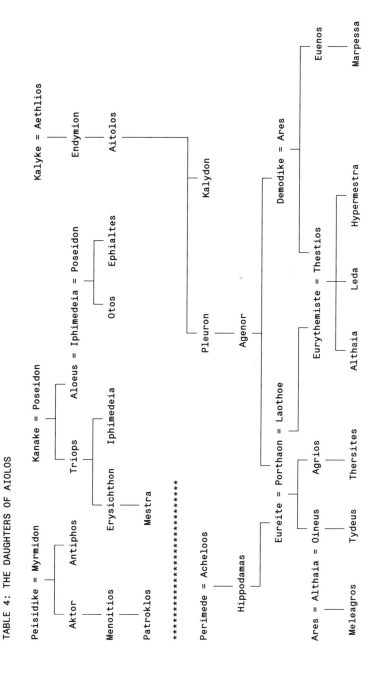

TABLE 5: THE SONS OF AIOLOS I

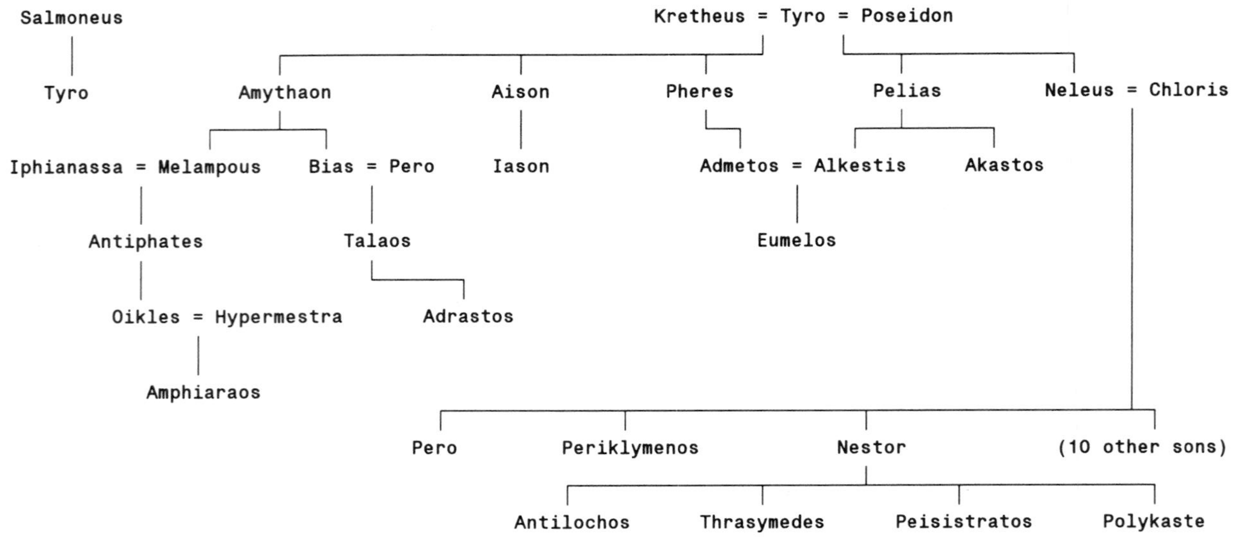

Salmoneus

Tyro

Kretheus = Tyro = Poseidon

Amythaon   Aison   Pheres   Pelias   Neleus = Chloris

Iphianassa = Melampous   Bias = Pero   Iason

Antiphates

Oikles = Hypermestra   Talaos

Amphiaraos   Adrastos

Admetos = Alkestis   Akastos

Eumelos

Pero   Periklymenos   Nestor   (10 other sons)

Antilochos   Thrasymedes   Peisistratos   Polykaste

TABLE 6: THE SONS OF AIOLOS II

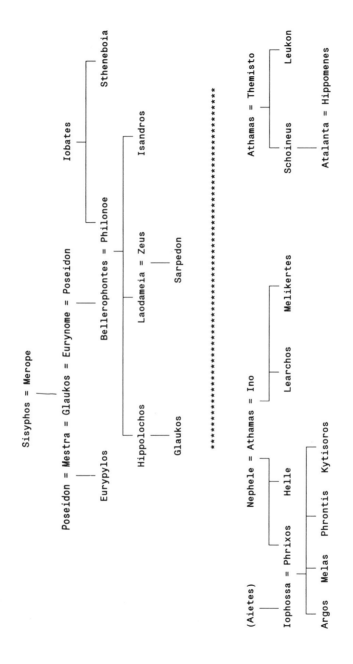

TABLE 7: THE SONS OF AIOLOS III

```
                              Perieres = Alkyone                      Halirrhothios

                                    Aphareus

                        Lynkeus    Idas = Marpessa

                                   Kleopatra = Meleagros

Leukippos                                                    Apollo = Philonis = Hermes

Phoibe   Hilaeira                                                  Autolykos

                    ************************************************    Antikleia = Laertes

Arsinoe                                                        Penelope = Odysseus = Kirke

                              Deion = Diomede                    Telemachos        Telegonos

                                Phylakos

                                Iphiklos               Philammon

                                Podarkes               Thamyris

Asterodeia           Aktor

                Protesilaos = Laodameia
```

TABLE 8: THE LINE OF INACHOS

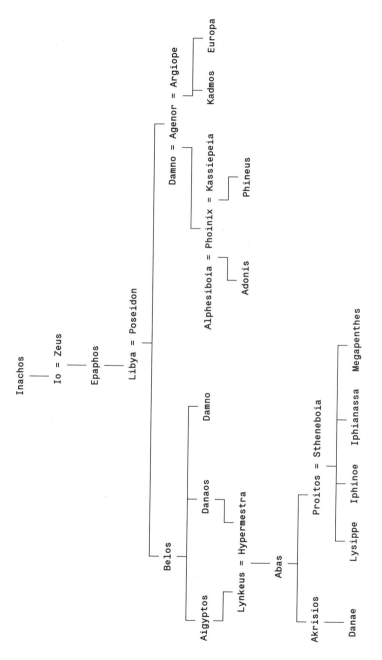

TABLE 9: THE DAUGHTERS OF ATLAS I

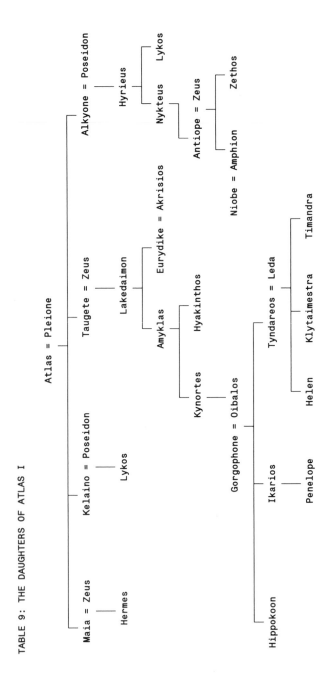

TABLE 10: THE DAUGHTERS OF ATLAS II

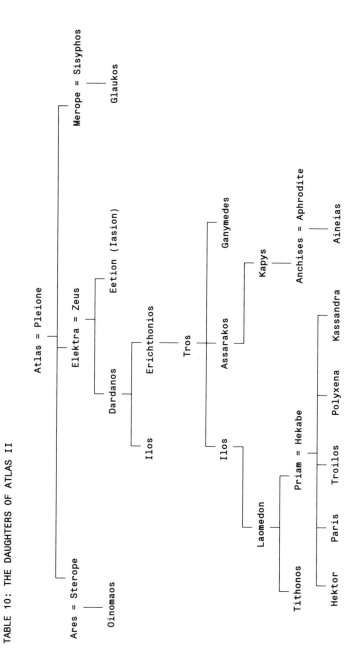

TABLE 11: THE DAUGHTERS OF ASOPOS

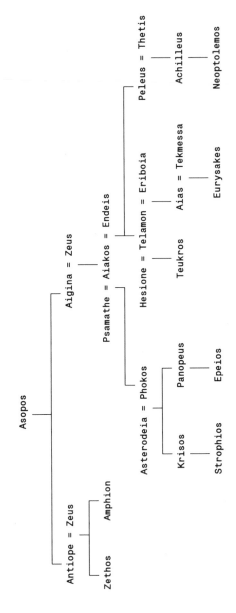

TABLE 12: THE HOUSE OF ATHENS

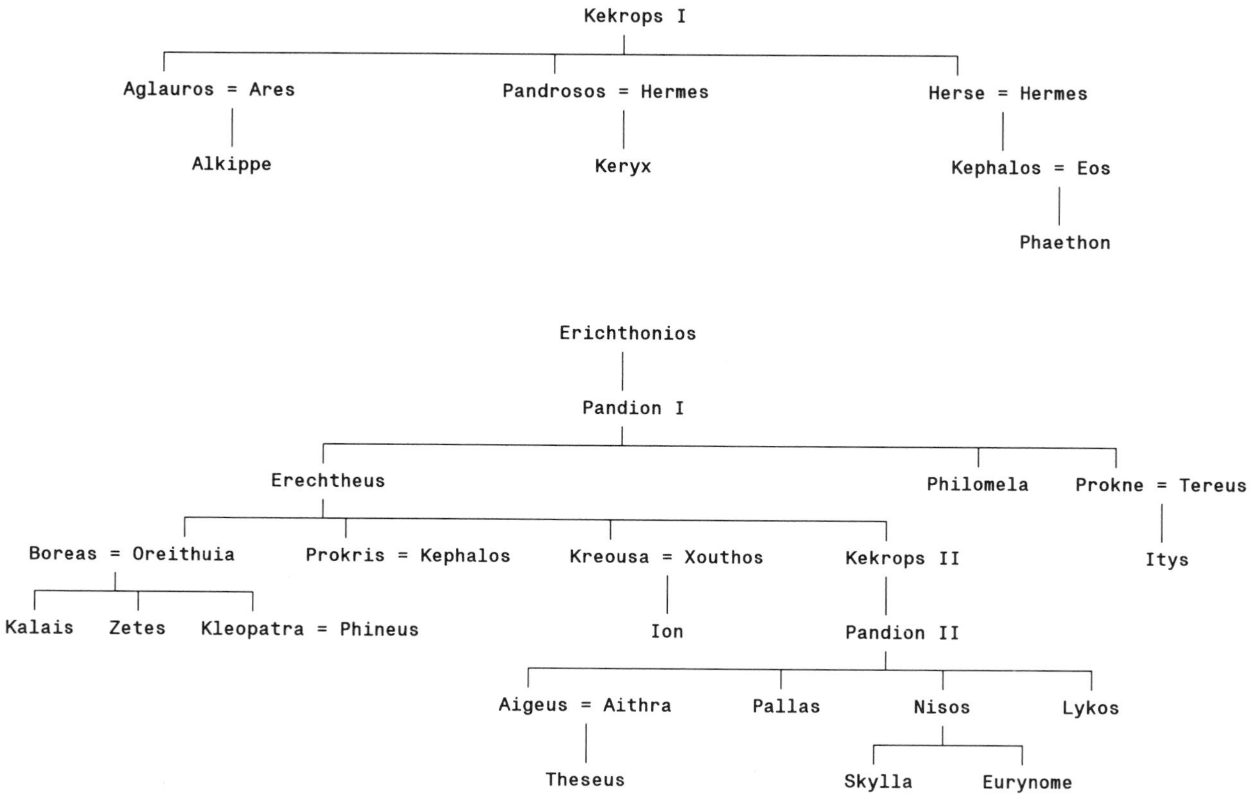

Kekrops I

Aglauros = Ares

Alkippe

Pandrosos = Hermes

Keryx

Herse = Hermes

Kephalos = Eos

Phaethon

Erichthonios

Pandion I

Erechtheus

Prokris = Kephalos

Boreas = Oreithuia

Kalais   Zetes   Kleopatra = Phineus

Kreousa = Xouthos

Ion

Kekrops II

Philomela   Prokne = Tereus

Itys

Pandion II

Aigeus = Aithra

Theseus

Pallas

Nisos

Skylla   Eurynome

Lykos

TABLE 13: THE LINE OF EUROPA

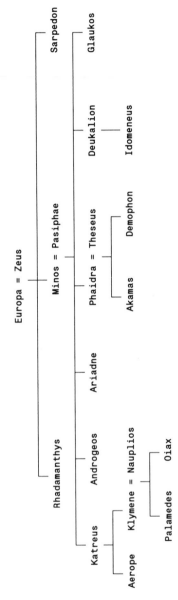

TABLE 14: THE LINE OF DANAE

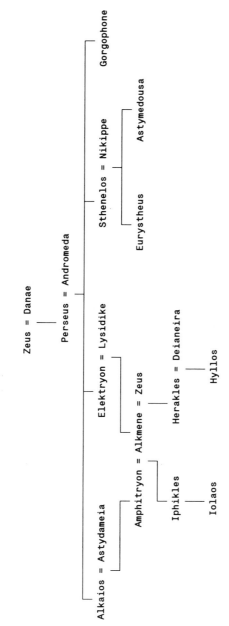

TABLE 15: THE LINE OF KADMOS

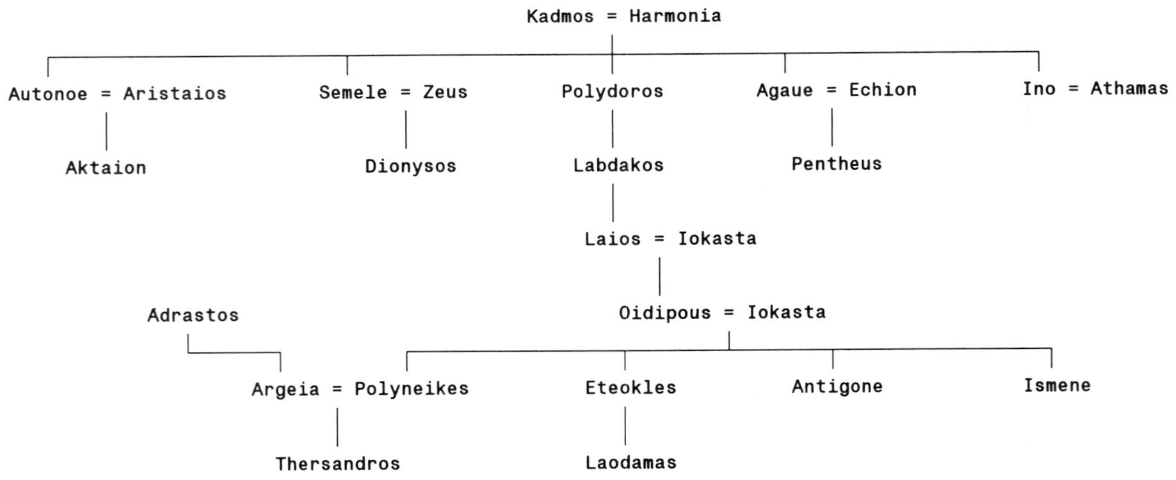

Kadmos = Harmonia

Autonoe = Aristaios   Semele = Zeus   Polydoros   Agaue = Echion   Ino = Athamas

Aktaion   Dionysos   Labdakos   Pentheus

Laios = Iokasta

Oidipous = Iokasta

Adrastos

Argeia = Polyneikes   Eteokles   Antigone   Ismene

Thersandros   Laodamas

TABLE 16: THE LINE OF TALAOS

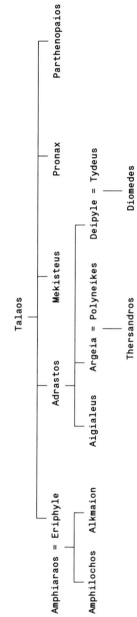

TABLE 17: THE LINE OF TANTALOS

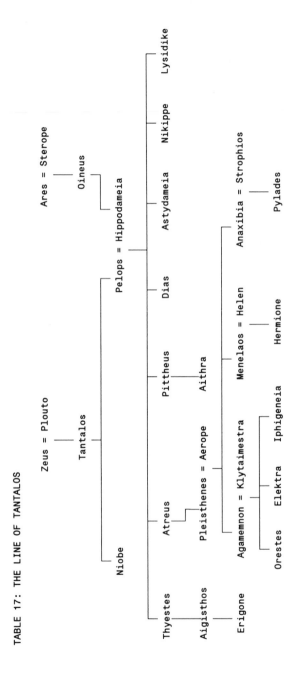

TABLE 18: THE LINE OF LYKAON

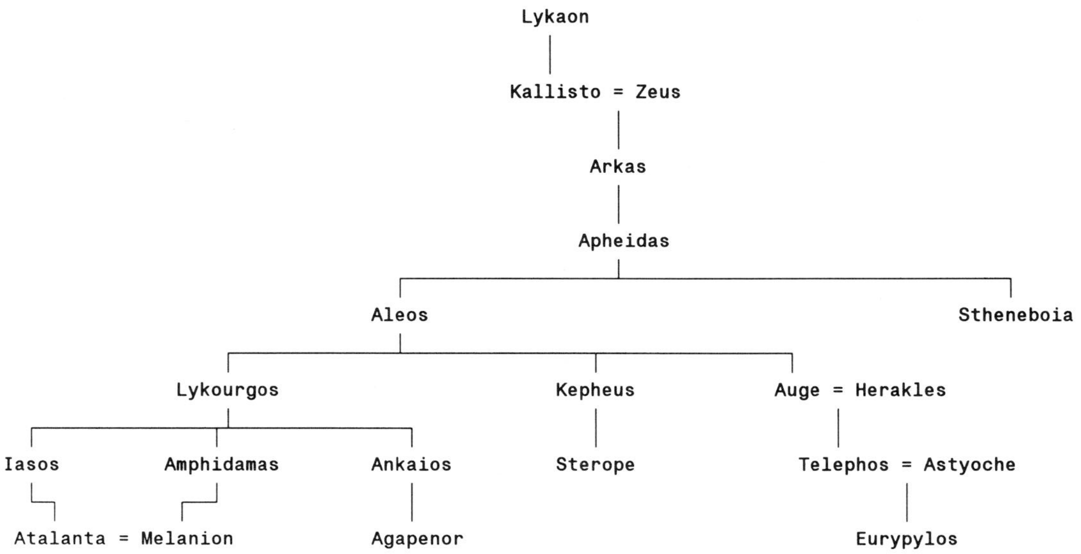

Lykaon

Kallisto = Zeus

Arkas

Apheidas

Aleos

Lykourgos

Ankaios

Agapenor

Amphidamas

Iasos

Atalanta = Melanion

Kepheus

Sterope

Auge = Herakles

Telephos = Astyoche

Eurypylos

Stheneboia

Abbreviations

A:*Hik*	Aischylos, *Hiketides (Supplices, Suppliants)*
AA	Ovid, *Ars Amatoria*
Ach	Statius, *Achilleis*
Ades	Adespota, that is, of uncertain authorship
AdvMath	Sextus Empiricus, *Pros Mathematikous (Adversus Mathematicos, Against the Scholars)*
Aen	Vergil, *Aeneid*
Ag	Aischylos, *Agamemnon*
Ai	Sophokles, *Aias*
Ais	Aischylos
Aith	*Aithiopis*
Akou	Akousilaos
Al	Alkaios
Alk	Euripides, *Alkestis*
Anab	Xenophon, *Anabasis*
And	Euripides, *Andromache*
Ant	Sophokles, *Antigone*
AntLib	Antoninus Liberalis
AP	*Palatine Anthology (Greek Anthology)*
Ap*B*	Apollodoros, *Bibliotheke (Library)*
Ap*E*	Apollodoros, *Epitome* (summary of last part of *Bibliotheke*)
Apl:*Met*	Apuleius, *Metamorphoses* (or *The Golden Ass*)
Apol	Plato, *Apologia*
ApTy	Flavius Philostratos, *Life of Apollonios of Tyana*
AR	Apollonios of Rhodes, *Argonautika*
Ar:*Lys*	Aristophanes, *Lysistrata*
Arat	Aratos, *Phainomena*
Arch	Isokrates, *Archidamos*

823

Aspis	*Aspis,* or *Shield of Herakles,* part of the Hesiodic Corpus
Astr	Hyginus, *De Astronomia*
Athen	Athenaios
AthPol	Aristotle, *Athenaion Politeia (Constitution of the Athenians)*
Aus	Recently discovered fragments of Euripides, cited according to Austin 1968
Ax	*Axiochos*
Bak	Bakchylides
Batr	Aristophanes, *Batrachoi (Ranae, Frogs)*
Bkch	Euripides, *Bakchai*
Bowra	Fragments of Pindar cited according to C. M. Bowra, *Pindari carmina* (Oxford 1947)
CarMin	Claudian, *Carmina Minora*
Cert	*Certamen Homeri et Hesiodi (The Contest between Homer and Hesiod)*
Chatzis	Fragments of Ptolemaios Chennos cited according to A. Chatzis, *Der Philosoph und Grammatiker Ptolemaios Chennos* (Paderborn 1914)
Cho	Aischylos, *Choephoroi*
Cl:*Pro*	Clement of Alexandria, *Protreptikos*
Coll	Collection
Cu	Vergil, *Culex*
Dar	Dares, *De Excidio Troiae Historia (Tale of the Fall of Troy)*
DD	Loukianos, *Dialogi Deorum (Dialogues of the Gods)*
Dem	Demosthenes
DH	Dionysios of Halikarnassos
Diehl	Fragments of Greek lyric poetry cited according to E. Diehl, *Anthologia Lyrica Graeca* 1–3 (Leipzig 1949–52)
Dik	Diktys, *Ephemeris Belli Troiani (Diary of the Trojan War)*
Div	Cicero, *De Divinatione*
DK	Testimonia and fragments of the Presocratic philosophers cited according to H. Diels and W. Kranz, *Die Fragmenta der Vorsokratiker* (6th ed., Berlin 1951)
DL	Diogenes Laertius
DMar	Loukianos, *Dialogi Marini (Dialogues of the Sea-gods)*
DMor	Loukianos, *Dialogi Mortuorum (Dialogues of the Dead)*
DP	Dion of Prusa
DS	Diodoros Siculus
E:*El*	Euripides, *Elektra*
E:*Hik*	Euripides, *Hiketides (Supplices, Suppliants)*
Ecl	Vergil, *Eclogues* (or *Bucolics*)
Epig	*Epigonoi*
Epitr	Menander, *Epitrepontes*

Eu-*Il*	Eustathios' commentary on the *Iliad*
Eu-*Od*	Eustathios' commentary on the *Odyssey*
Euag	Isokrates, *Euagoras*
Eum	Aischylos, *Eumenides*
Eum	Eumelos
Eur	Euripides
Fab	Hyginus, *Fabulae*
FGrH	Fragments of the Greek historians cited according to F. Jacoby, *Die Fragmente der griechischen Historiker* (Leiden 1923–58)
G	Vergil, *Georgics*
GLP	Fragments of more recent Greek literary papyri cited according to D. L. Page, *Select Papyri III* (London 1941)
Gomperz	Fragments of Philodemos cited according to T. Gomperz, *Herkulanische Studien 2* (Leipzig 1866)
H	*Hymn*
HAp	*Homeric Hymn to Apollo*
HAph	*Homeric Hymn to Aphrodite*
HDem	*Homeric Hymn to Demeter*
Hdt	Herodotos
Hek	Euripides, *Hekabe (Hecuba)*
Hel	Euripides, *Helen*
Hell	Hellanikos
Hepta	Aischylos, *Hepta epi Thebas (Septem contra Thebas, Seven against Thebes)*
Her	Ovid, *Heroides*
Hes	Hesiod, or rather the corpus of "Hesiodic" fragments, most of them from the *Ehoiai*, cited according to the edition of R. Merkelbach and M. L. West, *Fragmenta Hesiodea* (Oxford 1967)
HF	Euripides, *Herakles Mainomenos (Hercules Furens)*
HHerm	*Homeric Hymn to Hermes*
Hipp	Euripides, *Hippolytos*
Hkld	Euripides, *Herakleidai*
HN	Pliny, *Historia Naturalis*
HomH	*Homeric Hymn*
Hyg	Hyginus
IA	Euripides, *Iphigeneia at Aulis*
IG	Inscriptiones Graecae
Il	Homer, *Iliad*
IlMik	*Ilias Mikra (Little Iliad)*
Is	Pindar, *Isthmian Odes*

IT	Euripides, *Iphigeneia among the Tauroi*
Kaibel	Fragments of Epicharmos cited according to G. Kaibel, *Comicorum Graecorum Fragmenta* 1 (Berlin 1899)
Katast	Ps-Eratosthenes, *Katasterismoi*
Kenyon	Fragments of Hypereides cited according to the edition of F. G. Kenyon, *Hyperidis Orationes et Fragmenta* (Oxford 1907)
Kern	Fragments of Orphic writers cited according to O. Kern, *Orphicorum Fragmenta* (Berlin 1922)
Kock	Fragments of Greek comedy cited according to T. Kock, *Comicorum Atticorum Fragmenta* (Leipzig 1880–88)
Kyn	Xenophon, *Kynegetikos*
Kyp	*Kypria*
LL	Varro, *De Lingua Latina*
LP	Fragments of Sappho and Alkaios cited according to E. Lobel and D. L. Page, *Poetarum Lesbiorum Fragmenta* (Oxford 1955)
Lyk	Lykophron, *Alexandra*
Lys	Plutarch, *Lysandros*
Med	Euripides, *Medeia*
Mem	Xenophon, *Memorabilia*
Met	Ovid, *Metamorphoses*
Mim	Mimnermos
Mir	Aristotle, *Peri Thaumasiôn Akousmatôn (Mirabilia, Concerning Wondrous Things)*
Mor	Plutarch, *Moralia*
MW	Fragments of the Hesiodic Corpus cited according to R. Merkelbach and M. L. West, *Fragmenta Hesiodea* (Oxford 1967)
N²	Fragments of Euripides cited according to A. Nauck, *Tragicorum Graecorum Fragmenta* (2d ed., Leipzig 1889)
NA	Aelianus, *De Natura Animalium*
Nau	*Naupaktia*
ND	Cicero, *De Natura Deorum*
Nem	Pindar, *Nemean Odes*
Neph	Aristophanes, *Nephelai (Nubes, Clouds)*
OA	*Orphic Argonautika*
OCT	*Oxford Classical Texts*
Od	Homer, *Odyssey*
Oed	Seneca, *Oedipus*
Oik	Loukianos, *Peri tou Oikou (De Domo, On the Hall)*
OK	Sophokles, *Oidipous at Kolonos*
Ol	Pindar, *Olympian Odes*

Or	Euripides, *Orestes*
OT	Sophokles, *Oidipous Tyrannos (Oedipus Rex, Oedipus the King)*
Pa	Pindar, *Paians*
Pac	Pacuvius
Pal	Palaiphatos
Panath	Isokrates, *Panathenaikos*
Par	Parthenios
Paus	Pausanias
PCG	Fragments of Greek comedy cited according to R. Kassel and C. Austin, *Poetae Comici Graeci* (Berlin 1983-)
PD	Aischylos, *Prometheus Desmotes (Prometheus Vinctus, Prometheus Bound)*
PEG	Fragments of early Greek epic cited according to the edition of A. Bernabé, *Poetae Epici Graeci* 1 (Leipzig 1987)
Per	Plutarch, *Perikles*
Pf	Fragments of Kallimachos cited according to Pfeiffer 1949
Ph	Sophokles, *Philoktetes*
Pher	Pherekydes of Athens
PHerc	Papyrus fragments from Herculaneum
Phil	Philochoros
Pho	Euripides, *Phoinissai (Phoinician Women)*
PMG	Fragments of the Greek lyric poets cited according to D. L. Page, *Poetae Melici Graeci* (Oxford 1962)
Poet	Aristotle, *Poetics*
Pol	Plato, *Politikos*
Pow	Fragments of Euphorion and other Hellenistic poets cited according to J. U. Powell, *Collectanea Alexandrina* (Oxford 1925)
POxy	Papyrus fragments from Oxyrhynchus in Egypt, as published in the *Oxyrhynchus Papyri* series (London 1898-)
Prop	Propertius
Prot	Plato, *Protagoras*
PRylands	Papyrus fragments in the John Rylands Library in Manchester
PSI	Papyrus fragments published in the Papiri Greci e Latini series (Pubblicazioni della Societa italiana, Florence 1912-)
Py	Pindar, *Pythian Odes*
QS	Quintus of Smyrna
R	Fragments of Aischylos' or Sophokles' lost plays, cited according to S. Radt's *Tragicorum Graecorum Fragmenta* editions (Göttingen 1985, 1977)
Rep	Plato, *Republic*
Rh	Euripides, *Rhesos*

Rhet	Aristotle, *Rhetoric*
Rib	Fragments of Roman tragedy cited according to O. Ribbeck, *Tragicorum Romanorum Fragmenta* (Leipzig 1897)
Rose	Fragments of Aristotle cited according to V. Rose, *Aristotelis qui ferebantur librorum fragmenta* (Stuttgart 1886)
RP	Claudian, *De raptu Proserpinae*
S: *El*	Sophokles, *Elektra*
Sal	Loukianos, *De Saltatione*
Sen: *Ag*	Seneca, *Agamemnon*
Sen: *Med*	Seneca, *Medea*
Sen: *Ph*	Seneca, *Phaedra*
Sen: *Tro*	Seneca, *Troades*
Sim	Simonides
SLG	Recently discovered fragments of the Greek lyric poets cited according to D. L. Page, *Supplementum Lyricis Graecis* (Oxford 1974)
SM	Fragments of Pindar or Bakchylides cited according to the Teubner editions of B. Snell and H. Maehler (Pindar: Leipzig 1975 [4th ed.]; Bakchylides: Leipzig 1970 [10th ed.])
Sn	Fragments of minor Greek tragedians cited according to B. Snell, *Tragicorum Graecorum Fragmenta* 1 (Göttingen 1971)
Sol	Plutarch, *Solon*
Soph	Sophokles
Sph	Aristophanes, *Sphekes (Vespae, Wasps)*
St: *Theb*	Statius, *Thebais*
Stes	Stesichoros
Str	Strabo
Sym	Plato, *Symposion*
TD	Cicero, *Tusculan Disputations*
Tel	*Telegoneia*
test	*testimonia*
Th	Hesiod, *Theogony*
Theb	*Thebais*
Theog	Theognis
Theok	Theokritos
Ther	Nikandros, *Theriaka*
Thes	Plutarch, *Theseus*
Thouk	Thoukydides
Tib	Suetonius, *Tiberius*
Tim	Plato, *Timaios*
Tit	*Titanomachia*

Tr	Sophokles, *Trachiniai (Women of Trachis)*
Tro	Euripides, *Troades (Trojan Women)*
VF	Valerius Flaccus, *Argonautica*
VH	Aelianus, *Varia Historia*
VM	Vatican Mythographer
W	Fragments of elegiac and iambic poets cited according to M. L. West, *Iambi et Elegi Graeci* (Oxford 1971)
Westermann	Mythological texts (assigned to Libanius and Nonnos) cited according to Westermann 1843
W&D	Hesiod, *Works & Days*

Notes

Preface

1. H. J. Rose, *A Handbook of Greek Mythology*, 5th ed. (London 1953); K. Kerényi, *The Gods of the Greeks* (London 1951) and *The Heroes of the Greeks* (London 1959), both translated from the original German. Most exhaustive of all in this respect is the multivolume *Griechische Mythologie* (Preller and Robert 1894; Robert 1920–26). Here copious citations are given, sometimes in the text, sometimes in footnotes, and the present volume is much indebted to that work. Given its age, however, it is inevitably dated in some places, especially with regard to works of art, and it aims at reconstructions not attempted here. On the need to consider myths closely in the context of their sources, Wilamowitz's essay "Die griechische Heldensage I" (*SB* Berlin [1925] 41–62) is still the best account.

2. See now West 1985.

Chapter 1. The Early Gods

1. For the *Theogony*, M. L. West's introduction and commentary (West 1966) is still the most essential tool, and the present chapter is in various ways greatly indebted to it.

2. On this poem see, in addition to A. Bernabé's 1987 edition of the fragments, Gigon's essay on the literary evidence and its relationship to the *Theogony* in Dörig and Gigon 1961.

3. We do not in fact know whether the Epic Cycle was prefaced by a non-Hesiodic *Theogony* distinct from the *Titanomachia* ascribed to Eumelos or Arktinos; see bibliography in Bernabé 1987.8, and as well his Cyclus Epicus *testimonia* 6, where Philo speaks of Cyclic Theogonies *and* Titanomachies. West (1983.125–31) has recently argued that such a *Theogony* did exist, being made up from several "Orphic" accounts (see Appendix A of the present work), and was added to the rest of the Cycle in the Hellenistic period. The matter remains open, however.

4. On the nature and date of the material ascribed to Epimenides, see West 1983. 45–53.

5. Ibid., 39–44.

6. See n. 3 above.

7. Kirk, Raven, and Schofield 1983.34–44.

8. See Brommer 1967.34–35.

9. See Schefold 1981.199–201.

10. The manuscripts have for the last two names (or one name?) Hestia and Ere-

thousa, sometimes emended as one to Hesperethousa; for later sources with that form (ascribed to Hesiod) see Merkelbach and West on Hesiod fr 360 *(dubium)*.

11. So C. F. Russo, with arguments from F. Schwarz, in his commentary on the poem (1965.142–43).

12. On the difficult first line of this fragment with its notion that Helen is someone's third child, see the fuller discussion of Helen's birth in chapter 11; she is in any case surely not the third child of Nemesis.

13. For this reading of Philodemos' fragmentary text (now accepted by Bernabé), with Zeus in the form of a goose, not swan, see W. Luppe, *Philologus* 118 (1974) 193–202.

14. For the possibility that Eris also appears on one of the Foce del Sele metopes, see Van Keuren 1989.103–9.

15. So West (1966 at *Theogony* 18), with linguistic and morphological arguments cited for this conclusion.

16. So too Orphic fr 58 Kern, where only the males are swallowed.

17. West (1983.117–21) would make this work which the *Timaios* reflects his Orphic "Eudemian" Theogony of the last third of the fifth century, a poem which he believes may have begun with Nyx and made both Phorkys and Dione Titans in the place of Okeanos and Tethys: see Appendix A. Presumably he believes such material to go back in some form to Homer and beyond.

18. On this characteristic of the Homeric poems, see Griffin 1977.

19. See n. 17 above.

20. Although there is some debate on this topic. A. L. Brown (*CQ* 34 [1984] 260–76) summarizes the evidence for the cults of the three sets of goddesses and concludes that while Aischylos may have interpreted the Semnai Theai as "reformed Erinyes," Erinyes and Eumenides were not in fact equated by anyone until Euripides' *Orestes* of 408 B.C. By contrast, H. Lloyd-Jones (*Owls to Athens: Essays on Classical Subjects presented to Sir Kenneth Dover* [Oxford 1990] 203–11) argues that the Erinyes embraced the roles (and names) attributed to both the Semnai Theai and the Eumenides long before Aischylos.

21. The word *iris* also appears as a substantive twice in the *Iliad* with the meaning "rainbow" (*Il* 11.26–28; 17.546–48), but nothing suggests that this sense was associated with the goddess.

22. So too on a Red-Figure cup in the manner of the Pistoxenos Painter from the New York market Iris stands alone (or approached by Dionysos on the other side) holding a bull's tongue (Sotheby NY: 18 June 1991 no. 73). For the Boston and Berlin pots, see Brommer 1959.126–29 and figs. 17 and 18.

23. E. Simon, in *The Eye of Greece: Studies in the Art of Athens* (ed. D. Kurtz and B. Sparkes [Cambridge 1982], 125–29), argues in fact that Iris has been sent by Hera precisely to steal away the offerings to Zeus' son Dionysos, and that the Satyroi attack her for that reason, not out of lust. Moreover, Simon sees the two sides of London E65 as part of the same satyr play, with Hera on the reverse similarly threatened because of her jealousy against Dionysos, and Herakles saving the whole situation.

24. On this Porkos see Page (1951.38–40), who concludes that he is an early Lakonian sea god eventually equated with Nereus.

25. On the obvious possibilities that this Kentauros Medousa relates in some way to the mating with Poseidon and the birth of Pegasos, see the discussion in Hampe

1936.58–67, where such ideas are, I think, rightly rejected in favor of the Kentauros as a form indicating simply Medousa's monstrosity.

26. Hampe (1935/36.277–84) argues against these features as distorted and in fact would make the "Chrysaor" of the pediment in reality Perseus; the lack of distinctive iconography for the latter is not perhaps a serious problem so early, but the small size of such a Perseus vis-à-vis Medousa surely remains one. On the supposed Chrysaor birth of Louvre E857 (Tyrrhenian amphora), see Hampe 1935/36.296.

27. See West 1966.250–51 (at l. 304).

28. For this last possibility see E. Siegmann, *Hermes* 96 (1968–69) 755–57.

29. Moret (1984) offers an exhaustive catalogue of scenes portraying the Sphinx in the Oidipous legend, with numerous illustrations. See also the remarks of Vermeule 1979.171–73.

30. See West 1983.47–49.

31. Hyginus says (*Astr* 2.6.1) that Panyasis also spoke of a combat between the two, but it is not clear whether Zeus here intervened before Herakles could triumph.

32. Though Schefold (1981.320) objects that such a locally oriented Attic legend will not have been shown on a Korinthian artifact of this date; he supposes Pausanias mistaken and suggests Typhoeus or some such figure (but does Typhoeus ever carry off maidens?).

33. On Hekate's role in the *Theogony*, see now J. S. Clay, *GRBS* 25 (1984) 27–38.

34. Solmsen 1981; see the discussion of Iphigeneia's sacrifice in chapter 16.

35. On the Aischylos passage see in particular Friis Johansen and Whittle 1980 3.41–43.

36. For this triple form see Kraus 1960.102–12. S. Karouzou proposes another possible appearance of Hekate (in Hades) with her lower body turning into dogs on a Black-Figure lekythos of the fifth century (Athens 19765), and suggests such appendages as the original concept from which two additional human bodies developed (*JHS* 92 [1972] 64–73).

37. So G. Thomson (1932.151–32) and M. Griffith (1983.147) in their commentaries on the play, against views such as those expressed by Wilamowitz (1914.121) and Unterberger (1968.58–59) that Okeanos played a major role (with or against Zeus) in the Titanomachy.

38. On this problem see Taplin (1977.270–72), where it is argued that they remain with Prometheus.

39. See Diggle's arguments in the introduction to his edition of the fragments of Euripides' lost *Phaethon* (1970.10–15).

40. Though West (1985.105) prefers to assign this fragment to the Hesiodic *Astronomia*.

41. So first Wilamowitz in his reconstruction of the play (*Hermes* 18 [1883] 412–16), in part on the supposition that Euripides conflated the two separate Phaethons (Hesiod's Phaethon carried off by Aphrodite and the Phaethon son of Helios) to create his plot. Webster in his discussion of the play (1967.227–30) tends to agree, but Diggle rightly objects (1970.155–60) to the incredibility of such an unequal match, especially when Merops, the marriage's arranger, knows nothing of his son's real father. H. Weil's suggestion (revived by Diggle) that a daughter of Helios (thus Phaethon's half-sister?) was instead the proposed bride cannot be proved, but it provides a certain logical economy, and the correct answer must be a minor goddess of that sort.

42. For this *Fabula* and a full discussion of its possible relationship to both Hesiod and Aischylos, see Diggle 1970.15–32; the present summary owes much to his suggestions, particularly with regard to the possibility of an early (though for him not Hesiodic) version in which Phaethon has no father other than Helios.

43. Page (1955.273–74) suggests in fact two separate Endymions, a Western king of Elis taken up to Olympos (where he falls in love with Hera) and an Eastern youth of Asia Minor visited by Selene as he sleeps.

44. Schefold 1981.294–97.

45. This is usually, and I believe correctly, identified as Selene, but Schefold (ibid., 93–94) does object that she is more commonly shown on horseback; he would make the female figure in scenes with a chariot Nyx.

46. For this series of fifth-century vases see Kaempf-Dimitriadou 1979.81–86, 91–92, and discussion at 16–18.

47. Ibid., 87–90.

48. The one possible (but highly questionable) illustration of the birth in art occurs on a Theban relief amphora of the early seventh century: two smaller figures cling (one on each side) to a larger, frontally facing woman who holds her hands up in the air (Athens 5898). Hampe (1936.56–58) takes this woman to be a *potnia therôn*; Simon (1985.57–59) calls her Hera in the act of receiving a new garment from attendants.

49. See n. 16 above.

50. West 1983.195, adducing fifth- and fourth-century examples of the phrase *proskunôn tên Adrasteian* ("yielding to Necessity").

51. See Burkert 1985.177–79.

52. West 1983.75–101 and, for this point in particular, 93–94.

53. Note also *Iliad* 4.59, where Hera claims to be Kronos' oldest daughter. Presumably she means oldest after the disgorging, but perhaps Homer here is not thinking about the swallowing.

54. R. Mondi (*GRBS* 25 [1984] 325–44) makes the attractive suggestion that originally Zeus' personal defeat of Kronos and the war between all the Olympians and the Titans were separate and exclusive ways of describing the transfer of power from the older to the younger generation. Because in the latter account Kronos played no special role, being just one of many Titans, Hesiod had no tales to relate about his participation, and did not bother to create any. *Prometheus Desmotes* 201–3 may possibly reflect this latter situation, although I suspect that Aischylos there has reshaped the conflict into a more political situation for his own purposes. The Epimenides *Theogony*, on the other hand, may have Zeus alone in mind when it says that Aigikeros was with Zeus on Ida when he marched against the Titans (3B24).

55. On the Kerkyra pediment figures, see Dörig's assessment in Dörig and Gigon 1961.21–29. Here and elsewhere in his survey of evidence he strongly (and ingeniously) advocates the possibility of scenes from a Titanomachy, but I confess I am not convinced. The giant figure threatened by Zeus in the corresponding right corner of the pediment could at this early date surely be meant as a Gigas or Typhoeus, and even if it is a Titan, I do not believe that the left-corner scene need derive from the same series of events. In any event (as Schefold 1964.51 has already noted) the interpretation of the seated figure as Rheia (threatened by Poseidon) can scarcely be correct; Rheia has already placed herself squarely on the side of her children against their father. Nor is it credible that in her unarmed seated condition anyone would need to attack her (for convincing arguments that the figure is in fact male see Ridgway 1977.194). For the Lakonian cup in

Athens see now Pipili 1987.31–32 (cat. no. 88). Kronos is certainly possible here (two men seem to coerce an older, larger figure between them) but, as Pipili notes, several other interpretations are also quite feasible (she supports Menelaos and Proteus). The gap in the upper-right corner unfortunately prevents us from grasping the full significance of the gestures.

56. Gigon (n. 2 above) does everything that can reasonably be done toward assessing the value of the incidental details provided by these fragments.

57. Probably also Simonides, although the name of the person holding *ouranos* on his shoulders is missing (556 *PMG*). Atlas was also portrayed on the Chest of Kypselos, where Pausanias says he supports both earth and sky (5.18.4); probably he has misinterpreted the curved section or globe used by the artist to represent the sky (West 1966.311).

58. So in their editions or commentaries on the *Works & Days* Rzach (1913), Wilamowitz (1928), Mazon (1928), Sinclair (1932), Colonna (1959), West (1978, with the fullest commentary), and Verdenius (1985). The lines in some texts are numbered 169a-c, as their intended position is not always certain.

59. On these see Payne 1931.76–77.

60. Buschor (1934), followed by Schefold (1964.27) and Amyx (1988.367), among others, argues for Typhoeus, since Zeus attacking an ordinary Kentauros would be unparalleled (and pointless). Fittschen (1969.119–23) makes the objection to the supposed thunderbolt as unconventional in form; he would see here rather a firebrand, and the scene would be Herakles in the cave of Pholos. His point has some merit, but the grip on the object in question seems dubious for a firebrand. Dörig (Dörig and Gigon 1961.38–39) suggests from the lack of snakes that Zeus' opponent is actually Kronos. The interpretation of Zeus and Typhoeus has also been applied by Buschor to the Late Geometric bronze statuette group in New York showing a man and Kentauros (NY 17.190.2072). But here (with a sword tip visible on the thigh of the Kentauros), there is no compelling reason to think of Zeus rather than Herakles (save perhaps the group's findspot at Olympia).

61. On this scholion see Kirk, Raven, and Schofield 1983.59–60.

62. The belief of Schefold (1964.13; cf. Fittschen 1969.129–31) that this unusual scene is indeed the birth of Athena seems now confirmed by E. Simon's discovery of traces of a beard around the edges of the restored chin (*AntK* 25 [1982] 35–38).

63. So Friis Johansen and Whittle 1980 2.287, with full discussion of the alternatives.

64. Kirk (1985.217) suggests that maiming and deprivation should be understood together, thus that the Mousai somehow paralyze their victim and prevent him from playing his lyre.

65. For this scholion (at line 916 of a newly discovered page of a text of the play) see H. Rabe, *RhM* 63 (1908) 419–20.

66. For the theory that the scholiasts in question mistakenly derived the notion of wondrous eyes from the account of this mask, which in reality was designed to show the singer before (the black side) and after (the gray) blinding, see Pearson 1917 1.177–78, Séchan 1926.193 n. 9, Trendall and Webster 1971.69. I am not myself entirely convinced, in part because so many sources stress that the Mousai took Thamyris' eyes, rather than simply blinding him: see, for example, Konon 26F1.7, where they are gouged out.

Chapter 2. The Olympians

1. Despite Griffith's admirable reevaluation (1977) of the evidence for the author-ship of this play, I still believe that its basic plot is the work of Aischylos, even if the text has been reworked or completed by someone else (his son?). On the place of the play's characterization of Zeus within the overall framework of Aischylos' thought, see Gantz 1981.

2. Against interpretation of this and other passages in Aischylos as indications of an unusually elevated view of Zeus, see H. Lloyd-Jones, *JHS* 76 (1956) 55–67.

3. Asklepiades surely erred in attributing this passage to Aischylos' *Xantriai:* see K. Latte, *Philologus* 97 (1948) 47–56, and my arguments below in chapter 14 (plus Gantz 1981.25).

4. Kaempf-Dimitriadou 1979.26. See also chapter 7.

5. So Willcock (1978.192) and Kirk (1985.80) on the *Iliad* line in their commen-taries on the poem; Russo (1965.120) argues that Theseus in the *Aspis* is genuine, and that the line was transferred from there to the *Iliad.*

6. On the presumed original separation of Persephone and Kore see G. Zuntz, *Persephone: Three Essays on Religion and Thought in Magna Graeca* (Oxford 1971) 75–83, where Persephone is envisaged as a pre-Greek Underworld goddess with links perhaps to fertility.

7. For this Hymn, see N. J. Richardson's excellent 1974 introduction and commen-tary, the former including a very full account of later versions of the abduction (74–86).

8. Though Schefold (1981.259) suggests that fragments of a Black-Figure oinochoe from the Cahn Collection (912) in Basel should be so interpreted, based on the belief that the chariot into which the man lifts the woman is in process of entering a cave.

9. See Kaempf-Dimitriadou 1979.35–36, and for a survey of the theft in fifth-century and later art Lindner 1984.

10. Lindner 1984.45–46.

11. Jane Harrison (1922.276–83) suggests that a certain *contaminatio* has here taken place, with the hammers used for the creation of Pandora transferred to the break-ing up of the ground for Persephone. More recent discussion appears in Bérard (1974), who argues that rites of epiphany rather than an *anodos* proper (or any specific myth) are involved.

12. See Richardson 1974.194–96.

13. For the development of the Triptolemos-in-chariot motif see Peschlow-Bindokat 1972.78–85.

14. West ad loc. in his commentary (1978.276) offers other examples of a Zeus Chthonios who must be the sky god, and points out parallels for the separation of a god-plus-title from the god himself.

15. See H. von Prott, *AM* 24 (1899) 241–66, and especially 252; of the supposed dative *Ploutoni* only the letters -*ni* survive, followed by *theoin* ("the two goddesses").

16. See M. Robertson in *Greek Vases in the J. Paul Getty Museum* 5 (Malibu 1991) 75–98.

17. On this figure in art see Schauenburg 1953.38–60; he would identify the name "Plouton" exclusively with the Underworld god carrying a cornucopia, and suppose a development from Hades to Plouton similar to that of the Erinyes to Eumenides.

18. On all aspects of this god, in literature as well as in art, see Brommer 1978.

19. See West (1966.401–3), who suggests that this anger might have been due to

Teiresias' verdict on the relative enjoyment of sex by men and women in the *Melampodia*.

20. On Alkaios' poem, and especially the ascription of 349b LP to him rather than to Sappho, see Page 1955.268–71, where the text of "Libanius" is also quoted in full and translated.

21. On Hephaistos' return, see the list and discussion in Brommer 1937b, updated in Brommer 1978.198–204, and as well the discussion in Carpenter 1986.15–27. Regarding the amphoriskos in Athens, Carpenter objects that the interpretation cannot be certain when similarly crippled figures populate so much of Corinthian vase-painting (15–17).

22. Wilamowitz (*NGG* [1895] [Phil.-Hist. Klasse] 220–22) argues that this version goes back to Alkaios and ultimately to a major Ionic poem of the seventh century. His view that Ares would have received Aphrodite, had he succeeded in bringing back Hephaistos, creates however an awkward imbalance of logic, since not Dionysos but Hephaistos then wins her. We might better suppose that Zeus authorized Dionysos to promise Aphrodite's hand if Hephaistos came back; thus, at the mere sight of Hephaistos returning, the goddess knows she is lost.

23. So Schefold 1981.127, though the left-hand combatant is here named Daidalos, not Hephaistos. But since the other two figures are clearly inscribed as Ares and Hera, "Daidalos" as a epithet or alternate name for Hephaistos seems unavoidable.

24. For a complete list of Hephaistos' (relatively insignificant) children, see Brommer 1978.137 with preceding index.

25. Certainly he appears (left of Zeus, moving away with axe) on the Madrid puteal sometimes (but by no means always) taken as reproducing the pediment's composition: see Brommer 1963.108–9.

26. Lloyd-Jones 1957.541–56, working from the assumption that Hephaistos can be called Daidalos (see also n. 23 above).

27. Kirk (1985.114) suggests "curved . . . on both sides, that is, severely bow-legged." See also Hainsworth 1982.274. The scholia at *Odyssey* 8.300, after translating as "lame in both legs," note that some take the expression allegorically, because a dying fire is said to "limp."

28. Incompatible with all these accounts, it would seem, is the story in the Aristophanes scholia that Halirrhothios, son of Poseidon, tried to cut down Athena's olive tree on the Akropolis (because this cost his father patronage of the city) but struck himself by mistake and died (Σ *Neph* 1005). The same tale appears in Servius, where the blade of the axe comes loose as Halirrhothios swings it and cuts off his head; Poseidon charges Ares as in other versions (Σ *G* 1.18).

29. For a general catalogue and discussion of Ares in art, see Beck 1984.

30. Cicero, describing the various multiple figures denoted by the traditional names of Greek gods, includes an Athena, daughter of Pallas, who killed her father when he made an attempt on her virginity and is shown with wings on her ankles (*ND* 3.59). For Clement of Alexandria, in a similar context, this Athena (daughter of Pallas and the Oceanid Titanis) slew her father impiously *(dussebôs)* and wears his skin as a cloak or fleece (Cl:*Pro* 2.28). The scholia at Lykophron 355 include all these details (agreeing with Cicero that Pallas sought to rape his daughter); they add as well that Pallas had wings that Athena attached to her feet, and that she wore his skin as the aigis.

31. See Kirk 1985.394 and the scholia cited by him at *Iliad* 4.515 (A) and 8.39 (bT: Athena given to the river Triton to raise).

32. Kirk 1985.133.

33. Kirk (ibid., 162) suggests a shield covered with a goatskin, at least in Homer.

34. West 1978.366–68, pointing out as well that if the first part of the epithet referred to the aigis, the formation ought to be from *aigido-*, not *aigio-*. His own suggestion is that this first part (from *aix*) refers to a bird that served as an omen of coming storms, and which was imagined to be ridden by the sky god who brought those storms.

35. See n. 30 above for the idea in later authors that the aigis was the skin of Athena's father, Pallas.

36. On theriomorphic gods (or the lack of them) in Greek religion, see Burkert 1985.64–66.

37. For Orpheus, see chapter 18.

38. At line 212, the Medicean manuscript reads *Zênos ornis*, "bird of Zeus," emended in the *OCT* text of Page (and others) to *Zênos inis*, "child of Zeus," so that Apollo, not the eagle, becomes the entity compared to the sons. The manuscript reading is retained by Friis Johansen and Whittle (see their commentary at 1980 2.170–72) and in the new Teubner edition of Aischylos' plays by Martin West (Stuttgart 1990).

39. On the status of these as originally separate poems, see Janko 1982.99–100.

40. The so-called Creusa from the series of Etruscan terracotta acroterial sculptures found in the Portonaccio sanctuary at Veii (end of the sixth century B.C.) has also been taken to be Leto with the child Apollo on her shoulder, since the figure does carry a male child (only lower half preserved) and the series includes (in some context) fragments of a snake; see M. Pallottino, *ArchClass* 2 (1950) 122–78 and I. Krauskopf in *LIMC* 2:338.

41. Roughly the same scene appears on fragments of a stamnos by the Triptolemos Painter, with Idas, Marpessa, and Euenos all named and the latter seizing Apollo by the wrist to hinder his shot (fragments in Florence and the Louvre): see J. Beazley in *Charites: Studien zur Altertumswissenschaft*, ed. K. Schauenburg (Bonn 1957) 136–39.

42. See West 1985.69–72.

43. For the Cumaean Sibyl hanging in a jar *(ampulla)* and expressing the desire to die, our only source is Petronius' *Satyricon* 48; presumably she has shriveled up in the manner of Tithonos.

44. Kyrene and the lion may also have appeared in the pediment of the Treasury of Kyrene at Olympia: see Pipili 1987.37 and n. 376.

45. See West 1985.85–87. Janko (1982.248 n. 38) suggests, however, that even the transfer to Libya could have preceded the Theran colony.

46. Only in Ovid (where the girl is Chione, daughter of Daidalon: *Met* 11.301–27) do we receive any details of this mating with two gods. Predictably Apollo is the one there fooled: see below, pp. 109–10.

47. Schefold (1978.49) prefers Hyakinthos and Periboia, because of both the cup's provenance and the delicate appearance of the male. But see Pipili 1987.12.

48. For this and other such suggested scenes of Hyakinthos on vases see the discussion by H. Sichtermann (*JdI* 71 [1956] 116–23), who takes a properly cautious view of many of them.

49. For all phases of this myth in art see Schauenburg 1958.42–66.

50. For the Olympia tripod leg and a list of other early scenes showing a combat in the presence of a tripod, see Fittschen 1969.28–32. His own conclusion is that tripods would not have distinctively characterized Apollo before dedications of them to various other gods ceased (toward the end of the eighth century B.C.), and thus that such scenes are representations of athletic contests, be they from everyday life or myth.

51. See Burkert 1985.144–45; Hutchinson (1985.68–69) argues that the name was certainly taken to denote wolves in the Classical period.

52. So Lloyd-Jones 1983.119–21. I do not myself believe this to have been the reason, and Lloyd-Jones does not explain why Apollo in particular should be offended by such behavior, but it remains a possibility.

53. See Gantz 1981.21–22, 31–32.

54. From Ovid and Hyginus only survives the tale of her slaying of Chione (or Philonis), daughter of Daidalon, because the latter boasted of greater beauty (*Met* 11.321–27) or better skill in the hunt (*Fab* 200).

55. See West 1966.223–24.

56. Kirk (1990.94–95) suggests that this concentration may be due to metrical considerations arising out of Aphrodite's special role here.

57. See West 1966.88.

58. This seems the only preserved occasion on which a god pointedly lies to another god, although Zeus may have returned the favor by dissimulating on the subject of his relationship with Io in the *Ehoiai*: Hes fr 124 MW.

59. Theophrastos' earlier reference (*Characteres* 16) to someone frequently crowning the Hermaphroditoi refers presumably to the crowning of Herms, so that the term was perhaps originally used of these figures.

60. West (1978.368–69) revives the idea that the word means "dog-slayer," pointing out that watchdogs are the primary enemies of Hermes as nocturnal thief (or patron of such). He also suggests that Argos, the watcher of Io, may have originally been a dog.

61. Pausanias calls this Daidalon the real father of Autolykos, whom tradition makes the son of Hermes (8.4.6).

62. The "wedding" of Hermes and Dryops' daughter is perhaps shown on Bologna 236, a Red-Figure column krater of the mid-fifth-century on which the god leads a woman (elegantly clad, with covered head) by the hand while a Silenos follows with a chest and an old woman holds torches.

63. "Epimenides" makes him in fact an offspring of Zeus and one Kallisto (as a twin, with Arkas: 3B16). Brommer (1937.7) argues that in origin the Penelope credited as Pan's mother was a Nymph, and only subsequently was this figure forgotten and in consequence equated with Odysseus' wife.

64. The late Black-Figure neck-amphora by the Diosphos Painter (CabMéd 219: name vase) may show the birth even earlier, although here the child *stands* on his father's thighs and holds torches.

65. See the analysis of the evidence by K. Deichgräber, *NGG* (1938–39) 231–309.

66. For these and other illustrations see Séchan 1926.70–75, and Trendall and Webster 1971.49–52.

67. On such scenes in general see Carpenter's fine study (1986).

68. So Ps-Libanius; see above p. 75.

69. So Carpenter, rightly, I think (1986.24). He cites evidence here and elsewhere which makes likely the identification of women paired with Dionysos (in many if not most cases) as Aphrodite, even when a child is involved. Of such vases the best known is probably London B168, where the woman holds two children who are (despite the lack of any inscriptions) often claimed to be Staphylos and Oinopion.

70. Certainly he is the same in some later sources, for example, Σ *Aeneid* 10.763, where Oinopion calls upon his father Dionysos for help against Orion.

71. Gantz 1980.154–58.

72. See ibid. and Gantz 1981.25–26.

73. See Janko 1982.184–85.

74. For later sources see W. Burkert, *Homo Necans* (Berlin 1972) 307–8. According to the scholia at *Batrachoi* 479, during the festival of the Lenaia in Athens the god was summoned with the cry, "Semeleian Iakchos," so that here too some overlap was felt to exist, but we cannot say how much, or exactly when it began.

75. That Kallimachos probably did call the child Zagreus is endorsed by West (1983. 154), who argues for a verbal borrowing of fr 43.117 Pf by Nonnos at 6.165.

Chapter 3. Olympos, the Underworld, and Minor Divinities

1. On this topic see especially W. M. Sale, *AJP* 105 (1984) 1–28; the present brief assessment owes much to his collection and study of the evidence.

2. Ibid., 19–24.

3. So, for example, the Red-Figure versions of Oltos (Tarquinia RC 6848) and Sosias (Berlin:Ch F2278).

4. For this poem, which has been thought to concern Orpheus' descent to Hades, or Herakles' victory over Orchomenos, or even the exploits of the Argonautai, see Huxley 1969.118–20. The few fragments remaining seem to establish only that it had a substantial Underworld component that *may* have inspired a good deal of Polygnotos' painting.

5. For this and other representations of Charon, see Felten 1975.86–90.

6. Kurtz and Boardman 1971.166, 211.

7. So most scholars: see Mette 1963.170–72. The *Drapetes* was definitely satyric; one fragment alone is known from the *Petrokylistes*, and that also looks satyric, but perhaps an error has been made in attribution. Only the *Drapetes* appears in the Medicean Catalogue.

8. See West 1966.356–59, 364–65.

9. See the works cited by Heubeck 1983.302 and his own arguments for nevertheless regarding this section as structurally unified with the rest of the *Nekuia*.

10. So Russo 1965.141–42.

11. For these vases and their relationship to Polygnotos' painting, see Keuls 1974. 34–41; she herself argues against the Palermo lekythos as an Underworld scene, on the theory that purification rather than punishment is involved.

12. The question whether some heroes died and others went to the Isles of the Blessed, or all died and arrived there, seems unresolvable, given that Hesiod's grammar probably permits both: see Nicolai 1964.43–46 on the use of *men* and *de*. Those preferring the latter view argue that in its fate this fourth age should be treated as a unit, like the first three (see Bona Quaglia 1973.105–12), although Homer and the Epic Cycle certainly offer parallels for arbitrary selection. Against Solmsen's bracketing of line 166 in his *OCT* text, thus eliminating the "some" whom death covers over (arguments in *AJP* 103 [1982] 22–24), see West 1978.192.

13. See chapter 1, n. 58.

14. See Carpenter 1986.76–77.

15. For this Black-Figure dinos see R. Young, *Hesperia* 4 (1935) 430. The creature in question is ithyphallic and pursues a woman.

16. Naturally there are many other possibilities as well. Brommer, for example, suggests (1937a, *passim*) that the term *Satyros* originally applied only to the *Dichbauch-tänzer* of the seventh-century Peloponnese (referred to as such by the *Ehoiai*), while

Silênos denoted equine-tailed/-eared creatures of whatever type, both those with equine legs and those with human ones. According to this view the "Silenoi," though not at first connected with Dionysos, eventually found their way into early Attic tragedy, but when Pratinas brought them back for his farces he called them by the name familiar to him in the Peloponnese for Dionysos' companions, namely "Satyroi." The same author also has valuable material on later uses of the two terms (1937a.2–5).

17. For these metopes see Zancani Montuoro and Zanotti-Bianco 1954.141–66. Van Keuren (1989.57–66) argues, however, that the third metope is better interpreted as Elektra and Orestes, and that the real target of these Silenoi (Hera and Herakles with a bow, or less likely Iris or Amymone) was on a metope now lost.

18. See Brommer 1959.

19. See Brommer, *AA* (1941) 36–52.

20. For this uncertainty see chapter 14; the question is not relevant for present purposes.

21. Carpenter (1986.90) emphasizes rather the moment on the Amasis Painter neck-amphora in Paris when two women unaccompanied by any Satyroi and wearing leopardskins over their *peploi* offer Dionysos a rabbit (CabMéd 222). But he does not commit himself to these as necessarily mortal women rather than Nymphai (80 n. 17). The thyrsos is first wielded by a woman companion of the god (or by anyone, for that matter) on a cup by Oltos (Tarquinia RC 6848).

22. See above chapter 1, n. 60, and for Typhoeus in particular Schefold 1964.19.

23. See V. R. Desborough, R. V. Nicholls, and M. Popham, *BSA* 65 (1970) 21–30; Desborough assigns the date as between 950 and 850 B.C. (or more likely 925 and 875) based on associated pottery.

24. See the list of Fittschen 1969.93–103 with following discussion (note that these are his *Rossmenschen* only, "horse/men" not part of any story).

25. Beazley 1951, pl. 2.

26. R. V. Nicholls' original assessment on this point is understandably cautious: "four animal legs, the front pair of which may show faint concessions to human form about the knees" (p. 25; see n. 23 above).

27. *Perachora II*, pl. 22.

28. See Schiffler 1976.37–41.

29. For surviving illustrations of Kentauros families in the fourth century, see ibid., 168.

30. See D. S. Robertson, *JHS* 71 (1951) 150–55.

31. Or, accepting Wendel's emendation of *analuontes* to *metalleuontes* (Σ AR 1. 1126), miners.

32. On these figures see also Diodoros Siculus 5.64.3–5, 17.7.5, and the anonymous fragmentary hymn to them (pp. 171–72 Pow).

Chapter 4. Prometheus and the First Men

1. See West (1978.172–77) for the customary view that the Greek Heroic Age (with perhaps a preceding era of heroes vs. monsters) has intruded into an earlier metallic system, and as well for Near Eastern parallels and possible sources.

2. For later sources that do have men born from ash-trees, see West 1966.211. The same author in his commentary on this passage from the *Works & Days* suggests that the Doric form *melian* indicates something specifically feminine in gender and thus tips the scales toward the Nymphai (1978.187).

3. The question depends on several ambiguous pronoun referents in *Works &
Days* 161–68: see p. 133 above.

4. See chapter 1, n. 58, above.

5. For Prometheus' role at Mekone, see E. Wirshbro in *GRBS* 23 (1982) 101–10.
Note also the textual uncertainty of the pronouns at *Theogony* 538 and 540: West writes
tois in the latter line, so that Prometheus actually assigns to Zeus the better share, and
Zeus, seeing the stomach on top, rejects it.

6. See in *Hésiode et son Influence* (Fondation Hardt, vol. 7: Geneva 1962) the discussion on pp. 105–6, where W. J. Verdenius makes this suggestion and Waszink and
Solmsen approve, the latter adding that Aischylos has no doubt misunderstood the
passage.

7. Discussion in Pipili (1987.34–35), who rejects attempts to see here Tityos.

8. So West 1966.313, following F. Sittl in 1889. Like others he also suggests that
the release was Athenian-inspired, probably because of a Prometheus cult there which
made it impossible for the Titan to remain imprisoned.

9. See Robert 1914.25–26. Of his arguments the strongest is also the most obvious, that *pêma* at *Works & Days* 82 should be in apposition to *dôron*, not the entire
preceding idea.

10. For this interpretation see W. J. Verdenius, *Mnemosyne* 24 (1971) 225–31
(together with his commentary on the passage: 1985.66–71) and, more precisely,
V. Leinieks, *Philologus* 128 (1984) 1–8 (although I am not entirely in accord with the
latter's suggestion that the Elpis story was originally a separate *ainos*).

11. So Karlsruhe B2591; Florence 76359; Milan (*olim* Vidoni Coll). On a fourth
vase, where the impalement seems clearest, Prometheus holds out bound hands toward
his rescuer (Berlin:Ch F1722).

12. Furtwängler 1885.333. Schefold (1981.30) proposes rather Artemis.

13. See A. H. Smith, *JHS* 11 (1890) 279, and pl. 11, where a drawing makes the
whole composition clear.

14. See Griffith 1977 and West, *JHS* 99 (1979) 130–48. Conacher (1980.140–74)
puts a number of the former's arguments into clearer perspective, while his pp. 175–91
should be read in conjunction with West's expressed doubts on the ability of the *Desmotes* to be staged during Aischylos' lifetime.

15. So the scholia to *Desmotes* 511.

16. See, for example, F. Focke, *Hermes* 65 (1930) 263–69, and against his conclusions about the Medicean Catalogue, T. Gantz, *RhM* 123 (1980) 210–22.

17. See Conacher 1980.100–102 for discussion, and Radt 1985.329 for lists of the
scholars ranged on each side.

18. So the scholia at *Prometheus Desmotes* 1, admitting that this is a conjecture
from the text. The same scholia also claim that such a location diverges from the usual
view in which Prometheus is imprisoned in the Caucasians. For the belief that Prometheus in the course of the trilogy is moved to the Caucasians, see below.

19. So Wilamowitz 1914.142–47.

20. It is difficult to decide whether exterior and tondo are part of the same scene.
Simon (1985.223) argues that they are, with Prometheus (linked as he is to Hephaistos
in cult) perhaps advising Hera on the need for reconciliation with her son. We may or
may not wish to remember also that in one tradition (ΣAb *Il* 14.295; ΣT *Il* 14.296),
Prometheus is Hera's son.

21. Sometimes considered to be, strictly speaking, an adaptation of a *Prometheus* by Accius. But Cicero neither says nor implies this, and I see no reason to suppose it. See further Radt 1985.310–11.

22. This is the common assumption, and I think probably a correct one, but West (n. 14 above: pp. 141–42) does argue that Gaia's name was erroneously picked up from a (potential) marginal gloss in the *Desmotes* by the person compiling the cast list for that play.

23. Lloyd-Jones 1983.97–103.

24. See above, p. 147.

25. Robert, who believes Pandora to be released from the earth in this play, supposes (1914.34–37) that she then instructed Prometheus in the making of mortal women from mud. West for his part suggests (since Σ *W&D* 89 has Prometheus receive the jar of evils from Satyroi) that what the Satyroi of this play find in the earth (while toiling as slave laborers) is in fact that jar, rather than Pandora (1978.165).

26. So, for example, Arafat (1990.61–62) suggests that Epimetheus' hammer (and artisan's tunic) are simply the result of conflation with the familiar iconography of Pandora's creator, Hephaistos.

27. So West 1985.50–51, although earlier (1978.164–66) he suggests that originally Pandora and Prometheus were indeed married, with her transfer to Epimetheus concocted to defend Prometheus' supposed forethought.

28. See chapter 5 below.

29. Nor does the quote seem to come from the beginning of the poem, but rather from a later context with Lokros and Leleges under discussion and Deukalion mentioned only as part of their story.

30. The curious tale that Deukalion performed a lover's leap into the sea to resolve his mad passion for Pyrrha seems to survive only in Ovid (*Her* 15.167–70).

31. That Prometheus himself created mankind also survives first in the fourth century (e.g., Herakleides Ponticus, apud *Astr* 2.42.1).

Chapter 5. The Line of Deukalion

1. See West 1985.138–44 for speculation on how these eponymous ancestors might have been developed into a unified family under Deukalion.

2. West (ibid., 56) adds in favor of this probability the argument that the *Ehoiai* by its basic organizational principle must begin from a union of mortal woman and god, and since we know that the poem started with the Deukalionidai, Pyrrha loved by Zeus is the obvious choice. See his p. 53, n. 44, for other sources supporting this arrangement.

3. See above, p. 135, on the Satyroi for the evidence for this conclusion.

4. West (1985.57–58) suggests that Xouthos and Ion have together been brought from Euboia to Athens by his presumed Athenian author of the *Ehoiai* in order to convey to the Athenians precedence over the Ionians.

5. For the various sources that combine to give us the plot of this drama, see Webster 1967.157–60.

6. West (1985.32) reiterates earlier arguments that the *Nekuia's* source for the Aiolid section of its catalogue of woman is in fact Book 1 of the *Ehoiai*.

7. On Salmoneus as originating in Elis but somehow gravitating to the family of Kretheus and Thessaly (because both lands possess an Enipeus river?) see Robert 1916. 290–92; 1920–26.41); his links with Elis would then be explained by having him (as

here in Apollodoros) migrate back to that land. See also West (1985.140–42), who offers a more general picture of the amalgamation of Aiolos' family and supposes the Elean Enipeus to have been Tyro's original lover.

8. Schefold (1981.158) supposes the chain to indicate that Salmoneus has had himself fettered so that he might show off his strength. Earlier Robert (1920–26.203) had suggested the vase to mean that Salmoneus' people imprisoned him on Zeus' command, but that at the moment shown he has broken free and, wearing the greave like an aigis and brandishing a wooden thunderbolt, prompts Zeus' final punishment.

9. West (1985.142–43) suggests that Neleus alone (or with Amythaon?) was in origin the offspring of Salmoneus' daughter and the (Elean) Enipeus, and that only his mother's subsequent journey north to mate instead with the Thessalian river necessitated his migration back to the Peloponnese.

10. Robert (1916.298–301) hypothesizes, based on a Roman grave relief, that the plot of the first play was the discovery by Kretheus of the birth and exposure of Tyro's children soon after the fact, in contrast to the second where those children are reuinted with their mother only after they are grown, and must save her from Sidero (273–87). Pearson (1917 2.270–74) offers a more cautious assessment of the evidence which indicates some of the difficulties in supposing two separate plots, given what remains.

11. So Robert 1920–26.39.

12. In the paintings of the Etruscan François Tomb at Vulci, and possibly also in the Tomba dell' Orco (chamber II) at Tarquinia, a small winged figure likewise hovers over Sisyphos: see Steingräber 1984.380 and 334.

13. See Pipili 1987.35–36.

14. See Sinn 1979.114 (MB 58).

15. On this hypothesis and that for *Phrixos A* in the same papyrus see also the remarks of H. Lloyd-Jones, *Gnomon* 35 (1963) 441–42.

16. For this metope see de La Coste-Messelière 1936.172–74, 118–19; he suggests that it may have been paired with that showing Europa and the bull and with a conjectured third metope showing Bellerophontes and Pegasos (horse's leg only preserved).

17. Also of the fifth century, and earlier than this neck-amphora, are several representations on which Phrixos is likewise pulled along (through water?) by the ram, but without the stepmother: so, for example, a Melian relief (Athens 4196: see Jacobsthal 1931.38) and a Red-Figure cup (Berlin:PM VI 3289: Jacobsthal 1931.187 fig. 60). For Phrixos generally in Greek art see Schauenburg 1958.

18. Helle may possibly appear by herself on the ram on several other fifth-century Melian reliefs, if Jacobsthal's interpretation (1931.53) is correct. But of course we must ask why she would be so portrayed without Phrixos. Certainly, though, on coins of Halos in Thessaly she is shown alone with the ram in such a fashion: see Head 1911. 295–96, plus E. Rogers, *The Copper Coinage of Thessaly* (London 1932) 83–86.

19. So West 1985.67 n. 86; at 156 he suggests that Oibalos' marriage to Gorgophone is an attempt to link the Amyklaian dynasty with Perseus' prestigious Mycenaean clan.

20. Ibid., 65–66.

21. D. S. Robertson argues in fact that in the beginning the ram was always supposed to swim to Kolchis, rather than flying (*CR* 54 [1940] 1–8). Although he omits the references to Simonides and Akousilaos, he does cite numerous later writers (beginning with Palaiphatos) for whom the ram does indeed swim, and much of the artistic evidence

(see n. 17 above) points in the same direction. Apollodoros is perhaps the most notable source to claim that the creature could fly (ApB 1.9.1).

22. POxy 2245 frr 14 and 16 (= Hypothesis 31 Aus) offer scraps of a hypothesis for this play, beginning with the usual marriage to Ino after that to Nephele and the stepmother's plotting against Phrixos and Helle; thus we can say that the play, like the same poet's *Phrixos B*, depended upon the Nephele-Phrixos-Ino plot. But whether that plot was again the action of the drama or only the preface to it we do not know.

23. Both the *Nekuia* and the *Ehoiai* make clear that this Periklymenos (despite the gift of Poseidon in the latter work) is Neleus' actual son. Pindar does, however, mention a Periklymenos "of the race of Poseidon" as one of the Argonautai (*Py* 4.172–75), and a figure of the same name as one of the defenders of Thebes against the Seven (*Nem* 9.26). On the first of these two occasions the scholia take the Periklymenos in question to be Neleus' offspring (called "of the race of Poseidon" because he is the god's grandson: Σ *Py* 4.306), but on the second they claim the existence of a Periklymenos, son of Poseidon, by Chloris, daughter of Teiresias, in other words, a Theban whom they specifically differentiate from the Pylian son of Neleus (Σ *Nem* 9.57). Euripides' *Phoinissai* also names Periklymenos, son of Poseidon, as one of the defenders of Thebes (*Pho* 1156–58), and that play's scholia (at another point) note in passing Chloris as one of the daughters of Teiresias (with Peisandros as source: Σ *Pho* 834 = 16F9). Seemingly, then, there were two figures of the name "Periklymenos" whose background at some point overlapped, leading to the doublet of the mother Chloris. But whether Periklymenos, son of Neleus and Chloris, was ever in reality the son of Poseidon we cannot say.

24. Robert (1920–26.766) goes even further, envisioning as the oldest form of the Argo's voyage a version in which Iason makes the journey of his own accord, and lives peacefully in Iolkos after his return.

25. So Dugas (1944.9–10), arguing that Iason's participation in the games must mean that the tradition of an ignoble death begins after this vase.

26. See Schefold 1978.178.

27. So Schauenburg 1957.210–30, where a number of other possible early illustrations of this myth are also discussed. The Yale lekythos, if relevant here, shows a figure who is probably Apollo rather than Admetos stepping into the chariot drawn by a lion, boar, wolf, and panther as Artemis (?) watches. Other scenes of this type certainly portray Kadmos and Harmonia, as we shall see in chapter 14.

28. Louvre F60, a Black-Figure neck-amphora of *c.* 540 B.C., shows Hermes, Herakles, and an unnamed woman who *may* be Alkestis: see chapter 13 on this point.

Chapter 6. Other Early Families

1. Pausanias gives the following scheme: Inachos-Phoroneus-(Niobe)-Argos-Phorbas-Triopas-Iasos-Io (2.15.5–16.1).

2. See West 1985.145–46, 150. At 153 he takes this development back still further in time to a point when Io's journey extended no further than the Argolid.

3. See above, p. 158.

4. For reconstructions of this play, see W. M. Calder III, *GRBS* 1 (1958) 137–55, who regards it as a tragedy, and D. F. Sutton, *Sophocles' Inachus* (Meisenheim am Glan 1979), where it is considered a stayr play. Both scholars do agree in seeing as the core of the play Inachos' conflict with Zeus over the treatment of his daughter. The slaying of

Argos by Hermes may also have been included if, as Sutton believes, *PTebt* 692 belongs here.

5. West 1985.147–52.

6. On this fragment, and possible alternative interpretations of its contents, see Garvie 1969.1–28.

7. See ibid., 215–23; J. K. MacKinnon, *CQ* 28 (1978) 74–82; Friis Johansen and Whittle 1980 1.30–37.

8. Admittedly a personal interpretation of a much debated question: see, in addition to the discussions in the previous note, Gantz, *Phoenix* 32 (1978) 279–87.

9. On the various proposals for the identity of this chorus, see Garvie 1969. 191–97.

10. On these see Friis Johansen and Whittle 1980 1.48.

11. A controversial passage, since *himeros* could be construed with *paidôn* to mean "desire for children" rather than "passion (for a husband)." But Aischylos certainly does not mean that Hypermestra gives herself to a repugnant spouse solely to bear a child; rather, that wish is an inextricable part of her feeling for Lynkeus.

12. Cf. fr 2 of Euripides' lost *Archelaos* (p. 13 Aus) which may (there are gaps) say the same thing.

13. P. 220 (Inscr. b) of Drachmann's edition, vol. 2 (Leipzig 1910).

14. For other later traditions see Friis Johansen and Whittle 1980 1.49–50.

15. For these vases see Keuls 1974.84–100; she contends that the women shown here are either Danaides or figures who will eventually be merged with Danaides, and that they here serve as Nymphai of water and fertility, not the uninitiated or murderesses undergoing punishment. Certainly Danaides, in any event, are the women pouring water into a pithos on Policoro 38462, a mid-fourth-century Apulian hydria, *if* the figures on the shoulder above them are in fact Poseidon and Amymone; here though (given the reeds around the pithos) the setting is probably Argos rather than the Underworld. Earlier in her book Keuls takes the motif of water-carrying back to Aischylos, where she argues that it accomplishes an earthly purification of the Danaides from bloodshed before their new marriages (68–81).

16. Perhaps also, and earliest, Lucretius, but his rationalizing passage at 3.1003–10 does not name the young female watercarriers as Danaides, and just possibly they were not yet so considered.

17. On the respective attributions to the *Ehoiai* and Pherekydes, I follow here Jacoby and the manuscripts; Merkelbach and West alter *phasin* to *phêsin* and repunctuate so that Pherekydes is cited only for Phineus as Phoinix's son, and the *Ehoiai* for the other offspring.

18. West (1985.83) considers the possibility that before the search story evolved (it's not clear when he thinks this was) Kadmos might well have been the son of Agenor and brother of Phoinix, with Europa (daughter of Phoinix as in the *Iliad* and the *Ehoiai*) his niece.

19. Of the early seventh century is a relief amphora now in Paris (CabMéd 3003); mid-sixth-century in date are metopes from the Sikyonian *monopteros* at Delphi (Delphi, no #) and an unknown structure ("Temple Y") on the akropolis at Selinous (Palermo 3915).

20. Likewise, on a White-Ground cup of about 470 B.C. the bull on which Europa rides is named as Zeus (Munich 2686).

21. See West 1985.40, 42.

22. West 1978.255.

23. Diels and Kranz quote the version of the Germanicus scholia which says (surely a mistake: see Robert's emendation) Okeanos and Aithra; Hyginus (*Astr* 2.21.2) has the correct version, also assigned to Mousaios.

24. For this and other vases representing Zeus and Aigina (twice named) see Kaempf-Dimitriadou (1979.22–24), who supposes that many if not all scenes of this period showing Zeus in pursuit of an unidentified woman should be so interpreted. Cook's belief (1925.24–29), that those in which Zeus brandishes the thunderbolt intend rather Semele, does not really fit the myth as we know it; Zeus may destroy this mortal lover unwillingly, but he does not threaten her with his thunderbolt, any more than he does Hera when he comes to her bed.

25. An Aktaios is known to later sources as the father-in-law of Kekrops I and at times as the first king of Athens (Paus 1.2.6; ApB 3.14.2). One would think him though much too early in time to be the figure intended by Pherekydes.

26. See West 1985.163.

27. The Pindaric scholia do have one version that addresses this problem, however: Menoitios is made the son not of Aktor and Aigina, but of Aktor and Damokrateia, daughter of Aigina (by Zeus: Σ *Ol* 9.104a, 106b).

28. Elsewhere Pausanias relates that prior to his death at Peleus' hands Phokos visited Iaseus in Phokis and received from the latter a ring (9.30.4); he does not, however, actually say that the ring was the motive for the slaying.

29. See von Bothmer 1957.234 (index to Telamon in Amazon scenes) for a full list.

30. See Pearson on the lost *Daidalos* of Sophokles (1917 1.110) and note as well the Apulian calyx krater with "Daidalos" fighting Ares before an enthroned Hera (London F269: see p. 76 above).

31. For this myth in vase-painting see Krieger 1975.

32. Of about the same period, perhaps, is the engraved bronze tripod leg in New York with a similar scene (NY 58.11.6: see Fittschen 1969.169). Brommer (in Böhr and Martini 1986.13–14) now questions the authenticity of this piece.

33. See A. Stewart in Moon 1983.53–74.

34. So Severyns (1928.255–59), who suggests that this was the version of the *Kypria*.

Chapter 7. The Royal House of Athens

1. See Bernabé (1987.135–36) for what little remains of this work. Aristotle may have known several such poems (*Poet* 1451.a19). A number of scholars now suppose that such an epic was composed toward the end of the sixth century at the instigation of the Alkmeonidai for political purposes against the Peisistratidai and their use of Herakles (see Jacoby 1949.394–95 n. 23; Schefold, *MH* [1946] 65–67).

2. See Brommer (1957.152–64), who suggests in fact that even the tales themselves may have developed in the fifth century, given the lack of literary and artistic evidence from earlier periods.

3. For recent views on this problem see Kron 1976.37–39.

4. West 1985.90–91.

5. Admittedly, it has long been questioned whether Harpokration has not altered an original Erechtheus to Erichthonios in reporting on these two sources in order to

conform to later usage (since in neither instance is a verbatim quote involved); so most recently ibid., 106 n. 170. But this is perhaps an excess of caution.

6. Sophokles' *Aias* 202 is often cited as a third example, but Tekmessa here simply addresses the Salaminian sailors as "of the race of the chthonian Erechtheidai," which does not quite prove the point.

7. Disputed in some quarters, since this is essentially an Attic legend: see chap. 1, n. 32, above.

8. For a detailed assessment of what Hellanikos' work might have contained see Pearson (1942.1–26), who argues that for the earliest periods he had little real material and relied on explanations of local cults and topography to fill the gaps. Jacoby (1949.127) credits him with inventing much of the list of Attic kings.

9. See Preller and Robert 1894.200 n. 2.

10. For the birth of Erichthonios in art see Kron 1976.55–67.

11. So W. R. Letharby, *JHS* 50 (1930) 7; against this view Brommer 1963.32–33 and Kron 1976.97, among others.

12. Non-Attic evidence for this tradition would seem to come from the charming Melian relief in Berlin on which Gaia hands the child to Athena as a snake-tailed Kekrops watches (Berlin:PM TC 6281); the piece has however been judged a forgery in some quarters (so Jacobsthal 1931.96–98, opposed by W. Züchner, *JdI* 65/66 [1950–51] 199–203; see further the bibliography at *LIMC* Erechtheus 23).

13. Kron 1976.67–72.

14. Possibly also a chest, or at least a rectangular object, though this is on the other side of the vase (departure of Triptolemos) together with the snake's tail.

15. So Robert 1881.89. I confess that I do not see why such a relatively obscure and insignificant figure should be shown here (in preference to, say, Kekrops' wife), but I have no better suggestion to offer.

16. A human Kekrops (so inscribed) is also to be found on a Red-Figure scene of Boreas and Oreithuia by the Oreithyia Painter in which the abductee's sisters appeal to both Erechtheus and Kekrops for help (Munich 2345). Just possibly, as Brommer notes (1957.155–56), this is Kekrops II, the brother of Oreithuia, but more likely (as he himself concludes) we are dealing with the patriarch of the family, perhaps conceived to be Erechtheus' father.

17. Possibly, of course, in those scenes (Frankfurt:Lieb ST V 7, Basel BS 404) where snake and basket alone are shown (i.e., without child) the snake itself is meant to represent Erichthonios (so, e.g., M. Schmidt, *AM* 83 [1968] 200–202). But I remain doubtful that artists would so entirely transform a child, or that that child would be made (in any form) the agent of punishment against the Kekropides.

18. So R. Philippson, *Hermes* 5 (1920) 244; against his restoration of *Kalli-* to *Kallimachos* Pfeiffer objects (1949 2.484 [*apparatus* for fr 783]), but see now A. Henrichs (*BCPE* 13 [1983] 33–43), who reads the letter *mu* after *Kalli-* (based on a firsthand inspection of the papyrus) and considers the attribution to Kallimachos of Pandrosos' transformation extremely likely (42 n. 50). The text is now to be found in *Supplementum Hellenisticum* (ed. H. Lloyd-Jones and P. Parsons: Berlin 1983) as no. 307.

19. See the commentary on this line in Owens' edition of the play (1939.91).

20. For this detail see the close-up photograph and drawing of the metope in R. Hampe and E. Simon, *The Birth of Greek Art* (Oxford 1981) figs. 109, 110.

21. Most likely neither, as West in his 1990 Teubner edition now concludes; for

other guesses see his *apparatus* ad loc. Aristotle quotes as from Aischylos a passage describing Tereus' metamorphosis, which might mean that Aischylos wrote an entire play on this theme, or only alluded to it elsewhere; in any case the quote is now widely believed to come from Sophokles' *Tereus*: see Radt 1977.437–38.

22. See p. 167 above, and note that Ion's appearance here depends on a supplement (though some offspring with a very short name is certainly required). West (1985.106) suggests that the Catalogue Poet failed to mention Apollo's involvement here because the family under discussion is that of Xouthos, not Kreousa, and that he may have appeared when Erechtheus' family was considered in Book 4. But fragment 10a.23 as restored certainly says that Kreousa bore the child to Xouthos, and for the Catalogue Poet to mingle children of two different fathers in the same line would be most unusual.

23. See Conacher 1967.273–75.

24. Though much earlier in his work Apollodoros has attested to a Kephalos, son of Deion and husband of Prokris, who is carried off by Eos: ApB 1.9.4.

25. Assuming that Nikandros' version accurately survives in AntLib 41.

26. See p. 36 above.

27. See chapter 2, n. 5, above.

28. So H. Herter, *RE* Supp. 13 (1973) 1053–57, stressing the final result as a compromise between two separate traditions. See also Sourvinou-Inwood 1979.18–21.

29. Or perhaps she too fails to understand it, since subsequently in this interview she promises Aigeus that she knows *pharmaka* that will bring him children (*Med* 716–18), and we might have expected her to then counsel abstinence until her arrival in Athens. Euripides' intentions remain uncertain; we do not even know what role Medos, the child of Aigeus and Medeia, was meant to play here.

30. See the commentary of W. S. Barrett (1964.333–34) on this line and the rationale for such shifts.

31. For the literary and artistic tradition of this event see Sourvinou-Inwood 1971. 100–107.

32. On all this material see Brommer 1982.3–26.

33. For a list of these see Brommer 1973.211–12.

34. So C. H. Morgan, *Hesperia* 31 (1962) 212–14.

35. See Kron 1976.177–80, 182–85.

36. For these see Brommer 1982.22–23.

37. So now Sourvinou-Inwood 1979.32–35, convincingly I think, despite attempts to make this figure a local Nymph, at least in scenes before about 430 B.C., when the Oriental costume first appears (so B. B. Shefton, *AJA* 60 [1956] 159–63). See also Webster 1967.79–80; Trendall and Webster 1971.72–73.

38. Far earlier than any of these (mid-sixth-century) will be CabMéd 174 (Attic Black-Figure amphora: young man prepares to attack a bull while an older man watches). Kron (1976.128–29) and others do take this to be Theseus, with Aigeus watching, but, given the isolation of this piece, Herakles and the Kretan Bull must remain a possibility.

39. Fragmentary, but the essential elements are clear; see J. E. Harrison, *JHS* 10 (1889) 235, 238–39.

Chapter 8. Minos and Krete

1. The problem lies in the word *enneôros*, which in some way relates Minos' rule (or converse with Zeus) to nine years. See J. Russo 1985.234–35.

2. See Webster 1967.87–92.

3. For the passages as Euripidean, see Webster 1967.106; his chief argument is that, of the Sophoklean candidates, *Theseus* may not even have existed, while *Minos* is probably not different from his *Kamikoi,* and thus not about the Minotaur at all. Radt prints the fragments with others of Sophokles from plays unknown, but suggests tentatively the *Theseus;* see his notes (1977.497–98) for further bibliography.

4. See Fittschen 1969.167–68.

5. See Fittschen's discussion of this vase (ibid., 51–58) with bibliography on earlier views. He himself (with Hampe 1936.78–79, and others) argues that the circlet is probably a love token, and in any case not distinctive enough to characterize the scene, which he further believes could be either a carrying-off of the woman or a leave-taking.

6. See on this and the following shield-band Kunze (1950.131–32), who approves such an interpretation. Brommer (1982.42: cf. 44–45 on Attic vases), however, appears to reject the idea, and Herter (1112–14; see chap. 7, n. 28, above) seems likewise doubtful if we can find here anything more than a crown of victory.

7. Date uncertain, but certainly first or early second quarter of the sixth century. On the representation see Friis Johansen 1945.30–38.

8. Brommer 1982.56.

9. So Schefold 1964.71.

10. Friis Johansen 1945, especially 3–11, 18–25, 46–50. He stresses as well as the problems with the Delos interpretation the direct link between defeat of the Minotaur and dance in other artistic representations.

11. Sometimes cited in this connection is Vienna 1773, a Red-Figure stamnos showing Theseus abandoning Ariadne on one side and a woman consigning two children to a nurse on the other. But with only the nurse on this second side named (as "Nymphe"), the inference that these are Ariadne's children by Theseus (as opposed to Dionysos) seems perilous.

12. Poignant too is the scene on Tarquinia RC 5291: Theseus very gently picks up one of his sandals from the side of the sleeping Ariadne so as not to awaken her, while Hermes as his escort moves off to the left.

13. Cf. also (as discussed in chapter 2) Σ *Od* 11.325, where Dionysos accuses Ariadne of lying with Theseus in his precinct on Delos.

14. So Webster 1967.37–39, although the evidence is really quite frail, and Katreus may have been more of a major character.

15. See Radt 1977.312–13.

16. On this and later representations of Ikaros in art see J. D. Beazley, *JHS* 47 (1927) 222–33.

17. For the relief see Schmidt 1977.265–75 (discussion of both relief and metope, which she believes show the same myth, possibly Minos, more likely Iason); for the first publication of the metope, Zancani Montuoro and Zanotti-Bianco 1954.350–54 (Metope no. 32: Pelias). To be added here is a recently published shield-band from Olympia (B 4964) showing a man in a cauldron surrounded by two women, although few details are preserved: see Bol 1989.155–56 (cat. no. H 53) and pl. 72.

Chapter 9. Theseus' Later Exploits

1. See Thompson 1962.342–44; the suggestion goes back to K. O. Müller in the last century, followed by Wilamowitz and Robert. What sort of Gigantes naked men

with boulders might be remains unclear, however; certainly they are nothing like the armed Gigantes who challenge the gods.

2. See chap. 2, n. 5, above.

3. So Kirk 1985.235.

4. For speculation on earlier horse/man combat scenes as this battle, see Fittschen 1969.125–26.

5. On the problems of identification and on this myth in general in art, see Brommer 1982.104–10.

6. For a list of Kentauromachies set at the wedding, see B. B. Shefton, *Hesperia* 31 (1962) 365–67.

7. See Barron 1972.25–33. He supposes both the brawl at the wedding and the subsequent outdoor battle depicted on this mural.

8. Barron (ibid., 30–32) summarizes the rather slim evidence, which consists primarily of indications of rough terrain combined with the wedding fight.

9. So, e.g., Schefold 1964.71. Fittschen (1969.188 n. 889) objects on the grounds that in his opinion both "wrestlers" are male.

10. On illustrations of this theme in art, see von Bothmer 1957.124–30.

11. Seemingly therefore the same Hegias (or "Hagias" in Doric) credited with the epic *Nostoi*. But scholars are generally dubious; Robert (1920–26.731 n. 2) supposes a sixth-century epic *Theseis* intended, with authorship perhaps falsified.

12. Barrett 1964.8–9 and n. 3.

13. Judging from a fragmentary commentary, Stesichoros made Demophon the son of Theseus and Iope, daughter of Iphikles (this survives nowhere else), and Akamas Theseus' son by a second woman whose name is lost but who may well have been an Amazon (the letters *am*—— survive: 193 *PMG*).

14. Von Bothmer 1957.6–115.

15. Barron 1972.33–40.

16. Von Bothmer 1957.161–92 (index of inscribed names on 234).

17. See Barrett 1964.10–45; Webster 1967.64±76.

18. Probably the usual tradition did make this wish—to kill his son—Theseus' last, as Barrett (1964.39–40) supposes, even if that tradition was not always prepared to name the uses to which the first two had been put. So Seneca's Theseus declares that he has one wish left because he did not use it to escape from Hades (his most hopeless situation) but will not tell us what such wishes *are* good for, aside from cursing sons (Sen:Ph 948–53); this is simply rhetoric to intensify the present moment.

19. On this and other supposed representations of Helen with either Theseus and Peirithoos or the Dioskouroi or both, see Fittschen (1969.161–65), where it is argued that in no case are these stories certain or even likely. But the objection that an artist cannot show Theseus and Peirithoos present at Helen's rescue seems overly critical; cf. Kunze 1950.133. Ghali-Kahil (1955.309) makes the suggestion that perhaps in some accounts Theseus and his ally were in fact defeated by Helen's brothers, and that Athenian tradition altered this fact to spare Theseus' reputation.

20. See Kunze 1950.133–35. The types in question are Forms xxxvi and xliv; although only the lower half of each is preserved, Kunze argues that for a woman standing between two men the first abduction of Helen is the obvious interpretation. The inscriptions on Olympia shield-band B 4475 now prove conclusively that Menelaos and Helen constitute the correct interpretation on at least one of these types: see Bol 1989. 153–54 no. H 44 and fig. 9.

21. So Robert 1920–26.699 n. 1 and Ghali-Kahil 1955.310, among others.

22. Schefold (1978.157) suggests that Korone was a current hetaira's name, and that Theseus is here shown preferring her to Helen.

23. Sinn 1979.101–2 and fig. 7.3, with the observation that Helen struggles at the time of the abduction but seems quite willing to follow Theseus from Korinth to Athens.

24. Admittedly, Plutarch reports that according to Hereas of Megara (fourth or third century B.C.?) Peisistratos inserted this mention of Theseus into the *Nekuia* (*Thes* 20.2). Such a source will probably not have been immune to anti-Athenian bias, however, and we may wonder too how late reliable evidence on this point would have been available.

25. So Kunze 1950.112–13, probably rightly.

26. See Sutton 1987 for the most recent analysis; he concludes that there is little reason not to attribute the play to Euripides. Fragments, however, are cited from Snell's edition of the minor tragedians, since he assigns the play to Kritias.

27. H. M. Cockle's publication of the papyrus (*POxy* 50 [1983]) also contains a useful summary of other pieces of evidence and their possible significance for the play.

28. Just possibly such an idea might explain why Theseus holds the two swords in Polygnotos' painting: Peirithoos alone is unable to wield his (whatever the form of his binding). But in that case it will be strange that the artist has portrayed both men sitting on thrones, when only Peirithoos needs to do so.

29. To these we should perhaps add the name vase of the Niobid Painter, a calyx krater in the Louvre now frequently taken to present Herakles and these heroes rather than the Argonautai (Louvre G341: cf. J. Six, *JHS* 39 [1919] 130–35). Here Herakles stands by unconcernedly with bow and club while one possible candidate for Theseus or Peirithoos reclines on the ground holding two spears and the other perches casually on a rock, his knee drawn up by one hand. The two spears (found also on the Berlin lekythos) may or may not suggest the two swords held by Theseus in Polygnotos' painting at Delphi; on the New York krater Peirithoos (named) holds just one spear.

30. So, e.g., Kunze 1950.112 n. 2; Felten 1975.48–50. The latter suggests that Peirithoos' separate fate is an Attic innovation.

31. See *VL* 221, supplemented by 1982.100 n. 9.

32. See Fraenkel 1963.98–100; his arguments derive primarily from the awkward placement of the lines as Oidipous laments his wife and children, and the internal contradiction with Oidipous' previous uncertainty about his future (*Pho* 1687). Admittedly, not everyone is convinced: for challenges to this view that Oidipous' journey to Athens was not part of the *Phoinissai*, see H. Diller, *Gnomon* 36 (1964) 641, 646, and H. Erbse, *Philologus* 110 (1966) 20, 30.

33. For these (and the interpretation that here follows), see Sourvinou-Inwood 1979.3–7, 35–46.

34. See above, p. 255.

Chapter 10. Perseus and Bellerophontes

1. See Gantz 1980.149–51.

2. On the reconstruction of this play, see the very thorough treatment by M. Werre-De Haas, *Aeschylus' Dictyulci* (Leiden 1961).

3. Admittedly, these three titles have been thought by some scholars to represent less than three separate plays: see Pearson 1917.38 and Radt 1977.136 on the *Akrisios*.

4. See Webster 1967.94–95.

5. Schauenburg (1960a.3–12) surveys most of the following material in greater detail.

6. T. P. Howe, *AJA* 57 (1953) 269–75. Admittedly, such a trilogy would have to be one of Aischylos' earliest.

7. For illustrations and discussion of vases showing the arrival on Seriphos, see J. H. Oakley, *AJA* 86 (1982) 111–15. The Red-Figure pyxis in the Clairmont Collection is the most complete example, and shows Danae and Perseus (as a young boy) already out of the chest. That the figure next to Diktys on the Agora fragment is, as Oakley believes, Polydektes, is certainly possible, but such a juxtaposition need not necessitate a literary version in which the king meets Danae immediately after her arrival.

8. Schefold 1981.241.

9. J.-J. Maffre, *LIMC* 1.452.

10. Presumably this means that he intends to court her himself, but the words have also been taken to indicate a gift on the occasion of Hippodameia's marriage to someone else (so, e.g., Robert 1920–26.232–33 n. 7).

11. See A. de Ridder, *BCH* 22 (1898) 448–58.

12. The scholiast's preface to this ode says that Midas won in the twenty-fourth and twenty-fifth Pythiads, thus 490 and 486 B.C. As no mention is made of a second victory, 490 is regarded as the more likely date.

13. A third vase from earlier in the century (Metaponto 20145: *c.* 460 B.C.) may also represent the Graiai, if the three women on the reverse of a column krater showing Perseus' flight are correctly interpreted: see J. H. Oakley, *AJA* 92 (1988) 383–91. The women do appear to be blind, and hold out their hands in what might be gestures of despair; since there is no sign of eye or tooth the moment would be that *after* the theft, with the unseen Perseus waiting for their help or (more likely) long departed with the eye, as in Aischylos.

14. Perseus' use of a reflecting surface to protect him from Medousa's face also occurs in the scholia Parisina to Apollonios at 4.1515, the source for Pher 3F11. But the words do not occur in the earlier scholia tradition, and are excluded as an addition by both Wendel and Jacoby.

15. Schauenburg 1960a.77–82, with this interpretation which is surely correct.

16. See Webster 1967.197–99.

17. The question of Phineus' inclusion is, however, controversial: see Séchan 1926.269–73. Likewise uncertain is whether a divinity (Athena?) appeared at the end to resolve matters and promise elevation to the stars, as in Ps-Eratosthenes (*Katast* 15 [Kepheus], 16 [Kassiepeia], 17 [Andromeda], 32 [Perseus]).

18. For this last see H. P. Isler, *JdI* 98 (1983) 19–23, 29–31, where Perseus is preferred to Herakles and the *kêtos* at Troy. Hemelrijk (1984.141–42) suggests, rather than Perseus or Herakles, a lost myth about Phokaia.

19. The *Batrachoi* scholia (at 53) date the *Andromeda* to 412 B.C. (eight years earlier); cf. *Thesmophoriazousai* 1059–61.

20. On these and later representations of Andromeda see Phillips (1968.6–13), to which the following discussion is much indebted.

21. Ibid., 11, 20–21.

22. See Helbig 1969 3.596 no. 2641; Schauenburg 1960a.84. I have seen this vase only in the museum; to my knowledge it is not published.

23. So West 1985.110–11.

24. Apollodoros adds, as children of Perseus and Andromeda, two other sons, He-

leios and Mestor; the latter of these we will encounter again in chapter 13. As the mother of Alkaios' children two other women are suggested, Laonome, daughter of Gouneus, and Hipponome, daughter of Menoikeus, in addition to Astydameia, daughter of Pelops.

25. The scholia at *Odyssey* 11.326 call Proitos' wife Anteia, daughter of Amphianax; possibly this detail is from Pherekydes, who is cited at the end of the entry for the story of Proitos' daughter Maira.

26. The *Ehoiai* clearly named three daughters; the first, at the beginning of the line, is missing in our papyrus source, but surely to be supplied from Apollodoros, where the three are named in exactly the same order and Hesiod is immediately cited as the first source for their story.

27. For the ivory group see G.M.A. Richter in *AJA* 49 (1945) 261–69, where the two figures are interpreted as Aphrodite and Peitho; Schefold (1964.31) suggests simply two goddesses. For the identification as the Proitides (first proposed by Rumpf), see J. Dörig, *AM* 77 (1962) 72–91.

28. The cryptic words "portents of the gods" *(theôn teraessi)* are presumably too cryptic to call readily to mind Pegasos, but one is hard put to imagine any other device that would make possible Bellerophontes' heroics, and Homer here surely suppresses the full story. For other explanations, see Kirk 1990.184.

29. The B scholia at *Il* 6.200 offer other explanations for the gods' enmity (Bellerophontes became angry over the loss of his children, or the Solymoi were dear to them), but nothing very convincing.

30. See, in general, on this point Griffin 1977.

31. See P. Demargne, *RA* (1972) 35–46, who himself expresses considerable reserve about such an interpretation. The scene appears three times in succession on one band of the pithos; other scenes (on the neck) include two griffins and a standing male-female couple.

Chapter 11. The Daughters of Thestios

1. The evidence for Stesichoros is from POxy 2359, generally attributed to his *Suotherai* on the basis of meter and dialect. Prokaon and Klyti[os] are named and, since Eurytion immediately follows, were probably the only Thestiadai to participate; the previous lines suggest that other children (not named) were too young and remained at home.

2. To these Pausanias adds Prothous and Kometes as the brothers of Althaia shown fighting the Boar on the east pediment of the temple of Athena Alea at Tegea (8.45.6); where he got these names we do not know.

3. See Pearson 1917 2.119.

4. See below, p. 328, and West 1985.47.

5. See West's suggestion in the *apparatus* to fr 24, where the *Kypria* is substituted for Hesiod and Nemesis becomes the Okeanid in question.

6. That Zeus and Nemesis are in this fragment the parents of Helen is clear; the exact meaning of the first line is less so, given the word "thirdly" and the absence of an expressed subject for the verb *teke*. To supply here Nemesis as bearing a third child (who would be the first two, not to mention the problem of their father?) seems impossible, while if Zeus is the subject we may object that Helen is not strictly the third of his children raised by Leda because the *Kypria* makes Kastor mortal (thus presumably her son by Tyndareos). But perhaps the poet's logic was not that strict; on the whole ques-

tion and possible solutions (e.g., emendation of *teke?*), see Severyns 1928.267–68.

7. As seen in chapter 1, this is surely the correct interpretation of the text: Luppe 1974 (see above, chap. 1, n. 13).

8. To be fair, the reference to swans here (missing from Venetus Marcianus 444 [R]) has the look of an expansion of an original epitome in which the birds may well have been geese: so Olivieri, in the *apparatus* to his edition of the *Katasterismoi*. But at least we can say that *someone* concocted a version in which both Zeus and Nemesis became swans. What Asklepiades' source had Nemesis transform herself into (if anything) is unfortunately not specified.

9. Our text of Apollodoros does say that Zeus became a swan, but the word order and a pointless definite article (excised by Wagner and Frazer in their editions) may indicate an interpolation. If the word for "swan" is deleted along with the definite article, as Luppe (see n. 7 above) advocates, then Zeus and Nemesis will both become geese here, just as in the *Kypria.*

10. Schefold (1981.242) suggests, perhaps rightly, that behind the birth from Nemesis lies an Athenian attempt to associate Helen with Athens before she is taken to Sparta, so as to give the Athenians a greater part in the Trojan War. By contrast, Severyns (1928.270) regards Nemesis' parenthood as the older version of the story.

11. These lines have been bracketed by Murray and others; they are defended by A. M. Dale in her edition of the play (Dale 1967.83).

12. So too Hyginus, who borrows Euripides' motif by having Zeus as a swan flee an eagle (Aphrodite, suborned by Zeus for this purpose) and land in the lap of Nemesis, whom he mates with as soon as she has fallen asleep (*Astr* 2.8). Leda's role as real mother in human guise is thus transferred back to the goddess. Just possibly, however, this was the form of Zeus and Nemesis' story that Asklepiades found in tragedy.

13. Robert (1920–26.343) suggests that since Euripides drew the play's idea of the phantom Helen at Troy from Stesichoros, he derived Leda's swan suitor from that source as well; this is certainly possible, but in essence it remains a guess with nothing else to support it.

14. I confess that I do not know quite what to make of Horace's statement (*Epistulae* 2.3.147) that the Trojan War began from an *ovum geminum.* Possibly he refers to a double birth of Helen and Polydeukes from one egg, but since Helen is the only one who matters here the adjective seems slightly superfluous.

15. Unfortunately, the scholiast does not say who the other two were. The shadowy early lyric poet Xanthos apparently found room for Laodike too in later accounts by claiming that she was none other than Elektra, rechristened by the Argives to her more familiar name because of her unmarried state (700 *PMG*). In Sophokles, Iphianassa is listed with Chrysothemis as (it seems) living sisters of Elektra, though the scholiast hesitates over whether she might not be the same as Iphigeneia; the play's later references to the sacrificed sister never give her name.

16. West (1985.119) concludes that this child Nikostratos was born to Helen and Menelaos after the Trojan War. He suggests too that the two lines of fr 175 have been juxtaposed by the scholiast who cites them, with the first line simply a variantly recalled form of fr 204.94 (Hermione) and the second (Nikostratos) standing alone at a later point in the poem.

17. Iphigeneia, her child by Theseus in some accounts (pp. 289, 291, above), is presumably excluded for the *Ehoiai* by the fact that, as we have seen, Klytaimestra in this poem is mother of the Iphimede sacrificed at Aulis (Hes fr 23a.13–17 MW).

18. Note, however, that if the above interpretation of *Kypria* fr 9 is correct, and Zeus begets *his* third child rather than Nemesis hers, then we might (despite Kastor's mortality) have evidence that the *Kypria* supposed both Kastor and Polydeukes his.

19. On these family relationships see p. 181 above.

20. The *Iliad* scholion, we should note, closes with the remark that the story is found in Pindar. Conceivably the scholiast means that the details as he reports them were in a work of Pindar not preserved, but perhaps the reference is simply to that part of the story known already to us from *Nemean 9*.

21. See Schefold and Jung 1988.29–32.

22. For discussion of this last, see de La Coste-Messelière 1936.370–88.

23. See Severyns (1928.278–79), who argues in part that Apollodoros (like Proklos' summary of the *Kypria*) separates the abduction of the girls from the quarrel.

24. We remember that Leda's third daughter by Tyndareos, Phylonoe, is here made immortal by Artemis and has no children (Hes fr 23a.11–12).

25. Wilamowitz argued (*SB Berlin* [1925] 216 n. 2) that the play was set in Pleuron and thus could not have treated the death of Meleagros. But more likely the play's title refers to handmaidens brought by Althaia (a Pleuronian) with her to Kalydon on the occasion of her marriage to Oineus. Thus the play is set in Kalydon, and Althaia is as we might expect the central character who makes in the presence of these handmaidens the crucial decision to burn the brand. Those scholars who agree with Wilamowitz have yet to explain what other mythological narrative could be set in Pleuron or involve Pleuronian women.

26. See Willcock 1964.147–54, where it is argued that everything after Meleagros' slaying of his uncle(s) is Homer's own invention; March (1987.29–42) would eliminate even that event, so that the hero's demise in the earliest versions has nothing to do with his family. The opposite extreme is represented by Howald, who maintains (1924. 402–13) that virtually Phoinix's entire story represents a previously existing *Meleagris* poem after which Achilleus' anger in the *Iliad* has been modeled. For an intermediate position, with the death of Althaia's brother(s) and her curse part of the standard tradition but the withdrawal from battle and siege of Kalydon influenced by the *Iliad*, see, for example, Robert 1920–26.91–92.

27. March (1987.36–37) does question this point, preferring to see the Kouretes as an outside people involved in the Hunt, since otherwise Meleagros' withdrawal will support his mother's interests. But if the Kouretes are the Pleuronians (as all later sources assume), her interests will be compromised regardless of what happens.

28. Presumably *kasignêtoio phonoio* at *Iliad* 9.567 does mean "death of a brother," so that only one brother, rather than the two of later sources, is involved. But we cannot completely exclude Aristarchos' theory that *kasignêtoio* could be an adjective ("brotherly death"), with the number of victims thus left open (ΣA *Il* 9.567; so too bT).

29. Robert (1920–26.91), who grasps this point better than many, adds that the death of Meleagros in this *paradeigma* would scarcely constitute a good omen for Achilleus. In his view Homer simply reworks for the purposes of the moment an original story in which Meleagros dies on the battlefield as soon as his mother's curse is heard (as we would expect).

30. So too (and only so) is the parallel with Achilleus' situation properly completed; as Althaia undoes the damage that caused her son's anger, making it appropriate for him to return to battle, thus Agamemnon has undone the damage he caused by returning Briseis.

31. I have tried here to render Bakchylides' words as in the Greek, where taken strictly they guarantee only that *Agelaos* was Meleagros' brother. But the more normal assumption, given two names joined by the particle *te*, is that those names are closely linked as a pair, and we will see below other reasons to suppose that Bakchylides meant us to understand both victims as the hero's brothers.

32. See Radt 1977.345.

33. That Apollo could ever have been supposed to have slain Meleagros (or anyone) on the command of the Erinyes I take to be totally excluded.

34. There would seem basically two possibilities: (1) Homer replaced the brand with the curse (so, e.g., Willcock 1964.151–52); (2) someone after Homer replaced the curse with the brand (so Croiset 1898.77–80, suggesting Stesichoros). But some scholars have suggested that the version Homer adapted had neither curse nor brand, but only Apollo, in which case Homer would have had to invent Althaia's role altogether (see March 1987.34–36).

35. Slightly earlier perhaps are two Black-Figure dinoi, preserved only in fragments, on which Atalanta is named (and thus recognizable): Agora P334 (*Hesperia* 4 [1930] 430–41) and Blatter Coll (*AntK* 5 [1962] 45–47). On these also a national rather than local cast of hunters was probably featured, but the other fragments preserve only the dead Ankaios. Of interest would certainly be the metopes of the Sikyonian *monopteros* flanking that with the Boar, if only they had survived, since these very likely showed the hunters (with names); the same is true of the Amyklai Throne, if names were given there (Paus 3.18.15). For discussion of scenes of the Hunt in art, including those boar hunts without criterially distinctive features, see de La Coste-Messelière 1936.120–21, 130–52.

36. See n. 1 above.

37. See Robert, *Hermes* 33 (1898) 157–58. He supposes further, on the model of Bakchylides' poem, that in Homer and all earlier versions the killing of Althaia's brothers is accidental, and that first in Euripides does Meleagros deliberately slay them, spurred on by Atalanta's mistreatment.

38. To be precise, the inscription here reads "Antaios" rather than "Ankaios," but other inscriptions and the general tradition leave little doubt that this is a mistake.

39. For yet another Ankaios sometimes conflated with the Boar's victim, this one the Samian offspring of Poseidon and Astypalaia, see Σ Lyk 488. In Apollonios this son is a separate Argonaut (AR 1.185–89).

40. So Robert distinguishes them, suggesting in fact that the Arkadian Atlanta may have been modeled on the Boiotian one: Robert 1920–26.84.

41. For discussion of the problems with this passage, see M. L. West, *Studies in Greek Elegy and Iambus* (Berlin 1974) 165–67.

42. That these two Atalantas were *in origin* a single figure is, of course, quite possible. What I am concerned with here is solely their status in the myths of the Archaic and Classical periods, when they appear to have been understood and consistently distinguished as two separate individuals.

43. See Beazley, *AJA* 64 (1960) 221–24.

Chapter 12. Iason and the Argo

1. See Huxley 1969.63–64.

2. Wendel 1935.3.

3. See Radt 1985.135. A critical issue is what role Satyroi might play, if in fact the Argo refused to let servants come on board.

4. See Vojatzi 1982.39–48, plus 48–51 for other possible early Argo ship scenes.

5. De La Coste-Messelière 1936.195–97.

6. So ibid., 193–95, postulating a third metope to the right of the completed ship. Vojatzi (1982.47–48), more reasonably I think, considers the group a tableau, "ein epischer Argonautenkatalog" without specific narrative content.

7. On this point see Meuli 1921.1–24, where a number of parallels are cited for this version of the "Helpers" motif. His contention that many of these figures owe their origin to animal traits is perhaps less certain.

8. So T. P. Howe, *AJA* 61 (1957) 341–50.

9. Beazley, 221–25 (see chap. 11, n. 43).

10. Merkelbach and West ad loc. = Soph fr 705 R = Wendel 1935.140.

11. If "Apollo" here really does mean Apollo, and not Helios (as emended by Wendel), then the god perhaps acts out of jealousy over the competition to his own prophetic skills. If on the other hand Helios is meant, his role as god of light may be involved, as in Asklepiades (see below).

12. One other remark of the Apollonios scholia (at 2.178b), that Helios blinds Phineus because he chose long life rather than sight, makes no sense on any reading, unless perhaps Helios acts here as the agent of Zeus.

13. Omitted from this discussion is Aristotle's baffling reference to a *Phineidai* tragedy in which, on seeing a certain place, unidentified women infer that they are fated to die there, for there they were once set forth (presumably exposed as children). Who these women might be, and what they could possibly have to do with the sons of Phineus, remains totally unclear. Timotheos wrote a dithyramb and Accius a tragedy with the same title, but in both those cases the myth involved may have been much closer to that found in *Phineus* plays.

14. Something of the same sort appears in Dionysios Skytobrachion, where Herakles finds the sons out in the wilderness, having been exiled by their father on the accusation of the (Scythian) stepmother who has supplanted Kleopatra in Phineus' affections (32F5). Here, too, they seem not to be blind, and Herakles kills Phineus when the latter opposes their restoration.

15. On this and other representations of the myth, see Blome 1978.70–75 and Vojatzi 1982.51–87.

16. Samos: VM 1540, a slightly earlier cup by the same painter, preserves only the central part of one Harpuia.

17. Vojatzi 1982.71–86. The fragments are from Sane on the Pallene peninsula of Chalkidike, near Potidaia.

18. With which Sophokles was connected: see R. E. Wycherley, *The Stones of Athens* (Princeton 1978) 181–82.

19. Blome 1978.

20. See Trendall and Webster 1971.58–60.

21. For the view that this and other of Odysseus' adventures have been borrowed from an original utilization in the Argo's voyage, see Meuli 1921. 82–115.

22. For the Bonn alabastron, see Vojatzi 1982.118 no. 59 and pl. 11; for the Samos fragments, G. Kopcke, *AM* 83 (1968) 282 fig. 31.

23. Though here as elsewhere we must remember that Daidalos *might* represent another name for Hephaistos: see Pearson 1917.110 and p. 837, n. 23, above.

24. See C. M. Robertson, *JHS* 97 (1977) 158–60.

25. Keeping in mind, of course, that we do not know how much later than the *Theogony* proper this passage might be; West suggests for Medeios at least a date in the second half of the sixth century (1966.430).

26. The starting point will be earlier still, if the *Dreifuss* metope from Foce del Sele with the man in cauldron does in fact show the death of Pelias. But with so many other possibilities (Minos, Iason, Pelops, Tantalos), this identification is quite uncertain, and becomes more so when we consider that Pelias is never in the cauldron whole: see Schmidt 1977 and p. 275 above.

27. Dugas (1944.5–11) would make it the work of the Samian epic poet Kreophylos, Meyer (1980.121–23) of the Athenian Lasos. Neither is impossible, but both scholars surely err in claiming that prior to this point Iason and Pelias were on good terms.

28. For a more complete list of these and later representations see Meyer 1980. 3–16.

29. The early fifth century in Athens also brings three Black-Figure lekythoi showing a small child (rather than a ram) emerging from the fire-lit cauldron as women watch: ibid., 66–68, with previous literature. Meyer himself takes these to represent the rejuvenation of Iason, but Pelops is clearly a possibility as well. On the *Dreifuss* metope from Foce del Sele (which Meyer, following Schmidt, also takes to represent Iason), see n. 26 above, and for an Etruscan mirror on which Medeia offers an (aged?) Iason something to drink, Meyer 1980.106 and pl. 26.1.

30. Although, surprisingly, in Lykophron's sequence this occurs between the harnessing of the bulls and the securing of the Fleece, thus allowing Meyer (1980.105–9) to argue that in some early traditions Iason needs rejuvenation (if not resuscitation) after his encounter with the serpent. The Lykophron scholia are of no help here.

31. So Meyer 1980.70–71.

32. Dugas 1944.7–11, attributing this also to Kreophylos of Samos.

33. Page 1938.xxx–xxxvi.

Chapter 13. Herakles

1. So the hypothesis to the *Aspis*, which specifies that the first fifty-six lines of that poem are taken from the *Ehoiai*. That this juxtaposition was the work of the author of the *Aspis* is generally assumed (*contra* West 1985.136).

2. On the likelihood that this detail does go back to Pherekydes, even though some of the other material assigned to him by the scholia and assembled under 3F13 surely does not, see van der Valk 1963.382 and n. 279.

3. For possible explanations of this curious detail see Thummer's commentary ad loc. (1969 2.116–17). Webster (1967.93) suggests an allusion to it on London F149, where Alkmene on the altar is surrounded by such a rain, but there a different purpose altogether is surely intended: see below.

4. See Séchan 1926.242–48; Webster 1967.92–94.

5. See B. van Groningen, *Mnemosyne* 58 (1930) 134; no special arguments are there advanced or plot reconstruction attempted.

6. Thummer (1969 2.79) supposes, probably rightly, that Pindar here tries to modify the known tradition slightly in order to distance Herakles from the slaying of helpless, unarmed children.

7. On these omissions see Thompson 1962.339–40.

8. On the evidence for this canon see the discussion of Brommer (1972.53–63), where it is argued that Olympia did indeed play the determining role.

9. Pronoun referent at *Theogony* 326 not entirely certain; see West 1966 ad loc.

10. Catalogue of this and other possibilities in Fittschen 1969.83–84.

11. See Kunze 1950.99–100, where these examples are interpreted as representing a tradition in which the Lion is killed by the sword, one completely separate from the wrestling motif.

12. See n. 38 below.

13. For the earliest of these see Fittschen 1969.147–50.

14. See Amyx and Amandry 1982.102–16 for a full catalogue and discussion.

15. See Hampe 1936.42–43; Fittschen 1969.92 expresses the usual doubts, but does not exclude the possibility.

16. That the hunter here kills the Hind, as in Euripides, I doubt, *pace* Hampe (1936.44); the latter does, however, make the interesting suggestion that the tale was originally independent of Eurystheus, with the Hind needing to be brought back alive only when she became a Labor.

17. See. E. Dyggve, *Das Laphrion: Der Tempelbezirk von Kalydon* (Copenhagen 1948) 160–61, plus 153, fig. 164, and pl. XIX (Metope 2A). Only the man's head and part of a boar's back and bristles directly above the head are preserved.

18. See chap. 1, n. 60, above for the theory that the Boston Protocorinthian aryballos with "Zeus" and a Kentauros (Boston 95.12) also represents this myth, with the thunderbolt held by the former actually a firebrand.

19. Pyxis lid: *Perachora II*, 115 (cat. no. 1114) and pl. 48; Fittschen 1969.115 (SB 10). Thermon metope: Schiffler 1976.63 (K–S 6).

20. For illustrations of this myth (restricted, however, to examples on which Pholos or the cave and pithos are actually shown), see Brize 1980.52–54 and the catalogue at 146–50, as well as von Steuben 1968.26–28.

21. For this interpretation and the problem in general see B. Ashmole and N. Yalouris, *Olympia: The Sculptures of the Temple of Zeus* (London 1967) 29.

22. See Dörig, *JdI* 72 (1957) 19–43 (in particular 19–28).

23. See Fittschen (1969.64–65), who against general support for a Herakles interpretation objects that the figure (two figures, actually) with birds on the London fibula are female, and that the Copenhagen oinochoe represents a generic hunt.

24. On these see Pipili 1987.4–5. Cabinet des Médailles 174, a mid-sixth-century Black-Figure amphora with bull, older man, and young man sometimes taken to represent Herakles rather than Theseus, is discussed above, chap. 7, n. 38. The Labor may have appeared as well on a metope from the so-called Temple Y on the acropolis at Selinous: see Tusa 1983.113–14.

25. Probably: see previous note.

26. For this and the following cup, see D. C. Kurtz, *JHS* 95 (1975) 171–72.

27. See von Bothmer 1957.1–2; Fittschen 1969.177–78; Schefold 1964.22.

28. For the inscriptions on this alabastron see Amyx 1988.557, and von Bothmer 1957.3–4.

29. Pipili (1987.6) is skeptical, citing the lack of supporting evidence in art for this time period and arguing that Herakles simply extends his arm to seize the nearest Amazon. It must be admitted, too, that the other Amazon wears a similar belt.

30. See von Bothmer 1957.6–10, 30–69.

31. Schauenburg in his discussion of the *Gürtel* (1960b.1–13) cites two vases that he believes may show the belt (1 n. 7). But on one (London B533) the object raised by Herakles (while still fighting) is a circlet, not an unbuckled belt (von Bothmer [1957.47] suggests it may be a wreath), and on the other (London E45), although he certainly reaches toward a falling Amazon's waist, no belt is to be seen; probably he intends rather to intercept his opponent's half-drawn sword.

32. Schauenburg (1960b.2–3) concludes that the belt was probably always the purpose of the expedition, albeit long unrecognized in Attic art; by contrast, Boardman (see chap. 1, n. 23) speculates on a Western Greek (or Ionian) pedigree for this detail, with an entry into Athenian versions of the story only after 500 B.C.

33. As Robert (1920–26.463–64) well notes, stressing that the belt was military in nature, although he perhaps goes further than necessary in identifying it with a Mycenaean-Minoan *mitra*.

34. See the commentary of Bond (1981.172–73), who suggests that the word *pharos*, "robe," is perhaps the source of the problem and conceals a participle or infinitive of purpose.

35. For the following vases, see Schauenburg 1960b.6–8.

36. So ibid., 8.

37. Catalogue of illustrations and discussion in Brize 1980.41–51, 133–44.

38. See Brize, *AM* 100 (1985) 53–90.

39. At least 1,300 lines, since that number appears as a line marker on one papyrus fragment (27 *SLG*).

40. For the various weapons that Herakles uses (including a club in Red-Figure), and the possibility of a version (Stesichorean?) in which Herakles shoots one body of Geryoneus (plus Eurytion and/or Orthos) before closing in with sword or club, see M. Robertson, *CQ* 19 (1969) 207–14.

41. So ibid., 218–21, noting also Basel BS 428, a Black-Figure cup of the mid-sixth century with a band of Kentauroi (from the cave of Pholos?) above one with men driving cattle.

42. Catalogue and discussion in Brize 1980.51–52, 63, 145, to which add the same author's entry at *LIMC* Herakles 2545–52. Perhaps relevant here is NY 56.171.33, a Black-Figure lekythos of *c.* 515 B.C. on which Herakles is seen fishing in the company of Hermes and Poseidon. Schefold and Jung (1988.161) suggest that Hermes has guided Herakles to the Far East, and that they fish while waiting for Helios to appear.

43. Or probably so: G. Pinney and B. Ridgway (*JHS* 101 [1981] 141–44) would see here rather Herakles' preparations for the descent into Hades, with the hero making a sacrifice to win the gods' help, and a cave and dog to one side indicating the Underworld. In this view the joint appearance of Helios, Nyx, and Eos marks that misty realm beyond Okeanos where Day and Night exchange roles, in Hesiod near the gates of Hades. I would object only that while Day might appear in this context, a rising Helios seems out of place.

44. That arrows (fired by Herakles) are intended in these two scenes is maintained by Brommer (1984.106) and Schefold and Jung (1988.161), among others. Brize says nothing about them, and argues (*LIMC* V 85) that the side of Taranto 7029 with Herakles sitting shows the moment of his original request, and that where he climbs up the slope his arrival on Erytheia (presumably Helios is here sinking down into Okeanos). This is certainly possible, but since the means of the arrival is Helios' cup (not his chariot), one does not immediately see why Helios and not the cup should be shown.

45. Clement's statement (Cl:*Pro* 36.2) that in Panyasis Herakles wounds Elean Augeias is frequently emended to produce a wounding of Helios (see *apparatus* to fr 21 *PEG*), but this seems dubious, especially as the same author has Herakles obtain the cup from Nereus: see below.

46. On the form of the inscription see Kunze 1950.213. Nereus is so termed five times in the *Iliad* (1.538, etc.) and once each in the *Odyssey* (24.58) and *Theogony* (1003).

47. Likewise named as Nereus is the old man wrestling with Herakles on a fragment of a Late Corinthian krater, where the level of the combatants' heads in respect to the rest of the scene suggests for the sea god a lower fish body (Cahn Coll 1173: see Glynn 1981.122–23 and pl. 21.1).

48. First, it seems, on an unpublished Black-Figure neck-amphora by Exekias in Taranto: see Brize 1980.162 (NER III 40). Prior to this, the dividing line between fish/ man Nereus and fish/man Triton is somewhat uncertain, depending upon how much of a receding hairline we require for Nereus, and whether a lack of attached animal protomes is criterial. See also below, n. 49.

49. First on several pots by the Heidelberg Painter: Brize 1980.166. Glynn (1981.130–32) takes this new mode of presentation to mean that at this point Nereus becomes uniformly human in Attic tradition, with all Herakles and fish/man compositions henceforth representing Herakles and Triton in a completely different context (Athens' control of Sigeion?); Brize perhaps does better to see natural artistic shifts in illustrating the same myth at work here.

50. The logistics of this folktale motif are also difficult in the context of a Greek myth. If the heat is oppressive, Helios should be well up in the sky at midday, far from the earth and far from his cup, while Herakles (presumably in mid-journey) will be himself far from any part of Okeanos in which he could use the cup. A meeting of god and mortal on the banks of Okeanos to the far east, when Helios has just left his cup, resolves all these problems.

51. For (lost) second-century B.C. predecessors of these sources in relating the story (e.g., Gnaeus Gellius), and for Cacus' evolution from the Etruscan (or Italic?) seer Cacu, see J. P. Small, *Cacus and Marsyas in Etrusco-Roman Legend* (Princeton 1982) 3–36.

52. Jucker 1977.191–99.

53. The Basel relief is published by Jucker 1977 as plate 55.2 and in Schefold 1978 as figure 154; the Olympia relief appears in Bol 1989 as pl. 47.

54. Some scholars prefer the return of the Keryneian Hind (e.g., Schefold 1978. 102); but it is difficult to see how an audience would recognize such a scene without the presence of Artemis herself.

55. On artistic representations of the Garden in general and these scenes in particular, see Brommer 1942.

56. Note, however, that in contrast to Brommer (1972.49–50 and pl. 29), D. von Bothmer (supported, it seems, by Beazley) considers this albastron a forgery: "The drawing on the alabastron, as Beazley has seen, must be modern" (*AJA* 61 [1957] 106). Von Bothmer himself objects to the style of the apple tree, snake, and lionskin, as well as the bordering meander.

57. This is the lost vase listed as I 1a, b, c and figure 1 in Brommer's catalogue (1942.108).

58. For an earlier version of this story ascribed to one Polyidos in a dithyramb

(which, however, distinguishes its Atlas from the guardian of the tree), see the discussion of Atlas in chapter 1.

59. Boardman in Böhr and Martini 1986.127.

60. To Pindar's poem (his dithyramb *Kerberos?*) may belong POxy 2622, with its mention of Eleusis, Persephone, and Demeter; see H. Lloyd-Jones, *Maia* 19 (1967) 206–29.

61. See pp. 454–55 below.

62. For a drawing see Felten 1975, fig. 1.

63. Boardman suggests (1975.6–10), rightly or wrongly, that this shift reflects the creation of the Lesser Eleusinian Mysteries and Herakles' initiation by means of them; because he participates in these Mysteries his relationship with the powers of death (and rebirth) is now on a new footing, and his welcome in Hades considerably warmer. Such an initiation may be attested in literature as early as Pindar, and conceivably go back into sixth-century epic: see n. 60 above.

64. On the various possibilities for this metope, see now Van Keuren 1989.66–72.

65. For this idea as late-sixth-century in art (and perhaps literature), see n. 63 above.

66. See p. 456 below.

67. See Zancani Montuoro and Zanotti-Bianco 1954.204–9.

68. See *LIMC* I p. 805 (Antaios I 37, 39).

69. One of the three new metopes found in 1958. See Van Keuren 1989.72–77 for arguments supporting this identification and a review of other opinions.

70. See ibid., 74 and pl. 20a, b; Schmidt 1977.270–71 and pl. 72.3, 5. Of the two panels, the first is thought to show Athena putting Alkyoneus to sleep while Herakles converses with Hermes, and the second to show the actual attack.

71. On Herakles and Alkyoneus in vase-painting see B. Andreae, *JdI* 77 (1962) 162–203.

72. Or perhaps rather to Ares or Phobos, as we might expect, if a likely emendation is correct: see p. 206 of Malcolm Davies' new edition of the melic poets (Vol. 1, Oxford 1991).

73. See Beck 1984.44–56 and catalogue at 154–61; Vian 1945.5–32. The earliest Attic example seems to be Basel BS 428, a Black-Figure cup with in the tondo Herakles (in lionskin) stabbing a hoplite with a sword.

74. See D. von Bothmer, *The Amasis Painter and His World* (New York 1985) 236, with illustration.

75. So Furtwängler 1885.277. Thunderbolts do, however, appear at times in subsequent representations, either held by Zeus (not in an immediately threatening fashion: so Lugt Coll, no #) or descending from the sky (as in Apollodoros and Hyginus) as a substitute for a personal appearance by the god. On the Lugt lekythos, Kyknos falls backward as Ares moves forward above him; possibly here too, as on the Berlin oinochoe, Zeus' intention is to separate his two sons. Basel BS 498, a Black-Figure hydria by the Antimenes Painter, shows a seated Zeus with Hermes on the reverse as Herakles and Ares close over the defeated Kyknos (see Burow 1989.94 and pl. 128); if both sides are part of the same scene, as seems likely, then Zeus here perhaps sends Hermes to resolve the conflict.

76. Or Moline: on the form of the name see West 1985.63 n. 73. To avoid confusion with the mother in English transliteration, I have used throughout the plural form *Moliones* for the brothers rather than the dual *Molione*.

77. On the earliest of these (including krater, oinochoe, and fibula) see Fittschen 1969.68–75. He is properly cautious in some cases (so, e.g., the Attic Late Geometric krater in New York on which the three bands feature no less than four such *Zwitterwesen*: NY 14.130.15) but excessively so, I think, in others. This reduplicating of an (at times) stock element need not mean that such creatures were never intended to represent a specific character in myth, any more than is true of the Sphinx in Attic art.

78. On the problems in interpreting the myth of this poem see Page 1951.30–42.

79. For Telephos in both literature and art, see Bauchhenss-Thüriedl 1971.

80. See Gantz 1980.161–62.

81. See Bauchhenss-Thüriedl (1971.78–86) for a catalogue of these.

82. Conceivably, of course, Telephos could return from Mysia to Greece at a later time to fulfill this oracle; as we will see below, he does seem to come back to Arkadia (with his mother) in the Cyzicene Epigrams and in Hyginus. But this is a strangely deviant tradition that would seem to leave no room for his wounding by Achilleus and visit to Argos to be cured.

83. In Apollonios two sons of Aleos, Kepheus and Amphidamas, plus the offspring Ankaios of a third son, Lykourgos, are among the crew of the Argo (AR 1.161–67), while Apollodoros speaks of two sons, Kepheus and Lykourgos, born to Aleos and Neaira (Ap*B* 3.9.1; Amphidamas, like Ankaios, is here a son of Lykourgos). Neither source mentions any killing by Telephos.

84. Pearson (1917 1.47–48) suggests in fact that this formed the end of the *Aleadai*, with Telephos recognized only *after* he has killed Aleos' sons (for mocking his seemingly unknown birth).

85. For the vase see J. Kroll, *AntK* 11 (1968) 21–23. Both the attacking figure striding forward with sword and the victim reaching for his own sword wear mantles; in Kroll's view the name Telephos (TELAPHOS) was incised after firing by someone other than the artist.

86. So Pearson 1917 2.70–72.

87. See n. 79 above.

88. Attempts have been made to argue that Dion gives evidence for the bowshot across the river as first in Sophokles (so Lasserre 1950.198–99; Kamerbeek 1959.3). But Dion does not say that arrows were inappropriate to this situation nor (*pace* Lasserre) that Herakles might have struck Deianeira with them. Rather he objects that by shooting too soon in the Sophoklean version Herakles runs the risk of Nessos' dropping Deianeira and letting her drown. In fact Dion's words could mean that Archilochos used the bowshot more logically or not at all; but since Herakles must be some distance from Deianeira when Nessos makes his attempt, the river and the bowshot seem a reasonable assumption.

89. The scholiast's text here does say *en Euênôi*, which might, despite the foregoing argument, be thought to indicate that Nessos is shot in the river. But elsewhere *en* with a river clearly means "beside, on the banks, of": so *Iliad* 18.520–21, where the ambush on Achilleus' shield certainly takes place *by* the river, and likewise *Odyssey* 5.465–69, where Odysseus contemplates sleeping *by* the river, not in it.

90. March 1987.49–77 suggests in fact that bowshot, Nessos' gift to Deianeira, and her unwitting use of that gift to destroy Herakles are all inventions of an early *Trachiniai*, subsequently followed by Bakchylides' poem. In the earlier tradition of the *Ehoiai*, according to this view, Deianeira derived the poison from some more obvious source, and knew exactly what it was when she sent it to Herakles. I would object only

that her view of the narrative in Archilochos (following Lasserre: see n. 88 above) is arguable.

91. In person it does look like a horn. See Boardman 1968.46 cat. no. 75, 48.

92. Also interpreted by some as Zeus battling Typhoeus: see chap. 1, n. 60, above.

93. See Van Keuren 1989.81–90.

94. Zancani Montuoro and Zanotti-Bianco, who do link the archer-and-woman metope with that of the charging Kentauros, solve this problem by making the Kentauros Eurytion rather than Nessos (1954.167–77). But whether an audience would easily recognize such a (from our vantage point) little-known myth is open to question.

95. The *Iliad's* Catalogue of Ships places it (as Eurytos' city) clearly in inland Thessaly, under control of the Asklepiadai (*Il* 2.729–33); scholia claim that the *neôteroi* subsequently put it in Euboia (ΣA *Il* 2.596). Pausanias cites Hekataios (and Kreophylos) for the latter location but prefers himself to credit the claims of the Messenians (4.2.3), possibly influenced by *Iliad* 2.594–96, where Thamyris meets the Mousai in Messenia after leaving Oichalia. See Jacoby's commentary on 1F28. Pherekydes seems to have placed the city rather in Arkadia, next to Tiryns where Iphitos comes to look for the missing cattle (3F82a).

96. Skeptical, however, is Fittschen (1969.28–32 [F4 on 29]), who sees here a typical boxing contest, whether as part of a myth or everyday life.

97. For a survey of the myth in vase-painting see von Bothmer 1977.

98. For this (surely correct) identification of the central figure as Zeus rather than Athena, see B. S. Ridgway, *AJA* 69 (1965) 1–5.

99. For other vases on which Zeus appears in this capacity see von Bothmer 1977.52.

100. On this and other possible representations of Omphale in vase-painting see Schauenburg 1960c.66–76.

101. On these representations see Brommer 1944/45.69–78.

102. *Perachora II*, 262–63, cat. no. 2542, pls. 106, 110; Amyx 1988.565. One Kerkops' leg and part of a name (−*batos?*) survive.

103. Berlin:Ch F766 shows the central part of a striding Herakles with two smaller inverted figures, presumably suspended from a pole. Berlin:Ch F767 preserves only Herakles' head and one such inverted figure whom he appears to hold out with his arm (see Zancani Montuoro and Zanotti-Bianco 1954.187, fig. 36 and 190 n. 3). The date is perhaps, like that of the cup, Middle Corinthian.

104. For these texts see Allen 1912.159–60.

105. For discussion and illustration of many of these see Zancani Montuoro and Zanotti-Bianco 1954.185–95.

106. On the original distinction and ultimate confusion of these two groups see Vian 1952.169–74.

107. See Fraenkel (1950.332), where Hesychios' definition of *gigas* as great or powerful is cited as perhaps relevant.

108. On these and later representations of the combat see Vian 1951, updated now by his *LIMC* Gigantes article (written with M. B. Moore).

109. See M. B. Moore's valuable reconstructions and discussion in *AJA* 83 (1979) 79–99.

110. See M. B. Moore in *Greek Vases in the J. Paul Getty Museum*, Vol. 2 (Occasional Papers on Antiquities 3: Malibu 1985) 21–40.

111. Schefold (1978.61) argues that the mode of wearing the lionskin here, with the head inverted as a hanging element rather than set upon the wearer's own head, indicates Dionysos rather than Herakles.

112. Of these two metopes the excavators link that of the man with sword to the Silenoi, and the kneeling archer to the metope with the charging Kentauros left over from the Pholos section (Zancani Montuoro and Zanotti-Bianco 1954.141–66, 167–77). Van Keuren interprets the first of these as rather Orestes goaded on by Elektra; the opponents of the Silenoi (Hera and Herakles) she assumes to have appeared on a metope now lost (1989.57–66).

113. These are now assembled by Boardman as *LIMC* Herakles 3488–97, but with the cornucopia bearer identified as Palaimon (see below). Note, too, that 3488 (skyphos once on the Basel market: Herakles shaking hands with cornucopia bearer) is said to be Early Classical, in contrast to the rest of the group.

114. To these two should be added a Red-Figure cup fragment (Weimar, once Preller Coll) on which Herakles carries a man with staff; the cornucopia if present is broken away. See Metzger 1951.197 and pl. 26.3; Brommer 1984.104 fig. 50. Metzger (following Preller) supposes the staff a thyrsos and the figure Dionysos. For discussion of the problem of identification see Schauenburg 1953.50–56.

115. See Boardman as above, n. 113.

116. Kunze 1950.121–25.

117. See Brommer, *AA* (1952) 60–73.

118. For these illustrations see Boardman (in Böhr and Martini 1986.127–32), where it is suggested that on present evidence the pyre as an element of Herakles' death may well be fifth-century in conception.

119. So probably also Villa Giulia 11688 (RF bell krater fragments), where a man's legs are visible moving away from the slumping figure of Herakles on the pyre, and he does appear to hold (though not very prominently) a bow: see C. Clairmont, *AJA* 57 (1953) 85–89.

120. West 1966.397–99.

121. From a tomb excavated in 1981 in the Osteria district: see A. Sgubini Moretti (83–88) and M. Pandolfini (88–89) in *Archeologia nella Tuscia* 2 (Rome 1986).

122. Figures are from Brommer's *Vasenlisten*[3] (1973.159–73); see also Schefold 1978.35.

Chapter 14. Thebes

1. On the difficulties involved in this and other attributions to early mythographers see Vian 1963.21–26.

2. So Vian (ibid.), although he would exclude Kadmos' exile and servitude to Ares on the grounds that Zeus' resolution of the conflict between Kadmos and Ares precludes such exile. I confess I do not see why the two ideas are incompatible: on the scholiast's view Ares wants to destroy Kadmos, so that Zeus' resolution may well consist of letting the mortal off with a lighter sentence (certainly not inappropriate considering that Kadmos has dispossessed the original resident of the land). More skeptical on the question of Hellanikian origins are van der Valk (1963.305–6), who argues that the scholiast has simply attached Hellanikos' name to an Apollodoran account in order to look more scholarly, and Jacoby (commentary at 4F51).

3. So Vian (1963.44–45), pointing out armor, lack of pitcher, and lack of clear indication of fountain house. But these last two factors count against Achilleus as well; in

favor of Kadmos (or at least a myth concentrating on the snake), see Stibbe 1972.170, Schefold 1978.79–80, and now Prag 1985.45–46 (arguing that the Rider Painter derived this scene from that of Achilleus in ambush).

4. Catalogue of these and other artistic representations in Vian 1963.35–44.

5. On scenes of Kadmos and Harmonia in art, see Schauenburg 1957, where in addition to the Louvre neck-amphora the author tentatively suggests Göttingen R23, a Black-Figure oinochoe with a boar, two lions, and a wolf drawing a chariot sometimes thought to be that of Admetos.

6. See E. R. Dodds' note ad loc. in his edition of the play (Oxford 1960).

7. Actually only the last twelve lines of the Hymn are preserved in manuscript; the beginning (presumably from the same poem) comes from a citation in Diodoros.

8. See Carpenter (1986.22–29), however, where it is argued that Aphrodite disappears from such scenes after about 540, leaving us unsure about the identity of the women who sometimes replace her.

9. See Gantz 1980.154–58.

10. See Gantz 1981.29–30.

11. See p. 220 above, and Kaempf-Dimitriadou 1979.23.

12. = PMich 1447: see T. Renner, *HSCP* 82 (1978) 282–87.

13. To this scant information on Aktaion in the *Ehoiai* should perhaps be added *POxy* 2509, as Lobel thought. The hexameter text describes some goddess (Athena? Artemis?) coming to the cave of Cheiron to tell him something about Dionysos, son of Zeus and Semele, and about dogs, Aktaion, madness, and grief. Lobel supposed this to mean that Aktaion's death was prophesied, but subsequent scholars are surely right to think that Aktaion has just died, and that the goddess in question tells Cheiron that Dionysos himself will hunt with these dogs in future, until he goes up to Olympos. Either the goddess or Cheiron then removes the madness *(lussa)* from the dogs, and they are greatly upset to find their master dead (for this reconstruction see now R. Janko, *Phoenix* 38 [1984] 299–307). Much the same situation (without the goddess) appears in Apollodoros, where Artemis casts madness upon the dogs, and they do in fact come to Cheiron's cave after the slaying, to be mollified by an image of Aktaion which he makes for them (ApB 3.4.4). Whether this is sufficient to justify an attribution to the *Ehoiai* I do not know; the discursive tone, direct address, and concern for the future of the dogs might be thought to indicate epic proper rather than a catalogue poem.

14. On this version as perhaps earlier than we might have supposed (given that it appears only in Diodoros [and Hyginus]), see Lacy 1990.34–42. Among other arguments he suggests that Aktaion's intent to marry Artemis was suppressed by Kallimachos because such a circumstance gave Artemis more justification than was appropriate to a comparison with the "more merciful" Athena of *Hymn* 5.

15. The scene on an Apulian volute krater (Naples Stg 31), with Aktaion killing a deer in the presence of Artemis near a spring, has however been taken as an allusion to the goddess' bath: see ibid., 36–39.

16. For a very useful assessment that pulls together the different threads of Aktaion's story into a whole, see now Forbes-Irving 1990.80–90 together with 197–201.

17. See Radt 1985.116–17 for various other suggested possibilities. The (mistaken, I believe) notion of Asklepiades that Hera appeared in the *Xantriai* disguised as a temple priestess is discussed above, pp. 474–75.

18. For the following reconstruction see also Webster 1967.205–11.

19. Probably also on Athens 11798, a "Megarian" relief bowl with a representation

of a Satyros and woman in a cave, as well as two other scenes that may be part of Euripides' play (or at least the story): see Sinn 1979.109 (MB 51) and pl. 21.1, 2.

20. So Jacoby, who includes this and other fragments of the presumed Peisandros under heading 16 in his edition of the lost Greek historians; see also his comments in the corresponding *Kommentar* volume, where the scholion is supposed to derive from a single account, itself patched together from various sources, including tragedy (1957.493–96). Earlier Bethe (1891.1–28) had argued that almost the entire scholion (including the Chrysippos section) was drawn from the epic *Oidipodeia*. But Robert (1915.149–67) has well shown the insuperable problems therein, especially regarding the attempt to link Hera's wrath against Laios with the Sphinx; he himself regards the scholion as a conflation of numerous different sources, only a few of which come from the Peisandros cited.

21. See Lloyd-Jones 1983.120–21 and Thalmann 1978.16. The latter argues that the naming of the Sphinx as a "reproach to Thebes" (*Hepta* 539: *poleôs oneidos*) means that the Thebans had for Aischylos done something to merit her depredations. But perhaps the reproach lay in their inability to deal with her until Oidipous arrived. Thalmann's further point, that in Aischylos' *Sphinx* someone sends the monster (fr 236 R), is dubious, since the word *pempei* at *Batr* 1287 almost certainly goes with the parody of the *Agamemnon*.

22. See Robert 1915.155–57, 396–414, supported by L. Deubner, *Abh Berlin* 4 (1942) 3–27; the latter regards the entire first half of the Peisandros scholion as drawn from the *Chrysippos* (and culminating in Laios' death). More recently, K. Schefold (*Classica et Provincialia: Festschrift Erna Diez* [Graz 1978] 177–81) has returned to the theory of a Laios-Chrysippos tale in late Archaic epic, arguing that themes of transgression and hereditary atonement (by Laios and his descendants) are most appropriate to that period. Clearly much depends upon one's subjective reactions to the story and its place in Greek thought.

23. Conceivably this passage too allows Laios to avoid his fate by not begetting a child. But Iokaste's failure to mention that fact, plus the casual relegation of the birth to a subordinate clause, more naturally suggest that the child has already been conceived, so that exposure after its birth is Laios' only option.

24. See Sinn 1979.106 (MB 44) and pl. 21.3.

25. Robert (1915.94–97) cites in this connection the scholia at *Odyssey* 11.271, where the Sikyonian herdsmen care for Oidipous and he eventually sets out for Thebes (not Delphi) to find his parents, and postulates an Aischylean version in which Oidipous is not adopted by the king of any other land but knows from the beginning that he is a foundling, and knows as well the city where he may expect to find his parents, if not their identity. On this interpretation Laios himself is thought to be headed toward Kithairon in search of his son when the two meet and fail to recognize each other.

26. On this hydria's possible links to what we know as Chalkidian ware, see A. Collinge, *AA* (1988) 628–31.

27. Discussion in Robert 1915.48–58.

28. On the Sphinx of Thebes in art (with or without Oidipous) see the catalogue and discussion in Moret 1984. Two early items rightly (I think) discounted by him as generic man and Sphinx (if linked at all) are Thebes 50.265 (Boiotian kantharos) and Capua 183 (a Campanian amphora): see 81 n. 4.

29. On possible erotic motifs here see Vermeule 1979.171–73.

30. See M. L. West, *Greek Metre* (Oxford 1982) 98.

31. For other, less certain vases on which Oidipous defeating the Sphinx by force have been suspected, see Moret 1984.79–91. As he there notes (79), the painting on the Boston lekythos (97.374) which supported Robert's belief in the early existence of this version is probably modern. I omit here various other literary references that make Oidipous "destroy" or "kill" the Sphinx because such wording need mean no more than that the solving of the riddle caused the Sphinx to kill herself. But perhaps to be noted is Athenaios 6.253f, where as part of a song composed for Demetrios Poliorketes Oidipous is said to have thrown the Sphinx from a cliff.

32. See Webster's reconstruction (1967.242–46).

33. Published by P. Parsons (*ZPE* 26 [1977] 7–36) and now included by Malcolm Davies in volume 1 of his new edition of the melic poets (Oxford 1991) as Stesichoros 222b. The attribution to Stesichoros is not certain but seems very likely: on the metrics see M. Haslam, *GRBS* 19 (1978) 29–57.

34. See Severyns (1928.215), who believes that this can in fact be deduced (from the scholia and Eustathios at *Il* 23.681) as a conclusion of Aristarchos.

35. The T scholia at *Il* 23.679 seem in fact of the opinion that only in Homer and Hesiod (i.e., the *Ehoiai*) does Oidipous live on as king.

36. See n. 33 above.

37. Text uncertain, and *andrêlatên* has been emended to refer to Polyneikes (rather than Eteokles) as the future exiler of his brother. Even if the text is sound, we are probably dealing with a certain amount of emotional exaggeration.

38. Most notably F. Solmsen, *TAPA* 68 (1937) 197–211.

39. See A. Burnett, *GRBS* 14 (1973) 343–68.

40. Text not entirely certain, and one word (the corrupt *araias*) has been omitted; it is not certain with what it agreed. For an analysis of this passage with conclusions running counter to mine, see G. R. Manton, *BICS* 8 (1961) 81–83.

41. On a Tyrrhenian amphora in Basel, Eriphyle, Baton, and Oikles are all named as watching the departure (Cahn Coll 921). Other possible early representations of this scene include an ivory relief from the Halos deposit at Delphi and a bronze relief from Olympia (B 103).

42. The scholia at *Odyssey* 11.326 also state that Eriphyle received the necklace "from Polyneikes or Adrastos" but add no details. In Hyginus, surprisingly, Adrastos has the necklace made, and with it bribes Eriphyle to reveal the hiding place of her concealed husband (*Fab* 73). Bethe (1891.50–56) supposed from these accounts an epic version ("Der Amphiaraos Ausfahrt") in which Eriphyle had every right to prefer the necklace, not believing the predictions of her husband's death, and there was no matricide/revenge. Certainly this is a possible stage in the development of the story, but the evidence does not do much to support it. In Apollodoros, Polyneikes goes to Iphis, son of Alektor, who advises the necklace as a bribe to Eriphyle (Ap*B* 3.6.1).

43. Drachmann 1927.3.

44. The bulk of our information about this play derives from the text of a papyrus first published in 1908 and hence not included in Nauck. See Bond's edition of all this material, with commentary (Oxford 1963).

45. Kunze (1950.175) rather leans toward the view that this right-hand inscription does refer to an on-looker; he does not consider the possibility that the right-hand warrior was Tydeus.

46. The scene has also long been thought to represent Herakles killing Iphitos; if

the victim could be male (the outline of a female breast seems the main point of contention) I would suggest too as a possibility Orestes and Aigisthos.

47. For this interpretation see R. Hampe, *AntK* 18 (1975) 10–16; the reverse of the skyphos may show the departure of Tydeus from Deipyle in Argos.

48. Robert, for example, argues (1915.121–29) that Ismene is a priestess of Athena seduced by Periklymenos, son of Poseidon, and punished by the goddess for that reason (in a context completely separate from the expedition); see in any case his discussion of the evidence from art.

49. For this gem see Krauskopf 1974.43, 108 and pl. 20.1; Hampe and Simon 1964.27–28 and fig. 5.

50. See R. Meiggs, *The Athenian Empire* (Oxford 1972) 469–72.

51. Just previously, Pausanias has noted the presence, near this group, of seven statues of the original attackers, although he names, alas, only Polyneikes. The wording of his description of the Epigonoi group may suggest that he did not think of (or see before him) Mekisteus as one of the Seven.

52. See Krauskopf 1974.43–45.

53. J. Nicole, *Les scolies genevoises de l'Iliade* (Geneva and Basel 1891) II 63–64.

54. *ARV²* 1073.4. For both these vases and their subject matter see Beazley, *JHS* 67 (1947) 1–7.

55. See now the assessment and bibliography in Hutchinson 1985.209–11, plus R. D. Dawe, *CQ* 17 (1967) 16–28 and *Dionysiaca* (ed. R. D. Dawe, J. Diggle, P. Easterling: Cambridge 1978) 87–103.

56. So Lloyd-Jones, *CQ* 9 (1959) 87–92, in the context of an interpretation in which he supposes the word *ateknous* to be corrupt or else to imply something closer to "ill-begotten" than "without children."

57. See the arguments of Hutchinson (1985.195–96), who discounts this last possibility and excises the line, probably rightly.

58. On this vase see F. Hauser, *JdI* 8 (1893) 93–103 (where the scene is interpreted as the sacrifice of Polyxena), H. Thiersch, *"Tyrrhenische Amphoren"* (Leipzig 1899) 55–58, and among more recent discussions of the problems, J. P. Small, *RM* 83 (1976) 124–26.

59. On this reconstruction see Webster 1967.265–68.

Chapter 15. The Line of Tantalos

1. Admittedly there is no hard evidence for this conclusion, merely the fact that a *Atreidôn Kathodos* is attested only here and at one other point in Athenaios, where a battle is in progress (9.399a). Either way, Tantalos' appearance in this poem is puzzling; Wilamowitz (1884.157) was surely right to stress that even if the work did include Agamemnon's descent to Hades, we ought not to expect to find Tantalos and his rock there.

2. The serving of Pelops will be attested already in the sixth century, if E. Simon (1967.281–87) is right in supposing the Foce del Sele *Dreifuss* metope to represent the child in the cauldron. But we have seen that there are many other possible interpretations, including the death of Minos: see p. 275.

3. Gerber (1982.55–59) well discusses these problems, although I am not in accord with his belief that the cauldron and ivory shoulder of the opening scene are part of what Pindar means to reject. My own views appear in *RivStCl* 26 (1978) 31–35.

4. So now Gerber 1982.99–103, with earlier bibliography and full discussion.

5. For the idea that Tantalos claimed (or revealed?) the sun to be a mass of hot metal (so Σ *Ol* 1.91, DL 2.8), plus a possible origin of Euripides' version in Anaxagoras' views on meteorites, see R. Scodel, *HSCP* 88 (1984) 13–24.

6. I am not convinced by Van Keuren's interpretation (1989.139–46) of the Turtle-rider Foce del Sele metope as Tantalos, but her arguments are intriguing and demonstrate how little we really know on this subject.

7. For the tradition that Minos was the one to kidnap Ganymedes, see p. 559 below.

8. Schefold suggests, however, that the two accounts are to be seen on a *terra sigillata* fragment in Bruges from the second century A.D. (1981.218 and fig.299): the wing of an eagle shows that he has flown off with Ganymedes as a distressed Tantalos (in Phrygian dress) and a small Eros look on. This is possible, although I would have thought Tros himself losing his son a more likely conjecture.

9. See Willcock 1964.141–42.

10. See, e.g., J. Th. Kakridis (*Homeric Researches* [Lund 1949] 96–103) for a reiteration of the ancient view that Niobe's metamorphosis here is an interpolation designed to bring Homer's innovations into line with the more familiar tradition.

11. On the identification of these at times disputed figures (and interpretation of Pausanias' account) see Säflund 1970.112–21.

12. On all phases of the story in the (mostly late) artistic tradition see Säflund 1970. 131–42.

13. For useful discussion and reconstruction of the play (assuming Myrtilos' participation to have been central) see W. M. Calder, *Philologus* 118 (1974) 203–14, where it is argued that Myrtilos' betrayal of his master here is simply the carrying out of the will of Zeus against the murderous Oinomaos.

14. Calder (ibid.) supposes this motif to be the invention of Euripides.

15. For late Etruscan urns on which Myrtilos dies by some means other than falling from Pelops' chariot (but still at the hands of Oinomaos or Pelops), see Säflund 1970.142.

16. See Severyns 1928.231–34.

17. So Robert 1915.406–12, although he excludes the Dositheos version as plainly the invention of a later time. The evidence for a Sophoklean play of this name is a single quote by Stobaios (fr 472 R), who may intend by "Hippodameia" only the speaker of the lines (in the *Oinomaos?*), not the title of the work.

18. See p. 311 above.

19. On this scholion see n. 20 below.

20. From Wolfenbüttel Gudianus graec. 15, second hand (Gu). Not in Schwartz's edition of the scholia; text printed in Pearson 1917 1.92, Radt 1977.162. On the manuscript see A. Turyn, *The Byzantine Manuscript Tradition of the Tragedies of Euripides* (Urbana 1957) 20–21, 60–61.

21. Fraenkel, however, strongly defends the manuscript reading in his commentary (1950 3.758–60), arguing that the twelfth or thirteenth as saved is a folktale pattern on which our modern notions of seemliness should not be allowed to intrude.

22. In Hyginus' account something has fallen out, but both there and in Lactantius Placidus (who offers a fuller account drawn probably from the same source: Σ St:*Theb* 4.306) Pelopia seemingly knows her assistant and exposes the child for that reason; he is again suckled by goats, thus explaining his name.

23. Pelops' children here (which in fact match perfectly those reported by Σ *Or* 4)

are in the part omitted by Merkelbach and West. For the form "Kleolla" actually reported by Tzetzes, see West 1985.111–12.

24. For this text see M. Papathomopoulos, *Nouveaux fragments d'auteurs anciens* (Ioannina 1980) 11–26.

Chapter 16. The Trojan War

1. So Robert 1920–26.388–89, arguing that a patronymic can in Homer go back to the grandfather at most, and then only exceptionally.

2. For these see Kaempf-Dimitriadou 1979.7–12, plus catalogue at 76–79.

3. Strabo, who gives a fuller account of this expedition (with the attack by mice) speaks only of Teukroi, and says that the elegiac poet Kallinos told their story (13.604). We find Teukros as a Kretan also in the second-century Hegesianax's *Troika* (45F4), and of course in Vergil (*Aen* 3.104–10).

4. Servius at *Aeneid* 3.167 suggests that Dardanos is the child of Zeus and Elektra, Iasion that of Korythos and Elektra. In this scholion Dardanos founds Dardania while Iasion takes possession of Samothrace. For Iasion there see also Diodoros 5.48.4–49.4, where his mating with Demeter is integrated into the local mysteries.

5. For this hypothesis and other fragments of Euripides' play, see R. A. Coles, *A New Oxyrhynchus Papyrus: The Hypothesis of Euripides' Alexandros* (London 1974).

6. See in addition to ibid. on the fragments the reconstruction of Scodel 1980. 20–42.

7. Some Alexandrian scholars did attempt to find references to such an oath in several passages of the *Iliad* (e.g., 2.284–90, 2.337–41). But these clearly denote the boasts and promises warriors customarily make to each other when setting out for war.

8. In support of this point see now M. Davies, *JHS* 101 (1981) 56–62.

9. For the whole Greek artistic tradition of the Judgment see Raab 1972.

10. On the animals accompanying the goddesses (and the absence of the apple frequently assumed to have been held by Paris), see R. Hampe in *Neue Beiträge zur klassischen Altertumswissenschaft: Festschrift Bernhard Schweitzer* (Stuttgart 1954) 77–86.

11. So perhaps even earlier on NY 98.8.11, a Black-Figure neck-amphora by the Swing Painter on which the middle goddess of the procession holds up a very small round object. For these and other possible instances of the apple (and arguments against those [such as Clairmont 1951.102–4] who doubt its appearance in Attic art) see Raab 1972.49–60.

12. On this point see Stinton 1965.51–63.

13. On all these solutions, with bibliography, see Bernabé 1987.52–53 (*apparatus* to fr 14); he himself prefers the last-named possibility.

14. See the catalogue of Ghali-Kahil 1955.49–70.

15. For metrical arguments placing the *Elektra* in the 420s B.C., see G. Zuntz, *The Political Plays of Euripides* (Manchester 1955) 68–71. But even conceding the play's supposed link with Athens' Sicilian expedition, the work will date to 413, a year before the certain date of 412 for the *Helen*.

16. So in Apollodoros, and Tzetzes after correction; the *Odyssey* scholia (see below) have "Oinotropoi."

17. The text has the aorist of *peithô* here; presumably somewhere in transmission someone misconstrued a conative imperfect as representing a completed fact.

18. For the interpretation of the scene on this krater (there are no names) and a

slightly later loutrophoros by the same painter in a private collection in Naples, see Trendall in Böhr and Martini 1986.165–68.

19. See Radt 1985.343–44.

20. See Severyns 1928.291–95.

21. On the interpretation see Bauchhenss-Thüriedl 1971.16–18.

22. The A (and in part T) scholia at *Iliad* 9.668 claim the existence of a town Skyros in Phrygia as well, perhaps simply to eliminate conflict between Homer and the tale of the concealment in Lykomedes' court. But whether they know of such a town or are just guessing, Homer certainly could have intended something local here.

23. So Severyns (1928.285–91), claiming that an epitomator of Proklos substituted the storm version for that of the concealment in Proklos' text so as to create agreement with the account of the *Little Iliad*. The *Iliad* scholion in question (Σb *Il* 19.326) is now printed by Bernabé in his edition as *Kyp* fr 19.

24. In contrast to Severyns (previous note) Robert suggests (1881.34) that Polygnotos in fact introduced this version into Athens as a variant designed to rescue Skyros from the humiliation of a military conquest.

25. For the text of the papyrus see Austin 1968.95–96; for the reconstruction of the play, Webster 1967.95–97.

26. So already the *Iliad* scholia (A at 9.145).

27. Solmsen 1981.353–58.

28. For this date see P. Von der Mühll 1958.141–46; for 454 B.C., the other possibility offered by the scholia, Bowra 1964.402–5.

29. For supporters of these opposing views see Gantz, *HSCP* 87 (1983) 71–78.

30. For this and other suggested trilogies see Radt 1985.115.

31. See Lesky 1972.481–82.

32. See Mette 1963.101–3.

33. See, for example, Strabo 13.1.35, where the precinct is located at the point where the Thymbraios River empties into the Skamandros.

34. On this problem see Kunze 1950.141–42.

35. Although the interpretation of this rare instance of Troilos defending himself is questioned by von Bothmer (1957.11) on the grounds that the rider is bearded.

36. On these and several other sixth-century Lakonian examples see Pipili 1987. 27–30.

37. So Zancani Montuoro and Zanotti-Bianco 1954.275–88; in support of the Troilos interpretation see now Van Keuren (1989.95–103), who offers among other arguments the belief that the victim here is unbearded.

38. Text not entirely certain: see Erbse ad loc. and Radt 1977.453.

39. That he was also conceived as a warrior in Vergil's *Aeneid* has sometimes been supposed, given the scene on the Carthage temple doors in Book 1 with Troilos dragged behind his chariot, still holding the reins, his "weapons having been lost," and his "reversed spear dragging in the dust" (*Aen* 1.474–78). Mention of this chariot and lost weapons has been thought to mean that Troilos has challenged Achilleus to battle and been struck by the latter's spear. But the emphasis throughout this section is on the brutality of the Greeks; Troilos has more likely "lost" his arms because he has taken them off, thinking himself safe, and the "reversed spear" seems proved by a later passage in the *Aeneid* to be his own, used as a goad for his horses (*Aen* 9.609–10): see R. D. Williams, *CQ* 10 (1960) 145–48.

40. Presumably to pass the time. In Polygnotos' Nekuia painting for the Knidian

Lesche at Delphi, Pausanias reports seeing Palamedes and Thersites playing at dice (10.31.1); this might spring from an actual narrative or represent simply an artist's conceit.

41. For these sources (quoted in full) and very useful discussion see Scodel 1980. 43–54.

42. The Aischylean fragment 182 R is clearly an enumeration of Palamedes' accomplishments spoken by himself, and we know of no other play in which it could be placed. If it was part of the *Palamedes*, then Aischylos would seem to have staged both the execution (but probably not a trial) and Nauplios' protest in the same drama.

43. So Robert (1920–26.1134), who reminds us, however, that Oiax or even someone like Aias or Achilleus is also possible.

44. For this conclusion see Scodel 1980.51–54.

45. Virtually nothing survives of either play; the titles may well be two different appellations for the same drama.

46. Other such plays (about which nothing is known) include a *Priamos* by Philokles, a *Hektor* by Astydamas, son of Astydamas, and a *Ransoming of Hektor* by Dionysios I, tyrant of Syracuse.

47. See Webster 1967.84–85. The play is parodied as early as Aristophanes' *Acharnes* 421, where Euripides suggests to Dikaiopolis the rags of his blind Phoinix as a suitable costume.

48. For the arguments see W. Ritchie, *The Authenticity of the Rhesus of Euripides* (Cambridge 1964).

49. For a catalogue of such representations, with commentary, see K. Friis Johansen 1967.244–80.

50. Zancani Montuoro and Zanotti-Bianco 1954.250–59.

51. Ibid., 260–68.

52. Admittedly, Patroklos' tending has been taken by some to reflect a narrative moment from the *Kypria*, namely a wound sustained in the battle with Telephos (so Robert 1920–26.1148); there is really no evidence for or against this notion.

53. So Schefold 1964.42–43; K. Friis Johansen 1967.279–80, with bibliography.

54. For this (probably well-founded) skepticism, see Taplin 1977.431–33.

55. See Gantz 1980.220–21, 1981.146–48.

56. Adding probability to the interpretation of this scene as Achilleus and Paris is the fact that the other side almost certainly shows Achilleus, Hektor, and Athena.

57. Against this view Hampe (in Hampe and Simon 1964.47–49) argues that on the lost Chalkidian amphora Achilleus has been slain by the (much smaller) arrow in his side, the shot to the ankle having only incapacitated him. I would agree that Paris could make this shot, but Apollo should have no need for more than one arrow.

58. See P. Kakridis, *Hermes* 89 (1961) 288–97.

59. See Young 1979.12–17, in the context of an extremely valuable article on the transfer of motifs in myths.

60. The slaying of Achilleus with an arrow in the Thymbraion is also reported by Eustathios (Eu-*Il* p. 816), after which he notes that Hellanikos used the form "Dymbraios" of the god. Robert (1881.127) took this as proof that Achilleus' death in this fashion was actually related by Hellanikos, but that conclusion seems to me no more than possible.

61. What Homer meant by the term *paides Trôôn* was contested even in antiquity. Aristarchos supposed women of Troy, and thus athetised the line as contamination

from the similar version of the *Little Iliad*. But probably these are Trojan prisoners, whether male or female, as in the scholia.

62. For what it is worth, the Geneva scholia at *Iliad* 14.406 (first hand) attribute the notion of Aias' invulnerability to the *neôteroi*.

63. Against this initial interpretation of D. von Bothmer and in favor of Aias' suicide, see B. B. Shefton, *RA* (1973) 203–18 and M. I. Davies, *AntK* 16 (1973) 60–70, the latter incorporating significant new fragments of the cup not originally available to von Bothmer; these last eliminate any possibility that the woman is removing a robe from the corpse rather than covering it with one. The odd position of this corpse may be due to nothing more than a desire to show Aias' dead body face up, but just possibly a reference to a single vulnerable spot (more toward the back than the ribs?) is also involved.

64. See D. L. Thompson, *ArchClass* 28 (1976) 30–39.

65. See Sadurska 1964.27–28; the entire left side of the relief, and with it the left half of this particular scene, is broken away, so that we do not know how Philoktetes was armed.

66. Athenaios 9.393d.

67. Conceivably she appeared in Bakchylides, if the letters *Oin*[. . .] in fragment 20D Sm refer to her (as wife of Paris) rather than to Althaia, wife of Oineus. On this point see Stinton (1965.40–50), who suggests that the papyrus' subsequent reference to Niobe could imply Oinone just as well as Althaia, since both women (like Niobe) bring about the death of a loved one, Paris in the first case, Meleagros in the second. Stinton also interprets Paris' pre-Helen romantic attachment (minus Korythos) as very much a part of his shepherd *persona*, in contrast to his role as prince.

68. Admittedly, as Aristarchos noted, Deiphobos can be removed from the first of these scenes by the athetising of a single line. But in the second situation we must imagine that Menelaos' first thought will be to secure Helen, lest she escape or be killed by someone else; since he goes to Deiphobos' house, Homer surely means us to understand that she is there.

69. Earlier the plot of this play was taken to be the fetching of *Achilleus*, not Neoptolemos, from Skyros, as in the *Skyrioi* of Euripides, and the matter is not entirely certain, but see Pearson 1917 2.191–93 and Radt 1977.418–19.

70. For this papyrus fragment see A. S. Hunt, *Catalogue of the Greek Papyri in the John Rylands Library, Manchester* 1 (Manchester 1911) 40–42, and for the supplement Bernabé 1987.75. The papyrus relates three events as in the *Little Iliad*, although with the theft of the Palladion well out of the sequence Proklos reports; between the fetching of Neoptolemos (by Phoinix and someone) and the arrival of Eurypylos there is room for Achilleus' ghost, and some location seems to be specified.

71. Though note that Bernabé includes this among fragments he believes to come from a different *Little Iliad*. The *Iliad* scholia cite verses about the different medical skills of Machaon and his brother Podaleirios which they attribute to the *Iliou Persis* of Arktinos (ΣT *IL* 11.515); these *might* mean that the death of Machaon was also related in that poem.

72. Probably this last explanation is, as Severyns argues (1928.343–44), simply another Aristarchean attempt to separate Homer from what was to be found in later elaborations (i.e., the Cycle).

73. Aristotle (or an interpolation) mentions such a play, but without naming the author (*Poet* 23.1459b6). An *Oxyrhynchus papyrus* (*POxy* 1175 = frr 206a–222a R)

apparently drawn from it now suggests Sophoklean authorship, given similarities to the papyrus of the same poet's *Ichneutai*.

74. Proklos' summary of the *Little Iliad* does not in fact say that Helenos counseled the theft of the Palladion, although it seems a reasonable assumption, and admittedly is the case in the PRylands 22 account perhaps drawn from the same epic: see n. 70 above. Helenos is likewise responsible in Apollodoros' account (ApE 5.10).

75. Severyns claims that Apollodoros here follows the version of Arktinos, contaminating it, however, with Odysseus' disguise as a beggar taken from Lesches (1928. 349–52). Certainly this is possible, but the inclusion of the theft of the Palladion in Arktinos' poem remains questionable (see p. 644 below), and if there is only one foray, then Odysseus' daytime visit as a beggar in the *Odyssey* stands unexplained. We will see, too, below that the curious anomaly of Odysseus disguising himself to infiltrate Troy at night appears already in Aristophanes and Antisthenes, however that story was concocted.

76. On the *Little Iliad* scenes from the *Tabula Iliaca Capitolina*, Diomedes exits from the city holding the Palladion, followed by Odysseus with a shield, if the names are correctly assigned: see Sadurska 1964.28, 30. Even if this does come from Lesches' poem, it is no more than we would expect from later versions.

77. Although of course Athena may not favor Odysseus in every account: see Severyns for the suggestion (1928.351–52, 354–55) that Lesches consciously minimizes Odysseus' roles and accomplishments, compared with Arktinos and the *Odyssey*.

78. On the evidence of Proklos, Arktinos' poem began only with the debate over the Horse, that is, with events belonging to the actual Sack of Troy. We cannot, however, be sure that a summary of earlier events has not been cut from our text to avoid overlap with the summary from Lesches, much as seems to have been done in making that latter summary end well before the *Little Iliad* does. Another possibility is that the reference to the Palladion occurred in the course of the description of the Sack, with no detailed narration of the attempted theft. Conceivably in that case Arktinos omitted any prophecy, motivated perhaps by a desire to have the Palladion remain in Troy until the Sack in the belief that this statue (not another) was required for the impiety against Kassandra.

79. For the various Roman explanations of how the true Palladion reached Italy (including some that recognize the difficulty of allowing the Trojans to keep the statue and make Diomedes bring it to Italy instead), see R. G. Austin, *Aeneidos Liber Secundus* (Oxford 1964) 84–85.

80. For discussion of this material (with illustrations), see Moret 1975 1.71–84.

81. Polyainos adds a version in which the statue is deposited with Demophon, who sends it to Athens while feigning a defense against Agamemnon, after which he fools the latter with a copy (1.5).

82. For the theory that two Palladia were needed (and *both* taken to Athens) because the Athenians had two such cult statues to explain, see Robert 1920–26.1235–37.

83. For what it is worth he does not appear in the *Little Iliad* scenes on the *Tabula Iliaca Capitolina*: see Sadurska 1964.28. But other events of the poem are also omitted (i.e., Odysseus' infiltration of Troy as a beggar) and then too the scenes in question conclude with the bringing of the Horse into the city; if Laokoon's tale appeared in Lesches where it does in Arktinos (i.e., only *after* the Horse is inside) we should not expect to find it here. The *Tabula* does show Sinon (bound) and Kassandra (agitated?) at the Skaian gates as the Horse enters; if this last detail is not interpolated from the *Aeneid*

(see n. 90 below) it will constitute our first evidence of the seeress attempting to warn her people against the hidden Greeks.

84. Robert 1881.192–93.

85. One other artifact sometimes thought to represent the tale of Laokoon is a mid-fifth-century Red-Figure kantharos in London with a bearded figure at an altar being bitten by a snake and gazing with drawn sword at a just deceased youth (London E155). The bearded figure has been interpreted as Laokoon or the second of his sons (if he is not Ixion or Orestes), but either identification seems dubious (surely the man has slain the youth himself), and unless the winged figure holding the youth is a metamorphosed snake (rather than Thanatos) they offer in any case nothing noteworthy for our purposes. For arguments revising and bolstering earlier versions of this interpretation of the scene, see E. Buschor in A. Furtwängler, F. Hauser, and K. Reichhold, *Griechische Vasenmalerei*, Series 3 (Munich 1932) 274–76.

86. Severyns argues (*RBPh* 5 [1926] 317–21) that the original number was thirteen, although he also postulates that this was simply the number of Achaians (out of a larger total) actually *named* by the *Little Iliad*.

87. The improbability of Helen knowing the voices of the other Achaians' wives caused Aristarchos to athetise the line in question, but even without it Helen in tapping on the Horse is clearly aiming at the betrayal of those inside it.

88. Presumably Pausanias means that in Lesches Koroibos dies during the Sack by Diomedes' hand rather than Neoptolemos', but PRylands 22 has a Korybos, son of Mygdon of Phrygia, slain during the theft of the Palladion, so that possibly both slayer and point in time were different in the *Little Iliad:* see n. 70 above.

89. See Sadurska 1964.28–30.

90. For the Vergilian contamination of material supposedly drawn from Greek epic, and the probable working methods of the artist (Theodoros) in crediting sources, see Horsfall 1979a.35–43.

91. But see n. 83 above on her possible appearance in this role in the *Little Iliad.*

92. See M. Ervin, *AD* 18 (1963) 37–75, for the full publication of this pithos.

93. Robert in fact argues (1920–26.1268 n. 2) that works such as the *Odyssey* and the *Nostoi*, where Kassandra is Agamemnon's prize, must reject this tradition of the rape.

94. On this scene as representing the death of Astyanax see E. T. H. Brann, *AntK* 2 (1959) 35–37.

95. See Payne 1931.136 n. 3; Hampe 1935/36.272–77; Kunze 1950.158. This view is by no means proved, but Dörig's attempt to return to the theory of a Titanomachy (with Poseidon threatening Rheia) is not likely to be right: see above, chap. 1, n. 55.

96. Catalogue of early representations in Ghali-Kahil 1955.71–112. Not included here is the Mykonos relief pithos, which was discovered only in 1961.

97. See R. Förster, *Hermes* 18 (1883) 475–78, where it is also proposed that the mention of Polyxena's death well in advance of the fact might have occurred as a remark of the poet, perhaps on the occasion of Troilos' death and her flight.

Chapter 17. The Return from Troy

1. See above, pp. 574–75.

2. See D. F. Sutton, *Philologus* 128 (1984) 127–30.

3. On the Homeric version of Agamemnon's death see now Prag 1985.68–73. Against his separation of the various accounts into "Aigisthos alone" and "Aigisthos and

Klytaimestra" versions, I would argue that Homer stresses the complicity of each in accordance with the needs of the moment, but of course previous tellers of the tale may have themselves shifted responsibility one way or another as their tastes dictated. For an "Aigisthos alone" version much depends on how we understand *Odyssey* 3.269.

4. See S. West (1981.359–61) for objections to Agamemnon's unusual sea route and arguments that material has here been added.

5. Bowra 1961.112–14.

6. See Prag 1985.1–5.

7. In favor of these two points see Schefold (1964.44) and M. I. Davies (1969. 228–30), both of whom argue that Klytaimestra does hold a weapon in her right hand. More properly cautious, I think, are Fittschen, who doubts both net and weapon, supposing Aigisthos to commit the murder with his right hand (1969.189), and Prag, who does likewise but with Klytaimestra the assailant, operating with her left hand behind Agamemnon's back (1985.1–2).

8. See Kunze 1950.167–68.

9. In favor of this interpretation see Kunze 1950.168 and (with a new drawing) Prag 1985.2–3 and pl. 2b, c.

10. See Fittschen 1969.187; Prag 1985.58.

11. See Boardman 1963.128–29 and, for the interpretation of the scene as the death of Agamemnon, M. I. Davies 1969.224–28, 230–36.

12. See Schäfer 1957.75; Fittschen 1969.188, 191. Hampe (1936.71) argued that the three figures shown could only be Hekabe, Priam, and Neoptolemos, but Kunze (1950.157 and n. 3) thought to see traces of a throne in the center and suggested the death of Aigisthos or Agamemnon; so too Fittschen (preferring Agamemnon) and now Van Keuren 1989.120–22 (Agamemnon in bath: see below).

13. See n. 12 above and Prag (1985.32–33), who favors Herakles and Apollo.

14. For the theory that relief vessel and Foce del Sele metope present Agamemnon's death in his bath, see Van Keuren 1989.120–22. The same scholar, following Schmidt (1977.269 n. 19), also argues that traces of a bath (i.e., a pitcher) can be seen on the New York steatite seal discussed above.

15. For discussion of both the metope and the Basel relief see p. 275 above.

16. See Fittschen 1969.186–87.

17. M. I. Davies 1969.252–56, interpreting at the same time the scene on the reverse (usually taken to show Apollo and Artemis) as the death of Aigisthos.

18. Sinn 1979.101 (MB 36); see also C. Robert, *JdI* 34 (1919) 72–76.

19. See E. Vermeule, *AJA* 70 (1966) 1–22.

20. On 474 B.C. as the more likely date of *Pythian* 11 see chap. 16, n. 28, above.

21. March (1987.86–98) argues that since in the *Kypria, Ehoiai,* and Stesichoros Iphigeneia is saved by Artemis, her fate cannot have served as motivation for Klytaimestra's deeds; probably that is reasonable, although Agamemnon did *intend* to sacrifice her, and she is thereby lost to her mother. March further suggests, based on the sudden spate of Attic vase-paintings with the killing, that Simonides is responsible for Klytaimestra's greater involvement.

22. Of these sources, the *Iliad* scholion specifically assigns the device of the chiton with no outlet at the neck to the tragedians; whether the scholiast knew of a play in which this was actually dramatized, as opposed to just the allusion in Euripides' *Orestes,* we do not know.

23. Although there was as well a recognition by means of a lock of Orestes' hair, as in Aischylos: 217 *PMG*.

24. This is the standard interpretation; for bibliography and other suggestions (apart from his own of the death of Agamemnon) see M. I. Davies 1969.252 n. 1 and 253 n. 1.

25. For the publication of this mitra see H. Bartels in E. Kunze et al., *VIII. Bericht über die Ausgrabungen in Olympia* (Berlin 1967) 198–205, where it is suggested that an already dead Aigisthos (on throne?) might have occupied the missing left half. Fittschen (1969.187–88, 191) likewise interprets the scene as the matricide.

26. So H. Hoffmann in H. Hoffmann and A. Raubitschek, *Early Cretan Armorers* (Mainz 1972) 26, 39.

27. Kunze 1950.168–69.

28. See above, chap. 1, n. 55, and p. 656.

29. See Fittschen 1969.188–89.

30. In support of this interpretation see Fittschen 1969.191; Schefold 1964.89. Against it Prag objects (1985.35–36) that Tydeus and Ismene might be intended (although he admits that the dress of the figures is wrong) or else that the relief has been reworked, the artist having originally intended a male figure in place of the female victim.

31. Zancani Montuoro and Zanotti-Bianco 1954.269–74 (Metope no. 24: "Laodameia and Klytaimestra").

32. Ibid., 141–45 (Metope no. 7: "Herakles and Hera"). The excavators as we saw earlier associate this metope with two others showing attacking Silenoi; for the view that it represents Orestes and Elektra see Van Keuren 1989.57–64.

33. Zancani Montuoro and Zanotti-Bianco 1954.275–88 (Metope no. 25: "Orestes and Aigisthos").

34. For the identification of this metope as in fact Achilleus and Troilos see Van Keuren 1989.95–103.

35. So Zancani Montuoro and Zanotti-Bianco 1954.289–300, supported most recently by Van Keuren 1989.123–29.

36. See Prag 1985.47–48 and pls. 28d, 29a.

37. Against Simon's dubious opinion that Ixion could be portrayed (1955.25–26; 1967.280) there remains the difficult fact that no literary tradition records Ixion pursued by Erinyes; indeed, the crime he commits (killing his father-in-law) is not one that they properly punish, since the victim is not a real parent, or even a relative.

38. See most recently A. H. Somerstein in his commentary on the play (1989. 222–26), with argument that Athena votes as part of the jury and cogent discussion of previous views.

39. Discussion of these and other scenes of Aigisthos' death in Prag 1985.13–34.

40. See ibid., 106–7, and pl. 46.

41. Admittedly, Accius' *Erigona* does seem to have treated this figure (since Aigisthos and Orestes are mentioned), and presumably it had a Greek model. Pearson (1917.173–74) does suppose the subject of Sophokles' play the trial.

42. Stobaios is the sole source, citing a number of fragments (content of no help) from a play he calls *Aleites* and ascribes to Sophokles (see Pearson 1917.62–67). Modern opinion generally rejects the ascription (for the fragments in the new *Tragicorum Graecorum Fragmenta* see Ades fr 1b), and given Stobaios' spelling of the title even its link to the house of Atreus remains uncertain.

43. According to Pausanias, however, there was also such a statue, brought back by Iphigeneia when she left the Tauroi, at Brauron (1.33.1).

44. So H. Lloyd-Jones, *JHS* 103 (1983) 96.

45. We should remember that Aischylos' *Iphigeneia*—about which nothing whatever is known—*could* have dealt with these same events. Sophokles' *Iphigeneia* seems clearly to have dramatized the sacrifice at Aulis, but his *Chryses* has been suspected as a predecessor of Euripides' plot: see below.

46. The portent consists of finding a land where the houses have iron foundations, wooden walls, and roofs of wool; in Epeiros, Neoptolemos then encounters men who fix their spears in the ground and use their cloaks to form tents.

47. Schwartz in his edition of the *Orestes* scholia accepts the emendation to Machaireus; Jacoby in editing Pherekydes restricts it to the *apparatus*.

48. This conclusion will naturally be invalidated if, as some have thought, the controversial scene on London E155 (a Red-Figure kantharos of the early fifth century) does in fact represent Orestes with a just-slain Neoptolemos, rather than Laokoon and his sons, or Ixion. But the man on the altar (with snake and drawn sword) is bearded, while the dead person is not, and this is surely an impossible way in which to present the relationship between Orestes and a man his senior who has fought at Troy.

49. On the vexed question of what the contestant was supposed to shoot at after stringing the bow, see now the survey of views by Fernández-Galiano in Fernández-Galiano and Heubeck 1986.xviii–xxv.

50. See Gantz 1980.151–53.

51. Catalogue and discussion of the *Odyssey* in art in Touchefeu-Meynier 1968; see also the valuable compilation in Brommer 1983.56–109. For Polyphemos, Fellman (1972) now offers a separate study.

52. Against Schefold's view (1978.267–68) that this could be a non-Homeric version of the Odyssean tale see Amyx and Amandry 1982.113–15.

53. The eye of this rapidly falling Seiren seems clearly closed, leading to the suggestion that she is dead or dying, perhaps because in some accounts these creatures were fated to die when someone successfully resisted them: see Arafat 1990.1.

54. For this identification of the scene (cautiously advanced), see C. Weickert, *RM* 60/61 (1953–54) 56–61; he supposes the piece to be of Corinthian Late Geometric fabric.

55. Zancani Montuoro and Zanotti-Bianco 1954.301–15. The interpretation as Odysseus originates here (Zancani Montuoro). The same scholar argues her case in more detail in *PP* 14 (1959) 221–29.

56. For the theory (already noted in chapter 15) that the figure could be Tantalos, and a good discussion of other turtle riders in art, see Van Keuren 1989.139–46.

57. Earlier Pausanias also speculates that a scene on the topmost panel of the Chest—a man and woman on a couch in a grotto surrounded by attendants—represents Odysseus and Kirke (5.19.7); this he admits is wholly a guess on his part, and in this case at least we might think of numerous other possibilities.

58. So West (1966.433–36), arguing that this notion will derive from the sixth century, since before that time the Etruscans would not have been of sufficient interest to the Greeks, and after 510 B.C. Etruscans and Latins would have been more clearly differentiated. West also supposes the line mentioning Telegonos interpolated into this section, since it interrupts the link between the first two sons and their dominion.

59. According to the *Odyssey* scholia, Hephaistos makes this spear for Telegonos (at the request of Kirke) from a ray that Phorkys had slain; the shaft had parts of adamantine and gold.

60. H. Lloyd-Jones, in *CR* 14 (1964) 247, suggests that the words *ek toud'* in the third line of the quote might mean "after this" (the depositing of excrement) rather than "from this." The idea is attractive (and Sextus perhaps had no more evidence than we do), but in that case one must wonder that Aischylos would leave such an unfortunate ambiguity in his text.

61. See Sadurska 1964.24–37, in particular 29 (description of scenes in question), 30 (inscriptions), and 32–35 (survey of the [widely divergent] previous opinions and discussion of the problem). Her own conclusion, that the artist of the tablet has followed earlier pictorial models without introducing significant new elements, is not in my opinion compelling, nor does it take into account the fact that most (perhaps all) of the elements in question will be earlier than the *Aeneid*. A more properly skeptical analysis (on which many of the following arguments are based) appears in Horsfall 1979a.26–48; see also Galinsky, who suggests (1969.106–13) that Stesichoros may have left Aineias' westward goal quite vague, thus opening the door for later writers and artists to attribute an Italian (or Sicilian) landing to him. Most scholars seem now agreed that Stesichoros is not likely to have used the actual word *Hesperia*.

62. For these see S. Woodford and M. Loudon, *AJA* 84 (1980) 30–33, 38–39; K. Schauenburg, *Gymnasium* 67 (1960) 176–90.

63. In favor of the receptacle see Alföldi 1965.284–86; of the suitcase Horsfall 1979a.40.

64. Head 1911.214; M. Price and N. Waggoner, *Archaic Greek Coinage: The Asyut Hoard* (London 1975).

65. See Brommer 1967.220–21.

66. The problems in this passage are investigated at length by Horsfall (1979b. 377–83), although I am not sure I would agree that Aineias' arrival in Italy with Odysseus means that he left Troy as a captive. Horsfall's final judgment, that Aineias' link to Latium and Rome is probably no older than Timaios, remains the safest conclusion, although F. Solmsen (*HSCP* 90 [1985] 93–110) renews the arguments in favor of Hellanikos.

Chapter 18. Other Myths

1. See Gantz, *Hermes* 106 (1978) 14–26.

2. A fragmentary inscription from the Athenian Agora listing productions now increases the likelihood that Sophokles did write such a play (see B. Merritt, *Hesperia* 7 [1938] 116–18); the only other evidence is a one-word citation from the Apollonios scholia which some have thought might be in fact from Aischylos' version of the story.

3. For this interpretation see Robert 1881.210–12, subsequently supported by Simon 1955.5–14 and 1967.175–95. Both scholars concede that the victim cannot be Ixion's father-in-law, but argue that some other relative not known to us is intended.

4. See frr 293–96 Kern.

5. Sale (1962.122–31) argues, in fact, that nothing in this account after Kallisto's metamorphosis and the birth of Arkas is from "Hesiod," in part because Ps-Eratosthenes omits intervening material (the version of Amphis: see below) reported by our Latin derivatives of Eratosthenes. This cannot be certain, but Sale well points out the absurdities of a tale in which Arkas pursues his mother after they have grown up together.

Originally they must have been separated after his birth, so that he might come in time to threaten her (in ignorance of her identity) and to endanger himself in so doing.

6. On this variant as Hesiodic (from the *Ehoiai*, in fact), see Sale, who argues (1965.14 plus 1962.140–41) that the evidence of Ps-Eratosthenes and Apollodoros indicates two retellings in the Hesiodic Corpus, one making Kallisto a Nymph, the other making her the daughter of Lykaon. Her role as Nymph slain by Artemis he sees as the earlier, local account, since it serves to explain her grave at Trikolonoi in Arkadia (Paus 8.35.8).

7. For the reconstruction see Webster 1967.147–50.

8. For the *Xantriai* as dramatizing this myth see Séchan 1926.102 n. 2 and Mette 1963.146–47; the suggestion was first made by Boeckh in the last century.

Appendix A. Some "Deviant" Cosmogonies

1. For what follows see, in particular, Schibli 1990.

Bibliography

As a rule, the following list includes only items that are cited more than once in the notes or were found to be generally useful in the writing of this book. Editions of ancient authors and scholia are cited in Appendix B; they reappear here only if the notes refer to them in some special connection. Reference works to Greek art are cited at the beginning of Appendix C.

Alföldi, A. 1965. *Early Rome and the Latins.* Ann Arbor, Mich.

Allen. T. 1912. *Homeri Opera 5.* Oxford.

Amyx, D. 1988. *Corinthian Vase-Painting of the Archaic Period.* 3 vols. Berkeley.

Amyx, D., and P. Amandry. 1982. "Héraclès et l'Hydre de Lerne dans la céramique corinthienne." *AntK* 25:102–16.

Arafat, K. W. 1990. *Classical Zeus.* Oxford.

Austin, C. 1968. *Nova Fragmenta Euripidea in papyris reperta.* Berlin.

Barrett, W. S. 1964. *Euripides: Hippolytos.* Oxford.

Barron, J. P. 1972. "New Light on Old Walls. The Murals of the Theseion." *JHS* 92:20–45.

Bauchhenss-Thüriedl, C. 1971. *Der Mythos von Telephos in der antiken Bildkunst.* Würzburg.

Beazley, J. 1951. *The Development of Attic Black-Figure.* Berkeley.

Beck, I. 1984. *Ares in Vasenmalerei, Relief und Rundplastik.* Frankfurt.

Beckel, G. 1961. *Götterbeistand in der Bildüberlieferung griechischer Heldensagen.* Stiftland.

Bérard, C. 1974. *Anodoi: Essai sur l'Imagerie des Passages chthoniens.* Rome.

Bernabé, A. 1987. *Poetae Epici Graeci 1.* Leipzig.

Bethe, E. 1891. *Thebanische Heldenlieder.* Leipzig.

Blome, P. 1978. "Das gestörte Mahl des Phineus auf einer Lekythos des Sapphomalers." *AntK* 21:70–75.

Boardman, J. 1963. *Island Gems: A Study of Greek Seals in the Geometric and Early Archaic Periods.* London.

———. 1968. *Archaic Greek Gems.* Evanston, Ill.

———. 1975. "Herakles, Peisistratos and Eleusis." *JHS* 95:1–12.

Böhr, E. 1982. *Der Schaukelmaler.* Mainz am Rhein.

Böhr, E., and W. Martini. 1986. *Studien zur Mythologie und Vasenmalerei: Konrad Schauenburg zum 65. Geburtstag am 16. April 1986.* Mainz am Rhein.

Bol, P. 1989. *Argivische Schilder (Olympische Forschungen XVII).* Berlin.

Bona Quaglia, L. 1973. *Gli "Erga" di Esiodo.* Turin.

883

Bond, G. W. 1963. *Euripides: Hypsipyle*. Oxford.

———. 1981. *Euripides: Heracles*. Oxford.

Bowra, C. M. 1961. *Greek Lyric Poetry: From Alkman to Simonides*. 2d ed. Oxford.

———. 1964. *Pindar*. Oxford.

Brize, P. 1980. *Die Geryoneis des Stesichoros und die frühe griechische Kunst*. Würzburg.

Brommer, F. 1937a. *Satyroi*. Würzburg.

———. 1937b. "Die Rückführung des Hephaistos." *JdI* 52:198–219.

———. 1942. "Herakles und die Hesperiden auf Vasenbildern." *JdI* 57:105–23.

———. 1944/45. "Herakles und Syleus." *JdI* 59/60:69–78.

———. 1957. "Attische Könige." In *Charites: Studien zur Altertumswissenschaft*. Bonn.

———. 1959. *Satyrspiele*. 2d ed. Berlin.

———. 1963. *Die Skulpturen der Parthenon-Giebel*. Mainz am Rhein.

———. 1967. *Die Metopen des Parthenon*. Mainz am Rhein.

———. 1972. *Herakles: Die zwölf Taten des Helden in antiker Kunst und Literatur*. Darmstadt.

———. 1973. *Vasenlisten zur griechischen Heldensage*. 3d ed. Marburg.

———. 1978. *Hephaistos: Der Schmiedegott in der antiken Kunst*. Mainz am Rhein.

———. 1982. *Theseus: Die Taten des griechischen Helden in der antiken Kunst und Literatur*. Darmstadt.

———. 1983. *Odysseus: Die Taten und Leiden des Helden in antiker Kunst und Literatur*. Darmstadt.

———. 1984. *Herakles II: Die unkanonischen Taten des Helden*. Darmstadt.

Burkert, W. 1985. *Greek Religion*. Cambridge, Mass.

Burow, J. 1989. *Der Antimenesmaler*. Mainz am Rhein.

Buschor, E. 1934. "Kentauren." *AJA* 38:128–32.

Carpenter, T. H. 1986. *Dionysian Imagery in Archaic Greek Art*. Oxford.

Clairmont, C. 1951. *Das Parisurteil in der antiken Kunst*. Zurich.

Conacher, D. J. 1967. *Euripidean Drama*. Toronto.

———. 1980. *Aeschylus' Prometheus Bound: A Literary Commentary*. Toronto.

Cook, A. B. 1914. *Zeus: A Study in Ancient Religion* 1. Cambridge.

———. 1925. *Zeus: A Study in Ancient Religion* 2. Cambridge.

Croiset, A. 1898. "Sur les origines du récit relatif à Méléagre dans l'ode V de Bacchylide," 73–80. In *Mélanges Henri Weil*. Paris.

Dale, A. M. 1967. *Euripides: Helen*. Oxford.

Davies, M. 1991. *Poetarum Melicorum Graecorum Fragmenta*. Oxford.

Davies, M. I. 1969. "Thoughts on the *Oresteia* before Aischylos." *BCH* 93:214–60.

de La Coste-Messelière, P. 1936. *Au Musée de Delphes*. Paris.

Diggle, J. 1970. *Euripides: Phaethon*. Cambridge.

Dörig, J., and O. Gigon. 1961. *Der Kampf der Götter und Titanen*. Olten and Lausanne.

Drachmann, A. B. 1927. *Scholia vetera in Pindarum* 3. Leipzig.

Dugas, C. 1944. "Le premier crime de Médée." *REA* 46:5–11.

Fellman, B. 1972. *Die antiken Darstellungen des Polyphemabenteuers*. Munich.

Felten, W. 1975. *Attische Unterweltsdarstellungen*. Munich.

Fernández-Galiano, M., and A. Heubeck. 1986. *Omero: Odissea* 6. Milan.

Fittschen, K. 1969. *Untersuchungen zum Beginn der Sagendarstellungen bei den Griechen*. Berlin.

Forbes-Irving, P. 1990. *Metamorphosis in Greek Myth*. Oxford.

Fraenkel, E. 1950. *Aeschylus: Agamemnon*. 3 vols. Oxford.

———. 1963. *Zu den Phoenissen des Euripides*. Munich.

Friis Johansen, H., and E. W. Whittle. 1980. *Aeschylus: The Suppliants*. 3 vols. Copenhagen.

Friis Johansen, K. 1923. *Les vases sicyoniens*. Paris and Copenhagen.

———. 1945. *Thésée et la danse à Délos (Det Kgl. Danske Videnskabernes Selskab: Arkeologisk-Kunsthistoriske Meddelelser)* 3, no. 3. Copenhagen.

———. 1967. *The Iliad in Early Greek Art*. Copenhagen.

Furtwängler, A. 1885. *Beschreibung der Vasensammlung im Antiquarium*. 2 vols. Berlin.

Galinsky, G. K. 1969. *Aeneas, Sicily, and Rome*. Princeton.

Gantz, T. 1980. "The Aischylean Tetralogy: Attested and Conjectured Groups." *AJPh* 101:133–64.

———. 1981. "Divine Guilt in Aischylos." *CQ* 31:16–32.

Garvie, A. F. 1969. *Aeschylus' Supplices: Play and Trilogy*. Cambridge.

Gerber, D. 1982. *Pindar's Olympian One: A Commentary*. Toronto.

Ghali-Kahil, L. 1955. *Les enlèvements et le retour d'Hélène dans les textes et les documents figurés*. Paris.

Glynn, R. 1981. "Herakles, Nereus and Triton." *AJA* 85:121–32.

Griffin, J. 1977. "The Epic Cycle and the Uniqueness of Homer." *JHS* 97:39–53.

Griffith, M. 1977. *The Authenticity of Prometheus Bound*. Cambridge.

———. 1983. *Aeschylus: Prometheus Bound*. Cambridge.

Grimal, P. 1951. *Dictionnaire de la Mythologie grecque et romaine*. Paris.

Hainsworth, J. B. 1982. *Omero: Odissea* 2. Milan.

Hampe, R. 1935/36. "Korfugiebel und frühe Perseusbilder." *AM* 60/61:271–99.

———. 1936. *Frühe griechische Sagenbilder in Böotien*. Athens.

Hampe, R., and E. Simon. 1964. *Griechische Sagen in der frühen etruskischen Kunst*. Mainz am Rhein.

Harrison, J. E. 1922. *Prolegomena to the Study of Greek Religion*. 3d ed. Cambridge.

Head, B. 1911. *Historia Numorum*. 2d ed. Oxford.

Helbig, W. 1969. *Führer durch die öffentlichen Sammlungen klassischer Altertümer in Rom*. 3: *Die staatlichen Sammlungen*. 4th ed. revised by H. Speier and others. Tübingen.

Hemelrijk, J. M. 1984. *Caeretan Hydriae*. Mainz am Rhein.

Heubeck, A. 1983. *Omero: Odissea* 3. Milan.

Heydemann, H. 1872. *Die Vasensammlungen des Museo Nazionale zu Neapel*. Berlin.

Horsfall, N. 1979a. "Stesichoros at Bovillae?" *JHS* 99:26–48.

———. 1979b. "Some Problems in the Aeneas Legend." *CQ* 29:372–90.

Howald, E. 1924. "Meleager und Achill." *RhM* 73:402–25.

Hutchinson, G. 1985. *Aeschylus: Septem contra Thebas*. Oxford.

Huxley, G. L. 1969. *Greek Epic Poetry: From Eumelos to Panyassis*. Cambridge, Mass.

Jacobsthal, P. 1931. *Die melischen Reliefs*. Berlin-Wilmersdorf.

Jacoby, F. 1949. *Atthis: The Local Chronicles of Ancient Athens*. Oxford.

———. 1957. *Die Fragmente der griechischen Historiker* 1. 2 vols. 2d ed. Leiden.

Janko, R. 1982. *Homer, Hesiod and the Hymns*. Cambridge.

Jucker, H. 1977. "Herakles und Atlas auf einer Schale des Nearchos in Bern." In *Festschrift für Frank Brommer*. Mainz am Rhein.

Kaempf-Dimitriadou, S. 1979. *Die Liebe der Götter in der attischen Kunst des 5. Jahrhunderts v. Chr. (AntK* Beiheft 11). Bern.

Kamerbeek, J. 1959. *The Plays of Sophokles* 4: *The Trachiniai.* Leiden.

Kerényi, K. 1951. *Die Mythologie der Griechen; die Götter- und Menschheitsgeschichten.* Zurich.

———. 1958. *Die Heroen der Griechen.* Zurich.

Keuls, E. C. 1974. *The Water Carriers in Hades.* Amsterdam.

Kirk, G., J. Raven, and M. Schofield. 1983. *The Presocratic Philosophers.* 2d ed. Cambridge.

Kirk, G. S. 1962. "The Structure and Aim of the *Theogony.*" In *Hésiode et son Influence (Entretiens sur l'Antiquité classique VII).* Geneva.

———. 1985. *The Iliad: A Commentary* 1: Books 1–4. Cambridge.

———. 1990. *The Iliad: A Commentary* 2: Books 5–8. Cambridge.

Kossatz-Deissmann, A. 1978. *Dramen des Aischylos auf westgriechischen Vasen.* Mainz am Rhein.

Kraus, T. 1960. *Hekate: Studien zu Wesen und Bild der Göttin in Kleinasien und Griechenland.* Heidelberg.

Krauskopf, I. 1974. *Der thebanische Sagenkreis und andere griechischen Sagen in der etruskischen Kunst.* Mainz am Rhein.

Krieger, X. 1975. *Der Kampf zwischen Peleus und Thetis in der griechischen Vasenmalerei.* Münster.

Kron, U. 1976. *Die zehn attischen Phylenheroen (AM* Beiheft 5). Berlin.

Kunze, E. 1950. *Archaische Schildbänder (Olympische Forschungen II).* Berlin.

Kurtz, D., and J. Boardman. 1971. *Greek Burial Customs.* Ithaca, N.Y.

Lacy, L. 1990. "Aktaion and a Lost 'Bath of Artemis.'" *JHS* 110:26–42.

Lasserre, F. 1950. *Les Épodes d'Archiloque.* Paris.

Lesky, A. 1972. *Die tragische Dichtung der Hellenen.* Göttingen.

Lindner, R. 1984. *Der Raub der Persephone in der antiken Kunst.* Würzburg.

Lloyd-Jones, H. 1957. *Aeschylus* 2:523–603. Loeb Library, Cambridge, Mass.

———. 1983. *The Justice of Zeus.* 2d ed. Berkeley.

March, J. 1987. *The Creative Poet.* London.

Mette, H. J. 1963. *Der verlorene Aischylos.* Berlin.

Metzger, H. 1951. *Les représentations dans la céramique attique du IVᵉ siècle.* 2 vols. Paris.

Meuli, K. 1921. *Odyssee und Argonautika.* Berlin.

Meyer, H. 1980. *Medeia und die Peliaden.* Rome.

Moon, W. 1983. *Ancient Greek Art and Iconography.* Madison, Wis.

Moret, J.-M. 1975. *L'Ilioupersis dans la céramique italiote.* 2 vols. Rome.

———. 1984. *Oedipe, la Sphinx et les Thébains.* 2 vols. Rome.

Nicolai, W. 1964. *Hesiods Erga.* Heidelberg.

Owens, A. S. 1939. *Euripides: Ion.* Oxford.

Page, D. L. 1941. *Select Papyri III.* Loeb Library, Cambridge, Mass.

———. 1951. *Alcman: The Partheneion.* Oxford.

———. 1955. *Sappho and Alcaeus.* Oxford.

Payne, H. 1931. *Necrocorinthia.* Oxford.

Pearson, A. C. 1917. *The Fragments of Sophocles.* 3 vols. Cambridge.

Pearson, L. 1942. *The Local Historians of Attica.* Philadelphia.

Peschlow-Bindokat, A. 1972. "Demeter und Persephone in der attischen Kunst des 6. bis 4. Jahrhunderts." *JdI* 87 : 60–149.

Pfeiffer, R. 1949. *Callimachus.* 2 vols. Oxford.

Phillips, K. M. 1968. "Perseus and Andromeda." *AJA* 72 : 1–23.

Pipili, M. 1987. *Laconian Iconography of the Sixth Century B.C.* Oxford.

Prag, A.J.N.W. 1985. *The Oresteia: Iconographic and Narrative Tradition.* Chicago.

Preller, L. and C. Robert. 1894. *Theogonie und Götter (Griechische Mythologie 1).* 4th ed. Berlin.

Raab, I. 1972. *Zu den Darstellungen des Parisurteils in der griechischen Kunst.* Frankfurt and Bern.

Radt, S. 1977. *Tragicorum Graecorum Fragmenta 4: Sophocles.* Göttingen.

———. 1985. *Tragicorum Graecorum Fragmenta 3: Aeschylus.* Göttingen.

Ribbeck, O. 1875. *Die römische Tragödie im Zeitalter der Republik.* Leipzig.

Richardson, N. J. 1974. *The Homeric Hymn to Demeter.* Oxford.

Ridgway, B. S. 1977. *The Archaic Style in Greek Sculpture.* Princeton.

Robert, C. 1881. *Bild und Lied.* Berlin.

———. 1914. "Pandora." *Hermes* 49 : 17–38.

———. 1915. *Oidipus.* Berlin.

———. 1916. "Tyro." *Hermes* 51 : 273–302.

———. 1920–26. *Die griechische Heldensage (Griechische Mythologie 2).* 3 vols. Berlin.

Russo, C. F. 1965. *Hesiodi Scutum.* Firenze.

Russo, J. 1985. *Omero: Odissea 5.* Milan.

Sadurska, A. 1964. *Les Tables Iliaques.* Warsaw.

Säflund, M. L. 1970. *The East Pediment of the Temple of Zeus at Olympia.* Gothenburg.

Sale, W. 1962. "The Story of Callisto in Hesiod." *RhM* 105 : 122–41.

———. 1965. "Callisto and the Virginity of Artemis." *RhM* 108 : 11–35.

Schäfer, J. 1957. *Studien zu den griechischen Reliefpithoi des 8.-6. Jahrhunderts v. Chr. aus Kreta, Rhodos, Tenos und Boiotien.* Kallmünz.

Schauenburg, K. 1953. "Pluton und Dionysos." *JdI* 68 : 38–72.

———. 1957. "Zu Darstellungen aus der Sage des Admet und des Kadmos." *Gymnasium* 64 : 210–30.

———. 1958. "Phrixos." *RhM* 101 : 41–50.

———. 1960a. *Perseus in der Kunst des Altertums.* Bonn.

———. 1960b. "Der Gürtel der Hippolyte." *Philologus* 104 : 1–13.

———. 1960c. "Herakles und Omphale." *RhM* 103 : 57–76.

Schefold, K. 1964. *Frühgriechische Sagenbilder.* Munich.

———. 1978. *Götter- und Heldensagen der Griechen in der spätarchaischen Kunst.* Munich.

———. 1981. *Die Göttersage in der klassischen und hellenistischen Kunst.* Munich.

Schefold, K., and F. Jung. 1988. *Die Urkönige, Perseus, Bellerophon, Herakles und Theseus in der klassischen und hellenistischen Kunst.* Munich.

———. 1990. *Die Sagen von den Argonauten, von Theben und Troja in der klassischen und hellenistischen Kunst.* Munich.

Schibli, H. 1990. *Pherekydes of Syros.* Oxford.

Schiffler, B. 1976. *Die Typologie des Kentauren in der antiken Kunst.* Frankfurt.

Schmidt, M. 1977. "Zur Deutung der Dreifuss-Metope Nr. 32 von Foce del Sele," 265–75. In *Festschrift für Frank Brommer.* Mainz am Rhein.

Scodel, R. 1980. *The Trojan Trilogy of Euripides*. Göttingen.

Séchan, L. 1926. *Études sur la tragédie grecque dans ses rapports avec la céramique*. Paris.

Severyns, A. 1928. *Le cycle épique dans l'école d'Aristarque*. Liège and Paris.

Simon, E. 1953. *Opfernde Götter*. Berlin.

———. 1955. "Ixion und die Schlangen." *JÖAI* 42:5–26.

———. 1967. "Die vier Büsser von Foce del Sele." *JdI* 82:275–95.

———. 1985. *Die Götter der Griechen*. 4th ed. Munich.

Simon, E., et. al. 1975. *Führer durch die Antikenabteilung des Martin von Wagner Museums der Universität Würzburg*. Mainz.

Sinn, U. 1979. *Die homerischen Becher*. Berlin.

Solmsen, F. 1981. "The Sacrifice of Agamemnon's Daughter in Hesiod's *Ehoeae*." *AJP* 102:353–58.

Somerstein, A. 1989. *Aischylos: Eumenides*. Cambridge.

Sourvinou-Inwood, C. 1979. *Theseus as Son and Stepson*. London.

Steingräber, S. 1984. *Catalogo Ragionato della Pittura Etrusca*. Milan.

Stibbe, C. M. 1972. *Lakonische Vasenmaler des sechsten Jahrhunderts v. Chr.* Amsterdam and London.

Stinton, T. C. W. 1965. *Euripides and the Judgement of Paris*. London.

Sutton, D. F. 1987. *Two Lost Plays of Euripides*. Frankfurt.

Taplin, O. 1977. *The Stagecraft of Aeschylus*. Oxford.

Thalmann, W. 1978. *Dramatic Art in Aeschylus's Seven against Thebes*. New Haven.

Thompson, H. A. 1962. "The Sculptural Adornment of the Hephaisteion." *AJA* 66:339–47.

Thomson, G. 1932. *Aeschylus: The Prometheus Bound*. Cambridge.

Thummer, E. 1969. *Pindar: Die isthmischen Gedichte*. 2 vols. Heidelberg.

Touchefeu-Meynier, O. 1968. *Thèmes Odysséens dans l'art antique*. Paris.

Trendall, A. D., and T.B.L. Webster. 1971. *Illustrations of Greek Drama*. London.

Tusa, V. 1983. *La scultura in pietra di Selinunte*. Palermo.

Unterberger, R. 1968. *Der gefesselte Prometheus des Aischylos*. Stuttgart.

van der Valk, M. 1963. *Researches on the Text and Scholia of the Iliad: Part One*. Leiden.

Van Keuren, F. 1989. *The Frieze from the Hera I Temple at Foce del Sele*. Rome.

Verdenius, W. J. 1985. *A Commentary on Hesiod: Works & Days, vv. 1–382*. Leiden.

Vermeule, E. 1979. *Aspects of Death in Early Greek Art and Poetry*. Berkeley.

Vian, F. 1945. "Le combat d'Héraclès et de Kyknos." *REA* 47:5–32.

———. 1951. *Répertoire des Gigantomachies figurées dans l'art grec et romain*. Paris.

———. 1952. *La guerre des Géants: Le mythe avant l'epoque hellénistique*. Paris.

———. 1963. *Les Origines de Thèbes: Cadmos et les Spartes*. Paris.

Vojatzi, M. 1982. *Frühe Argonautenbilder*. Würzburg.

von Bothmer, D. 1957. *Amazons in Greek Art*. Oxford.

Von der Mühll, P. 1958. "Wurde die elfte Pythie Pindars 474 oder 454 gedichtet?" *MH* 15:141–56.

von Steuben, H. 1968. *Frühe Sagendarstellungen in Korinth und Athen*. Berlin.

Webster, T.B.L. 1967. *The Tragedies of Euripides*. London.

Wendel, C. 1935. *Scholia in Apollonium Rhodium vetera*. Berlin.

West, M. L. 1966. *Hesiod: Theogony*. Oxford.

———. 1978. *Hesiod: Works and Days.* Oxford.

———. 1983. *The Orphic Poems.* Oxford.

———. 1985. *The Hesiodic Catalogue of Women.* Oxford.

West, S. 1981. *Omero: Odissea* 1. Milan.

Westermann, A. 1843. *Mythographoi: Scriptores poeticae historiae graeci.* Brunswick.

Wilamowitz-Moellendorf, U. von. 1884. *Homerische Untersuchungen.* Berlin.

———. 1914. *Aischylos Interpretationen.* Berlin.

Willcock, M. M. 1964. "Mythological Paradeigma in the *Iliad.*" *CQ* 14:141–54.

———. 1978. *The Iliad of Homer: Books I–XII.* London.

———. 1984. *The Iliad of Homer: Books XIII–XXIV.* London.

Young, D. C. 1979. "The Diachronic Study of Myth and Achilles' Heel." *Journal of the California Classical Association: Northern Section* 4:3–34.

Zancani Montuoro, P., and U. Zanotti-Bianco. 1954. *Heraion alla Foce del Sele II: Il primo thesauro.* Rome.

Index

Boldface page numbers signify primary discussions.

908

Index

Designed by Glen Burris
Set in Aldus by G&S Typesetters, Inc.
Printed on 55-lb. Glatfelter Offset
by The Maple Press Company